THE PROCEEDS OF CRIME
Law and Practice of Restraint,
Confiscation, Condemnation and Forfeiture

THE PROCEEDS OF CRIME

Law and Practice of Restraint,
Confiscation, Condemnation and Forfeiture

SECOND EDITION

Trevor Millington *LLB(Hons) Wales*
Barrister of the Middle Temple

Mark Sutherland Williams *LLB(Hons) Exon*
Barrister of the Inner Temple

OXFORD
UNIVERSITY PRESS

OXFORD
UNIVERSITY PRESS

Great Clarendon Street, Oxford OX2 6DP

Oxford University Press is a department of the University of Oxford.
It furthers the University's objective of excellence in research, scholarship,
and education by publishing worldwide in

Oxford New York

Auckland Cape Town Dar es Salaam Hong Kong Karachi
Kuala Lumpur Madrid Melbourne Mexico City Nairobi
New Delhi Shanghai Taipei Toronto

With offices in

Argentina Austria Brazil Chile Czech Republic France Greece
Guatemala Hungary Italy Japan Poland Portugal Singapore
South Korea Switzerland Thailand Turkey Ukraine Vietnam

Oxford is a registered trade mark of Oxford University Press
in the UK and in certain other countries

Published in the United States
by Oxford University Press Inc., New York

© Trevor Millington and Mark Sutherland Williams 2007

The moral rights of the author have been asserted
Database right Oxford University Press (maker)

Crown copyright material is reproduced under Class Licence
Number C01P0000148 with the permission of OPSI
and the Queen's Printer for Scotland

First published 2003
Second Edition published 2007

All rights reserved. No part of this publication may be reproduced,
stored in a retrieval system, or transmitted, in any form or by any means,
without the prior permission in writing of Oxford University Press,
or as expressly permitted by law, or under terms agreed with the appropriate
reprographics rights organization. Enquiries concerning reproduction
outside the scope of the above should be sent to the Rights Department,
Oxford University Press, at the address above

You must not circulate this book in any other binding or cover
and you must impose the same condition on any acquirer

British Library Cataloguing in Publication Data

Data available

Library of Congress Cataloging in Publication Data

Millington, Trevor.
  The proceeds of crime : the law and practice of restraint, confiscation and
forfeiture / by Trevor Millington and Mark Sutherland Williams. — 2nd ed.
  p. cm.
  Includes index.
  ISBN 978-0-19-929864-8 (hardback : alk. paper) 1. Forfeiture—England. 2.
Forfeiture—Wales. 3. Great Britian.
Proceeds of Crime Act 2002. I. Williams, Mark Sutherland. II. Title.
KD8460.M55 2007
345.42'0773—dc22

2007006380

Typeset by Cepha Imaging Private Ltd, Bangalore, India
Printed in Great Britain
on acid-free paper by
Antony Rowe Ltd., Chippenham

ISBN 978-0-19-929864-8

1 3 5 7 9 10 8 6 4 2

If I hadn't seen such riches

I could live with being poor

'Sit down', James

For Angela

For Jayne

FOREWORD

In *R v Sekhon* [2003] 1 WLR 1655, Lord Woolf CJ began his judgment by noting that one of the most successful weapons that can be used to discourage offences that are committed in order to enrich the offender is to ensure that any profit which is made from the offending is confiscated. He went on to say that Parliament had repeatedly introduced legislation designed to enable the courts to confiscate the proceeds of crime. These comments were made in the context of a number of appeals against sentence in which errors had occurred in confiscation proceedings before the Crown Court. These appeals were themselves only some of the many which made their way to the Court of Appeal. The legislation had become a trap for the unwary. The difficulties were compounded by the fact that different statutory regimes existed for drug trafficking, other crime and terrorism. Moreover, which regime applied did not only depend upon the nature of the offence but also on the date of its commission. Now, the principal legislation is the Proceeds of Crime Act 2002, which runs to about 320 pages and which has been amended by, amongst other statutes, the Serious and Organised Crime and Police Act 2005. This combination of legislation amounts to a dense thicket of law and there are many problems still to be resolved.

Mark Sutherland Williams and Trevor Millington, who are both extremely able and experienced lawyers in this field, have performed an invaluable service to the law by producing a book which explains the legislation and the formidable body of case law it has accumulated. They are to be congratulated for producing a work that satisfies all the requirements of an enquiring and demanding reader. It is well written and even the most obscure statuory provisions are illuminated by the authors' knowledge and understanding. It is analytical and comprehensive, dealing with everything from absconding defendants to warrants of commitment. It contains helpful practical observations on the operation of the legislation and helpfully explains the rationale for many of the provisions. The précis of the case law is a model of its kind.

In short, it is a practical and accessible guide whose value will be as great as the care and effort the authors have taken over its preparation. All those who have the responsibility for advising on or resolving the intricate problems which arise in this field will be grateful for such an excellent work.

David Perry
6 King's Bench Walk
Temple
January 2007

FOREWORD TO THE FIRST EDITION

by the Honourable Mr Justice Maurice Kay
(now Lord Justice Maurice Kay)

Crime can be extremely profitable. Examples abound of fraudsters, drug dealers, racketeers and other professional criminals living lives of luxury on the proceeds of crime. In recent years the need to convict and sentence the guilty has been supplemented by the need to separate the criminal from his ill-gotten gains. The Proceeds of Crime Act 2002 is a statute of great size and importance. It is difficult. It is complex. It is a legal minefield. Moreover, it will impose burdens on judges in Crown Courts who will be required to fit countless urgent and complicated applications of a novel kind into their crowded lists. In addition, High Court judges will have to grapple with the new civil recovery provisions in cases where the Assets Recovery Agency seek to recover property which it alleges to be the proceeds of crime where no one has been convicted—and even where the defendant has been acquitted. All this calls for the most detailed examination by practitioners and judges. It requires the striking of a balance between the need to ensure that criminals do not prosper and the guarantee of fair treatment for defendants and third parties.

All those involved with this rapidly developing area of legal practice will benefit from this authoritative book. Trevor Millington and Mark Sutherland Williams are two acknowledged experts with great experience in the field. I welcome and pay tribute to the fruits of their labours.

The Honourable Sir Maurice Kay
The Royal Courts of Justice
July 2003

PREFACE TO THE SECOND EDITION

It is now some three years since the first edition of this book was published. In that time the law in relation to the proceeds of crime, and the legislation surrounding it, has developed at an ever increasing pace. It was therefore time for a second edition.

We have strived to keep to the original formula, namely that of a straightforward, easily digestible work on this at times complex area of the law. Whether we have succeeded we will leave for others to decide. The task of any textbook writer is inevitably complicated by the volume of case law that is generated within any given field, and the proceeds of crime field has seen more than its fair share in recent years. We trust therefore that where we have delved into more detail, and sometimes comment, we will be forgiven. This we feel was the most obvious way of explaining the sometimes conflicting authorities to the reader.

Practitioners in the proceeds of crime discipline have noticed in recent years a return to a more robust approach emanating from the higher courts. This has been particularly so in relation to case law revolving around civil recovery under Pt 5 of the Act, where the High Court has interpreted the legislation favourably (and probably as Parliament intended) when it comes to the recovery of the proceeds of unlawful conduct. Equally, the same court has been alert to arguments in relation to equality of arms, which led in part to a revision of the legislation by SOCPA to allow for the release of legal funds from frozen assets in ARA cases, thus ensuring respondents have proper access to representation.

Generally therefore the revised scheme has settled well. Some of the concerns expressed at the time of the introduction of POCA have proved misplaced, albeit there remains some anecdotal evidence that in the Crown Court the requirement for urgency in certain without notice applications is not always adhered to. Elsewhere, however, the legislature should not be complacent. The system inevitably still has many imperfections. We believe that there may in future years be scope for a confiscation tribunal or court, taking the restraint and receivership work recently transferred to the Crown Court back into a jurisdiction where it is, by virtue of its civil law roots, better understood. In practice this would have the advantage of allowing specialist judges to adjudicate on disclosure and receivership issues without trespassing on the criminal justice system or court time. Similarly issues such as certificates of increase and inadequacy and enforcement of confiscation orders could also come within the tribunals remit, whilst retaining the ultimate sanction of the matter being referred back to the Crown Court for the activation of any default sentence in apppropriate cases.

Such a tribunal could also take on the determination of Assets Recovery Agency claims, and extinguish the anomaly that at present lay magistrates' are entitled to determine, for example, that £1 million in cash seized under Pt 5 of POCA is the proceeds of unlawful conduct, but only a High Court judge, at much greater expense, may determine that a motor car worth £10,000 was purchased with the proceeds of unlawful conduct.

Preface to the Second Edition

The removal of the cash seizure and civil condemnation matters from the magistrates' courts would also have the benefit of making the hearings less associated with the criminal courts, and a tribunal that dealt with the issue of both condemnation and restoration would overcome Mr Justice Evans-Lombe's concern in *Weller* that the present system was both confusing and pregnant with the possibility of substantial injustice.

We have included in this edition, as in the last, extensive coverage of all three of the main Acts. Any notion on our part that the CJA and DTA would be winding down by this stage having proved optimistic. Once again we regret that we have been unable to incorporate in any great detail confiscation and civil recovery law in Scotland and Northern Ireland.

We are grateful to all those who rewarded our efforts with warm and encouraging words about the first edition. We have tried to incorporate what suggestions and improvements we have received into this volume, most notably a new chapter on Condemnation and Restoration. The mistakes are ours. Any views expressed are our own and are not representative of any government department or other organisation.

Trevor Millington would again like to thank his learned and delightful co-author, Mark Sutherland Williams for his support, friendship and encouragement: working with 'MSW' is a real pleasure and privilege for me. My thanks are also due to David Green QC, the Director of the Revenue and Customs Prosecutions Office, for his kindness and support throughout this project. I owe a particular word of thanks to the RCPO team at the Enforcement Task Force — Bode Ogunfemi, Marc Fisken, Emma Oettinger, Catherine Colquohoun, Shannyn Carty, Tejal Hirani-Vekaria, Rachel Lavery, John Iloenyosi, Hilda Owagboe and Ndidi Onyido — both for their many helpful comments on the first edition of this work and their loyalty and consideration since I started working with them just over a year ago. I must also say a special thank you to Sarah Kay and Steven Burton who have now left the ETF for pastures new. Most importantly, my sincere thanks go to those dearest to me — to Margaret whose unfailing support and understanding is beyond all praise and to John and Marion O'Loughlin who have been my close friends since my Call to the Bar 25 years ago this July. Finally, a special word of thanks goes to Angela whose kindness continues to be a source of inspiration and to whom, once again, I dedicate this book with my admiration, affection and grateful thanks.

Mark Sutherland Williams would like to thank: firstly my distinguished co-author, Trevor Millington, who continues to humble me with not only his command of this subject, but also his generosity in dispensing the knowledge he has collected over the years. Behind nearly all of the decisions that reach the higher courts is an instructing lawyer prepared to forge ahead and take risks with the development of the law. In the proceeds of crime field that lawyer is most often Trevor Millington and this area of the law owes a great debt of gratitude to him. Secondly, I thank all those I thanked in the first edition. I am indeed fortunate to have the opportunity to work with some of the best in this field, including Bode Ogunfemi and his collegaues at the ETF; John Pattinson and the Asset Forfeiture Department at the RCPO, particularly Alex Marine for all his help on a number of cases; Philip Mobedji at the SFO; Tania November and the case team on Operation Extend; the staff and Jane Earl at ARA, including Ambrose King and Anthony Kennedy for their kind assistance with the civil recovery chapters. My special thanks to Sue Pritchard at HMRC for her help and

Preface to the Second Edition

advice on condemnation and restoration. Finally my thanks to the clerks and members of the Proceeds of Crime Unit at 3 Paper Buildings for their continuing support. Above all I thank my wife Jayne. Always have and always will.

Both my and Trevor's thanks go to Annabel and Jane at OUP for their patience whilst we have wrestled to meet deadlines.

We congratulate Sir Maurice Kay on his elevation to the Court of Appeal, and particularly thank one of the true leading lights in this area of the law, David Perry QC, deputy High Court Judge and former Senior Treasury Counsel, for agreeing to pen the Foreword to this second edition.

Trevor Millington
New Kings Beam House
London

Mark Sutherland Williams
3 Paper Buildings
Temple
January 2007

PREFACE TO THE FIRST EDITION

When the idea for a book on the proceeds of crime was first discussed over a long lunch and a couple of bottles of wine in the late summer of 2002, it seemed to be a good one. Our intention then was to put together not only a comprehensive manual on the existing Acts, which we had both lived with for several years, but also to review and include the new Proceeds of Crime Act 2002.

It was, as they say, a good idea at the time. The Proceeds of Crime Act 2002 runs to 462 sections, with 12 accompanying schedules: a total of 323 pages, a book in itself. In addition a booklet of some 130 pages entitled 'Explanatory Notes' was published with it to assist in the understanding of the new Act. And in addition to all of that, over the last few months we have seen a variety of statutory instruments published, over 25 in total, to supplement the new Act. These govern everything from the Rules of the Crown Court in relation to confiscation hearings and restraint orders, to no less than five commencement and savings orders, to statutory instruments dealing with pension provisions, the Police and Criminal Evidence Act, Crown Servants, and various codes of practice. The difficulty we were left with was what to leave out rather than what to put in. We regret, as a result, that we have only been able to focus on the law in England and Wales, leaving out, at least for this edition, confiscation law in Scotland and Northern Ireland.

Whilst no one can doubt this present Government's sincerity and determination to deal firmly with offenders who benefit financially from their crimes, the result of all this new legislation is that the practitioner is left with something of a confused picture, and we were left with something of a mountain to climb, not least because, whilst the Proceeds of Crime Act attempts to consolidate previous legislation, it will, for the foreseeable future, run side by side with the existing Drug Trafficking Act and Criminal Justice Act. Many cases will remain therefore, as before, in the High Court; other cases will now be dealt with by the Crown Court.

The notion that Crown Court judges, prior to their normal sitting day, will be prepared to consider restraint and receivership applications is one that many judges themselves still find difficult to digest. This area of the law is extensively within the civil jurisdiction and it is therefore potentially foreign to those judges who will now deal with the majority of applications. Complaints have already been raised by certain members of the judiciary about the lack of training they have received prior to the implementation of the new Act. For many, it has consisted of no more than half a day or a day's course. Many anticipate that the work of the Crown Court judge will only have begun as a result of a restraint order made *ex parte* on a Monday morning. The risk is that by the following Thursday the case will be back in court *inter partes* to be argued. This will potentially disrupt and have further ramifications for the Crown Court list. We suspect also that the new Act will be truly tested in the courts, particularly in the light of the Human Rights Act 1998. The upshot is that with the volume

Preface to the First Edition

of new legislation that has been created by the new Act, which replaces two fairly self-contained sections in the Drug Trafficking Act and the Criminal Justice Act, far from having simplified the law, the new Act has gone some way to complicating it. We do not intend in any way to be the prophets of doom. Far from it, we suspect and hope that the new Act will work, and will work well. One can recall that not too long ago many in the legal profession were airing similar reservations about the Human Rights Act: and as we now know that Act fitted fairly easily into modern-day practice and is now accepted and accommodated by members of the Judiciary and most in criminal practice.

We trust we have fulfilled our initial objectives and that this book will serve as a useful touchstone for reference not only in relation to the new Act, which at the time of writing is yet truly to have effect, but also as a reference work for case law under the DTA and the CJA, both of which are likely to be around for some time to come. It will of course be noted that the views expressed herein are our own and are not representative of any government department or other organisation.

Trevor Millington would like to thank Mark Sutherland Williams, my most delightful and knowledgeable co-author who unhesitatingly agreed to take on the task of writing this work at a very busy time both personally and professionally, and all of Mark's colleagues at 3 Paper Buildings for their help and encouragement throughout. My particular thanks must go to members of the senior management team at HM Customs and Excise for their unfailing support, including, in particular, David Pickup, the Solicitor for Customs and Excise, David North, and Brett Welch. I must also thank Farah Sheikh for her invaluable research assistance. Above all, however, my thanks go to my dearest friends, John and Marion O'Loughlin, without whose support through the most difficult times none of this would ever have been possible, and to Angela and Roberto for their extraordinary kindness which has been a constant source of inspiration over the last year and to whom this book is dedicated with my affection, admiration, and gratitude.

Mark Sutherland Williams would like to thank his co-author, Trevor Millington, for not only suggesting the project but also for having the confidence in him to complete the task. Trevor Millington is undoubtedly one of the country's leading authorities on asset forfeiture law, and responsible for shaping and developing many aspects of it. It has been my pleasure to work with him on this project. Further I would like to thank my Head of Chambers, Michael Parroy QC, for the ride; Michael Brompton QC, for the highs and the lows; Oliver Sells QC, for recent successes; and Christina Gorna for the kick start. I must also thank Purvi Patel of the Assets Recovery Agency for her contribution to the chapter on Civil Recovery and interim receiving orders; and all of my Clerks at 3 Paper Buildings, now too many to mention, but particularly our Chief Clerk, Charles Charlick for his guidance over the years. I would also like to thank all of my friends at the Solicitor's Office of HM Customs and Excise and the Assets Recovery Agency, including Colin Jones, Emma Wotton, Carolyne Lamptey, Justine Holmes, Piers Doggart, Charles Birikorang, Sue Pritchard and Vinod Kalia, for their continued support, and to Terry Scarborough and Katie Hawe for many great times, they both having now taken to pastures new. Both my and Trevor's thanks go to Annabel and Meg at the Oxford University Press, for being so terrific about all of our missed deadlines. Lastly, I owe an enormous debt of gratitude to Barrie McKay, the

Preface to the First Edition

Assistant Treasury Solicitor, for his encouragement, a very big case, and for everything that followed. Above all I would like to thank my wife for her support throughout this project which meant we effectively lost a Christmas and many weekends together.

We both respectfully thank the Honourable Sir Maurice Kay, Head of the Administrative Court, for agreeing to pen a Foreword to this work.

Trevor Millington
New Kings Beam House
London

Mark Sutherland Williams
3 Paper Buildings
Temple
May 2003

BIOGRAPHIES

Trevor Millington

Trevor Millington is a Barrister and Senior Lawyer in the Asset Forfeiture Division of the Revenue and Customs Prosecutions Office (formerly the Solicitor's Office of HM Customs and Excise). He was responsible for setting up the Customs and Excise Asset Forfeiture Unit in 1989 and since that time has specialised exclusively in the law relating to the restraint and confiscation of the proceeds of crime. He has been involved in many of the reported cases concerning this increasingly complex area of law, including *Re T (Disclosure Orders)*, *Hare v Commissioners of Customs and Excise* (piercing the corporate veil of companies), *Commissioners of Customs and Excise v Hughes* (liability to pay costs of management receivers) and *Re S* (release of funds subject to a Proceeds of Crime Act restraint order to meet the defendant's legal fees). In 1994 he was seconded to Gibraltar, where he was responsible for drafting legislation to implement the EC Money Laundering Directive and to provide for the restraint and confiscation of the proceeds of crime. His first book, Restraint and Confiscation Orders, was published by FT Law and Tax in 1996. He has lectured widely on the subject to audiences as diverse as Interpol, Europol, the National Criminal Intelligence Service, police and customs officers, lawyers and receivers. His interests include a passionate love of opera and classical music.

Mark Sutherland Williams

Mark Sutherland Williams has appeared as counsel in a number of the most significant cases that have been decided in the proceeds of crime field in recent years. These include the Court of Appeal cases of: *Singh* (2004), *Capewell* (2005), *Re S* (2005), *Ashton* (2006), and the time to pay argument in *Soneji* (2006). He was the first counsel to be instructed by the Director of the Assets Recovery Agency to draft an interim receiving order under POCA and a property freezing order under SOCPA, and was the first counsel to be instructed by the Asset Forfeiture Unit to obtain a restraint order under the Act. In 2006 he drafted and obtained the first external restraint order under the new legislation. He regularly appears in both the High Court and the Court of Appeal in specialist forfeiture, receivership, restraint and confiscation order matters. He is head of his chamber's Proceeds of Crime Unit. His career has also been notable for his involvement in a number of the country's most high-profile drug importation cases, including Operations *Stealer* and *Extend*. In 1999 he was instructed to draft the witness statement of Baroness Thatcher and John Major for the BSE public inquiry, and in 2001 he was appointed to part time judicial office. He has recently completed the New York marathon.

CONTENTS — SUMMARY

Table of Cases — lv
Table of Legislation — lxix
List of Abbreviations — ci

1	Setting the Scene	1
2	Restraint and Charging Orders under the DTA and CJA	13
3	Management Receivers under the DTA and CJA	39
4	Ancillary Orders: Seizure, Disclosure and Repatriation of Assets	59
5	Applications to Vary or Discharge Restraint Orders made under the DTA and CJA	73
6	Enforcement of Restraint and Receivership Orders: Contempt of Court	91
7	Practice and Procedure in the High Court: DTA and CJA Cases	103
8	Restraint and Receivership under the Proceeds of Crime Act 2002	119
9	Preparing for Confiscation Hearings under the DTA	151
10	The DTA Confiscation Hearing	173
11	Preparing for Confiscation Hearings under the CJA	211
12	The CJA Confiscation Hearing	229
13	Variations to Confiscation Orders under the DTA and CJA	249
14	Preparing for Confiscation Hearings under POCA	263
15	The POCA Confiscation Hearing	283
16	Reconsideration of Confiscation Orders under POCA and the Defendant who Absconds	301
17	Enforcement of Confiscation Orders under the CJA, the DTA, and POCA	323
18	The Insolvent Defendant	355
19	Civil Recovery: Property Freezing Orders; Interim Receivers; and Legal Expenses	363
20	Civil Recovery: Recovery Orders; Pensions; and the ECHR	405
21	Recovery and Seizure of Cash under POCA	431
22	Third Parties and Confiscation Law	473
23	Investigations	509
24	Appeals	527
25	The International Element	549
26	Money Laundering	571

Contents — Summary

27 Disclosure of Suspicious Transactions	597
28 Costs and Compensation	619
29 Condemnation and Restoration	643
Appendix 1: Restraint Order	689
Appendix 2: Management Receivership Order	695
Appendix 3: Enforcement Receivership Order	699
Appendix 4: Letter of Agreement between Prosecutor and Receiver	703
Appendix 5: Variation of Restraint Order	707
Appendix 6: LSC Funding Arrangements	709
Appendix 7: Application Notice by Defendant seeking a Certificate of Inadequacy	711
Appendix 8: Certificate of Inadequacy	715
Appendix 9: Claim Form (CPR PART 8)	717
Appendix 10: Extract from the Practice Direction on POCA 2002 Parts 5 and 8: Civil Recovery: section III	719
Appendix 11: Extract from the Practice Direction on POCA 2002 Parts 5 and 8: Civil Recovery: section IV	721
Appendix 12: Schedule 6 to POCA 2002 Sections 247 and 257	725
Appendix 13: Draft Restraint, Disclosure and Repatriation Order under POCA	727
Appendix 14: Certificate of Service	733
Appendix 15: Interim Receiving Order under s 246 of POCA 2002	735
Appendix 16: Useful Websites on POCA 2002	743
Appendix 17: Property Freezing Order	745
Appendix 18: Civil Recovery by Consent Order	751
Appendix 19: Guidance to solicitors and applicants seeking Community Legal Service funding for proceedings under the Proceeds of Crime Act 2002 involving the Assets Recovery Agency	755
Appendix 20: Condemnation and Forfeiture of Goods	761
Appendix 21: ARA: Settlement of Civil Recovery and Tax Cases	765
Appendix 22: Guidance by the Secretary of State to the Director of the Assets Recovery Agency	767
Appendix 23: The House of Lords Decision in *Capewell*	769
Index	771

CONTENTS

Table of Cases   lv
Table of Legislation   lxix
List of Abbreviations   ci

1 Setting the Scene

A. Introduction	1.01
B. Why was Confiscation Law Enacted?	1.02
C. The Object of the Confiscation Regime	1.09
D. The Drug Trafficking Act 1994: A Summary	1.11
E. The Criminal Justice Act 1988: A Summary	1.13
F. The Proceeds of Crime Act 2002: A Summary	1.14
G. Agencies responsible for the Enforcement of the Legislation	1.17
(1) The Assets Recovery Agency	1.17
(2) The Crown Prosecution Service	1.23
(3) The Revenue and Customs Prosecutions Office	1.24
(4) HM Revenue and Customs	1.27
(5) The Serious Fraud Office	1.28
(6) The Serious Organised Crime Agency	1.30
(7) The Enforcement Task Force	1.33
(8) Regional Asset Recovery Teams	1.36
H. The International Element	1.37
I. Money Laundering	1.38
J. Recent Developments in Confiscation Law	1.39
(1) Release of restrained funds to meet legal expenses in POCA cases	1.40
(2) Management receivers—the *Capewell* decisions	1.41
(3) Restraint orders: failure to comply with the duty to give full and frank disclosure	1.43
(4) Release of restrained funds to pay unsecured third party creditors	1.44
(5) Confiscation orders: failure to follow the prescribed procedures	1.45
(6) Delay in enforcing confiscation orders	1.47
(7) The international element	1.48
(8) Civil recovery under the Proceeds of Crime Act 2002	1.49
(9) Amendments brought in by the Serious Organised Crime and Police Act 2005	1.50
(10) The Criminal Procedure Rules 2005	1.52

2 Restraint and Charging Orders under the DTA and CJA

A. Introduction	2.01
(1) Purpose of restraint and charging orders	2.02
(2) Freezing orders distinguished	2.03
B. Restraint Orders under the Drug Trafficking Act 1994	2.08
(1) Proceedings have been instituted or an application made	2.09
(2) What are drug trafficking offences?	2.11
(3) Section 25(1)(b): proceedings have not been concluded	2.12
(4) Section 25(1)(c): reasonable cause to believe the defendant has benefited from drug trafficking	2.15
(5) What is drug trafficking?	2.17
(6) Section 25(3): proceedings to be instituted in the future	2.19
C. Restraint Orders under Part VI of the Criminal Justice Act 1988	2.23
(1) Proceedings have been instituted in England and Wales	2.25
(2) Offences to which Part VI of the CJA applies	2.26
(3) Proceedings have not been concluded	2.27
(4) Proceedings may result or have resulted in a conviction for an offence of a relevant description from which the defendant may have benefited	2.33
(5) Benefit	2.34
D. Delay and Proving there is a Risk of Dissipation of Assets	2.40
E. The Standard of Proof on Restraint Order Applications	2.49
F. The Scope and Duration of Restraint Orders	2.50
(1) Parties restrained by the order	2.50
(2) Limited companies	2.53
(3) Property restrained by the order	2.64
(4) Legitimately acquired assets	2.67
(5) Leasehold interests	2.69
(6) Property that is not realisable under the legislation	2.73
(7) Meaning of property	2.74
(8) Overseas assets	2.76
(9) Duration of restraint orders	2.78
G. Terms and Conditions upon which Orders are Made	2.82
(1) Costs and expenses incurred in complying with the order	2.84
(2) Legal expenses	2.89
(3) Businesses	2.91
H. Charging Orders	2.93
(1) What is a charging order?	2.93
(2) When may a charging order be made?	2.94
(3) What property can be charged?	2.97
(4) Protecting the charging order	2.99
(5) Applications to vary or discharge charging orders	2.100
(6) Relationship between restraint and charging orders	2.102

3 Management Receivers under the DTA and CJA

A.	Introduction	3.01
B.	Jurisdiction to Appoint Management Receivers	3.07
C.	Exercising the Discretion to Appoint Management Receivers: The *Capewell* Guidelines	3.14
D.	Status of the Receiver on Appointment	3.18
E.	Powers, Duties and Liabilities of the Receiver	3.22
	(1) Duties and liabilities of the receiver	3.32
	(2) Employment of agents	3.36
	(3) Receiver's accounts	3.39
F.	Remuneration of Receivers	3.43
G.	Discharge of the Receiver	3.61
H.	Taxation and Receivers	3.64

4 Ancillary Orders: Seizure, Disclosure and Repatriation of Assets

A.	Introduction	4.01
B.	Seizure of Assets	4.02
C.	Disclosure Orders	4.06
	(1) Jurisdiction to make the order	4.07
	(2) The problem of self incrimination	4.15
	(3) Form of disclosure orders	4.29
	(4) Disclosure and third parties	4.30
	(5) Disclosure cannot be ordered against the prosecutor	4.31
	(6) Advising the defendant or third party required to disclose	4.33
D.	Repatriation of Assets	4.42
	(1) Jurisdiction to make repatriation orders	4.44
	(2) Form of repatriation order	4.49

5 Applications to Vary or Discharge Restraint Orders made under the DTA and CJA

A.	Introduction	5.01
B.	Applications for the Discharge of the Order	5.02
	(1) On the conclusion of proceedings	5.03
	(2) Procedural irregularities by the prosecutor	5.04
	(3) Failure to give full and frank disclosure	5.07
C.	Applications to Vary the Restraint Order	5.09
	(1) Legal expenses	5.10
	(2) General living expenses	5.20
	(3) Companies and other business entities	5.24
	(4) Burden of proof	5.25

	D. The Principles on which the Court Acts: The 'Legislative Steer'	5.27
	E. The Source of Payment of Legal Fees and General Living Expenses	5.47
	(1) Assets not legitimately acquired	5.48
	(2) Assets that are prosecution exhibits	5.49
	F. Release of Funds after a Confiscation Order has been Made	5.52

6 Enforcement of Restraint and Receivership Orders: Contempt of Court

A. Introduction	6.01
(1) Ways in which breaches may be committed	6.02
(2) Sanctions available for breach of restraint and receivership orders	6.03
B. Procedure on Applications	6.05
(1) Strict compliance necessary	6.05
(2) The burden and standard of proof	6.06
(3) Commencing proceedings	6.07
(4) Contents of the application notice	6.08
(5) The evidence in support of the application	6.11
(6) Proving service of the order	6.12
(7) Proving the breach	6.16
(8) Issuing and serving the application	6.17
(9) The defendant's response	6.19
C. The Hearing	6.21
(1) Preliminary matters	6.21
(2) Procedure at the hearing	6.28
(3) Sentence	6.30
(4) Suspended committals	6.35
(5) Effect of being in contempt	6.36
(6) Purging contempt	6.37
(7) Appeals	6.39

7 Practice and Procedure in the High Court: DTA and CJA Cases

A. Introduction	7.01
B. The Woolf Reforms and the Overriding Objective	7.03
(1) Structure of the Civil Procedure Rules	7.07
(2) Terminology	7.08
(3) Evidence	7.09
C. Procedure on Applications for Restraint Orders	7.13
(1) Allocation of business	7.13
(2) Title of the proceedings	7.14
(3) Preparation of documentation	7.15
(4) The claim form	7.16
(5) The draft order	7.17
(6) The witness statement	7.19
(7) The duty of full and frank disclosure	7.23
(8) What additional matters should be disclosed?	7.25
(9) The consequences of non-disclosure	7.27

D. The Hearing	7.34
(1) Service of the order	7.39
E. Procedure on Applications to Vary or Discharge the Order	7.42
(1) Variation by consent: consulting the prosecutor	7.43
(2) Applying to the court	7.46
(3) Drafting the witness statement or affidavit	7.48
(4) Drafting the order	7.50
(5) Issuing the application	7.51
(6) Service of the application	7.52
(7) Proof of service	7.53
(8) The hearing	7.54
(9) Costs	7.56
(10) After the hearing: drafting and serving the order	7.57
(11) Variation applications by the prosecutor	7.58
(12) Appeals	7.60

8 Restraint and Receivership under the Proceeds of Crime Act 2002

A. Introduction	8.01
(1) Overview	8.02
B. Restraint Orders	8.03
(1) When does POCA apply?	8.03
(2) Conditions for obtaining restraint orders under POCA	8.12
(3) The first condition: criminal investigations	8.13
(4) The second condition: criminal proceedings already started	8.17
(5) The third condition: application for reconsideration to be made	8.23
(6) The fourth condition: reconsideration of benefit	8.27
(7) The fifth condition: reconsideration of available amount	8.29
(8) Making the order	8.33
(9) Exceptions	8.38
(10) Legal expenses	8.40
(11) Ancillary orders	8.50
(12) Restrictions	8.52
(13) Variation and discharge of the order	8.55
(14) Charging orders	8.56
C. Management Receivers	8.57
(1) Powers of management receivers	8.59
(2) Restriction on the use of powers	8.62
D. Powers of the Court and Receiver: the 'Legislative Steer'	8.64
E. Procedure on Applications	8.69
(1) Applications for restraint orders	8.70
(2) The order	8.73
(3) Variation or discharge applications by persons affected by restraint orders	8.75
(4) Variation applications by the person who applied for the order	8.78
(5) Discharge applications by the person who applied for the order	8.80
(6) Receivership proceedings	8.81
(7) The application for appointment	8.82

	(8)	Applications for the conferment of powers on receivers	8.84
	(9)	Applications to vary or discharge receivership orders	8.86
	(10)	Security	8.87
	(11)	Remuneration of receivers	8.89
	(12)	Receiver's accounts	8.90
	(13)	Non-compliance by a receiver	8.91
F.	Provisions as to Hearings and Evidence		8.92
	(1)	Restraint and receivership hearings in the Crown Court	8.92
	(2)	Evidence	8.94
	(3)	Evidence should be in writing	8.96
	(4)	Hearsay evidence	8.99
	(5)	Expert evidence	8.100
	(6)	Disclosure and inspection of documents	8.102
	(7)	Court documents	8.103
	(8)	Service of documents	8.104
	(9)	Service by an alternative method	8.107
	(10)	Service outside the jurisdiction	8.108
	(11)	Proof of service	8.109
	(12)	Consent orders	8.110
	(13)	Slips and omissions	8.111
	(14)	Supply of documents from court records	8.112
	(15)	Preparation of documents	8.114
	(16)	Change of solicitor	8.116
	(17)	Costs	8.117
	(18)	Assessment of costs	8.119
	(19)	Time for complying with orders for costs	8.121
G.	Protecting POCA Restraint Orders in Relation to Real Property		8.122
H.	Enforcing POCA Restraint and Receivership Orders		8.123

9 Preparing for Confiscation Hearings under the DTA

A.	Introduction		9.01
	(1)	When does the DTA apply?	9.01
	(2)	The objectives of DTA proceedings	9.02
B.	Preparing for Crown Court DTA Confiscation Hearings		9.05
	(1)	Confiscation Orders	9.05
	(2)	When are DTA confiscation hearings held?	9.06
	(3)	Offences which constitute drug trafficking offences	9.11
	(4)	Postponement of the proceedings pending further enquiries	9.12
	(5)	Postponing the determination	9.13
	(6)	Postponing DTA hearings: analysis	9.14
	(7)	Conviction, not sentence	9.16
	(8)	What amounts to exceptional circumstances?	9.17
	(9)	No requirement to find further exceptional circumstances	9.33
	(10)	Postponement: absence of the defendant	9.34
	(11)	Six month rule: no retrospective extension	9.35
	(12)	Purpose of postponement: further information	9.36
	(13)	Failure to properly postpone	9.38

(14) Postponements: the case law applied		9.43
(15) Postponement pending appeal		9.45
(16) Application for postponement: procedure		9.47
(17) Sentence		9.49
C. Standard of Proof		9.51
D. Preparatory Steps for a DTA Hearing		9.54
(1) Statements relating to drug trafficking		9.54
(2) Section 11 statements generally		9.55
(3) The prosecutor's statement		9.56
(4) The purpose of the prosecutor's statement		9.57
(5) Form and content of prosecutor's section 11 statements		9.60
(6) When should the prosecutor's statement be served?		9.68
(7) Upon whom should the prosecutor's statement be served?		9.69
(8) The defendant's statement		9.70
(9) Requiring the defendant to respond to the prosecutor's statement		9.71
(10) Drafting the defendant's statement		9.73
(11) Defendant's acceptance conclusive		9.76
(12) The risk of self incrimination		9.80
(13) Further provision of information by the defendant		9.82
(14) Consequences of the defendant failing to respond to the prosecutor's statement		9.86
(15) Valuing the drugs		9.91
(16) Further statements by the prosecutor		9.92
(17) Securing the attendance of witnesses		9.93

10 The DTA Confiscation Hearing

A. Introduction		10.01
(1) Purpose of the hearing		10.01
(2) Procedure leading to the hearing		10.03
(3) The burden and standard of proof		10.04
(4) Basis of plea		10.10
B. Benefit from Drug Trafficking		10.11
(1) Statutory provisions as to benefit		10.16
(2) Payments or other rewards		10.18
(3) Joint apportionment/multiple defendants		10.19
(4) Are drugs seized from the defendant a payment or reward?		10.33
(5) The payment or other reward must be received in connection with drug trafficking		10.37
(6) Section 63(2) DTA		10.39
(7) Knowledge that the payment comes from drug trafficking		10.44
(8) Conspiracies		10.47
(9) Assessing the defendant's proceeds of drug trafficking		10.49
(10) Proceeds not profits		10.52
(11) Joint benefit		10.59

	C.	The Assumptions	10.63
		(1) When the assumptions must not be applied	10.65
		(2) No other assumptions may be made	10.72
		(3) When must the assumptions be applied?	10.73
		(4) At what stage are the assumptions applied?	10.74
		(5) Effect of applying the assumptions	10.75
		(6) Rebutting the assumptions	10.77
		(7) Certificates of benefit	10.79
		(8) A review of the authorities in relation to benefit: DTA and CJA	10.82
		(9) Determining the amount to be realised	10.91
		(10) Burden of proof	10.92
		(11) Hidden assets	10.94
		(12) Meaning of realisable property	10.100
		(13) Property held by the defendant	10.101
		(14) Margin for error	10.103
		(15) Costs of sale	10.104
		(16) Assets jointly held with third parties	10.105
		(17) Matrimonial homes	10.106
		(18) Assets held overseas	10.107
		(19) Gifts	10.108
		(20) When is a gift caught by the Act?	10.109
		(21) Obligations having priority	10.114
		(22) Valuing property	10.116
		(23) Market value	10.121
		(24) Confiscation orders and the forfeiture of drugs	10.122
		(25) Is the court limited to the prosecutor's statement?	10.123
		(26) Public interest immunity	10.124
	D.	Making the Confiscation Order	10.125
		(1) Relationship with forfeiture orders and other legislation	10.126
		(2) Relationship between the confiscation order and the sentence	10.127
		(3) Imprisonment in default	10.133
		(4) Time to pay	10.138
		(5) Orders for the payment of costs	10.143
		(6) Unreasonable delay in enforcement	10.144
		(7) Confiscation orders and the ECHR	10.145
	E.	Confiscation Orders against Defendants who Die or Abscond	10.153
		(1) Post-conviction orders	10.154
		(2) Pre-conviction cases	10.155
		(3) Rules of the Supreme Court	10.158
		(4) Procedural matters	10.164
	F.	Confiscation Hearings under the DTA: Index of Defined Expressions	10.166
	G.	Appeals	10.167
11	**Preparing for Confiscation Hearings under the CJA**		
	A.	Introduction	11.01
		(1) The purpose of CJA confiscation hearings	11.01

B.	Preparing for CJA Confiscation Hearings	11.05
	(1) When does the CJA apply?	11.05
	(2) Preliminary matters	11.07
	(3) When may a CJA confiscation hearing be held?	11.08
C.	Offences of a Relevant Description	11.09
	(1) Relevant criminal conduct	11.11
	(2) When does a defendant benefit from an offence?	11.12
	(3) The standard of proof	11.13
	(4) The burden of proof	11.15
	(5) The requirement to give notice	11.18
	(6) Failure to give notice under the CJA	11.20
	(7) Court may still proceed	11.23
	(8) Qualifying offences under section 72AA	11.24
	(9) The problem of victims	11.28
	(10) The jurisdiction of the Crown Court following committal	11.30
	(11) Offences where the CJA 1988 applies in the magistrates' court	11.32
D.	Postponement of the Proceedings	11.33
	(1) More than one postponement allowable	11.38
	(2) What constitutes exceptional circumstances?	11.39
	(3) Considerations to be applied when postponing confiscation hearings	11.44
	(4) Postponement runs from date of conviction	11.48
	(5) Postponement pending appeal	11.49
	(6) Sentence pending CJA hearing	11.52
E.	Section 73 Prosecutor's Statements	11.55
	(1) Form and content of the statement	11.59
	(2) Service of the statement	11.62
	(3) The defendant's statement	11.63
	(4) Importance of the defendant's reply	11.69
	(5) Defendant's acceptance conclusive	11.71
	(6) Obtaining information from the defendant 'at any time'	11.73
	(7) Prosecutor's acceptance conclusive	11.76
	(8) Consequences of the defendant failing to respond to the prosecutor's statement	11.78
	(9) Further statements by the prosecutor	11.79
	(10) Securing the attendance of witnesses	11.80
	(11) Relationship between disclosure statements and confiscation hearings	11.81
	(12) The risk of self incrimination	11.82

12 The CJA Confiscation Hearing

A.	Introduction	12.01
	(1) Amendments made by the Proceeds of Crime Act 1995	12.01
	(2) Purpose	12.02
	(3) Procedure leading to CJA confiscation hearing	12.03
	(4) Appeal pending	12.04
	(5) When to hold proceedings	12.05

B.	Jurisdiction to Hold a Confiscation Hearing under the CJA	12.07
	(1) The problem of victims	12.09
	(2) Purpose of the hearing	12.10
	(3) Burden and standard of proof	12.11
	(4) Prosecution and defence statements	12.17
	(5) Basis of pleas	12.20
	(6) Multiple defendants and apportionment of benefit	12.23
	(7) Conspiracies	12.24
C.	Benefit	12.25
	(1) Calculating benefit under the CJA	12.25
	(2) Relevant criminal conduct	12.26
	(3) Offences of a relevant description	12.29
	(4) Pecuniary advantage	12.31
	(5) Extended benefit—application of the assumptions	12.44
	(6) When may the assumptions be applied?	12.46
	(7) Qualifying offences	12.47
	(8) Relevant period	12.48
	(9) The assumptions that can be made	12.49
	(10) When the assumptions should not be applied	12.52
	(11) Gifts caught by the Act	12.55
	(12) Defendant does not have to be able to realise gift	12.58
	(13) Distinction between realisable property and gifts	12.61
	(14) Contract services	12.65
	(15) Determining the amount that might be realised	12.66
	(16) Hidden assets	12.67
	(17) Valuing property	12.68
D.	Realisable assets	12.69
	(1) The amount to be recovered	12.69
	(2) Realisable property	12.70
	(3) Assets not restricted to those derived from criminal activity	12.73
	(4) Proceeds, not profits	12.76
	(5) Inflationary adjustment	12.77
	(6) The reducing value of property	12.80
	(7) Costs of sale	12.81
	(8) Abolition of the £10,000 'minimum amount' requirement	12.82
	(9) Imprisonment in default	12.83
	(10) Serving the default sentence does not extinguish the debt	12.87
E.	Confiscation Orders and Sentencing for the Offence	12.88
	(1) Time to pay	12.90
	(2) Power to vary sentence	12.91
	(3) Prosecution costs	12.93
	(4) Third parties and confiscation law	12.94
	(5) Unreasonable delay in enforcement	12.95
	(6) Confiscation and the ECHR	12.96

13	**Variations to Confiscation Orders under the DTA and CJA**	
A.	Introduction	13.01
B.	Applications by the Prosecutor in Drug Trafficking Cases	13.05
	(1) Section 13: where the court has not proceeded under the Act	13.07
	(2) Time limits	13.10
	(3) Section 14: where the court determines the defendant has not benefited from drug trafficking	13.11
	(4) Section 15: revised assessment of the proceeds of drug trafficking	13.14
	(5) Procedure on applications	13.16
C.	Increase in Realisable Property	13.18
	(1) Introduction	13.18
	(2) Practice	13.19
	(3) Unfettered discretion	13.23
	(4) Procedure on applications	13.24
	(5) Certificates of increase: ECHR	13.26
D.	CJA Cases	13.27
	(1) Section 74A: review of cases where the proceeds of crime have not been assessed	13.28
	(2) Section 74B: revision of assessment of the proceeds of crime	13.32
	(3) Section 74C: revision of assessment of amount to be recovered	13.34
	(4) Increase in realisable property	13.35
E.	Applications by the Defendant for a Decrease in the Confiscation Order	13.36
	(1) Certificates of inadequacy	13.36
	(2) Burden and standard of proof	13.38
	(3) The Crown Court stage	13.40
	(4) Not a route to appeal	13.41
	(5) Assets difficult to realise	13.54
	(6) Certificates of inadequacy: procedure	13.55
	(7) Court must give its reasons	13.57
	(8) Certificate of inadequacy and legitimate expectation	13.58
14	**Preparing for Confiscation Hearings under POCA**	
A.	Introduction	14.01
	(1) The evolution of confiscation hearings	14.01
	(2) When do POCA confiscation hearings have to be held?	14.06
B.	Confiscation in the Magistrates' Court	14.07
	(1) Section 70: committal by a magistrates' court	14.09
	(2) The circumstances where a magistrates' court may commit	14.12
	(3) The discretion to commit	14.14
	(4) Committal: practice and procedure	14.22
C.	The Guiding Principles of Confiscation under POCA	14.24
	(1) If ss 6(1)–(3) are satisfied, how must the court proceed?	14.24
	(2) How is 'criminal lifestyle' defined?	14.25
	(3) What are 'lifestyle offences'?	14.26
	(4) 'Criminal lifestyle' and relevant benefit of not less than £5000	14.30
	(5) How is 'relevant benefit' defined?	14.31

	(6)	Criminal conduct and benefit	14.33
	(7)	General criminal conduct	14.34
	(8)	Particular criminal conduct	14.35
	(9)	The relationship between general and particular conduct	14.36
	(10)	When does a defendant's conduct form part of his criminal activity?	14.37
	(11)	When does a person benefit from criminal conduct?	14.38
	(12)	Transitional provisions	14.40
D.	Postponement of POCA Confiscation Hearings		14.45
	(1)	What is the 'permitted period'?	14.47
	(2)	Date of conviction	14.48
	(3)	Further postponements	14.49
	(4)	Postponement beyond two years	14.50
	(5)	Who may apply for a postponement?	14.56
	(6)	The effect of the court failing to follow the postponement provisions	14.57
	(7)	Postponement pending appeal	14.59
	(8)	Sentencing	14.60
	(9)	Power to vary sentence	14.62
E.	Preparatory Steps for a POCA Hearing		14.63
	(1)	Section 16 statements of information	14.63
	(2)	The purpose of s 16 statements	14.65
	(3)	The content of s 16 statements	14.67
	(4)	A duty of full and frank disclosure?	14.71
	(5)	When should the s 16 statement be served?	14.72
	(6)	Disclosure evidence inadmissible	14.74
	(7)	Upon whom should the prosecutor's statement be served?	14.75
	(8)	The defendant's statement	14.77
	(9)	Defendant's acceptance conclusive	14.81
	(10)	Failure to respond by the defendant	14.83
	(11)	Consequences of the defendant failing to respond to the prosecutor's statement	14.87
	(12)	The problem of self incrimination	14.92
	(13)	Further provision of information by the defendant	14.96
	(14)	Further protection against self incrimination	14.101
	(15)	Prosecutor's acceptance conclusive	14.102
	(16)	Failure to provide the information ordered	14.103
	(17)	Further statements by the prosecutor	14.104
	(18)	Securing the attendance of witnesses	14.106
	(19)	Joint control of assets and multiple defendants	14.107
	(20)	Expert evidence	14.108
	(21)	Service of documents	14.109

15 The POCA Confiscation Hearing

A.	Introduction		15.01
B.	A Mandatory Regime		15.03
	(1)	Confiscation orders made by magistrates' courts	15.05
	(2)	Basis of pleas	15.06

	C. The Burden and Standard of Proof	15.07
	D. The Defendant's Benefit	15.11
	(1) General criminal conduct	15.13
	(2) Rule against double counting	15.14
	(3) Particular criminal conduct	15.16
	(4) Recent case law	15.17
	(5) Proceeds, not profits	15.18
	(6) Value of property obtained from criminal conduct	15.19
	E. The Assumptions: Section 10	15.20
	(1) The four assumptions	15.24
	(2) The 'relevant day'	15.25
	(3) The 'date of conviction'	15.27
	(4) When the assumptions do not apply	15.28
	F. The Recoverable Amount	15.31
	(1) Recoverable amount: victims	15.33
	(2) The 'available amount'	15.34
	(3) Market value	15.38
	(4) Hidden assets	15.45
	(5) Court must give reasons	15.46
	(6) Costs of sale	15.47
	G. Tainted Gifts	15.48
	(1) When is a gift tainted?	15.49
	(2) Gifts and their recipients	15.55
	(3) Value of tainted gifts	15.59
	H. Time for Payment	15.61
	(1) Imprisonment in default	15.65
	(2) Interest on unpaid sums	15.69
	(3) Unreasonable delay in enforcement	15.70
	I. The Effect of a Confiscation Order on Sentence and the Court's Other Powers	15.71
	(1) The relationship between the confiscation order and compensation	15.72
	(2) The importance of following the provisions of POCA	15.74
	(3) Orders for the payment of costs	15.76
	J. Confiscation and the ECHR	15.77
	K. Appeals	15.79
	L. Interpretation: Confiscation and POCA	15.81
	M. Steps to Confiscation: A Summary	15.82
16	**Reconsideration of Confiscation Orders under POCA and the Defendant who Absconds**	
	A. Introduction	16.01
	B. Reconsideration of Case where no Confiscation Order was Originally Made	16.02
	(1) Time limit	16.05

	(2) How are the 'relevant date' and the 'date of conviction' defined?	16.06
	(3) The status of previous orders of the court and compensation	16.08
	(4) Procedure: applications under s 19 of POCA	16.09
	(5) Statements of information	16.10
C.	Reconsideration of Benefit where no Confiscation Order was Originally Made	16.11
	(1) The first condition	16.12
	(2) The second condition	16.13
	(3) The status of previous orders of the court	16.17
D.	Compensation	16.18
	(1) Procedure: applications under s 20 of POCA	16.19
	(2) Statements of information	16.20
E.	Where a Confiscation Order has been Made: Reconsideration of Benefit	16.21
	(1) When is the relevant time?	16.27
	(2) What is the relevant amount?	16.28
	(3) When is the date of conviction?	16.29
F.	The Assumptions	16.30
	(1) Revised benefit and relationship with the recoverable amount	16.31
	(2) The status of previous orders of the court	16.34
	(3) Exception to rule	16.35
	(4) Changes in the value of money	16.36
	(5) Procedure: applications under ss 19, 20, or 21 of the Act	16.37
G.	Statements of Information	16.38
H.	Increase in Available Amount	16.39
	(1) Where a confiscation order has been made: reconsideration of the available amount	16.39
	(2) What is the 'relevant amount' under s 22?	16.44
	(3) Changes in the value of money	16.46
	(4) Procedure: applications under s 22 of the Act	16.47
	(5) Certificates of increase: ECHR	16.48
I.	Inadequacy of Available Amount	16.49
	(1) Variation of the confiscation order	16.49
	(2) Inadequacy of available amount in bankruptcy cases	16.54
	(3) Procedure: variation of confiscation order due to inadequacy of available amount	16.55
	(4) Not a route to appeal	16.56
	(5) Burden and standard of proof	16.64
	(6) Assets difficult to realise	16.65
	(7) Court must give its reasons	16.66
	(8) Certificate of inadequacy and legitimate expectation	16.67
	(9) Inadequacy of available amount: discharge of confiscation order	16.68
	(10) Under s 24 what are 'specified reasons'?	16.70
	(11) Small amount outstanding: discharge of confiscation order	16.72
	(12) Procedure: application by Justices' Chief Executive to discharge a confiscation order	16.74
	(13) Procedure where the Crown Court discharges a confiscation order	16.76

J.	Defendants who Abscond or Die		16.77
	(1) Introduction		16.77
	(2) The defendant who dies		16.78
	(3) The defendant who absconds post-conviction		16.79
	(4) Procedure		16.80
	(5) The defendant who absconds pre-conviction		16.84
	(6) Two year rule		16.85
	(7) Procedure		16.86
	(8) What happens if the defendant later returns?		16.89
	(9) Variation and discharge of orders under s 28		16.90
	(10) Variation of order		16.91
	(11) What is the relevant period?		16.93
	(12) Procedure on applications for variation made by a former absconder		16.94
	(13) Powers of the court		16.96
	(14) Discharge of confiscation order where the defendant has absconded		16.98
	(15) Discharge of order: undue delay or proceedings not continuing		16.99
	(16) Procedure: application for discharge made by a former absconder		16.102
	(17) Compensation: confiscation order made against absconder		16.105
	(18) Increase in term of imprisonment in default		16.108

17 Enforcement of Confiscation Orders under the CJA, the DTA, and POCA

A.	Introduction		17.01
B.	Voluntary Satisfaction by the Defendant		17.03
C.	Enforcement Receivers under the DTA and CJA		17.13
	(1) DTA cases: meaning of 'a confiscation order is not satisfied'		17.18
	(2) CJA cases: meaning of 'proceedings have not been concluded'		17.19
	(3) Meaning of 'subject to appeal'		17.20
	(4) Powers of enforcement receivers		17.27
	(5) Ancillary orders		17.29
	(6) Procedure on applications		17.31
	(7) The evidence in support		17.33
	(8) The defendant's response to the application		17.36
	(9) Third parties		17.40
	(10) Advising third parties served with an application to appoint an enforcement receiver		17.44
	(11) The court's order		17.49
	(12) The matrimonial home: rights of spouses		17.50
	(13) Status of the receiver on appointment		17.51
	(14) Realisation of property		17.52
	(15) Remuneration of enforcement receivers		17.53
	(16) Dealing with the proceeds of realisation		17.57
	(17) Discharge of the receiver		17.61
D.	The Powers of the Magistrates' Court		17.62
	(1) Distress warrants		17.64
	(2) Third party debt orders		17.65
	(3) Warrants of commitment		17.66
	(4) Delay by the prosecutor in enforcing the confiscation order		17.78

		E. Enforcement under POCA 2002	17.87
		(1) Enforcement receivers	17.88
		(2) Powers of enforcement receivers	17.89
		(3) Director's receivers	17.92
		(4) Powers of Director's receivers	17.95
		(5) Procedure on applications for the appointment of enforcement receivers under POCA	17.96
		(6) Seized money	17.104
		(7) Implementing the default sentence: the Director not the enforcing authority	17.109
		(8) Implementing the default sentence: the Director appointed as the enforcement authority	17.110
18	**The Insolvent Defendant**		
	A.	Introduction	18.01
	B.	The Position under the DTA and CJA	18.02
	C.	Insolvency under POCA 2002	18.12
		(1) Winding up of companies	18.14
		(2) Floating charges	18.16
		(3) Limited liability partnerships	18.17
		(4) Protection of insolvency practitioners	18.18
	D.	Interaction Between Restraint and Insolvency Proceedings	18.19
	E.	Conclusion	18.23
19	**Civil Recovery: Property Freezing Orders; Interim Receivers; and Legal Expenses**		
	A.	Introduction	19.01
	B.	Overview in Relation to Civil Recovery	19.06
		(1) A power vested only in the ARA	19.07
		(2) Proceedings even on acquittal	19.08
		(3) Standard of proof	19.10
		(4) Civil proceedings	19.14
		(5) The distinction between recovery proceedings and confiscation proceedings	19.16
		(6) Civil recovery in the High Court: proceedings for recovery orders	19.18
		(7) Definitions within POCA	19.19
		(8) Definition of 'property'	19.20
		(9) Property obtained through unlawful conduct	19.24
		(10) Unlawful conduct	19.27
		(11) How is 'recoverable property' defined?	19.29
		(12) How is 'associated property' defined?	19.30
		(13) The tracing of property	19.34
		(14) Mixed property	19.35
		(15) Accruing profits	19.36
		(16) Granting interests	19.37

C.	Property Freezing Orders	19.38
	(1) Introduction	19.38
	(2) Definition	19.42
	(3) PFO without notice	19.43
	(4) Factors giving rise to the risk of dissipation	19.44
	(5) Duty of full and frank disclosure	19.46
	(6) Criteria for granting a Property Freezing Order	19.53
	(7) Variation and setting aside of the Property Freezing Order	19.57
	(8) Exclusions and variations	19.60
	(9) The legislative steer	19.65
	(10) Restriction on proceedings and remedies	19.68
	(11) Further SOCPA amendments	19.72
	(12) Ancillary orders	19.75
	(13) Undertakings for damages	19.76
	(14) Draft order	19.77
	(15) PFOs: practice and procedure	19.78
	(16) Exclusions when making a PFO: legal costs	19.87
	(17) Applications to vary or set aside a PFO	19.88
D.	Interim Receiving Orders	19.91
	(1) Application for an interim receiving order	19.92
	(2) Loss of power to investigate	19.95
	(3) Purpose and conditions	19.97
	(4) 'Good arguable case'	19.99
	(5) Application for an interim receiving order: practice and procedure	19.101
	(6) Interim receiving order made before commencement of claim for civil recovery	19.105
	(7) Duty of full and frank disclosure	19.106
	(8) The need for expedition	19.107
	(9) The legislative steer	19.108
	(10) The insolvent respondent	19.115
	(11) Insolvency and IROs	19.120
	(12) A stand alone claim	19.121
	(13) Powers of the High Court	19.123
	(14) Functions of an interim receiver	19.124
	(15) Contents of the order	19.126
	(16) Restrictions on dealing with property	19.133
	(17) Contents of the order in terms of reporting by the receiver	19.137
	(18) Protection against self incrimination	19.138
	(19) Protection for the receiver	19.139
	(20) Applications to clarify the receiver's powers	19.140
	(21) Applications for directions	19.141
	(22) The role and independence of the interim receiver	19.142
	(23) Power to vary or set aside	19.147
	(24) Application to vary or discharge an interim receiving order: practice and procedure	19.150
	(25) Non-specified recoverable property	19.153
	(26) Exclusion of property which is not recoverable	19.154
	(27) Exclusion of property to cover legal expenses	19.156

	(28)	Interim receiver's expenses	19.157
	(29)	Interim receiverships over land	19.159
	(30)	Restriction on exisiting proceedings and rights	19.162
	(31)	Reporting	19.167
	(32)	Compensation	19.170
	(33)	Time limit for compensation application	19.173
	(34)	The test the court should apply	19.175
E.	Legal Expenses in Civil Recovery Proceedings		19.177
	(1)	Introduction	19.177
	(2)	Background to the new provisions	19.189
	(3)	The new regulations	19.191
	(4)	Legal expenses at the conclusion of proceedings	19.192
	(5)	Expenses to be assessed if not agreed	19.195
	(6)	Two month time limit	19.196
	(7)	Practice and procedure	19.197
	(8)	Legal expenses at the commencement of proceedings	19.201
	(9)	Considerations for the court	19.205
	(10)	Practice and procedure: Part 3 of the regulations	19.209
	(11)	The Director's response	19.213
	(12)	Release of an interim payment	19.216
	(13)	Evidence for the purpose of meeting legal costs	19.218
	(14)	Ongoing opportunity	19.219
	(15)	Statement of assets	19.220
	(16)	Legal expenses following the making of a recovery order	19.222
	(17)	Part 4 of the regulations	19.224
	(18)	Other assets	19.225
	(19)	Costs judge assessment	19.226
	(20)	Basis for assessment of legal expenses	19.227
	(21)	Civil legal aid	19.234

20 Civil Recovery: Recovery Orders; Pensions; and the ECHR

A.	Introduction		20.01
	(1)	The Assets Recovery Agency	20.03
	(2)	The reduction of crime	20.07
B.	Recovery Orders		20.08
	(1)	Introduction	20.08
	(2)	Financial threshold	20.10
	(3)	Claims for a recovery order: practice and procedure	20.11
	(4)	Procedure the ARA must follow	20.14
	(5)	Settlement agreements	20.15
	(6)	Consent orders	20.16
	(7)	Summary judgment	20.20
	(8)	What the Director needs to prove	20.29
	(9)	What is a 'trustee for civil recovery'?	20.39
	(10)	What are the functions of the trustee?	20.41
	(11)	Powers of the trustee for civil recovery	20.43
	(12)	The 12 year limitation	20.45

(13)	Rights of pre-emption	20.46
(14)	The vesting of recoverable property	20.50
(15)	Associated and joint property	20.51
(16)	'Excepted joint owner'	20.53
(17)	Agreements about associated and joint property	20.55
(18)	How is the amount calculated?	20.58
(19)	Associated and joint property: default of agreement	20.63
(20)	'Interest'	20.65
(21)	Exclusions, exemptions and exceptions	20.66
(22)	Where the court must not make a recovery order	20.68
(23)	Related property	20.70
(24)	Forfeiture of cash	20.74
(25)	Victims of criminal conduct	20.75
(26)	Recovery orders and confiscation orders	20.76
(27)	Supplementary provisions to s 278	20.78
(28)	Declaration of exemption	20.80
(29)	Other exemptions	20.83
(30)	Exemptions or exceptions to property being 'recoverable'	20.85
(31)	Insolvency and recovery orders	20.93
(32)	Public interest immunity	20.96

C. The Impact of the European Convention on Human Rights on Civil Recovery — 20.99

(1)	Article 1—interference with property	20.100
(2)	Article 6(1)	20.101
(3)	Article 6(2)	20.102
(4)	Article 7—civil proceedings	20.104
(5)	Article 7—a criminal penalty?	20.108
(6)	Article 7—retrospectivity	20.115
(7)	Article 8	20.118

D. Pension Schemes — 20.119

(1)	Introduction	20.119
(2)	What does a pension scheme mean within this part of the Act?	20.123
(3)	'Trustees or managers'	20.125
(4)	The Proceeds of Crime Act 2002 (Recovery from Pension Schemes) Regulations 2003	20.126
(5)	Calculation and verification of the value of rights under pension schemes	20.127
(6)	Calculation and verification of the value of rights under destination arrangements	20.132
(7)	Approval of manner of calculation and verification of the value of rights	20.133
(8)	Time for compliance with a pension recovery order	20.135
(9)	Costs of the trustees or managers of the pension scheme	20.137
(10)	Consequential adjustment of liabilities under pension schemes	20.138
(11)	Consent order: pensions	20.141

21 Recovery and Seizure of Cash under POCA

A. Introduction	21.01
(1) The DTA	21.03
(2) The POCA regime	21.05
(3) Civil proceedings	21.10
B. The Seizure and Forfeiture of Cash	21.12
(1) Preliminary matters	21.12
(2) The circumstances in which cash may be seized	21.13
(3) The minimum amount that may be seized: £1000	21.14
(4) Does the minimum amount need to be in the possession of a single person?	21.15
(5) The meaning of 'cash'	21.17
(6) How is 'unlawful conduct' defined?	21.20
(7) Does the 'unlawful conduct' have to be specified?	21.21
(8) How is 'recoverable property' defined?	21.25
(9) The tracing of property	21.28
(10) Mixed property	21.29
(11) Property that is not 'recoverable'	21.30
(12) The re-seizure of cash	21.33
(13) Ongoing criminal proceedings	21.34
C. Practice and Procedure	21.35
(1) The initial enquiry	21.35
(2) Procedure prior to the first hearing and venue	21.39
(3) The first detention hearing for the seized cash	21.43
(4) Unattended despatches	21.47
(5) The 48 hour rule	21.51
(6) The test the court will apply at further detention hearings	21.56
(7) Interest	21.58
(8) Interest—What does 'at the first opportunity' mean?	21.60
(9) Release of money over which no suspicion attaches	21.64
D. Continued Detention Hearings: Practice	21.65
(1) Form A	21.65
(2) Form B	21.70
(3) Form C	21.72
(4) Service of documents	21.73
(5) Procedure at the continued detention hearing	21.74
(6) What if the correct forms have not been served or the proper procedure not followed?	21.75
(7) Insolvency and further detention hearings	21.83
(8) Early release of the cash—to person from whom the cash was seized	21.84
(9) Form D	21.87
(10) Applications for early release by victims or other owners	21.91
(11) Section 301(3): victims of unlawful conduct	21.94
(12) Form E: Order for release under s 301(3)	21.95
(13) Section 301(4): third party applications/other owners	21.96

(14)	Objection to release under s 301(4) from the person from whom the cash was seized	21.97
(15)	Form F: Order for release under s 301(4)	21.98
(16)	Joinder	21.99
(17)	Applications for the return of the cash: standard of proof	21.100
(18)	Can officers agree to the release of cash?	21.102
(19)	Transfer of proceedings	21.103
(20)	Transfer: what test is to be applied?	21.104

E. Applications for Forfeiture of Detained Cash — 21.105
   (1) Forfeiture proceedings — 21.105
   (2) Form G — 21.106
   (3) Effect of lodging an application — 21.112

F. The Hearing — 21.113
   (1) Hearing for Directions — 21.113
   (2) What type of Directions may be ordered? — 21.116
   (3) The forfeiture hearing — 21.119
   (4) Procedure at hearings made on complaint — 21.120
   (5) Order of evidence and speeches — 21.124
   (6) Matters to be sworn under oath — 21.128

G. Rules of Evidence — 21.129
   (1) Burden and standard of proof — 21.129
   (2) Are previous convictions admissible? — 21.132
   (3) Is there a need for direct evidence of the unlawful conduct? — 21.137
   (4) The drawing of inferences and illustrative cases — 21.138
   (5) Hearsay in civil cases — 21.143
   (6) Lies told by the defendant — 21.148
   (7) Mass Spec expert reports — 21.151
   (8) Record of proceedings — 21.159
   (9) Form H: order for forfeiture — 21.160
   (10) Sensitive evidence — 21.161
   (11) Joint owners — 21.163

H. Costs and Compensation — 21.165
   (1) Costs under s 64 of the Magistrates' Courts Act 1980 — 21.171
   (2) Legal Services Commission funding — 21.174
   (3) May funds be released from the detained cash to fund continued detention and forfeiture applications? — 21.178
   (4) Compensation — 21.179
   (5) Application for compensation — 21.186

I. Appeals — 21.187
   (1) Appeals against forfeiture — 21.187
   (2) Can the 30 day period for the date of the appeal be extended? — 21.191
   (3) Funding the appeal — 21.192
   (4) Costs in appeal proceedings — 21.193
   (5) Judicial review — 21.194

J.	Searches and Seizure of Cash	21.195
	(1) Cash on premises	21.196
	(2) The minimum amount: £1000	21.197
	(3) The definition of 'cash'	21.199
	(4) Cash on the suspect	21.201
	(5) 'Unlawful conduct'	21.204
	(6) Safeguards for the new search powers	21.205
	(7) Report on exercise of powers	21.210
	(8) The Code of Practice	21.211
	(9) Procedure at hearings	21.215
K.	Compatability of the Forfeiture Provisions with the ECHR	21.217

22 Third Parties and Confiscation Law

A.	Introduction	22.01
B.	Restraint Orders	22.03
	(1) Jurisdiction to bind third parties	22.03
	(2) Obligations of third parties	22.07
	(3) Rights of third parties	22.11
	(4) Reasonable costs and expenses	22.12
	(5) Restraint orders and the wife of the defendant	22.16
	(6) Living expenses	22.19
	(7) Legal expenses	22.21
	(8) Restraint orders and limited companies	22.22
	(9) The corporate veil	22.23
	(10) Prosecutor does not have to give an undertaking in damages	22.29
	(11) Unsecured third party creditors	22.30
	(12) Use of assets	22.57
	(13) What remedies are available to a person who denies the defendant has an interest in a restrained asset?	22.58
C.	Confiscation Orders	22.59
	(1) Receivership proceedings	22.62
	(2) The right to be given notice of the proceedings	22.64
	(3) The right to make representations	22.65
	(4) What steps should be taken on behalf of the third party on receipt of an application to appoint an enforcement receiver?	22.67
	(5) Seeking an adjournment	22.68
	(6) Powers of the court and receiver in relation to third parties under POCA	22.70
	(7) The role of the defendant	22.73
	(8) The hearing	22.74
	(9) The court's order	22.75
D.	Specific Third Party Claims	22.79
	(1) Wives and cohabitees	22.79
	(2) The matrimonial home	22.85
	(3) *Re Norris* and *HM Customs v MCA*	22.88
	(4) Developing matrimonial home case law	22.100

E.	Property Adjustment Orders	22.119
	(1) Property adjustment orders: does POCA oust the MCA?	22.125
	(2) Matrimonial homes where the conditions set out in *Re Norris* and *HM Customs and Excise v MCA* do not apply	22.127
	(3) Property should form part of the confiscation order	22.128
	(4) Equitable interests in the matrimonial home	22.131
	(5) Trusts	22.133
	(6) Application of sums and third parties	22.134
	(7) Banks	22.135
	(8) Banks: No duty of care	22.141
	(9) The insolvent defendant: the position of the trustee in bankruptcy	22.146
	(10) POCA and the insolvent defendant	22.148
F.	Conclusion	22.150

23 Investigations

A.	Introduction	23.01
B.	A Short History of the Legislative Provisions	23.03
C.	Defining Investigations	23.06
D.	Courts and Judges having Jurisdiction to Make Orders	23.07
	(1) Judges	23.07
	(2) Courts	23.09
E.	Production Orders	23.10
	(1) Jurisdiction to make the order	23.10
	(2) Requirements for making an order	23.12
	(3) Legal professional privilege	23.16
	(4) Excluded material	23.19
	(5) Government departments	23.20
	(6) Procedure on applications: Crown Court	23.21
	(7) Procedure on applications: High Court	23.25
	(8) Who may apply for a production order?	23.29
	(9) Complying with the order	23.31
	(10) Failure to comply with production orders	23.36
F.	Search and Seizure Warrants	23.39
G.	Judicial Discretion	23.40
H.	Overseas Investigations	23.46
I.	Customer Information Orders	23.48
	(1) Requirements for making orders	23.51
	(2) Discharge and variation	23.53
	(3) Offences	23.54
J.	Account Monitoring Orders	23.55
K.	Disclosure Orders	23.58
L.	Statements Made in Response to Orders	23.60
M.	Code of Practice	23.61

N. Financial Reporting Orders under the Serious Organised
   Crime and Police Act 2005 … 23.62
   (1) Jurisdiction to make the order … 23.63
   (2) Offences to which s 76 applies … 23.65
   (3) Duration of orders … 23.67
   (4) Effect of a financial reporting order … 23.68
   (5) Variation and revocation of financial reporting orders … 23.72
   (6) Failure to comply with financial reporting orders … 23.73

24 Appeals

A. Introduction … 24.01
   (1) Appeals distinguished … 24.02
   (2) Transfer of powers from the High Court to the Crown Court … 24.04

B. The Criminal Procedure Rules … 24.05

C. Restraint Order Appeals: Practice and Procedure … 24.06
   (1) Appeals to the Court of Appeal from restraint orders under
       the DTA and CJA … 24.06
   (2) Procedure for appeals from the High Court under the DTA and CJA … 24.07
   (3) Appeals to the Court of Appeal from restraint orders under POCA … 24.13
   (4) Leave … 24.19
   (5) Hearing the appeal … 24.23
   (6) The Proceeds of Crime Act 2002 (Appeals under Part 2) Order 2003 … 24.26
   (7) Restraint orders under POCA: appeal to the House of Lords … 24.27

D. Receivership Order Appeals: Practice and Procedure … 24.29
   (1) Appeals to the Court of Appeal in receivership proceedings under
       the DTA and CJA … 24.29
   (2) Appeals to the Court of Appeal in receivership proceedings under POCA … 24.30
   (3) Leave … 24.36
   (4) Hearing the appeal … 24.40
   (5) The Proceeds of Crime Act 2002 (Appeals under Part 2) Order 2003 … 24.43
   (6) The powers of the Court of Appeal on receipt of an appeal
       against a receivership order … 24.44
   (7) Appeal to House of Lords … 24.45
   (8) Appeals by financial investigators under POCA … 24.47

E. Confiscation Order Appeals: Practice and Procedure … 24.50
   (1) Appeals in confiscation order cases … 24.50
   (2) Procedure for confiscation order appeals under the DTA and CJA … 24.54
   (3) A right of appeal against the confiscation order in all cases … 24.55
   (4) Appeals involving the judge's discretion … 24.57
   (5) Attorney-General's appeal … 24.58
   (6) Confiscation orders: the Crown Court 'slip rule' … 24.59
   (7) Appeals in confiscation order cases to the Criminal Cases
       Review Commission … 24.61
   (8) Fresh evidence … 24.63
   (9) Confiscation appeals under POCA … 24.64
   (10) Leave … 24.66

		(11) Appeal by the prosecutor or the Director of ARA	24.67
		(12) Appeal by the prosecutor or the Director of ARA: the Court of Appeal's powers	24.70
		(13) The steps the court must take	24.73
		(14) Corresponding provisions	24.77
		(15) Appeal by the prosecutor or the Director of ARA: appeal to the House of Lords by either the defendant or the prosecutor	24.78
		(16) Powers of the House of Lords in such circumstances	24.81
		(17) Where the Crown Court proceeds afresh	24.82
	F.	The Proceeds of Crime Act 2002 (Appeals under Part 2) Order 2003	24.85
		(1) Practice and procedure: appeals to the Court of Appeal	24.85
		(2) Initiating procedure	24.86
		(3) Disposal of groundless applications for leave to appeal	24.88
		(4) Preparation of case for hearing	24.90
		(5) Right of defendant to be present	24.92
		(6) Rules of evidence in the Court of Appeal	24.93
		(7) General provisions	24.96
		(8) References to the European Court of Justice	24.97
	G.	Appeals against Forfeiture Orders	24.98
		(1) Forfeiture appeals under POCA from the magistrates' court	24.98
		(2) Procedure on forfeiture appeals under POCA	24.104
		(3) Appeals in condemnation cases from the magistrates' court	24.106
		(4) Appeal from the magistrates' court to the High Court by way of case stated	24.109
	H.	Appeals under Part 6 of POCA: Revenue Functions	24.111
	I.	The Criminal Cases Review Commission	24.113
	J.	Appeals against Findings of Contempt of Court	24.115
		(1) Appeals in cases of findings of contempt of court by the High Court	24.115
		(2) Appeals in cases of findings of contempt of court by the Crown Court	24.118
	K.	Thumbnail Guide to the Appeal Provisions within the Criminal Procedure Rules	24.120
25	**The International Element**		
	A.	Introduction	25.01
	B.	International Assistance under the DTA and CJA	25.03
		(1) Designated countries and territories	25.05
		(2) Appropriate authorities	25.06
		(3) Obtaining restraint orders in the UK on behalf of designated countries	25.07
	C.	Procedure on Applications for Restraint Orders in DTA and CJA Cases	25.16
		(1) The letter of request	25.17
		(2) Evidence in support	25.19
		(3) Ancillary orders	25.24
		(4) Applications for the variation and discharge of orders	25.25

D.	Enforcement of External Confiscation Orders	25.26
	(1) Registration of the order	25.27
	(2) Procedure for registration	25.30
	(3) Evidence in support of the application for registration	25.32
	(4) The application	25.33
	(5) Applications to vary or set aside registration	25.35
	(6) Register of orders	25.36
	(7) Effect of registration	25.37
	(8) Variation, satisfaction and discharge of registered order	25.38
	(9) Application of the proceeds of realisation	25.39
E.	Enforcement of DTA and CJA Confiscation Orders Overseas	25.40
F.	Reciprocal Enforcement with Scotland and Northern Ireland	25.43
	(1) Scotland	25.44
	(2) Northern Ireland	25.45
G.	Co-operation under POCA 2002	25.46
	(1) Action to be taken on receipt of an external request	25.49
	(2) Powers of the Crown Court to make restraint orders	25.50
	(3) Ancillary orders	25.54
	(4) Application, discharge and variation of restraint orders	25.55
	(5) Appeals	25.57
	(6) Hearsay evidence	25.58
	(7) Management receivers	25.59
	(8) Applications to give effect to external orders	25.60
	(9) Registration of the order	25.65
	(10) Appeals	25.67
	(11) Enforcement of the order	25.68
	(12) Procedure on applications	25.69
H.	Enforcement of POCA Confiscation Orders in Different Parts of the UK	25.70
	(1) Civil Recovery proceedings	25.71

26 Money Laundering

A.	Introduction	26.01
	(1) What is money laundering?	26.05
	(2) Why criminalise money laundering?	26.06
	(3) How is money laundered?	26.07
B.	Money Laundering under the Proceeds of Crime Act 2002	26.11
	(1) Introduction	26.11
	(2) Mens rea: 'suspects'	26.13
	(3) Inchoate offences	26.15
	(4) Conspiracy	26.16
	(5) The first money laundering offence: concealing etc	26.25
	(6) 'Criminal property'	26.29
	(7) 'Criminal conduct'	26.31
	(8) Defences to section 327(1)	26.33

	(9)	Threshold amounts	26.37
	(10)	The second money laundering offence: arrangements	26.43
	(11)	Defences to section 328(1)	26.45
	(12)	The third money laundering offence: acquisition, use and possession	26.51
	(13)	Defences to section 329(1)	26.53
	(14)	Maximum penalty	26.57
	(15)	Disclosure under s 338	26.58
	(16)	Disclosure to a nominated officer	26.62
	(17)	Appropriate consent	26.64
	(18)	'Notice period'	26.66
	(19)	'Moratorium period'	26.67
	(20)	Consent from a nominated officer	26.69
	(21)	'The prohibited act'	26.72
	(22)	Protected disclosures	26.73
	(23)	Form and manner of disclosures	26.76
	(24)	Mode of trial	26.78
C.	Money Laundering Offences under the DTA 1994 and CJA 1988		26.79
	(1)	Introduction: the proceeds of drug trafficking	26.79
	(2)	Concealing or transferring the proceeds of drug trafficking	26.81
	(3)	Assisting another person to retain the benefit of drug trafficking	26.84
	(4)	Disclosure of transactions to a constable	26.90
	(5)	Drafting the indictment	26.92
	(6)	Defences	26.95
	(7)	Disclosures by persons in employment	26.97
	(8)	Acquisition, possession, or use of the proceeds of drug trafficking	26.98
	(9)	Defences: adequate consideration	26.100
	(10)	Other defences	26.103
	(11)	Laundering the proceeds of other crimes under the Criminal Justice Act	26.104
	(12)	Meaning of criminal conduct	26.106
	(13)	Sentencing for money laundering offences	26.107
	(14)	Mode of trial decisions	26.112
D.	The EC Money Laundering Directives		26.113
	(1)	UK legislation to implement the Directive	26.116
	(2)	The Money Laundering Regulations	26.117
	(3)	The new Regulations	26.119
	(4)	Relevant businesses	26.126
	(5)	Other amendments	26.127
	(6)	The Third European Money Laundering Directive	26.128

27 Disclosure of Suspicious Transactions

A.	Introduction		27.01
	(1)	Background	27.05
B.	Disclosure of Suspicious Transactions under POCA		27.10
	(1)	Failure to disclose: regulated sector	27.10
	(2)	Businesses in the regulated sector	27.14
	(3)	Excluded businesses	27.17

	(4)	Defences to failing to disclose in the regulated sector	27.19
	(5)	What tests should the court apply?	27.26
	(6)	Legal privilege	27.29
	(7)	'Suspects'	27.32
	(8)	Failure to disclose: nominated officers in the regulated sector	27.33
	(9)	Defence available	27.38
	(10)	Considerations for the court	27.39
	(11)	Failure to disclose: other nominated officers	27.40
	(12)	Protected disclosures	27.41
	(13)	Defence available	27.42
C.	Professional Legal Advisers		27.43
	(1)	Introduction	27.43
	(2)	*Bowman v Fels*: the facts	27.45
	(3)	*Bowman v Fels*: the issues	27.47
	(4)	*Bowman v Fels*: the judgment	27.50
	(5)	*Bowman v Fels*: conclusion	27.57
	(6)	Consensual resolution in a litigious context	27.60
	(7)	'POCA Clauses'	27.63
	(8)	Protection for judges	27.69
D.	Suspicious Activity Reports: 'SARS'		27.70
	(1)	Review	27.70
	(2)	Form and manner of disclosures	27.72
	(3)	Submitting reports	27.73
E.	Tipping Off		27.76
	(1)	The offence of tipping off under POCA	27.76
	(2)	Defences available	27.80
	(3)	Maximum penalty under ss 330, 331, 332, and 333	27.82
	(4)	Consent	27.84
	(5)	Protected and authorised disclosures	27.85
	(6)	Threshold amounts	27.86
	(7)	Mode of trial decisions	27.87
F.	Disclosure of Suspicious Transactions under the DTA		27.88
	(1)	Failure to disclose knowledge or suspicion of drug money laundering	27.89
	(2)	Legal professional privilege	27.92
	(3)	Defences	27.94
	(4)	Tipping off	27.95
	(5)	Defences to tipping off	27.97
	(6)	Tipping off under the CJA 1988	27.98
	(7)	Penalties	27.103

28 Costs and Compensation

A.	Introduction		28.01
	(1)	Costs and compensation distinguished	28.03

B. Costs		28.04
(1) Costs: High Court/civil cases		28.04
(2) Court's discretion and circumstances to be taken into account when exercising its discretion as to costs		28.06
(3) Basis of assessment		28.07
(4) Factors to be taken into account in deciding the amount of costs		28.09
(5) Interim costs orders		28.10
(6) Costs: Crown Court		28.13
(7) The power of the magistrates' court to order costs		28.15
(8) The acquitted defendant and costs		28.22
(9) Orders for the payment of costs in confiscation order cases		28.23
(10) Confiscation orders: prosecution costs		28.24
(11) Costs of receivers		28.26
(12) Receiver's costs in litigation		28.29
(13) Payment of receiver's costs: High Court		28.34
(14) Civil Procedure Rules 69		28.36
(15) The judgment in *Capewell*		28.43
(16) Remuneration, not expenses		28.46
(17) *Capewell*: analysis		28.48
(18) Indemnities		28.55
(19) *Capewell*: conclusion		28.56
(20) Receiver's costs: Crown Court		28.59
(21) Release of restrained funds to cover legal expenses under the DTA and CJA		28.60
(22) Legal expenses and third parties		28.70
(23) Release of restrained funds to cover legal expenses under POCA		28.71
C. Compensation		28.78
(1) Compensation for the acquitted defendant under the DTA and CJA		28.78
(2) Other conditions		28.80
(3) Compensation for third parties		28.81
(4) How much compensation and by whom is it paid?		28.83
(5) Procedure on applications		28.84
(6) Compensation for the acquitted defendant under POCA 2002		28.85
(7) When a confiscation order is varied or discharged under POCA		28.91
(8) Other powers to order compensation under POCA		28.93
(9) Compensation in relation to interim receiving orders and property freezing orders		28.96
(10) Compensation for recovery of cash in summary proceedings		28.99
(11) Compensation and the victims of crime		28.103

29 Condemnation and Restoration

A. Introduction		29.01
B. The Condemnation and Forfeiture of Goods		29.07
(1) The statutory basis		29.07
(2) Duty payable, unless for own use		29.09
(3) Importations for a commercial purpose		29.10
(4) Civil proceedings		29.15

	(5) Legislative background	29.18
	(6) The revised legislative scheme	29.20
	(7) Gifts	29.24
	(8) Transfers for money's worth	29.25
	(9) EU reaction	29.27
	(10) What factors define 'commercial purpose'?	29.29
	(11) What are the minimum indicative levels?	29.37
	(12) Travelling to the UK from outside the EU	29.44
C.	Detention, Seizure and Condemnation	29.45
	(1) The forfeiture provisions	29.46
	(2) What does 'liable to forfeiture' mean?	29.48
	(3) Secondary forfeiture	29.51
	(4) More than one person involved	29.58
	(5) Proof of certain other matters	29.59
	(6) Stops at Coquelles	29.60
D.	Condemnation: Practice and Procedure	29.61
	(1) Initial seizure	29.61
	(2) Possible criminal proceedings	29.67
	(3) Notice of claim—the one month time limit to appeal	29.70
	(4) Six month time limit on HM Revenue and Customs once notice lodged	29.72
	(5) Preparation for the hearing—service of evidence	29.75
	(6) Preparation for the hearing—dutiable goods	29.79
	(7) The hearing—commercial purpose v own use	29.80
	(8) Court procedure: preliminary matters	29.86
	(9) Court procedure: condemnation by complaint	29.90
	(10) Order of speeches	29.92
	(11) The burden and standard of proof	29.97
	(12) Hearsay in civil cases	29.102
	(13) Previous convictions	29.106
	(14) Reasons for stopping the traveller	29.109
	(15) Power to stop the traveller	29.111
E.	Condemnation: Costs and Compensation	29.112
	(1) Costs	29.112
	(2) LSC funding	29.120
	(3) Compensation	29.122
F.	Condemnation Appeals	29.124
	(1) Procedure	29.125
	(2) Pre-hearing review	29.128
	(3) Pending the hearing of an appeal	29.129
G.	Condemnation in the High Court	29.130
H.	Condemnation and the ECHR	29.131
I.	Red Diesel Cases	29.135
	(1) Introduction	29.135
	(2) The legislative provisions	29.137
	(3) Excepted vehicles	29.143
	(4) Compounding	29.147

	(5) Procedural requirements	29.148
	(6) The vehicle and the fuel	29.150
	(7) The civil burden	29.152
	(8) Criminal offences	29.153
J.	Delivery Up	29.156
	(1) Introduction	29.156
	(2) The legislative provisions	29.157
	(3) Practice	29.161
K.	Restoration	29.162
	(1) The statutory basis	29.162
	(2) Appeals against non-restoration	29.164
	(3) Burden and standard of proof	29.165
	(4) Test of reasonableness	29.167
	(5) Proportionality	29.173
	(6) Jurisdiction	29.177
	(7) Personal/commercial use	29.180
	(8) Case law	29.192
L.	Restoration: Practice and Procedure	29.198
	(1) Formal departmental reviews	29.198
	(2) Tribunal procedure	29.199
	(3) Time limits	29.200
	(4) Lodging the appeal and the statement of case	29.202
	(5) Disclosure	29.206
	(6) Witness statements	29.212
	(7) Ongoing criminal proceedings	29.216
	(8) Failure to comply with directions	29.217
	(9) Pre-hearing reviews	29.219
	(10) Preparation for the hearing	29.222
	(11) The hearing	29.223
	(12) Judgment	29.229
M.	Restoration Appeals	29.231
N.	Restoration: Costs and Compensation	29.233
	(1) Compensation	29.233
	(2) Costs	29.234
O.	The ECHR and Restoration	29.237

Appendix 1: Restraint Order	689
Appendix 2: Management Receivership Order	695
Appendix 3: Enforcement Receivership Order	699
Appendix 4: Letter of Agreement between Prosecutor and Receiver	703
Appendix 5: Variation of Restraint Order	707
Appendix 6: LSC Funding Arrangements	709
Appendix 7: Application Notice by Defendant seeking a Certificate of Inadequacy	711
Appendix 8: Certificate of Inadequacy	715

Appendix 9: Claim Form (CPR PART 8)	717
Appendix 10: Extract from the Practice Direction on POCA 2002 Parts 5 and 8: Civil Recovery: section III	719
Appendix 11: Extract from the Practice Direction on POCA 2002 Parts 5 and 8: Civil Recovery: section IV	721
Appendix 12: Schedule 6 to POCA 2002 sections 247 and 257	725
Appendix 13: Draft Restraint, Disclosure and Repatriation Order under POCA	727
Appendix 14: Certificate of Service	733
Appendix 15: Interim Receiving Order under s 246 of POCA 2002	735
Appendix 16: Useful Websites on POCA 2002	743
Appendix 17: Property Freezing Order	745
Appendix 18: Civil Recovery by Consent Order	751
Appendix 19: Guidance to solicitors and applicants seeking Community Legal Service funding for proceedings under the Proceeds of Crime Act 2002 involving the Assets Recovery Agency	755
Appendix 20: Condemnation and Forfeiture of Goods	761
Appendix 21: ARA: Settlement of Civil Recovery and Tax Cases	765
Appendix 22: Guidance by the Secretary of State to the Director of the Assets Recovery Agency	767
Appendix 23: The House of Lords Decision in *Capewell*	769
Index	771

TABLE OF CASES

A Defendant, re *The Times*, 7 April 1987 . . . . 2.15, 2.102, 4.07, 4.15, 4.16, 7.22
A v A [2002] EWHC Admin 611; [2002] EWCA Civ 1039;
    [2003] Fam 55 . . . . 22.114, 22.116, 22.117
A v C (No 2) [1981] QB 961 . . . . 5.43, 28.65
A-G v Moran [2001] EWCA Crim 1770 . . . . 12.36
A-G v Punch Ltd [2002] UKHL 50 . . . . 22.143
A-G v Times Newspapers [1991] 2 WLR 994 . . . . 22.143
A-G of Hong Kong v Lee Kwong-Kut [1993] AC 951 . . . . 26.96
A-G's Reference (No.3 of 1999) [2001] 2 AC 91 . . . . 11.34
A-G's References Nos 114, 115, 116, 144 and 145 of 2002 . . . . 24.58
Adams, re (2005) *LS Gaz* January 13, 28, QBD 12.65
Adams v Cape Industries plc [1991] 1 All ER 929; [1990] Ch 433;
    [1990] 2 WLR 657 . . . . 2.56, 2.60
Ahmad v Ahmad [1998] EWCA Civ 1246; [1999] 1 FLR 317 . . . . 2.79, 8.74, 22.98, 22.105
Air Canada v UK (1995) 20 EHRR 150 . . . . 29.133
AJ and DJ, re (CA, 9 December 1992) 2.41, 2.44, 5.05, 7.28, 7.34, 8.37, 8.71
Alfred Crompton Amusement Machines Ltd v Customs and Excise Commissioners
    [1974] AC 405 . . . . 29.211
Ali v Best (1997) 161 JP 393 . . . . 21.133, 29.106
Allgemeine Gold-und Silberscheideanstalt v Customs and Excise Commissioners
    [1980] 2 All ER 138 . . . . 29.08
Andrews, re [1999] 1 WLR 1236 . . . . 3.45, 3.46, 3.48, 28.34, 28.35,
                                                                      28.36, 28.42, 28.43, 28.49, 28.59
Arcuri v Italy (Application No 52024–99) 20.100, 20.105
Assets Recovery Agency *see* Director of the Assets Recovery Agency
Associated Provincial Picture Houses Ltd v Wednesbury Corp
    [1948] 1 KB 223 . . . . 29.171, 29.172
Attorney-General *see* A-G
Aykut Ates v Customs and Excise Commissioners (2002) (EOO 188) 29.174

B (A Minor) (Contempt Evidence), re *The Times*, 11 November 1995 . . . . 6.19
B, re (QBD, 13 May 1991) 22.85
B v Chief Constable of Avon and Somerset [2001] 1 All ER 562;
    [2001] 1 WLR 340 . . . . 19.11, 21.101, 21.130, 29.101
Bank of Scotland v A [2001] 1 WLR 751 . . . . 26.01, 27.78
Barnes and Barnes, re [2004] EWHC Admin 2620 . . . . 17.11
Barnette v Government of the United States of America [2004] UKHL 37 . . . . 25.28
Bassick and Osborne v Customs and Excise Commissioners (1997)
    161 JP 377 . . . . 21.138, 21.140, 21.150
Bater v Bater [1950] 2 All ER 458 . . . . 19.11, 21.101, 29.101
Bekhor (AJ) & Co Ltd v Bilton [1981] QB 923 (CA) 19.75, 19.123
Beni Falkai Mining Company Limited, in re [1934] Ch 406 . . . . 3.67
Benn v R [2004] EWCA Crim 2100 . . . . 21.156
Bevins and Pyrah v Customs and Excise Commissioners [2005] (EO 00903) 29.98, 29.166
Boehm v Goodall [1911] 1 Ch 155 . . . . 28.34
Booker McConnell v Plasgow [1985] RPC 425 . . . . 5.01
Bowman v Fels [2005] EWCA Civ 226 . . . . 26.47, 27.08, 27.31, 27.44–69

Table of Cases

Boyce v Wyatt Engineering *The Times*, 14 June 2001 .... 21.127, 29.95
Bradford City Metropolitan District Council v Booth *The Times*, 31 May 2000 .... 29.117
Briggs-Price, re [2006] EWHC 2751 (Admin) 5.19
Brinks Mat Ltd v Elcombe [1988] 1 WLR 1350 .... 7.27, 7.32, 19.48, 19.50, 25.20
Brookes (Robert) v Customs and Excise Commissioners (2005) (E00847) 29.192
Bryan v Customs and Excise Commissioners (1998) 162 JP 251 .... 21.140
BS v A [2001] 1 WLR 751 .... 27.79, 27.101
Burgess v Stafford Hotel Ltd [1993] 3 All ER 222 .... 29.236
Butler v UK (Application 41661/98) (27 June 2002) 20.110, 21.11, 21.217
Butt v Customs and Excise Commissioners (2002) 166 JP 173 .... 21.130, 21.131, 21.137

C, re (1987) (QBD, 18 November 1987) 13.43, 13.44
C, re (1993) unreported 5.49
C, re [2001] EWHC Admin 768 .... 2.29
C, re (2004) (QBD, 14 May 2004) 24.62
C, re [2005] EWHC Admin 966 .... 13.58
C (Restraint Order: Disclosure), re (QBD, 4 September 2000) 4.23, 4.25, 4.40, 14.74, 14.94
C (Restraint Order: Identification), re *The Times*, 24 April 1995 .... 14.74
Cala Crystal SA v Emran Al-Borno *The Times*, 6 May 1994 .... 5.16
Campbell Mussells v Thompson *The Times*, 30 May 1984 .... 5.44
Capewell v Customs and Excise Commissioners [2005] EWCA Civ 964; [2005]
    1 All ER 900 .... 1.42, 3.04, 3.05, 3.15, 3.63, 28.34, 28.42,
                              28.43, 28.46, 28.48, 28.49, 28.56, 28.57, 28.58
Capewell v Customs and Excise Commissioners (No 2) [2005] EWCA Civ 964 .... 1.42, 3.06,
                                        3.55, 3.58, 3.59, 3.60, 8.60
Capewell v HM Revenue and Customs and another [2007] UKHL 2;
    The Times, 1 February 2007 .... App 23
CBS United Kingdom Limited v Lambert [1982] 3 All ER 237 .... 2.86
Chief Constable of Lancashire Constabulary v Burnley Magistrates' Court [2003]
    EWHC Admin 3308 .... 21.69, 21.81
Chief Constable of Merseyside Police v Hickman [2006] EWHC Admin 451;
    (QBD, 1 March 2006) 21.33
Chief Constable of Merseyside Police v Reynolds [2004] EWHC Admin 2862 .... 21.55, 21.78
Compton v CPS [2002] EWCA Civ 1720 .... 2.49, 2.60, 4.03, 8.35
Compton v R [2002] EWCA Crim 2835 .... 21.156
Cowcher v Cowcher [1972] 1 WLR 425 .... 22.131
CPS v Grimes and Grimes [2003] 2 FLR 510 .... 22.106
CPS v Richards and Richards [2006] EWCA Civ 849 .... 22.118
Crocker v Revenue and Customs Commissioners (18 October 2005) (EO0926) 29.193
Customs and Excise Commissioners v A, A v A [2002] EWHC Admin 611; [2002]
    EWCA Civ 1039; [2003] Fam 55 .... 22.116, 22.117
Customs and Excise Commissioners v Alzitrans SL [2003] All ER (D) 288 .... 29.205
Customs and Excise Commissioners v Atkinson, Dore and Binns [2003]
    EWHC Admin 421 .... 29.110
Customs and Excise Commissioners v Barclays Bank plc [2004] EWCA Civ 1555 .... 22.02
Customs and Excise Commissioners v Barclays Bank plc [2006] UKHL 28 .... 22.141
Customs and Excise Commissioners v Barratt [1995] STC 661 .... 29.231
Customs and Excise Commissioners v Bradley (Jack) (Accrington) Ltd [1959]
    1 QB 219 .... 29.57, 29.141, 29.150
Customs and Excise Commissioners v Carrier (1995) 4 All ER 38 .... 29.19
Customs and Excise Commissioners v Corbitt (JH) (Numismatists) Ltd [1980]
    STC 231 .... 29.170, 29.171, 29.172
Customs and Excise Commissioners v Demack and Eatock [2005]
    EWHC 330 (Ch) 29.182, 29.184
Customs and Excise Commissioners v Dickinson *The Times*, 3 December 2003 .... 29.184

Table of Cases

Customs and Excise Commissioners *v* Duffy TLR 5 April 2002 .... 21.15
Customs and Excise Commissioners *v* El Heri [2001] EWCA Civ 1782 .... 4.26
Customs and Excise Commissioners *v* Gus Merchandise Corp [1992] STC 776 .... 29.209
Customs and Excise Commissioners *v* Harris (1999) 163 JPR 408 .... 21.178
Customs and Excise Commissioners *v* MCA [2002] EWCA Civ 1039 .... 17.50, 22.85,
 22.86, 22.88, 22.93–5, 22.119, 22.120, 22.121, 22.125, 22.127
Customs and Excise Commissioners *v* Mukesh Shah (1999) 163 JP 759 .... 21.100
Customs and Excise Commissioners *v* Newbury [2003] 2 All ER 964 (DC) 29.50, 29.85,
 29.110, 29.151
Customs and Excise Commissioners *v* Newbury [2003] EWHC Admin 702 .... 29.14
Customs and Excise Commissioners *v* Norris [1991] 2 All ER 395 .... 5.10, 5.56, 28.63, 28.64
Customs and Excise Commissioners *v* S [2004] EWCA Crim 2374; [2005]
 1 WLR 1338 .... 1.40, 8.42, 8.74, 19.180, 25.52
Customs and Excise Commissioners *v* T (1998) 162 JP 193 .... 21.135, 29.108
Customs and Excise Commissioners *v* Togher [2005] EWCA Civ 274 .... 17.16
Customs and Excise Commissioners *v* Venn *The Times*, 24 January 2002 .... 29.74
Customs and Excise Commissioners *v* Weller (David) [2006]
 EWHC 237 (Ch) .... xii, 29.03, 29.185, 29.188, 29.191
Customs and Excise Commissioners *v* Young [1993] STC 394 .... 29.217

D, re (1995) *The Times*, 26 January 1995 .... 4.30
D, re [2001] EWHC Admin 668 .... 14.74
D, re [2006] EWHC Admin 254 .... 2.61, 2.62, 3.36, 5.16
D, re [2006] EWHC Admin 1519 .... 5.57, 22.21, 28.70
D and D, re (28 October 1992) 5.41, 5.48
D (UK) Ltd *v* Revenue and Customs Prosecutions Office [2005] EWCA Crim 2919 .... 8.34
Dadourian Group International Inc *v* Azuri Ltd [2005] All ER (D) 323 (Apr);
 (ChD, 22 April 2005) 22.02
De Keyser *v* British Railway Traffic and Electric Co Ltd [1936] 1 KB 224 .... 29.49
Deamer (see R (on the application of Deamer)) *v* Southampton
 Crown Court (DC, 13 July 2006) 10.144
Deamer (see R (on the application of Deamer)) *v* Southampton Magistrates' Court
 [2006] EWHC Admin 2221 .... 1.47, 17.83, 17.86
Derby & Co Ltd *v* Weldon (No 1) [1990] 1 Ch 48 (CA) 19.56
Derby *v* Weldon (No 6) [1990] 3 All ER 263 .... 4.44, 4.46
Director of the Assets Recovery Agency *v* (1) Ashton (2) Harrison [2005]
 All ER (D) 92 (May) 20.21
Director of the Assets Recovery Agency *v* Charrington [2005] EWCA Civ 334 ..... 20.22, 20.103,
 20.109, 20.110
Director of the Assets Recovery Agency *v* Creaven [2005]
 EWHC Admin 2726 .... 19.63, 19.121, 19.148
Director of the Assets Recovery Agency *v* Green (Jeffrey David) [2005]
 EWHC Admin 3168 .... 19.13, 20.34
Director of the Assets Recovery Agency *v* Keenan (Gerard Malachy) [2005] NIQB 67;
 (NIHC, 23 September 2005) 19.44, 19.52
Director of the Assets Recovery Agency *v* Molloy [2006] NIQB 49 .... 19.152
Director of the Assets Recovery Agency *v* Olupitan and Makinde [2006]
 EWHC Admin 1906 .... 20.28
Director of the Assets Recovery Agency *v* Personal Representative of
 Paul Patrick Daly (Dec'd) [2006] NIQB 36 .... 20.96, 20.98
Director of the Assets Recovery Agency *v* Prince [2006] EWHC Admin 1080 .... 20.38
Director of the Assets Recovery Agency *v* Singh (Satnam) [2004]
 EWHC Admin 2335 .... 1.49, 7.36, 8.92, 19.50, 19.52, 20.101
see also Singh (Satnam) *v* Director of the Assets Recovery Agency [2005] EWCA Civ 580

Director of the Assets Recovery Agency *v* Szepietowski [2006] EWHC Admin 2406 .... 19.96
Director of the Assets Recovery Agency *v* Walsh [2004] NIQB 21;
  (QBD NI, 1 April 2004) 19.14, 20.102, 20.109, 20.111
Dodds *v* Walker [1981] 1 WLR 1027 .... 21.80
DPP *v* Channel Four Television [1993] 2 All ER 517 .... 8.125
DPP *v* Scarlett [2000] 1 WLR 515 .... 4.47
DWP *v* Richards *The Times*, 11 March 2005 .... 12.39

E, re and Re H [2001] EWHC Admin 472; (24 May 2001) 4.25, 4.29, 9.86, 11.82, 14.94
Edwards *v* UK [2004] ECHR 39647/98 .... 20.97
Empire Stores Ltd *v* Customs and Excise Commissioners (1992) VAT TR 271 .... 29.228
Engel *v* Netherlands (No 1) (1976) 1 EHRR 647 .... 19.14, 20.105, 20.111

Forwell, re [2003] EWCA Civ 1608 .... 13.57, 16.66
Fox *v* Customs and Excise Commissioners (2002) 166 JP 578
  The Times, 20 July 2002 .... 29.58, 29.84, 29.89
Francis and Francis *v* Central Criminal Court [1988] 3 All ER 775 (HL) 27.30, 27.81, 27.93
Freight Transport Leasing Ltd *v* Customs and Excise Commissioners (1992)
  VAT TR 120 .... 29.218
Frost and Mason *v* Customs and Excise Commissioners (2005) (E00872) 29.197

G, re (30 July 2001) 2.87, 5.11
G, re [2001] EWHC Admin 606 .... 5.24
G, re; Manning *v* G (No 4) [2003] EWHC Admin 1732 .... 3.19, 3.23, 3.42
G (No 1), re [2002] EWHC Admin 2495 .... 12.57
G (restraint order), re [2001] EWHC Admin 606; QBD, 19 July 2001 .... 7.17, 7.18, 22.16,
                                                                  22.22, 22.24, 22.26
Gagnon *v* McDonald *The Times*, 14 November 1984 .... 6.05
Gascoyne *v* Customs and Excise Commissioners [2005] 2 WLR 222 .... 29.04, 29.177,
                                            29.181, 29.182, 29.184, 29.185, 29.187, 29.189
Gissing *v* Gissing [1970] 2 All ER 780 .... 22.131
Gokal *v* Serious Fraud Office [2001] EWCA Civ 368 .... 13.47, 16.53, 16.58
Goldsmith *v* Customs and Excise Commissioners *The Times*, 12 June 2001 .... 29.16, 29.131
Golobiewska *v* Customs and Excise Commissioners *The Times*, 25 May 2005 .... 29.165
Gora *v* Customs and Excise Commissioners [2003] EWCA Civ 525;
  [2004] QB 93 .... 29.02, 29.171, 29.180, 29.183, 29.187, 29.238
Gorgievski *v* Customs and Excise Commissioners [2003] EWHC Admin 2773 .... 21.81
Government of India *v* Ottavio Quattrocchi [2004] EWCA Civ 40 .... 25.15, 25.20
Government of the United States of America *v* Montgomery [2001]
  1 WLR 196 .... 25.12, 25.13, 25.14
Grant *v* Edwards [1986] 2 All ER 426 .... 22.131
Griffin *v* Griffin *The Times*, 28 April 2000 .... 6.35
Grimes *v* CPS [2003] EWCA Civ 1814 .... 17.47

H, re (1988) *The Times*, 1 April 1988 .... 6.04
H, re [2001] EWHC Admin 472; (24 May 2001) 4.25, 4.29, 9.86, 11.82, 14.94
H (restraint order: realisable property), re [1996] 2 All ER 391 ...... 2.54, 2.58, 2.60, 2.63, 22.25
Hadkinson *v* Hadkinson [1952] 2 All ER 567 .... 6.36
Halford and Brooks [Senior] *The Times*, 3 October 1991 .... 29.106
Halford *v* Colchester Magistrates' Court (QBD, 25 October 2000) 21.77, 21.79
Harman *v* Glencross [1986] Fam 81 .... 22.98
Harmsworth *v* Harmsworth [1988] 1 FLR 349 .... 6.09
HN, re [2005] EWHC Admin 2982 .... 17.15, 17.59
Hopping *v* Customs and Excise Commissioners (2001) (EOO170) 29.134, 29.239

Table of Cases

Hornal v Neuberger Products Ltd [1957] 1 QB 247 . . . . 9.52, 11.14, 12.12,
19.11, 21.101, 21.131, 29.101
Hossain v Customs and Excise Commissioners [2004]
EWHC 1898 (Ch) 29.215
Hoverspeed see R (Hoverspeed)
Hughes v Customs and Excise Commissioners [2002] 4 All ER 633; [2003]
1 WLR 177 . . . . 1.41, 1.42, 3.04, 3.06, 3.14, 3.26, 3.46, 3.48, 3.49, 3.55,
3.56, 8.60, 17.54, 28.34, 28.36, 28.42, 28.43, 28.48, 28.49, 28.59
Hunter v Chief Constable of West Midlands [1982] AC 529 (HL) 29.108

Interoute Telecommunications (UK) Ltd v Fashion Gossip Ltd [1999] TLR 762;
The Times, 10 November 1999 . . . . 7.36, 8.92, 19.50, 19.51
IRC v Dayman and Piacentini *The Times*, 10 February 2003 . . . . 3.64
Istel v Tully [1993] AC 45 . . . . 14.94

J, re [2001] EWHC Admin 713 . . . . 9.86, 11.81, 11.82, 14.94
J, re (2005) *The Times*, 12 July 2005 . . . . 10.89
Jennings v Crown Prosecution Service [2005] EWCA Civ 746; [2005]
4 All ER 391 . . . . 1.43, 2.39, 2.45, 2.46, 5.08, 7.30, 7.33, 19.52
John Dee Ltd v Customs and Excise Commissioners [1995] STC 941 . . . . 29.172
Johnson v Whitehouse [1984] RTR 38 . . . . 2.15
Johnstone v Customs and Excise Commissioners [2005] EWCA Admin 115 . . . . 29.182

K, re (1990) (HC, 6 July 1990) 10.87
K, re (1990) *The Times*, 30 September 1990 . . . . 2.36, 2.37, 2.64
K, re [2005] EWCA Crim 619 . . . . 2.60, 2.64
K Ltd v National Westminster Bank plc [2006] EWCA Civ 1039;
CLW 06/29/13 . . . . 26.14, 26.50
K (Restraint Order), re [1990] 2 All ER 562 . . . . 22.137
Katchis, re (2001) ACD 372, DC (21 December 2000) 10.81
Kirk (David) v Customs and Excise Commissioners (14042) VAT Tribunal 29.209
Kwik Fit (GB) Ltd v Customs and Excise Commissioners [1998] STC 167–9 . . . . 29.226

L, re (18 January 1996) 13.51, 16.60, 16.61
L, re *The Times*, 10 July 1996 . . . . 5.14, 8.48
L (Restraint Order, Legal Costs), re *The Times*, 19 July 1996 . . . . 28.62
Lama Ltd v Customs and Excise Commissioners (COO 189) 29.205
Lawal v Northern Spirit Ltd [2004] 1 All ER 197 . . . . 20.96
Leigh v Uxbridge Magistrates' Court [2005] EWHC 1828 (QBD) 21.114
Lindsay v Customs and Excise Commissioners [2002] EWCA Civ 267 . . . . 29.173, 29.178,
29.183, 29.233, 29.237
Lister v Perryman (1870) LR 4 HL 521 . . . . 2.15
Lloyd v Bow Street Magistrates' Court [2003] EWHC Admin 2294 . . . . 1.47, 10.144, 17.79
London Scottish Benefit Society v Chorley (1884) 12 QBD 452; 13 QBD 872 (CA) 28.30
Long v Clarke (1894) 56 JP 258 . . . . 17.64

M, re [1992] 1 All ER 537; [1992] QB 377 . . . . 3.13, 5.38, 5.40,
18.06, 19.116, 19.119, 22.46, 22.52, 22.147
M, re (1993) (HC, 9 July 1993) 22.138, 25.01
M v Bow Street Magistrates' Court *The Times*, 27 July 2005 . . . . 21.194
M v Italy (17 DR 59) 20.105
M v Italy (Application No 12386–86) 20.100
McGinty (JJ) v Customs and Excise Commissioners (1995) V&DR 193 . . . . 29.235
McGuiness (William) v Customs and Excise Commissioners [E00793] 29.184

Table of Cases

McIntosh v Lord Advocate [2001] 2 All ER 638; [2001] 3 WLR 107 .... 9.21, 10.146, 10.148, 10.149, 14.17
McKinsley, re [2006] EWHC Admin 1092 .... 13.53, 16.63
Manning v G (No 4) [2003] EWHC Admin 1732 .... 3.19, 3.23, 3.42
Manning and Sinclair v Glatt [2003] EWCA Civ 1977 .... 3.24, 3.63
Marleasing SA v LA Comercial Internacional de Alinentacion SA [1990] ECR I-4135 .... 27.08
Marren v Dawson Bentley & Co [1961] 3 All ER 270 .... 21.80
Merchandise Transport Ltd v British Transport Commission; Arnold Transport
    (Rochester) Ltd v British Transport Commission [1961] 3 All ER 495;
    [1962] 2 QB 173 .... 2.55, 2.60
Metcalfe and Metcalfe v R [2004] EWCA Crim 3253 .... 10.39, 10.42
Midland Bank plc v Cook [1995] 4 All ER 562 .... 22.131
Mirror Group Newspapers plc v Maxwell (1998) BCC 324 .... 3.51
Mori Mohal Indian Restaurant v Customs and Excise Commissioners (1992)
    VAT TR 188 .... 29.227
Mudie v Kent Magistrates' Court [2003] EWCA Civ 237; 2 All ER 631 .... 29.16, 29.121
Muneka v Customs and Excise Commissioners [2005]
    EWHC Admin 495 .... 21.24, 21.142, 21.148, 21.149

N, re [2005] EWHC Admin 3211 .... 13.46, 13.51, 16.57, 16.60
Nevin v Customs and Excise Commissioners (QBD, 3 November 1995) 21.141, 21.148
Newman v Modern Bookbinders [2000] 2 All ER 814 .... 6.24
Niedersachsen, The [1983] 2 Lloyd's Rep 600, 605A 19.55, 19.99
Norris, re [2001] 1 WLR 1388 .... 17.40, 17.41, 22.61, 22.63, 22.85,
                               22.86, 22.87, 22.88–92, 22.100, 22.104, 22.127
Nossen's Letter Patent, re [1969] 1 WLR 683 .... 28.29

O, re [1991] 1 All ER 330 .... 3.38, 4.08, 4.11, 4.12, 4.13, 4.16, 4.19, 4.23, 5.23, 7.44
O (Restraint Order), re [1991] 2 QB 520, 530 (CA) 11.81, 14.74
O'Donoghue, re [2004] EWCA Civ 1800 .... 13.48, 16.59
O'Donoghue, re [2004] EWHC Admin 176 .... 13.39, 16.64
Ozturk v Germany (1984) 6 EHRR 409 .... 19.14

P, re [1998] EWHC Admin 1049; (QBD, 6 November 1998) 5.56, 17.22, 17.23,
                                         24.61, 24.62, 24.114, 28.66
P (Restraint Order: Sale of Assets), re [2000] 1 WLR 473 .... 3.10, 3.14, 3.28, 3.30,
                  3.31, 4.05, 5.29, 5.30, 8.63, 8.65, 8.66, 8.68, 8.83, 10.30, 22.42
P v Customs and Excise Commissioners [2005] EWHC Admin 877 .... 13.49, 16.59
P v P (Ancillary Relief Proceeds of Crime) [2004] Fam 1 .... 27.48, 27.54, 27.55
PCW (Underwriting Agencies) Ltd v Dixon [1983] 2 All ER 158 (QBD) 19.66
Peters, re [1998] 3 All ER 46; [1988] 3 WLR 182; [1988] QB 871 .... 1.12, 2.03, 5.20,
                                     5.29, 5.31, 5.33, 5.53, 19.111, 22.19, 28.62
Phillips v UK (2001) 11 EHRC 280 .... 10.146, 14.17
Phillips v UK [2001] EHRR No 41087/98 .... 10.145, 10.152, 12.96,
                                        12.97, 15.77, 15.78, 20.108
Piper, re [2000] 1 WLR 473 .... 19.113, 22.50
Polly Peck International v Nadir [2006] All ER (D) 176 (Jan);
    (ChD, 25 January 2006) 28.68
Popischal v Phillips The Times, 20 January 1988 .... 6.31
Powell v Revenue and Customs Commissioners (2005)
    (EOO 900) VAT Tribunal 29.179, 29.233
Project Blue Sky Inc v Australian Broadcasting Authority (1998) 194 CLR 355 .... 9.24
Purves v Revenue and Customs Commissioners (2005) (EOO 924) VAT Tribunal 29.218

Q3 Media Ltd, re [2006] EWHC 1553 (ChD) 19.120

R (Chief Constable of Northamptonshire) v Daventry Magistrates' Court [2001]
    EWHC Admin 446 .... 29.117
R (Customs and Excise Commissioners) v Maidstone Crown Court [2004]
    EWHC Admin 1459 .... 29.127
R (on the application of Deamer) v Southampton Crown Court
    (DC, 13 July 2006) 10.144
R (on the application of Deamer) v Southampton Magistrates' Court [2006]
    EWHC Admin 2221 .... 1.47, 17.83, 17.86
R (on the application of the Director of the Assets Recovery Agency) v (1) Jia Jin He and
    (2) Dan Dan Chen [2004] EWHC Admin 3021 .... 1.49, 19.12, 19.14, 19.91,
                            19.107, 20.32, 20.100, 20.104, 20.107, 20.115, 20.118
R (on the application of the Director of the Assets Recovery Agency) v
    Ashton (Paul) [2006] EWHC Admin 1064; (2006) LS Gaz April 21 .... 19.17, 20.05,
                            20.103, 20.107, 20.116
R (Director of the Assets Recovery Agency) v Green The Times, 27 February 2006 .... 21.23
R (on the application of the Director of the Assets Recovery Agency) v H [2004]
    EWHC Admin 2166; The Independent, 8 November 2004 .... 19.104, 19.151
R (Hoverspeed) v Customs and Excise Commissioners [2002] EWCA Civ 1804; [2003]
    2 WLR 950 .... 21.162, 28.28, 29.14, 29.110
R (Hoverspeed) v Customs and Excise Commissioners [2002] EWHC Admin 1630;
    [2002] 4 All ER 912 (DC); [2002] 3 WLR 1219 .... 29.08, 29.14, 29.18, 29.23,
                            29.36, 29.97, 29.98, 29.166, 29.237
R (McCann) v Crown Court at Manchester [2003] 1 AC 787 .... 8.44
R (on the application of Miller Gardner Solicitors) v Minshull Street Crown Court [2002]
    EWHC Admin 3077 .... 23.18
R (Mudie) v Kent Magistrates' Court [2003] EWCA Civ 237; [2003]
    2 All ER 631 .... 29.61, 29.121
R, re (21 October 1992) 4.27, 8.112, 9.70
R, re The Independent, 4 November 2002 .... 13.54, 16.65
R, re [2004] EWHC Admin 621 .... 5.38, 22.46
R, re (2005) 154 NLJ 581 .... 28.69
R (Restraint Order), re [1990] 2 All ER 569 .... 2.06, 2.69, 8.52, 22.29
R v Ahmed (CA, 8 February 2000) 12.01
R v Ahmed and Quereshi [2004] EWCA Crim 2599 .... 22.103
R v Ajibade [2006] EWCA Crim 368; [2006] 2 Cr App R(S) 486 .... 10.121, 15.17, 15.39
R v Akengin [1995] Crim LR 88 .... 10.35, 10.36
R v Alagobola (2004) 2 Cr App R(S) 248 .... 10.22
R v Ascroft [2003] EWCA Crim 2365 .... 10.29, 12.43
R v Ashton [2006] EWCA Crim 794 .... 9.32, 9.40
R v Ashton, Draz and O'Reilly The Times, 18 April 2006; CLW/06/15/9 .... 11.36
R v Atkinson [1992] Crim LR 749; (1993) 14 Cr App R(S) 182 .... 9.09, 9.68,
                            10.15, 10.123, 11.77
R v Ayensu and Ayensu [1982] Crim LR 764 .... 10.128, 10.129
R v Bakewell [2006] EWCA Crim 2; (2006) SJ 93 .... 10.24, 12.42
R v Banks [1997] Crim LR 234 .... 10.54
R v Barnham [2005] EWCA Crim 1049 .... 10.98
R v Barwick (2001) 1 Cr App R(S) 129 .... 10.95, 11.15, 12.79, 15.08
R v Basra (2002) 2 Cr App R(S) 100 .... 26.111
R v Bates (CA, 5 April 2006) 13.23
R v Benjafield [2001] 3 WLR 75; (2001) 2 Cr App R(S) 221 .... 9.58, 11.57, 14.14, 14.66
R v Benjafield [2002] UKHL 2; [2002] 1 All ER 815; (2002)
    2 Cr App R(S) 70 .... 9.02, 9.21, 9.59, 10.96, 10.145,
                            10.146, 12.96, 12.97, 14.17, 15.77, 15.78, 20.108
R v Berry (2000) 1 Cr App R(S) 352 .... 9.92

R v Briggs (Crown Court, 31 October 2003) 13.40
R v Brown [2001] EWCA Crim 2761 .... 12.01
R v Bullen and Soneji [2006] EWCA Crim 1125 .... 17.23, 17.25
  see also R v Soneji
R v Butler [1993] Crim LR 320; (1993) 14 Cr App R(S) 537 .... 10.33, 10.34, 10.35, 10.36
R v Byatt [2006] EWCA Crim 904 .... 15.06
R v Cadman-Smith (David) [2002] 1 WLR 54; (2002) 2 Cr App R(S) 37 .... 2.38, 10.84,
                                                                  12.03, 12.33, 12.34
R v Cain [1985] 1 AC 46, 55g–56d 10.169, 14.82, 24.55
R v Callan [1994] Crim LR 198 .... 10.130
R v Carroll [1991] Crim LR 720 .... 9.53, 11.16, 15.08
R v Central Criminal Court *ex p* Francis and Francis [1988] 3 All ER 775 .... 23.17
R v Chapman *The Times*, 18 November 1991 .... 10.118
R v Chichester Magistrates' Court *ex p* Crowther [1998]
    EWHC Admin 960 .... 1.47, 10.144, 17.78
R v Chrastny (No 2) [1991] 1 WLR 1385 .... 2.68, 10.60, 10.101, 12.75
R v Chuni (2002) Cr App R(S) 420 .... 9.19
R v City of London Justices *ex p* Chapman (1998) 162 JP 359;
    The Times, 17 March 1998 .... 12.86, 17.76, 17.77
R v City of London Justices *ex p* Peracha (HC, 31 March 1998) 17.77
R v Clacton Justices *ex p* Customs and Excise (1987) 152 JP 129 .... 17.37
R v Clarke [2006] EWCA Crim 1196 .... 9.40
R v Clayton *The Times*, 11 April 2003 .... 11.20
R v Cokovic (1996) 1 Cr App R(S) 131 .... 10.94, 15.36
R v Cole *The Independent*, 30 April 1998 (CA) 9.17, 11.40, 14.52
R v Colle (1992) 95 Cr App R 67 .... 26.96
R v Comiskey (1990) 12 Cr App R(S) 562 .... 9.53, 10.55, 10.58
R v Comiskey (1991) 93 Cr App R 227 .... 9.55, 9.64, 9.73, 9.88,
                                              10.92, 11.70, 12.13, 13.38, 14.66, 14.88, 15.36
R v Copeland (Alfonso) [2002] EWCA Crim 736 .... 9.38
R v Crawley Justices *ex p* Ohakwe (1994) 158 JP Reports 78 .... 21.11
R v Croft *The Times*, 6 July 2000 (CA) 10.73
R v Crown Court at Lewes *ex p* Hill (1991) 93 Cr App R 60 .... 23.42
R v Crown Court at Lewis *ex p* Rogers [1974] 1 All ER 589 .... 28.21
R v Crown Court at Southwark *ex p* Customs and Excise Commissioners [1989]
    3 All ER 673 .... 23.40, 23.46
R v Crutchley and Tonks [1994] Crim LR 309; (1994) 15 Cr
    App R(s) 627 .... 10.168, 12.80, 22.128
R v Currey (1995) 16 Cr App R(S) 421 .... 10.83, 12.73
R v Customs and Excise Commissioners *ex p* Boxall (Kenneth Stephen)
    (15 February 1996) (CO 1902/95) 29.19, 29.66, 29.79
R v Customs and Excise Commissioners *ex p* Dangol [2000] STC 107 (QBD) 29.229
R v Customs and Excise Commissioners *ex p* Emu Tabac SARL [1998]
    All ER (EC) 402; [1998] QB 791 .... 29.12, 29.14
R v Customs and Excise Commissioners *ex p* Mortimer [1999] 1 WLR 17 .... 28.33, 28.34,
                                                              28.35, 29.61, 29.62, 29.69
R v Cuthbertson [1980] 2 All ER 401 .... 1.03
R v Da Silva [2006] EWCA Crim 1654 .... 26.14
R v Davies [2002] EWCA Crim 3110 .... 10.85
R v Davies [2004] EWCA Crim 3380 .... 10.104
R v Davis (Steven) [2002] Crim LR 224 .... 9.38
R v De Prince *The Times*, 16 March 2004 .... 10.70
R v Derby Magistrates' Court *ex p* B [1996] 1 AC 487 .... 27.56
R v Dickens [1990] 2 All ER 626; [1990] 2 QB 102 .... 1.11, 9.04, 9.55,
                                                        9.57, 10.05, 10.06, 10.11, 10.63

Table of Cases

R v Dillon and Jagdev (2005) Cr App R(S) 232 .... 10.135
R v Dimsey and Allen (2000) 1 Cr App R(S) 497 .... 12.35
R v Donohoe *The Times*, 20 October 2006 .... 14.61
R v Dore (1997) 2 Cr App R(S) 152 .... 10.121, 15.17, 15.39, 15.42
R v Dorrian (2001) 1 Cr App R(S) 135 .... 28.103, 28.104
R v Dover and East Kent Magistrates' Court *ex p* Steven Gore
   (QBD, 23 May 1996) 21.11, 21.139
R v Dover Magistrates' Court *ex p* Customs and Excise Commissioners
   The Times, 12 December 1995 .... 21.166, 21.167
R v Duff (2003) 1 Cr App R(S) 466 (88) (CA) 27.93, 27.100
R v Edwards (2000) 1 Cr App R(S) 98 .... 9.17, 9.35
R v El-Kurd [2001] Crim LR 234 .... 26.92, 26.93
R v Ellingham [2004] EWCA Crim 3446; (CA, 2 December 2004) 10.22, 12.38
R v Emmett [1997] 3 WLR 1119; [1998] AC 773 .... 10.169, 11.72, 14.82, 24.55, 24.56
R v Enwezor (1991) 93 Cr App R 233 .... 9.53, 10.05, 10.06
R v Everson (2002) 1 Cr App R(S) 132 .... 26.111
R v Finch (1992) 14 Cr App R(S) 226 .... 10.37, 10.51
R v Foggon [2003] EWCA Crim 270 .... 12.37
R v Forte [2004] EWCA Crim 3188 .... 10.88, 12.02
R v Foxley (Gordon) (1995) 2 Cr App R 523 .... 12.61, 12.63, 12.64
R v French (1995) 16 Cr App R(S) 841 .... 10.136, 15.68
R v Gabriel (2006) CLW 06/20/7 .... 26.30
R v Gadsby (2002) 1 Cr App R(S) 97 .... 9.19, 9.20
R v Ghadami [1997] Crim LR 606 .... 12.93, 28.24
R v Gibbons (2003) 2 Cr App R(S) 34 .... 10.23, 10.27
R v Gibson *The Times*, 3 March 2000 .... 26.101
R v Gill [2004] EWCA Crim 3245 .... 26.88
R v Glatt (CA, 17 March 2006) 10.29, 10.30, 28.81
R v Greenwood (1995) 16 Cr App R(S) 614 .... 26.110, 26.112
R v Greet [2005] EWCA Crim 205 .... 22.100, 22.102
R v Gregory *The Times*, 19 October 1995 .... 22.130
R v H [2003] 1 All ER 497 .... 19.15
R v Haisman (2004) 1 Cr App R(S) 383 .... 9.41
R v Hall (1985) 81 Cr App R(S) 260 .... 26.13
R v Hanna (1994) 15 Cr App R(S) 44 .... 26.108, 26.109
R v Harmer [2005] EWCA Crim 1 .... 26.19
R v Harper [1989] Crim LR 755; 11 Cr App R(S) 240 .... 10.129, 10.131
R v Harrow Crown Court *ex p* Dave [1994] 1 WLR 98 .... 24.105
R v Harrow Justices *ex p* DPP [1991] 1 WLR 395 .... 17.37, 17.38, 17.69, 17.70, 17.71
R v Hastings and Rother Justices *ex p* Anscombe (Div Ct, 5 February 1998) 17.66, 17.68,
                                                                                                   17.73, 17.83, 17.109
R v Hesketh (2006) 150 *SJ* 1468 .... 12.54
R v Highgate Justices *ex p* Petrou [1954] 1 All ER 406 .... 28.16, 29.118
R v Homer [2006] EWCA Crim 1559 .... 10.23, 10.24, 10.25, 10.26, 10.27
R v Houareau [2005] EWCA Crim 2106 .... 10.69, 12.40, 12.41
R v Huntington Magistrates' Court *ex p* Percy (1994) COD 323 .... 24.109
R v Hussain [2006] EWCA Crim 621 .... 10.121, 15.40, 15.44
R v Hussain (Ali) [2005] EWCA Crim 87 .... 21.158, 26.17, 26.20
R v Hussain Bhatti and Bhatt *The Times*, 31 January 2002 .... 26.93
R v Ilsemann (1990) 12 Cr App R(S) 398 .... 9.53, 11.15, 11.16, 15.08, 15.30
R v Ilsemann [1991] Crim LR 141 .... 10.94
R v Inland Revenue Commissioners *ex p* Unilever plc [1996] STC 681 .... 13.58
R v Institute of Chartered Accountants and Others, *ex p* Brindle and Others,
   The Times, 12 January 1994; [1994] BCC 297 .... 29.216
R v Isleworth Crown Court *ex p* Kevin Marland (1998) 162 JPR 251 .... 21.134

Table of Cases

R v Jagdev [2002] 1 WLR 3017 .... 9.21, 9.36, 11.39, 14.41, 14.51
R v Jay (2001) 1 Cr App R(S) 273 .... 10.67
R v Jenkins (Paul) [1991] Crim LR 481 .... 10.12, 10.14
R v Johannes [2002] Crim LR 147 .... 10.68
R v Johnson [1991] 2 All ER 428; [1991] 2 QB 249 .... 10.01, 10.77, 15.82, 24.52
R v Jones (Confiscation Orders) *The Times*, 8 August 2006 .... 10.71, 12.54, 15.30
R v Judge and Woodbridge (1992) 13 Cr App R(S) 685 .... 22.128
R v K [2005] EWCA Crim 619 .... 8.36
R v Kansal (No 2) [2002] 1 All ER 257 .... 10.146
R v Kelly [2000] Crim LR 392 (CA) 9.35
R v Kensington Income Tax Commissioners *ex p* de Polignac [1917]
   1 KB 486 .... 19.47, 19.49
R v Knights [2005] 3 WLR 330; (HL, 21 July 2005) 9.27, 9.31, 11.21, 11.35
R v Kramer (1992) 13 Cr App R(S) 390 .... 10.104
R v Layode (CA, 12 March 1993) 2.37, 9.89, 11.15, 11.70, 14.90, 15.08
R v Lazarus [2005] Crim LR 64 .... 10.10, 12.22, 15.06
R v Lemmon [1991] Crim LR 791; (1991) 12 Crim App R(S) 66 .... 10.103, 10.104
R v Levin *The Times*, 20 February 2004 .... 10.08, 12.14, 15.10
R v Lingham (2001) 1 Cr App R(S) 46 .... 9.15
R v Liverpool Magistrates' Court *ex p* Ansen [1998] 1 All ER 692 .... 13.54, 16.65, 17.72
R v Loizou *The Times*, 23 June 2005 .... 26.28
R v Lunnon (2005) 1 Cr App R(S) 24 .... 10.10, 12.21, 15.06
R v Luton Justices *ex p* Abecasis *The Times*, 30 March 2000 .... 21.76, 21.77, 21.79
R v McQueen (2002) 2 Cr App R(S) 9(3) 10.102
R v Magistrates' Court at Dover *ex p* Customs and Excise Commissioners (1995)
   160 JP 233 .... 28.20
R v Mallick *The Times*, 30 May 2000 .... 10.149
R v Martin (2002) 2 Cr App R(S) 34 .... 1.45
R v Martin and White (1998) 2 Cr App R 385 .... 4.19, 4.23, 14.94
R v May [2005] EWCA Crim 97; [2005] 3 All ER 523 .... 10.23, 10.24, 10.25,
                                                                           10.26, 10.29, 10.32, 10.124, 20.97
R v May [2005] EWCA Crim 367 .... 12.90, 17.24, 17.25
R v May, Lawrence [2005] EWCA Crim 97 .... 10.139
R v Mesco [1980] 1 WLR 96 .... 3.67
R v Metcalfe [2001] EWCA Crim 1343 .... 10.21, 10.22
R v Metcalfe *The Times*, 12 January 2005 .... 10.90
R v Middlesex Guildhall Crown Court *ex p* Salinger *The Independent*,
   26 March 1992 .... 23.21, 23.24
R v Montila [2004] 1 WLR 3141 (CA) 26.16, 26.24, 26.94
R v Montila [2004] UKHL 50 (HL) 26.03, 26.18, 26.20
R v Moran [2002] 1 WLR 253 .... 10.41
R v Moulden (2005) 1 Cr App R(S) 691 (121); CLW/05/21/30 .... 10.120
R v O'Connell [2005] All ER (D) 59 .... 12.16
R v October [2003] EWCA Crim 452; *The Times*, March 11 2003 .... 9.22, 9.34
R v Odewale (CA, 10 March 2005) 10.132
R v O'Meally and Morgan (1994) 15 Cr App R(S) 831 .... 26.109, 26.112
R v Osei [1988] Crim LR 775; (1988) 10 Cr App R(S) 289 .... 10.18, 10.38, 10.55
R v Owens and Owens (2006) 150 *SJ* 1188 .... 29.154
R v Palmer [2002] EWCA Crim 2202 .... 1.45, 11.20, 11.21
R v Patel (2000) 2 Cr App R(S) 10 .... 10.21
R v Payton (2006) 150 *SJ* 741 .... 21.34
R v Pisciotto [2002] Crim LR 678 .... 9.38
R v Pope [2002] 1 Crim LR 196 .... 11.30
R v Popple [1992] Crim LR 675 .... 10.135, 15.67

Table of Cases

R v Potter (1991) 92 Cr App R 126 .... 10.23
R v Pragason [1988] Crim LR 778 .... 10.128
R v Pwllheli Justices ex p Soane [1948] 2 All ER 815 .... 28.17
R v Quinn [1996] Crim LR 516 .... 24.56
R v R [2006] EWCA Crim 1974 .... 26.24
R v Redbourne [1992] 1 WLR 1182; (1992) 96 Cr App R 201; (1992)
    14 Cr App R(S) 162 .... 10.34, 10.36, 10.74, 10.75, 10.76, 12.53
R v Rees (Plymouth Crown Court, 19 July 1990) 12.19, 12.69
R v Rezvi [2002] UKHL 1; [2002] 1 All ER 801; (2002) 2 Cr
    App R(S) 70 .... 10.30, 10.145, 10.147, 12.96, 12.97, 15.77, 15.78, 20.108
R v Richards [1992] 2 All ER 572 .... 10.44, 10.46
R v Robson [1991] Crim LR 222 .... 22.132
R v Ross (Keith) (2001) 2 Cr App R(S) 109 .... 9.38
R v Rowbotham [2006] EWCA Crim 7470 .... 10.24
R v Ruddick *The Times*, 6 May 2003 (CA) 12.93
R v Saggar [2005] EWCA Civ 174 .... 13.26
R v Saik [2006] 2 WLR 993 .... 26.14, 26.16, 26.23, 26.24, 26.94, 26.105
R v Sakavickas [2004] EWCA Crim 2686 .... 26.22, 26.23
R v Satchell [1996] Crim LR 351 .... 10.122
R v Sekhon [2002] EWCA Crim 2954; [2003] 1 WLR 1655; [2003] 3 All ER 508;
    (2003) 1 Cr App R(S) 575 .... vii, 1.13, 1.46, 9.16, 9.22, 9.38, 11.01,
                                    11.03, 11.45, 11.46, 11.48, 14.54, 28.104
R v Sekhon (2005) UKHL 49 .... 9.23
R v Selby (QBD, 16 June 2006) 6.33
R v Sharma [2006] EWCA Crim 16 .... 10.28, 22.133
R v Shergill [1999] 1 WLR 1944 (CA) 9.17
R v Shevki *see* R v Steele and Shevki
R v Siddique (Afraz) (CA, 14 July 2005) 10.99
R v Simons (1994) 15 Cr App R(S) 126; (1994) 98 Cr App R 100 .... 2.16, 10.20, 10.55
R v Simpson (1998) 2 Cr App R(S) 111 .... 10.21, 10.57, 10.82
R v Simpson *The Times*, 26 May 2003 .... 11.20
R v Singh [2003] EWCA Crim 3712 .... 26.20
R v Smart (2003) 2 Cr App R(S) 384 .... 28.25
R v Smith (1989) 11 Cr App R(S) 290 .... 10.18
R v Smith [2004] EWCA Crim 1219 .... 10.140
R v Smith (David) [2001] UKHL 68: [2002] 1 WLR 54 .... 12.42, 28.82
R v Smith (Ian) [1989] 2 All ER 948 .... 10.52
R v Smith (Wallace Duncan) (1996) 2 Cr App R 1 .... 12.59, 12.60
R v Soneji [2005] UKHL 49; [2005] 3 WLR 303; CLW/05/28/9 .... 1.46, 9.22, 9.26,
                                  9.27, 9.31, 9.34, 9.35, 11.34, 11.35, 11.36
R v Soneji [2006] EWCA Crim 1125 .... 17.23, 17.25
R v Soneji (CA, 27 March 2006) 10.138
R v Southwark Crown Court ex p Bowles [1998] AC 641 .... 23.42, 23.45
R v Stannard [2005] EWCA Crim 2717 .... 22.133
R v Steele and Shevki (2001) 2 Cr App R(S) 40; [2001] Crim LR 153 .... 9.21, 9.22,
                                         9.33, 9.37, 11.41, 14.53
R v Stroud [2004] EWCA Crim 1048 .... 24.63
R v Stuart and Bonnett (1989) 11 Cr App R(S) 89; [1989] Crim LR 599 .... 10.126, 12.86, 15.75
R v Suchedina [2006] EWCA Crim 2543 .... 26.24
R v Suchedina *The Times*, 9 September 2004 .... 10.47
R v Szrajber (1994) 15 Cr App R(S) 821; Crim LR 543 .... 10.136, 10.143,
                                              12.85, 15.68, 28.23
R v T (QBD, 1 February 1996) 13.52
R v Tahir [2006] EWCA Crim 792 .... 9.42

Table of Cases

R v Thacker (1995) 16 Cr App R(S) 461 .... 10.122
R v Thomas [2004] EWCA Crim 1101 .... 10.137
R v Tighe [1996] Crim LR 69 .... 12.58
R v Tivnan (1999) 1 Cr App R(S) 92 .... 10.30, 13.21, 16.14
R v Tredwen (1994) 99 Cr App R 154 .... 10.167
R v Uxbridge Justices ex p Metropolitan Police Commissioner [1981] 1 QB 829 .... 29.117
R v Uxbridge Magistrates' Court ex p Henry [1994] Crim LR 581 .... 21.52, 21.54, 21.55
R v Uxbridge Magistrates ex p Webb (1998) 162 JP 198 (DC) 29.55, 29.56
R v Valentine [2006] EWCA Crim 2717 .... 10.98
R v Versluis [2004] EWCA Crim 3168 .... 10.58
R v Wadmore and Foreman [2006] EWCA Crim 686 .... 21.147, 29.105
R v Walbrook and Glasgow [1994] Crim LR 613 .... 2.75, 9.74, 10.78, 11.66, 14.80
R v Walls *The Times*, 6 November 2002 .... 10.86
R v West London Magistrates' Court ex p Rowland Omo Lamai (QBD, 6 July 2000) 21.191
R v Whellen (2000) 1 Cr App R(S) 200 .... 11.31
R v Wilkes [2003] EWCA Crim 848 .... 10.85, 11.27
R v Williams *The Times*, 11 January 2001 .... 10.72
R v Williamson [2003] EWCA Crim 644 .... 9.44
R v Wright [2006] EWCA Crim 1257 .... 10.95, 10.97
R v Young [2003] EWCA Crim 3481 .... 9.18, 11.42
R v Zelzele [2001] Crim LR 830; (2002) 1 Cr App R(S) 62 .... 9.20, 9.33
Radcliffe v Bartholomew [1892] 1 QB 161 .... 21.80
Raimondo v Italy (1994) 18 EHRR 237 .... 8.45
Razaq (Mohammed) v Customs and Excise Commissioners (14949) VAT Tribunal 29.230
Refson (PS) & Co Ltd v Saggars [1982] 3 All ER 111 .... 7.39
Renfrewshire BC v Revenue and Customs Commissioners (E00963) (2006) 29.146
Revenue and Customs Commissioners v Smith (QBD, 17 November 2005) 29.188, 29.191
Revenue and Customs Prosecutions Office v Hill [2005] EWCA Crim 3271 .... 8.06
Rigby v R [2006] EWCA Crim 1653 .... 10.90, 12.43

S, re [1999] EWHC Admin 466 .... 6.29
S, re [2005] 1 WLR 1338 .... 28.76
S v Customs and Excise Commissioners *see* Customs and Excises Commissioners v
     S S and W, re (QBD, 7 February 2000) 4.31, 4.38
Saggar [2005] EWCA Civ 174 .... 16.48
Salabiaku v France (1988) 13 EHRR 379 .... 10.149, 29.132
Salomon v Salomon [1897] AC 22, [1895–9] 2.54
Saunders v United Kingdom [1996] 23 EHRR 313 .... 4.23
SCF Finance Co Ltd v Masri [1985] 1 WLR 876 .... 22.58
Schmautzer v Austria (1995) 21 EHRR 511 .... 19.14
Scottish Ministers v McGuffie [2006] SC(D) 26/2 .... 20.113, 20.117
Searose Ltd v Seatrain UK Ltd [1981] 1 All ER 806 (QBD) 19.76
Sekhon v R *see* R v Sekhon
Serious Fraud Office v X [2005] EWCA Civ 1564 .... 5.25, 5.43, 5.44
Silcock v Levin [2004] EWCA Crim 408 .... 11.17
Simms v Moore [1970] 3 All ER 1 .... 29.75
Singh (Satnam) v Director of the Assets Recovery Agency [2005]
     EWCA Civ 580 .... 19.22, 20.73, 20.77, 20.90
     see also Director of the Assets Recovery Agency v Singh (Satnam) [2004]
     EWHC Admin 2335
Siporex Trade SA v Condel Commodities Ltd [1986] 2 Lloyd's Rep 428 .... 19.47
Sisu Capital Fund Ltd v Tucker and Wallace [2005] EWHC 2321 (Ch) 28.31
SL, re [1995] 3 WLR 830 .... 25.11
Southern Cross Commodities Proprietary Ltd v Martin (CA, 11 February 1986) 5.45

Table of Cases

Squirrel Ltd v National Westminster Bank plc (Customs & Excise Commissioners
    intervening) [2005] 2 All ER 784 .... 26.49
Szukala Trans Pthu Export-Import v Revenue and Customs Commissioners (2006)
    150 *SJ* 571 .... 29.165, 29.169

T, re (17 December 2002) 5.17, 5.19
T, re [2006] EWHC 2233 .... 13.39
T (Restraint Order: Disclosure of Assets), re [1992] 1 WLR 949;
    (1993) 96 Cr App R 194 .... 4.12, 4.18, 9.86, 10.30, 14.94
T v Customs and Excise Commissioners [2004] EWHC Admin 3256 .... 5.18
Taylor, re (CA, 25 June 1996) 13.42
Taylor v Commissioners of Customs & Excise (1975) VAT TR 147 .... 29.210
Thane Investments Ltd v Tomlinson *The Times*, 10 December 2002 (Ch) 19.51
Thomas (Disclosure Order), re [1992] 4 All ER 814 .... 11.82
Thomas v Customs and Excise Commissioners (1997) 161 JP 386 .... 21.155
Three Rivers DC v Bank of England (No 6) [2004] 3 WLR 1274 .... 27.56
Three Rivers DC (Respondents) v Governor of the Bank of England [2004]
    UKHL 48 .... 29.211
Togher v Customs and Excise Commissioners [2001] EWCA Civ 474 .... 6.24
Travell v Customs and Excise Commissioners (1997) 162 JP 181 .... 29.54, 29.56
Trustor AB v Smallbone [2001] 1 WLR 1177 .... 22.25

Villiers v Villiers [1994] 2 All ER 149 .... 6.35

W (Drug Trafficking) (Restraint Order: Costs), re *The Times*, 13 October 1994 .... 28.04
W, re (1990) *The Times*, 15 November 1990 .... 1.44, 2.05, 3.68, 5.33,
                                    5.34, 5.38, 5.40, 5.54, 19.110, 22.30, 22.32,
                                    22.34, 22.35, 22.36, 22.38, 22.46, 22.52
W, re (1992) (QBD, unreported) 5.17, 5.19
W, re (1998) (QBD, 29 January 1998) 13.44, 13.53, 16.62
Walsh v Customs and Excise Commissioners *The Times*, 4 July 2001 .... 21.54, 21.55
Walsh v Director of the Assets Recovery Agency [2005] NICA 6 .... 1.49, 20.111,
                                                          20.112, 20.113
Ware v Customs and Excise Commissioners (E00735) 29.170
Webb v UK (2004) App No 56054–00 .... 20.110
Welch v UK (1995) 20 EHRR 247; [1995] 1/1994/448/527 .... 10.30, 10.150, 10.151
Weston v Dayman [2006] EWCA Civ 1165 .... 7.45, 17.09, 17.10
White v White [2001] 1 AC 596 .... 22.110
WJT, re (QBD, 5 October 1992) 4.45, 4.48
Woodstock v Director of the Assets Recovery Agency (CA, 18 May 2006) 20.26, 20.27

X, re [2004] 3 WLR 906; [2004] EWHC 861 .... 1.44, 2.05, 5.34, 5.38, 5.54
                              19.110, 22.31, 22.34, 22.39, 22.48, 22.51, 22.56
X v UK (1984) 6 EHRR 136 .... 8.44
X v X [2005] EWHC Fam 296 .... 22.107, 22.117
X Ltd v Morgan Grampian [1990] 2 All ER 1 .... 6.36

Yukong Line [1998] 1 WLR 794 .... 2.60

Z Ltd v A-Z and Others, *sub nom* Mareva Injunctions [1982] QB 558; [1982]
    2 WLR 288; [1982] 1 Al ER 556 .... 22.10, 22.143

TABLE OF LEGISLATION

UK Statutes	lxix
UK Statutory Instruments	xc
Civil Procedure Rules	xcv
Rules of the Supreme Court	xcvi
Criminal Procedure Rules	xcvii
European Community	xcviii
European Convention on Human Rights	xcix
International	xcix

UK STATUTES

Access to Justice Act 1999 . . . . 8.43, 29.120
  s 6 . . . . App 15
    (6) 29.120
  Sch 2 . . . . 29.120
    para 1 . . . . App 19
    para 2 . . . . App 13
      (3) 21.174, 29.120
    para 3 . . . . App 19
    para 6 . . . . 29.121
Administration of Justice Act 1960
  s 4 . . . . 24.116
  s 13 . . . . 24.115, 24.118
    (3)–(4) 24.117
Administration of Justice (Miscellaneous
  Provisions) Act 1933
  s 2 . . . . 2.09
    (2)(b) 2.09
Alcoholic Liquor Duties Act 1979 . . . . . . 29.08
  s 5 . . . . 29.08
  s 36 . . . . 29.08
  s 54 . . . . 29.08
  s 62 . . . . 29.08
Anti-Terrorism, Crime and Security
    Act 2001 . . . . 21.04, 21.194

Banking Act 1987 . . . . 17.106
Banking and Financial Dealings
    Act 1971 . . . . 8.76
Building Societies Act 1986 . . . . 17.106

Cinemas Act 1985
  s 10(1)(a) 2.26, 11.32

Civil Evidence Act 1968
  ss 11–12 . . . . 29.107
Civil Evidence Act 1995 . . . . 21.144, 29.107
  s 1 . . . . 21.147, 29.105
    (1)–(2) 21.145, 29.103
  s 2 . . . . 25.57
    (1) 8.99
  s 3 . . . . 25.57
  s 4 . . . . 25.57
    (2) 21.146, 29.104
Commissioners for Revenue and
    Customs Act 2005 . . . . 4.02
  ss 5–6 . . . . 1.27
  s 34 . . . . 1.24
    (1) 1.24
  s 35(1)–(2) 1.24
  s 50 . . . . 1.27, 29.06
Constitutional Reform Act 2005 . . . . App 20
Contempt of Court Act 1981
  s 14 . . . . 6.35
    (1) 6.30
Copyright, Designs and Patents
    Act 1988 . . . . 14.28
  s 107(1)–(3) 2.26, 11.32
  s 198
    (1) 2.26, 11.32
    (2) 11.32
Courts Act 1971
  s 52 . . . . 21.168, 21.169, 28.19
    (3) 21.166
    (b) 28.19
Courts and Legal Services
    Act 1990 . . . . 19.231

Table of Legislation

Criminal Appeal Act 1968 . . . . 24.26,
  24.43, 24.65, 24.85
  s 9 . . . . 24.52, 24.53
  s 18 . . . . 24.87
  s 18A 24.118
    (3) 24.118
  s 19 . . . . 24.119
    (1)(b) 24.119
  s 20 . . . . 24.89
  s 21 . . . . 24.91
  s 22 . . . . 24.92
  s 23 . . . . 24.95
  s 33(3) 24.28, 24.46, 24.80
  s 50(1) 24.53
  s 89(3) 24.26, 24.43, 24.65, 24.77
Criminal Appeal Act 1995
  s 9 . . . . 24.113
  s 13 . . . . 24.113
Criminal Attempts Act 1981
  s 1 . . . . 2.11, 9.11
Criminal Justice Act 1967 . . . . 17.77
  s 9 . . . . 8.98
Criminal Justice Act
  1987 . . . . 1.28, 1.29
  s 2 . . . . 1.28, 1.29
Criminal Justice Act 1988
  Part VI 2.23, 2.24, 2.26, 2.29,
    4.46, 7.21, 9.60, 11.04, 12.08,
    12.47, 15.15, 22.16, 25.02,
    25.13, 25.17, 25.30, 26.106
  s 1 . . . . 10.28
  s 36 . . . . 24.58
  s 71 . . . . 2.27, 2.39, 7.31, 11.03,
    11.31, 11.74, 12.08, 12.38,
    12.43, 13.30, 13.34, 22.113
    (1) 9.09, 11.07, 11.08,
      11.09, 11.34, 12.05, 12.08,
      12.66, 14.03, 25.12
      (a) 11.20, 12.08, 12.18,
        12.26, 12.46
      (b) 11.23, 12.08, 12.18
      (c) 12.66
      (d) 12.27, 12.28
    (1A) 11.07, 13.32
    (1B) 11.07
      (a) 13.33
    (1C) 11.07, 11.28, 12.09
    (1D) 11.07, 11.11, 12.29
    (1E) 2.33, 11.09, 11.30,
      11.31, 12.29
      (a) 12.08
      (b) 11.32
    (4) 2.35, 2.39, 11.12, 12.25,
      12.33, 12.34, 12.35, 28.83

    (5) 2.35, 12.31,
      12.41, 28.83
    (6) 11.07, 12.66
    (7) 28.81
    (7A) 11.04, 11.13, 12.11
    (9) 12.08
      (c) 2.26, 11.25
      (i) 11.08
      (ii) 11.08, 11.09
    (9A) 11.30
  s 72 . . . . 11.03, 11.20
    (1) 11.20
    (4)(a) 9.47
    (5) 11.53, 12.88, 12.92
      (a) 9.47
      (b)–(c) 12.08
    (7) 12.89
  s 72A 9.23, 9.31, 9.41, 9.42,
    11.04, 11.33, 11.35, 12.08
    (1) 9.27, 11.33, 11.34,
      11.50, 12.04
    (2) 11.38
    (3) 9.23, 11.34, 11.38,
      11.41, 11.42, 12.08
    (4) 11.49, 11.50, 12.04
    (5) 11.49, 11.50, 12.04
      (a) 11.51, 12.04
    (6) 11.49, 11.50, 12.04
    (7) 11.49, 11.52, 12.08
    (9) 11.53
      (a)–(b) 12.08
    (9A) 11.54, 12.91
  s 72AA 11.24, 11.26, 11.27,
    12.08, 12.18, 12.25
    (1) 11.18, 12.46
      (c) 12.44
    (2) 11.24, 12.47
    (3) 12.49
    (4) 12.08, 12.50
    (5) 12.52
    (6) 11.11, 12.28
    (7) 12.48
  s 73 . . . . 9.60, 11.03, 11.55, 11.56,
    11.57, 11.59, 11.60, 11.62,
    11.70, 11.80, 12.17, 13.31,
    13.33, 13.34, 17.34, 17.70
    (1) 11.55, 11.56
      (a) 9.61
    (1A) 11.55, 11.63, 12.18
    (1B) 11.55, 11.79, 12.18
    (1C) 11.55, 11.59, 11.71, 12.18
    (2) 11.63, 11.78
    (3) 11.69, 11.78
    (5) 11.63

Criminal Justice Act 1988 (*cont.*)
- s 73A 4.25, 11.64, 13.33, 13.34
  - (1) 11.73, 11.74
  - (2) 11.73, 11.74, 11.75, 12.18
  - (3) 11.73, 12.18
  - (5) 11.73, 11.75, 12.18
  - (6) 11.76, 11.77, 12.18
- s 74 . . . . . . 12.43, 22.101, 22.102, 22.113
  - (1) 2.67, 12.59, 12.65, 12.80
    - (a) 12.70
    - (b) 12.70, 25.12
  - (2) 2.73
  - (3) 2.37, 12.59, 12.70
  - (4) 12.64, 12.72
    - (b) 12.62
  - (5) 12.77, 12.78, 12.79
  - (6) 12.77, 12.78
  - (7) 12.63, 12.64
  - (8) 12.64
  - (10) 12.56, 12.57, 12.59, 12.60, 12.70
  - (11) 12.57
- s 74A 2.24, 2.31, 2.32, 13.27, 13.28, 13.31, 13.33
  - (1)–(2) 13.28
  - (3)–(6) 13.30
  - (9)–(11) 13.31
  - (12) 13.29
- s 74B 2.24, 2.31, 2.32, 13.27, 13.32
  - (2) 13.32
  - (3) 13.33
  - (9)–(11) 13.33
- s 74C 2.24, 2.31, 2.32, 13.27, 13.34
  - (3) 2.24, 13.34
  - (7)–(9) 13.34
  - (11) 13.34
- s 75
  - (1) 12.83, 17.63
  - (3) 17.75
  - (5) 17.38
    - (b) 17.65
  - (5A) 12.87, 17.19, 17.38
- s 75A 17.03
- s 76 . . . . 2.23, 2.94, 7.34, 25.12
  - (1) 2.24
    - (b) 13.03
    - (c) 2.33
  - (3)(a) 7.14
- s 77 . . . . 2.39, 4.10, 4.46, 5.34, 22.16, 22.38
  - (1) 2.50, 2.88, 5.34, 22.03, 22.04, 22.38
  - (2) 22.38
  - (3) 2.51, 2.64
  - (4) 2.102, 7.33
  - (5)(c) 4.10
  - (6) 22.38
    - (b) 5.03
  - (8) 3.07, 3.08, 4.10, 8.58, 17.31
  - (9) 2.51
  - (10) 4.02
  - (11) 4.04
- s 78 . . . . 2.102, 8.59, 17.27, 17.89, 25.61
  - (1) 2.95
  - (4) 2.98
  - (5) 2.97
  - (6) 2.98
  - (7) 2.100, 5.03
    - (b)(ii) 5.03
  - (8) 2.100
- s 79 . . . . 2.99
- s 79A 25.20
- s 80 . . . . 17.13, 17.14, 22.64, 22.76, 22.114, 25.37, 25.39
  - (1) 17.14, 17.20
  - (1A) 25.37
  - (2) 17.14, 17.15
  - (3) 17.14, 17.27
    - (a) 2.93
  - (4) 17.14, 17.29
  - (5) 17.14, 17.27, 22.129
  - (6) 17.14, 17.29, 22.77
  - (7) 17.14, 17.30
  - (8) 17.14, 17.40, 22.65
- s 81 . . . . 17.57
  - (2) 2.04, 17.60
  - (5) 3.65, 3.67, 17.58
- s 82 . . . . 3.63, 5.40, 8.64, 8.65, 17.42, 22.38, 28.69
  - (1) 5.29
  - (2) 2.39, 2.88, 3.14, 4.05, 5.29, 5.33, 5.34, 5.35, 17.11, 17.15, 22.30, 22.32, 22.33, 22.39, 22.50
  - (3) 5.29, 17.42
  - (4) 5.29, 5.36, 5.39, 17.42, 22.21, 22.39, 22.40, 22.47
  - (6) 3.67, 5.29, 5.34, 5.35, 5.57, 22.32, 22.35, 22.38, 22.39, 22.49
- s 83 . . . . 13.37
  - (4) 13.56
- s 84 . . . . 18.02, 18.06, 19.115
  - (1) 18.02, 22.147
  - (2) 18.04
  - (5) 18.07

Criminal Justice Act 1988 (*cont.*)
　s 86 . . . . 18.08
　　(1)–(2) 18.10
　　(6) 18.10
　s 87 . . . . 18.11
　　(2) 17.57
　s 88(1) 3.33
　s 89 . . . . 2.06, 3.45, 7.23, 28.78
　s 93A 26.22, 26.43, 26.104, 26.107
　　(1)(a) 26.14
　　(7) 26.106
　s 93B 26.51, 26.104, 26.107
　　(1)–(2) 26.101
　s 93C 26.23, 26.25, 26.104,
　　　　　　　　　　　　　　26.105, 26.107
　　(2) 26.16, 26.17, 26.18,
　　　　　　　　　　　　　　　26.21, 26.93
　s 93D 27.77, 27.98, 27.100
　　(1)–(3) 27.98, 27.99
　　(6) 27.99
　　(9) 27.103
　s 93H 23.04, 23.42, 23.45
　ss 93I–93J 23.04
　s 96 . . . . 25.04
　s 97 . . . . 25.29
　　(1) 25.27, 25.28
　　(2) 25.27
　s 102 . . . . 22.113
　　(1) 2.74, 4.02, 12.33, 12.65
　　(3) 2.76, 4.42, 25.02
　　(7) 2.68
　　(11) 2.25, 25.12
　　(12) 2.27, 2.29
　　　(d) 17.19
　　(12A) 2.31
　　　(b) 17.19
　　(12B) 2.28
　　(13) 17.20
　s 102(B) 17.19
　Sch 4 . . . . 2.26, 2.33, 11.08,
　　　　　　　　　　　　　11.10, 11.25, 11.32
Criminal Justice Act 1991 . . . . 6.30
　s 33(1) 6.30
　s 45 . . . . 6.30
　s 51 . . . . 17.77
Criminal Justice Act 1993 . . . . 1.13, 11.06,
　　　　　　　12.11, 26.02, 26.03, 26.12, 26.80,
　　　　　　　26.104, 27.88, 28.22, 28.34, 28.58,
　　　　　　　28.60, 28.62, 28.67, 28.71, 28.78,
　　　　　　　　　　　　28.80, 28.87, 28.90
　Part III 11.04, 26.104
　Part VI 28.78
　s 27 . . . . 11.04
　s 28 . . . . 11.04, 11.33
　ss 29–30 . . . . 26.104
　s 31 . . . . 26.104, 26.105
　s 32 . . . . 27.98
　s 72(5) 28.87
　s 77 . . . . 28.69
　　(2) 28.69
　　(8) 28.69
　s 78(6) 11.06
　s 89
　　(1) 28.78
　　(2)–(3) 28.78, 28.80
　　(4) 28.78
　　(5) 29.80
Criminal Justice (International
　Co-operation) Act 1990 . . . . 1.06,
　　　　　　　　　1.07, 14.26, 26.02, 26.03
　Part III 1.06, 21.01
　s 12 . . . . 2.11, 2.17, 9.11, 14.26
　s 14 . . . . 2.11, 9.11, 26.79, 26.82
　ss 15–16 . . . . 1.06
　s 19 . . . . 2.11, 2.17, 9.11, 14.26
　s 26(1) 21.52
　Sch 2 . . . . 2.11, 9.11, 14.26
Criminal Justice and Public Order
　Act 1994
　Sch 9
　　para 53 . . . . 11.06
Criminal Law Act 1977 . . . . 1.03
　s 1 . . . . 2.11, 9.11, 10.47
　　(1) 26.93
　　(2) 26.22, 26.24, 26.94
Criminal Law (Consolidation) (Scotland)
　Act 1995
　s 44(2) . . . . App 12, App 15
Criminal Procedure (Scotland) Act 1975
　s 223 . . . . 2.73
　s 436 . . . . 2.73
Crown Proceedings Act 1947 . . . . 23.20
Customs and Excise Act 1979 . . . . 29.07,
　　　　　　　　　　　29.51, 29.59, 29.122
Customs and Excise Management
　Act 1979 . . . . 14.26, 21.200,
　　　　　　　　　　　21.203, 28.83, 29.74,
　　　　　　　　　　　29.110, App 4
　s 1(1) 29.29
　s 49 . . . . 29.02, 29.07
　　(1) 29.07, 29.79
　　(2) 29.07
　s 50(2)–(3) 2.11, 9.11, 14.26
　s 68(2) 2.11, 9.11, 14.26, 14.27
　s 78 . . . . 29.111
　s 139 . . . . 29.02, 29.45, 29.67,
　　　　　　　　　　　　29.135, App 20
　　(6) 29.45

Customs and Excise Management
    Act 1979 (cont.)
  s 141 .... 29.02, 29.53, 29.85,
                       29.89, 29.150
    (a)–(b) 29.54
    (1) 29.51, 29.52
    (b) 29.58
  s 143 .... App 20
  s 144......................... 29.123
    (1)–(2) 29.122
  s 145 .... App 20
  s 152(b) 29.02, 29.162,
                       29.182, 29.233
  s 154......................... 29.59
    (1) 29.59
  s 163A 29.111
  s 164 .... 21.202, 29.111
  s 170 .... 2.11, 9.11, 14.26, 14.27
    (1)–(2) 29.67
  Sch 3......... 29.02, 29.45, 29.46, 29.58,
             29.74, 29.131, 29.135, 29.180
    para 1(1)–(2) .... App 20
    para 2...................... App 20
    para 3........... 29.70, 29.71, 29.72,
                     29.74, 29.188, 29.189, App 20
    para 4 .... 29.71, 29.72, 29.74
      (1)–(2) .... App 20
    para 5 .... 29.163, 29.183, App 20
    para 6........... 29.49, 29.50, 29.72,
             29.79, 29.152, 29.163, 29.183, App 20
    para 7 .... 29.47, App 20
    para 8 .... 29.16, App 20
    para 9...................... App 20
    para 10..................... App 20
      (1) 29.86, 29.88
      (3) 29.86
    para 11 .... 24.106, 29.124, App 20
    para 12 .... 24.106, 29.129, App 20
    paras 13–15 .... App 20
    para 16 .... 29.157, App 20
    para 17
      (1)–(8) .... App 20

Data Protection Act 1998 .... 23.71
Debtors Act 1868 .... 6.03
Debtors Act 1869 .... 6.03
Drug Trafficking Act 1994
  Part I 15.15
  Part II.......................... 21.03
  Part III 10.112, 26.79, 26.116
  s 1
    (1) 2.17, 10.166
    (2) 2.18, 10.166
    (3) 1.11, 2.11, 2.17, 9.11, 10.166
  s 2 .... 9.12, 9.44, 9.84, 10.01,
              10.07, 10.55, 10.73, 13.08, 13.09,
              13.11, 13.14, 14.02, 25.11
    (1)........... 9.06, 9.09, 10.11, 10.15,
                       14.02, 25.11
    (2) 10.01, 10.11, 10.37,
                       10.74, 25.11
    (3).......... 2.16, 10.16, 10.44, 10.45,
                  10.51, 10.57, 10.82, 10.166
    (4)............... 9.07, 10.49, 13.15
    (5) 9.07, 10.125
      (b)(iii).................... 10.126
      (c) 10.127
    (7) 10.15
    (8) 9.51, 10.06
    (9) 10.166
  s 3 .... 9.15, 9.20, 9.21, 9.35, 9.44
    (1) 9.07, 9.12, 9.13,
                       9.14, 9.37, 9.46
    (2) 9.12, 9.13, 9.14, 14.45
    (3) 9.12, 9.13, 9.14, 9.21
    (4)............ 9.07, 9.13, 9.37, 9.45,
                       9.46, 9.47
    (5).................. 9.13, 9.15, 9.46
      (a)........................ 9.47
    (6).............. 9.13, 9.46, 14.59
    (7) 9.08, 9.13, 9.50, 14.61
    (8)–(9) 9.13
    (11) 9.13
  s 4 .... 10.55, 10.77, 13.09
    (1) 10.50
      (a)............ 10.57, 10.82, 10.166
      (b)............ 10.52, 10.80, 10.166
    (2) 10.64, 10.73, 10.77, 10.164
    (3).......... 2.16, 9.67, 10.64, 10.70,
                  10.72, 10.146, 12.51
      (a)........................ 10.86
      (b) 10.68
      (d) 10.67
    (4) 10.65, 10.73
    (5) 10.66
  s 5 .... 9.05, 10.55, 10.77,
                       10.125, 16.65
    (1) 10.01, 10.50, 10.166, 12.75
      (b) 16.65
    (2) 10.79, 10.80
    (3) 10.01, 10.50, 10.53, 10.91
  s 6........................... 10.108
    (1) 10.114, 10.166
    (2) 2.67, 10.93, 10.100,
                  10.108, 10.166, 13.59
      (a)....................... 10.102
    (3) 10.100
    (4) 10.115

Drug Trafficking Act 1994 (cont.)
  s 7 . . . . 10.116
    (1) 10.86, 10.116, 10.166, 15.39
    (b) 10.119
    (2) 10.116, 10.166
    (b) 10.116
    (3) 10.116
  s 8
    (1) 10.109, 10.166
    (2) 10.166
    (a) 10.110
  s 9 . . . . 10.145, 12.96, 15.77, 20.108
    (1) 10.133, 17.63
    (2) 10.135, 17.75
    (4)(b) 17.65
    (5) 10.133, 17.38
  s 10 . . . . 17.03
  s 11 . . . . 9.55, 9.56, 9.60, 9.67,
       9.68, 9.69, 9.70, 9.71, 9.72, 9.79,
       9.81, 9.87, 9.94, 10.160, 10.164,
       11.60, 11.62, 11.70, 13.08, 13.13,
       13.17, 14.66, 17.34, 17.70
    (1) 9.54, 9.56, 9.60
    (2)–(3) 9.54, 9.56
    (4) 9.54, 9.93, 14.105
    (5) 9.54, 9.72, 9.73, 9.86, 9.87
    (6) 9.54, 9.73
    (7) 9.54, 9.61, 9.77, 9.78,
                10.167, 11.59, 11.71
    (8) 9.54, 9.87
    (9) 9.54, 9.79
    (10) 9.54
    (11) 9.54, 9.81, 9.82, 14.93
  s 12 . . . . 9.83, 9.84, 9.86, 9.87,
                13.08, 13.13, 13.17, 14.96
    (1) 9.83
    (2) 9.83, 9.84, 9.91
    (3) 9.85
    (5) 9.91
  s 13 . . . . 2.08, 2.10, 2.14, 2.20,
       13.07, 13.08, 13.09, 13.13, 13.15,
       13.16, 13.19, 13.28, 13.31
    (2) 13.07
    (3)–(4) 13.08
    (5)–(6) 13.09
    (7) 13.13
    (8)–(9) 13.09
    (10) 13.10
    (12) 13.10
  s 14 . . . . 2.08, 2.10, 2.14, 2.20, 13.11,
                13.15, 13.16, 13.19, 13.32
    (2) 13.11
    (3) 13.12
    (5) 13.13
    (8) 13.13

  s 15 . . . . 2.08, 2.10, 2.14, 2.20,
       13.14, 13.16, 13.19, 13.34
    (2) 13.14
    (3) 13.15
    (4) 2.08, 13.15
    (10)–(15) 13.15
  s 16 . . . . 2.08, 2.10, 2.14, 2.20,
       13.16, 13.18, 13.19, 13.20, 13.23,
       13.25, 13.26, 13.35, 16.48
    (1) 13.18
    (2) 2.08, 13.18, 13.19
    (3)–(4) 13.18
  s 17 . . . . 10.168, 13.37, 13.46, 13.49,
                16.57, 16.59, App 7
    (1)–(3) 13.37
    (4) 13.37, 13.56
  s 18 . . . . 2.06, 7.23, 28.78
    (1) 28.78
    (2)–(3) 28.78, 28.80
    (4) 28.78
    (5) 28.80
  s 19 . . . . 2.08, 2.10, 2.14, 2.20,
       10.153, 10.158
    (1) 10.154
    (2) 10.154, 10.159
    (3) 10.155
    (4) 10.155, 10.159
    (5) 10.157
    (6) 10.164
    (a)–(b) 10.164
    (c)–(d) 10.165
  s 25
    (1) 2.08, 2.19, 2.20, 2.94, 25.08
    (a) 2.10, 13.03
    (b) 2.12
    (c) 2.15
    (2) 2.08
    (3) 2.19, 2.20, 2.21, 25.08, 25.19
    (4) 2.22
    (a) 7.14
    (5) 2.21
  s 26 . . . . 2.49, 2.102, 18.09,
                22.16, App 9
    (1) 2.50, 2.82, 10.166, 22.03
    (2) 2.51, 2.64
    (3) 2.102
    (5)(b) 5.03
    (7) . . . . 3.07, 8.58, 17.31, App 4
    (8) 2.51
    (9) 4.02
    (11) 4.04
  s 27 . . . . 8.59, 17.27, 17.89,
                18.09, 25.61
    (1) 2.95
    (2) 10.166

Table of Legislation

Drug Trafficking Act 1994 (*cont.*)
- (4) 2.98
- (5) 2.97
- (6) 2.98
- (7) 2.100, 5.03
  - (b)(ii) 5.03
- (8) 2.100
- s 28 .... 2.99, 18.09
- s 29 .... 17.13, 18.09, 22.63,
  22.64, 22.76, 25.37, 25.39
  - (1) 17.14, 17.20
  - (1A) 25.37
  - (2) 17.14, 17.15
  - (3) 17.14, 17.27
    - (a) 2.93
  - (4) 17.14, 17.29
  - (5) 17.14, 17.27, 22.63, 22.129
  - (6) 17.14, 17.29
    - (a)–(b) 22.77
  - (7) 17.14, 17.30
  - (8) 17.14, 17.40, 22.65
- s 29A 25.19
- s 30 .... 17.57, 18.09
  - (3) 17.60
  - (6) 17.58
- s 31 .... 2.61, 5.40, 8.64,
  8.65, 17.42, 22.96
  - (1) 5.28
  - (2) 2.04, 2.61, 2.88, 3.14,
    4.05, 5.28, 5.29, 22.19, 22.30,
    22.50, 22.94, 22.95, 22.97, 28.64
  - (3) 5.28, 17.42, 22.97
  - (4) 2.61, 5.28, 17.42,
    22.94, 22.95, 22.97
  - (5) 5.28, 5.57, 22.49, 22.97
  - (6) 22.97
- s 32 .... 18.02, 18.06, 19.115
  - (1) 18.02, 22.147
  - (2) 18.04, 22.147
  - (4) 18.07
- s 34 .... 18.08
  - (1) 18.08, 18.10
  - (2) 18.09, 18.10
  - (4) 18.10
- s 35 .... 17.57, 18.11
- s 36(1) 3.33
- s 39 .... 25.21
  - (1)–(6) 25.04
- s 40 .... 25.21
  - (1) 25.27, 25.28
  - (2) 25.27
- s 41
  - (2) 2.09, 2.25, 8.19,
    10.166, 25.09, 25.21
- (3) 2.12, 25.10
- (4)–(5) 2.14
- (6) 2.13, 10.166, 17.18, 25.10
- (7) 10.166
- (8) 10.166, 17.20, 25.10
- s 42 .... 21.04, 21.07, 21.54, 21.178
  - (1) 21.52
  - (2) 21.54
- s 43 .... 20.79, 21.07,
  21.130, 21.137, 21.151
- s 44 .... 21.07
  - (4) 21.192
- ss 45–48 .... 21.07
- s 49 .... 2.11, 2.17, 9.11,
  10.55, 10.66, 26.25, 26.83,
  26.99, 26.104, 26.107, 27.90
  - (1) 26.81, 26.83, 26.104
    - (a) 26.83
  - (2) 26.17, 26.18,
    26.19, 26.21, 26.83, 26.93
    - (a) 26.83
  - (3) 26.83
- s 50 .... 2.11, 9.11, 10.55,
  10.66, 26.43, 26.79, 26.82,
  26.97, 26.99, 26.104, 26.107,
  26.108, 26.109, 26.110, 27.90
  - (1) 26.84, 26.88, 26.96, 26.104
  - (2) 26.86, 26.100
  - (3) 26.90, 26.97, 26.103
    - (a)–(b) 26.91
  - (4) 26.95, 26.96, 26.97, 26.102
    - (c) 26.103
  - (5) 26.97, 26.103
  - (7) 26.103
  - (9) 26.103
- s 51 .... 2.11, 2.17, 9.11,
  10.55, 10.66, 26.51, 26.102,
  26.104, 26.107, 27.90
  - (1) 26.88, 26.98, 26.104
  - (2)–(4) 26.100
  - (6) 26.99
- s 52 .... 27.12, 27.97
  - (1) 27.89
  - (2) 27.92
  - (3) 27.94
  - (5) 27.94
  - (7) 27.90
  - (8) 27.92
  - (9) 27.93
- s 53 .... 27.77, 27.95
  - (1)–(3) 27.95
  - (4) 27.97
  - (6)–(7) 27.97
- s 54(2) 27.103

Drug Trafficking Act 1994 (cont.)
  ss 55–56 .... 23.03
  s 59 .... 23.03
  s 62
    (1) 2.74, 10.166
    (2) 2.76, 4.42, 10.107, 25.02
    (3) 2.73, 10.166
    (5)
      (a) 2.68, 10.101, 10.166
      (b) 10.110, 10.166
  s 63
    (1) 4.02, 10.166
    (2) 10.38, 10.39, 10.42
    (3) 10.90
  s 64 .... 10.166
  s 66(2) 9.01
  s 69(2) 9.01
  s 72(5) 28.87
  s 73(1C) 9.61
Drug Trafficking Offences Act 1986
  s 1 .... 14.01
    (3) 10.44
    (4) 9.49
  s 2 .... 9.53
    (3)(a) 10.77
  s 3 .... 9.55, 9.56
    (2) 9.55
  s 5 .... 13.54
    (1)(b) 13.54
    (4) 10.119
      (a) 10.119
  s 9 .... 8.59, 17.14, 17.89, 25.61
  s 11(8) 17.40
  s 13(2) 5.31
  s 15(2) 19.115
  s 24 .... 26.79, 26.82
  s 27 .... 23.03, 23.40
    (2) 23.40
    (4) 23.40
  s 27(1) 23.46
  s 28 .... 23.03
  s 30 .... 23.03
  s 38(1) 23.46

Finance Act 1989
  s 182 .... App 4
Finance Act 1994
  s 14
    (1) 29.200
      (d) 29.168
    (2) 29.198
    (3) 29.200
  s 15(2) 29.201
  s 16
    (1) 29.164

    (b) 29.200
    (2) 29.198
    (4) 29.167, 29.169,
                                29.178, 29.192
    (6) 29.165
  Sch 5
    para 2(r) 29.168
Financial Services and Markets Act 2000
  s 38 .... 27.18
Firearms Act 1968
  s 31 .... 14.27

Human Rights Act 1998 .... xv, 1.47,
                          10.144, 10.146, 19.185,
                                20.66, App 9
  s 2(1) 29.237
  Sch 10.146
Hydrocarbon Oils Duties
  Act 1979 .... 29.143
  s 1(3)–(4) 29.139
  s 12(2)–(3) 29.137
  s 13
    (1)(a)–(b) 29.155
    (6) 29.137, 29.139
  Sch 1 .... 29.143, 29.146
    para 1 .... 29.143
    para 12(1)–(4) 29.143, 29.144
  Sch 5 .... 29.148
    section 32 .... 29.148

Immigration Act 1971
  s 25
    (1) 14.27
Industrial and Provident Societies
  Act 1965 .... 27.18
  s 6 .... 27.18, 27.19
  s 7(3) 27.18
Industrial and Provident Societies
  Act (Northern Ireland) 1969 .... 27.18
  s 6 .... 27.18, 27.19
  s 7(3) 27.18
Insolvency Act 1986 .... 16.54, 18.04,
                  18.05, 18.12, 18.17, 20.94, 22.149
  Part 1 .... 19.119, 20.93
  Part 8 .... 19.119, 20.93
  Part 9 .... 18.02, 18.04,
                                 22.147, 22.148
  s 252 .... 18.06, 22.147
  s 280(2)(c) 22.147, 22.148
  s 286 .... 18.07, 20.93
  s 307 .... 18.04, 22.147, 22.148
  ss 308–308A 18.04, 22.147, 22.148
  s 380(2)(c) 18.04
  s 386 .... 10.115
  s 388 .... 27.15

Insolvency Act 1986 (*cont.*)
 Sch 1
  para 11(B) 19.120
 Sch B1
  para 11(A) 19.120
Insolvency Acts 19.117

Judgments Act 1838
 s 17 .... 15.69
Justice (Northern Ireland)
 Act 2002 .... App 20
 s 88 .... App 20

Knives Act 1997
 s 6 .... 20.79

Land Charges
 Act 1972 .... 2.99, 8.56, 19.159
Land Registration Act 1925 .... 8.56, 19.159
 s 57 .... 19.161
Land Registration
 Act 2002 .... 2.99, 8.56, 19.159
Limitation Act 1980 .... 20.45
 s 27A 20.45
  (2) 20.45
  (3) 19.72
Local Government (Miscellaneous
 Provisions) Act 1982 .... 2.26
 Sch 3
  paras 20–21 .... 11.32

Magistrates' Courts Act 1980
 s 1 .... 2.09
 s 38 .... 11.30, 11.31
 s 51 .... 21.122, 29.90
 s 52 .... 21.40, 21.123, 29.91
 ss 53–54 .... 21.123, 29.91
 ss 55–57 .... 21.115, 21.123, 29.91
 s 58 .... 21.123, 29.91
 s 62(2)–(3) 21.172, 29.113
 s 64 .... 21.168, 21.169,
         21.171, 28.15, 28.18
  (1) 21.167, 28.15, 29.112
  (2)–(3) 28.15
 s 75 .... 17.109
 s 76 .... 17.64, 17.66
 s 81 .... 17.109
 s 82 .... 17.66
  (3) 17.66
 s 84(3) 17.66
 s 85 .... 17.109
 s 87 .... 17.65, 17.109
  (3) 17.65
 s 111
  (1) 24.109

  (4) 24.109
 s 127 .... 29.73
 s 145A 21.173, 29.119
Matrimonial Causes
 Act 1973 .... 22.96, 22.97,
         22.98, 22.99, 22.107,
         22.115, 22.116, 22.117,
         22.118, 22.121, 22.123,
         22.124, 22.125
 Part II 22.98, 22.99,
         22.116, 22.120
 s 23 .... 22.106
 s 24 .... 22.96, 22.97,
         22.98, 22.119, 22.122,
         22.124, 22.125
  (1)(c) 22.112
 s 25 .... 22.120, 22.121,
         22.122, 22.125
Misuse of Drugs Act 1971 .... 14.26
 s 3 .... 2.11, 9.11, 14.26
  (1) 2.17
 s 4
  (1) 2.17
  (2)–(3) 2.11, 9.11, 14.26
 s 5
  (1) 2.17
  (3) 2.11, 9.11, 14.26
 s 8 .... 14.26
 s 19 .... 2.11
 s 20 .... 2.11, 14.26
 s 27 .... 1.03, 2.73, 10.34,
         10.100, 10.126, 11.53, 12.88,
         15.37, 15.71, 20.79
 s 36(1) 23.47

National Loans Act 1968 .... 27.15

Obscene Publications Act 1959
 s 3 .... 20.79
Official Secrets Acts 1911–1989 .... App 4

Pensions Schemes Act 1993 .... 20.123
 s 159 .... 20.122
Perjury Act 1911
 s 5 .... App 12, App 15
Police and Criminal Evidence
 Act 1984 .... xv, 21.36,
         21.200, 23.04, 23.19, 23.39,
         23.42, 23.44, 29.17, 29.67, 29.68
 s 9 .... 23.44, 23.45
 s 19 .... 17.104, 21.33
 s 78 .... 4.41, 23.45
 s 114(2) 17.104
 Sch 1 .... 23.44
  para 7 .... 23.44

Powers of Criminal Courts Act 1973
  s 42 .... 11.31
  s 43 .... 15.75
Powers of Criminal Courts (Sentencing)
  Act 2000 .... 10.133, 12.85,
         14.06, 14.12, 15.65
  s 3 .... 14.06, 14.12, 14.13,
         15.04, 16.04, 16.79
  s 4 .... 14.06, 14.13,
         15.04, 16.04, 16.79
  s 6 .... 14.06, 14.13,
         15.04, 16.04, 16.79
  s 108 .... 17.75
  s 116 .... 14.13
  s 130 .... 11.53, 12.88,
         13.30, 14.58, 14.60, 14.62, 15.71,
         16.18, 16.42, 16.43, 20.87,
         21.31, 28.104
  s 139 .... 17.109
    (1) 12.83, 17.63
      (b) 12.86
    (2) 12.83, 13.18,
         13.37, 17.63, 17.109
    (3) 12.83, 17.63, 17.109
    (4) 10.134, 12.83,
         12.84, 15.66, 17.63, 17.109
    (9) 17.109
  s 140 .... 17.109
    (1)–(3) 12.83, 17.63, 17.109
    (4) 17.109
  s 143 .... 2.73, 10.100,
         10.126, 11.53, 12.88, 15.37, 15.71
  s 148(2) 20.88
  s 155
    (1) 12.91, 24.59
    (2) 12.91
Prevention of Terrorism Act 1989
  Part III 25.12
Proceeds of Crime
  Act 1995 .... 1.13, 2.23, 23.04
  s 2 .... 11.24
  Sch 1
    para 2 .... 11.33
Proceeds of Crime Act 2002
  Part 1 .... 1.17, 20.07
  Part 2 .... 8.01, 14.07,
         14.109, 15.03, 15.05, 15.12,
         16.51, 19.109, 19.158, 24.19,
         24.28, 24.36, 24.46, 24.66,
         24.80, 24.86, 24.88, 24.90,
         24.91, 24.92, 24.93, 25.68, 28.89,
         App 6, App 19
  Part 3 .... 15.15
  Part 4 .... 15.05, 15.15, 19.158

Part 5 .... xi, 1.27, 16.78,
         19.01, 19.09, 19.12, 19.14, 19.19,
         19.63, 19.109, 19.117, 19.121,
         19.122, 19.149, 19.153, 20.29,
         20.45, 20.79, 20.102, 20.110,
         20.120, 21.10, 21.23, 21.26,
         21.103, 21.120, 21.128, 21.177,
         21.215, 28.93, App 6,
         App 12, App 19
Part 6 .... 24.111
Part 7 .... 26.02, 26.11,
         26.12, 26.36, 26.64, 26.73,
         26.116, 27.35, 27.86
Part 8 .... 19.95, 23.05,
         23.06, 23.07, 23.08, 23.61, 26.04,
         App 10, App 11, App 12, App 19
Part 10 .... 19.144
  s 1
    (1) 12.05
    (2) 12.09
    (4) 12.82
  s 2 .... 11.25, 12.45,
         12.47, 20.07, App 22
    (1) 1.17, 20.05
    (2)–(3) 27.72
    (5)–(6) .... 1.18, App 22
  s 3 .... 12.17
  s 3A 27.35
    (2)–(3) 27.36
    (5A) 27.37
  s 4 .... 12.17
  s 6 .... 8.05, 14.22, 14.23,
         14.60, 14.96, 14.97, 15.03, 15.04,
         15.12, 16.04, 16.10, 16.20, 16.24,
         16.31, 16.32, 16.38, 16.77, 16.80,
         16.86, 16.87, 16.89, 16.94, 16.98,
         22.148, 24.71, 24.72, 24.73, 24.75,
         24.76, 24.81, 24.82, 24.83
    (1) 14.06, 14.24, 15.82, 24.71
    (2) 14.06, 14.24,
         15.04, 16.04, 16.80, 24.71
      (a) 15.82
      (b) 14.12, 14.13
    (3) 14.06, 14.24, 24.71
      (a) 14.63, 14.96, 15.82, 16.38
      (b) 14.64, 14.96, 16.38
    (4) 14.24, 15.04
      (a) 15.82
      (b)–(c) 14.33, 14.39, 15.04, 15.82
    (5) 14.39, 15.04
      (a) 15.82
    (6) 15.04, 15.33
    (7) 15.07, 15.82
  s 7 .... 14.39, 15.31, 15.32

Proceeds of Crime Act 2002 (*cont.*)
   (1)–(2) 15.31, 15.33, 15.82
   (3) 15.33
   (5) 15.46
  s 8
   (1) 15.11
   (2) 15.11, 16.25
   (3) 15.13, 15.14
     (c) 15.26
   (4) 15.13, 15.14
   (5) 15.13, 15.14, 16.26
   (6) 15.13, 15.14, 17.14
   (7)–(8) 15.13, 15.15
  s 8(2) 24.75
  s 9. . . . . 15.37, 16.32,
                16.40, 16.50, 16.69
   (1) 15.34, 15.35, 15.82
   (2) 15.34, 15.36
  s 10. . . . . 15.20, 15.21,
        15.22, 15.39, 15.82, 16.30,
           16.81, 16.88, 24.75
   (1) 15.21, 15.82
   (2) 15.24, 15.82
   (3)–(5) 15.24
   (6) 15.28, 15.82
   (7) 15.29
   (8) 15.25, 15.26
   (9) 15.26
   (10) 15.27
  s 11. . . . . 15.61
   (1) 15.61
   (2) 15.61, 15.62
   (3) 15.61
   (4) 15.62, 15.64
   (5) 15.63
   (6) 15.64
  s 12. . . . . 17.03
   (1)–(2) 15.69
   (4) 15.69
  s 13. . . . . 15.73
   (2) 15.71
   (3) 14.58, 14.60,
        14.62, 15.71, 24.72, 24.82
   (4) 15.71
   (5) 15.72, 24.73, 24.74
   (6) 15.72, 16.18,
      16.35, 16.43, 17.91, 24.73, 24.74
  s 14
   (1) 14.22, 14.45
     (a) 14.46
   (2)–(3) 14.45
   (4) 14.47, 14.50
   (5) 14.22, 14.47
   (6) 14.59

   (7) 14.56
   (8) 14.49
   (9) 14.48
   (11) 1.46, 9.38, 11.46, 14.57
   (12) 14.58
  s 15
   (1) 14.22, 14.60
   (2) 14.60
   (3) 14.60, 14.62
   (4) 14.62
  s 16. . . . . 14.67, 14.70,
       14.72, 14.74, 14.106, 16.38
   (1) 14.63, 14.72, 14.75
   (2) 14.64, 14.72
   (3) 14.65, 14.81, 16.81, 16.88
   (4) 14.68, 14.71, 16.81, 16.88
   (5) 14.69, 14.81
   (6) 14.104, 14.105
  s 17 . . . . 14.74, 14.78, 14.86,
       14.87, 14.92, 14.94, 14.106,
        16.38, 16.81, 16.88
   (1) 14.77, 14.83, 14.86
     (a) 14.79
   (2) 14.81, 14.82
   (3) 14.83
   (6) 14.74, 14.93, 14.95
  s 18. . . . . 14.96, 14.97,
       14.98, 14.101, 16.38, 16.81, 16.88
   (1)
     (a) 14.96
     (b) 14.96, 14.97
   (2) 14.96, 14.103
   (4) 14.99, 14.103
   (5) 14.99
   (6) 14.102
   (9) 14.101
  s 19 . . . . 8.24, 16.02, 16.07,
      16.09, 16.10, 16.18, 16.37, 16.38,
      16.41, 16.82, 16.83, 16.88, 17.92,
        24.69, 24.76, 28.73
   (1) 16.03, 16.04
     (b) 16.06
     (c) 16.05
   (2)–(6) 16.04
   (7) 16.04
     (c)–(d) 16.34
   (8) 16.04, 16.18
   (9) 16.06
   (10) 16.06, 16.16, 16.29
  s 20 . . . . 8.24, 16.11, 16.18,
     16.19, 16.20, 16.37, 16.41, 16.82,
       16.88, 17.92, 24.69, 28.73
   (2) 8.04, 16.12
     (a) 8.04

Proceeds of Crime Act 2002 (cont.)

(3) 8.04, 16.14
   (a) 8.04
(4) 16.15
(11)(c)–(d) 16.34
(12) 16.18
(13) 16.16
s 21 .... 8.27, 8.28, 8.31,
    16.23, 16.25, 16.30, 16.31, 16.36,
    16.37, 16.38, 16.41, 16.45, 16.82,
    16.88, 24.74, 28.74, 28.75
(1) 16.21
   (d) 16.23
(2) 16.22
(3) 16.24
(4) 16.25
(6) 16.30
(7) 16.31
   (b) 16.33, 16.35
(8) 16.32
(9) 16.33
   (b) 16.33, 16.34
   (c) 16.33, 16.34, 16.35
(10) 16.35
(11) 16.36
(12) 16.27
(13) 16.28
(14) 16.29
s 22 .... 8.30, 8.31, 16.39,
    16.46, 16.47, 28.75
(1) 16.39
(3) 16.40
(4) 16.42
(5) 16.42
   (c) 16.43
(7) 16.46
(8) 16.44
s 23 .... 16.49, 16.50,
    16.55, 16.68, 17.109
(1) 16.49
(2) 16.50
(3) 16.52
(4) 16.54
(5) 16.51
(6) 16.54
s 24 .... 16.68, 16.70, 16.71, 16.74
(1) 16.68
(2)–(3) 16.69
(4) 16.70
s 25 .... 16.72, 16.74
(1)–(2) 16.72
s 26 .... 16.10, 16.20, 16.38, 24.76
(1) 16.38, 24.76
(2)(a)–(b) 16.38

s 27 .... 8.24, 16.77, 16.81,
    17.92, 24.69, 28.73
(2)–(3) 16.79
(5) 16.80
   (c) 16.80
   (e) 16.82
s 28 .... 8.24, 16.77, 16.84,
    16.85, 16.86, 16.88, 16.89, 16.90,
    16.94, 16.98, 16.99, 16.102,
    16.105, 17.92, 24.69, 28.73
(1) 16.84
(2) 16.84, 16.100
   (a) 16.97
   (b) 16.85
(3) 16.84
(4) 16.86
(5)
   (a) 16.86
   (b) 16.87, 16.88
   (c)–(e) 16.88
(7) 16.89
s 29 .... 16.90, 16.93,
    16.94, 16.97, 16.105, 28.91
(1) 16.92
(2) 16.96
(3) 16.93
(4) 16.97
s 30 .... 16.90, 16.98,
    16.101, 16.102, 16.105, 28.91
(1) 16.98
(2) 16.98, 16.101
(3) 16.99
(4) 16.101
(5) 16.90, 16.101
s 31 .... 8.22, 24.05,
    24.78, 24.79, 24.85, 24.86
(1) 15.80, 24.67
(2) 8.22, 15.80, 17.92, 24.67
(3) 24.69
s 32 .... 24.70
(1) 15.80, 24.70
(3) 24.72
(4) 24.72
   (b) 24.82
(6)–(7) 24.73, 24.83
(8) 24.73, 24.74, 24.83
(9) 24.73, 24.75, 24.83
(10) 24.73, 24.76, 24.83
(11) 24.76
s 33 .... 8.22, 17.92,
    24.05, 24.81, 24.84, 24.85
(1) 24.78
(2)–(3) 24.79
(4) 24.81

Proceeds of Crime Act 2002 (cont.)
 (5) 24.82
 (6)(b) 24.82
 (8)–(12) 24.83
 (13) 24.84
s 34 . . . . 16.47, 16.55, 16.95,
  16.103, 16.106, 16.108, 17.92
 (1) 17.92
s 35(2) 17.109
s 37 . . . . 17.110
 (2) 17.110, 17.111
 (4)–(5) 17.111
 (7) 17.111
 (9) 17.111
s 38
 (2) 15.65, 15.67
 (5) 15.65
s 39(5) 16.108
s 40 . . . . 8.33
 (1) 8.12
 (2) 8.13, 28.71, 28.72
  (a) 2.01, 8.08
 (3) 8.17, 28.71, 28.72
  (a) 2.01
 (4) 8.23, 8.24, 28.73
 (5) 8.27, 28.74
 (6) 8.29, 28.75
 (7) 8.18
 (8) 8.32
 (9) 8.16
s 41 . . . . 2.01, 8.04, 18.12,
  18.13, 20.89, 22.03, 22.05,
  22.16, 22.148, 24.48, 28.71
 (1) 8.33, 22.04
 (2) 8.33
 (3) 8.38, 8.39, 28.71
  (a) 8.40
  (c) 8.39, 8.48
 (4) 1.40, 5.19,
  8.40, 8.42, 8.44, 8.45,
  8.73, 8.74, 25.52
  (a) 8.41
 (5) 8.41, 28.71
 (6) 8.49
 (7) 4.01, 8.49,
  8.70, 8.72, 8.75, 8.78,
  8.80, 23.06, 24.16
s 42 . . . . 8.70, 18.13,
  22.148, 24.15, 24.48
 (1)(a)–(b) 8.37
 (2) 8.37
 (3) 8.55, 8.75, 8.78,
  8.80, 22.58, 24.16
 (7) 8.16, 21.112, 24.103

s 43 . . . . 8.08, 18.13, 22.148,
  24.05, 24.15, 24.20, 24.27,
  24.48, 24.85, 24.86
 (1) 24.14, 24.17
 (2) 24.16
 (3) 24.15
s 44 . . . . 18.13, 22.148,
  24.05, 24.27, 24.48, 24.85
 (3) 24.27
  (a)–(b) 24.27
ss 45–46 . . . . 18.13, 22.148
s 47 . . . . 8.56, 18.13, 22.148
s 48 . . . . 8.53, 8.57, 17.91,
  18.13, 22.148, 24.31, 24.48, 28.59
 (1) 8.57, 8.82
  (b) 8.58
 (2) 8.57
s 49 . . . . 8.57, 8.60, 17.90,
  18.13, 22.148, 24.31, 24.48
 (1) 8.59, 8.84
 (2) 8.59
  (b) 8.62
  (d) 3.60, 8.60,
   8.62, 17.91, 28.59
 (3) 8.59, 8.61
 (4)–(5) 8.59
 (6) 8.59, 8.62
 (7) 8.59
 (8) 8.59, 8.62
 (9)–(10) 8.59
s 50 . . . . 8.53, 8.54, 16.47,
  16.55, 16.74, 16.76, 17.88,
  17.91, 18.12, 18.13, 22.64,
  22.134, 22.148, 24.31, 28.59
 (1) 8.82, 17.88
 (2) 17.88
s 51 . . . . 17.88, 17.89, 18.13,
  22.76, 22.134, 22.148, 24.31
 (1) 8.84, 17.89
 (2) 17.89
 (3) 17.89
  (a) 22.65
 (4) 17.89
 (5) 17.89, 22.65
 (6) 17.89, 22.65, 22.78
  (a)–(b) 22.77
 (7) 17.89
 (8) 17.89, 17.90, 17.95, 22.65
 (9) 17.89, 22.129
 (10) 17.89
s 52 . . . . 8.53, 16.47, 16.55,
  18.12, 18.13, 22.148, 24.35, 28.59
 (3)–(4) 17.93, 17.94
 (5) 17.94

Proceeds of Crime Act 2002 (cont.)
s 53 . . . . 17.95, 18.13,
22.148, 24.31, 24.35
 (1) 8.84
 (8) 17.95
s 54 . . . . 17.91, 18.13,
22.134, 22.148
 (2)–(4) 22.134
s 55 . . . . 17.91, 18.13, 22.148
 (2) 17.91
 (4)(b) 17.103, 28.59
s 56 . . . . 18.13, 22.148
s 57 . . . . 18.13, 22.148
 (4)(b) 17.103, 28.59
s 58 . . . . 8.51, 8.54, 18.13, 22.148
 (2) 8.51
 (3) 2.72, 8.52
 (4) 8.52
 (5) 8.53, 22.125
 (6) 8.53
s 59 . . . . 8.54, 18.13, 22.148
ss 60–61 . . . . 18.13, 22.148
s 62 . . . . 18.13, 22.148,
24.33, 24.34
 (2)–(3) 24.33
s 63 . . . . 18.13, 22.148,
24.35, 24.48
s 64 . . . . 18.13, 22.148
s 65 . . . . 18.13, 22.148,
24.05, 24.37, 24.44, 24.45,
24.48, 24.85, 24.86
 (1) 24.31
 (2) 24.32
 (3) 24.33
 (4) 24.34
 (6) 24.44
s 66 . . . . 18.13, 22.148,
24.05, 24.48, 24.85
s 67 . . . . 17.104, 17.106,
17.107, 18.13, 22.148
 (1)–(3) 17.104
 (4) 17.105
 (6) 17.106
s 68 . . . . 8.70, 8.78,
8.82, 8.84, 24.47
 (1) 24.48
 (3)–(4) 24.49
s 69 . . . . 8.08, 8.54, 22.72, 22.125
 (1) 8.64
 (2) 8.64
  (b) 8.65
  (c) 19.109
 (3) 8.64
  (a) 22.70, 22.72, 22.126

  (c) 8.65
 (4) 8.64, 8.65
 (5) 8.64
s 70 . . . . 14.10, 15.04, 16.04
 (1) 14.09
  (a) 14.14
  (b) 14.10, 14.16
 (2) 14.09, 14.10
 (3) 14.09
 (4)(a) 14.23
 (5) 14.11
s 71 . . . . 1.45
 (3)(b) 14.11
s 72 . . . . 16.107, 28.90, 28.92
 (1) 28.85
 (3) 28.86
 (5)(b) 28.103
 (6) 28.89
 (9) 28.87, 28.88
s 72A(9) 28.103
s 73 . . . . 16.105
 (1) 28.91
 (3) 28.92
s 74 . . . . 8.04
s 75 . . . . 8.36, 14.30, 15.20, 15.81
 (1) 14.25
 (2) 14.25, 15.82
  (a) 14.25
  (b) 14.30, 14.31,
14.41, 14.43
  (c) 14.30, 14.32, 14.44
 (3) 14.37
  (a) 14.40, 14.41
  (b) 14.42, 14.43
 (4) 14.30
 (5) 14.31, 14.41, 14.43
  (c) 14.41
 (6) 14.32, 14.44
  (b) 14.44
s 76 . . . . 15.16, 15.81
 (1) 14.33, 15.82
 (2) 14.34, 15.13, 15.82
 (3) 14.35, 15.16
  (a) 15.82
 (4) 14.33, 14.38, 15.82
 (5) 14.33, 15.82
 (6) 14.33
 (7) 14.33, 14.38, 15.82
s 77 . . . . 15.81
 (1) 15.48
 (2) 15.49, 15.50, 15.51
 (3) 15.49, 15.51
 (4) 15.52
 (5) 15.52, 15.53

Table of Legislation

Proceeds of Crime Act 2002 (*cont.*)
   (6)–(7) 15.53
   (8) 15.54
   (9) 15.50
 s 78 .... 15.81
   (1) 15.55
   (3) 15.58
 s 79 .... 15.38, 15.42,
                15.60, 15.81, 15.82
   (1) 15.41, 15.82
   (2) 15.38, 15.39, 15.41, 15.82
   (3)–(4) 15.38
 s 80 .... 15.19, 15.81, 15.82
   (1)–(3) 15.19
 s 81 .... 15.60, 15.81
   (1)–(2) 15.59
   (3) 15.60
 s 82 .... 15.81
   (3) 15.37
 s 83 .... 15.81
 s 84 .... 8.34, 15.81, 22.72
   (1) 4.42, 8.34, 25.02
   (2)
     (a) 8.34
     (f) 8.34, 22.72
     (h) 8.34
 s 85 .... 8.26, 15.81
   (1) 8.19
   (3)–(5) 8.20
   (6) 8.20, 8.22
   (7)–(8) 8.22
 s 86
   (1) 8.25
   (2) 8.31
 s 87 .... 15.81
   (2) 24.64
 s 88 .... 15.81
   (2) 8.15
   (5) 14.06
 s 89 .... 15.80
   (1) 24.19, 24.36, 24.66
 s 90(1) 24.28, 24.46, 24.80
 s 91 .... 24.04
 s 92 .... 22.148
 s 120 .... 20.89
 s 128 .... 22.148
 s 156 .... 22.148
 s 190 .... 20.89
 s 198 .... 22.148
 s 200 .... 22.148
 s 232(1) 21.25
 s 240 .... 19.13
   (1) 21.10
     (b) 21.12, 21.129
   (2) 19.08
 s 241 .... 19.13, 21.204
   (1) 19.27, 21.20
   (2) 19.28, 21.20
   (3) 19.10, 20.32, 21.12
 s 242
   (1) 19.24
   (2) 19.25
     (a) 19.25
     (b) 20.33, 21.21
 s 243 .... 20.103
   (1) 19.18, 20.08
   (2) 20.14
   (4) 20.13
 s 245 .... 20.54
   (1) 19.30
   (2) 19.33
   (3) 19.33, 19.155
 s 245A .... 19.40, 19.41, App 17
   (1) 19.40
   (2) 19.42
   (3) 19.43, 19.80
   (5)–(6) 19.53
 s 245B .... 19.57, App 15, App 17
   (1) 19.57
   (2) 19.58, 19.59
   (3) 19.58, 19.59, 19.65
   (4) 19.59, 19.65
   (5)–(6) 19.59
 s 245C .... App 15, App 17
   (1) 19.60
     (b) 19.42
   (2) 19.42, 19.62
   (3)–(4) 19.62
   (5) 19.62, 19.74
   (6) 19.65
   (8)–(9) 19.65
 s 245D 19.68, 19.71
   (2) 19.69
   (3) 19.70
 s 246 .... 15.37, 19.54,
               19.104, 19.120, App 15
   (1) 19.41, 19.92
   (2) 19.97
   (3) 19.93, 19.97,
                 19.101, 19.139
   (5)–(6) 19.97
   (7) 19.124
   (8) 19.123
 s 247 .... 19.123, 19.143, App 12
   (1) 19.94, 19.125
     (b) 19.142
   (2) 19.142, 19.168
     (a)–(b) .... App 15

Proceeds of Crime Act 2002 (cont.)
 s 248 . . . . 19.123, 19.159
  (1) 19.159
   (a) 19.72
  (2) 19.159
  (3) 19.160
  (4) 19.161
 s 249. . . . . 19.123
 s 250 . . . . 19.123, App 15
  (1) 19.129
  (2) 19.130
 s 251 . . . . 19.123, 19.141
  (1)–(2). 19.140, 19.143
  (4) 19.147
 s 252. 8.43, 19.110,
          19.119, 19.123
  (1) 19.133
  (2)–(3) 19.134
  (4). 19.74, 19.177, 19.208
  (4A) 19.206
  (5) 19.136
  (6) 19.108, 19.109,
        19.111, 19.114, 19.119,
        19.149, 19.206, 19.207
 s 253 . . . . 19.123, 19.166
  (1) 19.162
  (2) 19.163
  (3) 19.165
  (4) 19.166
 s 254. . . . . 19.123
  (1) 19.154
  (2) 19.155
 s 255 . . . . 19.123, 19.167
  (1) . . . . 19.143, 19.167, App 15
  (2) . . . . 19.137, 19.169, App 15
 s 256. . . . . 20.113
 s 257 . . . . App 12
 s 266. . . . . 15.37, 20.50, App 18
  (1)–(2) 20.09
  (3) 20.66
   (a). 20.66
  (4). 20.66, 20.67, 20.86
  (7)–(8) 20.50
  (8A). 19.189, 19.222
  (8B) 19.189
   (a). 19.193
 s 267. . . . . 20.11
  (1)–(2) 20.39
  (3)–(4) 20.41
  (7) 20.44
 s 269 . . . . 19.175, 20.46
  (2) 19.174, 20.47
  (3) 20.48
  (6) 19.174

 s 270 . . . . 20.50, 20.52
  (1) 20.51
  (2)–(3) 20.51, 20.58, 20.59
  (4) 20.53, 21.163
 s 271. 20.50, 20.51,
          20.52, 20.55, 20.56
  (1) 20.56, 20.59
  (2)–(3) 20.59
  (4) 19.73, 20.60
  (6) 20.62
 s 272. 20.50, 20.51,
          20.52, 20.63
  (1) 20.63
  (2) 20.63, 20.64
   (a). 20.63
  (3) 20.63, 20.64
  (4) 20.64
   (a). 20.64
  (5) 19.73, 19.171
  (6) 19.172
 s 273. 19.33, 20.50,
          20.120, 20.139
  (1) 20.120
  (2). 20.120, 20.126, 20.138
   (a). 20.135
  (3) 20.121
  (4) 20.137
  (5) 20.122
 s 274. . . . . 19.33, 20.50, 20.120
  (1) 20.140
  (2) 20.139
  (3) 20.140
 s 275. . . . . 19.33, 20.50, 20.120
  (4) 20.123
  (5) 20.125
  (7) 20.125
 s 276. . . . . 19.171, 20.39,
       20.44, 20.50, 20.68, 20.69,
       20.120, 20.141, 28.94, App 21
  (1)–(2) 20.16
 s 277. . . . . 20.50, 20.120, 20.141
  (2) 20.141
  (6) 20.141
  (7) 20.142
 s 278. 20.50, 20.72,
          20.74, 20.120
  (1) 20.69
  (2) 20.70
  (3) 20.68
  (5) 20.70
  (6) 20.72
  (8) 20.75, 20.82
  (9)–(10). 20.76, 20.89
 s 279. . . . . 20.78

Proceeds of Crime Act 2002 (*cont.*)
  (2)–(3) 20.78
 s 280. . . . . 20.16
  (2) 19.158, 19.189,
                                       20.16, 20.17
   (aa). 20.17
  (3)–(4) 19.157
 s 281. . . . . 19.171, 20.67,
                     20.75, 20.80, 20.81, 28.94
  (1) 20.80
  (3) 20.80
   (c). 20.82
  (4) 20.81
 s 282 . . . . 20.67, 20.83
  (1) 20.74, 20.84
  (4) 20.83
 s 283. . . . . 19.73, 19.176,
                            20.80, 28.93, 28.96
  (1). 19.170, 28.94, 28.97
  (2) 19.171, 28.94
  (3) 28.95
   (a). 19.173
  (4) 19.173, 28.95
  (5) 19.175, 28.97
  (6) 20.49
  (8) 20.49
  (9) 19.176, 28.96
 s 286. . . . . 19.74
 s 286A. 19.62, 19.74, 19.188
 s 286B 19.190
 s 287. . . . . 20.10
 s 288. . . . . 20.45
 s 289 . . . . 21.07, 21.08, 21.205,
                                    21.210, 21.211
  (1). 21.196, 21.200, 21.203
  (2) 21.201, 21.203
  (3) 21.201
   (b) 21.202
  (4) 21.202
  (5) 21.203
  (6). 21.17, 21.25, 21.199
  (7). 21.19, 21.200
  (8) 21.202
 s 290 . . . . 21.07, 21.08
  (1) 21.205, 21.209
  (2) 21.206
  (3)(a) 21.206
  (4) 21.207
  (6)–(8) 21.208
 s 291. . . . . 21.07, 21.08, 21.210
  (2) 21.210
 s 292 . . . . 21.07, 21.08
  (6) 21.212
  (7) 21.213

s 293. . . . . 21.07
s 294. 21.07, 21.08,
                       21.12, 21.14, 21.29, 21.33,
                    21.36, 21.43, 21.195, 28.102
  (1) 21.13, 21.35
  (2) 21.13
   (b) 19.25
  (3) 21.14
s 295. 21.07, 21.08,
                             21.12, 21.83, 21.92,
                           21.98, 21.174, 28.102
  (1) 21.43
  (1B) 21.51
  (2) 15.37, 21.41,
                              21.67, 21.85, 21.107,
                                  21.108, 21.186
   (a). 21.44
  (3) 21.46
  (4) 21.39, 21.41,
                     21.56, 21.65, 21.68, 21.74, 21.106
  (5)–(6) 21.56, 21.84, 21.93
s 296. 21.07, 21.08,
                             21.12, 21.58, 21.181
  (1) 21.98
  (2) 21.18, 21.19,
                                    21.64, 21.181
  (3) 21.60
  (4) 21.182
s 297. 21.07, 21.08,
                        21.12, 21.72, 21.84, 21.174
  (2) 21.84, 21.98
  (3) 21.84, 21.85,
                                 21.86, 21.87, 21.95
  (4) 21.102
s 298. . . . . 20.74, 20.110,
                     21.07, 21.08, 21.12, 21.92,
                       21.105, 21.119, 21.142,
                        21.174, 21.187, 24.98
  (1) 21.106
  (2) 15.37, 21.98, 21.105,
                     21.119, 21.129, 21.160, 21.162
   (b) 19.25
  (3) 21.163
  (4) 21.90, 21.98
s 299. 21.07, 21.08,
                      21.12, 21.187, 21.192, 24.98
  (1) 21.187, 21.188,
                                        24.98, 24.99
  (2) 21.189, 24.100
  (3) 21.188, 21.192,
                                      24.99, 24.104
s 300. . . . . 21.07, 21.08, 21.12
s 301. 21.07, 21.12,
                               21.86, 21.91, 21.174

Proceeds of Crime Act 2002 (cont.)
   (1) 21.9, 21.93, 21.99
   (2) 21.92
   (3) 21.93, 21.94,
                                  21.95, 21.98
   (4) 21.93, 21.96,
                         21.97, 21.98, 21.111
     (c) 21.96
     (d) 21.97
s 302 . . . . 21.07, 21.12,
                  21.174, 21.184, 28.99
   (1) 21.180, 21.186
   (2) 21.63, 28.99
   (3) 21.63, 28.100
   (4) 21.181, 28.101
   (5) 21.182
   (6) 28.101
   (8) 28.102
s 303 . . . . 21.07, 21.12, 21.197
s 304 . . . . 19.19, 19.22,
              19.29, 21.25, 21.26, 21.30
s 305 . . . . 19.19, 19.22,
      19.34, 20.71, 21.26, 21.28, 21.30
s 306 . . . . 19.19, 19.22, 19.35,
                    21.26, 21.29, 21.30
s 307 . . . . 19.19, 19.22,
                    19.36, 21.26, 21.30
s 308 . . . . 19.19, 19.22,
                 20.85, 21.26, 21.30
   (1) 20.67, 20.86, 21.30
   (3)–(4) 20.87, 21.31
   (6)–(7) 20.88
   (8) 20.89
   (9) 20.77, 20.89, 20.90
s 309 . . . . 19.19, 19.22,
               20.85, 21.26, 21.30
   (1)–(2) 20.92
   (4) 20.92
s 310 . . . . 19.19, 19.22,
               20.85, 21.26, 21.30
   (1)–(2) 19.37
s 311 . . . . 19.117, 19.119,
                     20.94, 21.27
   (1) 20.93
   (2) 21.83
   (3) 19.117, 20.93, 21.83
   (4)–(5) 20.94
s 314 . . . . 19.19, 21.26
s 316 . . . . 19.22
   (1) 19.07, 19.41,
           19.135, 19.170, 20.65, 20.81
   (4) 19.19, 19.20
   (5)–(7) 19.23
s 320 . . . . 24.111

   (1) 24.111
   (4) 24.112
s 327 . . . . 14.27, 26.11, 26.13,
            26.25, 26.46, 26.83, 26.104,
             26.107, 27.53, 27.66
   (1) 26.26, 26.28,
              26.33, 26.34, 26.58,
              26.62, 26.64, 26.72
    (a)–(b) 26.27
    (D) 26.38
   (2) 26.33, 26.36
    (c) 26.34
   (2A)–(2B) 26.36
   (2C) 26.37
   (3) 26.27
s 328 . . . . 14.27, 26.11,
           26.13, 26.36, 26.47, 26.50,
         26.79, 26.97, 26.104, 26.107,
           27.45, 27.47, 27.48, 27.49,
           27.53, 27.54, 27.55, 27.57,
           27.58, 27.59, 27.61, 27.63,
                 27.66, 27.69
   (1) 26.43, 26.45,
            26.49, 26.58, 26.62, 26.64,
             26.72, 27.53, 27.63
   (2) 26.45
   (5) 26.48
s 329 . . . . 26.11, 26.13, 26.36,
           26.51, 26.52, 26.102, 26.104,
         26.107, 27.53, 27.66, 27.67
   (1) 26.51, 26.52, 26.58,
              26.62, 26.64, 26.72
   (2) 26.53
    (c) 26.54
   (2C) 26.56
   (3)
    (a)–(b) 26.54
    (c) 26.55
s 330 . . . . 26.76, 26.127,
            27.10, 27.11, 27.12, 27.17,
           27.33, 27.35, 27.38, 27.42,
           27.50, 27.53, 27.66, 27.82
   (1) 26.127, 27.24
   (3) 27.09, 27.13
    (c) 27.65
   (3A) 27.11
   (4) 26.127, 27.11, 27.65
   (5) 27.11
    (a) 27.13
   (6) 27.68
    (b) 27.20, 27.23, 27.24
   (7) 27.13, 27.19
    (B) 27.43
   (7A) 27.21

Table of Legislation

Proceeds of Crime Act 2002 (*cont.*)
   (8) 27.26, 27.27, 27.28
   (9A) 27.43
     (a) 27.23
   (10) 27.23, 27.29,
                              27.30, 27.53
   (11) 27.30
   (13) 27.27
   (14) 27.23
  s 331 . . . . 26.76, 27.33,
                         27.38, 27.39, 27.82
   (1)–(3) 27.33
   (4) 27.35
   (5) 27.34, 27.35
   (6) 27.35, 27.38
   (6A) 27.38
   (7) 27.39
   (9) 27.39
  s 332 . . . . 26.76, 27.40, 27.82
   (1)–(5) 27.40
   (6)–(7) 27.42
  s 333 . . . . 26.49, 27.65, 27.82
   (1) 27.76
   (3) 27.80, 27.81
   (4) 27.81
  s 334 . . . . 26.11, 26.107, 27.83
   (1)–(2) 26.57
   (3) 27.83
  s 335 . . . . 26.49, 26.66, 27.63
   (1) 26.64
     (b) 26.64
   (2)–(4) 26.65
   (5) 26.66, 26.68, 26.71
   (6) 26.67, 26.68, 26.71
   (7) 26.68
   (8) 26.64
  s 336
   (1) 26.69, 26.72
   (2)–(4) 26.69
   (5) 26.70
   (6)–(9) 26.71
   (11) 26.62
  s 337 . . . . 26.73, 26.74,
                         27.40, 27.76, 27.85
   (1) 26.74
   (2) 26.74, 26.75
   (3) 26.74
   (4A) 27.41
  s 338 . . . . 26.33, 26.35,
                  26.46, 26.49, 26.53,
              26.58, 26.61, 26.62, 26.64,
                  26.73, 26.76, 27.40,
              27.63, 27.76, 27.82, 27.85
   (1) 26.53, 26.58

     (a) 26.59
   (2) 26.58
   (2A) 26.39
   (3) 26.58
   (4) 26.60
   (5)(a) 26.63
   (6) 26.58
  s 339 . . . . 26.76, 27.34, 27.40,
                      27.72, 27.85, 27.86
   (1) 26.61
   (1A) 27.72, 27.83
   (3)–(4) 26.77
  s 340 . . . . 26.30
   (2) 26.31
   (3) 26.29, 27.67
   (4) 26.32
   (11) 26.15
   (13) 26.64
  s 341
   (1)–(2) 23.06
   (3) 19.96, 23.06
     (b) 19.144
   (4) 23.06
  s 342 . . . . 23.31, 27.77
   (3)(c) 27.65
   (4) 27.65
  s 343
   (2)(a) 23.07
   (3) 23.08
  s 344 . . . . 23.09
  s 345 . . . . 23.40
   (1) 23.10, 23.40
   (2)–(3) 23.10
   (4) 23.13
     (a)–(b) . . . . App 11
   (5) 23.14, 23.31
  s 346(1)–(5) 23.12
  s 347 . . . . 23.15, App 11
  s 348
   (1) 23.16
   (2) 23.16, 23.19
   (5) 23.15
   (6) 23.15, 23.35
   (7) 23.35
  s 349 . . . . 23.14, 23.32
   (1)–(3) 23.32
  s 350(1)–(2) 23.20
  s 351
   (1) 23.21
   (3) . . . . 23.23, App 19
   (7) 23.36
  s 352 . . . . 23.39, 23.40
   (1) 23.40
   (6) . . . . App 11

Proceeds of Crime Act 2002 (*cont.*)
s 353 . . . . 23.39
s 357 . . . . 19.96
  (1)–(2) 23.58
  (4) . . . . 23.58, App 11
s 358 . . . . 23.59
s 359 . . . . 23.59, App 11
s 360 . . . . 23.60
s 362(3) . . . . App 19
s 363(5) 23.48
s 364 . . . . 26.04
  (2) 23.48
  (4) 23.49
s 365 . . . . 23.51
  (2)–(3) 23.51
  (5)–(6) 23.51
s 366 . . . . 23.54, App 11
  (1)–(4) 23.54
s 367 . . . . 23.60
s 369
  (1) 23.52
  (3) . . . . 23.52, 23.53, App 19
  (7) 23.52
s 370 . . . . 23.55
  (2)–(3) . . . . App 11
  (6) 23.55
  (7) 23.56
s 371 . . . . 23.55, 23.57
s 372 . . . . 23.55, 23.60
s 373 . . . . 23.55, 23.57
s 374 . . . . 23.55
s 375 . . . . 23.55
  (2) . . . . 23.57, App 19
s 377 . . . . 23.61
  (6)–(7) 23.61
s 378 . . . . 23.29
  (1) 23.29
  (2) 23.52
  (3)–(4) 23.30
s 391(3) 19.96
s 414 . . . . 21.25
s 415 . . . . 26.04, 26.15
s 417 . . . . 22.148
  (2)(a)–(b) 18.12
s 418 . . . . 18.13, 22.148
  (2) 22.148
    (a) 18.13
  (3) 22.148
s 426 . . . . 18.14
  (2)(a) 18.14
  (4)–(6) 18.15
  (9) 18.14
s 430 . . . . 18.16
  (2) 18.16
  (4) 18.16
  (6) 18.16
s 431 . . . . 18.17
s 432 . . . . 17.91, 22.134
  (1)–(2) 18.18
  (10) 20.16
s 433 . . . . 20.83
s 443 . . . . 25.46, 25.48
s 444 . . . . 1.48, 25.46, 25.48
  (1)–(3) 25.46
s 447
  (2) 25.59, 25.61
  (4)–(6) 25.61
  (8) 25.61
  (10) 25.61
s 448 . . . . 3.66
s 453 . . . . 23.52, 24.47
s 459(6)(a) 20.84, 20.92
Sch 1 . . . . 1.17
Sch 2 . . . . 14, 14.26,
                           14.27, 14.28, 14.29,
                                    15.82, 23.65
  para 10 . . . . 14.29
Sch 6 . . . . 19.125, 19.126,
                           19.128, 19.143, App 15
  para 1 . . . . App 12
  para 2 . . . . 19.138, App 15
    (1)–(2) . . . . App 12
    (3) . . . . 19.138, App 12
    (4) . . . . App 12
      (b) 19.138
    (5) . . . . App 12
  para 3 . . . . 19.128
    (1)–(3) . . . . App 12
  para 4(1)–(2) . . . . App 12
  para 5(1)–(2) . . . . App 12
Sch 7 . . . . 20.43
Sch 9 . . . . 27.16
  Part 1
    para 2(g) 27.16
Sch 10 . . . . 3.66
Sch 11 . . . . 22.149
  para 16 . . . . 22.149
  para 36 . . . . 21.174, App 13
    (4) 8.43
Appendix 9 . . . . 27.14
  Part 3 . . . . 27.14
Proceeds of Crime (Scotland)
  Act 1995 . . . . 10.148
  Part II 2.73
  s 35 . . . . 25.44, App 1
  s 36 . . . . 25.44
Salmon and Freshwater Fisheries
  (Protection) (Scotland)
  Act 1951 . . . . 20.79

Table of Legislation

Sentencing Act (Compensation Orders)
   s 130 . . . . 24.73, 24.74
Serious Organised Crime and Police
   Act 2005. . . . . xi, xix, 1.30,
           1.31, 1.50, 14.07, 19.38,
           19.177, 19.184, 19.206, 20.17,
           21.51, 23.02, 23.62, 23.65,
           26.04, 26.48, 26.56, 26.122,
           27.04, 27.17, 27.42, 27.83,
           28.50, 28.67
   Part 2 . . . . 1.50
   s 2. . . . . 1.30
       (1) 1.31
   s 5(3) 1.31
   ss 38–39 . . . . 1.32
   s 73(3)(c) 23.66
   s 76. . . . . 23.62
       (1)–(2) 23.63
       (3). 23.63, 23.65
       (4) 23.66
       (5)–(7) 23.67
   s 79
       (1) 23.68
       (10) 23.73
   s 80(1)–(2) 23.72
   s 81(1) 23.69
   s 82
       (2)–(4) 23.69
       (5)–(6) 23.70
       (7) 23.71
   s 97 . . . . 14.07, 15.05
       (2) 14.07, 15.05
   s 98 . . . . 19.40, 19.177
   s 99. . . . . 19.157
   s 100. . . . . 21.51
   s 101 . . . . 21.187, 24.98
   s 102. . . . . 26.36
   s 103. . . . . 26.37
       (5) 27.86
   s 104. . . . . 27.11
       (3). 26.127, 27.23
       (4) 27.35
       (7) 27.41
   s 105(5) 27.72
   s 106
       (2) 27.21
       (5) 26.39
   s 107. . . . . 26.04
   Sch 6 . . . . 19.72, 19.188
       para 4 . . . . 19.73
       para 15 . . . . 19.189
       paras 16–17 . . . . 19.73
       para 18 . . . . 19.189
       para 20. . . . . 19.74, 19.190
   Sch 9 . . . . 26.127

Sexual Offences Act 1956 . . . . 14.28
Solicitors Act 1974
   s 70. . . . . 3.52
Supreme Court Act 1981
   s 16 . . . . 24.06, 24.29
   s 37
       (1) 8.59
       (3) 2.03
   s 45 . . . . 24.106, 29.124
       (1) 8.124
   s 46 . . . . 24.106, 29.124
   s 47 . . . . 24.106, 29.124
       (2) 28.103
   s 48 . . . . 24.106, 29.124
   s 49(2)(a) 24.23, 24.40, 24.65
   s 51. . . . . 28.35
   s 53(1). 24.23, 24.40, 24.65
   s 79(3) 21.188, 24.99,
                                          24.107, 29.125

Taxes Management Act 1970 . . . . 24.112
   s 75. . . . . 3.65
   s 108
       (1) 3.67
       (3) 3.67
Terrorism Act 2000. . . . . 20.79
   ss 15–18 . . . . 2.26
   s 23 . . . . 2.73, 10.100, 15.37, 15.71
   s 56. . . . . 14.27
   s 111. . . . . 2.73, 10.100, 15.37
Theft Act 1968
   s 15. . . . . 23.65
   s 15A 23.65
   s 16. . . . . 23.65
   s 20(2) 23.65
   s 21. . . . . 14.28
Theft Act 1978
   ss 1–2 . . . . 23.65
Tobacco Products Duty Act 1979
   s 2. . . . . 29.08
Trade Marks Act 1994. . . . . 14.28
   s 92(1)–(3). 2.26, 11.32
Trades Description Act 29.163
Tribunal Inquiries Act 1992
   s 11(1) 29.231

Value Added Tax Act 1994
   s 86. . . . . 29.232
   Sch 12(10) 29.218
Video Recordings Act 1984
   ss 9–10. . . . . 2.26, 11.32

Welfare Reform and Pensions Act 1999
   s 28(1) 20.129
   s 29(1)(b) 20.124

UK STATUTORY INSTRUMENTS

Beer Regulations 1993 (SI 1993/1228)
  reg 15
    (1) 29.09
    (1A) 29.09, 29.22
    (1B) 29.09
    (b) 29.24
    (c) 29.25
    (d) 29.11
    (e) 29.29, 29.38,
                 29.80, 29.81, 29.83

Channel Tunnel (Alcoholic Liquor
  and Tobacco Products) (Amendment)
  Order 2002 (SI 2002/
  2693) 29.09, 29.60
Civil Evidence Act (Commencement No 1)
  Order 1968 (SI 1968/1734) 29.107
Civil Recovery Proceedings
  PDs 19.78, 19.90, 19.150,
              19.188, 19.204, 23.25
  section III .... App 10
  section IV 23.11, 23.15,
          23.39, 23.50, 23.56, App 11
  para 4.1 .... 20.11
  para 4.4 .... 20.12
  para 5A 19.86, 19.105
  para 5B.1 .... 19.87, 19.201, 19.220
  para 5B.2 .... 19.202
  para 5.1 .... 19.101
  para 5.3 .... 19.80
    (2) 19.101
  para 5.4 .... 19.81
  para 5.5 .... 19.82, 19.102
  para 5.6 .... 19.83, 19.103
  para 6.1 .... 19.141
  para 7A.1 .... 19.219
  para 7A.3 .... 19.87, 19.218,
                19.220, 19.221
  para 7A.5 .... 19.226
  para 7B.2 .... 19.223
  para 7B.8 .... 19.222
  para 7.1 .... 19.88
  para 7.2 .... 19.150
  para 7.3 .... 19.218
  paras 8.1–8.2 .... 23.26, App 10
  paras 9.1–9.3 .... App 10
  para 10 .... 23.26
  para 10.1 .... App 10
  paras 10.2–10.3 .... 23.26, App 10
  para 11.1 .... 23.27, App 10
  para 12.1 .... 23.28, App 10
  para 12.2 .... App 10
  paras 12.3–12.4 .... 23.28, App 10
  paras 13.1–13.5 .... App 11

  paras 14.1–14.4 .... App 11
  paras 14.5–14.9 .... App 11
  paras 15.1–15.3 .... App 11
  paras 16.1–16.3 .... App 11
  paras 17.1–17.3 .... App 11
  Annex 19.218
Community Legal Service (Costs)
  Regulations 2000 (SI 2000/824)
  reg 18 .... App 19
  reg 20 .... App 19
Community Legal Service (Financial)
  Regulations 2000
  (SI 2000/516) .... App 19
  reg 13 .... App 19
Companies (Northern Ireland) Order
  1990 (SI 1990/593) (NI 5)
  art 28 .... 27.15
County Court Rules 7.07
Costs PD 28.12
  Section 8 .... 28.11
  paras 4.5–4.6 .... 28.12
  para 8.7 .... 28.12
  para 12.2 .... 28.12
  para 49A 19.223
Criminal Appeal (References to the
  European Court) Rules 1972
  (SI 1972/1786) 24.97
Criminal Defence Service Funding
  Order 2001 (SI 2001/855) .... App 6
Criminal Justice Act 1988 (Designated
  Countries and Territories) Order
  1991 (SI 1991/2873) 1.48, 25.05,
            25.12, 25.14, 25.15, 25.16,
            25.17, 25.37, 25.43, 25.62
  art 2 .... 25.06
  art 4 .... 25.21, 25.22
  art 5 .... 25.21, 25.22, 25.30
  art 6 .... 25.18
  art 7
    (1) 25.41, 25.42
    (2) 25.41
  art 8 .... 25.42
    (2) 25.42
  Schs 2–3 .... 25.05
Criminal Justice Act 1988 (Enforcement
  of Northern Ireland Confiscation
  Orders) Order 1995
  (SI 1995/1968) 25.45
Criminal Justice Act 1993
  (Commencement No. 8) Order 1995
  (SI 1995/43) 11.06
Criminal Justice (Confiscation) (Northern
  Ireland) Order 1990 (SI 1990/2588)
  (NI 17)
  art 14 .... 8.59, 17.88, 17.89, 25.61

Table of Legislation

Crown Court (Confiscation, Restraint and
    Receivership) Rules 2003
    (SI 2003/421) 1.52

Divorce etc. (Pensions) (Scotland)
    Regulations 2000 (SSI 2000/392)
    reg 3 . . . . 20.131
      (11) 20.131
Drug Trafficking Act 1994 (Designated
    Countries and Territories) Order 1996
    (SI 1996/2880) 1.48, 25.05,
                             25.08, 25.11, 25.15,
                             25.16, 25.17, 25.37,
                             25.43, 25.62
    art 2 . . . . 25.06
    art 4 . . . . 25.21, 25.22
      (1)–(2) 25.21
    art 5 . . . . 25.21, 25.22, 25.30
      (1)–(4) 25.21
    art 7 . . . . 25.18
    art 8
      (1) 25.41, 25.42
      (2) 25.41
    art 9 . . . . 25.42
      (2) 25.42
    Schs 2–3 . . . . 25.05
    Appendix 25.09
Drug Trafficking Act 1994 (Enforcement
    of Northern Ireland Confiscation
    Orders) Order 1995 . . . . 25.45
Drug Trafficking Offences (Enforcement
    in England and Wales) Order 1998
    (SI 1988/593) 25.44

Excise Duties (Personal Reliefs)
    (Amendment) Order 1999
    (SI 1999/1617) 29.18,
                                 29.19, 29.35
Excise Duties (Personal Reliefs) Order 1992
    (SI 1992/3155) 29.14, 29.18,
                                 29.19, 29.35
    art 5(3) 29.19
Excise Duties (Personal Reliefs)
    (Revocation) Order 2002
    (SI 2002/2691) 29.18
Excise Goods, Beer and Tobacco Products
    (Amendment) Regulations 2002
    (SI 2002/2692) 29.09, 29.20,
                                 29.22, 29.24
    subreg (1B)
      (b) 29.24
      (c) 29.25
      (d) 29.11
      (e) 29.29, 29.38,
                             29.80, 29.81, 29.83

Excise Goods (Holding, Movement,
    Warehousing and REDS)
    Regulations 1992 (SI 1992/3135)
    reg 4
      (1) 29.09
      (1A) 29.09, 29.20
      (1B) 29.09
        (b) 29.24
        (c) 29.25
        (d) 29.11
        (e) 29.29, 29.38,
                             29.80, 29.81, 29.83

Financial Services and Marketing Act 2000
    (Regulations relating to Money
    Laundering) Regulations 2001
    (SI 1001/1819) 26.122
Financial Services and Markets Act 2000
    (Regulated Activities) (Amendment)
    (No.2) Order 2006
    (SI 2006/2383) 27.16

Insolvency (Northern Ireland) Order 1989
    (SI 1989/2405) (NI 19)
    art 3 . . . . 27.15
Insolvency Practitioner Regulations 1990
    (SI 1990/439) . . . . App 4

Land Registration Rules 2003
    (SI 2003/1417)
    r 91(1) 2.99
    r 93(1) 8.122
    Sch 4 . . . . 2.99, 8.122

Magistrates' Courts (Costs Against
    Legal Representatives in Civil
    Proceedings) Rules 1991
    (SI 1991/2096) 21.173, 29.119
Magistrates' Courts (Detention and
    Forfeiture of Cash) (Amendment)
    Rules 2003 (SI 2003/638) 21.40
Magistrates' Courts (Detention and
    Forfeiture of Cash) Rules 2002
    (SI 2002/2998) 21.09, 21.73,
                            21.75, 21.82, 21.186
    r 4
      (2) 21.41
      (3) 21.42, 21.45
      (4) 21.47
      (5) 21.48
      (6) 21.49
      (7) 21.50
      (9) 21.45, 21.72
    r 5 . . . . 21.78, 21.79
      (1) 21.65

Magistrates' Courts (Detention and
   Forfeiture of Cash) Rules 2002
   (SI 2002/2998) (*cont.*)
   (2) 21.67
   (3) 21.66
   (6) 21.72
 r 6
   (1) 21.85, 21.93
   (3)
     (a). 21.85
     (c). 21.85
   (4) 21.85
   (5) 21.99
   (7) 21.98
 r 7
   (1) 21.106
   (3) 21.77
   (4) 21.113
   (5) 21.116
   (6) 21.114
   (7) 21.160
 r 8(1)–(3) 21.186
 r 10. . . . . 21.103
   (1)–(4) 21.103
   (5)–(6) 21.104
 r 11
   (1) 21.120, 21.215
   (2) 21.121
   (3) 21.128
   (4) 21.159
 Sch. 21.72
Magistrates' Courts (Detention and
   Forfeiture of Drug Trafficking Cash)
   Rules 1999 (SI 1999/1923) 21.77
 Sch. 21.76
Magistrates' Courts (Hearsay Evidence in
   Civil Proceedings) Rules 1999
   (SI 1999/681) 21.143, 21.144,
               21.147, 29.102, 29.105
 r 2(2) 21.145, 29.103
 r 3(1)–(5). 21.143, 29.102
 rr 4–6. . . . . 21.144, 29.102
Magistrates' Courts (Miscellaneous
   Amendments) Rules 2003
   (SI 2003/1236) 21.71, 21.72,
             21.75, 21.87, 21.95, 21.98,
                    21.106, 21.160
 r 9. . . . . 21.73
   (6) 21.72
 r 91. . . . . 21.09
 r 92. . . . . 21.09
   (2) 21.71
 r 93 . . . . 21.09, 21.65
   (2) 21.71
 rr 94–96 . . . . 21.09

Magistrates' Courts Rules 1981
   (SI 1981/552) 21.49, 21.74,
           21.147, 24.108, 29.105, 29.126
 r 14 . . . . 21.124, 29.92
Money Laundering Regulations 1993
   (SI 1993/1933) 26.03, 26.116,
             26.117, 26.118, 26.120
 reg 7 . . . . 26.117
 reg 9 . . . . 26.117
 reg 12 . . . . 26.117
 reg 14 . . . . 26.117
Money Laundering Regulations 2001
   (SI 2001/3641) 26.03, 26.97,
             26.116, 26.118, 26.120
Money Laundering Regulations 2003
   (SI 2003/3075) 1.38, 26.119,
           26.120, 26.122, 26.126, 26.128
 reg 2 . . . . 26.120
   (2) 26.126
 reg 3
   (1) 26.121
     (b) 26.121
   (2) 26.123
   (3) 26.121
 reg 4 . . . . 26.120
 regs 6–7 . . . . 26.120
 reg 8 . . . . 26.123
 reg 9 . . . . 26.124
 reg 10. . . . . 26.122, 26.124
 regs 11–13 . . . . 26.124
 regs 15–19 . . . . 26.124
 regs 20–23 . . . . 26.125
 reg 25 . . . . 26.125

Pension Sharing (Pension Credit Benefit)
   Regulations 2000 (SI 2000/1054)
 reg 24 . . . . 20.132
Pension Sharing (Pension Credit Benefit)
   Regulations (Northern Ireland) 2000
   (NISR 2000/146)
 reg 24 . . . . 20.132
Pensions on Divorce etc. (Provision of
   Information) Regulations 2000
   (SI 2000/1048) 20.128
 reg 3. . . . . 20.130, 20.131
Pensions on Divorce etc. (Provision of
   Information) Regulations (Northern
   Ireland) 2000 (NISR 2000/210)
 reg 3 . . . . 20.131
Perjury (Northern Ireland)
   Order 1979 (SI 1979/1714) (NI 19)
 art 10 . . . . App 12, App 15
Police and Criminal Evidence
   (Northern Ireland) Order 1989
   (SI 1989/1341) (NI 12) 23.39

Table of Legislation

Proceeds of Crime Act 1995
   (Commencement) Order 1995
   (SI 1995/2650) 11.06,
                                   12.47, 12.50
Proceeds of Crime Act 2002 (Appeals
   under Part 2) Order 2003
   (SI 2003/82) 24.26, 24.43,
                                   24.77, 24.85
   art 3 . . . . 24.87
     (1) 24.86
     (3) 24.87
   art 4 . . . . 24.88, 24.90
   art 5
     (1) 24.90
     (2)–(3) 24.91
   art 6(1)–(2) 24.92
   art 7
     (1) 24.93
     (2) 24.95
     (3) 24.94
Proceeds of Crime Act 2002 (Application
   of Police and Criminal Evidence Act
   1984 and Police and Criminal Evidence
   (Northern Ireland) Order 1989)
   Order 2003 (SI 2003/174) 23.39
Proceeds of Crime Act 2002 (Business in
   the Regulated Sector) Order 2006
   (SI 2006/2385) 27.16
Proceeds of Crime Act 2002 (Business in
   the Regulated Sector and Supervisory
   Authorities) Order 2003
   (SI 2003/3074) 26.127, 27.14
   art 2(2)–(5) 27.23
   Sch 27.18
Proceeds of Crime Act 2002 (Cash Searches
   Code of Practice) Order 2002
   (SI 2002/3115) 21.214
Proceeds of Crime Act 2002
   (Commencement No. 1 and
   Savings) Order 2002
   (SI 2002/3015) 20.53, 21.07,
                                 21.195, 24.04
Proceeds of Crime Act 2002
   (Commencement No. 2) Order 2002
   (SI 2002/3055) 1.17
Proceeds of Crime Act 2002
   (Commencement No. 4 Transitional
   Provisions and Savings) Order 2003
   (SI 2003/120) 19.06, 23.05,
                        26.02, 26.12, 26.80, 27.03
Proceeds of Crime Act 2002
   (Commencement No. 5, Transitional
   Provisions, Savings and Amendment)
   Order 2003 (SI 2003/333) 8.03,
                8.06, 9.01, 11.05, 14.05, 15.02

   art 3(1) 8.05
   art 5 . . . . 2.01, 8.04, 8.08
Proceeds of Crime Act 2002
   (Commencement No. 5) (Amendment
   of Transitional Provisions) Order 2003
   (SI 2003/531) 14.40,
                                   14.41, 14.44
Proceeds of Crime Act 2002 (Enforcement
   in different parts of the
   United Kingdom) Order 2002
   (SI 2002/3133) . . . . 25.69, App 13
   Part V 25.62
Proceeds of Crime Act 2002 (Exemptions
   from Civil Recovery) Order 2003
   (SI 2003/336) 20.79, 21.30
Proceeds of Crime Act 2002 (External
   Requests and Orders) Order 2005
   (SI 2005/3181) 1.48, 25.03,
                            25.48, 25.50, 25.68
   Part V 25.70
   art 2 . . . . 25.59
   art 6
     (1) 25.49
     (4) 25.49
   art 7(1)–(2) 25.50
   art 8 . . . . 25.50
     (1) 25.51
     (2) 25.51, 25.52
       (a) 25.52, 25.53
       (b)–(c) 25.53
     (4) 25.54
   art 9
     (1)(a)–(b) 25.55
     (5)–(7) 25.55
   arts 10–11 . . . . 25.56
   art 13 . . . . 25.57
   art 15 . . . . 25.58
     (1)(b) 25.58
   art 16 . . . . 25.58
   art 20 . . . . 25.59
     (1)–(3) 25.60
   art 21 . . . . 25.59, 25.61
     (1) 25.61
     (2) 25.61, 25.62
     (3)–(8) 25.61
   art 22 . . . . 25.59
     (1) 25.64
     (3)–(4) 25.65
   arts 23–24 . . . . 25.66
   art 27 . . . . 25.67
   art 147(3) 19.80
   art 177
     (10) 19.222
     (11)(a) 19.193
   art 178 . . . . 20.11

Proceeds of Crime Act 2002 (Failure to
  Disclose Money Laundering:
  Specified Training) Order 2003
  (SI 2003/171) 27.20
Proceeds of Crime Act 2002 (Financial
  Threshold for Civil Recovery) Order
  2003 (SI 2003/175) 20.10
Proceeds of Crime Act 2002
  (Investigations in different parts of
  the United Kingdom) Order 2003
  (SI 2003/425) 23.61
Proceeds of Crime Act 2002 (Investigations
  in England, Wales and
  Northern Ireland: Code of Practice)
  Order 2003 (SI 2003/334) 23.61
Proceeds of Crime Act 2002 (Legal Expenses
  in Civil Recovery Proceedings)
  Regulations 2005
  (SI 2005/3382) 19.188, 19.191,
           19.197, 19.201, App 15, App 17
  Part 2 .... 19.197
  Part 3 .... 19.192, 19.200,
           19.209, 19.224, App 15, App 17
  Part 4 .... 19.192, 19.200, 19.223, 19.224
  Part 5 .... 19.194, 19.215, 19.227
  reg 1 .... 19.191, 19.197
  reg 4 .... 19.197
  reg 5 .... 19.199
  reg 8 .... 19.210
  reg 9 .... 19.213
     (1) 19.214
     (3) 19.215
  reg 10 .... 19.216
  reg 12 .... 19.193
     (2)–(3) 19.194
  reg 13(2) 19.195, 19.196
  reg 16 .... 19.228
Proceeds of Crime Act 2002 and Money
  Laundering Regulations 2003
  (Amendment) Order 2006
  (SI 2006/308) 26.119, 26.127
  reg 2(2) 26.127
Proceeds of Crime Act 2002 (Recovery of
  Cash in Summary Proceedings:
  Minimum Amount) Order 2004
  (SI 2004/420) 21.14
Proceeds of Crime Act 2002 (Recovery of
  Cash in Summary Proceedings:
  Minimum Amount) Order 2006
  (SI 2006/1699) 21.197
Proceeds of Crime Act 2002 (Recovery from
  Pension Schemes) Regulations 2003
  (SI 2003/291) 20.126,
                      20.131, 20.139
  reg 2 .... 20.136

  (1) 20.127
  reg 3 .... 20.136
     (1) 20.132
     (3) 20.132
  reg 4 .... 20.133
     (3)–(4) 20.134
  reg 5 .... 20.135, 20.136
     (1)–(3) 20.135
Proceeds of Crime Act 2002 (References
  to Financial Investigators) Order 2003
  (SI 2003/172) 24.47
Proceeds of Crime (Northern Ireland)
  Order 1996 (SI 1996/1299)
  (NI 19) 25.45
  art 32 .... 8.59, 17.89, 25.61
Proceeds of Crime (Scotland) Act 1995
  (Enforcement of Scottish
  Confiscation Orders in England
  and Wales) Order
  2001 (SI 2001/953) 25.44

Serious Organised Crime and Police
  Act 2005 (Commencement No. 1,
  Transitional and Transitory Provisions)
  Order 2005 (SI 2005/1521)
  art 3 .... 14.07

Tobacco Products Regulations 2001
  (SI 2001/1712)
  reg 12
     (1) 29.09
     (1A) 29.09, 29.22
     (1B) 29.09
        (b) 29.24
        (c) 29.25
        (d) 29.11
        (e) 29.29, 29.38,
                        29.80, 29.81, 29.83
Traveller's Allowance Order 1994
  (SI 1994/955) 29.44
Travellers' Allowances Amendment
  Order 1995 (SI 1995/3044)
  art 2 .... 29.44

Value Added Tax Tribunal Rules 1986
  (SI 1986/590) 29.199
  r 2 .... 29.213
  r 3 .... 29.202
     (2)(e) 29.203
  r 4(1)–(2) 29.201
  r 6 .... 29.203
  r 8 .... 29.205
  r 9 .... 29.203, 29.210
  r 19
     (1) 29.201, 29.213, 29.217

Value Added Tax Tribunal Rules 1986
(SI 1986/590) (*cont.*)
   (3) 29.216
r 20. . . . . 29.206
   (1) 29.206
   (2) 29.207
   (3) 29.208
   (6) 29.208
r 21. . . . . 29.212
   (2)–(5) 29.212
   (6)(c) 29.213
r 23(3) 29.222
r 24
   (1) 29.223
   (2) 29.221
r 25(1) 29.224
r 26(2) 29.228
r 27
   (1) 29.224
   (3)–(4) 29.226
r 28(2) 29.225

CIVIL PROCEDURE RULES

Civil Procedure Rules 1998
   (SI 1998/3132). 4.06, 7.02,
      7.07, 7.09, 8.98, 8.102, 17.47,
      21.147, 23.25, 24.04, 27.60,
      28.02, 29.105, 29.130
Part 1
   r 1.1(1)–(3). 7.04
   r 1.3 . . . . 17.47
   r 1.4(1)–(2). 7.05
Part 2
   r 2.11 . . . . 6.03
Part 5
   r 5.4 . . . . App 10
Part 6
   r 6.8(1) 6.18, 7.41
Part 7
   PD 7A
      para 5B.1 . . . . 19.225
      para 8 . . . . 19.199
Part 8 . . . . 19.41, 20.11, App 9
Part 22 . . . . 28.84
   PD 22
      para 2.1 . . . . 7.09
      para 3.8 . . . . 7.11
Part 23 . . . . 7.46, 10.158, 19.79,
      19.101, 22.09, 25.32, 28.84, App 10
   rr 23.3–23.4 . . . . 19.79
   r 23.7(1). . . . . App 10
   r 23.8 . . . . 19.84
      (c). 19.84
   r 23.9 . . . . 19.85

r 23.11 . . . . 19.85
Part 24. . . . . 20.20, 20.22
   r 24.2 . . . . 20.20
Part 25
   r 25.1(1)(b). 27.101
Part 29 . . . . 29.234
Part 30
   r 30A 29.232
Part 31 . . . . 8.102
   r 31.22 . . . . 4.24
Part 32 . . . . 22.74
   r 32.14(1)–(2). 7.11
Part 40
   r 40.2 . . . . App 11
Part 43. . . . . 28.12, 28.40
Part 44 . . . . 28.12, 28.40, 29.130
   r 44.3
      (1)–(2) 28.06
      (4)–(6) 28.06
      (8) 28.06, 28.11
   r 44.4. . . . . 19.229, 28.07
   r 44.5
      (1) 28.09
      (3) 28.09
   r 44.13(1)(a). 28.10
Parts 45–46 . . . . 28.12, 28.40
Part 47 . . . . 19.196, 19.223,
      28.12, 28.40
   r 47.7 . . . . 19.196
   r 47.14(2) 19.196
Part 48 . . . . 28.12, 28.40, 28.61
   r 48.8. . . . . 5.13, 28.11, App 1, App 2
      (2) . . . . 5.13, 5.14, App 1, App 2
      (a)–(b) 28.61
Part 52. . . . . 24.08, 29.231
   r 52.3 . . . . 24.08, 24.09, 24.115
   r 52.4. . . . . 24.10, 24.11
      (3) 24.115
   r 52.11(3)(a)–(b) 24.10
   PD 52 . . . . 24.08, 29.231
      para 3.1 . . . . 24.10
      para 4.1 . . . . 24.09
      para 5 . . . . 24.10
      para 5.9 . . . . 24.11
      para 5.19 . . . . 24.11
      para 7 . . . . 24.12
      para 7.1 . . . . 24.12
      para 21.4 . . . . 24.115
Part 67
   r 67.7 . . . . 3.58
Part 69. . . . . 1.42, 3.06, 3.15,
      8.89, 8.90, 17.56, 19.102,
      28.36, 28.37, 28.42, App 4
   r 69.7. . . . . 3.54, 3.55, 17.58,
      28.37, 28.38, 28.46

Civil Procedure Rules 1998
(SI 1998/3132) (cont.)
  (1) 3.53
  (2) 3.06, 3.53,
                3.55, 3.57, 3.58, 28.38,
                28.42, 28.43, 28.44
    (a). 28.46
  (3) 3.53
  (4) 3.53, 28.39, 28.40
  (5) 3.53
r 69.8. . . . . 3.39, 3.40
  (2) 3.40
  (3) 3.40, 3.41
    (c). 3.41
  (4) 3.41
PD 69 . . . . 19.102, 28.37, 28.47
  para 2.1 . . . . 19.102
  paras 4.1–4.2 . . . . 19.102
  para 9.2 . . . . 28.40
  paras 9.4–para 9.6. . . . . 28.41
Part 72 . . . . 17.65

RULES OF THE SUPREME COURT

Sch 1, RSC. 7.07, 28.36
Ord.30. . . . . 28.43, 28.44
  r 3 . . . . 17.54, 28.36
    (1) 17.55
Ord.45
  r 5. . . . . 6.03
    (1) 6.03
  r 7
    (4) 6.13
    (6) 6.14
Ord.52 . . . . 6.05, 7.07, 8.127
  r 1(2)(ii) 6.04
  r 4(1) 6.11
  r 6. . . . . 6.21
    (1)(d) 6.21
    (4) 6.28
  r 7(1) 6.35
  r 8(1) 6.37
PD 52 . . . . 6.05, 7.07
  para 2. . . . . 6.07
  para 2.6
    (3) 6.09
    (4) 6.08
    (5) 6.10
  para 3.1 . . . . 6.19
  paras 3.3–3.4 . . . . 6.19
  para 4.2 . . . . 6.17
  paras 4.3–4.4 . . . . 6.22
  paras 4.5–4.6 . . . . 6.23
  para 10 . . . . 6.05

Ord.115. . . . . 7.07, 7.17, 7.20,
          7.21, 7.22, 7.23, 7.34, 7.52, 8.69,
          8.77, 8.80, 8.81, 10.158, App 4
  r 1. . . . . 7.16
  r 2. . . . . 7.13
  r 2A 7.14, 22.16
  r 2B
    (1) 10.158
    (2) 10.159
    (3) 10.160
    (4) 10.161
    (5) 10.162
  r 3. . . . . 8.71
    (1) . . . . 7.19, 7.34, App 9
    (2) 7.19, 7.20
  r 4. . . . . 8.74
    (1) 2.06, 2.82, 2.85,
          7.23, 22.12, 22.29, 28.62
    (2) 2.78, 8.74
    (3). 7.39, 22.17, 22.26
  r 5. . . . . 8.76
    (1). 5.01, 7.46, 22.09
    (2) 7.47, 7.52
  r 6. . . . . 8.79
    (1) 7.58
    (2)–(3) 7.59
  r 7
    (1) 17.31
    (2) 17.31
      (b) 17.32, 22.64
    (3) 17.33
    (4) 17.40
  r 8
    (1) 3.39
    (2) 8.88
  r 9. . . . . 13.55
  r 9A 13.24
  r 10. . . . . 28.84
  rr 12–13 . . . . 25.33
  r 15. . . . . 25.32
    (1)–(2) 25.32
  r 16(1)–(2) 25.36
  r 17(1)–(3) 25.34
  rr 18–19 . . . . 25.35
  r 20. . . . . 25.38
  r 23
    (a). 7.21
    (c). 7.20
PD 115 . . . . 2.65, 3.11, 3.58,
          5.11, 5.20, 7.07, 7.17, 7.18
  para 3.1(2)–(3) 2.65
  para 3.2 . . . . 2.65
  para 4. . . . . 2.87, 5.10
    (1) 2.87

Sch 1, RSC (*cont.*)
  (2) 2.89
  paras 5.1–5.3 . . . . 7.18
  para 6 . . . . 5.36
   (1) 2.91
   (2) 2.92
  para 7.2 . . . . 2.81
  para 8.2 . . . . 3.54
  para 8.3 . . . . 3.11, 3.12
   (1)–(2) 3.11
  para 8.4 . . . . 3.11, 3.12
  para 12(1) 5.10
  para 12(4) 5.10
Sch 2 . . . . 7.07

CRIMINAL PROCEDURE RULES

Criminal Procedure Rules 2005
 (SI 2005/384) 1.52, 8.69,
       8.81, 8.127, 9.69, 14.76,
       21.147, 22.74, 24.04,
       24.05, 24.96, 24.120,
       28.13, 29.105
Part 1
 r 1.1 . . . . 7.06
Part 52
 r 52.2(5) 22.12
Part 53
 r 53(1) 8.101
Part 56 . . . . 1.52, 19.17
 r 56.1 . . . . 9.64, 11.59
  (1)(b) 9.60, 9.70
  (2) 9.61
 r 56.2 . . . . 11.59
  (1)
   (a) 11.51, 12.04
   (b) 9.47, 11.51, 12.04
 r 56.3 . . . . 13.16, 13.25
  (2) 13.16
 r 56.4(2)–(3) 23.23
 r 56.6 . . . . 28.80
Part 57 . . . . 1.52, 25.68
 r 57.1 . . . . 8.76
 r 57.2 . . . . 8.76
  (2) 8.76
  (4) 8.76
 r 57.3 . . . . 8.76
 r 57.7 . . . . 14.73, 14.79, 14.100
  (1)–(2) 8.97
  (4) 8.98
 r 57.8 . . . . 14.74, 14.93, 14.101
 r 57.9 . . . . 8.101, 14.108
  (1) 8.100, 8.101
   (c)–(d) 8.101
 r 57.10 . . . . 8.101, 14.108

r 57.11 . . . . 14.109
 (2) 8.104
 (3) 8.105
 (4) 8.106
r 57.12 . . . . 8.107, 8.109, 14.109
 (2)–(3) 8.107
r 57.13 . . . . 8.108, 14.109
 (2)–(4) 8.108
r 57.14 . . . . App 14
 (1)–(3) 8.109
r 57.15 . . . . 25.68
Part 58 . . . . 1.52
r 58.1 . . . . 14.70, 14.78
 (2) 14.70
 (4) 14.96
r 58.2 . . . . 14.46
r 58.3 . . . . 16.37
 (3)–(4) 16.37
r 58.4 . . . . 16.47
 (1)–(4) 16.47
r 58.5 . . . . 16.55
r 58.6 . . . . 16.74
 (2) 16.74
 (3) 16.74, 16.75
 (4) 16.75
 (5) 16.76
r 58.7 . . . . 16.94
 (2) 16.94
 (3) 16.95
 (4) 16.95, 16.103
r 58.8 . . . . 16.102
 (3) 16.103
 (5) 16.104
r 58.9 . . . . 16.108
 (2)–(4) 16.108
r 58.10 . . . . 16.107
r 58.11
 (1)–(2) 16.105
 (3) 16.106
r 58.11(3) 16.106
r 58.12
 (1) 17.107
 (2)–(3) 17.108
Part 59 . . . . 1.52, 8.55, 25.68
r 59.1 . . . . 8.93
 (1)–(2) 8.70, 8.71
 (3) 8.70
  (c) 8.72
r 59.2 . . . . 8.74
 (1)–(2) 8.73, 8.74
 (3) 8.73
 (4) 8.73, 22.29
 (5)–(6) 8.73
 (7) 8.73, 8.74
 (8) 8.73, 22.17, 22.26

Table of Legislation

Criminal Procedure Rules 2005
  (SI 2005/384) (*cont.*)
  r 59.3 . . . . 22.09
    (1)–(4) 8.75
  r 59.4 . . . . 8.79
    (1)–(3) 8.78
  r 59.5(1)–(4). 8.80
Part 60 . . . . 1.52, 17.96, 25.68
  r 60.1 . . . . 8.93
    (1) 8.82
    (2). 8.82, 8.83, 17.98
    (3) 8.82, 17.96
    (4) 8.82, 17.97
    (5) 8.82
    (6). 8.82, 17.98, 22.64
    (7) 8.82, 17.99
  r 60.2 . . . . 8.84, 8.93
    (1) 8.84
    (2) 8.84, 8.85
    (3)–(7) 8.84
  r 60.3. . . . . 8.86, 17.100
    (3) 17.101
  r 60.4 . . . . 17.102
    (2)–(3) 17.102
  r 60.5 . . . . 8.87
    (2) 8.87
    (3) 8.88
  r 60.6. . . . . 8.89, 17.103
    (5) 3.60, 28.59
    (6) 17.103, 28.59
    (7) 28.59
  r 60.7. . . . . 8.90, 17.103
  r 60.8 . . . . 17.103
    (1) 8.91
Part 61. 1.52, 25.68
  r 61.2 . . . . 8.93
  rr 61.3–61.4 . . . . 8.92
  r 61.5
    (1) 8.94, 8.95
    (2)–(3) 8.95
  r 61.6(1)–(2). 8.96
  r 61.7 . . . . 8.96
  r 61.8 . . . . 8.99
  r 61.9 . . . . 8.102
    (3) 8.102
  r 61.10. . . . . 8.103, 8.114
    (1)–(3) 8.103
  r 61.11 . . . . 8.110
    (2) 8.110
    (4) 8.110
  r 61.12 . . . . 8.111
    (2) 8.111
  r 61.13(1)–(2). 8.112
  r 61.14(2)–(3). 8.113
  r 61.15 . . . . 8.114
    (1) 8.114
    (2)–(3) 8.115
  rr 61.16–61.18 . . . . 8.116
  r 61.19 . . . . 8.117
    (1)–(7) 8.117
  r 61.20
    (1) 8.119, 28.13
    (2) 8.119, 28.13
    (b) 8.120
    (3) 8.120
    (5) 8.120, 28.14
  r 61.21 . . . . 8.121
    (1) 28.13
Part 62 . . . . 1.52
  r 62.1 . . . . 23.57
    (2) 23.57
  r 62.2 . . . . 23.53
    (1) 23.53
Part 63 . . . . 24.120
  r 63.2 . . . . 24.107, 24.120, 29.125
  rr 63.3–63.9 . . . . 24.120
Part 64. . . . . 23.120, 24.110
  rr 64.1–64.7 . . . . 24.120
Parts 65–70. . . . . 24.120
Part 71. . . . . 24.120, 25.68
  rr 71.1–71.9. . . . . 24.96, 24.120
  r 71.10 . . . . 24.28, 24.45,
                     24.80, 24.96, 24.120
  r 71.11 . . . . 24.96, 24.120
Part 72 . . . . 24.120
  rr 72.1–72.3. . . . . 24.64, 24.120
Part 73 . . . . 23.120
  r 73.1 . . . . 24.20, 24.37, 24.120
  rr 73.2–73.3 . . . . 24.21,
                           24.38, 24.120
  rr 73.4–73.6 . . . . 24.22,
                           24.39, 24.120
  r 73.7 . . . . 24.24, 24.41, 24.120
    (4) 24.25
    (5) 24.25, 24.42
Part 74 . . . . 24.120
  r 74.1 . . . . 24.120
Part 75 . . . . 24.120
  r 75.1 . . . . 24.120
Parts 76–77. . . . . 28.14
Part 78 . . . . 28.14
  rr 78.1–78.2 . . . . 21.193
  r 78.3 . . . . 8.119

EUROPEAN COMMUNITY

Directive 91/308/EC (Money
  Laundering) 21.02, 26.113,
                    26.114, 26.120, 27.05,
                    27.06, 27.08, 27.09

Directive 91/308/EC (Money
    Laundering) (*cont.*)
  Preamble 26.113
  art 1 . . . . 26.115, 27.05, 27.07
  art 2 . . . . 26.114, 27.05
  arts 3–4 . . . . 26.114, 26.117
  arts 6–7 . . . . 26.114
  art 9 . . . . 26.03
  arts 10–11 . . . . 26.117
  arts 12–13 . . . . 26.118
  art 15 . . . . 26.115
Directive 92/12/EC 29.12, 29.14,
                                         29.18, 29.39
  art 6 . . . . 29.12
  art 7 . . . . 29.12
    (2) 29.12
  art 8 . . . . 29.10, 29.12, 29.14
  art 9 . . . . 29.12, 29.14
    (1) 29.13
  art 10 . . . . 29.12
Directive 92/83/EC
  art 17(1) 29.41
Directive 2001/97/EC (Money
    Laundering) 26.120, 26.128,
                                 27.05, 27.06, 27.07,
                                 27.08, 27.09, 27.23
  Recital
    paras 1–15 . . . . 27.06
Directive (Banking Consolidation)
  Annex 1 . . . . 27.15
Directive (Life Assurance Consolidation)
  art 4 . . . . 27.15
  art 51 . . . . 27.15
EC Treaty art 226 . . . . 29.28

EUROPEAN CONVENTION ON HUMAN RIGHTS

European Convention on Human
    Rights 3.47, 9.21,
                            10.145, 10.146, 13.26, 15.77,
                            16.48, 19.05, 20.01, 20.99,
                            20.110, 21.192, 21.217,
                            25.29, 25.63, 29.131,
                            29.133, 29.183, 29.221

  art 1 . . . . 1.49, 10.118
  art 6 . . . . 1.47, 4.23, 4.26,
                        8.44, 9.58, 10.99, 10.144, 11.57,
                        14.66, 20.96, 20.102, 20.103,
                        20.110, 25.28, 25.29, 29.16,
                        29.133, 29.238
    (1) 1.49, 10.98,
                        10.146, 10.152, 12.97,
                        13.26, 15.78, 16.48, 17.80,
                        17.81, 20.101, 20.112
    (2) 1.49, 10.146, 10.148,
                        10.149, 10.152, 12.97, 15.78,
                        20.102, 29.131
    (3) 8.44
  art 7 . . . . 1.49, 10.150,
                        20.104, 20.105, 20.106,
                        20.108, 20.109, 20.110,
                        20.114, 20.115, 20.116, 20.117
    (1) 10.149, 10.150
  art 8 . . . . 20.118, 22.103
  Protocol 1 . . . . 14.17
    art 1 . . . . 3.46, 8.45, 10.30,
                        10.146, 20.100, 25.29, 29.85,
                        29.133, 29.134, 29.173, 29.239

INTERNATIONAL

Hong Kong Bill of Rights 26.96
Hong Kong Drug Trafficking (Recovery
    of Proceeds) Ordinance 26.96
United Nations Convention Against
    Illicit Traffic in Narcotic Drugs
    and Psychotropic Substances
    (Vienna Convention) 26.115
  art 3
    (b) 26.79
    (1)(a) 26.115
Vienna Convention on Diplomatic
    Relations 1961 . . . . 23.46

LIST OF ABBREVIATIONS

The following abbreviations are used throughout this work:

ARA	Assets Recovery Agency
CCR	County Court Rules
CCRC	Criminal Cases Review Commission
CJA 1988	Criminal Justice Act 1988
CJA 1993	Criminal Justice Act 1993
CLS	Community Legal Service
CPR	Civil Procedure Rules
CPS	Crown Prosecution Service
DTA	Drug Trafficking Act 1994
DTOA	Drug Trafficking Offences Act 1986
ECHR	European Convention on Human Rights
HMRC	HM Revenue and Customs
LSC	Legal Service Commission
MCA 1973	Matrimonial Causes Act 1973
NCIS	National Criminal Intelligence Service
PCC(S)A	Powers of Criminal Courts (Sentencing) Act 2000
POCA 1995	Proceeds of Crime Act 1995
POCA	Proceeds of Crime Act 2002
RCPO	Revenue and Customs Prosecutions Office
RSC	Rules of the Supreme Court
SOCA	Serious Organised Crime Agency
SOCPA	Serious Organised Crime and Police Act 2005

1

SETTING THE SCENE

A. Introduction	1.01	
B. Why was Confiscation Law Enacted?	1.02	
C. The Object of the Confiscation Regime	1.09	
D. The Drug Trafficking Act 1994: A Summary	1.11	
E. The Criminal Justice Act 1988: A Summary	1.13	
F. The Proceeds of Crime Act 2002: A Summary	1.14	
G. Agencies responsible for the Enforcement of the Legislation	1.17	
(1) The Assets Recovery Agency	1.17	
(2) The Crown Prosecution Service	1.23	
(3) The Revenue and Customs Prosecutions Office	1.24	
(4) HM Revenue and Customs	1.27	
(5) The Serious Fraud Office	1.28	
(6) The Serious Organised Crime Agency	1.30	
(7) The Enforcement Task Force	1.33	
(8) Regional Asset Recovery Teams	1.36	
H. The International Element	1.37	
I. Money Laundering	1.38	
J. Recent Developments in Confiscation Law	1.39	
(1) Release of restrained funds to meet legal expenses in POCA cases	1.40	
(2) Management receivers—the *Capewell* decisions	1.41	
(3) Restraint orders: failure to comply with the duty to give full and frank disclosure	1.43	
(4) Release of restrained funds to pay unsecured third party creditors	1.44	
(5) Confiscation orders: failure to follow the prescribed procedures	1.45	
(6) Delay in enforcing confiscation orders	1.47	
(7) The international element	1.48	
(8) Civil recovery under the Proceeds of Crime Act 2002	1.49	
(9) Amendments brought in by the Serious Organised Crime and Police Act 2005	1.50	
(10) The Criminal Procedure Rules 2005	1.52	

A. Introduction

The purpose of this introductory chapter is to consider why Parliament decided to enact confiscation legislation and to give a brief overview of the mechanics of the Acts. We also outline the functions of the key law enforcement agencies having the conduct of restraint and confiscation cases under the legislation and provide a summary of some of the most significant recent decisions in this fast moving area of law which are considered in more detail later in the text. As this is essentially a practical work, we do not intend to consider in any great detail the philosophy behind confiscation legislation, or to give a full academic criticism of the provisions. The aim of this work is to consider the legislation against the background of the practical problems it is likely to cause, both to the prosecuting and defending lawyer.

1.01

B. Why was Confiscation Law Enacted?

1.02 The first confiscation enactment to reach the statute book was the Drug Trafficking Offences Act 1986 (the DTOA) which came into force on 10 January, 1987. It was introduced following a recognition by Parliament that the profits made from drug trafficking were so great that the deterrent effect of even lengthy terms of imprisonment were negligible: the convicted criminal could spend his sentence secure in the knowledge that his illgotten gains (often well invested in the meantime) would be available to him on his release. The legislation also reflected the recognition by Parliament that existing forfeiture provisions were inadequate for the purpose of depriving the offender of the fruits of his crime.

1.03 The inadequacy of the old law is well illustrated by the decision of the House of Lords in *R v Cuthbertson* [1980] 2 All ER 401. The defendants had been convicted of offences of conspiring to produce and supply LSD following a police exercise known as 'Operation Julie'. The investigating officers traced assets to the value of approximately £750,000, which represented the defendants' proceeds of drug trafficking. The judge made a forfeiture order under s 27 of the Misuse of Drugs Act 1971 in this amount. This section empowers the court to order anything shown to relate to the offence to be forfeited. The House of Lords, however, quashed the order because the defendants had not been convicted of 'an offence under the Act' but of statutory conspiracies contrary to the Criminal Law Act 1977. Further, their Lordships ruled that the power of forfeiture was restricted to the physical items used to commit the offence and not to choses in action or other intangibles. In the words of Lord Diplock, at page 406:

> ... section 27 can never have been intended by Parliament to serve as a means of stripping the drug traffickers of the total profits of their unlawful enterprises.

1.04 Accordingly, the monies remained the property of the defendants to do with as they pleased on their release from prison.

1.05 In 1984, a committee chaired by Mr Justice Hodgson recommended that the courts should be empowered to confiscate proceeds of criminal offences of which defendants have been convicted. This led to the enactment of the DTOA, which imposed a mandatory obligation on the court to confiscate the proceeds of drug trafficking of those convicted of such offences. Some two years later, Parliament passed the Criminal Justice Act 1988 (the CJA), which, in broad terms, extended the confiscation regime imposed by the 1986 Act to cover all indictable offences together with a small number of offences triable only summarily where the benefits accruing to the defendant were likely to be unusually high.

1.06 The DTOA confiscation regime was augmented by a number of provisions in the Criminal Justice (International Cooperation) Act 1990 which came into force on 1 July 1991. Section 15 of the Act provided for the payment of interest on unpaid confiscation orders and s 16 empowered the prosecutor to apply to the Court for confiscation orders to be increased where further realisable property was identified. Part III of the Act introduced entirely new provisions empowering Customs Officers to apply to a magistrates' court for the detention and forfeiture of drug trafficking money being imported or exported in cash.

1.07 On 3 February 1995, the Drug Trafficking Act 1994 (the DTA) came into force. It consolidated the provisions of the DTOA and the Criminal Justice (International Co-operation)

Act 1990. It also strengthened the provisions of the DTOA by implementing many of the recommendations of the Home Office Working Group on Confiscation.

1.08 In October 1998 the Performance and Innovation Unit of the Cabinet Office examined once again the UK's asset recovery arrangements with a view to improving the efficiency of the recovery process and increasing the amount of illegally obtained assets recovered. It proposed the creation of a new agency with lead responsibility for asset recovery and the consolidation of existing laws on confiscation and money laundering into a single piece of legislation, together with the introduction of new powers to recover criminal assets through civil proceedings, without, controversially, the need for a criminal conviction. As a result the Proceeds of Crime Act 2002 (POCA) consolidated the law and created the Assets Recovery Agency (ARA).

C. The Object of the Confiscation Regime

1.09 It is important to appreciate at the outset of any study of the law relating to restraint and confiscation orders that POCA, the DTA, and the CJA are concerned with confiscating the *value* of the defendant's proceeds of the offences of which he has been convicted and not the actual proceeds themselves. It follows from this that once the court has determined the amount by which the defendant has benefited, all assets in which he has an interest, whether legitimately acquired or not, are vulnerable to confiscation up to the amount of that benefit. The Crown Court (under POCA) and the High Court (under the DTA and CJA) is thus entitled, pre-conviction, to restrain the defendant from dissipating assets which have been acquired perfectly legitimately for the purpose of ensuring that they remain available to satisfy a confiscation order in the amount of his benefit.

1.10 It is also important to appreciate that, contrary to the position in some countries (eg the USA), a confiscation order is not an *in rem* order against the defendant's realisable property but an *in personam* order against the defendant himself. This has a number of important consequences. In particular, the mere making of a confiscation order does not divest the defendant of his legal title to whatever realisable property was taken into account by the court in making the order. Thus the making of a confiscation order does not, itself, entitle any person in possession of the defendant's property to pass the same over to the enforcing magistrates' court in satisfaction of the confiscation order. Unless the property is being handed over pursuant to a receivership order or the defendant has expressly consented to the property being forwarded to the court, any person who does so will be vulnerable to a civil action for conversion.

D. The Drug Trafficking Act 1994: A Summary

1.11 It is plain that the object of the Act is to ensure, so far as is possible, that the convicted drug trafficker is parted from the proceeds of any drug trafficking which he has carried out. The provisions are intentionally draconian.

R v Dickens [1990] 2 QB 102, Lord Lane CJ

Where a defendant is convicted of a drug trafficking offence, as defined by s 1(3) of the Act, the Crown Court must enquire as to whether he has at any time benefited from drug trafficking.

If the court answers in the affirmative, it must go on to assess the value of the defendant's proceeds from drug trafficking. The court must then make a confiscation order against the defendant in the amount by which he has benefited unless he proved on a balance of probabilities that the value of his realisable property is less than this amount. In assessing the defendant's proceeds of drug trafficking, the court is not only required to take into account his proceeds from the offences of which he has been convicted, but of any drug trafficking activities carried on by him at any time.

1.12 The High Court is also given jurisdiction to make certain orders under the Act. Firstly, the court is empowered, normally at the pre-conviction stage, to make restraint and charging orders to prevent a defendant dissipating assets that may be made the subject of a confiscation order. Restraint orders have been described by Lord Donaldson MR in *Re Peters* [1988] QB 871 as being 'closely analogous' to *Mareva* freezing injunctions. The court may also appoint a receiver for the purposes of preserving and maintaining the value of the defendant's realisable property pending the conclusion of the criminal proceedings. Once a confiscation order has been made which is no longer subject to appeal, a receiver may be appointed to realise the defendant's assets in satisfaction of the order. The monies are paid into the magistrates' court that committed the defendant for trial and the magistrates are given concurrent powers of enforcement, which entitle them to enforce confiscation orders, by similar means to fines and other financial penalties.

E. The Criminal Justice Act 1988: A Summary

1.13 One of the most successful weapons which can be used to discourage offences that are committed in order to enrich the offenders is to ensure that if the offenders are brought to justice, any profit which they have made from their offending is confiscated.

R v Sekhon, 16 December 2002, The Lord Chief Justice

The 1988 Act, in broad terms, extended the confiscation regime in respect of drug trafficking offences to cover all indictable offences together with a limited number of summary offences from which peculiarly high profits could be gained. There are, however, a number of differences between the two regimes and these will be considered in more detail in subsequent chapters. In general, the provisions of the CJA are less draconian than those of the DTA, although the Criminal Justice Act 1993, which came into force on 3 February 1995, and the Proceeds of Crime Act 1995, which came into force on 1 November 1995 removed many of the differences between the two regimes.

F. The Proceeds of Crime Act 2002: A Summary

1.14 The Proceeds of Crime Act 2002 received Royal Assent on 24 July 2002. It is designed to replace and improve the existing legislation, namely the DTA and the CJA. The main implementation date for Pt 2 of the Act, the Confiscation provisions, was the 24 March 2003. The transitional arrangement dictates that for all offences that commenced before or overlap that date, the 'old' Acts will apply, namely the DTA and the CJA. In effect, therefore, for some time to come one can expect the three Acts to co-exist side by side.

The other implementation dates on which POCA came into force are considered in the relevant chapters herein.

1.15 The new Act provides for confiscation orders in relation to persons who benefit from criminal conduct and for restraint orders to prohibit dealing with property. It also allows for the recovery of property that is or represents property obtained through unlawful conduct or is intended to be used in unlawful conduct; and it makes new provisions about money laundering and investigations relating to benefit from criminal conduct or to property that is or represents property obtained through unlawful conduct.

1.16 POCA will eventually provide a complete code governing confiscation law. Under it there is no distinction between drug trafficking offences and other offences (except in relation to the 'criminal lifestyle' provisions). Powers that were formerly exercised by the High Court in relation to restraint orders and the supervision and enforcement of confiscation orders will now be exercised by the Crown Court. It also introduces a new provision for 'civil recovery' where the defendant has not been convicted of a relevant offence.

G. Agencies responsible for the Enforcement of the Legislation

(1) The Assets Recovery Agency

1.17 Part 1 of POCA establishes the Assets Recovery Agency (ARA) and Sch 1 sets out the terms of appointment for the Director. The purpose of the ARA is to contribute to the reduction in crime and s 2(1) of the new Act requires the Director to exercise his powers in a way she considers best calculated to contribute to that reduction. The principle functions of the ARA are the recovery of criminal assets through confiscation; civil recovery; the exercise of revenue functions; and the accreditation and training of financial investigators. The provisions of Pt 1 came into force on 13 January 2003 by virtue of SI 2002/3055. On 11 January 2007 the Government announced a proposed merger between the ARA and the Serious Organised Crime Agency. As such a change will require legislation this text continues to consider ARA in its present form, as it is anticipated the actual merger will not take place for some time.

1.18 Section 2(5) requires the Director, in considering the way which is best calculated to contribute to the reduction of crime, to have regard to any guidance given to her by the Secretary of State. By s 2 (6), any such guidance by the Secretary of State must indicate that the reduction in crime is, in general, best secured by criminal investigations and criminal proceedings. The Secretary of State gave such guidance to the Director by letter dated 7 February, 2005. The Guidance emphasises the importance of prosecuting offenders where possible. By para of 3 of the Guidance, the Secretary of State indicates that the Director should, for the purpose of contributing to the reduction in crime:

(a) not normally act without a referral from the law enforcement or prosecution agencies;
(b) consult the relevant law enforcement or prosecution authority before exercising any of his operational functions, in order to enquire whether doing so would prejudice a criminal investigation or criminal proceedings, and give due weight to any advice so received;

Chapter 1: Setting the Scene

    (c) keep under review the extent to which taking, continuing or refraining from any course of action has a potential to prejudice a criminal investigation or criminal proceedings and avoid such prejudice where possible;

    (d) ensure where possible that information relevant to a criminal investigation or criminal proceedings is disclosed to the relevant law enforcement or prosecution authority at the earliest practical opportunity.

1.19 The Secretary of State also indicates in his Guidance that memoranda of understanding between the Director and law enforcement and prosecution agencies will help to give effect to these guidelines. Finally, the Secretary of State indicates that where a criminal conviction has been obtained, criminal confiscation of the proceeds of crime will best contribute to the reduction of crime.

1.20 The ARA website (<http://www.assetsrecovery.gov.uk>) sets out the criteria that must be met before a case will be considered for civil recovery proceedings. These criteria are as follows:

    (a) The case must normally be referred by a law enforcement agency or prosecution authority;

    (b) Criminal proceedings must have been considered and either failed or proved impossible to complete;

    (c) Recoverable property must have been identified and have an estimated value of at least £10,000;

    (d) Recoverable property must include property other than cash or negotiable instruments (although cash is recoverable if it is in addition to other property);

    (e) There must be evidence of criminal conduct that is supported to the civil standard of proof.

1.21 Additionally, the ARA must consider the potential impact of a successful civil recovery action in terms of crime reduction.

1.22 The ARA is also responsible for POCA taxation investigations in cases where the Director has reasonable grounds to suspect that income, gains, or profits are chargeable to a relevant tax and have arisen from criminal conduct. The Director then carries out the tax functions that would normally be discharged by HM Revenue and Customs.

(2) The Crown Prosecution Service

1.23 The Crown Prosecution Service (CPS) is responsible for the restraint and confiscation aspects of all prosecutions instituted by the police. The Central Confiscation Branch, located at CPS Headquarters, has the conduct of all restraint and confiscation proceedings brought under the DTA and CJA in police cases. POCA cases are generally dealt with locally in CPS area offices. The Central Confiscation Branch will also have the conduct of the restraint and confiscation aspects of cases brought by the Serious Organised Crime Agency in those cases where the CPS is the lead prosecuting authority.

(3) The Revenue and Customs Prosecutions Office

1.24 The Revenue and Customs Prosecutions Office (RCPO) was established under s 34 of the Commissioners for Revenue and Customs Act 2005 and came into existence on 18 April, 2005. The Office is headed by a Director appointed under s 34 (1) of the Act by the

G. Agencies responsible for the Enforcement of the Legislation

Attorney-General to whom he is accountable. Section 35 of the Act deals with the Director's functions and provides:

(1) The Director-
    (a) may institute and conduct criminal proceedings in England and Wales relating to a criminal investigation by the Revenue and Customs, and
    (b) shall take over the conduct of criminal proceedings instituted in England and Wales by the Revenue and Customs.
(2) The Director shall provide such advice as he thinks appropriate, to such persons as he thinks appropriate, in relation to-
    (a) a criminal investigation by the Revenue and Customs, or
    (b) criminal proceedings instituted in England and Wales relating to a criminal investigation by the Revenue and Customs.

1.25 The RCPO was established following much criticism of its predecessor, the Customs and Excise Prosecutions Office within the Solicitor's Office of HM Customs and Excise. A number of inquiries into failed prosecutions had criticised the lack of independence of the Office which reported through it's Solicitor to the Commissioners of Customs and Excise. The RCPO now enjoys the same degree of independence from officers of HM Revenue and Customs that the CPS enjoys from the police.

1.26 The restraint and enforcement aspects of all RCPO prosecutions, whether under the DTA, CJA or POCA, are dealt with by its Asset Forfeiture Division (AFD) working independently of, but in close liaison with, the prosecuting lawyer. The AFD will also have the conduct of the restraint and confiscation aspects of SOCA led investigations and prosecutions in those cases where RCPO is the lead prosecution agency.

(4) HM Revenue and Customs

1.27 On 18 April, 2005 the Inland Revenue and HM Customs and Excise merged to form one new Department known as HM Revenue and Customs (HMRC). HMRC is responsible for mounting criminal investigations into precisely the same offences for which its predecessors had responsibility including drug trafficking, money laundering and tax frauds. The one significant difference being that HMRC has no prosecution function: as noted above, this is now the responsibility of the Revenue and Customs Prosecutions Office. HMRC does, however, retain responsibility for applications before the magistrates' court for the detention and forfeiture of cash under Pt V of POCA. The effect of ss 5, 6 and 50 of the Commissioners for Revenue and Customs Act 2005 is such that references in any enactment, statutory instrument or other document to the 'Commissioners of Customs and Excise' is deemed to be a reference to the Commissioners of HM Revenue and Customs, and similarly references of 'Customs Officers' are deemed to be references to officers of HMRC.

(5) The Serious Fraud Office

1.28 The Serious Fraud Office (SFO) was established under the Criminal Justice Act 1987 to investigate and prosecute cases of serious fraud. The Act gives the SFO a number of investigatory powers not vested in other law enforcement agencies including the power under s 2 to require any person whom the Director has reason to believe has relevant information, or a person under investigation, to attend for interview and provide information and documentation.

1.29 The Act provides no definition of what constitutes a 'serious fraud' and the SFO does not take on every case referred to it. According to the SFO website (<http://www.sfo.gov.uk>), the following matters are taken into account in deciding whether to adopt a case:

(a) Does the value of the alleged fraud exceed £1,000,000?
(b) Is there a significant international dimension?
(c) Is the case likely to be of widespread public concern?
(d) Does the case require highly specialised knowledge, eg of financial markets?
(e) Is there a need to use the SFO's special powers such as those under s 2?
(f) Does the fraud appear to be complex and one where the use of the s 2 powers might be appropriate?

Offences prosecuted by the SFO are caught by the restraint and confiscation of the CJA and POCA and the office has its own specialist confiscation unit handling this aspect of their cases.

(6) The Serious Organised Crime Agency

1.30 The Serious Organised Crime Agency commenced operations on 1 April, 2006. It is a statutory body created by the Serious Organised Crime and Police Act 2005. Under s 2 of the Act, SOCA's functions are:

(a) preventing and detecting serious organised crime, and
(b) contributing to the reduction of such crime in other ways and to the mitigation of its consequences.

1.31 'Serious organised crime' is not defined in the Act and s 5(3) provides that notwithstanding the reference to 'serious organised crime' in s 2(1), SOCA may nonetheless carry on activities in relation to other crime provided they are carried on for the purposes of any of the functions conferred on SOCA by the Act. SOCA thus has a very broad remit and it is with some justification that it has been referred to in the media as a 'British FBI'.

1.32 It is likely that financially motivated crime such as drug trafficking, people smuggling, money laundering and tax frauds will henceforth be investigated by SOCA. This will include the financial aspects of the cases which will be handled by trained financial investigators. It should be noted, however, that SOCA has no prosecution function and will not be responsible for the conduct of criminal proceedings in relation to the offences it investigates. By s 38 of the Act, prosecutions of 'designated offences' will be conducted by the Director of the Revenue and Customs Prosecutions Office and prosecutions of 'non designated offences' by the Director of Public Prosecutions. The expression 'designated offences' is not defined in the Act, but s 39 provides that the Directors may give directions to enable SOCA to determine whether cases should be refered to the Director of Revenue and Customs Prosecutions or to the Director of Public Prosecutions.

(7) The Enforcement Task Force

1.33 The Enforcement Task Force (ETF) was established in December 2002 following widespread concern about the number of unenforced DTA and CJA confiscation orders that remained outstanding. It is a multi-disciplinary agency comprising CPS and RCPO lawyers, working alongside police officers and officers of HMRC. All DTA and CJA confiscation orders made in CPS and RCPO prosecutions are referred to the ETF for enforcement action to be taken. ETF staff enforce the outstanding confiscation orders by making applications for the appointment of enforcement receivers and by effective liaison with HM Prison Service and enforcing magistrates' courts.

ETF investigators also revisit old confiscation cases and, where appropriate, applications are made for confiscation orders to be increased to take account of subsequently acquired assets. **1.34**

Thus far, ETF has been incredibly successful having brought in over £100,000,000 since it opened for business. **1.35**

(8) Regional Asset Recovery Teams

Regional Asset Recovery Teams (RART) have been set up in London, Wales, North West and North East England, and the West Midlands. The teams are formed of police and customs officers as well as NCIS staff and provide advice, support and assistance to law enforcement authorities within their areas. They will take over the financial investigations in particular cases and prepare witness statements in support of restraint applications and, where the defendants are convicted, will prepare the prosecutor's statement of information. Many of the officers attached to the RARTs are accredited financial investigators under POCA. **1.36**

H. The International Element

Drug trafficking involves in nearly every case, at some stage, the smuggling of controlled drugs from one country to another. There is also an international element in many other organised criminal activities including tax frauds, people smuggling and money laundering. It is not surprising therefore that the various Acts make provision for assets held in the UK by defendants being prosecuted in other jurisdictions to be restrained and ultimately realised in satisfaction of a foreign confiscation order. Similarly all UK confiscation legislation applies to assets a defendant owns overseas and prosecuting authorities frequently seek the assistance of overseas jurisdictions, by means of letters of request, to restrain such assets and, after conviction, realise the same in satisfaction of a confiscation order. The High Court and Crown Court also has power to make a 'repatriation order' directing a defendant to bring within the jurisdiction of the Court assets he holds overseas. **1.37**

I. Money Laundering

Closely related to restraint and confiscation law is the law relating to money laundering. Those who participate in drug trafficking and other criminal offences that yield huge profits need to conceal their proceeds from law enforcement authorities to prevent confiscation and also to disguise the true source of their ill gotten gains. Consequently, confiscation legislation has criminalised money laundering activities and as the threat of money laundering has increased, so the provisions have become increasingly more draconian. The legislation now extends to financial institutions and others who hold money on behalf of clients. **1.38**

The Money Laundering Regulations 2003 make it a criminal offence not to report suspicious transactions to law enforcement authorities and impose a positive obligation to introduce systems and staff training with a view to detecting such transactions.

J. Recent Developments in Confiscation Law

1.39 The period since the first edition of this work was published in 2003 has seen many significant developments in confiscation law both in terms of statute and case law. We summarise below the most important developments which are considered in greater detail in the following chapters.

(1) Release of restrained funds to meet legal expenses in POCA cases

1.40 In *Customs and Excise Commissioners v S* [2005] 1 WLR 1338 the Court of Appeal held that the prohibition in s 41(4) of POCA on the release of restrained funds to meet legal expenses extends to costs incurred in the restraint proceedings and does not just relate to legal expenses incurred in defending the criminal prosecution.

(2) Management receivers—the Capewell decisions

1.41 One of the most significant developments in confiscation law in recent times concerns the appointment of management receivers at the pre-conviction stage. The courts have expressed considerable concern as to the costs incurred by management receivers which have, on occasion, been disproportionate to any benefit derived to the defendant's estate, particularly in the light of the decision in *Hughes v Customs and Excise Commissioners* [2002] 4 All ER 633 where the Court of Appeal held that the defendant is liable to meet the receiver's costs even when the order has been discharged following his acquittal.

1.42 In *Capewell v Customs and Excise Commissioners* [2005] 1 All ER 900 the Court of Appeal commended a number of guidelines that prosecutors should follow in making applications for the appointment of management receivers. These are dealt with in more detail in Chapter 3. In *Capewell v Customs and Excise Commissioners (No 2)* the Court of Appeal found that, the decision in *Hughes* notwithstanding, Part 69 of the Civil Procedure Rules gives the Court a discretion to require the prosecutor to pay the receiver's remuneration in appropriate circumstances. The House of Lords has given the prosecutor leave to appeal against this aspect of the *Capewell* decisions and the hearing is expected to take place in December 2006. (A summary of the House of Lords judgment is at Appendix 23.)

(3) Restraint orders: failure to comply with the duty to give full and frank disclosure

1.43 In *Jennings v CPS* [2005] 4 All ER 391 the Court of Appeal ruled that the public interest in restraining assets to make them available for confiscation was such that restraint orders should not always be discharged where there has been a failure by the prosecutor to give full and frank disclosure. The Court observed that in many such cases it is sufficient for the court to express its displeasure by penalising the prosecutor's actions in costs and that the remedy of discharging the order entirely should be reserved for cases whether the prosecutor's failure to disclose has been 'appalling'.

J. Recent Developments in Confiscation Law

(4) Release of restrained funds to pay unsecured third party creditors

The decision of Buckley J in *Re W* The Times, 15 November 1990 is authority for the proposition that restraint orders may not be varied to meet debts owed by the defendant to unsecured third party creditors. In *Re X* [2004] 3 WLR 906 Davis J ruled that *Re W* was wrongly decided and that the court did have a discretion to release restrained funds for such purposes in appropriate circumstances. This issue is considered in depth in Chapters 5 and 22.

1.44

(5) Confiscation orders: failure to follow the prescribed procedures

Failures by judges and prosecutors to follow the correct procedures have been the cause of many appeals in recent years and have resulted in a number of high value DTA and CJA confiscation orders being quashed. In *R v Palmer* [2002] EWCA Crim 2202 a £33 million confiscation order against a notorious time share fraudster was quashed due to errors by the prosecutor in drafting a notice under s 71 of the Act and in *R v Martin* (2002) 2 Cr App R (S) 34 a £10 million confiscation order made against an excise duty fraudster, who was able to carry on his trade from his prison cell while serving a sentence for an earlier excise evasion fraud, was quashed for the same reason. Confiscation orders have also been quashed as a result of mistakes by judges of a purely technical nature in following the statutory procedures for the postponement of confiscation hearings.

1.45

In *R v Sekhon* [2002] EWCA Crim 2954 the Court of Appeal, Lord Woolf CJ presiding, ruled that these cases were wrongly decided and that irregularities of a purely technical nature that neither prejudiced nor misled anyone could not affect the validity of a confiscation order. The issue was put beyond doubt in *R v Soneji* [2005] UKHL 49 where the House of Lords reinstated confiscation orders that had been quashed by the Court of Appeal because of a failure by the trial judge to follow the postponement procedures correctly. It seems that henceforth defendants will not be able to rely on these technical points. This in fact brings the position under the DTA and CJA into line with that under POCA where s 14(11) provides that confiscation orders must not be quashed merely on account of an irregularity that has occurred in relation to the postponement procedures.

1.46

(6) Delay in enforcing confiscation orders

There has been a significant change in the law concerning delays by prosecuting authorities in enforcing confiscation orders. In *R v Chichester Magistrates' Court ex p Crowther* [1998] EWHC Admin 960 the Divisional Court held that even where there has been a culpable delay by the prosecutor in taking steps to enforce a confiscation order, this does not act as a bar to the enforcing magistrates' court implementing the default sentence for non payment. This case was decided before the Human Rights Act 1998 came into force and in *Lloyd v Bow Street Magistrates' Court* [2003] EWHC Admin 2294, the Court ruled that an unreasonable delay on the part of the prosecutor in taking enforcement action would amount to a breach of the defendant's rights under Article 6 of the European Convention on Human Rights if an attempt was made to implement the default sentence. The Court made it plain however, that its decision applied only where enforcement action took the form of implementing the default sentence and had no application in respect of the use of civil remedies such as the appointment of an enforcement receiver. In the recent case of

1.47

Chapter 1: Setting the Scene

R (on the application of Deamer) v Southampton Magistrates' Court [2006] EWHC Admin 2221, the Divisional Court emphasised that a stay would only be granted where the delay is unjustified and unreasonable. This is considered in more detail in Chapter 17.

(7) The international element

1.48 After much delay the Proceeds of Crime Act 2002 (External Requests and Orders) Order 2005, SI 2005/3181, made under s 444 of POCA, came into force on 1 January 2006. It revoked the Drug Trafficking Act and Criminal Justice Act Designated Countries and Territories Orders and provides a comprehensive code for the enforcement of external orders in the UK and for the making of restraint orders in support of external investigations and proceedings. The most significant difference is that applications in relation to such orders and proceedings are now made to the Crown Court rather than the High Court. The effect of the Order is considered in more detail in Chapter 25.

(8) Civil recovery under the Proceeds of Crime Act 2002

1.49 The ability to finalise recovery order proceedings has been thwarted by legal challenges and delays in respondents obtaining LSC funding. As a result the Director has missed his targets in relation to civil recovery of the proceeds of crime. Nevertheless she has enjoyed a marked success in the courts in relation to legal challenges brought, particularly in respect of European Convention points, where the POCA legislation has been found to be generally compliant with Articles 1, 6(1), 6(2) and 7 (see *Director of the Assets Recovery Agency v (1) Jia Jin He (2) Dan Dan Chen* [2004] EWHC (Admin) 3021, *Director of the Assets Recovery Agency v Satnam Singh* [2004] EWHC (Admin 2335, *Walsh v Director of the Assets Recovery Agency* [2005] NICA 6, which are all considered in Chapter 20).

(9) Amendments brought in by the Serious Organised Crime and Police Act 2005

1.50 Part 2 of the 2005 Act makes a number of amendments to POCA making provision for confiscation orders to be made in the magistrates' court in certain circumstances, empowering the Director of the ARA to apply for property freezing orders pending the making of an application for a civil recovery order, allowing for the release of assets to fund legal expenses in ARA cases, and making a number of amendments to the money laundering provisions in the Act.

1.51 The Act also empowers judges sentencing defendants for certain specified offences to make a financial reporting order requiring the defendant to make reports giving specified information as to his financial affairs.

(10) The Criminal Procedure Rules 2005

1.52 Applications to the Crown Court under POCA for restraint, confiscation and receivership orders were initially governed by the Crown Court (Confiscation, Restraint and Receivership) Rules 2003. These Rules have now been revoked and have been consolidated in the Criminal Procedure Rules 2005. The relevant provisions may be found at Pt 56 to Pt 62 of the Rules and are quoted in the appropriate parts of the text.

2

RESTRAINT AND CHARGING ORDERS UNDER THE DTA AND CJA

A. Introduction	2.01	E. The Standard of Proof on Restraint Order Applications	2.49
(1) Purpose of restraint and charging orders	2.02	F. The Scope and Duration of Restraint Orders	2.50
(2) Freezing orders distinguished	2.03	(1) Parties restrained by the order	2.50
B. Restraint Orders under the Drug Trafficking Act 1994	2.08	(2) Limited companies	2.53
(1) Proceedings have been instituted or an application made	2.09	(3) Property restrained by the order	2.64
		(4) Legitimately acquired assets	2.67
(2) What are drug trafficking offences?	2.11	(5) Leasehold interests	2.69
(3) Section 25(1)(b): proceedings have not been concluded	2.12	(6) Property that is not realisable under the legislation	2.73
(4) Section 25(1)(c): reasonable cause to believe the defendant has benefited from drug trafficking	2.15	(7) Meaning of property	2.74
		(8) Overseas assets	2.76
		(9) Duration of restraint orders	2.78
(5) What is drug trafficking?	2.17	G. Terms and Conditions Upon which Orders are Made	2.82
(6) Section 25(3): proceedings to be instituted in the future	2.19	(1) Costs and expenses incurred in complying with the order	2.84
C. Restraint Orders under Part VI of the Criminal Justice Act 1988	2.23	(2) Legal expenses	2.89
(1) Proceedings have been instituted in England and Wales	2.25	(3) Businesses	2.91
		H. Charging Orders	2.93
(2) Offences to which Part VI of the CJA applies	2.26	(1) What is a charging order?	2.93
(3) Proceedings have not been concluded	2.27	(2) When may a charging order be made?	2.94
(4) Proceedings may result or have resulted in a conviction for an offence of a relevant description from which the defendant may have benefited	2.33	(3) What property can be charged?	2.97
		(4) Protecting the charging order	2.99
		(5) Applications to vary or discharge charging orders	2.100
(5) Benefit	2.34	(6) Relationship between restraint and charging orders	2.102
D. Delay and Proving there is a Risk of Dissipation of Assets	2.40		

A. Introduction

An application for a restraint order to prevent the dissipation of assets pending the determination of criminal proceedings against a defendant is frequently the first step a prosecutor will take in the confiscation process. Restraint orders are most commonly obtained shortly before or just after criminal proceedings are commenced, but they can be sought

2.01

at any stage prior to the conclusion of those proceedings. Indeed, it is by no means unusual for a restraint order to be obtained after a confiscation order has been made so as to protect assets against dissipation during the enforcement process. In this chapter we examine the powers of the court to make restraint orders under the DTA and CJA and the procedural steps that must be followed to obtain them. Section 41 of POCA (restraint orders under the new regime) does not have effect where the offence (mentioned in s 40(2)(a) or s 40(3)(a) of POCA) was committed before 24 March 2002 (SI 2003/333). For offences committed before that date the DTA and CJA still have effect. For cases under POCA, see Chapter 8.

(1) Purpose of restraint and charging orders

2.02 It is often many months after a defendant's arrest that he is brought to trial. The aims of the legislation would clearly be defeated if a defendant could deal with his assets in any manner he chooses while awaiting trial: he would be able to dispose of all his realisable property to ensure he was effectively 'judgment proof' by the time a confiscation hearing takes place. Accordingly both the DTA and the CJA give the High Court jurisdiction to make restraint and charging orders to prevent a defendant, subject to exceptions for the payment of reasonable amounts in living expenses and legal fees actually and properly incurred, from dealing in his realisable property pending the conclusion of the criminal proceedings to which he is subject. Restraint and charging orders may also be granted to prevent a defendant dealing in realisable property pending the determination of an application to the High Court for an increase in a confiscation order that has already been made.

(2) Freezing orders distinguished

2.03 Although the Court of Appeal held in *Re Peters* [1988] QB 871 that the jurisdiction to make restraint orders is 'closely analogous' to the jurisdiction to make freezing orders (formerly *Mareva* injunctions), there are a number of important distinctions between the two forms of relief. The jurisdiction to grant freezing orders stemmed initially from the inherent jurisdiction of the court before being enshrined in s 37(3) of the Supreme Court Act 1981 whereas the restraint order is exclusively a creature of statute. Further, the object of the freezing order is to preserve assets to meet any award of damages that might be made in favour of the claimant in a civil action. The restraint order, in contrast, is intended to preserve a defendant's assets to make them available to satisfy any confiscation order that might be made against him following conviction for a criminal offence.

2.04 Of most practical importance, the DTA and CJA impose strict limitations on the matters the court may take into account in deciding whether to grant a restraint order or allow any subsequent application for a variation. The provision is to be found in s 31(2) of the DTA and s 81(2) of the CJA and is in the following terms:

Subject to the following provisions of this section, the powers shall be exercised with a view to making available for satisfying the confiscation order or, as the case may be, any confiscation order that may be made in the defendant's case, the value for the time being of realisable property held by any person, by means of the realisation of such property.

2.05 This provision, which has become known as the legislative steer, persuaded Buckley J in *Re W* The Times, 15 November 1990 that the Court had no jurisdiction to vary a restraint order on the application of a bona fide third party creditor of the defendant to release funds to meet the outstanding debt. This is in marked contrast to the position in relation to freezing orders where the court will not allow a claimant who has not obtained judgment to gain priority over creditors of the defendant. It should, however, be noted that in *Re X* [2004] 3 WLR 906 Davis J concluded that *Re W* had been wrongly decided on this point. These judgments are considered in depth in Chapter 5.

2.06 A further important distinction between freezing orders and restraint orders is that the court has no power, when making a restraint order, to require the prosecutor to give an undertaking that he will indemnify third parties in respect of any liability which may flow from compliance with the order: see *Re R (Restraint Order)* [1990] 2 All ER 569. A freezing order, in contrast, will not normally be granted unless such an undertaking is given by the claimant. Similarly, as an essential prerequisite to obtaining a freezing order, the claimant will be required to give an undertaking to pay damages to the defendant if it later transpires that the order should not have been granted. In relation to restraint orders, however, sc115 r 4(1) provides that a prosecutor applying for a restraint order shall not be required to give any such undertaking. Further, s 18 of the DTA and s 89 of the CJA impose strict limitations on the circumstances in which an acquitted defendant can seek compensation against the prosecutor for any loss he has suffered as a result of being subject to the restraint order.

2.07 Another consequence of the legislative steer is that that court will take a more proactive stance in determining the reasonableness of sums released from restrained funds to meet legal and general living expenses than it does in cases where a freezing order has been made. Again, this is considered in more detail in Chapter 5.

B. Restraint Orders under the Drug Trafficking Act 1994

2.08 By s 25(1) of the DTA, the High Court may grant restraint and charging orders where the following conditions are satisfied:

(a) proceedings have been instituted against the defendant in England and Wales for a drug trafficking offence or an application has been made by the prosecutor in respect of the defendant under ss 13, 14, 15, 16 or 19 of the Act;
(b) the proceedings have not, or the application has not, been concluded; and
(c) the court is satisfied there is reasonable cause to believe:
   (i) in the case of an application under ss 15 or 16, that the court will be satisfied as mentioned in s 15(4) or, as the case may be, s 16(2); or
   (ii) in any other case that the defendant has benefited from drug trafficking.

Section 25(2) provides that the court shall not exercise its powers to make an order under s 25(1) where it is satisfied there has been undue delay in continuing the proceedings or application in question or that the prosecutor does not intend to proceed.

(1) Proceedings have been instituted or an application made

2.09 Section 41(2) of the DTA provides that proceedings are instituted in England and Wales in any of the following circumstances:

(a) where a justice of the peace issues a summons or warrant under s 1 of the Magistrates' Courts Act 1980 in respect of the offence;
(b) where a person is charged with the offence after being taken into custody without a warrant;
(c) where a bill of indictment is preferred under s 2 of the Administration of Justice (Miscellaneous Provisions) Act 1933 in a case falling within s 2(2)(b). This relates to circumstances where a bill of indictment is preferred by direction of the Criminal Division of the Court of Appeal or by direction, or with the consent of, a High Court Judge.

Where this would result in there being more than one time for the institution of proceedings, s 41(2) provides they shall be taken to have been instituted at the earliest of these times.

2.10 Sections 13, 14, 15, 16, and 19 of the Act empower the High Court, on the application of the prosecutor, to reconsider various decisions made during confiscation hearings at the Crown Court and, in certain circumstances, to make confiscation orders where none has been made or, where a confiscation order has been made, to increase the order in the light of newly acquired evidence. The powers of the High Court under these provisions are considered in more detail in Chapter 13. The effect of s 25(1)(a) of the DTA is to empower the High Court to make restraint orders when an application under any one of these sections has been made. Although the phrase 'application has been made' in s 25(1)(a) is not defined in the Act, it is submitted that the application is made when it has been issued out of the Administrative Court Office at the Royal Courts of Justice.

(2) What are drug trafficking offences?

2.11 In order to obtain a restraint order under the DTA, the prosecutor must establish that the criminal proceedings against the defendant are 'for a drug trafficking offence'. These are listed in s 1(3) of the Act and are as follows:

(a) an offence under ss 4(2) or (3) or 5(3) of the Misuse of Drugs Act 1971 (production, supply, and possession for supply of controlled drugs);
(b) an offence under s 20 of that Act (assisting in or inducing the commission outside the United Kingdom of an offence punishable under a corresponding law);
(c) an offence under:
 (i) s 50(2) or (3) of the Customs and Excise Management Act 1979 (improper importation),
 (ii) s 68(2) of that Act (exportation), or
 (iii) s 170 of that Act (fraudulent evasion)
 in connection with a prohibition or restriction on importation or exportation having effect by virtue of s 3 of the Misuse of Drugs Act 1971;
(d) an offence under s 12 of the Criminal Justice (International Co-operation) Act 1990 (manufacture or supply of substance specified in Sch 2 to that Act);
(e) an offence under s 19 of that Act (using a ship for illicit traffic in controlled drugs);
(f) an offence under ss 49, 50 or 51 of the DTA or s 14 of the Criminal Justice (International Co-operation) Act 1990 (which makes, in relation to Scotland and Northern Ireland, provision corresponding to s 49);

(g) an offence under s 1 of the Criminal Law Act 1977 of conspiracy to commit any of the offences in paragraphs (a) to (f) above;
(h) an offence under s 1 of the Criminal Attempts Act 1981 of attempting to commit any of those offences;
(i) an offence of inciting another to commit any of those offences whether under s 19 of the Misuse of Drugs Act 1971 or at common law.

The term also includes aiding and abetting, counselling or procuring the commission of any of the offences in paras (a) to (f) above.

(3) Section 25(1)(b): proceedings have not been concluded

2.12 Section 41(3) of the Act provides that proceedings for a drug trafficking offence are concluded when:
(a) the defendant is acquitted on all counts;
(b) the court decides not to make a confiscation order against a defendant who is convicted on one or more counts; or
(c) a confiscation order made against the defendant in those proceedings is satisfied.

2.13 It follows from this definition that proceedings do not conclude on the making of a confiscation order, but when the order has been satisfied. By s 41(6) the order is satisfied when no amount is due under it. Thus restraint and charging orders may be made for the first time after a confiscation order has been made but prior to it being satisfied. Further, restraint orders made pre-conviction are not discharged once a defendant is convicted and sentenced, but remain in force thereafter until such time as the confiscation order is satisfied. In practice, it is by no means uncommon for a restraint order to be made for the first time after a defendant has been convicted to prevent the dissipation of assets pending the determination of an appeal or the enforcement of the confiscation order.

2.14 By s 41(4) applications under ss 13, 14 and 19 are concluded:
(a) if the court decides not to make a confiscation order against the defendant, when it makes that decision; or
(b) if a confiscation order is made against him as a result of the application, when the order is satisfied.

Similarly, s 41(5) provides that applications under ss 15 and 16 are concluded:
(a) if the court decides not to vary the confiscation order in question, when it makes that decision; or
(b) if the court varies the confiscation order as a result of the application, when the order is satisfied.

(4) Section 25(1)(c): reasonable cause to believe the defendant has benefited from drug trafficking

2.15 The court must be satisfied there is reasonable cause to believe the defendant has benefited from drug trafficking. The term 'reasonable cause' has been held to impose an objective standard: see *Lister v Perryman* (1870) LR 4 HL 521. In *Johnson v Whitehouse* [1984] RTR 38 (a breathalyser case) the Divisional Court held that a higher standard of proof is required to establish 'reasonable cause to believe' than is necessary to establish 'reasonable cause to suspect'. The requirement for reasonable cause to believe does not, however, require the prosecutor to have substantial proof before applying for a restraint order and is clearly a lesser burden than having to establish the defendant has a case to answer. In many cases, it will suffice to show reasonable grounds for believing that the defendant has committed a drug trafficking offence, since the defendant's motive for committing such offences is almost invariably to benefit from them. In *Re A Defendant* The Times, 7 April 1987, Webster J held that evidence detailing police observations of the defendant trading in drugs gave rise to an 'almost inevitable' inference that he had benefited from drug trafficking.

2.16 In considering whether the prosecutor has established there is reasonable cause to believe the defendant has benefited from drug trafficking, the court is also entitled to bear in mind the assumptions in s 4(3) of the Act that must be made against the defendant at any confiscation hearing. The court must also have regard to the extended definition of benefit under s 2(3) to the effect that a person has benefited from drug trafficking if he has at any time received any payment or other reward in connection with drug trafficking carried on by him or another person. Thus if a defendant receives a sum of money in connection with drug trafficking, but forwards it on to a third party either because he is acting as a conduit (as in *R v Simons* (1994) 15 Cr App R(S) 126) or a money launderer he has still benefited from drug trafficking to the extent of that payment, notwithstanding that he did not keep it for his own use.

(5) What is drug trafficking?

2.17 The definition of 'drug trafficking' in s 1(1) DTA is entirely different from the definition of 'drug trafficking offence' as defined in s 1(3). Section 1(1) provides that 'drug trafficking' means doing or being concerned in any of the following whether in England, Wales or elsewhere:

(a) producing or supplying a controlled drug where the prohibition or supply contravenes s 4(1) of the Misuse of Drugs Act 1971 or a corresponding law;
(b) transporting or storing a controlled drug where possession of the drug contravenes s 5(1) of that Act or a corresponding law;
(c) importing or exporting a controlled drug where then importation or exportation is prohibited by s 3(1) of that Act or a corresponding law;
(d) manufacturing or supplying a scheduled substance within the meaning of s 12 of the Criminal Justice (International Co-operation) Act 1990 where the manufacture or supply is an offence under that section;
(e) using any ship for illicit traffic in controlled drugs in circumstances which amount to the commission of an offence under section 19 of that Act;
(f) conduct which is an offence under section 49 of the DTA or would be such an offence if it took place in England and Wales;
(g) acquiring, having possession of, or using property in circumstances which amount to the commission of an offence under s 51 of the DTA or which would amount to such an offence if it took place in England and Wales.

2.18 Section 1(2) provides that drug trafficking also includes:

a person doing the following, whether in England and Wales or elsewhere, that is entering into or being otherwise concerned in an arrangement whereby:

C. Restraint Orders under Part VI of the Criminal Justice Act 1988

(i) the retention or control by or on behalf of another person of the other person's proceeds of drug trafficking is facilitated, or

(ii) the proceedings of drug trafficking by another person are used to secure that funds are placed at the other person's disposal or are used for the other person's benefit to acquire property by way of investment.

(6) Section 25(3): proceedings to be instituted in the future

2.19 The provisions we have examined thus far only entitle the court to make a restraint order when criminal proceedings have been instituted against a defendant for a drug trafficking offence whether by his being charged at a police station, a summons or warrant being issued, or leave being given to prefer a voluntary bill of indictment. The court has no power under s 25(1) to make a restraint order prior to the institution of proceedings by one of these methods.

2.20 Section 25(3) allows the court to make restraint and charging orders in circumstances where a person is to be charged with a drug trafficking offence or an application under ss 13, 14, 15, 16 or 19 is to be made in respect of him and there is reasonable cause to believe he has benefited from drug trafficking. This is a useful weapon in the prosecutor's armoury where, for example, the mere arrest of a defendant is likely to lead to the dissipation of assets by family members or friends before the prosecutor is in a position to apply for an order under s 25(1).

2.21 As the DTA imposes no time limit within which proceedings must be instituted, s 25(3) is open to potential misuse. Some protection is provided by s 25(5), which provides that where the court has made a restraint or charging order under s 25(3) the court shall discharge the order if proceedings in respect of the offence are not instituted within such time as it considers reasonable. What constitutes a reasonable time is clearly an issue of fact for the court to determine, but the longer the period of time that elapses without the defendant being charged, the more difficult it is going to be for the prosecutor to prove that he has a settled intention of instituting proceedings against the defendant.

2.22 When the High Court makes a restraint order against a person prior to the institution of proceedings, s 25(4) provides that references in the Act to 'the defendant' shall be construed as references to that person; that references to 'the prosecutor' shall be construed as references to the person whom the court is satisfied is to have the conduct of the proposed proceedings; and references to 'realisable property' shall be construed as if, immediately before the time the court grants the order, proceedings have been instituted against that person for a drug trafficking offence.

C. Restraint Orders under Part VI of the Criminal Justice Act 1988

2.23 Part VI of the Criminal Justice Act 1988 as amended by the Proceeds of Crime Act 1995 gives the High Court power to make restraint orders in relation to defendants against whom criminal proceedings have been or are to be instituted for criminal conduct other than drug trafficking offences. As might be expected, the provisions are in very similar terms to those in the DTA and are to be found in s 76 of the Act.

Chapter 2: Restraint and Charging Orders under the DTA and CJA

2.24 Section 76(1) provides that the powers of the High Court to make restraint and charging orders are exercisable where:

(a) proceedings have been instituted in England and Wales against any person for an offence to which Part VI of the Act applies;
(b) the proceedings have not been concluded or (if they have) an application that has not been concluded has been made under s 74A, 74B or 74C in respect of the defendant in those proceedings; and
(c) the court is satisfied that there is reasonable cause to believe:
  (i) in a case where there is an application under s 74C, that the court will be satisfied as mentioned in s 74C(3);
  (ii) in any other case, that the proceedings may result or have resulted in, or that the application is made by reference to, a conviction for an offence of a relevant description from which he may be, or has been, shown to have benefited.

(1) Proceedings have been instituted in England and Wales

2.25 Section 102(11) defines 'proceedings have been instituted in England and Wales' in identical terms to s 41(2) of the DTA. This definition has been fully considered at para 2.09 above.

(2) Offences to which Part VI of the CJA applies

2.26 The proceedings instituted must relate to an offence to which Pt VI of the CJA applies. By s 71(9)(c) of the Act:

references to an offence to which this Part of this Act applies are references to any offence which:
 (i) is listed in Schedule 4 to this Act; or
 (ii) if not so listed, is an indictable offence, other than a drug trafficking offence or an offence under any of sections 15 to 18 of the Terrorism Act 2000.

There are only six offences listed in Sch 4 and they are:

(a) summary only offences relating to sex establishments contrary to the Local Government (Miscellaneous Provisions) Act 1982;
(b) supplying video recordings of unclassified works contrary to s 9 of the Video Recordings Act 1984;
(c) possession of such recordings for the purposes of supply contrary to s 10 of the same Act;
(d) using unlicensed premises for an exhibition which requires a licence contrary to s 10(1)(a) of the Cinemas Act 1985;
(e) trade mark offences contrary to s 92(1), (2), and (3) of the Trade Marks Act 1994; and
(f) copyright offences contrary to s 107(1), (2), and (3) and s 198(1) of the Copyright, Patents and Designs Act 1988.

In practice, the majority of restraint orders made under the CJA are in support of prosecutions for indictable offences other than drug trafficking and terrorism offences.

(3) Proceedings have not been concluded

2.27 By s 102(12) proceedings for an offence are concluded:

(a) when the defendant is acquitted on all counts or every charge against him is dismissed;
(b) if he is convicted, but the court decides not to make a confiscation order, when the court makes that decision;

C. Restraint Orders under Part VI of the Criminal Justice Act 1988

(c) if he is sentenced without the court having considered whether or not to proceed under s 71 in his case, when he is sentenced; and

(d) if a confiscation order is made against him in those proceedings, when the order is satisfied.

2.28 Thus, as with the DTA, once a confiscation order is made, proceedings only conclude for the purposes of the Act when that order is satisfied. By s 102(12B), a confiscation order is satisfied when no amount is due under it.

2.29 Restraint orders under the CJA are not offence specific and provided the defendant is charged with offences to which Part VI of the Act applies, proceedings have not concluded within the meaning of s 102(12) even if the original charges he faced at the time the restraint order was made have been withdrawn. In *Re C* [2001] EWHC Admin 768 CJA restraint and management receivership orders had been made against the defendant in support of alleged VAT fraud offences with which he had been charged in Cardiff on 12 April, 2000. On 30 November, 2000 the defendant was charged with with further VAT fraud offences in Nottingham for which he had been initially arrested in 1998. In May, 2001 the prosecution offered no evidence in relation to the Cardiff offences, leaving only the Nottingham offences which were not pending at the time the restraint order was made. The defendant applied for the restraint order to be discharged on the basis that the proceedings had concluded at the time of his acquittal in relation to the Cardiff offences. Burton J rejected this argument and ruled that the restraint order should remain pending the determination of the Nottingham charges. The defendant remained subject to charges to which Pt VI of the Act applied and proceedings had thus not concluded notwithstanding that the Nottingham charges had not been preferred at the time the restraint order was made.

2.30 Where this occurs, it is submitted that the proper approach is for the prosecutor, pursuant to his obligation of continuing full and frank disclosure, to serve a witness statement on the court and the defendant dealing with the circumstances in which the original charges were discontinued and new ones preferred. Further, the prosecutor must be vigilant to ensure that only sufficient assets to meet a confiscation order in the amount of benefit from the new offences remain restrained. If the alleged benefit from the new offences is less than that alleged to have been derived from the offences which have been withdrawn, and the case is not one to which the assumptions apply, the prosecutor must apply for the order to be varied to release assets no longer required to meet a confiscation order.

2.31 By s 102(12A) applications under s 74A, 74B, and 74C are concluded:

(a) if the court decides not to make or not to vary an order against the defendant on that application, when it makes that decision;

(b) if an order against the defendant is made or varied on that application, when the order is satisfied; and

(c) if the application is withdrawn, when the prosecutor notifies the withdrawal of the application to the court to which it was made.

2.32 Section 74A, 74B, and 74C gives the High Court jurisdiction to review and vary determinations made by the Crown Court during the course of confiscation hearings in the light of fresh evidence, and are considered in more detail in Chapter 13.

(4) Proceedings may result or have resulted in a conviction for an offence of a relevant description from which the defendant may have benefited

2.33 Section 76(1)(c) requires the court to consider two distinct issues: namely whether there is reasonable cause to believe the defendant will be convicted of an offence of a relevant description and whether there is reasonable cause to believe he may have benefited from it. As to the first issue, provided the prosecutor is able to supply a detailed summary of the case against the defendant the Crown will not normally have any difficulty in persuading the court that there is reasonable cause to believe the defendant may be convicted of an offence of a relevant description. For the purposes of the Act, s 71(1E) provides that offences are of a 'relevant description':

(a) in the case of an offence of which a person is convicted in any proceedings before the Crown Court or which is or will be taken into consideration by the Crown Court in determining any sentence, if it is an offence to which this Part of this Act applies; and
(b) in the case of an offence of which a person is convicted in any proceedings before a magistrates' court or which is or will be taken into consideration by a magistrates' court in determining any sentence if it is an offence listed in Schedule 4 to the Act.

(5) Benefit

2.34 In many cases it will be obvious from the circumstances of the alleged offence that there is reasonable cause to believe the defendant has benefited: for example the bank robber who makes off and spends the proceeds of his crime, or the business which spends the proceeds of its tax fraud have both clearly benefited. But there are many situations in relation to which the position is less clear—what for example of the professional man who launders the proceeds of a client's crime and only retains control of the money for a very short time? Or the tobacco smuggler who is intercepted and arrested by Customs and has his bounty seized before he has the chance to sell it on? The statute and the case law give considerable guidance on circumstances in which a defendant can be said to have benefited from his crimes.

2.35 Section 71(4) of the Act provides that a person benefits from an offence if he obtains property as a result of or in connection with its commission and that his benefit is the value of the property so obtained. This provision clearly catches the professional man who launders money on behalf of a client: he benefits to the extent of the value of the property he obtains and it matters not that he retains it only for a short period of time. Further assistance is provided by s 71(5) which provides that a person who obtains a pecuniary advantage as a result of or in connection with the commission of an offence is to be treated as if he had obtained as a result of or in connection with the commission of the offence a sum of money equal to the value of the pecuniary advantage.

2.36 The High Court first considered the meaning of 'benefit' for the purposes of restraint order proceedings in *Re K* The Times, 30 September 1990. The defendant had been charged with six alleged mortgage fraud offences. A police officer made an affidavit in support of an application for a restraint order in which he alleged the defendant had benefited from the offences to the extent of £242,744.78, being the sum advanced to him by way of mortgages from the building societies. The defendant sought the discharge of the restraint order contending that his true benefit from the offences was the value of the equity of redemption in the properties he had purchased which, given that most of the mortgages were for 100 per cent of their value, was negligible. McCullough J rejected this argument ruling that the question the court had to determine was 'What property did the defendant obtain as a result of or in connection with the commission of the offence and what was its value?' The answer to that question, the learned judge ruled, had to be 'the house' and the defendant's benefit was the value of the house and not the value of the equity of redemption. The judge observed:

> The Court is concerned with what the defendant received and not with any later diminution in what he received. If, for example, a bank robber steals £20,000, that £20,000 is the benefit he receives from the crime. The fact that some or all of the £20,000 is later dissipated is immaterial, even if he uses some of the money to repay his overdraft at the same bank.

2.37 The Court found that the defendant suffers no injustice from this construction because s 74(3) provides that a confiscation order cannot be made for an amount greater than the value of the realisable property held by him less, where there are obligations having priority at that time (eg mortgages), the total amounts payable in pursuance of such obligations. The decision of McCullough J in *Re K* was later upheld by the Court of Appeal (Criminal Division) in *R v Layode* (CA Crim Div, 12 March 1993).

2.38 The question of pecuniary advantage was considered by the House of Lords in *R v Cadman-Smith* [2002] 1 WLR 54. The defendant had pleaded guilty to an offence of being knowingly concerned in a fraudulent evasion of excise duty. He had attempted to smuggle 1.25 million cigarettes into the country in a boat which he sailed up the Humber estuary, past Customs posts at Immingham and Hull before he reached Goole, where the boat was stopped and searched and the contraband seized by Customs officers. The defendant was sent to prison for the offence and, at a confiscation hearing, the court determined he had benefited from the offence to the extent of £130,000, the amount of the duty evaded, and a confiscation order in the sum of £46,250 was made. The Court of Appeal quashed the confiscation order on the basis that the defendant had not benefited because the cigarettes had been seized by Customs officers before he had the opportunity of selling them. The prosecution appealed to the House of Lords, and in allowing the appeal, their Lordships ruled that the defendant had obtained a pecuniary advantage by evading duty on the cigarettes at the point of importation and it was immaterial that he had not been able to sell them on at the time of his arrest.

2.39 There have been many cases on the meaning of the term 'benefit' in the context of confiscation hearings and these are considered in more detail in Chapters 10 and 12. It needs to be borne in mind, however, that these cases are of limited relevance in the context of an application for a restraint order in the early stages of a prosecution. As Laws LJ observed in *Jennings v CPS* [2005] EWCA Civ 746:

> The sense to be attributed to 'benefit' in section 71 (4) of the Act of 1988 has been the subject of a good deal of authority. We have of course to consider this learning, not least given the divide in the positions taken by counsel, but it comes, so to speak, with a health warning. The cases are generally concerned with the court's function under s71 to make a confiscation order. But this appeal is about the prior stage arising under s77 relating to restraint orders, which is subject to the legislative steer given by s82 (2). I think it very important to have in mind that in deciding whether to make a restraint order under s77 (and, if so, in what terms)

the court's task is not to reach firm conclusions as to the precise extent of a respondent's benefit, or realisable property, for the purposes of s71; though of course if those matters are plain the facts will be put before the judge. Rather, under s 77 the court's duty is to decide whether to make a protective order so that in the particular case the satisfaction or fulfilment of any confiscation order made or to be made will be efficacious.

D. Delay and Proving there is a Risk of Dissipation of Assets

2.40 An applicant for a freezing order must satisfy the court that there is a real risk of assets being dissipated in order to be entitled to relief. Restraint orders, however, are creatures of statute and there is no express provision in the DTA or CJA requiring the prosecutor to establish that such a risk exists as a condition precedent to obtaining an order. As no such requirement appeared in the legislation, the various prosecuting authorities contended that, on an application for a restraint order, it was unnecessary for them to establish a risk of dissipation.

2.41 This argument was rejected by the Court of Appeal in *Re AJ and DJ* (CA, 9 December 1992). The defendants had been charged in July 1990 with various alleged mortgage fraud offences. They were granted bail and committal proceedings were continually adjourned until, in December 1990, a voluntary bill of indictment was preferred. During the time the defendants were on bail they made no attempt to dissipate assets but, shortly before the trial was due to commence, the CPS obtained restraint orders against them at an ex parte hearing. At a subsequent hearing inter partes, Laws J (as he then was) discharged the orders on the basis, amongst others, that the prosecutor had failed to establish there was a risk of assets being dissipated.

2.42 On an appeal by the CPS, the Court of Appeal upheld the decision of Laws J to discharge the restraint orders. Glidewell LJ observed at p 23C of the transcript:

> It follows in my judgment that Laws J was entirely correct to conclude that he had a discretion whether or not to make or discharge a restraint or charging order and to consider that such an order should only be made if there is a reasonable apprehension that, without it, realisable property may be dissipated. I agree with the judge that, to quote him, "If there is not such risk, or the risk is merely fanciful, the order ought not to be made, since *ex hypothesi* it would not be necessary for the achievement of its only proper purpose".

2.43 The Court considered that the major factor in determining whether a risk of dissipation existed was the very considerable period of time that had elapsed between the arrest of the defendants and the orders being sought. The charges had been hanging over the defendants for over three years with no restraint orders in place, yet no attempt had been made to dissipate realisable property during that time. This is not to say that restraint orders will never be appropriate after a delay of this nature and if the prosecutor has credible evidence that a defendant may be about to dissipate assets shortly before his trial is to commence an application for a restraint order may well be justified.

2.44 In many cases the risk of dissipation will speak for itself. As Glidewell LJ acknowledged in *Re AJ and DJ*:

> I accept that in many and perhaps the substantial majority of cases where offences involving a gain exceeding £10,000 are concerned, the circumstances of the alleged offences themselves will lead to a reasonable apprehension that, without a restraint or charging order, realisable

assets are likely to be dissipated. In drug trafficking offences, this is likely to be so in almost every case. Thus the onus on the prosecution will often not be difficult to satisfy.

2.45 Similarly, in relation to cases where there is an allegation of dishonesty, Longmore LJ observed in *Jennings v CPS* [2005] 4 All ER 391:

> In a case where dishonesty is charged, there will usually be reason to fear that assets will be dissipated. I do not therefore consider it necessary for the prosecutor to state in terms that he fears assets will be dissipated merely because he or she thinks there is a good arguable case of dishonesty. As my Lord has said, the risk of dissipation will generally speak for itself. Nevertheless prosecutors must be alive to the possibility that there may be no risk in fact. If no asset dissipation has occurred over a long period, particularly after a defendant has been charged, the prosecutor should explain why asset dissipation is now feared at the date of application for the order when it was not feared before.

2.46 In *Jennings v CPS* the defendant had been arrested on suspicion of conspiracy to defraud and fraudulent trading on 22 May 2003, was charged with conspiracy to defraud on 4 February 2004 and a CJA restraint order was made on 2 November 2004. The defendant applied to have the order discharged, amongst other things, on the grounds of delay. Leveson J refused to discharge the order on the basis that the delay notwithstanding the case was still in the early stages, the trial not being due to commence for some months and there was sufficient justification for a restraint order being in place in the meantime. The Court of Appeal held that this was the correct approach and dismissed the defendant's appeal. Laws LJ held:

> The principal question for the court must always be whether the protection of a restraint order is on the facts necessary to ensure so far as possible that any confiscation order will be efficacious. There remains the theoretical possibility of the eccentric case where the Crown delay on purpose for some collateral or mischievous reason. That, I am sure, can generally be discounted in the real world, as it can certainly be discounted in this case.

2.47 Similarly, Longmore LJ observed that:

> Delay will not usually be a significant fact on its own. It may be relevant if there has been delay between the defendant being charged and the date of the application, if there has been no dissipation of the assets meanwhile. It is then incumbent on the Crown to explain why dissipation was not initially seen as a major risk but now is.

2.48 As a general rule, however, the longer the prosecutor delays in making his application for a restraint order, the more difficult it will be to establish there is a risk of assets being dissipated and the greater will be the duty on him to justify the necessity for a restraint order. Those acting for defendants and affected third parties should be vigilant in ensuring the prosecuting authority has established a risk of dissipation in relation to restraint orders obtained without notice, particularly when there has been a considerable delay between the arrest of the defendant and the application for a restraint order being made.

E. The Standard of Proof on Restraint Order Applications

2.49 As we have seen, a restraint order is an interlocutory remedy to enable assets to be preserved pending the making or enforcement of a confiscation order. It is not therefore incumbent on the prosecutor to prove his case to the criminal, or even the civil, standard of proof on an application for a restraint order. As the Court of Appeal held in *Compton v CPS* [2002] EWCA Civ 1720, the test is the same as on an application for a civil freezing order, namely that the prosecutor can establish a good arguable case that the defendant has benefited from drug trafficking or other criminal conduct and that he has an interest in the assets in relation to which the application is made. As Simon Brown LJ (with whom May and Clarke LJJ agreed) noted in his judgment:

> If, on the documents, a good arguable case arises for treating particular assets as the realisable property of the defendant – here on the basis that the company's corporate veil should properly be pierced – then the relevant restraint (and possibly receivership) order(s) should ordinarily be made. That essentially is the test for the grant of *Mareva* relief. So too should it be the test for the exercise of the section 26 powers.

F. The Scope and Duration of Restraint Orders

(1) Parties restrained by the order

2.50 Section 26(1) DTA and s 77(1) CJA provide that a restraint order may:

prohibit any person from dealing with any realisable property, subject to such conditions and exceptions as may be specified in the order.

2.51 Section 26(8) DTA and s 77(9) CJA define the expression 'dealing with property' in the following terms;

For the purposes of this section, dealing with property held by any person includes (without prejudice to the generality of the expression)—
(a) where a debt is owed to that person, making a payment to any person in reduction of the amount of the debt; and
(b) removing the property from Great Britain.

Section 26(2) DTA and s 77(3) CJA provide that a restraint order may apply:

(a) to all realisable property held by a specified person, whether the property is specified in the order or not, and
(b) to realisable property held by a specified person, being property transferred to him after the making of the order.

2.52 These sections give the court very wide powers to restrain dealing in realisable property not only by the defendant, but by any other person or body holding assets in which he has an interest. Members of a defendant's family and business associates are the most common third parties to find themselves affected by restraint orders. Wives frequently find themselves restrained from dealing with the matrimonial home in which both spouses have a joint interest and in dealing with funds held in a joint bank account. Banks and other financial institutions holding accounts belonging to the defendant will also be bound by the terms of the restraint order. Business assets held by the defendant in conjunction with a business partner are equally vulnerable to restraint.

(2) Limited companies

2.53 Sometimes a defendant, subject to a restraint order, has an interest in a limited company incorporated under the Companies Acts. As limited companies enjoy a legal personality of their own their assets will not normally constitute 'realisable property' of the defendant within the meaning of the DTA and CJA. There are, however, a number of exceptions to this general rule. Firstly, assets that a defendant gifts to a company will be caught by the Acts

F. The Scope and Duration of Restraint Orders

in the same way as property gifted to any other third party. The second and most important exception relates to companies under the control of a defendant that have been used to facilitate the criminal activity with which he has been charged. This occurs most commonly in money laundering cases and in so-called VAT 'carousel' frauds where a series of buffer companies are frequently created to facilitate the fraudulent activity. In these circumstances, the court will lift the corporate veil of the company and treat the assets of the company as being the assets of the defendant and therefore capable of being restrained under the Acts.

2.54 The leading authority is *Re H (restraint order: realisable property)* [1996] 2 All ER 391. The three defendants had been charged with excise duty evasion offences in relation to which it was alleged there was a loss to the Exchequer in excess of £100 million. They owned, together with a third party, 100 per cent of the issued share capital of two family companies through which it was alleged the frauds had been committed. On this basis the High Court made restraint and management receivership orders that included the assets of the company. The defendants sought variations to the orders removing all references to the companies contending that the court had no jurisdiction to restrain them. The Court of Appeal rejected the defendants' contention, ruling that where a corporate structure had been used as a device or façade to conceal criminal activity, the court could lift the corporate veil and treat the assets of the company as the realisable property of the defendant for the purposes of the Acts. Rose LJ (with whom Aldous LJ and Sir Iain Glidewell agreed) said:

> As to the law, the general principle remains that which was enunciated in *Salomon v Salomon* [1897] AC 22, [1895–9] namely that a company duly formed and registered is a separate legal entity and must be treated like any other independent person with its own rights and liabilities distinct from those of its shareholders.

2.55 But a succession of cases throughout the twentieth century show, as Danckwerts LJ said in *Merchandise Transport Ltd v British Transport Commission, Arnold Transport (Rochester) Ltd v British Transport Commission* [1961] 3 All ER 495 at 518, [1962] 2 QB 173 at 206–207:

> ... where the character of a company, or the nature of the persons who control it is a relevant feature the court will go behind the mere status of the company as a legal entity, and will consider who are the persons as shareholders or even as agents who direct and control the activities of a company which is incapable of doing anything without human assistance.

2.56 In *Adams v Cape Industries plc* [1990] Ch 433; 2 WLR 657 Slade LJ, giving the judgment of the Court of Appeal (of which Mustill and Ralph Gibson LJJ were the other members) cited this passage and added,

> The correctness of this statement has not been disputed'. The Court also assumed to be correct the proposition that 'the court will lift the corporate veil where a defendant by the device of a corporate structure attempts to evade (i) limitations imposed on his conduct by law . . . .

2.57 Clearly, as a matter of law, the corporate veil can be lifted in appropriate circumstances.

2.58 The Court then went on to review the facts in *Re H* and concluded:

> As to the evidence, it provides a prima facie case that the defendants control these companies; that the companies have been used for fraud, in particular the evasion of excise duty on a large scale; that the defendants regard the companies as carrying on a family business, and that company cash has benefited the defendants in substantial amounts.

2.59 In these circumstances, the Court found it was appropriate to lift the corporate veil of the companies and treat them as the realisable property of the defendants.

2.60 The court is entitled to lift the corporate veil even if it is shown that the company in question is engaged in significant legitimate trading activity. In *Re K* [2005] EWCA Crim 619 (a POCA case) the judge found there was a substantial arguable case that the defendants had used various companies as a façade behind which they were hiding the proceeds of their smuggling. He proceeded to lift the corporate veil on the companies notwithstanding that he accepted they were also engaged in legitimate trading activity. The companies appealed contending that the judge had failed to ask himself the correct question, namely whether the companies were façades or shams set up by the defendants to conceal the true position. If he had done so, it was contended, he would have answered in the negative. The Court refused the companies leave to appeal on this point. Laws LJ observed in delivering the judgment of the Court:

> In our judgment, the judge's ruling here did no more than reflect the reality of the situation. There was a pressing case on the evidence that albeit none of the defendants had formal control of the companies as office holders they used the companies without the least let or hindrance to facilitate and execute their fraudulent designs. The judge's decision was, in our judgment, plainly in line not only with the dictum from *Re H* but also other authority, not least *Merchandise Transport Limited v British Transport Commission* [1962] 2 QB 173, *Adams v Cape Industries plc* [1990] 1 Ch 433, *Yukong Line* [1998] 1 WLR 794 and *Compton* to which we have already referred and which in truth replicated the test in *H*.

2.61 The Court held that the use of the expression 'lifting the corporate veil' may be somewhat misleading and in reality the true question is whether assets of the company may be treated as realisable property of the defendant.

This approach was followed by Ouseley J in *Re D* [2006] EWHC Admin 254. The facts of this case were somewhat unusual in that the application to lift the corporate veil was made for the first time long after the defendant had been convicted. The defendant had been convicted of drug trafficking offences and a confiscation order was made against him in the sum of £800,000. The order remained largely unsatisfied and in 2005 he was returned to prison to serve the default sentence for non payment. In 2004 or 2005 he set up a business with a Mr J known as X Limited which was engaged in property development. Each of them owned one of the two issued shares and both of them put some capital into the company – in the case of D in alleged breach of a restraint order. On discovering this, the Revenue and Customs Prosecutions Office applied, without notice, for the restraint order to be varied to include the assets of the company and for a management receiver to be appointed in relation to D's assets, including the company. After these orders were made, X Limited applied for them to be varied to remove therefrom references to the company's assets, contending that this was not an appropriate case in which the corporate veil should be lifted. Ouseley J rejected this contention observing that:

> In my judgment the real question which the judge faced with an application for a restraint or receivership order is whether the order of the extent sought and now obtained is appropriate or necessary in view of the two legislative objectives set out in section 31(2) and (4) of the 1994 Act. The question whether the effect of such an order is to pierce the corporate veil or whether some particular test related to that concept requires to be satisfied is not, in my judgment, the ultimate object of the inquiry the court has to carry out. The object of the Act is to enable proceeds of crime to be ascertained, protected and realised. The first question

F. The Scope and Duration of Restraint Orders

therefore is whether there are corporate assets which should be treated as the defendant's assets and the second question is whether, if that is the case, a restraint and receivership order of the extent sought is necessary. The position, in my judgment, is the same where there is an intermingling of the assets of a criminal, who is seeking to evade the effect of a confiscation order, with the assets of innocent business partners of a company. If it is established that some or all of the assets of the company are to be treated as assets of the defendant, the question of how their intermingling with the assets of someone who is innocent of wrongdoing is to be dealt with, is a matter for resolution by deciding whether an order should be made and if so on what terms, rather than a matter which has to be resolved by simply asking whether the corporate veil should be pierced. As I have said, the question is whether it is necessary to impose an order of the terms sought bearing in mind that there would be, necessarily, someone who is innocent whose interests would be adversely affected by such an order. This involves a balancing of interests as is inherent in the statutory provisions in section 31.

The cases to which I have been referred do not deal with the problem of the intermingling of a criminal's realisable assets with those of an innocent person in a company which has legitimate business activities but in part carries them out using the criminal's realisable assets. There would obviously be a very considerable lacuna in the ability of the Act to achieve its objective if in principle, because such a company was not a one man band or wholly criminal in its origin, funding or activites, assets held in it could not be subject to receivership or restraint order provisions.

2.62 The judge then went on to consider whether the restraint and receivership orders in relation to the assets of X Limited were necessary having regard to the particular facts of the case. He ruled that the orders were necessary saying:

The starting point is the background of Mr. D in crime with a substantial unsatisfied confiscation order. There is also evidence of a serious set of breaches by him of the restraint order and of the use by him of a personal account, the scale of transactions in which suggest that he was carrying on a business as he himself appeared to assert. There is evidence that Mr. D had a practice of putting property in the names of others but nonetheless controlling the destiny of the property and the assets with which it is purchased – in other words, there is a personal façade as opposed to a corporate façade in a number of transactions he has engaged in. There was evidence of investment in X Limited through the provision of cash, the shareholding, his role as an officer, his role as a signatory to accounts as director and as company secretary. He took part in the activities of the company and it represented some of the funds which he had sought to place beyond the R&CPO. The relationship of his loans to the company to those of Mr. J is unclear because there is no written documentary material, and nothing which could be described as a paper trail in relation to the loans made to the company. Although it is not said that Mr. J was involved in laundering or drug activities, the precise power or control relationship, the beneficial ownership of the assets is not wholly resolved and the documentary material or accounts in relation to that are rudimentary. There is no dispute but that Mr. D put money into the company and has a shareholding both of which are the proceeds of crime being dealt with through the company. In my judgment it would be absurd not to treat the company's assets as being his in part. Any other approach would enable, as I have said, somebody with criminal proceeds to incorporate himself with one other, who might be an innocent dupe, and thereby put his assets beyond the reach of the R&CPO.

2.63 Another avenue open to the prosecutor would, of course, be to institute criminal proceedings against the companies themselves. In this event they would become defendants in their own right and be liable to restraint and confiscation action. This did not, however, find favour with the Court of Appeal in *Re H*, Rose LJ observing:

In my judgment, the Customs and Excise are not to be criticised for not charging the companies. The more complex commercial activities become, the more vital it is for prosecuting authorities to be selective in whom and what they charge, so that issues can be presented in as clear and short a form as possible. In the present case, it seems to me that no useful purpose would have been served by introducing into criminal proceedings the additional complexities as to the corporate mind and will, which charging the companies would have involved. Conversely, there could have been justified criticism had the companies been charged merely as a device for obtaining orders under the Act in relation to their assets.

(3) Property restrained by the order

2.64 Sections 26(2) DTA and s 77(3) CJA empower the court to make restraint orders in respect of all realisable property whether specified in the order or not and to include property coming into the defendant's possession after the making of the order. In practice, prosecutors frequently rely on this provision to seek an order commencing in the purely general terms of paragraph (1) of the precedent at Appendix 1. Restraint orders are often obtained at an early stage of the proceedings before the full extent of the defendant's realisable property is known, but when restraint action is justified to prevent any dissipation. The only limitation is that the prosecutor must not seek a restraint order over assets greater in value than the amount by which the defendant has alleged to have benefited from his crimes: for example, if it is alleged that a defendant has benefited from a crime to the extent of £1 million, it would clearly be oppressive for the order to restrain assets worth over £5 million. In *Re K* The Times, 30 September 1990 the Court accepted that the prosecutor must be entitled to some latitude as, when he applies for the restraint order, it may not be possible to quantify the full extent of the defendant's benefit. Further, the prosecutor will be entitled to pray in aid the statutory assumptions that may be applied at a confiscation hearing. In *Re K* [2005] EWCA Crim 619 it was contended that the maximum amount of benefit of which there was prima facie evidence was £477,000 and there was no justification in making a restraint order to cover a greater amount. The judge rejected this argument ruling that he was entitled to have regard to the statutory assumptions which, if applied, may result in a confiscation order being made in a much larger amount. The Court of Appeal upheld the judge's ruling and rejected the contention that the restraint order should be restricted to assets to the value of £477,000. In delivering the judgment of the Court, Laws LJ said:

> In our view, the judge's reasoning demonstrates a common sense approach to the facts and we see no reason why this Court should interfere with it. It seems to us the judge was perfectly justified in looking to these assumptions as a feature of the case that might very well be in play at a later stage. The reality here is, in our judgment, that at the stage at which the judge was dealing with the matter in January 2005, and in the light of such information as he then had, he was entitled to make an order unlimited in amount. There was strong evidence of control of the companies by S and M. The companies were significantly engaged, on the Commissioners' evidence, in the defendants' criminality. We have already referred to the judge's finding, unchallenged here, that there is a substantial case that the defendants have used the companies as a façade behind which they were hiding the proceeds of smuggling. In our judgment, it would have been artificial for the judge to conclude that the realisable assets were to be treated as strictly limited to the ill gotten gains that were expressly demonstrated.

2.65 Where, however, in a CJA case the defendant's benefit can be readily ascertained and it is not a case in which the assumptions can be applied, the prosecutor should not seek to

F. The Scope and Duration of Restraint Orders

restrain assets in excess of the amount of that benefit. This principle is now enshrined in a Practice Direction made to supplement sc115. By para 3 of the Practice Direction:

3.1. A restraint order may, where appropriate, apply to—
   (1) all of the defendant's realisable property;
   (2) the defendant's realisable property up to a specified value; or
   (3) one or more particular specified assets.

3.2. Where—
   (1) a confiscation order or forfeiture order has already been made against the defendant in a particular amount; or
   (2) the prosecutor is able to make a reasonable accurate estimate of the amount of any confiscation order or forfeiture order that might be made against him,
and, in either case, it is clear that the defendant's realisable property is greater in value than the amount or estimated amount of that order, the court will normally limit the application of the restraint order in accordance with paragraph 3.1. (2) or (3).

3.3. In such cases the prosecutor's draft order should normally either include an appropriate financial limit or specify the particular assets to which the order should apply. Those acting for defendants subject to restraint orders should be vigilant in ensuring that the order does not restrain more assets than necessary and, if it does, require the prosecutor to consent to an appropriate variation.

2.66

(4) Legitimately acquired assets

It is a common misconception that restraint and charging orders may only be made in relation to assets that represent directly or indirectly the proceeds of the defendant's criminal activities. This view is erroneous because s 6(2) DTA and s 74(1) CJA define 'realisable property' as meaning:

(a) any property held by the defendant; and
(b) any property held by a person to whom the defendant has directly or indirectly made a gift caught by the Act.

2.67

Property is held by the defendant if he holds any interest in it: see s 62(5)(a) DTA and s 102(7) CJA. This definition makes no distinction between assets that have been acquired legitimately and those that have not, and all realisable property of the defendant is liable to restraint and ultimately to confiscation up to the full amount of his benefit, even if it is acquired many years before the commission of the offences. This was confirmed in *R v Chrastny (No 2)* [1991] 1WLR 1385 where Glidewell LJ commented in delivering the judgment of the court in a case under the Drug Trafficking Offences Act 1986:

2.68

> In our view it is quite clear that that definition embraces legitimately acquired property. We cannot read into the Act of 1986 any inference that that definition is limited to illegitimately acquired property; that is to say the proceeds of drug trafficking. The statute is undoubtedly draconian and the decision on that point may seem harsh; the statute is harsh. The statute is in essence one that seeks to ensure that anybody who has benefited from drug trafficking shall, to the extent to which he or she can do so, be deprived of the whole of that benefit.

(5) Leasehold interests

It is by no means unusual for a restraint order to cover a leasehold interest the defendant may hold in real property. Most leases contain a provision empowering the lessor to forfeit

2.69

the lease if the lessee fails to comply with its terms, for example by not paying ground rent or service charges when they become due. In *Re R (Restraint Order)* [1990] 2 All ER 569 Otton J held that a lessor is not in breach of the restraint order if he takes action to forfeit a lease when the lessee is in breach of its terms. He said:

> The right to forfeiture is a different matter and is an asset vested in the landlords. It is an unfettered right to determine the lease on the conditions contained and set out in clause 4 which I need not recite. I am satisfied that the exercise of the landlords' right would not be a breach of the restraint order.

2.70 It is submitted that the proper course in such circumstances would be for the landlord to liaise with the prosecutor before taking steps to forfeit the lease. The prosecutor may be able to assist by, eg applying for the restraint order to be varied to pay off any arrears or even to apply for the appointment of a receiver to manage the defendant's realisable property and ensure that future payments are made as and when they fall due.

2.71 It would, however, be a breach of the restraint order for the defendant lessee to agree to the lease being surrendered, particularly if such agreement was in consideration of the lessor waiving any charges that had fallen due under the lease. As Otton J observed:

> If the tenant were to surrender in consideration of the landlord extinguishing, either in whole or in part, his outstanding liabilities for rent, that also would be objectionable because he would be receiving a benefit from realisable property. Accordingly, and not surprisingly, the Customs and Excise required that any proceeds from the surrender of the lease should go into an account and not go to the landlords in extinguishment of past liabilities.

2.72 It should be noted that the position under the Proceeds of Crime Act, 2002 is different. Where a restraint order has been obtained under that Act the leave of the court is required under s 58 (3) before the lessor of any premises may exercise a right of forfeiture by way of peaceable re-entry.

(6) Property that is not realisable under the legislation

2.73 By s 62(3) DTA and s 74(2) CJA property is not realisable under the Acts if an order is in force in relation to it under any of the following provisions:
(a) s 27 of the Misuse of Drugs Act 1971 (forfeiture orders);
(b) s 143 of the Powers of Criminal Courts (Sentencing) Act 2000 (deprivation orders);
(c) ss 223 or 436 of the Criminal Procedure (Scotland) Act 1975 (forfeiture of property);
(d) s 23 of the Terrorism Act 2000 (forfeiture orders);
(e) Pt II of the Proceeds of Crime (Scotland) Act 1995 (forfeiture of property used in crime);
(f) s 111 of the Terrorism Act 2000 (forfeiture orders).

(7) Meaning of property

2.74 Property is defined in identical terms by s 62(1) DTA and s 102(1) CJA as: including money and all other property, real or personal, heritable or moveable, including things in action or other incorporeal property.

2.75 In *R v Walbrook and Glasgow* [1994] Crim LR 613, the Court of Appeal held that a contingent interest under a will was capable of constituting property.

F. The Scope and Duration of Restraint Orders

(8) Overseas assets

2.76 Realisable property of a defendant is subject to restraint and confiscation regardless of whether it is located within or without the jurisdiction of the courts of England and Wales. The relevant provisions of the DTA and CJA are worded in slightly different terms, but their effect is the same. Section 62(2) DTA provides that the Act applies to property 'whether it is located in England and Wales or elsewhere' and s 102(3) CJA provides that the Act applies to property 'wherever situated'.

2.77 Any dissipation of overseas assets by a defendant or third party having notice of a restraint order will therefore constitute a contempt of court punishable in England. This is, of course, only an effective remedy to the extent that the contemnor is amenable to the jurisdiction of the court: it would be of little concern to a person resident overseas who has no intention of coming to the United Kingdom. However, as will be seen in Chapter 25, procedures now exist in most countries whereby a restraint order made in England can be protected by the obtaining of a further order in the foreign jurisdiction in which the asset is located. This has the effect of making any breach of the order a punishable contempt in that jurisdiction. If an asset is located in a country where no such reciprocal arrangements exist, the prosecutor may apply to the court for a repatriation order, requiring the defendant to bring the asset within the jurisdiction of the court. The court's power to make repatriation orders is considered in more detail in Chapter 4.

(9) Duration of restraint orders

2.78 By sc115 Rule 4(2):

> Unless the Court otherwise directs, a restraint order made where notice of it has not been served on any person shall have effect until a day which shall be fixed for the hearing where all parties may attend on the application and a charging order shall be an order to show cause, imposing the charge until such day.

In practice, the court does in the majority of cases 'otherwise direct' and makes the restraint order 'until further order' without fixing a return date on which all parties may attend. The court will, however, invariably give all parties affected by the order permission to apply to vary or discharge the order upon giving the court and prosecutor two clear days notice in writing.

2.79 This procedure met with the approval of the Court of Appeal in *Ahmad v Ahmad* [1998] EWCA Civ 1246 when complaint was made by an appellant third party that a restraint order did not have a return date on which she could attend and argue why the order should not continue in that form. In rejecting this criticism, Thorpe LJ said:

> In my opinion that would not be a sensible practice since in the majority of cases I suspect that the return date, inter partes, would achieve little useful purpose. I can see no objection to the practice whereby the order obtained ex parte contains an obligation to serve with a liberty to apply on short notice. This is certainly the practice that obtains in ancillary relief litigation in the Family Division and it has proved to work effectively.

2.80 The majority of restraint orders will therefore remain in force either until the conclusion of proceedings or until they are varied or discharged by order of the court. This is not to say that the prosecutor should automatically seek a restraint order of indefinite duration: there may be special circumstances in which the justice of the case dictates that there should be an early hearing at which the court can determine whether it is appropriate for the order to continue in that form. In such an instance, it is submitted that a return date should always be obtained.

2.81 Paragraph 7.2 of the Practice Direction that supplements sc115 provides that where a return date is fixed, it should normally be no more than 14 days after the order is made. Where there is no return date, the order must always incorporate a provision giving the defendant or anyone affected by it permission to apply to vary or discharge it (see para 7.3).

G. Terms and Conditions upon which Orders are Made

2.82 Section 26(1) DTA and s 77(1) CJA provide that restraint orders may be granted 'subject to such conditions and exceptions as may be specified in the order'. Similarly sc115 Rule 4(1) provides that:

> A restraint order may be made subject to conditions and exceptions, including but not limited to conditions related to the indemnifying of third parties against expenses incurred in complying with the order, and exceptions relating to living expenses and legal expenses of the defendant, but the prosecutor shall not be required to give an undertaking to abide by any order as to damages sustained by the defendant as a result of the restraint order.

2.83 These provisions give the court a wide discretion as to what terms, conditions, and exceptions should be made on granting a restraint order. The conditions imposed will obviously depend upon the particular facts of individual cases and may be subject to further variation on the application of the defendant or affected third party, but the following are typical conditions imposed when a restraint order is made.

(1) Costs and expenses incurred in complying with the order

2.84 Third parties affected by restraint orders will frequently incur costs in ensuring they are properly complied with. Banks and other financial institutions, for example, will incur costs in identifying accounts affected by the order and freezing them in compliance with it. The court will invariably require an undertaking from the prosecutor to meet the costs involved in such an exercise. The defendant will be excluded from the terms of this undertaking as generally will be his spouse or partner, any company in relation to which the corporate veil has been lifted and the recipient of any gift caught by the Acts.

2.85 It should be noted that sc115 Rule 4(1) expressly provides that the prosecutor shall not be required to give an undertaking to abide by any order as to damages sustained by the defendant as a result of the restraint order. This is in marked contrast to the position in relation to freezing orders where an undertaking will be required as a condition precedent to making the order.

2.86 The court will also require the order to make provision for the release of funds (typically £300 per week) for the payment of general living expenses. As restraint orders are normally made at a time when the defendant has not been convicted and is therefore presumed to be innocent, it is only right and proper that he should be able to meet his general living

G. Terms and Conditions upon which Orders are Made

expenses pending the determination of the criminal proceedings. As Lawton LJ observed in *CBS United Kingdom Limited v Lambert* [1982] 3 All ER 237:

> Even if a plaintiff has good reason for thinking that a defendant intends to dispose of assets so as to deprive him of his anticipated judgment, the court must always remember that rogues have to live and that all orders, particularly interlocutory ones, should as far as possible do justice to all parties.

2.87 Similarly, where a restraint order prevents a spouse or partner of the defendant from dealing in realisable property in which they have a joint interest (eg money in a bank account), the order should also make provision for the release of funds to meet his or her legal and general living expenses as well unless there is evidence to show that he or she has access to adequate unrestrained funds: see *Re G* (30 July 2001). By para 4 of the Practice Direction supplementing sc115 a restraint order should, unless it is clear that the person restrained has sufficient assets not subject to restraint, include an exception permitting him to use assets for the purpose of meeting reasonable living expenses (see para 4(1)). The order should also make provision for the defendant to deal freely in any payments he receives from the Department of Work and Pensions by way of state benefit.

2.88 If the defendant or an affected third party considers the amount payable under the order by way of general living expenses is insufficient for his legitimate needs, he may invite the prosecutor to agree to the order being varied to enable greater amounts to be used for such purposes or, in default of agreement, make application to the court for the order to be varied. This subject is considered in more detail in Chapter 5 where it will be seen that the court has to achieve a difficult balance between ensuring the defendant has sufficient funds available to meet legitimate expenses on the one hand and complying with the 'legislative steer' under s 31(2) DTA and s 82(2) CJA to ensure that the value of the defendant's realisable property is made available to meet any confiscation order on the other.

(2) Legal expenses

2.89 The defendant and affected third parties are also entitled to have funds released to meet legal expenses incurred in connection with the restraint proceedings. Paragraph 4(2) of the Practice Direction provides that the order should, unless it is clear the restrained person has sufficient unrestrained assets available, include an exception allowing the release of funds to pay reasonable legal fees to take advice in relation to the order and, if so, advised to apply for its variation or discharge. The order will normally release £500 which should be sufficient to enable solicitors to advise generally on the terms of the order and to assist the defendant in drafting any witness statement as to his means that he may be required to file in compliance with the order. If further funds are required, an application to court will be necessary unless a variation can be agreed by consent with the prosecutor.

2.90 If the defendant is not legally aided, he is also entitled to have money released for the purpose of funding his defence in the associated criminal proceedings. The order will require the defendant or his solicitor to provide the prosecutor with a detailed bill setting out the general nature of the costs involved, the time spent and the grade of fee earner involved, the hourly rates applicable and the source of the fund to be used to meet them. If the prosecutor is unable to agree the amount claimed, the order will provide for detailed assessment on

(3) Businesses

2.91 The court will not, at the pre-confiscation stage, allow a restraint order to operate in such a way as to prevent a business in which the defendant has an interest from trading profitably and legitimately. This is now provided for in the Practice Direction supplementing sc115. Paragraph 6 provides:

6. If an application for a restraint order is made against a company, partnership or individual apparently carrying on a legitimate business—
   (1) the court will take into account the interests of the employees, creditors and customers of the business and, in the case of a company, any shareholders other than the defendant before making an order which would or might prevent the business from being continued; and
   (2) any restraint order made against that person will normally contain an exception enabling it to deal with its assets in the ordinary course of business.

2.92 Accordingly, most restraint orders will make provision for the release of company bank accounts for the purpose of facilitating legitimate trading activity subject to accounts, bank statements and related documentation being produced to the prosecutor on a regular basis. The standard form of words used appears in para 20 of the precedent restraint order at Appendix 1. In more complex cases, or where there is evidence to suggest the business may have been used to facilitate the commission of offences, the appointment of a management receiver to administer the business may prove necessary.

H. Charging Orders

(1) What is a charging order?

2.93 A charging order gives the prosecuting authority an interest in the property to which it relates. Unlike a restraint order, it does not prevent the property in question being sold, but any purchaser will take the property subject to the Crown's interest. In practice, little use of charging orders is made by prosecuting authorities and rarely, if ever, are they sought in relation to property other than land where the charge can be registered as a restriction at the Land Registry. A receiver appointed to realise assets in satisfaction of a confiscation order, may be empowered to enforce any charging order made under the Acts (see s 29(3)(a) DTA and s 80(3)(a) CJA).

(2) When may a charging order be made?

2.94 By s 25(1) DTA and s 76 CJA charging orders may be made in precisely the same circumstances as restraint orders. The criteria are considered in detail at paras 2.07 and 2.24 above respectively.

2.95 Provided these requirements have been met, the court may under s 27(1) DTA and s 78(1) CJA make a charging order on realisable property for securing payment to the Crown:

(a) where a confiscation order has not been made, of an amount equal to the value from time to time of the property charged; and

H. Charging Orders

(b) in any other case, of an amount not exceeding the sum payable under the confiscation order.

2.96 The extent of the charge is thus largely governed by the stage the proceedings have reached. If a confiscation order has been made, the charge must be limited to the amount of the order, whereas if no confiscation order has yet been made, the charge may extend to the full value of the property in question. In cases where the value of the benefit is readily ascertainable, the charge should be limited to the amount of that benefit notwithstanding that no confiscation order has yet been made.

(3) What property can be charged?

2.97 Section 27(5) DTA and s 78(5) CJA specify the types of property that are capable of being made the subject of charging orders:

(a) land in England and Wales; or
(b) securities of any of the following kinds:
   (i) government stock;
   (ii) stock of any body (other than a building society) incorporated within England and Wales;
   (iii) stock of any body incorporated outside England and Wales or of any country or territory outside the United Kingdom, being stock registered in a register kept at any place within England and Wales;
   (iv) units of any unit trust in respect of which a register of the unit holders is kept at any place within England and Wales.

2.98 Only a 'beneficial interest' in any of the above assets may be made the subject of a charging order and a bare legal interest is not sufficient: see s 27(4) DTA and s 78(4) CJA. The charge may, however, extend to any interest or dividend payable in respect of the property so charged: see s 27(6) DTA and s 78(6) CJA. A precedent for a charging order appears at paragraph 10 of the draft order at Appendix 1.

(4) Protecting the charging order

2.99 Section 28 DTA and s 79 CJA provide that the Land Charges Act 1972 and the Land Registration Act 2003 apply in relation to charging orders in respect of land as they apply to orders or writs issued or made for the purpose of enforcing judgments. This enables the prosecutor to make application to the Land Registry for a restriction to be registered against the title to the property. By r 92(1) of the Land Registration Rules 2003, SI 2003/1417 the application is made on Land Registry Form RX1. The making of a charging order on land does not deprive the registered owner of his title to the property and he is entitled to remain in possession of the property until such time as a receiver is appointed to enforce the charge after the making of a confiscation order. The restriction will be registered in Form N in Sch 4 to the Land Registration Rules 2003 and will preclude any disposition of the property without the consent of the prosecutor. If a person with an interest in the land wishes to have the restriction removed so that he may deal in it, he should approach the prosecutor to see if terms can be agreed on which the restriction may be discharged and, if no agreement can be reached, to make application to the court.

(5) Applications to vary or discharge charging orders

2.100 Section 27(7) DTA and s 78(7) CJA provide that the court may make an order discharging or varying the charging order, and must make an order discharging the same if the proceedings are concluded or the amount which is secured by the charge is paid into court. An application for the discharge or variation of a charging order may be made by the defendant or by any party affected by it: see s 27(8) DTA and s 78(8) CJA. Once a charging order has been discharged, any restriction registered by the prosecutor must be removed.

2.101 The most common circumstance in which an application to vary or discharge a charging order is contemplated is where a defendant or interested third party wishes to sell the property. It is unlikely that the court or prosecutor would raise any objection to this provided that adequate safeguards are incorporated in the discharge order to protect the proceeds of sale. The court will usually order that the property is to be sold to a bona fide purchaser for not less than the average of three valuations given by valuers who are members of a recognised trade association and that the net proceeds of sale are paid into an interest bearing account pending the conclusion of the proceedings. The court will usually require an undertaking to this effect to be given by the conveyancing solicitor. If any or all of the net proceeds of sale are to be used to purchase another property, the court will normally direct that the charge should be transferred to the new property.

(6) Relationship between restraint and charging orders

2.102 It will be noticed in the precedent charging order in paragraph 10 of the draft restraint order at Appendix 1 that the charged property is excluded from the general restraint provision in the order. This is because s 26(3) DTA and s 77(4) CJA provide that a restraint order may not be granted in respect of property subject to a charging order under s 26 DTA or s 78 CJA respectively. Thus in *Re A Defendant* The Times, 7 April 1987, where the prosecutor purported to restrain and charge the same property, Webster J ruled that one or the other had to come out of the order and the prosecutor was put to his election as to which it should be.

3

MANAGEMENT RECEIVERS UNDER THE DTA AND CJA

A.	Introduction	3.01	(1) Duties and liabilities of the receiver	3.32
B.	Jurisdiction to Appoint Management Receivers	3.07	(2) Employment of agents	3.36
			(3) Receiver's accounts	3.39
C.	Exercising the Discretion to Appoint Management Receivers: The *Capewell* Guidelines	3.14	F. Remuneration of Receivers	3.43
			G. Discharge of the Receiver	3.61
D.	Status of the Receiver on Appointment	3.18	H. Taxation and Receivers	3.64
E.	Powers, Duties and Liabilities of the Receiver	3.22		

A. Introduction

A restraint order, coupled with disclosure and repatriation provisions, will in most cases prove sufficient to preserve the value of realisable property pending the making and enforcement of a confiscation order. Banks will immediately freeze a defendant's accounts on being served with a copy of the order and the registration of a restriction at the Land Registry will effectively prevent any dealing in real property. As to the running of businesses, conditions requiring the defendant to deliver accounts, bank statements, and associated documentation at regular intervals will normally be sufficient to enable the prosecutor to satisfy himself the business is being properly run for legitimate trading activities. The defendant himself will also be aware that any dealing in realisable property in breach of the order will constitute a contempt of court for which he may be committed to prison. **3.01**

In some cases, however, a restraint order alone will not be an effective means of preserving the defendant's assets pending the determination of the proceedings. The defendant may, for example, be in custody or have absconded leaving valuable assets unmanaged. In consequence a house, often the most valuable asset available for confiscation, may be left unoccupied and fall into a state of disrepair or attract the attention of squatters, burglars, or vandals. It may be left uninsured and any mortgage payments may fall into arrears. Similar considerations may apply to other valuable assets such as cars, boats, and light aircraft. A business or company under the control of the defendant may need closer supervision **3.02** than that afforded by requiring the defendant to submit business records on a regular basis. Further, the prosecutor has neither the qualifications nor experience necessary to make important decisions relating to the management of the restrained business. He is not, for example, in a position to judge whether the release of a large sum of money from a restrained company bank account to fund a particular business venture represents a good business risk or not.

3.03 In circumstances such as these further measures need to be taken to manage and preserve the realisable property of the defendant while the restraint order remains in force. The Acts give the court power, on the application of the prosecutor, to appoint a receiver to take possession of and manage the defendant's realisable property pending the conclusion of the proceedings. Receivers appointed for such purposes are referred to as 'management' receivers to distinguish them from 'enforcement' receivers who are appointed after a confiscation order has been made to realise the defendant's assets in satisfaction of the order. The law relating to the appointment of management receivers under POCA is considered in Chapter 8.

3.04 In recent years, there have been significant developments affecting the law relating to the appointment of management receivers following the judgments of the Court of Appeal in the *Capewell* litigation. In *Hughes v Customs and Excise Commissioners* [2002] 4 All ER 633 the Court of Appeal held that the costs and disbursements of management receivers are to be paid from the estate under management even when the defendant is acquitted. Although the House of Lords later refused leave to appeal against that decision, it is clear that the courts have become increasingly concerned about the level of costs being incurred by management receivers and the potential injustice that may be caused as a result of such costs having to be met by an acquitted person.

3.05 In *Capewell v Customs and Excise Commissioners* [2005] 1 All ER 900 the Court of Appeal emphasised how management receivership orders can seriously interfere with the business and personal life of the defendant and that the costs of appointing a management receiver should always be proportionate to the benefits to be derived from the appointment. Once the overall objective of the receivership has been achieved and there is no further benefit to be derived without disproportionate cost, the receiver should be discharged. The Court also approved a number of guidelines drawn up by counsel which should be followed by prosecutors and the courts on the hearing of applications for the appointment of a management receiver, and which should be adhered to by all parties once the appointment has been made.

3.06 More controversially, in *Capewell v Customs and Excise Commissioners (No 2)* [2005] EWCA Civ 964 the Court of Appeal held the decision in *Hughes* had now to be considered in the light of Part 69 of the Civil Procedure Rules (CPR) and that Part 69.7(2) gave the court the discretion, in special circumstances, to order that the remuneration of the receiver should be paid by the prosecutor. The Crown has been given leave to appeal to the House of Lords against this decision and it is anticipated that the hearing will take place in December 2006. (A summary of the House of Lords judgment is at Appendix 23.)

B. Jurisdiction to Appoint Management Receivers

3.07 The power to appoint management receivers is to be found in s 26(7) DTA and s 77(8) CJA. The sections are worded in very similar terms. Section 26(7) DTA provides that:

Where the High Court has made a restraint order, the High Court or a county court—
(a) may at any time appoint a receiver—
   (i) to take possession of any realisable property, and
   (ii) in accordance with the court's directions, to manage or otherwise deal with any property in respect of which he is appointed,
subject to such exceptions and conditions as may be specified by the court; and
(b) may require any person having possession of property in respect of which a receiver is appointed under this section to give possession of it to the receiver.

3.08 Section 77(8) CJA provides that:

Where the High Court has made a restraint order, the court may at any time appoint a receiver—
(a) to take possession of any realisable property; and
(b) in accordance with the court's directions to manage or otherwise deal with any property in respect of which he is appointed,
subject to such exceptions and conditions as may be specified by the court and may require any person having possession of property in respect of which a receiver is appointed under this section to give possession of it to the receiver.

3.09 The only real difference between the two provisions is that under the DTA both the High Court and the county court have jurisdiction to appoint receivers, whereas under the CJA the jurisdiction is confined to the High Court. In practice prosecuting authorities invariably make all their applications for the appointment of management receivers to the High Court.

3.10 It is important to note that the court only has jurisdiction to appoint a management receiver in cases where there is a restraint order. If no restraint order is in force, the court has no jurisdiction to appoint a management receiver. A practice has developed whereby prosecuting authorities on occasion ask the court to appoint a receiver at the same time as making a restraint order. In *Re P (Restraint Order: Sale of Assets)* [2000] 1 WLR 473 the Court of Appeal found nothing improper in this practice, but indicated that it should be reserved for urgent cases. In delivering the judgment of the Court Simon Brown LJ said:

> But to justify the making of composite orders on an ex parte basis there must, in my judgment, be an urgency about the matter (or a need not to alert the defendant) such as to preclude putting the defendant on notice, and the order initially made should be in the narrowest terms necessary to meet the strict requirements of the situation.

3.11 This principle has now been incorporated in the Practice Direction supplementing sc115. By paras 8.3 and 8.4:

8.3. Where no confiscation order or forfeiture order has been made—
   (1) an application for the appointment of a receiver should not be made without notice, unless the application is urgent or there is some other good reason for not giving notice to the defendant; and

(2) if the application is made without notice, the prosecutor's written evidence should explain the reasons for doing so.

8.4. Where the court appoints a receiver on an application without notice in the circumstances set out in paragraph 8.3, the order will normally limit the receiver's powers to manage, deal with or sell property (other than with the defendant's consent) to the extent that is shown to be urgently necessary.

3.12 If the receiver seeks further powers, he should apply on notice for further directions. Applications for the appointment of management receivers without notice to the defendant should therefore be confined to genuinely urgent situations or where giving notice may result in the dissipation of assets. Where an application is made without notice, the powers given to the receiver should be limited to those strictly necessary to meet the justice of the situation. If further powers prove necessary, either the receiver or the prosecutor can apply to court, on notice, for the order to be varied at a later date.

3.13 Only the prosecutor may apply to the court for the appointment of a management receiver: neither the defendant nor an interested third party has the right to apply for the appointment of a receiver to manage restrained assets. This may seem an obvious point, but in *Re M* [1992] 1 All ER 537 a defendant did indeed apply to the court for the appointment of a management receiver. Otton J ruled that he had no locus standi to make the application saying:

> ... in my judgment, it is unthinkable that an application for the appointment of a receiver by or on behalf of an accused to preserve assets intended for the satisfaction of a confiscation order could be entertained by the court. A restraint order may only be made upon the application of a prosecutor and, bearing in mind that the making of an order appointing a receiver can only be exercised upon the making of a restraint order, it would follow, in my judgment, that an application for the appointment of a receiver can similarly only be made by a prosecutor.

C. Exercising the Discretion to Appoint Management Receivers: The *Capewell* Guidelines

3.14 The power to appoint a management receiver is a discretionary one, although the court must have regard to the 'legislative steer' in s 31(2) DTA and s 82(2) of the CJA in determining how that discretion should be exercised. While the need to preserve property to meet any confiscation order must carry great weight, it is not the only issue the court must take into account in the exercise of its discretion. As the Court of Appeal observed in *Re P (Restraint Order: Sale of Assets)* [2000] 1 WLR 473, a balance has to be struck between the preservation of property and allowing the defendant to continue with the ordinary course of his life at a time when he is presumed innocent. The court will need to be satisfied that a restraint order alone will be insufficient to prevent dissipation of the defendant's realisable property and the appointment of a receiver is an appropriate and proportionate measure in all the circumstances. The appointment of a receiver is inevitably an expensive exercise and the court will need to be satisfied that the costs involved do not outweigh the potential benefits to the defendant's estate. Further, in *Re Hughes v Customs and Excise Commissioners* [2002] 4 All ER 633 where the Court of Appeal held that, given the remuneration of a management receiver is in many cases met from the estate under management rather than paid by the prosecutor, the court must always take account of the fact that, if acquitted, significantly depleted assets

C. Exercising the Discretion to Appoint Management Receivers: The *Capewell Guidelines*

may be returned to the defendant on the conclusion of proceedings. Simon Brown LJ (with whom Laws and Arden LJJ agreed) said:

> Given that restraint orders can, as perhaps these very cases show, bear heavily upon the individuals involved and may leave acquitted defendants with substantially depleted assets, the court should, in deciding whether initially to make and whether thereafter to vary or discharge, such orders, weigh up the balance of competing interests with the greatest care. The Crown's concern to safeguard an accused's property against dissipation or removal abroad must always be weighed against the possibility that the price to be paid will fall upon an innocent man.

3.15 In *Capewell v Customs and Excise Commissioners* [2005] 1 All ER 900 at the Court's invitation, counsel on both sides prepared a set of Guidelines for the appointment of management receivers. Although the Court did not hear detailed argument on the Guidelines, it commended them as a 'useful checklist' for those involved in future cases. The Guidelines are in the following terms:

Application by the Prosecutor

1. Within the witness statement in support of the application to appoint a management receiver, the prosecutor should set out the reasons the prosecutor seeks the appointment of a receiver, and what purpose the prosecutor believes the receivership will serve.

2. The witness statement in support of the application should also give an indication of the type of work that it is envisaged the receiver may need to undertake, based on the facts known to the prosecutor at the time of the appointment.

3. The witness statement should specifically draw to the Court's attention the proposition that the assets over which the receiver is appointed will be used to pay the costs, disbursements and other expenses of the receivership (even if the defendant is acquitted or the receivership is subsequently discharged).

4. The letter of acceptance of appointment from the receiver, which must be exhibited to the applicant's witness statement, should contain the time charging rates of the staff the receiver anticipates he may need to deploy.

5. In appropriate cases, where it is possible, and this will not be in every case, the receiver should give in his letter of acceptance an estimate as to how much the receivership is likely to cost.

6. The prosecutor's witness statement in support of the application should inform the Court of the nature of the assets and their approximate value (if known) and the income the assets might produce (if known).

7. If the prosecutor or receiver is unable to comply with any of the above requirements the prosecutor should explain the reasons for the failure in the prosecutor's application to the court and the matter will be left at the discretion of the court.

Upon appointment

8. Upon the appointment of a receiver, the Judge should consider whether it is appropriate, in all the circumstances, to reserve any future applications to himself, with a view to minimising costs.

9. Upon the appointment of a receiver, the Judge should consider whether it is appropriate, in all the circumstances, to set a return date, balancing the need for such a hearing with the interests of the defendant, who ultimately will bear the costs of such a hearing.

10. The receiver should inform the parties by written report as soon as reasonably practicable, if it appears to him that any initial costs estimate will be exceeded, or receivership costs are increasing, or are likely to increase to a disproportionate level. Such a report should also be filed with the Court. In such circumstances the parties and the receiver shall be at liberty to seek directions from the Court.

Reporting requirements

11. Unless the Court directs otherwise, the receiver should report 28 days after his appointment and quarterly thereafter.

12. Unless the Court directs otherwise, the report should be served on the prosecutor and the defendant and filed with the Court.

13. Every report should set out the costs incurred to date; the work done; the projected costs until the next report; a summary of how those costs attach to the matters that led to the appointment or to the matters that may have arisen; and, where appropriate, an estimated final outcome statement.

14. Every report should contain a statement that the receiver believes that his costs are reasonable and proportionate in all the circumstances.

15. If the receiver is unable to fulfil any of the above reporting requirements, he should give, as soon as reasonably practicable, an explanation, by way of written report to be filed at Court and served on the parties, of why this is the case, and those parties shall be at liberty to seek directions from the Court.

Lawyers and other agents

16. The parties should always be told that lawyers or other agents have been instructed unless it is not practicable or in the interests of justice to do so (for example, to make an urgent without notice application to secure assets).

17. If lawyers or other agents are instructed the receiver should ask for monthly bills or fee notes. The receiver should endeavour to keep a close control on such fees and satisfy himself that the costs being incurred are reasonable and proportionate in all the circumstances.

18. The receiver should notify the parties as soon as reasonably practicable if it appears to him that any lawyers' or other agents' costs are rising to a disproportionate level, and those parties shall be at liberty to apply to the Court for directions.

General

19. Nothing in these guidelines should be read as surplanting the appropriate rules of court, particularly CPR 69, and the relevant statutory provisions.

20. Judges appointing receivers should always bear in mind that the costs of the receivership may fall on an innocent man. They should also bear in mind that the interests of justice dictate that receiverships are a necessary and essential tool of the criminal justice process for preserving and managing assets to satisfy confiscation orders if the defendant is convicted.

21. Management receivership orders should be endorsed with the appropriate penal notice. It will be a term of most orders that defendants should cooperate with and comply with, as soon as possible and forthwith, directions and requests of the receiver, so as to enable the receiver to efficiently and cost-effectively carry out the duties, functions and obligations of his office. It is therefore in the defendant's interest to avoid, as far as possible, the need for the receiver to return to Court for further orders or directions, the cost of which ultimately fall on the defendant's estate.

3.16 The *Capewell* Guidelines seek to achieve a balance between the rights of all concerned in management receivership cases: the prosecutor, concerned to protect the value of realisable property pending the determination of the proceedings; the defendant, anxious to prevent his business and personal life being unduly interfered with and the costs of the receivership escalating out of control; and the receiver's desire to have sufficient powers to act effectively and be properly remunerated for his work. The guidelines achieve this by making it clear that although the power to appoint a management receiver is an essential tool in the criminal justice system to ensure assets are properly preserved, prosecutors must give proper thought to the objectives the receivership is intended to achieve and consider whether the costs involved will be proportionate having regard to the benefits likely to accrue to the defendant's estate. The receiver too is enjoined to have proper regard to the principle of proportionality, to report regularly to the parties and the court on the state of progress with the receivership and the likely costs involved. He must also advise the parties promptly if costs are likely to increase to an amount beyond that estimated in his reports or to the extent that they cease to be proportionate. If a defendant fails to cooperate with the receiver in the proper discharge of his duties after being given due warning, the receiver should bring the matter promptly to the court's attention on an application for directions rather than allow the matter to drift with further unnecessary costs being incurred.

3.17 It should also be noted that the defendant has an important role to play in ensuring that receivership costs do not escalate out of control. As Guideline 21 makes plain, it is incumbent on the defendant to co-operate with the receiver by complying promptly and fully with his requirements to enable the receiver to discharge his duties, functions and obligations as an officer of the court efficiently and cost effectively. Indeed, it is in the defendant's best interests to cooperate in every way possible, because the consequence of any failure to do so is likely to be an application by the receiver for further directions requiring the defendant to take specific steps to enable the receiver to discharge his duties effectively. In particularly serious cases any such failure could result in the receiver or prosecutor instituting contempt proceedings.

D. Status of the Receiver on Appointment

3.18 The receiver appointed will in most cases be a chartered accountant or licensed insolvency practitioner with significant experience of asset and business management. The court will need to be satisfied of the suitability of the person put forward by the prosecutor for appointment as receiver and a person who has not acted in this capacity under the legislation on previous occasions will be required to give security together with an affidavit or witness statement from an independent person confirming his fitness for appointment.

3.19 On appointment, a management receiver becomes an independent officer of the court, accountable to the court for his actions. Although appointed on the application of the prosecutor, the receiver must act entirely independently and the prosecutor has no power to direct him to exercise his powers in a particular way. When the court appoints a receiver under the Act, it effectively assumes the management of the defendant's estate into its own hands and the receiver is entitled to refer to the court all issues arising about that management and about the nature and extent of the estate for it to determine: see *Re G, Manning v G (No 4)* [2003] EWHC Admin 1732. It is inevitable that the receiver will work very closely with the prosecuting authority because they will have access to a great deal of information as to the location and status of assets subject to the receivership order. Further, where there is no conflict of interest between the receiver and the prosecuting authority, they may arrange, with a view to saving costs, to be represented by the same counsel on the hearing of any subsequent applications in relation to the receivership. This practice was approved by Munby J in *Re G, Manning v G (No 4)*. The learned judge observed:

> I can see no overriding objection to HM Customs and Excise using the same counsel as the receiver where there is no reason to think there is any conflict of interest. Indeed, other things being equal, there are obvious financial advantages both to the receivership estate and to the public purse that duplication of work and effort should be avoided wherever possible.

3.20 As the receiver is entirely independent of the prosecutor, it follows that the prosecutor cannot be held liable for any default by the receiver.

3.21 It follows from the receiver's status as an officer of the court that any obstruction of the receiver in the performance of his duties under the court's order will constitute a contempt of court. It is for this reason that the standard practice is to endorse all receivership orders with a penal notice (see *Capewell,* Guideline 21). A wide range of acts and omissions can constitute obstruction of the receiver, including: putting assets beyond the receiver's reach; refusing to deliver up assets or documents to title relating to them; refusing to sign powers of attorney or other documents allowing the receiver to take control of assets; submitting false or forged documents to the receiver intending him to act on them as genuine and abusing; threatening or assaulting the receiver, members of his staff or agents.

E. Powers, Duties and Liabilities of the Receiver

3.22 Management receivers derive their powers from the order of the court appointing them and from the general law of receivership as it has developed. A precedent for a management receivership order at Appendix 2 shows that the following powers are normally incorporated in such orders:

(a) power to take possession of, preserve, manage, let, charge, and sell realisable property;
(b) power to appoint lawyers, accountants and other agents to advise and act on the receiver's behalf in any part of the world;
(c) power to discharge the costs, charges and expenses of the receivership from assets under the receiver's management;
(d) power to execute documents on behalf of the defendant;
(e) power to require the defendant and any person holding realisable property to take all reasonable and necessary steps to enable the receivership to be properly conducted and, in particular, to provide to the receiver information and documentation relating to realisable property, to sign letters of authority and powers of attorney authorising the receiver to receive information or effect a transfer of realisable property.

3.23 When a management receiver has been appointed, he assumes the power, and indeed the duty, to police compliance with the restraint order and to bring any breaches to the

E. Powers, Duties and Liabilities of the Receiver

attention of the court. In *Re G, Manning v G (No 4)* [2003] EWHC Admin 1732 Munby J said:

> Prior to the appointment of a receiver it is, no doubt, a matter for the prosecutor to 'police' the restraint order. But it is perfectly proper for the receiver, once he has been appointed, to police the order. So if it is said that there has been a breach of the restraint order by the defendant it is perfectly proper for the receiver to take steps to investigate the matter, whether for the purpose of locating and retrieving assets which he is entitled to have under his control and/or for the purpose of punishing the defendant for any contempt of court that can be proved. The receiver is simply acting in pursuance of his statutory duties, exercising powers which are conferred on him: those duties and powers are vested in the receiver, not the prosecutor, though the prosecutor will no doubt support the receiver as necessary. It is implicit in the entire statutory scheme that it is the receiver's duty to ensure that all realisable property is under his control, not the control of the prosecutor.

3.24 The powers of management receivers extend to intangible as well as tangible property. In *Manning and Sinclair v Glatt* [2003] EWCA Civ 1977 the Court of Appeal, in refusing an application for leave to appeal, rejected the contention that a management receiver's powers were confined to tangible property. Jacob LJ said:

> We explored with Counsel the various possibilities of different kinds of action that might involve receivers who have been appointed. Could they, if appointed as receivers over a lease, take proceedings for unpaid rent or for possession? Or could they defend proceedings if, for example, there was an application for a third party debt order? All those examples to my mind indicated very clearly that unless this Act was restricted to physical objects Counsel's argument disintegrated. I can think of no reason whatever why the Act should have been limited, as Counsel submitted. The power is to take possession of any realisable property. One focuses on anything, therefore, which can be converted into money. Almost all forms of property can be so converted. The word "possession" takes its flavour from the kind of property. The Act would serve no useful or meaningful purpose if confined to chattels. . . . once one has arrived at the position that the receiver can take possession of all realisable property it must follow that he has the power to look after that property by taking proceedings or defending them, as well as any other necessary action. Of course if the receiver acts in some improper way there may well be proceedings which can be taken, and if the receiver is ever in doubt as to what he should be doing he has, of course, express power to apply to the court. But that is much the same as the position of any other receiver appointed by the court, or indeed others concerned with insolvency, for example trustees in bankruptcy or liquidators of companies. The remedy lies not in challenging the receiver's powers, but in any misuse of them.

3.25 Sedley LJ, in agreeing with the judgment of Jacob LJ added:

> . . . receivers must have an implied power to resort to the courts in order to preserve the defendant's property. Once this is accepted there can be no bright line which restricts either the kinds of property which the receiver may bring or defend, or the kinds of realisable property to which the receivership may relate. The proper control of the receiver, precisely because he is an officer of the court, lies where necessary in the hands of the court. There is no reason why the defendant himself should not be able to alert the court to any possible irregularities of the kind with which Counsel is understandably concerned in the present case.

3.26 The powers of management receivers are not confined to those expressly set out in the DTA and CJA but include those vested in common law receivers save to the extent that the statutes provide otherwise. As Simon Brown LJ observed in *Hughes v Customs and Excise Commissioners* [2002] 4 All ER 633:

> Statutory receivers are to be treated precisely as their common law counterparts save to the extent that the legislation provides otherwise. The statute is not to be regarded as an entirely self contained code incorporating nothing from the common law.

3.27 The power to sell realisable property causes particular problems in relation to management receiverships. The primary role of a management receiver is of course to manage and preserve the defendant's realisable property. This is in contrast to the position of an enforcement receiver who is appointed to sell off realisable property and pay the proceeds into court in satisfaction of a confiscation order that has already been made and that is no longer subject to an appeal. Nonetheless, a situation may arise in which a management receiver wishes to sell a particular asset because, for example, it is depreciating in value. This course of action may be opposed by a defendant who claims that an asset is of sentimental value or irreplaceable and that sale would prevent him having the asset back in the event of his acquittal.

3.28 This problem was considered by the Court of Appeal in *Re P (Restraint Order: Sale of Assets)* [2000] 1 WLR 473. The defendant had been arrested and charged with drug trafficking offences in relation to which he had been remanded in custody and the High Court had, on the same occasion, made restraint and management receivership orders under the DTA without notice to him. The assets caught by the order included three race horses one of which, named 'Nipper Reed', apparently had race winning potential and was also alleged to be a 'much loved pet' by the defendant's family. The receiver, on assuming office, wished to sell the horses believing them to be depreciating assets. This course of action was strongly opposed by the defendant who made application to the High Court for an order directing the receiver not to sell the horses unless it proved necessary to satisfy any confiscation order made in the event of his conviction. The application was dismissed by Scott Baker J at first instance, but the defendant succeeded on appeal to the Court of Appeal.

3.29 Simon Brown LJ (with whom Chadwick LJ and Rattee J agreed) considered why the legislation gives the court power to appoint management receivers and said:

> In part, no doubt this is because appointment is to guard against attempts by determined defendants, less concerned than most at the thought of the sanctions attending breach of restraint orders, to salt away their assets beyond the reach of any eventual restraint order. In short, I see the primary task of an interim receiver as the safeguarding of the defendant's assets from dissipation and secretion rather than their realisation so as to maximise the amount of any confiscation order.

The learned judge concluded:

> On the material then before the judge I for my part would not have thought it right to allow these three horses to be sold. There was no suggestion that the defendant was dissipating his assets (in the sense of incurring excessive or unusual expenditure beyond what for him was the norm), still less that he was attempting to salt them away. While the defendant remains unconvicted, his assets should not be sold against his wishes except for compelling reason. The possibility, even the probability, that

E. Powers, Duties and Liabilities of the Receiver

these horses could be more profitably sold now than at some future date is not such a compelling reason.

3.30 The mere fact that an asset is depreciating will not normally be a sufficient basis for a receiver effecting sale. As the court observed, in *Re P* the purpose of the legislation is to impoverish the defendant and not to enrich the Crown. This is not to say that it will never be appropriate for a management receiver to sell assets. If a defendant is deliberately exposing his assets to the risk of dissipation, for example by not paying the mortgage and insurance premiums on a property or not effecting essential repairs, abandoning an asset or causing wanton damage, it may be appropriate for the court to order sale particularly if there are no liquid assets available within the receivership to enable these essential payments to be paid. Further, the decision in *Re P* only applies to the position of a defendant who has not been convicted where regard must be had to the defendant's right to have his property returned to him in the event of an acquittal. It has no bearing on the position of a defendant who has been convicted and it is submitted that a management receiver appointed in relation to a convicted defendant should be able to sell assets to prevent any further dissipation. Finally, it should be noted that the decision in *Re P* does not prevent the sale of assets for the purpose of making funds available to meet receivership costs and expenses and indeed to pay any sums required for the defendant's general living expenses and legal fees.

3.31 The Court in *Re P* also gave useful guidance as to the circumstances in which the Court should interfere with decisions made by a receiver in the exercise of his powers. At first instance, Scott Baker J ruled that it was only appropriate for the court to interfere where it was satisfied the receiver had 'clearly fallen into error'. The Court of Appeal ruled that this was not the correct approach and the court was entitled to interfere wherever the judge's view differs from that of the receiver. The Court was, however, at pains to emphasise that this should not be seen as a charter for every aggrieved defendant to complain to the court as to every decision made by the receiver. As Simon Brown LJ observed:

> All that said, a court faced with a dispute between the receiver and the defendant as to the proposed course of the receivership is likely to give great weight to the essentially disinterested views of the former, particularly where they are supported by professional advice and expertise. This judgment should certainly not be seen as a charter for niggling complaints by disgruntled defendants.

(1) Duties and liabilities of the receiver

3.32 Like all professionals a receiver owes a duty of care to those affected by his actions during the course of a receivership. This does not, however, mean that the receiver will be held liable in relation to every act or omission that results in loss to the estate. If, for example, the receiver is managing a business, he is entitled to take decisions in relation to the running of the business that involve an element of risk, provided that the risk is not such that no reasonable and prudent person in the receiver's position would have taken it. In order to succeed in an action against a receiver, the defendant or aggrieved third party would have to establish negligence on the part of the receiver.

3.33 Further, the legislation itself gives the receiver some protection against liability to the defendant and third parties. Section 36(1) DTA and s 88(1) CJA provide that where a receiver appointed under the Acts:

(a) takes any action in relation to property which is not realisable property, being action which he would be entitled to take if it were such property, and
(b) believes, and has reasonable grounds for believing, that he is entitled to take that action in relation to that property, he shall not be liable to any person in respect of any loss or damage resulting from his actions except in so far as the loss or damage is caused by his negligence.

3.34 Thus, even where the receiver acts in relation to property that turns out not to be realisable under the legislation, he will enjoy protection from liability for his actions provided that he was not negligent and had reasonable grounds for believing he was entitled to act in relation to the property in question.

3.35 The receiver will be personally liable in relation to any contracts he enters into in his capacity as receiver. He will not, however, be liable in relation to any contracts already in force prior to his appointment, save to the extent that he adopts them and allows them to continue.

(2) Employment of agents

3.36 In most management receivership cases, the receiver will need to instruct agents to assist and advise him in the proper discharge of his duties and the receivership order will normally empower him to do so. The receiver will frequently need to instruct a solicitor to provide legal advice and litigation support, expert valuers to value assets subject to the receivership and property management agents to manage real property. The receiver should, however, ensure that the costs of any agents he instructs are reasonable and proportionate having regard to the benefits that are likely to accrue to the receivership. It is the practice of many receivers to instruct City solicitors to advise them during the course of the receivership and, although most receivers are able to negotiate a discount on the firm's usual charge out rates, the costs of these firms can rapidly escalate. Although it may be entirely justifiable for the receiver to instruct a City firm in highly complex receivership cases, the use of such a firm to act on a straightforward conveyancing transaction in relation to a property located in the provinces, would not. In such a case the receiver would be expected to instruct a high street solicitor in the area where the property is located. In *Re D* [2006] EWHC Admin 254, solicitors acting for a company affected by restraint and management receivership orders sought the release of some £110,000 by way of legal fees for advising and representing the company. This amount represented a third of the company's entire asset base. Ouseley J ruled that this was disproportionate and released only £50,000 to the solicitors. It is submitted that the same principle applies to receivers and their agents: the services of agents must be obtained at a cost that is proportionate in all the circumstances and not necessarily from their first choice of professional advisers.

3.37 When the receiver intends to instruct an agent, he should notify the parties as soon as possible except where it is not practicable or in the interests of justice to do so (see *Capewell* Guideline 16). The receiver should also ask for monthly bills or fee notes and satisfy himself

E. Powers, Duties and Liabilities of the Receiver

that the amounts claimed are reasonable and proportionate (see *Capewell* Guideline 17). The duties of the receiver in this regard are considered in more detail at para 3.49 below. Finally, the receiver must notify the parties immediately if it appears to him that the costs of his agents are rising to a disproportionate level (see *Capewell* Guideline 18).

3.38 Receivers must, therefore, take great care to review the reasonableness and proportionality of their actions at all times. If they are unable to satisfy the court that their fees and disbursements are reasonable and proportionate, having regard to all the circumstances of the case, they run the risk of them being disallowed in whole or in part. The court will not expect them to get it right every time and, it is submitted, should be willing to give receivers appointed under the DTA and CJA rather more latitude than those appointed in civil cases because, as Lord Donaldson MR observed in *Re O* [1991] 1 All ER 330, the legislative contemplation is that some of those claiming an interest in realisable property may be of a 'dishonest disposition' who do their expert best to deal with it in such a way that it is outside the grasp of the court and the receivers whom it appoints.

(3) Receiver's accounts

3.39 Under CPR Part 69.8 (which sc115 Rule 8(1) provides shall apply to receivers appointed under the Acts) the court may order a receiver to prepare and serve accounts. The letter of agreement between the receiver and the prosecuting authority, on whose application he is appointed, will invariably require the preparation and service of accounts on the prosecutor and defendant at regular intervals and the receivership order itself will provide that the receiver must act in accordance with that letter of agreement.

3.40 CPR Part 69.8 gives all parties served with the receiver's accounts certain important rights. Firstly, under CPR 69.8(2), any party served with the accounts may apply for an order permitting him to inspect any document in the possession of the receiver relevant to those accounts. This does not entitle a defendant to have full access to the receiver's file, but merely to documents that are of relevance to the accounts he has submitted. Secondly, by CPR 69.8(3), any party may within 14 days of being served with the accounts, serve notice on the receiver:

(a) specifying any item in the accounts to which he objects;
(b) giving the reason for such objection; and
(c) requiring the receiver, within 14 days of receipt of the notice, either;
   (i) to notify all the parties who were served with the accounts that he accepts the objection; or
   (ii) if he does not accept the objection, to apply for an examination of the accounts in relation to the contested item.

3.41 By CPR Part 69.8(4), when the receiver applies for the examination of the accounts he must file the accounts and a copy of the notice served on him under para (3). If the receiver fails either to accept the objection or apply for an examination of his accounts under para (3)(c), any party may apply to the court for an examination of the accounts in relation to the contested item.

3.42 The duty of the receiver to serve accounts on the defendant also extends to any reports he may prepare for the prosecutor as to the progress of the receivership. If the receiver considers that particularly sensitive mattters in his report should be withheld from the defendant he should refer the matter to the court and be in a position to justify departing from the usual rule: see *Re G, Manning v G (No 4)* [2003] EWHC Admin 1732 and *Capewell*, Guideline 12.

F. Remuneration of Receivers

3.43 Receivers are generally speaking chartered accountants or licensed insolvency practitioners working in large accountancy firms. They accept appointments under the Acts because they are a commercially viable enterprise from which they are entitled to charge fees and make a profit for themselves or their employers. This gives rise to two fundamental questions namely: who is liable to pay the receiver's fees and who exercises control over the amounts claimed?

3.44 The receivership order will provide that the receiver is entitled to payments of his remuneration and related costs and expenses from the estate under management, and he will normally draw down his costs from receivership funds on a regular basis. The letter of agreement between the prosecutor and the receiver will provide that in the event of insufficient funds being available within the receivership estate, the prosecutor will indemnify the receiver in relation to those costs. This arrangement causes no difficulty in cases where the defendant is ultimately convicted and a confiscation order is made against him, but difficulties arise in cases that ultimately result in an acquittal. In such cases, where the receiver has taken his fees from the estate under management, the acquitted defendant may well find that the estate returned to him on the discharge of the receiver is worth rather less than at the time the receiver was appointed.

3.45 The position was considered by the Court of Appeal in *Re Andrews* [1999] 1 WLR 1236. In that case, the defendant found that following the discharge of the receiver on his acquittal, some £10,000 had been taken from his estate by way of receiver's fees. He sought an order that this sum be reimbursed to him by the prosecuting authority. The Court of Appeal ruled that it followed from the fact that on appointment a receiver became an officer of the court, that receivership fees should be paid from the estate under management rather than by the prosecutor. Accordingly, the Court refused to order the prosecutor to make the payment sought by the acquitted defendant. Ward LJ made it clear that he reached this conclusion with 'unfeigned reluctance' and that if he had any discretion in the matter he would have exercised it in the defendant's favour. Aldous LJ, who expressed no such regret in his judgment, agreed with the prosecutor's submission that in reality the defendant's claim for costs amounted to a claim for compensation 'dressed up as an application for an award of costs' because he could not bring himself within the strict requirements of s 89 of the CJA to enable him to claim compensation.

3.46 The Court of Appeal in *Andrews* made it clear that they had not considered the provisions of the European Convention on Human Rights in reaching its decision. The matter came before the Court of Appeal again in *Hughes v Customs and Excise Commissioners* [2002] 4 All ER 633, and on this occasion the court considered the matter afresh in the light of the Convention. In this case the acquitted defendant claimed that the costs of the receivership being met from the estate under management would represent a breach of his rights under Article 1 of the First Protocol to the Convention and that it would be disproportionate and arbitrary to deprive an unconvicted or acquitted defendant of his assets in the absence of provision for the payment of compensation. The Court upheld its earlier decision in *Andrews*, ruling that statutory receivers appointed under the DTA and CJA should be treated in precisely the same way as their common law counterparts except where the legislation provided to the contrary. Accordingly the costs of the receiver were to be met from the fund under management rather than by the prosecutor.

3.47 The Court went on to consider the human rights arguments and found nothing in their decision that conflicted with the European Convention. Simon Brown LJ said:

> It is common ground that acquitted defendants are not, save in the most exceptional circumstances, entitled to compensation for being deprived of their liberty while on remand or indeed for any other heads of loss suffered through being prosecuted. In my view, it is no more unfair, disproportionate or arbitrary that they should be uncompensated too for any effects that restraint and receivership orders may have had upon their assets.

3.48 The decisions in *Andrews* and *Hughes* may not be as harsh as they first appear. The defendant will have had the benefit of having a professional manager administering his assets and business. In many cases, following his acquittal, the defendant will get back assets that are far better managed and maintained than at the time the receiver took office. Further, in managing these assets, the receiver will incur much expenditure. Houses and other real property will need to be insured, kept in good repair, and mortgage repayments and council tax liabilities met. If there is a business to run, staff and public utility bills will need to be paid and proper accounts prepared and maintained. All these items of expenditure are essential to the proper management of the defendant's estate and would have to be met regardless of whether a receiver is in office.

3.49 In the *Hughes* case, the Court of Appeal ruled that receivers' costs must be approved by the Court and the practice that had developed of such fees being vetted and approved by the prosecutor was wrong. Arden LJ drew attention to para 22.6 of the Chancery Guide which provides that:

> The receiver's remuneration must be authorised by the Court. Unless the court directs it to be fixed by reference to some fixed scale, or percentage of rents collected, it is assessed by the court, but in the first instance the receiver should submit his remuneration claim to the parties for approval. If the claim is accepted by the parties, the court should not normally be concerned to intervene, but it must at least formally authorise the remuneration.

3.50 This is, it is submitted, a more equitable regime because it gives the defendant the right to make representations if he considers the receiver's claim is too high. The earlier system whereby fees were simply agreed between the prosecutor and the receiver left no avenue of redress open to a defendant who wished to challenge the receiver's claim.

3.51 Indeed, it must not be thought that a receivership order gives the receiver a 'blank cheque' to charge whatever fees he thinks appropriate, embark on whatever enquiries he chooses, or pay the fees of agents he engages without holding their invoices up to critical scrutiny. In *Mirror Group Newspapers plc v Maxwell* (1998) BCC 324, Ferris J described as 'profoundly shocking' a receivership in which nothing at all had been realised for the benefit of creditors in an estate valued in excess of £1.5 million, and the majority of the funds had been used to meet the costs of the receivers and their lawyers. He issued a timely reminder to receivers as to their duties as office holders and fiduciaries. He said that the test for determining whether a receiver had acted properly in undertaking particular tasks at a particular cost must be:

> whether a reasonably prudent man, faced with the same circumstances in relation to his own affairs, would lay out or hazard his own money in doing what the office-holders have done. It is not sufficient, in my view, for office-holders to say that what they have done is within the scope of the duties or powers conferred on them. They are expected to deploy commercial judgment, not to act regardless of expense. This is not to say that a transaction carried out at a high cost in relation to the benefit received, or even an expensive failure, will automatically result in the disallowance of expenses or remuneration. But it is to be expected that transactions having these characteristics will be subject to close scrutiny.

3.52 The learned judge took a similarly robust line in relation to the fees of lawyers and other professionals engaged to advise receivers. He said:

> At the very least they must subject the bills to critical scrutiny. If they simply pay them without such scrutiny they will obviously be vulnerable. They may be able to negotiate certain reductions, thus facilitating an argument that the negotiated reductions are preferable to the possibility of obtaining great reductions at greater cost. In an appropriate case (but, not I would expect one where the issues are as complex and the amounts as large as in this case) they may be able to obtain a certificate from the Law Society as to the proper amount of their solicitors' bill. Finally they can require the bills to be taxed pursuant to Section 70 of the Solicitors Act 1974.

3.53 The concerns expressed by Ferris J led to new rules being introduced in relation to the remuneration of receivers with effect from 2 December 2002. The new rules are to be found in CPR 69.7 which provides:

(1) A receiver may only charge for his services if the court—
  (a) so directs; and
  (b) specifies the basis on which the receiver is to be remunerated;
(2) The court may specify—
  (a) who is to be responsible for paying the receiver; and
  (b) the fund or property from which the receiver is to recover his remuneration;
(3) If the court directs that the amount of the receiver's remuneration is to be determined by the court—
  (a) the receiver may not recover any remuneration for his services without a determination by the court; and
  (b) the receiver or any party may apply at any time for such a determination to take place.
(4) Unless the court orders otherwise, in determining the remuneration of a receiver the court shall award such sum as is reasonable and proportionate in all the circumstances and which takes into account—
  (a) the time properly given by him and his staff to the receivership;
  (b) the complexity of the receivership;
  (c) any responsibility of an exceptional kind or degree which falls on the receiver in consequence of the receivership;
  (d) the effectiveness with which the receiver appears to be carrying out or to have carried out, his duties; and
  (e) the value and nature of the subject matter of the receivership.
(5) The court may refer the determination of a receiver's remuneration to a costs judge.

F. Remuneration of Receivers

3.54 Paragraph 8.2 of the Practice Direction supplementing sc115 specifically provides that CPR r 69.7 applies in relation to the remuneration of receivers appointed under the DTA and CJA.

3.55 In *Capewell v Customs and Excise Commissioners (No 2)* [2005] EWCA Civ 964 The Court of Appeal held that CPR 69.7 gives the court a discretion to require the prosecutor, in special circumstances, to pay the remuneration of the receiver, the decision in *Hughes* notwithstanding. Carnwarth LJ said:

> On its face, it gives us an unlimited discretion in respect of the receiver's remuneration. Without more detailed information as to the background, I am prepared to assume that this rule was not intended to make a radical change to the previous practice. However, it seems clearly designed to give the court some discretion in the matter, at least in special circumstances where application of the ordinary rule would cause unfairness or hardship. *Andrews* may have been one example in the draftsman's mind. Acordingly, if as I think justice requires that Customs should bear the receiver's costs from 1st June 2004, rule 69.7 (2) seems to give us the means to achieve it.

3.56 In a concurring judgment, Longmore LJ added:

> I would only add a reference to para 60 of the judgment of Simon Brown LJ in *Hughes v Customs and Excise Commissioners* [2003] 1 WLR 177 where he said this:-
>
> It is important that this legislation continues to be operated to strip criminals of their ill gotten gains. But it is important too that the court keeps a close control over those it appoints to act as receivers on its behalf and that costs are not too readily incurred, particularly before any confiscation order is made.
>
> It is only by making, in appropriate cases, orders of the kind we have decided to make in the present case that the courts can exercise the sort of control envisaged by Simon Brown LJ to be necessary.

3.57 It is submitted that r 69(2) CPR is also open to the interpretation, contended for by the Crown, that it is merely intended to give the court power to order which part of the restrained fund the receiver's remuneration should be paid. If, for example, a management receiver was appointed over a company in which the defendant is alleged to have an interest, the court would have power to order the order that the receiver's remuneration for managing the company be paid from the company's bank accounts rather than the personal accounts of the defendant. This issue will now have to be resolved by the House of Lords when the Crown's appeal is heard in December.

3.58 In the meantime, it should be noted that the scope of the Court of Appeal's decision in *Capewell* is not as great as it might first appear. Firstly, the decision only applies to the remuneration of the receiver and not to the costs and expenses he incurs during the course of the receivership. As Carnwath LJ noted in *Capewell*:

> As its heading makes clear, rule 69.7 is dealing with the "remuneration" of the receiver. In ordinary language, that would not include his expenses. Although rule 69.7 (2) (a) refers simply to responsibility for "paying the receiver" which in a different context might include payment of expenses, I do not think it is possible to read that sub-paragraph on its own as extending beyond the subject-matter of the rest of the rule. The Practice Direction confirms that the distinction between remuneration and expenses is deliberate. That may make sense in relation to rules directed to determining the amount of remuneration. It is less clear why the distinction should be relevant to responsibility for payment. Ordinarily one would

3.59 Secondly, it should be noted that the rule in *Capewell* only applies in special circumstances where requiring the defendant to pay the receiver's remuneration would cause unfairness or hardship. The general rule therefore is that the defendant remains liable to pay the remuneration of a management receiver save where he can show there are special circumstances. The Court did not indicate what might amount to special circumstances, but in *Capewell* they appear to have been influenced by the view that the management receiver should have been discharged by 1 June 2004 and it was therefore appropriate that the prosecutor should be liable to pay his remuneration from that date until he was discharged on 13 October, 2004. The Court does not appear to have been influenced by a defendant being acquitted, as the criminal proceedings against Mr Capewell were still pending at the time of the Court's judgment.

3.60 Finally, it should be noted that the *Capewell* ruling only applies to management receiverships under the DTA and CJA. Section 49(2)(d) of the Proceeds of Crime Act, 2002 and r 60.6(5) of the Criminal Procedure Rules 2005 make specific provision for the payment of the receiver's remuneration from the estate under management.

G. Discharge of the Receiver

3.61 Receivers and the prosecuting authorities that apply for their appointment should be vigilant in reviewing both the economic viability of the receivership and the continued necessity for having a receiver in office. If the point comes when it is apparent that the receivership would no longer serve any useful purpose or that it is no longer economically viable, an application should be made to the court for the receiver's discharge.

3.62 A defendant who considers that a management receivership should be discharged for these reasons should invite the receiver and prosecutor to justify why it is necessary for the receiver to stay in office. If he considers any response unsatisfactory, the defendant should apply to discharge the receivership. The defendant should serve a witness statement in support of his application setting out his grounds for seeking the discharge of the receiver and setting out his proposals for the effective management of his realisable property pending the conclusion of the proceedings.

3.63 In *Capewell v Customs and Excise Commissioners* [2005] 1 All ER 900, the Court gave guidance as to the issues the court should take into account in determining whether a management receivership order should be discharged. Carnwath LJ said:

> On the question of discharge, cost is of course a factor, but it is not the primary issue. The overriding consideration is whether the receivership is still serving a valid purpose, within the overall objective set by section 82. The relevant questions for the court are likely to be—
>
> (i) For what purposes, within the overall objective, was the receivership authorised?
> (ii) To what extent have those purposes been achieved or overtaken?

(iii) To the extent that they have not yet been achieved or overtaken, is the continuation of the receivership (as opposed to a restraint order or some other order) necessary to achieve them?

(iv) In any event, having regard both to the overall objective and to fairness to the defendant, is the additional cost of continuing the receivership proportionate to the likely financial gain?

We would add that fairness to the defendant cannot be measured purely in financial terms. Even without accepting all of Mr. Capewell's evidence, it requires little imagination to understand how a receivership of this kind can seriously interfere with the ordinary business and personal life of those affected and their families. The premise of the 1988 Act is that such a burden may have to be accepted in the public interest. But it is for the court to decide in individual cases where the balance lies, weighing all the benefits and burdens, both public and private.

Even if there are insufficient grounds to justify the discharge of the receiver, the defendant or an affected third party is always entitled to seek the court's directions if he considers the receiver is abusing his powers or is otherwise acting improperly: see *Manning & Sinclair v Glatt* [2003] EWCA Civ 1977 referred to at para 3.23 above.

H. Taxation and Receivers

Receivers appointed under the DTA and CJA, whether for management or enforcement purposes are not liable to pay income tax or capital gains tax in respect of realisations of or dealings in the receivership assets. In *IRC v Dayman and Piacentini* The Times, 10 February 2003, the defendant had been charged with tax fraud offences. He was ultimately convicted and a confiscation order was made against him in the sum of £2.1 million. A receiver was appointed initially to manage the defendant's assets pending his trial, and after conviction, to enforce the confiscation order by the realisation of those assets. The receiver was able to satisfy the confiscation order in full and sought the court's directions as to whether she was liable to pay income and capital gains tax in relation to her dealings with the defendant's assets.

3.64

The case involved consideration of two issues: whether the receiver incurs any personal liability to pay income tax or capital gains tax and secondly whether the tax liability is an expense for the purposes of s 81(5) CJA to be paid and discharged from the proceeds of realisation. Lightman J. answered both questions in the negative. As to the personal liability issue, the learned judge said:

3.65

> Common sense requires that where there is a realisation by the receiver the tax liability (whether for capital gains or income tax) should remain that of the Defendant alone and that the Receiver should not be assessable. Nothing in section 75 (of the Taxes Management Act, 1970) compels me to reach any other conclusion. This conclusion is reinforced by the absence of any provision in the scheme of the CJA for any such liability for tax for ring fencing of assets to meet that liability or for any indemnity. I accordingly hold that the Receiver is not assessable to capital gains tax or income tax.

As the learned judge noted, under the Proceeds of Crime Act 2002 there is express statutory provision to the effect that receivers appointed under the Act have no personal liability to pay tax in respect of their dealings in and realisations of realisable property pursuant to their orders of appointment (see s 448 and Sch 10 to POCA).

3.66

3.67 Lightman J then went on to consider whether the liability of the defendant to pay income and capital gains tax could constitute an 'expense' under s 81(5) CJA which should be discharged from the proceeds of realisation. The learned judge said:

> In my view the answer is clearly in the negative. First it is to be noted that the liquidator in *Mesco* was by reason of section 108(1) and (3) of the TMA the proper officer to pay the liability, it would and could not be discharged. In the case of a receivership such as the present there is no equivalent to section 108(1) or (3) making the Receiver the proper person to pay, and the liability of the Defendant continues unaffected by the receivership. Secondly, section 82(6) of the CJA provides that in exercising [the Receiver's] powers 'no account shall be taken of any obligation of the defendant . . . which conflicts with the obligation to satisfy the confiscation order'. This provision makes plain that the proceeds of realisation available for satisfaction of the confiscation order are not to be depleted by any application in discharge of the Defendant's liability for capital gains tax . . . Thirdly, having particularly in mind that the term 'expenses' is not a term of art (see Maughan J in *In Re Beni Falkai Mining Company Limited* [1934] Ch 406 at page 418–9) in the absence of any liability on the part of the Receiver to pay the capital gains tax, the term 'expense' of the Receiver is not apposite to a continuing liability of the Defendant. Fourthly, and finally, the whole scheme of the CJA is to place a strict limit on the items to be paid and discharged out of the proceeds of realisation, and it is not consistent with that scheme to make a payment in effect for the benefit and in discharge of a continuing liability of the Defendant.

3.68 Receivers accordingly have no liability to pay income and capital gains tax in relation to their dealings in a defendant's realisable property. It is submitted this must be the correct approach. Third parties with a legitimate claim against the defendant for monies due and owing have no right to seek a variation to a restraint order to allow funds to be released to meet their claims (see *Re W* The Times, 15 November 1990) and it would hardly be just and equitable for the Exchequer to be put in a more favourable position. Further, should a confiscation order be made in the proceedings, the proceeds of realisation will in any event go to the Crown when they are paid into Court by the receiver in satisfaction of that order.

4

ANCILLARY ORDERS: SEIZURE, DISCLOSURE AND REPATRIATION OF ASSETS

A. Introduction	4.01	(5) Disclosure cannot be ordered against the prosecutor	4.31
B. Seizure of Assets	4.02	(6) Advising the defendant or third party required to disclose	4.33
C. Disclosure Orders	4.06	D. Repatriation of Assets	4.42
(1) Jurisdiction to make the order	4.07	(1) Jurisdiction to make repatriation orders	4.44
(2) The problem of self incrimination	4.15	(2) Form of repatriation order	4.49
(3) Form of disclosure orders	4.29		
(4) Disclosure and third parties	4.30		

A. Introduction

4.01 Practitioners may be surprised, on seeing a restraint order for the first time, to note the extent and breadth of its terms. The majority of such orders go way beyond simply restraining the defendant's assets, but require him in addition to serve a witness statement on the prosecutor disclosing the full extent and location of his realisable property and even to repatriate assets held overseas. The DTA and CJA make no specific provision for such orders to be made. The power to make them flows from the inherent jurisdiction of the court to make such ancillary provision as is necessary to ensure that its orders are properly policed. In this chapter, we examine the powers of the court to make such orders and the conditions and limitations to which they are subject. Although this chapter focuses on the DTA and CJA it should be borne in mind that many of the principles set out herein apply equally to the POCA regime with s 41 (7) of the Act empowering the Crown Court to make any such order as it believes is appropriate for the purpose of ensuring the restraint order is effective.

B. Seizure of Assets

4.02 Unlike the majority of powers examined in this chapter the power to seize realisable property is to be found in the legislation itself. Section 26(9) of the DTA and s 77(10) of the CJA empower a constable, once a restraint order has been made, to seize any realisable property for the purpose of preventing it being removed from Great Britain. The reference in the Acts to 'a constable' includes an officer of Revenue and Customs (see s 63(1) of the DTA and s 102(1) of the CJA as amended by the Commissioners for Revenue and Customs Act 2005).

4.03 The legislation is silent as to the degree of proof the constable must have that the asset is going to be removed from Great Britain before he can seize it. It is submitted that the standard must be the same as that required to obtain a restraint order, namely there is a good arguable case that the asset is to be removed: see *Compton v CPS* [2002] EWCA Civ 1720. Substantial proof is not required and, it is submitted, there is no requirement that the evidence should be in a form that would be admissible in a criminal trial.

4.04 Once an asset has been seized, it must be dealt with in accordance with the court's directions (see s 26(11) of the DTA and s 77(11) of the CJA). Although no procedures are laid down in the legislation or in the rules of court, it is submitted that the proper course is for the prosecutor to issue an application notice seeking the court's directions as to how the asset should be dealt with. The application notice should be served on all parties who, to the prosecutor's knowledge, claim to have an interest in the property. If the asset is of particularly high value, it may be appropriate for the prosecutor to apply for the appointment of a management receiver to take possession of it pending the conclusion of proceedings.

4.05 It would seem that the legislation confers an almost unlimited jurisdiction on the court to give such directions as it sees fit as to how the seized property should be dealt with. The court will obviously need to have regard to the 'legislative steer' in s 31(2) of the DTA and s 82(2) of the CJA, although it would seem that the court's power to order sale is fettered by the decision of the Court of Appeal in *Re P (Restraint Order: Sale of Assets)* [2000] 1 WLR 473, considered in Chapter 3 above.

C. Disclosure Orders

4.06 The prosecutor should have full information of the nature, extent and location of all the defendant's realisable property to police the restraint order effectively. Although, at the time he applies for a restraint order, the prosecutor will have much information about the defendant's realisable property from a variety of sources, in the last analysis the extent of a defendant's assets is a matter uniquely within his own knowledge. Thus, from the very early days of restraint and confiscation legislation, prosecutors have asked the court, when exercising its jurisdiction to make restraint orders, to require the defendant to make an affidavit or witness statement supported by a statement of truth, disclosing the full extent of his realisable property. The early cases required the defendant to make disclosure on affidavit but, since the advent of the Civil Procedure Rules, the normal requirement is for the defendant to make the required disclosure in a witness statement verified by a statement of truth. The effect of statements of truth is considered in more detail in Chapter 7.

(1) Jurisdiction to make the order

4.07 The power to make disclosure orders stems not from the legislation, but from the court's inherent jurisdiction to make such orders as it considers just and convenient. The first reported case in which the court ruled it had jurisdiction to make a disclosure order is

C. Disclosure Orders

Re A Defendant The Times, 7 April 1987, a decision of Webster J at first instance. A restraint order, including a disclosure provision, had been made ex parte and, at a later hearing, inter partes. The defendant challenged the power of the court to make the disclosure order. He contended that if the power to order disclosure existed at all, it could only be granted in favour of a receiver because it was his function and not that of the prosecutor to get in property. Webster J rejected that argument ruling that the principal purpose to be achieved by the appointment of a receiver was the management of assets which, for whatever reason, the defendant could not manage himself.

4.08 The power of the court to require disclosure was first considered by the Court of Appeal in *Re O* [1991] 1 All ER 330. Restraint orders had been made against the defendants under the CJA containing an exception allowing the sum of £100 per week to be spent on general living expenses. The defendants applied to vary the order by increasing the amount payable to £500 per week. The prosecutor contended that the variation should not be entertained unless the defendants swore affidavits disclosing the extent of their assets. Macpherson J acceded to that submission and made an order requiring the defendants:

> to swear an affidavit disclosing the full value of any salary, money, goods or other assets whatsoever within and without the jurisdiction identifying with full particularity the nature of all such assets, their whereabouts and whether the same be held in their own names or jointly with some other person or person, or by nominees or otherwise howsoever on their behalf.

4.09 He then adjourned the application pending compliance with the disclosure order. The defendants appealed contending that the judge had no jurisdiction to make the disclosure order.

4.10 The Court of Appeal dismissed the appeal, finding that the court had an inherent jurisdiction to order disclosure of assets in support of restraint orders. Lord Donaldson of Lymington MR said:

> Equally in my judgment, the High Court must have been intended to have power to render effective a restraint order made under section 77 of the 1988 Act.
>
> Under that section notice of the order has to be given to persons affected by it (s 77(5)(c)). In addition there is power to appoint a receiver and manager of any realisable property (s 77(8)). Finally, there is an obvious necessity to be able to police compliance with the order. All these features dictate that there should be some means of identifying and ascertaining the whereabouts and the value of assets affected by the restraint order and this need is reinforced when it is realised that, whatever may be the position in an individual case, the legislative contemplation is that restraint orders will be made in circumstances in which it is thought that some of those having interests in the property may well be of a dishonest disposition. I therefore have no doubt that there is jurisdiction to make an order for disclosure in the nature of that made in this case.

4.11 Although *Re O* related to restraint orders made under the CJA it was assumed that the principle applied equally to orders made under the DTA and its predecessor, the Drug Trafficking Offences Act 1986 particularly, as Lord Donaldson commented in his judgment, that:

> The jurisdiction to make restraint orders under the Drug Trafficking Offences Act 1986 is mirrored by that under the Criminal Justice Act 1988 and a decision in relation to one Act will apply equally to the other.

4.12 An attempt was made, however, in *Re T (Restraint Order: Disclosure of Assets)* [1992] 1 WLR 949, to argue that *Re O* had no application in drug trafficking cases. In that case a restraint order under the 1986 Act had been made that contained a disclosure provision in precisely the same terms as that considered by the Court of Appeal in *Re O*. The defendant made an application to Schiemann J for the disclosure provision to be removed from the order. The learned judge refused the application, ruling that he could find no good reason for distinguishing between disclosure provisions included in restraint orders made under the 1986 Act from those in orders made under the CJA.

4.13 The defendant appealed to the Court of Appeal contending that notwithstanding the remarks of Lord Donaldson in *Re O*, given the material differences between the confiscations regimes in the two Acts, the decision did not apply in drug trafficking cases. The Court of Appeal dismissed the appeal, ruling that any differences there may be between the two Acts were of limited substance. Parker LJ said of Lord Donaldson's observations in *Re O*:

> It is in my view clear from the passage from Lord Donaldson's judgment immediately following the passage which I have quoted, that his reference to a "mirror image" related only to the sections in the two Acts dealing with jurisdiction of the High Court to make restraint and charging orders. Those sections are not identical but I can detect no difference in substance.

4.14 Concluding his judgment, Parker LJ said:

> The context of the restraint order provisions of the two Acts is certainly different, but the difference is such that it is in my judgment clearer under the Act of 1986 than under the Act of 1988 that the jurisdiction to make a disclosure order in support of a restraint order exists.

(2) The problem of self incrimination

4.15 There is a real risk that by requiring a defendant to disclose his assets he would be in danger of incriminating himself both in relation to the offence with which he has been charged and to other offences as well. Full compliance with a disclosure order might, eg result in the defendant admitting money laundering offences. The courts have from the outset been vigilant to protect the defendant's privilege against self incrimination by insisting that the prosecutor may not make any use of the disclosure statement during any criminal trial. In *Re A Defendant* The Times, 7 April 1987, Webster J ruled that the disclosure order was only to take effect upon the prosecutor giving an undertaking:

> not to use any of the information obtained as a result of compliance with the order for any purpose in or in connection with any criminal proceedings taken or contemplated against the defendant or for any purpose other than a purpose arising under the Drug Trafficking Offences Act, 1986.

4.16 The Court of Appeal made it clear in *Re O* [1991] 1 All ER 330 that the CJA could not be construed in such a way as to abrogate the privilege against self incrimination. The Court ruled, however, that the privilege was capable of protection by the imposition of conditions upon the use to which information provided in disclosure statements may be put. The Court considered the practice that had developed following *Re A Defendant* and Lord Donaldson MR said:

> We were told that in another case the CPS were required to give an undertaking limiting the class of person to whom the disclosed information could be given and the purposes for which

C. Disclosure Orders

it could be used. I would not wish to be taken to criticise such an approach, but consider it preferable to impose a condition in the order rather than seek an undertaking.

The Court suggested that the condition should be in the following terms: **4.17**

> No disclosure made in compliance with this order shall be used as evidence in the prosecution of an offence alleged to have been committed by the person required to make that disclosure or by any spouse of that person.

In *Re T (Restraint Order: Disclosure of Assets)* [1992] 1 WLR 949 the defendant contended **4.18** that this condition was insufficient to protect his privilege against self-incrimination in a drug trafficking case. It was contended that, by complying with the disclosure order, the defendant would suffer an enhanced penalty by increasing the size of the confiscation order that would be made against him and, in consequence, render him liable to serve a longer term of imprisonment than would otherwise be the case in the event of any default in payment. The Court of Appeal rejected this argument ruling that the purpose of the legislation is to compel the defendant to make reparation in respect of his unjust enrichment from his criminal activities and that by making such reparation he did not incur punishment. There was thus no question of self incrimination. Leggatt LJ summarised the position thus:

> Compliance with the order to swear an affidavit does not expose the defendant to any such risk: the condition to which the order is subject precludes the risk of further prosecution on that account; a confiscation order is different in nature from forfeiture: and even if it were right to regard a confiscation order as penal in character, disclosure on affidavit does not render the defendant liable to the imposition of a form of order to which he would not otherwise be subject.

> Disclosure of assets in conjunction with the statutory assumptions merely facilitates assessment of the amount to be recovered in the defendant's case, once it has been determined that he has benefited from drug trafficking, and does not in my view amount to self incrimination. Confiscation applies to the value of the defendant's proceeds of drug trafficking, whereas forfeiture extends to things used for the commission of crime and is therefore punitive. It is true that disclosure of assets exposes the defendant to the risk of a confiscation order greater in amount than could be made in the absence of disclosure. But it is not self incriminating because a person does not by making reparation incur punishment.

In *R v Martin and White* (1998) 2 Cr App R 385 the Court of Appeal had to consider a **4.19** complaint by a defendant that the condition approved in *Re O* had been breached by the prosecutor during the course of his trial. Prosecuting Counsel, who had been supplied with a copy of the disclosure affidavit by those instructing him, had cross-examined the defendant on inconsistencies between the evidence he gave on oath to the jury and the contents of the affidavit. The defendant contended that this represented a breach of the condition and, furthermore, there should be a species of 'Chinese Wall' preventing the affidavit coming into the possession of those having the conduct of the prosecution until such time as the defendant was convicted.

The Court of Appeal ruled that there had been no such breach by the prosecutor because **4.20** the affidavit had not been adduced as evidence in the prosecution of an offence, but merely in cross-examination as to credit. Rose LJ added that it would be an 'affront to common sense' if the defendant could make two wholly contradictory statements on oath and avoid being challenged in any way as to the inconsistency. Further, the Court rejected the suggestion that the disclosure affidavit should have been withheld from those having the conduct of the prosecution until after conviction, Rose LJ saying:

> We cannot accede to the submission that such an affidavit should remain detached from those engaged in prosecution. To attempt to debar the prosecution from sight of such an affidavit would be both impracticable and wrong, not least because the conduct of the prosecutor is or should be under the immediate supervision of the court. We are not prepared to contemplate the prosecution being kept in ignorance of any such affidavit until a confiscation order is sought.

4.21 It is clear, however, that the Court was troubled by the use to which the affidavit had been put and the circumstances in which it was used without prior reference to the judge. Rose LJ emphasised that:

> We cannot envisage circumstances in which any such affidavit could become admissible in evidence during a criminal trial at the behest of the Crown, either in the course of the prosecution or, as was thought to have happened here, by being purportedly proved by way of cross-examination of the accused. We would hope and expect that, in future cases, the Crown and the court will be alert to the limitations subject to which an order for disclosure by affidavit is made.

4.22 The Court also held that prosecuting counsel should not rely on the disclosure statement without first seeking the leave of the judge. Rose LJ said:

> Such use of the affidavit should be subject to safeguards aimed at reconciling the proviso with the immediate needs of the Crown. In our judgment, prosecuting counsel should seek prior directions from the judge as to the precise use which can be made of the affidavit. This will alert the judge and defence counsel to the situation and enable the judge to maintain an oversight that reconciles use of the affidavit with the proviso.

4.23 The wording of the condition as approved in *Re O* has subsequently been reviewed by the High Court in the light of the incorporation of the European Convention on Human Rights into English law. In *Re C (Restraint Order: Disclosure)* (4 September 2000) the prosecutor sought an order of committal against the defendant for failing to comply fully with disclosure provisions in a DTA restraint order. In response, counsel for the defendant expressed concern that compliance with the disclosure order might put those investigating the criminal case on the track of some evidence they would otherwise have been unaware of which might prove gravely prejudicial to the defendant. Collins J ruled that this submission had considerable force and that any such use of the disclosure statement would constitute a breach of the defendant's right to a fair trial under Article 6 of the Convention, given the ruling of the European Court of Human Rights in *Saunders v UK* [1996] 23 EHRR 313. The learned judge also expressed doubt as to whether the decision in *Martin and White*, which was made prior to the Convention being incorporated in English law, was consistent with Article 6. In delivering judgment, Collins J said:

> It does not matter in what form the information is used: whether as evidence, whether because it enables other evidence to be obtained which could not otherwise have been discovered or whether it is used merely as a weapon in cross-examination of the defendant. Whatever use in the criminal trial is prima facie a breach, as it seems to me, of Article 6.

4.24 Collins J ruled that the wording of the condition should be tightened to make it plain that the information disclosed should not be used against the defendant in the course of the

C. Disclosure Orders

criminal proceedings against him. The revised wording of the condition approved by the judge is in the following terms:

> Subject to any further order of the Court pursuant to CPR Part 31.22 any disclosure made or information given in compliance with this order shall only be used for the purpose of these proceedings or in the event that the defendant is convicted for the purpose of any confiscation hearing that may take place and thereafter in the event that a confiscation order is made for the purposes of enforcement of that order including any receivership proceedings. There shall be no disclosure of any material disclosed in compliance with this Order to any co-defendant in criminal proceedings. Nothing in this paragraph shall make inadmissible any disclosure made by the defendant in any proceedings for perjury to which any such disclosure made may relate.

4.25 This revised wording has now been adopted by all prosecuting authorities and appears in all restraint orders containing a disclosure provision. Collins J recognised that there may be circumstances in which the interests of justice dictate that the terms of a disclosure statement should be disclosed to a co-defendant. It may be, for example, that the contents of a disclosure statement by defendant A exonerate or at the very least assist the defence of defendant B. He emphasised, however, that the High Court must retain ultimate control over the use to which the disclosed information is put and that in circumstances such as these an application should be made to the Court for directions as to how, if at all, the disclosed information might be revealed to the co-accused.

It should be noted that the condition as revised by the ruling of Collins J in *Re C* does not preclude the use of the disclosure statement in any confiscation hearing that may take place after the defendant has been convicted. In *Re E and Re H* (24 May 2001) an application by the defendants for an order preventing the prosecutor relying on the disclosure statement at any confiscation order that might follow subsequent to conviction was robustly rejected by the High Court. In delivering his judgment Henriques J observed:

> The absurd consequence of Counsel's submission is that where a prosecuting authority are aware of assets disclosed and verified they would not be able to rely on that information in the confiscation proceedings. Nothing could be more absurd. If the defendant gave different information or no information when it was sought under section 73(A) known assets would have to be returned. Counsel suggests that it is a necessary consequence of Parliament not clearly revoking the privilege against self incrimination. He suggests, in any event, that individuals might themselves obtain Mareva injunctions. Such a course is fanciful and it would dismember a now sophisticated and highly developed procedure for recovering assets from criminals and returning them to their rightful source. The absurdity of the consequence exposes the fallacy of the argument which unhappily falls at the first hurdle of binding precedent.

4.26 Dyson LJ took a similar line in refusing the defendant leave to appeal against the decision of Henriques J. In *Customs and Excise Commissioners v El Heri* [2001] EWCA Civ 1782 the learned judge said:

> Counsel submits that unless the prohibition on the use of disclosed material is extended to the confiscation proceedings, then there will be a significant erosion of the privilege against self incrimination, an erosion for which there is no sufficiently clear statutory authority. I am not persuaded that the confiscation proceedings attract the privilege against self incrimination. I accept that the outcome of confiscation proceedings may properly be described as a penalty and may also be described as part of the sentencing process, since they

arise in criminal proceedings. But no authority has been cited to me which shows that the privilege against self incrimination extended to proceedings which take place following a conviction. Be that as it may, the authorities to which I have referred clearly point to the conclusion that the judge was right in this case. I do not accept that the law has been materially changed in this regard by Article 6 of the European Convention on Human Rights.

4.27 Disclosure orders are also subject to the usual rule of civil procedure to the effect that they may not be used for any ancillary or collateral purpose. In *Re R* (21 October 1992) a third party creditor of a defendant subject to a CJA restraint order had obtained an ex parte order from the Practice Master giving them leave to inspect the court file and copy the defendant's disclosure affidavit for the purpose of determining what assets he might have available for satisfying any judgment that might be made against him. The prosecutor, fearing that the use of disclosure affidavits for such purposes may cause defendants to be less than frank as to the extent of their assets, appealed against the order to a High Court Judge. In allowing the appeal, Macpherson J said:

> As a matter of general principle, it seems to me in the highest degree undesirable that these affidavits should go to anybody other than the court and the parties involved. The reasons for that are obvious. They may not be used in other criminal proceedings. There will be reticence, if not downright secretion of facts by individuals, if they feel that these affidavits may go elsewhere. In ordinary circumstances—this appears to be such a case—these affidavits should be kept locked in the Central Office and not disclosed to anyone.

4.28 Macpherson J also criticised the practice of seeking the order for inspection on an ex parte basis. He directed that henceforth if, for some exceptional reason, a third party wishes to seek inspection of the court file for such purposes, the application should be made on notice to the prosecutor and the defendant.

(3) Form of disclosure orders

4.29 A typical disclosure order appears at paras 11 and 12 of the draft restraint order at Appendix 1. It will be noted that the order imposes two distinct obligations on the defendant: firstly, to give initial disclosure in writing within 72 hours of the order being served and, secondly, within 14 days thereafter to serve a witness statement on the prosecutor, supported by a statement of truth, verifying the information provided in the initial disclosure. In *Re E and Re H* (24 May 2001) the defendant disputed the necessity for his disclosure statement to be supported by a statement of truth. In rejecting this submission Henriques J said:

> It is particularly appropriate in a case involving very large sums of money such as this that a disclosure of assets should be accompanied by a statement of truth. With prosecution for contempt as the only sanction and a two year maximum sentence discounted by way of good character, pleas and parole, many a fraudster would not be deterred from a partial or inaccurate disclosure of assets.

(4) Disclosure and third parties

4.30 It has been seen that restraint orders can bind third parties, not charged with any offence, who may be in control or possession of or who have an interest in any realisable property. In *Re D* The Times, 26 January 1995 the High Court held that the power to order disclosure extended to such third parties. The father of the defendant had been restrained from

C. Disclosure Orders

dealing with a number of bank accounts and was required to swear an affidavit disclosing details of transactions through accounts held in his name. Turner J dismissed the father's application to delete the disclosure order in so far as it affected him, ruling that the court did have jurisdiction to compel a third party to make disclosure. The learned judge held that as the purpose of requiring disclosure was to police compliance with the restraint order and that third parties could be restrained from dealing with realisable property, it followed that the inherent jurisdiction of the court to order disclosure applied equally to third parties as it did to the defendant.

(5) Disclosure cannot be ordered against the prosecutor

4.31 The defendant does not have the right to seek disclosure of information or documentation held by the prosecutor for the purpose of assisting him to comply with these disclosure obligations under the order. In *Re S and W* (QBD 7 February 2000) the defendants, who were both in custody, sought orders requiring the prosecutor to disclose documents they claimed were in his possession and which they required to assist in complying with the disclosure provisions in DTA restraint orders made against them. Tucker J dismissed the application saying:

> The point taken on behalf of Her Majesty's Customs and Excise is that if these defendants were aware of the information which Customs and Excise had obtained, they might have been tempted to tailor their own information to that which they were aware that Customs and Excise already had. I see the force in that submission. I rather doubt whether the court has the power, in any event, to order disclosure on the part of Her Majesty's Customs and Excise. Even if I had that power, I would not be minded in my discretion to exercise it.
>
> These orders are, and are intended to be, Draconian in their provisions. They are aimed at restricting the use by the defendants of ill-gotten gains obtained by them by allegedly criminal activities. The terms of the order are clear. The accounts may be numerous and it may be expensive for the defendants to obtain the information from their banks but the obligation is, nevertheless, laid on the defendants to do so. I am not going to relieve that obligation by making any order against Her Majesty's Customs and Excise; therefore, I decline to do so. It is for the defendants to obtain the information.

4.32 The judge did, however, make it plain that he had some sympathy with the defendants' position and, without making any order, invited the prosecutor to assist in so far as he felt able to do so. While the defendant must clearly use his best endeavours to provide full and complete disclosure, it is unlikely that minor discrepancies in a disclosure statement by a defendant who has genuinely attempted to give full disclosure would result in contempt proceedings being taken by the prosecutor.

(6) Advising the defendant or third party required to disclose

4.33 The practitioner's task in advising a client, whether he be a defendant or an affected third party, who is required under a restraint order to make disclosure, is an important and complex one. Serious consequences for the client may flow from a failure to give full and complete disclosure of his assets, whereas too much disclosure may cause unnecessary prejudice to the client at a later stage in the proceedings. Although each case must be considered on its own particular facts, we endeavour in this section to offer practical guidance to the practitioner faced with this important task.

4.34 The disclosure order usually requires compliance within a relatively short timescale: most orders require initial disclosure within 72 hours and full disclosure in a statement verified by a statement of truth within 14 or 21 days thereafter. The practitioner needs firstly to consider whether it will be physically possible for the client to comply within those time frames. There may be many legitimate reasons why compliance will not be possible: for example the client may be remanded in custody at a prison some distance from his solicitor's office and a legal visit may take some time to arrange. If it is not going to prove possible to comply with the time limits imposed by the order, the prosecutor should be approached as a matter of urgency and be asked to consent to the order being varied to extend the time for compliance. It is unlikely that the prosecutor will refuse provided a proper reason is advanced as to why the extension is necessary. However, given that the prosecutor requires the disclosure information to police the order effectively, a lengthy or open ended extension will probably not be acceptable and any extension of time agreed is likely to be expressed in terms of days rather than weeks or months. If the prosecutor will not consent, an application should be made to the court for an extension of time. The matter should not be left in abeyance, because the prosecutor may well institute contempt proceedings in the absence of proper compliance with the order or an application to court for further time to comply.

4.35 As far as initial disclosure is concerned, the client should be asked to list all his assets giving as much detail as possible. As initial disclosure has to be given within 72 hours, the prosecutor will not expect it to be full and comprehensive provided the defendant has identified all assets in which he has an interest to the best of his ability. If time permits, the list should be typed and the client invited to check it carefully and sign it before it is sent to the prosecutor. A handwritten list will suffice if there is insufficient time to provide the prosecutor with a typed version within the deadline.

4.36 Once the initial disclosure has been provided, work should begin on the preparation of the witness statement which will need to be served usually 14 days thereafter. Great care needs to be taken in the preparation of the statement because the order requires it to be verified by a statement of truth and potentially serious consequences will flow from any material inaccuracy: see Chapter 6, para 6.03.

4.37 When taking instructions from the client as to the contents of the disclosure statement, the practitioner should advise him very carefully of the potential consequences of any material inaccuracy. This includes not only the institution of proceedings for contempt of court, but the risk of serious damage to the defendant's credibility at any confiscation hearing if he has been shown to be untruthful in his disclosure statement. Further, the client should not assume that the full extent of the prosecutor's knowledge of a defendant's assets is set out in his witness statement in support of the restraint application. The prosecutor's investigations will inevitably continue right up until a confiscation hearing and those investigations may well lead to the identification of further assets. The client would therefore be well advised to disclose all of his assets at the outset, whether the prosecutor appears to be aware of them or not, in order to avoid any risk of contempt proceedings or his being embarrassed at the confiscation hearing.

4.38 The client should be taken through every subparagraph of the disclosure order and asked to set out all the assets he has caught by each provision. If he cannot remember the precise details, the relevant financial institution should be approached for confirmation of the position: banks may be contacted, for example, to advise as to account numbers and the balances outstanding on all the client's accounts. The restraint order only precludes the client dealing in his assets and does not prevent him making contact with the financial institutions concerned to enquire as to the present balance on his accounts. The prosecutor may also be approached for assistance if he has taken up documentation relating to the client's assets on his arrest, although the prosecutor may seek to rely on *Re S and W* (QBD 7 February 2000) as authority for the proposition that he is not required to provide copies of any documentation he may have relating to the client's affairs for the purpose of assisting him in complying with disclosure obligations.

4.39 Once the client has provided all the required information, work should commence on drafting the witness statement. It is submitted that the proper approach is to address each subparagraph of the disclosure order in turn, in the order in which they appear in the restraint order identifying each and every asset required to be disclosed. Once the draft has been completed and typed, the client should check it and the effect of his signing the statement of truth fully explained. If he is satisfied it sets out fully all the assets in which he has an interest, he should sign the statement of truth and it should be served on the prosecutor.

4.40 Once the disclosure statement has been served, the defendant's legal representatives should be vigilant in ensuring that it is not abused by the prosecutor and put to any improper use. The legal representative's suspicions should be aroused if, within a short time of a disclosure statement being made, the prosecutor serves further evidence in the criminal proceedings that appears to mirror facts disclosed by the defendant. In such circumstances, an enquiry of the prosecutor as to how the new evidence would be justified and, if it has been obtained perfectly legitimately and quite independently of the disclosure statement, the prosecutor should be able to demonstrate this through a proper audit trail. As Collins J said in *Re C (Restraint Order: Disclosure)* (4 September 2000):

> I am not prepared to assume that any prosecuting authority is going deliberately to fail to comply with the requirements and surreptitiously obtain evidence based on the material disclosed as a result of the order. I cannot approach my task, nor could any court, on that assumption. If there is a misuse, if there is an attempt to produce and rely on material obtained as a result of disclosure it would, I would have thought, normally be difficult to conceal that exercise because of the requirements of prior disclosure and because of the need for there to be a prima facie case before the High Court could be persuaded to make a restraint order.
>
> A restraint order is based upon an affidavit by the applicant which is itself based upon information given by the officer in the case. If further information suddenly came to light after disclosure, or something was alleged to come to light, and produced further material after disclosure it would indeed be suspicious. I do not doubt that the trial judge who could see among other things the affidavit of the officer which obtained the restraint order would be able to ascertain whether there had been bad faith, which is what it would amount to on the part of the prosecution. That, as I say, is not something I should take into account in my judgment in deciding whether the order in a particular form should or should not be made.

4.41 If the trial judge finds that there has been 'bad faith' on the part of the prosecutor, he has ample powers, it is submitted, to exclude any evidence obtained in consequence under s 78 of the Police and Criminal Evidence Act, 1984.

D. Repatriation of Assets

4.42 The legislation applies to realisable property of the defendant both within and without the jurisdiction of the court: see s 62(2) of the DTA, s 102(3) of the CJA and s 84(1) of POCA. As drug trafficking offences and organised crime frequently occur across international frontiers, it is by no means uncommon for a defendant arrested in England to have assets in overseas jurisdictions. Indeed, as money laundering operations have become more sophisticated and funds can be transferred from country to country more or less instantaneously by means of electronic transfer, those involved in criminal activity can invest the proceeds of their activities overseas with ease in an attempt to conceal them well away from the clutches of UK law enforcement agencies.

4.43 As we shall see in Chapter 25, international cooperation between countries can often facilitate the restraint and confiscation of assets in foreign jurisdictions in support of criminal proceedings brought in the UK. In CJA cases, however, the number of countries willing to cooperate in this way is comparatively small and, even in relation to those countries who are able to assist, the procedure for obtaining restraint orders overseas is often long and drawn out, giving the defendant ample opportunity to dissipate his assets. In such circumstances, the prosecutor may apply to the High Court for a repatriation order requiring the defendant to bring the asset in question within the jurisdiction of the court pending the determination of the proceedings.

(1) Jurisdiction to make repatriation orders

4.44 As with disclosure orders, the court's power to make repatriation orders stems from its inherent jurisdiction. The Court of Appeal first held that it had power to order the repatriation of assets when exercising its jurisdiction to make freezing orders in civil proceedings. In *Derby v Weldon (No 6)* [1990] 3 All ER 263 the Court of Appeal held that as the court's power to grant freezing orders depended not on its territorial jurisdiction but on its unlimited jurisdiction *in personam* against any person properly made a party to proceedings before it, the court had power to order the repatriation of assets held overseas. Dillon LJ, with whom the other members of the court agreed, said:

> I see no reason why that should not extend, in principle and in an appropriate case, to ordering the transfer of assets to a jurisdiction in which the order of the English court after the trial of the action will be recognised from a jurisdiction in which that order will not be recognised and the issue would have to be relitigated if, which may not be entirely the present case, the only connection of the latter jurisdiction with the matters in issue in the proceedings is that monies have been placed in that jurisdiction in order to make them proof against the enforcement, without a full retrial in the foreign court, of any judgment which may be granted to the plaintiffs by the English court in this action or indeed, if the only connection with the latter jurisdiction is financial, as a matter of controlling investments.

4.45 In *Re WJT* (QBD (Admin) 5 October 1992) the High Court considered the jurisdiction to make a repatriation order in support of a restraint order made under the CJA. The defendant had been charged with VAT fraud offences from which it was alleged he had benefited

D. Repatriation of Assets

to the extent of some £250,000. A restraint order was obtained after which it was discovered that a sum of £187,000 had been taken from an account in the defendant's name by his sister acting on his authority. May J made an order requiring the repatriation of this money to a bank account within the jurisdiction of the court. The defendant challenged the court's power to make this order, submitting that the Court should not take upon itself a jurisdiction which Parliament had not expressly given it.

4.46 Brooke J rejected this argument ruling that the court had an inherent jurisdiction to require the repatriation of assets held overseas. He said:

> In my judgment, in principle, the jurisdiction exists if the court considers it just and convenient to grant an injunction of the type to which the Court of Appeal referred in *Derby v Weldon (No. 6)* in aid of a restraint order made under section 77 of the Act. We are living in a world where money can be transferred very rapidly from one jurisdiction to another. On the face of it, it would be surprising if this court was powerless to make orders *in personam* against a defendant which had the effect of making safe assets and preventing them from being dissipated prior to the outcome of the criminal proceedings merely because the assets were outside the jurisdiction at the time the original restraint order was made. All I am concerned about is an application to make an order *in personam* against the defendant and, in my judgment, on an analogy with the judgment of the Court of Appeal in *Re O*, in order to achieve the purposes of Parliament in Part VI of the Criminal Justice Act 1988 and to render effective a restraint order made under section 77 of the Act, the court has the power to grant an injunction of the type which the Customs and Excise sought in this case. Accordingly, as a matter of principle, I am satisfied, as I have been told other judges sitting in chambers exercising jurisdiction under Part VI of the Criminal Justice Act 1988 have also been satisfied, that I have jurisdiction to make the type of order which May J made in this case.

4.47 Although WJT was given leave to appeal, the appeal was not pursued and it was not until the case of *DPP v Scarlett* [2000] 1 WLR 515 that the jurisdiction to make repatriation orders in support of restraint orders was considered by the Court of Appeal. The Court of Appeal had no hesitation in confirming that the jurisdiction to make such orders in restraint cases did indeed exist. Beldam LJ (with whom Roch and Judge LJJ agreed) said:

> If a power to order full disclosure of assets on affidavit is inherent in a restraint order, the order should also include the power to order the return of those assets within the jurisdiction. Both powers are essential to the purpose of the restraint order and to the realisation of those assets which is the purpose of the express statutory power given by Parliament. For these reasons I would hold that the court does have inherent power to make an order requiring a defendant to repatriate personal assets as part of its inherent power to enforce restraint orders.

4.48 The power to order repatriation is, of course, a discretionary one and it does not follow that the court will order it in every case where assets are located overseas. In *Re WJT*, by way of example, having satisfied himself that he had jurisdiction to make the repatriation order, Brooke J went on to discharge it on the basis that the defendant had sufficient assets within the jurisdiction to satisfy a confiscation order in the amount by which he was alleged to have benefited from criminal conduct. Further, the court will not make an order with which it is impossible for the defendant to comply given the possible sanctions available if the defendant breaches the order. The court will therefore need to satisfy itself that the defendant is actually capable of repatriating the asset to the jurisdiction before making an order.

Finally, the court may well require an explanation as to why it is not possible to take action in the country in which the asset is located pursuant to any bilateral agreement that might exist with the jurisdiction. There may be many reasons why such action would prove impractical: the country in question may not be prepared to assist in CJA cases, or the necessity to prevent threatened dissipation may require urgent action to be taken.

(2) Form of repatriation order

4.49 The draft restraint order in Appendix 1 incorporates repatriation provisions at para 13. The usual form of order is to require the asset to be brought within the jurisdiction within 21 days and for the prosecutor to be informed of its location within seven days thereafter. If the asset is in the form of money, the order will require it to be deposited in an interest-bearing account and for the prosecutor to be notified of its location within the same period on its arrival. As with disclosure orders, if compliance within the periods stipulated in the order is for any reason impossible, the prosecutor must be approached with a view to an extension of time being agreed to and, in default of agreement, an application to court must be made.

5

APPLICATIONS TO VARY OR DISCHARGE RESTRAINT ORDERS MADE UNDER THE DTA AND CJA

A. Introduction	5.01	(3) Companies and other business entities	5.24
B. Applications for the Discharge of the Order	5.02	(4) Burden of proof	5.25
(1) On the conclusion of proceedings	5.03	D. The Principles on which the Court Acts: The 'Legislative Steer'	5.27
(2) Procedural irregularities by the prosecutor	5.04	E. The Source of Payment of Legal Fees and General Living Expenses	5.47
(3) Failure to give full and frank disclosure	5.07	(1) Assets not legitimately acquired	5.48
C. Applications to Vary the Restraint Order	5.09	(2) Assets that are prosecution exhibits	5.49
(1) Legal expenses	5.10	F. Release of Funds After a Confiscation Order has been Made	5.52
(2) General living expenses	5.20		

A. Introduction

By sc115.5 (1), any person or body upon whom a restraint order is served or who is notified of the order may make application to the court for the same to be varied or discharged. Further, the order itself will invariably give permission to all parties affected by it to apply for its discharge or variation on giving two clear days notice in writing to the court and the prosecutor. Although it is possible to appeal against the making of a restraint order to the Court of Appeal, a party aggrieved by the order should always apply for the order to be discharged before embarking on an appeal: see *Booker McConnell v Plasgow* [1985] RPC 425. In this chapter we consider the grounds on which applications for the variation or discharge of orders might be made by prosecutors, defendants and affected third parties under the DTA and CJA. The position under POCA is considered in Chapter 8.

5.01

B. Applications for the Discharge of the Order

Cases in which it is appropriate to apply for the discharge of the entire order will, in practice, be comparatively rare. Further, even where an application for the discharge of an order is appropriate, it may not, in the long term, achieve the desired result for the defendant. If, eg an order is discharged because of some procedural irregularity by the prosecutor it is

5.02

always open to him to remedy the defect and apply to the court for a new order. In many cases, the most effective way of mitigating the harsher effects of a restraint order will be to apply for it to be varied by, for example releasing further funds to meet general living expenses. Nonetheless, there will be circumstances in which an application to discharge the order may be appropriate and these are considered below.

(1) On the conclusion of proceedings

5.03 Restraint and charging orders must be discharged when proceedings have concluded: see s 26(5)(b) of the DTA and s 77(6)(b) of the CJA in relation to restraint orders, and s 27(7) of the DTA and s 78(7) of the CJA in relation to charging orders. The meaning of 'proceedings have concluded' is considered in Chapter 2, paras 2.12 and 2.27 above. A charging order must also be discharged if the amount secured by the order is paid into court: see s 27(7)(b)(ii) of the DTA and s 78(7)(b)(ii) of the CJA.

(2) Procedural irregularities by the prosecutor

5.04 A procedural irregularity by the prosecutor in obtaining the restraint order may be a sufficient basis to seek its discharge although, as indicated above, this could prove a short lived victory for the defendant, because it is always open to the prosecutor to remedy the defect and apply for a new order. If the irregularity is of a minor or technical nature that can be easily remedied, the defendant and any affected third party would be well advised to take no point in relation to it as litigating the matter would prove costly and may serve no useful purpose.

5.05 If, however, the irregularity is a serious one an application to discharge the order may well be appropriate, particularly if it is not easily capable of remedy. A classic example of this is where the prosecutor has failed to establish there is any real risk of assets being dissipated. In *Re AJ and DJ* (9 December 1992) there had been a delay in excess of two years between the defendants being charged and an application for a restraint order being made, during which time no attempt had been made by the defendants to dispose of realisable assets other than by expending reasonable sums on normal living expenses. In these circumstances, the Court of Appeal found there was no evidence to establish there was a real risk of assets being dissipated and the decision of the judge to discharge the order was upheld. If there has been a lengthy delay by the prosecutor in applying for a restraint order, the witness statement in support should provide a detailed explanation as to why it is believed assets will be dissipated in the absence of a restraint order. It does not follow from the fact that there has been a delay that the prosecutor is not entitled to seek a restraint order and it may be that he can justify his actions. For example, at the time a defendant is charged there may be no evidence to show a real risk of dissipation, but some time later as his trial approaches he may start removing large sums of money from a bank account or put properties on the market. In these circumstances his actions would establish a real risk of assets being dissipated and the making of a restraint order may well be appropriate. But without an explanation for a lengthy delay in the prosecutor's witness statement in support of an application for a restraint order, an application to discharge the order may well be justified on the basis of insufficient evidence to establish a risk of dissipation.

C. Applications to Vary the Restraint Order

5.06 A discharge application may also be made when the statutory criteria that have to exist for a restraint order to be granted have not been established. Applications for the discharge of restraint orders on this basis should be confined to cases where there is no evidence at all to show that one or more of the statutory criteria exist. The High Court will not attempt to usurp the functions of the Crown Court by assessing the strengths or weaknesses of the criminal case—if the statutory criteria have been made out it is unlikely the court will consider discharging an order in the absence of evidence that the prosecutor has being guilty of some serious procedural irregularity.

(3) Failure to give full and frank disclosure

5.07 Applications for restraint orders made without notice to the defendant are subject to the usual rule of civil procedure that the applicant for such relief must give full and frank disclosure of all material facts. The defendant has neither the right nor the opportunity to be present or represented when the application is made and the procedure therefore constitutes an exception to the principle of natural justice that both sides should be heard before the court makes an order. In consequence, the prosecutor is required to give full and frank disclosure of all material facts. This obligation requires him to disclose any weaknesses in his case of which he is aware, any information that might be favourable to the defendant, and any innocent explanation that he may have advanced when being interviewed. The prosecutor's duties in this regard are considered in more detail in Chapter 7 below, and it will be seen that a serious failure by the prosecutor to comply with his duties of full and frank disclosure may result in the order being discharged. Some caution does, however, need to be exercised in considering whether an application to discharge the order should be made on this basis because it is always open to the prosecutor to apply for a further order on the basis of an amended witness statement that remedies any previous deficiencies in his case.

5.08 Further, in *Jennings v CPS* [2005] 4 All ER 391 the Court of Appeal held that the public interest in the restraint and confiscation of the proceeds of crime dictated that the court should not be too ready to discharge a restraint order where there has been a failure of give full and frank disclosure. Lloyd LJ noted:

> The fact that the Crown acts in the public interest does, in my view, militate against the sanction of discharging an order if, after consideration of all the evidence, the court thinks that an order is appropriate. That is not to say that there could never be a case where the Crown's failure might be so appalling that the ultimate sanction of discharge would be justified.

C. Applications to Vary the Restraint Order

5.09 In the majority of cases the most appropriate means of seeking to mitigate the harsher effects of a restraint order is to apply for it to be varied in some respect. Applications to vary restraint orders are most commonly made to release funds to pay legal fees and to increase the amount payable to the defendant and his dependants by way of general living expenses.

(1) Legal expenses

5.10 The defendant is entitled to have funds released to meet his legal expenses incurred in defending both the restraint proceedings and the criminal proceedings with which they are closely associated and also to fund any appeal: see *Customs and Excise Commissioners v Norris* [1991] 2 All ER 395 and para 4 of the Practice Direction supplementing sc 115. Most restraint orders will already have made provision for funds to be released for such purposes: the example restraint order appended to the Practice Direction makes such provision at para 12(1) and (4). If the order does not make such provision, an application for a variation may be appropriate.

5.11 The order will normally provide for a specific sum (normally £750) to be released to the defendant to meet his immediate needs. This is intended to cover initial advice on the effect of the order and assistance in complying with any mandatory obligations it imposes such as disclosure and repatriation requirements. Further, unless there is evidence they have adequate separate means, the order should contain similar provisions releasing funds for affected third parties (eg the defendant's spouse) to obtain legal advice: see *Re G* (30 July 2001) and the Practice Direction supplementing sc115.

5.12 The order will then make provision for the release of further funds to meet legal expenses actually, reasonably, and properly incurred in defending the High Court proceedings and the criminal proceedings with which they are associated. As a condition precedent to funds being released for such purposes, the order will provide that the following details must be provided to the prosecutor:

(a) the source of the fund to be used to meet the costs;
(b) the general nature of the costs incurred;
(c) the time spent and the grade of fee earners involved; and
(d) the hourly rate charged by each grade of fee earner.

5.13 The order also makes provision for the resolution of any dispute between the parties as to the amount sought by providing that in the event of the prosecutor considering that the amount claimed has not been actually, reasonably, and properly incurred the claim shall be subject to detailed assessment by a costs judge with 65 per cent of the amount claimed being paid in the interim. The assessment will be on the indemnity basis in accordance with CPR Part 48.8 but without the provisions of CPR Part 48.8(2) applying.

5.14 The authority for the inclusion of this provision is the decision of the High Court in *Re L* The Times, 10 July 1996. In that case, the prosecutor, while not disputing the defendant's right to have restrained funds released to meet his legal fees, sought the imposition of conditions to prevent any extravagant expenditure. Latham J ruled that given the DTA and CJA identify a clear public interest in ensuring that the defendant's assets should be secured in so far as is reasonable, the imposition of some safeguards to prevent extravagant expenditure was justified. The judge decided that the balance between allowing reasonable sums to be released by way of legal fees against the necessity to preserve assets to make them available to meet any confiscation order could be best achieved by directing that in default of agreement with the prosecutor the costs be assessed on the indemnity basis, but without the presumptions in CPR Part 48.8(2) applying. He rejected the prosecutor's contention that assessment should be on the standard basis as:

> It seems to me it gives inadequate expression to the defendant's right to use the funds which are prima facie his for the purpose of defending himself. In instructing his solicitor he should

be entitled, subject to proper safeguards against extravagance, to expect that his solicitor would be remunerated on a solicitor and own client basis, and not as constrained by a process of taxation based upon the protection of a losing litigant.

5.15 The judge went on to decide that where the claim was disputed by the prosecutor, the full amount claimed should not be released from the restrained fund pending determination of the assessment proceedings and upheld the prosecutor's submission that only 65 per cent of the amount claimed should be paid at that stage. He said:

> It seems to me to be unsatisfactory for there to be payment out of a protected fund of sums which might thereafter have to be recovered. It follows that the most satisfactory solution is to provide for retention of such amount as will obviate so far as is fair to both interests, the risk of that happening. In the circumstances of the present case, bearing in mind the amounts which have been mentioned as counsel's fees, which may well need close scrutiny on taxation, I consider that the suggested retention of 35% is entirely appropriate.

5.16 Further, and in contrast to the position in relation to freezing orders, where a defendant or affected third party seeks the release of funds to meet legal expenses in connection with restraint or management receivership proceedings, the expenditure incurred must be proportionate having regard to all the circumstances. Thus, so long as the party concerned has access to proper legal advice, he may not necessarily be entitled to call on the services of his preferred solicitors if the expense incurred would be disproportionate. In *Re D* [2006] EWHC Admin 254 a company, referred to as X Limited, obtained an order authorising the release of up to £35,000 to instruct a firm of solicitors based in the City of London to apply to vary restraint and management receivership orders by which it was affected. The solicitors exceeded the £35,000 ceiling without referring the matter back to the court and, by the hearing of their substantive application to vary the order, their costs had increased to £90,000 plus VAT. This sum represented approximately one third of the company's entire asset base. Ouseley J refused to increase the ceiling to £90,000 plus VAT and, adopting what he described as 'a fairly generous approach', permitted the release of only £50,000 plus VAT. The learned judge said:

> Counsel urged on me in relation to the consideration of costs the approach adopted by Ferris J. in *Cala Crystal SA v Emran Al-Borno, The Times, 6th* May 1994 in which, when dealing with freezing injunction and the dissipation of assets and costs, he said that the expenditure by a company on legal costs was not prima facie the dissipation of the assets and it was not for the parties or indeed the court to criticise either the rate of charge or the hours spent or the nature of the solicitors, city firm or otherwise, who had been chosen to represent the defendant. Hence, said Counsel, it did not lie in the mouth of the receiver to object to his application to the court for an increase in the sum of money which could be spent on legal fees in relation to the receivership and his application, by reference to the hourly rate, time spent or purposes upon which it was spent by the solicitor provided that it reasonably and properly related to the permitted objectives.

> Counsel's submissions seem to me to get very close to saying that the ceiling had no purpose other than excluding quite absurd expenditure. I do not accept that. The object of it is not merely to prevent money being spent unnecessarily, it is to avoid disproportionate expenditure in relation to the assets. The avoidance of disproportionate expenditure might very well involve a court saying there is to be a ceiling on the amount of money spent because of the relationship which that bears to the assets of the company; if that means that the preferred choice of solicitors is not available then, provided advice can properly be obtained, it has to be obtained within that ceiling.

Chapter 5: Applications to Vary or Discharge Restraint Orders

5.17 The court will look at claims for the release of funds to meet legal costs with some scepticism where they are made by a defendant who already has the benefit of legal aid or who has not yet made an application for public funding. In *Re W* (QBD (Admin), unreported 1992) prior to a DTA restraint order being served on him, the defendant had applied for and been granted legal aid subject to a contribution of £5,000. Once the restraint order had been served, he decided he no longer wished to have legal aid and would pay the full costs of his defence privately. He sought a variation to the restraint order to enable funds to be released for this purpose. Potts J upheld the prosecutor's view that having sought and been granted legal aid prior to the restraint order being made, the defendant was only entitled to have the amount of his legal aid contribution released from restrained funds rather than the full costs of his defence. Similarly, in *Re T* (17 December 2002) the defendant had an application for legal aid outstanding at the time he applied to the High Court for the release of funds to meet his legal expenses. Forbes J adjourned the matter pending the determination of the legal aid application.

5.18 Davis J adopted a similar approach in *T v Customs and Excise Commissioners* [2004] EWHC Admin 3256 where the defendant sought the release of restrained funds to seek legal advice and representation in relation to the prosecutor's application to appoint an enforcement receiver in relation to an outstanding DTA confiscation order for £800,000. After Mr T admitted that he had not made any application for civil legal aid, Davis J refused the application for the release of funds, saying:

> I can see where Mr. T is coming from but, unfortunately, as I see it, the difficulty for him is that he has produced no evidence before me to show that he has actually applied for civil legal aid and been turned down. Indeed, he frankly told me that he had not, although he did tell me that he had approached a number of firms of solicitors who, in view of the lack of funds, were not able to assist him. I must of course bear in mind the legislative steer behind the Act and I also note, although I do not perhaps need to attach much weight to it, Counsel's stated concerns that this is an attempt to open the door a little bit and thereafter the door will then be sought to be opened wide, giving rise to numerous applications with the eventual effect that such funds as there are available will be dissipated, thereby failing to achieve the statutory purpose behind restraint orders and confiscation orders.

> I do not think it right to accede to this application for the reasons I have given and not least because there is no evidence before me as to any application for civil legal aid having actually been pursued by Mr. T and also, I have to say, my unease at the lack of precise evidence as to whether or not other funds might not be available to him for this purpose.

5.19 A defendant seeking the release of restrained funds to pay legal expenses must therefore be able to satisfy the court that he does not have access to unrestrained funds to meet those expenses. On the basis of these authorities, the position also seemed to be that he must be able to show that LSC funding will not be available to him. In *Re Briggs-Price* [2006] EWHC 2751 (Admin) Wilkie J declined to follow *Re W* and *Re T* considering himself bound by the Court of Appeal's decision in *Norris*. In *Re Briggs-Price* the defendant, having initially instructed a solicitor privately, had the benefit of LSC funding for his trial. He sought permission to appeal against the confiscation order and instructed new solicitors. Notwithstanding having the benefit of LSC funding, he wished to instruct the new solicitors privately. A management receiver has been appointed and he sought directions from the court as to whether he should release funds for this purpose. The Revenue and Customs

C. Applications to Vary the Restraint Order

Prosecutions Office opposed the release of funds relying on *Re W* and *Re T*. Wilke J rejected this submission and gave the receiver permission to release restrained funds to meet the defendant's legal expenses saying:

> ... though I can perfectly understand the misgivings of the Receiver and have great sympathy with the policy concerns expressed by the RCPO and given effect by the Proceeds of Crime Act 2002 section 41 (4), I am bound by authority to disregard the availability of public legal funding when considering whether to give a direction that the receiver may release restrained funds for the purpose of funding the defendant's legal representation in connection with the making of the confiscation order, pursuing his appeal against the confiscation order, and in relation to these proceedings.

The Crown has been given permission to appeal against this ruling and, until the appeal is determined, there will inevitably be a degree of uncertainty as to the correct approach to applications of this nature. It is submitted that the approach of Davis J in *Re T* is more consistent with the legislative steer and the intention of Parliament as expressed in s 41 (4) of POCA and is the one to be preferred.

(2) General living expenses

5.20 Most restraint orders will make provision for the release of a weekly sum (usually £350) to a defendant not in custody for the purpose of meeting his general living expenses. This is a requirement of the practice direction supplementing sc115: see, in particular, para 4. At the time the prosecutor applies for a restraint order, the information he has as to the personal circumstances of the defendant may well be very limited. He may not know, for example whether the defendant is married or single or whether he has any dependant children to care for. It is also unlikely that he will know the extent of his legitimate financial commitments, such as mortgage repayments, public utility bills and the like. If the defendant considers the amount allowed by way of general living expenses is insufficient, he may ask the prosecutor to consent to an upward variation and, in default of agreement, can apply to the court for the restraint order to be so varied. The leading authority on the variation of restraint orders to meet general living expenses is *Re Peters* [1988] 3 WLR 182 where the Court of Appeal considered an application by the defendant for the release of restrained funds to meet school fees in relation to his children. In delivering his judgment, Lord Donaldson MR observed:

> Mr. Peters as an unconvicted accused person who might be acquitted, was entitled to ask that his son's education should not be interrupted, that he himself should be adequately clothed and that he should be able to pay the costs of his defence.

5.21 Similarly, Mann LJ said:

> In my experience a restraint order does not, and properly does not, prevent the meeting of ordinary and reasonable expenditure. That which is or is not ordinary expenditure may vary from time to time.

5.22 What constitutes 'ordinary and reasonable expenditure' is an issue to be determined having regard to the circumstances of each individual case and the principles on which the court acts are considered at para 5.27 below.

5.23 It is unlikely that the court or prosecutor will sanction any increase until the defendant has fully complied with his disclosure obligations under the order because until such time as the required information has been supplied it is unlikely that sufficient information will be available on which to reach a decision. Indeed, it will be recalled that in *Re O* [1991] 1 All ER 330 the Court specifically adjourned an application for an increase in the amount payable by way of general living expenses until such time as the defendants had sworn disclosure affidavits. A detailed breakdown of the expenditure the proposed variation is intended to fund will also be required so the court might be satisfied that it is genuinely necessary for the purpose of meeting ordinary and reasonable expenditure. A defendant who wishes to have funds released to meet such expenses as mortgage repayments, pension and life insurance policies etc is unlikely to encounter any resistance from the court or prosecutor: indeed in most cases it will be in the prosecutor's interests to ensure that mortgages do not fall into arrears as the properties to which they relate will then become liable to repossession by the lender and no longer available to meet any confiscation order. A defendant who seeks to have funds released to fund an extravagant lifestyle is likely to incur more resistance from the prosecutor and find the court reluctant to accede to his requests. The court will only sanction the release of such funds as are necessary to enable the defendant to meet ordinary and reasonable expenditure and not to enable him to continue pursuing the lifestyle he enjoyed prior to the making of the order.

(3) Companies and other business entities

5.24 Often it happens, particularly in CJA cases, that the defendant has an interest in a company or other business entity engaged in legitimate trading. In the absence of special provision in the order, the business bank accounts would be frozen and it would not be able to deal with its assets. This would have the effect of preventing the business trading and cause it to close down. The court will not, however, allow a restraint order to prevent a defendant or his business trading legitimately prior to him being convicted: see *Re G* [2001] EWHC Admin 606. If a restraint order does not provide for such a business to trade legitimately, the defendant would be entitled to apply to the court for the order to be varied appropriately. The court will, however, require safeguards to be incorporated to prevent any variation being abused. In particular, the court is likely to insist on accounts and other business records being produced to the prosecutor at regular intervals. The usual provisions for the release of business accounts and assets for such purposes appear in para 15 of the draft restraint order at Appendix 1. Where the affairs of a restrained business are unusually complex, or it has a very high turnover, or there is a suggestion that it has been used to facilitate the commission of criminal offences, the appointment of a management receiver may well be appropriate.

(4) Burden of proof

5.25 It is for the applicant for a variation to a restraint order to satisfy the court that he should be entitled to the variation he seeks. In *Serious Fraud Office v X* [2005] EWCA Civ 1564, a case concerning the release of restrained funds to meet legal expenses, Sir Anthony Clarke, MR (with whom Brooke and Buxton LJJ agreed) said:

> If a defendant against whom a restraint order has been made wishes to vary the order in order to enable him to use the funds or assets which are the subject of the order, which I will call

D. The Principles on which the Court Acts: The 'Legislative Steer'

"the restrained assets", in order to pay for his defence, it is for him to persuade the court that it would be just for the court to make the variation sought. I would call that the burden of persuasion.

As X had failed to show that he did not have assets overseas which could be used to meet his legal expenses, the Court held that the order should not be varied for this purpose. **5.26**

D. The Principles on which the Court Acts: The 'Legislative Steer'

In determining applications for the release of restrained funds for whatever purpose, the court has to achieve a difficult balance between ensuring assets are available to satisfy a confiscation order on the one hand and ensuring that the defendant has sufficient money available to meet legitimate expenditure on the other. The DTA and CJA contain mandatory provisions with which the court is required to comply when exercising its powers under the Acts and these are particularly relevant in the context of variation applications and it is therefore convenient to consider them here. **5.27**

Section 31 of the DTA provides as follows: **5.28**

(1) The following provisions apply to the powers conferred—
   (a) on the High Court or a county court by sections 26 to 30 of this Act; or
   (b) on a receiver appointed under sections 26 or 29 of this Act or in pursuance of a charging order.
(2) Subject to the following provisions of this section the powers shall be exercised with a view to making available for satisfying the confiscation order or, as the case may be, any confiscation that may be made in the defendant's case, the value for the time being of realisable property held by any person by means of the realisation of such property.
(3) In the case of realisable property held by a person to whom the defendant has directly or indirectly made a gift caught by the Act, the powers shall be exercised with a view to realising no more than the value for the time being of the gift.
(4) The powers shall be exercised with a view to allowing any person other than the defendant or the recipient of any such gift to retain or recover the value of any property held by him.
(5) In exercising the powers, no account shall be taken of any obligations of the defendant or of the recipient of any such gift which conflict with the obligation to satisfy the confiscation order.

Identical provisions appear in s 82(1), (2), (3), (4) and (6) of the CJA. These provisions were described in *Re Peters* [1988] 3 WLR 182 as amounting to a 'legislative steer' as to how the court's discretion should be exercised. In *Re P (Restraint Order: Sale of Assets)* [2000] 1 WLR 473 Simon Brown LJ considered the interpretation of the provision and, although the court was primarily concerned with the powers of a management receiver to sell assets, the judgment, with which Chadwick LJ and Rattee J agreed, is of considerable assistance in considering the effect of the 'legislative steer' on applications for variations to restraint orders. The learned judge said of s 31(2): **5.29**

Section 31(2), let it be said at once, it not an entirely easy provision to construe. One of its difficulties, of course, is that it addressed two very different situations, one at the stage of an interim restraint order and the other after a confiscation order has been made. The first situation is, of course, encompassed in the words 'or as the case may be, any confiscation order that may be made in the defendant's case', words which, as Counsel for the defendant suggested, may conveniently be placed in notional brackets by those attempting the task of construction.

The phrase 'for the time being' clearly refers to the time when the power falls to be exercised. Perhaps less immediately obvious, but ultimately I believe no less clear, is that the concluding phrase 'by means of the realisation of such property' is linked to the word 'satisfying', not to the earlier word 'exercised'. The provision, in short is not to be read as a requirement upon the court in all cases to appoint a receiver with full powers of sale and for the receiver then immediately to realise all assets. Rather the court and receiver are directed (at whichever stage the question arises) to seek to preserve the present value of the defendant's assets. But plainly that cannot be the only relevant consideration, least of all before the defendant comes to be tried and whilst, therefore, he is to be presumed innocent. Rather, as *In Re Peters* makes clear, a balance has to be struck between, on the one hand, preserving the worth of the defendant's realisable property against the possibility that he may be convicted and a confiscation order made against him, and on the other hand allowing him meantime to continue the ordinary course of his life. The problem in *In Re Peters* was in deciding just what expenses are reasonable, the point at which expenditure becomes dissipation. The difficulty in the present type of case is to decide whether certain assets ought properly to be retained so that the defendant may continue to enjoy them, not merely to the limited extent possible whilst in custody awaiting trial but in future were he ultimately to be acquitted and the restraint order and receivership accordingly discharged. It is at this stage that I would return to what I have already suggested is the central policy underlying this legislation—Parliament's desire to strip criminals of their present assets to the extent of their past criminal profits. The Act is designed essentially to impoverish defendants, not to enrich the Crown. That this is so, indeed, is arguably evident even from the language of section 31(2) itself. In a case like the present (and no doubt the great majority of cases) where the assumed proceeds of crime far exceed the defendant's realisable assets, the amount of the confiscation order will be dictated by the latter and not the former. The subsection speaks only of 'satisfying the confiscation order', not of producing assets equivalent to past criminal gains.

5.30 It is submitted that what the 'legislative steer' amounts to in the context of applications for the variation of restraint orders is this: the court's primary function must be to ensure that the defendant's assets are preserved for the purpose of meeting any confiscation order that might be made in his case. This, however, cannot be the sole consideration influencing the court. Particularly at the pre-trial stage, when the defendant is unconvicted and entitled to be presumed innocent, he is entitled to have reasonable sums released by way of general living expenses and legal fees to enable him to continue leading a normal life pending the determination of the proceedings. The court has to achieve the right balance between keeping assets restrained on the one hand and allowing reasonable expenditure on the other. In the words of Simon Brown LJ in *Re P*, the court has to decide what expenses are reasonable and when expenditure becomes dissipation.

5.31 In a number of judgments the court has ruled on how the legislative steer should be applied in considering applications to vary restraint orders. In *Re Peters* [1988] 3 WLR 182 the Court, while agreeing that it was appropriate to release funds to meet school fees payable in respect of the defendant's child, refused to allow them to be capitalised to take account of future payments that would not arise until after the case had concluded. The defendant had been ordered in divorce proceedings to make a lump sum payment to his son to cover the costs of his education and maintenance until he reached the age of 18. McNeil J varied the restraint order releasing funds to the defendant to enable him to comply with the order made in the divorce proceedings. On appeal by the prosecutor, the Court of Appeal ruled that it would be contrary to the 'legislative steer' (at that time contained in s 13(2) of the

D. The Principles on which the Court Acts: The 'Legislative Steer'

Drug Trafficking Offences Act 1986) to allow expenditure to be capitalised in this way. Lord Donaldson MR summarised the court's approach thus:

> But the anticipatory discharge of liabilities which could be expected to arise only after Mr. Peters has either been acquitted or convicted and, in the event of conviction, his property has been made subject to a confiscation order is quite another matter and is wholly contrary to section 13(2) and indeed the underlying purpose of the protective provisions on the 1986 Act.

Thus, as Nourse LJ indicated in his judgment, the proper course was to pay the expenses and fees on a term by term basis. The Court indicated that it understood the motives that had led to McNeil J making the variation order, but as Mann LJ observed: **5.32**

> I fully understand that McNeil J may have been influenced by the disruption in the son's education should a confiscation order ultimately be made, but in my judgment there is, in the light of section 13(2), no room for the intrusion of sympathy.

In *Re W* The Times, 15 November 1990 it was held that the 'legislative steer' precludes a restraint order from being varied to release funds for the purpose of satisfying a claim made by an unsecured third party creditor of the defendant. In that case a third party judgment creditor of the defendant applied for a CJA restraint order to be varied to allow funds to be released to satisfy the judgment. Buckley J refused the application, ruling that the effect of s 82(2) was to give the prosecutor priority over most creditors of the defendant. He said: **5.33**

> Counsel drew my attention to *Re Peters* and the analogy made there with Mareva injunctions. He submitted that under that jurisdiction the court would permit bonafide debts to third parties to be paid as they fell due. There is a fundamental difference between the two jurisdictions which did not concern the court in *Re Peters* but which is vital here. The object of Mareva injunctions is not to give priority or advantage to the plaintiff over other creditors of the defendant. The provisions to which I have referred in the 1988 Act do give priority to the satisfaction of a confiscation order at least over general creditors.

In *Re X* [2004] 3 WLR 906 Davis J declined to follow *Re W* ruling that it had been wrongly decided. In that case restraint and management receivership orders had been made against X under the CJA and the corporate veil of a company known as Y Limited had been pierced. Shortly after his appointment the receiver was asked to make payment to another company, Z Limited, of £873,972 in relation to goods allegedly supplied to Y Limited. Payment to an account at a Swiss bank in Zurich was requested. The receiver sought the court's directions as to how he should proceed and Z Limited made its own application for the release of the funds. The prosecutor contended, on the authority of *Re W* that the court had no jurisdiction to entertain the application for the release of funds to Z Limited. Davis J rejected this submission and found that he did have jurisdiction to entertain the application for the following reasons: **5.34**

1. Section 77 (1) CJA was phrased in wide terms providing that restraint orders may be made 'subject to such conditions and exceptions as may be specified in the order'. Davis J held that these words confer a wide discretion on the court empowering it to sanction the payment of creditors over and above living expenses and legal expenses.
2. Although the powers under s 77 had to be exercised in a way that was compatible with the legislative steer in s 82(2) the words 'with a view to making available' in the subsection

should not be construed as meaning 'to make available'. The words 'with a view to' in s 82(2) introduce a degree of elasticity.

3. Although s 82(6) CJA provides that no account shall be taken of any obligations of the defendant which conflict with the obligation to satisfy the confiscation order, this provision only applies after a confiscation order has been made and not at a stage prior thereto.

5.35 Davis J also rejected an alternative submission by the prosecutor that the court was only empowered to sanction the payment of creditors where this would not result in any diminution in the value of realisable property as, for example, where a defendant is allowed to continue making mortgage payments from restrained funds. The judge appears to have been influenced particularly by the fact that at the pre-conviction stage, the defendant is entitled to be presumed innocent. He said:

> A confiscation order is made after conviction. Before conviction there is a presumption of innocence. The person who is the subject of the restraint order may be acquitted. It is difficult to think that Parliament could have intended to restrict the court's powers as a matter of jurisdiction in the way now contended for when the consequence might be the bankruptcy or ruin of the individual concerned before he has been tried. That, indeed, to my mind is one explanation for the distinction between the wording of section 82 (2) and section 82 (6).

5.36 Davis J also drew attention to the provisions of s 82(4) which provides that the powers shall be exercised with a view to allowing any person other than the defendant or the recipient of a gift to retain or recover the value of any property held by him. He held that:

> ... on its natural reading, subsection (4) in itself indicates that the court is required to have regard to the position of creditors who may be trying to recover the debts owed to them by the person the subject of any restraint order. That also seems consistent with what is contemplated in paragraph 6 of the Practice Direction annexed to RSC Order 115.

5.37 Nonetheless, having found that he did have jurisdiction to release funds to Z Limited from the restrained assets of X Limited, Davis J in the exercise of his discretion declined to do so. As the judge refused to authorise payment, neither the Crown nor the receiver sought permission to appeal the judgment, with the result that there remain two conflicting High Court decisions as to whether there is jurisdiction to release restrained funds to pay third party creditors of the defendant.

5.38 It is submitted that there must be some doubts as to the correctness of the judgment in *Re X*. It appears to be inconsistent with the legislative steer and the language and purposes of the legislation. Further, it is worthy of note that Davis J did not only fail to follow *Re W*, but also *Re R* [2004] EWHC Admin 621 and *Re M* [1992] QB 377. In those cases it was made clear that whilst payments may be made that have the effect of preserving the value of the defendant's assets, no payments may be made that have the effect of diminishing that value unless they are specifically authorised by the legislation such as living expenses or legal costs.

5.39 Further it is submitted that the judge's interpretation of s 82(4) is a misreading of the section. It is not concerned with unsecured creditors, but rather with individuals who have an interest in the property concerned, such as a half share in real property.

5.40 Section 82 of the CJA and the identically worded provisions of s 31 of the DTA are difficult sections to construe and what is required, it is submitted, is to strike a fair balance

D. The Principles on which the Court Acts: The 'Legislative Steer'

between securing assets to make them available to meet any confiscation order that might be made in the defendant's case in the event he is convicted and allowing him to meet legitimate expenses at a time when he is presumed innocent. It is submitted that the proper approach is to allow such expenditure to be incurred where there will be no diminution in the value of the defendant's realisable property. There is no difficulty with a management receiver paying off trade debts with a view to retaining and preserving the value of the business of a company, because the payment of such a debt would preserve a greater asset in value. Similarly, there can be no objection to allowing rent or mortgage payments to be made either on the basis that it constitutes a living expense or because it preserves and maintains the defendant's interest in property. In both cases the value of the realisable property is not diminished or reduced in value overall because it allows a company to continue trading, continue making profits, and prevents the mortgagee foreclosing. This purpose concurs with *Re W* and *Re M* and is consistent with the purpose of maintaining assets to meet a final order if one should be made, and meeting the reasonable requirements of the owner in the meantime.

5.41 Another consequence of the legislative steer is that the court will not give effect to a proposed variation which allows a defendant to pursue a luxurious life style or live beyond his legitimate means: see *Re D and D* (28 October 1992). In that case Hutchison J commented:

> As I suggested, perhaps a court which is making a variation will think that he may have to content himself in the exigencies in which he finds himself with something less than a Rolls Royce lifestyle until his guilt or innocence is established.

5.42 The defendant may well find that he has to tighten his belt and economise on his normal expenditure while the restraint order remains in force.

5.43 Further, and quite independently of the legislative steer, the Court of Appeal held in *Serious Fraud Office v X* [2005] EWCA Civ 1564 that the authorities in relation to the variation of freezing orders (formerly Mareva injunctions) are also relevant to applications to vary restraint orders. The Court drew particular attention to the judgment of Robert Goff J in *A v C* (No 2) [1981] QB 962 at p 963:

> In the present case, I have had to consider the position where the defendant has, or may have, other assets from which the relevant payment may be made. I have still to apply the basic principle, i.e., that I can only permit a qualification to the injunction if the defendant satisfies the court that the money is required for a purpose which does not conflict with the policy underlining the *Mareva* jurisdiction. I do not consider that in normal circumstances a defendant can discharge that burden of proof simply by saying 'I owe someone some money'. I put to the defendants' counsel, in the course of argument, the example of an English based defendant with two bank accounts, one containing a very substantial sum which was not subject to the *Mareva* injunction, and the other containing a smaller sum which was. I asked counsel whether it would be sufficient for the defendant simply to say, 'I owe somebody some money, please qualify the injunction to permit payment from the smaller account, without giving any consideration to the possibility of payment from the larger account'. Counsel was constrained to accept that that would not be sufficient because it would not satisfy the court that the payment out of the smaller account would not conflict with the principle underlying the *Mareva* jurisdiction. The whole purpose of selecting the smaller account might be to prevent the money in that account from being available to satisfy a judgment in the pending proceedings. In my judgment, a defendant has to go further

that that; precisely what he has to prove will depend, no doubt, upon the circumstances of the particular case. At all events, in the present case, if the defendants making the application have other assets freely available – and I do not know, on the evidence, whether they have or not – it would be open to counsel for the plaintiffs to submit, on the evidence, that it would be wrong for the court to vary the *Mareva* injunction. All I can say at present is that, on the evidence before the court, the defendants have not discharged the burden of proof which rests upon them.

5.44 The Court in *Serious Fraud Office v X* also held that two judgments of Sir John Donaldson MR in relation to Mareva injunctions were relevant to applications to vary restraint orders. In *Campbell v Mussells v Thompson* The Times, 30 May 1984 Sir John said:

> ... if there is reason to believe that people are asking for money for solicitors costs ... simply as a means of avoiding bringing free money into this country, or as a means of not having to use other monies which have not been discovered and which they wish to keep out of the clutches of the court, of course they will be refused.

5.45 In a similar vein, in *Southern Cross Commodities Proprietary Ltd v Martin* (CA, 11 February 1986) Sir John said:

> It is quite clear that the court will not allow expenditure to be channelled into funds which are subject to a Mareva injunction where there are other free funds proved to be available to meet the expenditure. It is also clear that the courts should exercise a healthy scepticism over claims that the only moneys available are in the funds which are subject to a Mareva injunction.

5.46 A defendant seeking to have restrained funds released, whether for legal fees, general living expenses or other expenditure, must therefore produce credible evidence that he has no unrestrained assets, either within the jurisdiction or overseas, which might be used for this purpose.

E. The Source of Payment of Legal Fees and General Living Expenses

5.47 The order will require the defendant to nominate a source for the payment of any sums released by way of legal fees and general living expenses. As a general rule, he has an unfettered right to nominate any source he chooses for this purpose. He must however, bear in mind that if he fails to disclose the nominated asset in his disclosure statement or claims it does not belong to him, the court and prosecutor may have some difficulty in acceding to its release for these purposes.

(1) Assets not legitimately acquired

5.48 It would seem that a defendant is entitled to use assets the Crown alleges have not been legitimately acquired as the source for payment of any sums released to him by way of legal fees or general living expenses. In *Re D and D* (28 October 1992) large sums of money were found in the homes of the defendants when they were arrested. They were later charged with alleged drug trafficking offences and restraint orders were obtained that specifically listed the seized money as one of the restrained assets. The order further provided that the money was to be paid into an interest bearing account if it was not required as an exhibit in the criminal proceedings. The prosecutor decided that the money was not so required and

E. The Source of Payment of Legal Fees and General Living Expenses

duly paid it into an interest bearing account in accordance with the terms of the order. The defendants then applied for the money to be released to pay their legal fees and general living expenses. The prosecutor objected, contending that the money had not been legitimately acquired and should not therefore be released for these purposes.

Hutchison J overruled the prosecutor's objections and acceded to the defendants' application for the release of the seized funds. The learned judge ruled that it would breach the presumption of innocence for a finding to be made prior to the defendants' trial that the funds had not been legitimately acquired. In any event given that both legitimately and illegitimately acquired assets could be used to satisfy any confiscation order made in the event of conviction, it was inappropriate, the learned judge ruled, to restrict a defendant to using only assets the prosecutor was satisfied were legitimately acquired to pay his legal fees and living expenses prior to conviction.

(2) Assets that are prosecution exhibits

5.49 It happens from time to time that restrained assets (particularly cash taken up at the time of the defendant's arrest) become an exhibit in the criminal proceedings. In *Re C* (unreported, 1993) the Court considered the extent to which exhibited assets could be released to fund general living expenses and legal fees. The defendant was found in possession of substantial sums of money when he was arrested and which were duly included in a DTA restraint order. In due course the money became an exhibit in the criminal case, and at committal the prosecutor gave an undertaking to the examining magistrates to produce the money along with all the other exhibits at trial. Laws J ruled that the court did have a discretion to order the release of the money notwithstanding that it was an exhibit in the criminal case and notwithstanding the prosecutor's undertaking. The judge said:

> In my judgment, the court is not deprived of the jurisdiction to release money for living expenses simply upon the Crown's assertion that it intends to put the relevant cash before the jury. Nor do I accept that where money in cash form, or for that matter any other property, has been accorded the formal status of an exhibit, this court lacks all power to release it in whole or in part to permit living expenses within the general context of a restraint order. Any undertaking by the Crown given to the magistrates' court to produce exhibits at trial will surely be released pro tanto by the High Court's superior order. The question, therefore, is one of discretion.

5.50 The judge then went on to consider the manner in which the court should exercise its discretion. The crucial test seems to be whether it is essential that the original exhibit must be produced to the criminal court if the prosecutor is to do justice to his case. Laws J said:

> The court will certainly give great weight to what after proper consideration are said to be the evidential needs of the prosecution. There will be situations in which that weight is obviously conclusive. Not only that: in my judgment there can be no question of making allowances for living or other expenses within a restraint order if to do so would curtail or circumscribe the Crown's function of properly presenting, by evidence, the case to the jury.

5.51 The judge found in the instant case that there was no reason why the prosecution could not produce photographs of the money and describe in the fullest detail the circumstances in which it was found and still do justice to its case. He therefore ordered the release of some of the money to meet the general living expenses of the defendant's family.

F. Release of Funds After a Confiscation Order has been Made

5.52 The right of defendants and affected third parties to draw on restrained funds to meet general living expenses and legal fees does not continue indefinitely. It is submitted that this right comes to an end on the making of a confiscation order against defendant or, if there is an appeal against conviction and/or the confiscation order, once that appeal has been determined. S31 (5) DTA and s 80 (6) CJA, which form part of the 'legislative steer' as to how the Court's powers under the Acts shall be exercised, provide that-

> . . . no account shall be taken of any obligations of the defendant or of the recipient of any such gift which conflict with the obligation to satisfy the confiscation order.

Once a confiscation order has been made which is no longer subject to appeal, it is submitted that these subsections preclude the release of funds if the consequence will be that insufficient assests will remain to satisfy the confiscation order in full, together with any accrued interest.

5.53 Further, the authorities all make reference to the defendant being entitled to have funds released for general living expenses and legal expenses because at the time the restraint order is made he has nor been covicted and is therefore entitled to a presumption of innocence.

5.54 Once the defendant stands convicted and a confiscation order has been made, these considerations no longer apply. All parties who are dependant on restrained funds to meet general living expenses and legal fees would therefore be well advised to make contingency plans as to how such expenditure should be met in the event of a confiscation order being made. If the parties do not make such plans, they may well find that, once a confiscation order has been made, restrained funds are no longer available to them or, at the very least, the court significantly reduces the amount payable.

5.55 Clearly, once the defendant is convicted, these considerations no longer apply. All parties dependent on restrained funds to meet general living expenses would therefore be well advised to bear these principles in mind and make contingency plans as to how such expenses should be met in the event of the defendant being convicted. If parties affected by the order do not make plans to fund their general living expenses from another source in the event of the defendant being convicted, they may well find that in this eventuality restrained funds are no longer available for this purpose or, at the very least, the court significantly reduces the amount payable.

5.56 A defendant who is appealing against his conviction or confiscation order is entitled to have restrained funds released to meet the legal costs incurred in the appeal proceedings: see *Customs and Excise Commissioners v Norris* [1991] 2 All ER 395. However, once domestic appeal procedures have been exhausted, further funds will not be released to pursue an appeal to the European Court of Human Rights or to refer the matter to the Criminal Cases Review Commission (see *Re P* [1998] EWHC Admin 1049).

5.57 It is submitted that the legislative steer would also preclude the release of funds to a defendant or affected third party to resist an application for the appointment of an enforcement receiver to realise assets in satisfaction of a confiscation order. In *Re D* [2006] EWHC Admin 1519

F. Release of Funds After a Confiscation Order has been Made

a confiscation order had been made against the defendant which took into account his interest in a number of properties. On the Crown's application to appoint a receiver to realise the properties in satisfaction of the confiscation order, a number of third parties intervened claiming ownership of them. They applied for an order for the properties to be sold and for some of the proceeds to be used to meet their legal fees in making their claim. This application was decisively rejected by Collins J who said:

> The court is enjoined to ensure so far as possible (a) that the property is retained and its full value is available in order to meet the confiscation and (b) that anyone who has an interest in that property is able to have the opportunity to establish the existence of that interest. Counsel, as I understand the argument, submits that that extends in an appropriate case to ensuring that the third party has legal representation and the only way in which that can be achieved in certain circumstances is to provide him with monies available from the proceeds of the property the subject of the restraint order and in which he is asserting an interest. That seems to me, as I indicated, to be a quite hopeless submission.
>
> The powers must be exercised to ensure that the third parties have a proper opportunity of pursing their claim. That they will do in the way that any litigation is to be pursued. If they have the means, then they will have to pay for it: if they do not have sufficient means, then they may apply for public funding. But what they cannot do is to obtain funding from the property which they are asserting they have an interest in when that interest is being disputed.

5.58 Once the position is reached where the prosecutor is applying for the appointment of an enforcement receiver, the defendant not only stands convicted but all appeals against the order and the underlying conviction will have been dismissed. At this stage, it would seem entirely consistent with the legislative steer and the policy underlying the legislation for the defendant and affected third parties to rely on public funding or, if they are available, unrestrained assets for the purpose of securing advice and representation in relation to the receivership application or any associated litigation. Similarly, when this point has been reached neither the defendant nor any affected third party is entitled to continue drawing on the restrained fund for the payment of general living expenses.

6

ENFORCEMENT OF RESTRAINT AND RECEIVERSHIP ORDERS: CONTEMPT OF COURT

A. Introduction	6.01	(6) Proving service of the order	6.12
(1) Ways in which breaches may be committed	6.02	(7) Proving the breach	6.16
		(8) Issuing and serving the application	6.17
(2) Sanctions available for breach of restraint and receivership orders	6.03	(9) The defendant's response	6.19
		C. The Hearing	6.21
B. Procedure on Applications	6.05	(1) Preliminary matters	6.21
(1) Strict compliance necessary	6.05	(2) Procedure at the hearing	6.28
(2) The burden and standard of proof	6.06	(3) Sentence	6.30
(3) Commencing proceedings	6.07	(4) Suspended committals	6.35
(4) Contents of the application notice	6.08	(5) Effect of being in contempt	6.36
(5) The evidence in support of the application	6.11	(6) Purging contempt	6.37
		(7) Appeals	6.39

A. Introduction

6.01 Restraint and receivership orders can only serve their intended purpose to the extent that there are effective sanctions available to the court to deal with any breach of the order committed by a defendant or third party affected by it. In this chapter we examine the powers of the court to deal with breaches of restraint and receivership orders, the procedures that must be followed to bring a person before the court for contempt of court in relation to any such breach; and offer guidance to practitioners who are instructed to act on behalf of those against whom such proceedings are brought.

(1) Ways in which breaches may be committed

6.02 Breaches of restraint and receivership orders may be committed in a variety of ways. The most common types of breach brought before the court are:

(a) a defendant or affected third party dealing or attempting to deal in restrained assets;
(b) a defendant failing to comply with the terms of a disclosure order either by not disclosing at all or by failing to disclose his interest in a particular asset;
(c) a defendant failing to comply with the terms of a repatriation order;

(d) a defendant or affected third party failing to comply with the terms of a receivership order, for example by refusing to deliver up assets to the receiver or refusing to sign a power of attorney in favour of the receiver; and

(e) obstructing the receiver in the performance of his duties, for example by assaulting, threatening, or abusing him, producing forged documentation intending the receiver to act on it as being genuine, or making untruthful statements to the receiver as to the extent of his realisable assets.

(2) Sanctions available for breach of restraint and receivership orders

6.03 The DTA and CJA do not give the prosecutor or receiver any specific remedy for breaches of restraint and receivership orders. Any breach of the order is to be dealt with as a contempt of court in the same way as a breach of any other form of High Court order. As with other instances of disobedience to an order of the court, the ultimate sanction available to the court is an order committing the contemnor to prison or, if the contemnor is a body corporate, an order sequestrating the company's assets. The authority for this is sc 45 Rule 5 which provides as follows:

(1) Where:
   (a) a person required by a judgment or order to do an act within a time specified in the judgment or order refuses or neglects to do it within that time or, as the case may be, within that time as extended or abridged under a court order or CPR rule 2.11; or
   (b) a person disobeys a judgment or order requiring him to abstain from doing any act, then, subject to the provisions of these rules, the judgment or order may be enforced by one or more of the following means, that is to say—
      (i) with the permission of the court, a writ of sequestration against the property of that person;
      (ii) where that person is a body corporate, with the permission of the court, a writ of sequestration against the property of any director or other officer of the body;
      (iii) subject to the provisions of the Debtors Act 1869 and 1878, an order of committal against that person, or where that person is a body corporate, against any such officer.

6.04 Where committal is sought in respect of a criminal cause or matter the application is to be made to a divisional court and the permission of a single judge must first be obtained to bring the proceedings: see sc52 Rule 1(2)(ii). It has, however been held in *Re H* The Times, 1 April 1988, that a breach of a restraint order does not occur in a criminal cause or matter. Bingham LJ, as he then was, said that the committal application was for: 'breach of an order made in civil proceedings, albeit closely connected to criminal proceedings.'

The application is therefore made to a single judge sitting in the Administrative Court of the Queen's Bench Division and it is not necessary to obtain permission to bring the proceedings before they may be issued.

B. Procedure on Applications

(1) Strict compliance necessary

6.05 The procedural rules in relation to applications for committal for contempt of court are to be found in sc 52 and in the Practice Direction accompanying the rules which is cited in the White Book as scpd 52. At the outset it must be emphasised that the court has held on

B. Procedure on Applications

many occasions that, as the liberty of the subject is at stake, strict compliance with all the required procedures is essential: see, for example, *Gagnon v McDonald* The Times, 14 November 1984. Any failure by the prosecutor to comply with these procedures may result in the application being dismissed, although the court may waive any procedural defect in the commencement or conduct of a committal application if it is satisfied the defendant suffers no injustice as a result: see scpd 52.10.

(2) The burden and standard of proof

6.06 The burden is on the person bringing the contempt proceedings (ie the prosecutor or receiver) to prove his case. The respondent to the application cannot be compelled to adduce evidence in his defence, although in most cases he would be well advised to file an affidavit responding to the allegations of contempt made against him. The standard of proof is proof beyond reasonable doubt. This is an exception to the usual rule that the standard of proof in civil proceedings is proof on a balance of probabilities and is justified on the basis that in contempt proceedings the liberty of the subject is at stake.

(3) Commencing proceedings

6.07 Proceedings for contempt of court are normally instituted by the issue of a claim form, but where, as will inevitably be the case in restraint and receivership cases, the application is brought in existing proceedings, they may be commenced by the issue of an application notice: see scpd 52.2.

(4) Contents of the application notice

6.08 Firstly, the application notice must state that the application is made in the proceedings in question and set out its title and reference number which must correspond with the title and reference number of those proceedings. In accordance with scpd 52.2.6(4) the application notice must:

set out in full the grounds on which the committal application is made and must identify, separately and numerically, each alleged act of contempt, including, if known, the date of each of the alleged acts.

6.09 Once an application notice has been issued, it may only be amended with the court's permission: see scpd 52.2.6.(3). The test as to whether an application notice provides sufficient detail as to the alleged acts of contempt is set out in the judgment of Nicholls LJ in *Harmsworth v Harmsworth* [1988] 1 FLR 349:

The test is, does the notice give the person alleged to be in contempt enough information to enable him to meet the charge? In satisfying this test it is clear that in a suitable case if lengthy particulars are needed, they may be included in a schedule or other addendum either at the foot of the notice so as to form part of the notice rather than being set out in the body of the notice itself. The rules require that the notice itself must contain certain information. The information is required to be available to the respondent to the application from within the four corners of the notice itself. From the notice itself the person alleged to be in contempt should know with sufficient particularity what are the breaches alleged.

6.10 The application notice must also contain a prominent notice setting out the possible consequences of the court making a committal order and the respondent not attending the hearing: see scpd 52.2.6.(5). The annex to the Practice Direction incorporates a form of notice that might be used to comply with scpd 52.2.6.(5) that reads as follows:

'IMPORTANT NOTICE

The court has power to send you to prison and fine you if it finds that any of the allegations made against you are true and amount to a contempt of court.

You must attend court on the date shown on the front of this form. It is in your own interest to do so. You should bring with you any witnesses and documents which you think will help you put your side of the case.

If you consider the allegations are not true you must tell the court why. If it is established that they are true, you must tell the court of any good reason why they do not amount to a contempt of court, or, if they do, why you should not be punished.

If you need advice you should show this document at once to your solicitor or go to a Citizens Advice Bureau.'

It is submitted that this form of words should be used in every case so there can be no suggestion that the terms of the Practice Direction have not been complied with.

(5) The evidence in support of the application

6.11 The notice of application must be accompanied by an affidavit setting out the evidence relied upon in support of each and every allegation of contempt made against the defendant: sc 52.4(1). This is the only instance in restraint and confiscation proceedings in the High Court where a witness statement verified by a statement of truth will not suffice: the evidence must be in affidavit form.

(6) Proving service of the order

6.12 The first issue the affidavit must address is the service of the restraint or receivership order on the person who is alleged to be in breach of it. In all but the most exceptional circumstances, the prosecutor must be in a position to prove that the order was personally served on the person who is said to have disobeyed it. It is obviously only right and proper that a person should not face the loss of his liberty for disobeying an order unless it can be proved that he had knowledge of the terms of that order.

6.13 Further, the prosecutor must prove that the order was endorsed with a penal notice in accordance with sc 45 Rule 7(4) which provides that:

There must be prominently displayed on the front of the copy of an order served under this rule a warning to the person on whom the copy is served that disobedience to the order would be a contempt of court punishable by imprisonment or, (in the case of an order requiring a body corporate to do or abstain from doing an act) punishable by sequestration of the assets of the body corporate and by imprisonment of an individual responsible.

6.14 The penal notice appears at the head of the draft restraint and receivership orders at Appendices 1 and 2 respectively. In rare circumstances, the court will dispense with proof of personal service of the order. The court is given this discretion under sc 45 Rule 7(6) which provides that in respect of an order requiring the defendant to abstain from doing any act, the order may be enforced by committal, notwithstanding that service has not been effected in the prescribed manner where the party sought to be committed has notice of the order either by:

(a) being present when the order was made; or
(b) being notified of its terms, whether by telephone, telegram or otherwise.

6.15 It should be noted that this provision can only be used where the contemnor is alleged to be in breach of the prohibitory terms of a restraint order: ie the provisions restraining him from dealing with assets. Where it is sought to commit the defendant for breach of requirements of the order to perform a positive act (eg make a disclosure statement or repatriate assets), only personal service will suffice. The affidavit should provide full details of the circumstances in which the order was served on the defendant and, it is submitted, should exhibit a copy of the order to enable the court to be satisfied that it contains all the required information.

(7) Proving the breach

6.16 The prosecutor's affidavit should set out clearly and fully the facts relied on to prove each breach alleged in the application notice. The affidavit should also exhibit all documentation relied on by the prosecutor to establish the breach. As the liberty of the subject is in issue, the court will require the best evidence possible to establish the breach and, it is submitted, hearsay evidence should be avoided, particularly when direct evidence is readily available.

(8) Issuing and serving the application

6.17 Once the prosecutor has all the required documents completed, he should issue the application out of the Administrative Court office. Unless the court otherwise directs, the application notice and evidence in support must be served on the alleged contemnor at least 14 days prior to the hearing: see scpd 52.4.2. The hearing date must be set out in the body of the application notice or in a Notice of Hearing attached to it.

6.18 The application notice and supporting evidence must, unless the court otherwise directs, be served personally on the alleged contemnor. If it proves impossible for the prosecutor to effect personal service because, for example, the defendant is deliberately evading service, then an application should be made to the court for an order allowing service by an alternative method in accordance with CPR 6.8(1). Once service has been effected, the prosecutor should cause an affidavit of service to be sworn to enable the court to proceed in the alleged contemnor's absence should he fail to attend.

(9) The defendant's response

6.19 Any written evidence by the defendant in opposition to the contempt application must also be given by affidavit: see scpd 52.3.1. Even if the defendant has not filed any such affidavit evidence, he may still give oral evidence at the hearing if he so chooses, but if he does so he will be liable to cross-examination: see scpd 52.3.3. Further, he may, with the permission of the court, call witnesses to give oral evidence regardless of whether they have sworn an affidavit: scpd 52.3.4. The court does, however, have power to direct the alleged contemnor to swear affidavits or produce statements from witnesses of fact upon which he wishes to rely and serve them in sufficient time to enable the prosecutor to consider them and file any necessary evidence in reply. The alleged contemnor retains the right not to have such evidence adduced at the hearing; the wise course is normally to make a full and frank admission of the contempt or, if appropriate, to file evidence setting out his case in detail: see *Re B (A Minor) (Contempt Evidence)* The Times, 11 November 1995. Further, the rule in criminal proceedings precluding the prosecutor from commenting on the defendant's failure to give evidence does not apply in contempt cases and the judge is entitled to make appropriate inferences from the alleged contemnor's failure to offer any explanation to the court as to his conduct.

6.20 For all these reasons, it is submitted that the best course is for a person facing contempt proceedings for an alleged breach of a restraint or receivership order to file affidavit evidence addressing each and every allegation made by the prosecutor in his notice of application and accompanying affidavit. If the breach is admitted, an affidavit should be filed making full and frank admissions and setting out any facts relied on in mitigation. The affidavit should also offer an unequivocal apology to the court and an undertaking to commit no further breaches. If the breach is capable of remedy, the affidavit should set out the defendant's proposals in this regard.

C. The Hearing

(1) Preliminary matters

6.21 The hearing will take place before a High Court judge assigned to Administrative Court business, sitting in open court. Advocates should therefore be robed. The court is, however, given jurisdiction under sc 52.6(1)(d) to hear the application in private in the interests of the administration of justice or national security. A defendant in a high profile case that has attracted a lot of publicity may wish to ask the court to hear the application in private if there is a risk that hearing it in public could prejudice his defence in the criminal proceedings. If the court does decide to hear the application in private and decides to make a committal order, it must under sc 52.6 state in public:

(a) the name of the person committed;
(b) in general terms the nature of the contempt of court in respect of which the order of committal is being made; and
(c) the length of the period for which he is being committed.

6.22 The court may at any time give case management directions, including directions as to the service of written evidence by the alleged contemnor and written evidence in response by the prosecutor and may also hold a directions hearing: see scpd 52.4.3. By scpd 52.4.4., the court may, on the hearing date:

(1) give case management directions with a view to a hearing of the committal application on a future date; or
(2) if the committal application is ready to be heard, proceed forthwith to hear it.

6.23 The court must always have regard to the need for the alleged contemnor to have details of the alleged acts of contempt and the opportunity to respond to the application: see scpd 52.4.5. Further, by scpd 52.4.6., the court must also have regard to the need for the respondent to be:

C. The Hearing

(1) allowed a reasonable time for responding to the committal application including, if necessary, preparing a defence;
(2) made aware of the availability of assistance from the Community Legal Service and how to contact the service;
(3) given the opportunity, if unrepresented, to obtain legal advice; and
(4) if unable to understand English, allowed to make arrangements, seeking the assistance of the court if necessary, for an interpreter to attend the hearing.

In *Togher v Customs and Excise Commissioners* [2001] EWCA Civ 474 the Court of Appeal emphasised the importance of those facing contempt proceedings being legally represented whenever imprisonment was contemplated as the appropriate sanction for the breach. Robert Walker, LJ said: **6.24**

> I consider next the criticisms which Mr. Togher makes of the procedure followed at the committal hearing, including the absence of any legal representation for Mr. Togher in a matter in which his personal liberty was at stake. Counsel for the Commissioners has pointed out, correctly, that the restraint order gave Mr. Togher the opportunity of applying for a variation of the restraints on his bank accounts so as to enable him to pay for legal representation but that he did not make such an application, nor did he ask for an order for cross-examination of the Customs and Excise witnesses on their affidavits.
>
> These observations are no doubt correct but they seem to me rather to miss the point. Legal representation is important for defendants because lawyers understand the need for applications of that sort and defendants who are not lawyers may not do so, even assuming them to be hardened criminals. It is easy for anyone who is not a lawyer, especially if he is under stress, to overlook the need to interrupt counsel (which is what Mr. Togher would have had to do) in order to raise this sort of preliminary point. This court has said that in matters of civil contempt, as soon as it appears that there is an appreciable risk of imprisonment an unrepresented defendant should be asked by the judge whether he or she wishes to be represented: see *Newman v Modern Bookbinders [2000] 2 All ER 814, 822*. It does not appear that Mr. Togher was asked that question at the hearing on 15th November 1995.

The court may, either of its own motion or on the application of the alleged contemnor, strike out a committal application if it appears to the court: **6.25**

(1) that the committal application and the evidence served in support of it disclose no reasonable ground for alleging that the respondent is guilty of contempt of court,
(2) that the committal application is an abuse of the court's process or, if made in existing proceedings, is otherwise likely to obstruct the just disposal of those proceedings, or
(3) that there has been a failure to comply with a rule, practice direction or court order.

If the prosecutor brings a contempt application during the course of the criminal trial or shortly before it is due to commence, the defendant may be able to argue with some force that it would be oppressive to require him to respond to it at that time when all his resources need to be directed to defending the criminal proceedings. This is particularly so if it can be shown that the prosecutor has been aware of the facts giving rise to the committal application, but has been guilty of an unreasonable delay in bringing the proceedings. In such circumstances, the court would be entitled to strike out the committal application as an abuse of process or adjourn it pending the determination of the criminal proceedings. The court is, however, unlikely to strike out or adjourn a committal application where the alleged breach occurs shortly before or during the criminal trial. **6.26**

6.27 Once a committal application has been issued, it may only be discontinued with the permission of the court. Thus, the prosecutor is not entitled to withdraw a committal application, even if the defendant has remedied the breach complained of by, eg filing a disclosure statement or repatriating assets. The proper course is for the prosecutor to write to the court, enclosing a letter of agreement from the defendant, seeking permission to discontinue the application. If the court agrees, the application can be discontinued without the necessity for the parties to attend court and the hearing date can be vacated.

(2) Procedure at the hearing

6.28 The court associate will open proceedings by identifying the defendant, reading each of the allegations of contempt contained in the application notice to him and asking him whether he admits or denies them. The prosecutor, upon whom the burden of proving the contempt rests, will then open his case, read his affidavits and call any witnesses required to attend for cross-examination. The defendant will then have the opportunity of addressing the court, reading his affidavits, and calling evidence. By sc 52.6(4) if the person sought to be committed expresses a wish to give oral evidence on his own behalf, he shall be entitled to do so. The parties will then have the right to make closing addresses before the judge considers his decision. If the court concludes that the prosecutor has not proved his case beyond reasonable doubt, the committal application will be dismissed. If, however, the court finds the case has been proved to the criminal standard, it will proceed to consider the appropriate sentence.

6.29 It is important to appreciate that proceedings for contempt of course are separate and distinct from the criminal proceedings and serve entirely different purposes. In *Re S* [1999] EWHC Admin 466 a restraint order had been obtained against the defendant which included a term requiring him to repatriate funds held in a named bank account in Jamaica. The defendant failed to comply with this requirement and, in the meantime, a confiscation order was made against him at Nottingham Crown Court in the sum of £47,851.45 with a term of imprisonment of 18 months to be served in default of payment. The CPS took proceedings against him alleging that he was guilty of contempt of court by failing to comply with the repatriation requirement. In his defence, the defendant contended that the contempt proceedings exposed him to double jeopardy because he was already liable to serve the default sentence if he did not pay the sums held in the Jamaican bank account in satisfaction of the confiscation order. Ognall J rejected this argument saying:

> It seems to me that that argument, however ingeniously clothed, is doomed to failure. First, on a narrow question of fact, it fails because there is no material before me which serves to satisfy me that in making the confiscation order in the quantum that he did, the judge paid any account whatever to such assets as there might be in the Jamaican bank account. Even if I be wrong in that conclusion, the argument is fatally flawed because of this consideration. The jeopardy in which the Respondent before me stands (in relation to the order made at Nottingham) is a jeopardy which would be triggered by his failure to pay the monies the subject of the confiscation order. The jeopardy in which he stands before the High Court is by reason not of his failure to pay any money. It stems from his wilful failure to bring assets within that Jamaican bank account into this jurisdiction as required by the court. The fact that in the event were he to have done so or were he to do so now, any proceeds to be derived from it might go in satisfaction of the confiscation order is neither here nor there. The fact is, the contingency which put him in contempt of this Court is his failure to comply with an

order to bring the proceeds of that account within this jurisdiction. It is a quite different contingency from that which triggers the sanction imposed by way of a default term at Nottingham.

The judge ruled that the contempt had to be marked with a separate and consecutive term of imprisonment and imposed a sentence of six months.

(3) Sentence

6.30 If the defendant admits the contempt, or the court finds the case proved, the court must then proceed to sentence. The contemnor will of course have the right to address the court in mitigation before sentence is imposed. Any such mitigation should include an unequivocal apology, an undertaking not to commit any further breaches of the order, and, if possible, proposals for remedying the contempt. The maximum penalty that may be imposed for contempt of court is two years' imprisonment: see s 14(1) of the Contempt of Court Act 1981. Consecutive sentences may be imposed for separate contempts, so long as the total sentence imposed on any one occasion does not exceed the maximum. Sentences of imprisonment for contempt of court are subject to the early release provisions set out in the Criminal Justice Act 1991. By s 33(1), as substituted by s 45 of the Act, as soon as the contemnor has served one half of his sentence if he has been committed for less than 12 months, or one third of the sentence if he has been committed for more than 12 months, he must be released unconditionally.

6.31 The court will invariably treat breaches of restraint and receivership orders very seriously, especially where the dissipation of assets is involved. Unless the contemnor has taken prompt steps to recover assets so dissipated, the almost inevitable consequence will be an immediate sentence of imprisonment. Indeed, in relation to freezing orders, there is clear authority to the effect that any dissipation of assets should be visited by immediate imprisonment. In *Popischal v Phillips* The Times, 20 January 1988, the Court of Appeal stressed that it was:

> of the highest importance to the public as well as to the parties, that Mareva injunctions issued to prevent the dissipation of assets should be obeyed and not disregarded, and certainly not flouted.

6.32 The Court held that where property had been sold in breach of such an order, an immediate custodial sentence was appropriate, irrespective of whether it was necessary to ensure compliance with the injunction.

6.33 A similar approach was adopted by Stanley Burnton J in *R v Selby* (QBD (Admin) 16 June, 2006) where a six month sentence of imprisonment was imposed for dissipating assets in breach of a CJA restraint order. In passing sentence the learned judge said:

> Any order of this court is regarded by the court as a matter of the greatest importance. It is necessary that they be complied with and, if not complied with, that punishment follows, otherwise the orders become pointless; compliance with the law would fall into disrepute. The courts necessarily regard a breach of any court order, particularly an order of the kind involved in this case, as a serious matter.

6.34 If the contemnor is at liberty at the time of his committal for contempt of court he will be taken into custody by an officer of the court known as the Tipstaff who will escort him to prison: male prisoners are sent to Pentonville prison and female prisoners to Holloway.

If the contemnor is already in prison at the time he is committed, whether remanded in custody awaiting trial or sentence or is already serving a sentence of imprisonment, he will be returned to the prison where he is already incarcerated to serve the sentence. If he is an unconvicted remand prisoner at the time of being sentenced for contempt of court, on his return to prison he will lose the privileges to which a remand prisoner is normally entitled while serving his sentence for contempt of court. If he is already serving a sentence of imprisonment at the time of being sentenced for contempt of court, the contempt sentence will be consecutive to the earlier sentence unless the court otherwise directs.

(4) Suspended committals

6.35 The court has power under sc 52.7(1) to direct that the execution of an order for committal be suspended for such period or on such terms or conditions as it may specify. In the context of restraint orders, this provision gives the court jurisdiction to suspend the committal provided the defendant remedies his breach by, eg serving his disclosure statement or repatriating assets within a specified period of time. The court may also suspend the committal on terms that the defendant henceforth comply with the terms of the order, notwithstanding that the effect of this is to suspend the committal indefinitely: see *Griffin v Griffin* The Times, 28 April 2000. If the committal is suspended and the contemnor thereafter commits another breach of the restraint order, the court can activate the suspended committal and impose another sentence for the new contempt to be served consecutively, provided the overall limit of two years imposed by s 14 of the Contempt of Court Act 1981 is not exceeded (see *Villiers v Villiers* [1994] 2 All ER 149).

(5) Effect of being in contempt

6.36 The potential consequences of being in contempt go well beyond being sentenced to a term of imprisonment. The court has a discretion to refuse to hear a person who is in contempt until such time as the contempt has been purged: see *Hadkinson v Hadkinson* [1952] 2 All ER 567 and *X Ltd v Morgan Grampian* [1990] 2 All ER 1. The discretion may only be exercised on an application made by the contemnor and may not be used to prevent him defending an application brought by the prosecutor in the proceedings. This can be a powerful weapon against the defendant who flagrantly disobeys a restraint or receivership order as it can preclude him seeking a variation of the order while he remains in contempt.

(6) Purging contempt

6.37 A defendant imprisoned for contempt of court has the right under sc 52.8(1) to go back to court at any time and seek his discharge on the ground that he has purged his contempt. In order to convince the judge that it is appropriate to release him, the defendant will have to show that he is now suitably contrite and henceforth will comply with the terms of the order. The chances of a defendant being discharged will be enhanced if he is able to advance proposals as to how the harm caused by his breach of the order might be remedied.

6.38 The application for the contemnor's discharge should be made on application notice issued out of the Administrative Court office supported, it is submitted, by an affidavit setting out the grounds relied upon. If he is available, the application should be made to the judge who heard the original application but, in his absence, may be heard by any judge assigned to Administrative Court business. The judge has a complete discretion as to what course of action to take: the judge may refuse the application which will mean the original sentence remains unchanged; he may accede to it, in which case the contemnor will be released immediately; or alternatively he may direct the contemnor's release at a future date prior to the end of the original sentence.

(7) Appeals

The contemnor has the right of appeal to the Court of Appeal (Civil Division) either against the finding of contempt or the sentence imposed by the court. Permission is not required and the court has jurisdiction to grant bail pending the determination of the appeal. **6.39**

7

PRACTICE AND PROCEDURE IN THE HIGH COURT: DTA AND CJA CASES

A. Introduction	7.01	D. The Hearing	7.34
B. The Woolf Reforms and the Overriding Objective	7.03	(1) Service of the order	7.39
(1) Structure of the Civil Procedure Rules	7.07	E. Procedure on Applications to Vary or Discharge the Order	7.42
(2) Terminology	7.08	(1) Variation by consent: consulting the prosecutor	7.43
(3) Evidence	7.09	(2) Applying to the court	7.46
C. Procedure on Applications for Restraint Orders	7.13	(3) Drafting the witness statement or affidavit	7.48
(1) Allocation of business	7.13	(4) Drafting the order	7.50
(2) Title of the proceedings	7.14	(5) Issuing the application	7.51
(3) Preparation of documentation	7.15	(6) Service of the application	7.52
(4) The claim form	7.16	(7) Proof of service	7.53
(5) The draft order	7.17	(8) The hearing	7.54
(6) The witness statement	7.19	(9) Costs	7.56
(7) The duty of full and frank disclosure	7.23	(10) After the hearing: drafting and serving the order	7.57
(8) What additional matters should be disclosed?	7.25	(11) Variation applications by the prosecutor	7.58
(9) The consequences of non-disclosure	7.27	(12) Appeals	7.60

A. Introduction

One of the most striking features of the DTA and CJA is that they bestow jurisdiction on the High Court to make orders intended to enforce confiscation orders that have been made, or may be made, by the Crown Court in criminal proceedings. The Crown Court has no jurisdiction to make, vary, or discharge restraint orders under the DTA and CJA, or to appoint receivers for the purpose of enforcing its orders. All these matters are exclusively within the jurisdiction of the High Court under these Acts. As we shall see in Chapter 8, the position has changed in relation to offences committed after 23 March 2003 and to which the Proceeds of Crime Act 2002 applies. In these cases, restraint and receivership orders are made, varied and discharged by the Crown Court.

7.01

This division of responsibility between the High Court and Crown Court in DTA and CJA cases can create a dilemma for many experienced criminal practitioners who rarely, if ever,

7.02

have cause to venture into the civil courts. Court procedures and terminology are entirely different and the practitioner who gets it wrong runs the risk of a costs award being made against his client or even a wasted costs order made personally against him. In 1998 radical changes to the civil justice system took place to implement the recommendations of Lord Woolf's 'Access to Justice' Report. On 26 April 1999 the Civil Procedure Rules (CPR) came into force with the aim of making the civil procedure system simpler, more efficient and cost effective. In this chapter, we examine the rules and procedures in so far as they affect restraint and confiscation applications in the High Court to assist the practitioner in pursuing the right course from the outset, thereby avoiding incurring judicial wrath and the risk of adverse awards of costs.

B. The Woolf Reforms and the Overriding Objective

7.03 In civil proceedings, the parties are required, following the Woolf reforms, to do their utmost to resolve their differences without recourse to litigation and, in those cases where litigation is unavoidable, to narrow down the issues in dispute as much as possible. The parties are expected to serve their evidence on each other and on the court well before the hearing, together with skeleton arguments summarising the case they propose to advance. They will also be expected to agree bundles of documents and serve them on the court so the trial judge can have the opportunity of considering them in advance of the hearing. In many cases, at an interim hearing, the judge will give directions as to the various steps the parties must take and the timescale within which they must be completed. A party to the proceedings who does not comply with such directions risks sanctions being imposed in costs.

7.04 This principle comes from the 'overriding objective' set out in r 1.1 CPR which provides as follows:

(1) These Rules are a new procedural code with the overriding objective of enabling the court to deal with cases justly.
(2) Dealing with a case justly includes, so far as practicable—
   (a) ensuring that the parties are on an equal footing;
   (b) saving expense;
   (c) dealing with the case in ways which are proportionate—
      (i) to the amount of money involved;
      (ii) to the importance of the case;
      (iii) to the complexity of the issues; and
      (iv) to the financial position of each party;
   (d) ensuring that it is dealt with expeditiously and fairly; and
   (e) allotting to it an appropriate share of the court's resources while taking into account the need to allot resources to other cases.
(3) The parties are required to help the court to further the overriding objective.

7.05 Under the CPR, the court adopts a much more 'hands-on' approach to case management than has hitherto been the case. In the past, case management was largely in the hands of the parties who were able to agree amongst themselves how the case would progress, often granting one another significant extensions of time in which to carry out various steps in the litigation prescribed by the rules of court. Under r 1.4(1) CPR the court now has a duty

B. The Woolf Reforms and the Overriding Objective

to further the overriding objective by 'actively managing' cases. Rule 1.4(2) sets out some of the ways in which the court may actively manage cases and these include: encouraging the parties to cooperate in the conduct of the proceedings; identifying the issues at an early stage; deciding the order in which issues should be resolved; fixing timetables or otherwise controlling the progress of the case; dealing with as many aspects of the case as it can on the same occasion; making use of technology and giving directions to ensure the trial proceeds quickly and efficiently.

Rule 1.1. of the Criminal Procedure Rules 2005, SI 2005/384 imposes a similar 'overriding objective' on the parties in criminal proceedings in the magistrates' court, Crown Court and Court of Appeal (Criminal Division). **7.06**

(1) Structure of the Civil Procedure Rules

The Civil Procedure Rules have revoked most of the Rules of the Supreme Court (RSC) and County Court Rules (CCR) and contain one procedural code to be applied in all civil courts. Some of the old rules have been retained and these are to be found in Sch 1 (RSC) and Sch 2 (CCR) and are cited as 'sc' and 'cc' respectively. Order 115 (which deals with DTA and CJA applications) is one of the rules which has been retained and appears in Sch 1 to the CPR. Order 115 is supplemented by a Practice Direction imposing a number of obligations on a prosecutor applying for a restraint order and incorporating as an Appendix an example restraint order. Order 52, which deals with contempt applications, has also been retained and supplemented by the addition of a Practice Direction. **7.07**

(2) Terminology

In order to make civil procedure simpler and more user friendly, many of the archaic and Latin expressions used in the past have been abolished and court forms simplified. Proceedings are no longer commenced by the issue of a writ or originating motion: all proceedings begin by the issue of a claim form. Interlocutory applications in an existing action are commenced by issuing an application notice rather than a summons. Applications are heard 'in private' rather than 'in Chambers' and 'ex parte hearings' are referred to as 'hearings without notice'. 'Mareva injunctions' are referred to as 'freezing orders' and 'Anton Piller orders' as 'search orders'. Costs are subject to either 'summary assessment' or 'detailed assessment' rather than 'taxation' and taxing masters are referred to as 'costs judges'. Finally, 'substituted service' is referred to as 'service by an alternative method'. **7.08**

(3) Evidence

Written evidence has always been used in civil proceedings to a much greater extent than in criminal proceedings. Prior to the CPR coming into force, written evidence was invariably presented in affidavit form. The CPR dispensed with affidavit evidence for most purposes, and witness statements verified by a statement of truth are now used instead. Practice Direction 22 (PD 22) para 2.1 provides that the statement of truth shall be in the following terms: **7.09**

I believe that the facts stated in this witness statement are true.

7.10 Claim forms and application notices must also be verified by a statement of truth. The statement of truth may also be made by the legal representative of a party in which case it shall be in the following form:

> The (claimant/defendant) believes that the facts stated in this (name of document being verified) are true.

7.11 Rule 32.14(1) CPR provides that a person who makes a false statement in a document verified by a statement of truth, or who causes such a statement to be made, without an honest belief in its truth is guilty of contempt of court. Proceedings for such a contempt may, however, only be brought by the Attorney General or with the permission of the court: see r 32.14(2) CPR. Practitioners should exercise great care when signing statements of truth on behalf of clients because PD 22 para 3.8 provides that in such circumstances the contents and consequences of signing it are deemed, by virtue of the signature, to have been explained to the client and the signature will be taken by the court as an indication that the client has authorised him to sign. In order to protect himself against an allegation of contempt of court or professional misconduct, the practitioner would be well advised to ensure he has written instructions from the client before signing on his behalf.

7.12 The one exception to the use of witness statements in civil cases is proceedings for contempt of court. In such cases, the evidence, both for the claimant and the defendant, must be on affidavit.

C. Procedure on Applications for Restraint Orders

(1) Allocation of business

7.13 By sc115 Rule 2 the High Court's jurisdiction under the DTA and CJA is to be exercised by a judge of the Chancery Division or of the Queen's Bench Division sitting in private. A Practice Direction issued by Lord Justice Watkins, then Senior Presiding Judge, on 27 January 1987 provides that such applications should be issued out of the Administrative Court office and be heard by a judge of the Queen's Bench Division. The only exception is in cases where the judge directs that the application be heard by a judge of the Chancery Division.

(2) Title of the proceedings

7.14 Sc115 Rule 2A provides that the proceedings shall be entitled in the matter of the defendant, naming him and in the matter of the Act under which the proceedings are brought and all subsequent documents shall be so entitled. In cases where restraint orders are made before proceedings have been instituted, the person against whom the order is made is still referred to as 'the Defendant' (see s 25(4)(a) DTA and s 76(3)(a) CJA).

(3) Preparation of documentation

7.15 The first thing a prosecutor wishing to apply for a restraint order will need to do is draft the necessary documentation in support of the application. Three documents are required: a claim form, a draft order, and a witness statement in support of the application.

C. Procedure on Applications for Restraint Orders

(4) The claim form

By sc115(1) applications for restraint orders must be commenced by the issue of a claim form by the prosecutor. An application for the appointment of a receiver may also be added to the claim form. A draft claim form appears at Appendix 9. **7.16**

(5) The draft order

The prosecutor must also submit a draft order for approval by the court together with three copies to be sealed by the court in the event that the order is granted. This should be in the form of the example appended to the Practice Direction supplementing sc 115. In *Re G (restraint order)* [2001] EWHC Admin 606 Stanley Burnton J reminded prosecutors to take great care when drafting restraint orders to ensure they properly protect the interests of third parties. Where assets are held in the name of a third party either alone or jointly with the defendant, the order should also be addressed to the third party and proper provision should be made for the payment of legal and general living expenses, save where it appears that the third party has access to his or her own restrained funds. Similar principles apply when a company is restrained: the company should be named in the order and it should include exceptions allowing the company to trade legitimately and pay legal fees in connection with the proceedings. **7.17**

Many of Mr Justice Stanley Burnton's concerns, especially in relation to the position of third parties, have been addressed in the Practice Direction supplementing sc 115. By para 5: **7.18**

5.1. Where a restraint order applies to property held in the name of a person other than the defendant—
   (1) the order must be addressed to that person in addition to the defendant; and
   (2) in applying for the order, the prosecutor must consider the guidance given in the matter of *G (restraint order) [2001] EWHC Admin 606.*
5.2. Examples of additional persons to whom an order must, where appropriate, be addressed include—
   (1) a person who has a joint bank account with the defendant;
   (2) in proceedings under the 1988 Act or the 1994 Act, a person to whom the defendant is alleged to have made a gift which may be treated as realisable property of the defendant under the provisions of the relevant Act; or
   (3) a company, where the prosecutor alleges that assets apparently belonging to the company are in reality those of the defendant.
5.3. However, an order should not normally be addressed—
   (1) to a bank with whom a defendant has an account; or
   (2) to the business name of a defendant who carries on an unincorporated business (such business not being a separate legal entity from the defendant).

(6) The witness statement

Sc 115 Rule 3(1) provides that an application for a restraint order must be supported by an affidavit or witness statement. In practice, all applications for restraint orders are now supported by a witness statement verified by a statement of truth rather than by affidavit. The witness statement is the means by which the applicant for the restraint order gives evidence of the factual matters of which the court has to be satisfied to be able to make the restraint order. It will normally be made by a specially trained financial **7.19** investigator employed by the prosecuting authority. sc 115 Rule 3(2) prescribes the matters as to which the person making the witness statement must depose in applications under the DTA. It provides:

An application under paragraph (1) must be supported by a witness statement or affidavit which shall—
  (a) give the grounds for the application; and
  (b) to the best of the witness's ability, give full particulars of the realisable property in respect of which the order is sought and specify the person or persons holding such property.

7.20 Sc 115 Rule 23(c) modifies these provisions in relation to witness statements made in support of applications for restraint orders made under the CJA. It provides that sc 115 Rule 3(2) shall have effect as if the following sub-paragraphs were substituted for subparas (a) and (b):

  (a) state, as the case may be, either that proceedings have been instituted against the defendant for an offence to which Part VI of the 1988 Act applies (giving particulars of the offence) and that they have not been concluded or that, whether by the laying of an information or otherwise, a person is to be charged with such an offence;
  (b) state, as the case may be, either that a confiscation order has been made or the grounds for believing that such an order may be made.

7.21 Further sc 115 Rule 23(a) provides that references in sc 115 to drug trafficking offences shall, in CJA cases, be construed as references to offences to which Pt VI of that Act applies.

7.22 The witness statement must address all the issues prescribed by sc 115. The statement may, unless the court otherwise directs, contain statements of information or belief, provided the sources and grounds thereof are identified. In *Re A Defendant* The Times, 7 April 1987 Webster J ruled that it was sufficient in a drug trafficking case for the maker of the witness statement to depose as to the commission of a drug trafficking offence by the defendant, as this constitutes evidence from which the inference can almost inevitably be made that he has benefited from drug trafficking. The judge held that the court was entitled to take judicial notice of the fact that the object of drug trafficking was to make a profit rather than to provide users with a free source of supply. The learned judge also ruled, in so far as sources of information and belief were concerned, that it was not necessary to identify each and every police officer who had witnessed the defendant dealing in controlled drugs and that a general reference to officers of the drugs squad would suffice.

(7) *The duty of full and frank disclosure*

7.23 It should not, however, be thought that the prosecutor need do no more than provide in his witness statement the information required by sc 115. Applications for restraint orders are subject to the usual rule of civil procedure that a litigant who asks the court to make an order without giving notice to the other parties to the action must give full and frank disclosure of all material facts whether they support his case or not. The requirement to give full and frank disclosure is imposed because the defendant has no opportunity to attend and address the court as to why an order should not be made. If granted, a restraint order can have a drastic effect on the defendant, his family and business and, in contrast to the

C. Procedure on Applications for Restraint Orders

position in relation to freezing orders, he will only have very limited rights to obtain compensation in the event of his acquittal (see s 18 of the DTA and s 89 of the CJA which are considered in more detail in Chapter 28). Further, the prosecutor cannot be compelled to give an undertaking in damages as a condition precedent to the order being granted (see sc 115 Rule 4(1)). Full and frank disclosure is thus essential to enable the court to determine the application fairly.

The obligation to give full and frank disclosure is a strict one and applies not only to matters known to the person making the witness statement but also to all other matters known to other officers of the prosecuting authority. The duty also extends to matters which ought to have been known to the prosecuting authority if all proper enquiries had been made prior to making the application. It matters not that the deponent was unaware of, or did not believe the omitted facts to be relevant or important. Relevance is a matter to be determined by the court and not by the applicant or his legal advisers. Implicit in the duty of full and frank disclosure is an obligation to take proper care to ensure that all matters so disclosed are accurate. **7.24**

(8) What additional matters should be disclosed?

There can be no exhaustive list of the matters which should be disclosed as each case is different and must be judged on its own particular facts. It is submitted, however, that the following matters should be disclosed by the prosecutor if he is to comply properly with his duty of full and frank disclosure: **7.25**

(a) particulars of any defence put forward by the defendant in interview or which would appear to be available to him from the facts known to the prosecutor;
(b) details of any innocent explanation advanced by the defendant as to his possession of substantial assets that appear to be inconsistent with his known legitimate source of income;
(c) details of any legitimate business operated by the defendant, so the court can be satisfied any restraint order makes proper provision to enable the company to continue in bona fide trading pending the conclusion of the proceedings;
(d) details, in so far as they are known, of the defendant's domestic circumstances and financial commitments, including his marital status, details of any children or other dependent relatives he may have, and the extent of any mortgage obligations. If the defendant has at any time been adjudged bankrupt, this too should be disclosed;
(e) particulars of any interest held by a third party in realisable property in respect of which the order is being sought;
(f) where it is alleged that a company controlled by the defendant has facilitated the criminal conduct complained of, all the facts relied on in support of this contention should be disclosed together with full details of the corporate structure, including the date on which the company was incorporated, the share capital, the names of the company's officers and shareholders and, when known, the approximate annual turnover of the company;
(g) in CJA cases, details of any civil proceedings brought against the defendant by any victim of the offence;

(h) full details as to why the prosecutor believes that assets will be dissipated if a restraint order is not made; and

(i) where the prosecutor seeks the appointment of a management receiver at the same time as applying for a restraint order, the *Capewell* Guidelines (dealt with in detail in Chapter 3) must be fully complied with in the witness statement in support. If it is not possible for the prosecutor to comply with any one or more of the Guidelines a full explanation as to the reasons must be included in the witness statement.

7.26 Further, the duty to give full and frank disclosure is a continuing one that does not come to an end once a restraint order has been made. The duty extends to disclosing subsequently discovered facts, so if further information comes to light after the order has been made that could be relevant to the exercise of the court's discretion whether or not to make a restraint order and, if so, on what terms, the prosecutor must make full and prompt disclosure. The proper course in such circumstances is for the prosecutor to make a further witness statement deposing as to the new matters and then to refer the matter back to the court, on notice to the defendant and affected third parties, to enable the court to determine what action should be taken having regard to those matters.

(9) The consequences of non-disclosure

7.27 The usual consequence of material non-disclosure is that the court will discharge the order. The court will also be at pains to ensure that a prosecution authority who obtains a restraint order without full disclosure will be deprived of any advantage it may have derived from that failure to disclose. However, as the Court of Appeal made clear in *Brinks Mat Ltd v Elcombe* [1988] 1 WLR 1350, the court does have some discretion in the matter and if it considers any non-disclosure to be of a minor nature, it may either direct the order to continue, or discharge it and make a new order on the same or different terms.

7.28 In *Re AJ and DJ* (CA, 9 December 1992) the Court of Appeal upheld a decision by Laws J to discharge a restraint order inter alia on the basis of material non-disclosure where the prosecutor's affidavit wrongly deposed that:

(a) the benefit from the alleged offences amounted to £450,000 when in reality it was nearer £40,000;

(b) no civil proceedings had been instituted by the victims of the offences when one of the building societies affected had in fact instituted such proceedings;

(c) the defendants had been uncooperative with the police when this was not the case and there was evidence that the defendants were attempting to dissipate assets when in reality there was no such evidence.

7.29 The Court did, however, indicate that not every instance of non-disclosure would automatically result in the order being discharged. Leggatt LJ said:

> Even if there is material non-disclosure in applying for a restraint order, the court will hesitate to discharge the order on that ground alone. Instead, it will normally be content to vary the order so as to apply only to that realisable property which it has been satisfactorily proved should be subject to the order, and will mark the breach of duty to the court in swearing an exceptionable affidavit by an appropriate order for costs.

C. Procedure on Applications for Restraint Orders

The Court of Appeal took a similar approach in *Jennings v CPS* [2005] 4 All ER 391 and was at pains to stress the public interest in ensuring that assets were available to meet any confiscation order that might be made in the defendant's case. Longmore LJ said: **7.30**

> The fact that the Crown acts in the public interest does, in my view, militate against the sanction of discharging an order if, after consideration of all the evidence, the court thinks that an order is appropriate. That is not to say that there could never be a case where the Crown's failure might be so appalling that the ultimate sanction of discharge would be justified.

As Laws LJ observed, however, this has to be balanced against the importance of requiring the Crown to comply strictly with the rules. He said: **7.31**

> It seems to me that there are two factors which might point towards a different approach being taken to without notice applications for restraint orders in comparison to applications in ordinary litigation for freezing orders; but they pull in opposite directions. First, the application is necessarily brought (assuming of course that it is brought in good faith) in the public interest. The public interest in question is the efficacy of s 71 of the Act of 1988. Here is the first factor: the court should be more concerned to fulfil this public interest if that is what on the facts the restraint order would do, than to discipline the applicant – the Crown – for delay or failure of disclosure. But secondly, precisely because the applicant is the Crown, the court must be alert to see that its jurisdiction is not being conscripted to the service of any arbitrary or unfair action by the State, and so should particularly insist on strict compliance with its rules and standards, not least the duty of disclosure.

Prosecutors must therefore remain vigilant to ensure that witness statements in support of applications for restraint orders made without notice to the defendant give full and frank disclosure of all material facts. This is not to say that it is incumbent on him to disclose every minute detail of the case and the court must, it is submitted, give the prosecutor some latitude to reflect the fact that in many cases restraint orders have to be obtained as a matter of great urgency to prevent assets of significant value being dissipated. Indeed, in *Brinks Mat Ltd v Elcombe* [1988] 1 WLR 1350 Slade LJ deprecated the practice of applying for orders obtained without notice to be discharged alleging non-disclosure on very slender grounds. **7.32**

When material non-disclosure does occur in restraint cases, it is rarely attributable to mala fides on the part of the prosecutor. In most instances it arises because of a breakdown in communication between those responsible for the financial investigation and those dealing with the prosecution side of the case in the criminal courts at a time when there is an understandable concern to have a restraint order in place at the earliest opportunity to prevent any dissipation of assets. In such circumstances, it is perhaps not surprising that, from time to time, misunderstandings arise in the passing of information between those having the conduct of different aspects of the case. A classic example of this arose in *Jennings v CPS* [2005] 4 All ER 391 where the defendant's solicitors had written to the Greater Manchester CPS advising of his intention to re-mortgage his home in order to pay off some outstanding liabilities. This letter was not passed on to the Central Confiscation Branch of the CPS in London and consequently was not disclosed in the witness statement made in support of the restraint order application. In rejecting the contention that the restraint order should be discharged on this basis, the Court of Appeal described the failure to pass on the letter as 'unimpressive but, plainly, not malicious'. Further, as the Court pointed out, the letter did **7.33** not in any event necessarily assist the defendant as it tended to show he was living beyond his means. As Laws LJ said:

> Plainly the letter displayed a willingness on the appellant's part to disclose to the CPS transactions which he intended to carry out relating to his property. But it cuts both ways. The letter tends also to show that the appellant was living beyond his means. He was having to borrow to pay tax; and he was proposing to turn unsecured debt into a secured loan, thus giving the lender a statutory priority over the Crown (see s 77 (4) of the Act of 1988). At the very least Leveson J. was not plainly wrong to hold that the impact of disclosure of the letter would only have been "to increase the concern of dissipation of assets, rather than reduce it". And the failure to disclose it was inadvertent. In the circumstances I am quite unable to hold that the failure was such as to require the court to discharge the restraint order, and then consider as a separate exercise whether to impose a fresh order.

D. The Hearing

7.34 Once the prosecutor has completed all the necessary documentation he will lodge it together with the prescribed fee (currently £400) at the Administrative Court office at the Royal Courts of Justice. Sc115 Rule 3(1) provides that the claim form need not be served on any other party to the proceedings and the application may therefore proceed without notice to the defendant. Although sc115 makes provision for the application to be made without notice to the defendant, this does not mean that in every case the prosecutor should automatically proceed in this way. In many cases, the risk of assets being dissipated will be so great that the prosecutor will be entirely justified in proceeding without notice. In each case, however, the prosecutor should consider carefully whether the risk is so great that an application without notice is necessary. Where there is little risk of dissipation, the prosecutor should always proceed on notice. The position was summarised by Leggatt LJ in *Re AJ & DJ* (9 December 1992) in these terms:

> In the ordinary case the prosecution would no doubt be unwise not to proceed *ex parte*, and will need, in support of the application no more than an affidavit which concisely and truthfully summarises the facts, but in an unusual case such as the present in which it is not established that there was any need for a restraint order to be made the order will be discharged. Rare though such cases will be, this represents a cautionary reminder for all prosecutors that they are not entitled to assume that an order will be made automatically once the conditions of section 76 have been satisfied.

7.35 If the prosecutor decides to proceed without notice, the papers will be placed before a judge of the Queen's Bench Division assigned to Administrative Court business. The judge will consider the matter in his private room without the prosecutor being present. If the judge is content that a restraint order should be made on the terms sought by the prosecutor he will make the order. If, on the other hand, there are matters of concern to the judge or issues he requires to have clarified, the prosecutor will be asked to attend on him to make oral representations. Similarly, if there are any unusual aspects to an application for a restraint order, the prosecutor himself should request an oral hearing to explain any areas of difficulty to the judge personally. Where a hearing takes place on notice the defendant will have the opportunity to attend on the judge either in person or through his legal representatives to make representations as to why an order should not be made or, if one is to be made, as to any conditions or exceptions that should be imposed.

D. The Hearing

Where an oral hearing takes place, in accordance with the procedure established in *Interoute Telecommunications (UK) Ltd v Fashion Gossip Ltd* [1999] TLR 762 in relation to freezing order applications, the prosecutor should take a full note of the hearing and serve the same on the defendant along with a copy of the restraint order. *In Director of the Assets Recovery Agency v Singh* [2004] EWHC Admin 2335 McCombe J held that the *Interoute* principle in relation to freezing orders applies with equal force to applications by the Asset Recovery Agency for interim receivership orders under the Proceeds of Crime Act, 2002. He said: **7.36**

> I can see no reason why the common practice in relation to without notice applications in the High Court should not be followed in cases of this type, unless the judge hearing the application expressly decides that, for good reason, a note should not be served on affected parties and provided that that decision is recorded on the face of the order, so that all affected parties may know that that decision also is susceptible to the customary permission to apply to vary or discharge the order.

It is submitted that this principle should apply to applications for restraint orders made without notice and the best practice is for the prosecutor to prepare and serve a note of the hearing on the defendant. **7.37**

If the judge decides to make an order he will initial the draft order and any amendments he may have made. The Administrative Court office will then seal the orders and give the case an official reference number commencing 'DTA' or 'CJA' depending on the Act under which the order is made. This reference number should be quoted in all correspondence with the Administrative Court office and should appear at the top right hand corner of all subsequent orders, affidavits, witness statements, and application notices filed in the case. **7.38**

(1) Service of the order

Once a restraint order has been made, the prosecutor must serve it, together with the witness statement in support, on the defendant and on all other named persons restrained by the order and shall notify all other persons and bodies affected by the order of its terms: see sc115 Rule 4(3). Indeed, the court will usually require the prosecutor to give an undertaking to serve the order 'as soon as reasonably practicable'. In *PS Refson & Co Ltd v Saggars* [1982] 3 All ER 111, the High Court held that 'as soon as reasonably practicable' meant 'forthwith'. Nourse J, with the concurrence of the Vice Chancellor, gave a clear warning to the effect that any failure to comply with undertakings as to service constitutes a contempt of court and that solicitors acting on behalf of a party can also be held in contempt for failing to implement any such undertaking given on behalf of a client. **7.39**

The officer effecting service of the order should make a full note as to the date, time, and place of service of the order. This is important because, in the event of any subsequent breach of the order necessitating the institution of proceedings for contempt of court, it will be necessary for the prosecutor to prove the defendant had due notice of it. This applies equally to third parties affected named in the order. Similarly, all unsuccessful attempts to effect service should also be recorded in case any complaint is made that service was not effected as soon as reasonably practicable. **7.40**

The prosecutor should always endeavour to effect personal service of the order on the defendant and named third parties. It occasionally happens, however, that a defendant may **7.41** seek to obstruct the service of the order by, for example, refusing to come to his front door when the officer calls or, if he is in custody, by refusing to leave his prison cell to collect the order. Alternatively, the defendant may be away from home at the time the order is made because, for example, he is on holiday or has absconded. In such circumstances, the prosecutor may apply to court for an order for service by an alternative method under r 6.8(1) CPR. The court may then order service by another method which it believes will result in the order coming to the attention of the party in question, for example service on his solicitor, on a member of his family, or by putting the order through the letter box at his last known place of abode.

E. Procedure on Applications to Vary or Discharge the Order

7.42 In Chapter 5 we considered the grounds on which a defendant or affected third party might apply to the court for a restraint order to be varied or discharged. In this section we examine the procedures that should be followed by a defendant or affected third party in seeking the variation or discharge of an order. Applications to discharge a restraint or receivership order should be confined to those instances where the prosecutor's evidence appears to be insufficient to justify the making of the order or where there has been a serious breach of the duty to give full and frank disclosure of all material facts. In most cases, it will be more appropriate to make an application to vary the order to mitigate its harsher effects on the defendant or affected third parties. In practice the most commonly made applications for variations include:

(a) requests for more time to comply with disclosure and repatriation requirements;
(b) requests for an increase in the amount payable by way of general living expenses; and
(c) applications to release a particular asset from the terms of the order either on the ground that it does not constitute realisable property or to effect a sale.

(1) Variation by consent: consulting the prosecutor

7.43 Most restraint orders contain a provision enabling the parties to agree that the order might be varied in any respect without the necessity to make application to court provided the variation is reduced to writing. A typical such provision appears in para 15 of the draft restraint order in Appendix 1. Any person seeking a variation to a restraint or receivership order should always first approach the prosecutor to discover whether the proposed variation, or a mutually acceptable compromise, can be agreed on a 'by consent' basis. An applicant who applies directly to the court for the order to be varied without first consulting the prosecutor risks being penalised in costs and, if the application is made on the advice of his legal representatives, the court may be minded to make a wasted costs order against those responsible.

7.44 In approaching the prosecutor, the applicant should provide precisely the same information that he would incorporate in his evidence in support were the matter to be determined by the court. Further, if the variation requested is an increase in the amount payable by way of general living expenses, the applicant should ensure that he has first complied with his disclosure obligations under the order. It is unlikely the prosecutor will be in a position to

E. Procedure on Applications to Vary or Discharge the Order

accede to a request for an increase prior thereto because he will not have sufficient information on which to base a decision in the absence of full details of the defendant's financial position. In *Re O* [1991] 1 All ER 330 the Court of Appeal upheld the decision of Macpherson J not to entertain a variation application until the defendants had given full disclosure of their assets. If the parties are able to reach agreement, it is sufficient that the agreed variation is recorded in writing—there is no necessity for it to be embodied in a formal consent order. If the variation is to increase the amount payable to the defendant by way of general living expenses, it will be necessary for the prosecutor to contact the bank at which the nominated account is held to confirm it is in order for the defendant to be paid the increased amount.

Defendants, affected third parties and their legal advisors should take care in agreeing the terms of 'by consent' variations and only agree to the same if they are content to be legally bound by them. A consent order is treated as a binding contract between the parties and, as the Court of Appeal held in *Weston v Dayman* [2006] EWCA Civ 1165, the Court will only entertain an application to vary an order made by consent in exceptional circumstances. Arden LJ said: **7.45**

> I would accept that the court should accede to an application for variation where it is just to do so but in my judgment one of the aspects of justice is that a bargain freely made should be upheld. Mr. Weston clearly obtained benefits under the order. It may well be that those benefits are not as great as he thought, but that is not a matter for this court. In those circumstances I do not consider it would be right for this court to exercise its discretion to vary the order as sought.

(2) Applying to the court

Where an approach to the prosecutor does not result in agreement, the only way forward is for an application to be made to the court for the order to be varied. Sc115 Rule 5(1) provides that: **7.46**

> Any person or body on whom a restraint order or a charging order is served or is notified of such an order may make application in accordance with CPR Part 23 to discharge or vary the order.

Further, most orders will themselves give the defendant and affected third parties permission to apply to have the same varied or discharged. A draft application notice covering the most common variation applications appears at Appendix 7. The application notice and any witness statement or affidavit in support must be lodged with the court and served on the prosecutor and, where he is not the applicant, the defendant not less than two clear days prior to the hearing: see sc115 Rule 5(2). It should be noted that the expression 'two clear days' means that the day of service and the day of the hearing are disregarded. Thus, if an application is served on a Monday, the first day on which it might be heard would be the following Thursday. **7.47**

(3) Drafting the witness statement or affidavit

Nothing in the rules of court requires an application for the discharge or variation of an order to be supported by evidence in the form of a witness statement or affidavit. However, unless the application involves only the determination of an issue of law with no **7.48** factual issues arising, it is most unlikely that the court would entertain an application for a variation in the absence of supporting evidence. The contents of any supporting evidence will obviously depend on the nature of the variation being sought and must of course allude to every issue of fact upon which the applicant wishes to rely in support of the application. A witness statement or affidavit in support of an application to increase the amount payable by way of general living expenses should, it is submitted, depose as to the following matters:

(1) the applicant's personal circumstances—ie his marital status, the number and ages of any children, and details of any other dependent relatives;
(2) the regular monthly income of the defendant, exhibiting all relevant documentation (eg salary advices, bank statements etc);
(3) the regular monthly expenditure of the defendant, again exhibiting all relevant documentation (eg proof of mortgage or rental payments, public utility bills, school fees, etc);
(4) confirmation that the defendant has no unrestrained assets from which the expenses can be paid; and
(5) identification of a source for payment from which it is intended the expenditure should be met.

7.49 Where the variation sought is the release of a restrained asset on the basis that it does not constitute realisable property, the witness statement or affidavit must provide full details of the factual basis for that assertion exhibiting all relevant documentation. If the suggestion is that it belongs to someone other than the defendant, a witness statement from the true owner should be obtained, again exhibiting all available documentation establishing the true owner.

(4) Drafting the order

7.50 As a matter of good practice the application should always include a draft order setting out the precise wording of the variation sought. The order must be drafted in precise terms, specifying the amounts to be released, the accounts from which and the means by which they are to be paid. This is to prevent any possible abuse by the defendant applying funds for purposes not authorised by the court or attempting to have the same sum of money released from two or three different sources.

(5) Issuing the application

7.51 The application notice is issued out of the Administrative Court office in Room C314 at the Royal Courts of Justice. On no account should an attempt be made to issue the application out of the Action Department at the Central Office or at a District Registry of the High Court. The applicant or his solicitor should attend at the Administrative Court office with the application notice (duly stamped to show the correct fee—currently £100—has been paid), the affidavit or witness statement in support, and the draft order together with three copies of each document. The Administrative Court office will then issue the application notice by sealing it and inserting a return date. The original and one copy will be retained by the court and the others returned to the applicant for service.

E. Procedure on Applications to Vary or Discharge the Order

(6) Service of the application

The application notice and supporting documentation must be served on the prosecutor at least two clear days before the hearing. Further, where the applicant for the variation is a person other than the defendant, he must also ensure that the defendant, too is served a minimum of two clear days before the hearing: see sc 115 Rule 5(2). The prosecutor and any other person upon whom the application is served should always be given at least the minimum period of notice required by sc 115 to ensure they have a fair opportunity of considering the application and filing evidence in response. In particularly complex cases, solicitors acting for a respondent to a variation application may invite the applicant to agree an adjournment to give more time in which to respond. Reasonable requests for an adjournment should always be agreed as a party who unreasonably withholds consent risks being ordered to pay costs if the other party then successfully applies to court for an adjournment. **7.52**

(7) Proof of service

An applicant for a variation should always be in a position to prove service of the application notice on all the relevant parties. This is particularly so in relation to a person who is unlikely to attend or who may deny receipt of the documentation. If the only person to be served is the prosecuting authority there is unlikely to be a dispute, but in cases where any dispute as to service may arise, it is essential that a witness statement proving service is available to the court to satisfy the judge that the application notice has been properly served on any interested party who fails to attend the hearing. **7.53**

(8) The hearing

The hearing will take place before a High Court judge sitting in private. In order to protect the position of an unconvicted defendant, the case will appear in the Daily Cause list and on the Court Service website (<http://www.courtservice.gov.uk>) using only the DTA/CJA reference number assigned to the case together with the first letter of the defendant's surname—eg 'DTA1/2003 Re A'. As the hearing will take place in private it is not necessary for the advocates to be robed. **7.54**

The procedure adopted at the hearing will be the same as for any hearing before a judge sitting in private. The applicant will open the proceedings by explaining to the judge the nature of the application, the grounds relied upon and referring to the evidence in support. Oral evidence is only very rarely heard on such applications, but when witnesses are called they will be subject to the usual rules as to examination in chief, cross-examination etc. The respondents to the application will then have the opportunity of presenting their cases in the same way and all parties will be afforded the chance of making a closing address to the judge before he delivers judgment. If a point of law of some importance is likely to be involved, or an appeal may follow, the judge should be asked to summon the shorthand writer to take a verbatim note of the judgment so that it might be reported and appear with any appeal papers. **7.55**

(9) Costs

In most applications for variations to restraint orders, a summary assessment of costs will be appropriate: only in the most complex of cases should the matter be referred to a costs **7.56** judge for detailed assessment. At least 24 hours before the hearing, the parties should serve on one another and on the court a schedule of costs setting out the amounts claimed and how they are calculated. The successful party should then invite the court to make a summary assessment of costs in his favour. The court should give the unsuccessful party the opportunity of making representations both as to whether he should be required to pay costs at all and in respect of the amount claimed. The usual rule is that costs follow the event, ie the successful party will be entitled to his costs unless he has behaved improperly in some way.

(10) After the hearing: drafting and serving the order

7.57 In accordance with the usual rule of civil procedure, the onus is on the party taking out the application notice to draw up the order and arrange for it to be sealed by the Administrative Court office. Once drawn up and sealed, the variation should be served by the applicant or his solicitor on all parties affected by it, including the prosecutor, defendant, and affected third parties. It is particularly important to serve a copy on any bank or other financial institution affected by the order, as they are unlikely to agree to the release of any funds to the defendant unless and until they have been served with a sealed copy of the order. The terms of the variation should always be explained most carefully to the lay client. In particular his attention should be drawn to the maximum amounts released to him, the purposes for which they may be expended and any conditions precedent to the release of funds imposed by the order. The client should be left in no doubt that any failure to comply with such terms may result in proceedings for contempt of court being brought against him.

(11) Variation applications by the prosecutor

7.58 Sc115 Rule 6(1) also allows the prosecutor to apply for a restraint order to be varied. This occurs quite frequently where, for example, after a restraint order has been made, the prosecutor discovers additional items of realisable property (perhaps as a result of information provided by the defendant in his disclosure statement) which have not been included in the original order. In these circumstances he may apply to the court for the order to be varied to include the newly discovered assets.

7.59 Applications by the prosecutor must be made on notice to the defendant save where the case is one of urgency or where the giving of notice would cause a reasonable apprehension that assets may be dissipated. In these circumstances the application may be made without notice. The application must be supported by a witness statement or affidavit giving, to the best of the deponent's ability, full particulars of the realisable property in respect of which the order is sought and specify the person or persons holding the property: sc115 Rule 6(2). As with applications by the defendant or affected third parties, the prosecutor must serve his application notice together with the supporting evidence at least two clear days before the date fixed for the hearing: sc115 Rule 6(3).

(12) Appeals

7.60 Any party to the proceedings may appeal against the judge's decision to grantor refuse an application to vary or discharge a restraint order. The appeal lies to the Court of Appeal (Civil Division) and, as the proceedings are interlocutory, permission is required.

8

RESTRAINT AND RECEIVERSHIP UNDER THE PROCEEDS OF CRIME ACT 2002

A. Introduction	8.01
(1) Overview	8.02
B. Restraint Orders	8.03
(1) When does POCA apply?	8.03
(2) Conditions for obtaining restraint orders under POCA	8.12
(3) The first condition: criminal investigations	8.13
(4) The second condition: criminal proceedings already started	8.17
(5) The third condition: application for reconsideration to be made	8.23
(6) The fourth condition: reconsideration of benefit	8.27
(7) The fifth condition: reconsideration of available amount	8.29
(8) Making the order	8.33
(9) Exceptions	8.38
(10) Legal expenses	8.40
(11) Ancillary orders	8.50
(12) Restrictions	8.52
(13) Variation and discharge of the order	8.55
(14) Charging orders	8.56
C. Management Receivers	8.57
(1) Powers of management receivers	8.59
(2) Restriction on the use of powers	8.62
D. Powers of the Court and Receiver: the 'Legislative Steer'	8.64
E. Procedure on Applications	8.69
(1) Applications for restraint orders	8.70
(2) The order	8.73
(3) Variation or discharge applications by persons affected by restraint orders	8.75
(4) Variation applications by the person who applied for the order	8.78
(5) Discharge applications by the person who applied for the order	8.80
(6) Receivership proceedings	8.81
(7) The application for appointment	8.82
(8) Applications for the conferment of powers on receivers	8.84
(9) Applications to vary or discharge receivership orders	8.86
(10) Security	8.87
(11) Remuneration of receivers	8.89
(12) Receiver's accounts	8.90
(13) Non-compliance by a receiver	8.91
F. Provisions as to Hearings and Evidence	8.92
(1) Restraint and receivership hearings in the Crown Court	8.92
(2) Evidence	8.94
(3) Evidence should be in writing	8.96
(4) Hearsay evidence	8.99
(5) Expert evidence	8.100
(6) Disclosure and inspection of documents	8.102
(7) Court documents	8.103
(8) Service of documents	8.104
(9) Service by an alternative method	8.107
(10) Service outside the jurisdiction	8.108
(11) Proof of service	8.109
(12) Consent orders	8.110
(13) Slips and omissions	8.111
(14) Supply of documents from court records	8.112
(15) Preparation of documents	8.114
(16) Change of solicitor	8.116
(17) Costs	8.117
(18) Assessment of costs	8.119
(19) Time for complying with orders for costs	8.121
G. Protecting POCA Restraint Orders in Relation to Real Property	8.122
H. Enforcing POCA Restraint and Receivership Orders	8.123

A. Introduction

8.01 The Proceeds of Crime Act 2002 (POCA) received the Royal Assent on 24 July 2002. Part 2 of the Act, which came into force on 24 March 2003, made radical changes to the procedures for obtaining restraint, receivership, and confiscation orders, and to the methods by which confiscation orders might be enforced after they have been made. These provisions only apply in cases where the offences to which the proceedings relate are committed after 24 March 2003; cases that have been brought under the DTA and CJA will continue to be dealt with in accordance with those Acts, as will cases that relate to offences committed before that date.

(1) Overview

8.02 In this chapter we consider, in detail, the changes that POCA has made to the procedures for obtaining restraint and receivership orders. We summarise below, for ease of reference, the principal changes brought about by the new Act:

(a) the provisions relating to restraint and confiscation for all criminal offences are, for the first time, consolidated in one enactment: there is no any distinction between drug trafficking and other criminal offences;
(b) the jurisdiction to make restraint and receivership orders is transferred from the High Court to the Crown Court;
(c) a defendant is not entitled to have restrained funds released for the purpose of meeting his legal expenses incurred both in relation to the criminal proceedings and the restraint proceedings;
(d) restraint orders may be made as soon as a criminal investigation has started in England and Wales for an offence where there are reasonable grounds to believe that the defendant has benefited from his criminal conduct; and
(e) the Act created the Assets Recovery Agency (ARA) which is empowered to take a prominent role in the obtaining of restraint orders and the enforcement of confiscation orders.

B. Restraint Orders

(1) When does POCA apply?

8.03 Under the Proceeds of Crime Act 2002 (Commencement No. 5, Transitional Provisions, Savings and Amendment) Order 2003, SI 2003/333 from 24 March 2003, all applications for restraint orders are made to the Crown Court where it is alleged that the offences have been committed after that date. Cases that have been commenced in the High Court continue to be dealt with in that court even after the commencement date, and any applications for the variation or discharge of such orders, for the appointment of management and enforcement receivers, or for certificates of inadequacy continue to be brought in the High Court. Similarly, applications for restraint orders in cases where the offence is

B. Restraint Orders

alleged to have been committed before POCA came into force will continue to be brought in the High Court.

8.04 Difficult questions may arise whether it is appropriate to proceed under POCA where the offences charged or under investigation straddle the 24 March 2003 commencement date. Article 5 of the 2003 Order provides that:

Sections 41 (restraint orders) and 74 (enforcement abroad) of the Act shall not have effect where—
(a) the powers in those sections would otherwise be exercisable by virtue of a condition in section 20 (2) or (3) of the Act being satisfied; and
(b) the offence mentioned in section 20 (2) (a) or (3) (a), as the case may be, was committed before 24th March 2003.

8.05 Further, Art 3(1) provides that s 6 of POCA, which gives the court power to make confiscation orders, shall not have effect where any of the offences were committed before 24 March 2003.

8.06 It appeared that the combined effect of these provisions of the 2003 Order was that the old legislation applied wherever one or more the offences was committed prior to the implementation date. This interpretation was, however, held to be incorrect by the Court of Appeal in *Revenue and Customs Prosecutions Office v Hill* [2005] EWCA Crim 3271. In March 2003 HM Revenue and Customs began an investigation into the affairs of two companies allegedly involved in a dishonest scheme to perpetrate a fraud on the Revenue. In July 2005 search warrants were obtained and three potential defendants were arrested and interviewed. Initial analysis of the documentation suggested that between £6 and £10 million had been transferred overseas between 2003 and 2005. The prosecutor took the view that these transfers amounted to money laundering offences. It was clear, however, that if any offences of tax evasion had been committed, they had either been committed before 24 March, 2003 or were continuing offences which had begun before and had continued after 24 March 2003. Indeed, enquiries revealed evidence of tax evasion going back to 1999.

8.07 The prosecutor, wishing to take advantage of the provisions of POCA which allowed restraint orders to be obtained while the defendants were still subject to investigation, decided to focus on the money laundering offences which, with one exception, had taken place after 24 March, 2003. The prosecutor applied, without notice, for restraint and management receivership orders under POCA and these were granted by the Crown Court. The defendants subsequently applied for the orders to be set aside and, on an inter partes application, the Crown Court judge agreed the orders should be discharged ruling that the orders ought have been made by the High Court under the CJA.

8.08 The Crown then exercised its right of appeal under s 43 of POCA contending that the judge had erred in law in holding that the CJA regime applied. The Court of Appeal upheld the prosecutor's appeal ruling, in the words of Smith LJ:

In our view, the judge erred in his approach to the requirement of section 40 (2) (a) when read in conjunction with Article 5 of the Commencement Order. The test to be applied is whether an investigation has begun into an offence which took place after 24th March, 2003. In order to satisfy section 69, the offence must be one in respect of which a confiscation order may be made following conviction. For the purpose of establishing jurisdiction to make an order, it matters not whether the investigating authority is also investigating one or more offences which occurred before 24th March, 2003. Nor does it matter, for the purpose of jurisdiction, that there is criminal conduct occuring before 24th March 2003, which underlies the post March 2003 offences – as may occur with money laundering. In our view, the time at which the test is to be applied is the time when the application is made, not when the investigation began. That is clear from the words of section 40 (2) (a). All that is required therefore, to establish jurisdiction, is that an offence that may, following conviction, give rise to a confiscation order is under investigation at the time of the application.

8.09 The Court remitted the matter back to the Crown Court so the judge could determine whether it would be appropriate to make another restraint order having regard to the fact that the defendants' assets had subsequently been frozen in civil proceedings.

8.10 It is submitted that prosecutors should proceed with caution in relying on the restraint provisions of POCA when the alleged offences straddle the commencement date. If the prosecutor has a settled intention to prefer charges to which the DTA or CJA applies, applications for restraint orders should be made to the High Court under that legislation. Where, however, at the commencement of an investigation, the prosecutor intends to focus only on offences committed after 24 March 2003 he may properly proceed under POCA. If, at a later date, it becomes apparent to him that charges will be preferred to which the DTA or CJA applies, he should forthwith apply for an order under the appropriate Act and seek the discharge of the POCA order.

8.11 Those acting for individuals subject to POCA restraint orders should be vigilant to ensure the prosecutor has used the jurisdiction appropriately. Any attempt by a prosecutor to rely on POCA simply to obtain a restraint order when a defendant is still subject to investigation or to preclude the release of funds to meet legal expenses would, it is submitted, amount to an abuse of process to which the court should be alerted immediately.

(2) Conditions for obtaining restraint orders under POCA

8.12 By s 40(1) of POCA, the Crown Court may make a restraint order if any of the following conditions are satisfied.

(3) The first condition: criminal investigations

8.13 By s 40(2) the first condition is that:

(a) a criminal investigation has been started in England and Wales with regard to an offence, and
(b) there is reasonable cause to believe that the alleged offender has benefited from his criminal conduct.

8.14 This is an entirely new provision. Under the DTA and CJA a restraint order can only be made when the defendant had been charged with a criminal offence or the prosecutor is in a position to say that he will be so charged at a future date. This, in effect, requires the prosecutor to have a settled intention to charge the person against whom the order was to be sought.

B. Restraint Orders

8.15 A 'criminal investigation' is defined in s 88(2) of POCA in these terms:

A criminal investigation is an investigation which police officers or other persons have a duty to conduct with a view to it being ascertained whether a person should be charged with an offence.

8.16 The term extends to investigations conducted by all prosecution authorities and not just the police. By s 40(9) of POCA, references to 'the defendant' are to be construed as references to the alleged offender and references to 'the prosecutor' are to the person the court believes will have the conduct of any proceedings for an offence. The prosecuting authority conducting the investigation cannot rest on its laurels once a restraint order is made and must conduct the investigation expeditiously. Section 42(7) provides that the restraint order must be discharged if proceedings for an offence are not started within a reasonable time of the order being made. What constitutes a 'reasonable time' is an issue of fact to be determined having regard to the circumstances of individual cases. If the investigation being conducted relates to a complex fraud with a vast quantity of documentation to examine and overseas enquiries to be made, it is clearly reasonable for the investigation to take much longer to complete than a more straightforward investigation into an offence where all the evidence is to be found in the UK. Where an investigation is taking an unusually long time to complete, it is submitted the proper course is for the prosecutor to return to court from time to time to provide an update as to the state of progress and give the court the opportunity to determine whether it is appropriate for the restraint order to remain in force and, if so, on what terms.

(4) The second condition: criminal proceedings already started

8.17 By s 40(3) the second condition is that:

(a) proceedings for an offence have been started in England and Wales and not concluded, and
(b) there is reasonable cause to believe that the defendant has benefited from his criminal conduct.

8.18 By s 40(7), the second condition is not satisfied if the court believes there has been undue delay in continuing the proceedings or that the prosecutor does not intend to proceed. Again, 'undue delay' is an issue of fact to be determined by the court having regard to the circumstances of the particular case. It is submitted that the court is entitled to look at the conduct of all the parties in determining whether there has been undue delay and it would be entitled to take into account the extent to which the defendant's conduct has caused or contributed to any such delay.

8.19 The second condition closely mirrors the provisions of the DTA and CJA and is likely to be the provision under which most applications for restraint orders will be brought. Section 85(1) of POCA defines the phrase 'proceedings for an offence have been started' in precisely the same terms as the phrase 'proceedings have been instituted' in s 41(2) DTA (see Chapter 2, para 2.09).

8.20 Section 85(3) to (6) does, however, provide an entirely new definition of the term 'proceedings are concluded'. The section provides as follows:

(3) If the defendant is acquitted on all counts in proceedings for an offence, the proceedings are concluded when he is acquitted.

Chapter 8: Restraint and Receivership under POCA 2002

(4) If the defendant is convicted in proceedings for an offence and the conviction is quashed or the defendant is pardoned before a confiscation order is made, the proceedings are concluded when the conviction is quashed or the defendant is pardoned.

(5) If a confiscation order is made against the defendant in proceedings for an offence (whether the order is made by the Crown Court or the Court of Appeal) the proceedings are concluded:
   (a) when the order is satisfied or discharged, or
   (b) when the order is quashed and there is no further possibility of an appeal against the decision to quash the order.

8.21 Thus, as under the CJA and DTA, proceedings only conclude when a confiscation order has been satisfied and the restraint order may remain in force until no further sums remain due under the order. In practice, this may not occur until some years have elapsed since the confiscation order was made.

8.22 Section 85(6) introduces entirely new rules for determining when proceedings have concluded in circumstances where the prosecutor exercises his right of appeal under s 31(2) against the refusal of the Crown Court to make a confiscation order. Section 85(6) provides:

(6) If the defendant is convicted in proceedings for an offence but the Crown Court decides not to make a confiscation order against him, the following rules apply—
   (a) if an application for leave to appeal under section 31(2) is refused, the proceedings are concluded when the decision to refuse is made;
   (b) if the time for applying for leave to appeal under section 31(2) expires without an application being made, the proceedings are concluded when the time expires;
   (c) if on appeal under section 31(2) the Court of Appeal confirms the Crown Court's decision, and an application for leave to appeal under section 33 is refused, the proceedings are concluded when the decision to refuse is made;
   (d) if on appeal under section 31(2) the Court of Appeal confirms the Crown Court's decision and the time for applying for leave to appeal under section 33 expires without an application being made, the proceedings are concluded when the time expires;
   (e) if on appeal under section 31(2) the Court of Appeal confirms the Crown Court's decision, and on appeal under section 33 the House of Lords confirms the Court of Appeal's decision, the proceedings are concluded when the House of Lords confirms the decision;
   (f) if on appeal under section 31(2) the Court of Appeal directs the Crown Court to reconsider the case, and on reconsideration the Crown Courts decides not to make a confiscation order against the defendant, the proceedings are concluded when the Crown Court makes that decision;
   (g) if on appeal under section 33 the House of Lords directs the Crown Court to reconsider the case, and on reconsideration the Crown Court decides not to make a confiscation order against the defendant, the proceedings are concluded when the Crown Court makes that decision.

(7) In applying subsection (6) any power to extend the time for making an application for leave to appeal must be ignored.

(8) In applying subsection (6) the fact that a court may decide on a later occasion to make a confiscation order against the defendant must be ignored.

The effect of these provisions is to permit the restraint order to remain in force until appeal proceedings brought by the prosecutor or the Director have been determined by the Court of Appeal or House of Lords in accordance with ss 31 and 33 of the Act.

(5) The third condition: application for reconsideration to be made

8.23 By s 40(4) the third condition is that:

(a) an application by the prosecutor or the Director has been made under sections 19, 20, 27 or 28 and not concluded, or the court believes that such an application is to be made, and
(b) there is reasonable cause to believe the defendant has benefited from his criminal conduct.

8.24 Sections 19 and 20 allow the prosecutor or the Director to apply to the Crown Court to reconsider a case in the light of fresh evidence where no confiscation order was made. Sections 27 and 28 permit the prosecutor or the Director to apply to the Crown Court for confiscation orders to be made against defendants who abscond. Section 40(4) gives the court jurisdiction to make restraint orders to prevent assets being dissipated while such applications are pending.

8.25 By s 86(1) of POCA such applications are concluded:

(a) in a case where the court decides not to make a confiscation order against the defendant when it makes the decision;
(b) in a case where a confiscation order is made against him as a result of the application, when the order is satisfied or discharged, or when the order is quashed and there is no further possibility of an appeal against the decision to quash the order;
(c) in a case where the application is withdrawn, when the person who made the application notifies the withdrawal to the court to which the application was made.

8.26 The effect of this section is very similar to s 85 in that it defines the word 'concluded' to allow the restraint order to remain in force pending any appeal or until such time as any confiscation order has been satisfied.

(6) The fourth condition: reconsideration of benefit

8.27 By s 40(5), the fourth condition is that:

(a) an application by the prosecutor or the Director has been made under s 21 and not concluded, or the court believes that such an application is to be made, and
(b) there is reasonable cause to believe that the court will decide under that section that the amount found under the new calculation of the defendant's benefit exceeds the relevant amount (as defined in that section).

8.28 Section 21 permits the court, on an application by the prosecutor or the Director, to make a new calculation of benefit and increase the confiscation order accordingly in the light of evidence that was not available at the time the original order was made.

(7) The fifth condition: reconsideration of available amount

8.29 By s 40(6), the fifth condition is that:

(a) an application by the prosecutor or the Director has been made under section 22 and not concluded, or the court believes that such an application is to be made, and
(b) there is reasonable cause to believe that the court will decide under that section that the amount found under the new calculation or the available amount exceeds the relevant amount (as defined in that section).

8.30 Under s 22 the court may, on the application of the prosecutor, the Director, or an enforcement receiver, increase a confiscation order when it appears that the value of the defendant's realisable property exceeds that found to be available at the time the confiscation order was made. In such circumstances, the court may increase the order to such amount as it believes just, provided it does not exceed the amount found as the defendant's benefit from the conduct concerned.

8.31 By s 86(2) of POCA, applications under ss 21 and 22 are concluded:

(a) in a case where the court decides not to vary the confiscation order concerned, when it makes that decision;
(b) in a case where the court varies the confiscation order as a result of the application, when the order is satisfied or discharged, or when the order is quashed and there is no further possibility of an appeal against the decision to quash the order;
(c) in a case where the application is withdrawn, when the person who made the application notifies the withdrawal to the court to which the application was made.

8.32 Section 40(8) provides that the third, fourth, and fifth conditions are not satisfied if the court believes there has been undue delay in continuing the application or that the prosecutor or the director (as the case may be) does not intend to proceed.

(8) Making the order

8.33 By s 41(1) the Crown Court may make a restraint order prohibiting any specified person from dealing with any realisable property held by him. if it is satisfied that any of the five conditions set out in s 40 is satisfied. Under s 41(2) of POCA the order may apply to all realisable property held by a specified person whether described in the order or not, and also to realisable property transferred to the specified person after the order is made.

8.34 Section 84 contains a number of important provisions in relation to property. Section 84(1) provides that 'property' is all property wherever situated and, includes money, all forms of real and personal property and things in action and other intangible or incorporeal property. By s 84(2)(a) property is held by a person if he holds an interest in it and, by s 84(2)(h), references to an interest in relation to property other than land include reference to a right (including a right to possession). References to an interest in land are to any legal estate or equitable interest or power (see s 84(2)(f)). In determining whether a defendant has an interest in property for the purposes of making a restraint order the court will have regard to the practical realities of the situation. In *D (UK) Ltd v Revenue and Customs Prosecutions Office* [2005] EWCA Crim 2919 a restraint order was varied, on the prosecutor's application, to include some £366,000 held in the account of a company known as 'R' on the basis that it should be available for confiscation at the end of a trial involving an alleged fraudster, Mrs S. On appeal it was argued that the order should not have been so varied as Mrs S had no interest in the money in the company bank account. This argument was rejected by the Court of Appeal and, in dismissing the appeal, Longmore LJ said, delivering the judgment of the Court:

> If, therefore, Revenue and Customs can show that there is a good arguable case that the money in R's account in R's bank was part of the benefit obtained by the alleged

B. Restraint Orders

fraudster, Mrs. S, that money will be liable to restraint until a confiscation order is made. In our judgment, Revenue and Customs do not have to show that there is any enforceable right to the money as between the fraudsters. If they can show an arguable case of fraud in which R (or any other party which may claim entitlement to the money) were participating, money retained in the execution of the fraud is, for the purposes of the legislation, the fraudster's money. No doubt the legal title to the chose in action constituted by R's account at the bank while it is in credit is in R, but the beneficial interest lies with any of the fraudster participants in the fraudulent scheme. It is thus an existing beneficial interest which can be subject to a restraint order, not, as Counsel sought to persuade the full court in his supplemental skeleton argument in order to obtain leave to appeal 'an inchoate future benefit'.

As with DTA and CJA cases, the prosecutor applying for a POCA restraint order does not have to prove his case or provide conclusive evidence of the defendant's interest in a particular asset. A restraint order is an interim remedy intended to preserve the position pending the determination of the proceedings and it is sufficient at the restraint stage for the prosecutor to establish a good arguable case (see *Compton v CPS* [2002] EWCA Civ 1720). **8.35**

The court is entitled, when determining whether an order should restrain all the defendant's realisable property or be limited to the benefit derived from specific offences, to take account of the lifestyle provisions in section 75 of POCA. In cases where those provisions apply, the court is entitled to restrain all the realisable property in which the defendant has an interest (see *R v K* [2005] EWCA Crim 619). **8.36**

Only the prosecutor, the Director, or an accredited financial investigator may apply for a restraint order (see s 42(1)(a) and 42(2) of POCA). The application may be made ex parte to a judge in chambers (s 42(1)(b) of POCA), but the prosecutor should always consider whether an application without notice is really justified and only proceed without notifying the defendant in cases where there is a real risk of assets being dissipated: see *Re AJ and DJ* (9 December 1992). **8.37**

(9) Exceptions

As with High Court restraint orders, the order may be made subject to conditions and exceptions. Section 41(3) of POCA provides that an exception may in particular: **8.38**

(a) make provision for reasonable living expenses and reasonable legal expenses;
(b) make provision for the purpose of enabling any person to carry on any trade, business, profession, or occupation;
(c) be made subject to conditions.

Section 41(3) of POCA gives statutory effect to many of the practices of the High Court enshrined in case law as to the type of exceptions that can be made. As we have seen in Chapter 2, the High Court has for many years been making restraint orders, subject to exceptions to enable living and legal expenses to be paid and businesses in which the defendant has an interest to continue trading legitimately. Section 41(3)(c) allows the court to impose conditions when making exceptions to a restraint order. This provision would, for example, allow the court, when making an exception to enable a business to continue trading legitimately, to impose a condition that the defendant produce accounts to the prosecutor on a regular basis. **8.39**

(10) Legal expenses

8.40 Although s 41(3)(a) gives the court jurisdiction to make provision in a restraint order for the release of funds to meet reasonable legal expenses, s 41(4) imposes strict limits on the court's powers in this regard. It provides:

> (4) But an exception to a restraint order must not make provision of any legal expenses which:
>   (a) relate to an offence which falls within subsection (5), and
>   (b) are incurred by the defendant or by the recipient of a tainted gift.

8.41 Section 41(5) provides that the offences caught by s 41(4)(a) are:

> (a) the offence mentioned in section 40(2) or (3), if the first or second condition (as the case may be) is satisfied;
> (b) the offence (or any of the offences) concerned, if the third, fourth or fifth condition is satisfied.

8.42 In *Customs and Excise Commissioners v S* [2005] 1 WLR 1338 the Court of Appeal held that s 41(4) prohibited the release of funds to meet legal expenses incurred in relation to the restraint proceedings as well as such expenditure incurred in defending the criminal proceedings. The Court upheld the prosecutor's contention that the words 'relate to an offence' in s 41(4) were sufficiently wide to cover the restraint proceedings as no restraint order could be made unless an investigation was underway in relation to an offence or a person had been charged with an offence. In reaching this conclusion, the Court attached great weight to the fact that the prohibition in s 41(4) extended to legal expenses incurred by the recipient of a tainted gift. As Scott Baker LJ observed:

> This makes clear that the legislation is not directed simply at excluding legal expenses in connection with the defendant's criminal proceedings – the underlying offence – but at the restraint proceedings themselves, otherwise the provision in relation to recipients of tainted gifts would be unnecessary.

8.43 In reaching this conclusion, the Court was also influenced by the fact that Sch 11 para 36(4) to POCA expressly amended the Access to Justice Act 1999 to make public funding available in relation to restraint proceedings and that s 252 of the Act imposed a similar prohibition on the release of funds to meet legal expenses incurred in relation to proceedings for an interim receiving order brought by the ARA.

8.44 The Court also considered, but rejected, a submission by the defendant that s 41(4) amounted to a breach of his right to a fair trial under Article 6 of the European Convention on Human Rights. At the outset the Court observed that the defendant faced 'an overwhelming factual difficulty' because he was represented throughout and it was not suggested that he did not have a fair hearing. The Court noted that Article 6(3) applied only to criminal hearings where the defendant had been charged with an offence and found, following *R (McCann) v Crown Court at Manchester* [2003] 1 AC 787 that it was 'impossible to conceptualise the restraint proceedings as criminal'. Further, the Court noted that in *X v UK* (1984) 6 EHRR 136 the European Commission distinguised civil proceedings from criminal proceedings holding that:

> Only in exceptional circumstances, namely where the withholding of legal aid would make the assertion of a civil claim practically impossible, or where it would lead to an obvious unfairness of the proceedings, can such a right be involed by virtue of Article 6 (1).

8.45 Finally, the Court considered whether s 41(4) amounted to a breach of the defendant's right to peaceful enjoyment of his possessions under Article 1 of the First Protocol to the

8.46 Convention. Again, the Court answered the question in the negative, noting that *Raimondo v Italy* (1994) 18 EHRR 237 made it plain that there is a distinction to be drawn between depriving a person of his possessions and temporary measures to prevent him from using them. As Scott Baker, LJ said:

> A restraint order constitutes a control in the use of property which will be lawful if, as in the present case, it serves a legitimate aim, namely the preservation of property believed to be the proceeds of crime for confiscation so as to deprive offenders of their benefit from crime.

8.47 The Court was, however, plainly troubled by the possible consequences of its ruling on those affected by restraint orders. In the concluding paragraph of the judgment, Scott Baker LJ stressed that: 'This is not a conclusion we have reached with any enthusiasm.'

8.48 Further, the Court suggested that henceforth a number of safeguards should be adopted to protect the interests of those affected by POCA restraint orders. Scott Baker LJ said:

> We think these orders should state clearly on their face that public funding is available. It is plainly desirable that defendants to restraint orders should in the ordinary course of events have legal representation. It would also be helpful if such orders direct defendants to the central unit in which their public funding application will be processed. Time will often be of the essence: it is crucial that public funding applications in these matters should be dealt with, with the greatest expedition.
>
> It also seems to us, in the light of the statutory prohibition on the use of restrained funds for legal expenses, that these orders should ordinarily be made with a short return date rather than left open ended for the defendant to apply to vary or discharge. In that way the court can exercise close supervision over orders that are by their nature draconian.

8.49 The prohibition also precludes, it is submitted, the release of restrained funds to meet the costs of any appeal in such proceedings. Where the release of funds to meet legal expenses is permitted under s 41(3)(c), eg to meet the costs incurred in a wholly unrelated matter such as divorce proceedings, the court may impose conditions including, it is submitted, the imposition of the 65 per cent rule approved in *Re L* The Times, 10 July 1996 whereby only 65 per cent is released pending detailed assessment by a costs judge if the prosecutor is unable to agree the amount claimed is reasonable. For further on the availability of LSC funding, see Appendix 6.

(11) Ancillary orders

8.50 In Chapter 4 we considered how the High Court had made use of its inherent jurisdiction to include in restraint orders a wide range of ancillary provisions, such as disclosure and repatriation orders, for the purpose of ensuring they are properly policed. The Crown Court, however, as a creature of statute has no such inherent jurisdiction and may only make orders to the extent that it has a statutory power to do so. Accordingly, in the absence of some specific provision in POCA, the Crown Court would be powerless to include disclosure and repatriation provisions in restraint orders. Such provision is, however, made in s 41(6) and (7) of POCA which provides as follows:

(6) Subsection (7) applies if—
  (a) a court makes a restraint order, and
  (b) the applicant for the order applies to the court to proceed under subsection (7) (whether as part of the application for the restraint order or at any time afterwards).

(7) The court may make such order as it believes is appropriate for the purpose of ensuring that the restraint order is effective.

8.51 This provision will enable the court to continue making disclosure and repatriation orders in precisely the same way as the High Court together with any other form of order it considers necessary to ensure the restraint order is effective. An example of a POCA restraint order, including disclosure and repatriation provisions, is found at Appendix 13.

(12) Restrictions

8.52 Section 58 of POCA imposes a number of restrictions on third parties exercising certain rights they may otherwise have in relation to realisable property. By s 58(2), no distress may be levied against property subject to a restraint order except with the leave of the Crown Court and subject to any conditions it may impose.

8.53 Similarly, by s 58(3) and (4), where a restraint order applies to a tenancy of any premises, no landlord or other person to whom rent is payable may exercise a right of forfeiture by way of peaceable re-entry without the leave of the Crown Court. This is in contrast to the position under the DTA and CJA where it has been held that the exercise of a right to forfeiture by a landlord does not constitute a breach of any restraint order affecting the property (see *Re R (Restraint Order)* [1990] 2 All ER 569).

By s 58(5) where a court in which proceedings are pending in relation to any property is satisfied that a restraint order has been applied for or made in respect of that property, it may either stay the proceedings or allow them to continue on such terms as it thinks fit. Before the court exercises these powers it must, under s 58(6), give the applicant for the restraint order and any receiver appingted under ss 48, 50 or 52 an opportunity to be heard.

8.54 Section 59 makes similar provision to s 58 in relation to the position where an enforcement receiver has been appointed under s 50. Although the sections appear to give the Crown Court a wide discretion as to the terms on which it may permit the forfeiture of leases by way of peaceable re-entry or permit litigation in relation to restrained property to continue, it is submitted that it is a discretion that must be exercised in accordance with the legislative steer in s 69.

(13) Variation and discharge of the order

8.55 By s 42(3) of POCA an application to vary or discharge a restraint order may be made by the person who applied for the order or by anyone affected by it. The procedures to be followed on applications to vary POCA restraint orders are set out in r 59 of the Criminal Procedure Rules 2005 and are considered in more detail at para 8.75 below.

(14) Charging orders

8.56 It should be noted that POCA does not give the Crown Court jurisdiction to make charging orders and these are effectively abolished in relation to cases arising after POCA came into force. In practice, very little use was made of charging orders under the DTA and CJA with most prosecutors preferring to obtain restraint orders and, in cases where they affected real property, to protect the order by registering a restriction at the Land Registry. Section 47

C. Management Receivers

of POCA allows this practice to continue, providing that the 'registration acts' (defined as the Land Registration Act 1925, the Land Charges Act 1972, and the Land Registration Act 2002) shall apply to restraint orders as they apply in relation to orders which affect land and are made by the Court for the purpose of enforcing judgments and recognisances.

C. Management Receivers

Sections 48 and 49 of POCA give the Crown Court jurisdiction to appoint management receivers for the purpose of managing and preserving the value of realisable property pending the conclusion of the proceedings. By s 48 of POCA: **8.57**

(1) Subsection (2) applies if—
  (a) the Crown Court makes a restraint order, and
  (b) the applicant for the restraint order applies to the court to proceed under subsection (2) (whether as part of the application for the restraint order or at any time afterwards).
(2) The Crown Court may by order appoint a receiver in respect of any realisable property to which the restraint order applies.

Section 48(1)(b) gives express statutory effect to what had become the practice by prosecutors of applying for restraint and management receivership orders at the same time. Under the equivalent provisions of the DTA and CJA—ss 26(7) and 77(8) respectively—the High Court was given jurisdiction to appoint management receivers in any case where it 'has made a restraint order'. Thus in the High Court, the prosecutor had to apply first for his restraint order and, if it was granted, go on to apply for his management receivership order. Now the court may consider both applications simultaneously. **8.58**

(1) Powers of management receivers

Many of the powers given to management receivers by the High Court emanate from its inherent jurisdiction and the power under s 37(1) of the Supreme Court Act 1981 to appoint a receiver whenever it appears to be 'just and convenient to do so'. As we have seen, the Crown Court, being a creature of statute, has no such inherent jurisdiction and the powers the Court may confer on a management receiver are therefore set out in the Act itself. By s 49 of POCA: **8.59**

(1) If the court appoints a receiver under section 48 it may act under this section on the application of the person who applied for the restraint order.
(2) The court may by order confer on the receiver the following powers in relation to any realisable property to which the restraint order applies—
  (a) power to take possession of the property;
  (b) power to manage or otherwise deal with the property;
  (c) power to start, carry on or defend any legal proceedings in respect of the property;
  (d) power to realise so much of the property as is necessary to meet the receivers remuneration and expenses.
(3) The court may by order confer on the receiver power to enter any premises in England and Wales and to do any of the following—
  (a) search for or inspect anything authorised by the court;
  (b) make or obtain a copy, photograph or other record of anything so authorised;
  (c) remove anything which the receiver is required or authorised to take possession of in pursuance of an order of the court.

(4) The court may by order authorise the receiver to do any of the following for the purpose of the exercise of his functions—
   (a) hold property;
   (b) enter into contracts;
   (c) sue and be sued;
   (d) employ agents;
   (e) execute powers of attorney, deeds or other instruments;
   (f) take any other steps the court thinks appropriate.
(5) The court may order any person who has possession of realisable property to which the restraint order applies to give possession of it to the receiver.
(6) The court—
   (a) may order a person with an interest in realisable property to which the restraint order applies to make to the receiver such payment as the court specifies in respect of a beneficial interest held by the defendant or the recipient of a tainted gift;
   (b) may (on payment being made) by order transfer, grant or extinguish any interest in the property.
(7) Subsections (2), (5) and (6) do not apply to property for the time being subject to a charge under any of these provisions—
   (a) section 9 of the Drug Trafficking Offences Act 1986 (c32);
   (b) section 78 of the Criminal Justice Act 1988 (c33);
   (c) Article 14 of the Criminal Justice (Confiscation) (Northern Ireland) Order 1990 (SI 1990/2588 (NI17));
   (d) section 27 of the Drug Trafficking Act 1994 (c37);
   (e) Article 32 of the Proceeds of Crime (Northern Ireland) Order 1996 (SI 1996/1299 (N19)).
(8) The court must not—
   (a) confer the power mentioned in subsection (2)(b) or (d) in respect of property, or
   (b) exercise the power conferred on it by subsection (6) in respect of property, unless it gives persons holding interests in the property a reasonable opportunity to make representations to it.
(9) The court may order that a power conferred by an order under this section is subject to such conditions and exceptions as it specifies.
(10) Managing or otherwise dealing with property includes—
   (a) selling the property or any part of it or interest in it;
   (b) carrying on or arranging for another person to carry on any trade or business the assets of which are or are part of the property;
   (c) incurring capital expenditure in respect of the property.

8.60 The majority of the powers the court may vest in the receiver under s 49 of POCA merely reflect powers the High Court has conferred on receivers for many years pursuant to its inherent jurisdiction. Section 49(2)(d) gives statutory effect to the decision of the Court of Appeal in *Hughes v Customs and Excise Commissioners* [2002] 4 All ER 633 that the remuneration and expenses of a management receiver are to met from the estate under management rather than by the prosecutor. It is submitted that the wording of s 49(2)(d) makes it plain that the decision of the Court of Appeal in *Capewell (No 2) v Customs and Excise Commissioners* [2005] EWCA Civ 964 (A summary of the House of Lords judgment is at Appendix 23) does not apply to management receivership orders made under POCA and is confined to DTA and CJA cases.

8.61 Section 49(3) empowers the court to confer on the receiver a right of entry to property. This will enable the receiver to enter premises to value and take inventories and photographs of property, copy business records, and remove any property he is authorised by the court to take possession of. The court will, no doubt, wish to exercise some caution in allowing receivers to take possession of property, particularly at the pre-conviction stage where the defendant must be presumed innocent. But where there is a real risk of assets being removed or of their depreciating in value if they remain in the possession of the defendant it would, it is submitted, be an appropriate use of the power to authorise the receiver to enter property and take possession of such assets. Similarly, in relation to businesses, if the defendant or a third party is in possession of documentation or other property that the receiver properly required to run the business and he refused to hand it over voluntarily, it would, it is submitted, be a proper use of the power to give the receiver a power of entry to take possession.

(2) Restriction on the use of powers

8.62 Section 49(8) imposes an important restriction on the court's jurisdiction to confer powers on the receiver. The powers to manage or otherwise deal with property (s 49(2)(b)), to realise assets to meet the costs and expenses of the receivership (s 49(2)(d)), and to require a person holding realisable property to make payments to the receiver after which property rights may be granted, transferred, or extinguished, (s 49(6)), until persons having an interest in the property have been given a reasonable opportunity to make representations to the court. Thus, in cases where the receiver is appointed without notice to the defendant or interested parties, a further application on notice will have to be made before the receiver can be given any of the powers referred to in s 49(8).

8.63 This provision gives statutory effect to the decision of the Court of Appeal in *Re P (Restraint Order: Sale of Assets)* [2000] 1 WLR 473 to the effect that the powers given to management receivers appointed without notice to the defendant or interested parties should be 'in the narrowest terms necessary to meet the strict requirements of the situation', (see Chapter 3, para 3.11).

D. Powers of the Court and Receiver: the 'Legislative Steer'

8.64 In Chapter 5 we saw how the 'legislative steer' imposed by s 31 of the DTA and s 82 of the CJA imposed restrictions on the way the court and receivers were to exercise their powers under the Act with a view to ensuring the value of the defendant's realisable property was maintained so as to make it available to meet any confiscation order that might be made in his case (see Chapter 5, para 5.27 and following). POCA retains the 'legislative steer' and indeed expands it considerably to reflect the recent case law. By s 69 of POCA:

(1) This section applies to—
  (a) the powers conferred on a court by sections 41 or 60 and sections 62 to 67;
  (b) the powers of a receiver appointed under section 48, 50 or 52.
(2) The powers—
  (a) must be exercised with a view to the value for the time being of realisable property being made available (by the property's realisation) for satisfying any confiscation order that has been or may be made against the defendant;
  (b) must be exercised, in a case where a confiscation order has not been made, with a view to securing that there is no diminution in the value of realisable property;
  (c) must be exercised without taking account of any obligation of the defendant or a recipient of a tainted gift if the obligation conflicts with the object of satisfying any confiscation order that has been or may be made against the defendant;

(d) may be exercised in respect of a debt owed by the Crown.
(3) Subsection (2) has effect subject to the following rules:
  (a) the powers must be exercised with a view to allowing a person other than the defendant or a recipient of a tainted gift to retain or recover the value of any interest held by him;
  (b) in the case of realisable property held by a recipient of a tainted gift, the powers must be exercised with a view to realising no more than the value for the time being of the gift;
  (c) in a case where a confiscation order has not been made against the defendant, property must not be sold if the court so orders under subsection (4).
(4) If on an application by the defendant, or by the recipient of a tainted gift, the court decides that property cannot be replaced it may order that it must not be sold.
(5) An order under subsection (4) may be revoked or varied.

8.65 Most of these provisions are not new and merely re-enact s 31 of the DTA and s 82 of the CJA. The provisions in s 69(2)(b), (3)(c) and (4) are, however, entirely new and appear to be a response to the decision of the Court of Appeal in *Re P (Restraint Order: Sale of Assets)* [2000] 1 WLR 473. Section 69(2)(b) would appear to overrule the court's decision because it provides that powers shall be exercised with a view to ensuring there is no diminution in the value of realisable property. As the Guidance Notes to the Act say, this provision: 'requires the powers to be exercised with a view to maintaining the value available for confiscation'.

8.66 It will be recalled that in *Re P* the Court of Appeal found that the purpose of the Acts was to impoverish the defendant and not to enrich the Crown by selling assets to ensure they do not depreciate in value. It would seem that to this extent *Re P* is no longer good law in relation to restraint orders made under POCA.

8.67 POCA protects the position of unconvicted defendants in possession of property that 'cannot be replaced' in that it gives the court a power to order that it must not be sold. The reason for this new provision is set out in the Guidance Notes in these terms:

The provision has regard to the fact that the defendant has not been convicted at this stage and should not, therefore, be obliged to lose irreplaceable assets.

8.68 It should, however, be noted that the court is not compelled to order that irreplaceable assets should not be sold: the Act provides that the court 'may' order that the asset is not to be sold, not that it must do so. Unless, however, there were very compelling reasons to the contrary, such as a deliberate intention on the part of the defendant to dispose of property, it is submitted that the proper course would be to order that irreplaceable assets should not be sold prior to the defendant's conviction. It is likely therefore that the racehorses, the subject of *Re P*, described as 'well loved family pets', would not have been sold even if POCA had been in force at the time the decision was made.

E. Procedure on Applications

8.69 The procedures for applying for restraint and receivership orders under POCA and for the variation and discharge of such orders are to be found in the Criminal Procedure Rules 2005, SI 2005/384. Many of the Rules merely mirror sc 115 but, as we shall see, some of the provisions are entirely new.

E. Procedure on Applications

(1) Applications for restraint orders

By r 59.1: **8.70**

(1) This rule applies where the prosecutor, the Director or an accredited financial investigator makes an application for a restraint order under section 42 of the Act.
(2) The application may be made without notice.
(3) The application must be in writing and supported by a witness statement which must—
   (a) give the grounds for the application;
   (b) to the best of the witness's ability, give full details of the realisable property in respect of which the applicant is seeking the order and specify the person holding that realisable property;
   (c) give the grounds for, and full details of, any application for an ancillary order under section 41(7) of the Act for the purposes of ensuring that the restraint order is effective;
   (d) where the application is made by an accredited financial investigator, include a statement that he has been authorised to make the application under section 68 of the Act.

Rule 59.1(1) closely follows the provisions of sc 115 Rule 3 in relation to High Court restraint applications. Rule 59.1(2) expressly provides that the application may be made without notice to the defendant and persons holding realisable property. As the Court of Appeal emphasised in *Re AJ and DJ* (9 December 1992), the mere fact that applications 'may' be made without notice does not mean that the prosecutor should automatically make his application without notice in every case. Where there is little likelihood of assets being dissipated in the short period between notice of an application being given and the hearing taking place, the prosecutor should always consider whether it would be more appropriate for the application to be heard on notice. As a general rule, the longer the delay between the defendant being charged and the hearing of the application for a restraint order, the more difficult it will be for the prosecutor to justify proceeding without notice. **8.71**

By r 59.1(3)(c), the prosecutor's witness statement must specify the grounds for and full details of an application for an ancillary order under s 41(7). This provision serves as a useful reminder to prosecutors that they are not automatically entitled to have disclosure and repatriation provisions included in every restraint order, but must be able to justify why they are necessary. If, for example, the prosecutor has already identified sufficient assets to meet a confiscation order in the amount of the defendant's benefit from criminal conduct that are free of third party claims, there would be no need for the inclusion of disclosure provisions to make the order effective. Similarly, a repatriation order would not be necessary if sufficient assets are available within the jurisdiction of the court to meet a confiscation order in the amount of the defendant's benefit. **8.72**

(2) The order

By r 59.2 of the Criminal Procedure Rules 2005: **8.73**

(1) The Crown Court may make a restraint order subject to exceptions, including, but not limited to, exceptions for reasonable living expenses and reasonable legal expenses and for the purpose of enabling any person to carry on any trade, business or occupation.
(2) But the Crown Court must not make an exception for legal expenses where this is prohibited by section 41(4) of the Act.
(3) An exception to a restraint order may be made subject to conditions.

(4) The Crown Court must not require the applicant for a restraint order to give any undertaking relating to damages sustained by a person who holds realisable property as a result of the restraint order.
(5) The Crown Court may require the applicant for a restraint order to give an undertaking to pay the reasonable expenses of any person, other than a person who holds realisable property, which are incurred in complying with the restraint order.
(6) A restraint order must include a statement that disobedience of the order, either by a person to whom the order is addressed, or by another person, may be contempt of court and the order must include details of the possible consequences of being held in contempt of court.
(7) Unless the Crown Court directs otherwise, a restraint order made without notice has effect until the court makes an order varying or discharging the order.
(8) The applicant for a restraint order must—
　(a) serve copies of the restraint order and of the witness statement made in support of the application on the defendant and any person who holds realisable property to which the restraint order applies; and
　(b) notify any person affected by the restraint order of the terms of the restraint order.

8.74 Rule 59.2 mirrors very closely sc 115 Rule 4. A number of its provisions are, however, new. Rule 59.2(1) makes it clear for the first time that a restraint order may be made subject to an exception permitting a person to carry on any trade, business or occupation. Rule 59.2(2) limits the court's powers to make an exception for the payment of legal expenses where this is prohibited by s 41(4) of POCA. Rule 59.2(7), however, has entirely different terms to sc 115 Rule 4(2). By sc 115 Rule 4(2), a High Court restraint order is to have effect only until a return date for an inter partes hearing unless the court otherwise directs. Rule 59.2(7), on the other hand, provides that a restraint order has effect until the court makes an order varying or discharging it unless the Crown Court directs otherwise. In fact, this provision merely gives effect to what has been the practice of the High Court for some time and which was expressly approved by the Court of Appeal in *Ahmad v Ahmad* [1998] EWCA Civ 1246. As the Court remarked in that case, return dates were unnecessary because most restraint orders are not challenged by those affected by them, and, where variations are sought, many can be resolved by agreement with the prosecutor, and, provided defendants and affected third parties are able to apply for the order to be discharged at relatively short notice, they suffer no injustice from there being no return date. Rule 59. 2(2) must, however, be read in the light of the decision of the Court of Appeal in *Customs and Excise Commissioners v S* [2005] 1 WLR 1338 where the Court expressed the view that, given the prohibition on the release of restrained funds to meet legal expenses incurred in relation to the proceedings, POCA restraint orders should normally have a short return date rather than be left open ended.

(3) Variation or discharge applications by persons affected by restraint orders

8.75 By r 59.3 of the Criminal Procedure Rules 2005:

(1) This rule applies where a person affected by a restraint order makes an application to the Crown Court under section 42(3) of the Act to discharge or vary the restraint order or any ancillary order made under section 41(7) of the Act.
(2) The application must be in writing and may be supported by a witness statement.
(3) The application and any witness statement must be lodged with the Crown Court.
(4) The application and any witness statement must be served on the person who applied for the restraint order and any person who holds realisable property to which the restraint order applies

E. Procedure on Applications

(if he is not the person making the application) at least 2 days before the date fixed by the court for hearing the application, unless the Crown Court specifies a shorter period.

8.76 This Rule is in very similar terms to sc 115 Rule 5. The interpretation provisions in rr 57.1, 57.2 and 57.3 provide assistance in computing time. By Rule 57.2 (2):

A period of time expressed as a number of days shall be computed as clear days.
'Clear days' is defined in Rule 57.2 (3) in these terms:
(3) In this rule 'clear days' means that in computing the number of days—
   (a) the day on which the period begins; and
   (b) if the end of the period is defined by reference to an event, the day on which that event occurs
   are not included.

Further, under r 57.2(4), when the period is five days or less and includes a day that is not a business day, that day does not count for the purpose of computing time. 'Business day' is defined in rle 57.1 as being any day other than:

(i) a Saturday, Sunday, Christmas Day or Good Friday; or
(ii) a bank holiday under the Banking and Financial Dealings Act 1971 in England and Wales.

8.77 The effect of these rules is to provide very similar rules as to service as applied under sc 115. The position remains that two clear days notice must be given by the defendant or affected third party of any application to vary or discharge the restraint order. Thus if, for example, an application to vary or discharge a restraint order is served on the prosecutor on a Monday, the first day on which the same may be heard in the Crown Court would be the following Thursday.

(4) Variation applications by the person who applied for the order

8.78 By r 59.4 of the Criminal Procedure Rules 2005:

(1) This rule applies where the applicant for a restraint order makes an application under s 42(3) of the Act to the Crown Court to vary the restraint order or any ancillary order made under s 41(7) of the Act (including where the court has already made a restraint order and the applicant is seeking to vary the order in order to restrain further realisable property).
(2) The application may be made without notice if the application is urgent or there are reasonable grounds for believing that giving notice would cause the dissipation of realisable property which is the subject of the application.
(3) The application must be in writing and must be supported by a witness statement which must—
   (a) give the grounds for the application; and
   (b) where the application is for the inclusion of further realisable property in the order, to the best of the witness's ability, give full details of the realisable property in respect of which the applicant is seeking the order and specify the person holding that realisable property;
   (c) when the application is made by an accredited financial investigator, include a statement that he has been authorised to make the application under section 68 of the Act.
(4) The application and witness statement must be lodged with the Crown Court.
(5) Except where, under paragraph (2), notice of the application is not required to be served, the application and witness statement must be served on any person who holds realisable property to which the restraint order applies at least 2 days before the date fixed by the court for hearing the application, unless the Crown Court specifies a shorter period.
(6) If the court makes an order for the variation of a restraint order, the applicant must serve copies of the order and of the witness statement made in support of the application on—
   (a) the defendant;

(b) any person who holds realisable property to which the restraint order applies (whether before or after the variation); and
(c) any other person whom the applicant knows to be affected by the order.

8.79 Rule 59.4 is in very similar terms to sc 115 Rule 6 and introduces no procedural changes as to the way in which applications by prosecutors for variations should be made.

(5) Discharge applications by the person who applied for the order

8.80 By Rule 59.5 of the Criminal Procedure Rules 2005:
(1) This rules applies where the applicant for a restraint order makes an application under section 42(3) of the Act to discharge the order or any ancillary order made under section 41(7) of the Act.
(2) The application may be made without notice.
(3) The application must be in writing and must state the grounds for the application.
(4) The Crown Court may determine the application without a hearing.

This is an entirely new rule and no similar provision is to be found in sc 115. It gives effect to what has long been the standing practice for prosecutors to apply to the High Court immediately on the conclusion of proceedings for the discharge of a restraint order. Particularly if proceedings conclude with the acquittal of the defendant, there is always a need for the restraint order to be discharged promptly because, having been found not guilty, the defendant is entitled to deal with his assets as he chooses. This procedure enables the prosecutor to apply promptly for the discharge of the order without the necessity to give notice or for a formal hearing before the judge. It is submitted that the order should always make provision either for the payment of the defendant's costs of the restraint proceedings or give him permission to apply to the court for an order to be made.

(6) Receivership proceedings

8.81 The Criminal Procedure Rules make extensive provision in relation to applications for the appointment of management and enforcement receivers. Many of the provisions are entirely new and are not to be found in sc 115 in relation to applications to the High Court.

(7) The application for appointment

8.82 Rule 60.1 of the Criminal Procedure Rules 2005 provides:
(1) This rule applies to an application for the appointment of a management receiver under section 48(1) of the Act and an application for the appointment of an enforcement receiver under section 50(1) of the Act.
(2) The application may be made without notice if the application is—
    (a) joined with an application for a restraint order under rule 16; or
    (b) urgent; or
    (c) if there are reasonable grounds for believing that giving notice would cause the dissipation of realisable property which is the subject of the application.
(3) The application must be in writing and must be supported by a witness statement which must—
    (a) give the grounds for the application;
    (b) give full details of the proposed receiver;
    (c) to the best of the witness's ability give full details of the realisable property in respect of which the applicant is seeking the order and specify the person holding that realisable property;

E. Procedure on Applications

    (d) where the application is made by an accredited financial investigator, include a statement that he has been authorised to make the application under section 68 of the Act;
    (e) if the proposed receiver is not a member of staff of the Assets Recovery Agency, the Crown Prosecution Service or the Commissioners of Revenue and Customs and the applicant is asking the court to allow the receiver to act:
        (i) without giving security; or
        (ii) before he has given security or satisfied the court that he has security in place, explain the reasons why that is necessary.
(4) Where the application is for the appointment of an enforcement receiver, the applicant must provide the Crown Court with a copy of the confiscation order made against the defendant.
(5) The application and witness statement must be lodged with the Crown Court.
(6) Except where, under paragraph (2), notice of the application is not required to be served, the application and witness statement must be lodged with the Crown Court and served on—
    (a) the defendant;
    (b) any person who holds realisable property to which the application relates; and
    (c) any other person whom the applicant knows is affected by the application, at least 7 days before the date fixed by the court for hearing the application, unless the Crown Court specifies a shorter period.
(7) If the court makes an order for the appointment of a receiver, the applicant must serve copies of the order and of the witness statement made in support of the application on—
    (a) the defendant;
    (b) any person who holds realisable property to which the order applies; and
    (c) any other person whom the applicant knows to be affected by the order.

8.83 Rule 60.1(2) permits applications for the appointment of management receivers to be made without notice in urgent cases or where there are reasonable grounds to believe assets would be dissipated were notice to be given. In appropriate circumstances the application may be made at the same time as an application for a restraint order. Prosecutors should, however, have due regard to the decision of the Court of Appeal in *Re P (Restraint Order: Sale of Assets)* [2000] 1 WLR 473 where the Court emphasised that such applications should only be made in cases of genuine urgency and then the powers of the receiver should be confined to those strictly necessary to meet the justice of the situation.

(8) Applications for the conferment of powers on receivers

8.84 Rule 60.2 of the Criminal Procedure Rules 2005 deals with the conferment of powers on receivers and provides:

(1) This rule applies to an application for the conferral of powers on a management receiver under section 49(1) of the Act, an enforcement receiver under section 51(1) of the Act and a Director's receiver under section 53(1) of the Act.
(2) The application may be made without notice if the application is to give the receiver power to take possession of property and—
    (a) the application is joined with an application for a restraint order under rule 59.1;
    (b) the application is urgent;
    (c) there are reasonable grounds for believing that giving notice would cause the dissipation of the property which is the subject of the application.
(3) The application must be made in writing and supported by a witness statement which must—
    (a) give the grounds for the application;
    (b) give full details of the realisable property in respect of which the applicant is seeking the order and specify the person holding that realisable property;

(c) where the application is made by an accredited financial investigator, include a statement that he has been authorised to make the application under section 68 of the Act.
(4) Where the application is for the conferral of powers on an enforcement receiver or Director's receiver, the applicant must provide the Crown Court with a copy of the confiscation order made against the defendant.
(5) The application and witness statement must be lodged with the Crown Court.
(6) Except where, under paragraph (2), notice of the application is not required to be served, the application and witness statement must be served on—
   (a) the defendant;
   (b) any person who holds realisable property in respect of which a receiver has been appointed or in respect of which an application for a receiver has been made;
   (c) any other person whom the applicant knows to be affected by the application; and
   (d) the receiver (if one has already been appointed),
   at least 7 days before the date fixed by the court for hearing the application, unless the Crown Court specifies a shorter period.
(7) If the court makes an order for the conferral of powers on a receiver, the applicant must serve copies of the order on—
   (a) the defendant;
   (b) any person who holds realisable property in respect of which the receiver has been appointed; and
   (c) any other person whom the applicant knows to be affected by the order.

8.85 Although r 60.2(2) does make provision for applications for the conferment of powers on receivers to be made without notice in certain specified circumstances, it should be noted that only applications to give the receiver power to take possession of property may be made without notice. All applications for powers to manage and otherwise deal in realisable property must be made on notice to the defendant and affected third parties.

(9) Applications to vary or discharge receivership orders

8.86 The procedures for dealing with applications to vary or discharge receivership orders are set out in r 60.3 of the Criminal Procedure Rules 2005. These too must be made in writing on at least seven days notice unless the court specifies a shorter period and must be served on the defendant, the person who applied for the appointment of the receiver, any person who holds realisable property, and any other person whom the applicant knows is affected by the application.

(10) Security

8.87 Rule 60.5 of the Criminal Procedure Rules 2005 deals with the provision of security by receivers who are not members of the ARA, the Crown Prosecution Service or of the Commissioners of Revenue and Customs. By r 60.5(2):

(2) The Crown Court may direct that before the receiver begins to act, or within a specified time, he must either—
   (a) give such security as the Crown Court may determine; or
   (b) file with the Crown Court and serve on all parties to any receivership proceedings evidence that he already has in force sufficient security, to cover his liability for his acts and omissions as a receiver.

8.88 Under r 60.5(3), the Crown Court may terminate the receiver's appointment if he fails to give the security or satisfy the court as to the security he has by the date specified. It is to be noted that the Crown Court has a discretion whether or not to require the receiver to give security and does not have to order the provision of a security in every case. It is submitted that the Crown Court could properly dispense with the provision of security from an experienced receiver in the employ of a reputable firm of chartered accountants who has a proven track record for conducting receiverships in a proper manner. The purpose of the security is to ensure funds are available to meet any award of damages against the receiver if he acts improperly. If, in reality, there is no real risk that the receiver will abuse his position, it is submitted that security could properly be dispensed with. It is perhaps worthy of note that under sc 115 Rule 8(2), the High Court, when it appoints a receiver under the DTA and CJA, is not bound to require security in cases where the proposed receiver has already acted in previous cases under the Acts. The Crown Court, it is submitted, could properly apply the same rule in deciding whether or not to exercise its discretion in favour of requiring a security.

(11) Remuneration of receivers

8.89 Rule 60.6 of the Criminal Procedure Rules 2005 provides for the remuneration of receivers. As the rules are in all respects identical to CPR Part 69, which are considered in detail in Chapter 3 at para 3.43, they are not reproduced here.

(12) Receiver's accounts

8.90 Rule 60.7 of the Criminal Procedure Rules 2005 makes provision in relation to receiver's accounts which are again in identical terms to CPR Part 69, considered in more detail in Chapter 3 at para 3.39.

(13) Non-compliance by a receiver

8.91 Under r 60.8 (1) of the Criminal Procedure Rules 2005 a receiver who fails to comply with any rule, practice direction, or direction of the Crown Court may be ordered to attend a hearing to explain his non-compliance. At such a hearing, the court may make any order it considers appropriate, including an order terminating the receiver's appointment, reducing or disallowing the receiver's remuneration or requiring the receiver to pay the costs of any party.

F. Provisions as to Hearings and Evidence

(1) Restraint and receivership hearings in the Crown Court

8.92 By r 61.3 of the Criminal Procedure Rules 2005 applications in restraint and receivership proceedings are to be dealt with without a hearing unless the Crown Court orders otherwise. This rule gives effect to the practice that currently applies to applications for restraint orders in the High Court, whereby the judge considers the application without a hearing and only requires the prosecutor to attend if there are aspects of the application that concern him. Of course it is always open to the prosecutor to request a hearing and it is submitted he should do so where there are unusual features to the application that call for an explanation. Where a hearing is required, in restraint and receivership proceedings, it may take place in chambers: see Rule 61.4. If a hearing does take place, the prosecutor should ensure that a full note of it is taken and served on the defendant together with the order and supporting evidence: see *Interoute Telecommunications (UK) Ltd v Fashion Gossip Ltd* [1999] TLR 762 and *Director of the (Admin) Assets Recovery Agency v Singh* [2004] EWHC 2335.

8.93 An application for the appointment of a management receiver or an enforcement receiver under r 60.1 may be joined with an application for a restraint order under r 59.1 or an application for the conferral of powers on the receiver under r 60.2 (see r 61.2).

(2) Evidence

8.94 Rule 61.5(1) of the Criminal Procedure Rules 2005 gives the court power to control the evidence in restraint and receivership proceedings by giving directions as to:

(a) the issues on which it requires evidence;
(b) the nature of the evidence which it requires to decide those issues;
(c) the way in which the evidence is to be placed before the court

8.95 The court may use its powers under r 61.5(1) to exclude evidence that would otherwise be admissible (see r 61.5(2)); and may limit the scope of cross-examination (see r 61.5(3)).

(3) Evidence should be in writing

8.96 Rule 61.6(1) of the Criminal Procedure Rules 2005 imposes a general rule that unless the court otherwise orders, evidence in restraint and receivership proceedings should be in writing. The parties may apply under r 61.6(2) for permission to cross-examine a person who has submitted written evidence, and if a person is required to attend for cross-examination fails so to attend, his evidence may not be used unless the court gives permission. This accords with the procedures of the High Court in restraint and receivership proceedings under the DTA and CJA where evidence is normally given in witness statement or affidavit form. It is submitted that cross-examination should only be ordered in cases where there is a complete conflict of evidence between the parties. Rule 61.7 empowers the court, on the application of any party to the proceedings, to issue a witness summons requiring a witness to attend court to give evidence or produce documents to the court.

8.97 Witness statements required to be served under the Rules must be verified by a statement of truth contained in the statement itself (see r 57.7(1)). By r 57.7(2) a statement of truth is defined as:

> . . . a declaration by the person making the witness statement to the effect that the witness statement is true to the best of his knowledge and belief and that he made the statement knowing that, if it were tendered in evidence, he would be liable to prosecution if he wilfully stated in it anything which he knew to be false or did not believe to be true.

8.98 The effect of this provision appears to be that the statement of truth should be in the same form as that in witness statements tendered under s 9 of the Criminal Justice Act 1967 rather than the form required under the Civil Procedure Rules. If a person making a witness statement fails to verify the witness statement by a statement of truth, the court has a discretion to direct that it shall not be admissible in evidence (see r 57.7(4)).

F. Provisions as to Hearings and Evidence

(4) Hearsay evidence

8.99 Rule 61.8 of the Criminal Procedure Rules 2005 makes provision as to the admission of hearsay evidence in restraint and receivership proceedings, providing that the obligation imposed by s 2(1) of the Civil Evidence Act 1995 to give notice of an intention to rely on hearsay evidence does not apply to evidence in restraint and receivership proceedings.

(5) Expert evidence

8.100 By r 57.9(1) of the Criminal Procedure Rules 2005 a party to restraint or receivership proceedings who wishes to adduce expert evidence must, as soon as practicable:

(a) serve on the other parties a statement in writing of any finding or opinion which he proposes to adduce by way of such evidence; and
(b) serve on any party who requests it in writing, a copy of (or it if appears to the party proposing to adduce the evidence to be more practicable, a reasonable opportunity to examine)—
   (i) the record of any observation, test, calculation or other procedure on which the finding or opinion is based; and
   (ii) any document or other thing or substance in respect of which the observation, test, calculation or other procedure mentioned in sub-paragraph (i) has been carried out.

8.101 A party may waive his right to be served with evidence in accordance with r 57.9(1), but if he does not waive that right, expert evidence that has not been served in accordance with rule 53(1) may not be admitted without leave of the court (see r 57.9(c) and (d)). Rule 57.10 makes special rules to deal with the situation where a party fears that compliance with r 57.9 might lead to intimidation or attempted intimidation of the witness or the course of justice being otherwise interfered with. In such circumstances, he shall not be obliged to comply with r 57.9, but must serve a notice on the other party stating that the evidence is being withheld and the reasons for withholding it.

(6) Disclosure and inspection of documents

8.102 Under r 61.9 of the Criminal Procedure Rules 2005, where the Crown Court is in the course of restraint or receivership proceedings, and any issue arises as to whether any property is realisable property, it may make an order for the disclosure of documents. In such circumstances, Part 31 of the Civil Procedure Rules (CPR) has effect as if the proceedings were proceedings in the High Court (see r 61.9(3)). Part 31 is the provision in the CPR that provides for disclosure and inspection of documents and the service of lists of documents by the parties.

(7) Court documents

8.103 Rule 61.10 of the Criminal Procedure Rules 2005 makes various miscellaneous requirements as to court documents. These are primarily administrative provisions that give effect to the practices and procedures that apply in High Court proceedings under the DTA and CJA. Rule 61.10(1) provides that Crown Court orders must state the name and judicial title of the judge that made them, the date on which they are made. By r 61.10(2) the Crown Court may place the seal on the order by hand or by printing a facsimile of it on the order whether electronically or otherwise. A document purporting to bear the court's seal is admissible in evidence without further proof (see r 61.10(3)).

(8) Service of documents

8.104 By r 57.11(2) of the Criminal Procedure Rules 2005 unless the court directs otherwise, documents in restraint and receivership proceedings may be served by any of the following methods:

(a) in all cases, by delivering the document personally to the party to be served;
(b) if no solicitor is acting for the party to be served by delivering the document at, or by sending it by first class post to, his residence or his last known residence;
(c) if a solicitor is acting for the party to be served—
   (i) by delivering the document at, or sending it by first class post to, the solicitor's business address; or
   (ii) where the solicitor's business address includes a numbered box at a document exchange, by leaving the document at that document exchange or at a document exchange which transmits documents on every business day to that document exchange; or
   (iii) by sending a legible copy of the document by facsimile transmission to the solicitor's office.

8.105 By r 57.11(3) documents served by post or left at a document exchange are deemed to have been served on the second day after posting or being deposited at the document exchange. Where documents are served by fax, they are deemed to have been served on the same day, or if they were transmitted after 4pm, on the next business day.

8.106 Rule 57.11(4) allows orders made in restraint and receivership proceedings to be enforced against a defendant or party affected by it notwithstanding that it has not been served in accordance with the rules, provided the court is satisfied he had notice of it by being present when it was made.

(9) Service by an alternative method

8.107 Rule 57.12 of the Criminal Procedure Rules 2005 makes provision for service by an alternative method where there is good reason to do so. This would, for example, include cases where the defendant or affected third party is deliberately evading service. The application must be supported by evidence and may be made without notice (see r 57.12(2)). The court's order authorising service by an alternative method must specify the method of service allowed and the date when the document will be deemed to have been served (see r 57.12(3)).

(10) Service outside the jurisdiction

8.108 Rule 57.13 of the Criminal Procedure Rules 2005 allows documents to be served outside England and Wales with the permission of the court. The document may be served by any method permitted by the law of the country in which it is to be served (see r 57.13(2)). However, nothing in the rule or in any court order authorises or requires any person to do anything in the country where the document is to be served which is against the law of that country (see r 57.13(3)). Where a document is required to be served a certain time before the date of a hearing and the recipient does not appear at the hearing, that hearing must not take place unless the Crown Court is satisfied the document has been duly served (see r 57.13(4)).

F. Provisions as to Hearings and Evidence

(11) Proof of service

8.109 By r 57.14 (1) of the Criminal Procedure Rules 2005, where the rules require an applicant of an order to serve a document on another person, he must lodge a certificate of service with the Crown Court within seven days of the service of the document stating the method and date of service and, where the documents are served in accordance with an order under r 57.12, such other information as the court may require (see r 57.14(2)). A precedent for a certificate of service appears at Appendix 14. Where a document in restraint and receivership proceedings is to be served by the court, and the court is unable to serve it for any reason, it must send a notice of non-service stating the method attempted to the party who requested service (see r 57.14(3)).

(12) Consent orders

8.110 Rule 61.11 of the Criminal Procedure Rules 2005 makes provision in relation to consent orders. By r 61.11(2) any party to the proceedings may apply for a judgment or order in agreed terms and such an application may be dealt with without a hearing. By r 61.11(4) such a judgment or order must be drawn up in the terms agreed, must be expressed as being 'By Consent', and must be signed by the legal representative acting for each of the parties or by the party himself if he is a litigant in person.

(13) Slips and omissions

8.111 Rule 61.12 of the Criminal Procedure Rules 2005 introduces a 'slip rule' whereby the Crown Court may at any time correct an accidental slip or omission made in an order in restraint and receivership proceedings. A party may apply for a correction without notice (see r 61.12(2)).

(14) Supply of documents from court records

8.112 Under r 61.13(1) of the Criminal Procedure Rules 2005 no document relating to restraint or receivership proceedings may be supplied to any person to inspect or copy unless the Crown Court gives permission. Given the sensitivity of restraint proceedings, the court should normally be very reluctant to give such permission, especially at the pre-conviction stage. This is particularly so in relation to the defendant's disclosure statement or any other document he produces to the court under compulsion. The court should, it is submitted, follow the ruling given by Macpherson J in *Re R* (21 October 1992) to the effect that such statements should be held in the court office 'under lock and key' and disclosed to no one (see Chapter 4 para 4.16). An application for permission under r 61.13(1) must be made on notice to the parties to the proceedings (see r 61.13(2)).

8.113 Under r 61.14(2), the judge presiding at proceedings for the offence may be supplied with documents relating to restraint and receivership proceedings, but otherwise such documents must not be disclosed in the proceedings for an offence (see r 61.14(2) and (3)).

Chapter 8: Restraint and Receivership under POCA 2002

(15) *Preparation of documents*

8.114 Rule 61.15 of the Criminal Procedure Rules 2005 makes provision for the preparation of documents by the court and the parties. By r 61.15(1) orders in restraint and receivership proceedings should be drawn up by the Crown Court unless:

(a) the Crown Court orders a party to draw it up;
(b) a party, with the permission of the Crown Court, agrees to draw it up;
(c) the order is made by consent under rule 61.10.

8.115 Under r 61.15(2) the Crown Court may direct that orders drawn up by a party must be checked by the court prior to sealing, or that before an order is drawn up by the court the parties must lodge an agreed statement of its terms. It is submitted that the better course in most cases would be for the parties to draw up the order for the court's approval given the length and complexity of most restraint and receivership orders. Where an order is to be drawn up by a party to the proceedings, he must do so within seven days after the date on which he was ordered or permitted to draw it up and, if he fails to lodge it within that period, any other party may draw it up and lodge it at the court for sealing (see r 61.15 (3)).

(16) *Change of solicitor*

8.116 Rule 61.16 of the Criminal Procedure Rules 2005 requires a party who changes his solicitor to notify the court and all other parties to proceedings. Under r 61.17, a solicitor may apply to the court for an order that he has ceased to act for a party to restraint and receivership proceedings. If the solicitor has died, been made bankrupt, has ceased to practice, or cannot be found any other party to the proceedings may apply to the court for an order that he has ceased to act (see r 61.18).

(17) *Costs*

8.117 Rule 61.19 of the Criminal Procedure Rules 2005 make provision for the payment of costs in restraint and receivership proceedings. It provides:

(1) This rule applies where the Crown Court is deciding whether to make an order for costs under rule 78.1 in restraint proceedings or receivership proceedings.
(2) The court has discretion as to—
 (a) whether costs are payable by one party to another;
 (b) the amount of those costs; and
 (c) when they are to be paid.
(3) If the court decides to make an order about costs—
 (a) the general rule is that the unsuccessful party will be ordered to pay the costs of the successful party, but
 (b) the court may make a different order.
(4) In deciding what order (if any) to make about costs, the court must have regard to all of the circumstances including—
 (a) the conduct of all the parties; and
 (b) whether a party has succeeded on part of an application even if he has not been wholly successful.
(5) The orders which the court may make under rule 78.1 include an order that a party may include—
 (a) a proportion of another party's costs;
 (b) a stated amount in respect of another party's costs;
 (c) costs from or until a certain date only;
 (d) costs incurred before proceedings have begun;

F. Provisions as to Hearings and Evidence

    (e) costs relating to particular steps in the proceedings;
    (f) costs relating only to a distinct part of the proceedings; and
    (g) interest on costs from or until a certain date, including a date before the making of the order.
(6) Where the court would otherwise consider making an order under paragraph (5)(f), it must instead, if practicable, make an order under paragraph (5)(a) to (c).
(7) Where the court has ordered a party to pay costs, it may order an amount to be paid on account before the costs are assessed.

The rule gives the Crown Court a wide discretion as to whether it awards costs to a successful party or not and, if so, as to the amount it actually awards. If, for example a party makes an application in the course of restraint proceedings to which all the parties would have consented given the opportunity, the court could refuse to award any costs at all to the successful applicant, award only a proportion of those costs, or even order the applicant to pay costs to some or all of the other parties to the proceedings. **8.118**

(18) Assessment of costs

By r 61.20(1) of the Criminal Procedure Rules 2005, the court may either assess the costs or order assessment under r 78.3. In most cases that can be dealt with in less than a day, it is submitted that the appropriate course would be for the court to assess costs itself rather than refer them to the taxing authority for assessment under r 78.3. Rule 61.20(2) provides that the court or taxing authority must: **8.119**

(a) only allow costs which are proportionate to the matters in issue; and
(b) resolve any doubt which it may have as to whether costs were reasonably incurred or reasonable and proportionate in favour of the paying party.

In deciding whether costs were reasonable and proportionate the court or taxing authority must have regard to all the circumstances: see r 61.20(3). It would seem that the requirement in r 61.20(2)(b) to the effect that any doubt as to whether costs were reasonable and proportionate must be resolved in favour of the paying party, only gives the court jurisdiction to award costs on the standard basis, and that it has no power, as the High Court, to direct assessment on an indemnity basis. Finally, under r 61.20(5) the court or taxing authority is also required to have regard to: **8.120**

(a) the conduct of all the parties, including in particular, conduct before, as well as during, the proceedings;
(b) the amount or value of the property involved;
(c) the importance of the matter to all the parties;
(d) the particular complexity of the matter or the difficulty or novelty of the questions raised;
(e) the time spent on the application; and
(f) the place where and the circumstances in which work or any part of it was done.

(19) Time for complying with orders for costs

By r 61.21 of the Criminal Procedure Rules 2005 a party to restraint or receivership proceedings must comply with an order for the payment of costs within 14 days of the date of the order if it states the amount to be paid; if the amount is to be assessed by the taxing authority, within 14 days of the authority's decision; or, in either case, such later date as the Crown Court may specify. **8.121**

G. Protecting POCA Restraint Orders in Relation to Real Property

8.122 Under r 93(l) of the Land Registration Rules 2003, SI 2003/1417 a POCA restraint order may be registered as a restriction against the title to the property at the Land Registry. By Regulation 92(1) the application must be made by the prosecutor on Form RX1. The restriction will be entered in the charges register in Form EE set out in Sch 4 to the Land Registration Rules 2003 and will preclude any dealing in the property without the consent of the prosecutor or a further order of the Court.

H. Enforcing POCA Restraint and Receivership Orders

8.123 In Chapter 6 we saw that the DTA and CJA made no specific provision for dealing with breaches of restraint and receivership orders by defendants and affected third parties. Prosecutors who identify breaches of such orders have to rely on the ordinary law of contempt of court and apply to the Court for an order of committal or, where the contemnor is a body corporate, an order for sequestration of assets. The position is precisely the same under POCA and prosecutors must rely on the law of contempt of court to deal with any breach of a restraint or receivership order.

8.124 It seems that both the High Court and the Crown Court have jurisdiction to deal with contempt proceedings in relation to breaches of orders of the Crown Court. The powers of the High Court stem from its jurisdiction as a superior court of record and the jurisdiction of the Crown Court comes from s 45(1) of the Supreme Court Act 1981 which provides that:

> .... the Crown Court shall in relation to the attendance and examination of witnesses, any contempt of court, the enforcement of its orders and all other matters incidental to its jurisdiction, have the like powers, rights, privileges and authority as the High Court.

8.125 Thus, in *DPP v Channel Four Television* [1993] 2 All ER 517 it was held that the High Court and Crown Court had concurrent jurisdiction to deal with an alleged breach of a production order.

8.126 It is submitted that the appropriate venue for dealing with breaches of POCA restraint and receivership orders will almost always be the Crown Court. The clear intention of Parliament in enacting the Proceeds of Crime Act 2002 was to make the Crown Court a 'one stop shop' dealing with all matters in relation to restraint, receivership and confiscation orders and their enforcement. This dispensed with the somewhat cumbersome procedures under the DTA and CJA whereby cases passed to and fro between the High Court and Crown Court with the former responsible for making restraint, management and enforcement receivership orders and for determining applications for certificates of inadequacy and the latter being responsible for making confiscation orders and reducing the same when a certificate of inadequacy had been granted.

8.127 Unfortunately both POCA and the Criminal Procedure Rules 2005 are silent as to the procedures that should be followed on application for committal for contempt of court in relation to breaches of restraint and receivership orders. In the absence of specific procedural rules, it is submitted that the procedures set out in sc 52 and described in detail in

H. Enforcing POCA Restraint and Receivership Orders

Chapter 6, should be followed as closely as possible. Proceedings should be instituted by the service of an application notice accompanied by a schedule setting out the precise nature of the breaches alleged and an affidavit setting out the evidence relied on in support of those allegations. Any evidence upon which the alleged contemnor wishes to rely in his defence should also be in affidavit form.

9

PREPARING FOR CONFISCATION HEARINGS UNDER THE DTA

A.	Introduction	9.01	C. Standard of Proof	9.51
	(1) When does the DTA apply?	9.01	D. Preparatory Steps for a	
	(2) The objective of DTA proceedings	9.02	DTA Hearing	9.54
B.	Preparing for Crown Court DTA Confiscation Hearings	9.05	(1) Statements relating to drug trafficking	9.54
	(1) Confiscation Orders	9.05	(2) Section 11 statements generally	9.55
	(2) When are DTA confiscation hearings held?	9.06	(3) The prosecutor's statement	9.56
	(3) Offences which constitute drug trafficking offences	9.11	(4) The purpose of the prosecutor's statement	9.57
	(4) Postponement of the proceedings pending further enquiries	9.12	(5) Form and content of prosecutor's section 11 statements	9.60
	(5) Postponing the determination	9.13	(6) When should the prosecutor's statement be served?	9.68
	(6) Postponing DTA hearings: analysis	9.14	(7) Upon whom should the prosecutor's statement be served?	9.69
	(7) Conviction, not sentence	9.16	(8) The defendant's statement	9.70
	(8) What amounts to exceptional circumstances?	9.17	(9) Requiring the defendant to respond to the prosecutor's statement	9.71
	(9) No requirement to find further exceptional circumstances	9.33	(10) Drafting the defendant's statement	9.73
	(10) Postponement: absence of the defendant	9.34	(11) Defendant's acceptance conclusive	9.76
	(11) Six month rule: no retrospective extension	9.35	(12) The risk of self incrimination	9.80
	(12) Purpose of postponement: further information	9.36	(13) Further provision of information by the defendant	9.82
	(13) Failure to properly postpone	9.38	(14) Consequences of the defendant failing to respond to the prosecutor's statement	9.86
	(14) Postponements: the case law applied	9.43	(15) Valuing the drugs	9.91
	(15) Postponement pending appeal	9.45	(16) Further statements by the prosecutor	9.92
	(16) Application for postponement: procedure	9.47	(17) Securing the attendance of witnesses	9.93
	(17) Sentence	9.49		

A. Introduction

(1) When does the DTA apply?

9.01 The Drug Trafficking Act 1994 (DTA) came into force on 3 February 1995 (s 69(2)). It was replaced on 24 March 2003 by the Proceeds of Crime Act 2002 (POCA). However, for all drug trafficking confiscation cases where the offence, or any of the offences, were committed prior to 24 March 2003, the DTA regime will still apply (SI 2003/333). The practical effect of this is that the DTA is likely to remain with the criminal practitioner for at least some time to come. Under s 66(2) of the Act the DTA does not apply if the person accused of the relevant offence was charged with the offence before 3 February 1995, or if any proceedings were instituted before that date: in those circumstances the Drug Trafficking Offences Act 1986 (DTOA) applies.

(2) The objective of DTA proceedings

9.02 The importance of DTA hearings was considered by the House of Lords in *R v Benjafield* [2002] 1 All ER 815, when Lord Steyn commented that the 1994 Act pursued an important objective in the public interest and the legislative measures were rationally connected with the furtherance of this objective.

9.03 He commented:

> The procedure devised by Parliament is a fair and proportionate response to the need to protect the public interest.

9.04 In *R v Dickens* [1990] 2 All ER 626 Lord Lane stated:

> . . . it is plain that the object of the Act is to ensure, as far as possible, that the convicted drug trafficker is parted from the proceeds of any drug trafficking which he has carried out. The provisions are intentionally draconian. Since the amount of these proceeds and the size of his realisable assets at the time of conviction are likely to be peculiarly within the defendant's knowledge, it is not surprising perhaps if evidential burdens are cast upon him of a kind which are, to say the least, unusual in the area of the criminal law and this, despite the fact that the confiscation order and penalties for failing to comply with it, may be rigorous.

B. Preparing for Crown Court DTA Confiscation Hearings

(1) Confiscation Orders

9.05 Section 2 of the Act provides:

(1) Subject to subsection (7) below, where a Defendant appears before the Crown Court to be sentenced in respect of one or more drug trafficking offences (and has not previously been sentenced or otherwise dealt with in respect of his convictions for the offence or, as the case may be, any of the offences concerned) then:

    (a) if the Prosecutor asks the Court to proceed under this Section, or
    (b) if the Court considers that, even though the Prosecutor has not asked it to do so, it is appropriate for it to proceed under this Section, it shall act as follows:

(2) The Court shall first determine whether the Defendant has benefited from drug trafficking.
(3) For the purpose of this Act, a person has benefited from drug trafficking if he has at any time (whether before or after the commencement of this Act) received any payment or other reward in connection with drug trafficking carried out by him or another person.
(4) If the Court determines that the Defendant has so benefited, the Court shall, before sentencing or otherwise dealing with him in respect of the offence or, as the case may be, any of the offences concerned, determine in accordance with Section 5 of this Act, the amount to be recovered in his case by virtue of this section.

B. Preparing for Crown Court DTA Confiscation Hearings

(2) When are DTA confiscation hearings held?

9.06 Under s 2(1) of the DTA the court has a mandatory obligation to hold a DTA enquiry when a defendant appears for sentence if either the prosecution asks it to do so or the court considers it appropriate to do so.

9.07 If it is going to proceed with a DTA enquiry then the court will usually set an appropriate timetable for the purposes of proceeding under the DTA and secondly for sentencing the defendant. Section 2(4) and (5) of the DTA states that the court must conduct the DTA hearing before proceeding to sentence, but the DTA hearing may be postponed where the court requires more information, either in order to decide whether the defendant has benefited from drug trafficking or alternatively to determine the amount to be recovered (s 3(1)), or where the defendant appeals against his conviction under s 3(4).

9.08 Where the court has postponed a determination it may proceed to sentence the defendant for the offence (s 3(7)). It is submitted that caution should be exercised when a court is considering sentencing a defendant prior to conducting the DTA hearing because frequently matters emerge in DTA hearings which are either to the benefit of the defence, or to the Crown, and which properly should be taken into account when sentencing for the offence.

9.09 It will be noted that in *R v Atkinson* [1993] 14 Cr App R(S)182, the Court specifically disapproved of the tendency of some counsel to agree a confiscation order without the judge adjudicating upon the amount of the benefit and the realisable property available (see s 2(1) DTA and s 71(1) CJA 1998).

9.10 If the court establishes that it will not need to embark on a drug trafficking enquiry it may immediately proceed to sentence for the offence.

(3) Offences which constitute drug trafficking offences

9.11 Offences that constitute drug trafficking offences for the purposes of the DTA are set out in s 1(3):

(a) an offence under section 4(2) or (3) or 5(3) of the Misuse of Drugs Act 1971 (production, supply and possession for supply of controlled drugs);
(b) an offence under section 20 of the Act (assisting in or inducing commission outside the United Kingdom of an offence punishable under a corresponding law);
(c) an offence under:
   (i) section 50(2) or (3) of the Customs & Excise Management Act 1979 (improper importation);
   (ii) section 68(2) of that Act (exportation), or
   (iii) section 170 of that Act (fraudulent evasion), in connection with a prohibition or restriction on importation or exportation having effect by virtue of Section 3 of the Misuse of Drugs Act 1971;
(d) an offence under section 12 of the Criminal Justice (International Co-operation)Act 1990 (manufacture or supply of a substance specified in Schedule 2 to that Act);
(e) an offence under section 19 of that Act (using ships for illicit traffic in controlled drugs);
(f) an offence under sections 49, 50 or 51 of the DTA or section 14 of the Criminal Justice (International Co-operation) Act 1990 (which makes, in relation to Scotland and Northern Ireland, provision corresponding to section 49 of this Act);
(g) an offence under section 1 of the Criminal Law Act 1977 of conspiracy to commit any of the offences in paragraphs (a) to (f) above;

(h) an offence under section 1 of the Criminal Attempts Act 1981 of attempting to commit any of those offences; and
(i) an offence of inciting another person to commit any of those offences, whether under section 19 of the Misuse of Drugs Act 1971 or at common law, and includes aiding abetting counselling or procuring the commission of any of the offences in paragraphs (a) to (f) above.

(4) Postponement of the proceedings pending further enquiries

9.12 It frequently happens in more complex cases that the Crown is not in a position to proceed with a DTA confiscation hearing immediately following a defendant's conviction. This is particularly so in cases where a defendant may have many assets or connections overseas and where the results of international enquiries are not yet available. Previously, under the DTOA, the courts relied upon their inherent jurisdiction to grant adjournments pending the conclusion of such enquiries. The DTA put that jurisdiction on to a statutory footing. Section 3(1) provides that where the court is acting under s 2 of the Act, but considers it needs further information before either:

(a) determining whether the defendant has benefited from drug trafficking; or
(b) determining the amount to be recovered under the Act;

it may, to enable such information to be obtained, postpone the making of a determination for such period as it may specify.

Section 3(2) enables the court to order more than one postponement under s 3(1) but s 3(3) limits the court to allowing a maximum total adjournment of six months, save where it is satisfied there are exceptional circumstances.

(5) Postponing the determination

9.13 The relevant provisions of the Act are as follows:

Postponed determinations:

3(1) Where the Crown Court is acting under Section 2 of this Act but considers it requires further information before—
  (a) determining whether the Defendant has benefited from drug trafficking, or
  (b) determining the amount to be recovered in his case by virtue of that section, it may, for the purpose of enabling this information to be obtained, postpone making the determination for such period as it may specify.
(2) More than one postponement may be ordered under subsection (1) above in relation to the same case.
(3) Unless it is satisfied that there are exceptional circumstances, the court shall not specify a period under subsection (1) above which—
  (a) by itself, or
  (b) where there have been one or more previous postponements under subsection (1) above or (4) below, when taken together with the earlier specified period or periods, exceeds six months beginning with the date of conviction.
(4) Where the Defendant appeals against his conviction, the Court may, on that account—
  (a) postpone making either or both of the determinations mentioned in subsection (1) above for such period as it may specify, or
  (b) where it has already exercised its powers under this section to postpone, extend the specified period.
(5) A postponement or extension under subsection (1) or (4) above may be made—
  (a) on application by the Defendant or the Prosecutor; or
  (b) by the Court of its own motion.

B. Preparing for Crown Court DTA Confiscation Hearings

(6) Unless the Court is satisfied that there are exceptional circumstances, any postponement or extension under subsection (4) above shall not exceed the period ending three months after the date on which the Appeal is determined or otherwise disposed of.

(7) Where the Court exercises its power under subsection (1) or (4) above, it may nevertheless proceed to sentence, or otherwise deal with the Defendant in respect of the relevant offence or any of the relevant offences.

(8) Where the Court has so proceeded, section 2 of the Act shall have effect as if—
   (a) in subsection (4) the words 'before sentencing or otherwise dealing with him in respect of the offence, or as the case may be, any of the offences concerned' were omitted; and
   (b) in subsection (5)(c) after 'determining' there were inserted 'in relation to any offence in respect of which he has not been sentenced or otherwise dealt with'.

(9) In sentencing, or otherwise dealing with, the Defendant in respect of the relevant offence or any of the relevant offences at the time during the specified period, the Court shall not—
   (a) impose any fine on him; or
   (b) make any Order as is mentioned in section 2(5)(b)(ii) or (iii) in this Act.

(10) ...

(11) In this section 'the date of conviction' means—
   (a) the date on which the Defendant was convicted; or
   (b) where he appeared to be sentenced in respect of more than one conviction, and if those convictions were not all on the same date, the date of the latest of those convictions; and 'the relevant offence' means the drug trafficking offence in respect of which the Defendant appears ...

(6) Postponing DTA hearings: analysis

9.14 The court may postpone a determination under s 3(1) where it considers it requires further information for such period as it may specify. Section 3(2) states 'more than one postponement may be made under subsection (1) above in relation to the same case', and s 3(3) states that unless there are exceptional circumstances the court will not be allowed to specify a period which exceeds six months beginning from the date of conviction.

9.15 Postponements may be made on application by the defendant or the prosecutor, or of the court's own motion (s 3(5)). The only reason that a postponement may be made under s 3 is to enable 'further information to be obtained' and then only if that information is required for the making of the relevant determinations (see *R v Lingham* (2001) 1 Cr App R(S) 46). If the court cannot find that it requires further information, (or it cannot find there are exceptional circumstances in postponements exceeding six months), then the court should proceed to deal with the DTA hearing.

(7) Conviction, not sentence

9.16 In *R v Sekhon* [2002] EWCA Crim 2954, the Court of Appeal confirmed that the power to postpone a confiscation hearing for up to six months runs from the date of conviction and not the date of sentence.

(8) What amounts to exceptional circumstances?

9.17 What circumstances are exceptional is a judgment to be made by the court in considering whether to make the confiscation order. It must however be done before the six month period elapses (*R v Edwards* (2000) 1 Cr App R(S) 98 and *R v Shergill* [1999] 1 WLR

1944 (CA)). In *R v Cole* The Independent, 30 April 1998 (CA) the trial judge had become ill after a difficult and complex trial. The issue was whether this constituted exceptional circumstances in terms of the confiscation requirements of the DTA. Judge LJ stated:

> The judgment whether circumstances are exceptional or not must be made by the Court considering whether to make a confiscation order, and the decision must be made before the six month period has elapsed . . . here the Judge was in hospital on the date when he had indicated that he would determine the confiscation issue . . . Having studied the statutory code we do not consider that it was intended or drafted so as to preclude the Listing Officer making sensible arrangements for the conduct of the Crown Court business, normally after discussion with the Trial Judge or the Resident Judge.

9.18 A further example of listing difficulties equating to exceptional circumstances was given by the Court of Appeal in *R v Young* [2003] EWCA Crim 3481.

9.19 The Court of Appeal has shown a marked reluctance to interfere with the exercise of the discretion of the sentencing judge to find exceptional circumstances. It is not a question of whether or not the Court of Appeal would find the circumstances in question to be exceptional but whether the judge was entitled to conclude that they were (see *R v Gadsby* (2002) 1 Cr App R(S) 97). Nor is it necessary for the sentencing judge to use the expression 'exceptional circumstances' (although it is submitted it is better that he does) (see *R v Chuni* (2002) Cr App R(S) 420).

9.20 In *R v Gadsby* above the Court of Appeal concluded that the phrase 'exceptional circumstances' is one about which two judges may legitimately differ. In *Gadsby* the Court held that the judge had been entitled to hold that the refusal of the defendant's solicitors to accept service of the prosecutor's statement 21 days before the date of the hearing gave rise to 'exceptional circumstances' where the six month time limit was due to expire eight days later and there was not time to conclude the hearing. Accordingly the court held the judge had been justified in postponing the hearing for a further period of approximately six months. In *R v Zelzele* [2001] Crim LR 830 the judge postponed the confiscation hearing for a further eight days (and beyond the six month time limit) to allow him to conclude a long trial that he was involved in. He did so on the basis of exceptional circumstances. The Court of Appeal held that while the judge may have thought he was exercising the power under s 3, he was in fact exercising the general right of the court to control its own proceedings; and while there would be circumstances in which it would be appropriate to hear representations before adjourning a hearing, this was not a case that required the judge to have the matter listed simply so he could refer to the difficulties that had beset him arising from another case.

9.21 Exceptional circumstances have also been held to exist where there is yet to be a lengthy trial of a co-defendant (*R v Steel and Shevki* [2001] 2 Cr App R(S) 40; [2001] Crime LR 153) and where an important decision is pending in the criminal courts (see *R v Jagdev* [2002] 1 WLR 3017) where, at the date of sentence, the judge had required further information, and postponed the confiscation order proceedings under s 3 of the DTA. At a subsequent hearing the point was raised that the assumptions and reverse burden of proof provisions in the DTA might not be compliant with the European Convention of Human Rights. Decisions by both the Privy Council and Court of Appeal were awaited which were expected to deal with the point (namely *R v Benjafield* [2002] 1 All ER 815 and *McIntosh v Lord Advocate*

B. Preparing for Crown Court DTA Confiscation Hearings

[2001] 2 All ER 638, see Chapter 10, paras 10.146 et seq). The judge held those decisions were 'further information' fundamental to her own decision in the confiscation proceedings and that the potential impact of those decisions amounted to exceptional circumstances for the purposes of s 3(3) of the DTA for postponing the confiscation proceedings beyond a six month limit. She therefore adjourned the case to a date more than six months after the date of the defendant's conviction. The Court of Appeal upheld her ruling finding that the judge was entitled to regard the content of the expected judgment as 'further information' and to hold that there were exceptional circumstances. Accordingly, the judge had validly exercised the power to postpone under s 3 of the DTA beyond the six month period and had validly made a confiscation order).

9.22 In *R v Soneji and Bullen* [2003] Crim LR 738, a decision ultimately appealed to the House of Lords, the Court of Appeal held that where postponement of confiscation hearings required exceptional circumstances, the court proposing to postpone had to make enquiry into whether such circumstances in fact existed. Pill LJ, giving the judgment of the Court, said that if a court was proposing to adjourn confiscation proceedings more than 6 months from the date of conviction, it had to be satisfied that there were exceptional circumstances (see *R v Steele and Shevki* [2001] 2 Cr App R(S) 40; [2001] Crim LR 153). He further held that that requirement had been imported into the exercise of the common law power to postpone (see *R v October* The Times, March 11 2003). The Court stated that although confiscation orders should not be quashed for mere defects in procedure (see *R v Sekhon* (2003) 1 Cr App R(S) 575), nevertheless in order to give effect to the requirement of exceptional circumstances, it was a requirement that there should be enquiry into the circumstances that are stated to be exceptional and the possibility of a timely hearing. The Court of Appeal as a result held that since it was clear that there had been no such determination, the orders could not stand and the confiscation orders were therefore quashed.

9.23 As stated this decision was appealed by the Crown to the House of Lords ((2005) UKHL 49). The House of Lords held that non-compliance with the terms of s 72A(3) of the Criminal Justice Act 1988 (the mirror provisions under the CJA) did not deprive the court of its duty to consider the making of a confiscation order. The defendant had pleaded guilty to an offence of conspiracy to convert property and to remove it from the jurisdiction knowing or suspecting that it represented the proceeds of criminal conduct. The Court of Appeal had quashed the confiscation orders on the basis that they had been made more than 6 months beyond the date of conviction. The House of Lords were invited to consider two points:

(1) whether or not the court's common law jurisdiction to adjourn confiscation proceedings was subject to a mandatory time limit of 6 months from the date of conviction save where exceptional circumstances were present and

(2) whether or not, once the court had assumed jurisdiction, its jurisdiction was extinguished by a failure to comply with the provisions of s 72A of the CJA or any common law requirement relating to the postponement or adjournment of the proceedings.

9.24 The House of Lords held that when interpreting statutory provisions, the approach of distinguishing between mandatory requirements and directory requirements should not be applied, as it served to deflect attention from the real issue of whether an act done in breach of the legislative provision was invalid (see *Project Blue Sky Inc v Australian Broadcasting Authority* (1998) 194 CLR 355).

9.25 The House found that a purposive interpretation of the legislation was required, including considering the scope and object of the whole statute. It found generally that the argument of prejudice was over-stated and that Parliament's intention of a specific time limit would not be necessarily rendered ineffective because courts would still be able to police the scheme adopted by Parliament through the abuse of process jurisdiction.

9.26 In *Soneji and Bullen* there had been no suggestion of the Crown or Court having acted in bad faith and the House of Lords found that the potential prejudice was decisively outweighed by the overriding public interest in not allowing a convicted defender to escape confiscation for what were no more than bona fide errors in the judicial process. Their Lordships also found that there was no common law jurisdiction to adjourn confiscation proceedings. As a result, the court must comply with the six months' requirement wherever possible but, where difficulties arose, for example through listing, these could amount to exceptional circumstances and afford the court the power to postpone the proceedings beyond the six months' requirement.

9.27 In *R v Knights* [2005] 3 WLR 330, a CJA case, the judge purported to postpone the confiscation proceedings under s 72(A)(1) of the CJA by arranging for the case to be mentioned with a view to fixing a hearing. The appeal was heard immediately following the case of *Soneji and Bullen*. Both cases raised broadly similar questions as to whether non-compliance with the strict requirements of the 1988 Act (which correspond with the DTA) disabled the court from making confiscation orders.

9.28 The argument advanced suggested that the court was only allowed to postpone for a precise period of time and had to stipulate a date when the actual determination was to take place. It was argued that a date for mention was insufficient because it did not deal with the substantive hearing. Because it was anticipated that there would have to be a further postponement, it was argued that the initial postponement should not have been made without the court expressing itself satisfied that there were exceptional circumstances to justify such a course.

9.29 Lord Brown stated that when postponing the determination of one of the critical questions for determination in confiscation proceedings, the judge was required to specify the particular period of the postponement: he could not simply adjourn the proceedings generally. However, the judge was not bound to specify the very date when the substantive hearing was to begin, it was sufficient when postponing the proceedings to give directions for the service of statements and to specify a date when the proceedings were next to be listed, whether for disposal or for such further directions as might be needed (or to fix a final hearing date).

9.30 Only in exceptional circumstances should the need for postponement take the final date of any confiscation order beyond the six month time limit and the timetabling should reflect this.

9.31 In *Knights* the House of Lords held that it was only if the timetable initially set made it likely that the six month limit would ultimately be exceeded that the court had on the occasion of the first postponement to address the question of whether exceptional circumstances existed to justify the directions proposed. Although the House of Lords held that the judge *should* have addressed the question of exceptional circumstances, it found that that did not deprive the court of jurisdiction to make the confiscation order. Even if a judge were to postpone confiscation proceedings in a particular case without specifying any return date

B. Preparing for Crown Court DTA Confiscation Hearings

at all, the court would not, applying the approach now laid down in *Soneji*, be precluded from restoring the proceedings to the list for hearing and thereafter making an appropriate order (in *R v Soneji* [2005] 3 WLR 303, the House of Lords held that a failure to comply with the procedural requirements of s 72(A) of the CJA did not result in the invalidity of the proceedings, where a judge had made the order more than six months after conviction, owing to listing difficulties, without having made a finding of exceptional circumstances).

The meaning of 'exceptional circumstances' is further discussed in Chapter 11 para 11.39. See further *Ashton* at para 11.36.

9.32

(9) No requirement to find further exceptional circumstances

In *R v Steel and Shevki* [2001] 2 Cr App R(S) 40; [2001] Crim LR 153 it was held that once the court had postponed a determination beyond the six month date of conviction on the grounds that there are exceptional circumstances it is not then necessary for the court to find further exceptional circumstances for subsequent postponements (see also *R v Zelzele* (2002) 1 Cr App R(S) 62).

9.33

(10) Postponement: absence of the defendant

In *R v October* [2003] EWCA Crim 452, the Court of Appeal held that a defendant did not suffer prejudice where a judge had exercised common law powers to postpone the defendant's confiscation proceedings at a mention hearing in the defendant's absence (although note that the judge's common law powers are now called into question by *Soneji*).

9.34

(11) Six month rule: no retrospective extension

Subject to *Soneji* (above), an order for postponement beyond the six month period must be made before its expiry, ie there can be no retrospective extension (*R v Edwards* (2000) 1 Cr App R(S) 98 CA). The importance of this provision was emphasised in *R v Kelly* [2000] Crim LR 392 (CA) where the court held that where more than six months had elapsed from the date of conviction, a purported postponement of confiscation proceedings under s 3 of the DTA was a nullity and should be quashed.

9.35

(12) Purpose of postponement: further information

In *R v Jagdev* [2002] 1 WLR 3017 the Court held that the purpose of the power to postpone the confiscation proceedings was to enable the judge to reach a fair conclusion on the confiscation issue. If there was a real prospect the hearing might be wasted and an unjust order made if the judge proceeded to hear the case because of lack of information, (in *Jagdev* because of an awaited decision of the Court of Appeal); then the judge was entitled to find, if appropriate, that 'further information' was required and to hold that there were exceptional circumstances.

9.36

This reflects the view of Judge LJ in *R v Steel and Shevki* [2001] 2 Cr App R(S) 40; [2001] Crim LR 153 who concluded:

9.37

> Confiscation orders should normally form part of the ordinary sentencing process. For lack of appropriate information, this will often be impractical. If the conditions in section 3(1) or section 3(4) are satisfied, and within six months of conviction, the Court may decide that the

determination should be postponed. Unless the circumstances are exceptional this should not extend beyond six months after conviction. These decisions involve the Court's discretion, judicially expressed when the statutory conditions are present, taking full account of the preferred statutory sequence as well as the express direction in the statute that save in exceptional circumstances confiscation determinations should not be postponed for more than six months beyond conviction.

(13) Failure to properly postpone

9.38 The run of inconsistent case law (*R v Keith Ross* (2001) 2 Cr App R(S) 484 [109]; *R v Steven Davis* [2002] Crim LR 224; *R v Alfonso Copeland* [2002] EWCA Crim 736); *R v Pisciotto* [2002] Crim LR 678, considered fully in the first edition of this book), that had led to a large number of confiscation orders being quashed on technicalities was halted by the Court of Appeal in *Sekhon v R* [2002] EWCA Crim 2954. In *Sekhon* the Court suggested that it could not have been the intention of Parliament to exclude the jurisdiction of the court in relation to the making of confiscation orders because of procedural defects of a technical nature that caused no injustice to the defendant. It drew attention to the most recent legislation, namely s 14(11) of POCA, which provides: 'A confiscation order must not be quashed only on the ground that there was a defect or omission in the procedure connected with the application for or the granting of a postponement'.

9.39 The Court stated that it expected in future a procedural failure only to result in a lack of jurisdiction if this was necessary to ensure that the criminal justice system served the interests of justice and thus the public, or where there was at least a real possibility of the defendant suffering prejudice as a result of that procedural failure (para 29).

9.40 The rationale in *Sekhon* was confirmed in *R v Ashton* [2006] EWCA Crim 794 where the Court of Appeal stated at para 9:

> Absent a clear indication that parliament intended jurisdiction automatically to be removed following a procedural failure, the decision of the court should be based upon a wide assessment of the interests of justice, with particular focus on whether there was a real possibility that the prosecution or the defendant may suffer prejudice. If that risk is present, the court should then decide whether it is just to permit the proceedings to continue. (See also *R v Clarke* [2006] EWCA Crim 1196).

9.41 In *R v Haisman* (2004) 1 Cr App R(S) 383 (63), the Court of Appeal held that where prosecuting counsel invited a judge to postpone confiscation proceedings and the judge responded by saying, *'If everyone agrees to that, I will do that'* and there was no dissent from the counsel to that course, the judge had manifestly reached a decision to postpone the confiscation proceedings under s 72A of the CJA and the subsequent confiscation orders would be lawful.

9.42 This issue was once again considered in *R v Tahir* [2006] EWCA Crim 792, where the Court of Appeal stated that the correct approach to an alleged failure to comply with the provision (it was alleged the judge failed to comply with the postponement provisions of s 72(A) of the CJA was to ask whether it was the purpose of the legislature that an act done in breach of a statutory provision would be invalid and whether prejudice could be caused as a result of the failure to comply. In the instant case, the appellant had not suffered prejudice and therefore the appeal was dismissed.

B. Preparing for Crown Court DTA Confiscation Hearings

(14) Postponements: the case law applied

In conclusion, it appears that the courts have now settled that: 9.43

(1) When postponing the determination of one or other of the critical questions in confiscation proceedings, the judge is required to specify the particular period of the postponement and cannot simply adjourn the proceedings indefinitely.
(2) The judge is not obliged to specify the exact date on which the substantive hearing would begin or end. It is sufficient for him to give directions for the service of proceedings and to specify a date on which they are next to be listed, whether for disposal or for further directions.
(3) The Acts expressly envisage that more than one postponement could be necessary.
(4) Even if a judge has postponed confiscation proceedings without specifying a return date, the court is not precluded from restoring the proceedings to the list for hearing and making a confiscation order, provided that in postponing the proceedings the judge has acted in good faith and in the purported exercise of his power under the Acts.
(5) It is only if the timetable makes it likely that the six month statutory limit will be exceeded that the court has to address the question of whether exceptional circumstances exist.
(6) The court does not have to find that there are exceptional circumstances before the case can properly be postponed for further mention (rather than for final hearing) providing that the timetable is within the six month limit. If, when setting the timetable, it is apparent to the judge at the first postponement that the total period is likely to exceed the six month limit, the judge should address the question of exceptional circumstances at that time.
(7) Ineptness of the drafting of the prosecutor's notice does not render the court disabled from making the confiscation order and nor do defects therein.

It is important to note that one matter survives *Sekhon*, namely that the judge must 9.44 postpone the confiscation hearing prior to passing sentence. Failure to do so may still result in any subsequent confiscation order being quashed (see *R v Williamson* [2003] EWCA Crim 644, where confiscation orders were quashed because the sentencing judge failed to take a decision to postpone the drug trafficking enquiry prior to sentencing and thus had failed to comply with the provisions of ss 2 and 3 of the DTA).

(15) Postponement pending appeal

Section 3(4) enables the court, when the defendant appeals against his conviction, to: 9.45

(a) postpone making determinations under the Act for such period as it may specify; or
(b) where it has already exercised its powers to postpone, extend the specified period.

Section 3(6) provides that a postponement under s 3(4) shall not, save where the court is 9.46 satisfied that there are exceptional circumstances, exceed three months after the date on which the appeal is determined or otherwise disposed of. Section 3(5) empowers the court to grant postponements under s 3(1) and (4) either of its own motion or on application by the prosecutor or defendant.

(16) Application for postponement: procedure

9.47 Rule 56.2(1)(b) of the Criminal Procedure Rules states:

(1) Where an application to the Crown Court is made by the Defendant or the Prosecutor under section 3(5)(a) of the Drug Trafficking Act 1994 asking the Court to exercise its powers under section 3(4) of that Act (or under section 72(5)(a) of the Criminal Justice Act 1988 asking the Court to exercise its powers under section 72(4)(a) of that Act), such an application must be made in writing and a copy thereof must be served on the Prosecutor or the Defendant, as the case may be.

(2) A party which is served with a copy of an application under paragraph 1 shall, within 28 days of the date of service, notify the applicant and the appropriate officer of the Crown Court, in writing, whether or not it proposes to oppose the application, giving its reasons for any such opposition.

(3) After the expiry of the period referred to in paragraph (2), the Crown Court shall determine whether an application under paragraph (1) is to be dealt with—(a) without a hearing or (b) at a hearing at which the parties may be represented.

9.48 It should be noted that the relevant provisions of the 1988 and 1994 Acts were repealed on 24 March 2003, but they continue to have effect in respect of proceedings for offences committed before that date.

(17) Sentence

9.49 Previously, s 1(4) of the DTOA required the court to hold its enquiry under the Act before sentencing the defendant. This requirement was at the time criticised as leading to injustice because the defendant had to wait many months after conviction before he knew his fate in complex cases where there had to be a long adjournment before the enquiry could proceed.

9.50 This anomaly was remedied by s 3(7) of the DTA which provides that when the court exercises its powers of postponement, it may nevertheless proceed to deal with the defendant in respect of the offences for which he has been convicted.

C. Standard of Proof

9.51 Section 2(8) of the Drug Trafficking Act 1994 states:

(8) The standard of proof required to determine any question arising under this Act as to—
(a) whether a person has benefited from drug trafficking, or
(b) the amount to be recovered in his case by virtue of this Section, shall be that applicable in civil proceedings.

9.52 The standard of proof therefore is on the balance of probabilities. However it should be remembered that in civil cases the degree of probability required to establish proof may vary according to the allegation to be proved (see *Hornal v Neuberger Products Ltd* [1957] 1 QB 247) and the court may be reluctant, when considering claims by the Crown, to apply merely a 51/49 per cent test where an individual's property or other assets are in jeopardy.

9.53 It should also be noted that under the DTOA the burden and standard of proof was that of criminal proceedings (see R v *Ilsemann* (1990) 12 Cr App R(S) 398; *R v Carroll* [1991] Crim LR 720; *Comiskey* (1990) 12 Cr App R(S) 562; and *R v Enwezor* (1991)

D. Preparatory Steps for a DTA Hearing

93 Cr App R 233). Now, once the prosecution has proved to the civil standard the amount of benefit under s 2 of the Act, the burden of proof falls upon the defendant to satisfy the court that the 'amount that might be realised' is less than the amount of the benefit figure.

D. Preparatory Steps for a DTA Hearing

(1) Statements relating to drug trafficking

The Act provides: 9.54

11 (1) Where the Prosecutor asks the Court to proceed under Section 2 of this Act he shall give the Court, within such period as it may direct, a statement of matters which he considers relevant in connection with—
   (a) determining whether the Defendant has benefited from drug trafficking; or
   (b) assessing the value of his proceeds of drug trafficking.
(2) In this Section such a statement is referred to as a 'Prosecutor's Statement'.
(3) Where the Court proceeds under Section 2 of this Act without the Prosecutor having asked it to do so, it may require him to give it a Prosecutor's statement within such period as it may direct.
(4) Where the Prosecutor has given a Prosecutor's Statement—
   (a) he may at any time give the Court a further such Statement; and
   (b) the Court may at any time require him to give it a further such statement, within such period as it may direct.
(5) Where the Prosecutor's Statement has been given and the Court is satisfied that a copy of this Statement has been served on the Defendant, it may require the Defendant—
   (a) to indicate to it within such period as it may direct, the extent to which he accepts such allegations in the Statement; and
   (b) so far as he does not accept any such allegation, to give particulars of any matters on which he proposes to rely.
(6) Where the Court has given a direction under this Section it may at any time vary it by giving a further Direction.
(7) ... (Below) ...
(8) If the Defendant fails in any respect to comply with the requirements under subsection (5) above he may be treated for the purposes of this Section as accepting every allegation in the Prosecutor's Statement in question apart from—
   (a) any allegation in respect of which he has complied with the requirement; and
   (b) any allegation that he has benefited from drug trafficking or that any payment or any other reward was received by him in connection with drug trafficking carried on by him or another person.
(9) Where—
   (a) there is given to the Crown Court by the Defendant a Statement as to any matters relevant to determining the amounts that might be realised at the time the determination is made, and
   (b) the Prosecutor accepts to any extent any allegation in the Statement, the Court may, for the purposes of that determination, treat the acceptance by the Prosecutor as conclusive of the matters to which it relates.
(10) An allegation may be accepted or particulars of any matter may be given, for the purposes of this Section in such manner as may be described by the Rules of Court or as the Court may direct.
(11) ... (Below) ...

(2) Section 11 statements generally

9.55 Section 11 of the DTA (formerly s 3 of the DTOA) makes provision for the parties to submit written statements dealing with the matters that have to be determined at the DTA enquiry. These statements serve a number of useful purposes, including:

(1) Enabling each party to the proceedings to be put on notice of the other's case and thereby prevent one party being taken by surprise.

(2) Serving to identify the real issues in dispute, thereby saving court time in not having to hear evidence in relation to matters not really in issue.

In these respects, s 11 statements serve a similar purpose to pleadings in civil actions. It is perhaps not surprising that the courts have encouraged the parties, particularly the prosecution, to make full use of the provisions in s 11. In *R v Dickens* [1990] 2 All ER 626 Lord Lane CJ observed (at p 630A) that s 11 statements went 'a little way towards simplifying proceedings and crystallising the issues'. Further support for the use of s 11 statements came in the Court of Appeal's judgment in *R v Comiskey* (1991) 93 Cr App R 227 where Turner J, in delivering the judgment of the Court, said (at p 231):

> It is very desirable that those responsible for the prosecution of offences should make full use of this. It is also desirable that in appropriate cases the court should be invited to require the defendant to indicate to what extent he accepts the Crown's allegations and, so far as he does not do so, to indicate any matters he proposes to rely on (see s 3(2)). Unfortunately, this was not done in the present case.

(3) The prosecutor's statement

9.56 Section 3 of the DTOA did not provide a mandatory obligation on the prosecutor to serve a statement under the Act. This changed when the DTA came into force and the prosecutor is now required to provide a s 11 statement whenever he asks the court to proceed under the Act. Section 11(1) of the DTA provides that, in such circumstances, the prosecutor shall provide a statement of matters that he considers relevant in connection with:

(a) determining whether the defendant has benefited from drug trafficking; or
(b) assessing the value of his proceeds of drug trafficking.

The statement is referred to as a 'prosecutor's statement': (see s 11(2)). Section 11(3) empowers the court to require the prosecutor to provide such a statement where it decides of its own motion to proceed under the Act.

(4) The purpose of the prosecutor's statement

9.57 The purpose of the prosecutor's statement is to contain the ambit of the enquiry. In *R v Dickens* [1990] 2 All ER 626, the Court of Appeal held that where a defendant appears before the Crown Court to be sentenced in respect of a drug trafficking offence, the court, before sentencing him, must first make a preliminary assessment from the evidence at the trial or, if there was a plea, from the recital of facts, whether the defendant may have benefited from drug trafficking. Lord Lane went on to state that:

> the Prosecution have the task of proving both the fact that the Defendant has benefited from drug trafficking and the amount of such benefit . . . the evidence upon which the judgment

D. Preparatory Steps for a DTA Hearing

is based will come in part from the trial, if there has been one, in part from the statements tendered by the parties to the Court . . . and in part from evidence adduced before the Court.

9.58 The Court of Appeal also considered the purpose of prosecutor's statements in *R v Benjafield* (2001) 2 Cr App R(S) 221 para 107. In finding that such statements did not contravene Article 6 of the European Convention of Human Rights it held that:

> a Statement serves the useful purpose of forewarning the Defendant of the case of the Prosecution which he will have to meet from his assets. It should assist the Defendant by making it clear the matters with which he has to be prepared to deal. It is right that, as the rules require, the Prosecution should identify any information which will assist the Defendant.

9.59 The case of *Benjafield* progressed to the House of Lords ([2002] 1 All ER 815), where their Lordships endorsed the point that the defendant must know in advance the case he has to meet.

(5) Form and content of prosecutor's section 11 statements

9.60 Rule 56.1(1)(b) of the Criminal Procedure Rules deals with the form and content of s 11 statements:

(1) Where a prosecutor or defendant
   (b) tenders to the Crown Court any statement or other document under section 11 of the Drug Trafficking Act 1994 or section 73 of the 1988 Act in any proceedings in respect of a drug trafficking offence or in respect of an offence to which Part VI of the 1988 Act applies, he must serve a copy as soon as practicable on the defendant or the prosecutor, as the case may be.

9.61 Under r 56.1(2) any statement tendered to the Crown Court by the prosecutor under s 11 (or s 73(1)(a) of the CJA 1988) must include the following particulars:

(a) the name of the defendant;
(b) the name of the person by whom the statement is made and the date on which it was made;
(c) where the statement is not tendered immediately after the defendant has been convicted, the date on which and the place where the relevant conviction occurred; and
(d) such information known to the prosecutor as is relevant to the determination as to whether or not the defendant has benefited from drug trafficking or relevant criminal conduct and to the assessment of the value of his proceeds of drug trafficking or, as the case may be, benefit from relevant criminal conduct.

Rule 56.1 further provides:

(3) Where, in accordance with section 11(7) of the 1994 Act or section 73(1C) of the 1988 Act, the defendant indicates the extent to which he accepts any allegation contained within the prosecutor's statement, if he indicates the same in writing to the prosecutor, he must serve a copy of that reply on the court officer.
(4) Expressions used in this rule shall have the same meanings as in the 1994 Act or, where appropriate, the 1988 Act.

It will be noted that the relevant provisions of the 1988 and 1994 Acts were repealed on 24 March 2003, but they continue to have effect in respect of proceedings for offences committed before that date.

9.62 In practice the prosecutor's statement will normally include:

(1) the figures in summary form of why the Crown say the defendant has benefited from drug trafficking and what the Crown say are the defendant's current realisable assets;

(2) a short introduction to the defendant himself detailing his arrest and the charge itself. It will also include the date of his conviction, or his guilty plea, and details of his sentence (if appropriate);
(3) a brief summary setting out the details of the case against the defendant. There should also be a thumbnail sketch of what the defendant's role was in the charge;
(4) the defendant's personal history including his age, marital status, occupation, address;
(5) a summary of the law either within the statement or attached as an annex;
(6) a summary of proceedings before the High Court, and in particular whether or not a restraint order was granted and if so, on what date and by which judge;
(7) details of the financial investigation, including any examination of bank accounts and property;
(8) any other relevant financial enquiries, including assets that the defendant may hold either in this country or abroad and any expenditure on travel or lifestyle;
(9) the calculation of the proceeds of drug trafficking, setting out what assumptions the Crown rely upon and why;
(10) the calculation of benefit from the figures within the body of the statement, a summary of the total figure and how that figure has been reached;
(11) the amount that might be realised, setting out what realisable assets have been traced and their total figure. From a prosecutor's perspective, it is worthwhile including within the statement that 'the Crown does not necessarily accept that the assets identified are the only ones with which the Defendant holds an interest' to allow for the Crown to revert back to the court should any new evidence become available;
(12) the confiscation order sought. A short paragraph specifying what it is the Crown seeks from the court, ie a confiscation order in the sum of £100,000: a benefit of £100,000, realisable assets of £75,000 and hidden assets of £25,000.

9.63 It should be noted that r 56.1 imposes no obligation on the prosecutor to itemise the defendant's known realisable assets in the s 11 statement. This is in line with the decision of the Court of Appeal in *R v Comiskey* (1991) 93 Cr App R 227, where the Court ruled that once the amount of the benefit was determined, a confiscation order must be made in the full amount of that benefit unless the defendant proves that the value of his realisable property is less than that amount.

9.64 It is submitted, however, that in accordance with the prosecutor's general duty of disclosure, he should disclose particulars of such assets that are known to him. He may, of course, emphasise that the particulars given are only of known assets and that the Crown does not accept that the assets identified are the only ones in which the defendant holds an interest.

9.65 It is also good practice to exhibit to the prosecutor's statement the restraint order, any statement in support, the defendant's disclosure statement and any variation orders granted during the course of the proceedings together with any other relevant statements in support.

9.66 If the prosecutor seeks to rely on any of the assumptions in s 4(3) of the DTA, the s 11 statement should specify which assumptions are relied upon, together with the grounds upon which such reliance is sought.

D. Preparatory Steps for a DTA Hearing

The court is not restricted to making a confiscation order in the amount of the defendant's proceeds of drug trafficking as alleged in the prosecutor's s 11 statement. In *R v Atkinson* [1992] Crim LR 749, the Court of Appeal held that there was no such restriction on the court and if the court was satisfied that the amount of the defendant's sum was greater than that alleged by the prosecutor, the court would be obliged to make a confiscation order in the higher amount. **9.67**

(6) When should the prosecutor's statement be served?

Neither the DTA nor the Criminal Procedure Rules stipulate the stage at which the prosecutor's s 11 statement should be served, merely providing that it shall be served 'as soon as practicable'. This is no doubt because the appropriate time depends on the facts of individual cases. It is submitted, however, that best practice is to serve the s 11 statement prior to the trial whenever possible and, except in the most complex of cases, not later than the retirement of the jury. This will enable the trial judge to be in the best possible position to give directions as to how the DTA enquiry should proceed after conviction. In certain complex cases however the Crown may be unable to complete its s 11 statement prior to the retirement of the jury and it is not therefore unusual for the defence to only be served with it after the jury returns a verdict. **9.68**

(7) Upon whom should the prosecutor's statement be served?

Rule 56.1(1)(b)) of the Criminal Procedure Rules requires that the statement should be served on the defendant and on the Crown Court. There is no requirement that the statement should be served upon solicitors acting on behalf of a co-accused. It is submitted that (certainly prior to conviction) s 11 statements should not be served on those acting for a defendant's co-accused (and where appropriate a Public Interest Immunity application should be made). These statements frequently disclose personal matters relating to the defendant's financial affairs and exhibit his disclosure statement made in compliance with the restraint order. It is in the public interest that the defendant should be encouraged to make full and frank disclosure of all his realisable property in such statements, and he is not likely to do so if the statement is to be passed into the hands of third parties. It was on this basis that Macpherson J. in *Re R* (1992) refused to allow a defendant's (then) disclosure affidavit to be forwarded to a third party that was contemplating issuing unrelated civil proceedings against him. **9.69**

(8) The defendant's statement

The defendant's s 11 statement serves a similar purpose to a defence in a civil action; it indicates what matters set out in the prosecutor's statement are admitted and which are denied and sets out any matters relied upon by the defendant. **9.70**

(9) Requiring the defendant to respond to the prosecutor's statement

If the court had no power to compel the defendant to respond to the prosecutor's s 11 statement, he would be able to mount an 'ambush' to the Crown's case by not disclosing in advance what his case was, thereby taking the prosecution by surprise and giving them no **9.71** opportunity to make enquiries into the veracity of his assertions. Section 11(5) of the DTA enables the court to prevent such a situation occurring by ordering the defendant, where it is satisfied that the prosecutor's statement has been served on him:

(a) to indicate to it, within such period as it may direct, the extent to which he accepts each allegation in the statement; and

(b) so far as he does not accept any such allegation, to give particulars of any matters on which he proposes to rely.

9.72 When the prosecutor's statement has been served prior to the retirement of the jury, the judge will normally make an order under s 11(5) after a guilty verdict has been returned and thereafter will adjourn, pending compliance by the defendant within the period he specifies. It is a wise precaution for the prosecutor to draw up the judge's order and cause it to be served on the defendant. In view of the Court of Appeal's comments in *Comiskey*, there is little a defendant can say to resist the making of an order under s 11(5). Those representing defendants should, however, ensure that they are given sufficient time to respond to the prosecutor's statement. To do so before a jury's verdict may be viewed as a waste of public funds. The court may, under s 11(6) of the DTA, vary any direction it has given under the section by making a further direction.

(10) Drafting the defendant's statement

9.73 The prosecutor's statement should be considered paragraph by paragraph and each allegation admitted or denied. Where an allegation is denied, any facts relied on should be fully set out. If, for example, the defendant denies that monies in a particular bank account constitute a benefit from drug trafficking, the statement should not contain merely a bare denial, but also the defendant's assertions as to the source of the monies, corroborated wherever possible by independent evidence, for example, by an accountant's report. Similarly, if the defendant denies that he has an interest in a particular asset, details should be given as to the identity of those who do own the asset and, where possible, documents of title produced. The importance of obtaining independent corroboration of the defendant's assertions cannot be over-emphasised. In *R v Walbrook and Glasgow* [1994] Crim LR 613, the Court of Appeal held that where a defendant wished to show that the amount of his realisable assets available for confiscation were less than the amount of his benefit as certified by the court, 'he had to produce clear and cogent evidence: vague and generalised assertions unsupported by evidence would rarely, if ever, be sufficient'.

9.74 It has to be remembered that at this stage of the proceedings, whether on his guilty plea or by the verdict of the jury, the defendant stands convicted of drug trafficking offences and may therefore have something of a credibility problem with the court. This is particularly so in cases where the defendant pleaded not guilty and was disbelieved by the jury upon oath.

9.75 Although there is no rule that the defendant cannot rely on facts not pleaded in his statement, if the Crown are taken by surprise by suggestions or an account given for the first time from the witness box, the defendant runs the risk of an adjournment being ordered and his being required to pay costs. This process obviously involves taking careful and detailed instructions from the client and his financial advisers.

D. Preparatory Steps for a DTA Hearing

(11) Defendant's acceptance conclusive

Section 11(7) of the DTA reads: **9.76**

> (7) Where the Defendant accepts to any extent any allegation in any Prosecutor's Statement, the Court may, for the purposes of—
> (a) determining whether the Defendant has benefited from drug trafficking or
> (b) assessing the value of his proceeds of drug trafficking, treat his acceptance as conclusive of the matters to which it relates.

Great care should be taken only to admit assertions made in the prosecutor's statement that are genuinely accepted. The effect of s 11(7) of the DTA is such that where a defendant accepts to any extent any allegation contained in the prosecutor's statement, the court may, for the purposes of the DTA enquiry, treat that acceptance as being conclusive of the matters to which it relates.   **9.77**

Similarly, under s 11(9) of the DTA, any acceptance by the prosecutor of any allegation contained in a defendant's s 11 statement may be treated by the court as being conclusive for the purposes of the DTA enquiry.   **9.78**

However, it will be noted that such an acceptance of an allegation in a prosecutors statement need not be binding or conclusive on appeal (see para 10.169 of Chapter 10).   **9.79**

(12) The risk of self incrimination

The defendant should be assured that nothing he discloses in terms of payment or other reward received in connection with drug trafficking in his s 11 statement will be used as evidence in a trial. This is because s 11(11) of the DTA provides as follows: **9.80**

> (11) No acceptance by the defendant under this section that any payment or other reward was received by him in connection with drug trafficking carried on by him or another person shall be admissible as evidence in any proceedings for an offence.

The clear purpose of s 11(11) is to prevent the defendant invoking his privilege against self-incrimination as a justification for failing to respond to a prosecutor's statement. This provision is analogous to the condition subject to which disclosure orders are made in restraint order cases and which are designed to protect the defendant's privilege against self-incrimination.   **9.81**

(13) Further provision of information by the defendant

Section 12 of the DTA makes the obligations on a defendant at the DTA confiscation hearing even more draconian. The section applies where the prosecutor has asked the court to proceed under the Act, or the court has decided of its own motion to proceed under the Act (s 12(1)). Under s 12(2) of the DTA: **9.82**

> For the purpose of obtaining information to assist it in carrying out its functions, the court may at any time order the defendant to give it such information as may be specified in the order.

Although s 12(2) states that the court may 'at any time order the Defendant to give a Statement under section 12' it is submitted that that direction can only apply where the court is proceeding under s 2 of the DTA, ie after conviction. This is because s 12 only   **9.83**

Chapter 9: Preparing for Confiscation Hearings under the DTA

applies where the prosecutor has asked the court to proceed under the Act or the court has decided of its own motion to proceed under the Act.

9.84 Section 12(3) states:

> (3) an order under subsection (2) above may require all, or any specified part, of the required information to be given to the Court in such manner, and before such date, as may be specified in the order.

This gives the court the opportunity to specify the manner and the timeframe in which the defendant's statement should be provided.

9.85 In practice, the compiling of the prosecutor's statement and the defence's reply either under s 11(5) or s 12 is assisted when the defendant has already had to make a statement under the disclosure order provision of an existing restraint order. Leggatt LJ in *Re T (Restraint Order: Disclosure of Assets)* (1993) 96 Cr App R 194, held that disclosure of assets did not amount to self-incrimination; but merely facilitated an assessment of the amount to be recovered from a defendant who had benefited from drug trafficking. (On privilege against self incrimination, see *Re E and Re H* [2001] EWHC Admin 472 and *Re J* [2001] EWHC Admin 713).

(14) Consequences of the defendant failing to respond to the prosecutor's statement

9.86 The defendant who fails to respond to orders of the court made under ss 11 and 12 of the DTA runs the risk of having a confiscation order made in the full amount of his benefit from drug trafficking as alleged by the prosecution. Section 11(8) of the DTA provides that where a defendant has failed to comply with an order made under s 11(5):

> (8) ... he may be treated for the purposes of this section as accepting every allegation in the statement apart from:
> (a) any allegation in respect of which he has complied with the requirement; and
> (b) any allegation that he has benefited from drug trafficking or that any payment or other reward was received by him in connection with drug trafficking carried on by him or another person.

9.87 Further, in *R v Comiskey* (1991) 93 Cr App R 227, the Court of Appeal held that once the prosecution have proved benefit from drug trafficking and the amount of the defendant's proceeds, the burden then passes to the defendant to show, on a balance of probabilities, that the value of his realisable property was less than this sum. If he fails to discharge that burden, the court must make a confiscation order in the full amount by which it has certified he has benefited from drug trafficking. The Court of Appeal has shown a marked reluctance to interfere with confiscation orders made in circumstances where the defendant has failed to respond to the prosecutor's statement or failed to give evidence at the hearing. The Court in *Comiskey* held that the object of the Act was to oblige the defendant to reveal this information: there was no duty on the prosecution to satisfy the court that the amount that might be realised was less than the benefit.

9.88 In *R v Layode* (CA,12 March 1993) the defendant failed to respond to the prosecutor's financial statement or give evidence at the confiscation hearing. The Court of Appeal dismissed the defendant's appeal against a £133,891.00 confiscation order. Macpherson J in delivering the judgment of the court observed that:

D. Preparatory Steps for a DTA Hearing

If the judge was wrong about the realisable assets and the bank accounts or indeed about the true value of the 'benefits', the appellant had nobody but himself to blame in this regard.

9.89 In concluding his judgment, His Lordship observed that the case 'underlines the importance of a defendant submitting evidence'.

9.90 The position of a defendant who fails to provide information under s 12(2) of the DTA is dealt with in s 12(5) which provides as follows:

(5) If the defendant fails without reasonable excuse to comply with any order under this section, the court may draw such inference from that failure as it considers appropriate.

(15) Valuing the drugs

9.91 If the defendant gives no account of the price paid for the drugs he has in his possession, or the price that would have been obtained on their re-sale, the court is entitled to draw appropriate inferences from the evidence: *R v Berry* (2000) 1 Cr App R(S) 352. In such circumstances the court could consider ordering disclosure under s 12, and if the defendant failed to comply, draw the appropriate inference.

(16) Further statements by the prosecutor

9.92 A practice developed under the DTOA of the prosecutor submitting a further statement if there were matters in the defendant's statement with which he disagreed or which called for further comment. This practice gained statutory footing in s 11(4) of the DTA, which provides as follows:

Where the prosecutor has given a prosecutor's statement:
(a) he may at any time give the court a further such statement; and
(b) the court may at any time require him to give it a further such statement within such period as it may direct.

There is thus provision for further statements to be tendered by the prosecutor either acting of his own motion or in compliance with an order of the court.

(17) Securing the attendance of witnesses

9.93 Once all s 11 statements have been served, the parties should advise each other as to which witnesses are required to attend the hearing. It should particularly be borne in mind that many civilian witnesses, especially those employed by financial institutions, may not be prepared to attend court voluntarily. Further, as the financial enquiry is rarely complete by committal, few, if any, of such witnesses will be the subject of witness orders made by the magistrates. In such cases, witness summonses should be sought from the appropriate officer of the Crown Court.

10

THE DTA CONFISCATION HEARING

A. Introduction	10.01	
(1) Purpose of the hearing	10.01	
(2) Procedure leading to the hearing	10.03	
(3) The burden and standard of proof	10.04	
(4) Basis of plea	10.10	
B. Benefit from Drug Trafficking	10.11	
(1) Statutory provisions as to benefit	10.16	
(2) Payments or other rewards	10.18	
(3) Joint apportionment/multiple defendants	10.19	
(4) Are drugs seized from the defendant a payment or reward?	10.33	
(5) The payment or other reward must be received in connection with drug trafficking	10.37	
(6) Section 63(2) DTA	10.39	
(7) Knowledge that the payment comes from drug trafficking	10.44	
(8) Conspiracies	10.47	
(9) Assessing the defendant's proceeds of drug trafficking	10.49	
(10) Proceeds not profits	10.52	
(11) Joint benefit	10.59	
C. The Assumptions	10.63	
(1) When the assumptions must not be applied	10.65	
(2) No other assumptions may be made	10.72	
(3) When must the assumptions be applied?	10.73	
(4) At what stage are the assumptions applied?	10.74	
(5) Effect of applying the assumptions	10.75	
(6) Rebutting the assumptions	10.77	
(7) Certificates of benefit	10.79	
(8) A review of the authorities in relation to benefit: DTA and CJA	10.82	
(9) Determining the amount to be realised	10.91	
(10) Burden of proof	10.92	
(11) Hidden assets	10.94
(12) Meaning of realisable property	10.100
(13) Property held by the defendant	10.101
(14) Margin for error	10.103
(15) Costs of sale	10.104
(16) Assets jointly held with third parties	10.105
(17) Matrimonial homes	10.106
(18) Assets held overseas	10.107
(19) Gifts	10.108
(20) When is a gift caught by the Act?	10.109
(21) Obligations having priority	10.114
(22) Valuing property	10.116
(23) Market value	10.121
(24) Confiscation orders and the forfeiture of drugs	10.122
(25) Is the court limited to the prosecutor's statement?	10.123
(26) Public interest immunity	10.124
D. Making the Confiscation Order	10.125
(1) Relationship with forfeiture orders and other legislation	10.126
(2) Relationship between the confiscation order and the sentence	10.127
(3) Imprisonment in default	10.133
(4) Time to pay	10.138
(5) Orders for the payment of costs	10.143
(6) Unreasonable delay in enforcement	10.144
(7) Confiscation orders and the ECHR	10.145
E. Confiscation Orders Against Defendants who Die or Abscond	10.153
(1) Post-conviction orders	10.154
(2) Pre-conviction cases	10.155
(3) Rules of the Supreme Court	10.158
(4) Procedural matters	10.164
F. Confiscation Hearings Under the DTA: Index of Defined Expressions	10.166
G. Appeals	10.167

A. Introduction

(1) Purpose of the hearing

10.01 The purpose of the DTA confiscation hearing is to determine three distinct but inter-related issues with a view to a confiscation order being made in the amount that the defendant has benefited from drug trafficking. These issues are as follows:

(1) whether the defendant has benefited from drug trafficking: (see s 2(2) of the DTA);
(2) if so, the amount of the defendant's proceeds (benefit) of drug trafficking: (see s 2 and s 5(1) of the DTA);
(3) the value of his realisable property available to satisfy a confiscation order in the amount of his benefit: (see s 5(3) of the DTA);

Each of these three elements will be considered separately because it is important, as the Court of Appeal indicated in *R v Johnson* [1991] 2 All ER 428, that the necessary procedures should be followed step by step, and with the court stating at each stage the findings it has made. (See particularly para 10.31 in relation to purpose.)

10.02 The preparatory steps leading to the hearing itself are considered in detail in Chapter 9. It will have been noted from that chapter that the DTA will continue to have statutory effect over all drug trafficking confiscation hearings where the offence, or any of the offences, concerned were committed before 24 March 2003. It is only where the indictment does not reveal any alleged offence(s) committed prior to 24 March 2003 that POCA and the new regime will take effect. Where appropriate we have commented on the law as it applied under the DTOA 1986, although very few cases now arise under that Act. The primary purpose of making reference to the DTOA in this chapter is to consider the pre-existing case law that shaped and in some cases still binds the DTA.

(2) Procedure leading to the hearing

10.03 The practice and procedure in terms of preparation for a DTA confiscation hearing and the judicial and administrative steps required in that process are dealt with comprehensively in Chapter 9.

(3) The burden and standard of proof

10.04 In the early days of the DTOA it had been assumed by many that no burden of proof lay on the Crown at all, given that the hearing was only taking place because the Crown had succeeded in proving beyond reasonable doubt the defendant's guilt in respect of a drug trafficking offence. It was further considered that, in any event, the proceedings were not accusatorial in nature but involved the court holding an enquiry in which traditional concepts as to the burden and standard of proof were inappropriate.

10.05 This changed in *R v Dickens* [1990] 2 All ER 626, a DTOA case, where the Court of Appeal ruled that the burden of proof rested on the prosecution to prove to the criminal standard both that the defendant had benefited from drug trafficking and the amount of that benefit (see also *R v Enwezor* (1991) 93 Cr App R 233).

However in cases commenced after the DTA came into force, *Dickens* and *Enwezor* became superseded by statute because s 2(8) of the DTA provided that the standard of proof in determining: **10.06**

(a) whether a person has benefited from drug trafficking, or
(b) the amount to be recovered from him shall be that applicable in civil proceedings, namely proof on the balance of probabilities.

Under the DTA, once the prosecution has proved to the civil standard the amount of benefit under s 2 of the Act, the burden of proof falls upon the defendant to satisfy the court that the 'amount that might be realised' is less than the amount of the benefit figure. **10.07**

In *R v Levin* The Times, 20 February 2004, the Court of Appeal confirmed that the standard of proof to be applied in confiscation proceedings was that of the civil standard. As a result, when making a determination a judge was entitled to take into account both the evidence given at trial and any other information properly obtained either before or after the trial, including evidence inadmissible at trial. The Court held that the corresponding provisions under the CJA had been intended to change the procedural landscape in that: **10.08**

(1) the standard of proof was now the civil burden;
(2) the court could make far-reaching assumptions;
(3) the court could require the defendant to provide information and could draw inferences from the failure to do so; and
(4) the court might rely on evidence given at trial and any relevant information properly obtained either before the trial or thereafter in order to determine a defendant's benefit and the amount to be recovered.

The Court held that these changes did and were intended to separate the confiscation proceedings from the criminal proceedings. **10.09**

(4) Basis of plea

Care should be taken when drafting and agreeing to a basis of plea, particularly on behalf of the prosecution, to ensure nothing therein binds or purports to bind the hands of the court in the confiscation proceedings. See *R v Lunnon* (2005) 1 Cr App R(S) 24 and *R v Lazarus* [2005] Crim. LR 64, discussed further at para 12.20 of Chapter 12. **10.10**

B. Benefit from Drug Trafficking

Section 2(1) of the DTA states: **10.11**

(1) ... where a defendant appears before the Crown Court to be sentenced in respect of one or more drug trafficking offences (and has not previously been sentenced or otherwise dealt with in respect of his conviction for the offence or, as the case may be, any of the offences concerned), then:
  (a) if the prosecutor asks the court to proceed under this section or
  (b) if the court considers that, even though the prosecutor has not asked it to do so, it is appropriate for it to proceed under this section, it shall act as follows.
(2) The Court shall first determine whether the defendant has benefited from drug trafficking.

The first question the court has to determine is whether the defendant has benefited from drug trafficking. In many cases, this will be obvious from the evidence adduced during the trial. As Lord Lane CJ said in *Dickens* (at p 629D):

> The evidence on which the judgment is based will come in part from the trial, if there has been one, in part from the statements rendered by the parties to the court ... and in part from evidence adduced before the court.

10.12 It should be noted that there is no obligation on the Crown to recall evidence adduced in the trial for these purposes, the court being entitled to rely on that evidence in so far as it may be relevant to the issues it has to determine: see *R v Paul Jenkins* [1991] Crim LR 481–2.

10.13 Evidence adduced in the trial that the defendant has been observed selling drugs in the street or has been involved in commercial importations of drugs will, for example, provide almost irrefutable evidence of benefit from drug trafficking. The court will take judicial notice of the fact that the defendant participates in drug trafficking for the purpose of making a profit rather than a desire to keep drug addicts supplied with narcotics.

10.14 However, in *R v Paul Jenkins* (above) the Court was of the opinion that the defendant was entitled to give evidence at the confiscation stage to rebut whatever evidence the prosecution called, or the assumptions set out in the Act, and held that the defendant should not be deprived of his right to give evidence in the course of the enquiry, even though he had given evidence in the trial on related matters. Because in *Jenkins* there was doubt as to whether or not he had been allowed to do so, the Court of Appeal quashed the confiscation order.

10.15 The case of *R v Atkinson* [1992] Crim LR 749 confirms the view that the judge making a confiscation order under the DTA is not confined to the claims made by the prosecution. If the judge is satisfied that the defendant has benefited to a greater extent than the prosecution alleged, he may make an order in the amount which he judges to represent the value of the defendants proceeds of drug trafficking. It should be noted that under s 2(7), section 2(1) does not apply in relation to any offence for which a defendant appears before the Crown Court to be sentenced if:

> (b) the powers of the Court (apart from this section) to deal with him in respect of that offence are limited to dealing with him in any way in which a Magistrates' Court might have dealt with him in respect of the offence.

(1) Statutory provisions as to benefit

10.16 The DTA contains a number of provisions designed to assist the court in determining the question of benefit. Section 2(3) of the DTA provides that:

> For the purposes of this Act, a person has benefited from drug trafficking if he has at any time (whether before or after the commencement of this Act) received any payment or other reward in connection with drug trafficking carried on by him or another person.

10.17 The court is thus entitled to base its finding of benefit upon a payment or other reward from drug trafficking in addition to that for which the defendant has been convicted and further, where it was received by him prior to the commencement of the DTA. Nor does the payment the defendant receives need to emanate from his own drug trafficking activities to be caught by the provision.

(2) Payments or other rewards

10.18 Payments or other rewards from drug trafficking are not confined to money but extend to all property received by the defendant. In *R v Osei* [1988] Crim LR 775, a CJA case, the Court of Appeal held that 'payment or other reward' would include, for example, an air ticket or holiday. Glidewell LJ, in delivering the judgment of the court, said:

> Payment means payment. It means any payment. The dichotomy is between a payment which may be by way of reward or may be in some other way be in connection with drug trafficking or some other form of reward. An obvious instance of another form of reward is an air ticket paid for by the person who is arranging the trip with the intention that the courier shall get a free holiday in the UK and, in return, carry the drugs. That is the sort of matter which comes under 'other reward'. But 'payment' is apt to include not merely a payment which is going to be a profit or fee, so to speak for the courier, but also a payment such as that which was envisaged in what this appellant originally said to the Customs and in what she said through her Counsel to the court below: that is to say a payment to her to enable her to have money in her possession which would persuade the immigration authorities to allow her to enter the country so that she could bring in the drugs.

In *R v Smith* (1989) 11 Cr App R(S) 290 Lord Lane CJ said:

> the words 'any payment' are on the face of them clear. They must mean, indeed it is clear from the wording, any payment in money or kind. It does not mean, in the judgment of this court, net profit derived from the payment after the deduction of expenses, whether the expenses are those of purchase, travelling, entertainment, or otherwise. The same consideration applies to the words 'other rewards'. They also have to be valued. If for example the receiver of the drugs had rewarded the appellant by providing him with an expensive holiday or an expensive motor car, it would not, we think, be legitimate to construe the words 'value of the rewards' as meaning value of the holiday or motor car less the business expenses involved in earning the reward. It seems to us the section is deliberately worded so as to avoid the necessity, which the appellant's construction of the section would involve, of having to carry out an accountancy exercise which would be quite impossible in the circumstances of the case. It may be that the wording is draconian, and that it produces a draconian result, but it seems to us that if that is the case, it has a result intended by those who framed the Act.

(3) Joint apportionment/multiple defendants

10.19 It is not necessary that the payment or reward received by the defendant should be retained for his own use. Thus, if the defendant receives a payment from a co-accused in a drug trafficking conspiracy and passes it on to another conspirator he has still benefited from drug trafficking notwithstanding that he has not retained it for himself.

10.20 This construction received approval by the Court of Appeal in the case of *R v Simons* (1994) 15 Cr App R(S) 126, 98 Cr App R 100. A co-accused named Harvey had received the sum of £166,587 in connection with the conspiracy and forwarded it to Simons. Simons in turn forwarded it to another conspirator named Griffiths. On appeal against the trial judge's finding that these monies constituted a payment or other reward received in connection with drug trafficking and that Simons had thereby benefited from drug trafficking, it was contended that if such an interpretation were right each recipient of the payment would face having to pay a confiscation order in the amount of that payment. This argument did not find favour with the court, Henry J commenting as follows (at p 130):

For whatever that point may be worth, it is right. It would be equally right if there were no question of anyone being a conduit, but there having been a sale and then a re-sale at a profit at each stage. In such a situation there would undoubtedly be separate payments of the purchase price, separate proceeds, and the same result. If Parliament had wished to avoid this result, thinking it to be harsh or unfair, Parliament would have restricted the confiscatory powers to the profits made by drug dealing, though this would have presented great problems, and allowed drug traffickers to drive a coach and four through any attempt to strip them of the profits of their destructive trade. Intermediaries are useful to the principal and the purchasers of drugs. They can confuse the trail and distance the principal or, as in Mr. Simons' case, they can provide an expertise or spurious legitimacy which the principals may lack. That Parliament seeks to deter them by draconian measures is not a surprise.

It seems to us that the clear result is that where you have a chain of contracts, each purchase price is a 'payment'. That result cannot be avoided simply by the entrepreneur or middle man ensuring that the contractual situation was that he merely passed on as postman a payment from the consignee to the consignor and that what in the ordinary course of events would have been his profit was paid to him as a handling fee or something of that sort. As Parliament deprives drug dealers of proceeds of their sale, namely the payments made to them and not profits made from them, there is no reason why they should treat conduits any differently.

10.21 It follows that the Act is concerned with the confiscation of the proceeds of drug trafficking and not the profits. Further confirmation of this approach is found in *R v Patel* (2000) 2 Cr App R(S) (10), where the Court of Appeal held that the fact a conspirator did not retain the proceeds of his crime because it passed to a co-defendant was irrelevant and *R v Metcalfe* [2001] EWCA Crim 1343 where the Court of Appeal held that a money launderers benefit is the total amount that he launders (relying on the authority of *R v Simpson* (1998) 2 Cr App R(S) 111).

10.22 *Metcalfe* was confirmed in *R v Alagobola* (2004) 2 Cr App R(S) 248 where the Court of Appeal held that in respect to money laundering, each person through whom the property passes obtains the full amount of the property and therefore the full benefit. See also *R v Ellingham* [2004] EWCA Crim 3446 where (at para 20) Pill LJ said:

> On the face of it, however, his submission is an attractive one. It is said that the appellant derived no benefit; on the contrary, he sought to deprive himself of any benefit when he realised the possible source of the funds by ridding himself of them as soon as he could. It seems to us, however, that the submission is founded upon the fallacious assumption that when the appellant dealt with the money by transfer he derived thereby no benefit. On the contrary, it seems to us the appellant was now in possession of the funds in his account which he knew or suspected were the proceeds of criminal conduct. By dealing with it following the acquisition of that knowledge, upon the instructions of the alleged criminal, he was, in our view, and for the purpose of onward transmission, obtaining property in connection with the commission of an offence. He was exercising the right of the holder of the account to deal with the funds within it and he was dealing with those funds with a guilty mind. Accordingly, his benefit was the value of the property so obtained. Benefit from criminal conduct does not, for the purposes of s.71, mean personally to enjoy the fruits of criminal conduct.

10.23 Some question was cast over the apportionment (or otherwise) of the benefit from a criminal enterprise by the Court of Appeal where, eg there was a conspiracy between individuals, the court being prepared to allow for the division of benefit at least when making an order for the full amount obtained if the result would have led to recovery of more than the total amount obtained by the criminal conduct (see R v Potter (1991) 92 Cr App R 126, *R v Gibbons*

B. Benefit from Drug Trafficking

(2003) 1 Cr App R(S) 34 and *R v May* [2005] 3 All ER 523). However, in the most recent case *R v Homer* [2006] EWCA Crim 1559, this rationale itself has been called into question.

10.24 In *Homer* the appellant pleaded guilty to two counts of fraudulent evasion of duty chargeable on the importation of goods and two counts of keeping dutiable goods with intent to defraud. A confiscation order was made against him in the sum of £278,000 to be paid within 12 months with five years' imprisonment consecutive in default of payment. At the confiscation hearing the Appellant was found to have realisable assets of £278,000, whereas his co-defendants were found to have no assets and no confiscation order was sought against them (see para 10.25). The Crown's contention before the judge was that the appellant had benefited in the full amount of the loss of duty, namely £825,000. The defence contended that some lesser amount was appropriate to take account of the fact that others had benefited as well. Relying on the decision of *R v May* at first instance, the judge found that the appellant had indeed benefited to the extent of the full amount of the loss of duty and that apportionment was not appropriate, (there was no dispute that the matter represented a pecuniary advantage, the advantage being the evasion of duty by all of those involved with the contraband cigarettes from their initial importation from abroad through to their warehousing and subsequent distribution (see para 8)). The judge at first instance considered both the cases of *R v Bakewell* [2006] EWCA Crim 2 and *R v Rowbotham* [2006] EWCA Crim 7470, where Rose LJ said (at para 31):

> The Appellant's plea of 'guilty' . . . necessarily included an admission that he had evaded duty. The Appellant, by providing the warehousing facility, was, as (was) rightly conceded in the course of submissions, playing a part in the continuing process of keeping the cigarettes away from discovery.

10.25 The Court of Appeal in *Homer* found that the defendant had played an important organisational role in the evasion of duty by providing the essential link in the chain between importation and ultimate sale of the contraband up to which point no profit could actually be realised. The court distinguished the Court of Appeal's finding in *May* (at para 13) stating that it was 'a rather different case' in that it concerned a missing trader VAT fraud where the benefit was the actual VAT which should have been accounted for to Customs. (In *May* the unpaid VAT passed through a string of companies controlled by the principal defendants). In *Homer* the facts did not concern jointly held assets at all. It concerned a pecuniary advantage obtained by a number of offenders in various ways. Tuckey LJ stated:

> . . . but each offender who is sufficiently involved in the evasion of duty can properly be considered in our judgement to have obtained the whole of that advantage.

10.26 The Court in *Homer* referred itself to para 41 of the judgment in *May* where Keene LJ stated:

> . . . in some circumstances it may need the court to adopt an apportionment approach. For example, there may be cases where the defendants have substantial assets, with the result that making orders for the full benefit in each case would lead to the Revenue recovering far more than the conspiracy . . . had obtained. In such a case the court may be prepared to apportion the benefit.

10.27 In *Homer* the Court described these sentiments as 'a good starting point' but they nevertheless rejected the application of the apportionment principle as set out in *R v Gibbons* (2003) 2 Cr App R(S) 34 (para 17). Tuckey LJ holding:

The pecuniary advantage basis for assessing benefit in a case such as this is a further reason why it is not appropriate to make an apportionment in a case of this kind. If each principal participant in the . . . evasion of duty contributes to that evasion of duty, there is nothing intrinsically unfair to hold that the benefit he has obtained is the whole amount of that duty . . . We accept that at least at first sight this appears to be a harsh conclusion: a defendant who has assets can find himself having a liability to pay for the whole amount of the benefit obtained from this type of offence when he is not the only one who has been involved in it. But this legislation, as has been said many times, is designed to be tough and the fact that it is tough and may appear to produce a harsh result does not, it seems to us, provide any basis for saying that the conclusion we have reached and which the judge reached is wrong.

10.28 In *R v Sharma* [2006] EWCA Crim 16, the Court held that where money obtained by a fraud passes through the control of one offender before being shared with his accomplices, the offenders benefit is equal to the whole of the amount obtained by the fraud. The Court held that there was no room, where proceeds of crime were concerned, for the application of trust principles and the application of normal legal consequences that might flow from the receipt of money for others. It confirmed that where a member of a criminal enterprise fraudulently received money into a bank account on which he was the sole signatory, his benefit, for the purposes of s 1 of the CJA, was the whole of that money, notwithstanding that money from the account had been paid to other members of the enterprise. In the Court's view the amount of benefit that might be recovered in respect of an individual member of the enterprise was not affected by the amount which might be recovered from other members. Nor was the total amount that might be recovered from all members of the enterprise limited by the amount of the victim's loss.

10.29 Some of the above case law was returned to in *R v Glatt* (CA, 17 March 2006) where the Court considered the legislative framework surrounding the judge's discretion to impose a confiscation order pursuant to the unamended CJA 1988. In relation to apportionment of benefit, the court stated that it was clear that the effect of the legislation may be that the Crown receives payment from different individuals in respect of the same property. The effect may also be that each individual who is the subject of an order may lose more than the profit that he has made by his criminal conduct, and, in effect, pay twice over, (see para 41). The Court also acknowledged that the involvement of individuals could arise in a series or chain (where the proceeds of crime are passed from hand to hand or in parallel where individuals are jointly involved in the criminal acts). The Court gave the example of the thief who steals a ring with a market value of £3,000. He sells it to a handler H1 for £1,000. H1 sells it to another handler H2 for £1,500. It is found by police in H2's possession. All three are convicted. The fate of the ring itself may depend upon whether the true owner claims it or not: if she does, it will be restored to her by a restitution order, or she may claim for compensation in civil proceedings. If there is no traceable owner, or no claimant comes forward for some reason, there will be no order for restitution or compensation. In this example, on the Crown's case, a confiscation order may be made against T for £3,000. This is the benefit to him. As explained in *Ascroft* [2003] EWCA Crim 2365 (para 60), in cases where the goods acquired are not themselves illegal the value to the defendant is what it would have cost him to obtain legitimately the goods that he had in fact obtained dishonestly. On the Crown's case, a second confiscation order for £3,000 may be made against H1 and a third confiscation for £3,000 may be made against H2. In *R v May* [2005] EWCA Crim 97,

B. Benefit from Drug Trafficking

counsel accepted that there was this potential for multiple recovery in relation to chain cases and the Court held (at para 41) that it existed where defendants were jointly involved.

The Court in *Glatt* embarked on a thorough consideration of case law and concluded the following in relation to confiscation orders: **10.30**

(i) Confiscation orders are a penalty and are a measure to which Article 1 of Protocol 1 of the ECHR is applicable (see *Welch v UK* (1995) 20 EHRR 247).
(ii) Confiscation orders are designed to deter those who consider embarking upon criminal conduct (see *R v Rezvi* (2002) 2 Cr App R(S) 70).
(iii) Confiscation orders are designed to deprive a person of profits received from criminal conduct and to remove the value of the proceeds received from criminal conduct from possible future use in criminal conduct (see *Re T (Restraint Order: Disclosure of Assets)* [1992] 1 WLR 949; *R v Tivnan* (1999) 1 Cr App R(S) 92).
(iv) Confiscation orders are designed essentially to impoverish defendants, not to enrich the Crown (*P (Restraint Order: Sale of Asset), re* [2000] 1 WLR 473).

It held (at para 96) that:

> In cases involving very large sums of money, the disposal of the proceeds of crime (and civil wrongs) is difficult to achieve without the assistance of professional agents. The fact that they have not themselves profited from the crime to the full value of the loss is a point that arises on the issue of the contribution between defendants to civil proceedings. It is not normally a defence to a claim. If the financial risk to which they are exposed in the confiscation proceedings is limited by the amount of the reward they gain, the deterrent will be much less than if the financial risk is limited by the amount of the property they obtain, if multiple recoveries from different individuals, which in total exceed the value of the loss caused, is considered to create an injustice in a particular case, then that can be addressed under the [1988] Act (in its unamended form) in the exercise of the courts discretion.

The Court added that given that the object of the legislation includes a deterrent and penal element, and that there is in principle no objection to multiple recovery in the sense of recovery of the same sum from different individuals, it is difficult to attribute to the legislature the purpose of excluding such an important group of offenders from the scope of the legislation (see para 93). **10.31**

The case of *May* is being appealed to the House of Lords and it is therefore likely that the uncertainty that now arises as to how a court should be dealing with multiple defendants will be clarified. At present the majority of the case law seems to suggest that where property passes through multiple defendants' hands, each defendant has obtained and benefited from the whole amount. **10.32**

(4) Are drugs seized from the defendant a payment or reward?

It is sometimes suggested that drugs found in the possession of the defendant amount to a payment or other reward in connection with drug trafficking. The position was considered by the Court of Appeal in *R v Butler* (1993) 14 Cr App R(S) 537. The defendant was arrested on suspicion of handling stolen property and when his property was searched, a quantity of amphetamine found. He pleaded guilty to an offence of possessing controlled drugs with intent to supply. The judge found that the defendant had not previously been **10.33** involved in drug trafficking but nonetheless made a confiscation order against him incorporating, inter alia, the street level value of the drugs. The Court of Appeal ruled that the confiscation order should be set aside, Popplewell J in delivering the judgment of the court observing that:

> It is quite obvious that drugs held by a drug trafficker may be a payment or other reward if drugs have been sold and further drugs purchased. But in the instant case the learned judge took the view, having heard the evidence, that this was first time drug trafficking and that the drugs had been purchased on that single occasion. It is therefore, in our judgment, impossible to say that the drugs themselves are 'any payment or other reward' in connection with drug trafficking.

10.34 In the case of a person convicted of possession of drugs with intent to supply, a court may be entitled to assume (subject to the considerations explained in *R v Redbourne* (1992) 14 Cr App R(S) 162) that the drugs have been acquired with the proceeds of earlier drug trafficking, unless the defendant shows that this is not the case. If the court makes this assumption, it may be satisfied that the defendant has benefited from drug trafficking on the basis of this expenditure. If it is not satisfied that this is so, perhaps because, as in *Butler*, the defendant establishes that he bought the drugs with money which he had obtained legitimately, the court should not proceed further with the enquiry but should simply make an order under s 27 of the Misuse of Drugs Act 1971 for the forfeiture of the drugs, without attempting to value them (see the commentary to *R v Butler* in [1993] Crim LR 320).

10.35 In *R v Akengin* [1995] Crim LR 88, like *Butler*, the Court of Appeal ruled that the judge had been wrong to regard the sum of £54,647, being the value of the drugs in the country in which they were purchased, as constituting a benefit and reduced the confiscation order accordingly. Even though there was evidence that the appellant held the drugs, there was no evidence upon which the judge could come to the conclusion that they were themselves a payment or reward in connection with drug trafficking. There was no evidence that the heroin had come into the appellant's possession as a reward for acting as a courier or as a reward for past services in connection with drug trafficking. The sentencer had wrongly come to the conclusion that they were a benefit that should have been included in reaching his conclusion as to the amount of the confiscation order.

10.36 The decision in *Akengin* has been subject to some criticism, on the basis that given that there was no evidence that the appellant had received the drugs which were seized from him as a reward for drug trafficking, the court was correct to exercise its discretion (applying *Redbourne* (1992) 14 Cr App R(S) 162). The Court's expressed belief that the cost of the drugs had come from the appellant's and his confederates' profits of earlier drug trafficking was clearly a basis for making the assumption that any expenditure of his since the beginning of that period was met out of payments received by him in connection with drug trafficking carried on by him. It would then have been for the appellant to show that this was not the case, by calling evidence that the drugs had been purchased from other resources (as the appellant was able to do in *Butler* (1993) 14 Cr App R(S) 537). (See the commentary to *R v Akengin* in [1995] Crim LR 88.)

B. Benefit from Drug Trafficking

(5) The payment or other reward must be received in connection with drug trafficking

10.37 There is no 'benefit' unless the payment or reward is received in connection with drug trafficking (s 2(2)). If therefore the payment has been received in connection with some other activity, however criminal in nature it may be, there can be no benefit. In some cases the distinction may be far from clear (see *Finch* (1992) 14 Cr App R(S) 226 (below)).

10.38 The point is well illustrated by *R v Osei* [1988] Crim LR 775 where the defendant claimed monies had been given to her to assist in obtaining immigration clearance. The Court of Appeal held that the money was properly made the subject of a confiscation order, ruling that 'payment' meant any payment, whether by way of reward or in some other way in connection with drug trafficking. As the whole purpose of the defendant's visit was to smuggle drugs it is difficult to see, even on the defendant's account, how this payment did not constitute a payment or reward in connection with drug trafficking, particularly given the provisions of s 63(2).

(6) Section 63(2) DTA

10.39 Section 63(2) of the DTA provides:

> In this Act references to anything received in connection with drug trafficking includes a reference to anything received both in that connection and in some other connection.

The issue of the meaning of this section arose in the case of *Metcalfe and Metcalfe v R* [2004] EWCA Crim 3253. The Crown's case against the appellants was that they were involved in the large-scale manufacture and distribution of tablets which were sold as ecstasy and looked like ecstasy but were, in fact, not ecstasy. The prosecution did not seek to show that the appellants had benefited from drug trafficking, except to the substantial extent to which they had benefited from the indicted conspiracy. It was agreed that the benefit from the indicted conspiracy was £3.5 million and the judge accordingly so decided.

10.40 On appeal it was suggested that the benefit from the indicted conspiracy was not a benefit from drug trafficking and as such the finding that £3.5 million represented a benefit from drug trafficking obviously could not stand. Some of the tablets that the appellants supplied as ecstasy contained diazepam (which is a Class C drug). It was accepted by all parties that if there had been no diazepam in the tablets, which the appellants supplied in the course of the conspiracy, no confiscation order under the DTA could have been made. The question for the Court of Appeal was whether the presence of diazepam in some of the tablets supplied during the course of the conspiracy justified a finding that the appellants' benefit from drug trafficking was the whole benefit of the indicted conspiracy, namely £3.5 million.

10.41 In the Court of Appeal's view, the judge should have been asked to determine the benefit from the supply of this diazepam (para 8). If the judge had been asked to do that, the Court held, then the defence would have had an opportunity to present a case on the amount of diazepam although, of course, the section for assumptions may well have assisted the prosecution. That however did not happen. The Court of Appeal gained some assistance from the case of *R v Moran* [2002] 1 WLR 253 (a CJA case, see para 12.36 of Chapter 12).

10.42 In *Metcalfe* the Court of Appeal did not think it was necessary or desirable to attempt to list the kind of cases in which s 63(2) might be relevant. It did however give the example of a person who sells heroin cut with lactose, stating that s 63(2) would prevent the appellant from stripping out of the monies received for the heroin that proportion which related to lactose (or to other costs). The Court also held that the presence of the word 'both' in s 63(2) does limit its scope. If a person was to receive £100 from a drug addict, £20 of which represented the sale of heroin and £80 represented work done in the addict's garden, it would seem that s 63(2) would not bite. The £80 would not have been received in 'both' connections. The Court of Appeal therefore concluded that 's.63(2)' did not apply to the facts of the case of *Metcalfe*. They also accepted that s 63(2) does not, in the particular case, convert activity that was not drug trafficking into drug trafficking, (see para 19 per Hooper LJ):

> The notion that if only one tablet in one million consisted of a Class A, B or C drug, then the proceeds of the sale of the other 999,999 tablets became the benefit of drug trafficking seems to us to be very far fetched.

10.43 On that basis the appeal against the confiscation order succeeded, although the court was quick to comment that there may be other means by which the appellants may be deprived of their ill-gotten gains under the Proceeds of Crime Act 2002.

(7) Knowledge that the payment comes from drug trafficking

10.44 The Act is silent as to whether the Crown must prove that the defendant knew the payment or reward came from drug trafficking for it to be caught by s 2(3). In *R v Richards* [1992] 2 All ER 572, however, the Court of Appeal held that such knowledge must be proved. The appellant, who had pleaded guilty to involvement in the importation of 10 kg of cocaine, purchased a boat to facilitate the importation. £6,000 of the purchase price had been provided as a loan from a co-accused who had promised, but never paid, a further £5,000 towards the cost.

The judge ruled that the defendant had benefited from drug trafficking and that the amount of his benefit was £6,000. The judge made no express finding as to the defendant's knowledge when he received the payment. The court quashed the confiscation order, Rose J commenting in delivering the court's judgment (at p 575G):

> The fact that his co-accused knew that the money he paid was going to be used indirectly for drug trafficking does not, in our view, mean that the appellant so received it. If he received it believing it to be a loan unconnected with drug trafficking, he did not receive it within the terms of s 1(3) of the 1986 Act. We are strengthened in this approach by the words 'or other reward' which in our view serve to underline the need, when construing the words 'received any payment', for knowledge on the part of the recipient.

10.45 Accordingly knowledge that the payment or reward was made in connection with drug trafficking is an essential pre-condition to the operation of s 2(3) of the DTA.

10.46 However it should be noted that the Court went onto say in *Richards* that the circumstances of that case were somewhat unusual and if the judge had either made an express finding as to the appellant's knowledge when he received the £6,000 or had recourse to the statutory assumptions, the outcome might well have been different.

(8) Conspiracies

10.47 In *R v Suchedina* The Times, 9 September 2004, the Court of Appeal had to consider the situation where the trial judge had held that he was unable to determine which conspiracy

B. Benefit from Drug Trafficking

the offender had been convicted of (in circumstances where the defendant had been charged under s 1 of the Criminal Law Act 1977 with conspiracy to convert or transfer the proceeds of drug trafficking or criminal conduct), and therefore was unable to find that the offence fell within the definition of drug trafficking under the 1994 Act.

10.48 The Court of Appeal held that it was the agreement to conspire that constituted the offence, and not the way that agreement was to be implemented. Thus, an agreement to commit a number of different offences, or either of two offences, constituted an offence of conspiracy, even if only one, or even none of them was in fact committed. It followed that the offender was guilty of a conspiracy to commit offences under both the 1994 Act and the 1988 Act and the pre-condition for confiscation proceedings under the 1994 Act was therefore met. Latham LJ, giving the reasons of the Court, stated that the effect of the jury's verdicts was that they did not consider that the conspiracy was restricted to either the proceeds of drugs offences or the proceeds of crime, but was an agreement to launder the money whatever its provenance. The Court held that the judge was accordingly wrong to hold that he had no jurisdiction to entertain the confiscation proceedings.

(9) Assessing the defendant's proceeds of drug trafficking

10.49 If the court concludes that the defendant has not benefited from drug trafficking that is an end to the DTA enquiry and no confiscation order will be made. If, however, the court finds there has been benefit, it must then proceed in accordance with s 2(4) of the DTA, which provides that:

(4) If the court determines that the defendant has so benefited, the court shall, before sentencing or otherwise dealing with him in respect of the offence or, as the case may be, any of the offences concerned, determine in accordance with section 5 of this Act the amount to be recovered in his case by virtue of this section.

10.50 Section 5 of the DTA states:

(1) Subject to subsection (3) below, the amount to be recovered in the defendant's case under the confiscation order shall be the amount the Crown Court assesses to be the value of the defendant's proceeds of drug trafficking.
(2) ...
(3) If the court is satisfied that the amount that might be realised at the time the confiscation order is made is less than the amount the court assesses to be the value of his proceeds of drug trafficking, the amount to be recovered in the defendant's case under the confiscation order shall be:
   (a) the amount appearing to the Court to be the amount that might be so realised; or
   (b) a nominal amount, where it appears to the court (on the information available to it at the time) that the amount that might be so realised is nil.

At this second stage of the enquiry, having determined that there has been benefit, the court is concerned to determine the actual value of the defendant's proceeds (benefit) of drug trafficking. The Act's provisions in this regard are similarly draconian as s 4(1) illustrates:

(1) For the purposes of this Act:
   (a) any payments or other rewards received by a person at any time (whether before or after the commencement of this Act) in connection with drug trafficking carried on by him or another person are his proceeds of drug trafficking, and
   (b) the value of his proceeds of drug trafficking is the aggregate of the value of the payments or other rewards.

10.51 As with s 2(3), payments or rewards received in connection with drug trafficking at any time, whether related to the offences of which the defendant has been convicted or not,

Chapter 10: The DTA Confiscation Hearing

and whether received before or after the commencement of the DTA, are caught, as are payments or other rewards received by him in connection with drug trafficking carried on by other persons. Thus in *R v Finch* (1992) 14 Cr App R(S) 226, where the defendant alleged that he had received payment by 'ripping off a drug dealer', and therefore the money he had received was not the proceeds of drug trafficking but the proceeds of theft, the Court of Appeal ruled that the value of this payment was properly incorporated in his proceeds of drug trafficking.

(10) Proceeds not profits

10.52   It is important to note that the court is concerned at this stage to assess the defendant's proceeds of drug trafficking and not merely his profits. Consequently, in assessing the value of his proceeds, the court is not required to deduct the cost of any expenses of the enterprise such as the wholesale cost of the drugs or the travelling expenses incurred in their importation. In *R v Ian Smith* [1989] 2 All ER 948 the defendant was convicted of conspiracy to supply cannabis. The trial judge found that there had been four occasions on which he had received payments of £2,500 in connection with the conspiracy. The judge aggregated these payments in accordance with s 4(1)(b) and assessed the proceeds of drug trafficking at £10,000. On appeal it was submitted this was not a correct approach because the bulk of each payment received was invested in purchasing the next consignment and that the judge should only have taken into account the profit element of each successful trip. The Court rejected this argument, Lord Lane CJ commenting (at p 951B):

> The words 'any payment' are on the face of them clear. They must mean, indeed it is clear from the wording, any payment in money or in kind. It does not mean, in the judgment of this Court, net profit derived from the payment after the deduction of expenses, whether the expenses are those of purchase, travelling, entertainment or otherwise. The same consideration applies to the words 'other rewards'. They also have to be valued. If, for example, the receiver of the drugs had rewarded the appellant by providing him with an expensive holiday or an expensive motor car, it would not, we think, be legitimate to construe the words 'value of the rewards' as meaning the value of the holiday or motor car less the business expenses in earning the reward. It seems to us that the section is deliberately worded so as to avoid the necessity, which the appellant's construction of the section would involve, of having to carry out an accountancy exercise, which would be quite impossible in the circumstances of this case. It may be that the wording is draconian, and that it produces a draconian result. But it seems to us that, if this is the case, it was a result intended by those who framed the Act.

10.53   The Court went on to say that this draconian result was to some extent mitigated by the next stage of the procedure which required the court only to make a confiscation order in the value of the realisable property of the defendant if he is able to prove its value is less than his proceeds of drug trafficking (see s 5(3) of the DTA).

10.54   In *R v Banks* [1997] Crim LR 234 the judge assessed the value of the applicant's proceeds of drug trafficking at £200,000 and his realisable property as £37,000. The applicant claimed that his profits from drug trafficking were less than £37,000. It was argued that the judge was wrong to assess the value of the applicant's proceeds of drug trafficking on the basis of his gross receipts as opposed to his actual profits.

10.55   The applicant argued that as any property in the possession of any defendant could be treated as realisable property, even though it was wholly unrelated to drug trafficking, to make a confiscation order on the basis of gross receipts rather than profits would be to distort the purpose of the legislation. The Court however determined, refusing the application, that there were four insuperable objections to the applicant's interpretation of the legislation:

(1) The language of ss 2, 4, and 5 of the DTA. The Court found it was clear from the legislation that the defendant's benefit was to be the aggregate value of the payments or other rewards made to the defendant in connection with drug trafficking, and that the legislation did not direct attention to profit but to gross payments.
(2) There had been a series of decisions including *Osei* (1988) 10 Cr App R(S) 289 and *Comiskey* (1990) 12 Cr App R(S) 562 and *Simons* (1994) 15 Cr App R(S) 126, all of which held that the proceeds were not the profit achieved on a sale but the sale price.
(3) The provisions under the 1994 Act relating to the meaning of the value of the defendant's proceeds of drug trafficking had not been amended since the DTOA and the court was bound to proceed on the assumption that Parliament had re-enacted the same provisions, knowing of the decisions which had been made on them and intending that they should have effect.
(4) Later sections of the 1994 Act (ss 49, 50, and 51) dealt with money laundering and used the words 'proceeds' in a way which clearly related to the product of drug trafficking rather than the profits.

10.56 The Court found that it was clear that Parliament intended those who were engaged in the drug trade should suffer dire consequences.

10.57 In *R v Simpson* (1998) 2 Cr App R(S) 111, the Court of Appeal held that, based on the plain meaning of ss 2(3) and 4(1)(a) of the Act, proceeds must be understood as meaning the aggregate sum of payments which derive from drug trafficking.

10.58 In *R v Versluis* [2004] EWCA Crim 3168, the Court of Appeal stated that in a case where a defendant had adduced no evidence as to his realisable assets and as a result a confiscation order had been made in the sum of his benefit from the proceeds of drug trafficking, there was no need to make a deduction to reflect the expenses that must have been incurred by the defendant in the drug trafficking, pursuant to the concept of commercial reality observed in *R v Comiskey* (1990) 12 Cr App R(S) 562.

(11) Joint benefit

10.59 As drug trafficking tends to be a joint enterprise, it not infrequently happens that defendants derive a joint benefit from their activities.

10.60 In *R v Chrastny (No 2)* [1991] 1 WLR 1385 where the Court of Appeal had to consider the position where two defendants had benefited jointly from drug trafficking, but only one offender was before the court, the other having absconded. The defendant had been convicted, together with others, of conspiracy to supply cocaine. One of the co-accused was her husband, but he escaped from custody while on remand prior to trial and remained at large. The court held that where a defendant, jointly with a co-conspirator, had possession of property at the time of conviction and had sufficient control to be able to dispose of it, a confiscation order could properly be made in respect of the whole of that property notwithstanding that only one of the conspirators had been convicted.

10.61 It was suggested that this interpretation could lead to unfairness because, if the co-conspirator was ultimately apprehended and convicted, a confiscation order could be made against him in respect of the same property. This is not, however, the case because, as the Court pointed out, by the time the co-conspirator is apprehended, the property will already be the subject of a confiscation order and will no longer be within his possession or control.

10.62 For commentary on the joint control, apportionment or passing of assets where the proceeds have passed through more than one Defendant's hands, see para 10.19 above.

C. The Assumptions

10.63 We have seen that the burden is on the prosecution to prove the benefit and the value of the defendant's proceeds of drug trafficking. In cases commenced under the DTA the civil standard of proof applies. In *R v Dickens* [1990] 2 QB 102, Lord Lane CJ said (at p 106):

> What may thus seem at first sight to be a heavy burden on the prosecution is considerably lightened by the provisions of [section 4(2)].

10.64 Section 4(2) of the DTA requires the court to make a number of assumptions in determining the question of benefit and the amount of the proceeds from drug trafficking. Section 4(2) provides:

> (2) Subject to subsections (4) and (5) below, the Crown Court shall, for the purpose—
> (a) of determining whether the defendant has benefited from drug trafficking, and
> (b) if he has, of assessing the value of his proceeds of drug trafficking, make the required assumptions.

Section 4(3) goes on to set out the assumptions that can be made as follows:

> (3) The required assumptions are:
> (a) that any property appearing to the court:
> (i) to have been held by him at any time since his conviction, or
> (ii) to have been transferred to him at any time since the beginning of the period of six years ending when the proceedings were instituted against him, was received by him, at the earliest time which he appears to the court to have held it, as a payment or reward in connection with drug trafficking carried on by him;
> (b) that any expenditure of his since the beginning of that period was met out of payments received by him in connection with drug trafficking carried on by him; and
> (c) that, for the purposes of valuing any property received or assumed to have been received by him at any time as such a reward, he received the property free of any other interests in it.

(1) When the assumptions must not be applied

10.65 Section 4(4) provides that the court shall not make any required assumption if:

(a) that assumption is shown to be incorrect in the defendant's case; or
(b) the court is satisfied that a serious risk of injustice would arise if the assumption were to be made.

10.66 By virtue of s 4(5) the assumptions should not be applied in cases where the defendant appears to be sentenced in respect of offences contrary to ss 49, 50, or 51 of the DTA (concealing or transferring proceeds of drug trafficking, assisting another person to retain the benefit of drug trafficking, and acquisition, possession or use of proceeds of drug trafficking, respectively).

C. The Assumptions

In *R v Jay* (2001) 1 Cr App R(S) 273, the Court of Appeal held that if someone is found in possession of drugs, the normal inference is that he has acquired them by paying for them. However, where the judge's view in relation to a particular individual involved at a high level in a conspiracy of supplying drugs was that he had been entrusted with the drugs, it was not open to the judge to have inferred that he had paid for them and therefore s 4(3)(d) of the DTA (the assumption that any expenditure of the defendant since the beginning of the period was met out of payments received by him in connection with drug trafficking carried on by him), could not bite. Even if the inference relied on the facts that had been drawn, the Court of Appeal held that the confiscation order would be set aside to the extent that it was founded upon such inference because the defendant may have been misled as to the judge's view of his role by remarks which were made when passing sentence before the start of the confiscation proceedings, and in consequence of which he may have opted not to give evidence in the confiscation proceedings, so depriving himself of the opportunity of showing the assumption to be incorrect. **10.67**

In *R v Johannes* [2002] Crim LR 147, following a Newton hearing, the judge had found that the defendant was a minder of the drugs, that he had pleaded guilty to being in possession of with intent to supply, but that he held no beneficial interest in them. In those circumstances the court held that the usual inference that a person in possession of drugs will have paid for them could not be drawn. Accordingly there was no scope for the operation of the assumption provided for by s 4(3)(b) of the DTA in relation to his acquisition of the drugs. **10.68**

However, in *R v Houareau* [2005] EWCA Crim 2106, the Court of Appeal held that where someone had knowingly played his part in assisting in a fraudulent importation, it would be open to the judge, for the purposes of confiscation, to infer that that person had a beneficial interest in the goods in question, unless there was some evidence demonstrating the contrary. **10.69**

In *R v De Prince* The Times, 16 March 2004 the Court of Appeal held that where an assumption that the Crown Court is required to make under s 4(3) of the DTA had not been shown to be incorrect, but the court was satisfied that there would be a serious risk of injustice if the assumption were to be made in relation to the full value of the property held by the defendant, it would be appropriate, in certain cases, to make a percentage discount in order to guard against the remote possibility that a small part of the property held came from a legitimate source. **10.70**

In *R v Jones (Confiscation Orders)* The Times, 8 August 2006, (a POCA case) the Court of Appeal held that 'serious risk of injustice' does not refer to hardship that would be sustained by the offender by virtue of the making of the confiscation order, and it does not operate so as to confer discretion on the court to determine whether it is fair to make a confiscation order at all. **10.71**

(2) No other assumptions may be made

In *R v Williams*, The Times, 11 January 2001 the Court of Appeal held that while the Crown Court is bound to make the assumptions set out in s 4(3) of the DTA for the purposes of determining whether a defendant convicted of a drug trafficking offence has benefited from drug trafficking, and, if he has, of assessing the value of the proceeds, no other assumption other than those specifically provided for may be made. Any payment or rewards not covered **10.72**

Chapter 10: The DTA Confiscation Hearing

by the statutory assumptions must be proved (to the civil standard) to be a payment or reward made in connection with drug trafficking, as must the value of any such payment or reward.

(3) When must the assumptions be applied?

10.73 Where the Crown Court proceeds under s 2 of the DTA, it is bound for the purposes of determining whether the defendant has benefited from drug trafficking and if he has, of assessing the value of the proceeds therefrom, to make the required assumptions under s 4 (s 4(2): '... the Crown Court *shall*...'), unless the defendant satisfies him under s 4(4). If he fails to do so the judge has no discretion in the matter—as per *R v Croft* The Times, 6 July 2000 (CA). In short, the application of the assumptions is now mandatory under the DTA.

(4) At what stage are the assumptions applied?

10.74 The court may decide to apply the assumptions at any stage of the DTA enquiry, including before the defendant's case has commenced (*R v Redbourne* [1992] 1 WLR 1182. In delivering the judgment in *Redbourne*, a DTOA case, Staughton LJ said (at p 1187):

> The Act does not specify the stage of the proceedings at which the assumptions may be made. The concluding words of section 2(2), '... except to the extent that any of the assumptions are shown to be incorrect in the Defendant's case...' might be thought to indicate, grammatically, that no assumption may be made until the defendant's case is concluded. We do not believe that to be the meaning of the section. A judge's decision whether or not to make the assumptions is an interim one which falls to be made on his way to reaching his final decision, such final decision involving a full consideration of the defendant's case and whether (once fully deployed) it is sufficient to negate any assumptions made. In an appropriate case, the judge is entitled to make the assumptions at the start of his enquiry, for example, if he has reason to do so from the circumstances of the offence for which the defendant has been convicted. Or the judge may do so at any later stage, up to the time when he makes his final decision.

(5) Effect of applying the assumptions

10.75 In *Redbourne* Staughton LJ observed (at p 1188) that:

> An assumption, in this context is the acceptance of something as true which is not already known or proved, and therefore may or may not be true. If the Court is directed or empowered to make an assumption, that means that the Court must or may take the assumed fact as true. It matters not for that purpose whether the standard of proof is criminal or civil, whichever standard is appropriate, the assumed fact is still to be treated as true.

10.76 While *Redbourne* is now to a degree historic, as it was determined under the DTOA, it is submitted that it must be indicative of the law on the effect of the assumptions once applied, namely that the assumed fact is deemed to be true except to the extent that the defendant succeeds in rebutting it.

(6) Rebutting the assumptions

10.77 When the judge decides to apply one or more of the assumptions, this is not necessarily conclusive against the defendant. Section 4(2) of the DTA provides that the court must apply the assumptions except to the extent that they are shown to be incorrect in the defendant's case (ss 4 and 5). The burden of disproving an assumption rests on the defendant and the

C. The Assumptions

standard of proof is on a balance of probabilities. An example of where a defendant succeeded in disproving an assumption is *R v Johnson* [1991] 2 QB 249. In *Johnson*, the judge had made assumptions under s 2(3)(a) of the former DTOA in relation to a cheque received by the defendant for £6,750 and a motor vehicle she had purchased for £6,000. The evidence, however, was that the cheque was dishonoured on presentation and the purchase of the car had been funded by a loan from a finance company. The Court of Appeal ruled that in such circumstances the defendant had succeeded in showing that the assumptions were incorrect and the cheque and full purchase price of the car (but not a £400 deposit and £900 in repayments) should not have been taken into account in assessing her benefit from drug trafficking. Neill LJ commented (at p 259):

> It seems to us that, where it is possible for a defendant to demonstrate the actual source of the funds used to purchase an asset held by him at a material time, the statutory assumptions cannot be made. If the court is satisfied that the source of the sums is not from drug trafficking and does not represent a payment or reward. In the present case, there is no suggestion whatever that the loan provided by Forward Trust represented tainted money. It follows therefore in our view that the car cannot be assumed to have been received as a payment or reward in connection with drug trafficking.

Similarly, as regards the cheque, the Court ruled that the assumption was shown to be incorrect by evidence that it was dishonoured on presentation. If a defendant wishes to succeed in showing the assumptions are incorrect he must produce clear and cogent evidence: see *R v Walbrook and Glasgow* [1994] Crim LR 613, where the Court held: **10.78**

> vague and generalised assertions unsupported by evidence would rarely, if ever, be sufficient to discharge the burden on the defendant.

(7) Certificates of benefit

Section 5(2) of the DTA provides that: **10.79**

> (2) If the Court is satisfied as to any matter relevant to determining the amount that might be realised at the time the confiscation order is made (whether by reason of the acceptance of an allegation made in a statement given under Section 11 of this Act or made in the giving of information under Section 12 of the Act, or otherwise) the Court may issue a certificate giving the courts opinion as to the matters concerned, and shall do so if satisfied as mentioned in subsection (3) below.

Once the defendant's payments or other rewards from drug trafficking have been identified and assessed they are aggregated in accordance with section 4(1)(b) of the DTA to give the value of his proceeds of drug trafficking. When the court has determined the amount of the benefit, it may issue a certificate giving its opinion as to any matter relevant to the amount that might be realised from the defendant. It must issue such a certificate in circumstances where it is satisfied that the amount which can be realised is less than the amount of the defendant's benefit: see s 5(2) of the DTA. **10.80**

In *Re Katchis* (2001) ACD 372, DC (21 December 2000) the Court held a document recording the terms of a confiscation order and a default penalty should state the date of the making of the order and should be clear as to the fact that the time allowed for payment runs from that date. The document itself should be dated in such a way as to make it plain that that date is the date of the issue of the document, not the date of the order; and where there is an error in the document, any replacement should be endorsed with words stating that it replaces an incorrect copy. **10.81**

(8) A review of the authorities in relation to benefit: DTA and CJA

10.82 In the Court of Appeal's judgment in *R v Simpson* (1998) 2 Cr App R(S) 111, Dyson J held:

> We turn... to examine the language of sections 2(3) and 4(1)(a) of the Act. It is important to note the breadth of the language that has been used. Section 2(3) does not say 'if he has at any time... received any payment or other reward for his drug trafficking'. It refers to any payment or other reward received 'in connection with drug trafficking carried on by him or another person'. In our view the definition of proceeds of drug trafficking is not limited to the consideration received by one person (A) from another person (B) for his (A's) drug trafficking carried out for (B). The phrase 'in connection with' is wider than the word 'for'. As a matter of ordinary language, it would be right to say on the facts of the present case, that Simpson received the sum of £540,000 in connection with his drug trafficking (ie his drug money laundering). Nor is there any reason for construing the definition of proceeds of drug trafficking as requiring as a pre-condition that property in the payment or other reward should pass to the defendant.

10.83 In *R v Currey* (1995) 16 Cr App R(S) 421, the Court of Appeal held that the benefit figure was the total amount passing through a defendant's hands and that there was no requirement for it to be retained and the court should not become concerned in calculating profit.

10.84 In *R v Cadman-Smith* (2002) 2 Cr App R(S) 37, the House of Lords ruled that in a case where a defendant had imported a quantity of cigarettes which had been seized by Customs, he had still benefited under the Act because, when he passed the point of importation, a duty was evaded and that duty was still owed to Customs. (This was notwithstanding the fact that the cigarettes had been seized and that he had suffered the cost of buying the cigarettes themselves.) The benefit was the amount of the duty and it was irrelevant that the cigarettes were seized; if the cigarettes had been sold the benefit would be the aggregate of the duty evaded and the gross sale price.

10.85 A similar rationale was applied to the case of *R v Davies* [2002] EWCA Crim 3110, when the Court of Appeal held that where a defendant applies a false trade mark to goods with a view to sale, even though there had been no sale, he still benefited from the counterfeit goods. In *R v Wilkes* [2003] EWCA Crim 848, a burglar was held to benefit from property that he had obtained, notwithstanding the fact that that property had been immediately seized.

10.86 In *R v Walls* The Times, 6 November 2002 the Court of Appeal held that where a court is required to assume, pursuant to s 4(3)(a) of the DTA, that property held by the defendant was received by him as a payment or reward in connection with drug trafficking, s 7(1) of that Act ('value of property in relation to any person holding property is market value less amount required to discharge any encumbrance') requires the court, in assessing the value of the payment or reward, to take the value of the property less any 'clean money' known to the defendant and secured on the property by way of mortgage.

10.87 In *Re K* (HC, 6 July 1990), the Court held that in the circumstances of a mortgage fraud where a fraudulent advance was used to buy a house, the benefit would be the gross value of the house, and that the expenses incurred in carrying out the crime, and the redemption value of the house, should not be deducted.

10.88 In *R v Forte* [2004] EWCA Crim 3188, the Court of Appeal held that the confiscation provisions relating to benefit were a tight, comprehensive and specific statutory regime, where benefit is not in any way related to the profit or lack of profit which ultimately may be made.

C. The Assumptions

The Court of Appeal held in *Re J* The Times, 12 July 2005, that the word 'obtain' for the purposes of the confiscation regime did not mean retain or keep, it simply contemplated that the defendant should have been instrumental in getting property out of the crime. All that needs to be proved was that the defendant's act should have contributed to the obtaining of the proceeds of crime in a non-trivial way. **10.89**

In *R v Metcalfe* The Times, 12 January 2005, the defendant had been convicted for a drug trafficking offence although his benefit from drug trafficking only extended to receipts referable to the supply of diazepam which had been found in a few of the tablets and not the other tablets which contained no controlled drugs. The Court of Appeal held that s 63(3) of the 1994 Act could not operate so as to convert the proceeds of the conspiracy as a whole into receipts from drug trafficking. As a result the confiscation order was quashed. In *Rigby v R* [2006] EWCA Crim 1653 the Court determined the defendant did not obtain a benefit or a pecuniary advantage from a temporary increase in the value of shares he held. **10.90**

(9) Determining the amount to be realised

Once the defendant's proceeds of drug trafficking have been quantified, the court must next determine the amount to be recovered in accordance with s 5(3) of the DTA, which provides: **10.91**

> If the court is satisfied that the amount that might be realised at the time the confiscation order is made is less than the amount the court assesses to be the value of his proceeds of drug trafficking, the amount to be recovered in the defendant's case under the confiscation order shall be:
>
> (a) the amount appearing to the court to be the amount that might be so realised; or
> (b) a nominal amount, where it appears to the court (on the information available to it at the time) that the amount that might be so realised is nil.

It would clearly be inappropriate for a confiscation order to be made against a defendant in the full amount of his proceeds of drug trafficking if he did not have sufficient assets to meet an order in that sum.

(10) Burden of proof

Thus far, the burden of proof, at each stage, has been on the Crown. Once the Crown has discharged the burden of satisfying the court of the fact of benefit and the amount of the defendant's proceeds, the burden shifts onto the defendant to show that the value of his realisable assets is less than the amount of his benefit (see *R v Comiskey* [1991] 93 Cr App R 227). The reason for this rule is that the defendant is the person who is in the best possible position to know the extent and value of his own assets. As Tucker J said in delivering the judgment of the Court of Appeal (at p 231): **10.92**

> The Act was intended to avoid a situation where a drug dealer serves his sentence with equanimity, knowing that on his release substantial funds will be available to enable him to live in comfort. With this in mind, a successful drugs dealer will take care to ensure, so far as he can, that the proceeds of his trade will be hidden away so as to be untraceable. The Act is designed to oblige him to disclose his assets, or to face the risk that if he does not do so, the court will make certain assumptions against him, and that he may have to serve an additional sentence of imprisonment if he does not comply with an order.

As in all cases where the burden of proof rests upon the defendant, the standard of proof is on a balance of probabilities. If the defendant fails to participate in the hearing or fails to **10.93** discharge this burden, a confiscation order will be made in the full amount of his benefit. Where the defendant does choose to participate with a view to establishing that the value of his realisable property is less than the amount of his benefit, the court will have to consider two separate issues, namely whether assets constitute 'realisable property' within the meaning of s 6(2) of the DTA and, if so, their value.

(11) Hidden assets

10.94 In *R v Ilsemann* [1991] Crim LR 141 the Court of Appeal considered the mantra of 'hidden assets' and held:

> it was a misconception to say that the amount of the confiscation order should be limited to the amount which the prosecution could prove to be the value of the defendant's assets known to them. If the defendant wished to say that that was all that was realisable, it was for him to satisfy the court to this effect.

(See also *R v Cokovic* (1996) 1 Cr App R(S) 131.)

10.95 In *R v Wright* [2006] EWCA Crim 1257, the Court of Appeal returned to the subject of hidden assets. In *Wright* the judge at first instance had made a confiscation order in the sum of £100,000 but had not given specific reasons as to how he had come to that conclusion. A benefit figure of £4,630,823 had been identified and the appellant's realisable assets were put at a sum of just over £50,000. It was apparent and assumed therefore that the judge had concluded that the appellant must have hidden assets in the sum of the balance. The appellant appealed on the basis that there was no evidence that he had such hidden assets. The principles in *R v Barwick* (2001) 1 Cr App R(S) 129 were accepted by the Court of Appeal. They make clear that the burden of establishing that the realisable assets are in a lesser sum than the benefit is with the defendant. The question for the Court in *Wright* was whether the judge was entitled to add £50,000 by way of realisable assets upon the evidence before him. The Court of Appeal (Pill LJ) stated:

> Of course there are many ways in which assets can be hidden, including assets being held temporarily by some other person on the defendant's behalf. The burden was on the appellant, an appellant who hitherto had had a lavish lifestyle. It was for the judge to form a judgement on realisable assets in those circumstances. As he correctly pointed out, he had had no assistance from the appellant himself by way of oral evidence, or even by way of signed statements. (See para 20).

10.96 In *R v Benjafield* (2002) 2 Cr App R(S) 70, Lord Steyn confirmed (at para 12), 'The fact that the appellant did not testify is . . . a powerful point against him.'

10.97 The Court of Appeal concluded in *Wright* that the judge was amply entitled to reach the conclusion he did. There was, the Court said, no rule of law that a judge was not entitled to find on appropriate facts that there are hidden assets. The Court concluded that the judge had been modest in his assessment of the situation.

10.98 In *R v Barnham* [2005] EWCA Crim 1049, the Court of Appeal had to consider the issue of whether the Crown was required to make out a prima facie case that a defendant had hidden assets before a defendant could be expected to deal with such an allegation. The defendant submitted that Article 6(1) of the European Convention on Human Rights would be engaged in relation to the second stage of the confiscation proceedings, namely after a benefit figure had

C. The Assumptions

been found, contending that the assumptions flowed through to the second stage and accordingly the Crown should be required to establish a prima facie case of hidden assets before the burden of proof shifted to the defendant. The Court ruled that the correct approach was that once the prosecution had established the existence of benefit, there was no requirement on it to provide a prima facie case in relation to realisable or hidden assets. At the second stage, the burden of proof shifted to the defendant to establish, if he could, his realisable assets to the satisfaction of the court. By that stage the defendant would know exactly how the court had determined benefit attributable to him and he had to prove by evidence what his realisable assets were. It was for him to show why the confiscation order should not be the value of the proceeds of drug trafficking. The Court of Appeal held that to hold that the prosecution should, in some way, show a prima facie case that the defendant had hidden assets, would defeat the object of the legislation (which was designed to enable the court to confiscate the criminal's ill-gotten gains). It confirmed that the expression "hidden assets" was indicative of the fact that the prosecution could have no means of knowing how and where a defendant might have disposed of or dealt with the proceeds in question. See further *R v Valentine* [2006] EWCA Crim 2717.

In *R v Afraz Siddique* (CA, 14 July 2005), the Court held that in circumstances where a defendant had failed to provide evidence about his realisable assets for the purposes of the confiscation order, the judge was entitled to conclude that the appellant had not satisfied him that his realisable assets were less than the benefit of the drug trafficking. The Court held (at para 27) that: **10.99**

> The appellant had the opportunity of seeking to persuade the court about his realisable assets. He declined to take it, for no doubt the very good reason that either there was no, or no credible, evidence he could give and/or he would be exposed to penetrating cross-examination which could only make his position worse. The fact that his credibility may already have been badly damaged is not a shield behind which he can hide. If it were, defendants in the position of the appellant would refuse to give evidence and yet successfully maintain that their realisable assets were less than the benefit. Such a position would be nonsensical, given the structure of the DTA and its compliance with Article 6, and would place judges hearing confiscation proceedings in an impossible position.

(12) Meaning of realisable property

Realisable property is defined by s 6(2) as meaning, subject to s 6(3): **10.100**

(2) (a) any property held by the defendant, and
    (b) any property held by a person to whom the defendant has directly or indirectly made a gift caught by this Act.

Section 6(3) excludes from the definition of realisable property assets which have been made the subject of forfeiture orders under s 27 of the Misuse of Drugs Act 1971; deprivation orders under s 143 of the Powers of Criminal Courts (Sentencing) Act 2000; and forfeiture orders under ss 23 and 111 of the Terrorism Act 2000.

(13) Property held by the defendant

It has been seen that property is 'held' by a person if he holds any interest in it: s 62(5)(a) of the DTA. The term 'any interest' is clearly very wide and can, for example, include interests arising by reason of a constructive trust. Further, the definition covers all property held by **10.101** the defendant whether it has been legitimately acquired or represents the proceeds of drug trafficking. The Act makes no distinction between legitimately and illegally acquired assets and all realisable property of the defendant, whether innocently obtained or not, is liable to realisation to satisfy a confiscation order in the full amount of his benefit from drug trafficking. The authority for this is *R v Chrastny (No 2)* [1991] 1 WLR 1385 where Glidewell LJ in delivering the judgment of the Court said:

> In our view it is quite clear that that definition embraces legitimately acquired property. We cannot read into the Act . . . any inference that that definition is limited to illegitimately acquired property; that is to say, the proceeds of drug trafficking.

10.102 Cash in the possession of the defendant that had been loaned to him by another for a specific purpose (which had failed) was 'property held by the Defendant' within the meaning of s 6(2)(a) of the DTA. Where there had been no expectation on the part of either party that the loan would be repaid with the same notes, the cash became part of his 'realisable property'—as per the Court of Appeal in *R v McQueen* (2002) 2 Cr App R(S) 9(3).

(14) Margin for error

10.103 In *R v Lemmon* [1991] Crim LR 791, a DTOA case, the Court of Appeal held that the obligation of the court was to determine the value of the realisable property of the defendant at the time when the confiscation order was made. It held that the court must have in mind that estimating the value of real property was not a precise science and some safety margin for error must be allowed.

(15) Costs of sale

10.104 In *R v Davies* [2004] EWCA Crim 3380, the Court of Appeal held that it was 'quite right' to deduct the costs of any sale (eg estate agent's costs) from the value of the house that was to be sold in order to satisfy the confiscation order, (see para 15, reflecting *R v Kramer* (1992) 13 Cr App R(S) 390 and the terms of the order in *Lemmon* (1991) 13 Crim App R (S) 66).

(16) Assets jointly held with third parties

10.105 If the defendant owns an asset jointly with an innocent third party (eg a matrimonial home held jointly with his wife) it constitutes a realisable asset of the defendant to the extent of his interest in it. Thus, if the defendant has a 50 per cent interest in an asset with another party, 50 per cent of its value can be taken into account in assessing the amount to be realised. The means by which such assets are realised, procedure, and the rights of third parties in relation thereto are considered fully in Chapter 22. It should be emphasised at this stage that any third party claiming to have an interest in realisable property does not have the right to be heard or be legally represented at the confiscation hearing except in his capacity as a witness on behalf of the defendant, if he chooses to call him. The third party's right to be heard arises at the enforcement stage, in the High Court.

(17) Matrimonial homes

10.106 The issue of matrimonial homes and their fate in confiscation proceedings, together with case law relating thereto, is considered fully at para 22.85 of Chapter 22.

C. The Assumptions

(18) Assets held overseas

10.107 The Act extends to realisable property held in England and Wales 'and elsewhere': see s 62(2) of the DTA. Thus the court must take into account the value of property held by the defendant wherever it is located in the world in assessing the amount that might be realised. The means by which confiscation orders incorporating the value of overseas assets are enforced is considered in Chapter 25.

(19) Gifts

10.108 Property is realisable for the purposes of s 6 of the DTA even when not held by the defendant if it is held by a person to whom he has directly or indirectly made a gift caught by the Act (s 6(2)). If a defendant were able to gift all his property to other persons so that, in the event of his being convicted of drug trafficking offences, there would be no assets available to satisfy a confiscation order, the provisions of the DTA would soon be rendered ineffective. Accordingly, the legislation introduced the concept of 'a gift caught by the Act.'

(20) When is a gift caught by the Act?

10.109 Section 8(1) of the DTA provides that a gift, whether made before or after the coming into force of the Act, is caught by the Act if:

(1)(a) it was made by the defendant at any time since the beginning of the period of six years ending when the proceedings were instituted against him, or
  (b) it was made by the defendant at any time and was a gift of property:
    (i) received by the defendant in connection with drug trafficking carried on by him or another, or
    (ii) which in whole or in part directly or indirectly represented in the defendant's hands property received by him in that connection.

10.110 By s 8(2)(a) of the DTA, a defendant is treated as having made a gift where he transfers property to another for a consideration significantly less than that he provided when he acquired it. A defendant transfers property if he transfers or grants to another any interest in it: see s 62(5)(b) of the DTA.

10.111 It will thus be appreciated that this section makes a distinction between gifts of property that were received by the defendant in connection with drug trafficking and gifts which were not received by him in that connection. In the latter case, the gift may well only be caught by the Act if it was made in the six year period ending when the proceedings were instituted against the defendant, whereas in the former case, the gift will be caught by the Act whenever it was made.

10.112 Gifts take many forms and as confiscation law becomes more draconian, so the methods employed by drug traffickers to distance themselves from their ill-gotten gains become more sophisticated. The more straightforward methods used include investing money in bank or building society accounts in the names of the defendant's spouse or children and the purchase of real property in the names of family members. At the other end of the spectrum, the more sophisticated schemes used involve the creation of front companies and the transfer of funds to company bank accounts in the guise of legitimate commercial transactions. Potential recipients of such gifts should be aware that their acceptance of them might,

Chapter 10: The DTA Confiscation Hearing

in certain circumstances, constitute money laundering offences under Pt III of the DTA. This subject is considered in more detail in Chapter 26.

10.113 Finally, it should be noted that the gift provisions in the DTA are concerned with the confiscation of the value of the gift and not merely with the confiscation of the gift itself.

(21) Obligations having priority

10.114 By s 6(1) of the DTA the amount that might be realised at the time a confiscation order is made is:

(1)(a) the total of the values at that time of all the realisable property held by the defendant, less
    (b) where there are obligations having priority at that time, the total amounts payable in pursuance of such obligations, together with the total of the values at that time of all gifts caught by the Act.

10.115 Section 6(4) of the DTA defines 'obligations having priority' in very narrow terms as being sums due in respect of fines or other financial orders of the court made on conviction for an offence or preferential debts within the meaning of s 386 of the Insolvency Act 1986. This provision confines preferential debts to sums owing by way of various forms of taxation. The defendant is not, therefore, entitled to have deducted from the value of his realisable property, as assessed by the court, unsecured loans or other debts owing to third parties.

(22) Valuing property

10.116 Once the court has determined which assets are realisable, it must proceed to value the same. The value of property for DTA purposes is normally the market value. The position is dealt with in s 7 of the DTA which provides that:

(1) Subject to the following provisions of this section and to section 8 of this Act, for the purposes of this Act the value of property (other than cash) in relation to any person holding the property is the market value of the property, except that, where any other person holds an interest in the property, the value is:
    (a) the market value of the first-mentioned person's beneficial interest in the property, less
    (b) the amount required to discharge any encumbrance (other than a charging order on that interest).
(2) Subject to section 8(2) of this Act, references in this Act to the value at any time (referred to in subsection (3) below as 'the material time') of a gift caught by this Act or of any payment or reward are references to:
    (a) the value of the gift, payment or reward to the recipient when he received it, adjusted to take account of subsequent changes in the value of money, or
    (b) where subsection (3) below applies, the value there mentioned, whichever is the greater.
(3) Subject to section 8(2) of this Act, if at the material time the recipient holds:
    (a) the property which he received (not being cash), or
    (b) property which, in whole or in part, directly or indirectly represents in his hands the property which he received,

the value referred to in subsection (2)(b) above is the value to him at the material time of the property mentioned in paragraph (a) above or, as the case may be, of the property mentioned in paragraph (b) above so far as it so represents the property which he received, but disregarding in either case any charging order.

10.117 Thus, the court must determine the market value of the asset and deduct the amount required to discharge any encumbrance thereon obtained by a third party, so long as the same was obtained prior to a restraint order being granted or, where there is no restraint order, prior to the imposition of a confiscation order.

C. The Assumptions

10.118 A difficult problem regarding valuation arose in *R v Chapman* The Times, 18 November 1991. The defendant made a gift of £58,000 to his wife that she used as a part payment on a property that she purchased for £78,000, the balance coming from a £20,000 mortgage she obtained. The value of the property had increased to £150,000 at the time the confiscation order was made. The court calculated the value of the gift as being

$$£58,000/£78,000 \times £150,000 = £111,538.$$

10.119 On appeal the defendant contended that the court had erred in failing to take into account the mortgage debt, which at the time of the order was £20,353.32. The court ruled that it was bound to give effect to s 5(4)(a) of the DTOA (now s 7(1)(b) of the DTA) which provided that the relevant value was the market value less the amount required to discharge any encumbrance (ie the mortgage). The court held that giving effect to s 5(4), the appropriate calculation was

$$£150,000 - £20,353.32 \times 58/78$$

which reduced the value of the gift to £96,403.

10.120 In *R v Moulden* (2005) 1 Cr App R(S) 691 (121) the Court of Appeal held that where a defendant holds a property at the time that his benefit from drug trafficking is being valued, and where that property was financed in part by money received as a payment from drug trafficking and in part by way of a mortgage, the value of the payment is to be assessed at whichever is the greater of the payment adjusted for changes in the value of money or the equity in the property. The value is not limited to the amount of the payment adjusted pro rata according to the increase in the value of the property. For a commentary on *R v Moulden* see CLW/ 05/21/30.

(23) Market value

10.121 The words 'market value' were considered by the Court of Appeal in *R v Dore* (1997) 2 Cr App R(S) 152. In that case Lord Bingham stated that drugs which are illegal to buy and sell in this country had no market value for the purposes of the provisions of the DTA. This reasoning was recently confirmed in both *R v Ajibade* [2006] EWCA Crim 368 and *R v Hussain* [2006] EWCA Crim 621 (see para 15.38 of Chapter 15).

(24) Confiscation orders and the forfeiture of drugs

10.122 In *R v Satchell* [1996] Crim LR 351 the Court held that the Act allowed the judge to assume the purchase price of the drugs was made out of payments received in connection with drug trafficking. However the court was also concerned that the appellant might suffer double jeopardy if the appellant was ordered to pay a sum equal to the price paid for the drugs, and the drugs themselves were then forfeited. This issue arose in *R v Thacker* (1995) 16 Cr App R(S) 461 where it was held that drugs which had been seized from the appellant were not realisable property. In *Satchell* the court confirmed this and found that where it was inevitable that the drugs would be seized the court was under a duty to take into account the fact that nothing could be realised as proceeds from the drugs. The confiscation order was as a result quashed.

(25) Is the court limited to the prosecutor's statement?

10.123 In short, no. In *R v Atkinson* [1992] Crim LR 749, a DTOA case, the court held that the statute was imperative in its terms, which were mandatory. The court was obliged to determine the amount to be recovered under the Act, and the amount of the order was to be the amount which the court assessed to be the value of the defendant's proceeds of drug trafficking, and not the prosecutor's. The sentencer was therefore bound to reject any suggestion that the scope of the enquiry should be limited.

(26) Public interest immunity

10.124 In *R v May* [2005] EWCA Crim 97, the Court of Appeal held that where a judge was confident that he could put undisclosed material (namely, material subject to public interest immunity applications) out of his mind for the purposes of a decision in relation to confiscation proceedings, then he was neither obliged to recuse himself nor to appoint special counsel.

D. Making the Confiscation Order

10.125 Once the court has determined the amount to be recovered in accordance with s 5 of the DTA, it must make a confiscation order in that amount: see s 2(5) of the DTA. The order must be made in a monetary amount, and is an *in personam* order against the defendant. It does not name specific assets and does not take away the defendant's property rights in any of the realisable property that may have been taken into account in making the order.

(1) Relationship with forfeiture orders and other legislation

10.126 Under s 2(5)(b)(iii) of the DTA, the court must take account of the confiscation order before imposing any fine on the defendant or other order involving any payment by him. The court must also take account of the confiscation order before making a forfeiture order under s 27 of the Misuse of Drugs Act 1971 or a deprivation order under s 143 of the Powers of Criminal Courts (Sentencing) Act 2000 (PCC(S)A 2000). The clear legislative intention was that the DTA should take precedence and that forfeiture orders should only be made when an order under the DTA is inappropriate. So in *R v Stuart and Bonnett* (1989) 11 Cr App R(S) 89; [1989] Crim LR 599 where the trial judge had ordered the forfeiture of £2,500 in cash seized from the importer of cannabis under s 143 of the Powers of Criminal Courts Act 1973, (now replaced by s 143 PCC(S)A 2000), the Court of Appeal quashed the order, ruling that it was unlawful as the judge should have followed the confiscation provisions of the DTA. The court should always therefore follow the procedures of the DTA and not succumb to the temptation to make forfeiture orders under other legislation, no matter how small the amount involved may be and however much such a course may commend itself to the court in terms of simplicity.

(2) Relationship between the confiscation order and the sentence

10.127 Section 2(5)(c) of the DTA provides that the court must leave the confiscation order out of account when determining the appropriate sentence for the offence. Accordingly the court may not mitigate the sentence that would normally be imposed to reflect the fact that a confiscation order has been made.

D. Making the Confiscation Order

In *R v Ayensu and Ayensu* [1982] Crim LR 764 the Court held it was the duty of the Crown Court to pass sentence on the basis of the facts of the particular offence. It was not right, where the pleas had been accepted by the prosecution on the basis that they were, and the court having accepted those pleas, for the court to take into account matters which were later contested. Nor should the court take into account suggested early admissions or, in the circumstances of the case, assume that the affluent way of life enjoyed by the appellants was derived from smuggling cannabis on earlier occasions. See also *R v Pragason* [1988] Crim LR 778. **10.128**

The decision of *Ayensu and Ayensu*, is difficult to reconcile with *R v Harper* [1989] Crim LR 755, 11 Cr App R(S) 240 where the Court of Appeal held that if a sentencer had material on which he could find that there had been trafficking beyond the ambit of that shown in the evidence, it would be right for the sentencer to pay some regard to that evidence in the same way he might pay regard to general evidence placed before him as to the prevalence of trafficking in drugs. The court held that the correct approach was that the judge must sentence only on the counts that have been proven in the indictment. However, he could of course mitigate that sentence from what would be appropriate on the facts, for good character, or because the offence was shown to be an isolated incident. If there was evidence that it was not an isolated incident, then he should not mitigate from what would otherwise be the appropriate sentence. It seems, therefore, that the court is entitled to take into account evidence adduced in the confiscation hearing in determining the appropriate sentence. **10.129**

In *R v Callan* [1994] Crim LR 198, however, it was held to be inappropriate to deprive the defendant, who had no previous convictions, of the mitigation his previous good character would normally afford on the basis of findings made in the DTA hearing as a result of the court applying the assumptions. It would seem that the court might only act on findings made in the DTA hearing when imposing sentence if those findings were made on the basis of the evidence adduced rather than upon the application of the assumptions. **10.130**

In *R v Harper* (above) the Court of Appeal held that a judge would be entitled to have regard to the fact that he had made an order under the Act in the sense that there was then evidence before him to show that the accused offence was not an isolated one. **10.131**

In *R v Odewale* (CA, 10 March 2005) the Court held that where a judge knew that he was likely to conduct a fact-finding exercise in relation to a defendant, he should attempt not to express himself at a sentencing hearing or at an earlier stage in such a way in which it might sensibly be perceived to show that he was biased against the defendant and unlikely to believe anything he might tell him in the future. **10.132**

(3) Imprisonment in default

Under s 9(1) of the DTA, the provisions of the Powers of Criminal Courts (Sentencing) Act 2000 apply to the enforcement of a confiscation order in the same way as they apply to the imposition of a fine by the Crown Court. The effect of this provision is that the court must impose a prison sentence to be served in default of payment of the fine. It will be noted that a defendant must be present at the confiscation hearing, because the procedure involves the judge passing a sentence of imprisonment. It will also be noted that the serving of the sentence in default does not extinguish the debt (s 9(5) of the DTA). **10.133**

10.134 The penalties available for default in payment are set out in s 139(4) of the Powers of Criminal Courts (Sentencing) Act 2000 and are as follows:

An amount not exceeding £200—7 days
An amount exceeding £200 but not exceeding £500—14 days
An amount exceeding £500 but not exceeding £1,000—28 days
An amount exceeding £1,000 but not exceeding £2,500—45 days
An amount exceeding £2,500 but not exceeding £5,000—3 months
An amount exceeding £5,000 but not exceeding £10,000—6 months
An amount exceeding £10,000 but not exceeding £20,000—12 months
An amount exceeding £20,000 but not exceeding £50,000—18 months
An amount exceeding £50,000 but not exceeding £100,000—2 years
An amount exceeding £100,000 but not exceeding £250,000—3 years
An amount exceeding £250,000 but not exceeding £1,000,000—5 years
An amount exceeding £1,000,000—ten years

10.135 The imposition of a default sentence was held to be mandatory in *R v Popple* [1992] Crim LR 675, and s 9(2) of the DTA provides that the default sentence must be served consecutively to any sentence of imprisonment imposed for the substantive offence. It should be noted, however, that the above sentences are the maximum that may be imposed and it does not follow that the maximum sentence available for a particular amount should automatically be imposed in every case. (See also *Dillon and Jagdev* (2005) Cr App R (S) 232.)

10.136 In *R v Szrajber* (1994) Crim LR 543 a CJA confiscation order was made against the defendant in the sum of £407,188 and a five year sentence of imprisonment imposed for default in making payment, this being the maximum period that could be ordered in respect of a sum between £250,000 and £1 million. The trial judge imposed the maximum sentence assuming it was the fixed period that she was required to impose. The Court of Appeal confirmed that the periods set out in the table were maximum periods and the court had discretion to impose a period below the maximum. The normal procedure would be for the court to impose a default sentence that fell between the maximum and minimum. So, for a confiscation order in the sum imposed against the defendant, a default sentence between three and five years should normally be imposed. In determining the proper sentence the court had to have regard to the circumstances of the case, the overall seriousness of the matter and in particular to the purpose for which the default sentence was imposed, namely to secure payment of the sum ordered to be confiscated. It was not necessary to approach the matter on a strict arithmetical basis. In the circumstances, the court varied the default sentence to four years. See also *R v French* (1995) 16 Cr App R(S) 841, where the court held that the period of imprisonment in default should be such, within the maximum permitted, as to make it completely clear to the defendant that he had nothing to gain by failing to comply with the order.

10.137 In *R v Thomas* [2004] EWCA Crim 1101, the defendant had been convicted of conspiracy to supply cocaine and subsequently had a confiscation order in the sum of £24,000 made against him, which the court ordered was to be paid within six months, with a period of eighteen months set in default. The Court of Appeal found that the period of 18 months was manifestly excessive and reduced it to 12 months.

D. Making the Confiscation Order

(4) Time to pay

10.138 In *R v Soneji* (A, 27 March 2006) the issue concerned the time period that the defendants should be allowed in order to satisfy the confiscation orders made against them. At the Crown Court stage the judge had allowed 18 months from the date of any judgment of the Court of Appeal on the question of jurisdiction. However, the defendant was successful at the Court of Appeal stage and the Crown Court order was quashed. What had not been anticipated by the Crown Court judge was that the matter would then proceed to the House of Lords where the Crown's appeal was ultimately successful and the confiscation order reinstated. The question arose as to when did the 18 months start? The original date of the Court of Appeals decision? The date of the House of Lords decision? Or from some date in the future, pending any appeal to the ECHR? The matter was remitted back to the Court of Appeal who held that the obligation to pay the sums specified in the confiscation order within a specific period remained in force and the clock did not stop running unless the Court ordered to the contrary. The order of the House of Lords would be made an order of the Court of Appeal, whereby the confiscation orders would be restored. The Court concluded that, given the overall period of time since the confiscation orders were made, and since the successful appeal to the House of Lords, the defendants had had a sufficient and wholly fair opportunity to put their affairs in order and that the confiscation orders should therefore be paid within 28 days.

10.139 This robust approach was also reflected in the Court of Appeal case of *R v May, Lawrence* [2005] EWCA Crim 97, where Keene LJ held at para 5 that the:

> proposition that the time to pay a confiscation order runs from the date of the determination of an appeal was "unsound in law". In principle the fact that an appeal is pending does not operate so as to suspend the operation of any sentence or order.

He added at para 7 that:

> There is no reason why steps preparatory to the raising of the money specified in the confiscation order should not have been taken while in (the defendant May's) appeal was pending. The appellant was not entitled to assume that his appeal would be successful and, as indicated above, as a matter of law time was running during that period. Moreover, it would be wrong as a matter of principle for appellants to be encouraged to believe that bringing an appeal would be likely to lengthen the time given for payment, even if the appeal was unsuccessful.

10.140 In *R v Smith* [2004] EWCA Crim 1219, the judge at first instance rejected counsel's submission on the appellant's behalf that a period of two years be allowed for the sale of the principal asset, namely the former matrimonial home, which the appellant's ex-wife was still living in. The judge accepted that there might be difficulties in the appellant realising money from the former matrimonial home, but he concluded that the court did not know what attitude the appellant's ex-wife might take or what had transpired between the appellant and her when the appellant transferred his share in the former matrimonial home to her.

10.141 The appellant appealed on the basis that nine months was too short a period to enable the appellant to obtain a court order for the sale of the former matrimonial home and therefore effect the sale.

10.142 The Court of Appeal found that in the period that had elapsed since the hearing itself and the hearing of the appeal, no steps had been taken by the appellant to effect realisation of the asset. This, the court found to be a key facet in consideration of the merits of the appeal. The appellant had had many months to start the process whereby it would have been possible to take steps to realise the asset. In the light of the fact that there was no information before them or any explanation forthcoming as to why these steps were not taken within the period allowed by the judge, they concluded that there was no reason on the information before them to conclude that the period allowed by the judge at first instance of nine months was insufficient to enable the appellant to realise the assets and comply with the confiscation order he had made. The appeal was therefore dismissed.

(5) Orders for the payment of costs

10.143 Orders for the payment of costs should only be made where the defendant has the ability to pay them. If a confiscation order is made in what the court finds to be the full value of a defendant's realisable property, no order for costs should be made. In *R v Szrajber* (1994) Crim LR 543 the defendant's benefit from the offences was found to be £524,000, but his realisable property was valued at £407,188 and a confiscation order accordingly made in this lesser sum. In addition, an order for the payment of costs was made in the sum of £65,428. The Court of Appeal quashed the order for costs on the basis that a confiscation order had been made in the full amount of the defendant's benefit from the offence and accordingly he had no further assets at his disposal from which the order for costs could be paid.

(6) Unreasonable delay in enforcement

10.144 There has been a significant change in the law concerning delays by prosecuting authorities in enforcing confiscation orders. In *R v Chichester Magistrates' Court ex parte Crowther* [1998] EWHC Admin 960 the Divisional Court held that even where there has been a culpable delay by the prosecutor in taking steps to enforce a confiscation order, this does not act as a bar to the enforcing magistrates' court implementing the default sentence for non payment. This case was decided before the Human Rights Act 1998 came into force and in *Lloyd v Bow Street Magistrates' Court* [2003] EWHC Admin 2294 the Court ruled that an unreasonable delay on the part of the prosecutor in taking enforcement action would amount to a breach of the defendant's rights under Article 6 of the European Convention on Human Rights if an attempt was made to implement the default sentence. The Court made it plain however, that its decision applied only where enforcement action took the form of implementing the default sentence and had no application in respect of the use of civil remedies such as the appointment of an enforcement receiver. For further see para 17.78 of Chapter 17. This position has however been slightly modified by *R (on the application of Deamer) v Southampton Crown Court* (DC, 13 July 2006) where the Court held that where there had been no unexplained or unjustifiable delay on the part of the prosecutor a committal in default was not unreasonable even though six years had elapsed.

(7) Confiscation orders and the ECHR

10.145 It is now fairly well established that confiscation proceedings, following on and attaching to a criminal conviction, represent a penalty, not least because a prison sentence in default flows from non-payment, and the confiscation order itself is treated as a fine, pursuant to

D. Making the Confiscation Order

(eg) s 9 of the DTA (See *Benjafield* [2002] UKHL 2 (para 82); *Rezvi* [2002] UKHL 1 and *Phillips v UK* [2001] EHRR No 41087/98. Part of the reasoning in *Rezvi* was that the purpose of confiscation proceedings was to '... *punish convicted offenders.*')

In *R v Benjafield* [2002] UKHL 2 the House of Lords considered the relationship between confiscation orders under the DTA and the Human Rights Act 1998. The defendant had pleaded guilty to two counts of conspiracy to supply drugs, and was sentenced to a total of 14 years' imprisonment. Subsequently, the court made a confiscation order against him pursuant to the provisions of the DTA 1994. The order was imposed before the implementation of the Human Rights Act 1998. On the defendant's appeal against the confiscation order, which was heard after the implementation of the 1998 Act, the Court of Appeal considered whether the reverse assumptions in s 4(3) of the 1994 Act were compatible with the provisions of the ECHR (as set out in the Schedule to the 1998 Act), particularly Article 6(1) (the general right to a fair hearing) and Article 6(2) (the presumption of innocence in respect of those charged with a criminal offence). The House of Lords held that a defendant who was the subject of criminal proceedings before the implementation of the 1998 Act was not entitled to rely on Convention rights in an appeal after the implementation of that Act. It followed that in the case of *Benjafield* the defendant's Convention rights were not engaged, and his appeal was dismissed (applying *R v Kansal (No 2)* [2002] 1 All ER 257). However the House of Lords also held that Article 6(2) of the Convention does not apply to confiscation proceedings under the 1994 Act. Such proceedings, it held, are part of the sentencing process following a conviction, and are not a criminal charge within the meaning of Article 6(2). The Court held that although a person who is subject to confiscation proceedings had the full protection of Article 6(1), the reverse burden provisions in s 4(3) of the 1994 Act were compatible with that Article. Further, the Court held any interference with the right of peaceful enjoyment of possessions under Article 1 of the First Protocol of the Convention was also justified, (applying *McIntosh v Lord Advocate* [2001] 2 All ER 638 and *Phillips v UK* (2001) 11 EHRC 280).

10.146

In Lord Steyn's judgment he held (at para 8):

10.147

> Making due allowance for the differences between the confiscation procedures under the 1988 Act and under the 1994 Act, the reasoning in *R v Rezvi* (2002) 1 All ER 801 applies with equal force in this case. The 1994 Act pursues an important objective in the public interest and the legislative measures are rationally connected with the furtherance of this objective. The procedure devised by Parliament is a fair and proportionate response to the need to protect the public interest. The critical point is that under the 1994 Act, as under the 1988 Act, the judge must be astute to avoid injustice. If there is or might be a serious risk of injustice, he must not make a confiscation order. In these circumstances a challenge to the compatibility of the legislation must fail.

In *McIntosh v Lord Advocate* [2001] 3 WLR 107 the Privy Council had considered whether the assumptions set out in the Proceeds of Crime (Scotland) Act 1995 were incompatible with the presumption of innocence afforded by Article 6(2) of the ECHR. The court held that the presumption of innocence guaranteed by Article 6(2) applied only to persons 'charged with a criminal offence'; and that although a person against whom an application for a confiscation order was made faced a financial penalty with a custodial penalty in default of payment, it was a penalty imposed for the offence with which he had already

10.148

been convicted and involved no accusation of, or enquiry into, any other offence. Therefore in relation to the application for a confiscation order made against him the respondent was not a person entitled to rely on the presumption of innocence guaranteed by Article 6(2).

10.149 Further, on the assumption that Article 6(2) did apply to an application for a confiscation order following conviction, it was not unreasonable or oppressive to call on a proven drug trafficker to proffer an explanation for any significant discrepancy which could be established between his property and expenditure on the one hand and his known sources of income on the other. Accordingly, the assumptions that the court was entitled to make were not incompatible with the presumption of innocence under Article 6(2). The decision in *McIntosh* was confirmed by *R v Mallick* The Times, 30 May 2000, where the Court of Appeal held that the confiscation procedure under the DTA, particularly the making of an assumption of fact, does not conflict with the presumption of innocence under Article 6(2) of the ECHR. It held that case law established that any rule that applies a presumption operating against the accused must be confined within reasonable limits, but no more than that (applying *Salabiaku v France* 13 EHRR 379). The imposition of a term in default of payment of a confiscation order involved no violation of Article 7(1) 'nor shall a heavier penalty be imposed than the one that was applicable at the time the criminal offence was committed' since it was not a heavier penalty but simply a means of enforcement.

10.150 In *Welch v UK* [1995] 1/1994/448/527, the European Court of Human Rights held that the DTOA constituted a violation of Article 7 of the ECHR on the basis that Article 7(1) provides, inter alia, that a defendant may not be subject to a heavier penalty than that which was applicable at the time the offence was committed, and that the retrospective parts of the DTOA amounted to just that. It should be noted however that *Welch* concerned the DTOA and was principally decided in the way it was because prior to its introduction there had not been a comparative confiscation scheme. This had led to there being an inability within the Courts to forfeit property that had been converted from the proceeds of crime.

10.151 In *Welch* the Court specifically upheld the legality of the use of confiscation orders in combating drug trafficking; stating in its conclusion that it:

> ... does not call into question in any respect the powers of confiscation conferred on the courts as a weapon in the fight against the scourge of drug trafficking.

10.152 In conclusion, case law dictates that the confiscation procedure under the DTA does not involve the determination of a criminal charge (albeit a penalty) but is properly to be regarded as part of the sentencing procedures of the court, following conviction of a criminal offence. Accordingly Article 6(2) of the ECHR has no application as to the right to a fair trial under Article 6(1) or in respect of the determination of the defendant's civil obligations. The courts have found, for the time being, that the procedures under the 1994 Act contain sufficient safeguards (see *Phillips v UK* [2001] EHRR No 41087/98).

E. Confiscation Orders Against Defendants who Die or Abscond

10.153 Section 19 of the DTA gives the High Court jurisdiction, in certain circumstances, to make confiscation orders in relation to the realisable property of defendants who die or abscond.

E. Confiscation Orders Against Defendants who Die or Abscond

(1) Post-conviction orders

10.154 Section 19(1) and (2) of the DTA gives the High Court the power to make such orders post-conviction and provides as follows:

(1) Subsection (2) below applies where a person has been convicted of one or more drug trafficking offences.
(2) If the prosecutor asks it to proceed under this section, the High Court may exercise the powers of the Crown Court under this Act to make a confiscation order against a defendant if satisfied that the defendant has died or absconded.

(2) Pre-conviction cases

10.155 Section 19(3) and (4) deals with the position where proceedings have been instituted against the defendant, but at the relevant time there has been no conviction recorded against him and provides as follows:

(3) Subsection (4) below applies where proceedings for one or more drug trafficking offences have been instituted against a person but have not been concluded.
(4) If the prosecutor asks it to proceed under this section, the High Court may exercise the powers of the Crown Court under this Act to make a confiscation order against a defendant if satisfied that the defendant has absconded.

10.156 As one might expect, the powers given to the court when the case has reached the post-conviction stage are greater than those applicable when the case has not reached that stage. The most notable distinction is that at the post-conviction stage the court may make an order against a defendant who absconds or dies, whereas at the pre-conviction stage an order may only be made against the defendant who absconds. At the time it was no doubt considered too draconian a measure to make an order against a defendant who dies prior to conviction, when the presumption of innocence still applies, (but see now the powers of the ARA in relation to unconvicted defendants).

10.157 The defendant who absconds is, of course, in an entirely different position in that he absents himself voluntarily and has the means at his disposal to return at any time and face trial. Further, the very fact of his absconding is an act that may be viewed as inconsistent with innocence. The powers in relation to absconders are also more limited where the defendant absconds at the pre-conviction stage; if he absconds at the pre-conviction stage, under s 19(5) of the DTA the power to make a confiscation order may not be exercised until a period of two years following the date on which, in the opinion of the court, the defendant absconded. There is no such time restriction upon the making of an order in relation to a defendant who absconds after conviction.

(3) Rules of the Supreme Court

10.158 RSC Order 115 makes provision for applications under s 19 DTA. The application is to be made in accordance with CPR Part 23 where there have been proceedings in the High Court against the defendant, or where there are no such proceedings, by the issue of a claim form (see RSC Ord 115, r 2B(1)).

10.159 By RSC Ord 115 r 2B(2), the application must be supported by a witness statement or an affidavit giving particulars of the following matters:

(a) the grounds for believing that the defendant has died or absconded;
(b) the date or approximate date on which the defendant died or absconded;
(c) where the application is made under s 19(2), the offence or offences of which the defendant was convicted, and the date and place of conviction;
(d) where the application is made under s 19(4), the proceedings which have been initiated against the defendant (including particulars of the offence and the date and place of institution of those proceedings); and
(e) where the defendant is alleged to have absconded, the steps taken to contact him.

10.160 Rule 2B(3) requires that the prosecutor's s 11 statement must be exhibited to the witness statement or affidavit and must include the following particulars:

(a) the name of the defendant;
(b) the name of the person by whom the statement is given; and
(c) such information known to the prosecutor as is relevant to the determination whether the defendant has benefited from drug trafficking and to the assessment of the value of his proceeds of drug trafficking.

10.161 The witness statement or affidavit may, unless the court otherwise orders, contain statements of information and belief with their sources and grounds (RSC Ord 115 r 2B(4)).

10.162 By r 2B(5), the application and the witness statement or affidavit in support must be served on:

(a) the defendant (or on the personal representatives of a deceased defendant);
(b) any person who the prosecutor reasonably believes is likely to be affected by the making of a confiscation order; and
(c) the receiver, where one has been appointed in the matter.

10.163 If a person served with such an application considers that the seven-day period is insufficient to enable him to prepare his case it would, of course, be open to him to apply for an adjournment. It is unlikely that the prosecutor would oppose any reasonable request for an adjournment and the prosecutor should always be invited to agree the same on a 'by consent' basis before an application is made to the court.

(4) Procedural matters

10.164 Section 19(6) of the DTA deals with procedural matters. Under s 19(6)(a), the court may not apply any of the assumptions of s 4(2) when considering applications under the provision. The provisions of s 11 in relation to the provision of prosecutors' statements apply, but for obvious reasons the provisions requiring the defendant to respond thereto do not: see s 19(6)(b).

10.165 Section 19(6)(c) and (d) deal with the requirements as to giving notice of the application. Under s 19(6)(c) the court shall not make a confiscation order against an absconder unless it is satisfied that the prosecutor has taken reasonable steps to contact him. Third party rights are protected by s 19(6)(d), which provides that any person likely to be affected by the making of a confiscation order shall be entitled to appear before the court and make representations.

F. Confiscation Hearings Under the DTA: Index of Defined Expressions

The following is a thumbnail guide: **10.166**

   Amount that might be realised—s 6(1)
   Amount to be recovered—s 5(1)
   Benefit from drug trafficking—s 2(3)
   Charging order—s 27(2)
   Confiscation order—s 2(9)
   Defendant—s 63(1)
   Drug Trafficking—generally—s 1(1) and (2)
   Drug trafficking offence—s 1(3)
   Gift caught by the act—s 8(1)
   'Held', in relation to property—s 62(5)(a)
   Institution of proceedings for an offence—s 41(2)
   'Interest' in relation to property—s 62(3)
   Making a gift—s 8(2)
   Modifications—s 63(1)
   Proceeds of drug trafficking—s 4(1)(a)
   Property—s 62(1)
   Realisable property—s 6(2)
   Restraint order—s 26(1)
   'Satisfied', in relation to a confiscation order—s 41(6) and (7)
   'Subject to appeal', in relation to an order—s 41(8)
   'Transferred', in relation to property—s 62(5)(b)
   Value of a gift, payment or reward—s 7(2)
   Value of proceeds of drug trafficking—s 4(1)(b)
   Value of property—s 7(1)

For further defined expressions see s 64 of the DTA.

G. Appeals

The binding effect of s 11(7) (defendant's acceptance of allegations in prosecutor's statements conclusive, see para 9.77 of Chapter 9) appeared to be also conclusive on appeal. In *R v Tredwen* (1994) 99 Cr App R 154, a DTOA case, where the defendant, through his counsel, accepted at the DTOA enquiry that his benefit from drug trafficking was £1,245,150.74 and that the value of his realisable assets amounted to £186,979. These figures were put before the judge as agreed amounts. The defendant sought to challenge these previously agreed figures on appeal arguing that the word 'conclusive' did not mean conclusive on appeal against sentence. The Court of Appeal rejected this contention, Glidewell LJ saying, in delivering the judgment of the court (at p 154):   **10.167**

> In our view when Parliament said that figures accepted or agreed were to be conclusive for the purposes of the confiscation proceedings, it intended them to be conclusive for all stages of such proceedings, including appeal to this court.

10.168 The Court observed that the defendant suffered no unfairness from this interpretation because, if the value of his assets later proved to be insufficient to meet the confiscation order, he may apply for a certificate of inadequacy under s 17 of the DTA (see also *Crutchley and Tonks* [1994] Crim LR 309).

10.169 However, this position altered following *R v Emmett* [1997] 3 WLR 1119. In *Emmett*, another DTOA case, the defendants had pleaded guilty at the Crown Court. It had been agreed between Counsel that the benefit figure amounted to £100,000 and various sums were agreed in respect of the realisable assets. The judge was asked to make the agreed confiscation orders, which he did. In the Court of Appeal the Crown submitted that the general right to appeal against the confiscation order was excluded as a result of the defendant's acceptance of the allegations in the statement tendered by the prosecutor, which had been acted on by the Court. The Court of Appeal held, however, that there was a strong presumption that, except by specific provision, the legislature will not exclude a right of appeal as of right, or with leave, where such a right is ordinarily available (as per *R v Cain* [1985] 1 AC 46, 55g–56d). Lord Steyn held that unless the Act expressly or by necessary implication had excluded a right of appeal, there was, as a matter of jurisdiction, a right of appeal against a confiscation order *in all cases*. There is plainly no express ouster of the right of appeal.

10.170 In so doing he held that the focus was on the Crown Court to treat the defendant's acceptance as conclusive of the matters to which it relates. In that context it was capable of meaning no more. Lord Steyn added (at page 1123) that:

> it is of course true that if there is an appeal, the Court of Appeal may have to take account of the fact that a judge has decided to treat an acceptance of an allegation in a prosecution statement as conclusive and the Court of Appeal may have to give proper and due weight to the consideration.

10.171 Appeals in confiscation matters are considered more fully in Chapter 24 at paras 24.50–24.61.

11

PREPARING FOR CONFISCATION HEARINGS UNDER THE CJA

A. Introduction		11.01
(1) The purpose of CJA confiscation hearings		11.01
B. Preparing for CJA Confiscation Hearings		11.05
(1) When does the CJA apply?		11.05
(2) Preliminary matters		11.07
(3) When may a CJA confiscation hearing be held?		11.08
C. Offences of a Relevant Description		11.09
(1) Relevant criminal conduct		11.11
(2) When does a defendant benefit from an offence?		11.12
(3) The standard of proof		11.13
(4) The burden of proof		11.15
(5) The requirement to give notice		11.18
(6) Failure to give notice under the CJA		11.20
(7) Court may still proceed		11.23
(8) Qualifying offences under section 72AA		11.24
(9) The problem of victims		11.28
(10) The jurisdiction of the Crown Court following committal		11.30
(11) Offences where the CJA 1988 applies in the magistrates' court		11.32
D. Postponement of the Proceedings		11.33
(1) More than one postponement allowable		11.38
(2) What constitutes exceptional circumstances?		11.39
(3) Considerations to be applied when postponing confiscation hearings		11.44
(4) Postponement runs from date of conviction		11.48
(5) Postponement pending appeal		11.49
(6) Sentence pending CJA hearing		11.52
E. Section 73 Prosecutor's Statements		11.55
(1) Form and content of the statement		11.59
(2) Service of the statement		11.62
(3) The defendant's statement		11.63
(4) Importance of the defendant's reply		11.69
(5) Defendant's acceptance conclusive		11.71
(6) Obtaining information from the defendant 'at any time'		11.73
(7) Prosecutor's acceptance conclusive		11.76
(8) Consequences of the defendant failing to respond to the prosecutor's statement		11.78
(9) Further statements by the prosecutor		11.79
(10) Securing the attendance of witnesses		11.80
(11) Relationship between disclosure statements and confiscation hearings		11.81
(12) The risk of self incrimination		11.82

A. Introduction

(1) The purpose of CJA confiscation hearings

In *Sekhon v R* [2002] EWCA Crim 2954, [2003] 3 All ER 508, the then Lord Chief Justice considered the evolving history of the CJA and confiscation law, concluding that one of the most successful weapons that can be used to discourage offences that are committed in order to enrich offenders is to ensure that if the offenders are brought to justice any profit which they have made from their offending is confiscated. **11.01**

11.02 The Hodgson committee report, 'The Profits of Crime and their Recovery, Howard League for Penal Reform, 1984' made a number of recommendations which form the background of the confiscation provisions in the Criminal Justice Act 1988. The report recommended the repeal of the Criminal Bankruptcy Order and its replacement with confiscation and sentences in default, designed to catch the profits of major crime. Following these recommendations, a confiscation regime was introduced in relation to drug trafficking under the guise of the Drug Trafficking Offences Act 1986 (DTOA). As well as including the powers of restraint and confiscation, that Act also contained a statutory assumption to the effect that a drug trafficker's assets were the proceeds of crime and therefore liable to confiscation. The CJA 1988 introduced a new power to make a confiscation order in the case of certain crimes other than drug trafficking offences.

11.03 The former Lord Chief Justice noted in *Sekhon* that the confiscation provisions of the CJA, as originally enacted, applied mainly to offenders in the Crown Court and only in cases where the defendant had benefited by at least £10,000 from the offence (the 'old' s 71). In such cases the maximum amount of the confiscation order was the amount of the benefit or the extent of the realisable property, whichever was the lesser. The procedure for making a confiscation order involved the prosecution serving a notice (s 72) and, thereafter, was subject to a procedure requiring further statements and counter statements to establish the extent of the defendant's benefit (s 73).

11.04 Part III of the Criminal Justice Act 1993 made significant changes to Part VI of the CJA 1988. The principal changes were twofold:

(1) The standard of proof required to determine any question as to whether a person had benefited, and whether his benefit was at least the minimum amount, together with the amount to be recovered, was to be that applicable in civil proceedings (s 71(7A) of the 1988 Act as inserted by s 27 of the Criminal Justice Act 1993);
(2) The court was given the power to postpone a determination of the amount which might be recovered until after the court had sentenced the defendant (s 72A of the 1988 Act as inserted by s 28 of the Criminal Justice Act 1993).

B. Preparing for CJA Confiscation Hearings

(1) When does the CJA apply?

11.05 Under the Proceeds of Crime Act 2002 (Commencement No. 5, Transitional Provisions, Savings and Amendment) Order 2003, SI 2003/333, POCA 2002 applies where the offence or offences were committed on or after 23 March 2003. For cases where the indictment starts before that date the CJA or DTA will still apply. In effect, therefore, for at least a few years to come the three Acts, and their differing regimes, will live side by side with each other. The practical effect of this is that the criminal practitioner will continue to have to be alive to the issues and machinations of the CJA and the DTA, as well as POCA.

11.06 It should be noted that this chapter deals with the CJA as amended by the CJA 1993 and POCA 1995. If proceedings for the offences were commenced before 3 February 1995, then the CJA 1988 unamended applies, as neither the CJA 1993 nor the provisions of POCA 1995 have effect. Similarly, if an offence was committed before 1 November 1995 but the criminal proceedings against the defendant were not commenced until after 3 February 1995 then the CJA as amended by the CJA 1993 applies, but POCA 1995 is not applicable. However, if all the offences which the offender is charged with were carried out after 1 November 1995 then the CJA 1988 as amended by the CJA 1993 and POCA 1995 applies. (See SI 1995/43; and s 78(6) CJA 1993 as amended by the Criminal Justice and Public Order Act 1994 Sch 9 para 53; and SI 1995/2650).

(2) Preliminary matters

Section 71(1) of the CJA reads as follows: **11.07**

(1) Where an offender is convicted, in any proceedings before a Crown Court or Magistrates' Court, of an offence of a relevant description, it shall be the duty of the Court—
   (a) if the Prosecutor has given written notice to the Court that he considers that it would be appropriate for the Court to proceed under this section, or
   (b) if the Court considers, even though it has not been given such notice, that it would be appropriate for it so to proceed,
to act as follows before sentencing or otherwise dealing with the offence, in respect of that offence or any other criminal conduct.
(1A) The Court shall first determine whether the Defendant has benefited from any relevant criminal conduct.
(1B) Subject to subsection (1C) below, if the Court determines that the offender has benefited from any criminal conduct, it shall then—
      (a) determine in accordance with subs (6) below the amount to be recovered in his case by virtue of this section, and
      (b) make an order under this section ordering the Defendant to pay that amount.
(1C) [Para 11.28 below]...
(1D) [Para 11.11 below]...
(6) Subject to subsection (1C) above the sum which an order made by a Court under this section requires an offender to pay shall be equal to—
   (a) the benefit in respect of which it is made; or
   (b) the amount appearing to the Court to be the amount that might be real-ised at the time the order is made, whichever is the less.

(3) When may a CJA confiscation hearing be held?

A CJA hearing may be held in the Crown Court whenever a defendant has been convicted of an offence of a relevant description or an indictable offence other than a drug trafficking offence (see ss 71(1) and 71(9)(c)(ii) of the CJA 1988). CJA hearings may also be held in the magistrates' court where a defendant has been convicted of an offence listed in Sch 4 to the Act (see s 71(9)(c)(i) and para 11.32 below). **11.08**

C. Offences of a Relevant Description

Under s 71(1) the offender must be convicted of an offence of a 'relevant description' before a confiscation hearing may be held. Section 71(1E) specifies what offences are of a 'relevant description', namely: an offence for which a person is convicted in any proceedings before the Crown Court or which is or will be taken into consideration by the Crown Court in determining any sentence, providing it is an offence to which the CJA applies. Offences that apply to the CJA are all indictable offences, other than drug trafficking offences (see s 71(9)(c)(ii) of the CJA). **11.09**

11.10 In the case of an offence where the person is convicted before a magistrates' court (or which has been taken into consideration by a magistrates' court in determining any sentence), the CJA applies if it is an offence listed under Sch 4 to the CJA (offences listed under Sch 4 relate mainly to summary only offences—see para 11.32 below).

(1) Relevant criminal conduct

11.11 In this part of the CJA 'relevant criminal conduct', means:

(1D)... that offence taken together with any other offences of a relevant description which are either (a) offences of which he is convicted in the same proceedings, or (b) offences which the court will be taking into consideration in determining his sentence for the offence in question.
(See s 71(1D), and subject to s 72AA(6).)

(2) When does a defendant benefit from an offence?

11.12 Under s 71(4) for the purposes of confiscation orders:

a person benefits from an offence if he obtains property as a result of or in connection with its commission and his benefit is the value of the property so obtained.

(3) The standard of proof

11.13 The standard of proof required to determine any question arising under the CJA in relation to confiscation proceedings is that applicable in civil proceedings (see s 71(7A)).

11.14 The civil standard of proof is the balance of probabilities. However it should be remembered that in civil cases the degree of probability required to establish proof may vary according to the allegation to be proved (see *Hornal v Neuberger Products Ltd* [1957] 1 QB 247) and the court may be reluctant, when considering claims by the Crown, to apply merely a 51/49 per cent test where an individual's property or other asset is in jeopardy.

(4) The burden of proof

11.15 In *R v Barwick* (2001) 1 Cr App R(S) 129 the Court of Appeal held that in confiscation proceedings under the CJA it was for the prosecution to establish that the defendant benefited from an offence and the value of that benefit. Once that had been established, it was for the offender to prove, on a balance of probabilities, that the amount that might be realised is less than the value of his calculated benefit (see also *R v Layode* (CA, 12 March 1993) and *R v Ilsemann* 12 Cr App R(S) 398).

11.16 In *R v Carroll* [1991] Crim LR 720, the Court confirmed the principal established in *Ilsemann*, that once the prosecution has established that the defendant had benefited from the offence, in that case drug trafficking, and the value of his proceeds, it is for the defendant to satisfy the court that the amount that might be realised is less than the amount which the court has assessed as the value of his proceeds. If the defendant fails to satisfy the court of this, the confiscation order should be for the amount that has been assessed as the value of the defendant's proceeds.

11.17 In *Silcock v Levin* [2004] EWCA Crim 408, the Court of Appeal stated that the civil procedure was the correct approach to rules of evidence in confiscation proceedings.

C. Offences of a Relevant Description

(5) The requirement to give notice

11.18 Section 72AA states:

(1) This Section applies in a case where an offender is convicted, in any proceedings before the Crown Court or a Magistrates' Court, of a qualifying offence which is an offence of a relevant description, if—
   (a) the Prosecutor gives written notice for the purposes of subsection 1(a) of Section 71 above;
   (b) that notice contains a declaration that it is the Prosecutor's opinion that the case is one in which it is appropriate for the provisions of this section to be applied; and
   (c) the offender—
      (i) is convicted in those proceedings of at least two qualifying offences (including the offence in question); or
      (ii) has been convicted of a qualifying offence on at least one previous occasion during the relevant period.

11.19 There appears to be no requirement as to how long in advance of the hearing the notice must be served and it seems the notice provisions would be complied with if the prosecutor only gave notice on the day of the hearing, although it has to be written notice. Nor does there appear to be any requirement that a copy of the notice should be served on the defendant or his solicitors, although as a matter of good practice a copy of the notice should always be served on the defence.

(6) Failure to give notice under the CJA

11.20 In *R v Palmer* [2002] EWCA Crim 2202 a confiscation order was made in the sum of £33,243,812.46. The Court of Appeal quashed that confiscation order. Two notices under s 72 had been served by the prosecution. The Court of Appeal held that the first notice was invalid due to deficiencies and an inaccuracy on the notice (it referred to the wrong section), notwithstanding the fact that 'in substance everyone knew where they were going'. The second notice was served after the confiscation proceedings had commenced and therefore could not cure the absence of an effective notice at the outset. The consequence was that it was not possible for the trial court to postpone the confiscation proceedings and proceed to sentence. In *Sekhon* [2002] EWCA Crim 2954 the Court of Appeal held that it was difficult to conclude that Parliament had intended that technical failures of this sort should effect the jurisdiction of the court to make a confiscation order (the first notice in *Palmer* referred to the amended s 71(1)(a) when it should have referred to s 72(1)). In *Sekhon* the Court held that *Palmer* was per incuriam, wrongly decided, and should not be followed (see also now *R v Simpson* The Times, 26 May 2003 confirming the decision in *Sekhon* and *R v Clayton* The Times, 11 April 2003, where the Court of Appeal held a misdescription of the statutory basis underlying the proceedings on the prosecutor's notice would not deprive the Crown Court of its jurisdiction to proceed).

11.21 This decision was confirmed in the House fo Lords case of *R v Knights* [2005] 3 WLR 330, where Lord Brown stated:

> Can it seriously be said that the ineptness of the drafting [of the notices] invalidated all that followed? In my judgement, plainly not. In the first place it should be noted that, even without an effective notice from the prosecutor, the court would have been under a duty to proceed with confiscation proceedings had it considered them, as plainly it did, appropriate. Furthermore, now that the Court of Appeal's decsion in *R v Palmer* has been held to be wrongly decided . . . the present argument becomes more hopeless still.

11.22 As a result the House concluded that non-compliance with the strict requirements of the legislation does not disable the court from making confiscation orders.

(7) Court may still proceed

11.23 Where the court considers that the defendant has benefited from the offence charged it should still consider whether or not it would be appropriate to proceed with a confiscation hearing, even though it may not have been given notice by the prosecutor (see s 71(1)(b)) (a previous requirement that there be a minimum benefit of £10,000 before the court embarked on a CJA confiscation hearing was repealed by POCA 1995). (See *R v Nwangoro* [2006] EWCA Crim 3061.)

(8) Qualifying offences under section 72AA

11.24 Section 72 AA (2) states:

In this Section qualifying offence . . . means any offence in relation to which all the following conditions are satisfied, that is to say—
(a) it is an offence to which this part of the Act applies;
(b) it is an offence which was committed after the commencement of Section 2 of the Proceeds of Crime Act 1995; and
(c) that the Court is satisfied it is an offence from which the Defendant has benefited.

11.25 Offences to which this part of the Act applies are set out at s 71(9)(c) of the CJA, namely offences listed in Schedule 4 (see para 11.32 below) and indictable offences (other than drug trafficking offences). Section 2 of POCA 1995 commenced on 1 November 1995.

11.26 Where a defendant has committed two qualifying offences then the prosecution may invite the court to apply the statutory assumptions, provided that they have given notice in writing that in the prosecution's opinion it is appropriate for the provisions of s 72AA to be applied.

11.27 In *R v Wilkes* [2003] EWCA Crim 848, the Court of Appeal held that s 72(AA) of the CJA 1988 was triggered by the commission of qualifying offences and that the success or otherwise of those offences was irrelevant. Once the section had been triggered the property should be confiscated and it need not be referable to any particular piece of criminality or a successful outcome of the triggered offences.

(9) The problem of victims

11.28 Drug trafficking offences are victimless to the extent that no third party suffers a pecuniary loss as a result of the offence. The same cannot be said, however, of offences to which the CJA applies, where frequently an innocent third party has suffered loss, eg householders and insurance companies in burglary cases, building societies in mortgage fraud cases, HM Revenue and Customs in VAT and income tax frauds etc. The legislation dictates that it would be wrong for the defendant to have to meet a CJA confiscation order in the amount of his benefit from the offence and also face a civil claim from the victim for the loss suffered as a result of the offence. Accordingly, s 71(1C) of the CJA provides as follows:

(1C) If, in a case falling within subsection (1B) above, the Court is satisfied that a victim of any relevant criminal conduct has instituted, or intends to institute civil proceedings against the Defendant in respect of loss, injury or damage sustained in connection with that conduct—
(a) the Court shall have power, instead of a duty, to make an order under this section;

C. Offences of a Relevant Description

(b) subsection (6) below shall not apply for determining the amount to be recovered in that case by virtue of this section; and

(c) where the Court makes an order in exercise of that power, the sum required to be paid under that order shall be of such amount, not exceeding the amount which (but for paragraph (b) above) would apply by virtue of subsection (6) below as the Court sees fit.

11.29 In the above circumstances therefore the court shall have a discretion as to whether or not it proceeds to make an order under the CJA where an outstanding civil claim from a victim exists. If, for example, it transpires that a building society which has suffered loss as a result of a mortgage fraud has instituted civil proceedings against the defendant in which it is seeking the recovery of a sum equating to the benefit the defendant has derived from the offence, the court may form the view that it would not be proper to make a confiscation order against the defendant because of the element of double jeopardy involved.

(10) The jurisdiction of the Crown Court following committal

11.30 The jurisdiction of the Crown Court following committal from the magistrates' court, has been considered by both the Court of Appeal and the House of Lords in *R v Pope* [2002] 1 Crim LR 196. The defendant had pleaded guilty in the magistrates' court to offences relating to the procuring of valuable security by deception. It was alleged that he had diverted about £220,000 from his employers into his own bank account. The magistrates' court committed the defendant to the Crown Court for sentence, pursuant to s 38 of the Magistrates' Court Act 1980. The Crown Court sentenced him to a term of imprisonment and also imposed a confiscation order in the sum of £127,000. He appealed against the confiscation order on the grounds that the Crown Court had exceeded its jurisdiction. The Court of Appeal allowed the appeal and quashed the confiscation order on the grounds it was bound by a previous decision of the Court of Appeal and stated that a lacuna in the law had been created by the introduction of s 71(1E) of the CJA and until that lacuna was removed (which it was in September 1988 by the introduction of 71(9A)), when a defendant who had pleaded guilty in a magistrates' court was committed for sentence to the Crown Court, he could not be treated as if he had been convicted in the Crown Court and therefore the Crown Court had no power to make a confiscation order in respect of offences committed during that period.

11.31 The House of Lords overruled the Court of Appeal. They held that the purpose of s 38 of the 1980 Act was to enable the question of guilt in a case which was triable either way to be settled in the magistrates' court, but then to ensure that where the magistrates' court did not have the power to impose a sentence which adequately reflected the gravity of the offences, the question of sentence could be dealt with by the Crown Court. The words of s 42 of the Powers of Criminal Courts Act 1973 were clear and unambiguous and were not qualified by s 71 of the 1988 Act as originally enacted by the introduction of subs (1E). There was therefore no lacuna in the powers of the Crown Court to make confiscation orders, and it had throughout the power under s 42 to deal with an offender as if he had just been committed on indictment before the Crown Court. The Crown Court had an indictment from the Crown and accordingly the Crown Court had not exceeded its jurisdiction in making the confiscation order against the defendant (overruling *R v Whellen* (2000) 1 Cr App R(S) 200).

(11) Offences where the CJA 1988 applies in the magistrates' court

11.32 In the magistrates' court an offence is an offence of a 'relevant description' in cases where either the defendant is convicted in proceedings before the Magistrates' Court, or alternatively where an offence is or will be taken into consideration by a magistrates' court, providing in both cases that it is an offence listed in Schedule 4 of the Act (s 71(1E)(b)). Under Sch 4 the offences listed are:

(1) offences related to sex establishments contrary to the Local Government (Miscellaneous Provisions) Act 1982, Sch 3 paras 20 and 21;
(2) supplying a video recording of an unclassified work and possession of a video recording of an unclassified work for the purposes of supply, contrary to ss 9 and 10 of the Video Recordings Act 1984;
(3) use of unlicensed premises for exhibition which requires a licence contrary to s 10(1)(a) of the Cinemas Act 1985;
(4) use of places for dancing or entertainment;
(5) trade marks offences contrary to s 92(1), (2), and (3) of the Trade Marks Act 1994; and
(6) copyright offences contrary to s 107(1), (2), and (3) and s 198(1) or (2) of the Copyright, Designs and Patents Act 1988.

D. Postponement of the Proceedings

11.33 Section 72A(1) states:

Where a Court is acting under Section 71 above but considers it requires further information before—
(a) determining whether the Defendant has benefited from any relevant criminal conduct; or
(b) (repealed by PCA 1995 Schedule 1 paragraph 2);
(c) determining the amount to be recovered in the case,
it may, for the purpose of enabling that information to be obtained, postpone making that determination for such period as it may specify.

There will be many instances where the Crown will not be in a position to proceed with a CJA hearing immediately after conviction. The defendant, too, may require further time to prepare his case. Before s 28 of the CJA 1993, which introduced s 72A, the courts had met this problem by adjourning cases using their inherent jurisdiction to regulate their own proceedings. Section 72A(l) empowers the court to postpone making determinations under the Act when it considers it requires further information before determining any one or more of the following issues:
(1) whether the defendant has benefited from the offences;
(2) whether his benefit is at least the minimum amount; and
(3) the amount to be recovered in his case.

11.34 In *R v Soneji* [2005] 3 WLR 303, the House of Lords held that where a court was acting in accordance with its duty under s 71(1) of the CJA (considering whether to make a confiscation order) and where it had postponed proceedings under s 72A(1) but had not done so to a date which was more than six months from the date of conviction, the approach in determining whether the confiscation order was valid should be based on posing

D. Postponement of the Proceedings

the question whether Parliament could fairly be taken to have intended total invalidity, with reference to *A-G's Reference (No.3 of 1999)* [2001] 2 AC 91. The House of Lords found that the requirement of exceptional circumstances in s 72A(3) was not to be strictly construed, eg listing difficulties might amount to exceptional circumstances. Parliament could not have intended to disable the court from making a confiscation order after sentence merely because the time limits were not strictly adhered to. The House of Lords held that the time limits should not be ignored and any question of unfairness to the defendant was more properly considered under the abuse of process jurisdiction. The Court also held that there was no common law jurisdiction existing in parallel to the statutory jurisdiction to postpone the proceedings clearing up an issue which had for some time caused some uncertainty. For a commentary on *R v Soneji* see CLW/05/28/9.

In *R v Knights* (HL, 21 July 2005) the House of Lords held (applying the approach in *R v Soneji*, that Parliament would not have intended that a failure by a court to specify a period of postponement, when making an order for the postponement of confiscation proceedings under s 72A of the CJA, should disable the court from discharging its duty to complete the confiscation proceedings against the offender. It found that when postponing the proceedings, although a judge was required to specify the period of the postponement and not to simply adjourn the proceedings generally, he was not bound to specify the date when the substantive hearing was to begin and end. It is only in circumstances where the timetable being set makes it likely that the six month time limit will ultimately be exceeded that the court must, on the first postponement, address itself to the question as to whether exceptional circumstances exist to justify the directions proposed. **11.35**

In *R v Ashton, Draz and O'Reilly* The Times, 18 April 2006 the Court of Appeal held that whenever a court is confronted by a failure to take a required procedural step, unless it is clear that Parliament's intention is that the court's jurisdiction is removed in that particular situation, it should proceed to decide whether to allow the proceedings to continue having made a wide assessment of the interests of justice, with particular focus on whether there was a real possibility that the prosecution of the defendant may suffer prejudice (as per *R v Soneji*). For a full commentary on this case see CLW/06/15/9. **11.36**

The law in relation to the power to postpone, and the fact that procedural irregularities will no longer lead to confiscation orders being quashed, is further considered in detail at paras 9.12 eg seq of Chapter 9. **11.37**

(1) More than one postponement allowable

Under s 72A(2) more than one postponement may be made under subs (1) above in relation to the same case. However, under s 72A(3), unless there are exceptional circumstances, the court may not postpone the confiscation proceedings beyond six months: **11.38**

(3) Unless it is satisfied there are exceptional circumstances the Court shall not specify a period under subsection (1) above which—
 (a) by itself; or
 (b) where there have been one or more previous postponements under subsection (1) above or (4) below,

when taken together with the earlier specified period or periods, exceeds six months with the date of conviction. (See para 9.17 of Chapter 9.)

(2) What constitutes exceptional circumstances?

11.39 In *R v Jagdev* [2002] 1 WLR 3017 the Court held that the purpose of the power to postpone confiscation proceedings was to enable the judge to reach a fair conclusion on the confiscation issue; and that where there was a real prospect the hearing might have been wasted and an unjust order made if the judge had proceeded to hear the case (in *Jagdev* because of an awaited decision of the Court of Appeal), then the judge was entitled to hold, where 'further information' was required, that there were exceptional circumstances.

11.40 In *R v Cole* The Independent, 30 April 30 1998 (CA), the trial judge had become ill after a difficult and complex trial. The issue was whether this constituted exceptional circumstances. Judge LJ stated:

> The judgement whether circumstances are exceptional or not must be made by the Court considering whether to make a confiscation order, and the decision must be made before the six month period has elapsed . . . here the Judge was in hospital on the date when he had indicated that he would determine the confiscation issue . . . Having studied the statutory code we do not consider that it was intended or drafted so as to preclude the Listing Officer making sensible arrangements for the conduct of the Crown Court business, normally after discussion with the Trial Judge or the Resident Judge.

11.41 In *R v Steele and Shevki* [2001] 2 Cr App R(S) 40; [2001] Crim LR 153 Judge LJ returned to this subject and stated:

> unless the circumstances are exceptional they should not extend beyond six months after conviction. These decisions involved the Courts discretion, judicially exercised when the statutory conditions are present, taking full account of the preferred statutory sequence as well as the express directions in the statute that save in exceptional circumstances confiscation determinations should not be postponed for more than six months after conviction. . . For example, to take account of illness on one side or the other, or the unavailability of the Judge, without depriving a subsequent order for confiscation of its validity.

11.42 The position was further confirmed in *R v Young* [2003] EWCA Crim 3481, where the Court of Appeal held that difficulties in listing cases were capable of amounting to exceptional circumstances that justified the postponement of a determination beyond the six month period laid down by s 72(A)(3) of the Criminal Justice Act 1988; and in *Sekhon* where the Court of Appeal held that the decision as to whether to postpone and as to whether exceptional circumstances existed involved the consideration of the same types of issues that courts were regularly required to determine when engaged in case management and that the strict compliance with procedural requirements relating to issues of that nature would not normally be expected to go to jurisdiction.

11.43 The meaning of 'exceptional circumstances' is further discussed in Chapter 9, para 9.17.

(3) Considerations to be applied when postponing confiscation hearings

11.44 The difficult, at times unpredictable, case law history concerning the jurisdiction and manner in which confiscation hearings could be postponed has already been considered at para 9.38 of Chapter 9.

D. Postponement of the Proceedings

11.45 In *Sekhon v R* [2002] EWCA Crim 2954, [2003] 3 All ER 508, the Lord Chief Justice held that Parliament had not intended that the setting of a period of postponement was a condition precedent to the court's jurisdiction, particularly if it meant that the court lost its jurisdiction because of a failure to specify a date for the matter to return to court. The Court was of the opinion that all that is strictly required in order to give the court jurisdiction where a postponement is necessary is that there should be a decision to postpone (para 48). This requires no particular form of words, they held.

11.46 In *Sekhon* the Court also confirmed that it would not have been the intention of Parliament to exclude the jurisdiction of the court in relation to the making of confiscation orders because of procedural defects of a technical nature that caused no injustice to the defendant. It drew attention to the most recent legislation namely s 14(11) of POCA which provides:

A confiscation order must not be quashed only on the ground that there was a defect or omission in the procedure connected with the application for or the granting of a postponement'. The Court expected in future a procedural failure only to result in a lack of jurisdiction if this was necessary to ensure that the criminal justice system served the interests of justice and thus the public, or where there was at least a real possibility of the defendant suffering prejudice as a result of the procedural failure (para 29).

11.47 For further consideration of this area see para 9.43 of Chapter 9.

(4) Postponement runs from date of conviction

11.48 In *Sekhon* the Court of Appeal confirmed that the power to postpone a confiscation hearing for six months runs from the date of conviction and not the date of sentence.

(5) Postponement pending appeal

11.49 Section 72A (4) of the CJA states:

(4) Where the Defendant appeals against his conviction, the Court may, on that account—
  (a) postpone making any of the determinations mentioned in subsubsection (1) above for such period as it may specify; or
  (b) where it has already exercised its powers under this section to postpone, extend the specified period.
(5) The postponement or extension under subsection (1) or (4) above may be made—
  (a) on application by the Defendant or the Prosecutor; or
  (b) by the Court of its own motion.
(6) Unless the Court is satisfied there are exceptional circumstances, any postponement or extension under subsection (4) above shall not exceed the period ending three months after the date on which the appeal is determined or otherwise disposed of.
(7) Where the Court exercises its power under subsection (1) or (4) above, it may nevertheless proceed to sentence, or otherwise deal with the Defendant in respect of the offence or any offences concerned.

11.50 Section 72A(4) empowers the court to postpone the confiscation hearing pending the determination of an appeal against conviction. Except where there are 'exceptional circumstances' (see para 11.39 above), s 72A(6) restricts the period of postponement to a maximum period of three months after the determination of the appeal. Section 72A(5) provides that postponements under both s 72A(l) and (4) may be granted on the application of the prosecutor or defendant or by the court of its own motion.

11.51 See r 56.2(1)(b) of the Criminal Procedure Rules for the appropriate procedure and para 9.47 of Chapter 9. A similar provision is made for the magistrates' court under s 72A(5)(a) of the CJA by r 56.2(1)(a) of the Criminal Procedure Rules.

(6) Sentence pending CJA hearing

11.52 Section 72A(7) (above) provides that the court may proceed to sentence the defendant, notwithstanding there being a postponed confiscation hearing either while further information is sought or pending the determination of an appeal.

11.53 However, if the court sentences the defendant before the confiscation hearing, it may not impose a financial penalty. Section 72A(9) states:

In sentencing, or otherwise dealing with, the Defendant in respect of the offence, or any of the offences, concerned at any time during the specified period, the Court shall not—
(a) impose any fine on him; or
(b) make any such order as is mentioned in Section 72(5)(b) or (c).

This is because of the stipulation in s 72(5) which provides:
(5) Where a Court makes a confiscation order against a Defendant in any proceedings, it shall be its duty, in respect of any offence of which that Defendant is convicted in those proceedings, to take account of the confiscation order before
  (a) imposing any fine on him;
  (b) making any order involving any payment by him other than an order under Section 130 of the Powers of Criminal Courts (Sentencing) Act 2000 (compensation orders),
  (c) making any order under
    (i) Section 27 of the Misuse of Drugs Act 1971 (Forfeiture Orders); or
    (ii) Section 143 of the Powers of Criminal Courts (Sentencing) Act 2000 (Deprivation Orders).

11.54 If the court decides to sentence the defendant prior to the confiscation hearing, once the confiscation hearing has been made the court may vary the original sentence by imposing a financial penalty, see s 72A(9A). (It will be noted that it is not always desirable to pass sentence prior to the confiscation proceedings being resolved, particulalry if further relevant information is likely to surface during the course of the confiscation proceedings. On the other hand, it is equally undesirable to leave a defendant not knowing his fate in relation to the substantive offence for a prolonged period.)

E. Section 73 Prosecutor's Statements

11.55 The CJA has similar provisions to the DTA for the submission of statements by the parties dealing with the determination of matters relevant to the CJA enquiry, see paras 9.55 et seq of Chapter 9. The relevant provisions are found in s 73 of the CJA:

(1) Subsection 1(A) below applies in a case where a person has been convicted of an offence of a relevant description if—
  (a) the Prosecutor has given written notice to the Court for the purposes of subsection 1(a) of Section 71 above; or
  (b) the Court is proceeding in pursuance of subsection (1)(b) of that section and requires a statement under this section from the Prosecutor.

E. Section 73 Prosecutor's Statements

(1A) Where this subsection applies, the Prosecutor shall, within such period as the Court may direct, tender to the Court a statement as to any matters relevant—
    (a) to determining whether the Defendant has benefited from any relevant criminal conduct; or
    (b) to an assessment of the value of the Defendant's benefit from that conduct;
and, where such a statement is tendered in a case in which a declaration has been made for the purposes of subsection (1)(b) of Section 72AA above, that statement shall also set out all such information available to the Pros-ecutor as may be relevant for the purposes of subsections (4) and (5)(b) or (c) of that section.

(1B) Where a statement is tendered to the Court under this section—
    (a) the Prosecutor may at any time tender to the Court a further statement as to the matters mentioned in subsection (1A) above; and
    (b) the Court may at any time require the prosecutor to tender a further such statement within such period as it may direct.

(1C) Where
    (a) any statement has been tendered to any Court by the Prosecutor under this section and
    (b) the Defendant accepts to any extent any allegation in the statement,
the Court may for the purposes of determining whether the Defendant has benefited from any relevant criminal conduct or of assessing the value of the Defendant's benefit from such conduct, treat his acceptance as conclusive of the matters to which it relates.

11.56 In most cases the CJA confiscation machinery is initiated by the prosecutor giving notice under s 73(1); cases where the prosecutor does not then serve a statement under s 73 are very rare indeed.

11.57 The Court of Appeal, considered the purpose of s 73 statements in *R v Benjafield* (2001) 2 Cr App R(S) 221 para 107. In finding that such statements did not contravene Article 6 of the European Convention of Human Rights they held that:

> A statement serves a useful purpose by forewarning the Defendant of the case . . . . which he will have to meet as to his assets. It should assist the Defendant by making it clear the matters with which he has to be prepared to deal. It is right that, as the rules require, the prosecution should identify any information which would assist the Defendant.

11.58 The purpose of the prosecutor's statement is further considered at para 9.57 et seq. of Chapter 9.

(1) Form and content of the statement

11.59 The form and content of the s 73 statement is dealt with by Rules 56.1 and 56.2 of the Criminal Procedure Rules which provide that the statement, whether tendered by the prosecutor or defendant shall include the following details:
    (a) the name of the defendant;
    (b) the name of the person by whom the statement is made and the date on which it was made;
    (c) where the statement is not tendered immediately after the defendant has been convicted, the date on which and the place where the relevant conviction occurred; and
    (d) such information known to the prosecutor as is relevant to the determination as to whether or not the defendant has benefited from drug trafficking or relevant criminal conduct and to the assessment of the value of his proceeds of drug trafficking or, as the case may be, benefit from relevant criminal conduct.
(3) Where, in accordance with [section 11(7) of the 1994 Act] or section 73(1C) of the 1988 Act, the defendant indicates the extent to which he accepts any allegation contained within the prosecutor's

statement, if he indicates the same in writing to the prosecutor, he must serve a copy of that reply on the court officer.

(4) Expressions used in this rule shall have the same meanings as in the 1994 Act or, where appropriate, the 1988 Act.

11.60 As with s 11 DTA statements (see Chapter 9, para 9.63 for what in practice is included in prosecutor's statements), the purpose of s 73 statements is very similar to that served by pleadings in civil cases. Accordingly, the prosecutor's statement should set out all matters upon which he wishes to rely in support of the confiscation order sought, and the rules apply equally to both the Crown Court and the magistrates' courts. As with DTA cases, in accordance with his general duty of disclosure, the prosecutor should provide a list of the known assets while making it clear that this is not necessarily exhaustive.

11.61 It will be noted that the relevant provisions of the 1988 (and 1994 Acts) were repealed on 24 March 2003, but they continue to have effect in respect of proceedings for offences committed before that date

(2) Service of the statement

11.62 Exactly the same principles apply for persons upon whom, and the time at which, the s 73 statement should be served as apply to s 11 of the DTA statements (see Chapter 9, para 9.69).

(3) The defendant's statement

11.63 Where the prosecution serves a statement under s 73(1A), and the court is satisfied that a copy of that statement has been served on the defence (see s 73(2)), the court may then require the defendant to indicate to what extent he accepts each allegation in the statement and, so far as he does not accept any such allegation, to indicate any matters he proposes to rely on in rebuttal (as per s 73(2)). Section 73(5) adds:

(5) An allegation may be accepted or a matter indicated for the purposes of this section either—
   (a) orally before the Court; or
   (b) in writing in accordance with the rules of the court.

11.64 The defendant's s 73A statement serves a similar purpose to the defence in a civil action. In practice it should indicate which matters set out in the prosecutor's statement are admitted and which are denied and should also set out any matters relied upon by the defendant. Section 73A makes a provision similar to the DTA for compelling the defendant to respond to the prosecutor's statement, thereby preventing him from mounting an 'ambush' to the Crown's case at the hearing.

11.65 Where a defendant denies or fails to accept any part of the prosecutor's statement in relation to the facts alleged against him or denies that an asset has come from the proceeds of crime, then it is for the Crown to prove to the civil standard, ie the balance of probabilities, that that state of affairs or facts exist.

11.66 In *R v Walbrook and Glasgow* [1994] Crim LR 613, the court ruled that the defendant must produce: 'clear and cogent evidence; vague and generalised assertions unsupported by evidence would rarely if ever be sufficient to discharge the burden on the Defendant'.

E. Section 73 Prosecutor's Statements

11.67 It has to be remembered that at this stage of the proceedings, whether on his guilty plea or by the verdict of the jury, the defendant stands convicted of a criminal offence and may therefore have something of a credibility problem with the court. This is particularly so in cases where the defendant pleaded not guilty and was disbelieved by the jury upon oath.

11.68 Although there is no rule that the defendant cannot rely on facts not pleaded in his statement, if the Crown are taken by surprise by suggestions or an account given for the first time from the witness box, the defendant runs the risk of an adjournment being ordered and his being required to pay costs. This process obviously involves taking careful and detailed instructions from the client and his financial advisers.

(4) Importance of the defendant's reply

11.69 Section 73(3) states that:

(3) If the Defendant fails in any respect to comply with the requirement under subsection (2) above he may be treated for the purposes of this section as accepting every allegation in the statement apart from—
   (a) any allegation in respect of which he has complied with the requirement; and
   (b) any allegation that he has benefited from an offence or that any property was obtained by him as a result of or in connection with the commission of an offence.

11.70 It is submitted that the remarks of the Court of Appeal in *R v Comiskey* (1991) 93 Cr App R 227, in relation to the desirability of requiring the defendant to respond to s 11 DTA statements (in which the court ruled that once the amount of the benefit was determined, a confiscation order must be made in the full amount of that benefit unless the defendant proves that the value of his realisable property is less than that amount) apply with equal force to statements tendered under s 73 of the CJA. Support for this view can be found in the decision of the Court of Appeal in *R v Layode* (CA, 12 March 1993), in which their Lordships, in dismissing an appeal against a CJA confiscation order, observed that the case 'underlines the importance of a defendant submitting evidence'.

(5) Defendant's acceptance conclusive

11.71 The provision in s 11(7) of the DTA that the court may treat any acceptance by the defendant of an allegation contained in the prosecutor's statement as being conclusive is repeated in s 73(1C) of the CJA.

11.72 However, in *R v Emmett* [1997] 3 WLR 1119 the Court of Appeal held, in a DTOA case, that while the Crown Court may treat the defendant's acceptance as conclusive of the matters to which it relates, there was no necessary implication ousting the jurisdiction of the Court of Appeal to consider an appeal even though the defendant had accepted the allegation in the court below. Lord Steyn (at p 1123) went onto hold that:

> it is of course true that if there is an appeal the Court of Appeal may have to take account of the fact that a Judge has decided to treat an acceptance of an allegation in a prosecution statement as conclusive and the Court of Appeal may have to give proper and due weight to the consideration.

For further discussion on this topic see para 10.169 of Chapter 10.

(6) Obtaining information from the defendant 'at any time'

11.73 Section 73A states:
(1) This section applies in a case where a person has been convicted of an offence of a relevant description if—
  (a) the Prosecutor has given written notice to the Court for the purposes of subsection (1)(a) of Section 71 above; or
  (b) the Court is proceeding in pursuance of subsection (1)(b) of that section or is considering whether so to proceed.
(2) For the purpose of obtaining information to assist it in carrying out its functions under this Part of the Act, the Court may at any time order the Defendant to give it such information as may be specified in the Order.
(3) An Order under subsection (2) above may require all, or any specified part, of the required information to be given to the Court in such manner, and before such date, as may be specified in the Order.
(4) ...
(5) If the Defendant fails, without reasonable excuse, to comply with any order under this section, the Court may draw such inference from that failure as it considers appropriate.

11.74 While s 73A(2) provides that the court has the power 'at any time' to order the defendant to provide information, the provision only applies to cases where the defendant has been convicted and the court is proceeding under s 71 (s 73A(1)).

11.75 Where a defendant fails, without reasonable excuse, to comply with the court's order under s 73A(2) the court may draw such inferences from that failure as it deems appropriate (s 73A(5)).

(7) Prosecutor's acceptance conclusive

11.76 Section 73A(6) states:
Where the Prosecutor accepts to any extent any allegation made by the Defendant:
  (a) in giving to the Court information required by an Order under this section, or
  (b) in any other statement tendered to the Court for the purposes of this part of the Act,
the Court may treat that acceptance as conclusive of the matters to which it relates.

11.77 It should be noted that under s 73A(6) where the prosecutor accepts to any extent any allegation made by the defendant, the court may treat the acceptance by the prosecution as conclusive of the matters to which it relates. That does not mean to say that the Crown Court has to accept any agreement reached by the prosecution (*R v Atkinson* (1993) 14 Cr App R(S) 182), though most do.

(8) Consequences of the defendant failing to respond to the prosecutor's statement

11.78 If the defendant fails properly to comply with the court's order under s 73(2), he may be treated as having accepted every allegation in the statement except any allegation in respect of which he has complied with the requirement and any allegation that he has benefited from an offence or that any property was obtained by him as a result of or in connection with the commission of an offence: s 73(3) of the CJA.

E. Section 73 Prosecutor's Statements

(9) Further statements by the prosecutor

11.79 Under s 73(1B) the prosecutor may at any time tender to the court a further statement as to the matters set out in the defendant's statement and the court is en titled to order the prosecutor to submit such a statement under subs (1B). The court is entitled to take cognisance of any such statement that the prosecutor may tender of his own motion, pursuant to the court's inherent jurisdiction to regulate its own proceedings.

(10) Securing the attendance of witnesses

11.80 Once the s 73 statements have been served, the parties should advise each other as to which witnesses are required to attend the hearing. It should particularly be borne in mind that many civilian witnesses, especially those employed by financial institutions, may not be prepared to attend court voluntarily. Further, as the financial enquiry is rarely complete by committal, few, if any, of these witnesses will be the subject of witness orders made by the magistrates. In such cases, witness summonses should be sought from the appropriate officer of the Crown Court.

(11) Relationship between disclosure statements and confiscation hearings

11.81 Once the defendant is convicted there is nothing to prevent the Crown from relying upon a witness statement given by the defendant pursuant to a disclosure order made by the High Court in restraint proceedings. Indeed the object of those disclosure orders is to allow the Crown to begin the confiscation investigation at an early stage and to investigate any leads or audit trails as a result. The purpose of the disclosure statement when the restraint order is made is in fact threefold. Firstly, it provides supporting evidence at the confiscation hearing that may take place if the defendant is convicted; secondly, it forms the basis of any contempt application should the defendant fail to disclose an asset which the Crown is later able to prove he possesses. Thirdly, it renders the restraint order effective. (For the purpose of disclosure orders see also Glidewell LJ in *Re O (Restraint Order)* at p 531 and *Re J* [2001] EWHC Admin 713, paras 7 and 31.)

(12) The risk of self incrimination

11.82 The Court of Appeal considered the risk of self incrimination in *Re Thomas (Disclosure Order)* [1992] 4 All ER 814 and held that the disclosure requirement was made subject to a condition that no disclosure made in compliance with the order was to be used as evidence in the prosecution of the offence alleged to have been committed by the person required to make that disclosure. Lord Leggatt held the disclosure of assets did not amount to self-incrimination but merely facilitated an assessment of the amount to be recovered from a defendant who had benefited from drug trafficking while it exposed the defendant to the risk of a confiscation order greater in amount than could be made in the absence of disclosure, it was not self incriminating, because the person did not, by making it, incur punishment (for further on self incrimination and disclosure orders see *Re E and Re H* [2001] EWHC Admin 472 and *Re J* [2001] EWHC Admin 713, Chapter 4 and para 9.81 Chapter 9).

12

THE CJA CONFISCATION HEARING

A. Introduction	12.01	(11) Gifts caught by the Act	12.55
(1) Amendments made by the Proceeds of Crime Act 1995	12.01	(12) Defendant does not have to be able to realise gift	12.58
(2) Purpose	12.02	(13) Distinction between realisable property and gifts	12.61
(3) Procedure leading to CJA confiscation hearing	12.03	(14) Contract services	12.65
(4) Appeal pending	12.04	(15) Determining the amount that might be realised	12.66
(5) When to hold proceedings	12.05	(16) Hidden assets	12.67
B. Jurisdiction to Hold a Confiscation Hearing under the CJA	12.07	(17) Valuing property	12.68
(1) The problem of victims	12.09	D. Realisable Assets	12.69
(2) Purpose of the hearing	12.10	(1) The amount to be recovered	12.69
(3) Burden and standard of proof	12.11	(2) Realisable property	12.70
(4) Prosecution and defence statements	12.17	(3) Assets not restricted to those derived from criminal activity	12.73
(5) Basis of pleas	12.20	(4) Proceeds, not profits	12.76
(6) Multiple defendants and apportionment of benefit	12.23	(5) Inflationary adjustment	12.77
(7) Conspiracies	12.24	(6) The reducing value of property	12.80
C. Benefit	12.25	(7) Costs of sale	12.81
(1) Calculating benefit under the CJA	12.25	(8) Abolition of the £10,000 'minimum amount' requirement	12.82
(2) Relevant criminal conduct	12.26	(9) Imprisonment in default	12.83
(3) Offences of a relevant description	12.29	(10) Serving the default sentence does not extinguish the debt	12.87
(4) Pecuniary advantage	12.31	E. Confiscation Orders and Sentencing for the Offence	12.88
(5) Extended benefit—application of the assumptions	12.44	(1) Time to pay	12.90
(6) When may the assumptions be applied?	12.46	(2) Power to vary sentence	12.91
(7) Qualifying offences	12.47	(3) Prosecution costs	12.93
(8) Relevant period	12.48	(4) Third parties and confiscation law	12.94
(9) The assumptions that can be made	12.49	(5) Unreasonable delay in enforcement	12.95
(10) When the assumptions should not be applied	12.52	(6) Confiscation and the ECHR	12.96

A. Introduction

(1) Amendments made by the Proceeds of Crime Act 1995

12.01 When the CJA 1988 was enacted its provisions were far less draconian than the corresponding provisions in drug trafficking cases. To remedy this POCA 1995 made a number of important changes to the procedures adopted in CJA confiscation hearings commenced after 1 November 1995. The effect was to bring the confiscation procedures under the CJA more into line with those under the DTA (for an analysis of the impact of the amendments made by POCA 1995 to the CJA see *R v Ahmed* (CA, 8 February 2000) and *R v Brown* [2001] EWCA Crim 2761).

(2) Purpose

12.02 In *R v Forte* [2004] EWCA Crim 3188, the Court stated (at para 9):

> It has been argued, in this court and in the House of Lords, that the legislation operates unfairly. The House of Lords has emphasised, in particular in the recent case of *Cadman-Smith* (2002) 2 Cr.App.R (S.) 37, that the legislation has to be considered as having a dual purpose. It is aimed at depriving offenders of the proceeds of their criminal conduct, and it is also an act which has the purpose of punishing convicted offenders in order to deter the commission of further offences so as to reduce the profits available to fund further criminal enterprises. In that respect it is therefore described as penal, or indeed draconian in its operation.

(See also para 10.31 of Chapter 10)

(3) Procedure leading to CJA confiscation hearing

12.03 The practice and procedure for the preparation of a CJA confiscation hearing, including postponements, hearings, and statements, in set out in full within Chapter 11.

(4) Appeal pending

12.04 Section 72A(4) empowers the court to postpone the confiscation hearing pending the determination of an appeal against sentence. Except where there are 'exceptional circumstances', s 72A(6) restricts the period of postponement to a maximum period of three months after the determination of the appeal. Section 75A(5) provides that postponements under both s 72A(1) and (4) may be granted on the application of the prosecutor or defendant or by the court of its own motion. (See r 56.2(1)(b) of the Criminal Procedure Rules for the appropriate procedure and para 9.47 of Chapter 9. A similar provision is made for the magistrates' court under s 72A(5)(a) of the CJA by r 56.2(1)(a) of the Criminal Procedure Rules).

(5) When to hold proceedings

12.05 Section 1(1) of POCA 1995 amended s 71(1) of the CJA to provide that the court *shall* have a duty to hold a confiscation hearing:
  (a) if the prosecutor has given written notice to the court that he considers that it would be appropriate for the court to proceed under this section; or
  (b) if the court considers, even though it has not been given such notice, that it would be appropriate for it so to proceed.

12.06 Holding a CJA hearing, therefore, is no longer discretionary and, if the court considers it appropriate to do so, the court can conduct a hearing notwithstanding the fact that the prosecutor has failed to serve notice under the Act.

B. Jurisdiction to Hold a Confiscation Hearing under the CJA

The way in which the court, the prosecution, and the defence should consider their approach to such a hearing has already been considered in Chapter 11. **12.07**

In summary the main points in terms of jurisdiction are as follows: **12.08**

(1) The defendant must have been convicted before the Crown Court or a magistrates' court of an offence of a 'relevant description' (see s 71(1) and Chapter 11 para 11.09). An offence of a 'relevant description' means an offence to which part VI of the CJA applies (see s 71(1E)(a) and s 71(9), and Chapter 11 para 11.32).
(2) The prosecutor must have given written notice to the court (not the defendant) that he considers that it would be appropriate for the court to proceed (s 71(1)(a)). If the prosecutor is intending to invite the court to make any of the statutory assumptions under s 72AA(4), ie in a case where the defendant has two qualifying offences, the court and the defence should ensure that the prosecutor has included in the written notice a statement that in his opinion the assumptions of s 72AA should be applied.
(3) If this is not complied with the court is entitled to ask the prosecutor whether or not confiscation proceedings have been considered and, notwithstanding the reply, may itself proceed under s 71(1)(b) if it believes it is appropriate to proceed where it believes the offender may have benefited from any relevant criminal conduct (s 71(1)(a)).
(4) Section 71(1) envisages that the court shall consider confiscation proceedings before sentencing the offender, although under s 72A, where a court is acting under s 71 but considers that it requires 'further information' before determining whether the defendant has benefited from any relevant criminal conduct (or to determine the amount to be recovered in the particular case), it may postpone making the determination for such period as it may specify, providing that it does not postpone the hearing beyond six months (see s 72A(3)), unless there are exceptional circumstances (see Chapter 11 para 11.39).
(5) Once the court has postponed the confiscation hearing it may proceed to sentence under s 72A(7). However, having postponed the determination the court is not able to either fine the defendant (see s 72A(9)(a)) or make any compensation, forfeiture, or deprivation order as set out in s 72(5)(b) or (c) (see s 72A(9)(b)).

(1) The problem of victims

Where the court is satisfied that a victim has instituted, or intends to institute, civil proceedings against the defendant in respect of loss, injury, or damage sustained as a result of relevant criminal conduct, the court only has the power, rather than a duty, to make a confiscation order (see s 71(1C) of the CJA (as inserted by s 1(2) of POCA 1995) and see Chapter 11 para 11.28). **12.09**

(2) Purpose of the hearing

The CJA hearing serves a very similar purpose to the DTA enquiry in drug trafficking cases and deals with three distinct issues as follows: **12.10**

(1) whether the defendant has benefited from the offence(s) of which he has been convicted or asked to have taken into consideration;

(2) the amount of that benefit;
(3) the value of the defendant's assets available to meet a confiscation order in the amount of that benefit.

(3) Burden and standard of proof

12.11 The burden of proof rests upon the prosecution to prove (1) and (2) above. In cases which commenced before the CJA 1993 came into force (now few and far between), the standard of proof is the criminal standard, ie proof beyond reasonable doubt. In cases commenced after the 1993 Act came into force, the new s 71(7A) of the CJA 1988 reduces the standard of proof to the civil standard, ie proof on a balance of probabilities.

12.12 It will be remembered that in civil cases the degree of probability required to establish proof may vary according to the allegation to be proved (see *Hornal v Neuberger Products Ltd* [1957] 1 QB 247 and see Chapter 11 para 11.15).

12.13 As to (3), once the amount of the benefit has been determined, the burden shifts to the defendant to establish that the value of his realisable property is less than the amount of the benefit. Again, the standard of proof is proof on a balance of probabilities, see *R v Comiskey* (1991) 93 Cr App R 227.

12.14 In *R v Levin* The Times, 20 February 2004, the Court of Appeal confirmed that the standard of proof to be applied in confiscation proceedings was that of the civil standard. As a result, when making a determination a judge was entitled to take into account both the evidence given at trial and any other information properly obtained either before the trial or thereafter, including evidence inadmissible at trial. The Court held that the corresponding provisions under the CJA had been intended to change the procedural landscape in that:

(1) the standard of proof was now the civil burden;
(2) the court could make far-reaching assumptions;
(3) the court could require the defendant to provide information and could draw inferences from the failure to do so; and
(4) the court might rely on evidence given at trial and any relevant information properly obtained either before the trial or thereafter in order to determine a defendant's benefit and the amount to be recovered.

12.15 The Court held that these changes did and were intended to separate the confiscation proceedings from the criminal proceedings.

12.16 In *R v O'Connell* [2005] All ER (D) 59 the Court of Appeal held that the judge had been entitled to reach the conclusions that he had and his conclusions could not be challenged. The defendant had simply failed to discharge the burden of proof on him to prove his realisable assets. See also para 10.04 of Chapter 10 for further on the burden and standard of proof.

(4) Prosecution and defence statements

12.17 Sections 3 and 4 of POCA 1995 made important amendments to s 73 of the CJA. These amendments have the effect of making the procedures in relation to prosecution and defence statements almost identical to those under the DTA.

B. Jurisdiction to Hold a Confiscation Hearing under the CJA

The steps required by the Act in preparation for a CJA hearing are set out in more detail in Chapter 11. However the key features are as follows: **12.18**

(1) the prosecutor, within such period as the court may direct, tenders a statement dealing with matters relevant to determining whether the defendant has benefited and to an assessment of the value of that benefit. Where s 72AA is relied on, the statement must also set out all information available to the prosecutor that may be relevant for those purposes (s 73(lA));
(2) the prosecutor may at any time tender a further statement under s 73(lA) and the court may at any time require him to do so (s 73(lB));
(3) where the defendant accepts any allegation made in such a statement, the court may, for the purpose of determining whether he has benefited from any relevant criminal conduct or of assessing the value of that benefit, treat his acceptance as conclusive (s 73(1C));
(4) where the prosecutor has given written notice under s 71(1)(a), or the court is proceeding under s 71(1)(b) or is considering whether to so proceed, it may at any time order the defendant to give it such information as it may specify (s 73A(2));
(5) an order under s 73A(2) may require all or part of the required information to be given to the court in such manner and before such date as it may specify (s 73A(3));
(6) if the defendant fails without reasonable excuse to comply with such an order, the court may make such inference from that failure as it considers appropriate (s 73A(5)); and
(7) where the prosecutor accepts to any extent any allegation the defendant makes in such a statement, the court may treat that acceptance as being conclusive (s 73A(6)).

The effect of these provisions is that it is more essential than ever for the defendant to play a full part in the confiscation hearing. If he chooses to play no part or fails to comply with the court's orders to provide information he does so at his peril. It is significant that Parliament has not given the court any power to require the prosecutor to incorporate in his statement details of the realisable property of the defendant that he knows would be available to satisfy a confiscation order. Once the prosecutor has proved the fact of benefit and the amount of that benefit, the burden shifts onto the defendant to establish, if he can, that the value of his realisable assets is insufficient to meet a confiscation order in that amount (*R v Rees* (Plymouth Crown Court, 19 July 1990, Auld J)). **12.19**

(5) Basis of pleas

Care should be taken when drafting and agreeing to basis of pleas, particularly on behalf of the prosecution. **12.20**

In *R v Lunnon* (2005) 1 Cr App R(S) 24, the Court of Appeal quashed a confiscation order where the prosecution had agreed that the appellant had no role in drug trafficking before the rather limited role to which he pleaded guilty, in circumstances where he had not made any money from his drug trafficking role and where the assumptions could not be invoked. **12.21**

In *R v Lazarus* [2005] Crim LR 64, the Court of Appeal (Hughes J) stated: **12.22**

> In some cases the Crown may be in a position to make the kind of express acknowledgment that was made in Lunnon, that the indicated offence is the defendant's first involvement in relevant crime, and to do so knowing that that acknowledgment will be carried forward into

confiscation proceedings. In other cases . . . the Crown may be able to say no more than that for the purposes of sentence it does not and cannot dispute a particular assertion made by the defendant, but that it cannot say what information may arise in any subsequent confiscation proceedings . . . We have no doubt that the Crown ought, as a matter of good practice, when responding to a basis of plea which is advanced in a case where confiscation proceedings might follow, to bear in mind the question of whether it will be asking for a confiscation enquiry to be made and, if so, what if any admission is now being made which will apply to that enquiry.

(6) Multiple defendants and apportionment of benefit

12.23 The position and case law of where the benefit or funds of a criminal act are passed from one defendant to another (to sometimes another) in a criminal enterprise is considered fully at para 10.19 of Chapter 10.

(7) Conspiracies

12.24 A review of recent case law in relation to conspiracies and confiscation is found at para 10.48 of Chapter 10.

C. Benefit

(1) Calculating benefit under the CJA

12.25 Under the CJA there are two ways in which benefit is calculated:

(1) Simple benefit—calculating the benefit for the offences which the defendant has been convicted together with any which the defendant has asked to have been taken into consideration (s 71(4)).
(2) Extended benefit—where the court is not limited to the benefit from the offences of which the defendant has just been convicted, if the defendant has been convicted of two or more 'qualifying offences' (or convicted on at least one previous occasion in the relevant period). In such circumstances the court is entitled to apply the assumptions (s 72AA).

A review of recent case law in relation to benefit is found at paras 10.83–10.91 of Chapter 10.

(2) Relevant criminal conduct

12.26 The first issue to be determined is whether the defendant has benefited from any relevant criminal conduct (s 71(1)(a)). In this part of the Act 'relevant criminal conduct' means the offence for which the person was convicted before the court, taken together with any other offences which are either offences of which he is convicted in the same proceedings or offences which the court will be taking into consideration in determining his sentence for the offence in question (ie simple benefit).

12.27 Section 71(1)(d) states:

In this part of the Act 'relevant criminal conduct', in relation to a person convicted of an offence in any proceedings before a Court, means . . . that offence taken together with any other offences of a relevant description which are either—

C. Benefit

(a) offences of which he is convicted in the same proceedings, or
(b) offences which the Court will be taking into consideration in determining his sentence for the offence in question.

12.28 The definition of 'relevant criminal conduct' in s 71(1)(d) is subject to s 72AA(6), in cases where the extended benefit procedure applies (ie the defendant has been convicted of at least two qualifying offences or convicted on at least one previous occasion during the relevant period). Section 72AA(6) states:

(6) Where the assumptions specified in subsection (4) are made in any case, the offences from which, in accordance with those assumptions, the Defendant is assumed to have benefited, shall be treated as if they were comprised, for the purposes of this part of the Act, in the conduct which is to be treated, in that case, as relevant criminal conduct in relation to the Defendant.

(3) Offences of a relevant description

12.29 For the purposes of s 71(1D) of the CJA, an offence is an offence of a relevant description:

(a) in the case of an offence of which a person is convicted in any proceedings before the Crown Court or which is or will be taken into consideration by the Crown Court in determining any sentence, if it is an offence to which this part of the Act applies; and
(b) in the case of an offence of which a person is convicted in any proceedings before a Magistrates' Court or which is or will be taken into consideration by a Magistrates' Court in determining any sentence, if it is an offence listed in Schedule 4 of this Act.

12.30 Therefore in terms of simple benefit there can be no question of taking into account other criminal activity committed by the defendant from which he has benefited. The court may only take into account criminal activity in respect of which he has been convicted in the same proceedings or offences that the court will be taking into consideration in determining his sentence for the offence in question. This can cause a dilemma for prosecutors who, conscious of strictures from the Court of Appeal with regard to the overloading of indictments, content themselves with preferring a number of specimen counts which do not reflect the full degree of the defendant's offences. Although this course meets the court's objections in relation to overloading indictments, it can seriously prejudice the Crown's position in cases in which a confiscation order is sought. The answer, it is submitted, is for the prosecutor to prefer a conspiracy count wherever appropriate. This ensures that the indictment reflects the full extent of the defendant's offending for confiscation purposes, while avoiding any criticism about overloading the indictment. Defence solicitors should, however, be vigilant to ensure that confiscation orders are only made in respect of benefit derived from offences of which the defendant has been convicted or has asked to have taken into consideration.

(4) Pecuniary advantage

12.31 It often happens in CJA cases that, rather than obtaining property as a result of the offence, the defendant obtains a pecuniary advantage, for example the evasion of VAT which he would otherwise be liable to pay. This position is dealt with by s 71(5) of the CJA that provides as follows:

Where a person derives a pecuniary advantage as a result of or in connection with the commission of an offence, he is to be treated for the purposes of this Act as if he had obtained as a result of or in connection with the commission of the offence a sum of money equal to the value of the pecuniary advantage.

12.32 Thus the defendant is liable to have a confiscation order made against him in the amount of the pecuniary advantage he derived from the offence in the same way as if he had obtained property to that value.

12.33 In *R v David Cadman-Smith* [2002] 1 WLR 54 the House of Lords held that 'pecuniary advantage' should be given its ordinary natural meaning and that included cases where a debt was evaded or deferred. Under s 102(1) of the CJA 'property' includes 'money' and under s 71(4):

> For the purposes of this part of the Act the person benefits from an offence if he obtains property as a result of or in connection with its commission and his benefit is the value of the property so obtained.

12.34 In *Cadman-Smith* the House of Lords held that under s 71(4) the court was concerned simply with the value of the property as obtained by the defendant, and it made no difference if, after he had obtained it, it was destroyed or damaged or forfeited. In so finding they held that the defendant had derived a pecuniary advantage when he had evaded payment of an excise duty, even though the goods in question (cigarettes) had been forfeited before he had been able to dispose of them.

12.35 In *R v Dimsey and Allen* (2000) 1 Cr App R(S) 497 the main point argued was that failure to pay tax did not amount to a pecuniary advantage for the purpose of s 71(4) of the CJA because the tax remained payable. The court held that the deferment of payment of tax was a pecuniary advantage in the amount of the tax deferred. Allen was convicted of 13 counts of cheating the public revenue in an amount of £4 million. Laws LJ stated at page 501:

> Had these grave frauds succeeded then, in crude terms, Mr Allen would have been better off to the tune of £4 million. That represents in our judgement, the measure of his pecuniary advantage.

12.36 The Court of Appeal considered the question again in *A-G v Moran* [2001] EWCA Crim 1770. In *Moran* the defendant was a market trader. He traded in his own right and there was no company. For 20 years he had understated his income on his tax returns. There was no misappropriation of money *per se*. He was charged with cheating and making false statements. In confiscation proceedings it was alleged that the benefit he had received was the whole of his undeclared profits—£386,584. The judge rejected that submission and made a confiscation order in the sum of £190,000 representing the under payment of tax and interest. Mantell LJ stated (at para 8):

> What is plain and has been accepted before this court, as it was before the judge, is that we are dealing with the pecuniary advantage. On the face of things the pecuniary advantage would seem to be represented by the underpayment of tax which resulted from the failure to fully disclose profits. On the wording of the Act the pecuniary advantage must be taken to include any interest accrued or investment returned upon that sum. Giving the words of the Act their ordinary and natural meaning it is hard to see how the balance of the profits which are the product of lawful trading can be said to represent a pecuniary advantage which has resulted from or come about in connection with the commission of an offence. We reject the argument that where there has been systematic and persistent non-disclosure of profits the whole enterprise is to be regarded as fraudulent and the proceeds liable to forfeiture. It seems to us, therefore, that, authority apart, the judge was plainly right.

C. Benefit

In *R v Foggon* [2003] EWCA Crim 270 the Court of Appeal, including Mantell LJ, considering the above authorities held: **12.37**

> ... where a person misappropriates money from a company as an essential part of a fraud on the Inland Revenue, and is convicted of that fraud, he is liable to a confiscation order in the amount of the monies which he has misappropriated on the ground that the monies are property obtained as a result of or in connection with the fraud.

In *R v Ellingham* (CA, 2 December 2004) the Court held that where a defendant was responsible on behalf of others for the importation of goods in avoidance of Customs duty, it was he who obtained the pecuniary advantage of that avoidance for the purposes of confiscation proceedings, pursuant to s 71 of the CJA. The fact that he was only to receive a small financial advantage for arranging that importation was immaterial - the duty evaded was over £1 million and the defendant's benefit/pecuniary advantage was therefore over £1 million. **12.38**

In *DWP v Richards* The Times, 11 March 2005, the Court held that no allowance could be made for notional financial returns that might have been recovered from the victim in the absence of dishonest conduct. Accordingly, no deduction could be made in respect of an offender's notional entitlement to a sum under the Working Families Tax Credit Scheme, which the defendant would have been entitled to, had he not been fraudulently claiming social security benefits. **12.39**

In *R v Houareau* [2005] EWCA Crim 2106, the Court of Appeal held that the appellant had obtained a pecuniary advantage when his role had been to arrange the storing of cigarettes, although he had not been responsible for financing the operation. He was an importer on the facts if he had played a knowing part in assisting in the importation. **12.40**

In *Houareau*, the Court of Appeal held that where a person had knowingly played a part in assisting in the importation of goods on which excise duty was evaded, it was open to the judge to infer a beneficial interest in the goods in question, unless there was some evidence demonstrating to the contrary. Where such an inference was to be drawn, the defendant became an 'importer' of the goods and he was liable for the unpaid duty and had therefore obtained a pecuniary advantage within the meaning of s 71(5) of the CJA. His benefit therefore was the value of the pecuniary advantage. It will be noted that this decision is likely to carry across to POCA 2002. **12.41**

Similarly, in *R v Bakewell* (2006) 150 SJ 93, the Court of Appeal held that the judge had erred in assessing the defendant's benefit at £10,000. The Court found that his benefit was the value of any pecuniary advantage obtained, which in this case was the amount of duty evaded on the cigarettes that he had imported (see *R v David Smith*) [2002] 1 WLR 54). The Court held that the ultimate fate of the cigarettes was irrelevant. **12.42**

In *R v Ascroft* [2003] EWCA Crim 2365, the Court of Appeal held that where an offender stole substantial quantities of goods from containers in transit, the value of the property obtained by him for the purpose of the CJA (ss 71 and 74) was the amount that it would have cost the offender to obtain the goods lawfully wholesale, not the amount which he obtained for them on a dishonest re-sale (see Archbold News, Issue 8, 1 September 2003). **12.43**

For an illustration of where the Court did not find a pecuniary advantage see *Rigby v R* [2006] EWCA (Crim) 1653 (para 10.90 of Chapter 10).

(5) Extended benefit—application of the assumptions

12.44 It is important to remember when dealing with CJA cases that there is a second stage to be considered, ie the extended benefit calculation, where the defendant has been convicted of two 'qualifying offences' (see s 72AA(1)(c) below).

12.45 This second stage was added by s 2 of POCA 1995 and, for the first time, empowered the court to make assumptions at confiscation hearings in non-drug trafficking cases. There is no doubt that the application of the assumptions have had a very significant impact on CJA confiscation hearings, and the defendant who could, under the old provisions, sit back and make the prosecutor prove his case in relation to benefit and the proceeds of his criminal conduct, will now find himself having to adduce evidence as to the legitimacy of his acquisition of property and expenditure if he is to avoid having the assumptions made against him.

(6) When may the assumptions be applied?

12.46 By s 72AA(1) the assumptions may be applied if the following conditions are satisfied:

(1) the prosecutor has given written notice under s 71(1)(a);
(2) the notice contains a declaration that, in the prosecutor's opinion, the case is one in which it is appropriate for the assumptions to be made; and
(3) the offender
   (a) is convicted in those proceedings of at least two qualifying offences (including the offence in question); or
   (b) has been convicted of a qualifying offence on at least one previous occasion during the relevant period.

Case law and further commentary on the assumptions may be found at paras 10.63 *et seq* of Chapter 10.

(7) Qualifying offences

12.47 Section 72AA(2) defines a 'qualifying offence' as being one in respect of which all the following conditions are satisfied:

(1) it is an offence to which Pt VI of the CJA applies (see para 12.08 above);
(2) it was committed after the commencement of s 2 of POCA 1995 (1 November 1995, SI 1995/2650); and
(3) the court is satisfied the defendant has benefited from the offence.

(8) Relevant period

12.48 The 'relevant period' means a period of six years ending when the proceedings were instituted against the defendant (s 72AA(7) of the CJA).

C. Benefit

(9) The assumptions that can be made

Where the above conditions have been satisfied, the court may, if it thinks appropriate, determine that the assumptions should be applied for the purpose of determining whether the defendant has benefited from relevant criminal conduct and, if he has, of assessing the value of his benefit from that conduct (see s 72AA(3) of the CJA). **12.49**

The assumptions that can be made are set out in s 72AA(4) and are: **12.50**

(a) that any property appearing to the court:
  (i) to be held by the defendant at the date of conviction or at any time in the period between that date and the determination in question, or
  (ii) to have been transferred to him at any time since the beginning of the relevant period, was received by him, at the earliest time when he appears to the court to have held it, as a result of or in connection with the commission of offences to which this Part of this Act applies;
(b) that any expenditure of his since the beginning of the relevant period was met out of payments received by him as a result of or in connection with the commission of offences to which this Part of this Act applies; (1 November 1995(SI 1995/2650)) and
(c) that, for the purposes of valuing any benefit which he had or which he is assumed to have had at any time, he received the benefit free of any other interests in it.

The assumptions are thus in very similar terms to those applicable in drug trafficking cases under s 4(3) of the DTA. The distinction between the two provisions, however, is that under the DTA application of the assumptions is mandatory, whereas under the CJA the court has a discretion and may apply the assumptions 'if it thinks fit'. **12.51**

(10) When the assumptions should not be applied

Under s 72AA(5): **12.52**

Where the Court has determined the assumption specified in subsection (4) are to be made in any case it shall not in that case make any such assumption in relation to that particular property or expenditure if—

(a) that assumption so far as it relates to that property or expenditure, is shown to be incorrect in the Defendant's case or
(b) that assumption, so far as it so relates, is shown to be correct in relation to an offence the Defendant's benefit from which has been subject of a previous confiscation order or
(c) the court is satisfied that there would (for any other reason) be a serious risk of injustice in the Defendant's case if the assumption were to be made in relation to that property or expenditure.

In *R v Redbourne* (1992) 96 Cr App R 201 the Court of Appeal, when considering a DTOA case, held (as per Staughton LJ): **12.53**

> ... an assumption, in this context, is the acceptance of something which is true which is not already known or proved, and therefore may or may not be true. If the Court is directed or empowered to make an assumption, that means that the Court must or may take the assumed fact as true. It matters not for that purpose whether the standard of proof is criminal or civil; whichever standard is appropriate, the assumed fact is still to be treated as true. The exception ... allows the defendant to rebut an assumption, and places on him the burden of doing so. He has only the civil burden, on the balance of probabilities. If he fails to discharge that burden, the assumption stands as fact.

In *R v Jones (Confiscation Orders)* The Times, 8 August 2006, (a POCA case) the Court of Appeal held that 'serious risk of injustice' does not refer to hardship that would be sustained by **12.54** the offender by virtue of the making of the confiscation order, and it does not operate so as to confer discretion on the court to determine whether it is fair to make a confiscation order at all. (See also para 10.66 of Chapter 10). In *R v Hesketh* (2006) 150 SJ 1468, the Court of Appeal determined that where a defendant was able to show transfers in and out of a bank account were as a result of gambling activities, that would be sufficient to rebut the assumptions.

(11) Gifts caught by the Act

12.55 The CJA also makes provision in relation to gifts made by the defendant, but the provisions are less draconian than those contained in the DTA. The most important distinction between the gift provisions of the two Acts is that under the DTA gifts are caught if they were made during the six year period ending when the proceedings were instituted, or at any time if they related in any way to the defendant's drug trafficking activities; whereas under the CJA gifts are only caught if they are made after the commission of the offence. Further, under the CJA, the court is given discretion whether or not to take the gift into account, whereas no such discretion exists under the DTA.

12.56 By s 74(10) of the CJA, a gift is caught by the Act if:

(a) it was made by the defendant at any time after the commission of the offence or, if more than one, the earliest of the offences to which the proceedings for the time being relate; and

(b) the court considers it appropriate in all circumstances to take the gift into account.

12.57 References in s 74(10) to offences to which the proceedings relate include references to offences taken into consideration by the court in determining sentence (see s 74(11) of the CJA). See *Re G (No 1)* [2002] EWHC Admin 2495.

(12) Defendant does not have to be able to realise gift

12.58 In *R v Tighe* [1996] Crim LR 69 the Court of Appeal held that Parliament had contemplated that money might continue to be realisable even though it had been the subject of a gift or gifts by the defendant. The fact that a gift had been made would not save the offender from a confiscation order. The recovery of the money was only one factor of which the court must take account in exercising its discretion. In *Tighe* the appellant had deliberately put out of his control monies already outside of the jurisdiction. On that basis the judge had been correct in refusing to take account of the fact that the appellant might not be able to recover the money.

12.59 In *R v Wallace Duncan Smith* (1996) 2 Cr App R 1, the Court of Appeal held that in an appropriate case it was open to a judge to make an order against the defendant in relation to a disposal by way of a gift within s 74(10) of the 1988 Act, even though, at the time the order was made, the donor had disposed of the gift. Section 74(1) defines realisable property as:

(a) any property held by the Defendant; and

(b) any property held by a person to whom the Defendant has directly or indirectly made a gift caught by this Part of the Criminal Justice Act 1988.

Subsection (3) of s 74 provides

C. Benefit

...the amount that might be realised at the time the confiscation order is made is—
(a) the total of the values at that time of all the realisable property held by the Defendant, less
(b) where there are obligations having priority at that time, the total amounts payable in pursuance of such obligations, together with the total of the values at that time of all gifts caught by this Part of the Act.

In *Wallace Duncan Smith* it was in issue before the trial judge whether a gift made by the applicant of guns worth £49,000 to his son was a gift within subs 10 of s 74 of the Act. The Court of Appeal held that a judge does have power, by virtue of the provisions in the Act, to make a confiscation order against the defendant in relation to a gift made by him, notwithstanding the fact that at the time of the making of the order the guns were no longer realisable assets (as a result of the disposal by his son of the gift). Therefore, although a judge cannot make an order against the defendant in relation to assets which he does not have, it is open to him to make an order against a defendant in relation to a disposal by way of gift within s 74(10) of the Act, even though, at the time the order is made, the donee has, by whatever route, disposed of the gift. Notwithstanding the Court of Appeal's finding in relation to the law, as above, on the facts in *Wallace Duncan Smith* the Court found that the trial judge had accepted a statement made by the applicant's son that detailed what had happened to the guns and what had happened to the proceeds of the sale of those guns. The trial judge had accepted the content of the son's statement. No evidence had been called to contradict it. However the judge did not accept that the proceeds of the sale of the guns had gone to pay for 'family expenses'. The judge said he had taken that into account, but it could not persuade him that it would not be right to make an order in this case. In the judgment of the Court of Appeal, the trial judge having accepted the applicant's son's account of what had happened, had incorrectly imposed a confiscation order in the circumstances of the case as no further investigation had taken place as to the terms of the son's statement, which the judge had accepted; and therefore the making of the confiscation order was not a correct exercise of the power which the judge had. The court however emphasised that in a suitable case the court does have power to make such an order, even though the donee has disposed of that which was given to him.

12.60

(13) Distinction between realisable property and gifts

In *R v Gordon Foxley* (1995) 2 Cr App R 523 the Court of Appeal (Roch LJ) held:

12.61

...it is important in the construction of section 74 to keep in mind the distinction made by Parliament between realisable property held by the Defendant and the value of gifts caught by this part of the Act. Parliament no doubt appreciated the opportunities that could be created by dishonest persons to retain the benefit of their dishonesty by making gifts of their ill gotten gains to others and was, in our view, determined to close such a loop hole.

Section 74(4)(b) provides:

12.62

...the value of property (other than cash) in relation to any person holding the property—
...(b) in any other case, is its market value.

This subsection starts with the words: 'Subject to the following provisions of this section...' The gifts in the case of *Foxley* were gifts of money, not of property. Section 74(7) provides:

12.63

Subject to subsection (12) below [*subsection 12 sets out the circumstances in which a Defendant is to be treated as making a gift where there is a transfer of property at an undervalue*], references in

this part of the Act to the value at any time (referred to in subsection (8) below as 'the material time') of a gift caught by this Part of this Act are references to—
(a) the value of the gift to the recipient when he received it adjusted to take account of subsequent changes in the value of money; or
(b) where subsection (8) below applies, the value there mentioned, whichever is the greater.'

12.64 In s 74(8) the 'value therein mentioned' is the value to the receiver of the gift at the material time of the property which he received, or, if he no longer has the property given directly or indirectly to him by the defendant, the value of the property which in whole or in part, directly or indirectly, represents in his hands the property he received from the defendant, but disregarding any charging order. The Court held in *Foxley* that s 74(8) had no application because cash is expressly excluded from subs (8). The Court stated that the difficulty that the appellant faced was that s 74(4) is expressed to be 'Subject to the following provisions of this section'. Section 74(7) requires the court to take into account the greater of the two values ascertained in accordance with that subsection. In the case of *Foxley*, the greater of the two values was the value of the gift to the recipient when he received it, adjusted to take account of the subsequent changes in the value of money.

(14) Contract services

12.65 In *Re Adams* (2005) LS Gaz January 13, 28, QBD (Lightman J), the Court held that a consultancy contract entered into by the defendant under which he would be entitled to £52,000 p.a. for his services, was not 'realisable property' within s 74(1) and s 102(1) of the CJA, because the contract was for the provision of services where the identity of the provider was the essence and any entitlement to payment under the contract for services would only arise if the services were provided by the defendant. The Court found that such conditional and future entitlement 'was not property' but a chose in action personal to the party.

(15) Determining the amount that might be realised

12.66 Subject to s 71(1)(c) (where the court is satisfied that a victim of any relevant criminal conduct has instituted or intends to institute civil proceedings against the defendant in respect of loss, injury or damage sustained in connection with his conduct), the sum in which an order can be made by a court under s 71 shall be equal to:

(1) the benefit in respect of which it is made; or
(2) the amount appearing to the court to be the amount that might be realised at the time the order is made, whichever is the less (s 71(6)).

(16) Hidden assets

12.67 Recent case law in relation to the mantra of hidden assets is found at paras 10.94–10.99 of Chapter 10.

(17) Valuing property

12.68 See para 10.116 of Chapter 10.

D. Realisable Assets

(1) The amount to be recovered

12.69 The court will make a confiscation order in the full amount of the defendant's benefit unless he proves by evidence that the value of his realisable property is less than this amount. The authority for this proposition in CJA cases is the first instance decision of Auld J in *R v Rees*, (Plymouth Crown Court, 19 July 1990). In delivering his judgment, Auld J ruled as follows as to the burden of proof in relation to realisability:

> ... the 1988 Act, like the 1986 Act, was intended to be severe in its effect, and it would be incapable of effective application by the Courts if it were to impose a burden of proof upon the Crown whenever a defendant raises an issue as to the existence or extent of his realisable property, matters which are essentially within his personal knowledge. There is no reason to distinguish between the two statutes for this purpose, and it is noteworthy that the 1986 Act, for obvious reasons, operates more severely on a defendant raising such an issue since he will have to deal with any gifts made by him for many years before, not just since the first of the offences bringing him to court. I conclude, therefore, that in confiscation proceedings under the 1988 Act, once the prosecution has proved to the criminal standard [now *civil*] that a defendant has benefited as defined by the Act, and that the amount of the benefit exceeds the prescribed minimum, it is for the defendant to raise the issue of realisability and to satisfy the court that the 'amount that might be realised' is less than the amount which it has assessed as the value of the benefit. In accordance with the norm in criminal cases where the burden of proof is cast upon a defendant it is to the civil standard.

(2) Realisable property

12.70 Realisable property means:

(a) any property held by the defendant and
(b) any property held by a person to whom a defendant has directly or indirectly made a gift caught by ... this Act.

(See s 74(1)(a) and (b) and s 74(10)).

Under s 74(3):

For the purposes of this Part of the Act the amount that might be realised at the time the confiscation order is made is—

(a) the total of the values at that time of the realisable property held by the defendant less,
(b) where there are obligations having priority at that time, the total amounts payable in pursuance of such obligations, together with the total of the values at that time of all gifts caught by this part of the Act.

12.71 Therefore, the realisable property of a defendant is the totality of the defendant's assets, whereas the amount that might be realised is the totality of the defendant's assets less any encumbrances, (eg third party interests in a property).

12.72 Section 74(4) states:

> ... the value of property (other than cash) in relation to any person holding the property—
>
> (a) where any other person holds an interest in the property is—
>   (i) the market value of the first mentioned persons beneficial interest in the property, less

(ii) the amount prior to discharging any incumbrance, other than a charging order, on an interest; and

(b) in any other case, is its market value.

(3) Assets not restricted to those derived from criminal activity

12.73 As with DTA cases, any asset of the defendant, whether legitimately acquired or not, is vulnerable to confiscation in order to satisfy a confiscation order in the amount of the benefit. In *R v Currey* (1995) 16 Cr App R(S) 421 the defendant had been convicted of conspiring to import obscene articles and of being knowingly concerned in the importation of obscene articles. A confiscation order was made in the sum of £75,000 that represented in part the defendant's equity in a house. The defendant claimed that the property had been purchased prior to the commission of the offences and was not purchased from the profits of the obscene publication business. It was contended on his behalf that he had a legitimate business, that there was no evidence that he had personally benefited by high living or by retaining substantial sums of money and that the order had been made in respect of money which had merely passed through his hands. In these circumstances, it was contended, the court should have exercised its discretion not to make a confiscation order.

12.74 The Court ruled that this submission was based on a misconception as to the proper criteria for making confiscation orders. As Lord Taylor CJ said (at p 425):

> In our judgment, to accept the argument... that only if there is some remaining profit attributable to the appellant can a confiscation order properly be made would put a premium on offenders appearing before the court, stretching their hands wide and saying, "See, I have nothing left, you can't make a confiscation order against me, despite the fact that I have very substantial assets".

12.75 In *R v Chrastny (No 2)* [1991] 1 WLR 1385, a DTA case but of application in terms of the CJA, Glidewell LJ stated at p 1395:

> ... one of the questions that arises is if a defendant has legitimately acquired property which is not part of his or her proceeds of drug trafficking, and if the amount realisable from the proceeds of drug trafficking are less than the total proceeds attributable to her, whether an order can be made in the total sum of the proceeds of drug trafficking, which will mean that she has to turn to some of her legitimate assets in order to satisfy the order. I have read the definition of realisable property within section 5(1). In our view it is quite clear that that definition embraces legitimately acquired property. We cannot read into the Act of 1986 any inference that the definition is to be limited to illegitimately acquired property; that is to say, the proceeds of drug trafficking. This statute is undoubtedly draconian and the decision on that point may seem to be harsh; the statute is harsh. The statute is in essence one that seeks to ensure that everyone who has benefited from drug trafficking shall to the extent to which he or she can do so be deprived of the whole of that benefit.

(4) Proceeds, not profits

12.76 It is important to note that the court is concerned at this stage to assess the defendant's proceeds of crime and not merely his profits. Consequently, in assessing the value of his proceeds, the court is not required to deduct the cost of any expenses of the enterprise such as the travelling expenses incurred in their importation (see para 10.52 of Chapter 10).

D. Realisable Assets

(5) Inflationary adjustment

12.77 Section 74 states:

(5) References in this part of this Act to the value at the time (referred to in subsection 6 below as 'the material time') of any property obtained by a person as a result of or in connection with an offence are references to—
  (a) the value of the property to him when he obtained it adjusted to take account of any changes in the value of money or
  (b) where subsection 6 below applies, the value there mentioned, whichever is the greater.
(6) If at the material time he holds—
  (a) the property which he obtained (not being cash); or
  (b) the property which, in whole or in part, directly or indirectly, represents in his hands the property he obtained, the value referred to in subsection 5(b) above is the value at the material time of the property mentioned in paragraph (a) above or as the case may be, of the property mentioned in paragraph (b) above, so far as it so represents the property which he obtained, but disregarding any charging order.

12.78 The effect of s 74(5) and (6) is that if the defendant holds property which he obtained from his offending at the time of the confiscation hearing, the court should either assess the value as being the value to him at that time or the value of the property obtained when the defendant obtained it (adjusted to take into account changes in the value of money) whichever value is the greater.

12.79 In *R v Barwick* (2001) 1 Cr App R(S) 129 the Court of Appeal held that when a court is determining the value of property obtained by the defendant, it is correct to make an inflationary adjustment in accordance with s 74(5). When determining the amount that should be realised, the court should not assume the accused would in fact have invested the cash so as to keep pace with inflation. This however is open to the judge to find that he had done so, if the evidence and facts of the case as a whole support such a judgement.

(6) The reducing value of property

12.80 In *R v Crutchley and Tonks* [1994] Crim LR 309 the appellant claimed one of the properties which had been treated as part of his realisable property for the purposes of determining the amount that might be realised had been sold for significantly less than had been expected. The Court of Appeal would not receive evidence of the current values of the relevant properties, with a view to reducing the amount of the confiscation order. The Crown Court was empowered to make a confiscation order in 'the amount that might be realised at the time the order was made'. An appeal on the ground that the Crown Court had reached the wrong conclusion as to the amount that might be realised could relate only to the amount that might be realised at the time the order was made, on the evidence and figures submitted to the Crown Court. The realisable property as defined in s 74(1) included the appellant's own home, and there was no reason for not taking it into account in determining the amount that might be realised. The appeal against the confiscation order was therefore dismissed. (It should be noted that there does exist a route for reducing a confiscation order in these circumstances, ie by way of certificate of inadequacy).

(7) Costs of sale

12.81 See para 10.104 of Chapter 10.

(8) Abolition of the £10,000 'minimum amount' requirement

12.82 Section 1(4) of POCA 1995 abolished the requirement that CJA confiscation orders can only be made where the court is satisfied that the defendant's benefit was of at least the minimum amount of £10,000. Henceforth, as in DTA cases, confiscation orders can be made in any amount.

(9) Imprisonment in default

12.83 Section 75(1) states:

> Where the Crown Court orders the Defendant to pay an amount under this part of the Act, sections 139(1) to (4) and section 140(1) to (3) of the Powers of Criminal Courts (Sentencing) Act 2000 (powers of Crown Court in relation to an enforcement of Crown Court fines) shall have effect as if the amount were a fine imposed on him by the Crown Court.

12.84 The effect of this provision is the court must impose a prison sentence to be served in default of payment of the fine. The penalties available for default of payment are set out at s 139(4) of the Powers of Criminal Courts (Sentencing) Act 2000 as follows:

An amount not exceeding £200—7 days
An amount exceeding £200 but not exceeding £500—14 days
An amount exceeding £500 but not exceeding £1,000—28 days
An amount exceeding £1,000 but not exceeding £2,500—45 days
An amount exceeding £2,500 but not exceeding £5,000—3 months
An amount exceeding £5,000 but not exceeding £10,000—6 months
An amount exceeding £10,000 but not exceeding £20,000—12 months
An amount exceeding £20,000 but not exceeding £50,000—18 months
An amount exceeding £50,000 but not exceeding £100,000—2 years
An amount exceeding £100,000 but not exceeding £250,000—3 years
An amount exceeding £250,000 but not exceeding £1,000,000—5 years
An amount exceeding £1,000,000—10 years

12.85 It should be noted that the period set out in the Powers of Criminal Courts (Sentencing) Act 2000 (PCC(S)A) are maximum terms and it is within the judge's discretion to give a smaller term within the bracket where he feels it appropriate (*R v Szrajber* (1994) 15 Cr App R (S) 821).

12.86 It is desirable for the court to specify an end date for payment to be made under a confiscation order (see *R v City of London Justices ex p Chapman* The Times, 17 March 1998). The court may also direct payment of any amount ordered to be paid under a confiscation order by instalment (see s 139(1)(b) PCC(S)A). As to the necessity of the judge to follow the various steps set out in the Act see *R v Stuart and Bonnett* (1989) 11 Cr App R(s) 89; [1989] Crim LR 599.

(10) Serving the default sentence does not extinguish the debt

12.87 Under s 75(5A) where the defendant serves the term of imprisonment or detention in default of paying any amount due under a confiscation order, his serving that term does not prevent the confiscation order from continuing to have effect, so far as any other method of enforcement is concerned.

E. Confiscation Orders and Sentencing for the Offence

Section 72(5) provides: **12.88**

(5) Where a Court makes a confiscation order against the Defendant in any proceedings, it shall be its duty, in respect of any offence of which he is convicted in those proceedings, to take account of the order before—

  (a) imposing any fine on him;
  (b) making any order involving any payment by him, other than an order under Section 130 of the Powers of Criminal Courts (Sentencing) Act 2000 (compensation orders); or
  (c) making any order under
    (i) Section 27 of the Misuse of Drugs Act 1971 (forfeiture orders);
    (ii) Section 143 of the Powers of Criminal Courts (Sentencing) Act 2000 (deprivation orders), but subject to that shall leave the order out of account in determining the appropriate sentence or other manner of dealing with him.

Once the amount to be recovered has been determined, a confiscation order is made in that amount and the court must take account of the order before imposing any fine or other order requiring the payment of money by the defendant (other than a compensation order), or imposing any form of forfeiture or deprivation order in relation to property. Where the court makes a compensation order as well as a confiscation order and it appears that the defendant will have insufficient assets to meet both orders, the compensation order takes precedence (see s 72(7) of the CJA). **12.89**

(1) Time to pay

In *R v May* [2005] EWCA Crim 367, the Court of Appeal held that where a defendant appealed against a confiscation order, the time allowed for payment of the order ran from the making of the order, not from the conclusion of any appellant proceedings, Dyson LJ stated that: **12.90**

> The appellant was not entitled to assume that his appeal would be successful . . . It would be wrong as a matter of principle for appellants to be encouraged to believe that the bringing of an appeal would be likely to lengthen the time given for payment.

(See also para 10.138 of Chapter 10).

(2) Power to vary sentence

If the court decides to sentence the defendant prior to the confiscation hearing, once the confiscation hearing has been made the court may vary the original sentence by imposing a financial penalty. Section 72A(9A): **12.91**

Where the Court has sentenced the Defendant under subsection (7) above during the specified period it may, after the end of that period, vary the sentence by imposing a fine or making any such order as is mentioned in Section 72(5)(b) or (c) above so long as it does so within a period corresponding to that allowed by Section 155(1) or (2) of the Powers of Criminal Courts (Sentencing) Act 2000 (time allowed for varying a sentence) but beginning with the end of the specified period.

In effect this means the court has 28 days from the end of the period of postponement to vary the defendant's sentence by imposing a fine or by making one of the other orders under s 72(5), namely a compensation, forfeiture or deprivation order. **12.92**

(3) Prosecution costs

12.93 In *R v Ghadami* [1997] Crim LR 606 the Court of Appeal held that when it came to considering the question of an order to pay the costs of the prosecution, other debts should be taken into account (eg a confiscation order). It could then be seen that the appellant was a man without assets. In *Ghadami* the order to pay the costs of the prosecution was quashed (see also *R v Ruddick* The Times, 6 May 2003 (CA)). See also para 10.144 of Chapter 10.

(4) Third parties and confiscation law

12.94 While third parties have no rights of audience at the confiscation stage of proceedings at the Crown Court, they are entitled to pursue their interests in the High Court. A confiscation order is not a confiscation order in the literal sense. It is against the defendant. It is for him to pay the realisable sum. It is not against the third party who may have an interest in any of the assets identified in the confiscation hearing belonging to the defendant. They have the right to pursue those interests separately at the High Court stage. An extensive body of case law has developed in relation to third parties, the matrimonial home, and confiscation hearings. This area of the law is considered in detail in Chapter 22.

(5) Unreasonable delay in enforcement

12.95 See Chapter 10 para 10.145.

(6) Confiscation and the ECHR

12.96 It is now fairly well established that confiscation proceedings, following on and attaching to a criminal conviction, represent a penalty, not least because a prison sentence in default flows from non-payment, and the confiscation order itself is treated as a fine, pursuant to eg s 9 of the DTA. (See *Benjafield* [2002] UKHL 2 (para 82); *Rezvi* [2002] UKHL 1 and *Phillips v UK* [2001] EHRR No. 41087/98). Part of the reasoning in Rezvi was that the purpose of confiscation proceedings was to 'punish convicted offenders').

12.97 Case law however also dictates that the confiscation procedures do not involve the determination of a criminal charge (all be they a penalty) but are properly to be regarded as part of the sentencing procedures of the court, following conviction of a criminal offence. Accordingly Article 6(2) of the ECHR has no application as to the right to a fair trial under Article 6(1) or in respect of the determination of the defendant's civil obligations. The courts have found, for the time being, that the procedures under the 1994 Act contain sufficient safeguards (see also para 10.145 of Chapter 10.).

13

VARIATIONS TO CONFISCATION ORDERS UNDER THE DTA AND CJA

A.	Introduction	13.01	(1) Section 74A: review of cases where the proceeds of crime have not been assessed	13.28
B.	Applications by the Prosecutor in Drug Trafficking Cases	13.05	(2) Section 74B: revision of assessment of the proceeds of crime	13.32
	(1) Section 13: Where the court has not proceeded under the Act	13.07	(3) Section 74C: revision of assessment of amount to be recovered	13.34
	(2) Time limits	13.10	(4) Increase in realisable property	13.35
	(3) Section 14: where the court determines the defendant has not benefited from drug trafficking	13.11	E. Applications by the Defendant for a Decrease in the Confiscation Order	13.36
	(4) Section 15: revised assessment of the proceeds of drug trafficking	13.14	(1) Certificates of inadequacy	13.36
	(5) Procedure on applications	13.16	(2) Burden and standard of proof	13.38
C.	Increase in Realisable Property	13.18	(3) The Crown Court stage	13.40
	(1) Introduction	13.18	(4) Not a route to appeal	13.41
	(2) Practice	13.19	(5) Assets difficult to realise	13.54
	(3) Unfettered discretion	13.23	(6) Certificates of inadequacy: procedure	13.55
	(4) Procedure on applications	13.24	(7) Court must give its reasons	13.57
	(5) Certificates of increase: ECHR	13.26	(8) Certificate of inadequacy and legitimate expectation	13.58
D.	CJA Cases	13.27		

A. Introduction

13.01 When it makes a confiscation order the Crown Court will do its utmost to determine accurately the value of the defendant's realisable property. Nonetheless the valuation process is something of an inexact science and it frequently happens that the sum realised on sale of a particular asset is either less or more than that anticipated at the time a confiscation order is made. For example, fluctuations in the property market may mean that when a house is sold, perhaps up to two years after the confiscation order was made, following the determination of any appeal or third party claims, it may be worth significantly more or less than was originally anticipated. Further, as the objective of most criminals is to conceal the extent of their benefit from criminal conduct and the extent and location of their assets, it may well be that at the time of a confiscation hearing the prosecutor is unable to put before the court evidence which gives a full picture of a defendant's wealth.

13.02 Accordingly, both the DTA and the CJA give the prosecutor the right to apply to the court for the various determinations made during the course of a confiscation hearing to be revised in the light of new evidence. Similarly, both Acts give the defendant the right to seek a reduction in the amount of a confiscation order where the value of his realisable assets prove inadequate to satisfy the order in full.

13.03 The High Court has jurisdiction to make restraint orders in support of applications to review the determinations made by the Crown Court during the course of confiscation hearings under the DTA and CJA (see s 25(1)(a) DTA and s 76(1)(b) CJA referred to in Chapter 2 at paras 2.08 and 2.24 above respectively).

13.04 It will be noted that the relevant provisions of the 1988 and 1994 Acts were repealed on 24 March 2003 but they continue to have effect in respect of proceedings for offences committed before that date.

B. Applications by the Prosecutor in Drug Trafficking Cases

13.05 The DTA permits the prosecutor to seek a redetermination of the findings made during the course of a confiscation hearing with a view to the confiscation order being increased. The Act allows the prosecutor to make such applications in the light of new evidence in the following circumstances:

(1) where, on conviction, the court did not proceed under the Act at all;
(2) where the court has determined that the defendant did not benefit from drug trafficking;
(3) where it appears that the defendant's proceeds of drug trafficking are greater than that determined by the court; and
(4) where it appears that the value of the defendant's realisable assets is greater than that determined by the court.

13.06 It is necessary to consider each of these particular scenarios separately.

(1) Section 13: where the court has not proceeded under the Act

13.07 If, at the time of conviction, the prosecutor has no evidence to show that the defendant has benefited from drug trafficking, the court will not proceed under the DTA at all. Where this has occurred, s 13 of the DTA allows the prosecutor to return to the court and ask the court to make a confiscation order in the light of evidence obtained subsequently that shows the defendant has benefited from drug trafficking. By s 13(2) DTA:

If the prosecutor has evidence—
(a) which was not available to him when the defendant appeared to be sentenced (and accordingly was not considered by the court), but
(b) which the prosecutor believes would have led the court to determine that the defendant had benefited from drug trafficking if—
 (i) the prosecutor had asked the court to proceed under section 2 of this Act, and
 (ii) the evidence had been considered by the court,
he may apply to the Crown Court for it to consider the evidence.

13.08 It is an essential prerequisite to proceeding under s 13 that the evidence the prosecutor wishes the court to consider was not available to him at the time the defendant was sentenced. Once the court is satisfied the provisions of s 13 have been met, it shall proceed under s 2 if, having considered the evidence, it is satisfied it is appropriate to do so

B. Applications by the Prosecutor in Drug Trafficking Cases

(see s 13(3)). By s 13(4), in deciding whether it is appropriate to proceed under s 2, the court shall have regard to all the circumstances of the case. This gives the court an element of discretion in deciding whether to act under s 2 that it does not have if asked by the prosecutor to proceed under the Act immediately following conviction. If the court does decide to proceed under s 2, it has jurisdiction to order the parties to file prosecutor's and defendant's statements under s 11 and require the defendant to provide information in accordance with s 12.

13.09 In other respects, however, the provisions of s 13 are significantly less draconian than those that apply when the court proceeds under s 2 immediately after conviction. When the court decides to proceed under s 13, the confiscation order shall be for such amount as it thinks just in all the circumstances of the case: see s 13(5). The court may therefore make a confiscation order in a sum less than the defendant's benefit from drug trafficking. Further, in considering the circumstances of the case, s 13(6) requires the court to have regard, in particular, to the amount of any fine or fines imposed on the defendant in respect of the offences or offences in question. The court may take account of any payment or other reward received by the defendant on or after the date of his conviction, but only if the prosecutor shows that it is received by him in connection with drug trafficking carried on before that date: see s 13(8). Section 13(9) precludes the court from applying the assumptions under s 4 in relation to any such payment or reward.

(2) Time limits

13.10 Section 13(10) provides that no application under the section shall be entertained if it is made more than six years after the date of conviction. Section 13(12) defines 'date of conviction' as meaning the date on which the defendant was convicted or, where there appear to be sentences in respect of more than one conviction and those convictions were not all on the same date, the date of the latest conviction.

(3) Section 14: where the court determines the defendant has not benefited from drug trafficking

13.11 Section 14 of the DTA deals with the position where the court does proceed under s 2, but determines that the defendant has not benefited from drug trafficking and accordingly makes no confiscation order against him. By s 14(2):

If the prosecutor has evidence—
(a) which was not considered by the court in making the section 2(2) determination, but
(b) which the prosecutor believes would have led the court to determine that the defendant has benefited from drug trafficking if it had been considered by the court, he may apply to the Crown Court for it to consider that evidence.

13.12 Section 14(3) provides that if the court is satisfied, having considered the evidence, that it would have determined that the defendant had benefited from drug trafficking if the evidence had been available, the court:

(a) shall make—
   (i) a fresh determination under subsection (2) of section 2 of this Act; and
   (ii) a determination under subsection (4) of that section of the amount to be recovered by virtue of that section; and
(b) may make an order under that section.

13.13 The court again has jurisdiction to order the parties to serve statements under s 11 and to require the defendant to provide information under s 12 (see s 14(8)). Section 14(5) and (6) make the same provision as to the acceptance of payments and rewards by the defendant and the application of the assumptions as s 13. Again, a six year time limit from the date of conviction is imposed (see s 13(7)).

(4) Section 15: revised assessment of the proceeds of drug trafficking

13.14 Section 15 applies where the court proceeds under s 2, and it later appears to the prosecutor that the defendant's proceeds from drug trafficking are greater than the amount determined by the court. By s 15(2):

> Where the prosecutor is of the opinion that the real value of the defendant's proceeds of drug trafficking was greater than their assessed value, the prosecutor may apply to the Crown Court for the evidence on which the prosecutor has formed his opinion to be considered by the court.

13.15 If the court is satisfied, having considered the evidence, that the real value of the defendant's proceeds of drug trafficking is greater than their assessed value, the court must make a fresh determination under s 2(4) (see s 15(4)). Again, the court is given power to require the parties to serve statements and order the defendant to provide information (see s 15(3)). Section 15(10) and (11) make the same provision in relation to payments and rewards and the application of the assumptions as ss 13 and 14 (see Chapter 10 generally). If the amount of the fresh determination of the defendant's proceeds of drug trafficking exceeds the amount of the confiscation order, the court may increase the order to such greater sum as it thinks just in all the circumstances (see s 15(12)). The court may also make an appropriate increase in the default sentence to be served in the event of non-payment (see s 15(13)). Section 15(14), however, provides that this power may only be exercised in circumstances where the effect of the increase in the order would be to make the defendant liable to serve an increased default sentence. By way of example, an increase in a confiscation order from £150,000 to £200,000 would not necessarily make the defendant liable to an increased default sentence, but an increase from £150,000 to £275,000 would. Again, there is a six year time limit on applications from the date of conviction (see s 15(15)).

(5) Procedure on applications

13.16 By r 56.3 of the Criminal Procedure Rules, any application by the prosecutor under ss 13, 14, or 15 or under the equivalent sections in the CJA must be in writing and a copy served on the defendant. Rule 56.3 (2) requires that the application must include the following particulars:

(a) the name of the defendant;
(b) the date on which and the place where any relevant conviction occurred;
(c) the date on which and the place where any relevant confiscation order was made or, as the case may be, varied;
(d) the grounds on which the application is made;
(e) an indication of the evidence available to support the application.

C. Increase in Realisable Property

It is submitted that the most appropriate course is for the proper officer of the Crown Court, on receipt of such an application, to issue a summons requiring the defendant to attend on a particular date for the court to give directions as to how the application should proceed by, eg directing the service of s 11 statements by the parties and the provision of information by the defendant under s 12, within a specified timescale.

13.17

C. Increase in Realisable Property

(1) Introduction

Drug traffickers and others who commit financially motivated crime can be adept at concealing their true wealth from law enforcement authorities. It is therefore by no means uncommon for further assets to come to light after a confiscation order has been made in a sum considerably less than the sum by which the court certifies he has benefited from drug trafficking. Further, after a confiscation order is made against a defendant in a sum less than his certified benefit, he may acquire other assets that could be made available to meet the shortfall between the amount of the benefit and the amount of the order. This situation is dealt with in s 16 of the DTA which provides as follows:

13.18

(1) This section applies where, by virtue of section 5(3) of this Act, the amount which a person is ordered to pay by a confiscation order is less than the amount assessed to be the value of his proceeds of drug trafficking.

(2) If, on an application made in accordance with subsection 3 below, the High Court is satisfied that the amount that might be realised in the case of the person in question is greater than the amount taken into account in making the confiscation order (whether it was greater than was thought when the order was made or has subsequently increased) the court shall issue a certificate to that effect, giving the court's reasons.

(3) An application under subsection (2) above may be made either by the prosecutor or by a receiver appointed in relation to the realisable property of the person in question under section 26 or 29 of this Act or in pursuance of a charging order.

(4) Where a certificate has been issued under subsection (2) above the prosecutor may apply to the Crown Court for an increase in the amount to be recovered under the confiscation order; and on that application the court may—

  (a) substitute for that amount such amount (not exceeding the amount assessed as the value referred to in subsection (1) above) as appears to the court to be appropriate having regard to the amount now shown to be realisable; and

  (b) increase the term of imprisonment or detention fixed in respect of the confiscation order under subsection (2) of section 139 of the Powers of Criminal Courts (Sentencing) Act 2000 (as it has effect by virtue of section 9 of this Act) if the effect of the substitution is to increase the maximum period applicable in relation to the order under subsection 4 of that section.

(2) Practice

It should be noted that the practice and procedure under s 16 is significantly different from that under ss 13, 14, and 15. Under s 16, the Crown Court has no immediate jurisdiction to increase the confiscation order. An application must first be made to the High Court for a certificate under s 16(2) to reflect that the amount that might be realised is greater than

13.19

the amount of the order. Only when the High Court has issued such a certificate does the Crown Court have jurisdiction to increase the order. The application may be made by the prosecutor or by a receiver appointed under the Act.

13.20 The section applies to all property owned by the defendant, whether he acquired ownership of it before or after the making of the order. Further the prosecutor is not required to show that it represents the proceeds of drug trafficking or any other criminal activity. If the confiscation order is made for an amount less than the defendant's benefit from drug trafficking, any other assets he may acquire, whether legitimately or otherwise, may form the subject matter of a s 16 application until such time as the defendant has paid the full amount of his certified benefit.

13.21 In *R v Tivnan* (1999) 1 Cr App R(S) 92 the defendant had been convicted of importing cannabis. A confiscation hearing was held and the defendant's proceeds (benefit) of drug trafficking were certified as being £479,376. As the value of his realisable assets was found to be only £72,841 a confiscation order was made in this lesser amount with sentence of two years' imprisonment to be served in default of payment. It later transpired that the defendant owned a property in Hampshire, a motor vehicle, and funds in a bank account. The prosecutor applied for, and was granted, a certificate and the Crown Court duly increased the confiscation order to the amount of the benefit namely £476,376. The default sentence was also increased to four years' imprisonment. The defendant appealed to the Court of Appeal contending that the court had no jurisdiction to make the order in circumstances where the assets in question were 'not shown to be the proceeds of criminality or turpitude'. This argument was rejected by the court. Rose LJ, delivering the judgment of the Court, emphasised the purpose for which the legislation was enacted. He said:

> In our judgment, in relation to the question of statutory construction, the confiscation legislation relating to drug trafficking, as it is now principally enshrined in the Drug Trafficking Act 1994, is as has been repeatedly said previously by the courts, Draconian. It is intended to strip those who deal in drugs of any possible profit from so doing, by depriving them of their realisable assets whether or not these are the proceeds of drug trafficking, up to the amount by which they have benefited from drug dealing.

13.22 His Lordship concluded:

> We bear in mind that, as a penal statute, the 1994 Act must, in the case of ambiguity, be construed favourably to the defendant. But we see no ambiguity. The plain words of the statute, in our judgment, provide for the making of an application for a further certificate and for an increase in the amount to be recovered under the confiscation order at any time after the original confiscation order was made. By this means drug dealers can be deprived of their assets until they have disgorged an amount equivalent to all the benefit which has accrued to them from drug dealing. In those circumstances this appeal is dismissed.

(3) Unfettered discretion

13.23 In *R v Bates* [2007] 1 Cr App R 9(2) the Court of Appeal held that the Crown Court's discretion under s 16 of the DTA to increase the amount to be recovered under a confiscation order was unfettered. A judge could take into account certain matters, or reject them as being of little significance, depending on the circumstances of the case before him.

D. CJA Cases

(4) Procedure on applications

13.24 By sc115.9A, the High Court application for a certificate of increase must be served with any supporting evidence at least seven days before the hearing. The application must be served on the defendant and any receiver appointed under the Acts. Where the application is made by a receiver, he must serve it on the prosecutor. The application is issued out to the Administrative Court Office at the Royal Courts of Justice and is heard by a High Court Judge of the Queen's Bench Division assigned to Administrative Court business.

13.25 Rule 56.3 of the Criminal Procedure Rules does not apply to applications under s 16 and there appears to be no further guidance in the legislation as to the procedure to be followed in the Crown Court once a certificate has been granted. It is submitted that the proper course is for the prosecutor to write to the Crown Court providing all relevant information in relation to the defendant and the order and enclosing a copy of the High Court's certificate. The defendant should then be required to attend before the court for directions to be given as to the hearing of the prosecutor's application for the order to be increased.

(5) Certificates of increase: ECHR

13.26 In *Saggar* [2005] EWCA Civ 174, the Court of Appeal held that where the State had granted to itself the right to re-open the issue of confiscation under s16 of the DTA (for a certificate of increase), the reasonable time requirement under Article 6(1) of the European Convention of Human Rights was triggered and extended throughout the period starting from the original proceedings and not just from the institution of the s 16 application.

D. CJA Cases

13.27 The CJA as originally enacted did not make provision for the prosecutor to return to court to apply for the original determinations made in a confiscation hearing to be revised. This changed in 1995 when the Proceeds of Crime Act 1995 (POCA) added new ss 74A, 74B, and 74C to the CJA to give the prosecutor similar powers to those already in force under the DTA. Again, these provisions will be considered individually.

(1) Section 74A: review of cases where the proceeds of crime have not been assessed

13.28 Section 74A is in very similar terms to s 13 of the DTA and s 74A(1) applies where:

(1) a person has been convicted before the Crown Court or a Magistrates' Court of an offence of a specified description;
(2) the prosecutor did not give written notice under s 71(1)(a); and
(3) a determination was made under s 71(1)(b) not to proceed under that section or no determination was made for those purposes.

By s 74A(2), where these conditions are satisfied and the prosecutor has evidence:

(a) which, at the date of conviction or, if later, when any determination not to proceed under section 71 was made, was not available to the prosecutor (and, accordingly, was not considered by the court); but

(b) which the prosecutor believes would have led the court to determine, if—
  (i) the prosecutor had given written notice for the purposes of subsection (1)(a) of that section, and
  (ii) the evidence had been considered by the court,
  that the defendant had benefited from relevant criminal conduct, the prosecutor may apply to the relevant court for it to consider that evidence.

13.29 The relevant court is defined as meaning the Crown Court before which the defendant was convicted or, where he was convicted in a magistrates' court, any magistrates' court for the same area (see s 74A(12)).

13.30 By s 74A(3), where the court is satisfied on the evidence, the court shall proceed under s 71 as if it were doing so before sentencing the defendant. In considering whether it is appropriate so to proceed, the court must have regard to all the circumstances of the case (see s 74A(4)). If, having proceeded under s 71, the court determines the defendant did benefit from relevant criminal conduct, it then has a power rather than a duty to make a confiscation order and may make the order for such sum as it thinks fit, not exceeding the amount of that benefit: see s 74A(5). By s 74A(6), in considering the circumstances of the case either under subs (4) or (5) the court must have regard, in particular, to:

(1) any fine imposed on the defendant for any relevant criminal conduct; and
(2) any order made in connection with such conduct under s 130 of the Powers of Criminal Courts (Sentencing) Act, 2000 (compensation orders).

13.31 Section 74A contains many similar provisions to those in s 13 of the DTA. Section 74A(9) imposes similar restrictions in relation to the use of the assumptions and s 74(10) imposes the same six year time limit for the bringing of applications. Section 74A(11) gives the court jurisdiction to order the parties to file s 73 statements and require the defendant to provide information in the same way as if the hearing was taking place immediately after conviction.

(2) Section 74B: revision of assessment of the proceeds of crime

13.32 Section 74B is in similar terms to s 14 of the DTA and applies in circumstances where there has been a determination under s 71(1A) that the defendant has not benefited from any relevant criminal conduct. In such circumstances, by s 74B(2):

If the prosecutor has evidence—
(a) which was not considered by the court which made the original determination, but
(b) which the prosecutor believes would have led that court (if it had been considered) to determine that the defendant had benefited from relevant criminal conduct,
  the prosecutor may apply to the relevant court for it to consider that evidence.

13.33 If the court is satisfied these conditions are met, the procedure to be followed is very similar to that under s 74A. The court shall, by s 74B(3), proceed to make a fresh determination as to whether the defendant has benefited from relevant criminal conduct, make a determination under s 71(1B)(a) and then make an order requiring the defendant to pay such sum as it thinks fit. Similar restrictions on the use of the assumptions are imposed by s 74B(9) (see Chapter 12), and s 74B(10) again imposes a six year time limit for bringing applications.

E. Applications by the Defendant for a Decrease in the Confiscation Order

The court is given jurisdiction to order the parties to file statements under s 73 and to require the defendant to provide information under s 73A (see s 74B(11)).

(3) Section 74C: revision of assessment of amount to be recovered

13.34 Section 74C is in similar terms to s 15 of the DTA and applies where the prosecutor is of the opinion that the value of the defendant's benefit from relevant criminal conduct is greater than that assessed by the court. In these circumstances, the prosecutor can apply under s 74C for the court to consider the evidence on which he has formed this opinion. If the court is satisfied that the amount of the defendant's benefit is greater than that assessed by the court it may make a fresh determination under s 71 and has the power to increase, to such extent as it thinks just in all the circumstances, the amount to be recovered and vary the confiscation order accordingly (see s 74C(3)). The default sentence may also be increased (see s 74C(7) and (8)). There is again a six year time limit on bringing applications (see s 74C(9)) and the court is again given jurisdiction to order the parties to file s 73 statements and require the defendant to provide information under s 73A (see s 74C (11)).

(4) Increase in realisable property

13.35 Interestingly, the CJA contains no equivalent of s 16 giving the court jurisdiction to increase confiscation orders in circumstances where further realisable property is discovered. There does not seem to be any logical reason for this omission which has been remedied under the Proceeds of Crime Act 2002.

E. Applications by the Defendant for a Decrease in the Confiscation Order

(1) Certificates of inadequacy

13.36 There are many reasons why the assets of a defendant may fail to realise the amounts anticipated when a confiscation order is made. By way of example, property prices may fall in the period between an order being made and an enforcement receiver being appointed to sell the property with the result that when the defendant's assets have been realised there are insufficient funds available to satisfy the confiscation order in full. If no procedure existed whereby the defendant could apply to have the order reduced, the effect of this would be that he would have to serve part of the default sentence for non- payment. This could clearly be inequitable in circumstances where the defendant had not contributed in any way to the shortfall. The legislation has therefore made provision for applications to be made to the High Court for a certificate of inadequacy which can then form the basis of an application to the Crown Court for a reduction in the amount payable.

13.37 The relevant provisions are to be found in s 17 of the DTA and s 83 of the CJA. Section 17 of the DTA provides:

(1) If, on an application made in respect of a confiscation order by—
   (a) the defendant, or
   (b) a receiver appointed under section 26 or 29 of this Act or in pursuance of a charging order,

the High Court is satisfied that the realisable property is inadequate for the payment of any amount remaining to be recovered under the confiscation order, the court shall issue a certificate to that effect, giving the court's reasons.

(2) For the purposes of subsection (1) above—
   (a) in the case of realisable property held by a person who has been adjudged bankrupt or whose estate has been sequestrated the court shall take into account the extent to which any property held by him may be distributed among creditors; and
   (b) the court may disregard any inadequacy in the realisable property which appears to the court to be attributable wholly or partly to anything done by the defendant for the purpose of preserving any property held by a person to whom the defendant had directly or indirectly made a gift caught by this Act from any risk of realisation under this Act.
(3) Where a certificate has been issued under subsection (1) above, the person who applied for it may apply to the Crown Court for the amount to be recovered under the confiscation order to be reduced.
(4) The Crown Court shall, on an application under subsection (3) above—
   (a) substitute for the amount to be recovered under the order such lesser amount as the court thinks just in all the circumstances of the case; and
   (b) substitute for the term of imprisonment or of detention fixed under subsection (2) of section 139 of the Powers of Criminal Courts (Sentencing) Act 2000 in respect of the amount to be recovered under the order a shorter term determined in accordance with that section (as it has effect by virtue of section 9 of this Act) in respect of the lesser amount.

Section 83 of the CJA is in more or less identical terms and is therefore not reproduced here.

(2) Burden and standard of proof

13.38 The Acts are silent as to the burden and standard of proof, but it is submitted that the burden rests on the defendant to prove his case to the civil standard, that is to say on a balance of probabilities. In *R v Comiskey* (1991) 93 Cr App R 227 the Court of Appeal ruled that at a confiscation hearing, once the prosecutor had proved the amount of the benefit, the burden passed to the defendant to prove, if he could, that the value of his realisable property was less than the benefit. If he failed so to do, a confiscation order would be made in the full amount of the benefit. The Court observed, in coming to this decision, that the extent of a defendant's realisable property was uniquely within his own knowledge. It is submitted that precisely the same considerations apply to an application for a certificate of inadequacy and that the burden should therefore rest with the defendant to prove his case to the civil standard.

13.39 In *O'Donoghue* [2004] EWHC *Re (Admin)* 176, Lightman J confirmed that the burden of proof was on the defendant to establish that the value of his assets was inadequate to satisfy the whole value of the confiscation order. He added that it was not sufficient for him to merely state that his assets were inadequate, without demonstrating what had happened since the making of the confiscation order that had made them so. (See also *Re T* [2006] EWHC 2233.)

(3) The Crown Court stage

13.40 It should be noted that not every application for a certificate of inadequacy meets with unadulterated success. In *R v Briggs* (Crown Court, 31 October 2003), although the defence were successful in obtaining a certificate of inadequacy in the High Court, when the matter was referred to the Crown Court, the Crown Court judge took the view, on the particular facts, that the confiscation order in the sum of £40,586.97 should only be reduced by £1.

E. Applications by the Defendant for a Decrease in the Confiscation Order

(4) Not a route to appeal

13.41 A certificate of inadequacy should only be sought in cases where, since the making of the confiscation order, the value of the defendant's realisable property has decreased for some reason. It is not an appropriate remedy for a defendant who is aggrieved by the Crown Court's findings when it made the confiscation order: in such circumstances the defendant's remedy is an appeal to the Court of Appeal (Criminal Division). Indeed, as the authorities illustrate, the High Court will be vigilant in ensuring that the certificate of inadequacy procedure is not used as a device to appeal against the original findings of the Crown Court.

13.42 In *Re Taylor* (CA, 25 June 1996) the defendant had applied for a certificate of inadequacy, simply filing an affidavit saying that he did not have and never had had any realisable property as a result of his activities in the importation of drugs. The prosecutor resisted the application saying the defendant was simply trying to re-litigate the question of the amount of his realisable property without producing any additional evidence. McCullough J upheld the prosecutor's objections and refused the application. The Court of Appeal dismissed the defendant's appeal indicating they agreed with the following extract from McCullough J's judgment:

> I am not prepared to go behind the findings about the amount of his realisable property in November 1992. I have not been presented with any evidence of diminution in the value of his realisable assets since that date, despite the fact that the Commissioners have not been able to point to the existence of any particular assets of any appreciable value. I am not prepared to act on the applicant's assertion that he does not have such property. In the circumstances I am less than satisfied that he is unable to meet the confiscation order in full and the application is dismissed.

13.43 A similar view was taken by Dyson J in *Re C* (QBD (Admin), 18 November 1987). In that case the judge observed:

> It is not sufficient for a defendant simply to assert at the time of his application for a certificate of inadequacy that he has no realisable property. He must explain what has become of the realisable property whose existence formed the basis of the confiscation order. If a defendant is at liberty simply to rely upon the assertion of a present lack of realisable property to justify the issue of a certificate of inadequacy, then it is open to him, by a side wind, to subvert the decision which formed the basis of the confiscation order. That is plainly wrong in principle. The scheme of the Act is quite clear. If a confiscation order is to be challenged, that must be by way of appeal and only by way of appeal.

13.44 The decision of Dyson J in *Re C* was supported by Laws J in *Re W* (QBD (Admin) 29 January 1998). In that case Laws J said:

> In the result, I have concluded that I should dismiss this application. If the true position is that this applicant did not have £1,250 at the time of the hearing before the circuit judge and so likewise does not have £1,250 today, his remedy would then have been to appeal the confiscation order. There is, I repeat, no evidence of any change of circumstances since the confiscation order was made. It is of the greatest importance, as Dyson J indicated, that on an application of this kind the High Court should not be persuaded to go behind confiscation orders made in the Crown Court. I consider that in substance that is what this application invites me to do. I decline to do it.

13.45 It is important therefore that the certificate of inadequacy procedure should only be used where there has been a genuine change of circumstances since the confiscation order was made. It is not to be used as a means of challenging the original findings of the Crown Court.

13.46 In *Re N* [2005] EWHC QBD (Admin) 3211, Toulson J endorsed a 'hard-edged rule' in respect of certificate of inadequacy applications. He expressed concern that the provisions set out in s 17 of the DTA and the corresponding provisions of POCA, were being used by defendants as an appeal route, whereas the proper course would have been to pursue the matter in the Court of Appeal.

13.47 In *Gokal v Serious Fraud Office* [2001] EWCA Civ 368, Keene J considered a similar problem (paras 16 and 17):

> The evidence in support of the recent application for a certificate took the form of a witness statement . . . In the witness statement it is said that the appellant "seeks to prove that he has no realisable property to be applied in satisfaction of the confiscation order". Apparently an attempt was going to be made to produce evidence at this stage to show that the money which went into the appellant's personal bank account has been dissipated. This would take the form of schedules produced by accountants which were available at the time of the appeal to the Court of Appeal but not produced to that court. This is not a proper basis on which to seek a certificate. It amounts to an attempt to go behind the original confiscation order finding as to the amount of the defendant's realisable assets. Such a finding can only be challenged by way of an appeal against the confiscation order. . . . An application for a certificate does not provide an opportunity to try to make good deficiencies in the case presented at the time of the confiscation order or at the appeal against it.

13.48 In *Re O'Donoghue* [2004] EWCA Civ 1800, Lightman J said:

> It is clear that on an application for a certificate (of inadequacy) it is not possible to go behind the finding of the original confiscation order as to the amount of the defendant's realisable assets.

13.49 This was confirmed in *P v Customs and Excise Commissioners* [2005] EWHC (Admin) 877, where Beatson J stated (at para 18) that it was:

> . . . well established that the procedure under (s 17) . . . is not to be used as a device to appeal against the original finding that an item of property is realisable property within the legislation.

13.50 He added at para 20:

> In applying for a certificate of inadequacy, an applicant must show what has happened to the realisable property or to part of it since the making of the confiscation order.

13.51 While in *Re L* (QBD (Admin), 18 January 1996), Keene J refused to accept that there was any form of issue estoppel in relation to the way in which certificates of inadequacy were brought, Toulson J in *Re N* (above) stated that that approach had not been developed by the courts:

> The courts have adopted a hard-edge rule in this area and it would be inappropriate for me as a judge at first instance to seek to swim against the tide by going back to the approach of Keene J as he then was in *Re L*.

13.52 In *R v T* (QBD (Admin), 1 February 1996) McCullough J said:

> It is not sufficient for a defendant simply to assert at the time of his application for a certificate of inadequacy that he has no realisable property. He must explain what has become of the realisable property whose existence formed the basis of the confiscation order. If a defendant is at liberty simply to rely upon the assertion of the present lack of realisable property to justify the issue of a certificate of inadequacy, then it is open to him . . . to subvert the decision which formed the basis of the confiscation order. That is plainly wrong in principle. The scheme of the Act is quite clear. If a confiscation order is to be challenged, that must be by way of appeal and only by way of appeal.

E. Applications by the Defendant for a Decrease in the Confiscation Order

In *Re W* (QBD (Admin), 29 January 1998) Lord J stated: **13.53**

> It is of the greatest importance . . . that on an application of this kind the High Court should not be persuaded to go behind confiscation orders made in the Crown Court.

And these sentiments were recently re-affirmed in *Re McKinsley* [2006] EWHC 1092.

(5) Assets difficult to realise

The fact that particular assets prove difficult for a defendant to realise does not necessarily mean they cease to be realisable property under the Acts (see *Re R* The Independent, 4 November, 2002). In *R v Liverpool Justices ex p Ansen* [1998] 1 All ER 692 the assets taken into account in making a confiscation order included a deposit he had put down on a summer house in Turkey and held by German agents; a deposit he had put down and was entitled to reclaim in relation to some Waterford Wedgwood articles; and a loan he had apparently made to his junior counsel at trial. He had been unable to realise any of these amounts in satisfaction of a confiscation order and accordingly applied for a certificate of inadequacy. In refusing the defendant's application, May J said: **13.54**

> [Counsel for the prosecutor] submits that the fact that an asset may be difficult to realise is simply not relevant. The provisions of the Act, he submits, define 'realisable property' in terms of section 5 and do not address any question of whether in practical terms it is difficult to recover the money. I agree with that submission for two reasons. Firstly, the definition of 'realisable property' includes property held by the defendant and by definition 'property' is held by any person if he holds an interest in it and the 'interest' in property includes a right. Accordingly, if as Mr. Ansen's affidavit indicates, the sum of approximately £8,500 held by agents in Germany is an amount which he is entitled to recover, then it is realisable property by definition irrespective of any difficulty in its actual recovery. Secondly, s 5(1)(b) of the 1986 Act, referring, as it does, to "realisable property" including 'gifts caught by the Act', necessarily means that circumstances may arise where gifts made by an applicant has made may be practically, even legally, irrecoverable, but they are nevertheless still regarded as realisable property under this draconian Act. The purpose of these draconian procedures is obvious: they are intended, as has often been said, to make it as difficult as possible for those who traffic in drugs to get away with the proceeds of that traffic.

(6) Certificates of inadequacy: procedure

The procedure for making the application for the certificate of inadequacy to the High Court is set out in sc115.9. The application must be made by way of application notice which must be served together with any supporting evidence not less than seven days before the hearing on the prosecutor and, as the case may be, on either the defendant or the receiver, where one has been appointed. The application must be issued out of the Administrative Court Office at the Royal Courts of Justice. District Registries of the High Court have no jurisdiction to entertain such applications. The application should be accompanied by a witness statement from the defendant verified by a statement of truth setting out in detail why his assets have proved insufficient to meet the confiscation order in full. Any relevant documentation, including receiver's reports, should be exhibited to the statement. In some circumstances, particularly where any receiver that may have been appointed accepts that the assets are inadequate to meet the order, the prosecutor may be prepared to consent to the issue of a certificate without the necessity for a court hearing. **13.55**

13.56 Where the court grants a certificate of inadequacy whether by consent or otherwise, the defendant's solicitor must draw it up and arrange for it to be sealed by the Administrative Court Office. Care should be taken to ensure the order incorporates the court's reasons for granting the certificate. Once this has been done, the certificate should be lodged at the Crown Court where the order was originally made and arrangements made for the matter to be listed for the hearing of the defendant's application for the confiscation order to be reduced. At the hearing the court shall, by s 17(4) of the DTA and s 83(4) of the CJA substitute such lesser sum as it thinks just in all the circumstances and make any necessary reduction in the default sentence. It is submitted that at this stage the Crown Court can enquire into the reasons for the inadequacy and if, eg it transpires that it has been caused by the defendant dissipating assets to make them unavailable for confiscation, it would be entitled to reduce the order only by a nominal sum and leave the default sentence undisturbed. It will further be noted that in *Re T* [2005] EWHC 3359(Admin), Collins J heed that in an appropriate case the Court would consider bail pending a certificate of inadequacy application.

(7) Court must give its reasons

13.57 In *Re Forwell* [2003] EWCA Civ 1608, the Court of Appeal held that where a court, when issuing a certificate of inadequacy in the exercise of its discretion, decided to disregard any inadequacy, it was expressly required to set out its reasons for so doing. Conversely, there was a similar requirement implicitly imposed as a matter of fairness where there was a refusal to issue a certificate.

(8) Certificate of inadequacy and legitimate expectation

13.58 In *Re C* [2005] EWHC QBD (Admin) 966, the principle of 'legitimate expectation' was considered by Stanley Burnton J. At the Crown Court stage of the proceedings, the matrimonial home in which the defendant held an interest had been ignored by the judge for various reasons which were not challenged by Customs and Excise. The defendant argued that the principle of legitimate expectation therefore applied (citing *R v Inland Revenue Commissioners, ex p Unilever plc* [1996] STC 681) that the court could not depart from the legitimate expectation that the matrimonial home would not feature as a realisable asset, so as to cloud the application.

13.59 However, in his Lordship's judgment, on an application for a certificate of inadequacy, the fact that certain property had been excluded as it was in this case was not a matter to be taken into account, there being no discretion in the court. The words 'any property held by the defendant' set out in s 6(2) of the DTA (which defines realisable property) could not, in Burnton J's view, be clearer. They do not admit of any discretion on the part of the court which would, or could, entitle the court to disregard 'any property held by the defendant'.

13.60 Burnton J held that the judge at first instance had not decided that the matrimonial home was not realisable property within the meaning of the Act; he had merely decided to exercise the discretion conferred upon him by virtue of provisions elsewhere in the Act.

14

PREPARING FOR CONFISCATION HEARINGS UNDER POCA

A.	Introduction	14.01	(6) The effect of the court failing to follow the postponement provisions	14.57
	(1) The evolution of confiscation hearings	14.01	(7) Postponement pending appeal	14.59
	(2) When do POCA confiscation hearings have to be held?	14.06	(8) Sentencing	14.60
B.	Confiscation in the Magistrates' Court	14.07	(9) Power to vary sentence	14.62
	(1) Section 70: committal by a magistrates' court	14.09	E. Preparatory Steps for a POCA Hearing	14.63
	(2) The circumstances where a magistrates' court may commit	14.12	(1) Section 16 statements of information	14.63
	(3) The discretion to commit	14.14	(2) The purpose of s 16 statements	14.65
	(4) Committal: practice and procedure	14.22	(3) The content of s 16 statements	14.67
C.	The Guiding Principles of Confiscation under POCA	14.24	(4) A duty of full and frank disclosure?	14.71
	(1) If ss 6(1)–(3) are satisfied, how must the court proceed?	14.24	(5) When should the s 16 statement be served?	14.72
	(2) How is 'criminal lifestyle' defined?	14.25	(6) Disclosure evidence inadmissible	14.74
	(3) What are 'lifestyle offences'?	14.26	(7) Upon whom should the prosecutor's statement be served?	14.75
	(4) 'Criminal lifestyle' and relevant benefit of not less than £5000	14.30	(8) The defendant's statement	14.77
	(5) How is 'relevant benefit' defined?	14.31	(9) Defendant's acceptance conclusive	14.81
	(6) Criminal conduct and benefit	14.33	(10) Failure to respond by the defendant	14.83
	(7) General criminal conduct	14.34	(11) Consequences of the defendant failing to respond to the prosecutor's statement	14.87
	(8) Particular criminal conduct	14.35	(12) The problem of self incrimination	14.92
	(9) The relationship between general and particular conduct	14.36	(13) Further provision of information by the defendant	14.96
	(10) When does a defendant's conduct form part of his criminal activity?	14.37	(14) Further protection against self incrimination	14.101
	(11) When does a person benefit from criminal conduct?	14.38	(15) Prosecutor's acceptance conclusive	14.102
	(12) Transitional provisions	14.40	(16) Failure to provide the information ordered	14.103
D.	Postponement of POCA Confiscation Hearings	14.45	(17) Further statements by the prosecutor	14.104
	(1) What is the 'permitted period'?	14.47	(18) Securing the attendance of witnesses	14.106
	(2) Date of conviction	14.48	(19) Joint control of assets and multiple defendants	14.107
	(3) Further postponements	14.49	(20) Expert evidence	14.108
	(4) Postponement beyond two years	14.50	(21) Service of documents	14.109
	(5) Who may apply for a postponement?	14.56		

A. Introduction

(1) The evolution of confiscation hearings

14.01 Section 1 of the Drug Trafficking Offences Act 1986 (DTOA) imposed a mandatory obligation on the court to hold a financial enquiry whenever a defendant was convicted of a drug trafficking offence. This resulted in a considerable waste of court time, both in cases where it was patently obvious that there had been no benefit (or any benefit was of a purely nominal amount) and also in cases where the defendant was accepted to have no realisable property.

14.02 In cases that commenced after the Drug Trafficking Act 1994 (DTA) came into force (on 1 February 1995), the mandatory obligation on the court to hold a financial enquiry in every case was relaxed. Under s 2(1) of the DTA, the court was only obliged to hold a mandatory enquiry when either the prosecutor asked it to proceed under s 2 or, if the court considered it appropriate to proceed under s 2, even though the prosecutor had not asked it to do so.

14.03 Under s 71(1) of the Criminal Justice Act 1988 (CJA) a confiscation hearing could be held by the Crown Court whenever a defendant had been convicted of an indictable offence (other than a drug trafficking offence), but it was contingent upon the prosecutor giving written notice and/or the court considering it appropriate to proceed.

14.04 Under the Proceeds of Crime Act 2002 (POCA) the Crown Court must hold a confiscation hearing if a defendant has either been convicted of an offence in the Crown Court, or has been committed to the Crown Court for sentencing (or committed with a view to a confiscation order being considered), and the court has been asked to proceed by either the prosecutor or the Assets Recovery Agency (ARA), or where the court believes it is appropriate to do so. The POCA provisions therefore mirror the spirit of both the DTA and the CJA, but broaden the ambit of the enquiry to include a facility for the ARA to pursue confiscation proceedings.

14.05 The transitional arrangements anticipate that offences that were committed before the effective date of the legislation, 24 March 2003, should remain under the DTA or the CJA (SI 2003/333). Therefore, for some period to come, the three separate regimes will co-exist. The case law that has developed under the DTA and the CJA will remain persuasive in respect of POCA 2002. Wherever possible we have tried to incorporate that case law into the POCA legislation, however, the reader is also referred to the chapters that deal with preparation for both DTA and CJA hearings (Chapters 9 and 11 respectively) where, because of the embryonic state of the relatively new legislation, case law is dealt with in more detail.

(2) When do POCA confiscation hearings have to be held?

14.06 Under s 6(1) of POCA 2002 the Crown Court must proceed with a confiscation hearing if the following two conditions are satisfied:

6(2) The first condition is that a Defendant falls within any of the following paragraphs:
    (a) he is convicted of an offence or offences in proceedings before the Crown Court;
    (b) he is committed to the Crown Court for sentence in respect of an offence or offences under Section 3, 4 or 6 of the Sentencing Act;

(c) he is committed to the Crown Court in respect of an offence or offences under Section 70 of the Proceeds of Crime Act 2002 (committal with a view to a confiscation order being considered).

6(3) The second condition is that:
(a) the Prosecutor has asked the Court to proceed under [Section 6 of POCA]; or
(b) the Court believes it is appropriate to do so.

Section 6(1) therefore imposes a mandatory obligation on the court to hold a financial enquiry whenever subss (2) and (3) are satisfied. The Sentencing Act referred to is the Powers of Criminal Courts (Sentencing) Act 2000 (see s 88(5) of POCA).

B. Confiscation in the Magistrates' Court

14.07 From 1 July 2005, s 97 of the Serious Organised Crime and Police Act 2005 (SOCPA) has had effect. This permits magistrates' courts to make confiscation orders under Pt 2 of POCA 2002 in a sum less than £10,000, (for the enabling provision see SI 2005/1521, Art 3, and s 97(2)). As a result, magistrates now have the power to fix confiscation hearings pursuant to the POCA scheme following a trial or a guilty plea, where the sum to be confiscated is less than £10,000.

14.08 To some extent the new provisions in relation to the ability of magistrates' courts to make confiscation orders under the sum of £10,000 has eased the burden on prosecutors in determining whether or not to ask the magistrates to refer a case to the Crown Court. However, the issue of whether to commit will still arise in a number of cases, and this position is considered below.

(1) Section 70: committal by a magistrates' court

14.09 Section 70 states:

(1) This section applies if—
 (a) a Defendant is convicted of an offence by a Magistrates' Court, and
 (b) the Prosecutor asks the Court to commit the Defendant to the Crown Court with a view to a confiscation order being considered under Section 6.
(2) In such a case the Magistrates' Court must—
 (a) commit the Defendant to the Crown Court in respect of the offence and
 (b) may commit him to the Crown Court in respect of any other offence within subsection (3).
(3) An offence falls within this sub-section if—
 (a) the Defendant has been convicted of it by the Magistrates' Court or any other Court, and
 (b) the Magistrates' Court has power to deal with him in respect of it.

14.10 The effect of s 70 is that a defendant may be committed to the Crown Court for confiscation proceedings following a conviction of any offence, triable either way or summary, in the magistrates' court. The requirement to commit a defendant to the Crown Court is mandatory once the prosecutor has asked the magistrates' court to do so (see s 70(2)). (Unlike elsewhere in the POCA confiscation scheme, the power to have a person committed to the Crown Court for confiscation proceedings (under s 70(1)(b)) is granted only to the prosecutor and not to the Director of the ARA.)

14.11 Where the defendant is convicted of an either way offence, s 70(5) requires the magistrates' court to state whether it would have committed the defendant to the Crown Court for sentencing in any event. It appears this subsection is required because, under s 71(3)(b), the Crown Courts sentencing powers following a committal for confiscation are otherwise limited to the sentencing powers of the magistrates' court.

(2) The circumstances where a magistrates' court may commit

14.12 When considering s 6(2)(b) of POCA, the Powers of Criminal Courts (Sentencing) Act 2000 (PCC(S)A) gives the powers under which a magistrates' court may commit to the Crown Court. Section 3 of the PCC(S)A provides a general power to commit adult offenders summarily convicted of an offence triable either way; s 4 confers a power to commit adult offenders convicted of a triable either-way offence as a result of a guilty plea indicated before the mode of trial procedures have been embarked upon; and s 6 gives a general power to commit for sentence, which may be used to supplement a committal under the various provisions of the PCC(S)A.

14.13 It follows that defendants appearing before the Crown Court on appeal from decisions of the magistrates' court do not fall under s 6(2)(b) of POCA, nor do those defendants who are committed outside of ss 3, 4, and 6 of the PCC(S)A, eg committal for breach of a community order or return to custody under s 116 of PCC(S)A.

(3) The discretion to commit

14.14 Public policy considerations arise because s 70(1)(a) confers on the prosecutor a discretion as to whether he should ask the magistrates' court to commit following a defendant's conviction. How and when that discretion is exercised will ultimately depend on the circumstances of the individual case. The Code for Crown Prosecutors emphasises that deciding on what is in the public interest is not simply a matter of adding up factors on each side. It will be for the lawyer who has control of the case to determine how important each factor is in the circumstances of the individual case and go on to make an overall assessment. This approach was confirmed by the Court of Appeal in *R v Benjafield* [2001] 3 WLR 75, a DTA case, where the Court held that the discretion '*will have to be exercised taking into account all relevant considerations, so as to avoid the risk of injustice*'.

14.15 It has long been the view that it is not in the public interest to automatically make referrals; not least because such a course would entail no exercise of any discretion and would leave prosecutors exposed to potential judicial review actions (see para 5.6 of the Code for Crown Prosecutors).

14.16 However, there are a number of factors that are common to all confiscation matters, which may assist the prosecutor on the decision he is being asked to make in relation to s 70(1)(b):

  i. It is an established principle that prosecutors should seek to carry out a financial enquiry in every case where such an enquiry would be both relevant and appropriate. There is therefore a presumption that a case lawyer should consider whether the confiscation scheme is likely to be applicable.
  ii. The fact that Parliament has legislated for the prosecutor to seek confiscation orders in summary matters is a clear indication that this power is to be considered and *used* by prosecutors.

B. Confiscation in the Magistrates' Court

iii. It would not be in the public interest to allow a repeat offender to see the benefit from his criminality go unchecked.

14.17 Arguments concerning the First Protocol of the European Convention of Human Rights, proportionality and the protection of an individual's property, are somewhat diminished if one accepts that confiscating the proceeds of crime is in the overriding public interest. This view was confirmed by the House of Lords in *R v Benjafield* [2002] 1 All ER 815, applying *McIntosh v Lord Advocate* [2001] 2 All ER 638 and *Phillips v UK* [2001] 11 EHRC 280).

14.18 Whether it is a proportionate response to ask the magistrates' court to refer a case to the Crown Court will depend very much on the facts of the individual case, including the seriousness of the matter, whether the individual is a repeat offender, and the sums/loss involved.

14.19 The fact that the chances of recovering realisable assets ('the available amount') are very low is a consideration, but may not be determinative.

14.20 The burden of proof in confiscation proceedings rests on the prosecutor to demonstrate on the balance of possibilities that the defendant has benefited from his criminal conduct. Where the alleged benefit is not likely to be significant there will be instances when the benefit is so low that asking the bench to commit the case up to the Crown Court would be disproportionate. However to set a financial cut off point below which referrals should not be made would amount to a fettering of the prosecutor's discretion. Inevitably, internal resources may also be a factor in influencing matters.

14.21 It is useful to consider the Code for Crown Prosecutors in this regard. The decision to prosecute is in itself a serious step. It must be a fair and effective decision. The Code emphasises the following general principles, which can also serve as a useful guide to whether confiscation proceedings in the Crown Court should be sought:

- Each case is unique and must be considered on its own facts and merits.
- Crown Prosecutors must be fair, independent and objective.
- Each case must be properly reviewed. The evidence must be considered.
- Crown prosecutors must balance factors for and against carefully and fairly.

(4) Committal: practice and procedure

14.22 In relation to the confiscation proceedings themselves the timetable in the magistrates' court is likely to be as follows:

i. Defendant is convicted;
ii. The prosecutor asks the magistrates' court to commit;
iii. The matter is listed at the Crown Court for directions;
iv. The directions hearing deals with the serving of the prosecutor's statement, the defence reply, the time estimate for the confiscation hearing etc.
v. The defendant is sentenced. (NB the court may only proceed under s 6 of POCA *before* it sentences the defendant (ss 14(1) and 15(1)). So a timetable should be set and the matter postponed in relation to the confiscation hearing before sentence is passed.)

vi. A confiscation hearing may be postponed for upto two years from the date of conviction to allow for the financial reports etc. to be prepared (s 14(5)).

14.23 Once committed, the Crown Court will follow the confiscation procedure set out in s 6 et seq of POCA (see s 70(4)(a)).

C. The Guiding Principles of Confiscation under POCA

(1) If ss 6(1)–(3) are satisfied, how must the court proceed?

14.24 Section 6(4) states:

The court must proceed as follows:
(a) it must decide whether the defendant has a criminal lifestyle;
(b) if it decides that he has a criminal lifestyle it must decide whether he has benefited from his general criminal conduct;
(c) if it decides that he does not have a criminal lifestyle it must decide whether he has benefited from his particular criminal conduct.

Section 6(4) signals a departure from the CJA and DTA in relation to confiscation. Under s 6(4) the court must, when considering a confiscation hearing, decide whether the defendant has a 'criminal lifestyle'. If it decides he has (or presumably had) a criminal lifestyle the court must decide whether he has benefited from his 'general criminal conduct'. If the court decides that the offender does *not* have a criminal lifestyle, it must decide whether he has benefited from his 'particular criminal conduct'.

(2) How is 'criminal lifestyle' defined?

14.25 Section 75 of POCA provides:

(1) A Defendant has a criminal lifestyle if (and only if) the following condition is satisfied.
(2) The condition is that the offence (or any of the offences) concerned satisfies any of these tests —
  (a) it is specified in Schedule 2;
  (b) it constitutes conduct forming part of a course of criminal activity;
  (c) it is an offence committed over a period of at least six months and the Defendant has benefited from the conduct which constitutes the offence.

In respect of s 75(2)(a), the offences specified in Sch 2 are termed 'lifestyle' offences.

(3) What are 'lifestyle offences'?

14.26 Lifestyle offences are defined under Sch 2 to POCA, and include drug trafficking offences, namely:

(1) An offence under any of the following provisions of the Misuse of Drugs Act 1971—
  (a) Section 4(2) or (3) (unlawful production or supply of controlled drugs);
  (b) Section 5(3) (possession of controlled drugs with intent to supply);
  (c) Section 8 (permitting certain activities relating to controlled drugs);
  (d) Section 20 (assisting in or inducing the commission outside the UK of an offence punishable under a corresponding law).
(2) An offence under any of the following provisions of the Customs & Excise Management Act 1979 if it is committed in connection with a prohibition or restriction on importation or exportation which has effect by virtue of Section 3 of the Misuse of Drugs Act 1971—
  (a) Section 50(2) or (3) (improper importation of goods);

C. The Guiding Principles of Confiscation under POCA

    (b) Section 68(2) (exploration of prohibited or restricted goods);
    (c) Section 170 (fraudulent evasion).
(3) An offence under either of the following provisions of the Criminal Justice (International Co-operation) Act 1990—
    (a) Section 12 (manufacture or supply of a substance for the time being specified in Schedule 2 to that Act); or
    (b) Section 19 (using a ship for illicit trafficking of controlled drugs).

14.27 Other offences specified in Sch 2 include money laundering, particularly: s 327 of POCA (concealing, etc criminal property); and s 328 of POCA (assisting another to retain criminal property). Lifestyle offences also include: directing terrorism under s 56 of the Terrorism Act 2000; people trafficking under s 25(1) of the Immigration Act 1971; arms trafficking under s 68(2) of the Customs & Excise Management Act 1979 (exportation of prohibited goods), and s 170 of the same Act (fraudulent evasion); or an offence under s 31 of the Firearms Act 1968 (dealing in firearms or ammunition by way of trade or business).

14.28 Also included under Sch. 2 are: counterfeiting; intellectual property under the Copyright, Designs and Patents Act and the Trade Marks Act (unauthorised use of trade marks); offences relating to pimps and brothels under the provisions of the Sexual Offences Act 1956; and blackmail under s 21 of the Theft Act 1968.

14.29 Paragraph 10 of Sch 2 incorporates inchoate offences, namely: attempting; conspiring; inciting; aiding or abetting; or counselling or procuring, the commission of any offence specified in Sch 2.

(4) 'Criminal lifestyle' and relevant benefit of not less than £5000

14.30 Under s 75(4) an offence does not satisfy the test in s 75(2)(b) or (c) unless the defendant obtains a relevant benefit of not less than £5000. The term 'relevant benefit' is given two definitions under s 75, dependant upon whether or not the court is proceeding under s 75(2)(b) or s 75(2)(c).

(5) How is 'relevant benefit' defined?

14.31 Under s 75(5), 'relevant benefit' for the purposes of s 75(2)(b) (where the offence constitutes conduct forming part of a course of criminal activity), is defined as:

75 (5) (a) benefit from conduct which constitutes the offence;
    (b) benefit from any other conduct which forms part of the course of criminal activity and which constitutes an offence of which the Defendant has been convicted;
    (c) benefit from conduct which constitutes an offence which has been or will be taken into consideration by the Court in sentencing the Defendant for an offence mentioned in paragraph (a) or (b).

14.32 Under s 75(6), 'relevant benefit' for the purposes of subs (2)(c) (where the offence has been committed over a period of at least six months and the defendant has benefited from the conduct which constitutes the offence), is defined as:

75 (6) (a) benefit from conduct which constitutes the offence;
    (b) benefit from conduct which constitutes an offence which has been or will be taken into consideration by the court in sentencing the Defendant for the offence mentioned in paragraph (a).

(6) Criminal conduct and benefit

14.33 Section 6(4)(b) and (c) refers to 'criminal conduct'. Criminal conduct is defined at s 76(1) as being:

(1) ... conduct which (a) constitutes an offence in England and Wales; or (b) would constitute such an offence if it occurred in England and Wales.

Section 76 adds:

(4) A person benefits from conduct if he obtains property or a pecuniary advantage as a result of or in connection with the conduct.
(5) If a person obtains a pecuniary advantage as a result of or in connection with conduct, he is to be taken to obtain as a result of or in connection with the conduct a sum of money equal to the value of the pecuniary advantage.
(6) References to property or a pecuniary advantage obtained in connection with conduct include references to property or a pecuniary advantage obtained in both that connection and some other.
(7) If the person benefits from conduct his benefit is the value of the property obtained.

(7) General criminal conduct

14.34 Section 76(2) states:

General criminal conduct of the Defendant is all his criminal conduct, and it is immaterial—
(a) whether conduct occurred before or after the passing of this Act;
(b) whether property constituting a benefit from conduct was obtained before or after the passing of this Act.

The phrase 'general criminal conduct' therefore encompasses all of the defendant's criminal conduct, both conduct for the offence(s) in question and criminal conduct other than the offence in question on the basis that the defendant has a criminal lifestyle. It will be noted that said criminal conduct does not need to have been subject to prosecution to be captured by s 76(2).

(8) Particular criminal conduct

14.35 Section 76(3) defines the 'particular criminal conduct' of the defendant as being:

(3) ... all his criminal conduct which falls within the following paragraphs—
(a) conduct which constitutes the offence or offences concerned;
(b) conduct which constitutes offences of which he was convicted in the same proceedings as those in which he was convicted of the offence or offences concerned;
(c) conduct which constitutes offences which the court will be taking into consideration in deciding his sentence for the offence of offences concerned.

(9) The relationship between general and particular conduct

14.36 By virtue of its definition, 'general criminal conduct' is inclusive of 'particular criminal conduct'. Under the POCA regime courts must therefore consider the defendant's benefit from his general criminal conduct, where the court has found, upon conviction, that the defendant has a criminal lifestyle. If the court concludes that the defendant does not or has not had a criminal lifestyle, confiscation is by reference to his benefit from the particular criminal conduct on which he has been convicted (this is similar, although not identical, to the provisions of the CJA that dictate simple and extended benefit (see Chapter 12, para 12.25).

C. The Guiding Principles of Confiscation under POCA

(10) When does a defendant's conduct form part of his criminal activity?

14.37 Under s 75(3):

Conduct forms part of a course of criminal activity if the Defendant has benefited from the conduct and—
  (a) in the proceedings in which he was convicted he was convicted of three or more other offences, each of three or more of them constituting conduct from which he has benefited, or
  (b) in the period of six years ending with the day when those proceedings were started (or if there is more than one such day, the earliest day) he was convicted on at least two separate occasions of an offence constituting conduct from which he has benefited.

(11) When does a person benefit from criminal conduct?

14.38 Under s 76(4) a person benefits from criminal conduct if he obtains property as a result of or in connection with that conduct. If a person benefits from criminal conduct, his benefit is the value of the property obtained (s 76(7)).

14.39 Under s 6(5) of POCA, if the court decides under s 6(4)(b) or (c) that the defendant has benefited from criminal conduct, it must next decide the recoverable amount (see s 7 of POCA) and then make a confiscation order requiring him to pay that amount in full.

(12) Transitional provisions

14.40 Conduct shall not form part of a course of criminal activity under s 75(3)(a) of the Act where any of the three or more offences mentioned in s 75(3)(a) (see para 14.37 below) was committed before 24 March 2003 (SI 2003/531).

14.41 The transitional provisions set out in SI 2003/531 state that where the court is applying the rule in s 75(5) of the Act in relation to the calculation of relevant benefit for the purposes of determining whether or not the test in s 75(2)(b) is satisfied by virtue of conduct forming part of a course of criminal activity under s 75(3)(a), the court must not take into account benefit from conduct constituting an offence mentioned in s 75(5)(c) of the Act which was committed before 24 March 2003.

14.42 Conduct shall form part of a course of criminal activity under s 75(3)(b) of the Act if the offences that the defendant was convicted of on at least two separate occasions in the period mentioned in s 75(3)(b) were committed before 24 March 2003.

14.43 Similarly, where the court is applying the rule in s 75(5) in relation to the calculation of relevant benefit for the purposes of determining whether or not the test in s 75(2)(b) of the Act is satisfied by virtue of conduct forming part of a course of criminal activity under s 75(3)(b), the court may take into account benefit from conduct constituting an offence committed before 24 March 2003.

14.44 Under SI 2003/531, where the court is applying the rule in s 75(6) in relation to the calculation of relevant benefit for the purpose of determining whether or not the test in s 75(2)(c) of the Act is satisfied, the court must not take into account benefit from conduct constituting an offence mentioned in s 75(6)(b) of the Act which was committed before 24 March 2003.

D. Postponement of POCA Confiscation Hearings

14.45 Under s 14(1) of POCA the court may:

(1) (a) ... proceed under Section 6 before it sentences the Defendant for the offence (or any of the offences) concerned, or

(b) postpone proceedings under Section 6 for a specified period.

The court may order more than one postponement and the period of postponement may be extended (as per s 14(2) mirroring s 3(2) of the DTA). However a period of postponement must not end after the 'permitted period' has finished (s 14(3)).

14.46 As under the DTA and the CJA, where the court does not propose to postpone the making of the confiscation order, it must make the confiscation order *before* it sentences the defendant (see s 14(1)(a)).

It will be noted, pursuant to r 58.2 of the Criminal Procedure Rules the Crown Court may grant a postponement without holding a hearing.

(1) What is the 'permitted period'?

14.47 'Permitted period' is defined at s 14(5) as being a period of two years starting with the date of conviction. This section therefore extends the period of postponement previously permitted under the DTA and CJA from six months to two years. This will mean that the court will no longer have to find 'exceptional circumstances' to postpone beyond six months. Further it appears the court may now postpone a confiscation hearing under POCA for any reason, eg because no court is available. Previously it had to be on the grounds that 'further information' was required. Where the court is satisfied exceptional circumstances exist, the period may be extended beyond two years, adopting similar conditions to those that have developed under the DTA and CJA (see s 14(4) and below).

(2) Date of conviction

14.48 The defendant's date of conviction is defined in s 14(9) as being the date on which the defendant was convicted of the offence concerned, or where there are two or more offences and the convictions were on different dates, the date of the latest.

(3) Further postponements

14.49 Section 14(8) provides that where proceedings have been postponed already for a period and an application to extend the period further is made before the previous period of postponement ends, the application may be granted, even though the previous period (by the time the application is heard) may have ended. In effect this means that provided the application is submitted to the court before the postponed period comes to an end, the application may be granted, even though the end of the previous period of postponement has finished, eg because there were listing difficulties or the judge was unavailable.

D. Postponement of POCA Confiscation Hearings

(4) Postponement beyond two years

14.50 There is no limit to the period of postponement where the court finds that there are 'exceptional circumstances' (s 14(4)). The Act does not define when circumstances are exceptional, although some guidance may be found from previous case law in relation to the DTA or CJA.

14.51 In *R v Jagdev* [2002] 1 WLR 3017 the court held that the purpose of the power to postpone confiscation proceedings was to enable the judge to reach a fair conclusion on the confiscation issue; and that where there was a real prospect the hearing might have been wasted and an unjust order made if the judge had proceeded to hear the case (in *Jagdev* because of an awaited decision of the Court of Appeal), then the judge was entitled to hold that there were exceptional circumstances.

14.52 In *R v Cole* The Independent, 30 April 30 1998 (CA), the trial judge had become ill after a difficult and complex trial. The issue was whether this constituted exceptional circumstances. Judge LJ stated:

> The judgment whether circumstances are exceptional or not must be made by the Court considering whether to make a confiscation order . . . here the Judge was in hospital on the date when he had indicated that he would determine the confiscation issue . . . Having studied the statutory code we do not consider that it was intended or drafted so as to preclude the Listing Officer making sensible arrangements for the conduct of the Crown Court business, normally after discussion with the Trial Judge or the Resident Judge . . .

14.53 In *Steele and Shevki* [2001] 2 Cr App R(S) 40; [2001] Crim LR 153 Judge LJ returned to this subject and stated:

> These decisions involved the Courts discretion, judicially exercised when the statutory conditions are present, taking full account of the preferred statutory sequence . . . For example, to take account of illness on one side or the other, or the unavailability of the Judge, without depriving a subsequent order for confiscation of its validity.

14.54 In *Sekhon* [2003] 1 WLR 1655 the Court of Appeal held that the decision as to whether to postpone and as to whether exceptional circumstances existed involved the consideration of the same types of issues that courts were regularly required to determine when engaged in case management and that the strict compliance with procedural requirements relating to issues of that nature would not normally be expected to go to jurisdiction.

14.55 The meaning of 'exceptional circumstances' is further discussed in Chapter 9, para 9.17.

(5) Who may apply for a postponement?

14.56 A postponement or extension may be made upon application by either the defendant, or by the prosecutor or the Director of ARA, or alternatively by the court of its own motion, (see s 14(7)).

(6) The effect of the court failing to follow the postponement provisions

14.57 Section 14(11) states that a confiscation order *must not* be quashed on the sole ground that there was a defect or omission in the procedure connected with the application for the granting of a postponement.

14.58 In effect this prevents confiscation orders being quashed because of some procedural irregularity in the postponement procedures. There is an exception to this rule, if, before the court made the confiscation order, it imposed a fine on the defendant, or made an order falling within s 13(3) of POCA (ie a compensation order, a forfeiture order, or a deprivation order), or made an order under s 130 of the PCC(S)A (compensation orders), then, under s 14(12), a procedural irregularity of that type is likely to lead to the confiscation order being quashed.

(7) Postponement pending appeal

14.59 Under section 14(6) of POCA, if:

> 14 (6) (a) the Defendant appeals against his conviction for the offence (or any of the offences) concerned, and
> (b) the period of three months (starting with the day when the appeal is determined or otherwise disposed of) ends after the period found under sub-section (5), the permitted period is that period of three months.

Section 14(6) reflects s 3(6) of the DTA, and provides, where a defendant has appealed, that the postponement shall not, save where the court is satisfied there are exceptional circumstances, exceed three months after the date on which the appeal is determined or otherwise disposed of.

(8) Sentencing

14.60 If the court postpones proceedings under s 6 it may proceed to sentence the defendant for the offence (or any of the offences) concerned, by virtue of s 15(1). Section 15(2) provides:

> (2) In sentencing the Defendant for the offence (or any of the offences concerned) in the postponement period the Court must not (a) impose a fine on him, (b) make an order falling within section 13(3) [see para 14.58 above], or (c) make an order for the payment of compensation under Section 130 of the Sentencing Act.

14.61 The purpose of this section is to prevent sentencing being delayed while confiscation is being considered. This avoids criticism, previously levied under the DTOA and CJA, that delaying sentence until a confiscation order was made led to injustice because in certain cases the defendant was having to wait many months after his conviction before knowing his fate. This anomaly was remedied by s 3(7) of the DTA. It is submitted that in certain cases the defendant may benefit if the judge decides not to sentence until the confiscation hearing is over. For example, where new information surfaces concerning the defendant's criminal lifestyle, or lack of it, during the confiscation hearing, or where an assumption may have been made in respect of the defendant, which is also relevant to sentencing, and the defence are able to show at the confiscation hearing that it has no force. In those circumstances it may be to the defendant's benefit if the judge does not sentence until the confiscation hearing is over, and all of the facts have been considered. In *R v Donohoe* The Times, 20 October 2006, the Court of Appeal held that the making of a technically erroneous order for the forfeiture of illegal drugs did not have the effect of depriving the court of the jurisdiction to make a confiscation order. It would frustrate the object of the 2002 Act to hold that the erroneous imposition of a trivial fine rendered the court powerless to proceed with the substantive confiscation proceedings.

(9) Power to vary sentence

14.62 Under s 15(3), if the court decides to sentence the defendant for the offence concerned in the postponement period, once that period has ended the court may vary the sentence by imposing a fine on him, or making an order falling within s 13(3) (compensation, forfeiture, or deprivation orders), or making an order for the payment of compensation under s 130 of the PCC(S)A. However, the court may only proceed under s 13(3) within a period of 28 days starting from the last day of the postponement period (s 15(4)). In practice this means that a court may vary the sentence within 28 days of the end of the postponement period by making one or more of the orders referred to in s 13(3), ie a fine or ancillary order. This is intended to enable the court to order, for example, the forfeiture and destruction of drugs, if the court had not done so already.

E. Preparatory Steps for a POCA Hearing

(1) Section 16 statements of information

14.63 Under s 16(1) of POCA if the court is proceeding under s 6(3)(a) (where the prosecutor or Director of ARA has asked the court to proceed under the confiscation provisions), the prosecutor (or Director) must provide the court with a statement of information, within 'any period' that the court orders.

14.64 Alternatively, if the court is proceeding under s 6(3)(b) (where the court believed it was appropriate to proceed to a confiscation hearing without an invitation from the prosecutor), it may order the prosecutor to give it a statement of information, and the prosecutor must present such a statement within the time frame the court orders (see s 16(2)).

(2) The purpose of s 16 statements

14.65 Section 16(3) provides that if the prosecutor or the Director (as the case may be) believes the defendant has a criminal lifestyle, the statement of information should include matters the prosecutor or Director believes are relevant in connection with deciding the following issues:

16 (3) (a) whether the Defendant has a criminal lifestyle;
     (b) whether he has benefited from his general criminal conduct;
     (c) his benefit from the conduct.

14.66 The purpose of these statements is the same as under the DTA and CJA. Firstly, they enable the defence and the court to be put on notice of the Crown's case and prevent the defence from being taken by surprise. Secondly, they identify the real issues in terms of the Crown's case, thereby saving court time in relation to matters that are not really disputed. In *R v Comiskey* (1991) 93 Cr App R 227, Turner J, in delivering the judgment of the Court, said (at p 231): 'it is very desirable that those responsible for the prosecution of offences should make full use of this (section)' (when dealing with the use of s 11 statements under the DTA). Further, the Court of Appeal considered the purpose of prosecutor's statements in *R v Benjafield* (2001) 2 Cr App R(S) 221, para 107. In finding that such statements did not contravene Article 6 of the European Convention of Human Rights they held that:

> A statement serves the useful purpose of forewarning the Defendant of the case of the prosecution which he will have to meet as to his assets. It should assist the Defendant by making clear the matters with which he has to be prepared to deal. It is right that, as the rules require, the prosecution should identify any information which would assist the Defendant.

(3) The content of s 16 statements

14.67 Under s 16 of POCA the prosecutor or ARA should give to the court a statement with as much relevant detail as possible relating to the defendant's benefit from criminal conduct.

14.68 The full content of the statement will depend on whether the prosecutor alleges the defendant has a criminal lifestyle. Under s 16(4), the statement should also include information relevant to the making of the assumptions if the prosecutor believes that the defendant has had a criminal lifestyle.

14.69 If the prosecutor or the Director of the ARA (as the case may be) does not believe the defendant has a criminal lifestyle, the statement of information becomes a statement of matters the prosecutor or Director believes are relevant in deciding whether or not the defendant has benefited from his *particular* criminal conduct and, if so, his benefit from that conduct (see s 16(5)).

14.70 Under r 58.1 of the Criminal Procedure Rules, when the prosecutor or the Director of ARA is required, under s 16 of the Act, to give a statement to the Crown Court, the prosecutor or the Director, as the case may be, must also, as soon as practicable, serve a copy of the statement on the defendant. Any statement given to the Crown Court by the prosecutor or the Director under s 16 of the Act must, in addition to the information required by the Act, include the following information, pursuant to r 58.1(2) of the Criminal Procedure Rules:

(1) the name of the defendant;
(2) the name of the person by whom the statement is made and the date on which it is made; and
(3) where the statement is not given to the Crown Court immediately after the defendant has been convicted, the date on which, and the place where the relevant conviction occurred.

For further commentary on the form and content of the prosecutor's statements see Chapter 9, paras 9.60 et seq.

(4) A duty of full and frank disclosure?

14.71 If the prosecutor or Director of ARA believes that the defendant has a criminal lifestyle, under s 16(4) the statement must include information relevant to the making of the assumptions. To avoid criticism of the Crown/ARA, it is submitted that the statement should also include information about matters known to the prosecutor or ARA that might contribute to the court concluding that making an assumption would amount to a serious risk of injustice.

E. Preparatory Steps for a POCA Hearing

(5) When should the s 16 statement be served?

14.72 Under s 16(1) and (2) the prosecutor or Director of ARA must give the statement of information to the court 'within the period the Court orders'. It is submitted, however, that in matters flowing from criminal trials the best practice is to serve the s 16 statement prior to said trial whenever possible and, except in the most complex cases, not later than the return of the jury. This will enable the trial judge to be in the best possible position to give directions as to how the POCA enquiry should proceed after conviction or a timely guilty plea.

14.73 It will be noted, pursuant to r 57.7 of the Criminal Procedure Rules, that witness statements should be verified with a statement of truth in confiscation proceedings.

(6) Disclosure evidence inadmissible

14.74 A potential danger arises if information is passed to the prosecutor before the trial that reveals matters contained within the defendant's disclosure statement, if disclosure has been ordered pursuant to a restraint order. The prosecutor must be reminded that such disclosure is protected from cross examination by the Crown, pursuant to the restraint order itself and *Re O (Restraint Order)* [1991] 2 QB 520, 530 (CA); *Re C (Restraint Order: Identification)* The Times, 24 April 1995; *Re C (Restraint Order: Disclosure)* (4 September 2000) (DTA 7/2000) at paras 42, 43; and *Re D* [2001] EWHC Admin 668. A similar danger may arise if the prosecutor were allowed to utilise disclosures made in a defendant's reply to a s 16 statement, and may well offend against the principle of avoiding self incrimination. As a result some protection is included within the POCA statutory framework under s 17(6):

> No acceptance under section 17 (the defendant's response to the prosecutor's statement) that the Defendant has benefited from criminal conduct is admissible in evidence in proceedings for an offence.

This protection is also underlined by r 57.8 of the Criminal Procedure Rules. For further discussion on self incrimination, see para 14.92 below.

(7) Upon whom should the prosecutor's statement be served?

14.75 Section 16(1) of POCA states that the statement of information must be given to the court. At the same time as the court orders a statement to be prepared, it may also direct that a copy be served on the defendant and/or the defendant's solicitors.

14.76 There is no requirement in the Criminal Procedure Rules that a statement should be served on solicitors acting on behalf of the co-accused. This is because statements frequently disclose personal matters relating to the defendant's financial affairs and exhibit his disclosure statements sworn in compliance with a restraint order. Because it is in the public interest that the defendant should be encouraged to make full and frank disclosure of all his realisable property in such statements, it is submitted he is not likely to do so if the statement was to come into the hands of third parties.

(8) The defendant's statement

14.77 Section 17 of POCA reads as follows:

> (1) If the Prosecutor or the Director gives the Court a Statement of Information and a copy is served on the Defendant, the Court may order the Defendant—

(a) to indicate (within the period it orders) the extent to which he accepts each allegation in the statement, and
(b) so far as he does not accept such an allegation to give particulars of any matters he proposes to rely on.'

14.78 The purpose of s 17 is similar to that of defence statements under the DTA and CJA, namely to identify areas of dispute for the confiscation hearing, so that evidence may be adduced only in relation to the disputed points, thus narrowing the issues and saving court time. Under r 58.1 of the Criminal Procedure Rules where, under s 17 of the Act, the Crown Court orders the defendant to indicate the extent to which he accepts each allegation in a statement given by the prosecutor or the Director of the ARA, the defendant is then under a duty to state in writing to the prosecutor or the Director (as the case may be) his position and must give a copy to the Crown Court.

14.79 When considering s 17(1)(a), the defence should consider paragraph by paragraph the prosecutor's statement and state whether each allegation is admitted or denied. (This is analogous to a defence in civil proceedings and a similar approach should be adopted when drafting the defendant's statement). Where an allegation is denied, any facts relied upon to support that denial should be fully set out. The statement should also be verified by a statement of truth (r 57.7 of the Criminal Procedure Rules).

14.80 The importance of obtaining independent corroboration of the defendant's assertions cannot be overemphasised. In *R v Walbrook and Glasgow* [1994] Crim LR 613, the Court of Appeal held that where a defendant wanted to show the amount of his realisable assets available for confiscation was less than the amount of his benefit as certified by the court, he had to produce clear and cogent evidence; 'vague and generalised assertions unsupported by evidence would rarely if ever be sufficient'. It also must be remembered that at this stage the defendant is likely to stand convicted, whether by guilty plea or by verdict of a jury, of an offence and may therefore have something of a credibility problem. This matter is further discussed in Chapter 9, paras 9.74 et seq.

(9) Defendant's acceptance conclusive

14.81 Under s 17(2) of POCA, if the defendant accepts to any extent an allegation in the statement of information, the court may treat his acceptance as conclusive of the matters to which it relates for the purpose of deciding the issues referred to in s 16(3) (general criminal conduct) or s 16(5) (particular criminal conduct), as the case may be. Great care therefore should be taken only to admit assertions made in the prosecutor's statement that are genuinely accepted.

14.82 It should be noted however, that the defendant's acceptance will not necessarily be binding on appeal. In the case of *R v Emmett* [1997] 3 WLR 1119, a DTOA case, the defendant pleaded guilty at the Crown Court stage. It was agreed between counsel that the benefit figure amounted to £100,000 and various sums were agreed in respect of his realisable assets. The judge made an agreed confiscation order. In the Court of Appeal the Crown submitted that the general right to appeal against a confiscation order was excluded by virtue of the corresponding provision to s 17(2) of POCA, found in the then DTOA, in respect of the defendant's acceptance of any allegation in a statement tendered by the prosecutor

E. Preparatory Steps for a POCA Hearing

which had been acted upon by the court. However, the Court of Appeal ruled that there was a strong presumption that, except by specific provision, the legislature will not exclude a right of appeal as of right, or with leave, where such a right is ordinarily available (as per *R v Cain* [1985] AC 46, 55g–56d). In *Emmett* Lord Steyn held that unless the Act expressly or by necessary implication excluded a right of appeal, there is, as a matter of jurisdiction, a right of appeal against a confiscation order in all cases. However, he went on to state, at p 1123, that:

> it is of course true that if there is an appeal, the Court of Appeal may have to take account of the fact that a Judge has decided to treat an acceptance of an allegation in a prosecution statement as conclusive, and the Court of Appeal may have to give proper and due weight to that consideration.

(10) Failure to respond by the defendant

14.83 If the defendant fails in any respect to comply with an order under s 17(1) he may be treated, under s 17(3), as having accepted every allegation in the statement of information, apart from:

(a) any allegation in respect of which he has complied with the requirement;
(b) any allegation that he has benefited from his general or particular criminal conduct.

14.84 Thus, if the defendant fails to respond to a statement of fact, the fact may be deemed by the court to be true.

14.85 However, there should not be any automatic assumption that the defendant has accepted an allegation that he has benefited from general or particular criminal conduct. This is because, at the time this legislation was introduced, and as part of the explanatory notes that accompanied POCA, it was considered inappropriate that the defendant's silence should be conclusive of the two principle issues before the court.

14.86 One of the purposes of s 17 is to avoid the defendant ambushing the Crown by not disclosing in advance what his case is. In addition to this, s 17(1) anticipates giving the prosecution the opportunity of making enquiries into the correctness of the defendant's assertions.

(11) Consequences of the defendant failing to respond to the prosecutor's statement

14.87 The defendant who fails to respond to orders of the court made under s 17 of POCA runs the risk of having a confiscation order made in the full amount of his benefit from his criminal conduct as alleged by the prosecution.

14.88 In *R v Comiskey* (1991) 93 Cr App R 227, the Court of Appeal held that once the prosecution have proved benefit and the amount of the defendant's proceeds, the burden then passes to the defendant to show, on a balance of probabilities, the value of realisable property was less than this sum. If he fails to discharge that burden, the court must make a confiscation order in the full amount by which it has certified he has benefited from his crime.

14.89 Similarly, the Court of Appeal has shown a reluctance to interfere with confiscation orders made in circumstances where the defendant has failed to respond to the prosecutor's statement and has failed to give evidence at the confiscation hearing.

14.90 In *R v Layode* (CA, 12 March 1993) the defendant failed to respond to the prosecutor's financial statement or give evidence at the confiscation hearing. The Court of Appeal dismissed the defendant's appeal against the confiscation order. McPhearson J, in delivering the judgment of the court, observed that:

> 'if the Judge was wrong about the realisable assets and the bank accounts . . . the Appellant had nobody but himself to blame in this regard.'

14.91 He added that this case underlined the importance of a defendant submitting evidence.

(12) The problem of self incrimination

14.92 Within s 17 there is a perceived safety guard in respect of self incrimination. Section 17(6) provides as follows:

> no acceptance under this Section that the Defendant has benefited from conduct is admissible in evidence in proceedings for an offence.

14.93 A similar provision existed under the DTA (s 11(11)). One of the purposes of s 17(6) is to prevent the defendant invoking his privilege against self-incrimination as a justification for failing to respond to a prosecutor's statement. This provision is analogous to the condition subject to which disclosure orders are made in restraint orders and which are designed to protect the defendant's privilege against self-incrimination (see para 14.74 above and r 57.8 of the Criminal Procedure Rules).

14.94 The purpose of a s 17 defendant's statement in response is not to assist the prosecution to advance their case. The reality however, it is submitted, is that there will often be an overlap between the criminal investigation and preparation for the confiscation hearing, particularly in criminal cases involving financial investigations, and often to the detriment of the defendant (see further Chapter 4: *Re J* [2001] EWHC Admin 713 at para 20 challenging *R v Martin and White* (1998) 2 Cr App R 385, and *Re C (Restraint Order: Disclosure)*, (4 September 2000) (DTA/7/2000); and on self incrimination: *Re E and Re H* [2001] EWHC Admin 472; *Istel v Tully* [1993] AC 45 at pp 55–57; and *Re: T (Restraint Order: Disclosure of Assets)* (1993) 96 Cr App R 194).

14.95 Section 17(6) is intended to encourage the defendant to be more forthcoming in his disclosure, whereas if the protection afforded by s 17(6) did not exist, the defendant may be reluctant to admit benefit from criminal conduct that had not been the subject of a prosecution. For further see Chapter 9, paras 9.81.

(13) Further provision of information by the defendant

14.96 Like s 12 of the DTA, s 18 of POCA makes the obligations on the defendant at the POCA enquiry fairly draconian. Section 18 applies either where the court is proceeding under s 6 of POCA in a matter where s 6(3)(a) applies (ie the prosecutor or the Director of ARA have asked the court to proceed) or where s 6(3)(b) applies (ie the court believes it is appropriate

E. Preparatory Steps for a POCA Hearing

to do so), or in circumstances where the court is considering whether or not it will proceed itself under s 6, (see s 18(1)(a) and (b)). Under r 58.1(4) of the Criminal Procedure Rules where the Crown Court orders the defendant to give to it any information under s 18 of the Act, the defendant must provide the information in writing and must, as soon as practicable, serve a copy of it on:

(a) the prosecutor, if the prosecutor asked the court to proceed under s 6 of the Act; or
(b) the Director, if the Director asked the court to proceed under s 6 of the Act.

Under s 18(2), for the purpose of obtaining information to help the court to carry out its function the court may at any time order the Defendant to give it such information as specified in the order.

14.97 Whereas under the DTA and the CJA the expression 'at any time' meant after the court had made a decision to proceed, under s 18(1)(b) the wording is more far reaching, to include where the court 'is considering whether to proceed'. A court could be considering whether or not to proceed under s 6 of POCA before the defendant is found guilty, in which case it would appear that s 18 would bite.

14.98 The purpose of s 18 is to allow the court to make an order where the defendant is relying, or has relied, on certain matters, and the court considers it requires more information to assist it in determining the point in question.

14.99 If the defendant fails to comply with the court's order, without reasonable excuse, s 18(4) allows the court to draw any inference it believes appropriate. Section 18(5) states that:

(5) Subsection 4 does not affect any power of the Court to deal with the Defendant in respect of a failure to comply with an order under this section.

14.100 For example, the court's power to punish the defendant for contempt of court in refusing to comply with the order would exist in addition to the court's power to draw an inference or rely on an assumption as a result of the defendant's failure to comply.

It will be noted that pursuant to r 57.7 of the Criminal Procedure Rules statements provided should bear a statement of truth.

(14) Further protection against self incrimination

14.101 Section 18(9) contains a similar provision to that in s 17(6), in that it protects the defendant from incriminating himself and others in the making of any admission or reply to s 18 (see para 14.92 above and r 57.8 of the Criminal Procedure Rules). However if the information disclosed leads the prosecuting authority to other new information or evidence, s 18 does not appear to prevent the authorities from using that other evidence.

(15) Prosecutor's acceptance conclusive

14.102 Under s 18(6) of POCA, any acceptance by the prosecutor of any assertion contained in a defendant's statement may be treated by the court as being conclusive for the purposes of the POCA enquiry.

(16) Failure to provide the information ordered

14.103 The position of a defendant who fails to provide information under s 18(2) of POCA is dealt with in s 18(4) which provides as follows:

If the Defendant fails without reasonable excuse to comply with an order under this section the Court may draw such inference as it believes is appropriate.

(17) Further statements by the prosecutor

14.104 Section 16(6) provides:

(6) If the Prosecutor or the Director gives the Court a statement of information—
  (a) he may at any time give the Court a further statement of information;
  (b) he must give the Court a further statement of information if it orders him to do so and he must give it within the period the Court orders.

14.105 A practice developed under the DTA and the CJA of the prosecutor submitting a further statement if there were matters in the defendant's statement with which he disagreed or which called for further comment (see s 11(4) of the DTA). Section 16(6) of POCA endorses this practice and provides for a further statement to be tendered by the prosecutor either acting on his own volition or in compliance with an order of the court.

(18) Securing the attendance of witnesses

14.106 Once s 16 and s 17 statements have been served, the parties should advise each other of which witnesses they require at the hearing. It should be borne in mind that certain civilian witnesses, especially those employed by financial institutions, may not be prepared to attend the court voluntarily. In such cases witness summonses should be sought from the appropriate officer of the Crown Court.

(19) Joint control of assets and multiple defendants

14.107 For commentary on the joint control or passing of assets where the proceeds have passed through more than one defendant's hands (see para 10.19 of Chapter 10).

(20) Expert evidence

14.108 The procedure to be followed for adducing expert evidence in confiscation hearings and the exceptions to same are set out in r 57.9 and 57.10 of the Criminal Procedure Rules.

(21) Service of documents

14.109 The procedure relating to the service of documents in relation to Part 2 of POCA is set out in r 57.11 of the Criminal Procedure Rules. The procedure for alternative service and service outside of the jurisdiction is contained in rr 57.12 amd 57.13 of the Criminal Procedure Rules respectively.

15

THE POCA CONFISCATION HEARING

A.	Introduction	15.01	G. Tainted Gifts	15.48
B.	A Mandatory Regime	15.03	(1) When is a gift tainted?	15.49
	(1) Confiscation orders made		(2) Gifts and their recipients	15.55
	by magistrates' courts	15.05	(3) Value of tainted gifts	15.59
	(2) Basis of pleas	15.06	H. Time for Payment	15.61
C.	The Burden and Standard of Proof	15.07	(1) Imprisonment in default	15.65
D.	The Defendant's Benefit	15.11	(2) Interest on unpaid sums	15.69
	(1) General criminal conduct	15.13	(3) Unreasonable delay in	
	(2) Rule against double counting	15.14	enforcement	15.70
	(3) Particular criminal conduct	15.16	I. The Effect of a Confiscation	
	(4) Recent case law	15.17	Order on Sentence and the	
	(5) Proceeds, not profits	15.18	Court's Other Powers	15.71
	(6) Value of property obtained from		(1) The relationship between the	
	criminal conduct	15.19	confiscation order and	
E.	The Assumptions: Section 10	15.20	compensation	15.72
	(1) The four assumptions	15.24	(2) The importance of following	
	(2) The 'relevant day'	15.25	the provisions of POCA	15.74
	(3) The 'date of conviction'	15.27	(3) Orders for the payment of costs	15.76
	(4) When the assumptions do not apply	15.28	J. Confiscation and the ECHR	15.77
F.	The Recoverable Amount	15.31	K. Appeals	15.79
	(1) Recoverable amount: victims	15.33	L. Interpretation: Confiscation	
	(2) The 'available amount'	15.34	and POCA	15.81
	(3) Market value	15.38	M. Steps to Confiscation: A Summary	15.82
	(4) Hidden assets	15.45		
	(5) Court must give reasons	15.46		
	(6) Costs of sale	15.47		

A. Introduction

Whether the hearing is under the Proceeds of Crime Act 2002 (POCA), the Drug Trafficking Offences Act 1994 (DTA), or the Civil Justice Act 1988 (CJA), the purpose of the confiscation hearing remains very similar. It is to determine whether or not the defendant has benefited from the offences of which he has been convicted (or which have been taken into consideration); the amount of that benefit; and the value of the defendant's assets available to meet any confiscation order. Many of the considerations outlined in the DTA and CJA confiscation hearing chapters apply equally to POCA. Where possible we

15.01

have attempted to introduce the existing case law into this chapter, although to avoid some repetition the reader is also referred to the previous chapters for reference.

15.02 POCA took effect from 24 March 2003. Where an indictment starts before that date the old Acts will still apply (SI 2003/333).

B. A Mandatory Regime

15.03 Section 6 sets out the circumstances in which confiscation orders may be made under Part 2 of POCA. It is a mandatory regime. A confiscation order under s 6 is an order to a convicted defendant to pay a sum of money representing the defendant's benefit from crime. Section 6 is considered more fully in Chapter 14.

15.04 The principal points, however, are as follows:

(1) The Crown Court must proceed under s 6 if the following two conditions are satisfied:
   (a) the defendant falls within s 6(2) (ie he is convicted of an offence or offences in proceedings before the Crown Court; or he is committed to the Crown Court for sentence by a magistrates' court under ss 3, 4, or 6 of the Powers of Criminal Courts (Sentencing) Act 2000 (PCC(S)A); or he is committed to the Crown Court in respect of an offence or offences under s 70 of POCA (committal with a view to a confiscation order being made));
   (b) the prosecutor or the Director of the Assets Recovery Agency (ARA) has asked the court to proceed under s 6 or the court believes it is appropriate to do so.
(2) Once the above is satisfied, the court must proceed in the following way:
   (a) it must decide whether the defendant has a criminal lifestyle;
   (b) if it decides that he has a criminal lifestyle it must decide whether he has benefited from his general criminal conduct;
   (c) if it decides that he does not have a criminal lifestyle it must decide whether he has benefited from his particular criminal conduct (s 6(4)).
(3) If the court decides under s 6(4)(b) or (c) that the defendant has benefited from either general or particular criminal conduct it must:
   (a) decide the recoverable amount and
   (b) make an order (the confiscation order) requiring him to pay that amount (as per s 6(5)).
(4) Under s 6(6), the court must treat the duty in s 6(5) as a power (an option) if it believes that any victim of the conduct has at any time started or intends to start proceedings against the defendant in respect of loss, injury, or damage sustained in connection with the conduct (see Chapter 12, para 12.09 and para 15.33 below).

(1) Confiscation orders made by magistrates' courts

15.05 Section 97 of SOCPA allows for provision to be made for magistrates' courts to make confiscation orders under Pt 2 or 4 of POCA. Section 97(2) provides that the power of the magistrates' courts to make a confiscation order is subject to a restriction that the amount does not exceed £10,000. Orders above this amount can only therefore be made by the Crown Court. (See para 14.07 of Chapter 14.)

(2) Basis of pleas

15.06 Care should be taken when drafting and agreeing to basis of pleas, particularly on behalf of the prosecution. See *R v Lunnon* (2005) 1 Cr App R(S) 24 and *R v Lazarus* [2005] Crim LR 64, discussed further at para 12.20 of Chapter 12. In *R v Byatt* [2006] EWCA Crim 904, the defendant pleaded guilty to conspiracy to rob. In his basis of plea, not challenged by the prosecution, he stated he withdrew from the conspiracy prior to the robbery taking place. He did not obtain the cash stolen in any realistic way. In those circumstances the Court held there was no benefit under POCA.

C. The Burden and Standard of Proof

15.07 In line with both the DTA and the CJA the standard of proof in determining whether the defendant has a criminal lifestyle and the recoverable amount is on a balance of probabilities (s 6(7)).

15.08 The issue of whether the defendant has benefited from the offences of which he has been convicted and the amount of that benefit is a matter for the prosecution to prove. In terms of the value of the defendant's assets available to meet a confiscation order it is for the defendant to establish that the value of the realisable property is less than the amount of the benefit. In all circumstances, the standard of proof is on a balance of probabilities. (See *R v Barwick* (2001) 1 Cr App R(S) 129 where the Court of Appeal confirmed that in confiscation proceedings (under the CJA) it was for the prosecution to establish that the defendant had benefited from an offence and the value of that benefit. Once that had been established, it was for the offender to prove, on a balance of probabilities, that the amount that might be realised is less than the value of his calculated benefit (see also *R v Layode* (CA, 12 March 1993), *R v Carroll* [1991] Crim LR 720 and *R v Ilsemann* 12 Cr App R(S) 398)).

15.09 Unlike under the DTA and the CJA where the standard of proof is expressed as being 'to the civil standard', under POCA the standard is expressed as being on the 'balance of probabilities'. This imports that the courts will be entitled to apply a test which is more closely linked to satisfaction on a 51/49 per cent basis (see Chapter 9, para 9.51).

15.10 In *R v Levin* The Times, 20 February 2004 the Court of Appeal confirmed that the standard of proof to be applied in confiscation proceedings was that of the civil standard. As a result, when making a determination a judge was entitled to take into account both the evidence given at trial and any other information properly obtained either before the trial or thereafter, including evidence inadmissible at trial. The Court held that the corresponding provisions under the CJA had been intended to change the procedural landscape in that:

(1) the standard of proof was now the civil burden;
(2) the court could make far-reaching assumptions;
(3) the court could require the defendant to provide information and could draw inferences from the failure to do so; and
(4) the court might rely on evidence given at trial and any relevant information properly obtained either before the trial or thereafter in order to determine a defendant's benefit and the amount to be recovered.

The Court held that these changes did and were intended to separate the confiscation proceedings from the criminal proceedings. For further, see paras 10.04 of Chapter 10.

D. The Defendant's Benefit

15.11 Section 8(1) of POCA provides:

(1) If the court is proceeding under Section 6 this section applies for the purpose of—
   (a) deciding whether the defendant has benefited from conduct; and
   (b) deciding his benefit from the conduct.
(2) The court must—
   (a) take account of conduct occurring up to the time it makes its decision;
   (b) take account of property obtained up to that time.

15.12 Section 6 makes it clear that Pt 2 of POCA provides for confiscation of the defendant's benefit from either his 'general criminal conduct' or his 'particular criminal conduct'.

(1) General criminal conduct

15.13 Section 8(3) to (8) of POCA deal with the situation where the court is holding confiscation proceedings in respect of the defendant's general criminal conduct. General criminal conduct means any criminal conduct of the defendants, whenever the conduct occurred and whether or not it has ever formed the subject of any criminal prosecution (s 76(2)).

(2) Rule against double counting

15.14 In theory, where a defendant has been the subject of a confiscation order in the past, a court making a general criminal conduct confiscation order could confiscate the same benefit twice, unless the legislation prevented it. Section 8(4) prevents double counting by ensuring that a calculation of benefit once made in relation to an offence would apply for the purposes of any subsequent calculation of benefit in respect of general criminal conduct:

8(3) Subsection 4 applies if—
   (a) the conduct concerned is general criminal conduct,
   (b) a confiscation order mentioned in subsection (5) has at an earlier time been made against the defendant, and
   (c) his benefit for the purpose of that order was benefit from his general criminal conduct.
(4) His benefit found at the time of the last confiscation order mentioned in subsection (3)(c) was made against him must be taken for the purposes of this section to be his benefit from his general criminal conduct at that time.
(5) If the conduct concerned is general criminal conduct the court must deduct the aggregate of the following amounts—
   (a) the amount ordered to be paid under each confiscation order previously made against the defendant;
   (b) the amount ordered to be paid under each confiscation order previously made against him under any of the provisions listed in subsection 7.

Section 8(5) does not apply to an amount that has been taken into account for the purposes of a deduction of that subsection on any earlier occasion (s 8(6)).

D. The Defendant's Benefit

15.15 The provisions in s 8(7) include the Drug Trafficking and Offences Act 1986 (DTOA), Pt VI of the CJA, Pt I of the DTA and Pt 3 and 4 of POCA 2002. The reference to general criminal conduct in the case of a confiscation order made under any of the provisions listed in s 8(7) is a reference to conduct in respect of which the court is required or entitled to make one or more assumptions for the purpose of assessing the person's benefit from the conduct (see s 8(8)).

(3) Particular criminal conduct

15.16 Particular criminal conduct means the offences of which the defendant has been convicted in the current proceedings, together with any taken into consideration by the court in passing sentence (s 76(3)). For a definition of criminal conduct see s 76 (see Chapter 14, para 14.35 et seq for more detail about these provisions).

(4) Recent case law

15.17 For a review of recent case law under the sister DTA and CJA regimes, see para 10.82 of Chapter 10. In *R v Ajibade* [2006] 2 Cr App R(S) 486 it was determined that the principles in *R v Dore* [1997] 2 Cr App R(S) 152 (controlled drugs have no market value because they cannot be sold lawfully) applies in POCA cases. (See para 15.38 below.)

(5) Proceeds, not profits

15.18 It is important to note that the court is concerned at this stage to assess the defendant's proceeds of crime and not merely his profits. Consequently, in assessing the value of his proceeds, the court is not required to deduct the cost of any expenses of the enterprise such as the travelling expenses incurred in their importation (see para 10.52 of Chapter 10).

(6) Value of property obtained from criminal conduct

15.19 When deciding the value of property obtained by a person as a result of, or in connection with, his criminal conduct, s 80 of POCA applies. Section 80(1) states that the material time for valuing property is the time when the court makes its decision.

Section 80(2) provides:
(2) The value of the property at the material time is the greater of the following—
   (a) the value of the property (at the time the person obtained it) adjusted to take account of later changes in the value of money;
   (b) the value at the material time of the property found under subsection (3).
(3) The property found under this subsection is as follows:
   (a) if the person holds the property obtained, the property found under this subsection is that property;
   (b) if he holds no part of the property obtained, the property found under this subsection is any property which directly or indirectly represents it in his hands;
   (c) if he holds part of the property obtained, the property found under this subsection is that part and any property which directly or indirectly represents the other part in his hands.

See also para 10.116 of Chapter 10 and *R v Scragg* (2006) EWCA Crim 2916 where the Court of Appeal held that it ws not realistic to treat the purchase and sale of the same vehicle on separate criminal enterprises, and therefore there were not two separate benefits.

E. The Assumptions: Section 10

15.20 As we have seen the burden is on the prosecution to prove on the balance of probabilities the benefit and the value of the defendant's proceeds of criminal conduct. Section 10 of POCA creates a single scheme under which certain assumptions are mandatory. Under the DTA they were mandatory, but discretionary in all other confiscation cases. Now they are mandatory in all cases where a person has a criminal lifestyle (for a definition of criminal lifestyle see s 75 and para 14.25 in Chapter 14).

15.21 Section 10 therefore requires the court to make a number of assumptions in determining the question of benefit and the amount of proceeds from general criminal conduct. Section 10(1) provides:

> (1) If the court decides under Section 6 that the defendant has a criminal lifestyle it must make the following four assumptions for the purpose of (a) deciding whether he has benefited from his general criminal conduct, and (b) deciding his benefit from the conduct.

15.22 Section 10 applies where the court has decided that the defendant has a criminal lifestyle and it is, accordingly considering the defendant's benefit from general criminal conduct.

15.23 For further on the application of the assumptions generally, see para 10.63 of Chapter 10.

(1) The four assumptions

15.24 The four assumptions are as follows:

(1) That any property transferred to the defendant at any time after the relevant day was obtained by him:
   (a) as a result of his general criminal conduct, and
   (b) at the earliest time he appears to have held it (s 10(2)).
(2) That any property held by the defendant at any time after the date of conviction was obtained by him:
   (a) as a result of his general criminal conduct, and
   (b) at the earliest time he appears to have held it (s 10(3)).
(3) That any expenditure incurred by the defendant at any time after the relevant day was met from property obtained by him as a result of his general criminal conduct (s 10(4)).
(4) For the purpose of valuing any property obtained (or assumed to have been obtained) by the defendant, he obtained it free of any other interest in it (s 10(5)).

(2) The 'relevant day'

15.25 Under s 10(8), the 'relevant day' is the first day in the period of six years ending with:

(1) the day when proceedings for the offence concerned were started against the defendant, or
(2) if there are two or more offences and proceedings for them were started on different days, the earliest of those days.

15.26 However, where the defendant's benefit for the purposes of the confiscation order was a benefit from his general criminal conduct under s 8(3)(c), and that confiscation order was

F. The Recoverable Amount

made against the defendant at any time during the period mentioned in s 10(8), the 'relevant day' becomes the day when the defendant's benefit was calculated for the purposes of his last confiscation order; and the second assumption (relating to any property held by the defendant at any time after the date of conviction obtained by him as a result of his general criminal conduct) does not apply to any property which was held by him on or before the relevant day (as per s 10(9), with the intention, it is submitted of avoiding double counting).

(3) The 'date of conviction'

15.27 Under s 10(10) the date of conviction is:

(1) the date on which the defendant was convicted of the offence concerned, or
(2) if there are two or more offences and the convictions were on different dates, the date of the latest.

(4) When the assumptions do not apply

15.28 The court must not make a required assumption in relation to particular property or expenditure if:

(1) the assumption is shown to be incorrect, or
(2) there would be a serious risk of injustice if the assumption were made (see s 10(6)).

15.29 Under s 10(7) if the court does not make one or more of the required assumptions it must state its reasons. Where the court does not make any of the assumptions specified in the legislation, it must nevertheless continue to decide whether the defendant has benefited from general criminal conduct and decide the recoverable amount, albeit without the assistance of the assumptions.

15.30 In *R v Jones (Confiscation Orders)* The Times, 8 August 2006, the Court of Appeal held that 'serious risk of injustice' does not refer to hardship that would be sustained by the offender by virtue of the making of the confiscation order, and it does not operate so as to confer discretion on the court to determine whether it is fair to make a confiscation order at all. Parliament's plain intention was that a confiscation order should be made in every case where the court concludes that the offender has benefited from his general criminal conduct. See also para 10.65 of Chapter 10.

F. The Recoverable Amount

15.31 Section 7 of POCA provides that:

(1) The recoverable amount for the purposes of section 6 is an amount equal to the Defendant's benefit from the conduct concerned.
(2) But if the defendant shows that the available amount is less than that benefit the recoverable amount is—
    (a) the available amount, or
    (b) a nominal amount, if the available amount is nil.

15.32 It will be noted that under s 7 the method of calculation in terms of assessing the recoverable amount is the same as in the DTA and the CJA. The recoverable amount is the amount of the defendant's benefit from either his general criminal conduct or his particular criminal conduct (as the case may be). However, if the amount available for confiscation is, after consideration by the court, found to be less than the benefit in question, the confiscation order must be made in the lesser amount. The word 'nominal' is defined in the Oxford English Dictionary as meaning 'virtually nothing'.

(1) Recoverable amount: victims

15.33 Where the victim of the criminal conduct has started or intends to start proceedings against the defendant in respect of loss, injury, or damage sustained in connection with the conduct, the recoverable amount will be an amount which:

(1) the court believes is just, but
(2) does not exceed the amount found under s 7(1) or 7(2) as the case may be (see ss 6(6) and 7(3)).

(2) The 'available amount'

15.34 Section 9(1) and (2) of POCA provides:

(1) For the purposes of deciding the recoverable amount, the available amount is the aggregate of—
 (a) the total of the values (at the time the confiscation order is made) of all the free property then held by the Defendant minus the total amount payable in pursuance of obligations which then have priority, and
 (b) the total of the values (at that time) of all tainted gifts.
(2) An obligation has priority if it is an obligation of the defendant—
 (a) to pay an amount due in respect of a fine or other order of a Court which was imposed or made on conviction of an offence and at any time before the time the confiscation order is made, or
 (b) to pay a sum which would be included amongst preferential debts if the defendants bankruptcy had commenced on the date of the confiscation order or his winding up had been ordered on that date.

15.35 Under s 9(1) the 'available amount' is the value of all the defendant's property, minus certain prior obligations of the defendant, such as earlier fines, plus the value of all tainted gifts made by the defendant. It is, in effect, equivalent to the term 'the amount that might be realised' in the earlier confiscation legislation, and is calculated in the same way. The amount actually ordered to be confiscated is the 'recoverable amount', equivalent to 'the amount to be recovered' in the earlier confiscation legislation.

15.36 Section 9 (2) affirms a line of case law (*Comiskey, Ilsemann,* and *Cokovic*, see para 15.08 above) to the effect that the burden is on the defendant to show that the available amount is less than the benefit and to show the extent of that available amount.

15.37 Under s 9 the total of the values of all the free property held by the defendant may be taken into account. Section 82(3) defines free property as follows:

'Property is free unless an order is enforced in respect of it under any of these provisions:

(a) forfeiture orders under Section 27 of the Misuse of Drugs Act 1971;
(b) . . .
(c) . . .

F. The Recoverable Amount

(d) deprivation orders under Section 143 of the Sentencing Act;
(e) Section 23 or 111 of the Terrorism Act 2000 (forfeiture orders);
(f) Section 246, 266, 295(2) or 298(2) of this Act.

(3) Market value

15.38 Section 79 states that in deciding the value at any time of property held by a person, its value is the market value of the property at that time (s 79(2)). But if at that time another person has an interest in the property, its value, in relation to the person who holds the property, is the market value at the time of the person who holds the property's interest, ignoring any charging order (see s 79(3) and s 79(4) for the provisions relating to charging orders).

15.39 The words 'market value' in s 79(2) have the same meaning as that given in s 7(1) of the DTA. In *R v Dore* (1997) 2 Cr App R(S) 152, Lord Bingham CJ said (at p 158) that 'market value' means the market value if the property in question was lawfully sold; there is however no lawful market in drugs, so drugs themselves have no market value. In *R v Ajibade* [2006] EWCA Crim 368 the Court of Appeal quashed a confiscation order where the judge had taken into account the value of the drugs illegally imported by a courier as part of her benefit. It is submitted that the position would be different if there was evidence that the importer had purchased the drugs, as the price he had paid would be assumed (unless he satisfies the court to the contrary), to have been derived from earlier trafficking and that price therefore becomes part of the benefit figure, (see the third assumption under s 10 of POCA).

15.40 In *R v Hussain* [2006] EWCA Crim 621, the Court of Appeal had to consider whether or not the Crown Court judge had been correct to decline to make a confiscation order against a respondent who had been convicted of being knowingly concerned with the fraudulent evasion of the prohibition on the importation of a Class A controlled drug, namely diamorphine. The trial judge had indicated that there was no evidence as to how the defendant came into possession of the diamorphine, whether he bought it to sell as an investment, or whether he was acting with others. There was no evidence to indicate any previous involvement by him in the importing of illegal drugs.

15.41 The crucial issue for the Court of Appeal was whether the judge's decision was correct, having regard to the fact, undoubtedly, that the respondent had in his possession a quantity of drugs of considerable value if sold illicitly. The subsidiary question that arose was whether the drug had a 'market value' when it was acquired, or indeed at any subsequent time, the value being 'market value' by reason of the prescription in s 79(1) and (2) of POCA. Their Lordships held that the natural meaning of 'market value' is 'value in a lawful market'. The consequence in relation to something, which it is illegal to buy and to sell, is that it has no market value.

15.42 In *R v Dore* (above) Lord Bingham stated that drugs, which it was illegal to buy and to sell in this country, had no market value for the purposes of the provisions of the DTA. In their Lordships' opinion Parliament has recognised that the Court of Appeal had already decided that market value meant 'value in a lawful market', when it re-enacted the same expression into the 2002 Act. Different words could have been used, for example s 79 might have provided that the value of the property is the value to the defendant. It did not. In the Court's judgment therefore, Parliament must be taken to have advisedly and deliberately used an expression, which had already received an interpretation, by the Court of Appeal in that context (see para 14 of the judgment).

15.43 The result is not a result which is in any way offensive to common sense. In a case such as *Hussain*, the drugs having been seized, the defendant had received no benefit from the drugs themselves. Had he sold the drugs, the proceeds of sale, assuming them to be cash (or other property which it is lawful to buy and to sell in this country), would have been 'a benefit', which would have been the subject of confiscation proceedings.

15.44 Equally, if it could have been shown that the drugs in this case had been purchased with property, which was itself, the proceeds of drug trafficking, that property, which would normally be a sum in cash, would have been his benefit for the purposes of the Act. However, none of those circumstances applied *Hussain* (as per Stanley Burton J). The benefit therefore was nil and the judge's decision was upheld.

(4) Hidden assets

15.45 For a review of case law in relation to hidden assets under the DTA and CJA, see paras 10.94–10.99 of Chapter 10.

(5) Court must give reasons

15.46 Under s 7(5) if the court decides the available amount, it must include in the confiscation order a statement of its findings as to the matters relevant for deciding that amount.

(6) Costs of sale

15.47 See para 10.104 of Chapter 10.

G. Tainted Gifts

15.48 Under s 77(1) of POCA, the doctrine of tainted gifts applies if:
   (1) (a) no court has made a decision as to whether the Defendant has a criminal lifestyle or
      (b) the court has decided that the Defendant has a criminal lifestyle.

(1) When is a gift tainted?

15.49 Under s 77 of POCA, a gift becomes tainted if:
   (2) ... it was made by the defendant at any time after the relevant day.
   (3) A gift is also tainted if it was made by the defendant at any time and was of property—
      (a) which was obtained by the defendant as a result of or in connection with his general criminal conduct, or
      (b) which (in whole or in part and whether directly or indirectly) represented in the Defendant's hands property obtained by him as a result of or in connection with his general criminal conduct.

G. Tainted Gifts

15.50 Under s 77(9) the 'relevant day' referred to in s 77(2) is the first day of the period of six years ending with:
  (a) the day when proceedings for the offence concerned were started against the Defendant, or
  (b) if there are two or more offences and proceedings for them were started on different days, the earliest of those days.

15.51 Under POCA therefore a gift is tainted if it is made by the defendant to any person in the period beginning six years before the commencement of proceedings, (under s 77(2)) and is also tainted, if it was made by the defendant at any time and the gift was from the proceeds of crime (under s 77(3)).

15.52 Section 77(5) adds a further situation where a gift will be tainted, but, by virtue of s 77(4), it only applies if the court has decided that the defendant does not have a criminal lifestyle:
  (5) A gift is tainted if it was made by the defendant at any time after—
    (a) the date on which the offence concerned was committed, or
    (b) if his particular criminal conduct consists of two or more offences and they were committed on different dates, the date of the earliest.

15.53 For the purposes of s 77(5) an offence which is a continuing offence is committed on the first occasion when it is committed (as per s 77(6)), and the defendant's particular criminal conduct for the purposes of s 77(5), includes any conduct which constitutes offences which the court has taken into consideration in deciding his sentence for the offence or offences concerned (s 77(7)).

15.54 It should be noted that the gift might be a tainted gift whether it was made before or after the passing of POCA 2002 (as per s 77(8)). Further, like the earlier legislation, gifts made by the defendant to other persons may be placed under restraint at the restraint stage.

(2) Gifts and their recipients

15.55 Section 78(1) provides:
  (1) If the defendant transfers property to another person for a consideration whose value is significantly less than the value of the property at the time of the transfer, he is to be treated as making a gift.

15.56 This section is designed to prevent defendants from benefiting under the legislation if they sell property for an under value. Under POCA a 'gift' includes a transaction for a consideration which is significantly less than the value of the gift at the time of the transfer, eg if a defendant sells a painting worth £100,000 for £5,000.

15.57 This is a departure from the earlier legislation, where an undervalued transaction was defined as the difference between the value of the property when the defendant received it and its value at the time of the transfer.

15.58 References to a recipient of a tainted gift are to a person to whom the defendant has made the gift (s 78(3)).

(3) Value of tainted gifts

15.59 Under s 81 of POCA:
  (1) The value at any time (the material time) of a tainted gift is the greater of the following—

(a) the value at the time of the gift of the property given adjusted to take account of later changes in the value of money; and
(b) the value (at the material time) of the property found under subsection (2).
(2) The property found under this subsection is as follows:
   (a) if the recipient holds the property given, the property found under this subsection is that property;
   (b) if the recipient holds no part of the property given, the property found under this subsection is any property which directly or indirectly represents it in his hands;
   (c) if the recipient holds part of the property given, the property found under this subsection is that part and any property which directly or indirectly represents the other part in his hands.

15.60 Section 81 sets out how the court is to work out the value of property held by a person. These principles broadly reproduce the previous legislation. The references under s 81 to value are to the value found in accordance with s 79 (as per s 81(3)).

H. Time for Payment

15.61 Section 11 indicates how long the court may allow the defendant to pay the amount due under the confiscation order. Section 11(1) states that the amount ordered to be paid under a confiscation order must be paid on the making of the order (ie immediately) but this is subject to certain provisions:

(2) If the defendant shows that he needs time to pay the amount ordered to be paid, the court making the confiscation order may make an order allowing payment to be made in a specified period.
(3) The specified period—
   (a) must start with the day on which the confiscation order is made, and
   (b) must not exceed six months.

15.62 It is for the defendant to show that he needs more time to pay (eg because he envisages the sale of his home). If within the specified period the defendant applies to the Crown Court for the period to be extended and the court believes there are exceptional circumstances, it may make an order extending the period (see s 11(4)). However the court must not make an order under either s 11(2) or (4) unless it gives the prosecutor or the Director of the Assets Recovery Agency (ARA) a right to be heard and make representations at any such application.

15.63 Section 11(5) states the extended period:

(1) must start with the day on which the confiscation order is made, and
(2) must not exceed 12 months.

15.64 Similarly an order under s 11(4) may be made after the end of the specified period, but must not be made after the end of the period of 12 months starting on the day on which the confiscation order is made (see s 11(6)). Therefore, no more than 12 months may be granted from the day on which the confiscation order is made. For case law see para 10.138 of Chapter 10.

(1) Imprisonment in default

15.65 Under s 38(2) and (5) of POCA, the provisions of the PCC(S)A apply to the enforcement of a confiscation order in the same way as they apply to the imposition of a fine by the Crown Court. The effect of this provision is that the court must impose a prison sentence

H. Time for Payment

to be served in default of payment of the 'fine'. It will be noted that, as with the previous legislation, the serving of the sentence in default does not extinguish the debt.

15.66 The penalties available for default in payment are set out in s 139(4) of the PCC(S)A and are as follows:

An amount not exceeding £200—7 days
An amount exceeding £200 but not exceeding £500—14 days
An amount exceeding £500 but not exceeding £1,000—28 days
An amount exceeding £1,000 but not exceeding £2,500—45 days
An amount exceeding £2,500 but not exceeding £5,000—3 months
An amount exceeding £5,000 but not exceeding £10,000—6 months
An amount exceeding £10,000 but not exceeding £20,000—12 months
An amount exceeding £20,000 but not exceeding £50,000—18 months
An amount exceeding £50,000 but not exceeding £100,000—2 years
An amount exceeding £100,000 but not exceeding £250,000—3 years
An amount exceeding £250,000 but not exceeding £1,000,000—5 years
An amount exceeding £1,000,000—ten years

15.67 The imposition of a default sentence was held to be mandatory in *R v Popple* [1992] Crim LR 675 and s 38(2) of POCA provides that the default sentence must be served consecutively to any sentence of imprisonment imposed for the substantive offence. It should be noted, however, that the above sentences are the maximum that may be imposed and it does not follow that the maximum sentence available for a particular amount should automatically be imposed in every case.

15.68 In *R v Szrajber* (1994) 15 Cr App R (S) 821, Crim LR 543 a CJA confiscation order was made against the defendant in the sum of £407,188 and a five year sentence of imprisonment imposed for default in making payment, being the maximum period that could be ordered in respect of a sum between £250,000 and £1 million. The trial judge imposed the maximum sentence assuming it was a fixed period that she was required to impose. The Court of Appeal ruled, however, that the periods set out in the table were maximum periods and the court had discretion to impose a period below the maximum. The normal procedure would be for the court to impose a default sentence that fell between the maximum and minimum of the band being considered. So, for a confiscation order in the sum imposed against the defendant, a default sentence between three and five years should normally be imposed. In determining the proper sentence the court had to have regard to the circumstances of the case, the overall seriousness of the matter and in particular to the purpose for which the default sentence was imposed, namely to secure payment of the sum ordered to be confiscated. It was not necessary to approach the matter on a strict arithmetical basis. In the circumstances, the court varied the default sentence to four years. See also *R v French* (1995) 16 Cr App R(S) 841, where the court held that the period of imprisonment in default should be such, within the maximum permitted, as to make it completely clear to the defendant that he had nothing to gain by failing to comply with the order.

(2) Interest on unpaid sums

15.69 If the amount to be paid by a person under a confiscation order is not paid by the time it was required to be paid, the defendant must pay interest on that amount for any period after which it remains unpaid (see s 12(1)). Under s 12(2), the rate of interest is the same as that for interest on civil judgment debts (see s 17 of the Judgments Act 1838). The payment of interest is mandatory in all cases, the interest being treated as part of the amount to be paid under the confiscation order (s 12(4)).

(3) Unreasonable delay in enforcement

15.70 See Chapter 10 para 10.144.

I. The Effect of a Confiscation Order on Sentence and the Court's Other Powers

15.71 Once the court has made a confiscation order it must then proceed in respect of the offence or offences concerned in the terms set out in s 13(2) and (4) of POCA:

13(2) The court must take account of the confiscation order before—
(a) it imposes a fine on the defendant, or
(b) it makes an order falling within subsection (3).
(3) ...
(4) Subject to subsection (2) the court must leave the confiscation order out of account in deciding the appropriate sentence for the defendant.

Orders falling within subs (3) include compensation orders under s 130 of the Sentencing Act; forfeiture orders under s 27 of the Misuse of Drugs Act 1971; deprivation orders under s 143 of the Sentencing Act 2000; and forfeiture orders under s 23 of the Terrorism Act 2000.

(1) The relationship between the confiscation order and compensation

15.72 Under s 13(5):

(5) Subsection (6) applies if—
(a) the Crown Court makes both a confiscation order and an order for the payment of compensation under section 130 of the Sentencing Act against the same person in the same proceedings, and
(b) the court believes he will not have sufficient means to satisfy both the orders in full.
(6) In such a case the court must direct that so much of the compensation as it specifies is to be paid out of any sums recovered under the confiscation order; and the amount it specifies must be the amount it believes will not be recoverable because of the insufficiency of the person's means.

15.73 Section 13 requires the court to have regard to the confiscation order before imposing a fine or other order involving payment on the defendant, except for a compensation order, but otherwise to leave the confiscation order out of account in sentencing the defendant. In effect therefore it reproduces existing legislation.

(2) The importance of following the provisions of POCA

15.74 It is submitted that the confiscation provisions in POCA should be followed by courts as closely as possible, if the risk of the order being quashed by the Court of Appeal at a later date is to be avoided.

L. Interpretation: Confiscation and POCA

In *R v Stuart and Bonnett* (1989) 11 Cr App R(S) 89; [1989] Crim LR 599, the trial judge ordered the forfeiture of £2,500 in cash seized from the importer of cannabis under s 43 of the Powers of Criminal Courts Act 1973. The Court of Appeal quashed the order, ruling that it was unlawful, as the judge should have followed the confiscation provisions of the DTA. The court should always, therefore, follow the procedures of POCA and not succumb to the temptation to make forfeiture orders under other legislation, no matter how small the amount involved may be and however much such a course may commend itself to the court in terms of simplicity. **15.75**

(3) Orders for the payment of costs

See Chapter 10, para 10.143. **15.76**

J. Confiscation and the ECHR

It is now fairly well established that confiscation proceedings, following on and attaching to a criminal conviction, represent a penalty, not least because a prison sentence in default flows from non-payment, and the confiscation order itself is treated as a fine, pursuant to eg s 9 of the DTA. (See *R v Benjafield* [2002] UKHL 2 (para 82); *Rezvi* [2002] UKHL 1 and *Phillips v UK* [2001] EHRR No. 41087/98.) Part of the reasoning in *Rezvi* was that the purpose of confiscation proceedings was to '. . . *punish convicted offenders*'.) **15.77**

Case law however also dictates that the confiscation procedures do not involve the determination of a criminal charge (albeit a penalty) but is properly to be regarded as part of the sentencing procedures of the court, following conviction of a criminal offence. Accordingly Article 6(2) of the European Convention on Human Rights (ECHR) has no application as to the right to a fair trial under Article 6(1) or in respect of the determination of the defendant's civil obligations. The courts have found, for the time being, that the procedures contain sufficient safeguards. (See also para 10.145 of Chapter 10.) **15.78**

K. Appeals

The defendant's right of appeal in relation to POCA confiscation matters is considered fully at para 24.64 of Chapter 24. **15.79**

Under s 31(1) and (2) and s 89 of POCA, the prosecutor's right of appeal is without restriction, subject to leave. Section 32(1) confirms that on an appeal the Court of Appeal may confirm, quash or vary the confiscation order. **15.80**

L. Interpretation: Confiscation and POCA

Criminal lifestyle—s 75 **15.81**
Conduct and benefit—s 76
Tainted gifts—s 77
Gifts and their recipients—s 78
Value: the basic rule—s 79

Value of property obtained from conduct—s 80
Value of tainted gifts—s 81
Free property—s 82
Realisable property—s 83
Property: general provisions—s 84
Proceedings—s 85
Confiscation orders—s 87
Other interpretative provisions—s 88

M. Steps to Confiscation: A Summary

15.82 In *R v Johnson* [1991] 2 All ER 428 the Court of Appeal held that the necessary procedures should be followed step by step with the court stating at each stage the findings it has made.

1. The Crown Court must proceed to determine a confiscation application if the defendant is convicted of an offence before the court and the prosecution ask the court to proceed (ss 6(1),6(2)(a) and 6(3)(a) of POCA);
2. The court must decide whether the defendant has benefited from his particular criminal conduct, if it has determined that the defendant has not had a criminal lifestyle (s 6(4)(c));
3. In order to determine whether the defendant has benefited from his particular criminal conduct the court must decide the issue on the balance of probabilities (s 6(7)).
4. In order to determine whether the defendant has benefited from his particular criminal conduct from the offence concerned, the court must resolve whether the defendant received property as a result of or in connection with the conduct or obtained a pecuniary advantage as a result of or in connection with the conduct (which is equated to a sum of money equal to that advantage), whereby the benefit is the value of the property obtained (ss 76(3)(a), 76(4) and (5) and s 76(7));
5. The amount of the confiscation order which is the recoverable amount is the sum equal to the defendant's benefit from the conduct, unless the defendant shows that the available amount, which is all his free property together with any tainted gifts, is less than that sum (ss 7(1), 7(2), 9(1));
6. The court must find that the defendant had a criminal lifestyle if the offence concerned is specified in Sch 2 to POCA (s 75(2), s 6(4)(a));
7. The court must then decide whether the defendant has benefited from his general criminal conduct (s 6(4)(b), s 76(1) and (2));
8. A person benefits from conduct if he obtains property as a result or in connection with the conduct (s 76(4));
9. If the court decides the defendant has benefited from general criminal conduct, it must make the assumptions set out in s 10. The assumptions are not to be made if it is shown to be incorrect (ss 10(1), (2), (6));
10. The court then has to decide the 'recoverable amount' (s 6(5)(a));
11. The recoverable amount is an amount equal to the defendant's benefit from the conduct concerned (s 7(1));

M. Steps to Confiscation: A Summary

12. If a person benefits from criminal conduct his benefit is the value of the property obtained (s 76(7));
13. The determination of the 'value' of each property must be carried out in accordance with ss 79 and 80. Section 79(1) and (2) provides that the value of the property is 'the market value of the property'.

16

RECONSIDERATION OF CONFISCATION ORDERS UNDER POCA AND THE DEFENDANT WHO ABSCONDS

A. Introduction		16.01
B. Reconsideration of Case where no Confiscation Order was Originally Made		16.02
(1) Time limit		16.05
(2) How are the 'relevant date' and the 'date of conviction' defined?		16.06
(3) The status of previous orders of the court and compensation		16.08
(4) Procedure: applications under s 19 of POCA		16.09
(5) Statements of information		16.10
C. Reconsideration of Benefit where no Confiscation Order was Originally Made		16.11
(1) The first condition		16.12
(2) The second condition		16.13
(3) The status of previous orders of the court		16.17
D. Compensation		16.18
(1) Procedure: applications under s 20 of POCA		16.19
(2) Statements of information		16.20
E. Where a Confiscation Order has been Made: Reconsideration of Benefit		16.21
(1) When is the relevant time?		16.27
(2) What is the relevant amount?		16.28
(3) When is the date of conviction?		16.29
F. The Assumptions		16.30
(1) Revised benefit and relationship with the recoverable amount		16.31
(2) The status of previous orders of the court		16.34
(3) Exception to rule		16.35
(4) Changes in the value of money		16.36
(5) Procedure: applications under ss 19, 20, or 21 of the Act		16.37
G. Statements of Information		16.38
H. Increase in Available Amount		16.39
(1) Where a confiscation order has been made: reconsideration of the available amount		16.39
(2) What is the 'relevant amount' under s 22?		16.44
(3) Changes in the value of money		16.46
(4) Procedure: applications under s 22 of the Act		16.47
(5) Certificates of increase: ECHR		16.48
I. Inadequacy of Available Amount		16.49
(1) Variation of the confiscation order		16.49
(2) Inadequacy of available amount in bankruptcy cases		16.54
(3) Procedure: variation of confiscation order due to inadequacy of available amount		16.55
(4) Not a route to appeal		16.56
(5) Burden and standard of proof		16.64
(6) Assets difficult to realise		16.65
(7) Court must give its reasons		16.66
(8) Certificate of inadequacy and legitimate expectation		16.67
(9) Inadequacy of available amount: discharge of confiscation order		16.68
(10) Under s 24 what are 'specified reasons'?		16.70
(11) Small amount outstanding: discharge of confiscation order		16.72
(12) Procedure: application by Justices' Chief Executive to discharge a confiscation order		16.74
(13) Procedure where the Crown Court discharges a confiscation order		16.76
J. Defendants who Abscond or Die		16.77
(1) Introduction		16.77
(2) The defendant who dies		16.78
(3) The defendant who absconds post-conviction		16.79
(4) Procedure		16.80

(5)	The defendant who absconds pre-conviction	16.84	(13)	Powers of the court	16.96
(6)	Two year rule	16.85	(14)	Discharge of confiscation order where the defendant has absconded	16.98
(7)	Procedure	16.86	(15)	Discharge of order: undue delay or proceedings not continuing	16.99
(8)	What happens if the defendant later returns?	16.89	(16)	Procedure: application for discharge made by a former absconder	16.102
(9)	Variation and discharge of orders under s 28	16.90	(17)	Compensation: confiscation order made against absconder	16.105
(10)	Variation of order	16.91	(18)	Increase in term of imprisonment in default	16.108
(11)	What is the relevant period?	16.93			
(12)	Procedure on applications for a variation made by a former absconder	16.94			

A. Introduction

16.01 This chapter has been divided into two parts. Firstly we consider the various provisions concerning the reconsideration, variation, and discharge of confiscation orders under the Proceeds of Crime Act 2002 (POCA); and secondly we consider the rules in relation to defendants who abscond, both pre- and post-conviction.

B. Reconsideration of Case where no Confiscation Order was Originally Made

16.02 Section 19 of POCA applies where no confiscation hearing was held after the original conviction.

16.03 Section 19(1) states:

This section applies if—
(a) the first condition in Section 6 is satisfied, and no court has proceeded under that section;
(b) there is evidence which was not available to the Prosecutor on the relevant date;
(c) before the end of the period of six years starting with the date of conviction the Prosecutor or Director applies to the Crown Court to consider the evidence; and
(d) after considering the evidence the Court believes it is appropriate for it to proceed under Section 6.

16.04 The first condition of s 6 of POCA (s 6(2)) is that a defendant must fall within one of the following categories:

(a) he is convicted of an offence or offences in proceedings before the Crown Court;
(b) he is committed to the Crown Court for sentencing in respect of an offence or offences under ss 3, 4, or 6 of the Powers of Criminal Courts (Sentencing) Act 2000 (PCCSA); or
(c) he is committed to the Crown Court in respect of an offence or offences under s 70 of POCA (committal with a view to a confiscation order being considered).

Once the court has established that s 19(1) is satisfied the court must proceed under s 6 (s 19(2)) and in doing so must apply s 19(3) to (8).

C. Reconsideration of Benefit where no Confiscation Order was Originally Made

(1) Time limit

16.05 Importantly, it will be noted that in all cases, an application must be made to the Crown Court within six years of the original conviction (see 19(1)(c)),

(2) How are the 'relevant date' and the 'date of conviction' defined?

16.06 The 'relevant date' referred to in s 19(1)(b) is defined in s 19(9) as either:

(a) if the court made a decision not to proceed under section 6, the date of that decision; or,

(b) if the court did not make such as decision, the date of conviction.

Under s 19(10) the date of conviction is either:

(a) the date on which the defendant was convicted of the offence concerned; or

(b) if there were two or more offences and the convictions were on different dates, the date of the latest.

16.07 It should be noted that the purpose of s 19 is to allow the prosecutor to return to court when new evidence in relation to confiscation arises. It is therefore inappropriate for a prosecutor who had possession of evidence relating to the defendant's assets and conduct etc at the time of his trial and conviction, but chose not to apply for a confiscation order then, to apply for reconsideration under s 19 at a later date in circumstances where no new evidence has arisen.

(3) The status of previous orders of the court and compensation

16.08 See paras 16.17 and 16.34 below.

(4) Procedure: applications under s 19 of POCA

16.09 See para 16.37 below.

(5) Statements of information

16.10 Under s 26 of POCA if the court proceeds under s 6 (the making of a confiscation order) in pursuance of s 19, the prosecutor or the Director of the Assets Recovery Agency (ARA) (as the case may be) must give the court a statement of information within the period the court orders (see para 16.38 below).

C. Reconsideration of Benefit where no Confiscation Order was Originally Made

16.11 Section 20 of POCA applies when a confiscation hearing was originally held and the court decided on that occasion that the defendant had a criminal lifestyle but had not benefited from his general criminal conduct; or did not have a criminal lifestyle and did not benefit from his particular criminal conduct. Section 20 of POCA only applies if two specified conditions are satisfied.

(1) The first condition

16.12 Section 20(2) states:

The first condition is that in proceeding under Section 6 the Court has decided that
(a) the Defendant has a criminal lifestyle but has not benefited from his general criminal conduct, or
(b) the Defendant does not have a criminal lifestyle and has not benefited from his particular criminal conduct.

(2) The second condition

16.13 The second condition is split, depending upon whether it is an ARA case or whether it is a confiscation case brought by another prosecutor or under the court's own volition.

16.14 For the purpose of ARA cases, s 20(3) states:

(3) If the Court proceeded under Section 6 because the Director asked it to, the second condition is that—
(a) the Director has evidence which was not available to him when the Court decided the Defendant had not benefited from his general or particular criminal conduct,
(b) before the end of the period of six years starting with the conviction the Director applies to the Crown Court to consider the evidence, and
(c) after considering the evidence the court concludes that it would have decided that the Defendant had benefited from his general or particular criminal conduct (as the case may be) if the evidence had been available to it.

16.15 For the purpose of cases other than for ARA, s 20(4) states:

(4) If the Court proceeded under Section 6 because the Prosecutor asked it to or because it believed it was appropriate for it to do so, the second condition is that—
(a) there is evidence that was not available to the Prosecutor when the Court decided that the Defendant had not benefited from his general or particular criminal conduct;
(b) before the end of the period of six years starting with the date on which the Prosecutor or Director applies to the Crown Court to consider the evidence; and
(c) after considering the evidence the Court concludes that it would have decided that the Defendant would have benefited from his general or particular criminal conduct (as the case may be) if the evidence had been available to it.

16.16 The 'date of conviction' is defined at s 19(10) as the date on which the defendant was convicted of the offence concerned or, if there are two or more offences and the convictions were on different dates, the date of the latest (see s 20(13)).

(3) The status of previous orders of the court

16.17 See para 16.34 below.

D. Compensation

16.18 Sections 19(8) and 20(12) make it clear that where a compensation order under s 130 of the PCC(S)A was made following the trial the court cannot order payment of that compensation out of a confiscation order made at a s 19 or s 20 reconsideration hearing. It follows that the payment of any compensation should only be ordered out of confiscated

E. Reconsideration of Benefit

monies under s 13(6) of POCA where a confiscation order was also made in the original proceedings.

(1) Procedure: applications under s 20 of POCA

See para 16.37 below. **16.19**

(2) Statements of information

Under s 26 of POCA if the court proceeds under s 6 (the making of a confiscation order) in pursuance of s 20, the prosecutor or the Director of the ARA (as the case may be) must give the court a statement of information within the period the court orders (see para 16.38 below). **16.20**

E. Where a Confiscation Order has been Made: Reconsideration of Benefit

Section 21 of POCA applies if: **16.21**

(1) (a) the Court has made a confiscation order,
 (b) there is evidence which was not available to the prosecutor or the Director at the relevant time,
 (c) the prosecutor or Director believes that if the court were to find the amount of the Defendant's benefit in pursuance of this section, it would exceed the relevant amount,
 (d) before the end of the period of six years starting from the date of conviction the prosecutor or Director applies to the Crown Court to consider the evidence, and
 (e) after considering the evidence the court believes it is appropriate for it to proceed under this section.

When reconsidering the defendant's benefit, the court must make a new calculation of the defendant's benefit from the conduct concerned (s 21(2)). In effect this enables a confiscation order already made to be increased. **16.22**

Under s 21 there is no restriction as to the number of times that either the prosecutor or ARA may return to the Crown Court to seek an increase in the defendant's benefit figure, although it will have been noted that s 21(1)(d) imports a limitation date of six years starting from the date of conviction. **16.23**

If a court has already sentenced the defendant for the offence (or any of the offences) concerned, s 6 of POCA has effect as if the defendant's particular criminal conduct included conduct which constitutes offences which the court has taken into consideration in deciding his sentence for the offence or offences concerned (as per s 21(3)). **16.24**

When the court is reconsidering the defendant's benefit under s 21, s 8(2) of POCA does not apply. Instead the court must: **16.25**

(4) (a) take account of conduct occurring up to the time it decided the Defendant's benefit for the purposes of the confiscation order;
 (b) take account of the property obtained up to that time;
 (c) take account of property obtained after that time if it was obtained as a result of or in connection with conduct occurring before that time.

16.26 When applying s 8(5) of POCA in relation to reconsidering a defendant's benefit, the confiscation order previously made against the defendant must be ignored (s 8(5) concerns general criminal conduct and the deducting of aggregate amounts).

(1) When is the relevant time?

16.27 Under s 21(12) the relevant time is:

(a) when the court calculated the defendant's benefit for the purposes of the confiscation order, if s 21 has not applied previously;

(b) when the court last calculated the defendant's benefit in pursuance of s 21, if s 21 has applied previously.

(2) What is the relevant amount?

16.28 Under s 21(13) the relevant amount is:

(a) the amount found as the defendant's benefit for the purposes of the confiscation order, if s 21 has not applied previously;

(b) the amount last found as the defendant's benefit in pursuance of s 21, if s 21 has applied previously.

(3) When is the date of conviction?

16.29 The date of conviction is:

(a) the date on which the defendant was convicted of the offence concerned; or

(b) if there are two or more offences and the convictions are on different dates, the date of the latest (see s 21(14) applying s 19(10)).

F. The Assumptions

16.30 When considering s 10 of POCA (assumptions to be made in cases of criminal lifestyle) in s 21 cases:

(a) the first and second assumptions do not apply with regard to property first held by the defendant after the time the court decided his benefit for the purposes of the confiscation order;

(b) the third assumption does not apply with regard to expenditure incurred by him after that time;

(c) the fourth assumption does not apply with regard to property obtained (or assumed to have been obtained) by him after that time (see s 21(6)).

(1) Revised benefit and relationship with the recoverable amount

16.31 If the amount found under the new calculation of the defendant's benefit under s 21 exceeds the relevant amount, the court must make a new calculation of the recoverable

F. The Assumptions

amount for the purposes of s 6, and, if it exceeds the amount required to be paid under the confiscation order previously ordered, the court may vary the order by substituting for the amount required to be paid such amount as it believes is just (s 21(7)).

16.32 When making the new calculation for the recoverable amount for the purposes of s 6, the court must take the new calculation of the defendant's benefit and apply s 9 of POCA (the available amount), as if references to the time the confiscation order was made were to the time of the new calculation of the recoverable amount, and as if references to the date of the confiscation order were to the date of that new calculation (s 21(8)).

16.33 Under s 21(9), in applying s 21(7)(b) (where the court is considering varying an order to substitute it for an amount it believes 'just') the court must have regard to:

(a) any fine imposed on the Defendant for the offence (or any of the offences) concerned;
(b) any order which falls within Section 13(3) of POCA [compensation orders, forfeiture orders or deprivation orders] which have been made against the Defendant in respect of the offence (or any of the offences) concerned and have not already been taken into account by the court in deciding what is the free property held by him for the purposes of Section 9;
(c) any order which has been made against the defendant in respect of the offence (or any of the offences) concerned under Section 130 of the Sentencing Act (compensation orders).

The purpose of s 21(9)(b) and (c) is to avoid double recovery and equally to prevent a defendant from being allowed a reduction twice in respect of the same property.

(2) The status of previous orders of the court

16.34 Under ss 19(7)(c) and (d), 20(11)(c) and (d), and 21(9)(b) and (c), POCA requires the court to take into account certain orders already made against the defendant in the original proceedings, namely fines, forfeiture, and compensation orders.

(3) Exception to rule

16.35 Under s 21(10) the court cannot take a compensation order into account in one specified circumstance when reconsidering the defendant's benefit. If the court has made a direction under s 13(6) (compensation to be paid out of any sums recovered under the confiscation order), in applying s 21(7)(b) (where the defendant's benefit exceeds the amount required to be paid under the confiscation order) the court must not have regard to an order falling within s 21(9)(c) (compensation orders).

(4) Changes in the value of money

16.36 When deciding under s 21 whether one amount exceeds another, the court must take account of any change in the value of money (s 21(11)).

(5) Procedure: applications under ss 19, 20, or 21 of the Act

16.37 Where the prosecutor or Director of the ARA makes an application under s 19, 20, or 21 of the Act (application for reconsideration of a decision to make a confiscation order or benefit assessed for purposes of a confiscation order) the application must be in writing and give details of:

(a) the name of the defendant;
(b) the date on which and the place where any relevant conviction occurred;
(c) the date on which and the place where any relevant confiscation order was made or varied;
(d) the grounds for the application;
(e) an indication of the evidence available to support the application (see r 58.3 of the Criminal Procedure Rules). Under r 58.3 (3) any application for reconsideration of a decision to make a confiscation order or reconsideration of benefit assessed for the purposes of a confiscation order, must be lodged with the Crown Court and the application must be served on the defendant at least seven days before the date fixed by the court for hearing the application, unless the Crown Court specifies a shorter period (see r 58.3 (4)).

G. Statements of Information

16.38 Under s 26 of POCA if the court proceeds under s 6 (the making of a confiscation order) in pursuance of either s 19 (no order made: reconsideration of case) or s 20 (no confiscation order made: reconsideration of benefit) or the prosecutor or ARA applies under s 21 of POCA (where a confiscation order has been made and the court has to reconsider the benefit figure) the prosecutor or ARA must give the court a statement of information within the period the court orders (see s 26(1) and (2)(a)). Section 16 of POCA (the provision of a statement of information) applies accordingly (with appropriate modification where the prosecutor or Director of the ARA applies under s 21); as does s 17 (the defendant's response to the statement of information), and s 18 (the provision of information by the defendant) where s 6(3)(a) or s 6(3)(b) applies (ie the prosecutor or Director has asked the court to proceed under s 6 or the court believes it is appropriate for it to do so), or the court is considering whether or not to proceed under s 6 (s 26(2)(b)).

H. Increase in Available Amount

(1) Where a confiscation order has been made: reconsideration of the available amount

16.39 The purpose of s 22 of POCA is to allow the court to recalculate the available amount in circumstances where a confiscation order has been previously made in an amount lower than the defendant's assessed benefit because at that time there was insufficient realisable property to satisfy an order in the full amount. Section 22 of POCA applies if:

(1) (a) a court has made a confiscation order,
    (b) the amount required to be paid was the amount found under section 7(2) [where the Defendant was able to show that the available amount was less than the benefit figure], and
    (c) an applicant falling within section 22(2) [ie the prosecutor; the Director of the ARA; or a receiver appointed under s 50 or s 52 of POCA (an enforcement receiver or a Director's receiver)] applies to the Crown Court to make a new calculation of the available amount.

H. Increase in Available Amount

Where the above circumstances apply the court must make the new calculation, and in doing so it must apply s 9 of POCA (calculation of the available amount) as if references to the time the confiscation order is made were to the time of the new calculation, and as if reference to the date of the confiscation order were to the date of the new calculation (s 22(3)). This section operates in a similar way as the 'Certificate of Increase' provisions operated under the DTA. The purpose of these provisions was identified by Rose LJ in *R v Tivnan* (1999) 1 Cr App R(S) 92 who held:

16.40

> . . . we see no ambiguity. The plain words of the statute, in our judgment, provide for the making of an application for a further certificate and for an increase in the amount recovered under the confiscation order at any time after the original confiscation order was made. By this means drug dealers can be deprived of their assets until they have disgorged an amount equivalent to all the benefit which had accrued to them from drug dealing.

It will be noted that, unlike ss 19, 20, and 21, there is no limitation to the time when an application may be made and the prosecutor, the Director or a receiver may apply on more than one occasion.

16.41

Under s 22(4) if the amount found under the new calculation exceeds the relevant amount the court may vary the order by substituting for the amount required to be paid such amount as:

16.42

(a) it believes is just, but
(b) does not exceed the amount found as the defendant's benefit from the conduct concerned.

In deciding what is 'just' the court must have regard in particular to:

(5) (a) any fine imposed on the defendant for the offence (or any of the offences) concerned;
 (b) any order which falls within section 13(3) (compensation orders, forfeiture orders or deprivation orders) and has been made against him in respect of the offence (or any of the offences) concerned and has not already been taken into account by the court in deciding what is the free property held by him for the purposes of section 9 of POCA [the available amount];
 (c) any order which has been made against the Defendant in respect of the offence (or any of the offences) concerned under Section 130 of the Sentencing Act (compensation orders).

In deciding what is 'just' the court must have regard to an order falling within subs (5)(c) (orders made under s 130 of the Sentencing Act (compensation orders)) if a court has made a direction under s 13(6), to avoid the defendant being able to off-set the impact of the compensation order on both occasions (subs (6)).

16.43

(2) What is the 'relevant amount' under s 22?

Under s 22(8) the relevant amount is:

16.44

(a) the amount found as the available amount for the purposes of the confiscation order, if section 22 had not applied previously;
(b) the amount last found as the available amount in pursuance of section 22, if section 22 has applied previously.

The amount found as the defendant's benefit from the conduct concerned is:

16.45

(9) (a) the amount so found when the confiscation order was made, or
 (b) if one or more new calculations of the Defendant's benefit have been made under section 21 of POCA, the amount found on the occasion of the last such calculation.

(3) Changes in the value of money

16.46 When deciding under s 22 whether one amount exceeds another, the court must take account of any change in the value of money (see s 22(7)).

(4) Procedure: applications under s 22 of the Act

16.47 Under r 58.4 of the Criminal Procedure Rules, where the prosecutor, the Director, or a receiver makes an application under s 22 of the Act for a new calculation of the available amount in circumstances where a confiscation order has already been made, the application must be in writing and must be supported by a witness statement. That application and any witness statement must be lodged with the Crown Court and served upon:

(a) the defendant;
(b) the receiver, if the prosecutor or the Director is making the application and a receiver has been appointed under s 50 or 52 of the Act (either an enforcement receiver or a Director's receiver) and
(c) if the receiver is making the application:
   (i) the prosecutor; or
   (ii) if the Director is appointed as the enforcement authority under s 34 of the Act, the Director;

at least seven days before the date fixed by the court hearing the application, unless the Crown Court specifies a shorter period (see r 58.4 (1) to (4)).

(5) Certificates of increase: ECHR

16.48 In *Saggar* [2005] EWCA Civ 174, the Court of Appeal held that where the State had granted to itself the right to re-open the issue of confiscation under s 16 of the DTA (for a certificate of increase), the reasonable time requirement under Article 6(1) of the European Convention of Human Rights, was triggered and extended throughout the period starting from the original proceedings, and not just from the institution of the s 16 application.

I. Inadequacy of Available Amount

(1) Variation of the confiscation order

16.49 The intention of s 23 of POCA is to replace the previous procedure where defendants or the receiver had to apply to the High Court for a certificate of inadequacy. It applies if:

(1) (a) a court has made a confiscation order, and
    (b) the Defendant, or a receiver appointed under Section 50 or 52 of POCA [an enforcement receiver or a Director's receiver], applies to the Crown Court to vary the order under section 23.

16.50 Where an application is being considered under s 23, the Crown Court must calculate the available amount, and in doing so it must apply s 9 of POCA (calculation of the available amount) as if references to the time the confiscation order was made were to the time of the previous calculation and as if references to the date of the confiscation order were to the date of the previous calculation (see s 23(2)).

I. Inadequacy of Available Amount

16.51 The court may disregard any inadequacy which it believes is attributable (wholly or partly) to anything done by the defendant for the purpose of preserving property which is held by the recipient of a tainted gift from any risk of realisation under Pt 2 of POCA (the confiscation provisions) (s 23(5)).

16.52 Under s 23(3) if the court finds that the available amount (as so calculated) is inadequate for the payment of any amount remaining to be paid under the confiscation order it may vary the order by substituting it for a smaller amount as the court believes is just.

16.53 If the defendant or others are going to rely upon this provision they must demonstrate to the court firm and clear evidence of the reduced circumstances—see *Gokal* [2001] EWCA Civ 368 where Keene LJ stated:

> As has been said many times in the authorities, it is not enough for the defendant to come to court and say that his assets are inadequate to meet the confiscation order, unless at the same time he condescends to demonstrate what has happened since the making of the order to the realisable property found by the Trial judge to have existed at the time when the order was made...

(2) Inadequacy of available amount in bankruptcy cases

16.54 Section 23(4) states that if a person has been adjudged bankrupt or his estate has been sequestrated (or if an order for the winding up of a company has been made), the court must take into account the extent to which realisable property held by that person or that company may be distributed among creditors ('company' for these purposes means any company that may be wound up under the Insolvency Act 1986 (see s 23(6)).

(3) Procedure: variation of confiscation order due to inadequacy of available amount

16.55 Rule 58.5 of the Criminal Procedure Rules applies where the defendant or a receiver makes an application under s 23 of POCA for the variation of a confiscation order. Under r 58.5 the application must be in writing and may be supported by a witness statement, and any application and accompanying witness statement must be lodged with the Crown Court. That application and any witness statement must be served on:

(a) the prosecutor, or if the Director is appointed as the enforcement authority under s 34, the Director;
(b) the defendant, if the receiver is making the application; and
(c) the receiver, if the defendant is making the application and a receiver has been appointed under s 50 or 52 of POCA (enforcement or Director's receiver)

at least seven days before the date fixed by the court for hearing the application, unless the Crown Court specifies a shorter period.

It will also be noted that in *Re T* [2005] EWHC 3359 (Admin) Collins J held (in a DTA case) that the court did have jurisdiction to grant bail in an appropriate case.

(4) Not a route to appeal

16.56 A certificate of inadequacy should only be sought in cases where, since the making of the confiscation order, the value of the defendant's realisable property has decreased for some reason. It is not an appropriate remedy for a defendant who is aggrieved by the Crown Court's findings when it made the confiscation order: in such circumstances the defendant's remedy is an appeal to the Court of Appeal (Criminal Division) (see Chapter 13, para 13.41).

16.57 Recent case law has confirmed this to be the position. In *Re N* [2005] EWHC QBD (Admin), 3211, Toulson J endorsed a 'hard-edged rule' in respect of certificate of inadequacy applications. He expressed concern that the provisions set out in s 17 of the DTA and the corresponding provisions of POCA, were being used by defendants as an appeal route, whereas the proper course would have been to pursue the matter in the Court of Appeal.

16.58 In *Gokal v Serious Fraud Office* [2001] EWCA Civ 368, at paras 16 and 17 Keene J considered a similar problem:

> The evidence in support of the recent application for a certificate took the form of a witness statement ... In the witness statement it is said that the appellant "seeks to prove that he has no realisable property to be applied in satisfaction of the confiscation order". Apparently an attempt was going to be made to produce evidence at this stage to show that the money which went into the appellant's personal bank account has been dissipated. This would take the form of schedules produced by accountants which were available at the time of the appeal to the Court of Appeal but not produced to that court. This is not a proper basis on which to seek a certificate. It amounts to an attempt to go behind the original confiscation order finding as to the amount of the defendant's realisable assets. Such a finding can only be challenged by way of an appeal against the confiscation order. ... An application for a certificate does not provide an opportunity to try to make good deficiencies in the case presented at the time of the confiscation order or at the appeal against it.

16.59 In *Re O'Donoghue* [2004] EWCA Civ 1800, Lightman J said:

> It is clear that on an application for a certificate (of inadequacy) it is not possible to go behind the finding of the original confiscation order as to the amount of the defendant's realisable assets....

This was confirmed in *P v Customs and Excise Commissioners* [2005] EWHC (Admin) 877, where Beatson J stated (at para 18) that it was:

> ... well established that the procedure under [s 17] ... is not to be used as a device to appeal against the original finding that an item of property is realisable property within the legislation.

He added at para 20:

> In applying for a certificate of inadequacy, an applicant must show what has happened to the realisable property or to part of it since the making of the confiscation order.

16.60 While in *Re L* (QBD (Admin), 18 January 1996), Keene J refused to accept that there was any form of issue estoppel in relation to the way in which certificates of inadequacy were brought, Toulson J in *Re N* stated that that approach had not been developed by the courts:

> The courts have adopted a hard-edge rule in this area and it would be inappropriate for me as a judge at first instance to seek to swim against the tide by going back to the approach of Keene J as he then was in *Re L*.

16.61 In *R v T* (QBD (Admin), 1 February 1996) McCullough J said:

> It is not sufficient for a defendant simply to assert at the time of his application for a certificate of inadequacy that he has no realisable property. He must explain what has become of

the realisable property whose existence formed the basis of the confiscation order. If a defendant is at liberty simply to rely upon the assertion of the present lack of realisable property to justify the issue of a certificate of inadequacy, then it is open to him . . . to subvert the decision which formed the basis of the confiscation order. That is plainly wrong in principle. The scheme of the Act is quite clear. If a confiscation order is to be challenged, that must be by way of appeal and only by way of appeal.

In *Re W* (QBD (Admin), 29 January 1998) Lord J stated: **16.62**

> It is of the greatest importance . . . that on an application of this kind the High Court should not be persuaded to go behind confiscation orders made in the Crown Court.

And these sentiments were recently re-affirmed in *Re McKinsley* [2006] EWHC QBD (Admin), 1092. **16.63**

(5) Burden and standard of proof

In *Re O'Donoghue* [2004] EWHC (Admin) 176, Lightman J reaffirmed that the burden of proof was on the defendant to establish that the value of his assets were inadequate to satisfy the whole value of the confiscation order. He added that it was not sufficient for him to merely state that his assets were inadequate, without demonstrating what had happened since the making of the confiscation order that had made them so (see para 13.38, Chapter 13). **16.64**

(6) Assets difficult to realise

The fact that particular assets prove difficult for a defendant to realise does not necessarily mean they cease to be realisable property under the Acts (see *Re R*, The Independent, 4 November 2002). In *R v Liverpool Justices ex p Ansen* [1998] 1 All ER 692 the assets taken into account in making a confiscation order included a deposit he had put down on a summer house in Turkey and held by German agents; a deposit he had put down and was entitled to reclaim in relation to some Waterford Wedgwood articles; and a loan he had apparently made to his junior counsel at trial. He had been unable to realise any of these amounts in satisfaction of a confiscation order and accordingly applied for a certificate of inadequacy. In refusing the defendant's application, May J said: **16.65**

> [Counsel for the Prosecutor] submits that the fact that an asset may be difficult to realise is simply not relevant. The provisions of the Act, he submits, define 'realisable property' in terms of section 5 and do not address any question of whether in practical terms it is difficult to recover the money. I agree with that submission for two reasons. Firstly, the definition of 'realisable property' includes property held by the defendant and by definition 'property' is held by any person if he holds an interest in it and the 'interest' in property includes a right. Accordingly, if as Mr. Ansen's affidavit indicates, the sum of approximately £8,500 held by agents in Germany is an amount which he is entitled to recover, then it is realisable property by definition irrespective of any difficulty in its actual recovery.

> Secondly, s 5(1)(b) of the DTA, referring, as it does, to 'realisable property' including 'gifts caught by the Act', necessarily means that circumstances may arise where gifts which an applicant has made may be practically, even legally, irrecoverable, but they are nevertheless still regarded as realisable property under this draconian Act. The purpose of these draconian procedures is obvious: they are intended, as has often been said, to make it as difficult as possible for those who traffic in drugs to get away with the proceeds of that traffic.

(7) Court must give its reasons

16.66 In *Re Forwell* [2003] EWCA Civ 1608, the Court of Appeal held that where a court, when issuing a certificate of inadequacy in the exercise of its discretion, decided to disregard any inadequacy, it was expressly required to set out its reasons for so doing. Conversely, there was a similar requirement implicitly imposed as a matter of fairness where there was a refusal to issue a certificate.

(8) Certificate of inadequacy and legitimate expectation

16.67 For consideration of argumentsd in relation to legitimate expectation, see para 13.58 of Chapter 13.

(9) Inadequacy of available amount: discharge of confiscation order

16.68 Section 24 is a provision that previously did not exist under either the DTA or the CJA. It is not available to ARA in cases where ARA have appointed a receiver and where the more appropriate route would be under s 23.
Section 24 of POCA applies if:

(a) a court has made a confiscation order;
(b) a Justices' Chief Executive applies to the Crown Court for the discharge of the order; and
(c) the amount remaining to be paid under the order is less than £1,000 (s 24(1)).

16.69 In such a case the court must calculate the available amount and in so doing it must apply s 9 (calculation of available amount) as if references to the time the confiscation order is made were to the time of the original calculation and as if references to the date of the confiscation order were to the date of the original calculation (see s 24(2)).

Under s 24(3) if the court:

(a) finds that the available amount (as so calculated) is inadequate to meet the amount remaining to be paid, and
(b) is satisfied that the inadequacy is due wholly to a specified reason or a combination of specified reasons,

it may discharge the confiscation order.

(10) Under s 24 what are 'specified reasons'?

16.70 The specified reasons are:

(4) (a) in a case where any of the realisable property consists of money in a currency other than sterling, the fluctuations in currency exchange rates occurred;
 (b) any reason specified by the Secretary of State by Order.

16.71 For the procedure to be followed by Justices' Chief Executives for applications under s 24 see para 16.74.

(11) Small amount outstanding: discharge of confiscation order

16.72 Under s 25 of POCA, if:

(a) a court has made a confiscation order;

J. Defendants who Abscond or Die

(b) a Justices' Chief Executive applies to the Crown Court for the discharge of the order; and
(c) the amount remaining to be paid under the order is £50 or less, the court may discharge the order (see s 25(1) and (2)).

16.73 This section only applies where the magistrates' court is enforcing a confiscation order. The intention is that certain confiscation orders should be discharged where their final recovery becomes uneconomic.

(12) Procedure: application by Justices' Chief Executive to discharge a confiscation order

16.74 Under r 58.6 of the Criminal Procedure Rules, where a Justices' Chief Executive makes an application under s 24 or s 25 of POCA for the discharge of a confiscation order, the application must be in writing and supported by a witness statement which must give details of:

(a) the confiscation order;
(b) the amount outstanding under the order; and
(c) the grounds for the application (see r 58.6(2)).

That application and witness statement must be served on:

(a) the defendant;
(b) the prosecutor; and
(c) any receiver appointed under s 50 (enforcement receiver) of the Act, under r 58.6(3).

16.75 Once such an application has been made the Crown Court may determine the application without a hearing unless any of the persons listed in r 58.6(3) indicates, within the period of seven days beginning on the day after the day on which the application was served on him, that he would like to make representations (see r 58.6(4)).

(13) Procedure where the Crown Court discharges a confiscation order

16.76 Under r 58.6(5) of the Criminal Procedure Rules, if the Crown Court makes an order discharging the confiscation order, the appropriate court officer must at once send a copy of the order to:

(a) the Justices' Chief Executive who applied for the order;
(b) the defendant;
(c) the prosecutor; and
(d) any receiver appointed under s 50 of the Act (an enforcement receiver).

J. Defendants who Abscond or Die

(1) Introduction

16.77 Sections 27 and 28 of POCA gives the court jurisdiction, in certain circumstances, to make confiscation orders in relation to s 6 of POCA for defendants who abscond. It will be noted that previously these powers were vested in the High Court and that in effect the power to deal with absconded defendants now rests with the Crown Court.

(2) The defendant who dies

16.78 The existing provision for the High Court to make a confiscation order against a drug trafficker who dies after conviction but before the Crown Court can make a confiscation order is abolished under POCA (it was considered, according to the explanatory notes that accompany POCA, that the recovery of benefit where the perpetrator is dead is better dealt with under the Civil Recovery Procedures in Pt 5 of POCA).

(3) The defendant who absconds post-conviction

16.79 Section 27(2) and (3) of POCA gives the Crown Court the power to make confiscation orders post-conviction and provides as follows:

(1) The section applies if the following two conditions are satisfied.
(2) The first condition is that a defendant absconds after—
   (a) he is convicted of an offence or offences in proceedings before the Crown Court,
   (b) he is committed to the Crown Court for sentencing in respect of an offence or offences under s 3, 4 or 6 of the Sentencing Act, or
   (c) he is committed to the Crown Court in respect of an offence or offences under s 70 (committal with a view to a confiscation order being considered).
(3) The second condition is that—
   (a) the prosecutor or the director applies to the Crown Court to proceed under this Section and
   (b) the Court believes it is appropriate to do so.

(4) Procedure

16.80 If this section applies the court must then proceed under s 6 in the same way as it must proceed if the two conditions mentioned in s 6 are satisfied; but in the case of the absconded defendant this is subject to s 27(5):

(5) If the court proceeds under Section 6 as applied by this section, this Part has effect with these modifications—
   (a) any person the Court believes is likely to be affected by an order under Section 6 is entitled to appear before the court and make representations;
   (b) the court must not make an order under Section 6 unless the prosecutor or the Director (as the case may be) has taken reasonable steps to contact the defendant;
   (c) Section 6(9) applies if the reference to subsection (2) were to subsection (2) of this section;
   (d) sections 10, 16(4), 17 and 18 must be ignored;
   (e) ss 19, 20 and 21 must be ignored while the defendant is still an absconder.

Subsection (5)(c) imports that the defendant must fall within the paragraphs set out in 6(2).

16.81 For the purposes of s 27 the following sections of POCA must be ignored: s 10 (assumptions to be made cases of a criminal lifestyle); s 16(4) (the requirement that a statement of information by the prosecutor or the Director under s 16(3) must include information the prosecutor or Director believes is relevant in connection to the making of the required assumptions or for the purpose of enabling the court to decide if the circumstances are such that it must not make an assumption); s 17 (the defendant's response to the statement of information); and s 18 (provision of information by the defendant). It is submitted that the requirement that the defendant need not respond to the prosecutor's statement is not surprising in the circumstances.

J. Defendants who Abscond or Die

Furthermore, ss 19 (no order made: reconsideration of case), 20 (no order made: reconsideration of benefit), and 21 (order made: reconsideration of benefit) must be ignored while the defendant is still an absconder (see s 27(5)(e)). **16.82**

Once however the defendant ceases to be an absconder s 19 has effect as if subs (1)(a) read: **16.83**

(a) at a time when the first condition in Section 27 was satisfied the court did not proceed under Section 6.

Similarly if the court does not believe it is appropriate for it to proceed under s 27, once the defendant ceases to be an absconder, s 19 has effect as if subs (1)(b) read:

(b) there is evidence which was not available to the prosecutor or the Director on the relevant date.

(5) The defendant who absconds pre-conviction

Section 28 deals with the position where proceedings have been instituted against the defendant, but at the relevant time there has been no conviction recorded against him. Section 28 provides as follows: **16.84**

(1) This section applies if the following two conditions are satisfied.
(2) The first condition is that—
  (a) proceedings for an offence or offences are started against a defendant but are not concluded,
  (b) he absconds and
  (c) the period of two years (starting with the date the court believes he absconded) has ended.
(3) The second condition is that—
  (a) the prosecutor or the Director applies to the Crown Court to proceed under this section, and
  (b) the Court believes it is appropriate for it to do so.

(6) Two year rule

In circumstances set out in s 28 it will be noted that a confiscation order may only be made against an absconder if two years have elapsed from the time he absconds (s 28(2)(b)). **16.85**

(7) Procedure

If s 28 applies the court must proceed under s 6 in the same way as it must proceed if the two conditions mentioned in s 6 are satisfied (s 28(4)). Any person the court believes is likely to be affected by an order under s 6 is entitled to appear before the court and make representations (s 28(5)(a)). **16.86**

The court is not entitled to make an order under s 6 unless the prosecutor or the Director has taken reasonable steps to contact the defendant (s 28(5)(b)). **16.87**

Under s28(5)(b)–(e), the following sections of the confiscation provisions of POCA must be ignored when proceeding under s 28: s 10 of POCA (assumptions to be made in case of a criminal lifestyle); s 16(4) (the requirement that a statement of information by the prosecutor or the Director under s 16(3) must include information the prosecutor or Director believes is relevant in connection to the making of the required assumptions or for the purpose of enabling the court to decide if the circumstances are such that it must not make an **16.88** assumption); ss 17 to 20 (the defendant's response to a statement of information; provision of information by the defendant; and where no confiscation order is made: reconsideration of case and benefit); as must be s 21, while the defendant is still an absconder (confiscation order made: reconsideration of benefit). However, once the defendant had ceased to be an absconder s 21 does have effect.

(8) What happens if the defendant later returns?

16.89 If the court makes an order under s 6 as applied by s 28, and the defendant is later convicted in proceedings before the Crown Court of the offence or any of the offences concerned, s 6 does not apply so far as that conviction is concerned (s 28(7)). In other words, when a court has made a confiscation order under s 28 it cannot go on to make another confiscation order if the defendant returns and is convicted.

(9) Variation and discharge of orders under s 28

16.90 Section 29 deals with varying orders made under s 28, and s 30 deals with the discharging of orders made under s 28. If the court discharges a confiscation order under s 30 it may make such consequential or incidental order as it believes is appropriate (see s 30(5)).

(10) Variation of order

16.91 POCA identifies certain circumstances where, if the court makes a confiscation order in circumstances where the defendant has absconded, such an order may later be varied. The variation provisions have effect only where the defendant applies to the court on the grounds the original order, made in his absence, is too large.

16.92 These circumstances are set out in s 29(1) which applies if:

(a) the court makes a confiscation order under s 6 as applied by s 28 (where the defendant is neither convicted nor acquitted);
(b) the defendant ceases to be an absconder;
(c) he is convicted of an offence (or any of the offences) mentioned in s 28(2)(a) (ie he is now convicted of an offence where previously proceedings had been started against him but had not been concluded);
(d) the defendant believes that the amount required to be paid was too large (taking the circumstances prevailing when the amount was found for the purposes of the order), and
(e) before the end of the relevant period the defendant applies to the Crown Court to consider the evidence on which his belief is based.

(11) What is the relevant period?

16.93 Under s 29(3) the relevant period referred to in subs (1)(e) is the period of 28 days starting with:

(a) the date on which the Defendant was convicted of an offence mentioned in section 28(2)(a), or
(b) if there are two or more offences and the convictions were on different dates, the date of the latest.

It should be noted that the defendant only has 28 days from his conviction to apply for a variation of an order made in his absence under s 29.

J. Defendants who Abscond or Die

(12) Procedure on applications for a variation made by a former absconder

16.94 Under r 58.7 of the Criminal Procedure Rules, where the defendant makes an application under s 29 of the Act for a variation of a confiscation order that application must be made in writing and supported by a witness statement which must give details of:

(a) the confiscation order made against an absconder under section 6 of the Act as applied by section 28 of the Act;
(b) the circumstances in which the Defendant ceased to be an absconder;
(c) the Defendant's conviction of the offences concerned; and
(d) the reason why he believes the amount required to be paid under the confiscation order was too large.

(Rule 58.7(2))

16.95 That application and witness statement must be lodged with the Crown Court and must be served on the prosecutor or, if the Director of ARA is appointed as the enforcement authority under s 34 of the Act, the Director, at least seven days before the date fixed by the court for hearing the application, unless the Crown Court specifies a shorter period (r 58.7 (3) and (4)).

(13) Powers of the court

16.96 If (after considering the evidence) the court concludes that the defendant's belief is well founded:

29(2) (a) it must find the amount which should have been the amount required to be paid (taking the circumstances prevailing when the amount was found for the purposes of the order), and
(b) it may vary the order by substituting for the amount required to be paid such amount it believes is just.

16.97 However, in a case where s 28(2)(a) applies to more than one offence the court must not make an order under s 29 unless it is satisfied that there is no possibility of any further proceedings being taken or continued in relation to any such offence in respect of which the defendant has not been convicted (s 29(4)).

(14) Discharge of confiscation order where the defendant has absconded

16.98 Under s 30 of the new Act, if the court makes a confiscation order under s 6, as applied by s 28 (defendant neither convicted nor acquitted) and the defendant is later tried for the offence (or offences) concerned and acquitted on all accounts, and the defendant then applies to the Crown Court to discharge the confiscation order made in his absence, the court must discharge that confiscation order (see s 30(1) and (2)).

(15) Discharge of order: undue delay or proceedings not continuing

16.99 Under s 30(3) if the court makes a confiscation order under subs 6, as applied by s 28 (a confiscation order in circumstances where the defendant is neither convicted nor acquitted, ie pre-conviction), and the defendant ceases to be an absconder, and the defendant was never tried for the offence(s) concerned: the defendant may apply to the Crown Court to discharge the order.

16.100 The court may discharge the order if it finds that there has been undue delay in continuing the proceedings mentioned in s 28(2) (ie the proceedings for the offence(s) have been started against the defendant but have not been concluded), or the prosecutor does not intend to proceed with the prosecution.

16.101 Unlike s 30(2), s 30(4) is discretionary. If the court discharges a confiscation order under s 30 it may make such other consequential or incidental orders as it believes are appropriate (s 30(5)).

(16) Procedure: application for discharge made by a former absconder

16.102 Under r 58.8 of the Criminal Procedure Rules, if a defendant makes an application under s 30 of the Act for discharge of a confiscation order, that application must be in writing and supported by a witness statement which must give details of:

(a) the confiscation order made under section 28 of the Act;
(b) the date on which the Defendant ceased to be an absconder;
(c) the acquittal of the Defendant if he had been acquitted of the offences concerned; and
(d) if the Defendant has not been acquitted of the offence concerned—
　(i) the date on which the Defendant ceased to be an absconder;
　(ii) the date on which the proceedings taken against the Defendant were instituted; and a summary of steps taken in the proceedings since then; and
　(iii) any application given by the prosecutor that he does not intend to proceed against the Defendant.

16.103 Under r 58.8(3) once that application and witness statement has been made they must be lodged with the Crown Court. Further, under r 58.7(4) they must be served on the prosecutor or, if the ARA is appointed as the enforcement authority under s 34 of the Act, the Director, at least seven days before the date fixed by the court for hearing the application, unless the Crown Court specifies a shorter period.

16.104 If the Crown Court orders the discharge of the confiscation order, the court must serve notice on the magistrates' court responsible for enforcing the order if the Director has not been appointed as the enforcement authority (see r 58.8(5) Criminal Procedure Rules).

(17) Compensation: confiscation order made against absconder

16.105 Rule 58.11(1) of the Criminal Procedure Rules applies to an application for compensation under s 73 of the Act (where a confiscation order has been varied or discharged under either s 29 or s 30 of POCA and an application has been made to the Crown Court by a person who held realisable property and who has suffered a loss as a result of the making of that order). Under r 58.11(2) the application must be in writing and supported by a witness statement which must give details of:

(a) the confiscation order made under s 28 of the Act;
(b) the variation or discharge of the confiscation order under s 29 or s 30 of the Act;
(c) the realisable property to which the application relates; and
(d) the loss suffered by the applicant as a result of the confiscation order.

16.106 Once the application and witness statement are made they must be lodged with the Crown Court (r 58.11(3)) and served on the prosecutor or, if ARA is appointed as the enforcement

J. Defendants who Abscond or Die

authority under s 34 of POCA, the Director, at least seven days before the date fixed by the court for hearing the application, unless the Crown Court specifies a shorter period.

The rules applying to general compensation under s 72 of POCA are set out in r 58.10 of the Criminal Procedure Rules. **16.107**

(18) Increase in term of imprisonment in default

Under s 39(5) of POCA there is provision for the prosecutor or the Director to makes an application to increase the term of imprisonment in default of payment of a confiscation order. The Criminal Procedure Rules in relation to same are found at r 58.9, which provides: **16.108**

(2) The application must be made in writing and give details of —
 (a) the name and address of the defendant;
 (b) the confiscation order;
 (c) the grounds for the application; and
 (d) the enforcement measures taken, if any.
(3) On receipt of the application, the court must —
 (a) at once send to the defendant and, if the Director has not been appointed as the enforcement authority under section 34 of the 2002 Act, the magistrates' court responsible for enforcing the order, a copy of the application; and
 (b) fix a time, date and place for the hearing and notify the applicant and the defendant of that time, date and place.
(4) If the Crown Court makes an order increasing the term of imprisonment in default, the court must, at once, send a copy of the order to —
 (a) the applicant;
 (b) the defendant;
 (c) where the defendant is in custody at the time of the making of the order, the person having custody of the defendant; and
 (d) if the Director has not been appointed as the enforcement authority under section 34 of the 2002 Act, the magistrates' court responsible for enforcing the order.

17

ENFORCEMENT OF CONFISCATION ORDERS UNDER THE CJA, THE DTA, AND POCA

A. Introduction		17.01
B. Voluntary Satisfaction by the Defendant		17.03
C. Enforcement Receivers under the DTA and CJA		17.13
(1) DTA cases: meaning of 'a confiscation order is not satisfied'		17.18
(2) CJA cases: meaning of 'proceedings have not been concluded'		17.19
(3) Meaning of 'subject to appeal'		17.20
(4) Powers of enforcement receivers		17.27
(5) Ancillary orders		17.29
(6) Procedure on applications		17.31
(7) The evidence in support		17.33
(8) The defendant's response to the application		17.36
(9) Third parties		17.40
(10) Advising third parties served with an application to appoint an enforcement receiver		17.44
(11) The court's order		17.49
(12) The matrimonial home: rights of spouses		17.50
(13) Status of the receiver on appointment		17.51
(14) Realisation of property		17.52
(15) Remuneration of enforcement receivers		17.53
(16) Dealing with the proceeds of realisation		17.57
(17) Discharge of the receiver		17.61
D. The Powers of the Magistrates' Court		17.62
(1) Distress warrants		17.64
(2) Third party debt orders		17.65
(3) Warrants of commitment		17.66
(4) Delay by the prosecutor in enforcing the confiscation order		17.78
E. Enforcement under POCA 2002		17.87
(1) Enforcement receivers		17.88
(2) Powers of enforcement receivers		17.89
(3) Director's receivers		17.92
(4) Powers of Director's receivers		17.95
(5) Procedure on applications for the appointment of enforcement receivers under POCA		17.96
(6) Seized money		17.104
(7) Implementing the default sentence: the Director not the enforcing authority		17.109
(8) Implementing the default sentence: the Director appointed as the enforcement authority		17.110

A. Introduction

A confiscation order is an *in personam* order against the defendant requiring him to pay a sum of money, and is not an *in rem* order against the property taken into account by the court in making the order. A confiscation order does not therefore divest the defendant or any interested third party of title to the property and any person who attempts to realise the same in satisfaction of the confiscation order will be vulnerable to civil proceedings for conversion if they do so without his consent. This principle must be borne in mind by all those in possession of a defendant's realisable property, particularly officers of prosecuting authorities who may, eg be in possession of money taken up from the defendant on his arrest.

17.01

17.02 A further order of the court is necessary to enforce a confiscation order unless the defendant cooperates with the prosecuting authority in satisfying the order voluntarily. In this chapter we examine the various powers available to the courts under the Drug Trafficking Act 1994 (DTA), the Criminal Justice Act 1988 (CJA) and the Proceeds of Crime Act 2002 (POCA) to ensure that confiscation orders are satisfied.

B. Voluntary Satisfaction by the Defendant

17.03 In most circumstances, the defendant should be given the opportunity, in so far as he is able, to satisfy the confiscation order voluntarily. It is to the defendant's advantage to cooperate in the voluntary satisfaction of the order because the court's enforcement methods can prove costly and the defendant may well be required to meet some or all of those costs. The defendant will also be liable to pay interest on unpaid confiscation orders at the same rate applicable to civil judgments, currently eight per cent: see s 10 of the DTA, s 75A of the CJA and s 12 of POCA. These provisions also give the court power, on the application of the prosecutor, to increase the default sentence if the effect of adding interest to the sum due is to increase the maximum period of imprisonment for which he would be liable. Further, enforcement of a confiscation order pursuant to the court's powers of compulsion inevitably takes longer than voluntary satisfaction of the order by the defendant, and the defendant who refuses to cooperate may find himself serving the default sentence for non-payment, particularly in cases where the sentence imposed for the substantive offence is a relatively short one.

17.04 The prosecutor should normally give the defendant the opportunity to satisfy the confiscation order voluntarily. If he does not do so, the court may refuse to appoint an enforcement receiver to realise assets in satisfaction of the order. There may be circumstances where voluntary satisfaction is inappropriate: eg where a defendant has shown, by his previous conduct, that he cannot be trusted to realise assets himself or where the assets in question are subject to third party claims that need to be determined.

17.05 In many cases the defendant will be in some difficulty in satisfying the confiscation order voluntarily because he may be serving a lengthy prison sentence. This need not, however, prevent him signing letters authorising the prosecuting authority to pay over to the court money taken up at the time of his arrest or permitting banks to pay over money held in his bank accounts. Similarly, in so far as real property is concerned, there is no reason why the defendant cannot give his solicitor instructions to effect a sale notwithstanding the fact that he is in prison.

17.06 If a restraint order is in force, it may be necessary to seek a variation to authorise the payment of money to the enforcing magistrates' court, or to put a restrained property on the market to satisfy the confiscation order. It is important that those holding assets on behalf of a defendant or who are instructed to act for him in the sale of property should check the terms of the restraint order carefully before taking any action. It will not normally be necessary for the restraint order to be varied to enable money held by the defendant or a third party to be paid into court in satisfaction of the confiscation order. This is because most

B. Voluntary Satisfaction by the Defendant

restraint orders contain a provision to the effect that nothing in the order shall prevent the payment of money into court in satisfaction of a confiscation order: see para 16 of the draft restraint order at Appendix 1.

In so far as other assets are concerned, a variation to the restraint order will normally be necessary, and solicitors should be vigilant to ensure such a variation is obtained prior to taking steps to realise restrained property on behalf of a client. In the absence of such a variation a solicitor or any other professional person instructed to effect a sale of realisable property on behalf of a client could be vulnerable to proceedings for contempt of court if he assists in any way in the sale of an asset subject to a restraint order. In most cases the prosecutor will be prepared to agree that the restraint order should be varied by consent to allow a sale to take place, but he will want to be assured that the property is not sold at an under value, possibly to an associate of the defendant, and that once the sale is completed the proceeds are paid directly into court and not handed to the defendant. These concerns can normally be met by the inclusion of a number of conditions in the variation order. These usually include the following: **17.07**

(a) that the property shall be valued by at least two independent valuers who are members of a recognised trade association and be sold to a bona fide purchaser for value for not less than the average of the two valuations;
(b) an undertaking by the defendant to instruct a named solicitor to act for him in relation to the transaction and a further undertaking not to terminate that solicitor's retainer without the consent of the prosecutor or the permission of the court;
(c) an undertaking by the solicitor to pay the net proceeds of sale into court in satisfaction of the order forthwith on completion of the transaction;
(d) that all fees payable to solicitors, estate agents, and other professionals in relation to the transaction should be agreed with the prosecuting authority in advance of being incurred.

It is also usual for the prosecutor to give an undertaking to apply for the discharge of any caution or inhibition registered at HM Land Registry in relation to the property on being notified that the proceeds of sale have been paid into court. **17.08**

Defendants and affected third parties should take great care when agreeing consent orders with the prosecutor to check its terms and ensure they are content to be bound by them. Once a consent order has been agreed it has the status of a contract between the parties and will be interpreted as such. In *Weston v Dayman* [2006] EWCA Civ 1165 the claimant, who had been subject to CJA restraint and management receivership orders, agreed a consent order dealing with the discharge of the receiver on his acquittal. One of the terms of the consent order was that the receiver would not be liable for any failure by her to properly manage the claimant's estate after her discharge. Notwithstanding this provision, the claimant instituted proceedings against the receiver claiming damages alleging she had acted in breach of duty by failing to take proper care of a motor yacht. The Court of Appeal upheld the judge's ruling that summary judgment should be entered in favour of the defendant receiver, holding that he was bound by the terms of the consent order he had freely entered into whereby the receiver was released from any such liability. **17.09**

17.10 Although it would be open to a defendant to apply for a consent order to which he is party to be varied or set aside, it is submitted this would only be appropriate in exceptional circumstances. As Arden LJ observed in *Weston v Dayman* [2006] EWCA Civ 1165:

> I would accept that the court should accede to an application for variation where it is just to do so but in my judgment one of the aspects of justice is that a bargain freely made should be upheld. Mr. Weston clearly obtained benefits under the order. It may well be that those benefits are not as great as he thought, but that is not a matter for this court. In those circumstances I do not consider it would be right for this court to exercise its discretion to vary the order as sought.

17.11 A variation to the restraint order will not be sanctioned by the court if it does not result in the confiscation order being satisfied in full. In *Re Barnes and Barnes* [2004] EWHC Admin 2620 CJA confiscation orders were made against the defendants (who were husband and wife) in the sums of £42,845.73 and £63,320.73 respectively. The realisable assets of the defendants included their half shares in the matrimonial home which amounted to some £21,316.50. They sought a variation to the restraint order to permit them to take out a second mortgage on the property which would enable them to pay £38,715 into court in part satisfaction of the confiscation orders. They proposed to pay off the balance in monthly instalments of £60. Lightman J refused the defendants' application, ruling that the variation sought was incompatible with the legislative steer in s 82(2) CJA. He said:

> In my judgment, the language of section 82 (2) of the Criminal Justice Act 1988 is mandatory and requires the power to be exercised with a view to securing the full realisation of the realisable property, so far as necessary to secure the full satisfaction of the confiscation order. An exercise of power for the purpose of anything less than full realisation of value can only be sanctioned if it is clear that that exercise, or that exercise jointly with something else (for example, a further payment to the Crown) will fully discharge the debt due to the Crown.
>
> In this case, assuming – and this is a considerable assumption – that the building society, after being correctly informed as to the full and true facts, is prepared to agree to the proposed remortgage, there will be a shortfall due to the Crown of some £8,000 to £10,000, and this shortfall will arise because the defendants propose a remortgage and not a sale. I do not think that the court has jurisdiction to vary the restraint order with a view to authorising a transaction which does not realise the full value of the property, or at least sufficient tio enable the confiscation order to be satisfied. The adverse consequences for the defendants (which are the plight of their own criminal conduct) and the adverse consequences to the community in the cost of providing housing are nothing to the point.

17.12 If a defendant refuses to cooperate in the voluntary satisfaction of a confiscation order or, for whatever reason, it is inappropriate to allow him to do so, it will be necessary to invoke the powers of the court to ensure the order is paid and we examine below the various sanctions available to the court.

C. Enforcement Receivers under the DTA and CJA

17.13 Section 29 of the DTA and s 80 of the CJA empower the court to appoint receivers for the purpose of enforcing confiscation orders. In contrast to the position in relation to management receivers, the primary purpose of an enforcement receiver is to realise assets in satisfaction of the confiscation order, although an enforcement receiver will inevitably have to

C. Enforcement Receivers under the DTA and CJA

manage assets pending realisation. As the two sections are worded somewhat differently, it is necessary to consider each in turn.

By s 29 of the DTA: **17.14**

(1) Where a confiscation order—
   (a) has been made under this Act,
   (b) it is not satisfied, and
   (c) is not subject to appeal,
   the High Court or a county court may, on an application by the prosecutor, exercise the powers conferred by subsections (2) to (6) below.
(2) The court may appoint a receiver in respect of realisable property.
(3) The court may empower a receiver appointed under subsection (2) above, under section 26 of this Act or in pursuance of a charging order—
   (a) to enforce any charge imposed under section 27 of this Act on realisable property or on interest or dividends payable in respect of such property; and
   (b) in relation to any realisable property other than property for the time being subject to a charge under section 27 of this Act to take possession of the property subject to such conditions or exceptions as may be specified by the court.
(4) The court may order any person having possession of realisable property to give possession of it to any such receiver.
(5) The court may empower any such receiver to realise any realisable property in such manner as the court may direct.
(6) The court may—
   (a) order any person holding an interest in realisable property to make to the receiver such payment as it may direct in respect of any beneficial interest held by the defendant or, as the case may be, the recipient of a gift caught by this Act; and
   (b) on the payment being made, by order transfer, grant or extinguish any interest in the property.
(7) Subsections (4) to (6) above do not apply to property for the time being subject to a charge under section 27 of this Act or section 9 of the Drug Trafficking Offences Act, 1986.
(8) The court shall not in respect of any property exercise the powers conferred by subsection (3)(a), (5) or (6) above unless a reasonable opportunity has been given for persons holding any interest in the property to make representations to the court.

By s 80 of the CJA (as amended by s 8(6) of POCA 1995):

(1) Where—
   (a) a confiscation order is made in proceedings instituted for an offence to which this Part of this Act applies or an order is made or varied on an application under section 74A, 74B or 74C above;
   (b) the proceedings in question have not, or the application in question has not been concluded; and
   (c) the order or variation is not subject to appeal;
   the High Court may, on an application by the prosecutor, exercise the powers conferred by subsections (2) to (6) below.
(2) The court may appoint a receiver in respect of realisable property.
(3) The court may empower a receiver appointed under subsection (2) above, under section 77 above or in pursuance of a charging order—
   (a) to enforce any charge imposed under section 78 above on realisable property or on interest or dividends payable in respect of such property;
   (b) in relation to any realisable property other than property for the time being subject to a charge under section 78 above, to take possession of the property subject to such conditions or exceptions as may be specified by the court.

(4) The court may order any person having possession of realisable property to give possession of it to any such receiver.

(5) The court may empower any such receiver to realise any realisable property in such manner as the court may direct.

(6) The court may order any person holding an interest in realisable property to make such payment to the receiver in respect of any beneficial interest held by the defendant or, as the case may be, the recipient of a gift caught by this Part of this Act as the court may direct and the court may, on the payment being made, by order transfer, grant or extinguish any interest in the property.

(7) Subsections (4) to (6) above do not apply to property for the time being subject to a charge under section 78 above.

(8) The court shall not in respect of any property exercise the powers conferred by subsection (3)(a), (5) or (6) above unless a reasonable opportunity has been given for persons holding any interest in the property to make representations to the court.

17.15 Under both statutes the remedy is a discretionary one and the court is not bound to appoint a receiver even when the provisions of s 29(2) DTA or s 80(2) CJA have been satisfied. The court may, for example, consider whether the defendant could reasonably satisfy the order voluntarily and, if so whether he has been given sufficient opportunity to do so. The court may also consider whether other less expensive methods of enforcement might be equally effective. The court must, however, exercise its discretion judicially and in accordance with the legislative steer. It is submitted that the correct approach is that outlined by Munby J in *Re HN* [2005] EWHC Admin 2982. He said:

> On the face of it, once a confiscation order has been made, the Crown is entitled to demand the appointment of an enforcement receiver in order to realise the funds with which to discharge the confiscatiion order. That, after all, is no more than the "legislative steer" in section 82 (2) would normally demand. On the other hand, since the effect of my ruling is potentially to throw onto the defendant's assets the burden of meeting the receiver's costs, disbursements and fees, it may be proper in an appropriate case, to defer the appointment of a receiver for a short period to give the defendant the opportunity himself (subject of course to suitable safeguards) to realise the assets – something he may perhaps be able to do more advantageously and at lesser expense than a receiver.

17.16 The court will not, on an application for the appointment of an enforcement receiver, entertain any challenge by the defendant to the validity of the confiscation order to which it relates. In *Customs and Excise Commissioners v Togher* [2005] EWCA 274 the defendant contended that a confiscation order made against him under the DTA was invalid because it should have been made under the Drug Trafficking Offences Act, 1986. Sedley LJ, in refusing the defendant leave to appeal, said:

> This submission is, in my judgment, entirely misconceived. The confiscation order exists. It has the authority of the Criminal Division of the Court of Appeal and of the Crown Court. Customs & Excise are not only entitled but are required, as a matter of public duty, to enforce it if they can. The time for challenging its validity is past. The place for challenging its validity, in any event is not the receivership proceedings consequent upon it.
>
> I am tempted to go into the reasons why it seems to me that the underlying argument is a bad one. But to do so would be to accept the very thing that I do not accept, which is that it is open to the Administrative Court, or therefore to this court, in receivership proceedings, to embark upon the question whether the order upon which Customs & Excise rely is a properly made order. The time and place for such a challenge are not here and are not now.

C. Enforcement Receivers under the DTA and CJA

It is worthy of note that the sections do not require any time allowed for payment by the Crown Court to elapse before an enforcement receiver can be appointed. An application to appoint an enforcement receiver may therefore be made before the time allowed for payment has expired. Although this will be a matter the court will wish to take into account in exercising its discretion whether or not to accede to the application, it is submitted there is nothing wrong in principle in applying for the appointment of a receiver before time to pay has expired so as to ensure that the order is satisfied within the period allowed for payment. This is particularly so in cases where assets are going to take a considerable time to realise and the defendant fails to advance his own proposals for the voluntary satisfaction of the order. 17.17

(1) DTA cases: meaning of 'a confiscation order is not satisfied'

By s 41(6) of the DTA: 17.18

A confiscation order is satisfied when no amount is due under it. It should be noted that a DTA confiscation order is not satisfied by the defendant serving the default sentence for non payment. By s 9(5) of the DTA, serving a default sentence for non payment does not expunge the debt and the order can continue to be enforced by, for example, the appointment of a management receiver.

(2) CJA cases: meaning of 'proceedings have not been concluded'

The meaning of this term is fully considered at para 2.28 above and, for the purposes of enforcing a confiscation order, proceedings only conclude when the confiscation order is satisfied (see s 102(12)(d) and s 102(12A)(b) of the CJA). As with DTA cases, under s 102(B) of the CJA, the order is satisfied when no amount remains due under it and, by virtue of s 75(5A), serving the default sentence for non-payment does not expunge the debt. 17.19

(3) Meaning of 'subject to appeal'

Section 29(1) of the DTA and s 80(1) of the CJA preclude the appointment of enforcement receivers while the confiscation order is still 'subject to appeal'. The phrase is defined in s 41(8) of the DTA and s 102(13) of the CJA in these terms: 17.20

An order is subject to appeal until (disregarding any power of a court to grant leave to appeal out of time) there is no further possibility of an appeal on which the order could be varied or set aside.

A confiscation order is therefore only subject to appeal if an appeal has been lodged within the time limits prescribed by rules of court or if permission to appeal has been granted out of time. If an application for permission to appeal has been lodged but not determined, or if the defendant merely indicates an intention to appeal out of time, the order will not be 'subject to appeal' within the meaning of the Acts. Although a confiscation order will not technically be 'subject to appeal' if an application for permission to appeal out of time has been made, the fact that such an application has been lodged will be a matter the court will wish to consider in exercising its discretion whether or not to appoint an enforcement receiver. If a confiscation order is properly 'subject to appeal' there would be nothing to 17.21

prevent the prosecutor applying for the appointment of a management receiver to manage and preserve realisable property pending the determination of the appeal. A management receiver would not, however, have power to realise assets and pay the proceeds into court in satisfaction of the confiscation order.

17.22 In *Re P* [1998] EWHC Admin 1049 it was held that a confiscation order is not 'subject to appeal' within the meaning of the Acts if there is a pending application to the Criminal Cases Review Commission or the European Court of Human Rights in relation to it. Laws J said:

> The fact is that, so far as the domestic criminal litigation is concerned in this case Mr. P is well past the end of the road. The Commission may, of course, investigate a matter after all other criminal legal processes have been exhausted. Indeed, that is their very role. However, it is quite clear to me that while they are doing so, and the fact that they are doing so, are no basis for altering, suspending or varying the effect of a restraint order and therefore, in effect, the execution of a confiscation order once that has been made. The same applies in relation to his application to the European Court of Human Rights.

17.23 *Re P* was followed in *R v Bullen and Soneji* [2006] EWCA Crim 1125 where the Court of Appeal expressed itself as being:

> ... wholly unimpressed by the suggestion that the period allowed for payment should be extended uncertainly into the future so that the defendants can pursue their petition before the European Court of Human Rights.

17.24 Further, it is important to appreciate that in the absence of a specific order of the court, a pending appeal does not suspend the obligation to pay the confiscation order and time continues to run. In *R v May* [2005] EWCA Crim 367 the Crown Court made a confiscation order for £3,264,277 and ordered the defendant to pay within three years. He appealed against the order to the Court of Appeal, but his appeal was dismissed. He then contended that the three year period for payment should run from the date on which his appeal was dismissed and not from the date on which the confiscation order was made. Keene LJ described this proposition as 'unsound in law' and said:

> We do not find this argument persuasive. There is no reason why steps preparatory to the raising of the money specified in the confiscation order should not have been taken while May's appeal was pending. The appellant was not entitled to assume that his appeal would be successful and, as indicated above, as a matter of law time was running during that period. Moreover, it would be wrong as a matter of principle for appellants to be encouraged to believe that the bringing of an appeal would be likely to lengthen the time given for payment, even if the appeal was unsuccessful.

17.25 The decision in *May* was followed by the Court of Appeal in *R v Bullen and Soneji* [2006] EWCA Crim 1125. In that case confiscation orders were made against the defendants in the sums of £375,000 and £30,284 respectively. The trial judge, being aware of the defendants' intention of appealing against the orders, allowed 18 months to pay from the date on which the Court of Appeal determined the appeals. In due course the Court of Appeal allowed the appeals and quashed the confiscation orders.

17.26 The Crown thereafter successfully appealed to the House of Lords and the confiscation orders were reinstated. The defendants contended that the eighteen month period should run from the date on which the House of Lords allowed the Crown's appeal. The Court of

C. Enforcement Receivers under the DTA and CJA

Appeal rejected this argument and ordered the defendants to pay in full within 28 days. In delivering the judgment of the Court, Fulford J said:

> ... in our view, they have had ample time to raise, speedily, adequate funds. Given the time that has elapsed, it is our a view a sufficient – indeed generous – opportunity has been afforded to the defendants to put their affairs in order so that they can pay these sums. As the decision of this Court in *R v May [2005] EWCA Crim 367* makes clear, the obligation to pay a confiscation order within a specified period remains in force from the date it was imposed. The clock does not stop running whilst an appeal is pending, save by judicial authorisation, in other words, time continues to run unless there is a court order to the contrary. Defendants subject to confiscation orders who appeal against the order, or against the conviction which resulted in the order being made, should be advised to make contingency plans for the prompt satisfaction of the order in the event that the appeal is unsuccessful. If they do not do so, they may find enforcement action being taken shortly after the appeal is dismissed.

(4) Powers of enforcement receivers

17.27 The powers that may be given to enforcement receivers are set out in s 29(3) and (5) of the DTA and s 80(3) and (5) of the CJA. They are:

(a) power to enforce any charge imposed on realisable property or on interest or dividends payable on such property;
(b) power to take possession of any realisable property except property subject to a charging order under s 27 DTA or s 78 CJA, subject to such conditions and exceptions as the court may specify; and
(c) power to realise any realisable property in such manner as the court may direct.

17.28 It should be noted that where the receiver is given power to enforce a charging order on realisable property he cannot be given power to take possession of the property. The reason for this is that his interest in the property is sufficiently protected by the charge and there is no need for him to take physical possession of the property pending the enforcement of the charge.

(5) Ancillary orders

17.29 In order to enable the receiver to discharge his duties effectively, the court is empowered to make the following ancillary orders:

(a) that any person having possession of realisable property deliver it up to the receiver (see ss 29(4) of the DTA and 80(4) of the CJA);
(b) that any person holding an interest in realisable property make such payment to the receiver in respect of any beneficial interest held by the defendant as the court may direct and, on payment being made, the court may transfer, grant or extinguish any interest in the property (see s 29(6) of the DTA and s 80(6) of the CJA).

17.30 Again, these powers may not be exercised in respect of property subject to a charging order (see s 29(7) of the DTA and s 80(7) of the CJA). Further, the powers may not be exercised unless any third party holding an interest in the property is afforded a reasonable opportunity to make representations to the court. This is considered further at para 17.40 below.

(6) Procedure on applications

17.31 Applications for the appointment of an enforcement receiver are made to a High Court Judge by the issue of an application notice or, where there have been no previous High Court proceedings in the matter, by the issue of a claim form (see sc 115 Rule 7(1)). The application notice or claim form must be served, together with the evidence in support, at least seven days prior to the date of the hearing on:

(a) the defendant;
(b) any person holding an interest in any of the property to which the application relates; and
(c) if a receiver has already been appointed (that is to say a management receiver under s 26(7) of the DTA or s 77(8) of the CJA), on that receiver (see sc 115 Rule 7 (2)).

17.32 If the prosecutor entertains any doubts as to whether a person has an interest in any of the property to which the application relates, it is submitted that he should resolve that doubt in favour of the person concerned and serve the application on him in accordance with sc 115 Rule 7(2)(b).

(7) The evidence in support

17.33 By sc 115 Rule 7(3):

The application shall be supported by a witness statement or affidavit which shall, to the best of the witness's ability, give full particulars of the realisable property to which it relates and specify the person or persons holding such property, and a copy of the confiscation order, of any certificate issued by the Crown Court under section 5(2) and of any charging order made in the matter shall be exhibited to such witness statement or affidavit.

17.34 The prosecutor should also, it is submitted, exhibit any statements under s 11 of the DTA or s 73 of the CJA tendered at the Crown Court confiscation hearing together with any disclosure statements made by the defendant or affected third parties in accordance with the requirements of the restraint order.

17.35 The witness statement should also exhibit all relevant correspondence passing between the prosecutor and the proposed receiver. This will include the letter of agreement in which the prosecutor sets out the terms of the proposed receivership and the receiver's reply agreeing to accept the proposed appointment and abide by those terms. A precedent letter of agreement appears at Appendix 5. Save in cases where the proposed receiver has previously acted in this capacity under the DTA or CJA, he must provide a fidelity bond and affidavit of fitness. The affidavit, sworn by a reputable person known to the proposed receiver, confirms his fitness to act and the fidelity bond is a form of insurance policy should the defendant's assets go astray whilst in the receiver's possession as a result of his default. Where these documents are required, they should also be exhibited to the prosecutor's witness statement.

(8) The defendant's response to the application

17.36 It is important that the defendant should determine well in advance of the application what his response is to be. Where a defendant has been sentenced to a long term of imprisonment and has a substantial confiscation order to meet he will, in most instances, have no defence to the application for the appointment of an enforcement receiver, and where this is the case he should promptly write consenting to the application, thereby saving a considerable amount of court time. If the defendant is in a position to satisfy the order voluntarily, he should make a witness statement setting out realistic proposals as to how this might be achieved. The court will, however, need to be satisfied that any such proposal is genuine and the defendant who wishes to satisfy his confiscation order voluntarily will have to offer very clear and detailed proposals as to how he intends to pay the order and the timescale within which he intends to do so.

One argument that will find little favour with the court is that the defendant intends to serve the default sentence for non-payment rather than satisfy the order. As the Divisional Court made very clear in *R v Harrow Justices ex p DPP* [1991] 1 WLR 395 this is not an option open to the defendant. In delivering the judgment of the court, Stuart-Smith LJ said: **17.37**

> (1) The object of a confiscation order is to divest the defaulter of money or other realisable assets. Consequently, (2) it is not a matter of choice for the defaulter to 'buy' his way out of such an order by serving the term of imprisonment imposed in default of responding to the order for confiscation: see *R v Clacton Justices ex parte Customs and Excise* (1987) 152 JP 129.

In any event, since *Harrow Justices* was decided, new legislation provides that serving the default sentence no longer expunges the debt (see s 9(5) of the DTA and s 75(5A)(5) of the CJA). **17.38**

If the defendant contends that an asset the prosecutor wishes to have incorporated in the receivership order does not constitute realisable property, this should be dealt with in the witness statement and documentary evidence exhibited to confirm the position. Ideally, evidence should also be obtained from the person the defendant alleges to be the true owner of the property. Indeed, wherever possible, independent evidence should be obtained to corroborate the defendant's testimony. It has to be remembered that at this stage the defendant stands convicted and, particularly if he pleaded not guilty and was convicted after a trial, he may well face something of a credibility problem with the court, having been disbelieved by the jury. **17.39**

(9) Third parties

Section 29(8) of the DTA and s 80(8) of the CJA preclude the court from empowering receivers to realise assets in which a third party has an interest until such time as the person in question has had the opportunity of making representations to the court. This is an important protection for third parties because they have no right to appear or be represented at the confiscation hearing in the Crown Court when the court is determining the extent and value of the defendant's realisable property. Indeed, the only opportunity the law allows a third party to prevent property in which he claims an interest being realised by a receiver to satisfy a confiscation order is in the High Court proceedings. This was confirmed by the House of Lords in *Re Norris* [2001] 1 WLR 1388, a case concerning the DTOA. Mr Norris had been convicted of drug trafficking offences and a confiscation hearing was held under the 1986 Act. There was a dispute as to whether the matrimonial home (registered in the name of Mrs Norris) belonged beneficially to her or to her husband. **17.40**

Mrs Norris was called as a witness by her husband and gave evidence on his behalf to the effect that she was the beneficial owner of the property. Her evidence was rejected by the trial judge and the value of the property was incorporated in the confiscation order. The prosecutor then applied to the High Court for the appointment of an enforcement receiver to sell the property in part satisfaction of the confiscation order. After the receiver was appointed Mrs Norris made application to the High Court for the order to be varied to recognise her interest in the property. The prosecutor objected, contending that Mrs Norris had already litigated the issue before the Crown Court and that it was an abuse of process for her to attempt to re-litigate it before the High Court. The High Court upheld the prosecutor's objection and the application was dismissed, as was an appeal to the Court of Appeal. The House of Lords, however, unanimously allowed a further appeal by Mrs Norris. In considering the different roles of the Crown Court and High Court in the confiscation process, Lord Hope of Craighead said:

> The scheme of the Act, so far as third party interests are concerned, is for their claims to be resolved in the High Court. The question for the High Court, when proceedings reach this stage, relates not to the amount of money which the defendant must pay—that has already been fixed by the order made in the Crown Court—but to the powers which the receiver is to be authorised to exercise. It is at this stage that third parties are entitled to have their claims heard and determined. This is when, as a matter of both substance and procedure, representations may be made as to their interests, if any, in the property which the receiver wishes to realise. This is provided for expressly by section 11(8) of the Act, consistently with which RSC Ord 115, r7(4) lays down the procedure by which those holding any interest in the realisable property are to be notified.
>
> Provisions designed to protect the interests of third parties are conspicuously absent from the rules of procedure that apply at the stage of the hearing in the Crown Court. Third parties are not entitled to participate in the criminal proceedings in that court. But the issue for the Crown Court is not whether any property in which a third party might have an interest is to be confiscated. The order which it makes is an order which is directed against the defendant only, and it is simply an order for the payment of a sum of money. The question of realisation, if the exercise of powers by a receiver is needed in order to make good the order which the defendant is required to satisfy, is reserved for the High Court.
>
> I do not therefore, with respect, agree with the observation by Tuckey LJ that the situation which has arisen in this case is exactly that which the doctrine of abuse of process is designed to prevent. The scheme of the Act itself shows that this proposition must be unsound. It cannot be an abuse of process for a third party holding an interest in property, to whom a right is given by section 11(8) of the (1986) Act to make representations to the High Court, to seek to exercise that right just because he or she gave evidence in the Crown Court in support of the defendant's case that the property was not to be valued and taken into account as realisable property.

17.41 Further, as Lord Hobhouse of Woodborough observed, at a confiscation hearing before the Crown Court, the interests of the defendant and a third party are not necessarily identical. He said:

> It was wrong to say that her interests were identical with those of her husband. Indeed their proprietary interests were in principle opposed to each other. There were competing rights of property giving rights to one spouse against the other. It was in the interest of the defendant to put forward in the Crown Court the interest of his wife because he could use it to get a reduction in the confiscation order which was going to be made against him. But the wife's

C. Enforcement Receivers under the DTA and CJA

interests were not and are not the same as those of her husband. She wishes to preserve for herself and her children the right to live at [the matrimonial home] against her husband if necessary and against anyone claiming through him. The defendant also had an interest in mitigating the sentence of imprisonment which he was going to receive. The proceedings in the Crown Court were for the benefit of the defendant and the Customs and Excise and not Mrs Norris.

17.42 The legislative steer in s 31 of the DTA and s 82 of the CJA provides further protection for third parties and the recipients of gifts caught by the Acts in the way they require the court and receivers to exercise their powers under the Act. Section 31(3) and (4) of the DTA and s 82(3) and (4) of the CJA provide:

(3) In the case of realisable property held by a person to whom the defendant has directly or indirectly made a gift caught by this Act, the powers shall be exercised with a view to realising no more than the value for the time being of the gift.
(4) The powers shall be exercised with a view to allowing any person other than the defendant or the recipient of any such gift to retain or recover the value of any property held by him.

17.43 The protection third parties are given by these subsections is not absolute. They do not prevent the court from empowering receivers to sell assets in which the defendant and a third party have a joint interest: instead they are concerned with protecting the value of the third party's interest in such property. If, eg a defendant and a third party each have a half share in a property, although the court will be vigilant to protect the third party's interest, it will not preclude the court ordering a sale to ensure the defendant's share is realised in satisfaction of the confiscation order. The court will merely direct that an amount of money proportionate to the third party's interest should be paid to him from the proceeds of sale with the balance being paid into court in satisfaction of the confiscation order. An alternative way of proceeding would be to give the third party the option of buying out the defendant's interest in the property. In this event, the court would order the third party to pay to the receiver a sum of money equivalent to the value of the defendant's interest in the property and, on payment being made, would direct that the defendant's interest in the property be transferred to the third party.

(10) Advising third parties served with an application to appoint an enforcement receiver

17.44 As soon as a solicitor is instructed by a third party affected by an application to appoint an enforcement receiver, he should notify the court, then the prosecuting authority, and any solicitor acting on behalf of the defendant, of his interest in the matter. If the client is unable to fund the case privately and meets the eligibility criteria, an emergency application for public funding should be made. As third parties, like the defendant, are only entitled to seven days notice of the hearing of an application to appoint an enforcement receiver, the solicitor may find it necessary to seek an adjournment. Although the court will view such a request sympathetically, given that the public interest dictates that the confiscation order should be satisfied promptly, the court may well not be prepared to adjourn the entire receivership application. In many such cases, the court will proceed to appoint the receiver to enable him to realise assets that are free from third party claims, but will impose a stay on the receiver's powers of realisation of those assets in which the third party claims an interest pending the determination of his claim. At the same time, the court may exercise its case management functions to impose directions as to how the third party claim should proceed, issuing directions, eg as to the timescale within which the third party's evidence must be served, along with any response by the prosecutor and the defendant.

17.45 Once any necessary adjournment has been obtained and funding secured, the third party's witness statement in support of his claim should be prepared. Where documentary evidence exists to support the claim, it should be exhibited to the witness statement. If there are other persons who are in a position to confirm the veracity of the third party's claim, witness statements should also be taken from them. Such independent evidence is particularly important in cases where no documentary evidence exists to support the third party claim.

17.46 Once the third party's evidence has been served, it may be prudent to enter into 'without prejudice' negotiations with the prosecutor and the defendant. In many cases, the fact of the third party having an interest in the asset in question will be beyond dispute. The real issue is more commonly the extent of that interest. As all the parties will be anxious to resolve the matter expeditiously with the minimum of costs, and the court will encourage the parties to reach agreement wherever possible, it may well be that all concerned would be willing to take a commercial view and not press for the highest amount for which they could contend.

17.47 Although the prosecutor acts in the public interest in taking proceedings to enforce a confiscation order, this does not mean he should not negotiate with the defendant and interested third parties to reach a mutually acceptable compromise where this is justified by the evidence. In *Grimes v CPS* [2003] EWCA Civ 1814 the Court of Appeal accepted that the prosecutor had public duties to perform in relation to the confiscation order but, in the words of Brooke LJ:

> That does not in my judgment mean that the CPS were entitled to behave, as litigants far too often behaved before the CPR came in, by simply standing back and saying "We will make no offer at all for the court to consider when it decides what order as to costs is a reasonable one to make. We will simply see you in court.
>
> The CPS has a duty under CPR 1.3 to help the court to further the overriding objective, and it would be the reverse of justice if the court were to be perceived to be upholding a policy which led the CPS to think that it did not have to make any offer at all and could come to court for an expensive contested hearing, simply leaving the successful party to lose much of its success by an order for costs which it could not recover.

He added:

> To some extent both parties were at fault for not doing all they could to resolve this dispute without the uneconomic costs of a hearing before a High Court judge, and it may well be that mediation is a more appropriate way of resolving many of these disputes now that experieince of mediation, and of successful mediation, has grown so much.

17.48 All parties to receivership proceedings should, it is submitted, bear these remarks very much in mind and should be willing to make what Brooke LJ described as 'a well pitched offer' to compromise the proceedings. A party to the proceedings who refuses to accept such an offer is at risk of having costs awarded against him.

C. Enforcement Receivers under the DTA and CJA

(11) The court's order

17.49 If the parties cannot reach agreement, the application for the appointment of a receiver will proceed to a full contested hearing before the judge. In most cases, where there is a substantial confiscation order to be met involving significant third party interests or where the defendant has made little effort to satisfy the order voluntarily, or it is impracticable to allow him to do so, the court will exercise its discretion to appoint a receiver. The precise terms of the appointment will depend on the findings the court makes in determining any third party claims. If a third party is successful in satisfying the court that a particular asset belongs entirely to him, it will form no part of the receivership order, and neither the prosecutor nor the defendant will have any claim over it. If, however, the court finds that an asset is jointly owned, it will determine the extent of the respective interests of the defendant and third party and may then proceed in one of two ways:

(1) The court may direct that the defendant and third party give possession of the asset to the receiver to realise and that the receiver should pay to the third party a sum of money from the proceeds of sale proportionate to his interest in it; or
(2) The court may direct the third party to pay to the receiver a sum of money equivalent to the defendant's interest in the property. On payment of this sum, the court may direct that the defendant's interest in the property should be extinguished and transferred to the third party. The court will need to be satisfied that the third party has sufficient funds before making an order in these terms, but will usually be prepared to give the third party a reasonable time in which to raise any necessary finance.

(12) The matrimonial home: rights of spouses

17.50 It should be noted that following the decision of the Court of Appeal in *Customs and Excise Commissioners v MCA* [2002] EWCA Civ 1039, different rules apply in relation to the matrimonial home and, in appropriate circumstances, the spouse of a defendant may be allowed to remain in the matrimonial home notwithstanding that he or she has less than a 100 per cent interest in it. This subject is considered in more detail in Chapter 22.

(13) Status of the receiver on appointment

17.51 As with a management receiver, on appointment an enforcement receiver becomes an officer of the court accountable only to the court for his actions. Although appointed on the application of the prosecutor, an enforcement receiver is entirely independent of the prosecutor who has no power to direct the receiver to act in a particular way. This is not to say that the prosecutor and receiver should not work closely together during the course of the receivership. Indeed, in practice, the prosecuting authority's financial investigation officers will work very closely with the receiver and his staff, as they are in the best possible position to advise as to the realisable property owned by the defendant and its current location. Similarly, where during the course of the receivership the defendant or an interested third party makes an application to the court, the prosecutor frequently liaises closely with the receiver because he may well have access to information and documentation relevant to the court's consideration of the claim. Where no conflict of interest exists, the prosecutor and the receiver frequently instruct the same counsel with a view to saving costs. It is submitted that these practices are perfectly proper provided the receiver does nothing to compromise his objectivity and independence as an officer of the court.

(14) Realisation of property

17.52 The receivership order places the receiver in the same position as the defendant and enables him to sell all the defendant's assets in satisfaction of the order. The receiver will normally appoint agents to assist him, eg estate agents and solicitors to arrange the sale of a house. The receiver is not under a duty to obtain the best possible sale price for assets, so long as the price obtained is reasonable in all the circumstances. In order to protect himself against any possible claim for negligence, the receiver will often obtain at least one independent valuation before agreeing a sale price for any assets of significant value such as houses, motor vehicles, boats, jewellery, etc.

(15) Remuneration of enforcement receivers

17.53 As with management receivers, an enforcement receiver has the right to be remunerated for his work and to have his fees paid from the proceeds of realisation of the defendant's assets. The letter of agreement between the prosecutor and the receiver will normally set out the basis on which the receiver is to be remunerated. The letter of agreement will give the receiver an indemnity under which the prosecutor will agree to meet the receiver's remuneration and expenses in the event that he realises insufficient assets to pay these in full. It is usual for the prosecutor to impose a 'cap' on the indemnity in a specified sum and to require the receiver to give him immediate notice if it is likely that he will need to rely on the indemnity.

17.54 In the past such letters of agreement have usually provided for the receiver's fees to be approved by the prosecutor, and paid from the proceeds of realisation. In default of agreement the fees were assessed by a costs judge. The defendant had no role in the process and had little redress open to him if he considered the receiver's fees to be excessive. In *Hughes v Commissioners of Customs and Excise* [2002] 4 All ER 633 the Court of Appeal made it clear that the procedure whereby receiver's fees were approved by the prosecutor was wrong and that they should be approved by the court. Simon Brown LJ, with whom Laws and Arden LJJ agreed, said:

> Paragraph 6 of the letter of agreement in the *Hughes* case incorporated into the court's restraint and receivership order by para 11 of that order, both in common form, provides for the receiver's remuneration to be agreed between the receiver and the commissioners and only in default of that by the High Court. As we observed during the course of the hearing, this arrangement is difficult to reconcile with RSC Order 30, r3. Although the issue is not strictly before us on these appeals, first instance judges who make these orders should be alerted to the need under r3 to retain control over the way the receiver's remuneration is fixed.

17.55 Arden LJ reinforced these concerns, drawing attention to the procedures that applied in the Chancery Division. She said:

> I agree with what Simon Brown LJ has said about the terms of any order of the court as to the receiver's remuneration. The practice of the Chancery Division is set out in the 'Guide for Receivers in the Chancery Division' referred to at para 22.6 of the Chancery Guide (see Civil Court Practice (2002) vol 1, p1787 (Green Book). This states:

C. Enforcement Receivers under the DTA and CJA

The receiver's remuneration must be authorised by the Court. Unless the court directs it to be fixed by reference to some fixed scale, or percentage or rents collected, it is assessed by the court, but in the first instance the receiver should submit his remuneration claim to the parties for approval. If the claim is accepted by the parties, the court should not normally be concerned to intervene, but it must at least formally authorise the remuneration.

Rule 3 (1) is an important provision which should not be overlooked.

It is submitted that the proper approach is for the receiver to submit his claims for remuneration to the parties at regular intervals for approval. If agreement can be reached then the receiver should submit his claim to the enforcing magistrates' court, who is responsible for paying the reciever, together with the letters of approval from the parties, for the court to formally authorise payment. If agreement cannot be reached, the claim will be subject to examination in accordance with CPR Part 69. **17.56**

(16) Dealing with the proceeds of realisation

The sole purpose of an enforcement receivership is to realise assets in satisfaction of the confiscation order. The proceeds of realisation will ultimately fall to be paid to the magistrates' court responsible for enforcing the confiscation order. The appropriate magistrates' court will generally be the court from which the defendant was sent for trial at the Crown Court. Section 30 of the DTA and s 81 of the CJA make provision as to how the receiver should deal with the proceeds of realisation. The sections provide that payments should be made in the following order: **17.57**

(1) the receiver should first meet any expenses incurred by a licensed insolvency practitioner dealing with realisable property under s 35 of the DTA or s 87(2) of the CJA;
(2) the receiver should make any payments that may have been ordered to be made by the High Court. This would include, for example, payments to third parties who have an interest in realisable property sold by the receiver;
(3) the balance is paid to the appropriate magistrates' court in satisfaction of the confiscation order.

The responsibility for paying the receiver rests with the Justices' Chief Executive (see s 30 (6) DTA and s 81 (5) CJA). It follows from this that the receiver is not entitled to deduct his fees before paying the proceeds of realisation to the court. He must pay the full amount to the Justices' Chief Executive who will then pay the receiver's remuneration and expenses. The JJustices Chief Executive does not, however, have any role to play in the assessing the reasonableness of the receiver's costs. This is a matter within the exclusive jurisdiction of the High Court in accordance with CPR 69.7. **17.58**

Rarely, if ever, will it be appropriate for the prosecutor to be held responsible for the payment of the remuneration and expenses of an enforcement receiver. As Munby J said in *Re HN* [2005] EWHC Admin 2982: **17.59**

> If it becomes necessary to have a receiver, why should the Crown be left paying his costs, disbursements and fees? On the contrary, in most such cases, at least where there is a sufficiency of assets, the only proper order is that the burden of meeting those costs, disbursements and fees should be thrown on the defendant rather than on the Crown. Why, after all, should the

public purse be expected to pay for something necessitated by a solvent criminal's failure to discharge a confiscation order? I can think of no good reason.

17.60 If the receiver has brought in more funds than are required to satisfy the confiscation order and his costs of realisation, he must apply to the High Court under s 30(3) of the DTA or s 81(2) of the CJA for directions as to how the surplus should be distributed amongst interested parties.

(17) Discharge of the receiver

17.61 Once the receiver has completed his work, either by satisfying the confiscation order in full or realising all the available assets in part satisfaction of the order, he should be discharged from office. The application may be made either by the receiver himself or by the prosecuting authority that sought his appointment.

D. The Powers of the Magistrates' Court

17.62 The appointment of a receiver, although a highly effective remedy to secure payment of the confiscation order, is also an expensive one. Its use should normally be confined to the larger confiscation orders and those where there are houses or other substantial assets to be sold, overseas properties to be dealt with, third party claims to be determined, or other compelling reasons why the magistrates' court's powers are inadequate. In cases where there are no third party claims and the assets are easy to realise, such as money held in bank accounts or by the prosecutor, or jewellery or motor vehicles of a relatively low value, recourse should always be had to the sanctions available to the magistrates' court responsible for enforcing the order before the appointment of a receiver is considered.

17.63 Magistrates' courts are involved in the enforcement process because s 9(1) of the DTA and s 75(1) of the CJA provide that ss 139(1) to (4) and 140(1) to (3) of the Powers of Criminal Courts (Sentencing) Act 2000 (PCC(S)A) shall apply in relation to the enforcement of confiscation orders in the same way as they apply to the enforcement of fines. In consequence, all the powers of that magistrates' court that are available for the enforcement of fines are also available to them for the purpose of enforcing confiscation orders.

(1) Distress warrants

17.64 Section 76 of the Magistrates' Courts Act 1980 empowers the court to issue a distress warrant. Such a warrant empowers bailiffs to take possession of and sell property belonging to the defendant to satisfy the confiscation order. It is particularly useful in relation to motor vehicles, jewellery, and other goods belonging to the defendant, providing as it does a quick and inexpensive means of realisation. It should be noted, however, that a distress warrant does not give the bailiff any authority to enter by force the premises where the goods are held for the purpose of taking possession of them. Entry may, however, be gained through an unsecured door or window: see *Long v Clarke* (1894) 56 JP 258. Distress warrants are also useful in cases where the prosecutor is in possession of property taken up from the defendant at the time of his arrest which the defendant will not authorise the prosecutor to

D. The Powers of the Magistrates' Court

hand over to the court. In such circumstances, the issue of a distress warrant protects the prosecutor from any civil claim for conversion if he hands the property over to the bailiff.

(2) Third party debt orders

By s 87 of the Magistrates' Courts Act 1980, the clerk to the justices may enforce the order in the High Court or the county court otherwise than by the issue of a writ of *fieri facias*, imprisonment, or attachment of earnings. This, in effect, restricts the court to applying for a third party debt order (formerly known as a 'garnishee order') under CPR Part 72. Section 9(4)(b) of the DTA and s 75(5)(b) of the CJA provide that s 87(3) of the Magistrates' Courts Act 1980 does not apply in relation to the enforcement of confiscation orders and it is therefore not necessary for the clerk to obtain authorisation from the court after a means enquiry before making application for a third party debt order: he may act entirely of his own motion. Third party debt orders are particularly useful where a defendant has money in a bank account which he will not voluntarily pay into court or where the prosecutor is in possession of money belonging to the defendant which he will not permit the prosecutor to pay into court.

17.65

(3) Warrants of commitment

Section 76 of the Magistrates' Courts Act gives the court power to issue a warrant of commitment committing the defendant to prison to serve the default sentence imposed by the Crown Court in the event of non-payment. Although the court is under an obligation to conduct a means enquiry prior to committing a defendant to prison for failing to pay a fine, and may only then commit him if it finds there has been a wilful refusal or culpable neglect to pay, no such obligation exists in relation to a confiscation order. In *R v Hastings and Rother Justices ex p Anscombe*, (Div Ct, 5 February 1998) the Divisional Court refused to quash a warrant of commitment where no means enquiry had been conducted. Schiemann, LJ said:

17.66

> The basic submission on behalf of the applicant is that the Magistrates had no power to commit the applicant to prison without first holding a means enquiry. That submission was based on section 82 of the 1980 Act. I would reject it for the simple reason that the inhibition in section 84(3) only bites if the Magistrates' Court is bound by section 82(3) to inquire into the offender's means. They are only so bound if they have not on a previous occasion fixed a term of imprisonment to be served in default of payment. In the present case a term of imprisonment in default of payment had been fixed on conviction by the Crown Court. The effect of the legislation is to treat this term as having been fixed by the Magistrates.

The only duty of the justices is to enquire into the defendant's proposals for payment and to determine whether any of the other methods of enforcement might be effective. If the defendant advances no such proposals or no other methods of enforcement appear to the court to be effective, it is entitled to issue the warrant of commitment.

17.67

When the Justices are determining whether or not to issue the warrant of commitment, they are entitled to hear representations from the prosecuting authority as to the position in relation to the confiscation order. In *R v Hastings and Rother Justices ex p Anscombe* (Div Ct, 5 February 1998) Schiemann LJ observed:

17.68

> The applicant also seeks to quash the decision of the Justices to hear the representative of the Customs and Excise who informed them as to the current situation as best it was known to

him and who informed them amongst other things of the undisputed fact that, in breach of bail, the applicant had previously left the jurisdiction. I see nothing wrong either in the fact that the representative was heard or that he saw it appropriate to put this fact before the magistrates who were being asked to adjourn the proceedings. Had they adjourned Mr Anscombe would have been released from prison and might have chosen this opportunity to go abroad again.

17.69 Similar sentiments were expressed by the Divisional Court in *R v Harrow Justices ex p DPP* [1991] 1 WLR 395. In that case Stuart-Smith LJ observed:

> Given the inter partes nature of the procedure leading to the making of a confiscation order, it will be in the nature of things that the prosecution will in all prob-ability have information available which would be relevant for the justices consideration. More compellingly, the prosecution has a legitimate interest in being heard before the Justices' come to any decision.

17.70 It is submitted that justices should as a matter of course liaise with the prosecutor before deciding whether to issue a warrant of commitment and give him the opportunity of making representations. In the *Harrow Justices'* case the court reminded the justices that two Home Office circulars numbered 98/1986 and 10/1988 advised that such consultation with the prosecutor should take place. The latter circular advises that in every case where either a confiscation order for a sum in excess of £10,000 is made or it appears that a restraint order is in force, the justices should always liaise with the prosecutor prior to taking enforcement action. In cases involving an amount less than £10,000 the circular states that it might be assumed, unless the prosecutor contacts the court to indicate otherwise, that no High Court action is involved and the order may be enforced solely by the magistrates. The court would, however, always be well advised to contact the prosecutor who may be in a position to provide a considerable amount of information including copies of s 11 and s 73 statements, disclosure statements and the like which will assist in identifying assets that may be the subject of garnishee orders or distress warrants.

17.71 It is important that the justices should resist the temptation to act as any form of appeal court against the making of the confiscation order. The court is only concerned with the enforcement of the order and if the defendant is aggrieved by it he has the right to appeal to the Court of Appeal and, if he claims that his assets are insufficient to meet the confiscation order, he may apply to the High Court for a certificate of inadequacy. As Stuart-Smith LJ observed in the *Harrow Justices* case:

> The mere fact that a confiscation order has been made is evidence that, at the date of its imposition, there were realisable assets available to meet the requirements of the order. Even if at the date when the Justices' have to consider the question of enforcement, the value of realisable assets are less than they were at the date of the confiscation order, it is open to the defendant to apply for a certificate of inadequacy . . . which will lead to a reduction in the amount of the original order.

17.72 The commencement of enforcement proceedings by the justices often results in the defendant seeking a certificate of inadequacy from the High Court. The mere fact that the defendant asserts that he is taking such steps does not, however, mean that the justices must adjourn the hearing at which they are considering the issue of the warrant of commitment pending the outcome of the application to the High Court. The justices must, of course, exercise their discretion judicially and, if there has been an inordinate delay by the defendant in making his application for a certificate of inadequacy, they would be quite entitled to refuse an application for an adjournment. If, on the other hand, the High Court application has already been issued and a hearing date fixed when the justices are considering whether to issue a warrant of commitment, the better course may be to adjourn to await the outcome of the High Court proceedings. In *R v Liverpool Magistrates' Court ex p Ansen* [1998] 1 All ER 692 there had been a delay of two years between the confiscation order being made and the justices issuing the warrant of commitment, during which time no application had been made by the defendant for a certificate of inadequacy. He brought judicial review proceedings against the justices, inter alia, for refusing his application for the hearing to be adjourned to enable him to apply for a certificate of inadequacy. In rejecting this argument, May J said:

> The next matter relied upon is that the magistrate did not adjourn the matter before him so that the applicant could be given time to make an application to the High Court for a certificate of inadequacy. The evidence of the magistrate here is that he did not do so because he reckoned that the applicant had had quite adequate time to do this and that an adjournment for that purpose should be refused. In my judgment, that was a perfectly proper decision for the magistrate to make.

17.73 The Court took a similar view in *R v Hastings and Rother Justices ex p Anscombe* (Div Ct, 5 February 1998) where an application for a certificate of inadequacy would have had no prospect of success. Schiemann LJ said:

> The Justices could have adjourned the proceedings in front of them in order to see whether or not the High Court would issue a certificate of inadequacy and, if so, whether an application would be made by the defendant to the Crown Court to reduce the amount of the order and of the period to be served in default. An application for an adjournment was made to them. The only grounds put forward appear to have been the promised application to the High Court for the certificate of inadequacy which in turn seems to have been based on the contention that the sums which the Crown Court had held had been salted away had never been salted away. That assertion was not open to the appellant as I have indicated earlier in this judgment. I see no error of law in the failure by the Justices to exercise in Mr Anscombe's favour their discretion to adjourn.

17.74 It is submitted that each case must be determined on its own particular facts and the result in both these two cases may well have been different if the Justices had refused to adjourn in circumstances where the defendant had made a prompt application for a certificate of inadequacy as soon as the deficiency came to his attention and that application was still pending at the time the justices decided to issue the warrant of commitment.

17.75 Where the warrant of commitment is issued by the Justices, the sentence is to be served consecutively to the sentence imposed for the substantive offence. The authority for this is s 9(2) of the DTA and s75(3) of the CJA. The sections are in more or less identical terms, s 9(2) of the DTA providing:

'Where—
(a) a warrant of commitment is issued for a default in payment of an amount ordered to be paid under section 2 of this Act in respect of an offence or offences, and
(b) at the time the warrant is issued, the defendant is liable to serve a term of custody in respect of the offence or offences,

the term of imprisonment or of detention under section 108 (of the Power of Criminal Courts (Sentencing) Act 2000) (detention of persons aged 18 to 20 for default) to be served in default of payment of the amount shall not begin to run until after the term mentioned in paragraph (b) above.

17.76 In *R v City of London Justices ex p Chapman* (1998) 162 JP 359 the defendant sought to argue that where he had been released on licence from the sentence of imprisonment imposed for the substantive offence, the default sentence could not start until the end of the licence period since he was still 'liable to serve' the remainder of his sentence. The Divisional Court rejected this argument, Gage J (with whom Pill LJ agreed) observing:

> It seems to me that the scheme of the Drug Trafficking Offences Act was to require that sentences in default be served consecutively immediately following the period in custody in respect of the offence or offences . . . In my judgment, 'liable to serve a term of custody in respect of the offence' is to be construed as currently liable to serve a term of imprisonment. It is not apt to include a prisoner who is released on licence.

17.77 The decision in *ex p Chapman* was followed by the High Court in *R v City of London Justices ex p Peracha* (HC, 31 March 1998). In that case Rose LJ said:

> For my part, I see no reason to regard *Chapman* as having been wrongly decided. On the contrary, I agree with those passages in the judgments of Mr Justice Gage and Lord Justice Pill which I have cited in relation to the construction of section 6; that is to say, 'liable' in section 6 means, 'presently liable'. The history of the legislation, in so far as it provides any assistance, to my mind suggests that the words 'liable to serve' which appear in section 6(3) should, if anything, be given a restricted meaning, because they are no longer immediately preceded by the word 'serving'.
>
> In any event, for my part, I am satisfied that 'liable' means 'bound to serve' and not 'exposed to the risk of serving'. There is a separate regime for sentences for substantive offences and default terms imposed if confiscation orders are not complied with. This is demonstrated, to my mind, both by the definition of sentence of imprisonment in the 1967 Act, which is repeated in the 1991 Criminal Justice Act section 51, and by the separate regime which is provided in the 1991 Act for default terms as compared with sentences of imprisonment.
>
> To my mind, it would be absurd to suppose that in the draconian provisions in relation to drug trafficking, Parliament intended that a person, subject to a default term, should be able to avoid serving that term by taking advantage of a period of liberty stretching to months or, as in the present case, to years, in order to abscond either in this country or abroad. If this were the case, there would, as it seems to me, never be any practical purpose in a court making an order for committal in default, for it would not have the effect of encouraging regurgitation of drug profits.

(4) Delay by the prosecutor in enforcing the confiscation order

17.78 Cases occasionally arise in which there has been a long delay before the prosecuting authority takes action to enforce a confiscation order. The creation of the Enforcement Task Force (see Chapter 1) has significantly reduced the number of cases in which such delays occur, but it is inevitable that whether through administrative error or a breakdown in communication with the enforcing authority delays will occur from time to time. The decision of the High Court in *R v Chichester Magistrates' Court ex p Crowther* [1998] EWHC Admin 960 was authority for the proposition that even if there was a cuplable delay in enforcing a confiscation order, it did not act as a bar to implementing the default sentence for non-payment.

17.79 All this changed, however, following the decision of the Divisional Court in *Lloyd v Bow Street Magistrates' Court* [2003] EWHC Admin 2294. A CJA confiscatiion order was made against the defendant on 21 June, 1996 for £33,236 with an 18 month sentence of imprisonment to be served in default of payment. On 10 July, 1997 when £26,897.37 was still outstanding, the CPS wrote to the defendant advising him of their intention of applying for the appointment of an enforcement receiver unless the amount owing was paid within 14 days. No further payments were made, but it was not until 30 November 1998 that the CPS issued an application for the appointment of a receiver who was duly appointed by order of the court dated 15 January 1999. Thereafter it appears there was a breakdown of communication between the CPS and the receiver, the latter claiming never to have received a copy of the order appointing him. The CPS did not write to the receiver to establish what progress had been made in realising the defendant's assets, but on 6 December 1999 wrote to the enforcing magistrates' court saying that no assets had been realised and inviting the court to issue the warrant of commitment. In January, 2001 the court issued a summons requiring the defendant to attend for consideration to be given to the warrant being issued, but the hearing did not take place until 9 October, 2002 when the defendant was duly committed to prison.

17.80 The Court quashed the warrant of commitment, ruling that the delay constituted a breach of the defendant's right under Article 6.1 of the European Convention on Human Rights to a fair trial within a reasonable time. At first sight this might seem surprising, because the primary obligation to satisfy a confiscation order is on the defendant and not on the prosecuting authority or enforcing magistrates' court. If there is a delay it is normally the result of the defendant failing to comply with the terms of the order. This contention was, however, firmly rejected by Dyson LJ who said:

> We do not see how the fact that the defendant is in breach of his continuing duty to satisfy the confiscation order can be relevant. In our view, the conduct of the defendant can have no bearing on the question whether he has a right to have proceedings against him in respect of that conduct instituted and determined within a reasonable time. It is common ground that a defendant is entitled to have a substantive criminal charge against him determined within a reasonable time. That right is predicated on the basis that the defendant is alleged to have broken the law by committing a crime. The fact that a defendant is alleged to have committed a crime is plainly not a reason for denying him the right to have the criminal charge determined within a reasonable time. Indeed, the existence of the criminal charge is the very reason why he has that right. Similarly, in our view, the fact that a defendant is alleged to be in breach of a confiscation order is no reason to deny him the right to have proceedings brought to enforce the order by commitment to prison determined within a reasonable time.

He added:

> Convicted criminals who are the subject of confiscation orders do not attract sympathy and are not entitled to favoured treatment. But there is nothing surprising about a requirement that, if the prosecuting authorities/magistrates court seek to enforce a confiscation order, they should do so within a reasonable time. It is potentially very unfair on a defendant that he should be liable to be committed to prison for non-payment of sums due under a confiscation order

many years after the time for payment has expired, and long after he has been released from custody and resumed work and family life.

In a clear warning to enforcement agencies, Dyson LJ concluded:

> If the authorities whose task it is to enforce confiscation orders are so slow in communicating with one another or in activating enforcement mechanisms that they become in breach of Article 6.1, then the appropriate remedy may well be (as in this case) that the weapon of imprisonment in default is lost. The sooner this is appreciated by all agencies of the criminal justice system, the better.

17.81 This case is a cautionary reminder to all prosecuting authorities and magistrates' courts charged with the enforcement of confiscation orders to proceed with due expedition or the remedy of committal to prison may no longer be available. If, however, the defendant is responsible for the delay or, due to the complexity of his financial affairs, his assets take an unusually long time to realise, Article 6.1 will not assist him. As Dyson LJ observed:

> It follows that, in deciding what is a reasonable time, regard should be had to the efforts made to extract the money by other methods, for example (as in the present case) by the appointment of a receiver. If a receiver has been appointed within a reasonable time and has proceeded with reasonable expedition, then the fact that all of this may hve taken some time will not prevent the court from concluding that there has been no violation of the defendant's Article 6.1 rights if the unsuccessful attempts to recover the money have led to delay in the institution of proceedings to commit. Likewise, if the defendant has been evasive and has avoided diligent attempts to extract the money from him, he will be unable to rely on the resultant delay in support of an argument that his right to a determination within a reaonable time has been violated.

17.82 Finally, the court made it plain that its ruling applied only to enforcement of confiscation orders by means of committal to prison and not to civil methods of enforcement such as the appointment of a receiver.

17.83 In *R (on the application of Deamer) v Southampton Magistrates' Court* [2006] EWHC Admin 2221, the High Court reiterated that a stay would only be granted where the delay by the enforcing authority was unreasonable and unjustified. In that case a confiscation order was made against the claimant on 1 March 1999 in the sum of £5,448,200. The order was to be paid in full by 29 January 2000 and the claimant was ordered to serve an additional six years imprisonemnt in default of payment. On 18 February 2000 an enforcement receiver was appointed, but he only succeeded in bringing in £5,456.06 before his discharge on 24 May, 2001. On 23 January 2002 a further £350,182.85, representing funds taken up by HM Customs and Excise (as it was then known) at the time of the defendant's arrest, was also paid into court in part satisfaction of the order.

17.84 Thereafter, between 2002 and 2006 extensive correspondence passed between the Revenue and Customs Prosecutions Office (RCPO) and the claimant's solicitors concerning the payment of the balance due under the order. At various points the solicitors suggested they were intending making an application for a certificate of inadequacy and were pursuing enquiries as to the availability of assets in the USA to satisfy the order. In the event, no application for a certificate of inadequacy was made and the order remained unsatisfied. On a number of occasions RCPO warned the claimant's solicitors that in the absence of acceptable proposals for payment the matter would be referred to the enforcing magistrates' court.

17.85 On 3 April, 2006, one day before the claimant was eligible for release on parole, he appeared before the enforcing magistrates' court for consideration to be given to implementing the default sentence. He contended that having regard to the delay in enforcing the order, the court should order the proceedings to be stayed, relying on the ruling in *Lloyd*. The District Judge held that the mere passage of time was not enough to order a stay and there had to be some delay that is 'unjustifiable and unreasonable'. The District Judge concluded that the period while the receiver was in office should be disregarded because it was proper for the receiver to have been appointed and the time allowed for him to bring in the assets was reasonable. As to the period between May 2001 and February 2006 the District Judge reviewed the correspondence between RCPO and the claimant's solicitors and concluded that the prosecutor had not been indolent. She found that the prosecutor had regularly sought information from the claimant's solicitors and the correspondence made it plain that is was their continuing intention to enforce the order. Although RCPO may have been naïve in accepting some of the assurances given by the claimant's solicitors, the District Judge found they had not allowed the case to become dormant and their decision to await further information from the claimant as to the availability of further assets was neither unreasonable nor unjustifiable. The District Judge refused a stay of proceedings and activated the six year default sentence.

17.86 The claimant applied for judicial review of the District Judge's decision. The Court dismissed the application, Aikens J observing:

> In my view, the District Judge cannot be criticised for her conclusion that the period up to the end of the appointment of the Receiver is unexceptional. As to the period when Mr. Deamer's solicitors were apparently seeking evidence for the application of a Certificate of Inadequacy, it seems to me that they were trying to get information to back such an application. At the same time, the RCPO were hoping that the information would provide material to show that Mr. Deamer indeed had assets to pay the confiscation order. I agree with the District Judge's tentative view that the RCPO might have been naïve in this regard. But I have reached the firm conclusion that it cannot be said that the District Judge's finding on the facts was in any way unreasonable. The solicitors for Mr. Deamer did indicate that investigations were going on in the USA, even if they had produced no results.
>
> In my view, it cannot be said that the District Judge's conclusion on the reasonableness of the RCPO's activity and their stance in relation to these investigations is either irrational or perverse or unreasonable.

The decision in *Deamer* makes it clear that mere delay by itself will not be sufficient to justify a stay of the enforcement proceedings. The delay must be one for which the enforcement agency is responsible and which is unreasonable and unjustifiable on the facts. If the defendant causes or contributes to any such delay, it will not normally be appropriate to order a stay of proceedings. This is particularly so where, as in *Deamer*, the enforcement agency had throughout made its intention of enforcing the order abundantly clear.

E. Enforcement under POCA 2002

17.87 POCA 2002 makes provision for the enforcement of confiscation orders made under that Act. It is important to note that these provisions do not have retrospective effect and do not apply in relation to confiscation orders made under the DTA and CJA.

(1) Enforcement receivers

17.88 POCA 2002 makes very similar provision to the DTA and CJA for the appointment of enforcement receivers. The relevant provisions are found in ss 50 and 51 of the Act. Section 50 provides:

(1) This section applies if—
   (a) a confiscation order is made,
   (b) it is not satisfied, and
   (c) it is not subject to appeal.
(2) On the application of the prosecutor the Crown Court may by order appoint a receiver in respect of realisable property.

(2) Powers of enforcement receivers

17.89 The powers the Crown Court may give an enforcement receiver are set out in some detail in s 51 of the Act. This is because, in contrast to the High Court, the Crown Court being a creature of statute has no inherent jurisdiction and all the powers the court may bestow on a receiver must therefore be set out in the Act itself. Section 51 provides:

(1) If the court appoints a receiver under section 50 it may act under this section on the application of the prosecutor.
(2) The court may by order confer on the receiver the following powers in relation to the realisable property—
   (a) power to take possession of the property;
   (b) power to manage or otherwise deal with the property;
   (c) power to realise the property, in such manner as the court may specify;
   (d) power to start, carry on or defend any legal proceedings in respect of the property.
(3) The court may by order confer on the receiver power to enter any premises in England and Wales and to do any of the following—
   (a) search for or inspect anything authorised by the court;
   (b) make or obtain a copy, photograph or other record of anything so authorised;
   (c) remove anything which the receiver is required or authorised to take possession of in pursuance of an order of the court.
(4) The court may by order authorise the receiver to do any of the following for the purpose of the exercise of his functions—
   (a) hold property;
   (b) enter into contracts;
   (c) sue and be sued;
   (d) execute powers of attorney, deeds or other instruments;
   (e) take any other steps the court thinks appropriate.
(5) The court may order any person who has possession of realisable property to give possession of it to the receiver.
(6) The court—
   (a) may order a person holding an interest in realisable property to make to the receiver such payment as the court specifies in respect of a beneficial interest held by the defendant or the recipient of a tainted gift.
   (b) may (on the payment being made) by order transfer, grant or extinguish any interest in the property.
(7) Subsections (2), (5) and (6) do not apply to property for the time being subject to a charge made under any of these provisions—
   (a) section 9 of the Drug Trafficking Offences Act 1986 (c32);
   (b) section 78 of the Criminal Justice Act 1988(c33);

E. Enforcement under POCA 2002

   (c) Article 14 of the Criminal Justice (Confiscation) (Northern Ireland) Order 1990 (SI 1990/2588 (NI 17));
   (d) section 27 of the Drug Trafficking Act, 1994(c37);
   (e) Article 32 of the Proceeds of Crime (Northern Ireland) Order 1996 (SI 1996/1299 (NI 9)).
(8) The court must not—
   (a) confer the power mentioned in subsection (2)(b) or (c) in respect of property, or
   (b) exercise the power conferred on it by subsection (6) in respect of property,
   unless it gives the persons holding interests in the property a reasonable opportunity to make representations to it.
(9) The court may order that a power conferred by an order under this section is subject to such conditions and exceptions as it specifies.
(10) Managing or otherwise dealing with property includes—
   (a) selling the property or any part of it or interest in it;
   (b) carrying on or arranging for another person to carry on any trade or business the assets of which are or are part of the property;
   (c) incurring capital expenditure in respect of the property.

17.90 These powers are in very similar terms to those given to management receivers under s 49 of the Act and which are considered in Chapter 8 above. Section 51(8) of the Act provides the same protection for third parties as provided for by the DTA and CJA in that certain powers cannot be conferred on the receiver unless and until they have been given the opportunity to make representations.

17.91 Sections 54 and 55 of POCA deal with the application of sums realised by an enforcement receiver and make identical provision to the DTA and CJA as to the order in which liabilities must be satisfied and as to the obtaining of directions as to how any surplus funds should be dealt with. The receipt of the sums by the Justices' Chief Executive reduces the amount payable under the order (s 55(2)) and they must be applied in the following order:

(1) to meet the fees of a licensed insolvency practitioner appointed under s 432;
(2) to meet the fees of a management receiver appointed under s 48 to the extent that they have not already been paid under a power conferred on the receiver under s 49(2)(d);
(3) to meet the remuneration of an enforcement receiver appointed under s 50;
(4) to pay any compensation order to be paid from the amount recovered under s 13(6);
(5) any balance is paid into the consolidated fund in the same way as a fine.

(3) Director's receivers

17.92 In certain circumstances s 34 of POCA requires the court to appoint the Director of ARA as the enforcement authority. By s 34 (1) these circumstances are:

(a) where the court proceeded to make a confiscation order after being asked to do so by the Director;
(b) where the court made a confiscation order in consequence of an application by the Director under ss 19, 20, 27, or 28;
(c) where the court proceeded to make a confiscation order as a result of an appeal by the Director under ss 31(2) or 33; or
(d) where, before the court made the confiscation order, the Director applied to the court to be appointed as the enforcement authority.

Chapter 17: Enforcement of Confiscation Orders under the CJA, the DTA, and POCA

17.93 Where the Director has been appointed as the enforcement authority, the court must, under s 52(3), make an order appointing a receiver in respect of the defendant's realisable property. By s 52(4):

An order under subsection (3)—

(a) must confer power on the Director to nominate the person who is to be the receiver, and
(b) takes effect when the Director nominates that person.

17.94 The procedures for appointing a Director's receiver are therefore entirely different from those applicable in relation to the appointment of an enforcement receiver. In contrast to the position in relation to enforcement receivers, where the Director has been appointed the enforcement authority, the court has no discretion under the Act other than to appoint the receiver, and it is entirely a matter for the Director to decide who the receiver shall be once the order is made. The court has no jurisdiction to determine who the receiver shall be. The person the Director nominates to act as receiver under an order made under s 52(3) may be a member of the staff of the ARA, or a person providing services under arrangements made by the Director. The Director may not make a nomination under s 52(4) if the confiscation order is subject to appeal (see s 52(5)).

(4) Powers of Director's receivers

17.95 By s 53, the court may, on the application of the Director, confer on a Director's receiver precisely the same powers that it may give a conventional enforcement receiver. Section 53(8) protects the position of third parties in the same way as s 51(8) protects third party interests on applications for the conferment of powers on enforcement receivers, by requiring that persons holding an interest in realisable property must be given a reasonable opportunity to make representations.

(5) Procedure on applications for the appointment of enforcement receivers under POCA

17.96 The procedures to be followed on applications for the appointment of enforcement receivers are set out in Part 60 of the Criminal Procedure Rules 2005. By r 60.1 (3) the application must be in writing supported by a witness statement which must:

(a) give the grounds for the application;
(b) give full details of the proposed receiver;
(c) to the best of the witness's ability, give full details of the realisble property in respect of which the applicant is seeking the order and specify the person holding it;
(d) if the proposed receiver is not a member of staff of the Assets Recovery Agency, the Crown Prosecution Service or the Revenue & Customs Prosecutions Office and the applicant is asking the court to allow the receiver to act-
　(i) without giving security, or
　(ii) before he has given security or satisfied the court that he has security in place, explain the reasons why that is necessary.

17.97 The applicant must provide the Crown Court with a copy of the confiscation order it is sought to enforce against the defendant (see r 60.1(4)). It is submitted that the

E. Enforcement under POCA 2002

best practice is to exhibit a copy of the order to the witness statement in support of the application.

17.98 Although r 60.1(2) allows all applications for the appointment of receivers to be made without notice, it is submitted that it would rarely be appropriate for enforcement receivership applications to be made other than on notice to the defendant and affected third parties. Where the application is made on notice, the application and witness statement in support must be lodged with the Crown Court and served on the defendant, any person who holds realisable property to which the application relates and any other person whom the applicant knows to be affected by it at least seven days before the date of the hearing (see r 60.1(6)).

17.99 Where the court appoints a receiver the applicant must serve a copy of the order and the witness statement in support on the defendant, any person who holds realisable property to which the order relates and on any other person the applicant knows is affected by it (see r 60.1(7)).

17.100 Rule 60.3 makes similar provision in relation to applications to vary or discharge the receivership order. Again, any such application must be made in writing and served on:

(a) the person who applied for the receiver to be appointed;
(b) the defendant;
(c) any person holding realisable property in relation to which the receiver was appointed;
(d) the receiver; and
(e) any other person whom the application knows to be affected by the application.

17.101 The application must be served at least seven days before the hearing date unless the Crown Court specifies a shorter period (see r 60.3(3)). There does not appear to be any requirement for the application to be accompanied by a witness statement in support but, unless the application is of a purely formal nature or is being made by consent, the best practice is to file and serve a such a statement. It is perhaps unlikely that a court would accede to an application by a defendant or affected third party to vary or discharge an order unless he is prepared to set out the factual basis for the application in a witness statement.

17.102 Rule 60.4 deals with the position where a receiver is still holding funds after a confiscation order has been satisfied. In these circumstances, he must make application to the Crown Court for directions as to how such funds are to be distributed (see r 60.4(2)). Again the application must be made in writing and served, together with any evidence in support, on all affected parties at least seven days before the hearing unless the Court specifies a shorter period (see r 60.4(3)).

17.103 Rules 60.6, 60.7 and 60.8 deal with remuneration, accounts and non-compliance by receivers respectively. As these provisions are considered in detail in Chapter 8, they are not reproduced in detail here. Rule 60.6 (6) provides that an enforcement receiver is to receive his remuneration by applying to the enforcing magistrates' court under s 55(4)(b) of POCA and a Director's receiver by applying to the Director for payment under s 57(4)(b).

(6) Seized money

17.104 Section 67 of POCA gives the enforcing magistrates' court power to direct banks and building societies holding money belonging to a defendant to pay it to the Justices' Chief

Executive in satisfaction of the confiscation order. Section 67(1) to (3) sets out the money to which the section applies and is in the following terms:

(1) This section applies to money which—
   (a) is held by a person, and
   (b) is held in an account maintained by him with a bank or building society.
(2) This section also applies to money which is held by a person and which—
   (a) has been seized by a constable under section 19 of the Police and Criminal Evidence Act 1984 (c.60) (general power of seizure, etc), and
   (b) is held in an account maintained by a police force with a bank or a building society.
(3) This section also applies to money which is held by a person and which—
   (a) has been seized by a customs officer under section 19 of the 1984 Act as applied by an order made under section 114(2) of that Act, and
   (b) is held in an account maintained by the Commissioners of Customs and Excise with a bank or building society.

17.105 If the seized cash falls into any of these categories, the Justices may make an order requiring the bank or building society to pay the money to the Justices' Chief Executive provided the conditions set out in s 67(4) of POCA have been satisfied. These are:

(a) a restraint order has effect in relation to money to which this section applies;
(b) a confiscation order is made against the person by whom the money is held;
(c) the Director has not been appointed enforcement authority for the confiscation order;
(d) any period allowed under section 11 for payment of the amounts ordered to be paid under the confiscation order has ended.

17.106 The use of this new provision will obviate the need for the Justices' clerk to adopt the cumbersome procedure of applying to the county court for a third party debt order in relation to such money. If the bank or building society fails to comply with an order under s 67 of POCA it may be fined up to £5,000 (see s 67(6)). For the purpose of the section, a bank is a deposit taking business within the meaning of the Banking Act 1987 and 'building society' has the same meaning as in the Building Societies Act 1986.

17.107 Rule 58.12 (1) of the Criminal Procedure Rules 2005 makes provision as to the information that an order under section 67 must contain. It provides:

An order under section 67 of the Proceeds of Crime Act 2002 requiring a bank or building society to pay money to a magistrates' court officer ('a payment order') shall-

(a) be directed to the bank or building society in respect of which the payment order is made;
(b) name the person against whom the confiscation order has been made;
(c) state the amount which remains to be paid under the confiscation order;
(d) state the name and address of the branch at which the account in which the money ordered to be paid is held and the sort code of that branch, if the sort code is known;
(e) state the name in which the account in which the money ordered to be paid is held and the account number of that account, if the account number is known;
(f) state the amount which the bank or building society is required to pay to the court officer under the payment order;
(g) give the name and address of the court officer to whom payment is to be made; and

E. Enforcement under POCA 2002

(h) require the bank or building society to make payment within a period of seven days beginning on the day on which the payment order is made, unless it appears ot the court that a longer or shorgter period would be appropriate in the particular circumstances.

17.108 By r 58.12(2) the order shall be served by leaving it at, or sending it by first class post to the principal office of the bank or building society in question. If the order is served by first class post, unless the contrary is proved, it is deemed to have been served on the second business day after posting: see r 58.12(3).

(7) Implementing the default sentence: the Director not the enforcing authority

17.109 Where the Director has not been appointed the enforcing authority, by s 35(2) of POCA, ss 139(2) to (4) and (9) and 140(1) to (4) of the PCC(S)A apply to the enforcement of the order in the same way as they do to fines. These provisions empower the Justices' to implement the default sentence imposed by the Crown Court to be served in the event of non payment. The provisions of ss 139 and 140 are subject to the following modifications in relation to the enforcement of confiscation orders:

(a) the magistrates may not dispense with the requirement for immediate payment by ordering payment by instalments under s 75 of the Magistrates' Courts Act 1980;
(b) the provisions of s 81 of the Magistrates' Courts Act 1980 that modify the provisions in relation to the enforcement of fines in relation to young offenders to not apply;
(c) there is no power to remit the confiscation order in the same way as a fine under s 85 of the Magistrates' Courts Act 1980. If the defendant claims he has insufficient assets to meet the order, his remedy is to apply to the Crown Court for a variation of the order under s 23 of POCA; and
(d) the Justices do not have to hold a means enquiry under s 87 of the Magistrates' Courts Act 1980. This confirms the ruling of the Divisional Court in *R v Hastings and Rother Justices ex p Anscombe* (Div Ct, 5 February 1998).

(8) Implementing the default sentence: the Director appointed as the enforcement authority

17.110 Section 37 of POCA contains entirely new provisions as to the implementation of the default sentence in cases where the Director has been appointed the enforcement authority. If the conditions set out in s 37(2) are met, the Director may apply to the Crown Court for a summons to be issued ordering the defendant to appear before the court. The conditions set out in s 37(2) are:

(a) a confiscation order has been made;
(b) the Director has been appointed as the enforcement authority for the order;
(c) because of the defendant's wilful refusal or culpable neglect the order is not satisfied;
(d) the order is not subject to appeal;
(e) the Director has done all that is practicable (apart from this section) to enforce the order.

17.111 If the defendant fails to appear in answer to the summons, the Crown Court may issue a warrant for his arrest (see s 37(4)). If the defendant does appear in answer to the summons and the court is satisfied that the conditions in s 37(2) have been satisfied, it may issue a warrant committing him to prison or detention in default of the amount ordered to be paid under the confiscation order (see s 37(5)). If only part of the confiscation order remains unsatisfied the term of the default sentence is reduced proportionately (see s 37(7)). If, having been committed to prison, the defendant pays the full amount outstanding, he must be released unless he is also in custody for another reason (see s 37(9)). Finally, if he pays some of the amount outstanding the remaining default term will be reduced proportionately.

18

THE INSOLVENT DEFENDANT

A. Introduction	18.01	(3) Limited liability partnerships	18.17
B. The Position Under the DTA and CJA	18.02	(4) Protection of insolvency practitioners	18.18
C. Insolvency under POCA 2002	18.12	D. Interaction Between Restraint and Insolvency Proceedings	18.19
(1) Winding up of companies	18.14		
(2) Floating charges	18.16	E. Conclusion	18.23

A. Introduction

It is not unusual for a defendant to become insolvent either before or during the course of restraint and confiscation proceedings. There are a number of reasons for this. A defendant who has a business experiencing cash flow problems may be tempted to commit criminal offences as a means of alleviating the problems. He may, eg commit income tax or VAT offences, or become involved in other criminal activities such as drug trafficking in the hope of raising funds to overcome his financial difficulties. Further, once a defendant has been charged with serious criminal offences and remanded in custody, he will be unable to work and earn sufficient funds to meet his ongoing liabilities. It is also not uncommon for a defendant to try and make himself insolvent with a view to rendering any restraint or confiscation proceedings ineffective. A third party creditor may take action in an attempt to ensure he is paid in priority to any restraint or confiscation order. Finally, in cases where the Crown has suffered a significant loss, for example in a VAT carousel or 'MTIC' fraud as it has become known, law enforcement agencies sometimes seek to mitigate those losses by bringing civil proceedings and seeking the appointment of a provisional liquidator in relation to the companies involved. In this chapter we examine the various provisions of the Drug Trafficking Act 1994 (DTA), the Criminal Justice Act 1988 (CJA) and the Proceeds of Crime Act 2002 (POCA) in relation to the insolvent defendant.

18.01

B. The Position Under the DTA and CJA

The relevant provisions appear in s 32 of the DTA and s 84 of the CJA and are in identical terms. Section 32(1) of the DTA and s 84(1) of the CJA deal with the position where the restraint comes first in time. Section 32(1) provides:

18.02

(1) Where a person who holds realisable property is adjudged bankrupt—
   (a) property for the time being subject to a restraint order made before the order adjudging him bankrupt; and

(b) any proceeds of property realised by virtue of section 26(7) or 29(5) or (6) of this Act for the time being in the hands of a receiver appointed under section 26 or 29 of this Act,

is excluded from the bankrupt's estate for the purposes of Part IX of the Insolvency Act 1986 ('the 1986 Act').

18.03 Thus, if a restraint order is in force and the defendant is later made bankrupt, any assets subject to the order or any proceeds of realisation held by a management or enforcement receiver, do not form part of the defendant's estate for the purpose of the bankruptcy proceedings.

18.04 Section 32(2) of the DTA and s 84(2) of the CJA deal with the position where the bankruptcy order comes first in time. Again the two sections are in identical terms. Section 32(2) provides:

(2) Where a person has been adjudged bankrupt the powers conferred on the High Court or a county court by sections 26 to 30 of this Act or on a receiver so appointed shall not be exercised in relation to—
(a) property for the time being comprised in the bankrupt's estate for the purposes of Part IX of the 1986 Act;
(b) property in respect of which his trustee in bankruptcy may (without leave of the court) serve a notice under sections 307, 308 or 308A of that Act (after acquired property and tools, clothes etc exceeding value of reasonable replacement and certain tenancies); and
(c) property which is to be applied for the benefit of creditors of the bankrupt by virtue of a condition imposed under section 380(2)(c) of that Act;
but nothing in that Act shall be taken as restricting or enabling the restriction of, the exercise of those powers.

18.05 If the bankruptcy order pre-dates the restraint order, the court may not include in the order any property that forms part of the bankrupt's estate for the purposes of the Insolvency Act 1986 and a management or enforcement receiver appointed under the DTA or CJA may not exercise his powers in relation to such property. The rule is therefore essentially one of 'first come, first served': if the restraint order is made first it takes priority and, conversely, if the bankruptcy order is first in time it takes priority over the restraint order.

18.06 A defendant subject to a restraint order may not enter into a voluntary arrangement under s 252 of the Insolvency Act 1986. In *Re M* [1992] 1 All ER 537 the defendant, who was already subject to a restraint order, purported to enter into a voluntary arrangement. The prosecutor thereupon applied to the High Court for the appointment of a management receiver. The Court held that the defendant's actions in entering into the voluntary arrangement did not preclude the prosecutor applying for a receiver to be appointed since voluntary arrangements were not provided for in s 32 of the DTA and s 84 of the CJA. The Court also ruled that the defendant had no locus standi to apply to the court for the appointment of a management receiver himself.

18.07 Where an interim receiver has been appointed under s 286 of the Insolvency Act 1986 in relation to a debtor, and any property of the debtor is already subject to a restraint order, the powers conferred on the receiver do not apply to property for the time being subject to that order (see ss 32(4) of the DTA and 84(5) of the CJA).

C. Insolvency under POCA 2002

Section 34 of the DTA and Section 86 of the CJA make similar provision in relation to the winding up of companies holding realisable property. Again, the sections are in identical terms. By s 34(1):

18.08

(1) Where realisable propoerty is held by a company and an order for the winding up of the company has been made or a resolution has been poassed by the company for the voluntary winding up of the company, the functions of the liquidator (or any provisional liquidator) shall not be exercisable in relation to-
   (a) property for the time being subject to a restraint order made before the relevant time; and
   (b) any proceeds of property realised by virtue of section 26 (7) or 29 (5) or (6) of this Act for the time being in the hands of a receiver appointed under section 26 or 29 of this Act.

By s 34 (2) where a winding up order has been made or a winding up resolution has been passed, the powers under section 26 to 30 of the DTA shall not be exercisable in relation to any realisable property held by the company in relation to which the functions of the liquidator are exercisable:

18.09

(a) so as to inhibit him from exercising those functions for the purpose of distributing any property held by the company to the company's creditors; or
(b) so as to prevent the payment out of any property or expenses (including the remuneration of the liquidator or any provisional liquidator) properly incurred in the winding up in respect of the property.

Thus, a similar rule applies in relation to the winding up of companies holding realisable property, namely that the order which comes first in time takes priority. If the restraint order is first in time, by virtue of s 34(1) DTA and s 86(1) CJA, the powers of the liquidator or provisional liquidator shall not be exercisable in relation to restrained assets or those in the hands of a receiver. If, on the other hand the winding up has come first in time s 34 (2) and s 86(2) provide that the restraint order may not bite on assets in the hands of the interim liquidator for the purposes identified above. Section 34 (4) DTA and s 86(6) CJA define the 'relevant time' for the purposes of the sections as meaning:

18.10

(a) where no order for the winding up of the company has been made, the time of then passing of the resolution for the voluntary winding up;
(b) where—
   (i) such an order has been made, but
   (ii) before the presentation of the petition for the winding up of the company by the court, such a resolution has been passed by the company,
   the time of the passing of the resolution; and
(c) in any other case where sucvh an order has been made, the time of the making of the order.

Section 35 DTA and s 87 of the CJA give insolvency practitioners who mistakenly deal in realisable property some protection, providing that they will only be liable in damages if it can be shown they have been negligent. The sections also allow them to recover their remuneration from property they hold and give them a lien over it for the purposes of securing payment.

18.11

C. Insolvency under POCA 2002

A similar regime applies under POCA 2002 whereby, in most circumstances, the order that comes first in time has priority. By s 417(2)(a) of POCA, property is excluded from a

18.12

bankrupt's estate for the purposes of the Insolvency Act 1986 if it is the subject of a restraint order under s 41 made before the order adjudging him bankrupt. The same restriction applies in relation to property subject to an enforcement or Director's receivership order made under ss 50 and 52 respectively (see s 417(2)(b) of POCA).

18.13 Similarly, s 418 restricts the powers of the court and management, enforcement, and Director's receivers, in cases where the bankruptcy order comes first in time. In such cases, the court may not, in respect of property that forms part of the bankrupt's estate, exercise the powers conferred on it by ss 41 to 67 and a receiver may not exercise any powers conferred on him in relation to the property (see s 418(2)(a) of POCA).

(1) Winding up of companies

18.14 Section 426 makes similar provision in relation to the winding up of companies. By s 426(2)(a) where a court has made a winding up order or the company passes a resolution for its voluntary winding up, the functions of the liquidator (or any provisional liquidator) may not be exercised in relation to property subject to a restraint order made before the relevant time. Section 426(9) defines the relevant time as:

(a) if no order for the winding up of the company has been made, the time of the passing of the resolution for voluntary winding up;
(b) if such an order has been made, but before the presentation of the petition for the winding up of the company by the court such a resolution has been passed by the company, the time of the passing of the resolution;
(c) if such an order has been made, but paragraph (b) does not apply, the time of the making of the order.

18.15 Section 426(4) and (5) deal with the situation where the order or resolution for winding up pre-dates the restraint order and provides that the powers of the court to make restraint orders and management, enforcement, and director's receivers must not be exercised in a way mentioned in s 426(6) in relation to property held by the company and in relation to which the functions of the liquidator are exercisable. Section 426(6) provides:

(6) The powers must not be exercised—
    (a) so as to inhibit the liquidator from exercising his functions for the purpose of distributing property to the company's creditors;
    (b) so as to prevent the payment out of any property of expenses (including the remuneration of the liquidator or any provisional liquidator) properly incurred in the winding up in respect of the property.

(2) Floating charges

18.16 Creditors, particularly financial institutions, frequently hold a floating charge over a company's assets as security for a loan. The terms of the charge will normally empower the creditor to appoint an administrative receiver, without the necessity to make an application to court, for the purpose of taking control of the assets subject to the charge. The relationship between such charges and restraint and court appointed receivers are provided for in s 430 of POCA. Again, the rule is generally one of 'first come, first served'. By s 430(2) the functions of a receiver appointed pursuant to a floating charge are not exercisable in relation to property subject to a restraint order made prior to the appointment of the receiver. Similarly, if the receiver is appointed prior to the application for the restraint order, s 430(4) provides that the administrative receivership shall take precedence and the powers of the court to make restraint orders and of management, enforcement, and Director's receivers shall not be used in the way mentioned in s 430(6). By s 430(6):

> The powers shall not be exercised—
> (a) so as to inhibit the receiver from exercising his functions for the purpose of distributing property to the company's creditors;
> (b) so as to prevent the payment out of any property of expenses (including the remuneration of the receiver) properly incurred in the exercise of his functions in respect of the property.

(3) Limited liability partnerships

By s 431 of POCA, the same provisions as to winding up and floating charges apply equally to limited liability partnerships that are capable of being wound up under the Insolvency Act 1986.

18.17

(4) Protection of insolvency practitioners

Section 432 (1) and (2) give protection to insolvency practitioners who mistakenly deal in realisable property, providing that they will only be liable in damages for their actions if they are negligent. The section also empowers them to recover their remuneration and expenses and gives them a lien over the property and the proceeds of sale for payment.

18.18

D. Interaction Between Restraint and Insolvency Proceedings

As noted above, it is by no means uncommon for restraint and insolvency proceedings to proceed concurrently in respect of companies holding realisable property. This is particularly common in VAT 'carousel' or 'MTIC' fraud cases where there has been a signficant loss – often many millions of pounds – to the Exchequer. It is understandable that, in such circumstances, the Government Department suffering the loss, usually HM Revenue and Customs, wishes to pursue every remedy at its disposal to recoup the loss that has been sustained. In circumstances where the restraint and insolvency proceedings are serving separate and distinct purposes, it is submitted this course of action is entirely unobjectionable.

18.19

Problems can, however, arise when – perhaps due to a lack of communication between the prosecutor and those having the conduct of the insolvency proceedings – both a management receiver appointed under the DTA, CJA or POCA and a liquidator or provisional liquidator are pursuing the same assets. Both the liquidator and the receiver will be seeking to claim their remuneration and expenses from the assets under their control and both may well have City solicitors and other agents acting for them at considerable expense. In such circumstances there is a real risk of a duplication of effort or the receiver and liquidator fighting over the same assets which, one way or the other, will all go to the benefit of the Crown if the proceedings are successful, whether in the liquidation proceedings or by way

18.20

of the satisfaction of a confiscation order. Clearly, it cannot be in the public interest for this to occur.

18.21 It is submitted that proper communication between those having the conduct of the two sets of proceedings is vital to prevent such duplication occurring. If a restraint order has been obtained, possibly coupled with the appointment of a management receiver over all the realisable assets of a defendant, including a company in respect of which the corporate veil has been lifted, careful consideration needs to be given to the question of whether proceeding down the insolvency route at the same time will serve any useful purpose.

18.22 Similarly, if the insolvency route has been pursued first, prosecutors need to consider carefully whether there will be any added value to lifting the corporate veil on a company involved in fraudulent activity. If a restraint and/or management receivership application is pursued in such circumstances it is vital that the prosecutor, in compliance with his duties of full and frank disclosure, informs the court of the existence of the insolvency proceedings and explains why a restraint order is still considered necessary: it may be, for example, that there are other personal assets of the defendant not caught by the insolvency proceedings that can properly be restrained. If the appointment of a mangement receiver is to be sought, the prosecutor must comply fully with the *Capewell* guidelines considered in Chapter 3 and explain clearly why the order is required when a liquidator is already in office, provide details of the estimated costs of the exercise and their proportionality in terms of the likely benefits to the defendant's estate.

E. Conclusion

18.23 Although the general rule in relation to insolvency proceedings is one of first come, first served, creditors of defendants subject to restraint orders and the insolvency practitioners and other professional advisers they employ to advise them should always take the greatest possible care in dealing with assets belonging to a defendant under restraint. Firstly, it cannot be too strongly emphasised that if a restraint order is in force in relation to particular assets, its terms must be complied with even if it appears to have been made in error. If, notwithstanding the provisions of the Act, a restraint order is in force in relation to a defendant who has already been made bankrupt or in respect of a company already in liquidation, this does not justify a a trustee in bankruptcy or liquidator proceeding to administer the estate regardless of the order. If an order of the court has been made in relation to property, even in error, it must be obeyed until such time as it is varied or set aside. It is not the place of any individual to decide that an order has been made in error and to disregard it. In such circumstances an application should be made to the court either for the order to be set aside or varied to the extent that references to any assets caught by a pre-existing bankruptcy or winding up order are deleted. It may well be that if the prosecutor is given advance notice of any such application and is provided with a copy of the pre-existing order, he will readily agree to a proposed variation and the matter can be dealt with on a 'by consent' basis without the necessity to trouble the court.

18.24 Creditors and their advisers should also pay close attention to their obligations under money laundering and 'suspicious transaction' reporting legislation. The fact that a defendant is

E. Conclusion

subject to a restraint order must, in most circumstances, give rise to a suspicion that assets in his possession represent the proceeds of drug trafficking or other criminal conduct. Great caution should therefore be exercised in taking possession of a defendant's assets, particularly when a large amount of cash is involved. Any suspicion should be reported immediately to the appropriate authority, and no attempt should be made to use such funds to pay creditors until the permission of that authority has been obtained.

19

CIVIL RECOVERY: PROPERTY FREEZING ORDERS; INTERIM RECEIVERS; AND LEGAL EXPENSES

A. Introduction		19.01
B. Overview in Relation to Civil Recovery		19.06
(1) A power vested only in the ARA		19.07
(2) Proceedings even on acquittal		19.08
(3) Standard of proof		19.10
(4) Civil proceedings		19.14
(5) The distinction between recovery proceedings and confiscation proceedings		19.16
(6) Civil recovery in the High Court: proceedings for recovery orders		19.18
(7) Definitions within POCA		19.19
(8) Definition of 'property'		19.20
(9) Property obtained through unlawful conduct		19.24
(10) Unlawful conduct		19.27
(11) How is 'recoverable property' defined?		19.29
(12) How is 'associated property' defined?		19.30
(13) The tracing of property		19.34
(14) Mixed property		19.35
(15) Accruing profits		19.36
(16) Granting interests		19.37
C. Property Freezing Orders		19.38
(1) Introduction		19.38
(2) Definition		19.42
(3) PFO without notice		19.43
(4) Factors giving rise to the risk of dissipation		19.44
(5) Duty of full and frank disclosure		19.46
(6) Criteria for granting a Property Freezing Order		19.53
(7) Variation and setting aside of the Property Freezing Order		19.57
(8) Exclusions and variations		19.60
(9) The legislative steer		19.65
(10) Restriction on proceedings and remedies		19.68
(11) Further SOCPA amendments		19.72
(12) Ancillary orders		19.75
(13) Undertakings for damages		19.76
(14) Draft order		19.77
(15) PFOs: practice and procedure		19.78
(16) Exclusions when making a PFO: legal costs		19.87
(17) Applications to vary or set aside a PFO		19.88
D. Interim Receiving Orders		19.91
(1) Application for an interim receiving order		19.92
(2) Loss of power to investigate		19.95
(3) Purpose and conditions		19.97
(4) 'Good arguable case'		19.99
(5) Application for an interim receiving order: practice and procedure		19.101
(6) Interim receiving order made before commencement of claim for civil recovery		19.105
(7) Duty of full and frank disclosure		19.106
(8) The need for expedition		19.107
(9) The legislative steer		19.108
(10) The insolvent respondent		19.115
(11) Insolvency and IROs		19.120
(12) A stand alone claim		19.121
(13) Powers of the High Court		19.123
(14) Functions of an interim receiver		19.124
(15) Contents of the order		19.126
(16) Restrictions on dealing with property		19.133

(17)	Contents of the order in terms of reporting by the receiver	19.137	E.	**Legal Expenses in Civil Recovery Proceedings**	19.177
(18)	Protection against self incrimination	19.138	(1)	Introduction	19.177
(19)	Protection for the receiver	19.139	(2)	Background to the new provisions	19.189
(20)	Applications to clarify the receiver's powers	19.140	(3)	The new regulations	19.191
(21)	Applications for directions	19.141	(4)	Legal expenses at the conclusion of proceedings	19.192
(22)	The role and independence of the interim receiver	19.142	(5)	Expenses to be assessed if not agreed	19.195
(23)	Power to vary or set aside	19.147	(6)	Two month time limit	19.196
(24)	Application to vary or discharge an interim receiving order: practice and procedure	19.150	(7)	Practice and procedure	19.197
			(8)	Legal expenses at the commencement of proceedings	19.201
(25)	Non-specified recoverable property	19.153	(9)	Considerations for the court	19.205
(26)	Exclusion of property which is not recoverable	19.154	(10)	Practice and procedure: part 3 of the regulations	19.209
(27)	Exclusion of property to cover legal expenses	19.156	(11)	The Director's response	19.213
			(12)	Release of an interim payment	19.216
(28)	Interim receiver's expenses	19.157	(13)	Evidence for the purpose of meeting legal costs	19.218
(29)	Interim receiverships over land	19.159	(14)	Ongoing opportunity	19.219
(30)	Restriction on existing proceedings and rights	19.162	(15)	Statement of assets	19.220
			(16)	Legal expenses following the making of a recovery order	19.222
(31)	Reporting	19.167	(17)	Part 4 of the regulations	19.224
(32)	Compensation	19.170	(18)	Other assets	19.225
(33)	Time limit for compensation application	19.173	(19)	Costs judge assessment	19.226
			(20)	Basis for assessment of legal expenses	19.227
(34)	The test the court should apply	19.175	(21)	Civil legal aid	19.234

A. Introduction

19.01 Civil recovery of the proceeds of unlawful conduct includes both recovery in the High Court (under Chapter 2 of Pt 5 of the Proceeds of Crime Act 2002 (POCA)) and the recovery of cash in summary proceedings (under Chapter 3 of Pt 5 of POCA). As a result, Pt 5 of the Act has two purposes: firstly, to enable the ARA to recover in civil proceedings before the High Court property that is, or represents, property obtained through unlawful conduct; and secondly, to enable cash which is, or represents, property obtained through unlawful conduct, or which is intended to be used in unlawful conduct, to be forfeited in civil proceedings before a magistrates' court.

19.02 The second of these objectives is considered fully in Chapter 21, Recovery and Seizure of Cash under POCA.

19.03 The first objective, to enable the Assets Recovery Agency (ARA) to recover property in civil proceedings before the High Court, is considered in this and the next chapter.

19.04 For ease of reference we have divided civil recovery into two parts. Firstly, in this chapter, we give an overview of the legislation in relation to civil recovery and then look at the two interim measures anticipated by the Act, namely Property Freezing Orders and Interim Receiving Orders, before considering how to obtain the release of funds to cover legal expenses in ARA cases.

B. Overview in Relation to Civil Recovery

19.05 In the next chapter we consider recovery orders themselves; recent decisions concerning the ECHR and lastly, as part of the recovery order scheme, the complex pension provisions. At the time of going to press the Government announced that the Assets Recovery Agency was to be merged with the Serious and Organised Crime Agency. This change is likely to take place in April 2008 but is unlikely to affect the substance of the legislation.

B. Overview in Relation to Civil Recovery

19.06 The civil recovery provisions came into force on 24 February 2003, SI 2003/120.

(1) A power vested only in the ARA

19.07 The power to recover in civil proceedings before the High Court is reserved to the 'enforcement authority'. The definition of enforcement authority is limited in England and Wales to the Assets Recovery Agency and does not include any of the more familiar prosecuting authorities (s 316(1)).

(2) Proceedings even on acquittal

19.08 Under s 240(2) it is possible to invoke civil recovery and cash forfeiture proceedings even though proceedings have not been brought for a criminal offence in connection with the property, eg where there may be insufficient grounds for a prosecution, or the suspect is outside of the jurisdiction, or has died:

> (2) The powers conferred by this Part are exercisable in relation to any property (including cash) whether or not any proceedings have been brought for an offence in connection with that property.

19.09 It should be added that cases where criminal proceedings have been brought include cases where a defendant has been acquitted, as they too fall within the scheme of Pt 5. In *Director of the Assets Recovery Agency v Taher and Ors* [2006] EWHC 3402 (Admin), Collins J confirmed the effect of the legislation:

> The legislation provides that if the Director is able to establish on the balance of probabilities that assets are the proceeds of crime, they are recoverable even if there has been a prosecution, which has not succeeded and even if there has been no prosecution, because for example the view has been taken that evidence would not be sufficient to establish criminality beyond reasonable doubt.

(3) Standard of proof

19.10 Section 241(3) states:

> The court . . . must decide on *a balance of probabilities* whether it is proved:
> (a) that any matters alleged to constitute unlawful conduct have occurred, or
> (b) that any person intended to use any cash in unlawful conduct.

19.11 The standard of proof applicable is that which normally applies to civil matters, ie the balance of probabilities, and not the criminal standard of beyond reasonable doubt. Some commentators have already observed that the Act is specific in that it states that the burden is on 'the balance of probabilities' and not to the 'civil standard'. In many civil cases the degree of probability required to establish proof may vary according to the allegation to be proved (see *Hornal v Neuberger Products Ltd* [1957] 1 QB 247) and the court is often reluctant, when considering claims by the Crown, to apply merely a 51/49 per cent test where an individual's property or other assets are in jeopardy (see *Bater v Bater* [1950] 2 All ER 458 and *B v Chief Constable of Avon and Somerset* [2001] 1 All ER 562). POCA however, is proactively encouraging the courts to apply a strict 51/49 per cent 'balance of probabilities' test. Hence the difference in drafting between the DTA, CJA (the civil standard) and POCA (the balance of probabilities).

19.12 The standard of proof appropriate in deciding whether matters alleged to constitute unlawful conduct have occurred was considered by Collins J in *R (on the application of the Director of the Assets Recovery Agency) v (1) Jia Jin He and (2) Dan Dan Chen* (2004) EWHC Admin 3021, in which he found that 'cogent' evidence, although no gloss, was required. He stated:

> As a general rule, no doubt, criminal conduct may be regarded as less probable than non-criminal conduct. But where there is evidence from which a court can be satisfied that it is more probable than not that criminal conduct has been involved, it does not seem to me that that is something that is so improbable as to require a gloss on the standard of proof. However, I recognise, and it is no doubt right, that since it is necessary to establish that there has been criminal conduct in the obtaining of the property, the court should look for cogent evidence before deciding that the balance of probabilities has been met. But I have no doubt that Parliament deliberately referred to the balance of probabilities, and that the court should not place a gloss upon it, so as to require that the standard approach is that appropriate in a criminal case. Apart from anything else, if that were necessary, then the effectiveness of, in particular, Part 5 of the Act would be to a considerable extent removed . . . It is plain that Parliament deliberately imposed a lower standard of proof as the standard appropriate for these proceedings.

19.13 In the *Director of the Assets Recovery Agency v Jeffrey David Green* [2005] EWHC (Admin) 3168 Sullivan J stated (at para 19) that when read in the context of s 240 and the remainder of s 241, it was plain that Parliament envisaged that in civil recovery proceedings the Director would identify the matters alleged to constitute unlawful conduct in sufficient detail to enable the court not to decide whether a particular crime had been committed by a particular individual, but to decide whether the conduct so described was unlawful under the criminal law of the UK (or the criminal law of the United Kingdom and the foreign country in question). He stated that any litigant in civil proceedings seeking to recover property upon the basis that it had been obtained by unlawful conduct would be expected to identify (a) the property, and (b) the conduct that was said to be unlawful (para 23).

(4) Civil proceedings

19.14 In *Jia Jin He* Collins J stated that there was 'no doubt' that in domestic law proceedings under Pt 5 are classified as civil proceedings (para 47). In so finding, he adopted the decision of Coghlin J in the *Director of the Assets Recovery Agency v Walsh* [2004] NIQB 21 where his Lordship considered the three principal criteria identified in *Engel v The Netherlands (No 1)* (1976) 1 EHRR 647 (para 13) for civil proceedings namely:

> (i) the manner in which the domestic state classifies the proceedings, [although this normally carries comparatively little weight and is regarded as a starting point rather than determinative – see *Ozturk v Germany (1984) 6 EHRR 409 at 421 and 422*];

B. Overview in Relation to Civil Recovery

(ii) the nature of the conduct in question classified objectively bearing in mind the object and purpose of the Convention;
(iii) the severity of any possible penalty – severe penalties, including those with imprisonment in default and penalties intended to deter are pointers towards a criminal classification of proceedings – see *Schmautzer v Austria (1995) 21 EHRR 511.*

19.15 Having applied the approach in *Engel* (confirmed as appropriate by the House of Lords in *R v H* [2003] 1 All ER 497) Coghlin J found the civil recovery scheme to be civil in nature, a view Collins J in *Jia Jin He* concurred with.

(5) The distinction between recovery proceedings and confiscation proceedings

19.16 There are a number of fundamental differences between these two schemes, including the distinct procedural requirements that govern the appropriate proceedings.

19.17 In the *Director of the Assets Recovery Agency v Ashton* [2006] EWHC 1064 Newman J endorsed (at para 50) the following distinctions between civil recovery and confiscation proceedings:

- No conviction is necessary in recovery order proceedings (indeed civil recovery proceedings may be brought where no offence has been charged or where a Defendant has been tried and acquitted), whereas a confiscation order can only be made if there has been a conviction.
- No one stands in jeopardy.
- Enforcement is through a Trustee, as opposed to an enforcement magistrates' court.
- Confiscation proceedings are dealt with by criminal courts (albeit operating on the civil standard – see the Criminal Procedure Rules, SI 2005/384 r 56 et seq) and often by the Judge who oversaw the criminal trial.
- Confiscation proceedings are initiated by the prosecutor, or the judge of his own motion.
- A confiscation order is not directed towards particular assets per se. A defendant may use any resource to satisfy the order made against him. Whereas in civil recovery the property itself is the target of the claim.

(6) Civil recovery in the High Court: proceedings for recovery orders

19.18 Proceedings for a recovery order may be taken by the Director of the ARA in the High Court against any person who the enforcement authority (the Agency) thinks holds recoverable property (see s 243(1)).

(7) Definitions within POCA

19.19 Chapter 4 of Pt 5 of POCA sets out various definitions which apply to both the civil recovery scheme and the cash forfeiture provisions. It deals particularly with recoverable property, namely:

Property obtained through unlawful conduct—s 304
Tracing property—s 305
Mixing property—s 306
Recoverable property accruing profits—s 307
General and other exceptions and exemptions—ss 308 and 309

Granting interests—s 310
Obtaining and disposing of property—s 314
Property — s 316(4)

These sections are considered more closely below.

(8) Definition of 'property'

19.20 Under s 316(4) property is all property wherever situated and includes:

(a) money;
(b) all forms of property, real or personal, heritable or moveable;
(c) things in action and other intangible or incorporeal property.

19.21 It should be noted that under s 308(9) the property is not recoverable if it has been taken into account in deciding the amount to be paid under a confiscation order.

19.22 Under s 316 'recoverable property' (defined in s 304 as 'property obtained through unlawful conduct') is to be read in accordance with ss 304–310 which deal with property obtained through 'unlawful conduct'; tracing property; mixing property; recoverable property and accruing profits; and general exceptions and exemptions including the granting of interests. In short, recoverable property is property that has been obtained through unlawful conduct or property that represents such property (see *Singh* [2005] EWCA Civ 580).

19.23 Under s 316(5) any reference to a person's property (whether expressed as a reference to the property he holds or otherwise) is to be reads as follows:

(1) In relation to land, it is a reference to any interest which he holds in the land.
(2) In relation to property other than land it is a reference to the property (if it belongs to him), or to any other interest which he holds in the property (s 316(5) to (7)).

(9) Property obtained through unlawful conduct

19.24 Under s 242(1) a person obtains property through unlawful conduct (whether his own conduct or another's) if he obtains property by or in return for that conduct.

19.25 In deciding whether any property was obtained through unlawful conduct, it is immaterial 'whether or not any money, goods or services were provided in order to put the person in question in the position to carry out the conduct in question' (s 242(2)(a)); nor is it necessary to show that the conduct was of a particular kind, if it can be shown that the property was obtained through conduct of one of a number of kinds, each of which would have fallen within the definition of 'unlawful conduct' (see s 242(2)). This will have an important impact on the forfeiture provisions of Pt 5 (s 294(2)(b) and s 298(2)(b)).

19.26 It follows that a person will obtain property through unlawful conduct if he obtains it by his conduct, eg by stealing, or if he obtains it in return for unlawful conduct, eg by taking a bribe to award a contract.

(10) Unlawful conduct

19.27 Conduct occurring in any part of the UK is unlawful conduct if it is unlawful under the criminal law of that part of the UK (s 241(1)).

B. Overview in Relation to Civil Recovery

Furthermore, under s 241(2) conduct which: **19.28**

(a) occurs in a country outside the United Kingdom and is unlawful under the criminal law of that country, and
(b) if it occurred in a part of the United Kingdom, would be unlawful under the criminal law of that part, is also unlawful conduct.

The effect of s 241(2) is to enable property obtained through unlawful conduct abroad to be recovered.

(11) How is 'recoverable property' defined?

'Recoverable property' is defined as property obtained though unlawful conduct (s 304). The definitions of 'property' and 'unlawful conduct' are set out above. **19.29**

(12) How is 'associated property' defined?

Associated property is defined by s 245(1): **19.30**

(1) 'Associated property' means property of any of the following descriptions (including property held by the Respondent which is not itself the recoverable property)—
   (a) any interest in the recoverable property,
   (b) any other interest in the property in which the recoverable property subsists,
   (c) if the recoverable property is a tenancy in common, the tenancy of the other tenant,
   (d) if (in Scotland) the recoverable property is owned in common, the interest of the other owner,
   (e) if the recoverable property is part of a larger property, but not a separate part, the remainder of that property.

This broad definition is intended to deal with circumstances in which only part of the property is recoverable, or where there is more than one interest in the property and some of it is not recoverable. In those circumstances the non-recoverable part is described as 'associated property'. **19.31**

The guidance notes that accompanied POCA give the following examples in terms of (a) to (e) above: **19.32**

> In paragraph (a) the associated property might be a tenancy in a recoverable freehold. In paragraph (b), where a lease in a freehold block of flats has been purchased with recoverable property, another lease in the same block bought with legitimate money would be associated property. In paragraphs (c) and (d) where two people buy a car together, one with recoverable cash and one with legitimate cash, the share of the person who bought with legitimate cash is the associated property. In paragraph (e), where a painting is recoverable property but it had been framed using legitimate money, the frame would be associated property.

Section 245(2) adds that references to property 'being associated with recoverable property' are to be read accordingly, and that no property is to be treated as associated with the recoverable property where the recoverable property consists of rights under a pension scheme (within the meaning of ss 273 to 275 of POCA) (see s 245(3)). **19.33**

(13) The tracing of property

The Act envisages under s 305 the tracing of property, which may include an audit trail exercise. Where property was originally obtained through unlawful conduct (or would have been recoverable property), property that also represents the original property is also **19.34** recoverable. For example, a person steals a valuable painting (the original property), it is sold and the cash received from the sale is later used to purchase a Mercedes motor car. The Mercedes becomes recoverable property, being representative of the proceeds of a crime.

(14) Mixed property

19.35 The Act also stipulates that where a person's 'recoverable property' is mixed with other property, the portion of the mixed property that is said to relate to unlawful conduct becomes 'recoverable property' (see s 306—mixing property). For example, where there are two joint company directors, one uses the company account for legitimate monies, the other to launder the proceeds of crime. The 'honest' director withdraws a large sum of cash and as part of an investigation that cash is seized. The portion of the cash which he has on him that relates to legitimate money from the business does not fall within the recovery scheme; however, the portion which was paid in as part of the proceeds of a crime does stand to be forfeited, whether that particular director knew about it or not.

(15) Accruing profits

19.36 As one might expect, where a person who has 'recoverable property' obtains further property because of profits that have accrued on that recoverable property, those profits also become recoverable and are to be treated as 'property obtained through unlawful conduct' (eg increase in the value of an investment or in the value of a house) (see s 307—Accruing Profits).

(16) Granting interests

19.37 Section 310 provides:
(1) If a person grants an interest in his recoverable property, the question of whether the interest is also recoverable is determined in the same manner as it is in any other disposal of recoverable property.
(2) Accordingly, on his granting an interest in the property in question,
　(a) where the property in question is property obtained through unlawful conduct, the interest is also to be treated as obtained through that conduct;
　(b) where the property in question represents property, in his hands, obtained through unlawful conduct, the interest is also to be treated as representing, in his hands, the property so obtained.

In other words, gifting a property or granting an interest in any other way is unlikely to save the property from civil recovery.

C. Property Freezing Orders

(1) Introduction

19.38 The Serious Organised Crime and Police Act 2005 (SOCPA) introduced various amendments to the Civil Recovery Scheme. The Assets Recovery Agency (ARA) had at an early stage taken a conscious decision not to appoint an interim receiver in every case, eg where the location and the value of the assets said to be the proceeds of unlawful conduct were known and where the functions therefore of an interim receiver were limited. By avoiding the appointment of an interim receiver the Director also avoided the costs incurred by such an appointment, the costs of which fell upon the ARA.

C. Property Freezing Orders

19.39 To get around this problem the ARA started using freezing orders (formerly known as Mareva orders) as an interim remedy to restrain respondents from dealing with their assets and from removing them from the jurisdiction, pursuant to CPR 25.1. However, the use of freezing orders in this way was not something originally envisaged by the legislation and as a result SOCPA introduced a purpose built freezing order, known as a Property Freezing Order (PFO), as a device to be utilised by the Agency.

19.40 Section 98 of SOCPA inserts s 245A into POCA. Section 245A(1) states:

Where the enforcement authority may take proceedings for a recovery order in the High Court, the authority may apply to the court for a property freezing order (whether before or after starting the proceedings).

19.41 Section 245A reflects s 246(1) of POCA, in that it anticipates that the Director will be at liberty to apply for a property freezing order before she has started her CPR Part 8 claim for civil recovery. (Section 316(1) defines enforcement authority, in relation to England and Wales, as meaning the Director of the ARA.)

A draft PFO is found at Appendix 17.

(2) Definition

19.42 Section 245A(2) defines a property freezing order as an order that:

(a) specifies or describes the property to which it applies, and
(b) subject to any exclusions (see s 245C(1)(b) and (2)), prohibits any person to whose property the order applies from in any way dealing with the property.

(3) PFO without notice

19.43 By s 245A(3) the Director may apply for a PFO without giving notice, if the circumstances are such that notice of the application would prejudice any right of ARA to obtain a recovery order in respect of any property. This provision, like interim receiving orders and restraint orders under POCA, is to safeguard against the possibility that a respondent may attempt to either secrete his assets or transfer them out of the jurisdiction once put on notice that the Director intends to seek a PFO. Clearly, whilst that risk is always a possibility, it is still incumbent upon the Director to at least state what his belief is in relation to the risk of dissipation and the facts upon which he bases it, when making an ex parte application.

(4) *Factors giving rise to the risk of dissipation*

19.44 One of the purposes of seeking a property freezing order is the risk that assets may be lost which would otherwise be the subject of a civil recovery order. In *Assets Recovery Agency v Keenan* [2005] NIQB 67, Coughlin J stated that assets obtained by the proceeds of crime were '. . . by their very nature assets likely to be at particular risk of dissipation'.

19.45 In many cases the risk of dissipation will speak for itself. But of relevance will be the nature of the allegations against the respondent; whether or not those allegations have been proven and therefore the impact upon his credibility and integrity as a result; the ease with which the assets can be transferred including whether or not the respondent has any bank accounts or connections overseas; and whether or not he has attempted to deal with his assets in the past. His cooperation with the authorities may also be relevant particularly if he has a history of either evading court orders or failing to cooperate with the authorities. The respondent's geographical residence may also be a factor. It should be remembered that a defendant who is either out of the country or being detained in prison is still able to deal with his assets fairly fluidly through the cooperation of others, particularly bearing in mind the technological age in which we live.

(5) Duty of full and frank disclosure

19.46 It is important to remember that a person applying for an injunction without notice is under a duty of full and frank disclosure of all the material facts. The grant of either a PFO (or an IRO) is a discretionary remedy, and the Director is not therefore entitled to either order as of right. Accordingly, it is very important that the evidence put before the court should be as complete as possible and should demonstrate compelling reasons why such relief is necessary.

19.47 In *R v Kensington Income Tax Commissioners ex p de Polignac* [1917] 1 KB 486, the Court held that there was a duty on all applicants to make full and fair disclosure of all material facts. In *Siporex Trade SA v Condel Commodities Ltd* [1986] 2 Lloyd's Rep 428, Bingham J (as he then was) said:

> The scope of the duty of disclosure of a party applying ex parte for injunctive relief is, in broad terms, agreed between the parties. Such an applicant must show the utmost good faith and disclose his case fully and fairly. He must, for the protection and information of the defendant, summarise his case and the evidence in support of it . . . must identify the crucial points for and against the application, and not rely on general statements and the mere exhibiting of numerous documents.

19.48 In *Brinks Mat Ltd v Elcombe* [1988] 1 WLR 1350, Ralph Gibson LJ said that the duty to make full and frank disclosure encapsulated the following duties and principals:

(1) the duty of the applicant to make a full and fair disclosure of all material facts;
(2) the material facts are those which it is material for the judge to know in dealing with the application as made, materiality is to be decided by the court and not by the assessment of the applicant or his legal advisers;
(3) the applicant must make proper inquiries before making the application;
(4) the extent of the inquiries which will be proper and therefore necessary, must depend on all the circumstances of the case;
(5) if material non-disclosure is established the court will be astute to ensure that a plaintiff who obtains an ex parte injunction without full disclosure is deprived of any advantage he may have derived by that breach of duty;
(6) whether the fact was not disclosed is of sufficient materiality to justify or require immediate discharge of the order without examination of the merits, depends on the importance of the fact to the issues which were to be decided by the judge on the application;
(7) It is not for every omission that the injunction will be automatically discharged. The court has a discretion, notwithstanding proof of material non-disclosure which justifies or requires the immediate discharge of the ex parte order, nevertheless to continue the order or to make new terms.

C. Property Freezing Orders

19.49 Lord Justice Slade added to the above remarks:

> ... the principle is, I think a healthy one. It serves the important purposes of encouraging persons who are making ex parte applications to the court diligently to observe their duty to make full disclosure of all material facts and to deter them from any failure to observe this duty, whether through deliberate lack of candour or innocent lack of due care. Nevertheless, the nature of the principle, as I see it, is essentially penal and in its application the practical realities of any case before the court cannot be overlooked. By their very nature ex parte applications usually necessitate the giving and taking of instructions and the preparation of the requisite drafts in some haste. Particularly, in heavy commercial cases, the borderline between material facts and non-material facts may be somewhat uncertain. While in no way discounting the heavy duty of candour and care which falls on persons making ex parte applications, I do not think the application of the principle should be carried to extreme lengths. In one or two other recent cases coming before this court, I have suspected signs of a growing tendency on the part of some litigants against whom ex parte injunctions have been granted or of their legal advisers to rush to the *R v Kensington Income Tax Commissioners (1917) 1 KB 486* principle ... alleging material non-disclosure on sometimes rather slender grounds, as representing substantially the only hope of obtaining the discharge of injunctions in cases where there is little hope of doing so on the substantive merits of the case or on the balance of convenience.

19.50 In *Director of the Assets Recovery Agency v Satnam Singh* [2004] EWHC Admin 2335 McCombe J considered the above authorities (at para 42 of the judgment) and the duty upon the Director to make full and frank disclosure at the time of a without notice hearing (in *Singh* the Court was considering an application for an interim receiving order). Having considered the authorities, His Lordship found that there had been a failure to disclose certain things to the court, but that this did not afford grounds to discharge the order. He stated he considered it a situation to one which the remarks of Slade LJ in *Brinks Mat* were particularly applicable. The non-disclosure was attributable to an innocent lack of knowledge on the part of the Director and her advisers and the order should therefore be maintained. He did however adopt the procedure established in *Interoute Telecommunications (UK) Ltd v Fashion Gossip Ltd* The Times, 10 November 1999, which establishes that the applicant should provide to the respondent a note of what has taken place during the ex parte hearing. McCombe J stated (para 47):

> For the future, I can see no reason why the common practice in relation to without notice applications in the High Court should not be followed in cases of this type, unless the judge hearing the application expressly decides that, for good reason, a note should not be served on affected parties and provided that that decision is recorded on the face of the order, so that all affected parties may know that the decision also is susceptible to the customary permission to apply to vary or discharge the order.

19.51 It follows that if the Director is going without notice for an application it is important that notes are made during the hearing and that those notes are provided to any party affected by the injunction. In *Interoute* Lightman J. said that this was essential so that each party might know exactly what had occurred, and the basis for granting the injunction, in order to be able to make an informed application for discharge. It should also be noted that the duty to provide full notes applies regardless of whether the respondent asks for them (see *Thane Investments Ltd v Tomlinson* The Times, 10 December 2002 (ChD). (While these cases relate to freezing orders one can see that there must be an overlap between the jurisdictions and it is submitted that they represent good practice in relation to applications for both PFOs and IROs.)

Chapter 19: Civil Recovery: PFOs; Interim Receivers; and Legal Expenses

19.52 The reasoning of McCombe J in *Singh* was adopted by Coghlin J in *Director of the Assets Recovery Agency v Gerard Malachy Keenan* (NIHC, 23 September 2005) (para 23). See also *Jennings v CPS* [2005] 4 All ER 391 for full and frank disclosure in relation to restraint orders.

(6) Criteria for granting a Property Freezing Order

19.53 The court may make a PFO if it is satisfied that the conditions in s245A(5), and where applicable s 245A (6) are met.

Section 245A(5) states:

The first condition is that there is a good arguable case
(a) that the property to which the application for the order relates is or includes recoverable property, and
(b) that if any of it is not recoverable property, it is associated property.

Section 245A(6) reads:

The second condition is that, if
(a) the property to which the application for the order relates includes property alleged to be associated property, and
(b) the enforcement authority has not established the identity of the person who holds it, the authority has taken all reasonable steps to do so.

19.54 Once again, these conditions mirror those that relate to an application for an interim receiving order under s 246 of the Act.

19.55 Whilst the expression 'good arguable case' is not defined in the Act, it is a familiar expression to practitioners seeking injunctions under the freezing order scheme. In *The Niedersachsen* [1983] 2 Lloyd's Rep 600, 605A it was held a good arguable case related to the merits of the substantive claim, '*a case which is barely more than capable of serious argument, and yet not necessarily one that the Judge believes to have a better than 50% chance of success*' (p 605).

19.56 In *Derby & Co Ltd v Weldon (No 1)* [1990] 1 Ch 48 (CA) Parker LJ stated that a freezing injunction would only be made if the applicant could demonstrate that: (1) there is a good arguable case; (2) the respondent has assets (either in or outside the jurisdiction) over which such an order can bite; (3) there is a real risk that, if the freezing injunction is not granted, the respondent will remove assets from the jurisdiction or otherwise deal with or dispose of assets so as to render worthless any judgment subsequently obtained by the applicant.

(7) Variation and setting aside of the Property Freezing Order

19.57 Pursuant to s 245B of the amended Act, the court may at any time vary or set aside a PFO (s 245B(1)).

19.58 Section 245B(2) requires the court to set aside a PFO if it subsequently makes an interim receiving order that applies to all of the same property which a PFO covers. Where the court makes an IRO that applies to some *but not all* of the property to which the PFO applies, it must vary the PFO so as to exclude any property to which the IRO applies (s 245B(3)). It is therefore also apparent that as a result of s 245B(3), the new legislation anticipates that IROs and PFOs will not be mutually exclusive and may operate in tandem with each other.

C. Property Freezing Orders

19.59 If the court decides upon application that any property to which the PFO applies is neither recoverable property nor associated property it must vary the order so as to exclude the property (s 245B(4)). This subsection is directory and clearly affords the court little discretion once property has been identified as no longer being recoverable. However, before exercising any power to vary or set aside a PFO, the court must (as well as giving the parties to the proceedings an opportunity to be heard) give such an opportunity to any person who may be affected by the court's decision (see s 245B(5)) (although this sub-section does not apply where the court is acting as required by s 245B(2) or (3) (see subsection (6)). For practice and procedure in applying for variations see paras 19.78-19.90 below.

(8) Exclusions and variations

19.60 The power to vary a PFO includes (in particular) power to make certain exclusions. These include:

(a) power to exclude property from the order, and
(b) power, otherwise than by excluding property from the order, to make exclusions from the prohibition on dealing with the property to which the order applies. (See s 245C(1).)

19.61 Exclusions from the prohibition on dealing with the property to which the order applies may also be made when the order is made. Such exclusions may make provision for the purpose of enabling any person to:

(a) meet his reasonable living expenses, or
(b) carry on any trade, business, profession or occupation.

19.62 However, such an exclusion may be made subject to conditions (see s 245C (2)–(4)). Section 245C(5) states that where the court exercises the power to make an exclusion for the purpose of enabling a person to meet legal expenses that he has incurred, or may incur, in proceedings under this part of the Act (note, not legal expenses in relation to other proceedings), it must ensure that the exclusion;

(a) is limited to the reasonable legal expenses that the person has reasonably incurred or that he reasonably incurs,
(b) specifies the total amount that may be released for legal expenses in pursuance of the exclusion, and
(c) is made subject to the required conditions (see s 286A (below)) in addition to any conditions imposed under sub-section (4).

19.63 The court has a discretion in deciding whether to make an exclusion for the purpose of enabling a person to meet legal expenses and in exercising that discretion it:

(a) must have regard (in particular) to the desirability of the person being represented in any proceedings under Pt 5 of the Act in which he is a participant, and
(b) must, where the person is the respondent, disregard the possibility that legal representation of the person in any such proceedings might, were an exclusion not make, be funded by the Legal Services Commission. The test the court is likely to apply was set out by Stanley Burnton J in *Director of the Assets Recovery Agency v Creaven* [2005] EWHC Admin 2726 (see para 19.148 below). For practice and procedure in applying for exclusions see paras 19.78-19.87 below.

19.64 The issue of obtaining funding from frozen assets to meet legal expenses is considered in detail at para 19.177 below.

(9) The legislative steer

19.65 What can be described as a 'legislative steer' is found at s 245C(8), where the amended Act states that the power to make exclusions must, subject to s 245C(6), be exercised with a view to ensuring, so far as practicable, that the satisfaction of any right of the enforcement authority to recover the property obtained through unlawful conduct is not unduly prejudiced. (Section 245C(8) does not apply where the court is acting as required by s 245B(3) or (4), (see s 245C(9).)

19.66 It is perhaps worthy of note that whilst judicial precedent is sometimes useful when looking at freezing orders/Mareva injunctions and considering them in the light of the new powers of the ARA, it must be borne in mind that unlike the freezing order jurisdiction, POCA contains this legislative steer that courts are required to consider. Courts are also likely to have regard to the overall purpose of the Act: namely to recover the proceeds of crime. So for example, whilst in *PCW (Underwriting Agencies) Ltd v Dixon* [1983] 2 All ER 158 (QBD) Lloyd J stated 'justice and convenience require that [the frozen respondent] should be able to pay his ordinary bills and continue to live as he has been accustomed to live before' the same considerations may not necessarily apply in a POCA matter.

19.67 See para 19.108 below for further on the legislative steer.

(10) Restriction on proceedings and remedies

19.68 Under s 245D, while a PFO has effect, the court must stay any action, execution or other legal process in respect of the property to which the order applies and no distress may be levied against the property to which the order applies accept with the leave of the court and subject to any terms the court may impose.

19.69 Similarly, under s 245D(2), if a court (whether the High Court or any other court) in which proceedings are pending in respect of any property is satisfied that a PFO has been applied for or made in respect of the property, it may either stay the proceedings or allow them to continue on any terms it thinks fit.

19.70 If a PFO applies to the tenancy of any premises, no landlord or other persons to whom rent is payable may exercise the right of forfeiture by peaceable re-entry in relation to the premises in respect of any failure by the tenant to comply with any terms or conditions of the tenancy, except with the leave of the court and subject to any terms the court may impose (see s 245D(3)).

19.71 Before exercising any power conferred by s 245D of the amended Proceeds of Crime Act 2002, the court must (as well as giving the parties to any of the proceedings concerned an opportunity to be heard) give such an opportunity to any person who may be affected by the court's decision.

(11) Further SOCPA amendments

19.72 Schedule 6 to SOCPA makes various amendments to legislation affected by the changes it introduces. Section 27A(3) of the Limitation Act 1980 (time limits for bringing proceedings for recovery orders) inserts para (aa) to include an application made for a PFO. POCA is further amended by paras 4 et seq of Sch 6 to SOCPA to incorporate, where appropriate, property freezing orders into the legislation. See, eg s 248 which is amended at subs (1)(a) to read 'Property freezing orders, and in relation to interim receiving orders' to allow for PFOs to be registered at Land Registries.

19.73 Similarly, paras 16 and 17 of Sch 6 amend ss 271(4) and 272(5) to allow certain payments to trustees for civil recovery to be reduced to take account of loss caused by PFOs and the compensation for loss caused by PFOs respectively (see also para 19 in relation to s 283).

19.74 Paragraph 20 of Sch 6 to SOCPA 2005 also inserts after s 286 of POCA new conditions in relation to legal expenses excluded from freezing. Section 286A allows for the Lord Chancellor to make regulations specifying the conditions which exclude legal expenses from being frozen pursuant to ss 245C(5) or 252(4) and those conditions may restrict who can receive sums released in pursuance of the exclusion (by, eg, requiring released sums to be paid to professional legal advisers) or be made for the purpose of controlling the amount of any sum released in pursuance of the exclusion in respect of an item of expenditure (discussed fully at para 19.177 below).

(12) Ancillary orders

19.75 In *AJ Bekhor & Co Ltd v Bilton* [1981] QB 923 (CA) the Court held that it had an inherent power to make such ancillary orders (including disclosure) as appears to be just and convenient in order to ensure that a freezing order was effective.

(13) Undertakings for damages

19.76 Under the new legislation (it should be borne in mind that PFOs are creatures of statute, unlike freezing injunctions) there appears to be no requirement on the Director to give an undertaking to pay the reasonable costs incurred by anyone other than the respondent as a result of the injunction (known as a 'Seatrain proviso' after the case of *Searose Ltd v Seatrain UK Ltd* [1981] 1 All ER 806 (QBD) in the freezing injunction jurisdiction).

(14) Draft order

19.77 A draft property freezing order is found at Appendix 17.

(15) PFOs: practice and procedure

19.78 The amended Civil Recovery Proceedings Practice Direction sets out the procedure to be followed in relation to proceedings in the High Court under POCA.

19.79 Paragraph 1 stipulates that the venue for issuing applications should be the Administrative Court. Paragraph 5.1 states that an application for a PFO must be made to a High Court judge in accordance with Part 23 of the Civil Procedure Rules. Under CPR r 23.3 the general rule is that an applicant must file an Application Notice which must then be served on each respondent (see r 23.4).

Chapter 19: Civil Recovery: PFOs; Interim Receivers; and Legal Expenses

19.80 Paragraph 5.3 of the Practice Direction allows for applications to be made without notice pursuant to s 245A(3) of the Act, and Art 147(3) of the Order in Council (meaning the Proceeds of Crime Act 2002 (External Requests and Orders)) Order 2005.

19.81 Paragraph 5.4 provides that an application for a PFO must be supported by written evidence which must:

(1) set out the grounds on which the order is sought; and
(2) give details of each item or description of property in respect of which the order is sought, including:
  (a) an estimate of the value of the property; and
  (b) the additional information referred to in para 5.5

19.82 The additional information referred to in para 5.5 requires that the written evidence must state in relation to each item or description of property in respect of which the PFO is sought:

(a) whether the property is alleged to be (i) recoverable property or (ii) associated property, and the facts relied upon in support of that allegation; and
(b) in the case of any associated property (i) who was believed to hold the property; or (ii) if the Director is unable to establish who holds the property, the steps that have been taken to establish their identity.

19.83 Paragraph 5.6 of the Practice Direction stipulates that a draft of the order which is sought must be filed with the Application Notice. This should, if possible, also be supplied to the court in an electronic form compatible with the word processing software used by the court.

19.84 Rule 23.8 CPR deals with situations where applications may be dealt with without a hearing, and it was not unheard of in relation to restraint orders under the DTA and the CJA for High Court judges to make orders without requiring the attendance of counsel on behalf of the prosecuting authority (see r 23.8(c) CPR). However, while some judges will be prepared to deal with PFO applications on the papers alone, many still require the attendance of counsel on behalf of the Director to explain the history and necessity of the order being applied for.

19.85 Rule 23.9 CPR deals with the service of the application and r 23.11 sets out the powers of the court to proceed in the absence of a party.

19.86 Paragraph 5A of the Practice Direction states that where a PFO is made before a claim for a recovery order has been commenced it must:

(1) specify a period within which the Director must either start the claim or apply for the continuation of the order while he carries out his investigation; and
(2) provide that the order shall be set aside if the Director does not start the claim or apply for its continuation before the end of that period.

(16) Exclusions when making a PFO: legal costs

19.87 Paragraph 5B.1 of the Civil Recovery Practice Direction sets out the court's power to make exclusions for the purpose of enabling a respondent to meet his reasonable legal costs so that

D. Interim Receiving Orders

he may: (1) take advice in relation to the order (2) prepare a statement of assets in accordance with para 7A.3; and (3) if so advised, apply for the order to be varied or set aside. The total amount specified in the initial exclusion will not, according to the Practice Direction, normally exceed £3,000. This exclusion is dealt with in detail at para 19.201 below.

(17) Applications to vary or set aside a PFO

19.88 Pursuant to para 7.1 of the Practice Direction an application to vary or set aside a PFO can be made at any time by (1) the Director or (2) any person affected by the order.

19.89 Unless the court otherwise directs or exceptional circumstances apply, a copy of the application notice must be served on every party to the proceedings and any other person who may be affected by the court's decision.

19.90 This is an important proviso as it appears that the Practice Direction accompanying the new legislation does not make any provision for return dates where applications for discharge and variation might otherwise be argued.

D. Interim Receiving Orders

19.91 In *R (on the application of the Director of the Assets Recovery Agency) v (1) Jia Jin He and (2) Dan Dan Chen* (2004) EWHC Admin 3021, Collins J stated:

> One of the weapons in the Director's armoury is an interim receiving order. Such an order appoints a receiver who may be authorised to take a number of steps for the purposes of identifying relevant property and ensuring that it is preserved.

(1) Application for an interim receiving order

19.92 Where the ARA is considering taking proceedings for a recovery order in the High Court, the ARA may apply to the court for an interim receiving order (whether before or after starting proceedings) (see s 246(1)). An example of such an order is found at Appendix 15.

19.93 An application for an interim receiving order (IRO) may be made without notice if the circumstances are such that notice of the application would prejudice any right of the ARA to obtain a recovery order in respect of any property (see s 246(3)). For example, because of the risk of dissipation (see para 19.44 above (PFOs)).

19.94 It is a requirement of the Act that an IRO must require the interim receiver to take any steps which the court thinks necessary to establish:

(a) whether or not the property to which an order applies is recoverable property or associated property;
(b) whether or not any other property is recoverable property (in relation to the same unlawful conduct) and if it is, who holds it (s 247(1)).

(2) Loss of power to investigate

19.95 It should be noted that up to the issuing of the claim form or until an IRO is made the ARA has access to the civil investigation powers set out in Pt 8 of POCA. Once an IRO is made or a claim form for civil recovery is issued the ARA ceases to have the powers set out in Part 8 and the duty of taking further steps to establish facts about the property is placed with the interim receiver acting under the court's direction.

19.96 The ARA also loses the power to obtain a disclosure order under s 357. This is because s 391(3) provides that an application for a disclosure order must state that certain property specified in the application is subject to a civil recovery investigation. Section 341(3) provides that an investigation is not a civil recovery investigation if an interim receiving order applies in relation to the property. Therefore the only person who can use compulsory questioning powers is the interim receiver. The ARA would thus be prohibited from doing so. In *Director of the Assets Recovery Agency v Szepietowski* [2006] EWHC (Admin) 2406, Silber J held however that the ARA was entitled to rely on information about property which had come to light only as a result of investigations conducted pursuant to a previous IRO which related to different wrongdoing by the proposed defendant.

(3) Purpose and conditions

19.97 Under s 246(2) an interim receiving order is an order for:

(a) the detention, custody, or preservation of property; and
(b) the appointment of an interim receiver.

A court may make an IRO on the application of the Director of the ARA if it is satisfied that either of the following two conditions is met:

(1) That there is a good arguable case that the property to which the application for the order relates is or includes 'recoverable property', and that, if any of it is not recoverable property, it is 'associated property' (see s 246(5)).
(2) That if the property to which the application for the order relates includes property alleged to be associated property, and the enforcement authority has not established the identity of the person who holds it, the authority has taken all reasonable steps to do so (see s 246(6)).

If either of these conditions is met, an application can be made to the High Court to make an IRO and this may be done before the Director of the ARA issues a claim form for a recovery order. The application may also be without notice if the ARA believes that giving notice would prejudice the ARA's right to recover the property (s 246(3)).

19.98 Often it may be necessary to apply ex parte in circumstances where alerting the potential parties may cause the property to be either hidden or dissipated (see paras 19.43-19.44 above, (PFOs)).

(4) 'Good arguable case'

19.99 The expression 'good arguable case' is not defined in the Act although it is already used in applications for injunctions to freeze disputed property in civil courts under the freezing injunction regime formerly known as Mareva injunctions. In *The Niedersachsen* [1983]

2 Lloyd's Rep 600, 605A it was held a 'good arguable case' related to the merits of the substantive claim:

> a case which is more than barely capable of serious argument, and yet not necassarily one which the Judge believes to have a better than 50 per cent chance of success (p 605).

(See para 19.55 above, (PFOs).) **19.100**

(5) Application for an interim receiving order: practice and procedure

Under para 5.1 of the Civil Recovery Proceedings Practice Direction, an application for an interim receiving order must be made: **19.101**

(1) to a High Court judge; and
(2) in accordance with CPR Part 23.

Rule 23 CPR requires both written evidence in support and a draft order.

The application may be made without notice in the circumstances set out in s 246(3) of the Act (para 5.3(2)).

Under para 5.5, CPR Part 69 (the court's power to appoint a receiver) and its Practice Direction apply to an application for an IRO with the following modifications: **19.102**

(1) paragraph 2.1 of the PD supplementing Part 69 does not apply;
(2) the Director's written evidence must, in addition to the matters required by paragraph 4.1 of that PD, also state in relation to each item or description of property in respect of which the order is sought—
   (a) whether the property is alleged to be—
      (i) recoverable property;
      (ii) associated property,
   and the facts relied upon in support of that allegation; and
   (b) in the case of any associated property—
      (i) who is believed to hold the property;
      (ii) if the Director is unable to establish who holds the property, the steps that have been taken to establish their identity; and
(3) the Director's written evidence must always identify a nominee and include the information in paragraph 4.2 of that PD [claim form for a recovery order].

There must, under para 5.6, be filed with the application notice a draft of the order sought. This should if possible also be supplied to the court in electronic form. An example draft order is found at Appendix 15. **19.103**

In *R (on the application of the Director of the Assets Recovery Agency) v H* The Independent, 8 November 2004, McCombe J held that it is important that the jurisdiction within s 246 of POCA should be exercised carefully, so that people are not wrongfully injuncted, or injuncted for a period longer than is required. Equally, a court should not permit an individual to attack the basis upon which the order is made simply by choosing a snapshot in time where the evidence remains incomplete and thereby 'crawl away' from the consequences of various suspicions until the investigation is complete and matters are capable of clear resolution. **19.104**

(6) Interim receiving order made before commencement of claim for civil recovery

19.105 Pursuant to para 5A of the Civil Recovery Proceedings Practice Direction an IRO which is made before a claim for a recovery order has been commenced must:

(1) specify a period in which the Director must either start the claim or apply for the continuation of the order while she carries out her investigations; and

(2) provide that the order shall be set aside if the Director does not start the claim or apply for its continuation before the end of that period.

(7) Duty of full and frank disclosure

19.106 This is considered fully at para 19.46 above.

(8) The need for expedition

19.107 In *Director of the Assets Recovery Agency v (1) Jia Jin He (2) Dan Dan Chen* [2004] EWHC (Admin) 3021 Collins J commented at para 81:

> ... It is plain that there is a need for expedition. The receiver has an obligation to report as soon as practicable and there is a serious interference with Mr. He's property and his ability to carry on business if the reality is that he is not in any way involved in criminal conduct and this is not to be regarded as recoverable property. The matters which the receiver has to investigate are of some complexity, and it is not surprising that she has taken some time to resolve them. But the time is nigh when enquiries must be brought to a conclusion. It seems to me that in the very early part of next year those conclusions must be reached.

(9) The legislative steer

19.108 Section 252(6) of POCA states:

> The power [of the Court] to make exclusions [regarding the general prohibition against dealing with receivership property] must be exercised with a view to ensuing, so far as is practicable, that the satisfaction of any right of the enforcement authority to recover the property ... is not unduly prejudiced.

19.109 There is a distinct contrast between s 69(2)(c) of POCA (which deals with the legislative steer under Pt 2 of the Act (restraint and confiscation) and s 252(6) under Pt 5. This may well be deliberate and designed to reflect that one section is concerned with confiscation of a criminal's benefit, whereas the other concerns the civil recovery of property.

19.110 As a result it may be inappropriate to draw too much upon the case law that has arisen in relation to, for example, the payment of third party debts/creditors, under the earlier legislation. It goes without saying that in 1990, when *Re W* The Times, 15 November 1990 was decided, Buckley J could not have possibly anticipated the provisions of section 252 of POCA. Similarly, in *Re X* [2004] EWHC 861 Davis J stated in terms that he was not considering POCA or s 252, and *Re X* can be further distinguished because of Davis J's overriding concern about the presumption of innocence, whereas no such consideration applies in IRO cases.

19.111 The question therefore arises should s 252(6) of POCA be interpreted by reference to case law in the civil law jurisdiction of freezing/Mareva injunctions? It is submitted that the answer is no, and that s 252(6) is sui generis. Under freezing order/Mareva injunctions a bona fide creditor can recover their debts. This was confirmed by Lord Donaldson in *Re Peters* at p 879, who stated:

> The interest of the potential judgement creditor has to be balanced against those of actual creditors, whether secured or unsecured, and of the defendant himself who may succeed in the action and should be fettered in his dealing with his own property to the least possible extent necessary to ensure the interests of justice are not frustrated.

In IRO and PFO matters it is submitted that it is appropriate for the court or the receiver to consider all approaches for the settlement of secured or unsecured debts (which are bona fide) on their merits. It would not however be appropriate, it is submitted, to release property from civil restraint when that property was the probable proceeds of unlawful conduct, because to do so would be to frustrate the purpose of the Act. **19.112**

An interim receiver will often be able to assist the court with this question, and where a court is faced with a dispute between the receiver and a respondent (or third party) as to the proposed course of a receivership, the court is likely to give greater weight to the disinterested views of the receiver, particularly if supported by professional advice and expertise (see *Re Piper* [2000] 1 WLR 473). **19.113**

Although s 252(6) may not be particularly robust, it must still be considered by the court, and the approach of the Court therefore cannot be as liberal as that which a court might adopt when considering freezing order injunctions. A distinction may also be drawn in cases where the nexus to unlawful conduct has not yet been established in relation to any given asset and where the possibility at least must exist that that property will not be subject to civil recovery. **19.114**

(10) The insolvent respondent

It should first be noted that receiverships where an individual has been adjudged bankrupt have always been subject to different rules in proceeds of crime legislation – see eg s 15(2) of the DTOA and its corresponding provisions, together with s 32 of the DTA and s 84 of the CJA. In such cases the powers of a receiver have never been exercisable in relation to property within the bankrupts estate or to property that is to be applied for the benefit of creditors. **19.115**

Voluntary arrangements were not similarly protected (see *Re M* [1992] QB 377 at p 381). So a receiver can enjoy full powers before a defendant is adjudged bankrupt under the CJA or DTA. In restraint cases realisable property is defined as *'any property held by the defendant'* – and the restraint order prevents any person from dealing with any realisable property. In *Re M*, Otton J concluded that the restraint order prohibits 'any person' from dealing with any realisable property, *'This prevents the debtor from petitioning for his own bankruptcy'* (p 382). **19.116**

Section 311 of POCA deals with Insolvency in Civil Recovery proceedings under Part 5. Proceedings for a recovery order may not be taken or continued in respect of property that is an asset of a company which is being wound up; where the company or an individual has entered into a voluntary arrangement; where an interim trustee has already been appointed over it, pursuant to the Insolvency Acts; or where it is an asset comprised in the estate of an individual who has been adjudged bankrupt (see s 311(3) of POCA). **19.117**

19.118 A potential flaw exists in that knowing this, an individual may prefer to rack up debts/force his petition for bankruptcy rather than be subjected to civil recovery proceedings.

19.119 Unlike the situation in *Re M*, s 311 does not merely provide for a Respondent who has actually been adjudged bankrupt, but also for individuals and companies who have entered into a voluntary arrangement under Part 1 or Part 8 of the Insolvency Act 1986. As a result, the diluted legislative steer in s 252 and the broadening of the categories to include voluntary arrangements has potentially made it easier for respondents to avoid civil recovery. Whether in practice individuals would pursue such a line is a moot point. Any suggestion of contrivance would be likely to be viewed dimly by the court, and might lead to the court interpreting s 252(6) in a more robust fashion.

(11) Insolvency and IROs

19.120 In *Q3 Media Ltd* [2006] EWHC 1553 (Ch D) Rimer J considered the issue of insolvency where an interim receiver had been appointed. The effect of a company being subject to an IRO and the supremacy of such an order was underlined in the court's judgment. In relation to an application by a company's prospective creditor for an administration order over the company, although the court was satisfied that the company was unable to pay its debts, it was not satisfied that an order was likely to achieve the purpose of administration, as the company was subject to an IRO under s 246 of POCA. It was likely that all the company's assets were recoverable property and not available to creditors. Rimer J held that the basis of W's claim was that X were creditors and their claim was a claim in restitution, not a claim for a debt. Therefore it might be that W's claim was on behalf of prospective creditors, not creditors, and Q was waiting to see how X would make good their claim. However, in the circumstances, the court was satisfied that Q was unable to pay its debts as even if the applicants were regarded as prospective creditors, the unexplained failure to pay justified the inference that it was unable to pay. There was a good arguable case that all of Q's assets were recoverable property, given the IRO, and that Q was unable to pay its debts, so that the Insolvency Act 1986, Sch B1, para 11(A) had been satisfied. However, the court could not be satisfied under para 11(B), Sch 1 to the 1986 Act that the making of the administration order would be reasonably likely to achieve the purpose of administration, because if Q's assets were recoverable property they would be available to meet the creditors' demands. An administration order therefore was not granted at that stage.

(12) A stand alone claim

19.121 In *Director of the Assets Recovery Agency v Creaven* [2005] EWHC Admin 2726, the applicants applied to vary an interim freezing injunction that restrained them from dealing in property that they controlled in the UK. Although the respondent was acquitted of his role in a VAT Missing Trader fraud, the ARA decided to pursue him on the basis that his assets were derived from unlawful conduct within the meaning of Pt 5 of POCA. Stanley Burnton J held that a claim under Pt 5 of the Act differed from both the conventional personal and conventional proprietary claim. It differed from a conventional personal claim in that it was confined to identified property, although not all of the property needed to be identified when the claim was brought. It differed from a conventional proprietary claim in that a respondent held no personal liability.

D. Interim Receiving Orders

After an order was made the property was transferred to a trustee for civil recovery. Accordingly, a claim under Pt 5 was to be regarded as sui generis, a statutory creation of a special kind. **19.122**

(13) Powers of the High Court

The High Court has an inherent discretion in civil proceedings to make such and any orders in law that it considers appropriate when making interlocutory injunctions (see *AJ Bekhor & Co Ltd v Bilton* [1981] QB 923 (CA)). This discretion is reflected in s 246(8) which states that the power to make an interim receiving order is not limited by ss 247 to 255 of POCA. **19.123**

(14) Functions of an interim receiver

The Director of the ARA must nominate a suitably qualified person for appointment as an interim receiver. This will usually be an independent licensed insolvency practitioner. It may not be a member of the staff of the ARA (s 246(7)). **19.124**

The interim receiving order made by the High Court may authorise or require the interim receiver to: **19.125**

(a) exercise any of the powers mentioned in Sch 6 to POCA;
(b) take any other steps the court thinks appropriate,
    for securing the detention, custody or preservation of the property to which the order applies or of taking any steps under subsection (2).

(Section 247(1).)

(15) Contents of the order

Schedule 6 to POCA is reproduced at Appendix 12 of this book. The powers it invests in an interim receiver include the following: **19.126**

(1) The power to seize property to which the order applies.
(2) The power to obtain information or require a person to answer any questions.
(3) The power to enter any premises in the UK to which the interim order applies and take the following steps:
    (a) carry out a search or inspection of anything described in the order;
    (b) make or obtain a copy, photograph, or other record of anything so described, and
    (c) remove anything which the receiver is required to take possession of in pursuance of the order.
(4) The power to manage any property to which the order applies, including selling or otherwise disposing of assets comprised in the property which are perishable or which ought to be disposed of before their value diminishes, or where the property comprises assets of a trade or business, or incurring capital expenditure in respect of the property.

The power to sell depreciating assets remains the most controversial of these, and can include cars and other high value items. In such circumstances it is submitted the receiver **19.127** should give the respondent/owner sufficient notice of the sale to allow them the opportunity to make representaions, either by correspondence or by way of an application to the High Court, if the costs of such a course are not prohibitive.

19.128 Schedule 6 also anticipates the order may make provision to give the interim receiver access to any premises which he may need to enter in pursuance of Sch 6 para 3. The order may also require any person to give the interim receiver any assistance he may need for taking the steps mentioned above.

19.129 An IRO may also require any person to whose property the order applies to bring or repatriate the property to a place in England and Wales specified by the interim receiver, or place it into the custody of the interim receiver (if, in either case the person to whose property the order applies is able to do so), and/or to do anything he is reasonably required to do by the interim receiver for the preservation of the property (see s 250(1)).

19.130 The interim receiving order may also require any person to whose property the order applies to bring any documents relating to the property which are in his possession or control to a place (in England and Wales) specified by the interim receiver or to place them in the custody of the interim receiver. For these purposes 'document' means anything in which information of any description is recorded (s 250(2)).

19.131 These 'duties of the respondent' graphically illustrate just how far reaching the powers of the interim receiver actually are, and that they extend to dictating the control of assets held outside of the UK.

19.132 These provisions of the Act reflect very closely matters that would ordinarily be set out in management receivership orders made under the DTA or CJA. As under those receivership orders, a person who ignores or contravenes such an order would be potentially liable to committal proceedings in the High Court for contempt.

(16) Restrictions on dealing with property

19.133 Under s 252(1) of POCA:

(1) An interim receiving order must, subject to any exclusions made in accordance with this section, prohibit any person to whose property the order applies from dealing with the property.

19.134 Exclusions may be made when the IRO is made or on an application to vary the order (see s 252(2)). Under s 252(3) an exclusion may, in particular, make provision for the purpose of enabling any person:

(a) to meet his reasonable living expenses or
(b) to carry on any trade, business, profession or occupation, and may be made subject to conditions.

19.135 The purpose of this section is to ensure that IROs prevent any dealing with the property that they cover. It also anticipates that from time to time there will be exclusions to that rule. 'Dealing' with property includes disposing of it, taking possession of it, or removing it from the UK (see s 316(1)).

19.136 Any excluded property must either be specified or described in general terms in the order (s 252(5)).

D. Interim Receiving Orders

(17) Contents of the order in terms of reporting by the receiver

19.137 Section 255(2) states that an IRO must require the interim receiver to report his findings to the court and serve copies of his reports to the enforcement authority, and on any person who holds any property to which the order applies or who may otherwise be effected by the report. This requirement is considered in more detail at para 19.167 below.

(18) Protection against self incrimination

19.138 Under Sch 6 para 2(3) to POCA, any answer given by a person in pursuance of the requirements set out in para 2 may not be used in evidence against him in criminal proceedings (see also para 2(4)(b)).

(19) Protection for the receiver

19.139 Section 246(3) provides legal protection for the receiver if he mistakenly, but honestly, deals with property that is not the property specified in the order, providing that those dealings are not caused by his or her own negligence.

(20) Applications to clarify the receiver's powers

19.140 The interim receiver, any party to the proceedings, and any person affected by any action taken by the interim receiver, or who may be affected by any action proposed to be taken by him, may at any time apply to the court for directions in relation to the interim receiver's functions. Once such an application has been made and the matter is before the court, before giving any directions the court must (as well as giving the parties to the proceedings an opportunity to be heard) give such an opportunity to the interim receiver and to any person who may be interested in the application (see s 251(1) and (2)). Such directions may be used to clarify the powers of the receiver in relation to certain property.

(21) Applications for directions

19.141 Under para 6.1 of the Practice Direction, an application for directions in relation to the interim receiver's functions may, under s 251 of the Act, be made at any time by:

(1) the interim receiver;
(2) any party to the proceedings; and
(3) any person affected by any action taken by the interim receiver, or who may be affected by any action proposed to be taken by him.

The application must always be made by application notice, which must be served on:

(1) the interim receiver (unless he is the applicant);
(2) every party to the proceedings; and
(3) any other person who may be interested in the application.

(22) The role and independence of the interim receiver

19.142 The role of the interim receiver is two-fold. Firstly, there is a management role which is to secure the detention, custody or preservation of property to which the order applies (s 247(1)(b)) (similar to that of a management receiver appointed while a restraint order is extant). Secondly, there is an investigative role whereby the interim receiver should investigate on behalf of the court: (a) whether the property to which the order applies is recoverable property; and (b) whether there is any other recoverable property (related to the same unlawful conduct) and, if there is, who holds it (see s 247(2)).

19.143 Interim receivers should be considered as independent officers of the court. It is the court that appoints them. Their independence is underlined in that the Act stipulates they must not be a member of ARA's staff. The interim receiver is under a duty to report to *the court* any material change in circumstances (s 255(1)). It is the court that determines the receiver's powers on a case by case basis within the framework prescribed by s 247 and Sch 6 to POCA. At any time, the interim receiver can apply to the court for directions as to the exercise of his powers (s 251(1)), only the court is able to direct an interim receiver, and it follows that he or she should be beyond the direction of the parties. In addition, the court may vary or set aside an interim receiving order at any time (s 251(2)). It will also be noted that there is no requirement for an independent person to supervise when the interim receiver is exercising the powers conferred by Sch 6.

19.144 Once an interim receiving order is made, the Director is deemed no longer to be carrying on a civil recovery investigation (s 341(3)(b)). While the Director may still receive information by virtue of the Gateway provisions in Pt 10 of POCA, in practice it is generally the position that the investigation will cease on the granting of an IRO. The imposition of the investigative function upon the Interim Receiver confers a unique role amongst receivers in UK jurisprudence. A vital aspect of the scheme is that the interim receiver is not a witness for the Agency and is not supervised by the ARA. He is the court's investigator and it can be expected that the report will be used to determine which issues can be agreed and which remain in dispute. However, the role of the interim receiver is not that of a single joint expert and civil recovery is not litigation by expert witness. Whilst an interim receiver may have some similarities with that of a single joint expert, the powers they have vested in them places them outside of that remit. This interpretation is confirmed by the Explanatory Notes to POCA that state the report will 'be capable of being used as a basis to establish agreed facts and to identify disputed matters that will fall to be resolved at the time of hearing' (para 325).

19.145 If a party wishes to dispute the correctness of the findings of an interim receiver, they should in the first instance notify the receiver in writing of the matter that they take issue with for the receiver to consider. Similar considerations apply where a party believes that a receiver has taken account of evidence which is either not relevant or is incorrect. Thereafter the interim receiver should either reply in writing or prepare a further report for the court. Whether it is desirable for interim receivers to meet with the parties in the absence of the other parties is a moot point. Clearly there will be occasions where it is appropriate to give the other party notice that a meeting is going to take place and to invite their observations and/or attendance. On the other hand, to require a third party to attend on every occasion not only will lead to additional cost for that party, as well as potential inconvenience, but may well inhibit the subject matters that need to be discussed. The interim receiver is not acting as mediator but is trying to establish the facts in order to report them to the court.

D. Interim Receiving Orders

The minutes of any such meeting, if a party has not attended, can thereafter be circulated, subject to the agreement of the party attending.

19.146 Occasionally, respondents may wish to appoint their own forensic accountant or expert witness to deal with issues that arise. Whether such reports should be publicly funded or funded from the frozen assets will be something that will need to be determined on the facts of any given case. What clearly should be avoided is funding for an expert witness when that witness is simply embarking on a mere fishing expedition, in circumstances where the interim receiver has already reported on the property in question and where there is no genuine dispute. The court will clearly want to ensure that such expenditure is reasonably incurred and the interim receiver's report will usually constitute compelling independent evidence in itself.

(23) Power to vary or set aside

19.147 The court may at any time vary or set aside an interim receiving order (see s 251(3)). However, before exercising that power the court must give such opportunity to the interim receiver, and to any person who may be affected by the court's decision, an opportunity to be heard, including the parties to the proceedings themselves (s 251(4)).

19.148 In *Director of the Assets Recovery Agency v Creaven* [2005] EWHC Admin 2726, Stanley Burnton J held it was the clear policy of the Act to deprive respondents of property obtained through unlawful conduct (unless they could establish a statutory defence), and for that property to be transferred for the benefit of the community.

19.149 Section 252(6) of POCA provides that the power to make exclusions to an interim receiving order has to be exercised with a view to ensuring that the satisfaction of any right of the Agency to recover property obtained through unlawful conduct is not unduly prejudiced. The power to make exclusions to a freezing order made in support of a claim under Part 5 should be exercised on that basis. In general a court is unlikely to permit a respondent who has property available that is not recoverable property to use property that is claimed to be recoverable property to meet his expenditure pending the hearing.

(24) Application to vary or discharge an interim receiving order: practice and procedure

19.150 Under the Practice Direction that accompanies the Act an application to vary or discharge an interim receiving order may be made at any time by:

(1) the Director; or
(2) any person affected by the order.

Paragraph 7.2 of the Practice Direction states that a copy of the application notice must be served on:

(1) every party to the proceedings;
(2) the interim receiver; and
(3) any other person who may be affected by the court's decision.

19.151 In *R (on the application of the Director of the Assets Recovery Agency) v H* [2004] EWHC (Admin) 2166, McCombe J held that since the making of IROs was a Draconian power, it was very important for the jurisdiction to be exercised carefully so that people were not wrongly injuncted, or injuncted for a longer period than was required. He added however, it should not be permitted for any respondent, when faced with what was an inherently suspicious business activity, to 'crawl away' from the consequences of the various suspicions simply by choosing a snapshot in time when the evidence remained incomplete.

19.152 The difficulty in making an application for discharge prematurely was illustrated in *Director of the Assets Recovery Agency v Molloy* [2006] NIQB 49, where Coghlin J dealt with an application to discharge in circumstances where it was suggested the ARA had not identified any relevant unlawful conduct on the part of the Respondent, nor identified any property alleged to have been obtained as a result of such unlawful conduct. Coghlin J held that although no property had been specifically identified as representing the product of unlawful conduct, such an identification may have been unlikely at the stage of the application he was dealing with because of extensive and complex property arrangements. He added:

> it is the specific task of the interim receiver to investigate that property for the purposes of establishing whether or not it is recoverable property. . . .a good deal of progress has already been made and it has become necessary to amend Sch 2 of the original receiving order so as to exclude a substantial amount of property which is no longer regarded as recoverable. However, at this stage, I remain of the view that there is a good arguable case that the property to which this interim receiving order relates is or includes recoverable property . . . and, accordingly, I dismiss this application.

(25) Non-specified recoverable property

19.153 As soon as an interim receiver believes that property not specifically referred to in the order is recoverable then he should take steps to seize and take possession of that property. It is only by doing this that the risk of dissipation is minimised pending an application to the court to seek directions in respect of the non-specified property. Such an application therefore should be made forthwith in order to protect the interests of all the parties affected, as well as to inform the court as to what has happened. It may also be that the interim receiver will be required to give evidence and be cross-examined in relation to the property itself. The court may then order either that the property be returned or extend the order itself to specifically include it and in so doing clarify that the newly discovered asset is potentially recoverable property. Such a conclusion is essential to the effective working of Pt 5 of POCA and its purpose of recovering the proceeds of crime.

(26) Exclusion of property which is not recoverable

19.154 If the court decides that any property to which an IRO applies is neither recoverable property nor associated property, it must vary the order so as to exclude it (s 254(1)).

19.155 Under s 254(2) the Court may (importing a discretion) also exclude property providing the ARA's rights to recover the remaining property is not prejudiced:

> (2) The court may vary an interim receiving order so as to exclude from the property to which the order applies any property which is alleged to be associated property if the court thinks the satisfaction of

D. Interim Receiving Orders

any right of the enforcement authority to recover the property obtained through unlawful conduct will not be prejudiced.

Under s 245(3) the court may exclude any property within this section on any terms or conditions, which the court thinks 'necessary or expedient'.

(27) Exclusion of property to cover legal expenses

19.156 The issue of release of restrained funds to cover a respondent's legal costs is set out in detail at para 19.189 below.

(28) Interim receiver's expenses

19.157 Section 99 of the Serious Organised Crime and Police Act 2005 (SOCPA) amended s 280 of POCA (civil recovery orders: applying realised proceeds) to insert after subs (2):

(3) the Director may apply a sum received by him under sub-section (2) in making payment of the remuneration and expenses of
   (a) the trustee or
   (b) any interim receiver appointed in, or in anticipation of, the proceedings for the recovery order.
(4) Sub-section (3)(a) does not apply in relation to the remuneration of the trustee if the trustee is a member of the staff of the Agency.

19.158 This effectively allows for the Director of the ARA to recompense the interim receiver (and the trustee for civil recovery) from sums which represent the realised proceeds of property following a successful civil recovery order claim after payments referred to in s 280(2) of POCA have been made. This directly mirrors the manner in which receivers are paid pursuant to Pts 2 and 4 of the Act.

(29) Interim receiverships over land

19.159 The purpose of s 248 of POCA is to ensure that where an IRO is made over land, its effect may be reinforced by taking action at the Land Registry to prevent the disposal or dissipation of the land in question. The 'Registration Acts' (namely the Land Registration Act 1925, the Land Charges Act 1972, and the Land Registration Act 2002) apply in relation to IROs as they would apply in relation to orders which affect any other land where an order is made by the court for the purpose of enforcing judgments or other pending land actions (see s 248(1) and (2)).

19.160 Section 248(3) prohibits the registering of title under the Land Registration Act 2002 in respect of property covered by an IRO.

19.161 It should be noted that a person applying for an IRO should be treated for the purposes of s 57 of the Land Registration Act 1925 (inhibitions) as an interested person in relation to any registered land to which the application relates (see s 248(4)).

(30) Restriction on existing proceedings and rights

19.162 Whilst an interim receiving order has effect, the court may stay any action, execution, or other legal process in respect of the property to which the order applies. Nor may any distress be levied against the property to which the order applies except with the leave of the court and subject to any terms the court may impose (see s 253(1)).

19.163 Section 253(2) states:

(2) If a court (whether the High Court or any other court) in which proceedings are pending in respect of any property is satisfied that an interim receiving order has been applied for or made in respect of the property, the court may either stay the proceedings or allow them to continue on any terms it thinks fit.

19.164 This section allows the court in which proceedings are pending in respect of the property to stay them or impose terms on their continuation.

19.165 Section 253(3) deals with the situation where IROs apply to tenancies on premises and thereby a landlord may not exercise a right of forfeiture by peaceful re-entry on a property affected by an order.

19.166 When exercising the powers conferred by s 253 the court must give the opportunity to the interim receiver (if appointed) and any other person who may be affected by the court's decision, including the parties, to be heard (s 253(4)).

(31) Reporting

19.167 Section 255(1) reads:

(1) An interim receiving order must require the interim receiver to inform the enforcement authority and the court as soon as reasonably practicable if he thinks that—
   (a) any property to which the order applies by virtue of a claim that it is recoverable property is not recoverable property,
   (b) any property to which the order applies by virtue of a claim that it is associated property is not associated property,
   (c) any property to which the order does not apply is recoverable property (in relation to the same unlawful conduct) or associated property or
   (d) any property to which the order applies is held by a person who is different from the person it is claimed holds it, or if he thinks that there has been any other material change of circumstances.

This therefore lays a pro-active duty upon the receiver to inform both the ARA and the court of circumstances where, eg he believes that property covered by an IRO claimed to be recoverable property, is in fact not recoverable. By virtue of this section, it is submitted, there must also be on an on-going duty within the receivership to keep matters under review to ensure that s 255 is complied with.

19.168 This duty is a corollary to s 247(2) which requires the interim receiver to take any steps which the court thinks are necessary to establish whether or not the property in which the order applies is recoverable property or associated property.

19.169 Under s 255(2) an interim receiving order must require the interim receiver:

(a) to report his findings to the court
(b) to serve copies of his reports to the enforcement authority and on any person who holds any property to which the order applies or who may otherwise be effected by the report.

D. Interim Receiving Orders

This formalises the receiver's duty to produce a formal report of his findings and ensure that he serves copies of that report on all those who may be affected by it. These reports may then be used as a basis to establish agreed facts in relation to disputed matters.

(32) Compensation

19.170 Where an IRO is made by the court, and the court later decides that the property is neither recoverable property nor associated property, the person whose property it is may make an application to the High Court for compensation (see s 283(1) and s 316(1)).

19.171 The ability to claim compensation does not extend to property in respect of which a declaration has been made under s 281 (victims of theft), or in circumstances where an order under s 276 has been made (a consent order) (see s 283(2)).

Under s 272(5):

(5) If—
  (a) an interim receiving order . . . applied at any time to the associated property or joint tenancy and
  (b) the court is satisfied that the person who holds the associated property or who is an excepted joint owner has suffered loss as a result of the interim receiving order . . . , a recovery order making any provision by virtue of subsection (2) or (3) [of section 272] may require the enforcement authority to pay compensation to that person.

19.172 The criterion which the court is to apply is set out in s 272(6) and it is an amount the court thinks reasonable, having regard to the person's loss and any other relevant circumstance.

(33) Time limit for compensation application

19.173 Where the court has decided that no recovery order should be made in respect of property the application for compensation must be made within a period of three months beginning:

283(3)(a) . . . in relation to a decision of the High Court, with the date of the decision, or if any application is made for leave to appeal, with the date on which the application is withdrawn or refused or, (if the application is granted) on which any proceedings on appeal are finally concluded.

If the proceedings in respect of the property have been discontinued, the application for compensation must be made within the period of three months beginning with the discontinuance (see s 283(4)).

19.174 If, but for s 269(2) (circumstances where a right of pre-emption, right of irritancy, right of return, or other similar right does not operate as a result of the vesting of any property under a recovery order), any right would have operated in favour of, or become exercisable by any person, that person may make an application to the court for compensation. Such an application must be made within three months beginning with the vesting referred to in s 269(2) as per (s 269(6)).

(34) The test the court should apply

19.175 If the court is satisfied that the applicant has suffered loss as a result of the IRO, it may require the ARA to pay compensation to him under s 283(5). Similarly if the court is satisfied that in consequence of the operation of s 269, the right of the applicant can no longer be operated or exercised by him, it may require the ARA to pay compensation to him. (It will be noted that these are discretionary awards and will clearly depend on the facts and evidence in the case.)

19.176 The amount of compensation to be paid under s 283 is the amount that the court 'thinks reasonable' having regard to the loss suffered and any other relevant circumstances (see s 283(9)).

E. Legal Expenses in Civil Recovery Proceedings

(1) Introduction

19.177 Section 98 of SOCPA allows respondents, who are subject to civil proceedings, to have access to their frozen assets in order to fund the costs of their legal representation. It is supplemented by Chapter 6 of SOCPA which contains what are described as 'minor and consequential amendments', including the turn-around proviso that allows respondents to meet their legal costs from frozen funds (originally prohibited by s 252(4) of POCA).

19.178 The Act as originally drafted heralded a sea change in the way in which funding for responding to applications made by prosecuting authorities and the Director of the ARA in restraint and civil recovery proceedings would operate, by making a specific exclusion that those subject to such orders would be unable to withdraw from frozen assets funds in order to pay their legal representatives privately.

19.179 There had always been a tension between prosecuting authorities and defence firms, (and for that matter receivers appointed by the court), in connection with the release of funds, with a burden being placed on the defence to show that they were being properly and reasonably incurred. Whilst some defence firms resented the previous regime as it equated to having to go 'cap in hand' to prosecuting authorities for their fees, other commentators pointed towards the fact that tens of thousands of pounds and sometimes hundreds of thousands of pounds of money that would otherwise have been used in confiscation proceedings were being diverted to pay sometimes exorbitant defence fees.

19.180 The new Act sought to overcome both these difficulties, and the Court of Appeal in *Customs and Excise Commissioners v S* [2004] EWCA Crim 2374 upheld Parliament's intention in this regard, with the result restraint orders under POCA have no exception for defence legal expenses.

19.181 However, the ARA ran into a number of obstacles with their cases, particularly in relation to persuading the LSC to award civil funding (see Appendix 19 for guidance in relation to same).

19.182 Although in relation to restraint and receivership matters under the confiscation regime, defendants appear to have been able to attract LSC funding, respondents attempting to claim LSC funding under the civil recovery regime encountered a series of difficulties. The LSC civil legal aid scheme is fairly restrictive and as a result respondents faced great difficulties in obtaining funding to defend claims. This had the knock-on effect of causing delays in progressing matters through courts with High Court judges insisting that claims for civil recovery should not proceed without the respondents having proper legal advice and being properly represented. Whilst efforts were made to relax the LSC funding rules to allow for ARA cases to be expedited, there still existed long delays, with a number of ARA cases being referred for 'special investigation'. This resulted in targets not being met.

19.183 Those delays had the result of creating a backlog of cases within the Agency. Similarly, respondents were able to frustrate the process by being slow to provide information to the LSC and there was anecdotal evidence that this too was leading to lengthy delays.

19.184 The impasse was broken with the introduction of SOCPA, which now allows for the release of legal expenses in certain restricted and controlled circumstances.

19.185 The amended legislation is aimed at resolving funding difficulties and allowing matters to proceed at a faster pace. It has the advantage of avoiding frustrating delays whilst LSC funding is explored. Equally, it has the disadvantage that defence firms must now go to the Director and in effect make their case for funding arrangements in which the Director is not only a party, but the claimant of the property concerned. The concept of what are 'reasonable' legal expenses is left somewhat open by the amended legislation. It is intended that the courts will resolve any disagreement between the parties, although one can see that this has the potential to give rise to yet more delay, with foreseeable arguments being made in relation to both the Human Rights Act and judicial review, particularly bearing in mind that the new legislation appears to afford employees of the Director a discretion.

19.186 It is important to note that the regulations are designed to ensure that the assets can only be used to fund what is described as 'a reasonable defence', and presumably therefore not to fund proceedings that extend and frustrate the legal process by unjustifiably diminishing the assets on legal fees. At the time of their introduction the Legal Aid Minister, Bridget Prentice, said:

> These measures will achieve a balance that will ensure that the tax payer does not foot the bill for defendants who can afford to pay their own legal costs, while also ensuring that frozen assets are not misused to fund a "champagne defence". They will ensure that funds are only released for legal costs where reasonable and proportionate.

19.187 In a press release issued at the time it was anticipated that the new measures would save around three million pounds a year from the Legal Aid budget.

19.188 Whilst the intention of the legislation may be sound, it is submitted that Sch 6 to SOCPA which seeks to amend s 286A of POCA and the amended Practice Direction in civil recovery proceedings together with the Proceeds of Crime Act 2002 (Legal Expenses in Civil Recovery Proceedings) have made this process unnecessarily complicated. The new system appears to lack control and regulation. As will be seen, defence firms are expected to carry out the work and only then submit their invoices to the Director for consideration of payment. Although the regulations anticipate a controlled and staged cost plan, clearly some work undertaken will lead to other enquiries which may not be anticipated at the beginning of an application. Furthermore, a respondent's solicitors may not wish to disclose every aspect of the work that they anticipate they will carry out to the person bringing the claim against them. It is anticipated that there are likely to be a number of teething problems with the operation of the new system. It is of some interest that in Scotland respondents will continue to be prevented from using frozen assets to fund the cost of legal representation and that it is still anticipated that legal aid will continue to be available to them, where eligible.

(2) Background to the new provisions

19.189 Paragraph 15 of Sch 6 to SOCPA inserts into s 266 (Recovery Orders) subs 8(A) and 8(B), which state:

8(A) A recovery order made by a court in England and Wales or Northern Ireland may provide for payment under s 280 of reasonable legal expenses that a person has reasonably incurred, or may reasonably incur, in respect of
   (a) the proceedings under this Part in which the order is made, or
   (b) any related proceedings under this Part.
8(B) If regulations under s 286B apply to an item of expenditure, a sum in respect of the item is not payable under s 280 in pursuance of provision under s 8(A) unless
   (a) the enforcement authority agrees to its payment, or
   (b) the court has assessed the amount allowed by the regulations in respect of the item and the sum is paid in respect of the assessed amount.

Section 280(2) (application of the realised proceeds of a recovery order) is amended by para 18 of Sch 6 to SOCPA to insert after para (a)

(aa) Next, any payment of the legal expenses which, after giving effect to s 266(8B), are payable under this sub-section in pursuance of a provision under s 266(8A) contained in the recovery order.

19.190 Paragraph 20 of Sch 6 inserts a new para 286B into POCA which sets out the Lord Chancellor's powers in terms of making provision for the purposes of remuneration allowable to representatives for work undertaken in ARA cases (which he has done, see below).

(3) The new regulations

19.191 The new regulations were introduced by the Proceeds of Crime Act 2002 (Legal Expenses in Civil Recovery Proceedings) Regulations 2005, SI 2005 3382, which came into force on the 1 January 2006 (see reg 1).

(4) Legal expenses at the conclusion of proceedings

19.192 Part 4 of the Regulations deals with the agreement or assessment of expenses at the conclusion of civil recovery proceedings. It sets out the procedure for determining the amount payable in respect of legal expenses once the High Court has made a recovery order which vests property in the trustee for civil recovery and provides for the payment of those expenses out of that property. If the expenses are not agreed with the Director, proceedings must be commenced for them to be assessed by the court. Part 4 applies regardless of whether interim payments have been made under Pt 3, and the amount which must be paid is reduced by the amount of any interim payments.

19.193 Regulation 12 applies where a person seeks the Director's agreement to the payment of a sum in respect of his legal expenses pursuant to s 266(8B)(a) of the 2002 Act or Art 177(11)(a) of the Proceeds of Crime Act 2002 (External Requests and Orders) Order 2005.

E. Legal Expenses in Civil Recovery Proceedings

In determining the amount which may be paid in respect of legal expenses with his agreement, the Director must have regard to the provisions of Pt 5 of the Regulations which apply on the assessment of those expenses by the court (reg 12(2)). Reg 12(3) states: **19.194**

Where the Director agrees to the payment of the sum which a person seeks in respect of his legal expenses –
(a) he shall give that person and the trustee for civil recovery notice of the agreed sum; and
(b) the sum payable in respect of those expenses shall be the agreed sum.

(5) Expenses to be assessed if not agreed

Unless the Director agrees to the payment of the sum which a person seeks in respect of his legal expenses pursuant to a provision made in a recovery order, that person must commence proceedings for the assessment of those expenses in accordance with reg 13(2). **19.195**

(6) Two month time limit

Regulation 13(2) states: **19.196**
(a) In relation to civil recovery proceedings in England and Wales, [a person] must commence proceedings for the detailed assessment of those expenses in accordance with CPR Part 47, subject to the modifications that
  (i) r 47.7 shall have effect as if it provided that he must commence those proceedings not later than two months after the date of the recovery order; and
  (ii) r 47.14(2) shall have effect as if it is provided that he must file a request for a detailed assessment hearing not later than two months after the expiry of the period for commencing the detailed assessment proceedings.

(7) Practice and procedure

The Proceeds of Crime Act 2002 (Legal Expenses in Civil Recovery Proceedings) Reg. 2005 came into force on the 1 January 2006 (see para 1 of SI 2005/3382). Part 2 of those Regulations set out the general conditions required before money can be released to pay legal fees. Pursuant to reg 4 an exclusion must specify: **19.197**

(a) the stage or stages in civil recovery proceedings to which it relates; and
(b) the maximum amount which may be released in respect of legal expenses for each stage to which it relates.

If the solicitor acting for the person to whose legal expenses the exclusion relates, becomes aware that: **19.198**

(a) that person's legal expenses in respect of any stage in civil recovery proceedings have exceeded or will exceed the maximum amount specified in the exclusion for that stage; or
(b) that person's total legal expenses in respect of all the stages to which the exclusion relates have exceeded or will exceed the total amount that may be released pursuant to the exclusion,

the solicitor must give notice to the Director and the court as soon as reasonably practicable.

19.199 This obviously places a pro-active duty upon the solicitor and the respondent's legal advisers. (See reg 5 and PD7A.8.)

19.200 Where a person has incurred legal expenses in relation to a stage in civil recovery proceedings specified in an exclusion:

(a) during any period when a property freezing order or interim receiving order has effect, a sum may only be released in respect of those expenses in accordance with Pt 3 of the Regulations;

(b) where the court makes a recovery order which provides for the payment of that person's reasonable legal expenses in respect of civil recovery proceedings, the sum payable in respect of his legal expenses shall be determined in accordance with Pt 4 of the Regulations, regardless of whether a sum has been released in respect of any of these expenses under Pt 3.

(8) Legal expenses at the commencement of proceedings

19.201 Paragraph 5B.1 of the Civil Recovery Proceedings Practice Direction (not to be confused with the Legal Expenses in Civil Recovery Proceedings Regulations) sets out the court's power to make exclusions for the purpose of enabling a respondent to meet his reasonable legal costs so that he may:

(1) take advice in relation to the order
(2) prepare a statement of assets in accordance with para 7A.3; and
(3) if so advised, apply for the order to be varied or set aside.

19.202 As a result, when a court makes a PFO or an IRO it may also make an exclusion to enable the respondent to meet his reasonable legal costs so that (for example) when the claim is commenced: (1) he may file an Acknowledgment of Service and any written evidence on which he intends to rely; or (2) he may apply for a further exclusion for the purpose of enabling him to meet his reasonable costs of the proceedings. (see PD 5B.2).

19.203 The total amount specified in the initial exclusion will not, according to the Practice Direction, normally exceed £3,000. This clearly affords both the Director and the court some latitude in relation to the amount and there may be instances where initial exclusions will exceed that figure (particularly, for example, if the respondent will have to make inquiries overseas or if a preliminary hearing or conferences are envisaged which require further work, or, if the respondent is divorced from the individual who now holds the appropriate records).

19.204 The Practice Direction also provides that an exclusion made for the purpose of enabling a person to meet his reasonable legal costs should specify:

(1) the stage or stages in civil recovery proceedings to which it relates;
(2) the maximum amount which may be released in respect of legal costs for each specified stage; and
(3) the total amount which may be released in respect of legal costs pursuant to the exclusion (para 7A.7).

E. Legal Expenses in Civil Recovery Proceedings

(9) Considerations for the court

The court, in deciding whether to make an exclusion for the purpose of enabling a person to meet legal expenses in respect of proceedings must: **19.205**

(a) have regard (in particular) to the desirability of the person being represented in any proceedings under this Part in which he is a participant, and
(b) where the person is the respondent, disregard the possibility that legal representation of the person in any such proceedings might, were an exclusion not made, be funded by the Legal Services Commission.

The steer set out at s 252(6) of POCA is amended so that the requirement that the power to make exclusions must be exercised with a view to ensuring that the satisfaction of any right of the enforcement authority to recover the property obtained through unlawful conduct is not unduly prejudiced, is now caveated by making that requirement subject to s 252(4A) introduced by SOCPA. **19.206**

Section 252(6) requires the court to have regard to equality arms arguments and the desirability of persons being legally represented. It tells the court to disregard the possibility that legal representation might be funded by the LSC. **19.207**

The amended subs (4) states as follows: **19.208**

(4) Where the court exercises the power to make an exclusion for the purpose of enabling a person to meet legal expenses that he incurred, or may incur, in respect of proceedings under this Part, it must ensure that the exclusion (a) is limited to reasonable legal expenses that the person has reasonably incurred or that he reasonably incurs, (b) specifies the total amount that may be released for legal expenses in pursuance of the exclusion, and (c) is made subject to the required conditions (see s 286A) in addition to any conditions imposed under sub-section (3).

(10) Practice and procedure: part 3 of the regulations

Part 3 sets out the procedure for the release of frozen property to make interim payments of legal expenses during civil recovery proceedings. Once expenses have been incurred, the person may seek the Director's agreement to the release of an interim payment in respect of those expenses. The amount which may be released is the amount which the Director agrees or 65 per cent of the amount claimed, whichever is the greater. **19.209**

A request for the Director's agreement to the release of a sum in respect of legal expenses must be made in writing to the Director by the person to whose expenses the exclusion relates (see reg 8). **19.210**

The request must describe the stage or stages in the civil recovery proceedings in relation to which the legal expenses were incurred; summarise the work done in connection with each stage; be accompanied by any invoices, receipts or other documents which are necessary to show that the expenses have been incurred; and identify any item or description of property from which the person making the request wishes the sum to be released. **19.211**

A person may not make a request under this regulation in respect of legal expenses which he has not yet incurred; or more than once in any two month period. **19.212**

(11) The Director's response

19.213 Pursuant to reg 9 the Director is required to respond to a request to release legal fees not later than 21 days after he receives the request and such a response must set out: (a) whether he agrees to the release of the requested sum; and (b) if he does not agree to the release of the requested sum (i) the amount (if any) which he agrees may be released; and (ii) the reasons for his decision.

19.214 Where an IRO applies to the property from which it is proposed that the requested sum should be released, the Director must at the same time send copies of the request and the notice referred to in reg 9(1) to the interim receiver.

19.215 In determining the amount which may be released in respect of legal expenses with his agreement, the Director must have regard to the provisions of Pt 5 of the Regulations which set out the basis for assessment of legal expenses and which apply on the assessment of those expenses by the court (reg 9(3)).

(12) Release of an interim payment

19.216 Pursuant to the Legal Expenses Regulations, (reg 10) the sum which may be released is the greater of:

(a) the amount which the Director agrees may be released; and
(b) 65 per cent of the requested sum.

The sum may only be released to (a) the solicitor who is instructed to act in the civil recovery proceedings for the person to whose legal expenses the exclusion relates; or (b) where appropriate, to the solicitor who was so instructed when the legal expenses to which the sum relates were incurred.

19.217 There is no provision for the sum that is to be released to go to the respondents themselves. If the Director does not agree the amount to be released, only 65 per cent of the requested sum may be released at this stage.

(13) Evidence for the purpose of meeting legal costs

19.218 Pursuant to para 7.3 of the Practice Direction, the evidence in support of an application for the purpose of enabling a person to meet his reasonable legal costs must:

(1) contain full details of the stage or stages in civil recovery proceedings in respect of which the costs in question have been or will be incurred;
(2) include an estimate of the costs which the person has incurred and will incur in relation to each stage to which the application relates (see precedent H of the Costs Precedent annexed to the Practice Direction);
(3) include a statement of assets containing the information set out in para 7A.3 (unless the person has previously filed such a statement in the same civil recovery proceedings and there has been no material change in the facts set out in the statement);

E. Legal Expenses in Civil Recovery Proceedings

(4) where the court has previously made an exclusion in respect of any stage to which the application relates, explain why the persons costs will exceed the amount specified in the exclusion for that stage; and

(5) state whether the terms of the exclusion have been agreed with the Director.

(14) Ongoing opportunity

19.219 The Practice Direction goes on to say that when the court makes an order or gives directions in civil recovery proceedings, it will at the same time consider whether it is appropriate to make or vary an exclusion for the purpose of enabling any person affected by the order or directions to meet his reasonable legal costs (see para 7A.1).

(15) Statement of assets

19.220 The court will not make an exclusion for the purpose of enabling a person to meet his reasonable legal costs (other than as provided for by para 5B.1) unless that person has made and filed a statement of assets. Para 7A.3 defines a statement of assets as being a witness statement which sets out all the property which the maker of the statement owns, holds or controls or in which he has an interest, giving the value, location and details of all such property. To that extent it is similar to a disclosure statement provided in restraint proceedings, albeit without the requirement to give details dating back six years. Such a statement must bear a statement of truth.

19.221 Paragraph 7A.3 also provides that the information given in a statement of assets under the Practice Direction will be used only for the purpose of the civil recovery proceedings. What it does not do is provide that the maker of the statement will be afforded some form of guarantee that the information that he or she supplies will not then be utilised by the ARA in terms of pursuing further assets.

(16) Legal expenses following the making of a recovery order

19.222 Pursuant to para 7B.8 of the Civil Recovery Proceedings Practice Direction, where the court:

(1) makes a recovery order in respect of property which was the subject of a property freezing order or interim receiving order; and
(2) had made an exclusion from the property freezing order or interim receiving order for the purpose of enabling a person to meet his reasonable legal costs, the recovery order will make provision under s 266(8A) of POCA or Art 177(10) of the External Requests Order.

19.223 Effectively where the court makes a recovery order which provides for the payment of a person's reasonable legal costs in respect of civil recovery proceedings, it will at the same time make an order for the detailed assessments of those costs, if they are not agreed. Parts 4 and 5 of the Regulations, Part 47 of the Civil Procedure Rules and r 49A of the Practice Direction on Costs apply to a detailed assessment pursuant to such an order (see para 7B.2)

(17) Part 4 of the regulations

19.224 Part 4 sets out the procedure for determining the amount payable in respect of legal expenses once the High Court has made a recovery order which vests property in the trustee for civil recovery and provides for the payment of those expenses out of that property. If the expenses are not agreed with the Director, proceedings must be commenced for them to be assessed by the court. Part 4 applies regardless of whether any interim payments have been made under Pt 3, and the amount which must be paid is reduced by the amount of any interim payments.

(18) Other assets

19.225 The court may set aside any exclusion which it has made for legal expenses or reduce any amount specified in such an exclusion, if it is satisfied that the person has property which the PFO or IRO does not apply to and from which he may meet his legal costs. (PD 7A.4 para 5B.1).

(19) Costs judge assessment

19.226 Where there is dispute, the court will normally refer to a costs judge any question relating to the amount which an exclusion should allow for reasonable legal costs in respect of proceedings or a stage of the proceedings (7A.5).

(20) Basis for assessment of legal expenses

19.227 Part 5 of the Legal Expenses Regulations provides that the court is to assess legal expenses on the standard basis (which is defined in the Rules of Court). It also specifies the hourly rates of remuneration which may be allowed in respect of work done by legal representatives. Higher rates may be allowed for cases involving substantial novel or complex issues of law or fact, and the rates are increased for legal representatives whose offices are situated in certain London post code areas and districts.

19.228 Pursuant to reg 16, the court must give effect to (a) any provision made in the recovery order for the purpose of enabling a person to meet his reasonable legal expenses in civil recovery proceedings; and (b) subject to subpara (a), the terms of any exclusion made for the purpose of enabling that person to meet those legal expenses (including the required conditions).

19.229 The standard basis of assessing a person's legal expenses is set out in CPR r 44.4.

19.230 Remuneration for work done by a legal representative may only be allowed by the appropriate hourly rate shown in the table below:

Table: Rates of remuneration for legal representatives

Category of fee earner	Standard hourly rate (excluding VAT)	Higher hourly rate (excluding VAT)
Solicitors and their employees		
Senior solicitor (of at least 8 years' standing)	£187.50	£225.00
Solicitor (of at least 4 years' and less than 8 years' standing)	£150.00	£187.50
Junior solicitor (of less than 4 years' standing)	£107.50	£131.25

E. Legal Expenses in Civil Recovery Proceedings

Table: Rates of remuneration for legal representatives *(cont.)*

Category of fee earner	Standard hourly rate (excluding VAT)	Higher hourly rate (excluding VAT)
Solicitors and their employees		
Trainee solicitor, paralegal or other fee earner	£75.00	£93.75
Counsel		
Queen's counsel	-	£275.00
Senior junior counsel (of at least 10 years' standing)	£150.00	£225.00
Junior counsel (of less than 10 years' standing)	£100.00	£150.00

19.231 Several points arise from this table. Firstly, in relation to England and Wales, a reference to a number of years standing as a solicitor or counsel is to be interpreted as referring to the number of years of general qualification within the meaning of the Courts and Legal Services Act 1990.

19.232 Secondly, the higher hourly rates as specified in the third column may only be allowed where the case involves substantial novel or complex issues of law or fact. These are not defined further in the Regulations, however, most courts will be adept at recognising same.

19.233 Thirdly, the rates specified in the Table can be increased by 20 per cent for legal representatives whose offices are situated in central London, namely EC1-4, SW1, W1 and WC1-2 and increased by 10 per cent for legal representatives whose offices are situated in outer London (meaning all other post code districts and post code areas including BR, CR, DA, E, N, NW, SE, SW, UB and W).

(21) Civil legal aid

19.234 It is important to note that civil legal aid remains available for cases where access to assets is not possible. Official guidance to solicitors and applicants seeking Community Legal Service funding for proceedings under POCA involving ARA is set out at Appendix 19 of this book. See also Appendix 6 for further information on the availability of LSC funding.

20

CIVIL RECOVERY: RECOVERY ORDERS; PENSIONS; AND THE ECHR

A. Introduction		20.01
(1) The Assets Recovery Agency		20.03
(2) The reduction of crime		20.07
B. Recovery Orders		20.08
(1) Introduction		20.08
(2) Financial threshold		20.10
(3) Claims for a recovery order: practice and procedure		20.11
(4) Procedure the ARA must follow		20.14
(5) Settlement agreements		20.15
(6) Consent orders		20.16
(7) Summary judgment		20.20
(8) What the Director needs to prove		20.29
(9) What is a 'trustee for civil recovery'?		20.39
(10) What are the functions of the trustee?		20.41
(11) Powers of the trustee for civil recovery		20.43
(12) The 12 year limitation		20.45
(13) Rights of pre-emption		20.46
(14) The vesting of recoverable property		20.50
(15) Associated and joint property		20.51
(16) 'Excepted joint owner'		20.53
(17) Agreements about associated and joint property		20.55
(18) How is the amount calculated?		20.58
(19) Associated and joint property: default of agreement		20.63
(20) 'Interest'		20.65
(21) Exclusions, exemptions and exceptions		20.66
(22) Where the court must not make a recovery order		20.68
(23) Related property		20.70
(24) Forfeiture of cash		20.74
(25) Victims of criminal conduct		20.75
(26) Recovery orders and confiscation orders		20.76
(27) Supplementary provisions to s 278		20.78
(28) Declaration of exemption		20.80
(29) Other exemptions		20.83
(30) Exemptions or exceptions to property being 'recoverable'		20.85
(31) Insolvency and recovery orders		20.93
(32) Public interest immunity		20.96
C. The impact of the European Convention on Human Rights on Civil Recovery		20.99
(1) Article 1—interference with property		20.100
(2) Article 6(1)		20.101
(3) Article 6(2)		20.102
(4) Article 7—civil proceedings		20.104
(5) Article 7—a criminal penalty?		20.108
(6) Article 7—retrospectivity		20.115
(7) Article 8		20.118
D. Pension Schemes		20.119
(1) Introduction		20.119
(2) What does a pension scheme mean within this part of the Act?		20.123
(3) 'Trustees or managers'		20.125
(4) The Proceeds of Crime Act 2002 (Recovery from Pension Schemes) Regulations 2003		20.126
(5) Calculation and verification of the value of rights under pension schemes		20.127
(6) Calculation and verification of the value of rights under destination arrangements		20.132
(7) Approval of manner of calculation and verification of the value of rights		20.133
(8) Time for compliance with a pension recovery order		20.135
(9) Costs of the trustees or managers of the pension scheme		20.137
(10) Consequential adjustment of liabilities under pension schemes		20.138
(11) Consent order: pensions		20.141

A. Introduction

20.01 For ease of reference we have divided Civil Recovery into two parts. In this chapter we consider recovery orders themselves; recent decisions concerning the ECHR; and lastly, as part of the Recovery Order scheme, the complex pension provisions.

20.02 In the previous chapter we gave an overview of the legislation in relation to civil recovery and considered the two interim measures anticipated by the amended Act, namely Property Freezing Orders (PFOs) and Interim Receiving Orders (IROs), together with the provisions for the release of funds to cover legal expenses in Assets Recovery Agency cases.

(1) The Assets Recovery Agency

20.03 By June 2005 the Assets Recovery Agency (ARA) had collected £4.6 million since its inception with 200 people being targeted. In addition, the Agency had been given recovery orders to liquidate assets amounting to a further £5.5 million against a target of £13 million, and had frozen assets of a further £16.8 million.

20.04 Objectively the ARA has enjoyed a measurable success before the courts (particularly with challenges to the legislation) but has nevertheless collected less than half of its target figure of £10 million. One of the problems cited was delays with legal aid which created a considerable backlog in applications. The cost of the ARA to June 2005, which employs 162 staff, was £29 million, leading some commentators to question its value for money's worth.

20.05 The purpose of the legislation was considered in *R (on the application of the Director of the Assets Recovery Agency) v Ashton (Paul)* [2006] EWHC (Admin) 1064, where Newman J stated (at para 41):

> What, in my judgment, Parliament is here doing is indeed seeking to enforce some measure of recovery for the benefit of the State. It is seeking to make a recovery for the State which is in the public interest of the State, so that the proceeds of crime should not be at large in society for the benefit of those who happen to be in possession of it at the time.
>
> Crime, when it is committed, is not simply a crime against the individual victim of the crime. Crime, when it occurs, is an offence against the good order of the State and, apart from the victim, it puts the State to enormous expense to resolve questions in connection with crime.

He added at para 46:

> Obviously one of the purposes of this Act is to ensure that those people who are criminals and are in possession of the proceeds of crime, should not be able to continue, according to their criminal propensity, to use the assets that they have acquired in order to further more crime. Thus I find it wholly consistent with the preventative purpose that this statute has, that in s 2(1) the Director's general functions are described as follows:
>
>> The Director must exercise his functions in the way which he considers is best calculated to contribute to the reduction of crime. (see para 46).

20.06 For further on the duties of the Director of the ARA, see para 1.17 of the Introduction to this work. At the time of going to press the Government announced that the Assets Recovery Agency was to be merged with the Serious Organised Crime Agency. This change is likely to take place in April 2008 but is unlikely to affect the substance of the legislation.

B. Recovery Orders

(2) The reduction of crime

20.07 The Director's functions are set out in Pt 1 of the Proceeds of Crime Act 2002 (POCA) and s 2 of the Act, which provides that the Director must exercise his functions in a way that he considers is best calculated to contribute to the reduction of crime. The Secretary of State had issued specific guidance to the Director in relation to this, and the full text of that guidance may be found at Appendix 22 of this book. On 11 January 2007 the Government announced a proposed merger between the ARA and the Serious Organised Crime Agency. As such a change will require legislation this text continues to consider ARA in its present form, as it is anticipated the actual merger will not take place for some time.

B. Recovery Orders

(1) Introduction

20.08 Proceedings for a recovery order may be taken by the Director of the ARA in the High Court against any person who the enforcement authority (the Agency) thinks holds recoverable property (see s 243(1) POCA).

20.09 Section 266(1) of POCA enables the court, if satisfied that any property is recoverable, to make a 'recovery order'. Once made, the recovery order must vest the recoverable property in the 'trustee for civil recovery' (see s 266(2)). In practice this will either be the interim receiver (an insolvency practioner) or an employee of the Director of ARA.

(2) Financial threshold

20.10 Section 287 of the Act anticipates the setting of a figure below which the ARA will not be able to seek a recovery order. That figure has been set at £10,000 (see SI 2003/175).

(3) Claims for a recovery order: practice and procedure

20.11 Under the Civil Recovery Proceedings Practice Direction a claim by the Director for a recovery order must be made using the CPR Part 8 procedure (see para 4.1). The claim form must:

(1) identify the property in relation to which a recovery order is sought;
(2) state, in relation to each item or description of property:
   (a) whether the property is alleged to be recoverable property or associated property; and
   (b) either—
      (i) who is alleged to hold the property; or
      (ii) where the Director is unable to identify who holds the property, the steps that have been taken to try to establish their identity;
(3) set out the matters relied upon in support of the claim; and
(4) give details of the person nominated by the Director to act as trustee for civil recovery in accordance with s 267 of the Act (or article 178 of the External Requests Order).

20.12 The evidence in support of the claim must include the signed, written consent of the person nominated by the Director to act as trustee for civil recovery if appointed by the court (PD4.4)

20.13 References to the claim form also include the Particulars of Claim when they are served subsequently (s 243(4)).

(4) Procedure the ARA must follow

20.14 Under s 243(2) the enforcement authority (ARA) must serve a claim form:
(a) on the respondent, and
(b) unless the court dispenses with service, on any other person who the authority thinks holds any associated property which the authority wishes to be subject to a recovery order, wherever domiciled, resident or present.

(5) Settlement agreements

20.15 The Director will be prepared to settle matters, providing that they are suitable for settlement, and the settlement does not abuse the ARA's strategic aims. With this in mind the ARA has produced a document entitled 'Settlement of Civil Recovery and Tax Cases: Issues for Consideration' which forms the basis for policy in relation to agreeing terms. That full document is reproduced at Appendix 21 of this Book, and a draft Civil Recovery agreement may be found at Appendix 18.

(6) Consent orders

20.16 The court may make an order staying any proceedings for a recovery order on terms agreed by the parties for the disposal of proceedings if each person to whose property the proceedings, or the agreement, relates, is a party both to the proceedings and the agreement (s 276(1)). A consent order, as well as staying the proceedings, may make provision under 276(2) for:
(a) ... any property which may be recoverable property to cease to be recoverable,
(b) [and] make any further provision which the court thinks appropriate.

Section 280 applies to property vested in the trustee for civil recovery, or money paid to him, in pursuance of an agreement. Under s 280(2) the trustee must pay out of the sums that he receives:
(a) first, any payment required to be made by him by virtue of section 272,
(b) second, any payment or expenses incurred by a person acting as an insolvency practitioner which are payable ... by virtue of section 432(10)
and any sum which remains to be paid to the enforcement authority.

(Section 432(10) confirms that whether or not the insolvency practitioner has ceased or disposed of any property, he or she is entitled to payment of their expenses under s 280.)

20.17 This section should now also be read in the light of amendments made to s 280(2) by the Serious Organised Crime and Police Act 2005 (SOCPA), which inserts subpara (aa) and allows for payment of a respondent's agreed legal expenses (see para 19.177 of Chapter 19).

20.18 For consent orders involving pensions see para 20.141 below.

20.19 A draft civil recovery agreement and ARA's settlement policy may be found at Appendicies 18 and 21 respectively.

B. Recovery Orders

(7) Summary judgment

20.20 The Director has adopted the policy of applying for summary judgment, pursuant to Part 24 of the Civil Procedure Rules, in cases where the evidence lodged reveals that a respondent has no real prospect of succeeding on the claim or issue, and there is no other compelling reason why the case should not be disposed of before a hearing (see CPR r 24.2).

20.21 The case of *Director of the Assets Recovery Agency v (1) Ashton (2) Harrison* [2005] All ER(D) 92(May) illustrates the point. Mitting J made a civil recovery order against the second respondent on the basis that there was no real prospect of her showing that certain property represented anything other than assets derived either from her housing benefit fraud or from her son-in-law's criminal activity. This was notwithstanding the fact that the respondent was unrepresented. The Director submitted that it would be fair and just to hear the application nonetheless, as correspondence with the Legal Services Commission suggested that public funding had been granted in principle, although it had yet to receive information that it had requested from the second respondent to finalise the position. His Lordship held that although the principle of equality of arms required that a reasonable opportunity to obtain legal representation be given, public funding was available to the second respondent in principle and would be available if the requested information was provided. The fact that she was not represented was her responsibility, and not that of the State.

20.22 In *Director of the Assets Recovery Agency v Brian Colin Charrington* [2005] EWCA Civ 334, the Court of Appeal considered the position of summary judgments following a decision of Collins J where an order for summary judgment under Part 24 of the CPR had been made. The genesis of the Director's claim was a seizure by Customs in June 1992 of some £2.25 million in cash at the respondent's home after the respondent had been arrested in connection with the importation of very substantial quantities of cocaine into the UK. Factually, the respondent had been an informant and had told officers at the time he was interviewed that he had been acting as an informant and that he had been asked to launder money from the sale of drugs. A note had been found at his premises which appeared to corroborate this. Partly as a result of this a decision was taken that the respondent should not be prosecuted (see para 4 of their Lordships' judgment). The burden therefore fell on the Director to prove that the cash in question was the proceeds of crime.

20.23 The defence put forward by the respondent was that the cash represented a commission paid to him for his part in a legitimate transaction concerning diamonds and had nothing whatsoever to do with the importation of drugs or laundering the proceeds of criminal drug sales. Two statements were deployed in support of this case. Collins J held at first instance that:

> It is a strong thing to give summary judgment without the matter being tested by the giving of evidence and cross-examination of relevant witnesses. But it is necessary for me to form a view if this application is brought before me. It seems to me that the story that is now given is truly incredible. Everything that was said at the material time and the note that was discovered (and I of course recognise that he now says it was a fabrication) all point in the direction that Charrington was indeed involved and heavily involved in these importations of cocaine and was laundering the money on behalf of those who were behind the importation. That is what he admitted, that is what he told a number of officers, that was the information that he

himself gave in order to enable himself not to be prosecuted. At no time was the diamond suggestion raised until the question arose of seeking this confiscation, for want of a better word, on behalf of the Director of the Assets Recovery Agency.

20.24 Collins J stated that in the circumstances he had no hesitation whatever in rejecting the evidence that was now sought to be relied upon. He said:

'I cannot imagine that any judge would believe it, were it to be put forward.'

20.25 In the Court of Appeal, Laws LJ held that in his judgment, on the material before him, Collins J was not only right but 'obviously right' to dismiss the respondent's explanation out of hand for all the reasons which he had given.

20.26 In *Woodstock v Director of the Assets Recovery Agency* (CA, 18 May 2006), however, the Court of Appeal held that where at a summary judgment stage it was not possible to say that a respondent was bound to be disbelieved, on his contention that the source of his money was loaned from friends as opposed to being from unlawful conduct, there was a triable issue that needed to be determined and in such circumstances summary judgment was not an appropriate remedy.

20.27 In *Woodstock* the respondent had been in custody for a substantial part of the period during which he had been directed to supply evidence as to his assets, and LSC funding had not been in place for most of that time. In their Lordships' opinion the ARA had a prima facie case that the source of the money must have been from unlawful conduct given the absence of any known legitimate source; but this needed to be balanced with the fact that the respondent also had a prima facie case that the money had been borrowed from friends.

20.28 There is nothing to prevent respondents also seeking summary judgment in a civil recovery claim (or its striking out) if the particulars of claim are not sufficiently clear or pertinent, or contain insufficient material to support the claim. However where inferences may be drawn from the particulars, or where the pleadings were sufficiently clear such an application would be unlikely to succeed (see *Director of the Assets Recovery Agency v Olupitan and Makinde* [2006] EWHC (Admin) 1906).

(8) What the Director needs to prove

20.29 It is submitted that the language of Pt 5 is somewhat equivocal in terms of what the Director must identify and prove in relation to the alleged unlawful conduct. On the one hand it may be suggested that the Director must prove the unlawful conduct and show its nexus to the funds that have been used to purchase the property sought by way of civil recovery. On the other hand, it may be argued that it is sufficient for the Director to prove that there is no lawful source for the respondent's assets and lifestyle leading to an inference that his property was obtained through unlawful conduct.

20.30 The purpose and object of the Act is to ensure that individuals who are enjoying the benefit of their crime are deprived of the proceeds. It should be remembered that the Director does not normally act without a referral from a law enforcement or prosecuting agency and this will usually follow an investigation or a failed prosecution. It should also be remembered that the burden of proof that the property is recoverable is with the Director, albeit on a civil standard.

20.31 Often proving an unlawful source where it has been heavily disguised will be a difficult task, whereas for the respondent it will usually be easy to demonstrate that a particular asset has come from a lawful source.

20.32 In *Director of the Assets Recovery Agency v He and Chen*, Collins J held (at p 66) that the standard of proof required under s 241(3) is the balance of probabilities, a standard to which the court 'should not place a gloss upon, so as to require that the standard approach is that appropriate in a criminal case'.

20.33 Section 242(2)(b) provides in terms that it is not necessary to show that the conduct was a particular kind if it is shown that the property was obtained through conduct of one of a number of kinds, each of which would have been unlawful conduct.

20.34 In the *Director of the Assets Recovery Agency v Green* [2005] EWHC (Admin) 3168 Sullivan J held that the Director need neither allege nor prove the commission of any specific criminal offence. However, nor should he merely set out the matters that are alleged to constitute the particular kind or kinds of unlawful conduct. He must prove that, on the balance of probabilities, the property was obtained by or in return for a particular kind or one of a number of kinds of unlawful conduct (para 50).

20.35 He also held that a claim for civil recovery could not be sustained solely upon the basis that a defendant had no identifiable lawful income to warrant his lifestyle.

20.36 > The purpose of the Act was to strike a fair balance between the interests of the State and society in general and the civil rights of the individual. If Parliament had wished the Agency to be able to recover property simply by alleging and thereafter persuading the court on the balance of probabilities that it had been obtained by or in return for some unspecified unlawful conduct, it could have said so, but it had not.

20.37 Criminal conduct is by its nature committed in secrecy and direct evidence is often lacking. Juries are regularly invited to infer facts from the evidence. It is submitted therefore that a court in a civil action may also draw inferences from circumstantial evidence as to the fact of unlawful conduct of one sort or another and it follows there is no further requirement to identify any particular crime. Nor is there any obvious need for a respondent to know the specific or general nature of the crime complained of in order to be able to explain the lawful provenance or legitimacy of the property in question.

20.38 In *Director of Assets Recovery Agency v Prince* [2006] EWHC (Admin) 1080, Silber J held that the Director of the ARA was entitled to a recovery order in circumstances where although the first respondent was only convicted of possessing cannabis with intent to supply, there was evidence that he was an active drug dealer who made substantial sums from those activities. It could also be shown that the properties were obtained using those proceeds. Other elements of the account put forward were not credible in his Lordship's opinion. (For proceedings on acquittal see *Director of Assets Recovery Agency v Taher and Ors* [2006] EHWC 3406 (Admin).)

(9) What is a 'trustee for civil recovery'?

20.39 A trustee for civil recovery is a person appointed by the court to give effect to a recovery order (s 267(1)). Whenever a court makes a recovery order or a consent order under s 276, the

Chapter 20: Civil Recovery: Recovery Orders; Pensions; and the ECHR

court must also appoint a trustee for civil recovery. It is the duty of the enforcement agency (the ARA) to nominate a suitably qualified person for the appointment (see s 267(2)).

20.40 The person nominated is likely to be the interim receiver in situ, or an insolvency practitioner (the Director retains an 'approved' list of suitably qualified individuals and firms), or an employee of the ARA. Much will depend upon the complexity and issues involved in realising the assets in question. If, for example, assets are held outside of the jurisdiction, a Trustee in the form of an insolvency practioner is likely to be appointed, because of the jurisdictional issues involved. If, on the other hand, the realisation is a straightforward matter over a modest number of assets, the Director is likely to nominate a member of his staff, not least because it is more cost effective to do so.

(10) What are the functions of the trustee?

20.41 The functions of the trustee are:

267(3)(a) to secure the detention, custody or preservation of any property vested in him by the recovery order,
   (b) in the case of property other than money, to realise the value of the property to the benefit of the enforcement authority, and
   (c) to perform any other functions conferred on him by virtue of [Chapter 5].

Under s 267(4) of the Act, in performing his functions the trustee acts on behalf of the enforcement authority and must comply with any directions given by that authority. This gives rise to the question of independence. In the case of receivers they will be not only dependent on the ARA for instructions, but also dependent on the ARA for future work.

20.42 The trustee's duty is to realise the value of the property vested in him by the recovery order, so far as practicable, in the manner best calculated to maximise the amount payable to the enforcement authority. In this regard the duty is very similar to an enforcement receiver under the DTA and CJA.

(11) Powers of the trustee for civil recovery

20.43 Schedule 7 to POCA sets out the powers of the trustee for civil recovery. They are as follows:

(1) The power to sell the property or any part of it or interest in it.
(2) The power to incur expenditure for the purpose of—
   (a) acquiring any part of the property, or any interest in it, which is not vested in him,
   (b) discharging any liabilities, or extinguishing any rights, to which the property is subject.
(3)
   (a) The power to manage property;
   (b) Managing property involves doing anything mentioned in paragraph 5(2) of Schedule 6. [See Appendix 13].
(4) The power to start, carry on or defend any legal proceedings in respect of the property.
(5) The power to make any compromise or other arrangements in connection with any claim relating to the property.
(6)
   (a) For the purposes of or in connection with, the exercise of any of his powers—
      (i) power by his official name to do any of the things mentioned in subparagraph (2),
      (ii) power to do any other act which is necessary or expedient.

(b) Those things are—
  (i) holding property,
  (ii) entering into contracts,
  (iii) suing and being sued,
  (iv) employing agents,
  (v) executing a power or attorney, deed or other instrument.

20.44 It has already been noted that references to a recovery order include an order under s 276 (consent orders) and references to 'property vested in a trustee by a recovery order' include property vested in him in pursuance of an order under s 276 (see s 267(7)).

(12) The 12 year limitation

20.45 Section 288 of POCA adds s 27A to the Limitation Act 1980. It deals with actions for recovery of property obtained through unlawful conduct and states that none of the time limits given in the Limitation Act apply to any proceedings under Chapter 2 of Pt 5 of POCA 2002 (civil recovery of the proceeds of unlawful conduct). Under s 27A(2):

Proceedings under that chapter [Chapter 2 of Pt 5 of POCA] for a recovery order in respect of any recoverable property shall not be brought after the expiration of the period of 12 years from the date on which the Director's cause of action accrued.

Proceedings are brought when (a) a claim form is issued, or (b) an application is made for an interim receiving order, whichever is the earlier.

(13) Rights of pre-emption

20.46 Under s 269 of POCA, recovery orders take precedence and have effect in relation to any property, despite circumstances where provision (of whatever nature) would otherwise prevent, penalise, or restrict the vesting of the property.

20.47 The right of pre-emption, the right of irritancy, the right of return, or other similar rights do not operate or become exercisable once property has been vested under a recovery order (see s 269(2) which defines a right of return as any right under a provision for the return or aversion of property in specified circumstances).

20.48 It follows that a person who has the first right to buy a property when it changes hands will not be able to exercise his right to prevent the vesting of recoverable property in the trustee by the recovery order. He should, however, have first right to buy the property when the trustee comes to sell it (s 269(3)).

20.49 Under s 283(6) if a person holding any such right suffers a loss as a result of the property vesting in the trustee he is entitled to apply to the court for compensation and the court may order compensation to be paid (s 283(8)).

(14) The vesting of recoverable property

20.50 Under s 266(8) a recovery order may impose conditions as to the manner in which the trustee for civil recovery may deal with any property vested in the order for the purpose of realising it, and under s 266(7) a recovery order may sever any property. It should be noted that s 266 is subject to both s 270, which deals with associated and joint property (below) and ss 271 to 278, which deal with associated and joint property, payments in respect of pension schemes, consent orders, and limits on recovery.

(15) Associated and joint property

20.51 Section 271 of POCA (agreements about associated and joint property) and s 272 (associated and joint property: default of agreement) apply if the court makes a recovery order in respect of any recoverable property which falls within the following four categories (see s 270(1) to (3)):

(a) the property to which the proceedings relate includes property which is associated with the recoverable property and is specified or described in the claim form and
(b) if the associated property is not the respondent's property the claim form or application form has been served on the person whose property it is or the court has dispensed with service,
(c) the recoverable property belongs to joint tenants, and
(d) one of the tenants is an excepted joint owner.

20.52 Sections 270 to 272 have been created because joint tenants are, as a matter of law, treated as though they are the single owner of the property in issue. That would also include joint bank accounts or real property held jointly.

(16) 'Excepted joint owner'

20.53 Under s 270(4) which came into force on 30 December 2002 (SI 2002/3015):

(4) An excepted joint owner is a person who obtained the property in circumstances in which it would not be recoverable as against him; and references to the excepted joint owner's share of the recoverable property are to so much of the recoverable property as would have been his if the joint tenancy had been severed.

20.54 For a definition of associated property see s 245 and para 19.30 of Chapter 19.

(17) Agreements about associated and joint property

20.55 Section 271 is intended to deal with situations where an agreement can be reached with the ARA so that the recovery order may require a person to make a payment to the trustee rather than vesting property in the trustee.

20.56 Where s 271 of POCA applies, and the ARA and the person who holds the associated property who is the excepted joint owner agree, the recovery order may, instead of vesting the recoverable property in the trustee for civil recovery, require the person who holds the associated property or who is the excepted joint owner to make a payment to the trustee (s 271(1)).

20.57 A recovery order which makes such a requirement may, so far as is required for giving effect to the above agreement, include provision for vesting, creating, or extinguishing any interest in property. In effect the joint owner is buying out the interest the enforcement authority has in the property.

(18) How is the amount calculated?

20.58 The amount of the payment is the amount which the enforcement authority and the person who holds the associated property or who is the excepted joint owner agree represents:

B. Recovery Orders

(a) in a case within s 270(2), the value of the recoverable property,
(b) in a case within s 270(3), the value of the recoverable property less the value of the excepted joint owner's share.

20.59 Section 270(2) deals with situations (a) and (b) mentioned at para 20.51 above. Section 270(3) deals with (c) and (d) also mentioned at para 20.51 above (s 271(1) to (3)).

20.60 However, if an IRO applied at any time to the associated property or joint tenancy, and the ARA agrees that the person has suffered a loss as a result of the IRO, the amount of the payment may be reduced by any amount the ARA and that person agree is reasonable, having regard to that loss and to any other relevant circumstances (see s 271(4)).

20.61 If there is more than one such item of associated property or excepted joint owner, the total amount to be paid to the trustee and the part of that amount which is to be provided by each person who holds any such associated property or who is an excepted joint owner, is to be agreed between both (or all of them) and the ARA.

20.62 Upon agreement, the recovery order must provide that the property concerned ceases to be recoverable (see s 271(6)).

(19) Associated and joint property: default of agreement

20.63 Section 272 applies where no agreement can be reached in relation to either associated or joint property, but the court thinks it would be just and equitable to make provision concerning that property (see s 272(1)). Under s 272(2) the recovery order may provide:

(a) for the associated property to vest in the trustee for civil recovery or (as the case may be) for the excepted joint owners interest to be extinguished or,
(b) in the case of an excepted joint owner, for the severance of his interest.

In relation to s 272(2)(a) above, a recovery order may also provide:

(a) for the trustee to pay an amount to the person who holds the associated property or who is an excepted joint owner, or
(b) for the creation of interests in favour of that person, or the imposition of liabilities or conditions, in relation to the property vested in the trustee, or for both. (See s 272(3))

20.64 Pursuant to s 272(4), when making provision in a recovery order for subss (2) or (3) the court must have regard to the following:

(a) the rights of any person who holds the associated property or who is an excepted joint owner and the value to him of that property or, as the case may be, of his share (including any value which cannot be assessed in terms of money),
(b) the enforcement authority's interest in receiving the realised proceeds of the recoverable property.

Section 272(4)(a) particularly acknowledges the rights of third parties and directs the court ot take into account those rights.

(20) 'Interest'

20.65 'Interest' in relation to land held in England and Wales means any legal estate and any equitable interest or power. In relation to property other than land, 'interest' includes any right 'including a right of possession of the property' (see s 316(1)).

(21) Exclusions, exemptions and exceptions

20.66 Exclusions to recovery orders are provided for under s 266(3):

(a) any provision in respect of any recoverable property if each of the conditions in subsection (4) . . . is met and it would not be just and equitable to do so, or

(b) any provision which is incompatible with any of the convention rights (within the meaning of the Human Rights Act 1998).

Under s 266(4) the conditions referred to in subs (3)(a) are that:

(a) the respondent obtained the recoverable property in good faith,

(b) he took steps after obtaining the property which he would not have taken if he had not obtained it or he took steps before obtaining the property which he would not have taken if he had not believed he was going to obtain it,

(c) when he took the steps he had no notice that the property was recoverable,

(d) if a recovery order were made in respect of the property, it would, by reason of the steps, be detrimental to him.

20.67 In deciding whether it would be 'just and equitable' to make a provision in the recovery order where the conditions set out in s 266(4) are met, the court must have regard to:

(6) (a) the degree of detriment that would be suffered by the Respondent if the provision were made,
(b) the enforcement authority's interest in receiving the realised proceeds of the recoverable property.

(See also s 308(1).)

It should be further noted that the exemptions set out at s 281 (victims of theft) and s 282 (other exemptions) apply to this section of the Act.

(22) Where the court must not make a recovery order

20.68 Under s 278(3) the court is not to make a recovery order if it thinks that the enforcement authority's right to recover the original property has been satisfied by a previous recovery order under s 276 (a consent order).

20.69 Section 278(1) applies if ARA seeks a recovery order in respect of both property which is or represents property obtained through unlawful conduct and related property; or in respect of property which is or represents property obtained through unlawful conduct where a recovery order (or an order under s 276—consent orders) has previously been made in respect of related property.

(23) Related property

20.70 Under s 278(2):

(2) For the purposes of this section—
(a) the original property means the property obtained through unlawful conduct,
(b) the original property, and any items of property which represent the original property, are to be treated as related to each other.

Under subs (5), the court may, in order to satisfy the enforcement authority's right to recover the original property, make a recovery order in respect of:

(a) only some of the related items of property, or
(b) only part of any of the related items of property, or both.

B. Recovery Orders

In other words, the power to make a recovery order still subsists with the court, and any property which has not been the subject to a previous recovery order within the claim is not itself excluded. The court may act under subs (5) if it thinks that:

(4) (a) . . . a recovery order may be made in respect of two or more related items of recoverable property, but
(b) the making of a recovery order in respect of both or all of them is not required in order to satisfy the enforcement authority's right to recover the original property.

It will be noted that under s 305 (the provision that deals with the tracing of property), where property obtained through unlawful conduct ('the original property') is or has been recoverable, property which represents the original property is also recoverable property. **20.71**

Under s 278(6) where the court has made the recovery order in respect of any property, s 278 does not prevent the recovery of any profits which have accrued in respect of that property. **20.72**

In *Satnam Singh v Director of the Assets Recovery Agency* [2005] EWCA Civ 580, it was held that if an order were quashed on appeal (in *Singh* a confiscation order), for example on a technicality, the fact the order was made over the property in question once before did not prohibit the ARA from making a further claim (see para 20.90 below). **20.73**

(24) Forfeiture of cash

If an order is made under s 298 for the forfeiture of cash, and the enforcement authority (ARA) subsequently seeks a recovery order in respect of related property, the order under s 298 is to be treated, for the purposes of s 278, as if it were a recovery order obtained by the ARA in respect of the forfeited property. This avoids double counting and/or the proceeds of the same criminal conduct being recovered twice (see also s 282(1)). **20.74**

(25) Victims of criminal conduct

Section 278(8) is designed to ensure that where a victim of unlawful conduct has recovered, through civil litigation, property which was obtained through unlawful conduct, the enforcement authority cannot secure an order under the civil recovery scheme for that property (see also s 281). **20.75**

(26) Recovery orders and confiscation orders

Sections 278(9) and (10) deal with the circumstance where property has been taken into account in deciding the amount of the person's benefit from criminal conduct for the making of a confiscation order and the ARA subsequently seek a recovery order in respect of the same property. For the purposes of s 278(9) the confiscation order is to be treated as if it were a recovery order. This again avoids double counting and/or the proceeds of the same criminal conduct being recovered twice. **20.76**

In *Satnam Singh v Director of the Assets Recovery Agency* [2005] EWCA Civ 580, it was held that if a confiscation order was quashed on appeal, for example on a technicality, the ARA would not be prevented from making a Civil Recovery claim (see para 20.90 below and s 308(9)). **20.77**

(27) Supplementary provisions to s 278

20.78 Section 279 gives examples of the satisfaction of the enforcement authority's right to recover original property. Section 279(2) states:

(2) If—
   (a) there is a disposal, other than a part of disposal, of the original property, and
   (b) other property (the representative property) is obtained in its place, the enforcement authority's right to recover the original property is satisfied by the making of a recovery order in respect of either the original property or the representative property.

(3) If—
   (a) there is a part disposal of the original property and
   (b) other part property (the representative property) is obtained in place of the property disposed of, the enforcement authority's right to recover the original property is satisfied by the making of a recovery order in respect of the remainder of the original property together with either the representative property or the property disposed of.

20.79 The Proceeds of Crime Act 2002 (Exemptions from Civil Recovery) Order 2003, SI 2003/336 provides that certain property is not recoverable property for the purposes of Pt 5 of POCA 2002, eg s 27 of the Misuse of Drugs Act 1971, s 6 of the Knives Act 1997, s 43 of the DTA, s 3 of the Obscene Publications Act 1959, and s 23 of the Terrorism Act 2000 and less used statutes such as the Salmon and Freshwater Fisheries (Protection) (Scotland) Act 1951 and other enactments. This is because these sections make particular provision for forfeiture themselves.

(28) Declaration of exemption

20.80 Sections 281 and 283 set out exemptions to the recovery order scheme. Unders 281(1) where a person affected by a recovery order claims that any property alleged to be recoverable property, or any part of the property, belongs to him, he may apply for a declaration under s 281. The court may make a declaration to the effect sought by the person claiming the property providing the following conditions are met:

(3) (a) the person was deprived of the property he claims, or of property which it represents, by unlawful conduct
   (b) the property he was deprived of was not recoverable property immediately before he was deprived of it, and
   (c) the property he claims belongs to him.

20.81 It follows that if the court makes a declaration, the property is not recoverable property (subs (4)). Section 281 therefore gives a true owner precedence over the ARA for property which, for example, has been stolen in the past. 'The court' means the High Court (see s 316(1)).

20.82 Any unlawful conduct will suffice, and it does not have to be the subject matter which the ARA have been investigating or bringing proceedings under. However, the person who makes the claim must have true title to the property concerned (s 281(3)(c) and s 278(8)).

(29) Other exemptions

20.83 Section 282 lists the circumstances in which proceedings for a recovery order may not be taken. They include:

B. Recovery Orders

(1) Proceedings in respect of cash found at any place in the UK, unless the proceedings are also taken in respect of property other than cash which is property of the same person. This means that the ARA may not take civil recovery proceedings in respect of cash alone; unless they are simultaneously taking proceedings against other property held by the same person. (Cash seizures fall within the domain of either the police or HM Revenue and Customs.)

(2) Proceedings against the Financial Services Authority in respect of any recoverable property held by the Authority.

(3) Proceedings which relate to a collateral security charge; a market charge; a money market charge; or a system charge (s 282(4)).

(4) Proceedings against any person in respect of any recoverable property which he holds by reason of his acting, or having acted, as an insolvency practitioner ('acting as an insolvency practitioner' is defined by s 433).

20.84 Further the Secretary of State may add to this list of exemptions in a prescribed order (see s 282(1)). Any such order must be approved by both Houses of Parliament (see s 459(6)(a)).

(30) Exemptions or exceptions to property being 'recoverable'

20.85 Under ss 308–310 there are certain general exceptions and exemptions to the civil recovery rules, some of which appear to be repetitive of the above.

20.86 General exceptions include a situation where a person disposes of recoverable property and the person who obtains it on the disposal does so in good faith, for value and without notice that it was recoverable property. In such circumstances the property may not be followed into the persons hands and, accordingly it ceases to be recoverable (s 308(1) and s 266(4)).

20.87 Similarly, if in pursuance of a judgment in civil proceedings the defendant makes a payment to the claimant or the claimant otherwise obtains property from the defendant (which may otherwise have been recoverable property), that payment (property) ceases to be recoverable (see s 308(3)). Alternatively, if a payment is made to a person in pursuance of a compensation order under s 130 of the PCC(S)A 2000, the payment (property) ceases to be recoverable (s 308(4)).

20.88 If a payment is made to a person in pursuance of a restitution order under s 148(2) of the PCC(S)A 2000 or a person otherwise obtains any property/money in pursuance of such an order, the property ceases to be recoverable. A similar provision applies in respect of restitution orders under s 308(6) and (7).

20.89 Under s 308(8), the property is not recoverable while a restraint order applies under ss 41, 120, or 190 of POCA. Nor is it recoverable if it has already been taken into account in deciding the amount a person has benefited from for the purpose of making a confiscation order (see s 308(9) and s 278(9) and (10)).

20.90 In *Satnam Singh v Director of the Assets Recovery Agency* [2005] EWCA Civ 580, the Court of Appeal held (at para 18) that where a previous court had quashed a confiscation order it must inevitably follow that no order was made 'under the corresponding provision' of a relevant enactment for the purposes of s 308(9) of POCA. This, in the view of Latham LJ, was 'precisely what Parliament intended'. The purpose of s 308(9) was to prevent double recovery. He stated at para 19:

Its effect is to ensure that the only mechanism for recovery in relation to property taken into account if a confiscation order has been made is that provided for under the confiscation order. But if criminal proceedings are brought, but no confiscation order is made or the property in question has not been taken into account in determining benefit for the purpose of any confiscation order that has been made, I can see no justification under the 2002 Act for precluding the respondent from seeking to obtain a recovery order in relation to the proceeds of crime.

20.91 He went on to hold that the clear intention of Parliament was to ensure that, so far as possible, criminals should be deprived of the possibility of benefiting from their own crimes:

> To permit the technicality which resulted in the confiscation order being quashed to preclude recovery by the civil recovery route would be to perpetrate a mischief which the 2002 Act was clearly designed to prevent.

20.92 Other exemptions within the Act include where an order provides that property is not recoverable if it is prescribed property or if it is disposed of in pursuance of a prescribed enactment (see s 309(1) and (2)). 'Prescribed property' means prescribed by an order made by the Secretary of State, (see s 309(4)). (Any order made by the Secretary of State is subject to the affirmative resolution procedure provided under s 459(6)(a) of POCA.)

(31) Insolvency and recovery orders

20.93 Proceedings for a recovery order may not be taken or continued in respect of property which falls under the following categories, unless the appropriate court gives leave and the proceedings are taken (or as the case may be) continued in accordance with the terms imposed by that court (see s 311(1) and (3)):

(a) an asset of a company being wound up;
(b) an asset of a company and a voluntary arrangement under Part 1 of the Insolvency Act 1986;
(c) an order under s 286 of the Insolvency Act 1986;
(d) an asset comprised of an estate of an individual who has been adjudged bankrupt;
(e) an asset of an individual and a voluntary arrangement under Part 8 of the Insolvency Act 1986.

20.94 An application under s 311, or under any provision of the Insolvency Act 1986, for leave to take proceedings for a recovery order may be made without notice to the person, (an *ex p* application). That however does not affect any requirement for notice of an application to be given to any person acting as an insolvency practitioner or to the official receiver (see s 311(4) and (5)).

20.95 Insolvency and civil recovery is also considered at para 19.115 of Chapter 19.

(32) Public interest immunity

20.96 The issue of public interest immunity in civil recovery proceedings arose in the case of *Director of the Assets Recovery Agency v Personal Representative of Paul Patrick Daly (Dec'd)* [2006] NIQB 36, where Coghlin J was shown some 87 intelligence documents referred to in an affidavit. It was thereafter submitted that having carried out an ex parte exercise he should recuse himself from sitting as a judge for the purpose of determining the substantive recovery order proceedings. Coghlin J accepted that the concept of fairness enshrined in Article 6 of the ECHR should be considered in this context. He balanced the interests of the parties with the efficient operation of the justice system, including additional delays,

C. The Impact of the European Convention on Human Rights on Civil Recovery

expense and frustration on the part of other litigants which were likely to result from a decision to split the function of determining disclosure from that of determining the substantive issues (paras 8 and 9). Taking those matters into account, he stated that the basic test remained that set out by Lord Steyn in *Lawal v Northern Spirit Ltd* [2004] 1 All ER 197 at para 22, namely the 'indispensable requirements of public confidence in the administration of justice'.

He observed that in *R v May* [2005] 3 All ER 523, the judge had dealt with several PII applications and then went on to deal with confiscation proceedings brought under the Criminal Justice Act 1988. In that case the appellant had relied upon the decision of the Strasbourg Court in *Edwards v UK* [2004]ECHR 39647/98. In the Court of Appeal, Keene LJ attributed considerable importance to the judge's statement in *May* that he had ignored anything revealed to him which attracted public interest immunity, and felt able to distinguish the case of *May* from *Edwards v UK*. 20.97

In *Edwards* the court had not been pronouncing upon a situation in which the judge had expressly stated that he had ignored the undisclosed material for the purpose of a subsequent ruling, but had been concerned with a situation in which the judge made a determinative ruling on an issue of fact which he had decided by reference to undisclosed material.

And there it seems the distinction lies. As a result in *Daly*, Coghlin J was quite satisfied that he could exclude from his consideration the reports/observations that he had been shown in ex parte hearings, and thus was able to go on and consider the recovery order claim. 20.98

C. The Impact of the European Convention on Human Rights on Civil Recovery

The ECHR has featured in a number of ARA cases, as perhaps it inevitably would bearing in mind the controversial nature of the legislation. 20.99

(1) Article 1— interference with property

In *Director of the Assets Recovery Agency v (1) Jia Jin He (2) Dan Dan Chen* [2004] EWHC (Admin) 3021 Collins J considered Article 1 of the First Protocol which prohibits interference with property. He referred to the Italian cases of *Arcuri v Italy (Application No 52024–99)* and *M v Italy (Application No 12386–86)*, where the European Court had held that recovery provisions did not fall foul of Article 1, provided that the measure in question was regarded as proportionate. At para 74 Collins J stated, in upholding the principle: 20.100

> Whilst the situation in this country is not, I hope, as dire as that represented by the activities of the Mafia in Italy, nonetheless Parliament has quite clearly decided that these measures are necessary in order to fight crime, and in particular to ensure, as far as possible, that those involved in crime should be unable to enjoy the fruits of their criminal activities.

(2) Article 6(1)

In the *Director of the Assets Recovery Agency v Satnam Singh* [2004] EWHC Admin 2335 McCombe J rejected an argument advanced in relation to Article 6(1) of the European Convention that sought to join the overall length of the criminal proceedings with those of 20.101

the recovery proceedings (a total of nine years from arrest for the substantive matter). While Article 6(1) provides that in the determination of the civil rights and obligations of an individual (or in criminal proceedings), everyone is entitled to a fair and public hearing 'within a reasonable time', McCombe J was inclined to the view that the recovery proceedings represented separate civil proceedings in which no question of relevant delay arose (para 40).

(3) Article 6(2)

20.102 In *Director of the Assets Recovery Agency v Walsh* [2004]NIQB 21, Coghlin J held that proceedings under the 2002 Act were civil proceedings to which Article 6(2) did not apply. Coghlin J held:

> It seems to me that, in substance, proceedings by way of a civil recovery action under the provisions of Part 5 of POCA differ significantly from the situation of a person charged with a criminal offence within the meaning of Article 6.

20.103 In R *(on the application of the Director of the Assets Recovery Agency) (Paul) v Ashton* [2006] EWHC (Admin) 1064, Newman J held that the imposition of a civil recovery order under s 243 of POCA was not punitive and could not therefore violate Article 6 of the ECHR (no punishment without law). He held that civil recovery orders had a compensatory aspect in that they are a manifestation of Parliament's intention to recover expenses incurred in investigating crime, and the fact that deprivation of property is involved does not constitute a penalty because the holder of the property to which the order relates had no right to hold it in the first place. (See also *Charrington* [2005] EWCA Civ 334).

(4) Article 7—civil proceedings

20.104 Article 7 was specifically referred to in the case of *Director of the Assets Recovery Agency v (1) Jia Jin He (2) Dan Dan Chen* [2004] EWHC (Admin) 3021. In that matter Collins J held that there was 'no doubt' recovery proceedings were civil, and that Article 7 did not apply as no penalty was involved (para 69).

20.105 In a considered judgment, His Lordship reviewed the structure and basis of the Act (para 1 et seq), together with the tests in *Engel v Netherlands (No 1)*(1976) 1 EHRR 647 (at 678–679) which dictate whether proceedings should be classified as civil or criminal (para 49). Furthermore he considered two European authorities, namely *Arcuri v Italy* and *M v Italy (17 DR 59)*, where the European Court settled that preventative confiscation measures that did not involve a finding of guilt do not constitute a penalty (and therefore were not in contravention of Article 7) (see para 56 of the judgment).

20.106 His Lordship went on to consider (in some detail) the standard of proof required in such claims, and concluded that Parliament had intentionally imposed a lower standard in civil recovery proceedings, namely that of the balance of probabilities (para 66).

20.107 In R *(on the Application of the Director of the Assets Recovery Agency) v Paul Ashton* [2006] EWHC (Admin) 1064, Newman J adopted the decision of Collins J in *Jia Jin He* and noted that his Lordship had rejected the suggestion that a heightened civil standard of proof applied where criminal conduct was said to be involved. At para 39 Newman J stated that he regarded the judgments which had preceded this matter to be '*an impeccable catalogue of features which are relevant when considering the issue of Article 7*'.

C. The Impact of the European Convention on Human Rights on Civil Recovery

(5) Article 7—a criminal penalty?

20.108 It is now established that confiscation proceedings, following on and attaching to a criminal conviction, represent a 'penalty', not least because a prison sentence in default flows from non-payment, and the confiscation order is treated as a fine, pursuant to (eg) s 9 of the Drug Trafficking Act 1994. (See *R v Benjafield* [2002] UKHL 2 (para 82); *Rezvi* [2002] UKHL 1 and *Phillips v UK* [2001] EHRR No 41087/98). Part of the reasoning in *Rezvi* was that the purpose of confiscation proceedings was to '... *punish convicted offenders*'.

20.109 The impact of Article 7 and the issue of 'penalty' in civil recovery proceedings was considered by the Court of Appeal in *Director of Assets Recovery Agency v Charrington* [2005] EWCA Civ 334, where Laws LJ embraced the argument that it was untenable to suggest that recovery orders should be treated as criminal (para 17). He described as 'entirely right' both Collins J's ruling (which was not appealed), and that of Coghlin J in the case of *Director of Assets Recovery Agency v Walsh* (QBD NI, 1 April 2004), (first instance) where Coghlin J said:

> ... what seems to me of greater importance is the fact that there is no arrest nor is there any formal charge, conviction, *penalty* or criminal record... (para 18).

20.110 Laws LJ roundly dismissed the argument that the case of *Charrington* should be classified as criminal proceedings for the purposes of Article 6 and Article 7 of the European Convention on Human Rights (para 14). His Lordship adopted the submissions of David Barnard of Counsel who maintained that the argument that proceedings for recovery orders should be treated as criminal for Convention purposes was untenable. He cited the fact that the ECtHR has twice considered and rejected that argument in cash forfeiture proceedings under the DTA, (see *Butler v UK* (2002) App No 41661-98 and *Webb v UK* (2004) App No 56054-00). It was submitted by Mr Barnard that it was inconceivable that the reasoning of the ECHR would not apply equally to the cash forfeiture provisions in Pt 5 of POCA (s 298) which replaced the DTA provisions. It followed that the argument being advanced on behalf of *Charrington* involved inviting the Court of Appeal to decide that the High Court civil recovery procedures under Pt 5 were 'criminal' in nature, whereas the magistrates' court procedures under Pt 5 were to be regarded as 'civil'. Mr Barnard submitted that there was no prospect of the court so holding and Laws LJ concurred with that view and adopted it in his judgment.

20.111 The case of *Walsh* went to appeal in Northern Ireland (Kerr LCJ, Nicholson LJ and Campbell LJ, *Walsh v Director of the Assets Recovery Agency* [2005] NICA 6), and the Court found, applying the three tests set out in *Engel v Netherlands* that:

(1) all the available indicators point strongly to recovery cases being classified as a form of civil proceedings.

> 'the Appellant is not charged with a crime... He is not liable to imprisonment or fine if the recovery action succeeds. There is no indictment and no verdict. The primary purpose of the legislation is restitutionary rather than penal. [para 27]

(2) In terms of the nature of the proceedings the allegation made does not impute guilt and there is no prosecutorial function [para 29].

(3) The primary purpose of the legislation is to recover the proceeds of crime; it is not to punish the appellant in the sense normally entailed in a criminal sanction [para 39].'

20.112 The Court in *Walsh* (which was primarily considering Article 6(1)) refrained from expressing any final view as to whether recovery of assets was penal within the autonomous meaning of the term (see para 39)).

20.113 Subsequently, the matter was further considered in *Scottish Ministers v McGuffie* [2006] SC(D) 26/2, in which the Court was invited to find that the petitioners were seeking to impose a criminal penalty retrospectively by asking for the appointment of an interim administrator pursuant to s 256 of the Act. It was accepted by the respondent that if there were no criminal penalty then his challenge to the petition would fail. Lord Kinclaven, having considered *Walsh* above, stated (see para 127):

> The proceedings are directed against property (*in rem*) rather than against Mr. McGuffie's person. The recovery procedures are under the control of the civil court. Mr. McGuffie's guilt is not in issue. He is not facing a criminal charge. He is not an accused person. He cannot be arrested or remanded or compelled to attend. There has been no formal accusation by the prosecuting authorities. He will not be subject to a criminal conviction or finding of guilt. He will not be imprisoned. He will not receive a sentence. A civil recovery order will not form any part of his criminal record.

20.114 Lord Kinclaven went on to list further features which distinguished civil recovery proceedings:

- The orders sought by the petitioners did not amount to a retrospective criminal penalty within the meaning of art 7 of the Convention.
- The orders sought by the petitioners were part of a regime for the civil recovery of property that was, or represented, property obtained through unlawful conduct rather than a regime of punishment.
- They were not at the instance of the Lord Advocate or a prosecuting authority.
- They had been initiated by civil petition.
- They were being heard in a civil court.
- The procedures involved for making and implementing the order were clearly civil rather than criminal.
- The proceedings were directed against property rather than against the respondent's person.
- The respondent would not be subject to a criminal conviction or a finding of guilt.
- A civil recovery order would not form any part of his criminal record.

For features that distinguish confiscation and civil recovery proceedings see para 19.17 of Chapter 19.

(6) Article 7—*retrospectivity*

20.115 In *Jia Jin He* Collins J held (at para 69):

> The authorities to which I have already referred make it plain that there is no question of any penalty involved in these proceedings. Furthermore, there has been no conviction of a criminal offence leading to a penalty. Of course, property cannot be recoverable unless, at the time it was acquired, it was obtained through unlawful conduct. That conduct must have been criminal at that time. To that extent, the prohibition against retrospectivity will apply, but only because the Act says that the property must be property which was obtained by criminal conduct. In those circumstances, it is quite clear that Article 7 has no application.

In *R (on the Application of the Director of the Assets Recovery Agency) v Paul Ashton* [2006] **20.116**
EWHC (Admin) 1064 Newman J also considered whether the civil recovery procedure
offended Article 7 of the ECHR governing retrospectivity, and found that it did not. (Leave
to appeal his judgment was subsequently refused.)

Similarly in *McGuffie* Lord Kinclaven, stated (at para 127): **20.117**

> In my opinion, on a fair valuation of all the circumstances, the orders sought by the Scottish Ministers in the present case do not amount to a retrospective criminal "penalty" within the meaning of Article 7.

(7) Article 8

In relation to Article 8, the right to family and personal life, Collins J in *Jia Jin He* held it **20.118**
added nothing to what he had said about proportionality in relation to Article 1.

D. Pension Schemes

(1) Introduction

Pension policies can be of great value, but their actual value is often, pursuant to the terms **20.119**
of the pension policy, unrealisable until a certain age, or until the policy itself dictates or
matures. Money paid into a policy tends to become locked in – with even the policy
holder powerless to realise it, or in the alternative, an ability to realise it, but at a considerable undervalue due to the excessive penalties involved and incurred. Parliament appears
to have acknowledged this practical problem and legislated for it accordingly within
POCA. Not only is the realisation of pension schemes and policies at their real value
important to the success of the Act and the recovery of the proceeds of crime, but it would
also represent a considerable loophole in the legislation if those involved in criminal activity were aware that they could pay £10,000s into pension schemes in the safe knowledge
that it would place those funds beyond the reach of the ARA and that in years to come
those individuals could look forward to living off a nest egg representing the proceeds of
ill-gotten gains.

Section 273(1) and (2) of POCA applies to recoverable property consisting of rights under **20.120**
a pension scheme. A recovery order in respect of the property must, instead of vesting the
property in the trustees for civil recovery, require the trustees or managers of the pension
scheme to pay to the trustee within a prescribed period, the amount determined by the
trustees or managers of the pension scheme to be equal to the value of the right, and to give
effect to any other provision made within ss 273, 274, and 275. This is subject to what is
said later in Pt 5 of the Act concerning consent orders (s 276), consent orders and pensions
(s 277), and the limit on recovery (s 278).

The requirement of the trustee or managers of the pension scheme to pay to the trustee for **20.121**
civil recovery an amount equal to the value of the rights of the pension scheme overrides the
provisions of the pension scheme itself, to the extent that if they conflict with the provisions
of the order, the order must take priority (see s 273(3)).

20.122 Subsection (5) of s 273 provides that any statutory provisions, eg s 159 of the Pension Schemes Act 1993, will not frustrate the ARA's or the interim receiver's ability to pursue the recovery of the value of pension rights.

(2) What does a pension scheme mean within this part of the Act?

20.123 A pension scheme means an occupational pension scheme or a personal pension scheme; under s 275(4), these expressions have the same meaning as in the Pension Schemes Act 1993.

20.124 References to a pension scheme also includes retirement annuity contracts; and annuity or insurance policies purchased or transferred for the purposes of giving effect to rights under an occupational pension scheme or a personal pension scheme and/or an annuity purchase, for the purpose of discharging any liability in respect of a pension credit under s 29(1)(b) of the Welfare Reform and Pensions Act 1999.

(3) 'Trustees or managers'

20.125 In relation to an occupational pension scheme or a personal pension scheme, the 'trustees or managers' mean either:

(a) in the case of the scheme established under a trust, the trustees
(b) in any other case, the managers (s 275(5)).

In relation to a retirement annuity contract or other annuity, references to the trustees or managers are to the provider of the annuity, and in relation to an insurance policy references to the trustees or managers are to the insurer (see s 275(7)).

(4) The Proceeds of Crime Act 2002 (Recovery from Pension Schemes) Regulations 2003

20.126 The Proceeds of Crime Act 2002 (Recovery from Pension Schemes) Regulations 2003 were introduced by SI 2003/291 and came into force on 17 March 2003. These Regulations make provision as to the exercise by trustees or managers of pension schemes of their powers when a civil recovery order is made under s 273(2) of POCA and requires them to make a payment to the trustee for civil recovery in respect of the rights of a member of that scheme.

(5) Calculation and verification of the value of rights under pension schemes

20.127 Regulation 2(1) applies where the High Court makes a pension recovery order (other than in respect of rights derived from a pension sharing transaction under a destination arrangement) in a pension scheme.

20.128 It provides for the calculation and verification of the cash equivalent of the value of pension rights which are recoverable property under the Act. This is by reference to the method applying for the purposes of the provision of information in respect of pensions on divorce, separation, and nullity under the Pensions on Divorce etc. (Provision of Information) Regulations 2000, SI 2000/1048 and the equivalent regulations applying in Scotland and Northern Ireland.

D. Pension Schemes

A 'destination arrangement' means a pension arrangement under which some or all of the rights are derived, directly or indirectly, from a pension sharing transaction. A 'pension sharing transaction' means an order or provision falling within s 28(1) of the Welfare Reform and Pensions Act 1999 (activation of pension sharing)). **20.129**

The trustees or managers of the pension scheme in respect of which the pension recovery order has been made must calculate and verify the cash equivalent of the value (at the valuation date of the rights which are the subject of the pension recovery order) and must pay to the trustee for civil recovery a sum equal to that cash equivalent (Regulation 3). **20.130**

In relation to the calculation and verification by the trustees or managers of the cash equivalent referred to above: **20.131**

(a) in the case of a pension scheme wholly or mainly administered in England and Wales, reg 3 of the Pensions on Divorce etc. (Provision of Information) Regulations 2000 (information about pensions and divorce: valuation of pension benefits), except para (2) thereof, shall have effect as it has effect for the valuation of benefits in connection with the supply of information and in connection with domestic and overseas divorce etc. in England and Wales, with the modification that, for 'the date on which the request for the valuation was received' in each case where it appears in that regulation, there shall be substituted 'the valuation date for the purposes of the Proceeds of Crime Act 2002 (Recovery from Pension Schemes) Regulations 2003';

(b) in the case of a pension scheme wholly or mainly administered in Scotland, reg 3 of the Divorce etc. (Pensions) (Scotland) Regulations 2000 (valuation), except para (11) thereof, shall have effect as it has effect for the valuation of benefits in connection with the supply of information in connection with divorce in Scotland, with the modification that, for 'the relevant date' in each case where it appears in that regulation, there shall be substituted 'the valuation date for the purposes of the Proceeds of Crime Act 2002 (Recovery from Pension Schemes) Regulations 2003'; and

(c) in the case of a pension scheme wholly or mainly administered in Northern Ireland, reg 3 of the Pensions on Divorce etc. (Provision of Information) Regulations (Northern Ireland) 2000 (information about pensions on divorce: valuation of pension benefits), except para (2) thereof, shall have effect as it has effect for the valuation of benefits in connection with the supply of information in connection with domestic and overseas divorce etc. in Northern Ireland, with the modification that, for 'the date on which the request for the valuation was received' in each case where it appears in that regulation, there shall be substituted 'the valuation date for the purposes of the Proceeds of Crime Act 2002 (Recovery from Pension Schemes) Regulations 2003.

(6) Calculation and verification of the value of rights under destination arrangements

As stated above, 'destination arrangement' means a pension arrangement under which some or all of the rights are derived, directly or indirectly, from a pension sharing transaction. Regulation 3(1) of the Proceeds of Crime Act 2002 (Recovery from Pension Schemes) Regulations 2003 applies where the High Court makes a pension recovery order in respect of rights derived from a pension sharing transaction under a destination arrangement in a **20.132** pension scheme. The trustees or managers of the pension scheme in respect of which the pension recovery order has been made must calculate and verify the cash equivalent of the value at the valuation date of the rights which are the subject of the pension recovery order and must pay to the trustee for civil recovery a sum equal to that cash equivalent. Regulation 3 provides:

(3) In relation to the calculation and verification by the trustees or managers of the cash equivalent referred to in paragraph (2)—
  (a) in the case of a pension arrangement in a scheme that is wholly or mainly administered in either England and Wales or Scotland, regulation 24 of the Pension Sharing (Pension Credit Benefit) Regulations 2000 (manner of calculation and verification of cash equivalents) shall have effect as it has effect for the calculation and verification of pension credit for the purposes of those regulations; and
  (b) in the case of a pension arrangement in a scheme that is wholly or mainly administered in Northern Ireland, regulation 24 of the Pension Sharing (Pension Credit Benefit) Regulations (Northern Ireland) 2000 (manner of calculation and verification of cash equivalents) shall have effect as it has effect for the calculation and verification of pension credit for the purposes of those regulations.

(7) Approval of manner of calculation and verification of the value of rights

20.133 Regulation 4 makes provision for circumstances where the person with the pension rights which are recoverable property is a trustee or manager of the scheme in question. In such circumstances, an actuary must approve the method of calculation and verification of the cash equivalent value.

20.134 The manner in which the trustees or managers have calculated and verified the value of the rights must be approved by:

(a) a Fellow of the Institute of Actuaries (the Institute of Actuaries is at Staple Inn Hall, High Holborn, London WC1V 7QJ); or
(b) a Fellow of the Faculty of Actuaries (the Faculty of Actuaries is at Maclaurin House, 18 Dublin Street, Edinburgh EH1 3PP).

Regulation 4 goes on to provide:

(3) Where the person referred to in paragraph (2) is not able to approve the manner in which the trustees or managers have calculated and verified the value of the rights which are the subject of a pension recovery order, he must give notice in writing of that fact to the trustee for civil recovery and the trustees or managers of the scheme.
(4) Where the trustees or managers of the scheme have been given notice under paragraph (3), they must re-calculate and re-verify the value of the rights which are the subject of a pension recovery order for the purposes of regulation 2 or 3.

(8) Time for compliance with a pension recovery order

20.135 Regulation 5 prescribes the period for paying the amount of those pension rights to the trustee for civil recovery:

5 (1) In this regulation, 'the prescribed period' means the period prescribed for the purposes of section 273(2)(a) of the Act.

D. Pension Schemes

(2) Subject to paragraphs (3) and (4), the prescribed period is the period of 60 days beginning on the day on which the pension recovery order is made.

Under reg 5(3) where an application for permission to appeal the pension recovery order is made within the period referred to in para (2), the prescribed period is the period of 60 days beginning on:

(a) the day on which permission to appeal is finally refused;
(b) the day on which the appeal is withdrawn; or
(c) the day on which the appeal is dismissed, as the case may be.

5(4) Where the person referred to in regulation 4(2) gives notice, in accordance with regulation 4(3) and within the period referred to in paragraph (2), to the trustee for civil recovery and trustees or managers of the scheme that he is unable to approve the manner in which the trustees or managers have calculated the value of the rights which are the subject of the pension recovery order, the prescribed period is the period of 60 days beginning on the day on which such notice is given.

20.136 'Valuation date' means a date within the period prescribed by regulation 5 in respect of which the trustees or managers of the pension scheme decide to value the relevant person's pension rights in accordance with reg 2 or 3.

(9) Costs of the trustees or managers of the pension scheme

20.137 The trustees or managers of the pension scheme may recover costs incurred by them in:

(a) complying with the recovery order, or
(b) providing information, before the recovery order was made, to the enforcement authority [the ARA], or interim receiver.

(See s 273(4).)

(10) Consequential adjustment of liabilities under pension schemes

20.138 A recovery order made by virtue of s 273(2) must require the trustees or managers of the pension scheme to make such reduction in the liabilities of the scheme as they think necessary in consequence of a payment made in pursuance of s 273(2).

20.139 Accordingly, by s 274(2), the order must require the trustees or managers to provide for the liabilities of the pension scheme to cease in respect of the respondent's recoverable property to which s 273 applies. For provision as to the exercise by trustees or managers of pension schemes of their powers see the Proceeds of Crime (Recovery from Pension Schemes) Regulations 2003, SI 2003/291.

20.140 Section 274(1) envisages that the recovery order itself will include a condition that stipulates that the trustees or managers of the pension scheme will reduce their liabilities to the extent they think necessary following the payment made under the order. Section 274(3) states that the trustees' or managers' powers include the power to reduce the amount of any benefit or future benefit to which the respondent is or may be entitled under the scheme, and any future benefit to which any other person may be entitled under the scheme in respect of that property.

(11) Consent order: pensions

20.141 Section 277 of POCA envisages orders by consent being made where recoverable property includes rights under a pension scheme. Section 277(2) states that:

> A consent order made under section 276—[which deals with consent orders generally in civil recovery, see para 20.16 above]
> (a) may not stay the proceedings on terms that the rights are vested in any other person, but
> (b) may include provision imposing the following requirement, if the trustees or managers of the scheme are parties to the agreement by virtue of which the order is made.

The requirement is that the trustees or managers of the pension scheme make a payment in accordance with the agreement and give effect to any other provision made by virtue of s 277 in respect of the scheme (s 277(3)). Section 277(4):

> (4) The trustees or managers of the pension scheme have power to enter into an agreement in respect of the proceedings on any terms on which [a consent] order made under Section 276 may stay the proceedings.

Section 277(6) makes it clear that a consent order made under s 276 overrides the provisions of the pension scheme to the extent that they conflict with the requirements of the order.

20.142 The consent order may provide for the recovery by the trustees or managers of the scheme (whether by deduction from any amount for which they are required to pay in pursuance of the agreement or otherwise) of costs incurred by them in complying with the order, or providing information before the order was made to the enforcement authority or interim receiver (s 277(7)).

21

RECOVERY AND SEIZURE OF CASH UNDER POCA

A. Introduction	21.01	(9) Release of money over which no suspicion attaches	21.64
(1) The DTA	21.03	D. Continued Detention Hearings: Practice	21.65
(2) The POCA regime	21.05	(1) Form A	21.65
(3) Civil proceedings	21.10	(2) Form B	21.70
B. The Seizure and Forfeiture of Cash	21.12	(3) Form C	21.72
(1) Preliminary matters	21.12	(4) Service of documents	21.73
(2) The circumstances in which cash may be seized	21.13	(5) Procedure at the continued detention hearing	21.74
(3) The minimum amount that may be seized: £1000	21.14	(6) What if the correct forms have not been served or the proper procedure not followed?	21.75
(4) Does the minimum amount need to be in the possession of a single person?	21.15	(7) Insolvency and further detention hearings	21.83
(5) The meaning of 'cash'	21.17	(8) Early release of the cash—to person from whom the cash was seized	21.84
(6) How is 'unlawful conduct' defined?	21.20	(9) Form D	21.87
(7) Does the 'unlawful conduct' have to be specified?	21.21	(10) Applications for early release by victims or other owners	21.91
(8) How is 'recoverable property' defined?	21.25	(11) Section 301(3): victims of unlawful conduct	21.94
(9) The tracing of property	21.28	(12) Form E: Order for release under s 301(3)	21.95
(10) Mixed property	21.29	(13) Section 301(4): third party applications/other owners	21.96
(11) Property that is not 'recoverable'	21.30	(14) Objection to release under s 301(4) from the person from whom the cash was seized	21.97
(12) The re-seizure of cash	21.33	(15) Form F: Order for release under s 301(4)	21.98
(13) Ongoing criminal proceedings	21.34	(16) Joinder	21.99
C. Practice and Procedure	21.35	(17) Applications for the return of the cash: standard of proof	21.100
(1) The initial enquiry	21.35	(18) Can officers agree to the release of cash?	21.102
(2) Procedure prior to the first hearing and venue	21.39	(19) Transfer of proceedings	21.103
(3) The first detention hearing for the seized cash	21.43	(20) Transfer: what test is to be applied?	21.104
(4) Unattended despatches	21.47		
(5) The 48 hour rule	21.51		
(6) The test the court will apply at further detention hearings	21.56		
(7) Interest	21.58		
(8) Interest—What does 'at the first opportunity' mean?	21.60		

E.	**Applications for Forfeiture of Detained Cash**	21.105	H. **Costs and Compensation**	21.165
	(1) Forfeiture proceedings	21.105	(1) Costs under s 64 of the Magistrates' Courts Act 1980	21.171
	(2) Form G	21.106	(2) Legal Services Commission funding	21.174
	(3) Effect of lodging an application	21.112	(3) May funds be released from the detained cash to fund continued detention and forfeiture applications?	21.178
F.	**The Hearing**	21.113	(4) Compensation	21.179
	(1) Hearing for Directions	21.113	(5) Application for compensation	21.186
	(2) What type of directions may be ordered?	21.116	I. **Appeals**	21.187
	(3) The forfeiture hearing	21.119	(1) Appeals against forfeiture	21.187
	(4) Procedure at hearings made on complaint	21.120	(2) Can the 30 day period for the date of the appeal be extended?	21.191
	(5) Order of evidence and speeches	21.124	(3) Funding the appeal	21.192
	(6) Matters to be sworn under oath	21.128	(4) Costs in appeal proceedings	21.193
G.	**Rules of Evidence**	21.129	(5) Judicial review	21.194
	(1) Burden and standard of proof	21.129	J. **Searches and Seizure of Cash**	21.195
	(2) Are previous convictions admissible?	21.132	(1) Cash on premises	21.196
	(3) Is there a need for direct evidence of the unlawful conduct?	21.137	(2) The minimum amount: £1000	21.197
	(4) The drawing of inferences and illustrative cases	21.138	(3) The definition of 'cash'	21.199
	(5) Hearsay in civil cases	21.143	(4) Cash on the suspect	21.201
	(6) Lies told by the defendant	21.148	(5) 'Unlawful conduct'	21.204
	(7) Mass Spec expert reports	21.151	(6) Safeguards for the new search powers	21.205
	(8) Record of proceedings	21.159	(7) Report on exercise of powers	21.210
	(9) Form H: order for forfeiture	21.160	(8) The Code of Practice	21.211
	(10) Sensitive evidence	21.161	(9) Procedure at hearings	21.215
	(11) Joint owners	21.163	K. **Compatibility of the Forfeiture Provisions with the ECHR**	21.217

A. Introduction

21.01 The UK's first cash seizure provisions came into force on 1 July 1991 when Pt III of the Criminal Justice (International Co-operation) Act 1990 was enacted. That legislation proved to be necessary because the Drug Trafficking Offences Act, together with similar provisions in other countries, became a victim of their own success. Drug traffickers and money launderers could no longer risk transferring money from country to country by means of the electronic bank transfer system for fear of being detected, or the location of their money being discovered if they were arrested.

21.02 The money launderer became even more vulnerable following implementation of the First EC Money Laundering Directive, which required Member States to introduce legislation requiring financial institutions to keep proper records of transactions and report on money laundering. In consequence, Customs officers at ports and airports noticed that it was becoming increasingly common for large sums of money derived from drug trafficking to be imported into and exported from the UK in cash. They were powerless to intervene and detain such monies unless there was a prosecution for a drug trafficking offence ongoing in which case the money could be the subject of restraint and confiscation orders.

A. Introduction

(1) The DTA

Part II of the DTA 1994 gave the police and Customs officers the power to seize and detain for up to 48 hours drug trafficking money being imported or exported in cash. Magistrates' courts were given the power to order its further detention for periods of up to two years and, ultimately, to order its forfeiture. **21.03**

Although the provisions of s 42 et seq of the DTA were considered extensively in the first edition of this work, we do not propose to deal with those provisions once again in this edition. This is because the POCA regime has now been in operation for over three years, and so the number of remaining cases under the old legislation are very few and far between (as are the cash seziure provisions under the Anti–Terrorism, Crime and Security Act 2001). However, where appropriate we have imported into this chapter any relevant case law that we believe is likely to transcend both schemes. **21.04**

(2) The POCA regime

While undoubtedly the DTA scheme for the seizure and forfeiture of cash met with some success in terms of both the amounts seized and the message it sent out to would be drug smugglers and their money couriers (not least because of its draconian nature), it was nevertheless restricted to money that represented or was intended for drug trafficking. In this regard the scheme was viewed by many as flawed, because it made no provision for the forfeiture of cash being imported or exported in relation to other forms of criminal conduct. **21.05**

As a result, a new scheme under POCA was enacted which expanded the DTA regime to include cash related to *all* unlawful conduct, and which went further, by expanding the meaning of 'cash', allowing cash found anywhere in the UK to be seized (not just that which was being imported or exported) and by adding in new search provisions. **21.06**

In this chapter we will consider the revised regime governing the law relating to the seizure, detention, and forfeiture of cash under ss 289–303 of POCA. These sections came into force on 30 December 2002 (SI 2002/3015) and replace the earlier provisions found in ss 42–48 of the DTA 1994. They affect all cash seizures made on or after that date. **21.07**

Sections 289–292 of POCA deal with the power to search premises and persons for cash (see the second part of this chapter), and ss 294–300 deal with the seizure and forfeiture of cash generally. **21.08**

The relevant court forms in relation to cash seizures under POCA are found in the Magistrates' Court (Detention and Forfeiture of Cash) Rules 2002, SI 2002/2998, as amended by rr 91–96 of the Magistrates' Courts (Miscellaneous Amendments) Rules 2003, SI 2003/1236. **21.09**

(3) Civil proceedings

Although some debate ensued under the previous statutory provisions as to whether forfeiture provisions were civil or criminal, it is submitted that the new Act draws a line under such discussion. The Introduction to Pt 5 of POCA (Civil Recovery of the Proceeds Etc **21.10** of Unlawful Conduct) states in terms that forfeiture proceedings will be civil proceedings before the magistrates' court:

S.240(1) This Part has effect for the purposes of—
(a) ....
(b) enabling cash which is, or represents, property obtained through unlawful conduct, or which is intended to be used in unlawful conduct, to be forfeited in civil proceedings before a magistrates' court or (in Scotland) the sheriff.

21.11 This accords with the findings of courts under the DTA that the cash seizure provisions were civil in nature (see *R v Dover and East Kent Magistrates' Court ex p Steven Gore* (QBD, 23 May 1996); *R v Crawley Justices ex p Ohakwe* (1994) 158 JP Reports 78; and *Butler v UK (Application 41661/98)* (27 June 2002)).

B. The Seizure and Forfeiture of Cash

(1) Preliminary matters

21.12 The provisions under ss 294–303 of POCA establish a civil procedure by which money suspected of being either recoverable property or intended by any person to be used in unlawful conduct may be seized, detained, and forfeited (see s 294). The proceedings for forfeiture are civil (see s 240(1)(b)), the burden being on either the police or Revenue and Customs to demonstrate that the property is recoverable or the conduct is unlawful, on the balance of probabilities (s 241(3)).

(2) The circumstances in which cash may be seized

21.13 Section 294(1) states:

(1) A Revenue and Customs Officer or constable may seize any cash if he has reasonable grounds for suspecting it is—
(a) recoverable property, or
(b) intended by any person for use in unlawful conduct.

An officer may also seize an entire consignment of cash where he has reasonable grounds for suspecting part of it to be:

(a) recoverable property, or
(b) intended by any person for use in unlawful conduct, in circumstances where it is not reasonably practicable to seize only the 'suspicious' part (s 294(2)).

(3) The minimum amount that may be seized: £1000

21.14 Section 294 does not authorise the seizure of cash if it is for less than the 'minimum amount' (see s 294(3)). The minimum amount was originally set at £10,000, but was subsequently reduced on 16 March 2004 to £5000 (SI 2004/420), and on 31 July 2006 to £1000 following the introduction of the Proceeds of Crime Act 2002 (Recovery of Cash in Summary Proceedings: Minimum Amount) Order 2004, SI 2004/420.

(4) Does the minimum amount need to be in the possession of a single person?

21.15 It is possible to foresee, particularly for inland seizures, the practical difficulties of linking cash seized from separate individuals and treating it as one amount. However some judicial guidance may be derived from the decision of *Customs and Excise Commissioners v Duffy* TLR 5 April 2002 (decided under the DTA) where the defendants, who had all been travelling to Malaga, were stopped by a Customs officer at Gatwick Airport. They were found with £20,000 collectively in cash. Of the three defendants stopped, it was found they were carrying £7,000, £7,000 and £6,000 respectively (the minimum amount under the DTA being £10,000). The Divisional Court held that a court should approach the Act having in mind that the cash might be with one individual, more than one individual, or in fact no individuals at all. Kennedy LJ said that the sums should not be aggregated if the individuals are otherwise apparently unconnected, but if it can be shown that the money comes from a common source or has a common destination, that may lead the court to conclude that in reality it is a single amount of cash.

21.16 It is submitted that the alternative would give rise to a situation developing where an individual involved in transferring large sums of cash could ask three individuals to, eg carry £950 each (in total £2850) in the knowledge that they would be able to avoid the bite of this legislation. Clearly it is important that Revenue and Customs or the police should be able to show a nexus between the individuals or the cash concerned, eg that the contamination of the money in terms of residue of drugs matches, or that the travellers' tickets were booked at the same time, or that the individuals know each other, or have other ties. Any combination of these may suggest that the individuals were operating together and that the source of the money was therefore linked.

(5) The meaning of 'cash'

21.17 The meaning of cash has been expanded under s 289(6) to include:

- notes and coins in any currency;
- postal orders;
- cheques of any kind including traveller's cheques;
- banker's drafts;
- bearer bonds and bearer shares.

21.18 Unlike the previous DTA regime, this entitles officers to seize, cheques where the cheque is under suspicion. Where, only part of the value of the cheque in question is under suspicion, s 296(2) allows an officer to pay that cheque into an interest bearing account, and release the part of the value of the cheque to which the suspicion does not relate (s 296(2)).

21.19 Cash also includes 'any kind of monetary instrument' (s 289(7)). Although 'monetary instrument' is yet to be defined by statutory instrument, it is submitted a 'monetary instrument' must be in such a form that it can be paid into an interest bearing account, so as to comply with the requirements of s 296(2). It follows that if it cannot be, then it is likely to fall outside of the seizure powers under this Act.

(6) How is 'unlawful conduct' defined?

21.20 Under s 241 of the Act 'unlawful conduct' is defined as either:

(1) Conduct occurring in any part of the United Kingdom which is unlawful under the criminal law of that part of the UK (s 241(1)); or,
(2) Conduct which
   (a) occurs in a country outside the United Kingdom and is unlawful under the criminal law of that country, and
   (b) if it occurred in a part of the United Kingdom, would be unlawful under the criminal law of that part [of the UK] (s 241(2)).

(7) Does the 'unlawful conduct' have to be specified?

21.21 It is submitted that there is a requirement for the police or Revenue and Customs to satisfy the court that the cash relates to unlawful conduct, although that need not be limited to identifying one particular kind. Section 242(2)(b) reads:

(2) In deciding whether any property was obtained through unlawful conduct—
   (a) ...
   (b) it is not necessary to show that the conduct was of a particular kind if it is shown that the property was obtained through conduct of one of a number of kinds, each of which would have been unlawful conduct.

21.22 Provided the court is satisfied, on the balance of probabilities, that the cash relates therefore to unlawful conduct of one kind or another, it is not necessary to narrow the test to a single particular type. However, in practice most cases are likely to involve an allegation of a particular form of unlawful conduct, because the facts will dictate same, eg income from a shop where no tax has been declared, or cash with an unusually high contamination for drugs. It is also submitted that such a course is also preferable if the defendant is to know, notwithstanding these being civil proceedings, the case he has to answer.

21.23 This approach also appears to be in line with *R (Director of Assets Recovery Agency) v Green 2006* The Times, 27 February 2006, where Sullivan J held that in civil proceedings under Pt 5 of POCA, the applicant did not need to allege the commission of any specific criminal offence, but did have to set out the matters alleged to constitute the particular kind of unlawful conduct by which the property was obtained. He stated that if Parliament had wished the applicant to be able to recover property by simply alleging, and thereafter persuading the court, that, on the balance of probabilities, it had been obtained by some unspecified unlawful conduct, it could have said so, but did not. It follows to merely allege that the defendant has no identifiable lawful income, and therefore the cash 'must be the proceeds of unlawful conduct' is not enough, some evidence is required.

21.24 However, the decision of Sullivan J does not sit entirely comfortably with another first instance decision. In *Muneka v Customs and Excise Commissioners* [2005] EWHC (Admin) 495 Moses J dismissed the suggestion that it was for the 'prosecution' (sic) to identify the criminal activity, the source of the money or the criminal offence for which it is intended to use the money:

> All that has to be shown is that the source of the money was a criminal offence in the United Kingdom and (*sic. or*) that it was intended for a criminal use either in the United Kingdom or elsewhere.

It is submitted that if there is a difference in emphasis, *Green* is to be preferred.

(8) How is 'recoverable property' defined?

'Recoverable property' is defined as property obtained though unlawful conduct (s 304) (ie property obtained through conduct which is unlawful under UK criminal law or/and the criminal law of a country outside the UK—see para 21.20 above). It is submitted to make full sense of this definition in the context of cash seizures; 'property' should be read as meaning 'cash' (and its various meanings under s 289(6)) (see s 232(1): 'Property is all property wherever situated and includes—(a) money . . .' and s 414). **21.25**

Chapter 4 of Pt 5 of POCA sets out various definitions that apply to both the civil recovery scheme and the cash forfeiture provisions. It deals particularly with recoverable property, namely: **21.26**

  Property obtained through unlawful conduct—s 304
  Tracing property—s 305
  Mixing property—s 306
  Recoverable property accruing profits—s 307
  General and other exceptions and exemptions—ss 308 and 309
  Granting interests—s 310
  Obtaining and disposing of property—s 314

Under s 311, if the cash concerned is 'an asset of a company being wound up' or if there is a prima facie/arguable case that it is (or one of the other terms imposed by s 311), then an application for further detention may not be made unless the court that is dealing with the winding up petition/bankruptcy gives leave. **21.27**

(9) The tracing of property

The Act envisages under s 305 the tracing of property. Where property was originally obtained through unlawful conduct (or would have been recoverable property), that original property falls within the definition of 'recoverable property'. For example, a person steals a valuable painting (the original property), it is sold and the cash received from the sale is later seized at an airport under POCA. Following an investigation the cash can be traced back to the stolen painting. The cash therefore becomes recoverable property, being the proceeds of a crime. **21.28**

(10) Mixed property

The Act also stipulates that where a person's 'recoverable property' is mixed with other property, the portion of the mixed property that is said to relate to unlawful conduct becomes 'recoverable property' (see s 306—Mixing Property). In terms of s 294 the recoverable property is likely to be mixed cash. For example, where there are two joint company directors, one uses the company account for legitimate monies, the other to launder the proceeds of crime. The 'honest' director withdraws a large sum and he is stopped going through the airport and the cash is seized. The portion of the cash which he has on him that relates to legitimate money from the business does not fall within the scheme; however, the portion which was paid in as part of the laundered proceeds of a crime does stand to be forfeited, whether that particular director knew about it or not. **21.29**

(11) Property that is not 'recoverable'

21.30 POCA also affords certain 'defences', under which property should not be considered recoverable (see ss 304–310, SI 2003/336 and Chapter 19). General exceptions include a situation where a person disposes of recoverable property and the person who obtains it on the disposal does so in good faith, for value and without notice that it was recoverable property. In such circumstances the property may not be followed into the person's hands and, accordingly it ceases to be recoverable (s 308(1)).

21.31 Similarly, if in pursuance of a judgment in civil proceedings the defendant makes a payment to the claimant or the claimant otherwise obtains property from the defendant, that property ceases to be recoverable (see s 308(3)); or if a payment is made to a person in pursuance of a compensation order under s 130 of the PCC(S)A 2000, the property ceases to be recoverable (s 308(4)).

21.32 In cash seizure cases these are all matters that in practice will need to be raised by the defence/traveller. It may be that as part of their enquiries the police or Revenue and Customs (or the court) will enquire of the defendant/traveller as to whether or not any of the exemptions or exceptions apply to the cash seized. Unless the court, police, or Customs are positively advised otherwise, they are likely to assume that they do not.

(12) The re-seizure of cash

21.33 In *Chief Constable of Merseyside Police v Hickman* [2006] EWHC (Admin) 451; (QBD, 1 March 2006) Mitting J held that money that had been seized pusuant to a criminal enquiry and s 19 of the Police and Criminal Evidence Act 1984, could be re-seized at any time under s 294 of POCA. There were no time limits on the exercise of the power to seize money under the cash forfeiture provisions of POCA and there was no reason why the police should be prevented from 'seizing' cash already in their possession, the postion being analogous to that of property found on an individual after arrest.

(13) Ongoing criminal proceedings

21.34 In *R v Payton* (2006) 150 SJ 741, the Court of Appeal considered the difficulty of where cash seizure proceedings may be ongoing and taking place either in advance of or contemporaneously with a defendant's criminal trial. The concern was that such proceedings would lead to a potential unfairness to a defendant in the criminal proceedings if he had been required to give or call evidence. To ensure that a defendant's entitlement to a fair trial was not compromised, the Court of Appeal stated that it was essential that there should be proper liaison between the police/cash seizing authority and the prosecuting authority.

C. Practice and Procedure

(1) The initial enquiry

21.35 The money may only be seized if the officer has reasonable grounds, upon enquiry, for suspecting the money is recoverable property or is intended by any person for use in unlawful

C. Practice and Procedure

conduct (s 294(1)). If the officer, or his senior officer, as the case may be, believes 'reasonable grounds' for such a suspicion do not exist, or conversely the explanation is credible, the cash should not be detained. It must be borne in mind that 'cash' also means traveller's cheques, cheques, and any other kind of monetary instrument.

21.36 In ascertaining whether the cash is recoverable or is intended by any person for use in unlawful conduct a short interview is often held. While the provisions of the Police and Criminal Evidence Act do not apply in civil proceedings, officers should nevertheless consider what is best practice, particularly bearing in mind that at this stage it remains a possibility that, subject to further investigation, a criminal charge (eg money laundering) may arise. The signing/witnessing of an officer's notebook that 'the contents have been read back to me and I agree that they are true and accurate' therefore remains important for all parties, particularly if one considers that very often the person being questioned may subsequently change his story. The caution is not appropriate when acting solely under s 294.

21.37 At this preliminary stage there is no compulsion for an individual to stay and answer questions. If the individual elects to continue their journey or does not wish to answer any questions, that is their prerogative.

21.38 Once the decision to seize has been made, the individual should be informed that the matter will be listed before a magistrates' court within 48 hours.

(2) Procedure prior to the first hearing and venue

21.39 The first application under s 295(4) for the extension of the period for which the cash (or any part of it) may be detained beyond the initial 48 hours may be made on Form A, and sent to the Justices' Chief Executive for the Petty Sessions Area of the court for which the applicant wishes to make the application. Unlike the previous legislation under the DTA, there is therefore no restriction on which magistrates' court the applicant may use.

21.40 This is also reflected in SI 2003/638, which amends the magistrates' jurisdiction so that for the purposes of s 52 of the Magistrates' Courts Act 1980, any magistrates' court has jurisdiction to hear such an application, whether or not it relates to a matter arising within the commission area for which the court is appointed.

It is a matter of choice and no doubt convenience for the officer concerned.

21.41 Where the reasonable grounds (under s 295(4)) for the suspicion which led to the seizure of the cash in question are connected to the reasonable grounds for suspicion which led to the seizure of other cash to which a previous order has been made under s 295(2) of the Act, then the application is likely to be/may be sent to the Justices' Chief Executive for the Petty Sessions Area of the court which made the previous order (r 4(2) of the Magistrates' Court (Detention and Forfeiture of Cash) Rules 2002, SI 2002/2998).

21.42 Under r 4(3) of the same rules, a copy of the written application and notification of the hearing of the application should be given by the applicant to the person from whom the cash was seized (except where cash is seized by a means of unattended despatch, eg an unattended letter or parcel, or where unattended cash is seized).

(3) The first detention hearing for the seized cash

21.43 Under s 295(1) of POCA, while the police or a Revenue and Customs officer continue to have reasonable grounds for his suspicion that the cash seized falls under s 294, he may detain it, initially, for a period of 48 hours (to allow further enquiries to be made).

21.44 At the first detention hearing the period for which the cash (or any part of it) may be detained may be extended by an order made by the magistrates' court, but not for a period of beyond three months beginning with the date of the order (s 295(2)(a)); after which the period of detention may be extended on a three monthly basis, but not beyond the end of a period of two years beginning from the date of the first order. In other words, the maximum order for continued detention, before having to return to the magistrates' court for a further order, is three months. The maximum period for the investigation is two years.

21.45 It should be noted that at this stage there is no obligation to notify any third party who may be affected by the first application (see r 4(3) Magistrates' Court (Detention and Forfeiture of Cash) Rules 2002, SI 2002/2998). However, the rules envisage the Justices' Chief Executive giving notice of any order made by the court to not only the person from whom the cash was seized but also to any other person known to be affected by the order (see r 4(9) as above).

21.46 Under the Act a single justice of the peace may exercise the powers of the magistrates' court to make the first order extending the period (s 295(3)).

(4) Unattended despatches

21.47 Where seized cash is found in a means of unattended despatch (eg an unattended letter or parcel), copies of the written application and notification of the hearing of the application must be sent by either the police or Revenue and Customs to the sender and intended recipient of the unattended despatch (r 4(4)).

21.48 Where the seized cash is contained in an 'unattended despatch', and the sender or intended recipient is not known, the applicant (understandably) is not required to send out copies of the written application and notification (see r 4(5)).

21.49 Under the Magistrates' Courts Rules it is not in the court's power to decline to hear an application solely on the ground that it has not been proved that the sender and intended recipient have been given a copy of the written application and notification of the hearing in cases where the seized cash is found in a means of unattended despatch (see r 4(6)).

21.50 Where unattended cash is seized (other than where the cash is found in an unattended despatch) the applicant need not give a copy of the written application and notification of the hearing to any person (see r 4(7)).

(5) The 48 hour rule

21.51 The 48 hour rule should be complied with in all cases. The Serious Organised Crime and Police Act 2005 (SOCPA) however has amended the rule to allow for greater latitude in

C. Practice and Procedure

relation to the meaning of '48-hours'. Section 100 of SOCPA inserts into s 295 of POCA the following provision:

(1B) In calculating a period of 48 hours in accordance with this subsection, no account shall be taken of—
(a) any Saturday or Sunday,
(b) Christmas Day,
(c) Good Friday,
(d) Any day that is a bank holiday ...
(e) Any day prescribed ... as a court holiday ... [in Scotland].

21.52 This new section avoids the pitfall that arose under the DTA in relation to the difficulty law enforcement officers had in getting the matter before magistrates within 48 hours when the seizure took place at weekends. Under the previous legislation the courts established that the application for continued detention should be made within the 48 hour period during which the police or Customs officer is entitled to detain the money. In the case of *R v Uxbridge Magistrates' Court ex p Henry* [1994] Crim LR 581 (a case decided under s 26(1) of the Criminal Justice (International Co-operation) Act 1990, the corresponding provision to s 42(1) of the DTA prior to its enactment) the facts were as follows: the defendant had been referred to Customs officers at 7.15am on 8 June. At 9.44 the same morning he was taken to a Customs room at Heathrow Airport where he was told he was free to leave if he wished, but that the money would not be released until the result of a Customs investigation. The applicant chose to remain and during the course of the morning the Customs officers counted the money and made various enquiries. Customs officers made the application to extend the 48 hour period on the morning of 10 June. The justice concluded that from 9.44am until approximately 12.30pm on 8 June the cash was in the possession of the applicant at all times; and that at approximately 12.30pm Customs officers took possession of the money and served the applicant with a notice of seizure. It was agreed by all parties that if the time of detention by the Customs officers was at 12.30pm on 8 June then the order of the Uxbridge Magistrates to order continued detention would have been properly made. The issue that arose for the Divisional Court to decide was whether the seizure had in fact taken place at 9.44am on the 8 June, in which case the Customs officers were out of time. Scott Baker J in his judgment found that by 9.44am on the 8 June the Customs officers had:

> ample grounds for suspecting that this very substantial sum of money (£47,000) in the possession of the Applicant was connected in one way or another with drugs,

(on the facts of the case the defendant had maintained that he was going to Amsterdam to buy a Mercedes motorcar; although the defendant had maintained he would be returning with the car by ferry, he and his girlfriend were found to have two return air tickets). The Court found that Parliament had prescribed a specifically limited period, a period to be measured in hours. In these circumstances it was particularly important, they held, that the provisions should be strictly complied with. They added:

> 48 hours is the period given to the Customs & Excise to make their further enquiries, and if they require more time than that they have to go to the Magistrates to seek an appropriate order.

21.53 In Baker J's judgment, the seizure and detention took place at 9.44am and not as found by the magistrates, at 12.30pm. That being the case, the subsequent detention of the money was unlawful and the order was set aside.

21.54 In *Walsh v Customs and Excise Commissioners* The Times, 4 July 2001, the Divisional Court reiterated the decision in *Henry*, holding that the 48hour time limit for authorising the continued detention of money seized under s 42 of the Drug Trafficking Act 1994 had to be strictly complied with. In *Walsh* the defendants had given what was described as an 'inherently unlikely and unsatisfactory explanation' as to the purpose of their visit to Paris, when £17,500 was found in their possession on their outbound journey on Saturday 2 December 2000. At 10.25am that day Customs and Excise officers told the two defendants involved that they were free to leave without the money, which would be formally seized. Formal seizure of the money took place at 11.30am and the defendants' were told that Customs would make an application for continued detention at 10am on Monday 4 December 2000. On 4 December the information in support of a Customs application was lodged at the magistrates' court at 9.55am. The Deputy District Judge was informed at 10.30am and the application was called on at 10.45am. A short adjournment was granted and authorisation of continued detention was made at 1.20pm. The Deputy District Judge who dealt with the application found that the time of seizure was 11.30am on 2 December and therefore the time limit of s 42(2) had been met. However, Latham LJ, applying *ex p Henry*, held that the money had been seized at 10.25am. He observed that magistrates must make their order *before* the end of the 48 hour period. While acknowledging the practical difficulties that might cause to Customs officials due to the constraints of time, his Lordship said that he could see no escape from the conclusion that the section authorised seizure only up to 48 hours.

21.55 Whether the decisions in *Henry* and *Walsh* survive POCA is yet to be seen. The overriding purpose of POCA is to recover the proceeds of crime. To return, for example, £100,000 of cash that can be linked to unlawful conduct, on the basis that an officer was 10 minutes late in lodging an application, or on some other technicality, may, it is submitted, be considered to offend against the overall intention of Parliament. (See also *Chief Constable of Merseyside Police v Reynolds* [2004] EWHC (Admin) 2862.)

(6) The test the court will apply at further detention hearings

21.56 Under s 295(4), once an application has been made it is for the court to decide whether or not to make an order, if satisfied, in relation to any cash to be further detained, that either of the following conditions are met:

Condition 1:

(5) ... that there are reasonable grounds for suspecting that cash is *recoverable property* and that either—
  (a) its continued detention is justified while its *derivation* is further investigated, or consideration is given to bringing (in the UK or elsewhere) proceedings against any person for an offence with which the cash is connected, or
  (b) proceedings against any person for an offence with which the cash is connected have been started and have not been concluded.

If there are such reasonable grounds, that test/condition is met and the court may order a period of further detention.

Condition 2:

(6) ... that there are reasonable grounds for suspecting that the cash is intended to be used in *unlawful conduct* and that either—

C. Practice and Procedure

(a) its continued detention is justified while *its intended use is further investigated* or consideration is given to bringing (in the United Kingdom or elsewhere) proceedings against any person for an offence with which the cash is connected, or

(b) proceedings against any person for an offence with which the cash is connected have been started and have not been concluded.

Under s 295(4) either of the above conditions must be met. It is not necessary for both conditions to be met.

21.57 It is important to reiterate, therefore, that the officer must not only show that he has reasonable grounds for suspecting that either the cash is recoverable property or the cash is intended to be used in unlawful conduct, but also that its continued detention is justified pending further investigation into its derivation or intended use; or consideration is being given to bringing proceedings against any person for an offence with which the cash is connected (or that proceedings against any person for an offence with which the cash is connected have been started and have not been concluded).

(7) Interest

21.58 Under s 296, if cash is detained for more than 48 hours, it must be, at the first opportunity, paid into an interest bearing account and held there; and the interest accruing on it must be added to it on its forfeiture or release.

21.59 It is submitted that this requirement will initially present some difficulty to law enforcement officers. The banking of cash is not likely to present a problem; the banking of bearer bonds, banker's drafts, cheques and the like, is. In practical terms cheques can be 'stopped'. They are likely to be made payable to third parties. The above requirement, therefore, requires special arrangements to be put in place with the banks to ensure acceptance of any monetary instrument, without, presumably, adopting usual banking protocols.

(8) Interest—What does 'at the first opportunity' mean?

21.60 Section 296(3) states that payment of money into an interest bearing account at the earliest opportunity does not apply if the cash or, as the case may be, the part to which the suspicion relates, is required as evidence of an offence or evidence in proceedings under Chapter 3 of the Act.

21.61 This slightly ambiguous subsection states that if the cash is required as evidence in proceedings under Chapter 3, ie recovery of cash and summary proceedings, it need not be banked at the first opportunity. One assumes that would cover the situation where the evidence was still being gathered, eg forensic testing of the money.

21.62 It follows that, if the police or Revenue and Customs want to submit the money for forensic testing for traces of drugs, they would not be obliged to pay it into an interest bearing account until the results were back and the defence had been given the opportunity to test the money themselves (affording the defence the opportunity of testing the money themselves was always considered best practice in DTA cases, and avoids any argument that the defence were not given such an opportunity).

21.63 In cases where no forensic testing is required, and the cash is not required as a physical exhibit, a strict interpretation of POCA appears to dictate that at the first opportunity after 48 hours have passed, in other words as soon as the banks open, the cash should be banked. It is submitted that an element of reasonableness should be implied, ie as soon as reasonably practicable. While that more lenient interpretation may afford the police or Revenue and Customs officers some further time, the failure to pay the money in at the first opportunity could later lead to criticism and potential compensation as s 302(2) provides:

(2) If for any period beginning with the first opportunity to place the cash in an interest bearing account after the initial detention of the cash for 48 hours, the cash was not held in an interest bearing account while detained, the Court may order an amount of compensation to be paid to the applicant.

(3) The amount of compensation to be paid under subsection (2) is the amount the Court thinks would have been earned in interest in the period in question if the cash had been held in an interest bearing account.

While in many cases the loss of interest will only be for a relatively nominal amount, in cases where the cash seized is a more significant sum the potentially accruing interest is likely to be of more significance.

(9) Release of money over which no suspicion attaches

21.64 Under s 296(2) the police or Customs officer must, on paying the seized cash into a bank account, release any part of that cash to which the suspicion does not relate.

D. Continued Detention Hearings: Practice

(1) Form A

21.65 Applications for the continued detention of seized cash under s 295(4) may be made on Form A (see r 5(1) of the Magistrates' Court (Detention and Forfeiture of Cash) Rules 2002, SI 2002/2998, as amended by r 93 of the Magistrates' Courts (Misc. Amendments) Rules 2003, SI 2003/1236).

21.66 On receipt of Form A the justices' clerk should fix a date for the hearing of the application, which, unless he directs otherwise, shall not be earlier than seven days from the date on which it is fixed, and the Justices' Chief Executive must then notify that date to Revenue and Customs and every person to whom notice of the previous orders has been given (r 5(3)). It will be noted that because the justices' clerk is required to give seven days notice for continued detention hearings, Form A should not only reach the clerk prior to the existing order running out, but also at least eight or nine days earlier than that date, to allow them time to issue the hearing notice and comply with the seven day requirement.

21.67 It is then the duty of the applicant to send a copy of the application to every person to whom notice of previous related orders made under s 295(2) of the Act has been given (see r 5(2)).

D. Continued Detention Hearings: Practice

The Act, like the DTA before it, envisages a period of up to two years for the investigation to take place. The magistrates may state a period up to a maximum of three months from the date of the order, but not beyond the end of a period of two years from the date of the first order (s 295(4)). It should be noted that, as in the initial detention application, the magistrates are entitled to conclude that only part of the cash seized should be continued to be detained. **21.68**

If the court refuses to grant a further detention that will not necessarily lead to the release of the cash. The applicant is still at liberty to bring an application for forfeiture within 48 hours and/or an appeal. The effect of the magistrates' decision being to refuse a further extension, as opposed to ordering its release (see *Chief Constable of Lancashire Constabulary v Burnley Magistrates' Court* [2003] EWHC (Admin) 3308). **21.69**

(2) Form B

Form B requires the court to record the date of the seizure, the time of the seizure, the place of the seizure, the date of the latest order for continued detention of seized cash (if any), the amount detained under the last order for continued detention, and amounts released since the last order for continued detention (if any). **21.70**

Under the Magistrates' Courts (Misc. Amendments) Rules 2003, SI 2003/1236, the requirement to make an order for the continued detention of cash on Form B is omitted and is no longer a requirement of the rules (r 92(2) and r 93(2)). **21.71**

(3) Form C

Form C relates to rr 4(9) and 5(6). It is a notice to persons affected by an order for continued detention of seized cash. It reflects the Act, in that the person from whom the cash was seized may apply for the release of the detained cash or any part of it under s 297 of the Act. Under the Magistrates' Courts (Misc. Amendments) Rules 2003, SI 2003/1236, Form C is omitted from the Schedule and is no longer a mandatory requirement of the rules (r 9(6)). **21.72**

(4) Service of documents

Under r 9 any notification or document required to be given or sent to any person under the new Magistrates' Court (Detention and Forfeiture of Cash) Rules 2002, SI 2002/2998 may be given by post or by fax to his last known address, or to any other address given to that person for the purpose of service of documents under the rules (presumably including solicitors). **21.73**

(5) Procedure at the continued detention hearing

Although the Magistrates' Courts Rules are themselves silent, Form A envisages the police or Revenue and Customs officer applying for the order, and stating on oath that at least one of the two grounds in s 295(4) is satisfied. **21.74**

(6) What if the correct forms have not been served or the proper procedure not followed?

Caution should be taken to ensure that the proper procedures set out in the Magistrates' Court (Detention and Forfeiture of Cash) Rules 2002 are followed. However, since the **21.75**

Chapter 21: Recovery and Seizure of Cash under POCA

introduction of the Magistrates' Courts (Misc. Amendments) Rules 2003, SI 2003/1236 the requirement to use any of the forms is considerably diluted and in cases other than Form A and G, omitted This reflects the case law that had developed in relation to cash seizure cases, which dictated that use of the forms was directory rather than mandatory.

21.76 In *R v Luton Justices ex p Abecasis* The Times, 30 March 2000, the Court of Appeal held that Form C under the DTA was no more than a request to continue the existing order and that it did not have to be served on the person whose cash has been seized. All that was required, the Court held, is that the clerk to the justices should fix a date for the hearing and notify the person whose cash had been seized that the hearing was so listed. Where that was done, the substance of the rule was complied with. May LJ, who delivered the judgment of the court, stated:

> Form C, which appears in a Schedule to the Magistrates' Courts (Detention and Forfeiture of Drug Trafficking Cash) Rules, is a simple little document occupying less than half a page of A4 paper in the form in which it appears in the statutory instrument . . . the form is simply, and no more, a means of telling the Justices that the Applicant wants an order for continued detention; and, by inference, a request for a date to be fixed.

21.77 In *Halford v Colchester Magistrates' Court* (QBD, 25 October 2000) the service of Form C under the Magistrates' Courts (Detention and Forfeiture of Drug Trafficking Cash) Rules 1999, SI 1991/1923 again arose. On 18 January 2000 Customs wrote to the court informing them of their application to seek the further detention of seized cash and enclosed Form C. The application was listed on the 24 January 2000 although the court failed to notify the applicant of the hearing and its purpose. That failure to notify, Customs accepted, was not in accordance with the requirements of r 7(3), although it was established that the defendant had nevertheless been aware of the hearing and was able to make representations. Potts J delivering the judgment of the court, and adopting the first instance judgment of Owen J, in *Abecasis*, stated:

> it seems to me that if the procedure laid down to be followed by HM Customs in relation to notifying the Justices was directory rather than mandatory, then equally the requirement that the Justices should inform the applicant of the hearing was directory also.

Potts J added:

> the service by Customs of Form C as late as 18 January, a matter of days before the date of the hearing was unsatisfactory and may well have contributed to the failure on the part of the Justices' to observe the requirements of Rule 7(3). The Clerk to the Justices failure to observe the rules was particularly unfortunate. Rules are there to be followed. Had they been in this case, this particular litigation would have been avoided.

21.78 More recently a similar problem arose in the POCA case of *Chief Constable of Merseyside Police v Reynolds* [2004] EWHC (Admin) 2862. In *Reynolds* an order for continued detention was made at 10am on 11 February 2004 for a further period of 90 days. It was argued, by way of case stated, that the order must have expired at midnight on 10 May 2004. The hearing for further detention had taken place on the morning of 11 May 2004. Furthermore, the request for an extension of time had not been served seven days prior to the hearing, as is required by r 5 of the Magistrates' Courts (Detention and Forfeiture of Cash) Rules 2002, SI 2002/2998.

D. Continued Detention Hearings: Practice

21.79 In relation to the latter point the Court (Rose LJ and Leveson J) held that the requirement in r 5 was merely directory and not mandatory (following *Halford* and *Abecasis*) and as such had no merit.

21.80 In terms of the expiry period the Court held 11 February should be excluded when calculating the 90 day period. It did do by adopting the decisions in *Marren v Dawson Bentley &Co* [1961] 3 All ER 270 and *Radcliffe and Bartholomew* [1892] 1 QB 161, which establish that the day a cause of action arises or an offence is committed is to be excluded in computing a limitation period and that the principle applied whether the statute in question was dealing with civil or criminal cases (see also *Dodds v Walker* [1981] 1 WLR 1027).

21.81 For a similar decision on the application of the *Abecasis* principle, and the refusal of further detention on the merits, see *Chief Constable of Lancashire Constabulary v Burnley Magistrates' Court* [2003] EWHC (Admin) 3308 and *Gorgievski v Customs and Excise Commissioners* [2003] EWHC Admin 2773.

21.82 These cases should not of course be regarded as an invitation to the police or Customs officers to not comply with the Rules. Leveson J commented in *Reynolds* that such arguments 'are entirely avoidable if the application is not made at the last moment'.

(7) Insolvency and further detention hearings

21.83 An application for an order for the further detention of any cash for which s 311(3) applies (assets subject to insolvency proceedings) may not be made under s 295 unless the appropriate court gives leave (s 311(2)).

(8) Early release of the cash—to person from whom the cash was seized

21.84 Section 297(2) of POCA authorises the court to release the cash prior to the expiration of a detention order. A magistrates' court may only direct the release of the cash under s 297 (either in whole or in part), if the following condition is met: the court must be satisfied, on an application from the person *from whom the cash was seized*, that the conditions in s 295(5) and (6) for the detention of the cash are no longer met in relation to the cash to be released (s 297(2) and (3)).

21.85 An application under s 297(3) of the Act for the release of detained cash must be made in writing and sent to the Justices' Chief Executive (see r 6(1)). If the applicant (the person from whom the cash was seized) has been given notice of an order under s 295(2) (continued detention) in respect of the detained cash, then the application should be sent to the Justices' Chief Executive who sent him that notice. Once an application has been received, the Justices' Chief Executive must send a copy of the application to the Commissioners (r 6(3)(a)), and every person to whom notice of the order made under s 295(2) of the Act has been given (r 6(3)(c)). The Justices' Clerk must then fix a hearing date (see r 6(4)).

21.86 Only a person from whom the cash was seized is entitled to make such an application under s 297(3). A third party affected by the order therefore will have no right to do so (but does under s 301).

(9) Form D

21.87 The requirement for the magistrates' court to make a direction for the release of the detained cash on Form D if it is satisfied that the condition set out in s 297(3) has been met is omitted by the Magistrates' Courts (Misc. Amendments) Rules 2003, SI 2003/1236 and is no longer a requirement, although in practice courts are still using the forms for administrative convenience.

21.88 Form D appears to envisage that the court will hear oral evidence and representations.

21.89 The court may either order the immediate release of the money or the release of the money on a date not more than seven days from the date of the direction, unless a later date is agreed by the applicant.

21.90 Cash cannot be released where s 298(4) of POCA applies (ie while forfeiture proceedings are ongoing).

(10) Applications for early release by victims or other owners

21.91 Section 301 is part of the supplementary provisions to the cash forfeiture regime, and allows a person who claims that any cash detained under Chapter 3 of POCA belongs to him, to apply to a magistrates' court for the release of the cash (or a part of it) (s 301(1)).

21.92 The application may be made in the course of proceedings under s 295 (detention of seized cash) or s 298 (forfeiture) or 'at any other time' (s 301(2)).

21.93 An application under s 301(1) of the Act for the release of detained cash must be made in writing and sent to the Justices' Chief Executive (see r 6(1)).

Section 301 is divided into two parts:

(a) for victims of unlawful conduct (s 301(3)); and
(b) for other owners of the cash where s 295(5) and (6) is no longer met (s 301(4)).

(11) Section 301(3): victims of unlawful conduct

21.94 Section 301(3) states:

(3) If it appears to the Court . . . concerned that—
  (a) the applicant was deprived of the cash to which the application relates, or of property which it represents, by unlawful conduct,
  (b) the property he was deprived of was not, immediately before he was deprived of it, recoverable property, and
  (c) that cash belongs to him,
the Court may order the cash to which the application relates to be released to the applicant.

All three stipulations must be met. An example of where s 301(3) may apply would be if a third party was to come forward who claimed that the money had been stolen from him at an earlier time, ie he is a victim of an unlawful event.

D. Continued Detention Hearings: Practice

(12) Form E: Order for release under s 301(3)

21.95 The requirement for the magistrates' court to make a direction for the release of the detained cash on Form D if it is satisfied that the condition set out in s 297(3) has been met, is omitted by the Magistrates' Courts (Misc. Amendments) Rules 2003, SI 2003/1236 and the form itself is no longer a requirement.

(13) Section 301(4): third party applications/other owners

21.96 Section 301(4) states:

(4) If—
 (a) the applicant is not the person from whom the cash to which the application relates was seized,
 (b) it appears to the Court . . . that that cash belongs to the applicant,
 (c) the Court . . . is satisfied that the conditions in Section 295 for the detention of the cash are no longer met or, if an application has been made under Section 298 [forfeiture], the Court decides not to make an order under that section in relation to that cash, and
 (d) no objection to the making of an order under this subsection has been made by the person from whom the cash was seized,

 the Court . . . may order the cash to which the application relates to be released to the applicant or to the person from whom it was seized.

All four criteria must be met before release can be sanctioned. Section 301(4)(c) is implicit that there must no longer be any reasonable grounds for suspecting the cash is recoverable property and no longer any reasonable grounds for suspecting that the cash is intended for use in unlawful conduct.

(14) Objection to release under s 301(4) from the person from whom the cash was seized

21.97 Section 301(4)(d) is important because if the person from whom the cash was seized objects to the third party's claim to being the true owner of the money, whatever the merits of the third party's claim, the court will not be able to release it. It is in effect a veto, held by the person from whom the cash was seized. Section 301(4)(d), according to the explanatory notes that accompany POCA, is intended to prevent the court from becoming embroiled in a complicated ownership dispute between the party from whom the cash was seized and the rightful owner of the cash prior to the forfeiture hearing.

(15) Form F: Order for release under s 301(4)

21.98 Although the importance of Form F has diminished since its omission from the Magistrates' Courts (Misc. Amendments) Rules 2003, SI 2003/1236, in practice courts are still using the form for the purposes of administrative convenience where it appears to the court that:

(a) the sum was not seized from the applicant;
(b) the sum (whether in full or in part) belongs to the applicant;
(c) the conditions in s 295 of POCA for detaining the sum are no longer met;
(d) the court has decided not to order forfeiture of the sum under s 298(2) of POCA; and
(e) no objection to the making of the order was made by the person from whom the sum was seized or alternatively the cash was unattended.

Chapter 21: Recovery and Seizure of Cash under POCA

Form F anticipates that any release of the sum under s 301(4) will include any interest accruing thereon, as per s 296(1). Under Rule 6(7):

A Direction under section 297(2) of the Act and an Order under Section 301(3) or (4) of the Act shall provide for the release of the cash within seven days of the date of the making of the Order or Direction, or such longer period as, with the agreement of the Applicant, may be specified, except that cash shall not be released while section 298(4) [where a forfeiture application has been made and proceedings have not been concluded] applies.

(16) Joinder

21.99 Under r 6(5) at the hearing of an application under s 301(1) the court may, if it thinks fit, order that the applicant be joined as a party to all the proceedings in relation to the detained cash.

(17) Applications for the return of the cash: standard of proof

21.100 In *Customs and Excise Commissioners v Mukesh Shah* (1999) 163 JP 759 (a DTA case) the Court accepted that it was for the applicant to satisfy the magistrates on the balance of probabilities to release the cash if they were satisfied that there are no, or no longer any, grounds for its detention or, on an application made by any other person, the detention of the cash is not for that or any other reason justified.

21.101 In many civil cases the degree of probability required to establish proof may vary according to the allegation to be proved (see *Hornal v Neuberger Products Ltd* [1957] 1 QB 247) and the court is often reluctant, when considering claims by the Crown, to apply merely a 51/49 per cent test where an individual's property or other assets are in jeopardy (see *Bater v Bater* [1950] 2 All ER 458 and *B v Chief Constable of Avon and Somerset* [2001] 1 All ER 562). This topic is considered further at para 21.129 below.

(18) Can officers agree to the release of cash?

21.102 Yes. Under s 297(4) of POCA a police or Revenue and Customs officer may (after notifying the magistrates' court under whose order the cash is being detained) release the cash in whole or in part if he is satisfied the detention of the cash is no longer justified. It is always advisable therefore for a defendant to first write to either the police or Revenue and Customs and set out the defendant's case for the return of the cash prior to contemplating court action.

(19) Transfer of proceedings

21.103 Under r 10 of the Magistrates' Court (Detention and Forfeiture of Cash) Rules 2002, SI 2002/2998 any person who is a party to, or affected by, proceedings under Chapter 3 of Pt 5 of POCA may, at any time, make application to the court dealing with the matter for the proceedings to be transferred to a different petty sessions area (r 10(1)). Applications should be made in writing (r 10(2)) and should specify the grounds on which they are made. The Justices' Chief Executive must send a copy of the application to the parties to the proceedings and any other people affected by the proceedings and fix a date for the hearing of the application under rr 10(3) and (4).

E. Applications for Forfeiture of Detained Cash

(20) Transfer: what test is to be applied?

21.104 Under r 10(5) the court may grant the application for transfer if it is satisfied that it would be more convenient or fairer for proceedings to be transferred to a different petty sessions area. Rule 10(6) sets out the steps that the Justices' Chief Executive should follow if the application is granted.

E. Applications for Forfeiture of Detained Cash

(1) Forfeiture proceedings

21.105 When the police or Revenue and Customs have completed their enquiries into the provenance of the detained monies and consider they have sufficient evidence to establish the cash or any part of it is:

(a) recoverable property or
(b) intended by any person for use in unlawful conduct,

an application for forfeiture on Form G should be made (see s 298 of POCA). Under s 298(2):

(2) The Court . . . may order the forfeiture of the cash or any part of it if it is satisfied that the cash or part—
   (a) is recoverable property, or
   (b) is intended by any person for use in unlawful conduct.

(2) Form G

21.106 An application under s 298(1) for forfeiture of the detained cash may be made on Form G (r 7(1), as amended by the Magistrates' Courts (Misc. Amendments) Rules 2003, SI 2003/1236 and sent to the Justices' Chief Executive to whom applications for the continued detention of the cash under s 295(4) of the Act have been sent (if no applications in respect of the cash have been made under s 295(4) then the application must be sent to the Justices' Chief Executive of the court before which the police or Customs wish to make the application).

21.107 Where the 'reasonable grounds for suspicion' which led to the seizure of the cash initially are connected to the 'reasonable grounds for suspicion' which led to the seizure of cash under another order (made under s 295(2)), the application should be sent to the Justices' Chief Executive for the magistrates' court which made the first order.

21.108 Form G should then be sent to every person to whom notice of any order made under s 295(2) (continued detention) has been given, and to any other person identified by the court as being affected by the application.

21.109 Form G requires the police or Revenue and Customs officer to state the grounds for his belief that the cash is recoverable property or is intended by any person for use in unlawful conduct.

21.110 It is the applicant's responsibility and not the court's to send a copy of the application to the various parties. This may well therefore require an enquiry by the applicant to the court.

21.111 If the recipient of that notification is not the person from whom the cash was seized, but someone who claims that the cash belongs to him, and the court decides not to make a forfeiture order, the recipient 'third party' of Form G may then apply to the court under s 301(4) for the release of the cash to them (as per Form G).

(3) Effect of lodging an application

21.112 Once an application for forfeiture (Form G) has been made the cash may not be released until any proceedings in pursuance of that application (including any proceedings on appeal) are concluded. This differs from the previous legislation (s 42(7)) under which the money was not to be released until the application or criminal proceedings were concluded.

F. The Hearing

(1) Hearing for Directions

21.113 Once Form G has been issued the justices' clerk must set a date for a directions hearing (see r 7(4)). At the directions hearing, the court may give directions relating to the management of the proceedings, including directions as to the date of the hearing of the application.

21.114 Importantly, under r 7(6) if neither the person from whom the cash was seized, nor any other person who was affected by the detention of the cash, seeks to contest the application, the court may decide the application at the directions hearing. It is therefore imperative that parties attend directions hearings, or at least make it clear on the record that they intend to contest the hearing. Failure to do so may well lead to the court making an order in the defendant's absence. This rule was tested in *Leigh v Uxbridge Magistrates' Court* [2005] EWHC (QBD) 1828 where Goldring J, while expressing no principle, quashed an order for forfeiture made by the magistrates' court and remitted the matter back to the justices in circumstances where it was apparent that the defendant had made it clear through his solicitors and counsel on previous occasions that he would be contesting the hearing, but nevertheless failed to attend the directions hearing.

21.115 For the non-appearance of the defendant, complainant or both at the hearing of the complaint: see ss 55–57 of the Magistrates' Court Act 1980.

(2) What type of Directions may be ordered?

21.116 Rule 7(5) appears to give the court a wide discretion:

> The Court may give Directions relating to the management of the proceedings, including Directions as to the date of the hearing of the application.

21.117 The court will be concerned to ensure that any witnesses who may be required are available and therefore parties should be prepared to notify the court of what witnesses they are likely to be calling and the length of their evidence. Enquiries should be made as to whether or not any evidence can be agreed and reduced to admissions, eg the date of the seizure and the amount of the cash. An enquiry should be made as to whether or not witness statements

F. The Hearing

can be disclosed to any of the parties involved and if so on what date (by way of mutual disclosure).

Enquiries should be made as to whether or not any expert witnesses will be called (eg forensic scientists), and whether or not any translators are required. **21.118**

(3) The forfeiture hearing

The purpose of the hearing is to determine whether, in accordance with s 298(2), the detained cash is recoverable property; or is intended by any person for use in unlawful conduct. If the court is so satisfied, it may order its forfeiture under s 298. **21.119**

(4) Procedure at hearings made on complaint

Rule 11(1) states: **21.120**

At the hearing of an application under Chapter 3 of Part 5 of the Act (either searches for cash or seizure of cash), any person to whom notice of the application has been given may attend and be heard on the question of whether the application should be granted. The fact that any such person does not attend should not prevent the Court from hearing the application.

Rule 11(2) states: **21.121**

. . . proceedings on such an application shall be regulated in the same manner as proceedings on a Complaint, and accordingly for the purposes of these rules the application shall be deemed to be a Complaint, the Applicant a Complainant, the Respondents to be Defendants, and any notice given by the Justices' Chief Executive under Rules 5(3), 6(4), 7(4), 8(4) or 10(4) to be a Summons: but nothing in this rule should be construed as enabling a Warrant of Arrest to be issued for failure to appear to any such Notice.

The rules in relation to the hearing of a complaint, procedure and the jurisdiction of the magistrates' court are set out at s 51 et seq of the Magistrates' Courts Act 1980. **21.122**

Section 52 confirms jurisdiction; s 53 deals with procedure, and states that at the hearing of a complaint, the court shall, if the defendant appears, state to him the substance of the complaint; s 54 sets out the adjournment provisions, which may take place 'at any time'; and s 55 confirms that if a defendant does not appear the court may proceed in his absence. Similarly, under s 56 where at the time and place appointed for the hearing or adjourned hearing of a complaint the defendant appears but the complainant does not, the court may dismiss the complaint or, if evidence has been received on a previous occasion, proceed in the absence of the complainant. By s 57, where neither party attends, the court may dismiss the complaint; and s 58 deals with the transfer of proceedings. **21.123**

(5) Order of evidence and speeches

The Magistrates' Courts Rules (1981) r 14 sets out the order of evidence and speeches in civil cases made on complaint. **21.124**

(1) On the hearing of a complaint the complainant shall call the evidence and before doing so may address the court.
(2) At the conclusion of the evidence for the complainant, the defendant may address the court, whether or not he afterwards calls evidence.

(3) At the conclusion of the evidence, if any, for the defence, the complainant may call evidence to rebut that evidence.
(4) At the conclusion of the evidence for the defence and the evidence, if any, in rebuttal, the defendant may address the court if he has not already done so.
(5) Either party may, with the leave of the court, address the court for a second time, but where the court grants leave to one party it shall not refuse leave to the other.
(6) Where the defendant obtains leave to address the court for a second time, his second address shall be made before the second address, if any, of the complainant.

21.125 It is important to note in the above rules that the applicant's only opportunity to fully address the court without leave comes when he opens his case. From the applicant's point of view therefore it is important that he gives as full an opening as he can, although depending on the facts of the case, he may apply for leave to address the court again for a second time.

21.126 Similarly if the defendant chooses to address the court in opening and before he calls evidence he loses his opportunity to make a closing speech without further leave. The usual rules apply, in that either party may address the court on a point of law at any time.

21.127 Although the defendant is at liberty to make a submission of no case to answer after the applicant's case, some caution should be exercised, because if it fails and the defendant has been asked to choose between calling evidence and making a submission, he will not be entitled to call evidence thereafter. See *Boyce v Wyatt Engineering* The Times, 14 June 2001.

(6) Matters to be sworn under oath

21.128 By r 11(3):

At the hearing of an application under Chapter 3 of Part 5 of the Act, the Court shall require the matters contained in the application to be sworn by the Applicant under oath, may require the Applicant to answer any questions under oath and may require any response from the Respondent to the application to be made under oath.

G. Rules of Evidence

(1) Burden and standard of proof

21.129 The burden is on the applicant, to prove the criteria set out in s 298(2). The standard of proof however is that applicable in civil proceedings (ie proof on the balance of probabilities (see s 240(1)(b)). Once the applicant has satisfied the court to the required standard, it is for the defendant to show, also on the balance of probabilities, that the suggestion advanced by the applicant is incorrect.

21.130 In *Butt v Customs and Excise Commissioners* (2002) 166 JP 173 money in the possession of the appellant's nephew was seized by Customs officers. The appellant's nephew had been travelling to Amsterdam on a single ticket with a large sum of cash in brown paper packages in a locked case. The defence argued that the justices had not born in mind the remarks

G. Rules of Evidence

made by Lord Bingham in *B v Chief Constable of Avon and Somerset* [2001] 1 WLR 340 to the effect that in serious cases the difference between civil and criminal standards is 'in truth largely illusory'. In dismissing the appeal the Court held that Parliament had explicitly provided that the civil standard of proof should apply in proceedings under s 43 of the DTA, namely 'more probable than not'. A forfeiture order made under the 1994 Act, they stated, involved no aspersions on the character of the applicant. Indeed, in this case the justices made no finding that the monies actually belonged to the appellant. The proceeding was effectively an action *in rem*, the courts findings only applying to the cash.

While the case of *Butt* suggests that the standard of proof need only be on the balance of probability, in accordance with the civil standard under which POCA operates, some caution needs to be exercised. In *Butt* the Court was of the view that since it had not been established that the money belonged to the appellant, who was a third party applicant, the order for forfeiture could not involve aspersions on the character of the owner. If, on the facts, a case cast aspersions on the character of the owner, it is submitted, the consequences might demand the application of a slightly higher standard of proof than the mere balance of probabilities. Support for this view is drawn from *Hornell v Neuberger* [1957] 1 QB 247 where Morris LJ said: 21.131

> it is, I think, clear from the authorities that a difference of approach in civil cases has been recognised (in terms of the burden of proof). Many judicial utterances show this. The phrase "balance of probabilities" is often employed as a convenient phrase to express the basis upon which civil issues are decided . . . in some civil cases the issues may involve questions of reputation which can transcend in importance even questions of personal liberty . . . In English law the citizen is regarded as being a free man of good repute. Issues may be raised in a civil action which affect character and reputation, and these will not be forgotten by judges and juries when considering the probabilities in regard to whatever misconduct is alleged. There will be reluctance to rob any man of his good name: there will also be reluctance to make any man pay what is not due or to make any man liable who is not or not liable who is.

(2) Are previous convictions admissible?

In contrast to the position in criminal proceedings, any previous conviction of a person claiming an interest in the money is admissible and adverse inferences may be made against him in relation to same.   21.132

The effect the admission of such a conviction can have was illustrated in the DTA case of *Ali v Best* (1997) 161 JP 393. In March 1992 the appellant had been convicted of an offence of possessing one ounce of heroin with intent to supply. In August 1994 Customs officers at Dover stopped him as he was about to leave the country and a holdall in the boot of his car was found to contain £48,830 in cash. No drugs were found in the vehicle and no traces of drugs were found on the bank notes. The justices ordered the money to be forfeited, and the appellant appealed by way of case stated. The High Court dismissed the appeal, McCowan J commenting in delivering the judgment of the court: 21.133

> In my judgment, evidence of that previous conviction and the facts of it were clearly admissible. The question that remains is, how cogent was it? In my judgment, it did have some cogency. It certainly called for an answer. The answer that he gave, apparently in interview, was that the money had come from trading in Cypriot antiques and, as he told the Customs

officer when stopped, he was intending to use it to buy a Mercedes or two. He did not, however, go into the witness box. In my judgment [counsel for the respondent] is entitled to rely on that fact that he did not choose to give any explanation on oath. This is not a criminal case, this is a civil case and in my judgment in those circumstances, this is a matter which can properly be relied upon by the respondent.

21.134 In *R v Isleworth Crown Court ex p Kevin Marland* (1998) 162 JPR 251 the Court held that in civil cases the rules concerning the admission of previous convictions were less circumscribed because the underlying intention is not to protect one side but to be fair to both sides. If the facts of the previous conduct are sufficiently similar to the facts sought to be proved in the instant case as to be logically probative, then evidence of previous conduct is admissible and that would include spent convictions, subject only to the judge's discretion to exclude them on such grounds as oppression, unfairness or surprise. Mrs Justice Smith held:

> it matters not whether the evidence is of a conviction or whether it is of past conduct which has not resulted in the conviction . . . When exercising its discretion to admit spent convictions the Court must be satisfied that justice cannot otherwise be done. Justice means justice to both parties. These convictions were plainly of some relevance to the issues in the case . . . because of the lapse of time, they may be said to have less probative value than if they were more recent. Some tribunals might well have considered the prejudicial effect out-weighed the probative value. However that is not to say that I think the decision to admit them was obviously wrong—I do not.

21.135 In *Customs and Excise Commissioners v T* (1998) 162 JP 193, Customs and Excise sought to produce evidence that the defendant had previously been charged with the importation of drugs, albeit that when the matter came to trial the prosecution had offered no evidence against him. The Luton Magistrates had ruled that that evidence was not admissible. The magistrates were asked to state a case. In Lord Justice Staughton's judgment Customs and Excise were not precluded from relying on the evidence of the previous incident. There were no estoppels against them because of the acquittal, and the standard of proof required in the forfeiture proceedings was the civil and not the criminal standard. In so finding he ruled that the lower court had not been correct to rule that the evidence of the earlier incident was inadmissible, although what weight the court should have given that evidence would have clearly been dictated by the facts of the case.

21.136 Once, therefore, a previous conviction or previous alleged criminal conduct can be shown to be relevant to the issues to be determined under the cash forfeiture provisions it may be admitted.

(3) Is there a need for direct evidence of the unlawful conduct?

21.137 No. In *Butt v Customs and Excise* (2002) 166 JP Reports173, the court held that in applications under s 43 of the DTA, there was no need for direct evidence of connection to drugs for the purpose of discharging the burden of proof.

(4) The drawing of inferences and illustrative cases

21.138 The drawing of inferences was a common thread through a number of cases under the DTA. In *Bassick and Osborne v Customs and Excise Commissioners* (1997) 161 JP 377, the magistrates came to the conclusion, having paid particular regard to the circumstances surrounding Bassick's possession of the cash seized, that it was more likely than not that the money directly or indirectly represented a person's proceeds of, or was intended by any person for use in, drug trafficking. Bassick was unemployed at the time he was stopped and on his way to Amsterdam with £21,520 in cash in various denominations, with a single flight ticket that had been bought shortly before the departure time of the aircraft. He possessed a note giving him instructions on how to reach an address in Amsterdam, and he had made no arrangements for his return journey or for his accommodation abroad. The magistrates had also noted his evasive demeanour and that of his witnesses when they testified. Accordingly the magistrates ordered forfeiture. There was nothing to suggest that either of the two defendants had been convicted of criminal offences involving drugs. There was nothing to suggest that they had been associated with people who were known to be connected with drug trafficking, nor was there anything to suggest that they were known to a person or persons in Amsterdam who were known to be so involved. On appeal Watkins LJ said:

> I can see no flaw in the way in which they (the Justices) approached it, and none in the decision which they reached upon it. It seems to me that there was ample material to allow them to come to the conclusion which they did . . . the overbearing fact is that these Justices simply did not believe Osborne and Bassick.

21.139 A similar decision was reached in *R v Dover and East Kent Magistrates' Court ex p Steven Gore* (QBD, 23 May 1996) where Auld LJ held:

> the Magistrates were entitled and indeed bound, to take into account all the circumstances (of the case): the circumstances in which the money was seized; the amount of the money; the fact that it was contaminated albeit slightly, with traces of cannabis or cannabis resin; the refusal of the applicant before caution to give an explanation as to who had given him the money, at a time when it might be expected that he would or could have given an explanation. The Magistrates were entitled to take into account the answers he gave in interview that I have summarised, an account which, putting aside any refusals to answer, raised more questions than it answered. I have no doubt that the Magistrates were entitled to apply the civil burden of proof to conclude as they did and to order the forfeiture of the money accordingly.

21.140 The case of *Bryan v Customs and Excise Commissioners* (1998) 162 JP 251 also re-enforces the decision in *Bassick and Osborne*. In *Bryan* the appellant had been observed carrying a large amount of cash out to Amsterdam. On his return no drugs were found but Customs officials recovered £15,000 in the appellant's money belt. The appellant's case was that he had been to Amsterdam to buy a diamond for his mother. He worked in buying and selling and valeting cars. His passport revealed he had travelled to Thailand twice and also Jamaica. He was asked if he had used any drugs in Amsterdam and he said that he had some cannabis spliffs and a piece of space cake. The money was packed in bundles of £1,000 in £50 notes. The Customs officer gave evidence about Amsterdam, stating it was the European warehouse for the distribution of drugs. Also evidenced was the fact that several years prior to the seizure of the cash, in April 1993, the appellant had been stopped by Customs officers and found in possession of two small packets of cannabis. The defence submitted on appeal that the court's conclusion was illogical because the appellant had taken the money out of the country and brought it back again without using it for the purchase of drugs. Mrs Justice Smith concluded that there was no merit in that submission. The magistrates had rejected as untruthful the appellant's evidence as to the origins of the money. They had rejected as untruthful his account of the purpose of his visit to Amsterdam. In her judgment, 'There was ample evidence upon which the Court was entitled to reach its conclusion.'

21.141 In *Nevin v Customs and Excise Commissioners* (QBD, 3 November 1995) the defence complained that the justices, in saying that the defendant could not prove the origin of the money conclusively, were in effect placing the burden on him to explain the origins of the cash. In the judgment of the court, delivered by Simon Brown LJ, it was held that that criticism was misplaced:

> The reality of the position is plain, namely that the justices were wholly unsatisfied with (the defendant's) explanation of the origins of the cash and altogether more importantly, of course, Mr Nevin's intentions with regards to its future.

21.142 In *Muneka v Customs and Excise Commissioners* [2005] EWHC (Admin) 495, a case that was dealt with under s 298 of POCA and concerned an appellant who was stopped at Heathrow with £22,760 in cash in his possession while on his way to Albania via Hungary, Moses J held:

> In my judgement, in this context the fact that there was no explanation for the source of that money, no reasonable explanation as to why he was taking that cash to Albania, the fact that there were discrepencies in his explanations as to the source of the money and as to its final destination, taken together, did establish, both source and intention. . . on the balance of probabilities.

(5) Hearsay in civil cases

21.143 The Magistrates' Courts (Hearsay Evidence in Civil Proceedings) Rules 1999, SI 1999/681 set out the rules applying to hearsay in magistrates' courts.

Those rules provide as follows:

3 (1) Subject to paragraphs (2) and (3), a party who desires to give hearsay evidence at the hearing must, not less than 21 days before the date fixed for the hearing, serve a hearsay notice on every other party and file a copy in the court by serving it on the justices' clerk.
3 (2) Subject to paragraph (3), the court or the justices' clerk may make a direction substituting a different period of time for the service of the hearsay notice under paragraph (1) on the application of a party to the proceedings.
3 (3) The court may make a direction under paragraph (2) of its own motion.
3 (4) A hearsay notice must-
    (a) state that it is a hearsay notice;
    (b) identify the proceedings in which the hearsay evidence is to be given;
    (c) state that the party proposes to adduce hearsay evidence;
    (d) identify the hearsay evidence;
    (e) identify the person who made the statement which is to be given in evidence; and
    (f) state why that person will not be called to give oral evidence.
3 (5) A single hearsay notice may deal with the hearsay evidence of more than one witness.

21.144 These Rules make provision for the requirements of the Civil Evidence Act 1995 in relation to hearsay evidence in civil proceedings in magistrates' courts. They also make provision for:

- the procedure to call a witness for cross-examination on hearsay evidence (r 4);
- a notice requirement where a party tenders hearsay evidence but does not call the person who made the statement to give oral evidence, and another party wishes to attack the

G. Rules of Evidence

credibility of the person who made the statement or allege that he has made another statement inconsistent with it (r 5);
- the service of documents required by the Rules (r 6).

21.145 However, a failure to comply with the duty to give notice should not affect the admissibility of hearsay evidence (see s 1(1) of the Civil Evidence Act 1995 and s 1(2) which is specifically adopted by r 2(2)). It then becomes a question of weight for the justices to determine. In assessing the weight, all the relevant circumstances should be considered including the fact that the individual who makes the statement has not been tendered in cross-examination and therefore has not been tested. The desirability of serving a hearsay notice is obvious, as a party may find itself liable for costs if a witness statement tendered at the hearing reveals new evidence that the other side has not had the opportunity of exploring, or evidence that amounts to an ambush.

21.146 Section 4(2) of the Civil Evidence Act 1995 gives some guidance that may or may not assist the court when assessing what weight should be given to hearsay. That guidance includes:

(i) Whether it would have been reasonable and practicable to have produced the person who made the statements rather than relying on a hearsay report of them;
(ii) Whether the person who originally made the statements made them contemporaneously with the matters stated;
(iii) Whether the evidence is multiple hearsay, in other words whether the hearsay witness is in fact repeating something which itself is hearsay;
(iv) Whether anyone involved has a motive to conceal or misrepresent matters;
(v) Whether the original statement was made for some purpose or produced in collaboration with others;
(vi) Whether the attempt to rely on hearsay rather than calling the person who made the original statement is designed to prevent a proper valuation of its weight by the court.

21.147 In the Crown Court the position in slightly different, although the same principle appears to apply. In *R v Wadmore and Foreman* [2006] EWCA Crim 686, a case that concerned an application for an anti-social behaviour order, the Court of Appeal held that ASBO's amounted to civil proceedings in a criminal court. The Criminal Procedure Rules 2005 do not apply to civil cases. The Civil Procedure Rules 1998 do not apply in criminal courts. The Magistrates' Courts (Hearsay Evidence in Civil Proceedings) Rules 1999, SI 1999/681 do not apply to the Crown Court. The Court of Appeal therefore assumed without deciding that, as the case was civil in nature, hearsay evidence was admissible under s 1 of the Civil Evidence Act 1995. There were no applicable procedural rules and the Court thought that the Magistrates' Court Rules should be applied by analogy.

(6) Lies told by the defendant

21.148 In *Nevin v Customs and Excise Commissioners* (QBD, 3 November 1995), Smedley J stated:

> While the prescribed Civil Standard of proof would not, of course, allow the Justices to act without satisfactory evidence on the intended use of the money, they are not required to direct themselves, for example, in relation to lies told by a defendant, as the Judge would direct a jury in a criminal trial. That is not to say that they should overlook the possibility that

lies may have the purpose of concealing something other than the misconduct presently alleged. But a suspect who gives an account of his reasons for carrying the money which the Justices reject as untruthful cannot complain if the Justices go on to infer from other relevant evidence, that by itself might not have been enough to satisfy them, that the true reason was for the use of [drug trafficking].

This passage was specifically referred to and approved by Moses J in *Muneka v Customs and Excise Commissioners* [2005] EWHC (Admin) 495, in which he stated:

Those comments apply with added force in the context of this case where it is not necessary to identify any criminal activity such as drug trafficking; all that has to be identified is that the source was criminal activity or the intended destination was use for criminal activity. A lie in that context may well entitle the fact-finding body to infer what the source or intention for which the cash was to be used was in reality on the balance of probabilities.

21.149 In *Muneka* the appellant sought judicial review of a district judge's decision on the grounds that the fact he may have lied in his account to Customs was not sufficient evidence to establish that the money was obtained as a result of unlawful conduct or was intended for use in unlawful conduct. In Moses J's judgment the fact that the appellant had lied was evidence upon which the district judge was entitled to conclude that the suggestions in relation to unlawful conduct being put to him were in fact true on the balance of probabilities:

The District Judge was entitled to ask herself: why should this appellant have lied about the source and destination of that cash? He must have appreciated that such lies could have had no reasonable explanation, other than that the suggestions made to him as to their source and as to destination were in fact true.

21.150 Moses J went on to cite *Bassick and Osborne* [1993] 161 JP 377 as authority for the proposition that lies in a particular context may establish a positive case as to the source of the money.

(7) Mass Spec expert reports

21.151 Previously, under the DTA regime, it would be commonplace in most s 43 applications for Customs to rely upon an expert's report from Mass Spec Analytical to demonstrate that the cash seized had traces, all be they microscopic, of drugs. That practice continues to operate in cases where the unlawful conduct may be related to drugs. The police have also used Mass Spec and their own Forensic Science Services to show traces of drugs on cash seized.

21.152 Mass Spec Analytical Ltd is a company that has for many years specialised in chemical analysis using a method known as mass spectral analysis. The technique is extremely sensitive. It can detect one nanogram of a drug, that has been described in layman's terms as being approximately one million times less that a single grain of sugar. It cannot identify the precise quantity of the drug, although it can determine orders of magnitude.

21.153 It is now universally recognised by the forensic science services that all UK notes in general circulation are likely to be contaminated with cocaine. This is not necessarily so with Ecstasy (MDMA) or cannabis (Tetrahydrachlorine). A study of drugs on notes in general

G. Rules of Evidence

circulation conducted by Mass Spec Analytical Ltd, by Sleeman, Burton, Carter, and Roberts, 'Rapid Screening for the Presence of Controlled Substances by Thermal Disorption Atmospheric Pressure Chemical Ionisation Tandem Mass Spectrometry' (1999) 124 The Analyst 103–108, found that cocaine, heroin (and two related opiates) were generally present on sterling bank notes from general circulation, although differences in both the frequency and degree of contamination were apparent between bundles of bank notes from general circulation and those suspected of being associated to the trafficking of drugs. A 'significant' number of bundles of bank notes confiscated by Customs were also found to be contaminated with detectable levels of THC (cannabis) and 3,4—Methylenedioxymethylamphetamiamine (MDMA/Ecstasy).

21.154 The real question therefore that arises is whether or not the money which has been seized has levels of drug contamination which are significantly higher than what would normally be expected for cash in normal circulation (for further reading see also Sleeman, Burton, Carter, Roberts, and Hulmston, 'Drugs on Money' (2000) June Anal. Chem. 397a–403a).

21.155 In *Thomas v Customs and Excise Commissioners* (1997) 161 JP 386, the defence argued that when considering whether the cash was *intended* for use in drug trafficking the magistrates had been wrong to pay attention to evidence of traces of drugs on the notes. That could, it was submitted, only be relevant if the cash *represented* the proceeds of drugs trafficking. In *Thomas* the suggestion was that the cash was to be exchanged for drugs in the future. The Court rejected this argument on the basis that, although such evidence would normally relate to past dealing, it could also show that a source near to the carrier of the cash had contaminated the notes.

21.156 In *Compton v R* [2002] EWCA Crim 2835, a case which sought to criticise the methods employed by Mass Spec, the Court of Appeal held that the range and weight of Mass Spec's database was 'sufficient for comparisons safely to be based on it'. A similar conclusion was reached in *Benn v R* [2004] EWCA Crim 2100 where doubts as to the validity of the methodology employed by Mass Spec and doubts as to the robustness of the findings because of the risks of innocent contamination were raised. (For further reading on drug contamination of bank notes see Archbold News, Issue 7, 16 August 2006.)

21.157 Mass Spec is currently developing the technology of identifying traces of explosives and other prohibited substances on cash, as well as the linking of traces of drugs on money to drugs discovered in other police and Revenue and Customs operations.

21.158 For the value in criminal proceedings of Mass Spec reports see *R v Ali Hussain* [2005] EWCA Crim 87.

(8) Record of proceedings

21.159 Under r 11(4) there is a duty for the legal advisor and/or the court to keep a record of any statement made under oath that are not already recorded in the written application. In other words the court must keep a record of proceedings, which may be later referred to in any appeal.

(9) Form H: order for forfeiture

21.160 The requirement for the magistrates' court to use Form H is omitted by the Magistrates' Courts (Misc. Amendments) Rules 2003, SI 2003/1236, and it is no longer necessary for an order for the forfeiture of detained cash under s 298(2) and r 7(7) to be made on Form H.

(10) Sensitive evidence

21.161 Although PII applications do not feature in magistrates' courts, exclusion of evidence on the grounds of public policy applies equally to civil proceedings as it does in criminal. The test is whether the production of a document or other piece of evidence would be 'injurious to the public interest'; ie whether the withholding of a document/information is necessary for the proper functioning of a government department. For example, the disclosure of the document may jeopardise an ongoing operation, or the methods deployed, or co-operation received from others in the investigation of an offence.

21.162 It is important to remember that the issue the court is having to decide is that set out in s 298(2), namely whether the seized cash is recoverable property; or is intended by any person for use in unlawful conduct. Considerations such as why the individual was stopped in the first place, or what information the police held on that individual, therefore fall away as being largely irrelevant to the test the court is having to apply, which focuses on the cash and its intended/previous purpose. (By analogy see *Hoverspeed v Customs and Excise Commissionners* [2002] EWCA Civ 1804 at paras 44–49.)

(11) Joint owners

21.163 Under s 298(3) where the recoverable property belongs to joint owners, the order for forfeiture of the cash may not apply to so much of the cash as the court thinks is attributable to the joint owner's share. Section 270(4) states:

> (4) An excepted joint owner is a person who obtained the property in circumstances in which it would not be recoverable as against him; and references to the 'excepted joint owner's share' of the recoverable property are to so much of the recoverable property as would have been his if the joint tenancy had been severed.

21.164 In other words, the court must not forfeit the cash that is attributable to the innocent partner's share (eg if two business partners have a joint bank account, and one of those partners has been trading legitimately and paying legitimate money into it whereas the other one, unbeknown to the other, has been paying in drug trafficking proceeds, if the illegitimate partner were to withdraw all of the cash in the account and it was subsequently seized, the court would have to distinguish between the clean and the 'dirty' money. The court would be entitled to return to the innocent partner his share of the money.).

H. Costs and Compensation

21.165 The successful party may apply for his costs against the unsuccessful party, and as the proceedings are civil in nature the usual rule that costs follow the event applies, sometimes rather crudely expressed as 'winner takes all'. As in all matters of costs, however, the court does have an element of discretion and would, for example, be entitled to refuse costs against a successful party whose behaviour had led the applicant to believe his case was stronger than it really was or where the case has been dismissed on a technicality rather than on the merits.

21.166 In *R v Dover Magistrates' Court ex p Customs and Excise Commissioners* The Times, 12 December 1995, a series of orders were made by the magistrates' court for continued detention of the money. During that period notice was given that an application for forfeiture had been lodged by Customs. Having put in that notice of application for forfeiture, Customs then gave notice that they did not intend to proceed with their application. Those representing the defendant applied for an order from the magistrates that Customs should pay the defendant's costs. The magistrates made the order, and said that if costs could not be agreed then they would assess the costs themselves. Subsequently, the magistrates made an order that the costs should be paid in accordance with the bill submitted by the defendant's solicitors. On appeal to the Divisional Court the issue was whether the defendant's bill included costs not only in relation to the proposed forfeiture hearing but also in relation to the earlier continued detention hearings. Section 52(3) of the Courts Act 1971 provides that where:

> (b) a complaint is made to a Justice of the Peace acting for any area but the complaint is not proceeded with, a Magistrates' Court for that area may make such order as to costs to be paid by the Complainant to the Defendant as it thinks just and reasonable.

21.167 In the *Dover* case there was a complaint made to the justices asking for forfeiture. Under s 64(1) of the Magistrates' Courts Act 1980:

> (1) On the hearing of a complaint a Magistrates' Court shall have power in its discretion to make such order as to costs that—
>
> > (a) on making the order for which the complaint is made, to be paid by the Defendant to the Complainant;
> >
> > (b) on dismissing the complaint, to be paid by the Defendant to the Complainant, as it thinks just and reasonable . . .

21.168 The distinction between the two is that s 64 of the Magistrates' Courts Act deals with cases where the complaint has been heard and determined, whereas s 52 of the Courts Act deals with cases where the complaint is not proceeded with.

21.169 The Divisional Court had to determine whether or not there was one complaint initiated by the first detention proceedings and continued up to and including the forfeiture proceedings; or whether there were separate complaints in respect of continued detention and forfeiture. Staughton LJ in the judgment of the Court held that it was clear that there was more than one complaint: 'There was a complaint for forfeiture and at least one complaint if not more for detention'. He explained:

> First, in the circumstances of this case the costs of detention proceedings fall to be dealt with under section 64. That says that where a complaint has succeeded the Court may award the costs to the Complainant, and where it has failed it may award the costs to the Defendant. That seems to me inconsistent with the court, in this case, awarding the costs of the detention proceedings, which have succeeded, to the Defendant. The second reason is this: it seems to

me implicit in section 52 that what the Court may award is the cost of the proceedings in question. I cannot accept that section 52 gives the Magistrates carte blanche to award any other costs on any other matter whatsoever if they think it just and reasonable to do so. In my opinion the power relates to the cost of the proceedings in question.

21.170 It is therefore incumbent on the parties to ensure that costs are dealt with at the end of each individual application for continued detention. Costs may not be 'reserved' to later hearings, although it should be noted that once a forfeiture application has been lodged any hearing that takes place following the lodging of the application, eg a pre-trial review, forms part of the same application and therefore costs need not be dealt with until the hearing itself.

(1) Costs under s 64 of the Magistrates' Courts Act 1980

21.171 The court has a discretion to make an award of costs in favour of the successful party. The successful party must specify the sum and such order must be such costs as the court thinks 'just and reasonable'. The magistrates' court does not enforce these costs. There is no imprisonment in default. It is not treated as a fine. They merely create a civil debt between the applicant and the defendant. Enforcement is a matter for the county court if the successful party thinks it is worth enforcing. When considering a costs order against a defendant, his means may be a relevant factor, because the court has to consider what sum is just and reasonable in the circumstances of the case. At this stage of the proceedings the court may be minded to infer that the defendant is of sufficient means if they have sat through a hearing where details of money being moved around the country or continent relating to unlawful conduct have been given. Conversely, if the applicant has just been awarded, by virtue of the court's finding, a large amount of money, then the court may not be minded to grant costs at all.

21.172 Pursuant to s 62(2) the amount ordered to be paid shall be specified in the order and s 62(3) confirms that the costs ordered shall be enforceable as a civil debt.

21.173 The power of the magistrates' court to make a wasted costs order is governed by s 145A of the Magistrates' Court Act 1980 and SI 1991/2096. Costs are further considered at para 28.15 of Chapter 28.

(2) Legal Services Commission funding

21.174 Pursuant to Sch11 para 36 to the Proceeds of Crime Act 2002, the Access to Justice Act 1999 (AJA) was amended by POCA to insert at Sch 2 para 2(3) of the AJA a provision that allows for LSC funding to be obtained for an order or direction under ss 295, 297, 298, 301 or 302 of POCA (The Cash Forfeiture and Supplementary Matters Provisions). Particularly, this allows for advocacy to be met by LSC funding.

21.175 The practical procedure is that solicitors should complete a LSC Merits form (APP 1) and also the appropriate Means form (for a passported individual on income support or JSA, a Means 2; for an individual who is working or on other benefits a Means 1; or for a business a Means 1 and a Means 1A. For a foreign national a Means 3 should be completed). This may then be submitted to the relevant LSC office who will then decide whether or not it should be granted. See Appendix 6 for further information in relation to same.

H. Costs and Compensation

21.176 Anecdotally the evidence has been that there has been a variation in how regional offices have dealt with such applications. Notwithstanding it being one of the stated aims of the LSC to produce consistent and justifiable decisions throughout its regional offices and amongst its contracted suppliers.

21.177 The practical difficulties include the fact that claimants on LSC funding have just had a large amount of cash seized from them. This obviously gives rise to a question in relation to their means and will often lead to delay while the LSC investigate matters. Often as a result defendants in cash seizure cases are left either defending themselves or with sometimes their advisers acting on a conditional fee arrangement. Quite why the cash seizure provisions are dealt with differently to those for civil recovery elsewhere under Pt 5 of the Act is not immediately clear. In civil recovery matters heard before the High Court judges were fairly robust in resisting applications from the Assets Recovery Agency whilst LSC funding was being determined. It was in part as a result of the robust attitude of the judiciary that the amendments to the Serious Organised Crime and Police Act that now allow for restrained funds to be utilised to fund representation were introduced. (Based on arguments such as equality of arms etc.) It may be in due course that it will be argued that it is unfair for a defendant to have to respond to a complaint made by either the police or the Commissioners for Revenue and Customs until his LSC funding has been determined.

(3) May funds be released from the detained cash to fund continued detention and forfeiture applications?

21.178 The short answer appears to be No. In *Customs and Excise Commissioners v Harris* (1999) 163 JPR 408 Forbes J held:

> I am satisfied that there is no proper basis for extending to the Magistrates a power to make any order for the release of lawfully detained cash which has been seized pursuant to the provision of Section 42 of the 1994 Act, because of the absence of any specific Statutory power to make such an order and it is plain that the 1994 Act contains no provision empowering the Magistrates to make any such order.

And nor does POCA 2002.

(4) Compensation

21.179 One of the main changes to the legislative scheme under POCA, as distinct from the DTA, is that it envisages payment in terms of compensation to either the person from whom the cash was seized or the person to whom the cash belongs.

21.180 Section 302(1) states:

> If no forfeiture order is made in respect of any cash claimed under this Chapter, the person to whom the cash belongs or from whom it was seized might make an application to the Magistrates' Court for compensation.

21.181 Under s 302(4) if the court is satisfied, presumably on the balance of probabilities, that, taking account of any interest to be paid under s 296 or any amount to be paid under sub s (2), (see para 21.58 above) the applicant has suffered a loss as a result of the detention of the cash, and that the circumstances are 'exceptional', the court may order compensation, or additional compensation, to be paid to him.

21.182 The amount of compensation to be paid under subs 4 is the amount the court thinks reasonable, having regard to the loss suffered and any other relevant circumstances (see s 302(5)).

21.183 This section applies to compensation for loss incurred as a result of the detention of the cash. Therefore, if an individual has suffered loss for any other reason, there is no recourse under this section.

21.184 Section 302 does not define what 'exceptional circumstances' are, nor does it give any indication as to the type of losses that would be considered appropriate. For example, ordinarily in any civil case the successful party would be entitled to claim their legal costs in any event. That clearly does not come under the heading of compensation. Loss of earnings however, in having to attend court, in order to defend the forfeiture application, may fall outside the traditional costs regime. The question is whether or not loss of earnings would constitute 'exceptional circumstances'. 'Exceptional' has a dictionary meaning of 'not ordinary; uncommon; rare; hence, better than the average; superior; unusual; beyond the norm'. It will also be noted that the Act uses the word 'circumstances' and not 'consequences'.

21.185 The court will also need to satisfy itself, again on the balance of probabilities that the loss was 'as a result of the detention of the cash'.

(5) Application for compensation

21.186 Under r 8(1) an application for compensation under s 302(1) must be made in writing and sent to the Justices' Chief Executive for the Petty Sessions Area of the court before which the applicant wishes to make the application, but under r 8(2) if the applicant has been given notice of an order under s 295(2) of the Act in respect of the cash which is the subject of the application, then the application must be sent to the Justices' Chief Executive who sent him that notice. The Justices' Chief Executive will also send a copy of the application to either the police or Revenue and Customs and then fix a date for the hearing of the application (see r 8(3)). Clearly therefore the Rules anticipate a separate and distinct hearing—the pre-requisite being an application in writing. (For further discussion see para 28.99 of Chapter 28.)

I. Appeals

(1) Appeals against forfeiture

21.187 Section 299 of POCA was amended by s 101 of the Serious Organised Crime and Police Act 2005 (SOCPA) because of an ambiguity as to its meaning. While the original s 299(1) appeared to allow 'any party to the proceedings' the ability to appeal against an order made under s 298, this was qualified by the words 'for the forfeiture of cash'. This meant that while any party may appeal an order for forfeiture there was no provision for the complainant to appeal a refusal to grant forfeiture, although somewhat ironically a complainant could appeal an order for forfeiture.

I. Appeals

The substituted s 299 now states: 21.188

(1) Any person to proceedings for an order for the forfeiture of cash under section 298 who is aggrieved by an order under that section or by the decision of the court to make such an order may appeal . . ..

In other words, both the complainant and the defendant now have a right of appeal from the magistrates' court hearing to the Crown Court. Such a hearing will normally be de novo (s 79(3) of the Supreme Court Act 1981), with the facts being re-examined in the court above, and with the opportunity for both parties to serve further evidence before the hearing takes place (while the original s 299(3) expressly stated that the appeal was by way of re-hearing, the substituted legislation does not).

The appeal is to the Crown Court and notice must be lodged before the expiration of 30 days from when the order or decision was made (substituted s 299(2)). 21.189

This section also has the effect of allowing the Appeal Court, and the Crown Court, to hear an appeal in an appropriate way, for example, on a point of law. 21.190

(2) Can the 30 day period for the date of the appeal be extended?

It appears not. In *R v West London Magistrates' Court ex p Rowland Omo Lamai* (QBD, 6 July 2000), a DTA case, the High Court held that the 30 day period could not be extended by either a Crown Court or a magistrates' court; and that the 30 day deadline was a deadline without flexibility. 21.191

(3) Funding the appeal

The provision under s 44(4) of the DTA for the release of cash in order to fund an appeal in DTA cases no longer exists under the corresponding provisions of s 299 (although it should be noted that substituted s 299(3) states that the court hearing the appeal may make 'any order it thinks appropriate'. It is anticipated that there is likely to be argument as to whether this can be extended to ordering release of part of the cash in order to fund the appeal, particularly where the appellants arguments have merit, he can demonstrate that he has no other available funds, and that he requires representation, ie 'equality of arms' at the Crown Court. By implication ECHR arguments arise if such a request were refused without proper consideration). 21.192

(4) Costs in appeal proceedings

For the Crown Court's powers to award costs in appeals brought from the magistrates' court, see rr 78.1 and 78.2 of the Criminal Procedure Rules 2005, SI 2005/384. 21.193

(5) Judicial review

While there remains obvious scope for judicial review proceedings in cash seizure cases, in *M v Bow Street Magistrates' Court* The Times, 27 July 2005 the Court held that in proceedings under the Anti-Terrorism, Crime and Security Act 2001 it was premature to seek permission to challenge by way of judicial review a district judge's decision on a preliminary ruling when the judge had not yet determined any of the factual issues or received evidence 21.194

in relation to the substantive matter. The Divisional Court held that it would be impossible to know precisely how the legal issues would arise until the evidence was heard and the facts were found. Appeals in cash seizure cases are further considered at paras 24.98 – 24.111 of Chapter 24.

J. Searches and Seizure of Cash

21.195 The second part of the regime under POCA deals with the power to search and seize cash found on either premises or on an individual. These provisions also came into force on 30 December 2002 (SI 2002/3015). Many of the procedural rules that apply to cash seizures under the seizure and detention provisions of s 294 apply equally to cash searches.

(1) Cash on premises

21.196 Section 289 states:

(1) If a Revenue and Customs Officer or constable who is lawfully on any premises has reasonable grounds for suspecting that there is on the premises cash—

(a) which is recoverable property or is intended by any person for use in unlawful conduct, and

(b) the amount of which is not less than the minimum amount, he may search for the cash there.

(2) The minimum amount: £1000

21.197 Under s 303 the 'minimum amount' is defined as the amount in sterling specified in an order made by the Secretary of State (£1000 —SI 2006/1699) and for that purpose the amount of any cash held in a currency other than sterling must be taken to be the sterling equivalent.

21.198 These search powers can only be exercisable therefore if the suspected cash is thought to exceed the threshold of £1,000.

(3) The definition of 'cash'

21.199 Under s 289(6) cash means:

(a) notes and coins in any currency,
(b) postal orders,
(c) cheques of any kind (including travellers cheques),
(d) bankers drafts,
(e) bearer bonds and bearer shares

found at any place in the UK.

21.200 Under s 289(7):

Cash also includes any kind of monetary instrument which is found at any place in the United Kingdom, if the instrument is specified by the Secretary of State by an Order . . .

J. Searches and Seizures of Cash

Section 289(1) is only exercisable on private premises where the police or Revenue and Customs have lawful authority to be present (see PACE 1984 and Customs & Excise Management Act 1979 (CEMA)). An officer could also be lawfully present on private premises if he is there at the invitation of the owner.

(4) Cash on the suspect

Under s 289(2): **21.201**

(2) If a Revenue and Customs Officer or constable has reasonable grounds for suspecting that a person (the suspect) is carrying cash—
  (a) which is recoverable property or is intended by any person to be used in unlawful conduct, and
  (b) the amount of which is not less than the minimum amount [£1,000], he may exercise the following powers.
(3) The officer or constable may, so far as he thinks it necessary or expedient, require the suspect—
  (a) to permit a search of any article he has with him;
  (b) to make a search of his person.

This section does not require the person to submit to an intimate search or a strip search (within the meaning of s 164 CEMA 1979) (see s 289(8)). However, under s 289(4) an officer exercising his powers under s 289(3)(b) may detain the suspect for 'so long as is necessary for the exercise'. **21.202**

Under s 289(5) the powers conferred by s 289(1) and (2) are exercisable only so far as is reasonably required for the purpose of finding cash and are exercisable by a Revenue and Customs officer only if he has reasonable grounds for suspecting the unlawful conduct in question relates to an assigned matter within the meaning of CEMA 1979. Areas within the meaning of CEMA include drug trafficking, money laundering, and excise evasion. **21.203**

(5) 'Unlawful conduct'

See s 241 at para 21.20 above. **21.204**

(6) Safeguards for the new search powers

The powers conferred by s 289 may only be exercised when the appropriate approval has been given unless it is not practicable to obtain that approval before exercising the power (s 290(1)). **21.205**

The appropriate approval means the approval of a judicial officer or, if that is not practicable, the approval of a senior officer (s 290(2)). Under s 290(3)(a) a judicial officer means a justice of the peace. **21.206**

A senior officer means, in relation to the exercise of the power by a Revenue and Customs officer, a Revenue and Customs officer of a rank designated by HM Revenue and Customs as equivalent to that of a senior police officer and in relation to the exercise of the power by a constable, a senior police officer (an inspector or above) (see s 290(4)). **21.207**

21.208 If judicial approval is not obtained prior to a search, and cash is either not seized or is released before the matter comes before a court (ie within 48 hours) the officer concerned must prepare a written statement giving the particulars of the circumstances which led him to believe that the powers were exercisable and why it was not practicable to obtain the approval of a judicial officer (ie a magistrate). Once that is prepared they must submit it to 'the person appointed by the Secretary of State' (see s 290(6) to (8)).

21.209 There is therefore in effect a three stage process in exercising these searches in terms of prior approval:

(1) the officer concerned must seek the approval of a judicial officer (a magistrate) before exercising the power;
(2) if it is not practicable to obtain a magistrate's approval, the officer concerned should seek the approval of a senior officer; and
(3) the power to search may still be exercised if, in the circumstances, it is not practical to obtain the approval of either of the above before exercising the power (s 290(1)).

(7) Report on exercise of powers

21.210 The report submitted to the 'appointed person', where judicial approval has not been sought, forms the basis of an annual report (s 291). The appointed person may draw general conclusions and make appropriate recommendations as to the circumstances and manner in which the powers conferred by s 289 are being exercised (see s 291(2)).

(8) The Code of Practice

21.211 A Code of Practice exists for officers in connection with the exercise of the search powers conferred by s 289 of POCA.

21.212 Under s 292(6) a failure by an officer to comply with a provision of the Code does not of itself make him liable to criminal or civil proceedings.

21.213 Under 292(7) the Code is admissible in evidence in criminal or civil proceedings and is to be taken into account by a court or tribunal in any case in which it appears to the court or tribunal to be relevant.

21.214 The Code of Practice was introduced by The Proceeds of Crime Act 2002 (Cash Searches: Code of Practice) Order 2002, SI 2002/3115 and came into force on 30 December 2002.

(9) Procedure at hearings

21.215 Rule 11(1) states:

> At the hearing of an application under Chapter 3 of Part 5 of the Act (either searches for cash or seizure of cash), any person to whom notice of the application has been given may attend and be heard on the question of whether the application should be granted. The fact that any such person does not attend should not prevent the Court from hearing the application.

21.216 For further on procedure following the discovery and seizure of cash under the search powers see para 21.120 et seq above.

K. Compatibility of the Forfeiture Provisions with the ECHR

In *Butler v UK* (Application 41661/98) (27 June 2002) the ECHR took the view that a forfeiture order was a preventative measure and could not be compared to a criminal sanction. (See para 20.110 in Chapter 20.) The Court further held that the court proceedings: **21.217**

> afforded the applicant ample opportunity to contest the evidence against him and to dispute the making of a forfeiture order and that the complaint before them was "manifestly ill-founded".

In short therefore, for the time being, this area of the law appears to be ECHR friendly.

22

THIRD PARTIES AND CONFISCATION LAW

A. Introduction	22.01	
B. Restraint Orders	22.03	
(1) Jurisdiction to bind third parties	22.03	
(2) Obligations of third parties	22.07	
(3) Rights of third parties	22.11	
(4) Reasonable costs and expenses	22.12	
(5) Restraint orders and the wife of the defendant	22.16	
(6) Living expenses	22.19	
(7) Legal expenses	22.21	
(8) Restraint orders and limited companies	22.22	
(9) The corporate veil	22.23	
(10) Prosecutor does not have to give an undertaking in damages	22.29	
(11) Unsecured third party creditors	22.30	
(12) Use of assets	22.57	
(13) What remedies are available to a person who denies the defendant has an interest in a restrained asset?	22.58	
C. Confiscation Orders	22.59	
(1) Receivership proceedings	22.62	
(2) The right to be given notice of the proceedings	22.64	
(3) The right to make representations	22.65	
(4) What steps should be taken on behalf of the third party on receipt of an application to appoint an enforcement receiver?	22.67	
(5) Seeking an adjournment	22.68	
(6) Powers of the court and receiver in relation to third parties under POCA	22.70	

(7) The role of the defendant	22.73
(8) The hearing	22.74
(9) The court's order	22.75
D. Specific Third Party Claims	22.79
(1) Wives and cohabitees	22.79
(2) The matrimonial home	22.85
(3) *Re Norris* and *HM Customs v MCA*	22.88
(4) Developing matrimonial home case law	22.100
E. Property Adjustment Orders	22.119
(1) Property adjustment orders: does POCA oust the MCA?	22.125
(2) Matrimonial homes where the conditions set out in *Re Norris* and *HM Customs and Excise v MCA* do not apply	22.127
(3) Property should form part of the confiscation order	22.128
(4) Equitable interests in the matrimonial home	22.131
(5) Trusts	22.133
(6) Application of sums and third parties	22.134
(7) Banks	22.135
(8) Banks: No duty of care	22.141
(9) The insolvent defendant: the position of the trustee in bankruptcy	22.146
(10) POCA and the insolvent defendant	22.148
F. Conclusion	22.150

A. Introduction

The draconian nature of confiscation law is such that restraint and confiscation orders will inevitably have an effect on parties other than the defendant who are in possession of, or hold an interest in, his realisable property. The purpose of this chapter is to consider the rights and obligations of third parties who find themselves holding realisable property subject to restraint and confiscation proceedings. **22.01**

Chapter 22: Third Parties and Confiscation Law

22.02 There is a body of case law within the Mareva/freezing injunction jurisdiction that suggests that the court's jurisdiction to make a freezing order against a third party is 'undoubted' (see *Dadourian Group International Inc v Azuri Ltd* [2005] All ER(D) 323 (April); (ChD.22 April 2005) and is exercised as, in effect, ancillary relief granted by the court in aid of, and as part of, the freezing relief granted against the defendant to the substantive claim. Exercise of the jurisdiction could occur where there is good reason to suppose that the assets of the third party were, in truth, the assets of the injuncted defendant.

B. Restraint Orders

(1) Jurisdiction to bind third parties

22.03 The power to restrain parties other than the defendant from dealing in his realisable property is found in s 26(1) of the DTA, s 77(1) of the CJA and s 41 of POCA. Section 26(1) of the DTA reads:

> The High Court may by order (in this Act referred to as a 'Restraint Order') prohibit any person from dealing with any realisable property, subject to such conditions and exceptions as may be specified in the Order.

22.04 Section 77(1) of the Criminal Justice Act 1988 is in exactly the same terms. Section 41(1) of POCA 2002 is in similar terms, namely:

> If any condition set out in Section 40 is satisfied the Crown Court will make an order (a Restraint Order) prohibiting any specified person from dealing with any realisable property held by him.

22.05 The obvious difference is that s 41 of POCA refers to 'any specified person' whereas previously the legislation had referred to 'any person'. Nevertheless the intention of the legislation remains the same, ie a restraint order may be made both against the defendant (or the person under investigation), and any other person holding realisable property.

22.06 These sections are intended to empower the court to prohibit third parties from dealing with any realisable property. They are clearly wide enough to restrain parties (other than the defendant) from dealing in assets in which the defendant holds an interest. It is, of course, an essential prerequisite to restraining a third party that the defendant has some interest in the property: the prosecutor may not restrain assets in which the defendant has no interest whatever except where the asset in question is a gift caught by the Acts.

(2) Obligations of third parties

22.07 Once a third party is given notice or served with a copy of a restraint order, he must not allow the defendant to deal with any realisable property caught by the order in a manner inconsistent with its terms. Any failure to do so will render the third party vulnerable to proceedings for contempt of court. If the order contains any exceptions, the third party should only allow the defendant to avail himself of that exception once he has satisfied himself that any conditions precedent have been satisfied. For example, the release of monies to pay a defendant's general living expenses is frequently conditional upon him giving notice to the prosecutor of the source of any monies he intends to use for this purpose.

A financial institution should always check with the prosecuting authority that conditions of this nature have been fulfilled before releasing money for such purposes.

22.08 The third party should also check whether he holds other assets belonging to the defendant which, although not specifically named in the order, are caught by the general restraint provision. These assets too should not be released to the defendant. A restraint order may, eg specifically restrain the defendant from dealing with monies held in a current account at a particular bank. It may transpire, however, that the defendant also holds a deposit account at the same bank of which the prosecutor was unaware when he obtained the restraint order. In such circumstances the bank should also take steps to freeze this account.

22.09 A third party served with a restraint order would be well advised to seek legal advice on its terms at an early stage. The third party has to steer a difficult course between preventing any dealing with assets properly caught by the order on the one hand, and allowing defendants access to assets that are not strictly within its terms on the other. Any failure to do the former may result in contempt proceedings being brought by the prosecutor, and any failure to do the latter may result in an action being brought against the third party by the defendant for breach of contract or other relief. In order to prevent being caught in this 'Catch 22' position, the third party should when in doubt make an application to court under either sc 115.5(1) (High Court CJA/DTA, in accordance with Pt 23 of the Civil Procedure Rules) or r 59.3 of the Criminal Procedure Rules (Crown Court/POCA).

22.10 In *Z Ltd v A-Z and Others,* sub nom *Marera Injunction* [1982] QB 558; [1982] 2 WLR 288, Lord Denning MR gave good advice to third parties holding assets subject to Mareva (now freezing) injunctions, and similar principles, it is submitted, apply to restraint orders. At p 563 he said:

> As soon as the bank is given notice of the *Mareva* injunction, it must freeze the defendant's bank account. It must not allow any drawings to be made on it, neither by cheques drawn before the injunction nor by those drawn after it. The reason is because, if allowed any such drawings, it would be obstructing the course of justice as prescribed by the court granting the injunction, and it would be guilty of contempt of court. I have confined my observations to banks and bank accounts. But the same applies to any specific asset held by a bank for safe custody on behalf of the defendant, be it jewellery, stamps, or anything else and to any other person who holds any other assets of the defendants. If the asset is covered by the terms of the *Mareva* injunction, that other person must not hand it over to the defendant or do anything to enable him to dispose of it. He must hold it pending further order.

Specific guidance to the various kinds of third party most commonly affected by restraint and confiscation orders is given later in this chapter.

(3) Rights of third parties

22.11 Restraint and confiscation law has to strike a balance between ensuring that realisable property in the hands of third parties are properly restrained on the one hand and ensuring that the third party does not suffer loss on the other. Inevitably this is a difficult balance to achieve, the two aims being to some extent in conflict. Third parties should, however, be aware of the rights they have in order to keep any potential loss suffered as a result of complying with the order to a minimum.

(4) Reasonable costs and expenses

22.12 Most third parties will inevitably incur costs in complying with the terms of the order. In most cases, it will be necessary to take legal advice on the terms of the order, and in the case of orders affecting commercial organisations, the time of fee-earning staff will be occupied in setting up systems to ensure the order is complied with. Banks, for example, will have to put a 'freeze' on the defendant's bank accounts to prevent money being withdrawn from its branches by cheque or cash card. By sc 115.4(1) the court is given power to make a restraint order:

> Subject to conditions and exceptions including, but not limited to conditions relating to the indemnifying of third parties against expenses incurred in complying with the order . . .

A similar provision is made in POCA cases by the Criminal Procedure Rules r 52.2(5).

22.13 It is usual for the prosecutor to give an undertaking to pay the reasonable costs and expenses of third parties (except the recipients of gifts caught by the Act), which are incurred:

(a) in ascertaining whether any assets caught by the order are within his possession or control; or

(b) in securing compliance with the terms of the order.

Typically such an undertaking is in the following terms:

> [The Prosecutor] will pay the reasonable costs of anyone other than the Defendant (and his wife) which have been incurred as a result of compliance with this Order including the costs of ascertaining whether that person holds any of the Defendant's assets SAVE THAT [the Prosecutor] will not pay any legal or accountancy costs so incurred without first giving their consent in writing.

22.14 The undertaking only extends to costs incurred for these purposes and for no other reason and only 'reasonable costs and expenses' are caught.

22.15 In the majority of cases, such issues can be resolved by agreement between the prosecutor and the third party concerned. Where the parties are unable to resolve any dispute as to liability or quantum, the third party should make an application to the court.

(5) Restraint orders and the wife of the defendant

22.16 In *Re G (Restraint Order)* (QBD, 19 July 2001) Burnton J laid down guidelines for what should and should not be included in restraint orders. In respect of the wife of the defendant he found that s 77 of the CJA (which corresponds with s 26 of the DTA and s 41 of POCA) empowered the High Court (and now under POCA the Crown Court) to make a restraint order prohibiting any person from dealing with any realisable property. He stated such a person might be someone other than the defendant, provided he or she holds realisable property. He added:

> There are therefore two possible bases under the 1988 Act for making a restraint order prohibiting the wife of a defendant from dealing with a bank account in their joint names: (a) that

B. Restraint Orders

the credit balance in the bank account constitutes realisable property; and (b) that the wife's interest in the joint bank account may be the result of a gift or gifts caught by Part VI of the 1988 Act. On the same basis the real property in joint names may also be made the subject of a Restraint Order prohibiting both husband and wife from dealing with the property. Of course, in many cases basis (b) will be inapplicable, either because no gift has been made (as where the wife's interest results from her own earnings) or because of the requirement of section 74(10) that the gift must have been made after the earliest of the offences in question. In addition if a joint bank account is used for domestic expenses and has a modest credit balance, it is debatable whether the payments into the account made by the Defendant are a 'gift' . . . if, as in the present case, a wife is to be prohibited from dealing with any property, the order should make clear on its face that she is the subject of the order. In the case of civil proceedings, this may be done by making her a Respondent to the application, and a Defendant in the proceedings. RSC Order 115 Rule 2A would seem to prevent making the wife, against whom no criminal proceedings have been instituted and, as far as I am aware, is not to be charged, a Defendant to proceedings such as the present. However, the 'Notice to the Defendant' at the beginning of the Restraint Order should be supplemented so as to become 'Notice to the Defendant and to (the wife)', giving the full name of the wife. It is not sufficient for the application of the Order for the wife to be found only in the operative paragraphs of the Order.

22.17 Burnton J went on to add that unless there is evidence that the wife has adequate separate means, it is essential that the order permits her to spend an adequate weekly sum on ordinary living expenses, and to pay for her separate legal advice and representation. It is not appropriate, he held, to rely on her right to apply to vary the order for this purpose. Lastly, he stated the order should include an undertaking by the prosecutor to serve the order and the witness statement in support on the wife as soon as practicable. Sc 115.4(3) (High Court DTA/CJA) and Criminal Procedure Rules r 59.2(8) now makes such service mandatory.

22.18 Burnton J added that the above considerations are equally applicable to anyone who is a cohabitee of the defendant.

(6) Living expenses

22.19 A wife is entitled to a sum from restrained funds in order to meet her weekly and monthly outgoings. If the defendant is in prison a figure will be fixed with her. If the defendant is at liberty a figure will be fixed for both him and his wife. 'Reasonable costs and expenses' will be met. School fees may, eg be payable. But such items would cease to be allowable once the defendant was convicted, as per *Re Peters* [1998] 3 All ER 46 where the Court of Appeal held that payment for school fees for the defendant's son for a period after the result of his trial was known could not be allowed. As Mann LJ said at p 52:

> I fully understand that [the court below] may have been influenced by the disruption of the son's education should a confiscation order be made, but in my judgment there is, in the light of section 31(2) no room for the intrusion of sympathy.

22.20 In the majority of cases, such issues can be resolved by agreement between the prosecutor and the third party concerned. Where the parties are unable to resolve any dispute as to liability or quantum, the third party should make an application to court.

(7) Legal expenses

22.21 In *Re D* [2006] EWHC (Admin) 1519, the question of whether third parties who assert an interest in property that is the subject of a restraint order and which was due to be considered as part of a confiscation order, have a right to receive legal funding from that property arose. There were a number of properties that were in the name of members of the defendant's family. It was part of the case against the defendant that that had been done deliberately in order to conceal the true situation, (namely that they were actually his benefit from his unlawful conduct). Counsel suggested that by virtue of s 82(4) of the CJA everyone who has an alleged interest in property should have the opportunity to establish the existence of that interest, and be provided with monies from the proceeds of the property, to pay for legal representation. Collins J described this as a 'quite hopeless submission'.

He stated:

> The powers must be exercised to ensure that the third parties have a proper opportunity of pursuing their claim. That they will do in the way that any litigation is to be pursued. If they have the means, they will have to pay for it: if they do not have sufficient means, then they may apply for public funding. But what they cannot do is to obtain funding from the property which they are asserting they have an interest in when their interest is being disputed.

(8) Restraint orders and limited companies

22.22 In *Re G (Restraint Order)* (2001) Stanley Burnton J held, leaving gifts aside, that there were two bases upon which a prosecutor may apply for a restraint order prohibiting dealings in the assets of a company controlled by a defendant but against which no criminal charge is to be made. Namely:

(1) that the company holds realisable property within the meaning of (the applicable Act); and

(2) that the company has no genuine separate existence from the defendant, and is used by him as a device for fraud.

(9) The corporate veil

22.23 In the case of (2) above, the court treats the assets of the company as if they were in the name of the defendant. The court is said to 'lift the corporate veil'. The application to lift the corporate veil will often come in the witness statement that supports the application for the restraint order. The wording will be in similar terms to the following:

> I invite the honourable court to lift the corporate veil in respect of Tosca Limited as I believe the sole purpose of the company and its bank accounts was and continues to be to perpetrate the fraud and provide a conduit for its proceeds.

22.24 In *Re G* Burnton J held that while the phrase 'lifting the corporate veil' was helpful shorthand, it had no place in an injunction (in the restraint order itself), because the object of that was to set out clear and specific prohibitions effecting the defendant and the other persons effected by the order and to impose equally clear obligations on the applicant. He stated as follows:

> If the evidence before the court raises a prima facie case justifying a lifting of the corporate veil, and to treat the property of the company as the property of the Defendant, the order should prohibit the company, in addition to the Defendant, from dealing with its property.

Notwithstanding Burnton J's above observation, it is commonplace to find within a restraint order the following additional injunction:

> AND IT IS ORDERED THAT: The assets of Tosca Limited be treated as the personal assets of the Defendant

thus reflecting the fact that the court has in fact lifted the corporate veil over that company.

22.25 The principles relating to the lifting of the corporate veil in this context are no different from those applicable in other areas of the law: see *Re H (Restraint Order: Realisable Property)* [1996] 2 All ER 391 and, more recently, *Trustor AB v Smallbone* [2001] 1 WLR 1177, (especially at para 23). In many cases, in addition it will be appropriate to appoint a receiver under the power conferred by the relevant statute to take possession of the property of the company and to manage it (see *Re H* above).

22.26 It should also be noted that at the stage of the application for a restraint order without notice, the courts will have no more than a prima facie case before it. The company may subsequently be able to establish that it has a legitimate existence as a legal person carrying on a lawful business. The order must therefore also be addressed to the company and the applicant's witness statement served on it, as required by sc 115.4(3) and the Criminal Procedure Rules r 59.2(8). The order should provide that the company should be entitled to spend up to a maximum sum (which is liable to be increased) on its separate legal advice and representation (as per Burnton J in *Re G*).

22.27 Burnton J also held that particular caution was required if it appears that, in addition to engaging in fraudulent transactions, the company is carrying on a legitimate business that may be closed down by the order. In those circumstances it may not be appropriate to treat the assets of the company as those of the defendant. Freezing injunctions and civil proceedings normally contain an exception to the prohibition against dealing with property to enable the person restrained to deal with his assets in the ordinary course of business. A restraint order may be made subject to such a specified exception where appropriate.

22.28 Where the company is not a company limited by guarantee but is merely a company which is a trading name for the defendant, eg Alfredo Germont trading as Alfredo Germont Fuels, it has no separate legal identity because it is not a registered company. It is therefore incorrect and unnecessary for it to be separately restrained. The restraint order itself would prevent the defendant from dealing with the assets of Alfredo Germont Fuels because he is prohibited from dealing with any assets that he holds.

(10) Prosecutor does not have to give an undertaking in damages

22.29 In contrast to the position in relation to freezing injunctions, the prosecutor cannot be required to give an undertaking in damages. This provision is to be found in sc 115.4(1) and the Criminal Procedure Rules r 59.2(4) (POCA cases) which states as follows:

> (4) The Crown Court must not require the applicant for a restraint order to give any undertaking relating to damages sustained as a result of the restraint order by a person who is prohibited from dealing with realisable property by the restraint order.

The sister provision under sc 115.4(1) was considered by Otton J in *Re R (Restraint Order)* [1990] 2 All ER 569. The third party was the landlord of industrial premises let to the defendant who had installed plant machinery in them. When the defendant was charged with drug trafficking offences, a restraint order was made prohibiting him, inter alia, from disposing of or dealing in the plant machinery at the premises leased from the applicants. The landlord sought to distrain the plant machinery for arrears of rent, and arranged for it to be sold by auction. The landlord became aware of the restraint order two days before the auction, cancelled it, and sought an order against the prosecutor to be indemnified in respect of their loss. Otton J refused to make such an order ruling that the court had no jurisdiction either by statute or in the exercise of its inherent jurisdiction to grant such relief.

(11) Unsecured third party creditors

22.30 In *Re W* The Times, 15 November 1990, Buckley J held that the effect of s 31(2) of the DTA and s 82(2) of the CJA was such as to give the prosecutor priority against unsecured creditors, whereas in contrast the plaintiff who has obtained freezing order relief has no such priority. If, of course, the prosecutor has assets to a greater value than any likely confiscation order restrained, a variation may be ordered. In refusing Mrs W's application for a variation to a CJA restraint order, Buckley J ruled as follows:

> There is one fundamental difference between the two jurisdictions . . . which is vital here. The object of *Mareva* injunctions is not to give any priority or advantage to the plaintiff over other creditors of the defendant. The provisions to which I have referred in the 1988 Act do give priority to the satisfaction of a confiscation order at least over general creditors. If that is the ultimate purpose of the Act, it must be wrong to make any order at an intermediate stage which might thwart such purpose.

22.31 The decision in *Re W* was cast into doubt however by *Re X* [2004] EWHC 861. The issue in *Re X* concerned a claim by a third party 'Z Ltd' that the company the receiver controlled as part of his appointment ('Y Ltd'), owed Z Ltd almost £874,000, pursuant to written invoices previously rendered. The receiver had in his control sufficient funds to make such a payment. The question was whether it was appropriate for the receiver to do so.

22.32 The receiver submitted that when a restraint order was made, the court was not empowered to pay general creditors in priority over the interests of the Crown which had obtained the order, by reference to s 82(2) ('the legislative steer') and s 82(6) of the CJA and *Re W*. Section 82(2) and (6) state as follows:

> . . . (2) subject to the following provisions of this section, the powers shall be exercised with a view to making available for satisfying the confiscation order or, as the case may be, any confiscation order that may be made in the defendant's case, the value for the time being of realisable property held by any person by the realisation of such property . . .
>
> (6) in exercising those powers, no account shall be taken of any obligations of the defendant . . . which conflict with the obligation to satisfy the confiscation order.

Davis J rejected that submission. He concluded it could not be right because it would mean:

i. that a receiver appointed over assets of a company under the CJA would have no power to pay off trade debts with a view to retaining the value of the business of the company (para 18), or

ii. that a receiver appointed over assets of a company under the CJA would have no power to pay a landlord for rent, thus losing the value of the property if it became forfeit and therefore lost,

and that the submission must be wrong, in any event, because a Court was empowered by virtue of the Act, to sanction debts in the form of living expenses and legal expenses to be paid.

The first submission therefore having failed, the receiver argued that the court was only empowered to order a payment to creditors where the value of the realisable property, as defined, is not reduced. It was argued that unless this was so the statutory purpose of s 82(2) ('the legislative steer') would be defeated. **22.33**

This second argument drew support from the case of *Re W*. Until Davis J's decision in *Re X*, prosecuting authorities and the courts had followed the earlier decision. *Re W* effectively holds that a restraint order should not be varied on the application of a bona fide third party judgment creditor so as to permit the judgment sum to be paid. **22.34**

Buckley J's reasoning in *Re W* was that the purpose of the restraint order was to make available the value of realisable property to satisfy a confiscation order that had or might be made. The applicant had no interest in the frozen monies, per se, in terms of ownership of it. And s 82(6) was clear that no account was to be taken of any 'obligations' of the defendant (Buckley J was prepared to assume that 'obligations' included debts and the satisfaction of the confiscation order took priority.) **22.35**

In *Re W* the Court's attention had been drawn to the analogy between restraint orders and freezing orders. Under its Mareva jurisdiction the Court would have permitted bona fide debts of third parties to be paid as they fell due. Under its Mareva/freezing order jurisdiction the court is not working to a 'legislative steer'. **22.36**

This highlights one of the fundamental differences between the two jurisdictions. The object of freezing orders is not to give any priority or advantage to the plaintiff over other creditors of the defendant. However, the provisions of the DTA and CJA do give priority to the satisfaction of the confiscation order at least over general creditors. As a result, Buckley J refused to make an order that might thwart the Act's purpose. **22.37**

However, Davis J came to the view that the interpretation Buckley J had given to the statutory provisions in *Re W* were incorrect, for the following three reasons: **22.38**

1. Section 77(1) was phrased in wide terms ('The High Court may by order (a Restraint Order) prohibit any person from dealing with any realisable property, subject to conditions and exceptions as may be specified in the order') and this discretion was preserved by s 77(2) (living expenses and legal expenses) and the unfettered discretion of s 77(6) (a Restraint Order may be varied in relation to any property);
2. While Davis J accepted that the s 77 powers were subject to s 82 (the legislative steer), the phrase, 'with a view to' in that section introduced a degree of elasticity;
3. Although s 82(6) of the CJA provides that no account shall be taken of any obligations of the defendant which conflict with the obligation to satisfy the confiscation order, s 82(6) only applies where a confiscation order has already been made; not at an earlier stage.

22.39 What further influenced Davis J in *Re X* was 'the clear distinction between after a Confiscation Order has been made and the position before one has been made'. A confiscation order is made after conviction. Before conviction Davis J was keen to stress that there was a presumption of innocence:

> The person who is the subject of the Restraint Order may be acquitted. It is difficult to think that Parliament could have intended to restrict the court's powers as a matter of jurisdiction in the way now contended for when the consequence might be the bankruptcy or ruin of the individual concerned before he has even been tried. That, indeed, to my mind in one explanation for the distinction between the wording of section 82(2) and section 82(6).

Furthermore he states, '*Moreover, I would draw attention to section 82(4). The wording of that section is apt to extend to debts, given the wide definition of the word "property" in section 102*' (para 22).

22.40 Section 82(4) states that the powers of the court shall be exercised with a view to allowing any person other than the defendant to retain or recover the value of any property held by the defendant.

22.41 In relation to the 'legislative steer' Davis J concludes:

> That will always, indeed, be a highly material and important consideration. But it is not, in my view . . . a conclusive consideration in all cases (para 23).

22.42 In relation to 'discretion' he affirmed Simon Brown LJ's view in the case of *Re P* [2000] 1 WLR 473 that:

> a balance has to be struck between, on the one hand preserving the worth of the defendant's realisable property against the possibility that he may be convicted and a confiscation order made against him, and on the other hand allowing him meantime to continue the ordinary course of his life.

22.43 As a result of his findings, Davis J held that he did have the power to grant the relief sought by Z Ltd, but (and this may be a clue as to why this decision was never appealed) refused to do so (factually it was submitted that the claimed debt was not as a result of legitimate or bona fide trading, and therefore the payment requested should not be permitted) – in effect therefore the applicants were unsuccessful on their cause of claim.

22.44 Importantly, Davis J makes it clear that he is expressing no view as to whether or to what extent the court has jurisdiction to vary a restraint order made after conviction has resulted.

22.45 It is submitted that there maybe certain reservations about the Davis J judgment. It appears not only inconsistent with the legislative steer, but also with the language and purpose of the Act.

22.46 It should also be noted that Davis J did not only fail to follow *Re W*, but also *Re R* [2004] EWHC Admin 621 and *Re M* [1992] QB 377. In those cases it was made clear that while payments may be made that have the effect of preserving the value of the defendant's assets, no payments may be made that have the effect of diminishing that value (save unless they are specifically authorised by statute, like living expenses or legal costs).

22.47 Davis J's interpretation of s 82(4) is a misreading of that section. That section is not concerned with unsecured creditors, rather individuals who have an actual interest in the actual property concerned (eg a half share, or some other type of ownership).

22.48 For these reasons elements of Davis J's judgment in *Re X* may be flawed (see Criminal Law Week (04/22/6)).

22.49 Contrary to this view is that of Stephen Gee QC, *Commercial Injunctions* (5th edn, 2004). He states Buckley J's decision is difficult to support because the wording of s 82(6) of the CJA (and s 31(5) of the DTA – allowing persons to recover the value of any property held by the defendant) does not lead to the conclusion that the Crown/confiscation order should be given priority, and relates to situations that arise solely after a confiscation order has been made, because the section refers only to the 'confiscation order', and unlike ss 82(2) and 31(2) not also to 'any confiscation order that may be made'.

22.50 This highlights one of the difficulties Davis J faced, namely that s 31(2) of the DTA and s 82(2) of the CJA (the legislative steer) are not entirely easy provisions to construe. They address two very different situations; one at the restraint order stage and one at the stage after a confiscation order has been made. Hence a balance has to be struck. It is perhaps for this reason that Simon Brown LJ concluded in *Re Piper* [2000] 1 WLR 473 that:

> the primary task of an interim receiver was the safeguarding of the defendant's assets from dissipation and secretion rather than their realisation so as to maximise the amount of any future confiscation order.

22.51 One of the questions in *Re X* was whether the court is empowered to order payment to creditors when the value of the realisable property will be reduced as a result. There is no difficulty with a receiver paying off trade debts with a view to retaining and preserving the value of the business of a company, because the payment of such a debt would preserve a greater asset in value, similarly rent can be paid – either on the basis that it is a living expense or to preserve and maintain the defendant's interest in a property. In both cases the value of the realisable property is not diminished or reduced in value overall, because it allows a company to continue trading, continue making profits, forestalls closure etc. The court/receiver is complying with the legislative steer because they are exercising their powers with a view to making available for satisfying the confiscation order, or any confiscation order that may be made, the value for the time being of the realisable property.

22.52 That purpose concurs with *Re W* and *Re M* and is consistent with the purpose of maintaining assets to meet a final order if one should be made, and meeting the reasonable requirements of the owner in the meantime.

22.53 In short, a receiver may and will pay off debts where not to do so would place an otherwise profitable company in jeopardy. They should hestitate to payoff debts where there is no risk to the company, its value or other assets. In such cases those owed the debt have to stand in line. The distinction is the role and purpose of the receiver: they are appointed to preserve and maintain the value of the defendant's assets.

22.54 Davis J also considered whether the payment of debts could be justified in terms of the exclusion that exists in relation to living expenses. Notwithstanding Davis J's conclusions, living expenses do not constitute debts and vice versa for these purposes.

22.55 The fact that a judgment has been obtained cannot be conclusive, and a fair balance has to be struck. Restraint orders are preservative in nature, although they should be operated so that a defendant who has not yet been tried is forced into bankruptcy.

22.56 Finally it will be noted that *Re X* concerned a restraint order and management receivership under the CJA. It did not concern a restraint order and management receivership under POCA. Davis J in *Re X* clearly states that '*that statute [POCA] was not examined in argument before me*' and it was common ground that the provisions of POCA did not apply (paras 8 and 9).

(12) Use of assets

22.57 The restraint order only prevents dealing in the property. Hence, a third party may continue to use an asset in such a way that does not constitute dealing in it. A wife may therefore continue to reside in a restrained property pending the making and enforcement of a confiscation order, and may continue to drive round in a restrained motor vehicle. What she may not do is attempt to sell the asset without first obtaining a variation order from the court.

(13) What remedies are available to a person who denies the defendant has an interest in a restrained asset?

22.58 It may happen that a third party denies that the defendant has an interest in a restrained asset. If this is correct, and the asset does not constitute a gift caught by the Acts, then the asset will not constitute 'realisable property'. A third party who so contends would be entitled to apply to the High Court under the pre-POCA regime, and now the Crown Court under s 42(3) of POCA, for a variation releasing the asset in question from the terms of the order. It should be borne in mind that the function of the restraint order is to preserve the status quo pending the making and enforcement of a confiscation order. It does not take away title to property, but merely restrains any dealing in it. Accordingly, previously the High Court, and now for POCA cases the Crown Court, will not normally be willing to become embroiled in an argument as to ownership of property at the restraint stage, but will prefer issues as to the ownership of property to be resolved at the confiscation and enforcement stage. Applications for the release of property should be confined at the restraint stage to those cases where the prosecution's evidence fails to establish any interest in the asset or where the applicant has clear and incontrovertible evidence that the defendant has no interest whatever in the asset. In *SCF Finance Co Ltd v Masri* [1985] 1 WLR 876 the Court of Appeal emphasised, in relation to freezing injunctions, that a mere assertion that a third party owns an asset need not be accepted without proper enquiry, and the court had jurisdiction in appropriate circumstances to order the trial of an issue in relation to any such dispute.

C. Confiscation Orders

22.59 It has already been observed that a confiscation order is an '*in personam* order' against the convicted defendant and not an '*in rem*' order against specific items of property. The consequence of this is that third parties who hold an interest in realisable property do not have a right to be heard at the confiscation hearing in the Crown Court or to have counsel make representations to the court on their behalf. If, however, the defendant wishes the third party to be called as a witness on his behalf for the purpose of establishing the extent of his interest in realisable property he may of course do so (see *Re Norris* below).

22.60 This may at first sight seem to be a denial of natural justice. However, this is not the case, because the mere making of a confiscation order does not take away the owner's title to the property. It may be that the defendant will be able to satisfy the confiscation order by realising assets other than those in which a third party claims to have an interest. In this event the third party concerned will not be troubled further. It is only if the defendant fails to satisfy the order voluntarily and the Crown seeks the appointment of a receiver that a third party holding an interest in realisable property need become involved as a party to the proceedings.

22.61 In *Re Norris* [2001] 1 WLR 1388 the House of Lords held that having convicted a person of a drug trafficking offence the Crown Court had to assess the value of his proceeds of drug trafficking and the amount of his realisable property for the purpose of making the necessary confiscation order. At that hearing the defendant's wife, who was not a party to the proceedings, had given detailed evidence on the defendant's behalf that the matrimonial home belonged either wholly or substantially to her. The judge disbelieved her evidence and made a confiscation order against the defendant on the basis that the house formed part of his realisable property. The House of Lords held that the assertion of an interest in the property by a third party (namely the wife) should be resolved by the High Court, a third party not being precluded from asserting his or her interest by reason of having previously made assertions as to the ownership of the property when called as a witness for the defence in the criminal proceedings (for further on matrimonial homes see para 22.85 below).

(1) Receivership proceedings

22.62 When this stage of the proceedings is reached third parties claiming to hold an interest in realisable property have a right to be heard, because a receivership order effectively extinguishes the property rights of those holding realisable property. However, the rights of third parties are protected in a number of ways.

22.63 Where, eg the Crown Court makes a confiscation order under the drug trafficking legislation which is not satisfied, and the prosecution applies to the High Court under s 29 of the DTA for it to exercise its power under s 29(5) ('the Court may empower the receiver to realise any realisable property'), the court has the power to allow a third party claiming an interest in the property to reopen the question of ownership previously determined in the confiscation proceedings in the Crown Court, but should not permit the re-litigation of issues which had been decided in the Crown Court on the same, or substantially the same, evidence and submissions (see *Re Norris* [2001] 1 WLR 1388).

(2) The right to be given notice of the proceedings

22.64 Sc 115.7(2)(b) provides that the process seeking the appointment of a receiver under s 29 of the DTA (or s 80 of the CJA) or in the case of s 50 of POCA, Criminal Procedure Rules r 60.1(6)) must be served, inter alia, upon:

> Any person holding any interest in the realisable property to which the application relates.

And the application, together with the evidence in support, must be served not less than seven days prior to the hearing date.

(3) The right to make representations

22.65 Section 51(8) of POCA states:

> The court must not—
> (a) confer the power mentioned in subsection (2)(b) or (c) in respect of property, or
> (b) exercise the power conferred on it by subsection (6) in respect of property,
>
> unless it gives persons holding interest in the property a reasonable opportunity to make representations to it.

A right merely to be given notice of the proceedings would, by itself, not be sufficient to protect the third party's interest in the property. Accordingly, s 29(8) of the DTA (and s 80(8) of the CJA and s 51(8) of POCA) provides that the court shall not exercise the powers given to it under subss (3)(a), (5) or (6) unless a reasonable opportunity has been given to persons holding an interest in the property to make representations to the court.

22.66 It should be noted that the only persons who have a right to be given notice of and make representations in receivership proceedings are those who have an interest in the defendant's realisable property. Thus, a bank holding a deposit account in the name of the defendant would have no right to make representations, whereas the defendant's spouse in whose name the matrimonial home was jointly held with the defendant clearly would.

(4) What steps should be taken on behalf of the third party on receipt of an application to appoint an enforcement receiver?

22.67 The solicitor should firstly go on the record by notifying the court, the prosecuting authority that issued the application, and the solicitors for the defendant, of his interest in the case. If the client is unable to fund the case privately and meets the eligibility criteria, an emergency application for Legal Service Commission (LSC) funding should be made. Once funding has been resolved work should commence on preparing a witness statement setting out in detail the precise nature of the third party's interest in the property. Where documentary evidence supporting the third party's claim exists (eg in relation to a spouse's interest in the matrimonial home) this should be produced and exhibited to the witness statement. If there are other persons who are in a position to confirm the extent of the third party's claim, witness statements should also be taken from them. Such independent corroboration is particularly important in cases where no documentary evidence exists confirming the third party's claim.

C. Confiscation Orders

(5) Seeking an adjournment

22.68 As third parties are only entitled to seven days notice of the hearing, there may be insufficient time to obtain LSC funding (formerly legal aid), conduct all the necessary enquiries, draft and serve witness statements, and brief counsel before the return date on the application. In these circumstances an adjournment should be sought. As the public interest requires that confiscation orders should be satisfied promptly, it may well be that the court would not be prepared to adjourn the entire receivership application. It is becoming increasingly common for the court to appoint a receiver to enable him to start realising assets that are free of third party claims. In order to protect the position of the third party, the court will then go on to order a stay on the receiver's powers of realisation in respect of those assets in which he claims an interest pending the determination of the claim. In order to ensure that the third party claim is determined expeditiously, the court may make directions as to how the case should proceed. The court may, eg direct that the third party should serve his evidence in support within a specific time and that the prosecutor and defendant be at liberty to serve evidence in rebuttal within a specified period thereafter.

22.69 Before the hearing, it may be prudent for the third party to enter into negotiations with the prosecutor and defendant. In many cases, the fact of the third party having an interest in the asset will be beyond question, as, eg where the defendant and third party own a house in joint names. The real issue is more commonly the extent of the third party's interest. As all parties will be anxious to resolve the matter expeditiously and at minimum cost, it may well be that the prosecutor and defendant would be prepared to take a commercial view and not press for the highest amount for which they could argue.

(6) Powers of the court and receiver in relation to third parties under POCA

22.70 Under s 69(3)(a) of POCA 2002, the powers of a receiver must be exercised with a view to allowing a person, other than the defendant or a recipient of a tainted gift, to retain or recover the value of any interest held by him. It follows that the confiscation and enforcement powers conferred on the court and the receiver by the Act must be exercised with a view to allowing an innocent third party to retain or recover the value of any interest in realisable property held by him. Unlike the CJA and the DTA, it is now the duty of the Crown Court to ensure that the value of the third party's interests in realisable property is preserved, and that duty is in priority to the duty of the court to preserve assets for payment of a confiscation order.

22.71 It is important to remember that while there is no right to be heard at the confiscation hearing a third party may be heard at the restraint stage of proceedings and then again at the enforcement stage.

22.72 It should also be noted that under s 84 of POCA references to an interest in relation to land in England and Wales are to a legal estate, or equitable interest or power (see s 84(2)(f)). This means that mere rights such as a right of occupation are not protected under s 69(3)(a). The statutory steer under s 69 therefore requires a court to exercise its powers with a view to avoiding the remuneration of the value of the defendant's assets or realisable property.

(7) The role of the defendant

22.73 It has been stressed throughout that the third party should serve his application and evidence on the defendant as well as the prosecutor and should also involve him in any negotiations. The reason for this is that the defendant has a clear interest in the outcome of the proceedings. The greater the interest the court rules the third party has in the asset, the less the defendant will have from the proceeds of sale to satisfy the confiscation order. Accordingly, he may well wish either to dispute the third party's claim in its entirety or at least argue that the extent of the third party's interest is not as great as that claimed. As there is such a potential conflict of interest between the defendant and third party, the practice of their being represented by the same solicitors should generally be discouraged, even when there remains a close relationship between the defendant and the third party.

(8) The hearing

22.74 If the parties are unable to agree, the matter will usually be listed for hearing before a judge in chambers (unrobed) to determine:

(a) whether the third party has any interest in the asset at all; and
(b) if so, the extent of that interest.

The third party, as applicant for relief, will normally open the proceedings and call his evidence, followed by the prosecution and defendant. Witness statement evidence will be admissible except to the extent that the court has required witnesses to attend for cross-examination under r 32 CPR or the Criminal Procedure Rules. Once all the evidence has been heard, the parties will have the right to make a closing address to the court in the usual way.

(9) The court's order

22.75 The order the court makes will depend on its findings of law and fact. If the court finds that the third party is the sole owner of the property in dispute, then clearly it cannot be incorporated in the receivership order because it is not a realisable asset of the defendant. Equally, if the court rules that the defendant is the sole owner of the asset, the entire net proceeds of sale will be applied to the satisfaction of the confiscation order and the third party will get nothing. These situations are relatively simple, but the matter becomes increasingly more complex when the court rules that the third party does have some interest in the asset.

22.76 In such circumstances, the court has a number of options under s 51 of POCA (or s 29 of the DTA and s 80 of the CJA). Firstly, it could order the receiver to sell the asset and pay to the third party out of the net proceeds of sale an amount proportionate to his interest in the property. If, eg the net proceeds of sale of a property were £50,000 and the third party's interest in the property was found to be 50 per cent, £25,000 would go to the third party and £25,000 towards the satisfaction of the confiscation order.

22.77 Alternatively, where the third party has the means to 'buyout' the defendant's interest in the property, the court may, under s 51(6)(a) of POCA (or s 29(6)(a) of the DTA and s 80(6) of the CJA), order the third party to pay to the receiver an amount equivalent to the value of the beneficial interest of the defendant in that property or, as the case may be, of the recipient of a gift caught by the Act. The court may order under s 51(6)(b) of POCA (or s 29(6)(b) of the DTA and s 80(6) of the CJA) that once such payment has been made the defendant's interest in the property be transferred to the third party, that an interest in the property be granted to a third party, and/or that the defendant's interest in the property be extinguished.

Section 51(6) of POCA states: **22.78**

The court—
(a) may order a person holding an interest in realisable property to make to the receiver such payment as the Court specifies in respect of a beneficial interest held by the Defendant or the recipient of a tainted gift;
(b) may (on the payment being made) by order transfer, grant or extinguish any interest in the property.

D. Specific Third Party Claims

(1) Wives and cohabitees

Wives and cohabitees enjoy little more protection under the Acts than other third parties, and their rights to realisable property are proportionate to the interest they hold therein. Practitioners are perhaps more likely to find themselves advising wives on their position under confiscation legislation than any other third party. The first approach a solicitor is likely to get is immediately after a restraint order has been served. At this stage, the wife may well be in a state of some distress; not only may her husband be in custody facing serious criminal charges, but she finds herself served with a restraint order freezing all of her husband's realisable property, including items in which she may hold a joint interest. It is possible to give her some reassurance at this stage. **22.79**

Firstly, although the matrimonial home may be subject to restraint or charging orders, she is entitled to remain in residence pending the conclusion of the proceedings. The restraint order merely prevents her from disposing of realisable property and does not prevent its use pending the determination of the proceedings against her husband. The same principle would apply to motor vehicles, namely that they may continue to be used by the wife, but not sold. The wife should be advised that if at any time she wishes to sell an asset, she must not do so but return to the solicitor forthwith. It may well be that if, eg she wishes to move to a smaller house or buy a smaller motor vehicle, the prosecution and defendant would readily consent to a variation of the restraint order to enable her to do so, subject to the new asset being immediately made subject to restraint and any surplus funds being paid into an interest-bearing account pending the conclusion of the proceedings. As well as being warned of the potential consequences of an unlawful sale, a wife should also be advised that, in so far as she is able, she should ensure that the asset is properly maintained in the interim. If eg she were to allow a property to deteriorate, or fail to keep up mortgage payments, this could provide a basis for the prosecution applying to appoint a pre-conviction receiver. **22.80**

22.81 Joint bank accounts can create particular problems when they are restrained. It may well be that the wife's salary is paid into such an account, or that they contain other monies belonging solely to her. Firstly, she should be advised to open a bank account in her sole name and arrange for all future salary payments, together with any other payments to which she alone is entitled to be paid into that account. The prosecution should be notified that she intends to do this. Secondly, as to any monies belonging solely to her that are already in the account at the time the restraint order is served, she should be asked to provide documentary evidence (eg salary advice, letter from her employer, etc) to prove her entitlement. This should then be forwarded to the prosecution who will normally consent to the order being varied to release from the account monies belonging solely to her that do not constitute realisable property of the defendant. If the prosecution will not agree, an application to court should be considered.

22.82 The wife is also entitled, pending the conclusion of the criminal proceedings, to expect her reasonable needs to be provided for. She would, therefore, be entitled to ask the court to vary the restraint order to allow reasonable sums to be released from the restraint order to pay the reasonable living expenses of herself and her family.

22.83 Restraint orders typically contain a proviso that spending limits for living expenses may be increased on the following terms:

> The Defendant and Mrs Germont may agree with the (Prosecutor) that the above spending limits for living expenses should be increased, and the Defendant (and the Prosecutor) may agree this order may be varied in any respect but any such agreement must be in writing.

22.84 Where agreement cannot be reached in relation to living expenses the matter should be listed before the court for determination. The principles on which the court acts and the procedure to be followed are fully set out in Chapter 2.

(2) The matrimonial home

22.85 Once a confiscation order has been made, the position of the wife becomes less secure because, as Henry J pointed out in *Re B* (QBD, 13 May 1991), the Acts make no special provision to protect the rights of the wife in the matrimonial home. However, if it is necessary to sell the matrimonial home in order to satisfy the confiscation order, the wife's interest will be protected to an extent. If she has young children to provide for, while she will not necessarily be able to prevent the property being sold, her interest will be converted to the proceeds of sale, and she will receive an amount proportionate to her interest in the property (if the conditions in *Customs and Excise Commissioners v MCA* [2002] EWCA Civ 1039 and *Re Norris* [2001] 1 WLR 1388 are not made out).

22.86 Of some comfort to wives caught in the above situation however are the judgments in *MCA* and *Norris*. In *MCA*, which is considered in detail at para 22.93 below, the Court held it would be disproportionate to any legitimate public interest to make an order, the practical effect of which would be to throw onto the innocent wife the burden of meeting from assets which were wholly untainted by criminality and which would otherwise be treated by the court as hers, the burden of discharging the liabilities to which the defendant has exposed himself by virtue of his offending. In those circumstances the appropriate course, the Court

D. Specific Third Party Claims

held, was to order the defendant to transfer his entire beneficial and legal interest in the house and the policies to the wife, and not to make an order that would force the wife to leave the home.

22.87 In *Re Norris* the House of Lords held that since it was the intention of the Act that questions of third party interests should be resolved in the High Court, a third party was not precluded from asserting his interest before the High Court by reason of having previously made assertions as to the ownership of the property when called as a witness for the defence in the criminal proceedings. Since in *Norris* the wife had evidence to raise an arguable case she had at least an interest in the matrimonial home, the court held that she was making proper use of the civil jurisdiction to protect her proprietary rights within the intention of the Act, and there was no misuse of the litigational process such as would require her application to be dismissed as an abuse of process.

(3) Re Norris *and* HM Customs v MCA

22.88 The judgments in *Re Norris* and *MCA* are now so fundamental to this area of the law we consider both below in more detail: In *Re Norris* [2001] 1 WLR 1388 Customs obtained a restraint order over the property of a defendant charged with drug offences, and following his conviction they applied to the Crown Court for a confiscation order. At that hearing, the defendant's wife, who was not a party to the proceedings, gave detailed evidence on the defendant's behalf that the matrimonial home belonged either wholly or substantially to her, since she had contributed to the purchase price of earlier matrimonial homes and the proceeds of which had been used to buy the house in question. The judge at the confiscation hearing disbelieved her evidence and made the confiscation order against the defendant on the basis that the house formed part of his realisable property. The defendant, who did not appeal the order, failed to discharge it, and Customs applied to the High Court to enforce the confiscation order. The judge appointed a receiver to realise the defendant's assets which, having made a declaration that the defendant held a beneficial interest in the house, included that property in question.

22.89 The wife made an application to vary the order on the grounds that she had an interest in the home, and sought to give evidence in support of her application. The judge held that he had no jurisdiction to reopen the issue of ownership, which had already been determined by the Crown Court, and dismissed the application. The wife appealed to the Court of Appeal.

22.90 The Court of Appeal held that persons holding an interest in property liable to be realised must be given a reasonable opportunity to make representations to the court before the court could exercise the powers of enforcement conferred on it. However, it added that it would be an abuse of process to allow a third party to re-litigate issues that had already been decided in the court below on substantially the same evidence and submissions, and where the third party, although not a party to the criminal proceedings and not separately represented, had had a fair opportunity to put her case. Accordingly the Court of Appeal dismissed her appeal.

22.91 The wife lodged a further appeal to the House of Lords which was allowed. The House of Lords found that the duty of the Crown Court, having convicted a person of a drug trafficking offence, was to assess the value of his proceeds of drug trafficking and the amount of his realisable property, which could extend to property he had given away, for the purpose of making the necessary confiscation order against him in the criminal proceedings. However, the subsequent enforcement of that order by way of empowering a receiver to take possession of the realisable property made subject to the order was a matter for the High Court as part of its civil jurisdiction, and allowed a third party to re-assert any interest in the property before its disposal; it being the intention of the legislation that the questions of third party interests be resolved by the High Court.

22.92 The House of Lords thus confirmed that a third party was not precluded from asserting his or her interests before the High Court by reason of having previously made assertions as to the ownership of the property when called as a witness for the defence in the criminal proceedings to support the defendant's case that the property was not his. Accordingly, since the wife had evidence to raise an arguable case that she had at least an interest in the matrimonial home, she was making proper use of the civil jurisdiction to protect her proprietary rights within the intention of the Act and there was no misuse of the litigation process such as would be required for an application to be dismissed as an abuse of process. Lord Hope stated:

> The proceedings in the Crown Court and those in the High Court are designed to serve different purposes and the interests of Mrs Norris and her husband in the matrimonial home are not the same. Mrs Norris was not a party to the proceedings in the Crown Court, nor did the procedure which the statute lays down require her case that she had a beneficial interest in the property to be put at that stage. At the stage when the proceedings were in the Crown Court the only question that had to be resolved was the value of the husband's interest in the house. The question for that Court was the amount of the Defendant's realisable property, and this was the upper limit on the amount of money which he could be ordered to pay . . . it was not the function of the Crown Court to make any order which effected the interests that any third parties might have in the realisable property whose value it took into account when determining the amount of the Defendant's realisable property. The scheme of the Act, so far as third party interests are concerned, is for their claims to be resolved in the High Court. The question for the High Court, when the proceedings reached this stage, relates not to the amount of money which the Defendant must pay, that has already been fixed by the order made in the Crown Court, but to the powers which the receiver is to be authorised to exercise. It is at this stage that third parties are entitled to have their claims heard and determined. This is when as a matter of both substance and procedure, representations may be made as to their interests, if any, in the property which the receiver wishes to realise.

Lord Hobhouse, in giving the judgment of the Court, stated:

> . . . the confiscation order does not override or confiscate the interests of others in the value of that property . . . this would be implicit even in the absence of an express provision since the confiscation order only applies to the convicted defendant, and indirectly through such a defendant, donees caught by the Act. To apply it so as to confiscate the property of innocent third parties would be not only exorbitant but also outside the purpose of the Act. Any such confiscation would now also raise human rights issues.

22.93 In *Customs and Excise Commissioners v MCA* [2002] EWCA Civ 1039 a receiver was appointed on 24 March 1998. On 4 December 1998, the day following the defendant's conviction,

D. Specific Third Party Claims

the Crown Court issued a confiscation certificate certifying that the value of the defendant's proceeds of drug trafficking was £197,639.94. The amount that might be realised was set at £47,868.22. On the same day the Crown Court made a confiscation order ordering the defendant to pay £47,868.22 by the 5 November 1999 and set the term of custody he might be liable to serve in default of payment at 21 months' imprisonment consecutive to another sentence. On 12 October 1999 the court made an order discharging the earlier management receivership order and appointed a new receiver over all the defendant's assets, save for the matrimonial home and the surrender value of certain insurance policies, to enforce the confiscation order made against the defendant by the Crown Court. The order conferred on the receiver power to sell the defendant's assets, apart from the house and the policies, and to apply the net proceeds of sale towards the satisfaction of the confiscation order.

On 20 July 2000, the receiver applied for a further order that the order made by the Court on 12 October 1999 be varied so that the house and the defendant's interests in the surrender value of the policies be included in the realisable property over which the receiver was appointed and the receiver be empowered to take possession of and sell the house for the purpose of realising the defendant's interest in the net proceeds of the sale. The defendant's wife had given evidence that she had no knowledge of her husband's criminal activities, that she never saw anything to alert her to what he was doing, and that it all came as an incredible shock when he was arrested. Customs and Excise accepted that no part of the equity in either the house or the policies was acquired with the proceeds of drug trafficking and that the couple had separated before the husband had begun his drug trafficking activities. The Court in *MCA* held it was of critical importance that not only was the wife innocent of any involvement in drug trafficking, but she also lived in the house and enjoyed the benefit of the policies which were untainted by drug trafficking. In Schiemann LJ's judgment, the critical issue, identified by the judge below, was the true meaning and interactive effect of s 31(2) and 31(4) of the DTA. Section 31(2) states: **22.94**

> Subject to the following provisions of this section the power shall be exercised with a view to making available for satisfying the Confiscation Order, or as the case may be, any Confiscation Order that may be made in the Defendant's case, the value for the time being of realisable property held by any person, by means of the realisation of such property.

Section 31(4) states the powers shall be exercised with a view to allowing any person other than the defendant or the recipient of any such gift to retain or recover the value of any property held by him. In the court below in *MCA*, the judge had found that s 31(2) of the 1994 Act took effect subject to s 31(4). Accordingly, in the case of conflict, the effect of the 1994 Act is to protect the claims of those whose rights are safeguarded by s 31(4) against the operation of the confiscation regime. Section 31(2) does not make the satisfaction of the confiscation order the overriding objective. **22.95**

In Schiemann LJ's judgment, there was nothing in the provisions of either the Matrimonial Causes Act 1973 (MCA 1973) or the DTA 1994 which required the court to hold that either statute takes priority over the other when the provisions of each are invoked in relation to the same property. He held that both the statutes confer discretion on the court, **22.96** which the court may or may not choose to exercise when making orders. The terms of those orders he said would depend on the facts of the individual case:

> Equally, it does not seem to me to be axiomatic that it is more in the public interest to enforce an order under s 31 of the DTA 1994 than to make a property adjustment order under s 24 of the MCA 1973. If the former has the effect of forcing a spouse to sell her home and become dependent on the state for housing and financial support in order to meet a confiscation order in relation to property which was not acquired by the profits of crime; if the wife has made a substantial financial or other contribution to the position of that property; if the crime involved is one of which she was ignorant and by which she is untainted; it seems to me that the public policy argument may well go the other way. Each case must depend on its facts.

22.97 As a result, the fact that s 31(2) to (6) of the DTA requires the court's powers for the realisation of property to be exercised in a particular way in enforcement proceedings under that Act, does not mean by necessary implication that those subsections either exclude or take priority over the powers of the court under the MCA 1973, particularly s 24. In the Court's judgment, the assumption that the provisions of the DTA exclude the operation of s 24 of the MCA 1973 is capable of leading to an injustice which parity between the statutes would prevent.

22.98 Schiemann LJ held that once it is accepted that neither the MCA 1973 nor the DTA have priority over the other, any need to identify a claim under s 24 of the MCA 1973 as a right in or in relation to property becomes unnecessary. What matters is that the wife's rights in relation to the property should be preserved until such time as the court can adjudicate upon them under s 24 of the MCA 1973 (see *Ahmad v Ahmad* [1999] 1 FLR 317 and *Harman v Glencross* [1986] Fam 81 for two leading judgments for the court's jurisdiction under Pt II of the MCA 1973 and for charges against the matrimonial home in favour of the judgment creditor).

22.99 In Judge LJ's judgment:

> The property with which we are concerned was the former matrimonial home. The couple are now divorced. For convenience I shall refer to them as husband and wife. Their interests in the matrimonial home were acquired long before the husband became involved in drug dealing. The starting point in the argument on behalf of HM Customs & Excise is that under the statutory framework the property innocently acquired by the offender is not exempt from the confiscation process. I agree. However, the wife enjoyed an interest in the matrimonial home, independently of and greater than her husband, acquired from her own sources, without involvement in drug or criminal activity, and before her husband's criminality began. Moreover, in her proceedings under the MCA, she was not seeking to collusively protect his interests in the matrimonial home. To the contrary, she was looking for a clean break from him, so that as part of the arrangements on the ending of their marriage, her financial links to him would be severed, and he would be excluded from enjoying any benefit of his original interest in the property.

He went on to hold:

> The determination to deprive drug dealers of their profits does not, however, carry with it the corollary that the property belonging to third parties ought to be considered as part of the realisable property.... It was submitted that the wife would be guaranteed her full share of the proceeds of sale of the former matrimonial home. She would not lose a penny of the value of

her interest in it. Accordingly her rights would be preserved. This submission overlooks two critical and linked considerations. The first, a Portia-like distribution of the proceeds of sale of the property would not preserve Mrs A's home for her, or if she had dependent children, for them. She would be forced to leave it and in effect start again. In this context, half or even three quarters of the proceeds of sale would represent a substantial loss. Second, however the provisions of the 1994 Act may apply in this context, the property jointly owned by the criminal and someone other than his spouse, the marriage, and the dissolution of the marriage, and the consequent rights of the innocent spouse, are not subsumed by the 1994 Act. 'Innocent' in this context is not a reference to the circumstances in which the marriage broke down, but underlines that the acquisition of the same was untainted by criminality by either party to the marriage, and that the wife herself enjoyed no personal benefit, direct or indirect, from her husband's drug dealing.'

Wall J in his judgment held:

> I am strongly of the opinion that the judges of the family division in dealing with future applications of the type exemplified by this case will be astute to balance the public interest represented by the DTA 1994 with the public interest in the protection of the rights of spouses under Part II of the MCA 1973. There can be no question of MCA 1973 being used as a means to circumvent the provisions of the DTA 1994, and I am confident that the judges will be acutely alert to ensure this is not the case.

(4) Developing matrimonial home case law

22.100 The case of *Re Norris* was revisited in *R v Greet* [2005] EWCA Crim 205 where the defendant's matrimonial home remained the main asset of his second wife, the property itself having been purchased with the proceeds from the sale of an earlier property that had been owned jointly by them. Initially the original property had been owned jointly by the defendant and his first wife, but she had subsequently transferred her half-share of the property to his second wife.

22.101 In determining the defendant's realisable assets, the judge found that the defendant's first wife had surrendered her half-share of the first property to the defendant who had been the conduit through which it had been transferred to the second wife. The judge therefore concluded the whole of the net equity transferred to the second property was the defendant's or amounted to a gift from the defendant to his second wife, which was caught by s 74 of the Criminal Justice Act (the gift provisions). The judge therefore took that gift into account when making the confiscation order.

22.102 The question that arose was whether the transfer of the first property from the first wife to the second wife had amounted to a gift for the purposes of the Act and whether it was appropriate to take that gift into account. Their Lordships allowed the appeal, finding that seeking to capture the gift of an innocent third party's property did not advance the purpose of the statute. On the facts in *Greet* it was clear that when the transfer of the property was made the first wife had been willing to give up what she had thought was a worthless interest in order to free her from a liability in respect of the mortgage. In such circumstances the Court of Appeal found that there was no reason to conclude that there had been an indirect gift with the defendant as the conduit. However, the judge retained discretion under s 74 to determine whether it was appropriate to take into account a gift to a donee wife in the form of a share in the matrimonial home in the instant case. Nevertheless, it remained appropriate to take into account the defendant's half-share of the matrimonial home. The proper time for the second wife to make representations, the Court held, was in enforcement proceedings before the High Court.

22.103 In *R v Ahmed and Quereshi* [2004] EWCA Crim 2599 the question of matrimonial homes once again arose. In the case of Quereshi the judge had assessed the benefit figure at £12,257,135.88, and in the case of Ahmed the benefit figure was assessed at £1,385,000. The judge made confiscation orders based on his assessment of their respective realisable assets. In calculating their realisable assets he took into account the value in each case of the defendant's half-share in the matrimonial home. He accepted from the families that in each case the probability was that the homes would have to be sold to meet the confiscation order. The appellants submitted to the judge that he had a discretion as to whether or not to include the value of those shares. The judge accepted those submissions but nonetheless concluded that there were no exceptional circumstances which justified him excluding them. The Court of Appeal was concerned with the next stage of the process, which was the assessment of the value of the realisable property. It seemed to the Court that the provisions of the Act prescribed that exercise. The court, it found, was merely concerned with the arithmetic exercise of computing what is, in effect, a statutory debt. That process did not involve any assessment of the way in which the debt may ultimately be paid, anymore than the assessment of any other debt. In the Court's opinion therefore no question arose under Article 8 of the ECHR at the realisable asset stage of the process. Different considerations however may arise if the debt was not met and the prosecution decided to take enforcement action, for example by obtaining an order for the receiver.

22.104 As the House of Lords explained in *Re Norris* [2001] 1 WLR 1388, the High Court was the stage of the procedure in which third parties' rights cannot only be taken into account, but resolved. If the court is asked at that stage to make an order for the sale of the matrimonial home, Article 8 rights are clearly engaged. It would be at that stage that the court would have to consider whether or not it would be proportionate to make an order selling the home in the circumstances of the particular case.

22.105 That is a decision that can only be made on the facts at that time. The court would undoubtedly be concerned to ensure that proper weight is given to the public policy objective behind the making of confiscation orders, which is to ensure that criminals do not profit from their crime, and the court will have a range of enforcement options available with which to take account of the rights of third parties, such as the members of the family. The Court of Appeal in *Ahmed* concluded that they considered that the judge's decision was right albeit that he had wrongly concluded that he had a discretion in the matter, (see para 12 of the judgment).

22.106 In *CPS v Grimes and Grimes* [2003] 2 FLR 510, Wilson J held that where the net proceeds of sale of a former matrimonial home were held in an account in the name of two firms of solicitors; and the CPS, on the one hand, sought a direction that they be paid in partial satisfaction of a confiscation order made against the husband, and the wife, on the other hand, sought a direction either that she was the beneficial owner of one half of the fund or, alternatively, that half of the sum should be paid to her as a lump sum under s 23 of the Matrimonial Causes Act 1973, the factors to be weighed against these competing arguments were (against the wife): (1) that she already had a home, (2) that some at least of the

D. Specific Third Party Claims

fund had effectively been contributed to by the husband's illicit income, (3) the fact that the confiscation order had been made with reference to the whole fund; and (for the wife) (1) that she had no participation or knowledge of her husband's activities, (2) that she had contributed to the ancillary costs of the property on the mortgage, (3) her state of health, (4) her poor financial position, (5) the fact that a significant period of cohabitation proceeded the marriage, (6) she could expect no maintenance from her husband. Wilson J found that the fact that the husband had not argued before the Crown Court that the wife had an interest in the property was of no significance. On the facts, the wife had established her equitable entitlement to a half-share, or in the alternative, an order for half a share would be made under s 23 of the 1973 Act.

22.107 In *X v X* [2005] EWHC Fam 296, the problems inherent in ancillary relief claims where the spouse concerned was also subject to a confiscation order for the recovery of assets gained through criminal activity, was once again considered. In *X v X* Moses J was considering both a cross-application by the wife and the husband for ancillary relief under the MCA 1973 and confiscation proceedings in the Administrative Court under the CJA.

22.108 The facts of the matter were fairly simple and not in dispute. The couple had been married since 1969 and the husband had spent most of his whole life working as a businessman running an entirely legitimate and successful business. In about 1998 however, he embarked upon a course of criminal conduct allowing his business to be used for professional money laundering. It was common ground that the wife was entirely innocent of any wrongdoing and that up until the moment of her husband's arrest she had not had the faintest suspicion of her husband's criminal activities. In October 2003 a Crown Court judge made a confiscation order in the sum of £1,427,316 against the husband and the family assets were said to be worth £2,559,119 including a former matrimonial home in London valued at £873,000, a house in France valued at £402,550; and various other interests in commercial property and bank accounts.

22.109 The CPS accepted that the only assets that were tainted by the husband's criminal activities were the business's bank account and the cash that was recovered at the time of his arrest.

22.110 The wife's position was very simple in that she wanted no part of the tainted assets, but asserted, subject to that, that she wanted an equal division of the family assets in accordance with *White v White* [2001] 1 AC 596.

22.111 Initially the preferred view of the CPS had been that the confiscation order should be paid in full, with only the balance of the assets being divided thereafter between the husband and the wife (para 11).

22.112 The husband's preferred solution was that the judge exercise his powers under s 24(1)(c) of the 1973 Act, to vary what he described as a post-nuptial settlement created when he acquired the house in France and put it into his wife's name. He invited the court to settle the sum of £300,000 on trust to enable suitable accommodation to be provided for the husband during his lifetime (see para 14). The husband's alternative proposal was that the family assets should first be applied in payment of the confiscation order and that he should receive a lump sum of £200,000 and the income from his pension fund, and that whatever remained after payment of capital gains tax should then go to his wife.

22.113 Moses J stated that the 1988 Act was, and was intended by Parliament to be, harsh, indeed draconian. He identified the three features which brought out the stringency of the statutory scheme:

(i) Confiscation is not limited to the profits of crime. The benefit from an offence, as that phrase is used in s.71, extends to all the money which passes through the defendant's hands in the course of his criminal behaviour. It is not confined to what sticks to his fingers or is left in his hands at the end of the day. It extends, as it were, to the turnover and not just the profits of his criminal activities (see para 18).

(ii) The property which is liable to be seized, what in the 1988 Act is referred to as realisable property, extends, by virtue of s 74 and 102, to every species of property, of whatever nature, in or in relation to which the defendant has either an interest or a right.

(iii) So far as is material absolutely nothing is excluded from the defendant's realisable property, neither his home nor his personal belongings, nor even the tools of his trade. The effect of the 1988 Act, therefore, is that the defendant may be completely stripped of all his property and possessions and left quite literally homeless, penniless and destitute.

22.114 At para 20 Moses J stated that whatever the ambit of the discretion in s 80 of the Act, the court did not have any general discretionary power to exonerate the defendant from the consequences of a confiscation order, or to ameliorate those consequences, merely because the judge thought it might be fair or just to do so. As such, he held he was not sitting on an appeal from the Crown Court. It was not for him to inquire whether the Crown Court had properly gone about its task and properly exercised its powers (see *Customs and Excise Commissioners v A, A v A* [2002] EWHC Admin 611 at paras 132 to 133 and [2002] EWCA Civ 1039. He stated his task was limited to the enforcement process relating to an unsatisfied confiscation order and that the same went for the Family Division.

22.115 In his judgment the proper exercise of the court's jurisdiction under the 1973 Act may have the effect of immunising an innocent wife from what would otherwise be the effect of the confiscation order made against her husband under the 1988 Act. But that, he said, was very different from saying that the jurisdiction under the 1973 Act could properly be exercised in such a way as to exonerate the defendant husband from the consequences of the confiscation order, or to ameliorate those consequences, merely because the family judge thinks it is right to do so. In *Webber v Webber and CPS* [2006] EWHC 2893 (Fam) the President of the Family Division held that the jurisdiction to deal with matters of restraint and confiscation resided solely with the Crown Court under POCA. Therefore where an innocent wife had sought for her ancillary relief application to be dealt with at the same time, the appropriate course was for the ancillary relief matter to be disposed of first by the High Court, thus enabling the Crown Court judge to make the appropriate determination in relation to what assets remained. (See also *W v H* (2004) EWHC 526 Fam, (2006) 2 FLR 258.)

22.116 In *Customs and Excise Commissioners v A, A v A* [2002] EWCA Civ 1039, [2003] Fam 55 at para 101, Wall J stated:

The judges of the Family Division in dealing with future applications of the type exemplified by this case will be astute to balance the public interest represented by the (CJA 1988) with the public interest in the protection of the rights of spouses under Part II of the MCA 1973. There can be no question of MCA 1973 being used as a means to circumvent the provisions of (the CJA), and I am confident that the judges will be acutely alert to ensure this is not the case.

22.117 In *X v X* Moses J concurred with the view that in this kind of case the legislation can properly be used as a shield to protect an innocent wife but not as a device to improve the guilty husband's position or to insulate him from the consequences of a confiscation order (para 21). The judge asked rhetorically why should a criminal who is married, and who as such may be able to invoke the 1973 Act, be in a better position than a criminal who is unmarried? The judge concluded that what the husband was proposing was the very kind of artificial contrivance that judges must be alert to prevent (para 30). He stated that he had to strike a proper balance between the competing interests of the Crown, the husband and the wife as per the principles set out in *Customs and Excise Commissioners v A, A v A*. In his judgment there was only one appropriate outcome which was to endorse the agreement that had been reached between the wife and the CPS, which allowed the wife to retain the London property, her bank accounts and her pension, in addition to receiving a lump sum of £262,500, (in all an award worth £1,191,374). He stated:

> To deprive this wife, in the circumstances of this case, of what she would otherwise be entitled to in order to enable the confiscation order to be satisfied ahead of her claims would be effectively to punish this innocent wife for her husband's crimes . . . There is a limit to how far one can press "for better or for worse" – and what this husband in this case is demanding of this wife goes far beyond that limit. . . . In all the circumstances it would in this case be wrong as a matter of principle to allow the husband's understandable need for accommodation – a need which in financial terms has been generated entirely because of the confiscation order – to turn the wife's *White v White* claim into a claim based merely on her needs.

22.118 In *CPS v Richards and Richards* [2006] EWCA Civ 849 the Court of Appeal held that where matrimonial assets were tainted with the proceeds of crime and subject to confiscation, they should ordinarily, as a matter of justice and public policy, not be distributed. At first instance the court had ordered the sale of properties, including the former matrimonial home, to allow for a lump sum payment to the defendant's former wife. Their Lordships found that although the judge found that all the assets were tainted as the proceeds of drug dealing and had considered the decision in *A v A* [2003] Fam 55, he failed to give sufficient weight to the inevitable consequences of that finding. While the court was not deprived of jurisdiction under the 1973 Act in most cases the fact that the assets were tainted would be the decisive factor in any balance. The Court of Appeal went on to say that the error of the judge lay in thinking that the requirement to conduct a balancing exercise meant that in every case, all factors were relevant. The Court stated that in a case such as this, the knowledge of the wife, throughout her married life, that the lifestyle and the assets she enjoyed were derived from drug trafficking was determinative.

E. Property Adjustment Orders

22.119 In *Customs and Excise Commissioners v MCA* [2002] EWCA Civ 1039, the Court of Appeal considered whether or not the court was precluded from making a property adjustment order under s 24 of the MCA 1973 when the property in question was also the subject of proceedings by HM Customs & Excise to enforce a criminal confiscation order made against the defendant in proceedings under the DTA following his conviction and imprisonment for a drug trafficking offence.

22.120 In concluding that it was not so precluded, the Court found that Pt II of the MCA 1973 enables the court to make a wide range of orders, including financial provision orders (that is, orders for periodical payment and lump sums) as well as property adjustment orders, designed, on divorce, to regulate the financial position of the parties to the marriage. The basis upon which the court exercises its discretion to make financial provision and property adjustment orders is set out in s 25 of the MCA 1973. In cases of divorce, Pt II of the MCA 1973 gives the parties to a marriage an unfettered right to apply to the court for financial provision and property adjustment orders. It follows, the Court held in *MCA*, that the court plainly has jurisdiction to entertain applications for ancillary relief by drug dealers or former spouses of drug dealers.

22.121 In *MCA*, the primary contention of the appellant (Customs & Excise) was that the exercise of jurisdiction under the MCA 1973 is effectively ousted by and must take second place to proceedings to enforce orders made under the DTA. The court was able to extract the following propositions from s 25 of the MCA 1973 namely:

(1) the court is not obliged to exercise its powers under ss 23 or 24: s 25(1) gives it discretion to do so;
(2) the fact that one or both of the parties to the marriage had been engaged in or convicted of trafficking in drugs is plainly a material circumstance of the case within s 25(1); and drug trafficking is almost certainly conduct which would be inequitable to ignore;
(3) the court would plainly be bound to have regard to any drug trafficking confiscation order and financial obligation that one or both of the parties had under such an order;
(4) the court equally plainly must have regard to the extent to which the assets to the parties were the product of drug trafficking; and the extent to which their standard of living and respective financial contributions to the marriage derived from drug trafficking.

22.122 In short, the Court held that, in exercising its powers to make a property adjustment order under s 24 of the MCA 1973, the court would be bound fully to take into account any order made under the DTA in deciding whether or not, in all the circumstances of the case, it was appropriate to exercise the discretion under s 25 of the MCA to make a property adjustment order under s 24, or whether it was appropriate to decline to make such an order and to allow the DTA order to be enforced.

22.123 The Court held it was not difficult to envisage cases in which the latter would be the correct course, an obvious example, it said, being where the matrimonial assets were the fruits of drug dealing in which both parties were engaged or complicit. The point the Court emphasised, however, was that that was a wholly different question on whether the terms of the DTA prevented the court exercising its MCA 1973 jurisdiction at all.

22.124 The Court also held that it was not correct (as a general proposition) that an order under s 24 of the 1973 Act would be unassailable if the consequent transfer pre-dated an application under the 1994 Act. Such a conclusion would give open season to collusive agreements between dishonest former spouses. In such a situation, it would be open to the prosecution to apply for the order under the 1973 Act to be set aside on the grounds that the court had

E. Property Adjustment Orders

not been given full disclosure by the parties, or had not been told the assets transferred represented the proceeds of criminal conduct.

(1) Property adjustment orders: does POCA oust the MCA?

22.125 Under s 58(5) of POCA, if a court in which proceedings are pending in respect of any property is satisfied that a restraint order has been applied for or made in respect of the property, the court may either stay the proceedings or allow them to continue on any terms it thinks fit. Thus s 69 powers may be applicable in family court proceedings where the court is considering a property adjustment order under s 24 or 25 of the MCA 1973. This has important significance following the case of *Customs and Excise Commissioners v MCA*. In *MCA* the court concluded that the DTA and the MCA were on an equal footing. It is now arguable that the provisions of POCA oust the provisions of the MCA and therefore the effect of that part of the decision in *Customs and Excise Commissioners v MCA* is questionable in relation to the new Act.

22.126 Under s 69(3)(a) the powers of the court and receiver must be exercised with a view to allowing a person other than the defendant or recipient to retain or recover the value of any interest held by him. If s 69(3)(a) is not applicable, ie there is no need to protect any interest held by a third party, then the duty to preserve any realisable asset to pay the confiscation order would take priority over any other statutory power.

(2) Matrimonial homes where the conditions set out in Re Norris and HM Customs and Excise v MCA do not apply

22.127 We now turn to consider the law as it stood prior to *Re Norris* and *Customs and Excise Commissioners v MCA* and where it stills applies, eg in circumstances where the home was purchased in full or in part with the proceeds of crime and/or with the wife's/cohabitee's knowledge. In such circumstances the wife will not necessarily be able to prevent the home from being sold, even if she has children. Her interest will be converted to the proceeds of sale and ring fenced so that she receives an amount proportionate to her interest in the property.

(3) Property should form part of the confiscation order

22.128 In *R v Judge and Woodbridge* (1992) 13 Cr App R(S) 685, the Court rejected the defendant's contention that it was 'unfair and oppressive' to make a CJA confiscation order in an amount which would necessitate the sale of the matrimonial home. Similarly in *R v Crutchley and Tonks* (1994) 15 Cr App R(S) 627 the Court of Appeal ruled that the offender's home may be incorporated in a confiscation order to the extent that it forms part of his realisable property.

22.129 The court may give the wife the option of buying out her husband's interest in the property. She may be able to persuade the court to exercise its discretion under s 51(9) of POCA (or s 29(5) of the DTA or s 80(5) of the CJA) to direct that the house should not be realised for a specific period to give her a reasonable opportunity either of finding alternative accommodation or raising the finance to buy out her husband's interest in the property.

She may well also find the receiver, anxious to avoid a forced sale, will have some sympathy for her position and will be prepared to negotiate.

22.130 In *R v Gregory* The Times, 19 October 1995, the Court of Appeal emphasised the importance of exercising caution when incorporating the value of a defendant's equity in the matrimonial home in a confiscation order. In that case, the judge had accepted the figure of £11,640.20 as representing the value of the defendant's realisable property. This figure was essentially half the apparent equity in the defendant's home, which he owned jointly with a cohabitee. The defendant and his cohabitee were joint tenants rather than tenants in common, and it appeared that the joint tenancy had not been severed. Further the property had been valued solely by means of an estate agent looking at it from the road and no attempt had been made to enquire about the contribution each party had made to the property so as to ascertain the extent of their respective interests. In these circumstances, the court excluded the property from the defendant's realisable property and reduced the confiscation order accordingly. It should be emphasised that the court here was not discouraging the incorporation of the defendant's interest in the matrimonial home in a confiscation order, but was merely issuing a timely reminder that the value of the property and the extent of the defendant's interest therein must be properly assessed before an order can be made.

(4) Equitable interests in the matrimonial home

22.131 In *Midland Bank plc v Cook* [1995] 4 All ER 562 the Court of Appeal held that where a partner in a matrimonial home without legal title had established an equitable interest through direct contribution, the court would assess (in the absence of express evidence of intention) the proportion the parties were assumed to have intended for their beneficial ownership by undertaking a survey of the whole course of dealing between the parties relevant to that ownership and occupation of the property, and their sharing of its burdens and advantages. The court, the Court of Appeal held, should take into consideration all conduct that threw light on the question what shares were intended. In particular, the Court held that a court was not bound to deal with the matter on the strict basis of a trust resulting from the cash contribution to the purchase price, and was free to attribute to the parties an intention to share the beneficial interest in some different proportions. The fact that the parties had neither discussed nor intended any agreement as to the proportions of their beneficial interest did not preclude the court from inferring one on general equitable principles (the Court of Appeal applying *Gissing v Gissing* [1970] 2 All ER 780 and *Grant v Edwards* [1986] 2 All ER 426). In *Cowcher v Cowcher* [1972] 1 WLR 425 the Court held that contributions to mortgage payments were to be treated as contributions to the purchase price of the property.

22.132 In *R v Robson* [1991] Crim LR 222 a DTOA confiscation order had been based in part on the finding that the appellant had an equitable interest in a house where he was living at the time of his arrest. The appellant's mother had bought the house. She had paid a deposit and contributed towards improvements. The appellant lived in the house for 13 months, during which period 14 mortgage payments were made. A number of lodgers also lived in the house during that period, paying rent. The mother never lived in the house. The appellant

E. Property Adjustment Orders

was involved in drug trafficking for about eight of the 13 months that he lived there. The judge concluded that the appellant had an interest in the house; on the basis that he was satisfied that there was a common intention between the appellant and his mother that he should have an interest. However, the Court of Appeal concluded that the judge had not been justified in deciding that there was a common intention that the appellant should have an interest. He had not made a finding that the outgoings paid by the appellant were referable to the purchase of the house, and the fact that the appellant contributed sums to his mother, which she applied to the mortgage, did not establish the intention that such payments should be allocated to the cost of the capital acquisition. On that basis the confiscation order was reduced.

(5) Trusts

22.133 For confiscation orders and family trusts see *R v Stannard* [2005] EWCA Crim 2717. In *R v Sharma* [2006] EWCA Crim 16, the Court of Appeal held that there was no room, where proceeds of crime were concerned, for the application of trust principles and the application of the normal legal consequences that might flow from the receipt of money for others.

(6) Application of sums and third parties

22.134 Under s 54 of POCA sums held by the receiver appointed by the Crown Court under s 50 of POCA which are the proceeds of the realisation of property under s 51, or sums in which the defendant holds an interest, must be applied as follows:

(1) they must be applied in payment for such expenses incurred by a person acting as an insolvency practitioner as are payable under this subsection by virtue of s 432;
(2) they must be applied in making any payments directed by the Crown Court; and
(3) they must be applied on the defendant's behalf towards satisfaction of the confiscation order.

(See s 54(2).) It follows therefore that where a third party had been successful in establishing their interest, that interest should be satisfied in terms of the repayment of any money owing in priority to satisfaction of the confiscation order but second to the payment of the receiver's fees itself. Under s 54(3) if the amount payable under the confiscation order has been fully paid and any sums remain in the receiver's hands he must distribute them:

(3) (a) among such persons who held (or hold) interest in the property concerned as the Crown Court directs, and
    (b) in such proportions as it directs.
(4) Before making a direction under subsection (3), the Court must give persons who held, or hold, interests in the property concerned, a reasonable opportunity to make representations to it.

(7) Banks

22.135 Banks and other financial institutions frequently find themselves affected by the terms of restraint orders, as they remain a popular repository for the proceeds of crime. The bank should, on receiving a restraint order, ensure that any accounts specified in the order which they hold are frozen forthwith. Further, if the restraint order is in purely general terms, any further accounts in which the defendant holds an interest of which they are aware should be similarly restrained. The bank is not, however, under an obligation to search through its records in an attempt to trace any other accounts the defendant may hold unless the prosecuting authority are prepared to pay for the reasonable costs of such an exercise. If the order contains exceptions allowing, eg the defendant to draw a specific weekly sum for general living expenses, the bank should ensure (by checking with the prosecution) that any preconditions to the release of such sums, such as the giving of notice to the prosecutor, have been complied with. Once such confirmation is forthcoming, the bank may release the sum allowed by the order and are not under any obligation to enquire into the purpose for which the defendant expends the money.

22.136   The bank is also entitled to look to the prosecutor for reimbursement of its reasonable costs and expenses in complying with the order. Inevitably, however, there will from time to time be cases that are of greater than average complexity and involve the bank in more work. In such cases the bank would be justified in seeking a higher payment.

22.137   The restraint order does not prevent the bank from exercising any existing rights it may have in relation to set off or to combine accounts. This principle is well illustrated by *Re K (Restraint Order)* [1990] 2 All ER 562. A restraint order was served on the Bank of India in respect of bank accounts that contained a total of £639,541.87. A separate account, however, had an overdraft of £337,585.59 and the bank applied to the court for a variation to the restraint order to enable it to combine the deposit and overdraft accounts so that the overdraft would be paid off leaving some £320,000 in the deposit accounts. Otton J allowed the application, ruling that a bank had an inherent right to combine the accounts and that by doing so it was merely carrying out an accounting exercise to determine the customer's indebtedness to the bank. The Court also ruled that, on the facts of the case, the bank had a right of set off and that the exercise of that right did not constitute disposing of or diminishing or in any way dealing with the money and that by so doing the bank was not in contravention of the restraint order.

22.138   A more difficult problem arises in relation to a bank that has an office within the jurisdiction of the court, but the account of the defendant is held at a branch overseas. If there is an agreement in force with the country in question, the account can be restrained by an order made in the courts of that jurisdiction, but considerable problems arise in relation to the defendant whose account is in a country where no such agreement exists. This problem arose in *Re M* (HC, 9 July 1993). M was charged with offences of VAT evasion and a restraint order was obtained under the CJA restraining him from dealing in any of his assets. M, who had been admitted to bail, subsequently absconded to Eire and pre-conviction receivers were appointed to manage and preserve his assets. M had an account at a branch of the Bank of Ireland in Southampton and a copy of the order was subsequently served on that branch. He also had accounts at two branches of the Bank of Ireland in Ireland. Although a reciprocal enforcement agreement was in force between the UK and Ireland in relation to drug trafficking cases, no such agreement existed in relation to the CJA. This placed the bank in an invidious position; if they refused to pay the money

E. Property Adjustment Orders

out to M, they would be vulnerable to an action for breach of contract by him, and if they did payout they would have been vulnerable to proceedings for contempt of court by the prosecution. The bank therefore sought the court's directions, contending that they were not obliged to concern themselves with the order in so far as it concerned the accounts in Ireland.

22.139 Ognall J rejected the bank's argument that they need not concern themselves with the order at all, ruling that they must do everything lawfully within their power to restrain the monies held at their branches in Ireland. Ognall J said, at para 11E:

> We live in an age when funds may be transferred from jurisdiction to jurisdiction as rapidly as it takes me to speak this sentence and when banks are increasingly multi-national operations. In so far as a foreign bank sets up operations and registers within this jurisdiction, it not only submits itself *pro tanto* to the jurisdiction; in my judgment it should be treated as implicitly undertaking to do all that is necessary to cooperate to the fullest extent with the courts and law enforcement agencies of this country.
>
> I do not think it would be right to ease in any way the undoubtedly onerous burden resting upon the Bank to ensure that they do nothing that they are not strictly obliged to do under Irish law which would abet M's breach of that order and would allow him the benefit of his allegedly ill-gotten gains.
>
> Public policy dictates that third parties such as banks operating in an international arena must play a responsible part in giving full effect to orders of the court. If that, from time to time, involves them in costs, that is part of the overheads and obligations of any person or body trading within, enjoying the commercial benefits of, and submitting itself to, the jurisdiction.

22.140 Ognall J refused the variation in the terms sought by the bank and only varied the order to the extent that it added the word 'lawfully' to that paragraph in the order dealing with its extraterritorial effect. It would quite clearly have been inappropriate to expect the bank to do anything in relation to the accounts in Ireland which it could not do lawfully under Irish law, but it is now established that merely because an order relates to an account at an overseas branch of a bank does not mean that a financial institution served with a restraint order at its office within the jurisdiction can wholly disregard its terms.

(8) Banks: No duty of care

22.141 In *Customs and Excise Commissioners v Barclays Bank plc* [2006] UKHL 28, Barclays Bank appealed against the decision that it owed a duty of care to Customs (a third party) to take reasonable care to ensure that no payments were made out of customer accounts that were subject to freezing injunctions. Customs had frozen two accounts while they sought payment of outstanding VAT and the restraints specifically prohibited disposal of or dealing with any of the debtor companies' assets. The bank had been notified of the injunctions by fax. Only a matter of hours after receiving the freezing injunctions Barclays had authorised transfers of substantial sums from the accounts. As a result Customs attempted to claim damages against Barclays for the sums paid out in breach of the freezing order.

22.142 The bank submitted that it did not owe a duty of care to avoid causing financial harm to another unless one had voluntarily undertaken responsibility towards that other person.

22.143 The House of Lords held that the presence or absence of a voluntary assumption of responsibility did not necessarily provide the answer in all cases. When the court granted Customs their application, the purpose was to protect Customs by preventing the companies from parting with their assets. The freezing injunctions were directed at the companies as opposed to the bank. Barclays, itself a third party, would be in contempt of court only if it knowingly failed to freeze customer accounts subject to the freezing injunctions and authorised transfers of sums from the accounts after being notified of the court orders, (see *Z Ltd v A-Z and Others, sub nom Marera Injunction* [1982] QB 558; [1982] 2 WLR 288, *A-G v Times Newspapers* [1991] 2 WLR 994 and *A-G v Punch Ltd* [2002] UKHL 50).

22.144 The Court held the failure to operate a system for freezing accounts did not mean that Barclays was liable to Customs who had obtained the orders. Notification of the order placed a duty on Barclays to respect the order of the court, but it did not of itself generate a duty of care to Customs. Having obtained a freezing order and notified the bank, Customs could expect that any responsible bank would respect the order, but it could not rely on the bank doing so.

22.145 Ultimately, Customs had to rely on the court to ensure that Barclays did not flout the orders and to punish Barclays if it did so. There was nothing that could be regarded as a voluntary assumption of responsibility by the bank for the way in which it would go about freezing the companies' accounts and there was nothing that involved Barclays in entering into any kind of relationship with Customs that required it to exercise such care as the circumstances required. The Court held that Barclays and Customs were about as far from being in a relationship 'equivalent to contract' as they could be, and therefore the court held that in the circumstances it would not be fair to hold that Barclays owed a duty of care to Customs.

(9) The insolvent defendant: the position of the trustee in bankruptcy

22.146 It happens from time to time that defendants involved in offences to which POCA, the DTA, and the CJA apply are made bankrupt. There are a variety of reasons for this. If the defendant is in custody, he will not be earning any income and will be unable to run any business he might own. Further, he may well already be in financial difficulty at the time of committing the alleged offences and, indeed his impecunious state may well provide an explanation for his offending in the first place.

22.147 The position is dealt with in s 32(1) of the DTA and s 84(1) of the CJA, which provide that where a person holding realisable property is adjudged bankrupt, property subject to a restraint order made prior to the bankruptcy order and any property realised by a receiver under the Acts is excluded from his estate for the purposes of Pt IX of the Insolvency Act 1986. Section 32(2) in both sections goes on to provide that where a person has been adjudged bankrupt, the powers of the court or of a receiver, may not be exercised in relation to:

(a) property for the time being comprised in the bankrupt's estate;
(b) property in respect of which the trustee in bankruptcy may serve a notice under ss 307, 308 or 308A of the Insolvency Act 1986 relating to after acquired property and clothes etc exceeding the value of reasonable replacements; and

E. Property Adjustment Orders

(c) property which is to be applied for the benefit of creditors of the bankrupt by reason of a condition imposed under s 280(2)(c) of that Act.

The rule therefore is basically one of 'first come, first served'. If the restraint order is obtained first, any property caught by its terms is excluded from the defendant's estate when the bankruptcy order is made and cannot become vested in the trustee in bankruptcy. If, however, the bankruptcy order pre-dates the restraint order, it will take precedence to the extent that the defendant's assets are required to satisfy the debt. In *Re M* [1992] 1 All ER 537 it was held that an interim order made under s 252 of the Insolvency Act 1986 which precluded the institution of bankruptcy proceedings did not prevent the prosecutor from applying for the appointment of a receiver in respect of realisable property caught by a restraint order which had been made prior to the commencement of the s 252 proceedings.

(10) POCA and the insolvent defendant

22.148 POCA 2002 modifies the position under the DTA and the CJA (see s 417 of the new Act). Under s 418 of POCA if a person is adjudged bankrupt in England and Wales the powers conferred on a court by ss 41 to 67 of POCA, and the powers of a receiver appointed under ss 48, 50, or 52 (Enforcement Receivers), must not be exercised in relation to:

(a) property which is for the time being comprised in the bankrupt's estate for the purposes of Part 9 of the Insolvency Act 1986;
(b) property in respect of which his trustee in bankruptcy may, (without leave of the court), serve a notice under section 307, 308 or 308a of the 1986 Act (after acquired property, tools, tenancies etc);
(c) property which is to be applied for the benefit of creditors of the bankrupt by virtue of the condition imposed under section 280(2)(c) of the Insolvency Act 1986;
(d) in a case where a confiscation order has been made under section 6 or 156 of [POCA], any sums remaining in the hands of the receiver appointed under section 50, 52, 198 or 200 of [POCA] after the amount required to be paid under the confiscation order has been fully paid;
(e) in a case where a confiscation order has been made under section 92 of [POCA], any sums remaining in the hands of an administrator appointed under section 128 of [POCA] after the amount required to be paid under the confiscation order has been fully paid.

(See s 418(2) and (3).)

22.149 The basic rule is that if at the time a person is adjudged bankrupt under the Insolvency Act 1986, a restraint order has previously been made, or a receiver or administrator has previously been appointed in respect of any of his property, that property is excluded from his estate for the purpose of the bankruptcy. So any of that property first goes to satisfy the confiscation order, rather than being dispersed to creditors. In so doing the legislation prevents defendants from attempting to use the insolvency legislation to defeat the purpose of the confiscation regime. Under Sch 11 to POCA if a restraint or receivership action is underway when the bankruptcy order is made, any unconfiscated property can be given to the creditors at a later date (see para 16 of Sch 11).

F. Conclusion

22.150 Anecdotally, prosecuting authorities are very conscious of the difficulties that restraint orders can cause to innocent third parties and, in so far as the legislation allows, endeavour to deal with them fairly and in a way which least encroaches upon their property rights. In the first instance, third parties and their solicitors who have any doubts as to their position, or who wish to deal with a particular asset would be well advised to contact the prosecuting authority which obtained the restraint order to see if a mutually acceptable agreement can be reached.

23

INVESTIGATIONS

A.	Introduction	23.01	G. Judicial Discretion	23.40
B.	A Short History of the Legislative Provisions	23.03	H. Overseas Investigations	23.46
			I. Customer Information Orders	23.48
C.	Defining Investigations	23.06	(1) Requirements for making orders	23.51
D.	Courts and Judges having Jurisdiction to Make Orders	23.07	(2) Discharge and variation	23.53
			(3) Offences	23.54
	(1) Judges	23.07	J. Account Monitoring Orders	23.55
	(2) Courts	23.09	K. Disclosure Orders	23.58
E.	Production Orders	23.10	L. Statements Made in Response to Orders	23.60
	(1) Jurisdiction to make the order	23.10		
	(2) Requirements for making an order	23.12	M. Code of Practice	23.61
	(3) Legal professional privilege	23.16	N. Financial Reporting Orders Under the Serious Organised Crime and Police Act 2005	23.62
	(4) Excluded material	23.19		
	(5) Government departments	23.20		
	(6) Procedure on applications: Crown Court	23.21	(1) Jurisdiction to make the order	23.63
			(2) Offences to which s 76 applies	23.65
	(7) Procedure on applications: High Court	23.25	(3) Duration of orders	23.67
			(4) Effect of a financial reporting order	23.68
	(8) Who may apply for a production order?	23.29	(5) Variation and revocation of financial reporting orders	23.72
	(9) Complying with the order	23.31		
	(10) Failure to comply with production orders	23.36	(6) Failure to comply with financial reporting orders	23.73
F.	Search and Seizure Warrants	23.39		

A. Introduction

If investigations by law enforcement agencies to trace the proceeds of criminal conduct are to be truly effective, it is essential that they should have powers to compel third parties such as financial institutions, solicitors, accountants, etc to disclose information and produce documentation that may be relevant to their investigations. Indeed, following the trail of the money often leads investigators to evidence of the substantive offence to which it relates. **23.01**

In this chapter we examine the powers of the court under POCA to make production orders, account monitoring orders, customer information orders and search and seizure warrants requiring third parties to hand over material they hold to law enforcement authorities to assist their investigations into drug trafficking and other criminal conduct. We also examine the entirely new powers given to the Crown Court and a magistrates' court under **23.02** the Serious Organised Crime and Police Act 2005 (SOCPA) to make financial reporting orders against persons convicted of certain criminal offences.

B. A Short History of the Legislative Provisions

23.03 Section 27 of the Drug Trafficking Offences Act 1986 gave circuit judges power to make production orders requiring persons to make material available to a constable to take away, or requiring them to give the constable access to it if it was likely to be of substantial value to an investigation into drug trafficking. Section 28 made similar provision for a search warrant to be made authorising a constable to enter and search premises for material likely to be of substantial value to such an investigation. Section 30 empowered the High Court, on an application by a prosecutor, to make an order for the production of material in the possession of a government department. These provisions were re-enacted in ss 55, 56 and 59 of the Drug Trafficking Act 1994.

23.04 Parliament chose not to make similar provision in relation to investigations into criminal conduct other than drug trafficking when it enacted the Criminal Justice Act, 1988. In consequence, law enforcement agencies wishing to obtain material relevant to financial investigations into such offences had to rely on the more general provisions contained in the Police and Criminal Evidence Act, 1984. This lacuna was remedied by the Proceeds of Crime Act, 1995 which inserted new ss 93H to 93J into the 1988 Act making identical provision in relation to investigations into non-drug trafficking offences.

23.05 The relevant provisions are now to be found in Part 8 of POCA which came into force on 24 February, 2003: see the Proceeds of Crime Act 2002 (Commencement No. 4 Transitional Provisions and Savings) Order 2003, SI 2003/120. In addition to giving the Crown Court power to make production orders, Pt 8 also adds a number of additional powers to the investigator's amoury, in particular the power to apply for account monitoring orders and customer information orders.

C. Defining Investigations

23.06 Part 8 prescribes three types of investigation in relation to which these orders may be obtained: a confiscation investigation; a money laundering investigation; and a civil recovery investigation. These are defined in s 341 in the following terms:

(1) For the purposes of this Part a confiscation investigation is an investigation into—
   (a) whether a person has benefited from his criminal conduct, or
   (b) the extent or whereabouts of his benefit from his criminal conduct.
(2) For the purposes of this Part a civil recovery investigation is an investigation into—
   (a) whether property is recoverable property or associated property,
   (b) who holds the property, or
   (c) its extent or whereabouts.
(3) But an investigation is not a civil recovery investigation if—
   (a) proceedings for a recovery order have been started in respect of the property in question,
   (b) an interim receiving order applies to the property in question,

(c) an interim administration order applies to the property in question, or
(d) the property in question is detained under section 295.
(4) For the purposes of this Part a money laundering investigation is an investigation into whether a person has committed a money laundering offence.

It would seem that this definition of "confiscation investigation" precludes law enforcement agencies from seeking production orders to obtain information for the purpose of identifying legitimately acquired assets for the purpose of making them available to satisfy a confiscation order. The information sought would neither relate to whether a person has benefited from criminal conduct nor the extent or whereabouts of his benefit from such conduct. In such circumstances, the appropriate remedy would be for the prosecutor to apply for a disclosure order in support of a restraint order under section 41 (7) of POCA or, in a case to which the DTA or CJA applies, relying on the Court's inherent jurisdiction. Disclosure orders are considered in more detail in Chapter 4. Further, if a management or enforcement receiver can compel a defendant or affected third party to cooperate in the identification of realisable property. After conviction, an application for a financial reporting order can also be considered: see section N below.

D. Courts and Judges having Jurisdiction to Make Orders

(1) Judges

23.07 In relation to a confiscation or money laundering investigation in England and Wales, a judge entitled to exercise the jurisdiction of the Crown Court is empowered to make orders under Pt 8: see s 343(2)(a) of POCA.

23.08 In relation to a civil recovery investigation, only a judge of the High Court has jurisdiction to make orders under Pt 8: see s 343(3) of POCA.

(2) Courts

23.09 Similarly, s 344 of POCA provides that the court having jurisdiction in relation to confiscation or money laundering investigations is the Crown Court and, in relation to civil recovery investigations, the High Court.

E. Production Orders

(1) Jurisdiction to make the order

23.10 Section 345(1) of POCA gives a judge power to make a production order if he is satisfied that all the requirements for making an order have been fulfilled. By s 345(2), the application for the order must state that:

(a) a person specified in the application is subject to a confiscation investigation or a money laundering investigation, or
(b) property specified in the application is subject to a civil recovery investigation.

The application must also, in accordance with s 345(3) state that:

(a) the material is sought for the purpose of the investigation;
(b) the order is sought in relation to material, or material of a description, specified in the application;
(c) a person specified in the application appears to be in possession or control of the material.

23.11 For specific provisions for applications for production orders see Practice Direction: Civil Recovery (Proceeds of Crime Act 2002) Parts 5 and 8 (2003), s IV, reproduced at Appendix 11.

(2) Requirements for making an order

23.12 These are set out in s 346 of POCA which provides as follows:

(1) These are the requirements for the making of a production order.
(2) There must be reasonable grounds for suspecting that—
   (a) in the case of a confiscation investigation, the person the application for the order specifies as being subject to the investigation has benefited from his criminal conduct;
   (b) in the case of a civil recovery investigation, the property the application for the order specifies as being subject to the investigation is recoverable property or associated property;
   (c) in the case of a money laundering investigation, the person the application for the order specifies as being subject to the investigation has committed a money laundering offence.
(3) There must be reasonable grounds for believing that the person the application specifies as appearing to be in possession or control of the material so specified is in possession or control of it.
(4) There must be reasonable grounds for believing that the material is likely to be of substantial value (whether or not by itself) to the investigation for the purposes of which the order is sought.
(5) There must be reasonable grounds for believing that it is in the public interest for the material to be produced or for access to it to be given having regard to—
   (a) the benefit likely to accrue to the investigation if the material is obtained;
   (b) the circumstances under which the person the application specifies as appearing to be in possession or control of the material holds it.

23.13 Most of these requirements are similar to those for obtaining production orders under the previous legislation. In particular, there is no requirement that a person should be charged with a criminal offence—it is sufficient that there is a confiscation, money laundering or civil recovery investigation. By s 345(4) the production order once made is an order either:

(a) requiring the person the application for the order specifies as appearing to be in possession or control of material to produce it to an appropriate officer for him to take away, or

(b) requiring that person to give an appropriate officer access to the material, within the period specified in the order.

23.14 The period specified for compliance is seven days unless the judge considers, on the facts of a particular case, that a longer or shorter period would be appropriate (see s 345(5)). Section 349 requires information held on a computer to be produced in a visible and legible form.

23.15 Section 347 empowers the judge to make an order to grant entry to allow an appropriate officer to enter premises to obtain the material required to be produced under the order. For specific provisions relating to applications under s 347 see Practice Direction: Civil Recovery (Proceeds of Crime Act 2002) Parts 5 and 8 (2003), s IV, at Appendix 11. By s 348(5) the appropriate officer may take copies of any material produced or to which access is given in compliance with a production order. Section 348(6) provides that material produced in compliance with a production order can be retained for as long as necessary in connection with the investigation for the purposes of which the order was made. If the appropriate officer has reasonable grounds for believing that the material may be required for the purpose of any legal proceedings and it might otherwise be unavailable for those purposes, he may retain it until the proceedings are concluded.

(3) Legal professional privilege

23.16 Section 348 (1) provides that a production order does not require a person to produce or give access to privileged material. By s 348 (2) 'privileged material' is defined as:

> any material which the person would be entitled to refuse to produce on grounds of legal professional privilege in proceedings in the High Court.

23.17 The mere fact that a lawyer is holding documentation on behalf of a client does not, however, automatically mean that it is subject to legal professional privilege. In *R v Central Criminal Court ex p Francis and Francis* [1988] 3 All ER 775 the House of Lords held that documents were not subject to legal professional privilege if they were held with the intention of furthering a criminal purpose. This applied regardless of whether the intention was that of the person holding the documents or of any other person. Thus, a solicitor's file in relation to a conveyancing transaction on a property would not be subject to legal privilege in circumstances where the property was being purchased for a criminal purpose, eg to launder the proceeds of drug trafficking.

23.18 Similarly, in *R on the application of Miller Gardner Solicitors v Minshull Street Crown Court* [2002] EWHC Admin 3077 the Divisional Court held that personal records held by a firm of solicitors such as the client's name and address, telephone number and date of birth was not subject to legal professional privilege.

(4) Excluded material

23.19 Section 348 (2) of POCA provides that a production order does not require a person to produce or give access to excluded material within the meaning of the Police and Criminal Evidence Act 1984.

(5) Government departments

23.20 A production order may be made in relation to material held by a government department as defined in the Crown Proceedings Act 1947 (see s 350 (1) of POCA). The order may require any officer of the department (whether named in the order or not) who may for the time being be in possession or control of the material to which it relates to comply with it (see s 350 (2)).

(6) Procedure on applications: Crown Court

23.21 Applications for production orders may be made ex parte to a judge in chambers (see s 351(1)). Although there is no formal requirement either in the Act or in rules of court, a practice has developed whereby applications to the Crown Court are made in the form of a written information prepared by the officer which is substantiated on oath by him in the presence of the judge. This procedure appears to have been given judicial approval in *R v Middlesex Guildhall Crown Court ex p Salinger* The Independent, 26 March 1992, a case involving similarly worded provisions in prevention of terrorism legislation. The Court issued the following guidelines:

(a) The application should be accompanied by a written statement upon which the officer wishes to rely to persuade the judge that the statutory conditions have been fulfilled. The statement need not disclose the nature or source of sensitive information. The officer should appear before the judge and be prepared to supplement the statement by oral evidence. The judge should not normally enquire into the nature and identity of the source of information, but it may be necessary for the officer to amplify the nature of the information itself, particularly if it has not been fully disclosed in the written statement.

(b) If the judge decides to make the order, he should give directions as to what, if any, information should be served with the order. In normal circumstances this information should be in writing and take the form of the written statement from the officer in support of the application. The information the judge requires the officer to give should be as full as possible without compromising security.

(c) If the judge decides it is inappropriate for any such information to accompany the order, he should consider whether it ought to be made available in the event of an application being made to vary or discharge the order.

23.22 The Court emphasised in its concluding words that the aim should be to provide as much information as possible, provided this is consistent with the security of the operation.

23.23 Any person affected by a production order may apply to have it varied or set aside under s 351(3). By r 56.4(2) of the Criminal Procedure Rules 2005 a person who proposes to apply for the variation or discharge of a production order must give a copy of the application, not later that 48 hours before the making application, to a constable at the police station specified in the order or, where the application for the order was not made by a constable, to the office of the appropriate officer who made that application. Rule 56.4(3) the judge may direct that these requirements need not be complied with if he satisfied that the person making the application has good reason to seek a discharge or variation of the order as soon as possible and it is not practicable to comply with them.

E. Production Orders

In *R v Middlesex Guildhall Crown Court ex p Salinger* The Independent, 26 March 1992, **23.24**
the Divisional Court ruled that applications to vary or set aside production orders should, if possible, be made before the same judge who made the ex parte order, and it was desirable that the same officer that gave evidence at the ex parte hearing should attend. The Court said that questions as to the nature or identity of the source of information should not be permitted and, if the nature or the information is sensitive in the sense that it may compromise the security of the investigation, the judge should not allow the questions. He should tell the respondent in such circumstances that he had been given information which satisfies him that the conditions are met, but that such information cannot be disclosed.

(7) Procedure on applications: High Court

Applications by the Director of the Assets Recovery Agency (ARA) for production orders **23.25**
or search warrants in support of civil recovery proceedings are made to the High Court and are governed by the Civil Recovery Proceedings Practice Direction accompanying the Civil Procedure Rules.

The application must be made to a High Court judge by filing an application notice(see **23.26**
para 8.1). By para 8.2 the application may be made without notice to the respondent. Paragraph 10 requires that the application must be supported with written evidence which must be filed with the application notice. Paragraph 10.2 provides that the evidence must set out all the matters on which the Director relies in suport of the application including the matters required to be stated in the Act and all material facts of which the court should be aware. By para 10. 3 the Director must also file with the application notice a draft of the order sought. If possible, this should be supplied to the court on disk in a form compatible with any word processing software used by the court.

The application will be heard and determined in private unless the judge directs otherwise **23.27**
(see para 11.1).

An application for the variation or discharge of a production order or search warrant **23.28**
obtained on the application of the Director may be made by any person affected by it (see para 12.1). Any person making such an application must first notify the Director under para 12.3. Paragraph 12.4 provides that any application for the variation of a production order or search warrant should be made to the judge who made the order or, if he is unavailable, to another High Court judge.

(8) Who may apply for a production order?

An application for a production order must be made by 'an appropriate officer'. This phrase **23.29**
is defined in s 378 of POCA and varies in accordance with the nature of the investigation in relation to which the application is made. By s 378(1), in relation to confiscation investigations, the following are appropriate officers:

(a) the Director of the Assets Recovery Agency (ARA);
(b) an accredited financial investigator;
(c) a constable; and
(d) an officer of Revenue and Customs.

23.30 In relation to money laundering investigations, s 378(4) provides that accredited financial investigators, constables, and officers of Revenue and Customs are appropriate officers. As to civil recovery investigations, only the Director of ARA is an appropriate officer (see s 378(3)).

(9) Complying with the order

23.31 Once the order has been sealed by the court, the officer should serve it promptly on the person or company to whom it is addressed who will normally have seven days in which to comply with it unless the judge has exercised his discretion under s 345(5) to order a longer or shorter period. On no account should a person served with a production order divulge to a third party, particularly a client in relation to whom he is required to produce information, the fact that the order has been made. Any such disclosure could constitute an offence of prejudicing an investigation contrary to s 342.

23.32 It sometimes happens that information required to be disclosed under a production order is held on a computer. This is dealt with in s 349 of POCA which provides:

(1) This section applies if any of the material specified in an application for a production order consists of information contained in a computer.

(2) If the order is an order requiring a person to produce the material to an appropriate officer for him to take away, it has effect as an order to produce the material in a form in which it can be taken away by him and in which it is visible and legible.

(3) If the order is an order requiring a person to give an appropriate officer access to the material, it has effect as an order to give him access to the material in a form in which it is visible and legible.

23.33 A person served with a production order may therefore have to print out the information covered by the order which he holds on computer or transfer it onto a disk, memory stick or another similar medium to enable the officer to take it away with him or have access to it.

23.34 In contrast to the position with restraint orders, there is no requirement for the prosecutor to give an undertaking to pay the costs of innocent third parties such as financial institutions, professional advisers etc incurred in complying with a production order. Any such costs will therefore have to be met by those named in the order and may not be reclaimed from the applicant for the order.

23.35 Once the appropriate officer has obtained material pursuant to a production order, it may be retained by him for so long as it is necessary to retain it (as opposed to copies of it) in connection with the investigation for the purposes of which the order was made (see s 348 (6)). However, by s 348 (7):

(7) But if an appropriate officer has reasonable grounds for believing that—
 (a) the material may need to be produced for the puroposes of any legal proceedings, and;
 (b) it might otherwise be unavailable for those purposes,
it may be retained until the proceedings are concluded.

(10) Failure to comply with production orders

23.36 By s 351 (7) of POCA:

Production orders and orders to grant entry have effect as if they were orders of the court.

G. Judicial Discretion

The effect of this provision is that any breach of the terms of a production order may be dealt with by the Crown Court as a contempt of court and may lead to imprisonment, the imposition of a fine or the sequestration of assets. The jurisdictiion of the Crown Court to deal with breaches of its orders as a contempt of court is dealt with fully in Chapter 6 above. **23.37**

Where the production order is made by the High Court in civil recovery proceedings, any failure to comply with the order will, of course, fall to be dealt with by the High Court rather than the Crown Court. **23.38**

F. Search and Seizure Warrants

Section 352 gives the court power to make search and seizure warrants empowering appropriate officers to enter premises and seize material likely to be of substantial value to the investigation for the purpose of which the order is made. The requirements that must be fulfilled before a warrant may be issued are that a production order has already been made and has not been complied with, and there are reasonable grounds for believing that the required material is on the premises, or that the requirements of s 353 have been met (see s 352(6)). For specific provisions about the issuing of applications for search and seizure warrants under the new Act, see Practice Direction: Civil Recovery (Proceeds of Crime Act 2002) Parts 5 and 8 (2003), section IV, at Appendix 11. Section 353 allows the court to issue search and seizure warrants in circumstances where it is not possible to make a production order. These instances include cases in which it is not practicable to communicate with a person in relation to whom a production order could be made, where consent would not be given without a warrant, or where the investigation might be seriously prejudiced if immediate entry to the premises could not be effected. Order SI 2003/174 applies for the purposes of a confiscation investigation or a money laundering investigation, and powers of seizure under them, modifying certain provisions under PACE and SI 1989/1341. **23.39**

G. Judicial Discretion

Even where the conditions set out in s 345 or s 352 have been met, the court retains a discretion as to whether or not a production order or search warrant should be granted: note the use of the phrase 'a judge may' in ss 345 (1) and 352 (1). This was confirmed by the Divisional Court in *R v Crown Court at Southwark ex p Customs and Excise Commissioners* [1989] 3 All ER 673, where similar provisions in s 27 of the DTOA 1986 were considered. Watkins LJ said: **23.40**

> ... We see nothing in the words of section 27(2) of the 1986 Act to suggest that Parliament did not intend the circuit judge to have a discretion either to grant or to refuse an order although he be persuaded that the conditions contained in subsection (4) are satisfied. While we acknowledge that it is not easy to identify circumstances in which a judge might properly refuse to make an order when those conditions have been satisfied, we are not persuaded that this is a subsection in which 'may' can be construed as meaning "must" or "shall".

The judge had imposed a condition that the material obtained under the production order should not be removed from the jurisdiction without the leave of the court. The judge imposed the condition on the basis of evidence from an official of a bank affected by the **23.41** order to the effect that there was a risk of reprisals against members of the bank's staff in Panama, their families, and properties. The court indicated that this evidence was 'unimpressive' and should not influence the court to exercise its discretion in favour of those who would use it to avoid compliance with an embarrassing order. Watkins LJ observed:

> The courts of this country are not to be deflected from making orders in aid of the international battle against drug trafficking for fear of reprisals no matter from where the threat of them emanates.

23.42 In *R v Southwark Crown Court ex p Bowles* [1998] AC 641 the House of Lords in considering the powers under s 93H of the CJA to make production orders, emphasised the intrusive nature of such orders and the need for judges to scrutinise applications carefully before exercising the discretion to grant an order. Lord Hutton cited the judgment of Bingham LJ in *R v Crown Court at Lewes ex p Hill* (1991) 93 Cr App R 60 where, in relation to similar powers under the Police and Criminal Evidence Act 1984, the court referred to the importance of achieving a balance between competing public interests. Bingham LJ said:

> The Police and Criminal Evidence Act governs a field in which there are two very obvious public interests. There is, first of all, a public interest in the effective investigation and prosecution of crime. Secondly there is a public interest in protecting the person and property rights of citizens against infringement and invasion. There is an obvious tension between these two public interests because crime could be most effectively investigated and prosecuted if the person and property rights of citizens could be freely overridden and total protection of the personal and property rights of citizens would make investigation and prosecution of many crimes impossible or virtually so.

23.43 As Lord Hutton pointed out, Bingham LJ emphasised that circuit judges must exercise their powers with great care and caution to ensure the proper balance between these two competing public interests is maintained.

23.44 The court must also take great care to ensure that the production order procedure is not abused by its use in cases where an application under s 9 and Sch 1 to the Police and Criminal Evidence Act, 1984 (PACE) is more appropriate. The statutory requirements for obtaining a production order are less stringent than those for an order under PACE and there must therefore be a considerable temptation for investigators to rely on the production order whenever possible. In particular:

(i) Applications for production orders can be made without notice whereas Sch 1 para 7 to PACE requires that applications under s 9 must be made on notice;
(ii) Section 9 applications must relate to a 'serious arrestable offence'; there is no such requirement in relation to applications for production orders;
(iii) A s 9 order can only be made where there are reasonable grounds for believing that an offence has been committed; whereas a production order involves a lower threshold test, namely that there are reasonable grounds for suspecting that a person has benefited from criminal conduct;
(iv) Applications under s 9 are further limited by a requirement that other methods of obtaining the material have failed or have not been tried because there were bound to fail; there is no similar requirement in relation to an application for a production order.

The House of Lords held in *R v Southwark Crown Court ex p Bowles* that a 'dominant purpose' test should be applied in determining whether a production order application or an application under s 9 is the most appropriate means of obtaining the required material. If the dominant purpose of the application is to obtain information in furtherance of a criminal investigation, s 9 should be used. If, however, the dominant purpose of the application is to obtain evidence in relation to an investigation into the proceeds of criminal conduct a production order application may properly be made. Further, the House of Lords ruled that provided a production order had been obtained because the dominant purpose of the application was to progress an investigation into the proceeds of criminal conduct, it mattered not that evidence was found that assisted the criminal investigation: this could still be relied upon in a criminal trial. Lord Hutton said: 23.45

> I consider that if the true and dominant purpose of an application under section 93H is to enable an investigation to be made into the proceeds of criminal conduct, the application should be granted even if an incidental consequence may be that the police will obtain evidence relating to the commission of an offence. But if the true and dominant purpose of the application is to carry out an investigation whether a criminal offence has been committed and to obtain evidence to bring a prosecution, the application should be refused.
>
> I further consider that if the police discover evidence of the commission of an offence in the course of an investigation consequent upon an order properly made under section 93H, the fact that the evidence was discovered in this way would not be an reason for the exclusion of the evidence under section 78 of PACE on the ground of unfairness at a trial where the prosecution sought to adduce such evidence.

H. Overseas Investigations

The Divisional Court held in *R v Crown Court at Southwark ex p Customs and Excise Commissioners* [1989] 3 All ER 673 that a production order may be made for the purpose of obtaining material for use in an investigation into drug trafficking being undertaken overseas. On the application of a Customs officer, production orders were made requiring the Bank of Credit and Commerce International to produce documents held by them in relation to General Manuel Noriega of Panama for use in proceedings in the USA. Although the judge made the orders, she imposed a condition requiring the Commissioners of Customs and Excise to undertake not to remove any documents obtained under the orders from the jurisdiction or to show or read them to a representative of any overseas law enforcement agency without the leave of the court. On an application for judicial review by the Commissioners, the Court ruled that the judge had no power to attach this condition to the order. Watkins LJ said: 23.46

> In our judgment there is nothing in section 27(1) of the 1986 Act which requires that the relevant investigation should necessarily be one being conducted by our customs officers. Suppose an investigation into drug trafficking be entirely into breaches of corresponding drug trafficking laws of other convention countries. In that situation it is surely not surprising that Parliament, in this day and age, should have legislated to permit a customs officer here to apply to a circuit judge for a production order in respect of the suspected passage of money laundered from drug trafficking abroad into a London bank account, no matter that such conduct only forms a comparatively small part of the trafficking being enquired into by a foreign law enforcement agency. It would, we think, be contrary to one of the purposes for

which the 1986 Act was made which are, we believe to advance the international cooperation to which this country is bound by the 1961 [Vienna Convention on Diplomatic Relations] to restrict the effect of section 27(1) in the manner for which the bank contended. There are no words either in section 27(1) or in section 38(1) which suggest that the effect of section 27(1) should be so limited.

23.47 The Court did, however, rule that where the application is made either solely or partly to assist an overseas investigation, this must be made clear in the information laid by the application in support of his application and that evidence must be adduced to show that the investigation is into possible breaches of a corresponding law as defined in s 36(1) of the Misuse of Drugs Act 1971. Further, the Court ruled that the applicant may not send any original documents to an overseas law enforcement agency without the leave of the court. Copies may, however, be provided.

I. Customer Information Orders

23.48 Customer information orders are a new concept introduced by POCA and put further powers at the disposal of investigators. Production orders on bank accounts can only be effective if the investigator has at least some information as to the identity of the account and the financial institution at which it is maintained. A customer information order requires a financial institution covered by the order to provide to an appropriate officer any customer information it has in relation to the person specified in the order (see s 363(5)). In relation to an individual, s 364(2) defines 'customer information' as information as to whether the person holds or has held an account with the institution named in the order and, if so information as to:

(a) the account or account numbers;
(b) the person's full name;
(c) his date of birth;
(d) his most recent address and any previous addresses;
(e) the date or dates on which he began to hold the account or accounts and, if he has ceased to hold the account or any of the accounts, the date or dates on which he did so;
(f) such evidence of his identity as was obtained by the financial institution under or for the purposes of any legislation relating to money laundering;
(g) the full name, date of birth and most recent address and any previous addresses of any person who holds or has held an account at the financial institution jointly with him;
(h) the account number or numbers of any other account or accounts held at the financial institution to which he is a signatory and details of the person holding the other account or accounts.

23.49 Section 364(4) defines customer information in similar terms in relation to companies or limited liability partnerships or similar bodies incorporated or otherwise established outside the UK.

23.50 Specific provisions for the issuing of applications for customer information orders are found in Practice Direction: Civil Recovery (Proceeds of Crime Act 2002) Parts 5 and 8 (2003), section IV (see Appendix 11).

I. Customer Information Orders

(1) Requirements for making orders

23.51 The requirements are set out in s 365. In all cases, there must be reasonable grounds for believing that the information will be of substantial value to the investigation (s 365(5)) and that it is in the public interest for the information to be provided having regard to the benefit likely to accrue to the investigation if the information is obtained (s 365(6)). The other requirements vary according to the nature of the investigation in relation to which the information is required:

(a) in a confiscation investigation, there must be reasonable grounds for suspecting that the person named in the application has benefited from criminal conduct (s 365(2));
(b) in a civil recovery investigation, there must be reasonable grounds for suspecting that the property specified in the application is recoverable or associated property and that the person holds some or all of the property (s 365(3));
(c) in a money laundering investigation, there must be reasonable grounds for suspecting that the person specified in the application has committed a money laundering offence.

23.52 Applications for customer information orders may be made ex parte to a Crown Court judge and any person affected by an order once it is made may apply for it to be varied or set aside (see s 369(1) and (3) respectively). Section 369(7) provides that an accredited financial investigator, constable, or an officer of Revenue and Customs may only apply for a customer information order if he is a 'senior appropriate officer' or has been authorised to make the application by such an officer. Section 378(2) defines a 'senior appropriate officer' as being the Director of ARA, a police officer not below the rank of superintendent, an officer of Revenue and Customs designated by the Commissioners of Revenue and Customs as being of equivalent rank to superintendent, and an accredited financial investigator designated in an order made by the Secretary of State under s 453.

(2) Discharge and variation

23.53 By s 369 (3) of POCA an application to vary or discharge a customer information order may be made by the person who applied for the order or by any person affected by it. The procedures to be adopted on such applications are set out in r 62.2 of the Criminal Procedure Rules 2005. By r 62.2 (1), where the application is made by a person other than the person who applied for the order he must, not later than 48 hours before the application is to be made, give a copy of the application to a police officer at the police station specified in the order or, where the application for the order was not made by a police officer, to the office of the appropriate officer who made the application. The notice must indicate the time and place at which the application will be made.

(3) Offences

23.54 It is an offence under s 366 for a financial institution to fail to comply with a customer information order without reasonable excuse (s 366(1)) or to knowingly or recklessly make a false statement when complying with such an order (s 366(3)). An offence contrary to s 336(1) is punishable by a fine not exceeding level 5 on the standard scale (see s 366(2) and an offence contrary to s 366(3) in punishable on indictment with an unlimited fine (see s 366(4).

J. Account Monitoring Orders

23.55 The court is empowered under ss 370 to 375 of POCA to make account monitoring orders on the application of an appropriate person. The particular value of these orders to investigators is that they impose an ongoing duty on the financial institution named in the order to provide information for a period of up to 90 days from the day on which it is made. In contrast, production orders merely require the disclosure of information in the possession of the financial institution when the order is served. If the officer requires further information after a production order has been complied with, he will have to apply to the court for another production order. An account monitoring order is defined in s 370(6) as:

> an order that the financial institution specified in the application for the order must, for the period stated in the order, provide account information of the description specified in the order to an appropriate officer in the manner, and at or by the time or times stated in the order.

23.56 The period stated in the order must not exceed 90 days (see s 370(7)).

Practice Direction: Civil Recovery (Proceeds of Crime Act 2002) Parts 5 and 8 (2003), section IV contains specific provision for the issuing of applications for account monitoring orders (see Appendix 11).

23.57 The requirements that must be fulfilled before an account monitoring order can be made are set out in s 371 and are identical to those for making customer information orders. Again the application may be made ex parte to a judge in chambers and affected parties have the right to apply to set aside and vary the order (see ss 373 and 375(2) respectively). Rule 62.1 of the Criminal Procedure Rules sets out the procedures that must be followed by affected parties who intend to apply for the order to be varied or discharged. As with customer inforamtion orders, the applicant must give at least 48 hours notice to the person who applied for the order (see r 62.1(2)).

K. Disclosure Orders

23.58 A further power is available only to the Director of ARA. By s 357(1) a judge may, on an application by the Director make a disclosure order which is defined in s 357(4) as:

> an order authorising the Director to give to any person the Director considers has relevant information notice in writing requiring him to do, with respect to any matter relevant to the investigation for the purposes of which the order is sought, any or all of the following—
>
> (a) answer questions, either at a time specified in the notice or at once, at a place so specified;
>
> (b) provide information specified in the notice, by a time and in a manner so specified;
>
> (c) produce documents, or documents of a description, specified in the notice,
>
> either at or by a time so specified or at once, and in a manner so specified.

Applications for disclosure orders may not be made in relation to money laundering investigations (see s 357(2)).

N. Financial Reporting Orders under the SOCPA

23.59 The requirements that must be fulfilled before an order can be made are set out in s 358 and are identical to those in relation to customer information orders and account monitoring orders, save that, as indicated above, they may not be made in relation to money laundering investigations. A person commits an offence under s 359 if he fails to comply with a disclosure order or knowingly or recklessly makes a false or misleading statement in response to such an order.

L. Statements Made in Response to Orders

23.60 POCA restricts the use to which statements made pursuant to disclosure orders, customer information orders, and account monitoring orders may be put. By s 360, a statement made by a person in response to a requirement imposed on him under a disclosure order may not be used against him in criminal proceedings. Similar protection is afforded to financial institutions complying with customer information orders (see s 367) and account monitoring orders (see s 372). These immunities do not, however, extend to confiscation proceedings, proceedings for contempt of court or perjury, or for an offence where, in giving evidence, a person makes a statement which is inconsistent with a statement made in complying with the order.

M. Code of Practice

23.61 Section 377 imposes an obligation on the Secretary of State to prepare a code of practice as to the use of the powers referred to in this chapter by the Director of ARA and members of his staff, accredited financial investigators, and officers of Revenue and Customs. This code was brought into force by virtue of SI 2003/334 on 24 March 2003. By s 377(6) a failure to comply with the Code does not of itself constitute a criminal offence, but by s 377(7) the code will be admissible in evidence and the court is entitled to take into account any failure to comply with its provisions in determining any question in the proceedings. SI 2003/425 makes provision for orders and warrants made or issued in one part of the UK under POCA Pt 8 to be enforced in another part of the UK.

N. Financial Reporting Orders under the Serious Organised Crime and Police Act 2005

23.62 Section 76 of the Serious Organised Crime and Police Act 2005 gives the Crown Court and a magistrates' court jurisdiction to make a financial reporting order. Unlike production orders, account monitoring orders and customer information orders, a financial reporting order may only be made after a defendant has been convicted of certain specified criminal offences. The explanatory note accompanying the Act describes the purpose of financial reporting orders in these terms:

> Such orders may be imposed as ancillary orders for certain trigger offences and would enable the financial affairs of serious acquisitive criminals to be monitored from the point of sentence.

(1) Jurisdiction to make the order

23.63 By s 76(1) a court sentencing or otherwise dealing with a person convicted of an offence specified in s 76(3), may also make a financial reporting order. Section 76(2) restricts the court's jurisdiction to make the order to cases where it is:

> satisfied that the risk of the person's committing another offence mentioned in subsection (3) is sufficiently high to justify the making of a financial reporting order.

23.64 In order to assess the risk of re-offending, it is submitted that the proper course is for the court to look at the circumstances of the offence of which the defendant has been convicted, his role in its commission and any previous convictions he may have.

(2) Offences to which s 76 applies

23.65 By s 76(3) the offences are:

(a) an offence under any of the following provisions of the Theft Act 1968-

Section 15 (obtaining property by deception),

Section 15A (obtaining a money transfer by deception),

Section 16 (obtaining a pecuniary advantage by deception),

Section 20 (2) (procuring execution of a valuable security, etc),

(b) an offence under either of the following provisions of the Theft Act 1978-

section 1 (obtaining services by deception),

section 2 (evasion of liability by deception),

(c) any offence specified in Schedule 2 to the Proceeds of Crime Act 2002 ('lifestyle offences').

23.66 The 'lifestyle offences' referred to in s 76(3)(c) are set out in detail in para 14.26 above and include most drug trafficking and money laundering offences. The Secretary of State may by order add or delete offences from this list (see s 76(4)).

(3) Duration of orders

23.67 By s 76(5) the order comes into force when it is made and has effect for the period specified in it, beginning on the date on which it is made. If the order is made by a magistrates' court the duration of the order must not exceed five years (see s 76(6)). If the order is made by the Crown Court its duration must not exceed 15 years, or 20 years if the defendant is sentenced to imprisonment for life (see s 76(7)). The duration of the order must be proportionate to the risk of re-offending and a lengthy order will rarely be justified against a defendant with few previous convictions who has not been convicted of a particularly serious offence.

(4) Effect of a financial reporting order

23.68 By s 79(1), a person against whom a financial reporting order has been made must do the following:

(2) He must make a report, in respect of—

N. Financial Reporting Orders under the SOCPA

(a) the period of a specified length beginning with the date on which the order comes into force; and

(b) subsequent periods of specified lengths, each period beginning immediately after the end of the previous one.

(3) He must set out in each report, in the specified manner, such particulars of his financial affairs relating to the period as may be specified.

(4) He must include any specified documents with each report,

(5) He must make each report within the specified number of days after the end of the period in question.

(6) He must make each report to the specified person.

23.69 By s 81 (1) 'the specified person' means the person to whom reports under the order are to be made. Section 82(2) empowers the specified person, for the purpose of doing either of the things mentioned in s 82(4), to disclose a report to any person who he reasonably believes may be able to contribuite to doing either of those things. Similarly, by s 82(3), any other person may disclose information to the specified person or to a person to whom the specified person has disclosed a report, for the purpose of contributing to doing either of the things mentioned in s 82(4). Section 82 (4) provides:

The things mentioned in subsections (2) and (3) are—

(a) checking the accuracy of the report or of any other report made pursuant to the same order,

(b) discovering the true position.

23.70 By s 82 (5) the specified person may also disclose a report for the purpose of the prevention, detection, investigation of criminal offences in the UK and elsewhere. Section 82 (6) provides that any disclosure made under the section does not breach:

(a) any obligation of confidence owed by the person making the disclosure, or

(b) any other restriction on the disclosure of information (however imposed).

23.71 This is subject to an important proviso in s 82(7) to the effect that the section does not authorise any disclosure in contravention of the Data Protection Act 1998 of personal data which is not exempt from its provisions.

(5) Variation and revocation of financial reporting orders

23.72 By s 80(1), an application for the variation or revocation of a financial reporting order may be made by the person in respect of whom it was made or by the person to whom reports are to be made under it. The application must be made to the court which made the order (s 80(2)) or, if the order was made on appeal, to the court which originally sentenced the person in respect of whom it was made.

(6) Failure to comply with financial reporting orders

23.73 It is an offence under s 79(10) to include false or misleading information in a report or otherwise to fail to comply with the order without reasonable excuse. The offence is punishable by imprisonment for a maximum of 51 weeks, a fine not exceeding level 5 on the standard scale or both.

24

APPEALS

A. **Introduction**	24.01	
(1) Appeals distinguished	24.02	
(2) Transfer of powers from the High Court to the Crown Court	24.04	
B. **The Criminal Procedure Rules**	24.05	
C. **Restraint Order Appeals: Practice and Procedure**	24.06	
(1) Appeals to the Court of Appeal from restraint orders under the DTA and CJA	24.06	
(2) Procedure for appeals from the High Court under the DTA and CJA	24.07	
(3) Appeals to the Court of Appeal from restraint orders under POCA	24.13	
(4) Leave	24.19	
(5) Hearing the appeal	24.23	
(6) The Proceeds of Crime Act 2002 (Appeals under Part 2) Order 2003	24.26	
(7) Restraint orders under POCA: appeal to the House of Lords	24.27	
D. **Receivership Order Appeals: Practice and Procedure**	24.29	
(1) Appeals to the Court of Appeal in receivership proceedings under the DTA and CJA	24.29	
(2) Appeals to the Court of Appeal in receivership proceedings under POCA	24.30	
(3) Leave	24.36	
(4) Hearing the appeal	24.40	
(5) The Proceeds of Crime Act 2002 (Appeals under Part 2) Order 2003	24.43	
(6) The powers of the Court of Appeal on receipt of an appeal against a receivership order	24.44	
(7) Appeal to House of Lords	24.45	
(8) Appeals by financial investigators under POCA	24.47	
E. **Confiscation Order Appeals: Practice and Procedure**	24.50	
(1) Appeals in confiscation order cases	24.50	
(2) Procedure for confiscation order appeals under the DTA and CJA	24.54	
(3) A right of appeal against the confiscation order in all cases	24.55	
(4) Appeals involving the judge's discretion	24.57	
(5) Attorney-General's appeal	24.58	
(6) Confiscation orders: the Crown Court 'slip rule'	24.59	
(7) Appeals in confiscation order cases to the Criminal Cases Review Commission	24.61	
(8) Fresh evidence	24.63	
(9) Confiscation appeals under POCA	24.64	
(10) Leave	24.66	
(11) Appeal by the prosecutor or the Director of ARA	24.67	
(12) Appeal by the prosecutor or the Director of ARA: the Court of Appeal's powers	24.70	
(13) The steps the court must take	24.73	
(14) Corresponding provisions	24.77	
(15) Appeal by the prosecutor or the Director of ARA: appeal to the House of Lords by either the defendant or the prosecutor	24.78	
(16) Powers of the House of Lords in such circumstances	24.81	
(17) Where the Crown Court proceeds afresh	24.82	
F. **The Proceeds of Crime Act 2002 (Appeals under Part 2) Order 2003**	24.85	
(1) Practice and procedure: appeals to the Court of Appeal	24.85	
(2) Initiating procedure	24.86	
(3) Disposal of groundless applications for leave to appeal	24.88	
(4) Preparation of case for hearing	24.90	
(5) Right of defendant to be present	24.92	
(6) Rules of evidence in the Court of Appeal	24.93	
(7) General provisions	24.96	

Chapter 24: Appeals

(8)	References to the European Court of Justice	24.97	I. The Criminal Cases Review Commission	24.113
G.	Appeals against Forfeiture Orders	24.98	J. Appeals Against Findings of Contempt of Court	24.115
(1)	Forfeiture appeals under POCA from the magistrates' court	24.98	(1) Appeals in cases of findings of contempt of court by the High Court	24.115
(2)	Procedure on forfeiture appeals under POCA	24.104	(2) Appeals in cases of findings of contempt of court by the Crown Court	24.118
(3)	Appeals in condemnation cases from the magistrates' court	24.106	K. Thumbnail Guide to the Appeal Provisions within the Criminal Procedure Rules	24.120
(4)	Appeal from the magistrates' court to the High Court by way of case stated	24.109		
H.	Appeals under Part 6 of POCA: Revenue Functions	24.111		

A. Introduction

24.01 The purpose of this chapter is to consider in more detail the practice and procedure of making an appeal against the various orders available to the court, including restraint and confiscation. It should be noted that the law relating to appeals generally is beyond the scope of this particular work.

(1) Appeals distinguished

24.02 It is vital that the difference between an appeal and an application to vary should be fully appreciated. An appeal is appropriate where there is a legal challenge to the order either in whole or in part. An application to vary is appropriate where, eg in confiscation cases, assets are sold and those assets realise a different amount than that which was anticipated when the confiscation order was made.

24.03 The distinction is important because the Court of Appeal is not likely to view sympathetically an appeal made on the basis that assets to the value of the order are no longer available, when the same could be dealt with more expeditiously and economically by a judge on an application for a certificate of inadequacy (the application to vary in confiscation matters is usually referred to as either a certificate of inadequacy or a certificate of increase). Equally, a judge will not take kindly to being asked to act as a Court of Appeal by having to consider matters of law on the validity of the confiscation order that should more appropriately be determined by the Court of Appeal. (For further discussion see para 13.41 of Chapter 13.)

(2) Transfer of powers from the High Court to the Crown Court

24.04 Restraint and receivership applications are currently dealt with by the High Court in DTA and CJA cases and fall under civil law jurisdiction; therefore the appropriate rules of court relating to appeals are the Civil Procedure Rules (CPR). Section 91 of POCA makes it clear that in future, restraint and receivership applications made before the Crown Court will be dealt with by the Crown Court, where the Criminal Procedure Rules now govern. The procedure on appeal to the Court of Appeal and the procedure on appeal to the House of Lords came into force on 30 December 2002 under SI 2002/3015.

B. The Criminal Procedure Rules

The Criminal Procedure Rules make provision for the procedure to be followed in the criminal division of the Court of Appeal for the purposes of three types of appeals introduced by the Proceeds of Crime Act 2002 (POCA). The first is an appeal under s 31 of POCA to the Court of Appeal (and from there to the House of Lords under s 33 of POCA) by the prosecutor or Director of the Assets Recovery Agency (ARA) against a confiscation order or a failure of the Crown Court to make a confiscation order. The second is an appeal under s 43 of POCA to the Court of Appeal (and from there to the House of Lords under s 44 of POCA) in respect of decisions of the Crown Court about restraint orders. The third is an appeal under s 65 of POCA 2002 to the Court of Appeal (and from there to the House of Lords under s 66 of POCA) in respect of decisions of the Crown Court about receivers. These new Rules are considered at the relevant stages of the appeal process set out below, and a thumbnail guide is included at the conclusion of this chapter at para 24.120. 24.05

C. Restraint Order Appeals: Practice and Procedure

(1) Appeals to the Court of Appeal from restraint orders under the DTA and CJA

Under both the DTA and CJA restraint orders are dealt with exclusively by the High Court and there is a general right of appeal against any such order made by the High Court to the Court of Appeal under s 16 of the Supreme Court Act 1981. 24.06

(2) Procedure for appeals from the High Court under the DTA and CJA

Notwithstanding the introduction of POCA, the High Court will retain jurisdiction for all cases begun under the DTA and CJA. Inevitably this will mean that certain cases will remain under the umbrella of the High Court for a number of years to come. 24.07

Part 52 of the Civil Procedure Rules and Practice Direction 52, which relates to appeals, govern appeal procedure in the High Court. In the Queen's Bench Division an appeal from the High Court Judge lies to the Court of Appeal. Permission is required to appeal from a decision of a High Court Judge except where the appeal is in respect of a committal order (ie contempt and certain insolvency appeals and certain statutory appeals) (see r 52.3 CPR). 24.08

Permission should be sought at the hearing at which the decision to be appealed against is made. If it is not, or if it is sought and refused, permission should be sought from the Court of Appeal. If permission is sought from the appeal court, it must be requested in the appellant's notice. Permission may be granted or refused, or granted in part and refused as to the rest (for obtaining permission to appeal see Practice Direction 52 para 4.1 and r 52.3 CPR). 24.09

Rule 52.11(3)(a) and (b) sets out the circumstances in which the appeal court will allow an appeal. The grounds of an appeal should set out clearly the reasons why r 52.11(3)(a) or (b) is said to apply (see Practice Direction 52 r 3.1). Rule 52.4 and para 5 of the Practice Directions deal with the appellant's notice (N161), which must be filed and served in all cases. 24.10

24.11 The appellant must file his notice at the appeal court either within the period specified by the High Court or, if no such period is specified, within 14 days of the date of the decision appealed from. The notice must be served on each respondent as soon as practicable, and in any event not later than seven days after it is filed (Practice Direction 52 para 5.19 and r 52.4). Skeleton arguments must be filed with the appellant's notice unless it is impractical for the appellant's skeleton argument to accompany the appellant's notice, in which case it must be lodged and served on all respondents within 14 days of filing the notice (Practice Direction 52 r 5.9 and 5.19).

24.12 A respondent who wishes to ask the appeal court to vary the order of the lower court in any way must appeal, and permission will be required on the same basis as for an appellant (Practice Direction 52 para 7.1). The respondent's notice must be filed either within a period specified by the lower court or, if no such period is specified, within 14 days (Practice Direction 52 para 7). The respondent's notice is form N162.

(3) Appeals to the Court of Appeal from restraint orders under POCA

24.13 Now that the powers to make restraint orders have been transferred to the Crown Court under POCA, the general right of appeal that existed under the DTA and CJA no longer exists. Therefore a specific right of appeal has been incorporated into the Act.

24.14 If on an application for a restraint order under POCA the Crown Court decides not to make one, the person who applied for the order may appeal to the Court of Appeal against the decision (s 43(1)).

24.15 It is important that this provision is not confused with the power to apply for discharge or variation of a restraint order under s 42. Section 43 applies where the Crown Court decides not to make a restraint order for whatever reason. On an appeal under s 43 the Court of Appeal may either confirm the decision or make such order as it believes is appropriate (see s 43(3)).

24.16 If an application is made under s 42(3) to discharge or vary a restraint, or an order under s 41(7) is made (an order for the purpose of ensuring that the restraint order is effective), the following persons may appeal to the Court of Appeal in respect of the Crown Court's decision on that application: '(a) the person who applied for the order; (b) any person affected by the order (s 43(2)).'

24.17 Section 43(1) is specifically directed at circumstances where a Crown Court decides not to make a restraint order. There is no right of appeal therefore against the Crown Court's decision to make a restraint order. The aggrieved defendant may only appeal against the Crown Court's decision not to vary or discharge the restraint order on their application. In effect therefore this becomes a two tier process: firstly, a dissatisfied defendant must apply to the Crown Court for the variation or discharge of the restraint order; if that application fails then the second stage is to appeal to the Court of Appeal.

24.18 It is important to realise that the application to vary or discharge is often the first time the Crown Court judge will have the opportunity of listening to and understanding the

C. Restraint Order Appeals: Practice and Procedure

defendant's objections to the restraint order. This is because the restraint orders are usually applied for on an ex parte basis so as to maintain the element of surprise and avoid any dissipation of assets prior to the matter being listed for an inter partes hearing.

(4) Leave

24.19 Under s 89(1) of POCA an appeal to the Court of Appeal under Pt 2 of POCA lies only with the leave of that court.

24.20 Under r 73.1 of the Criminal Procedure Rules, leave to appeal to the Court of Appeal under s 43 of POCA will only be given where:

(a) the Court of Appeal considers that the appeal would have a real prospect of success; or (b) there is some other compelling reason why the appeal should be heard.

24.21 Rule 73.2 of the Criminal Procedure Rules sets out the procedure for giving notice of appeal. The notice of appeal must be served on each respondent, any person who holds realisable property to which the appeal relates, and any other person affected by the appeal no later than seven days after the notice of appeal is served on the appropriate officer of the Crown Court. Rule 73.3 sets out the procedure for where a respondent is seeking leave to appeal, or wishes to ask the Court of Appeal to uphold the Crown Court's decision for different reasons from or additional to those given by the Crown Court.

24.22 Rules 73.4–73.6 of the Criminal Procedure Rules explain the procedure for amending, abandoning, staying, and striking out appeals.

(5) Hearing the appeal

24.23 Subject to the rules made under s 53(1) of the Supreme Court Act 1981 (distribution of business between civil and criminal divisions), the criminal division of the Court of Appeal is the division to which appeals should be made (s 49(2)(a)).

24.24 Under r 73.7 of the Criminal Procedure Rules, every appeal will be limited to a review of the decision of the Crown Court unless the Court of Appeal considers that in the circumstances of an individual appeal it would be in the interests of justice to hold a re-hearing. The Court of Appeal will allow an appeal where the decision of the Crown Court was:

(a) wrong; or
(b) unjust because of a serious procedural or other irregularity in the proceedings in the Crown Court.

24.25 The Court of Appeal may draw any inference of fact which it considers justified on the evidence (Criminal Procedure Rules r 73.7(4)). At the hearing of the appeal a party may not rely on a matter not contained in his notice of appeal unless the Court of Appeal gives permission (Criminal Procedure Rules r 73.7(5)).

(6) The Proceeds of Crime Act 2002 (Appeals under Part 2) Order 2003

24.26 The Secretary of State has made certain corresponding provisions to the Criminal Appeal Act 1968 to allow for the adoption of general procedures such as obtaining leave to appeal and transcripts (s 89(3)). The Proceeds of Crime Act 2002 (Appeals under Part 2) Order

2003, SI 2003/82 came into force on 24 March 2003. For a detailed consideration analysis of this order see para 24.85 below.

(7) Restraint orders under POCA: appeal to the House of Lords

24.27 Following an appeal to the Court of Appeal under s 43, a further appeal lies to the House of Lords under s 44 of POCA. The appeal may be made by any person who is a party to the proceedings before the Court of Appeal (and therefore includes the prosecution). The powers of the Court of Appeal are set out in s 44(3) and are either: '(a) to confirm the decision of the Court of Appeal; or (b) to make such order as it believes is appropriate.'

24.28 An appeal to the House of Lords only follows from a decision of the Court of Appeal and only the parties to the Court of Appeal proceedings may appeal. Section 33(3) of the Criminal Appeal Act 1968 (limitation on appeal from the Criminal Division of the Court of Appeal) does not prevent an appeal to the House of Lords under Pt 2 of POCA (as per s 90(1)). For the procedure to be adopted when applying to appeal to the House of Lords see r 71.10 of the Criminal Procedure Rules.

D. Receivership Order Appeals: Practice and Procedure

(1) Appeals to the Court of Appeal in receivership proceedings under the DTA and CJA

24.29 Under s 16 of the Supreme Court Act 1981 any person wishing to appeal a receivership order in any of its forms under the DTA or CJA has a general right of appeal to the Court of Appeal. For the procedure to be followed in bringing such an appeal, see para 24.07 above.

(2) Appeals to the Court of Appeal in receivership proceedings under POCA

24.30 In respect of receivership order appeals under POCA, the general right of appeal under the DTA and the CJA no longer exists now that the receivership provisions have been transferred to the Crown Court.

24.31 Under POCA if, on an application for a receivership order made under ss 48 to 51 or 53 of POCA, the court decides *not* to make such a receivership order, the person who applied for the order may appeal to the Court of Appeal against the decision (s 65(1)). Applications under s 48 to 51 are for: the appointment of a management receiver by the Crown Court; the powers given to the management receiver by the Crown Court; the appointment of an enforcement receiver by the Crown Court; the powers given to an enforcement receiver by the Crown Court; or the powers given to a Director's receiver (under s 53) (but not the decision to appoint a Director's receiver).

24.32 If, on the other hand, the court makes an order under any of the above sections, the person who applied for the order or any person affected by the order may appeal to the Court of Appeal in respect of the court's decision (s 65(2)).

24.33 On an application for an order under s 62 of POCA, namely an application by either the receiver to the Crown Court for an order giving directions as to the exercise of the receiver's

D. Receivership Order Appeals: Practice and Procedure

powers under s 62(2); or, any person affected by action taken by the receiver, or any person who may be affected by the action the receiver proposes to take (s 62(3)), if the court decides *not* to make the order applied for, the person who applied for the order may appeal to the Court of Appeal against that decision under s 65(3).

24.34 Similarly, if on the other hand, the court makes an order under s 62, then the person who applied for the order or any person affected by the order, including the receiver, may appeal to the Court of Appeal in respect of the court's decision (s 65(4)).

24.35 Where an application is made to discharge or vary the powers of the receiver under s 63 of POCA, an appeal may be made to the Court of Appeal against the decision of the Crown Court by the person who applied for the order in respect of which the application was made (or if the order was made under ss 52 or 53 the Director of ARA); or any person affected by the court's decision; or the receiver.

(3) Leave

24.36 As in restraint cases, under s 89(1) of POCA an appeal to the Court of Appeal under Pt 2 of POCA lies only with the leave of that court.

24.37 Under r 73.1 of the Criminal Procedure Rules 2003 leave to appeal to the Court of Appeal under s 65 of POCA will only be given where:

(a) the Court of Appeal considers that the appeal would have a real prospect of success; or
(b) there is some other compelling reason why the appeal should be heard.

24.38 Rule 73.2 of the Criminal Procedure Rules sets out the procedure for giving notice of appeal. The notice of appeal must be served on each respondent, any person who holds realisable property to which the appeal relates and any other person affected by the appeal, no later than seven days after the notice of appeal is served on the appropriate officer of the Crown Court. Rule 73.3 sets out the procedure for where a respondent is seeking leave to appeal or wishes to ask the Court of Appeal to uphold the Crown Court's decision for different reasons from or additional to those given by the Crown Court.

24.39 Rules 73.4 to 73.6 of the Criminal Procedure Rules explain the procedure for amending, abandoning, staying, and striking out appeals.

(4) Hearing the appeal

24.40 Subject to the rules made under s 53(1) of the Supreme Court Act 1981 (distribution of business between civil and criminal divisions) the criminal division of the Court of Appeal is the division to which appeals should be made (see s 49(2)(a)).

24.41 Under r 73.7 of the Criminal Procedure Rules every appeal will be limited to a review of the decision of the Crown Court unless the Court of Appeal considers that in the circumstances of an individual appeal it would be in the interests of justice to hold a re-hearing. The Court of Appeal will allow an appeal where the decision of the Crown Court was:

(a) wrong; or
(b) unjust because of a serious procedural or other irregularity in the proceedings in the Crown Court.

24.42 The Court of Appeal may draw any inference of fact that it considers justified on the evidence. At the hearing of the appeal a party may not rely on a matter not contained in his notice of appeal unless the Court of Appeal gives permission (r 73.7(5) of the Criminal Procedure Rules).

(5) The Proceeds of Crime Act 2002 (Appeals under Part 2) Order 2003

24.43 The Secretary of State has made certain corresponding provisions to the Criminal Appeal Act 1968 to allow for the adoption of general procedures such as obtaining leave to appeal and transcripts (s 89(3)). The Proceeds of Crime Act 2002 (Appeals under Part 2) Order 2003, SI 2003/82 came into force on 24 March 2003. For a detailed analysis of this new order see para 24.85 below.

(6) The powers of the Court of Appeal on receipt of an appeal against a receivership order

24.44 On an appeal under any of the heads of s 65, the Court of Appeal may either confirm the decision or may make such order as it believes is appropriate (s 65(6)).

(7) Appeal to House of Lords

24.45 An appeal also lies to the House of Lords from a decision of the Court of Appeal on an appeal under s 65 relating to receivers. It may be made by any person who was a party to the proceedings before the Court of Appeal and on an appeal the House of Lords may confirm the decision of the Court of Appeal or make such order as it believes is appropriate. For the procedure to be adopted when applying to appeal to the House of Lords see r 71.10 of the Criminal Procedure Rules.

24.46 It has already been noted that s 33(3) of the Criminal Appeal Act 1968 (limitation on appeal from the Criminal Division of the Court of Appeal) does not prevent an appeal to the House of Lords under Pt 2 of POCA (s 90(1)).

(8) Appeals by financial investigators under POCA

24.47 Section 68 of POCA extends appeals under restraint orders and management receivership orders to 'accredited financial investigators'. 'Accredited financial investigators' are defined as being:

(a) a police officer who is not below the rank of superintendent;
(b) a Revenue and Customs officer who is not below such grade as is designated by the Commissioners of Revenue and Customs as equivalent to that rank, or
(c) a person who falls within a description in SI 2003/172, eg certain employees of the Inland Revenue; the Financial Services Authority; the Department for Work and Pensions etc (specified by an order of the Secretary of State made under s 453 of POCA).

24.48 Section 68(1) gives the accredited financial investigator the power to make an application for a restraint order under ss 41 or 42 or the power to appeal a restraint order under ss 43 or 44. Similarly it gives the accredited financial investigator the power to apply for the appointment of a management receiver under ss 48 or 49 of POCA or appeal under ss 65 or 66 following an application for the appointment of a management receiver. It also extends to the accredited financial investigator the power to apply for variation or discharge of a management receiver under s 63 of POCA.

24.49 If such an application is made or appeal brought by an accredited financial investigator, any subsequent step in the application or appeal, or any further application or appeal relating to the same matter may be taken, made, or brought by a different accredited financial investigator providing they fall into or are authorised by the definitions set out in s 68(3) (as per s 68(4)). The purpose of this subsection is to ensure that no problems are created by, for example, the subsequent ill health of an investigator who makes an initial appeal concerning a restraint order.

E. Confiscation Order Appeals: Practice and Procedure

(1) Appeals in confiscation order cases

24.50 Appeals against confiscation orders lie to the Court of Appeal from both the High Court and the Crown Court. The main difference is that in Crown Court cases the appeal will be to the Criminal Division, whereas in High Court confiscation order cases the appeal will be to the Civil Division.

24.51 The grounds must be drafted in terms of either mistake of law or mistake of fact. An appeal to the Court of Appeal must not be used merely to seek a re-hearing where a confiscation ruling has been adverse to the client.

24.52 An appeal against a confiscation order lies as part of the sentencing process. In *R v Johnson* [1991] 2 QB 249 the Court of Appeal held that by virtue of s 9 of the Criminal Appeal Act 1968 (as amended) a person who has been convicted of an offence or indictment:

> ... may appeal to the Court of Appeal against any sentence (not being a sentence fixed by law) passed on him for the offence, whether passed on his conviction or in subsequent proceedings.

24.53 'Sentence' in relation to an offence is defined in s 50(1) of the Criminal Appeal Act 1968 as including:

> Any Order made by a court when dealing with an offender...

In *Johnson* the court therefore concluded that a confiscation order does form part of a sentence for the purpose of s 9 of the Criminal Appeal Act 1968.

(2) Procedure for confiscation order appeals under the DTA and CJA

24.54 For appeals made under the DTA and CJA the procedure to be followed for appeals to the Court of Appeal is considered at para 24.07 above.

(3) A right of appeal against the confiscation order in all cases

24.55 The right of appeal exists as a right against all matters determined by the Crown Court at the confiscation hearing proceedings (*R v Emmett* [1998] AC 773) where Lord Steyn stated that there was a strong presumption that except by specific provision the legislature will not exclude a right of appeal as of right or with leave. He stated the starting point is that, unless the Act expressly or by necessary implication excludes a right of appeal there is as a matter of jurisdiction a right of appeal against the confiscation order in all cases. In confiscation order matters there is no express ouster of the right of appeal contained in the various relevant Acts (as per Lord Scarman in *R v Cain* [1985] 1 AC 46, 55G–56D).

24.56 In *Emmett* the appellant asserted that his acceptance of an allegation in a prosecutor's statement was the result of a mistake of law or fact, and therefore that acceptance should not be binding upon him on appeal. The Court of Appeal held that the burden rests upon an appellant who asserts that his acceptance of any allegation in a prosecutor's statement was the result of a mistake of law or fact to persuade the Court of Appeal that his assertion was correct. Lord Steyn added (at p 783):

> Lest it be thought, however, that my observations are some kind of open sesame to such appeals I would mention four matters. First, the question in such cases will not be what mistake Counsel made but what mistake the Defendant made. Secondly, and particularly in regard to matters peculiarly within the knowledge of the Defendant, the burden on the Defendant of proving a mistake may not easily be discharged. Thirdly, the focus in such cases will be on a material and causatively relevant mistake viz. a material mistake which in fact induced the Defendant to accept the correctness of a [prosecutor's] statement. Fourthly, even if the Defendant can persuade the Court of Appeal on these three points, the Court of Appeal may still have to consider whether, absent a material mistake, the particular confiscation order would nevertheless have been inevitable. If that is the case, the appeal may have to be dismissed on the grounds that on a global view of the case no injustice can be shown.

(4) Appeals involving the judge's discretion

24.57 The Court of Appeal has shown a marked reluctance to interfere in appeals that hinge on a judge's power of discretion. Although the Court of Appeal does have the power to consider and interfere in matters involving the discretion of the trial judge, it will only do so in the following circumstances:

(1) where there has been a failure to exercise a discretion; or
(2) where the judge has failed to take into account a material consideration; or
(3) where the judge in the court below has taken into account an immaterial consideration (see *R v Quinn* [1996] Crim LR 516).

(5) Attorney-General's appeal

24.58 In *A-G References Nos 114, 115, 116, 144 and 145 of 2002* the Court of Appeal held that it could properly hear applications by the Attorney General to refer a sentence under s36 of the Criminal Justice Act 1988, on the basis that a judge had wrongly refused to make a confiscation order and could consider evidence as required.

(6) Confiscation orders: the Crown Court 'slip rule'

24.59 Under s 155(1) of the Powers of Criminal Courts (Sentencing) Act 2000 both the defendant and the Crown may apply to the Crown Court on the basis that the factual conclusions determined by the Crown Court can be shown to be incorrect.

E. Confiscation Order Appeals: Practice and Procedure

Subject to the provisions of this section, a sentence imposed, or other order made by the Crown Court when dealing with an offender may be varied or remedied by the Crown Court within the period of 28 days beginning with the day on which the sentence or other order was imposed or made. **24.60**

It will be noted that applications must be made within 28 days of the order.

(7) Appeals in confiscation order cases to the Criminal Cases Review Commission

In *Re P* (QBD, 6 November 1998) the defendant had been convicted in February 1995 of a conspiracy offence relating to drugs. On 17 July 1995 the court gave the receiver the right to sell properties owned by the defendant. Following that, on 6 October 1995, the Crown Court made a confiscation order against the defendant in the sum of £557,000 with an order that he serve four years' imprisonment in default of payment. In June 1997 the Court of Appeal dismissed the defendant's appeal against his conviction. On that occasion his counsel did not pursue any complaint against the confiscation order. In 1998 the defendant sought to pursue the claim that he was innocent of the offence he had been convicted of, and that, as a result, the confiscation order was wrongly made, with the Criminal Cases Review Commission. He also lodged an application to the European Court of Human Rights. The defendant made an unsuccessful application to the court to have funds released from the bite of the restraint order to enable him to meet the expenses associated with those two applications. Laws J held: **24.61**

> The fact is that, so far as the domestic criminal litigation is concerned in this case, Mr P is well past the end of the road. The Commission may, of course, investigate a matter after all other legal processes have been exhausted. Indeed that is their very role. However, it is quite clear to me that whilst they are doing so, and the fact that they are doing so, are no basis for altering, suspending or varying the affect of the restraint order and therefore, in effect, the execution of a confiscation order once that has been made. The same applies in relation to his application to the European Court of Human Rights.

In Re C (QBD, 14 May 2004), Owen J, relying on the dicta of Laws J in *Re P* held that the fact the matter had been referred to the CCRC *'does not afford a reason why the law should not take its course'*. **24.62**

(8) Fresh evidence

In *R v Stroud* [2004] EWCA Crim 1048, the Court of Appeal held that where a defendant sought to adduce fresh expert evidence on appeal against a confiscation order, the same considerations as to admissibility were to be considered as applied in appeals against conviction. **24.63**

(9) Confiscation appeals under POCA

Under s 87(2) of POCA, a confiscation order is subject to appeal until there is no further possibility of an appeal on which the order could be varied or quashed (for these purposes any power to grant leave to appeal out of time must be ignored). Provisions for giving notice of appeal are set out in r 72.1 of the Criminal Procedure Rules. Where a defendant is served with a notice of appeal under r 72.1, and wishes to oppose the granting of leave he **24.64** must, not later than 14 days after the date on which he received the notice of appeal, serve on the registrar and on the appellant a notice under Form 2 (see r 72.2). Rule 72.3 of the Criminal Procedure Rules outlines the procedure to be followed when an appeal is to be either amended or abandoned.

24.65 Subject to the rules made under s 53(1) of the Supreme Court Act 1981 (distribution of business between Civil and Criminal Divisions) the Criminal Division of the Court of Appeal is the division to which appeals should be made (see s 49(2)(a)). The Secretary of State has made certain corresponding provisions to the Criminal Appeal Act 1968 to allow for the adoption of general procedures such as obtaining leave to appeal and transcripts (s 89(3)).

(10) Leave

24.66 Like restraint and receivership appeals, under s 89(1) of POCA an appeal to the Court of Appeal under Pt 2 of POCA lies only with the leave of that court.

(11) Appeal by the prosecutor or the Director of ARA

24.67 If the Crown Court makes a confiscation order the prosecutor or the Director of the Asset Recovery Agency (ARA) may appeal to the Court of Appeal in respect of that order (s 31(1)). If the Crown Court decides not to make a confiscation order the prosecutor or the Director of ARA may appeal to the Court of Appeal against that decision (s 31(2)).

24.68 This is a new power to appeal against a confiscation order under POCA which is directed at the prosecutor. It may be an appeal on any ground (either a point of law or fact), for example, that the court has failed to take account of property that should be taken account of.

24.69 There is, however, no right of appeal against an order or decision made by virtue of s 19 (no confiscation order made: reconsideration of case); s 20 (no confiscation order made: reconsideration of benefit); s 27 (where the defendant has absconded and he has been convicted or committed) or s 28 (where the defendant has absconded but he has neither been convicted nor committed) (see s 31(3)).

(12) Appeal by the prosecutor or the Director of ARA: the Court of Appeal's powers

24.70 Under s 32 of POCA an appeal by the prosecutor (or Director, as the case may be) to the Court of Appeal gives the Court of Appeal the power to confirm, quash, or vary the confiscation order (s 32(1)).

24.71 If the appeal is on the grounds that the Court of Appeal has decided not to make a confiscation order the Court of Appeal may confirm the decision, or if it believes the decision is wrong it may itself proceed under s 6 of POCA to make a confiscation order (but in doing so ignoring s 6(1) to (3)), or it may direct the Crown Court to proceed afresh under s 6.

24.72 If the Crown Court is directed to proceed afresh, it must comply with any other directions the Court of Appeal may make in relation to the hearing (s 32(3)). Under s 32(4), if the Court of Appeal makes or varies a confiscation order, or directs the Crown Court to go through the confiscation procedures afresh under s 6, and the Crown Court has, in the meantime,

E. Confiscation Order Appeals: Practice and Procedure

imposed a fine or an ancillary order set out within s 13(3) of POCA, eg a compensation order, then the court is required to have regard to the fine or order made.

(13) The steps the court must take

24.73 If the Court of Appeal proceeds under s 6 or the Crown Court proceeds afresh pursuant to a direction by the Court of Appeal then s 32 (6) to (10) apply:

(6) If a court has already sentenced the Defendant for the offence (or any of the offences) concerned, section 6 has effect as if his particular criminal conduct included conduct which constitutes offences which the court has taken into consideration in deciding his sentence for the offence or offences concerned.

(7) If an order has been made against the Defendant in respect of the offence (or any of the offences) concerned under Section 130 of the Sentencing Act (Compensation Orders)—
   (a) the Court must have regard to it and,
   (b) Section 13(5) and (6) . . . do not apply.

24.74 Section 13(6) states that the court must specify that so much of the compensation is to be paid out of any sums recovered under the confiscation order; and the amount it specifies must be the amount it believes will not be recoverable because of the insufficiency of the person's means. This subsection only applies if the Crown Court makes both a confiscation order and an order for the payment of compensation under s 130 of the Sentencing Act against the same proceedings, and the court believes he will not have sufficient means to satisfy both the orders in full (s 13(5)).

(8) Section 8(2) does not apply, and the rules applying instead are that the court must—
   (a) take account of conduct occurring before the relevant date;
   (b) take account of property obtained before that date;
   (c) take account of property obtained on or after that date if it was obtained as a result of or in connection with conduct occurring before that date.

24.75 Section 8(2) limits the court to taking into account conduct occurring at the time that it makes its decision and taking account of property obtained at that time. Those restrictions do not apply where the Court of Appeal is proceeding under s 6 or the Crown Court is proceeding under s 6 as a result of a direction by the Court of Appeal following a successful appeal by the prosecutor or Director of ARA.

(9) In Section 10—
   (a) the first and second assumptions do not apply with regard to property first held by the Defendant on or after the relevant date; or
   (b) the third assumption does not apply with regard to expenditure incurred by him on or after the date;
   (c) the fourth assumption does not apply with regard to property obtained or assumed to have been obtained by him on or after that date.

Section 10 of POCA sets out the assumptions to be made in cases of criminal lifestyle.

24.76 Under s 32(10), s 26 of POCA applies in the circumstances mentioned in s 26(1), ie the court is proceeding under s 6 in pursuance of either s 19 (where no confiscation order has been made and the court is reconsidering the case, or where no order has been made and the court is reconsidering the benefit there is) or the prosecutor or the Director of ARA applies under s 21, namely where an order has been made and the prosecutor or Director is asking the court to reconsider the benefit.

The 'relevant date' for these purposes is the date on which the Crown Court decided not to make a confiscation order (s 32(11)).

(14) Corresponding provisions

24.77 The Secretary of State has made certain corresponding provisions to the Criminal Appeal Act 1968 to allow for the adoption of general procedures such as obtaining leave to appeal and transcripts (s 89(3)). The Proceeds of Crime Act 2002 (Appeals under Part 2) Order 2003, SI 2003/82 came into force on 24 March 2003. For a detailed consideration of this order see para 24.85 below.

(15) Appeal by the prosecutor or the Director of ARA: appeal to the House of Lords by either the defendant or the prosecutor

24.78 Under s 33(1) an appeal lies to the House of Lords from a decision of the Court of Appeal on an appeal under s 31 of POCA.

24.79 An appeal under this section lies at the instance of either the defendant or the prosecutor (if the prosecutor appealed under s 31); or the defendant or the Director (if the Director appealed under s 31) (see s 33(2)). On such an appeal from a decision of the Court of Appeal to confirm, vary, or make a confiscation order, the House of Lords may itself confirm, quash, or vary the order (s 33(3)).

24.80 It will have been noted already that s 33(3) of the Criminal Appeal Act 1968 (limitation on appeal from the Criminal Division of the Court of Appeal) does not prevent an appeal to the House of Lords under Pt 2 of POCA (s 90(1)). For procedure to be adopted when applying to appeal to the House of Lords see r 71.10 of the Criminal Procedure Rules.

(16) Powers of the House of Lords in such circumstances

24.81 On an appeal from the decision of the Court of Appeal to confirm the decision of the Crown Court not to make a confiscation order or from the decision of the Court of Appeal to quash a confiscation order the House of Lords may:

(a) confirm the decision, or
(b) direct the Crown Court to proceed afresh under s 6 if it believes the decision was wrong (s 33(4)).

It will be noted that the House of Lords has no power itself to proceed under s 6, unlike the Court of Appeal. Its powers under s 33 are limited to confirming, quashing, or varying the order of the Court of Appeal. If it elects to quash the order then it may remit the case to the Crown Court with directions to proceed afresh under s 6.

(17) Where the Crown Court proceeds afresh

24.82 If proceeding afresh in pursuance of this section the Crown Court must comply with any directions the House of Lords may make (s 33(5)). In similar terms to if the Court of Appeal orders the Crown Court to proceed afresh under s 6, if the Crown Court varies the confiscation order, or makes a confiscation order in pursuance of a direction by the House of Lords it must have regard to any fine imposed on the defendant in respect of the offence concerned or in respect of any ancillary orders (which fall within s 13(3) of POCA). However the Crown Court is not required to take account of an order if it has already taken account of the order in working out what the free property held by the defendant is (to avoid double counting) (ss 33(6)(b) and 32(4)(b)).

Sections 33(8)–(12) are in identical terms to s 32(6) to (10) above and apply where the Crown Court is proceeding afresh under s 6 in pursuance of an election by the House of Lords.

24.83

For the purposes of s 33 the 'relevant date' is:

(a) in a case where the Crown Court made a confiscation order which was quashed by the Court of Appeal, the date on which the Crown Court made the order;
(b) in any other case, the date on which the Crown Court decided not to make a confiscation order (s 33(13)).

24.84

F. The Proceeds of Crime Act 2002 (Appeals under Part 2) Order 2003

(1) Practice and procedure: appeals to the Court of Appeal

The Proceeds of Crime Act 2002 (Appeals under Part 2) Order 2003, SI 2003/82 came into force on 24 March 2003. It makes provisions that correspond with the provisions of the Criminal Appeal Act 1968 for the purposes of the three new appeal routes introduced by POCA, namely:

24.85

(1) an appeal under s 31 of POCA to the Court of Appeal (and from there to the House of Lords under s 33) by the prosecutor or Director of ARA against a confiscation order or a failure of the Crown Court to make a confiscation order;
(2) an appeal under s 43 of POCA to the Court of Appeal (and from there to the House of Lords under s 44 of POCA) in respect of decisions of the Crown Court about restraint orders; and
(3) an appeal under s 65 of POCA to the Court of Appeal (and from there to the House of Lords under s 66 of POCA) in respect of decisions of the Crown Court about receivers.

(2) Initiating procedure

Under Art 3(1) of the Proceeds of Crime Act 2002 (Appeals under Part 2) Order, a person who wishes to obtain the leave of the Court of Appeal to appeal to the Court of Appeal under Pt 2 of POCA, ie confiscation, restraint, and appointment of receivers, shall give notice of application for leave to appeal, in the manner directed by the Rules of Court. Such a notice of application for leave to appeal shall be given within:

24.86

(a) 28 days from the date of the decision appealed against, in the case of an appeal under s 31 of the Act (confiscation); or
(b) 14 days from the date of the decision appealed against, in the case of an appeal under s 43 (restraint) or s 65 (receiverships) of the Act.

24.87 Under 3(3) the time for giving notice under this Article may be extended by the Court of Appeal. Article 3 reflects the provisions previously set out in s 18 of the Criminal Appeal Act 1968.

(3) Disposal of groundless applications for leave to appeal

24.88 Under Art 4 of the Proceeds of Crime Act 2002 (Appeals under Part 2) Order, if it appears to the Registrar that a notice of application for leave to appeal to the Court of Appeal under Pt 2 of the Act does not show any substantial ground for appeal, he may refer the application for leave to the Court of Appeal for summary determination.

24.89 Where the case is so referred to the Court of Appeal, it may, if it considers that the application for leave is frivolous or vexatious and can be determined without adjourning it for a full hearing, dismiss the application for leave summarily, without calling on anyone to attend the hearing. This provision corresponds with s 20 of the Criminal Appeal Act 1968.

(4) Preparation of case for hearing

24.90 Once an application has been received, and subject to Art 4, Art 5 states as follows:

(1) The Registrar shall—
  (a) take all necessary steps for obtaining a hearing of any application for leave to appeal to the Court of Appeal under Part 2 of the Act of which Notice is given to him and which is not referred and dismissed summarily under Article 4;
  (b) where an application for leave to appeal to the Court of Appeal under Part 2 of the Act is granted, take all necessary steps for obtaining a hearing of an appeal; and
  (c) obtain and lay before the Court of Appeal in proper form all documents, exhibits and other things which appear necessary for the proper determination of the application for leave to appeal under Part 2 of the Act or the appeal under Part 2 of the Act.

24.91 This article corresponds with s 21 of the Criminal Appeal Act 1968 and provides that the Registrar must organise hearings for applications for leave to appeal and appeals. In the case of appeals in respect of confiscation orders, the Registrar must also organise documents and exhibits for the appeal and provide them, in accordance with the Rules of Court, to the parties. Under Art 5(2) a party to an appeal under Pt 2 of the Act may obtain from the Registrar any document or things, including copies or reproductions of documents, required for his appeal, in accordance with the Rules of Court. The Registrar may make charges in accordance with such rules for those documents (see Art 5(3)).

(5) Right of defendant to be present

24.92 Under Art 6(1) of the Proceeds of Crime Act 2002 (Appeals under Part 2) Order 2003, the defendant will be entitled to be present, if he wishes, at the hearing of any appeal to the Court of Appeal under Pt 2 of POCA to which he is a party, even though he may be in custody. However if the defendant is in custody, he will not be entitled to be present:

(a) where the appeal is on some grounds involving a question of law alone; or
(b) on an application for leave to appeal; or
(c) on any proceedings preliminary or incidental to an appeal, unless the Court of Appeal gives him leave to be present (see Art 6(2)).

F. The Proceeds of Crime Act 2002 (Appeals under Part 2) Order 2003

This article corresponds to s 22 of the Criminal Appeal Act 1968.

(6) Rules of evidence in the Court of Appeal

24.93 For the purposes of an appeal under Pt 2 of POCA, the Court of Appeal may, if they think it necessary or expedient in the interests of justice:

(a) order the production of any document, exhibit or other thing connected with the proceedings, the production of which appears to them necessary for the determination of the appeal;
(b) order any witness to attend for examination and be examined before the Court of Appeal; and
(c) receive any evidence which was not adduced in the proceedings from which the appeal relies.

(See Art 7(1) of the Proceeds of Crime Act 2002 (Appeals under Part 2) Order.)

24.94 The Court of Appeal may, if they think it necessary or expedient in the interests of justice, order the examination of any witness whose attendance might be required under para (1)(b) to be conducted before any judge or officer of the court or other person appointed by the court for the purpose, and allow the admission of any depositions so taken as evidence before the court (See Art 7(3) of the Proceeds of Crime Act 2002 (Appeals under Part 2) Order).

24.95 Under Art 7(2) of the Proceeds of Crime Act 2002 (Appeals under Part 2) Order the Court of Appeal must, in considering whether to receive any evidence, have regard in particular to:

(a) whether the evidence appears to the court to be capable of belief;
(b) whether it appears to the court that the evidence may afford any ground for allowing the appeal;
(c) whether the evidence would have been admissible in the proceedings from which the appeal lies on an issue which is the subject of the appeal; and
(d) whether there is a reasonable explanation for the failure to adduce the evidence in the proceedings giving rise to the appeal.

The above provisions reflect s 23 of the Criminal Appeal Act 1968.

(7) General provisions

24.96 The Criminal Procedure Rules set out certain other general provisions to be adopted where the circumstances dictate; the relevant rules are listed below:

- Extension of time—r 71.1
- Applications relating to bail, leave to be present, reception of evidence—r 71.2
- Examination of witnesses in court—r 71.3
- Supply of documentary and other exhibits—r 71.4
- Registrar's power to require information from court of trial—r 71.5
- Hearing by single judge—r 71.6
- Determination by full court—r 71.7
- Notice of determination—r 71.8

- Record of proceedings and transcript—r 71.9
- Appeal to House of Lords—r 71.10
- Service of Documents—r 71.11

(8) References to the European Court of Justice

24.97 The Court of Appeal has power to refer a case to the European Court of Justice at any time before the determination of an appeal (see the Criminal Appeal (References to the European Court) Rules 1972, SI 1972/1786).

G. Appeals against Forfeiture Orders

(1) Forfeiture appeals under POCA from the magistrates' court

24.98 Section 299 of POCA was amended by s 101 of the Serious Organised Crime and Police Act 2005 (SOCPA) because of an ambiguity as to it's meaning. While the original s 299(1) appeared to allow 'Any party to the proceedings' to appeal against an order made under s 298, this was qualified by the words 'for the forfeiture of cash'. This meant that while any party may appeal an order for forfeiture their was no provision for the complainant to appeal a *refusal* to grant forfeiture, although somewhat ironically a complainant could appeal an order *for* forfeiture.

24.99 The substituted s 299 now states:

(1) Any person to proceedings for an order for the forfeiture of cash under section 298 who is aggrieved by an order under that section or by the decision of the court to make such an order may appeal....

In other words, both the complainant and the defendant now have a right of appeal from the magistrates' court hearing to the Crown Court. Such a hearing should be *de novo* (s 79(3) Supreme Court Act 1981), with the facts being re-examined in the court above, and with the opportunity for both parties to serve further evidence before the hearing takes place (whilst the original s 299(3) expressly stated that the appeal was by way of re-hearing, the substituted legislation does not).

24.100 The appeal is to the Crown Court and notice must be lodged before the expiration of 30 days from when the order or decision was made (substituted s 299(2)).

24.101 This section also has the effect of allowing the Appeal Court, and the Crown Court, to hear an appeal in an appropriate way, for example, on a point of law.

24.102 Appeals in relation to the cash seizure provisions, including whether the 30 day period can be extended; funding the appeal and judicial review, are further considered at paras 21.187 – 21.194 of Chapter 21.

24.103 It will have been seen from the chapter on forfeiture of cash under POCA that once an application for forfeiture has been made, the seized cash may not be released until any proceedings in pursuance of that application (including any proceedings on appeal) are concluded. Under the previous legislation (s 42(7)) the money was not to be released until the application or criminal proceedings were concluded.

G. Appeals against Forfeiture Orders

(2) Procedure on forfeiture appeals under POCA

The appeal is to the Crown Court; and notice must be lodged before the expiration of 30 days from when the order was made. It is a *de novo* hearing the appeal being by way of rehearing (s 299(3)). **24.104**

The judge sits usually with two lay magistrates. The judge must give reasons for the court's decision. The reasoning required will depend on the circumstances of the case but must be enough to show that the court has identified the main issues and how it has resolved them (see *R v Harrow Crown Court ex p Dave* [1994] 1 WLR 98). The Rules on hearing a complaint should be adopted as the procedure of the court for such a hearing. **24.105**

(3) Appeals in condemnation cases from the magistrates' court

Both HM Revenue and Customs and the defendant may appeal from the magistrates' court decision to the Crown Court, or in the alternative invite the court to state a case for the High Court on a matter of law (see Sch 3 para 11 to CEMA). The Crown Court's jurisdiction and powers of disposal are set out in ss 45-48 of the Supreme Court Act 1981. **24.106**

On appeal to the Crown Court the hearing is *de novo* (s 79(3) Supreme Court Act 1981) and involves a complete re-hearing of the original case, including oral evidence. Rule 63.2 of the Criminal Procedure Rules 2005, SI 2005/38, sets out the time limit (21 days) and the procedure (written notice to the magistrates' court), appears to have been adopted for use in complaint appeals, albeit the appeal is civil. **24.107**

The procedure adopted at the hearing is the same as set out in the Magistrates' Courts Rules above. Pending the re-hearing, there is no restriction on either Revenue and Customs or the defence obtaining more evidence and adducing new evidence at the appeal. Appeals in condemnation cases, including procedure, are further considered at para 28.15 et seq of Chapter 29. **24.108**

(4) Appeal from the magistrates' court to the High Court by way of case stated

Under the Magistrates' Court Act 1980, s 111(1): **24.109**

'Any person who was a party to any proceedings before a Magistrates' Court or is aggrieved by the conviction, order, determination or other proceeding of the Court may question the proceeding on the ground that it is wrong in law or in excess of jurisdiction by applying to the Justices to state a case for the opinion of the High Court on a question of law or jurisdiction involved . . .

The following points should be noted:

(1) The application must be made in writing within 21 days of the sentence and must state the point of law upon which the opinion of the High Court is sought.
(2) There is no power to state a case until the magistrates have reached a final decision in the matter.
(3) The right to appeal to the Crown Court is lost once an application to state a case to the High Court is made (see Magistrates' Court Act 1980 s 111(4)).
(4) The magistrates are entitled to refuse to state a case once requested to do so but that decision is itself reviewable by the High Court on an application for judicial review (see *R v Huntington Magistrates' Court ex p Percy* (1994) COD 323.

Chapter 24: Appeals

24.110 The relevant Criminal Procedure Rules are set out at Part 64, and deal with, inter alia, the making of the application; extension of the time limit; service of documents and content.

H. Appeals under Part 6 of POCA: Revenue Functions

24.111 An appeal in respect of the exercise by the Director of general revenue functions shall be to the 'Special Commissioners' (s 320(1)). An assessor nominated to assist the Special Commissioners must have special knowledge and experience in the matter to which the appeal relates and must be selected from a panel of persons appointed for the purposes of s 320 by the Lord Chancellor.

24.112 This right of appeal is equivalent to those available to taxpayers subjected to decisions made by the Inland Revenue. All of the rules against actions arising from the exercise of his powers by the Director of his revenue functions will be to the Special Commissioners and not to General Commissioners. The Taxes Management Act 1970 enables the Lord Chancellor to regulate by secondary legislation the administration of the Special Commissioner's hearing (s 320(4)).

I. The Criminal Cases Review Commission

24.113 The Criminal Cases Review Commission (CCRC) may refer to the Court of Appeal any conviction or sentence. Such a reference is treated as an appeal by the person concerned under the Criminal Appeal Act 1995 s 9, provided that the conditions set out in s 13 of that Act are met. That entails that there is a real possibility that the conviction, finding, or sentence would not be upheld if the reference is made and, in the case of a sentence, on the basis of an argument on a point of law or information not raised in the proceedings. The appeal procedure must have been followed without success, or leave to appeal must have been refused, or there are exceptional circumstances that justify a reference, for a reference to be made.

24.114 If the CCRC forms a negative view about an application it will invite further representations or comments, usually within 20 working days. This period is non-statutory and may be extended upon application to the Commission. However, if further representations are not received within 20 working days (or any extension), or the representations raise no new issues, the case will be closed (see also *Re P* (QBD, 6 November 1998) at para 24.61 above).

J. Appeals against Findings of Contempt of Court

(1) Appeals in cases of findings of contempt of court by the High Court

24.115 Under para 21.4 of CPR Practice Direction 52, if an appeal under s 13 of the Administration of Justice Act 1960 is to be made (appeals in cases of contempt of court), the appellant must serve the appellant's notice on the court from whose order or decision the appeal is brought (r 52.4(3)). In the case of appeals from the Queen's Bench Division the notice must be served on the Senior Master of the Queen's Bench Division, and service may be affected by leaving a copy of the notice of appeal with the clerk of the lists. Permission is not required to appeal a committal for contempt of court; the defendant has the right of appeal to the Court of Appeal (Civil Division) either against the sentence imposed for contempt or the finding of contempt itself (see r 52.3 CPR).

K. Thumbnail Guide to the Appeal Provisions within the Criminal Procedure Rules

The High Court has the power to grant bail pending the outcome of any appeal. See s 4 of the Administration of Justice Act 1960. **24.116**

The powers of the Court of Appeal are found in s 13(3) of the Administration of Justice Act 1960, which reads: **24.117**

> The court to which an appeal is brought under this section may reverse or vary the order or decision of the court below, and make such other order as may be just; and without prejudice to the inherent powers of any report referred to in subsection 2 of this section, provision may be made by rules of court authorising the release on bail of an appellant under this section.

There is a further provision for an appeal to the House of Lords under s 13(4) subject to leave.

(2) Appeals in cases of findings of contempt of court by the Crown Court

Section 18A of the Criminal Appeal Act 1968 states that a person who wishes to appeal under s 13 of the Administration of Justice Act 1960 from any order or decision of the Crown Court in the exercise of its jurisdiction to punish for contempt of court shall give notice of appeal in such manner as may be directed by the rules of court. Notice of appeal shall be given within 28 days from the date of the order or decision appealed against. The time for giving notice under this section may be extended either before or after expiry by the Court of Appeal (s 18A(3)). **24.118**

The Court of Appeal may, if they think fit, grant an appellant bail pending the determination of his appeal (s 19 of the Criminal Appeal Act 1968). They may also revoke it (s 19(1)(b)). **24.119**

K. Thumbnail Guide to the Appeal Provisions within the Criminal Procedure Rules

Part 63–Appeals from the Magistrates Court to the Crown Court against conviction or sentence **24.120**

Notice of appeal	rule 63.2
Documents to be sent to Crown Court	rule 63.3
Entry of appeal and notice of hearing	rule 63.4
Abandonment of appeal - notice	rule 63.5
Abandonment of appeal - bail	rule 63.6
Number and qualification of justices - appeal from youth court	rule 63.7
Number and qualification of justices - dispensation	rule 63.8
Disqualification of justices	rule 63.9

Part 64 – Appeal to the High Court by Way of Case Stated

Application to magistrates' court to state case	rule 64.1
Consideration of a draft case by magistrates' court	rule 64.2
Preparation and submission of final case for magistrates' court	rule 64.3
Extension of time limit by magistrates' court	rule 64.4
Service of documents on application to magistrates' court	rule 64.5
Content of case stated by magistrates' court	rule 64.6
Application to the Crown Court to state case	rule 64.7

Chapter 24: Appeals

Part 65 – Appeal to the Court of Appeal against ruling in Preparatory Hearing

Part 66 – Appeal to the Court of Appeal Against Ruling Adverse to the Prosecution

Part 67 – Appeal to the Court of Appeal against order restricting reporting or public access

Part 68 – Appeal to the Court of Appeal against Conviction or Sentence

Part 69 – Reference to the Court of Appeal on a Point of Law

Part 70 – Reference to the Court of Appeal of Unduly Lenient Sentence

Part 71 – Appeal to the Court of Appeal under the POCA 2002: General rules

Extension of time	rule 71.1
Other applications	rule 71.2
Examination of witness by court	rule 71.3
Supply of documentary and other exhibits	rule 71.4
Registrar's power to require information from court of trial	rule 71.5
Hearing by single judge	rule 71.6
Determination by full court	rule 71.7
Notice of determination	rule 71.8
Record of proceedings and transcript	rule 71.9
Appeal to House of Lords	rule 71.10
Service of documents	rule 71.11

Part 72 – Appeal to the Court of Appeal under POCA 2002 – Prosecutor's Appeal regarding Confiscation

Notice of appeal	rule 72.1
Respondent's notice	rule 72.2
Amendment and abandonment of appeal	rule 72.3

Part 73 – Appeal to the Court of Appeal under POCA 2002: Restraint or Receivership Orders

Leave to appeal	rule 73.1
Notice of appeal	rule 73.2
Respondent's notice	rule 73.3
Amendment and abandonment of appeal	rule 73.4
Stay	rule 73.5
Striking out, setting aside and imposing conditions	rule 73.6
Hearing of appeals	rule 73.7

Part 74 – Appeal to the House of Lords

Application for leave to appeal from the Court of Appeal	rule 74.1

Part 75 – Reference to the European Court

Reference to the European Court	rule 75.1

25

THE INTERNATIONAL ELEMENT

A. Introduction	25.01	(9) Application of the proceeds of realisation	25.39
B. International Assistance Under the DTA and CJA	25.03	E. Enforcement of DTA and CJA Confiscation Orders Overseas	25.40
(1) Designated countries and territories	25.05	F. Reciprocal Enforcement with Scotland and Northern Ireland	25.43
(2) Appropriate authorities	25.06	(1) Scotland	25.44
(3) Obtaining restraint orders in the UK on behalf of designated countries	25.07	(2) Northern Ireland	25.45
C. Procedure on Applications for Restraint Orders in DTA and CJA Cases	25.16	G. Co-operation under POCA 2002	25.46
		(1) Action to be taken on receipt of an external request	25.49
(1) The letter of request	25.17	(2) Powers of the Crown Court to make restraint orders	25.50
(2) Evidence in support	25.19	(3) Ancillary orders	25.54
(3) Ancillary orders	25.24	(4) Application, discharge and variation of restraint orders	25.55
(4) Applications for the variation and discharge of orders	25.25	(5) Appeals	25.57
D. Enforcement of External Confiscation Orders	25.26	(6) Hearsay evidence	25.58
(1) Registration of the order	25.27	(7) Management receivers	25.59
(2) Procedure for registration	25.30	(8) Applications to give effect to external orders	25.60
(3) Evidence in support of the application for registration	25.32	(9) Registration of the order	25.65
(4) The application	25.33	(10) Appeals	25.67
(5) Applications to vary or set aside registration	25.35	(11) Enforcement of the order	25.68
(6) Register of orders	25.36	(12) Procedure on applications	25.69
(7) Effect of registration	25.37	H. Enforcement of POCA Confiscation Orders in Different Parts of the UK	25.70
(8) Variation, satisfaction and discharge of registered order	25.38	(1) Civil Recovery proceedings	25.71

A. Introduction

Organised crime transcends national frontiers more than ever before. Improvements to the public transport system make it easier to travel between countries, the advent of the internet and e-mail allows for virtually instantaneous communication between members of criminal gangs across the world, and, as Ognall J observed in *Re M* (unreported, 9 July 1993): **25.01**

> We live in an age when funds may be transferred from jurisdiction to jurisdiction as rapidly as it takes me to speak this sentence.

25.02 It is increasingly common to find a person prosecuted for criminal offences in one country owning assets in another. The purpose of the legislation would soon be defeated if criminals could invest their ill-gotten gains in an overseas country without fear of the same being restrained and ultimately realised in satisfaction of a confiscation order. It is not surprising that the Acts bite on assets held all over the world and provide for restraint and confiscation orders made in overseas countries to be enforced against assets held in the UK. All three Acts contain express provisions to the effect that they apply to assets held anywhere in the world: by s 62(2) of the DTA the Act 'applies to property whether it is situated in England and Wales or elsewhere' and s 102(3) of the CJA provides that Pt VI of the Act 'applies to property wherever situated.' Similarly, s 84 (1) of POCA defines property as being 'all property wherever situated'.

B. International Assistance under the DTA and CJA

25.03 The provisions of the DTA and CJA and the relevant subordinate legislation continue to apply to cases where international assistance requests were made before 1 January, 2006. The Proceeds of Crime Act, 2002 (External Requests and Orders) Order 2005 applies to international requests made after this date and is considered at para 25.46 and following.

25.04 The DTA and CJA empower the High Court to make restraint orders in support of prosecutions being conducted overseas against assets held in this country and to enforce overseas confiscation orders against such assets. By s 39 of the DTA:

(1) Her Majesty may by Order in Council—
   (a) direct in relation to a country or territory outside the United Kingdom designated by the Order (a 'designated country') that, subject to such modifications as may be specified, the relevant provisions of this Act shall apply to external confiscation orders and to proceedings which have been or are to be instituted in the designated country and may result in an external confiscation order made there;
   (b) make—
      (i) such provision in connection with the taking of action in the designated country with a view to satisfying a confiscation order;
      (ii) such provision as to the evidence or proof of any matter for the purposes of this section and section 40 of this Act, and
      (iii) such incidental, consequential and transitional provision, as appears to Her Majesty to be expedient, and
   (c) (without prejudice to the generality of this subsection) direct that, in such circumstances as may be specified, proceeds which arise out of action taken in the designated country with a view to satisfying a confiscation order shall be treated as reducing the amount payable under the order to such extent as may be specified.

(2) In this section 'external confiscation order' means an order made by a court in a designated country for the purpose of recovering or recovering the value of, payments or other rewards received in connection with drug trafficking.

(3) An Order in Council made under this section may make different provision of different cases or classes of case.

(4) The power to make an Order in Council under this section includes power to modify the relevant provisions of this Act in such a way as to confer power on a person to exercise a discretion.

B. International Assistance under the DTA and CJA

(5) An Order in Council under this section shall be subject to annulment in pursuant of a resolution of either House of Parliament.

(6) For the purposes of this section 'the relevant provisions of this Act' are this Part, except sections 10 and 16 and Part IV.

A similar provision is contained in s 96 of the CJA in respect of overseas orders made in cases concerning offences other than drug trafficking offences.

(1) Designated countries and territories

25.05 Orders in Council have been made both under the DTA and CJA: the Drug Trafficking Act 1994 (Designated Countries and Territories) Order 1996, SI 1996/2880 has been made under the DTA; and the Criminal Justice Act 1988 (Designated Countries and Territories) Order 1991, SI 1991/2873 has been made under the CJA. These Orders designate countries on whose behalf restraint orders may be obtained and enforcement action taken to enforce overseas confiscation orders. Subsequent Orders have been made adding additional designated countries. The Orders modify the terms of the Acts for the purpose of empowering the courts to make restraint orders and enforce confiscation orders on behalf of designated countries. Sch 2 to each Order lists the amendments made to the principal Act, and Sch 3 then reproduces the entire Act as amended.

(2) Appropriate authorities

25.06 If law enforcement agencies throughout the world were able to make direct contact with their opposite numbers in other countries to obtain restraint orders and enforce confiscation orders, a state of chaos would rapidly ensue in which no one authority was in overall charge or responsible for the coordination of the action designated countries take on behalf of one another. Accordingly both orders make provision for an 'appropriate authority' in each designated country through which all requests for restraint and enforcement action must be channelled: see Art 2 of both Orders.

(3) Obtaining restraint orders in the UK on behalf of designated countries

25.07 As in domestic cases, in most circumstances the first step that will need to be taken on behalf of a designated country is to obtain a restraint order to prevent the dissipation of assets pending the making and enforcement of a confiscation order. The procedures for obtaining such orders are very similar to those applicable in domestic cases.

(a) Drugs cases
25.08

By s 25(1) of the DTA as modified by the Order, the High Court may make a restraint order when:

(a) proceedings have been instituted against the defendant in a designated country;
(b) the proceedings have not been concluded; and
(c) either an external confiscation order has been made in the proceedings or it appears to the High Court that there are reasonable grounds for believing that such an order may be made in them.

By s 25(3) as modified, a restraint order may also be made where it appears to the court that proceeds are to be instituted against the defendant in a designated country and there are reasonable grounds to suspect that an external confiscation order will be made.

25.09 *Meaning of 'proceedings have been instituted'*

By s 41(2) of the DTA as modified, proceedings are instituted when:

(a) under the law of the designated country concerned one of the steps specified in relation to that country in column 2 of the Appendix hereto has been taken there in respect of alleged drug trafficking by the defendant; or

(b) where no steps have been specified in relation thereto as mentioned in paragraph (a) above, the defendant has been notified in writing in accordance with the laws of the designated country that the competent authorities of that country have begun proceedings against him in respect of alleged drug trafficking, or

(c) an application has been made to a court in a designated country for an external confiscation order,

and where the application of this subsection would result in there being more than one time for the institution of proceedings, they shall be taken to have been instituted at the earliest of those times.

The time at which proceedings are instituted may thus vary from country to country. This is inevitable given the differences in the legal systems of designated countries throughout the world. In order to determine the position in relation to any particular designated country, reference must be made to the Appendix to the Order.

25.10 *Meaning of 'proceedings have not been concluded'*

By s 41(3) as modified proceedings are only concluded:

(a) when (disregarding any power of a court to grant leave to appeal out of time) there is no further possibility of an external confiscation order being made in the proceedings;

(b) on the satisfaction of an external confiscation order made in the proceedings, whether by the recovery of all property liable to be recovered or the payment of any amount due.

By s 41(6) an order is satisfied when no property remains liable to be recovered under it or no amount is due under it; and by s 41(8), an order is subject to appeal until (disregarding any power to grant leave to appeal out of time) there is no further possibility of an appeal on which the order could be varied or set aside.

25.11 *Definition of 'external confiscation order'*

Section 2 of the DTA as modified defines 'external confiscation order' in these terms:

(1) An order made by a court in a designated country for the purpose of recovering payments or other rewards received in connection with drug trafficking or their value is referred to in this Act as an 'external confiscation order'.

(2) In subsection (1) above, the reference to an order includes any order, decree, direction or judgment, or any part thereof, however described.

It is important to note that s 2 does not require the order to have been made in criminal proceedings in the designated country for it to fall within the definition of 'external confiscation order'. The only requirement is that the order was made for the purpose of 'recovering payments or other rewards received in connection with drug trafficking or their value'. An order *in rem* made in civil proceedings in a designated country may therefore constitute an 'external confiscation order' if it is made for this purpose. This point arose in *Re SL* [1995] 3 WLR 830 where the Court of Appeal held that the powers of the High Court to make restraint orders in support of proceedings where an external confiscation order has been or may be made in a designated country were not confined to proceedings *in personam* against a particular individual, but could extend to proceedings *in rem* against particular assets. SL, a Colombian national, was under investigation in the USA for drug trafficking offences and a number of bank accounts in London were identified into which, it was alleged, his proceeds of drug trafficking had been paid. There was no prospect of criminal proceedings being instituted for an offence because SL had never been arrested and was believed to be resident in Colombia, with which country the USA had no extradition treaty. Accordingly, *in rem* proceedings against the monies in the bank accounts were instituted in New York. This action was entitled: *'United States of America (Plaintiff) v All funds on deposit in any accounts maintained in the names of H or E and all funds traceable thereto at the National Bank of Greece in London, England, et al (Defendants)'*. It was contended that a restraint order could not be made in support of such proceedings and that the funds in the account could not constitute a 'defendant' within the meaning of the Designated Countries and Territories Order. The Court held that the word 'defendant' in the Act, as modified by the Order, should not be construed as requiring proceedings *in personam*. The Court also held that weight had to be given to the purpose for which the Order was made and that an *in rem* order clearly fell within the definition of external confiscation order. There was no requirement that any person had to be charged or convicted of an offence for an order to come within that definition.

(b) Cases involving other criminal conduct 25.12

The Criminal Justice Act 1988 (Designated Countries and Territories) Order 1991 gives the High Court jurisdiction to make restraint orders in support of proceedings brought in designated countries involving criminal conduct other than drug trafficking. By s 76 of the CJA, as modified by the Order, a restraint order may be made in precisely the same circumstances as in drug trafficking cases, save that the proceedings in the designated country must be in respect of alleged conduct by the defendant to which the Act applies (see s 102(11) of the Act as modified). By s 74(1)(b) of the CJA as modified:

> references to conduct to which this part of this Act applies are references to conduct corresponding to any offence which—
>
> (i) is listed in Schedule 4 to this Act; or
>
> (ii) if not listed, is an indictable offence, other than a drug trafficking offence or an offence under Part III of the Prevention of Terrorism Act 1989.

For CJA purposes an 'external confiscation order' is defined in s 71(1) of the Act as modified in these terms:

An order made by a court in a designated country for the purpose—

(a) of recovering—
  (i) property obtained as a result of or in connection with conduct to which this Part of this Act applies; or
  (ii) the value of property so obtained; or
(b) of depriving a person of a pecuniary advantage so obtained,

is referred to in this Part of this Act as an 'external confiscation order . . .'

As with external confiscation orders made under the DTA, there is no requirement that the order was made in criminal proceedings upon the conviction of the defendant. It is the purpose for which the order was made that brings it within the definition of 'external confiscation order' rather than the nature of the proceedings in which it was made. As Lord Hobhouse of Woodborough observed in *Government of the United States of America v Montgomery* [2001] 1 WLR 196:

> The appellants submit that the order for the forfeiture of US$ 7.8 million was by way of punishment for civil contempt and thus outside the definition and was arrived at by making a calculation of notional damages for the delayed payment of money. I agree that this argument was rightly rejected by the Court of Appeal. The scope of the definition is widely drawn. It looks at the purpose of the relevant order of the foreign court. One of the purposes may be the purpose '(b) of depriving a person of a pecuniary advantage' obtained as a result of or in connection with the relevant criminal conduct, that is to say, the frauds practised by Mr Barnette. Mrs Montgomery had had the benefit of having the 900 shares since August 1983. It is clear that the US court was seeking to deprive her of the pecuniary advantage that she had thereby enjoyed and had resorted to the interest calculation as the best available way of assessing and quantifying that advantage. This is a legitimate approach under the common law as is illustrated by, for example, the law of restitution.

25.13 The House of Lords also held in *Government of the United States of America v Montgomery* that the High Court proceedings taken on behalf of a designated country are civil rather than criminal in nature. Lord Hoffman observed:

> It may be right, and possibly in most cases would be right, to regard orders made by way of enforcement of orders made or to be made in criminal proceedings as part and parcel of those proceedings . . . But I would not accept what I regard as the extreme proposition of (Counsel for the appellants) that the nature of the proceedings in which the original order was made will necessarily determine whether the machinery of enforcement through the courts is a criminal cause or matter. Modern legislation, of which Part VI of the 1988 Act is a good example, confers powers upon criminal courts to make orders which may affect rights of property, create civil debts or disqualify people from pursuing occupations or holding office. Such orders may affect the property or obligation not only of the person against whom they are made but of third parties as well. Thus the consequences of an order in criminal proceedings may be a claim or dispute which is essentially civil in character. There is no reason why the nature of the order which gave rise to the claim or dispute should necessarily determine the nature of the proceedings in which the claim is enforced or the dispute determined.

25.14 Further, their Lordships also ruled in *Government of United States of America v Montgomery* that restraint and enforcement proceedings could be brought in the UK

C. Procedure on Applications for Restraint Orders in DTA and CJA Cases

under a Designated Countries and Territories Order notwithstanding that the country in question was not a designated country at the time the external confiscation order was made. In that case the USA had become a designated country for the purposes of the Criminal Justice Act 1988 on 1 August 1994, whereas the external confiscation order to which the proceedings related was made as long ago as 1984. Lord Hoffman noted that there was no suggestion that the confiscation order was made by the American court in respect of an offence committed before the power to make the order came into force and said:

> In my opinion the enforcement in this country of rights conferred upon the United States by an order made before the DCO came into force is a very different matter from the retrospective imposition of a penalty. Even if there was nothing which the United States government could have done before 1 August 1994 to recover its assets from Mr or Mrs Montgomery by proceedings in this country, I can see no unfairness in it now being allowed to do so.

25.15 The court will not, in deciding whether or not to make a restraint order, allow itself to become embroiled in detailed argument as to the merits of the proceedings brought in the designated country in question. In *Government of India v Ottavio Quattrocchi* [2004] EWCA Civ 40 Buxton LJ (with whom Lord Phillips MR and Keene LJ agreed) said of the requirement in the Orders that an external confiscation may be made in the proceedings:

> Further, the statute says "may". That does not mean "will be made". All that is required is that in the future such an order may be made. Without trying to paraphrase the Act further, I would say in general terms that an external confiscation can be made when the English court concludes, on evidence, that there is a reasonable possibility of an Indian confiscation order eventually occurring. That the matter should be put comparatively low is only to be expected when one is dealing with what is a preliminary act, that is to say a restraint or charging order. If it were necessary to obtain the level of proof for which Counsel argued, these valuable provisions would be rendered largely ineffective.

C. Procedure on Applications for Restraint Orders in DTA and CJA Cases

25.16 As with domestic provisions, applications for restraint orders on behalf of overseas countries under the DTA and CJA Designated Countries and Territories Orders are made to the High Court. The procedures to be followed are very similar to those applicable in relation to domestic cases. There are, however, a number of important differences in the procedures which are considered below.

(1) The letter of request

25.17 The procedure is initiated by the relevant prosecuting authority in the designated country submitting a letter of request to its appropriate authority as defined in the Orders. The appropriate authority will in turn forward it to the appropriate authority for the UK which is the Central Authority based at the Home Office. There are no legal requirements as to the contents of a letter of request, but it is submitted that as a matter of good practice they should contain the following information:

(1) the name of the defendant (including any aliases by which he may be known), his last known address and date and place of birth;
(2) a certificate confirming that proceedings have been instituted for a drug trafficking offence or an offence corresponding to one to which Pt VI of the Criminal Justice Act applies and they have not been concluded or, as the case may be, that such proceedings are to be instituted. If an external confiscation order has already been made this should be stated in the certificate and a copy of the order annexed to it;
(3) a summary of the relevant law in the designated country, the facts of the case and any other matters which give rise to a belief that an external confiscation order may be made against the defendant;
(4) full particulars of the realisable property in respect of which the order is sought, including as much information as possible as to the nature, location and extent of such property;
(5) if a restraint order has already been made in the designated country, it is helpful, although not obligatory, for a copy together with an English language translation, to be appended to the letter of request.

25.18 When a letter of request is received by the UK appropriate authority from the appropriate authority in a designated country, it will be forwarded either to the Crown Prosecution Service (CPS) or to the Revenue and Customs Prosecutions Office (RCPO) to institute the necessary High Court proceedings. By Art 6 of the CJA Designated Countries and Territories Order and Art 7 of the DTA Order, the letter of request is deemed, unless the contrary is shown, to constitute the authority of the designated country for the CPS or RCPO to act on its behalf in any proceedings in the High Court under the Acts.

(2) Evidence in support

25.19 As with applications for restraint orders in domestic cases, an affidavit or witness statement in support of the application will be required. Section 29A of the DTA as modified makes provision as to the information which any such affidavit or witness statement should contain. It shall:

(a) state, where applicable, the grounds for believing that an external confiscation order may be made in the proceedings instituted or to be instated in the designated country concerned;
(b) to the best of the deponent's ability, give particulars of the realisable property in respect of which the order is sought and specify the person or persons holding such property;
(c) in a case to which section 25(3) of this Act applies, indicate when it is intended that proceedings should be instituted in the designated country concerned, and the affidavit may, unless the court otherwise directs, contain statements of information or belief with the sources and grounds thereof.

25.20 Section 79A of the CJA as modified makes similar provision as to the contents of affidavits and witness statements made in support of applications for restraint orders under that enactment. The duty of full and frank disclosure applies equally to applications for restraint orders made on behalf of overseas jurisdictions as it does to applications in domestic cases. The prosecuting authority should therefore be vigilant in ensuring that the overseas authority on whose behalf it is making the application has provided all the information the court will require to discharge this duty. The court will not, however, discharge a restraint order on this basis unless the failure

C. Procedure on Applications for Restraint Orders in DTA and CJA Cases

to give full and frank disclose goes to a matter central to the proceedings. As Buxton LJ said in *Government of India v Ottavio Quattrocchi* [2004] EWCA Civ 40:

> Complaint was made in the court below, and initially before us, that there had been non-disclosure of various matters, in particular before Moses J. First, there had been late disclosure of the Indian statutory provisions, secondly, there had been a mistake about when Mr. Quattrocchi left India; and, thirdly, that Moses J had not been properly informed as to the status of these matters by the Crown Prosecution Service. All those matters did not affect the outcome of the case, as Counsel was fair enough to accept. If one needs to go further than that, one merely needs to refer to the authority of this court of *Brinks Mat Ltd v Elcombe* [1988] 1 WLR 1350 in which the principles to be followed by the court are set out: in particular that non-disclosure is not in itself a ground for refusing the application provided that it does not go to a central matter.

25.21 Articles 4 and 5 of both orders make further provision in relation to evidence in applications to the High Court. By Art 4 of the DTA Order:

(1) For the purposes of sections 39 and 40 of the Act, and of the other relevant provisions of the Act, as applied under article 3(2) of this Order—

   (a) any order made or judgment given by a court in a designated country purporting to bear the seal of that court or to be signed by any person in his capacity as judge, magistrate or officer of the court shall be deemed without further proof to have been duly sealed or, as the case may be, to have been signed by that person; and

   (b) a document duly authenticated, which purports to be a copy of any order made or judgment given by a court in a designated country shall be deemed without further proof to be a true copy.

(2) A document purporting to be a copy of any order made or judgment given by a court in a designated country is duly authenticated for the purpose of paragraph (1)(b) above if it purports to be certified by any person in his capacity as a judge, magistrate or officer of the court in question or by or on behalf of the appropriate authority in a designated country.

Article 5 makes further provision in relation to proceedings and orders in a designated country as follows:

(1) For the purposes of sections 39 and 40 of the Act, and of the other relevant provisions of the Act as applied under article 3(2) of this Order, a certificate purporting to be issued by or on behalf of the appropriate authority of a designated country, stating—

   (a) that proceedings have been instituted and have not been concluded, or that proceedings are to be instituted there;

   (b) in a case to which section 41(2) of the Act, as modified by Schedule 2 to this Order applies, that the defendant has been notified as specified in that paragraph;

   (c) that an external confiscation order is in force and not subject to appeal;

   (d) that all or a certain amount of the sum payable under an external confiscation order remains unpaid in the designated country, or that other property recoverable under an external confiscation order remains unrecovered there;

   (e) that an order (however described) made or to be made by a court of the designated country has the purpose, or, as the case may be, will have the purpose of recovering payments or other rewards received in connection with drug trafficking or their value;

shall, in any proceedings in the High Court, be admissible as evidence of the facts so stated.

(2) In any such proceedings a statement contained in a document, duly authenticated, which purports to have been received in evidence or to be a copy of a document so

received, or to set out or summarise evidence given in proceedings in a court in a designated country, shall be admissible as evidence of any fact stated therein.

(3) A document is duly authenticated for the purposes of paragraph (2) above if it purports to be certified by any person in his capacity as a judge, magistrate or officer of the court in a designated country, or by or on behalf of the appropriate authority of the designated country, to have been received in evidence or to be a copy of a document so received or, as the case may be, to be the original document containing or summarising the evidence or a true copy of that document.

(4) Nothing in this article shall prejudice the admission of any evidence, whether contained in any document or otherwise, which is admissible apart from this article.

25.22 Articles 4 and 5 of the CJA Order make similar provision in relation to proceedings under that Act. It is submitted that the best course is for any documentation relied on under Arts 4 and 5 of the Orders to be exhibited to the affidavit or witness statement filed in support of the application.

25.23 Once the affidavit or witness statement is complete, it should be lodged at the Administrative Court office together with a claim form, the court fee, and a draft order in the same way as with an application for a domestic restraint order. The application will be considered on the papers by a High Court judge assigned to Administrative Court business and only if the judge has some concern in relation to the application in respect of which he requires an explanation will the appropriate prosecuting authority acting on behalf of the designated country be called on to attend before him.

(3) Ancillary orders

25.24 The court has the same powers as in domestic cases to make ancillary orders such as disclosure and repatriation orders and orders for the appointment of a management receiver. Indeed, given that in many cases the order is being made in relation to realisable property in England and Wales held by a defendant who is presently outside the jurisdiction, the appointment of a management receiver may well be appropriate.

(4) Applications for the variation and discharge of orders

25.25 The defendant and any third party affected by the order may apply for the order to be varied or discharged on the same grounds and by means of the same procedures as in domestic cases.

D. Enforcement of External Confiscation Orders

25.26 If an external confiscation order has been made by a designated country, it will be open to the appropriate authority of that country to request that enforcement action be taken in this country in relation to any realisable property held by the defendant in the UK.

(1) Registration of the order

25.27 The first stage in the enforcement process is for an application to be made to the High Court for the registration of the external confiscation order. The court has power under s 40(1) of the DTA and s 97(1) of the CJA to direct that the external confiscation order be registered if:

D. Enforcement of External Confiscation Orders

(a) it is satisfied that at the time of registration the order is in force and not subject to appeal;
(b) it is satisfied, where the person against whom the order is made did not appear in the proceedings, that he received notice of the proceedings in sufficient time to enable him to defend them; and
(c) it is of the opinion that enforcing the order in England and Wales would not be contrary to the interests of justice.

'Appeal' includes, for these purposes, any proceedings by way of discharging or setting aside a judgment and an application for a new trial or a stay of execution (see s 40(2) of the DTA and s 97(2) of the CJA).

25.28 In *Barnette v Government of the United States of America* [2004] *UKHL 37* the House of Lords considered the 'interests of justice' criteria in s 40(1) and s 97(1) and the extent to which registration of an external confiscation order might constitute a breach of Article 6 of the European Convention on Human Rights. It was suggested it was not in the interests of justice to register the external confiscation order because the US Courts of Appeal had summarily dismissed an appeal by the appellant without considering it on the merits because the defendant's wife, Mrs Montgomery, with whom he was co-accused, had fled from the jurisdiction and he had failed to comply with an orders requiring him to give information and discovery. In consequence, the US Courts applied the 'fugitive disentitlement doctrine' to dismiss the appeal. The US Courts of Appeal justified this doctrine in these terms:

> The rationales for this doctrine include the difficulty of enforcement against one not willing to subject himself to the court's authority, the inequity of allowing that "fugitive" to use the resources of the courts only if the outcome is an aid to him, the need to avoid prejudice to the non fugitive party, and the discouragement of flights from justice.

25.29 It was submitted on behalf of the appellant that it was not in the interests of justice to register an external confiscation order under s 97 of the CJA because, if the European Convention on Human Rights had been applied in the USA, the order would have been in breach of Article 6 and Article 1 of Protocol 1. The House of Lords held that it was necessary for the Court to consider whether registration of an external confiscation order would constitute a breach of Article 6 but, on the facts on the particular case, no such breach had occurred. Firstly, the Court noted that it was difficult to see how registration of the US order could constitute a direct breach of Article 6 since there could be no suggestion that the hearing afforded to the appellant in the registration proceedings failed to meet the requirements of the article. The Court also found that the application of the fugitive disentitlement doctrine did not amount to a breach of the appellant's human rights. Lord Carswell said:

> The fugitive entitlement doctrine is not an arbitrary deprivation of a party's right to a hearing, but is intended to be a means of securing proper obedience to orders of the court.

As Lord Woolf said:

> Where a party is guilty of contempt there may be no other sanction available if he is outside the jurisdiction of the court. The reason for the doctrine being applied by the United States Court of Appeal in Mrs. Montgomery's case was not to vindicate the dignity of the court, but because the court thought that it was the only available sanction which could achieve obedience to the orders of the court.

Although the application of the fugitive entitlement doctrine may be regarded as failing to secure all of the protection required by article 6 of the Covention, it is a rational approach which has commended itself to the Federal jurisdiction of the United States. As such it could not in my opinion be described by any stretch as a flagrant denial of the appellant's article 6 rights or a fundamental breach of the requirements of that article. It follows that the appellant's argument based on the indirect engagement of the responsbility of the United Kingdom must fail. The same reasons are relevant in considering the issue whether it was contrary to the interests of justice to enforce the confiscation order by registering the judgment of the US district court. As Stanley Burnton J and the Court of Appeal have pointed out in their judgments, the appellant was by no means shut out from taking part in the proceedings. The merits of her contentions had been fully considered at first instance and on appeal she filed a brief and was represented by counsel. When the issue of fugitive disentitlement was raised by the court she was able to file a brief relating to this issue. Moreover, it seems to me a material consideration that the US Court of Appeals found that she had been taking active steps to hide assets and transfer funds in an effort to evade the forfeiture judgment.

(2) Procedure for registration

25.30 As with applications for restraint orders, the procedure is commenced by a letter of request being sent by the appropriate authority in the designated country to the UK Central Authority. The letter should give the defendant's full name (including any aliases by which he is known), his last known address, a summary of the facts of the case, and full details of the external confiscation order it is sought to enforce in this country. A copy of the order should be annexed to the letter of request. Additionally, the letter should be accompanied by a certificate, duly authenticated in accordance with Art 5, confirming the following:

(a) that an external confiscation order has been made in the designated country and is not subject to appeal;
(b) that all or part of the amount due under the order remains unpaid or that other property recoverable under the order remains unrecovered in the designated country;
(c) that any person required to be notified of the proceedings in accordance with the law of the designated country has been duly notified; and
(d) that the order (however described) was made for the purpose of recovering payments or rewards received in connection with drug trafficking or, as the case may be, an offence to which Pt VI of the CJA, as modified, applies or their value.

25.31 The Central Authority will forward the letter of request either to the CPS or RCPO to make the application for registration and take any further enforcement action required. If a restraint order has already been obtained, the letter of request will invariably be referred to whichever authority obtained that order on behalf of the designated country in question.

(3) Evidence in support of the application for registration

25.32 On receipt of a letter of request from the Central Authority, the appropriate prosecuting authority will prepare a witness statement or affidavit in support of the application for registration. The procedure is governed by sc 115.15 which provides as follows:

D. Enforcement of External Confiscation Orders

(1) An application for registration of an external confiscation order must be made in accordance with CPR Pt 23, and be supported by a witness statement or affidavit;
   (a) exhibiting the order or a verified or certified or otherwise duly authenticated copy thereof and, where the order is not in the English language, a translation thereof into English certified by a notary public or authenticated by witness statement or affidavit; and
   (b) stating—
      (i) that the order is in force and is not subject to appeal;
      (ii) where the person against whom the order was made did not appear in the proceedings that he received notice thereof in sufficient time to enable him to defend them;
      (iii) in the case of money, either that at the date of the application, the sum payable under the order has not been paid or the amount which remains unpaid, as may be appropriate, or, in the case of other property, the property which has not been recovered; and
      (iv) to the best of the witness's knowledge, particulars of what property the person against whom the order was made holds in England and Wales, giving the source of the witness's knowledge.
(2) Unless the court otherwise directs, a witness statement or affidavit for the purposes of this rule may contain statements of information or belief with the sources and grounds thereof.

(4) *The application*

The witness statement or affidavit is then lodged at the Administrative Court office with a notice of application, the appropriate court fee, and a draft order. The application may be heard either by a High Court judge or a Master of the Queen's Bench Division (see sc 115.12). The application may be made without notice to the defendant or interested third parties (see sc 115.13). **25.33**

If the court is minded to register the external confiscation order, the order of registration must specify a period within which an application may be made to vary or set aside the registration (see sc 115.17(3)). Notice of registration of the order must be served on the person against whom it was obtained by delivering it to him personally or by sending it to his last usual address or place of business or in such other manner as the court may direct (see sc 115.17(1)). Service outside the jurisdiction is permissible without leave (see sc 115.17(2)). **25.34**

(5) *Applications to vary or set aside registration*

The person against whom the order was obtained may make application to the High Court for the registration to be varied or set aside within the period prescribed in the order. Any such application is to be made to a judge on application notice and supported by an affidavit or witness statement (see sc 115.18). Where such an application is made, no enforcement action may take place until such time as the application has been determined (see sc 115.19). **25.35**

(6) Register of orders

25.36 By sc 115.16(1), a register of orders registered under the Acts is kept in the Central Office of the High Court under the direction of the Master of the Crown Office. The register must include particulars of any variation or setting aside of a registration together with particulars of any execution issued on a registered order (see sc 115.16(2)).

(7) Effect of registration

25.37 The effect of an external confiscation order being registered in the High Court is that it becomes enforceable by similar means to confiscation orders made in this country. The court thus has jurisdiction under s 29 of the DTA and s 80 of the CJA (as duly modified) to appoint receivers to realise assets in the same way as in domestic cases. The High Court also has jurisdiction to make garnishee orders for the purpose of realising monies due under external confiscation orders, a power it does not have in domestic cases (see s 29(1A) of the DTA and s 80(1A) of the CJA as duly modified by the Designated Countries and Territories Orders). In contrast to the position in relation to garnishee orders made in civil proceedings, however, the order will require the funds to be paid into the High Court rather than to the applicant for the order.

(8) Variation, satisfaction and discharge of registered order

25.38 Sc 115.20 provides that where the court is notified by the applicant for registration that the order has been varied, satisfied, or discharged, the particulars thereof shall be entered on the register.

(9) Application of the proceeds of realisation

25.39 The proceeds of realisation are paid into the High Court either by a receiver appointed under s 29 of the DTA or s 80 of the CJA, or pursuant to a garnishee order. This is in contrast to the position in relation to confiscation orders made in domestic cases where the proceeds of realisation are paid into the enforcing magistrates' court. Where the funds have been realised by a receiver, he will need to seek the court's approval of his remuneration and expenses which will then be paid from the estate. The general rule is that the proceeds of realisation are retained by the enforcing country. However, many countries, including the UK, participate in an asset sharing scheme whereby the proceeds of realisation are split between the requesting and enforcing countries and used by those countries in the fight against crime.

E. Enforcement of DTA and CJA Confiscation Orders Overseas

25.40 As a condition precedent to being designated under the DTA and CJA, overseas countries were required to reciprocate and provide a mechanism whereby UK confiscation orders can be enforced in their jurisdictions. The procedures by which this is achieved inevitably vary in accordance with the laws and procedures of the designated country in question, but in all cases will be instigated by the relevant UK prosecution agency sending a letter of request to the Central Authority for onward transmission to the appropriate authority in the designated country concerned.

25.41 Where a domestic confiscation order is enforced in a designated country and assets are realised in that jurisdiction, the confiscation order is treated as having been reduced by the value of the property so recovered (see Art 7(1) of the CJA Designated Countries and Territories Order and Art 8(1) of the DTA Order). A certificate issued by the appropriate authority in a designated country stating that property has been recovered there pursuant to the order, the value of that property and the date on which it was recovered, is admissible as evidence of those facts in any court in England or Wales (see Arts 7(2) and 8(2) respectively).

25.42 Where the value of property recovered in a designated country is expressed in a foreign currency, the amount by which the confiscation order is reduced under Art 7(1) or Art 8(1) shall be calculated on the basis of the exchange rate prevailing on the date the property was recovered in the designated country concerned (see Art 8 of the CJA Order and Art 9 of the DTA Order). A certificate signed by an officer of any bank in the UK stating the exchange rate prevailing on a specified date is admissible evidence of that fact (see Art 8(2) and Art 9(2) respectively).

F. Reciprocal Enforcement with Scotland and Northern Ireland

25.43 The legislation makes special provision for the enforcement of orders made in Scotland and Northern Ireland and for the enforcement of orders made in England in the courts of Scotland and Northern Ireland. The relevant procedures are somewhat simpler than those under the Designated Countries and Territories Orders.

(1) Scotland

25.44 In so far as the orders made in Scotland are concerned the relevant provisions are to be found in the Drug Trafficking Offences (Enforcement in England and Wales) Order 1988 in relation to drugs cases and in the Proceeds of Crime (Scotland) Act 1995 (Enforcement of Scottish Confiscation Orders in England and Wales) Order 2001 in relation to other criminal conduct. The effect of these provisions is that the Scottish equivalent of restraint orders (interlocutors) and receivership orders (administration orders) are effective in England and Wales as soon as they are made without further order of the court. Additionally, if the orders are registered in the High Court in England they can be enforced in precisely the same ways as English restraint and receivership orders. Sections 35 and 36 of the Proceeds of Crime (Scotland) Act 1995 make similar provision in relation to the enforcement of orders made by the High Court under the DTA and CJA in the Court of Session in Scotland.

(2) Northern Ireland

25.45 Similar legislative provisions have been made in relation to Northern Ireland. Orders of the English courts may be enforced in Northern Ireland pursuant to the Proceeds of Crime (Northern Ireland) Order 1996 and orders made in Northern Ireland may be enforced in England and Wales under the Drug Trafficking Act 1994 (Enforcement of Northern Ireland Confiscation Orders) Order 1995 in relation to drugs cases and, in respect of other criminal conduct, the Criminal Justice Act 1988 (Enforcement of Northern Ireland Confiscation Orders) Order 1995. These orders make very similar provision to those in relation to Scotland.

G. Co-operation under POCA 2002

25.46 Sections 443 and 444 of POCA permit Orders in Council to be made permitting the enforcement in the United Kingdom of orders made in other jurisdictions.

Section 443 relates to Scotland and Northern Ireland and s 444 to other jurisdictions. It is worthy of note that nothing in s 444 requires overseas countries to be designated before orders made in its courts may be enforced in the United Kingdom. The section provides as follows:

(1) Her Majesty may by Order in Council—

   (a) make provision for a prohibition on dealing with property which is the subject of an external request;

   (b) make provision for the realisation of property for the purpose of giving effect to an external order.

(2) An Order under this section may include provision which (subject to any specified modifications) corresponds to any provision of Part 2, 3 or 4 or Part 5 except Chapter 3.

(3) An Order under this section may include—

   (a) provision about the functions of the Secretary of State, the Lord Advocate, the Scottish Ministers and the Director in relation to external requests and orders;

   (b) provision about the registration of external orders;

   (c) provision about the authentication of any judgment or order of an overseas court and of any document connected with such a judgment or order or any proceedings relating to it;

   (d) provision about evidence (including evidence required to establish whether proceedings have been started or are likely to be started in an overseas court);

   (e) provision to secure that any person affected by the implementation of an external request or the enforcement of an external order has an opportunity to make representations to a court in the part of the United Kingdom where the request is being implemented or the order is being enforced.'

25.47 The removal of the requirement for designation is intended to expedite the process of obtaining restraint orders on behalf of overseas countries, enabling any country that identifies assets in the United Kingdom to forward a letter or request seeking a restraint order and, ultimately, confiscation of the property concerned.

25.48 After ss 443 and 444 came into force on 24 March, 2003 there was a considerable delay in preparing the necessary secondary legislation to give effect to the provisions. Accordingly, for some time thereafter prosecuting authorities continued to rely on the DTA and CJA and the secondary legislation made thereunder. On 1 January, 2006, however, the Proceeds of Crime Act, 2002 (External Requests and Orders) Order 2005, SI 2005/3181 (the 2005 Order) came into force and all international requests made after that date are now dealt with under its provisions.

(1) Action to be taken on receipt of an external request

25.49 When an external request is received by the Secretary of State in connection with criminal investigations or proceedings in the country from which the request was made and concerning relevant property in England and Wales he may, under Art 6 (1) refer it to:

G. Co-operation under POCA 2002

(a) the Director of the Assets Recovery Agency (ARA);
(b) the Director of Public Prosecutions (DPP);
(c) the Director of Revenue and Customs Prosecutions (DRCP),

to be processed. Where the request appears to the Secretary of State to be made in connection with criminal investigations or proceedings which relate to an offence involving serious or complex fraud he may refer it to the Director of the Serious Fraud Office to be processed. The Director to whom the request is referred is described in the Order as 'the relevant Director': see Art 6 (4).

(2) Powers of the Crown Court to make restraint orders

25.50 The 2005 Order follows the scheme of POCA by transferring the jurisdiction to make restraint orders and enforce external confiscation orders from the High Court to the Crown Court. By Art 7(1) the Crown Court may exercise the powers conferred by Art 8 to make restraint orders if either of the following conditions are satisfied:

(2) The first condition is that-
  (a) relevant property in England and Wales is identified in the external request;
  (b) a criminal investigation has been started in the country from which the external request was made with regard to an offence, and
  (c) there is reasonable cause to believe that the alleged offender named in the request has benefited from his criminal conduct.

(3) The second condition is that-
  (a) relevant property in England and Wales is identified in the external request;
  (b) proceedings for an offence have been started in the country from which the external request was made and not concluded, and
  (c) there is reasonable cause to believe that the defendant named in the request has benefited from his criminal conduct.

25.51 If either of these conditions is satisfied, the Crown Court may make a restraint order under Art 8 (1) 'prohibiting any specified person from dealing with relevant property which is identified in the external request and specified in the order.' By Art 8 (2) the order may be made subject to exceptions and such exceptions may in particular:

(a) make provision for reasonable living expenses and reasonable legal expenses in connection with the proceedings seeking a restraint order or the registration of an external order;
(b) make provision for the purpose of enabling any person to carry on any trade, business, profession or occupation;
(c) be made subject to conditions.

25.52 The terms of Art 8(2)(a) represent a significant departure from the position under the Act itself where, as we have seen, Section 41 (4) precludes the release of funds to meet legal expenses incurred in relation to the proceedings. It was held in *Customs and Excise Commissioners v S* [2005] 1 WLR 1338 that this prohibition included the restraint proceedings as well as the criminal prosecution. Article 8(2) represents a departure from this rule in relation to restraint orders sought pursuant to external requests, but only in relation to the proceedings seeking the restraint order or registration of an external order. The defendant would not, under Art 8(2) be able to apply for the release of restrained funds to defend the criminal proceedings in the overseas jurisdiction making the request.

25.53 Article 8(2)(c) empowers the court to impose conditions subject to which funds are released under Art 8 (2)(a) and (b). This would enable the court to release funds for legal expenses subject to the '65 per cent rule' described in Chapter 5. Similarly, Art 8(2)(c) empowers the court to require a defendant to provide the prosecutor with banking records on a regular basis as a condition precedent to releasing funds to allow a business to continue trading legitimately pending the conclusion of the proceedings.

(3) Ancillary orders

25.54 Article 8(4) empowers the court to make such order as it believes is appropriate for the purpose of ensuring the restraint order is effective. This would include the powers, considered in detail in Chapter 4 above, to make disclosure and repatriation orders.

(4) Application, discharge and variation of restraint orders

25.55 By Art 9(1)(a) applications for restraint orders under the Order can only be made by the Director of the ARA, the DPP, the DRCP or the Director of the Serious Fraud Office. The application may be made ex parte to a judge in chambers (see Art 9(1)(b)).

25.56 The relevant Director and any person affected by the Order may apply for the restraint order to be varied or discharged. The order must be discharged if no external confiscation order is made (Art 9(5)), if no external confiscation order is registered within a reasonable time (Art 9(6)) or if proceedings for an offence are not started within a reasonable time when the order has been obtained on the basis that the defendant is subject to a criminal investigation (Art 9(7)).

(5) Appeals

25.57 Article 10 makes provision for the relevant Director and parties affected by restraint orders to appeal against decisions of the Crown Court to the Court of Appeal and Art 11 provides for a further appeal to the House of Lords.

(6) Hearsay evidence

25.58 Article 13 makes provision for the admissibility of hearsay evidence in restraint proceedings subject to the terms of ss 2 to 4 of the Civil Evidence Act 1995.

(7) Management receivers

25.59 Articles 15 and 16 empower the Court to appoint management receivers on the same basis as under the 2002 Act itself. The provisions are not therefore considered in detail in this chapter. The application may be made at the same time as the application for a restraint order or at any time after (see Art 15(1)(b)).

(8) Applications to give effect to external orders

25.60 Articles 20 to 22 make provision for giving effect to external orders. By Art 2, 'external order' has the meaning given to it in s 447(2) of POCA. Section 447(2) provides as follows:

G. Co-operation under POCA 2002

(2) An external order is an order which—

(a) is made by an overseas court where property is found or believed to have been obtained as a result of or in connection with criminal conduct, and

(b) is for the recovery of specified property or a specified sum of money.

25.61 By Art 20(1) the relevant Director may make application to the Crown Court to give effect to an external order. The application shall include a request to appoint the relevant Director as the enforcement authority for the order and the application may be made ex parte to a judge in chambers (see Art 20(3)). By Art 20(2), no application to give effect to an external order may be made otherwise than in accordance with Art 20(1). This provision effectively precludes overseas law enforcement agencies from making their own direct applications to the Crown Court to give effect to their orders; such applications may only be made by the relevant Director.

25.62 Article 21 sets out the conditions that must be satisfied for the Crown Court to give effect to external orders. It provides:

(1) The Crown Court must decide to give effect to an external order by registering where all of the following conditions are satisfied.

(2) The first condition is that the external order was made consequent on the conviction of the person named in the order and no appeal is outstanding in respect of that conviction.

(3) The second condition is that the external order is in force and no appeal is outstanding in respect of it.

(4) The third condition is that giving effect to the external order would not be incompatible with any of the Convention rights (within the meaning of the Human Rights Act 1998) of any person affected by it.

(5) The fourth condition applies only in respect of an external order which authorises the confiscation of property other than money that is specified in the order.

(6) That condition is that the specified property must not be subject to a charge under any of the following provisions-

(a) section 9 of the Drug Trafficking Offences Act 1986;

(b) section 78 of the Criminal Justice Act 1988;

(c) Article 14 of the Criminal Justice (Confiscation) (Northern Ireland) Order 1990;

(d) section 27 of the Drug Trafficking Act 1994;

(e) Article 32 of the Proceeds of Crime (Northern Ireland) Order 1996.

(7) In determining whether the order is an external order within the meaning of the Act, then Court must have regard to the definitions in subsections (2), (4), (5), (6), (8) and (10) of section 447 of the Act.

(8) In paragraph (3) 'appeal' includes-

(a) any proceedings by way of discharging or setting aside the order; and

(b) an application for a new trial or stay of execution.

25.63 The first condition, set out in Art 21(2) represents a major change from the position that applied under the previous legislation in that it requires that the external order was made on the conviction of the person named in it. This is in contrast to the position under the DTA and CJA Designated Countries and Territories Orders where orders could be registered even if they were made in civil proceedings. Part V of the 2002 Order creates a separate regime for the enforcement of external orders made in civil recovery proceedings. Applications in relation to the enforcement of such orders can only be made by the Director of ARA and are made to the High Court.

25.64 The third condition specifically requires the court to satisfy itself that giving effect to the order would not be incompatible with the Convention rights of any person affected by it.

(9) Registration of the order

25.65 Where the Crown Court decides to give effect to an external order, Article 22(1) provides that the court must:

(a) register the order in that court;
(b) provide for notice of the registration to be given to any person affected by it; and
(c) appoint the relevant Director as the enforcement authority.

25.66 By Art 22(3), the Crown Court may cancel the registration of the order or vary the property to which it applies on the application of the relevant Director or any person affected by it and, under Art 22(4) must cancel the registration if it appears that the order has been satisfied.

(10) Appeals

25.67 Article 23 makes provision for the relevant Director and any person affected by a registration to appeal to the Court of Appeal, and Art 24 provides for a further appeal to the House of Lords.

(11) Enforcement of the order

25.68 Once an external order has been registered, it may be enforced in similar ways to domestic confiscation orders: in particular Art 27 gives the court power to appoint enforcement receivers. As these provisions are in identical terms to those in relation to the appointment of enforcement receivers in domestic cases, considered in detail in Chapter 17 above, they are not considered separately in this chapter.

(12) Procedure on applications

25.69 Part 57.15 of the Criminal Procedure Rules provides that Pts 57, 59, 60, 61 and 71 shall apply with the necessary modifications to applications under the 2005 Order in the same way as they apply to the corresponding provisions under Part 2 of POCA.

H. Enforcement of POCA Confiscation Orders in Different Parts of the UK

25.70 Under the Proceeds of Crime Act 2002 (Enforcement in different parts of the United Kingdom) Order 2002, SI 2002/3133 orders made in England, Wales, Scotland, and Northern Ireland automatically have effect throughout the UK, but enforcement proceedings can only be brought if the orders are registered:

H. Enforcement of POCA Confiscation Orders in Different Parts of the UK

(a) in the Crown Court for England and Wales;
(b) the Court of Session for Scotland;
(c) the High Court for Northern Ireland.

Once registration is effective the court has the same powers of enforcement as if it had made the same order itself.

(1) Civil Recovery proceedings

Part V of the 2005 Order makes provision for the Assets Recovery Agency to take proceedings in the High Court to restrain and recover assets located in the UK in support of civil recovery proceedings taken in an overseas jurisdiction. **25.71**

26

MONEY LAUNDERING

A. Introduction	26.01
(1) What is money laundering?	26.05
(2) Why criminalise money laundering?	26.06
(3) How is money laundered?	26.07
B. Money Laundering under the Proceeds of Crime Act 2002	26.11
(1) Introduction	26.11
(2) Mens rea: 'suspects'	26.13
(3) Inchoate offences	26.15
(4) Conspiracy	26.16
(5) The first money laundering offence: concealing etc	26.25
(6) 'Criminal property'	26.29
(7) 'Criminal conduct'	26.31
(8) Defences to section 327(1)	26.33
(9) Threshold amounts	26.37
(10) The second money laundering offence: arrangements	26.43
(11) Defences to section 328(1)	26.45
(12) The third money laundering offence: acquisition, use and possession	26.51
(13) Defences to section 329(1)	26.53
(14) Maximum penalty	26.57
(15) Disclosure under s 338	26.58
(16) Disclosure to a nominated officer	26.62
(17) Appropriate consent	26.64
(18) 'Notice period'	26.66
(19) 'Moratorium period'	26.67
(20) Consent from a nominated officer	26.69
(21) 'The prohibited act'	26.72
(22) Protected disclosures	26.73
(23) Form and manner of disclosures	26.76
(24) Mode of trial	26.78
C. Money Laundering Offences under the DTA 1994 and CJA 1988	26.79
(1) Introduction: the proceeds of drug trafficking	26.79
(2) Concealing or transferring the proceeds of drug trafficking	26.81
(3) Assisting another person to retain the benefit of drug trafficking	26.84
(4) Disclosure of transactions to a constable	26.90
(5) Drafting the indictment	26.92
(6) Defences	26.95
(7) Disclosures by persons in employment	26.97
(8) Acquisition, possession, or use of the proceeds of drug trafficking	26.98
(9) Defences: adequate consideration	26.100
(10) Other defences	26.103
(11) Laundering the proceeds of other crimes under the Criminal Justice Act	26.104
(12) Meaning of criminal conduct	26.106
(13) Sentencing for money laundering offences	26.107
(14) Mode of trial decisions	26.112
D. The EC Money Laundering Directives	26.113
(1) UK legislation to implement the Directive	26.116
(2) The Money Laundering Regulations	26.117
(3) The new Regulations	26.119
(4) Relevant businesses	26.126
(5) Other amendments	26.127
(6) The Third European Money Laundering Directive	26.128

A. Introduction

26.01 No study of the law relating to the proceeds of crime would be complete without considering the provisions in the legislation that make the laundering of money a criminal offence. The importance of this area of the law was underlined in *Bank of Scotland v A* [2001] 1 WLR 751 where the Court of Appeal stated:

> Money laundering is an increasingly common problem of large scale crime. It is of the greatest importance, in the public interest, that the police should be supported by financial institutions in their attempts to prevent money laundering and to detect it when it happens.

26.02 The money laundering sections under Pt 7 of the Proceeds of Crime Act 2002 (POCA) came into force on 24 February 2003 (SI 2003/120). These principal money laundering offences do not have effect where the conduct constituting the offence began before 24 February 2003. In those cases the previous legislation, namely the Drug Trafficking Act 1994 (DTA), the Criminal Justice Act 1993 (CJA), and the Criminal Justice (International Co-operation) Act 1990, continue to have effect.

26.03 All of these Acts were introduced to meet the UK's obligation under Article 9 of the 1991 European Community Directive on the Prevention of the Use of the Financial System for the purpose of Money Laundering, which required contracting states to establish drug money laundering offences. This Directive, together with the Money Laundering Regulations 1993 were supplemented by the Money Laundering Regulations 2001, SI 2001/3641. (The international and domestic history of offences relating to laundering drugs' money is considered in some detail by the House of Lords in *R v Montila* [2004] UKHL 50.)

26.04 As will be seen, the money laundering provisions of POCA were significantly amended by the Serious Organised Crime and Police Act 2005 (SOCPA). From the 1 April 2006 the National Criminal Intelligence Service ceased to exist and its functions and staff were absorbed into the Serious Organised Crime Agency (SOCA). One of the difficulties with the reporting regime was that NCIS was inundated with insignificant and unnecessary suspicious activity reports (SARS) in relation to suspected money laundering or terrorist property offences. That burden is unlikely to be eased for SOCA. Sections 364 and 415 of POCA are amended by s 107 of SOCPA so that the meaning of money laundering offences includes the principal money laundering offences that were in force before the 2002 Act. This will enable the investigation powers in Pt 8 of the Act to be used in investigating old money laundering offences.

(1) What is money laundering?

26.05 Money laundering is the process by which monies derived from criminal activities are converted into funds or assets which appear to have an apparently legitimate source. Money laundering was first made a criminal offence in relation to monies derived from drug trafficking by the Drug Trafficking Offences Act 1986 (DTOA). Subsequent legislation, notably the CJA 1988 and the DTA 1994 have extended the number and ambit of these offences. POCA 2002 was intended to simplify and will in time replace the above Acts.

A. Introduction

(2) Why criminalise money laundering?

26.06 It has often been said that there would be fewer burglary offences committed if there were not those willing and able to receive and dispose of stolen property. Similarly, there would be less financially motivated crime committed if the criminal did not have at his disposal the means of concealing the origin of the proceeds of such offences by money laundering. The absence of legislation to prevent money laundering can result in a loss of confidence in a country's financial institutions as criminals invest and transfer the proceeds of crime through banks with impunity. Furthermore, legitimate banks do not wish to have accounts they maintain tainted with the proceeds of crime, and many have withdrawn from countries where money laundering has not been made illegal and where they are powerless to report suspicious transactions to law enforcement agencies without fear of an action for breach of confidence by the client. The absence of money laundering legislation can also serve to destabilise the political system of a country. The success of any terrorist organisation, for example, depends on its ability to raise and launder monies to fund their activities.

(3) How is money laundered?

26.07 Money laundering techniques vary in their degree of sophistication from the most simplistic to the highly complex. In its simplest form, money laundering occurs where a relative of a criminal, motivated by a misplaced sense of loyalty, agrees to pass the proceeds of a criminal enterprise through a bank account. The most sophisticated laundering operations involve the creation of front companies, trusts, etc, and the creation of bogus transactions to give the impression that monies come from a legitimate source. Most money laundering schemes can, however, be divided into three stages regardless of the degree of complexity: placement, layering and integration.

(a) Placement

26.08 At the placement stage, the launderer disposes of the so called 'dirty money'. Cash is the most common medium of exchange used for many types of criminal transactions, particularly those related to drugs. As cheques, credit cards, and other non-cash means are now used to finance the majority of legitimate transactions, the money launderer who carries out a large financial transaction in cash risks drawing undesired attention to his illegally acquired money. He thus attempts through placement to put his funds in to the financial system unnoticed, for example by engaging a number of people to make a series of small deposits on his behalf (a process known as 'smurfing') or by physically transporting the cash out of the country. It is at the placement stage that illegally acquired funds are most vulnerable to detection.

(b) Layering

26.09 After the funds have entered the financial system, the launderer further separates the illicit proceeds from their illegal source through layering. Layering occurs by conducting a series of financial transactions that, by reason of their frequency, volume, or complexities resemble legitimate financial transactions. The ultimate aim at this stage of the laundering process is to make tracing the funds back to their 'dirty' source as difficult as possible.

(c) Integration

26.10 At the final integration stage, the launderer integrates the illicit funds into the economy. He does this in such a way that the funds at this juncture appear to have originated from an entirely legal source, such as legitimate business earnings. At this stage the launderer has provided a legitimate explanation for the criminally derived funds, and distinguishing between legitimate and illicit funds proves extremely difficult, if not impossible to achieve. The profits may then be reinvested in the criminal enterprise, invested in other assets, or used to support an extravagant lifestyle.

B. Money Laundering under the Proceeds of Crime Act 2002

(1) Introduction

26.11 Part 7 of POCA 2002 introduces three principle money laundering offences: s 327, concealing, disguising, converting, transferring, or removing from England and Wales criminal property; s 328, becoming concerned in an arrangement which a person knows or suspects facilitates the acquisition, retention, use, or control of criminal property by or on behalf of another person; and s 329, acquiring, using, or having possession of criminal property. All of these money laundering offences apply to the laundering of an offender's own proceeds of crime as well as those of someone else. The maximum sentence for these money laundering offences is 14 years' imprisonment (see s 334).

26.12 As has already been noted, Pt 7 of POCA came into force on 24 February 2003 (SI 2003/120). The DTA and CJA money laundering offences will continue to be the principal Acts for all offences committed before that date (or which cross over that date). Because money laundering offences often contain historic transactions, the criminal courts can expect to be dealing with all three Acts for some time to come.

(2) Mens rea: 'suspects'

26.13 Sections 327-329 require proof that the conduct concerned involves 'criminal property'. Property is criminal property if it constitutes a person's benefit from criminal conduct, or it represents such a benefit (whether directly or indirectly), and the alleged offender knows or suspects that it constitutes such a benefit. The word 'suspect' is given various meanings in the Oxford English Dictionary. These include:

(1) an impression of the existence or presence of;
(2) believe tentatively without clear ground;
(3) be inclined to think;
(4) be inclined to mentally accuse; doubt the innocence of;
(5) doubt the genuineness or truth of a suspected person.

In *R v Hall* (1985) 81 Cr App R(S) 260 (CA) the Court suggested that 'suspicion encompassed where an individual suspected that goods were stolen, but it may be on the other hand, that they are not.'

26.14 In *K Ltd v National Westminster Bank* [2006] EWCA Civ 1039 the Court noted that there was no legal definition within the Act of what 'suspicion' or 'suspect' should be held to

B. Money Laundering under the Proceeds of Crime Act 2002

mean. In *R v Da Silva* [2006] EWCA Crim 1654 the Court of Appeal had said that for a defendant to be convicted of an offence under s 93A(1)(a) of the CJA, he or she must think that there is a 'possibility, which is more than fanciful, that the relevant facts exist'. This is subject, the Court held, to the further requirement that the suspicion so formed should be of 'a settled nature'. In *K Ltd* the Court held that if that definition was sufficient for criminal cases, it was also sufficient for civil cases (para 16). For further commentary on *K Ltd* see para 26.50 and *R v Saik*, para 26.16.

(3) Inchoate offences

26.15 Under s 340(11) of POCA money laundering is an act which is not only defined by the three substantive offences, but is extended to all inchoate offences relating to them:

(11) Money laundering is an act which—
   (a) constitutes an offence under sections 327, 328 or 329
   (b) constitutes an attempt, conspiracy or incitement to commit an offence specified in paragraph (a);
   (c) constitutes aiding, abetting, counselling or procuring the commission of an offence specified in paragraph (a), or
   (d) would constitute an offence specified in paragraph (a), (b) or (c) if done in the United Kingdom.

See also s 415 where money laundering offences are also defined.

(4) Conspiracy

26.16 In *R v Saik* [2006] 2 WLR 993, the House of Lords held that a mere suspicion that property might be the proceeds of crime was insufficient to establish guilt of conspiracy to engage in money laundering. To establish guilt, the Court held the accused had to be aware that the property involved was in fact the proceeds of crime or, in the case of unidentifiable property, intend that it should be. Lord Nicholls held that Parliament could not have intended that a person would be liable for conspiracy where he lacked the knowledge required to commit the substantive offence. When knowledge of a material fact was an ingredient of a substantive offence, it was also an ingredient of the crime of conspiracy to commit that offence. He went on to state that the ingredient of the substantive offence in s 93C(2) of the 1988 Act was that the property in question had to emanate from a crime (*R v Montila* [2004] 1 WLR 3141). The prosecution had to prove that the conspirator had intended or known that that fact would exist when the conspiracy was carried out. Hence, where the property had not been identified when the conspiracy agreement had been reached, the prosecution had to prove that the conspirator had intended that it would become the proceeds of criminal conduct.

26.17 In *R v Ali Hussain* [2005] EWCA Crim 87, the Court of Appeal held that offences under s 49(2) DTA and s 93C(2) CJA, required proof that a defendant was in fact dealing with the proceeds of drug trafficking or other criminal conduct. A jury could only convict of conspiracy if the defendant knew he was dealing with the proceeds of drug trafficking or other criminal conduct and mere grounds to suspect were not enough. The Court stated (at para 151) that the consequence of their decision was that the prosecution has a heavier burden to discharge than it would have in order to prove the substantive offence.

26.18 In *R v Montila* [2004] UKHL 50 the House of Lords decided that for offences under s 49(2) of the DTA 1994 and s 93C(2) of the CJA 1988, it must be proved that the property was in fact the proceeds of respectively drug trafficking or of other criminal conduct (reversing the Court of Appeal's decision). It was not enough that the defendant has reasonable grounds to suspect that the property was the proceeds of drug trafficking or of other criminal conduct, when in fact it is not (or could not be proved to be so). Lord Hope, giving the considered opinion of the committee said at para 27:

> Sub-section (2) states that a person is guilty of an offence "if knowing or having reasonable grounds to suspect that any property is . . . another person's proceeds of drug trafficking (s 49(2) of the 1994 Act) or of criminal conduct (s 93C(2) of the 1988 Act)" he does one or other of the things described to "that property" for the purpose which the sub-section identifies. A person may have reasonable grounds to suspect the property is one thing (A) when in fact it is something different (B). But that is not so when the question is what a person knows. A person cannot know that something is A when in fact it is B. The proposition that a person knows that something is A is based on the premise that it is true that it is A. The fact that the property is A provides the starting point. Then there is the question whether the person knows that the property is A.

26.19 The opening words of s 49(2) of the DTA 1994 thus provide a strong indication that it is directed to activities in relation to property which is in fact 'another person's proceeds of drug trafficking' or 'another person's proceeds of criminal conduct', as the case may be. The Court said a further indication is to be found in the absence of any defence if the property which the defendant is alleged to have known or had reasonable grounds to suspect was another person's proceeds turns out to be something different. Subsequent events may show that the property that he was dealing with had nothing whatever to do with any criminal activity at all, but was the product of a windfall, such as a win on the National Lottery. See also *R v Harmer* [2005] EWCA Crim 1.

26.20 In *R v Hussain* the Court of Appeal concluded that *R v Singh* [2003] EWCA Crim 3712, did not survive *Montila*. An intention to launder illicitly-obtained money is not enough. The money must be proved to have been the proceeds of drug trafficking or other criminal conduct.

26.21 If the property has been specifically identified when the conspirators make their agreement, the prosecution has to prove that the conspirators knew that the property was the proceeds of crime. Knowledge means true belief. As applied to s 93C(2) CJA 1988 (or s 49(2) DTA) this means that, in the case of identified property, the prosecution has to prove that the conspirator knew that the property was in fact the proceeds of crime.

26.22 This rationale is also reflected in *R v Sakavickas* [2004] EWCA Crim 2686, where the Court of Appeal held that s 1(2) of the Criminal Law Act 1977 did not apply to an offence contrary to s 93A of the CJA. Therefore, in a case where the allegation was one of conspiracy to assist another to retain the benefit of criminal conduct, the jury had to be sure, inter alia, that the defendant had agreed with others to retain control of criminal proceeds, knowing or suspecting that they were criminal proceeds.

26.23 However, in *R v Saik* the House of Lords called into question the analysis in *R v Sakavickas*. It found a conspiracy to commit an offence involved an agreement and under s 93C of the CJA that agreement was to convert another person's proceeds of criminal conduct.

B. Money Laundering under the Proceeds of Crime Act 2002

The agreement must be an agreement to do one or more of these acts for one or more of the stated purposes.

26.24 As stated above another ingredient of the substantive offence is that the property in question must emanate from a crime: *R v Montila* [2004] 1 WLR 3141. Lord Nicholls held that the criminal provenance of the property is in fact necessary for the commission of the offence. Hence, where the property has not been identified when the conspiracy agreement is reached, the prosecution must prove the conspirator intended that the property would be the proceeds of criminal conduct (para 23). The phrase 'intend or know' in s 1(2) is a provision of general application to all conspiracies: in this context the word 'know' should be interpreted strictly and not watered down. Finally, in *R v Suchedina* [2006] EWCA Crim 2543, the Court of Appeal held that where a conviction for conspiracy to commit money laundering offences had been obtained in circumstances where the jury had been directed that the offence was made, as to mens rea, by proof either of knowledge or of reasonable grounds for suspicion as to the illicit origins of the money, such a conviction could no longer be regarded as safe, in the light of the ruling in *R v Saik*. See also *R v R* [2006] EWCA Crim 1974.

(5) The first money laundering offence: concealing etc

26.25 The intention of s 327 is to simplify and replace s 49 of the DTA and s 93C of the CJA. In so doing POCA no longer distinguishes between the proceeds of drug trafficking in relation to money laundering and the proceeds of other crimes.

26.26 Under s 327(1) of POCA a person commits a money laundering offence if he:

(a) conceals criminal property
(b) disguises criminal property
(c) converts criminal property
(d) transfers criminal property
(e) removes criminal property from England or Wales or from Scotland or Northern Ireland.

26.27 In relation to s 327(1)(a) and (b) 'concealing' or 'disguising' criminal property includes concealing or disguising its nature, source, location, disposition, movement, or ownership of any rights with respect to it (s 327(3)).

26.28 In *R v Loizou* The Times, 23 June 2005 the Court of Appeal held, obiter, that the natural meaning of s 327(1) of POCA is that the property in question had to be criminal property at the time of the transaction. It was not sufficient that the property became criminal property within the meaning of the Act as a result of the transaction.

(6) 'Criminal property'

26.29 Criminal property is defined under s 340(3) as follows:

(3) Property is criminal property if—
 (a) it constitutes a person's benefit from criminal conduct or it represents such a benefit (in whole or part and whether directly or indirectly), and
 (b) if the alleged offender knows or suspects that it constitutes or represents such a benefit.

26.30 In *R v Gabriel* (2006) (CLW 06/20/7) the Court of Appeal held that where a person in receipt of state benefits failed to declare income from a legitimate trade in goods to the Inland Revenue and the DWP, his profits from the trade itself could not be said to constitute 'criminal property' within the meaning of s 340 of POCA. The failure to declare profits for the purposes of income tax may give rise to an offence, but that did not make the legitimate trading in goods an offence itself. The court also held that where the prosecution allege that property is criminal property, it was sensible, by giving particulars either in advance or in opening, to set out the facts upon which they rely in the inferences that the jury will be invited to draw.

(7) 'Criminal conduct'

26.31 Criminal conduct is conduct which either constitutes an offence in any part of the UK, or would constitute an offence in any part of the UK if it occurred there (s 340(2)).

26.32 It is immaterial who carried out the conduct, who benefited from it, or whether the conduct occurred before or after the passing of POCA (see s 340(4)).

(8) Defences to section 327(1)

26.33 Under s 327(2) a person does not commit such an offence if:

(a) he makes an authorised disclosure under s 338 of POCA and (if the disclosure is made before he does the act mentioned in s 327(1)) he has the appropriate consent;
(b) he intended to make such a disclosure but has a reasonable excuse for not doing so;
(c) the act he does is done in carrying out a function he has relating to the enforcement of POCA or of any other enactment relating to criminal conduct or benefit from criminal conduct.

26.34 Occasionally either the police or other enforcement authorities will themselves take possession of criminal property in the course of their duties and either convert or transfer it pending or as part of a further investigation. Section 327(2)(c) gives such authorities an appropriate exemption from the s 327(1) offence.

26.35 For the disclosure provisions of s 338 and the definition of 'appropriate consent', see paras 26.58 and 26.64 below respectively.

26.36 Section 102 of the Serious Organised Crime and Police Act 2005 (SOCPA) amends Pt 7 of POCA to introduce a new defence where overseas conduct is legal under local law. The amendment came into force on 1 July 2005. Section 327(2) has inserted into it the following defence:

(2A) Nor does a person commit an offence under sub-section (1) if (a) he knows, or believes on reasonable grounds, that the relevant criminal conduct occurred in a particular country or territory outside the United Kingdom, and (b) the relevant criminal conduct (i) was not, at the time it occurred, unlawful under the criminal law then applying in that country or territory, and (ii) is not of a description prescribed by an order made by the Secretary of State.
(2B) In sub-section (2A) 'the relevant criminal conduct' is the criminal conduct by reference to which the property concerned is criminal property.

B. Money Laundering under the Proceeds of Crime Act 2002

Section 328 (Arrangements) and s 329 (Acquisition, Use and Possession) are amended in identical terms.

(9) Threshold amounts

26.37 Section 103 of SOCPA amends the threshold amounts in relation to money laundering. Section 327 (Concealing etc) has inserted a new subsection (2C), which reads as follows:

> (2C) A deposit-taking body that does an act mentioned in para (C) or (D) of sub-section (1) does not commit an offence under that sub-section if – (a) it does the act in operating an account maintained with it, and (b) the value of the criminal property concerned is less than the threshold amount determined under s 339A for the act.

26.38 Under section 327(1)(D) of POCA, a bank or other deposit-taking body would need to make a disclosure to obtain consent before proceeding with any transaction that was suspected of involving criminal property. The new amendments will, in certain circumstances, allow deposit-taking bodies to continue to operate accounts without the need to seek consent in each case.

26.39 The new amendments do not apply to the duty to make a disclosure in respect of the initial opening of an account or, as the case may be, the time when the deposit-taking body first suspects that the property is criminal property (see s 338(2A) of POCA, s 106(5) of SOCPA).

26.40 A bank or other deposit-taking body would not commit an offence in operating an account of a person suspected of money laundering when the amount of money concerned in the transaction is below £250 or such higher threshold amount as may be specified by a constable or Customs' officer (or by a person authorised by the Director General of SOCA).

26.41 Where a deposit-taking body requests a threshold amount higher than the £250 default threshold, one may be specified. This threshold amount of £250 may be varied by the Secretary of State.

26.42 Where a threshold amount (above the £250 default level) has been specified for an account, the specified amount may be varied by any of the officers who could have specified it. Different thresholds may be specified in relation to the operation of the same account (for example, a threshold could be specified for deposits that is higher than the threshold specified for withdrawals).

(10) The second money laundering offence: arrangements

26.43 This section is intended to replace s 50 of the DTA and s 93A of the CJA. Under s 328 of POCA a person commits an offence:

> (1)... if he enters into or becomes concerned in an arrangement which he knows or suspects facilitates (by whatever means) the acquisition, retention, use or control of criminal property by or on behalf of another person.
>
> It is for the prosecution to show not only that the person entered into an arrangement which he knew or suspected would facilitate another person to acquire, retain, use, or control criminal property, but also that that person also knew or suspected that the property constituted or represented a benefit from criminal conduct.

26.44 For an interpretation of the the word 'suspects', see para 26.13 above.

(11) Defences to section 328(1)

26.45 Under s 328(2) certain defences are afforded to a person who it is alleged committed such an offence as follows:

(a) he makes an authorised disclosure under s 338 and (if the disclosure is made before he does the act mentioned in subsection (1)) he has the appropriate consent;
(b) he intended to make such a disclosure but has a reasonable excuse for not doing so;
(c) the act he does is done in carrying out a function he had relating to the enforcement of any provision of POCA or of any other enactment relating to criminal conduct or benefit from criminal conduct.

26.46 The defences available and the requirement for authorised disclosure under s 338 mirrors those found under s 327 (for the disclosure provisions of s 338 and the definition of 'appropriate consent', see paras 26.58 and 26.64 below respectively).

26.47 For a full consideration of the duties of disclosure in relation to s 328 and the Court of Appeal decision in *Bowman and Fels* see para 27.43 of Chapter 27.

26.48 Section 328 has after subsection (4) inserted a new defence, pursuant to SOCPA, which reads as follows:

(5) A deposit-taking body that does an act mentioned in sub-section (1) does not commit an offence under that sub-section if (a) it does the act in operating an account maintained with it, and (b) the arrangement facilitates the acquisition, retention, use or control of criminal property of a value that is less than the threshold amount determined under s 339A for the act.' (See para 26.36 above.)

26.49 In *Squirrel Ltd v National Westminster Bank plc (Customs & Excise Commissioners intervening)* [2005] 2 All ER 784, Laddie J held that once a bank suspected that a customer's account contained the proceeds of crime, it was obliged to report the matter to the relevant authority and not to carry out any transaction in relation to that account. Failing to do so would amount to an offence under s 328(1). That obligation remains the position unless and until consent to the transaction was given under s335 of POCA, or if it were not, the relevant time limit had expired. Equally, if the bank told the customer why it blocked the transaction or account it would breach the tipping-off provisions set out at ss 333 and 338 of POCA. Laddie J noted that although the statutory provisions might cause hardship to companies, to force the bank to unblock the account would be tantamount to compelling it to commit a criminal offence and therefore sympathy for the company/customer's position could not override that consideration. For further commentary see CLW/05/21/8.

26.50 Questions of construction in relation to the money laundering provisions were further considered in *K Ltd v National Westminster Bank plc* [2006] EWCA Civ 1039, in particular s 328. The bank found itself in a predicament when its customer asked it to make a payment which the bank suspected would facilitate the use of criminal property and leave it open to the allegation of becoming 'concerned in an arrangement'. The customer, following the bank's refusal, made a claim for an interim injunction requiring the bank to comply with its instructions. It was argued on behalf of the customer that the bank, by refusing to honour its customer's instructions, was acting in breach of the contract whereby the bank had agreed to honour its customer's instructions. The Court found that there could be no doubt that, if a banker knows or suspects that money in a customer's account is criminal property

B. Money Laundering under the Proceeds of Crime Act 2002

and, without making disclosure or without authorised consent (if disclosure is made), he processes a customer's cheque in such a way as to transfer the money in question into the account of another person, then he was facilitating the use or control of that criminal property, and thus committing an offence under s 328 of the 2002 Act. The Court held it would be no defence to a charge under that section that the bank was contractually obliged to obey its customer's instructions (see para 9):

> If the law of the land makes it a criminal offence to honour the customer's mandate in these circumstances there can be no breach of contract for the bank to refuse to honour its mandate...

For further commentary on *K Ltd*, see CLW 06/29/13.

(12) The third money laundering offence: acquisition, use and possession

26.51 Section 329(1) states that a person commits an offence if he:

(a) acquires criminal property;
(b) uses criminal property;
(c) has possession of criminal property.

26.52 Section 329 replaces s 51 of the DTA and s 93B of the CJA. In *Wilkinson, R (on the application of) v DPP* [2006] EWHC 3012 (Admin) an issue arose over the CPS's increasingly common practice of charging offences under s 329 as opposed, to the offence of handling stolen goods. Arguably it is easier to prove a s 329 offense, because the mens rea is 'knowing or suspecting' as opposed to 'knowing or believing' (s 22 Theft Act 1968). The Court held that if an offence was inappropriately charged the court should express a view and encourage (but no more) the CPS to charge a lesser offence. However, it was ultimately a matter for them and their own internal guidance.

(13) Defences to section 329(1)

26.53 The offence under s 329 is only committed if the person concerned knows or suspects the property which has been acquired or used or which he has in his possession, constitutes or represents his own or another's benefit from criminal conduct.

Under s 329(2) there are four specified defences available, as follows:

(a) [the person] makes an authorised disclosure under s 338 and (if the disclosure is made before he does the act mentioned in s 338(1)) he has the appropriate consent;
(b) he intends to make such a disclosure but has a reasonable excuse for not doing so;
(c) he acquired or used or had possession of the property for adequate consideration;
(d) the act he does is done in carrying out a function he has relating to the enforcement of any provision of this Act or of any other enactment relating to criminal conduct or benefit from criminal conduct.

26.54 In relation to s 329(2)(c) a person 'acquires property for inadequate consideration' if the value of the consideration is significantly less than the value of the property (see s 329(3)(a)). A person also uses or has possession of property for inadequate consideration if the value of the consideration is significantly less than the value of the use or possession (see s 329(3)(b)).

26.55 Further it should be noted that the provision by a person of goods or services which he knows or suspects may help another to carry out criminal conduct is not 'consideration' under s 329(3)(c).

26.56 Section 329 is also amended by SOCPA from 1 July 2005 to include a new defence (2C), as follows:

(2C) A deposit-taking body that does an act mentioned in sub-section (1) does not commit an offence under that sub-section if (a) it does the act in operating an account maintained with it, and (b) the value of the criminal property concerned is less than the threshold amount determined under s 339A for the act.

(14) Maximum penalty

26.57 Section 334 states:
(1) A person guilty of an offence under section 327, 328 or 329 is liable—
   (a) on summary conviction, to imprisonment for a term not exceeding six months or to a fine not exceeding the statutory maximum or to both, or
   (b) on conviction on indictment, to imprisonment for a term not exceeding 14 years or to a fine or to both.
(2) A person guilty of an offence under section 330, 331, 332 or 333 is liable—
   (a) on summary conviction, to imprisonment for a term not exceeding six months or to a fine not exceeding the statutory maximum or to both, or
   (b) on conviction on indictment, to imprisonment for a term not exceeding five years or to a fine or to both.

For further on sentencing see para 26.107 below.

(15) Disclosure under s 338

26.58 All three of the new money laundering offences afford a defence to an individual if disclosure is authorised under s 338 of POCA. Section 338 states that disclosure will be authorised if:
(1) (a) it is a disclosure to a constable, Revenue and Customs officer or nominated officer by the alleged offender that property is criminal property,
   (b) it is made in the form and manner (if any) prescribed for the purposes of this subsection by order under s 339, and
   (c) the first or second condition (set out below) is satisfied.
(2) The first condition is that the disclosure is made before the alleged offender does the prohibited act.
(3) The second condition is that:
   (a) the disclosure is made after the alleged offender does the prohibited act,
   (b) there is good reason for his failure to make the disclosure before he did the act, and
   (c) the disclosure is made on his own initiative and as soon as it is practicable for him to make it.

Under s 338(6) references to 'the prohibited act' in the second condition (subsection (3)), are to:

(a) an act mentioned in s 327(1) (ie the concealing, disguising, converting, transferring, or removing of criminal property), or
(b) an act mentioned in s 328(1) (where a person knows or suspects that an arrangement he has entered into will facilitate the acquisition, retention or use or control of criminal property), or
(c) an act mentioned in s 329(1) (where a person acquires criminal property, uses criminal property or has it in his possession).

B. Money Laundering under the Proceeds of Crime Act 2002

26.59 For this defence to be successful the disclosure must be made in the course of the defendant's employment and in accordance with the procedures established by the employer for the purpose (see s 338(1)(a)).

26.60 It should be noted that an authorised disclosure is not to be taken to breach any restriction on the disclosure of information (however imposed) (see s 338(4)).

26.61 By s 339(1) the Secretary of State may prescribe the form and manner in which a disclosure under s 338 must be made, that order may include a request to the discloser to provide additional information specified in the form. This is considered more fully in Chapter 27.

(16) Disclosure to a nominated officer

26.62 A nominated officer is a person nominated to receive disclosures under s 338 (see s 336(11)), ie a person nominated to receive authorised disclosures relating to the money laundering offences under ss 327(1), 328(1), or 329(1), as the case may be.

26.63 The nominated officer will often be the person nominated by the alleged offender's employer to receive authorised disclosures (see s 338(5)(a)). See also para 26.69.

(17) Appropriate consent

26.64 The three new principal money laundering offences envisage that a person will have a defence if the disclosure is authorised under s 338 and the person involved has 'appropriate consent'.

Under s 335 the appropriate consent is defined as:

(1) (a) the consent of a nominated officer to do a prohibited act if an authorised disclosure is made to the nominated officer;
    (b) the consent of a constable to do a prohibited act if an authorised disclosure is made to a constable;
    (c) the consent of a revenue and customs officer to do a prohibited act if an authorised disclosure is made to a revenue and customs officer.

References to a 'prohibited act' are references to the offences mentioned in s 327(1), 328(1), or 329(1), as the case may be, (see s 335(8)).

Under s 335(1)(b) a constable includes a person authorised for the purposes of Pt 7 of POCA by the Director General of SOCA (see s 340(13)).

26.65 By s 335(2),(3), and (4), a person must be treated as having the appropriate consent if he makes an authorised disclosure to a constable or a revenue and customs officer and he does not receive, before the end of the 'notice period', a notice from a constable or Revenue and Customs officer that consent to the doing of the act is refused. Or alternatively, before the end of 'the notice period' he does receive notice from a constable or Revenue and Customs officer that consent to the doing of the act is refused, but the 'moratorium period' has expired. POCA therefore envisages time limits under which Revenue and Customs or the police must respond to requests for consent.

(18) 'Notice period'

26.66 Section 335(5) states:

> (5) The notice period is the period of seven working days starting with the first working day after the person makes the disclosure.

Section 335 puts a proactive duty on the nominated officer or law enforcement agency concerned to respond within the time limit of seven days. Failure to do so will mean the person who has disclosed the information can go ahead with what may otherwise be a prohibited act and without an offence being committed.

(19) 'Moratorium period'

26.67 Under s 335(6) the moratorium period is the period of 31 days starting with the day on which the person receives notice that consent to the doing of the act is refused.

26.68 The effect of the moratorium period is that if a Revenue and Customs officer or constable withholds consent within the seven working day period under s 335(5) then they are entitled to a further 31 calendar days in which to take further action in relation to the disclosures, for example seeking a court order to restrain the assets in question. However, if the discloser hears nothing more after the 31 day period envisaged by s 335(6) then they can proceed with the transaction at no risk of committing any offence (a working day is defined as any day other than Saturday, Sunday, Christmas Day, Good Friday, or a Bank Holiday (see s 335(7)).

(20) Consent from a nominated officer

26.69 Nominated officers must not give the appropriate consent to the doing of a prohibited act unless certain conditions set out in s 336(2)–(4) are satisfied (see s 336(1)). Those conditions are as follows:

(1) The discloser makes a disclosure that property is criminal property to a person authorised for the purposes of Part 7 by the Director General of SOCA, and such a person gives consent to the doing of the act (s 336(2)).
(2) The discloser makes a disclosure that property is criminal property to a person authorised for the purposes of Part 7 by the Director General of SOCA, and before the end of the notice period he does not receive notice from such person that consent to the doing of the act is refused (s 336(3)).
(3) The discloser makes a disclosure that property is criminal property to a person authorised for the purposes of Part 7 by the Director General of SOCA before the end of the notice period he receives notice from such a person that consent to the doing of the act is refused, and the moratorium period has expired (s 336(4)).

26.70 The nominated officer must very carefully adhere to the above conditions. Failure to do so may itself result in the committing of an offence by the nominated officer, for example, if he gives consent to a prohibited act in circumstances where none of the conditions are satisfied and the nominated officer knows or suspects that the act is prohibited under the money laundering regime (s 336(5)).

26.71 A nominated officer found to be guilty of such an offence stands liable, on summary conviction, to imprisonment for a term not exceeding six months, or to a fine not exceeding

B. Money Laundering under the Proceeds of Crime Act 2002

the statutory maximum, or to both; or on conviction on indictment, to imprisonment for a term not exceeding five years, or to a fine, or to both (see s 336(6)). The notice period and the moratorium period are identical to that set out under s 335(5) and (6), namely seven working days and 31 calendar days respectively (see s 336(7), (8), and (9)).

(21) 'The prohibited act'

26.72 The prohibited act referred to in s 336(1) is an act which falls under either s 327(1) (concealing etc), s 328(1) (arrangements for money laundering), or s 329(1) (acquisition, use, and possession of criminal property for money laundering) as the case may be.

(22) Protected disclosures

26.73 Disclosures under Pt 7 of POCA fall into two specified categories, either protected disclosures (under s 337) or authorised disclosures (under s 338). Authorised disclosures are considered above (para 26.58).

26.74 Section 337 sets out three conditions under which disclosure will not be taken to breach any restriction on the disclosure of information (however imposed). The three conditions, all of which must be satisfied, are as follows:

(1) That the information or other matter disclosed came to the person making the disclosure (the discloser) in the course of his trade, profession, business, or employment (s 337(2));
(2) That the information or other matter:
    (a) causes the discloser to know or suspect, or
    (b) gives him reasonable grounds for knowing or suspecting, that another person is engaged in money laundering (s 337(3)); and
(3) That the disclosure is made to a constable, a Revenue and Customs officer, or a nominated officer as soon as is practicable after the information or other matter comes to the discloser (s 337(4)).

26.75 The first condition, s 337(2), exempts a person who receives information in the course of his trade or profession from any legal or other obligations that would otherwise prevent him from making disclosure to the authorities. This protection extends beyond the regulated sector to include, eg accountants or solicitors giving free advice.

(23) Form and manner of disclosures

26.76 Under s 339 of the Act, the Secretary of State is permitted to prescribe the form and manner in which a disclosure under ss 330, 331, 332, or 338 must be made. An order under this section may also provide that the form may include a request for the discloser to provide additional information specified in the form. (See also Chapter 27.)

26.77 While s 339(3) anticipates that the Secretary of State may ask for the discloser to provide additional information, it does not create any criminal offence if the discloser refuses to supply that additional information. Any additional information supplied appears, under s 339(4), to have been given immunity from any restriction on the disclosure of information, such as confidentiality clauses in contracts.

(24) Mode of trial

26.78 See para 26.112 below

C. Money Laundering Offences under the DTA 1994 and CJA 1988

(1) Introduction: the proceeds of drug trafficking

26.79 The first money laundering offence to be created in the UK was in relation to the laundering of the proceeds of drug trafficking and was found in s 24 of the now repealed Drug Trafficking Offences Act 1986. It was re-enacted in s 50 of the DTA, which itself has now been revised by s 328 of POCA 2002. Other offences were created by s 14 of the Criminal Justice (International Co-operation) Act 1990 and these, together with the former s 24 offence, were consolidated into Pt III of the DTA 1994. These offences were introduced in compliance with the UK's obligations under Article 3(b) of the United Nations Convention Against Illicit Traffic in Narcotic Drugs and Psychotropic Substances ('the Vienna Convention'), which required contracting states to establish drug money laundering offences.

26.80 As a result of the transitional provisions governing POCA, all principal money laundering offences where the conduct commenced prior to 24 February 2003 (and ended before or after that date) will still be dealt with under the previous legislation of the DTA or CJA, as the case may be (SI 2003/120).

(2) Concealing or transferring the proceeds of drug trafficking

26.81 By s 49(1) of the DTA, a person is guilty of an offence if he:

(a) conceals or disguises any property which is, or in whole or in part directly or indirectly represents, his proceeds of drug trafficking, or
(b) converts or transfers that property or removes it from the jurisdiction,

for the purpose of avoiding prosecution for a drug trafficking offence or the making or enforcement in his case of a confiscation order.

26.82 This offence was originally enacted in s 14 of the Criminal Justice (International Co-operation) Act 1990 and was introduced to close a loophole in s 24 of the DTOA 1986 (now s 50 of the DTA 1994) whereby it was not an offence to launder one's own proceeds of drug trafficking.

26.83 Section 49(2) makes it an offence for a person, knowing or having reasonable grounds to suspect that any property is, or in whole or in part directly or indirectly represents another person's proceeds of drug trafficking, to conceal or disguise that property, or convert or transfer it, or remove it from the jurisdiction. This section criminalises the same conduct as s 49(1), the only difference being that under s 49(1), the laundering is done by the drug trafficker himself, whereas under s 49(2) the launderer is a third party acting on behalf of

C. Money Laundering Offences under the DTA 1994 and CJA 1988

the trafficker. In both instances the money laundering activity must be performed for the purpose of avoiding prosecution for a drug trafficking offence or the making or enforcement of a confiscation order. If it is done with some other object in mind, the offence is not committed. By s 49(3), references in subss (1)(a) and (2)(a) to concealing or disguising property include references to concealing or disguising its nature, source, location, disposition, movement, or ownership, or any rights with respect to it. For conspiracy see para 26.16 above.

For offences where the conduct begins on or after 24 February 2003, s 49 of the DTA 1994 has been replaced by s 327 of POCA 2002.

(3) Assisting another person to retain the benefit of drug trafficking

26.84 By section 50(1) of the DTA:

. . . a person is guilty of an offence if he enters into or is otherwise concerned in an arrangement whereby—
(a) the retention or control by or on behalf of another person (call him 'A') of A's proceeds of drug trafficking is facilitated (whether by concealment, removal from the jurisdiction, transfer to nominees or otherwise); or
(b) A's proceeds of drug trafficking—
    (i) are used to secure that funds are placed at A's disposal; or
    (ii) are used for A's benefit to acquire a property by way of investment

and he knows or suspects that A is a person who carries on or has carried on drug trafficking or has benefited from drug trafficking.

26.85 The actus reus of the offence can thus be committed in two ways, either by being concerned in an arrangement whereby the retention or control by or on behalf of another of that other's proceeds from drug trafficking is facilitated, or whereby that other's proceeds from drug trafficking are used to secure that funds are placed at his disposal or are used to acquire property by way of investment.

26.86 References to a person's proceeds from drug trafficking include property which in whole or in part directly or indirectly represent his proceeds of drug trafficking (see s 50(2) of the DTA).

26.87 The mens rea of the offence is knowing or suspecting that A is a person who carries on or who has carried on, or benefited from, drug trafficking. Thus the section catches not only the professional money launderer who knows full well that the money he receives is the proceeds of drug trafficking, but also the banker, solicitor, accountant, or other professional who handles clients' money suspecting that it has come from drug trafficking.

26.88 In *R v Gill* [2004] EWCA Crim 3245, the Court of Appeal held that where a person was charged with an offence of assisting in the retention of the proceeds of drug trafficking and with an offence of acquiring the proceeds of drug trafficking, contrary to ss 50(1) and 51(1) of the DTA, respectively, the prosecution were not bound to identify different sums of money alleged to be the proceeds of drug trafficking in order to lay both offences.

26.89 For a definition in relation to 'suspects', see para 26.13 above.

(4) Disclosure of transactions to a constable

26.90 Section 50(3) of the DTA provides important protection for persons who disclose to a constable transactions that they know or suspect relate to the proceeds of drug trafficking. The subsection provides as follows:

(3) Where a person discloses to a constable a suspicion or belief that any funds or investments are derived from or used in connection with drug trafficking, or discloses to a constable any matter on which such a suspicion or belief is based:
   (a) the disclosure shall not be treated as a breach of any restriction upon the disclosure of information imposed by statute or otherwise; and
   (b) if he does any act in contravention of subsection (1) above and the disclosure relates to the arrangement concerned, he does not commit an offence under this section if:
      (i) the disclosure is made before he does the act concerned and the act is done with the consent of the constable;
      (ii) the disclosure is made after he does the act, but is made on his initiative as soon as reasonable for him to make it.

26.91 This section thus affords two distinct forms of protection to the person who discloses such a transaction. Firstly, s 50(3)(a) protects him from any action by his customer for breach of any restriction upon the disclosure of the information. This is essential, otherwise a bank that discloses a suspicious transaction to a constable would be vulnerable to civil proceedings at the suit of the customer for breach of the contractual duty of confidentiality. Secondly, s 50(3)(b) protects the person making disclosure from criminal liability where the disclosure is made before he does the act concerned and it is done with the consent of the constable or, where he makes the disclosure after the act, it is made on his initiative and as soon as reasonable thereafter. This is a useful investigative tool for law enforcement-authorities as it enables them to authorise the person making the disclosure to proceed with the transaction so that it may be followed through to its conclusion and those involved in the laundering operation identified.

(5) Drafting the indictment

26.92 In *R v El-Kurd* [2001] Crim LR 234 it was held that where there was evidence that the accused was party to both a conspiracy to launder the proceeds of drug trafficking and party to a conspiracy to launder the proceeds of criminal conduct, the appropriate course was not to have alternative counts, but to have a single count of conspiracy to commit both offences. The Court decided this on the basis that it would avoid the necessity of the jury having to make a choice if it was satisfied that the defendant was party to a conspiracy to launder the illicit proceeds of either drug trafficking or criminal conduct. One of the difficulties with the Court's decision in *El-Kurd* is that it does not necessarily assist the jury who are sure that the proceeds of crime in question are from the illicit proceeds of criminal conduct or drug trafficking but are not sure which. A jury would have to be agreed about at least one of the offences to return a verdict.

26.93 In *R v Hussain Bhatti and Bhatt* The Times 31 January 2002, the Court of Appeal held, adopting the *obiter* observations of the Court of Appeal in *El-Kurd*, that an indictment, the statement of offence on which read 'conspiracy to contravene Section 49(2) of the Drug Trafficking Act 1994, alternatively Section 93C(2) of the Criminal Justice Act 1988,

C. Money Laundering Offences under the DTA 1994 and CJA 1988

contrary to section 1(1) of the Criminal Law Act 1977' was not bad for duplicity. The Court held that duplicity was a matter of form, and it was theoretically possible that two men might enter an agreement 'to rape or rob' where, for example, they agreed that if the next person to come around the corner were a woman, they would rape her, but if it were a man, they would rob him. The Court, however, also stated that an indictment in a form such as in the case of *Hussain* was not necessarily to be encouraged. The Court felt it was significant that the essential ingredients of the two substantive offences were identical, save that one referred to the proceeds of drug trafficking and the other referred to the proceeds of criminal conduct. Clearly the prosecution would still have to prove that an agreement existed in relation to at least one of the two offences. The difficulty with the ruling of the Court of Appeal in *Hussain* is that it presents uncertainty for the prosecution, the defence, and the jury by charging alternative conspiracies. A single conspiracy to contravene s 49(2) of the 1994 Act and a single conspiracy to contravene s 93C(2) of the 1988 Act would have avoided this problem.

In *R v Saik* [2006] 2 WLR 993, Lord Nicholls commented that charges in relation to conspiracy to convert the proceeds of drug trafficking and/or criminal conduct were not happily framed, post *R v Montila* [2004] 1 WLR 3141. Such charges might be taken to suggest that for the purpose of the conspiracy charge 'Having reasonable grounds to suspect' was an alternative to proving knowledge. That, in his Lordship's judgment, was not so. The effect of s 1(2) of the Criminal Law Act 1977 was that the prosecution had to prove intention or knowledge. See para 26.16 above. 26.94

(6) Defences

By s 50(4) of the DTA it is a defence for the defendant to prove: 26.95

(a) that he did not know or suspect that the arrangement related to any person's proceeds of drug trafficking;
(b) that he did not know or suspect that by the arrangement the retention or control by or on behalf of 'A' of any property was facilitated or, as the case may be, that by the arrangement any property was used as mentioned in subsection (l)(b); or
(c) that—
  (i) he intended to disclose to a constable such a suspicion, belief or matter as is mentioned in subsection (3) in relation to the arrangement but,
  (ii) there is reasonable excuse for his failure to make any such disclosure in the manner mentioned in paragraph (b)(i) or (ii) of that section.

The burden of proving these defences rests with the defendant but, as in all cases where a burden rests on the defence, the standard of proof is the civil standard. The burden is on the prosecution to prove the *mens rea* of the offence as set out in the concluding words of s 50(1), but if the defendant wishes to raise a defence under s 50(4) to the effect that he did not know or suspect the nature of the transaction, the burden of proof is upon him to do so on a balance of probabilities (see *R v Colle* (1992) 95 Cr App R 67). The decision in *Colle* was approved by the Judicial Committee of the Privy Council in *A-G of Hong Kong v Lee Kwong-Kut* [1993] AC 951. In that case, the Judicial Committee ruled that an identically worded provision in the Hong Kong Drug Trafficking (Recovery of Proceeds) Ordinance did not contravene a provision in the Hong Kong Bill of Rights to the effect that persons 26.96

charged with criminal offences 'shall have the right to be presumed innocent until proved guilty according to law'. The burden of proof in relation to the *mens rea* remained on the prosecution and the burden imposed on the defendant by s 50(4) was justifiable in the context of the war against drug trafficking.

(7) Disclosures by persons in employment

26.97 By s 50(5), it is sufficient for the purposes of s 50(3) and (4) that a person in employment at the time in question discloses his suspicion or belief to an appropriate person in accordance with the procedure established by his employer. The Money Laundering Regulations impose an obligation on financial and other institutions to appoint a person within the organisation to whom such transactions may be reported, and the effect of s 50(5) is that it will be sufficient to report in accordance with procedures established by the employer under those regulations. Section 328 of POCA replaces s 50 of the DTA 1994.

(8) Acquisition, possession, or use of the proceeds of drug trafficking

26.98 By s 51(1) of the DTA:

> A person is guilty of an offence if, knowing that property is, or in whole or in part directly or indirectly represents, another person's proceeds of drug trafficking, he acquires or uses that property or has possession of it.

26.99 This offence is aimed at those coming into possession of or using property that, in whole or in part represents another's proceeds of drug trafficking. It does not have to be proved that legal title to the property has been transferred to the defendant—mere use will suffice. The provisions as to mens rea are much stricter than those in relation to the other offences created by the Act. Actual knowledge has to be proved in order for a defendant to be convicted, whereas suspicion is sufficient to establish liability under ss 49 and 50. By s 51(6), having possession of any property shall be taken to be doing any act in relation to it.

(9) Defences: adequate consideration

26.100 Section 51(2) provides that it is a defence that the person acquired or used the property or had possession of it for adequate consideration. This provision has to be read in the light of s51(3) and (4) which make provision for what constitutes adequate consideration. Subsection (3) provides that, for the purposes of s 50(2):

(a) a person acquires property for inadequate consideration if the value of the consideration is significantly less than the value of the property; and
(b) a person uses or has possession of property for inadequate consideration if the value of the consideration is significantly less than the value of his use or possession of the property.

26.101 In *R v Gibson* The Times, 3 March 2000 the Court of Appeal ruled that on a prosecution for an offence contrary to s 93B(1) of the CJA 1988 (which is in identical words to the DTA: acquisition, possession, or use of proceeds of criminal conduct) it is for the defendant to raise, and prove on a balance of probabilities, the defence afforded under s 93B(2), ie that the property was acquired, possessed, or used for 'adequate consideration'.

C. Money Laundering Offences under the DTA 1994 and CJA 1988

This is subject to an important proviso in s 50(4) to the effect that the provision of goods or services for any person, which are of assistance to that person in drug trafficking, shall not be treated as consideration. Section 329 of POCA unifies and replaces s 51 of the DTA. **26.102**

(10) Other defences

Section 50(5) provides an identical defence to that provided by s 50(3) in relation to the offence committed under that section and provides the same protection to persons who disclose suspicious transactions to law enforcement agencies; and s 50(7) provides an identical defence to that given by s 50(4)(c). Finally s 50(9) provides that no constable or other person shall be guilty of an offence under the section in respect of anything done in connection with the enforcement or intended enforcement of any provisions in the Act or another enactment relating to drug trafficking or the proceeds of drug trafficking. **26.103**

(11) Laundering the proceeds of other crimes under the Criminal Justice Act

It is equally culpable to launder the proceeds of criminal offences other than those relating to drug trafficking. Part III of the Criminal Justice Act 1993 thus added a number of sections to the CJA 1988 which created identically worded offences to the DTA in relation to the proceeds of other criminal conduct. Section 29 adds s 93A to the CJA, which makes it an offence to assist another to retain the benefit of criminal conduct (the corresponding provision of the DTA is s 50(1)). Section 30 adds s 93B which makes acquisition, possession, or use of the proceeds of criminal conduct an offence (the corresponding provision of the DTA is s 51(1)); and s 31 adds s 93C which makes it an offence to conceal or transfer the proceeds of criminal conduct (the corresponding provision of the DTA is s 49(1)). In view of the identical wording of these offences to those contained in ss 49, 50, and 51 of the DTA, it is not intended to consider their provisions in greater detail, save to say that s 327 of POCA replaces s 93C of the Criminal Justice Act 1988, s 328 replaces s 93A of the CJA, and s 329 replaces s 93B of the CJA. **26.104**

In *R v Saik* [2006] 2 WLR 993, a case decided under s 93C of the Criminal Justice Act 1988, as inserted by s 31 of the CJA 1993, their Lordships ruled that to establish guilt on a conspiracy charge, the accused had to be aware that the property involved was in fact the proceeds of crime or, in the case of unidentified property, intend that it should be. Whilst reasonable grounds for suspicion were sufficient for the substantive offence of money laundering, they were not sufficient for conspiracy. **26.105**

(12) Meaning of criminal conduct

By s 93A(7) 'criminal conduct' means conduct which constitutes an offence to which Pt VI of the CJA 1988 applies or would constitute such an offence if it had occurred in England or Wales. **26.106**

(13) Sentencing for money laundering offences

By s 334 of POCA, offences contrary to ss 327, 328, and 329 are punishable with up to 14 years' imprisonment and an unlimited fine on indictment and to a maximum of six months **26.107** imprisonment and a fine up to the statutory maximum on summary conviction. Identical penalties are available for the similar offences contrary to ss 93A, 93B, and 93C of the CJA and ss 49, 50, and 51 of the DTA.

26.108 These offences vary enormously in their gravity. At the lower end of the scale is the spouse or cohabitee of the criminal who launders a relatively modest sum of money through a bank account. At the opposite end of the spectrum is the professional money launderer who sets up 'dummy' companies, trusts, off-shore bank accounts and the like for the sole purpose of facilitating a money laundering operation. Under the DTA the Court of Appeal declined the invitation to give sentencing guidelines to judges. The indications are, however, that custodial sentences are considered appropriate in all but the most exceptional circumstances. In *R v Hanna* (1994) 15 Cr App R(S) 44 the defendant pleaded guilty to an offence under s 50 of the DTA. She had opened a building society account in her own name into which she had paid some £16,000 given to her by a Miss G and which represented the proceeds of heroin trafficking carried on by G's cohabitee. Some 10 days later Hanna withdrew the entire sum and returned it to G. The judge sentenced her to 12 months' imprisonment. In upholding this sentence, the Court of Appeal indicated that it entirely agreed with the judge's sentencing remarks when he commented:

> friends of drug dealers and their wives must also understand that if they suspect that money which is coming into their hands is coming from drug dealing then the thing to do is to have nothing to do with it because if you have anything to do with it imprisonment will almost automatically follow.

26.109 In *R v O'Meally and Morgan* (1994) 15 Cr App R(S) 831 the defendants were also convicted of offences under s 50 of the DTA. O'Meally had opened a building society account into which he had paid £6,000 which represented the proceeds of another's drug trafficking and was sentenced to nine months' imprisonment. Morgan travelled to Jamaica to deposit some £30,000, which again represented the proceeds of drug trafficking. He later withdrew £6,000, which was never traced. The Court of Appeal declined to give general sentencing guidelines on the basis that the offences vary so much in their gravity, but upheld the sentences imposed on both defendants indicating that they were entirely appropriate in the circumstances.

26.110 In *R v Greenwood* (1995) 16 Cr App R(S) 614 the defendant pleaded guilty to an offence under s 50 of the DTA in relation to the laundering of £22,000 and was sentenced to three years' imprisonment. The Court allowed the defendant's appeal and reduced the sentence to 21 months on the basis that his sister, who had been involved in the actual dealing in the drugs, had only been sentenced to two years' imprisonment. In delivering the judgment of the court, Gage J said (at p 616):

> 'We agree with the learned judge when he says that launderers 'are nearly as bad', but not quite so bad, as those who actually do the dealing.'

26.111 The Court of Appeal has ruled that there should be an element of proportionality in sentencing in money laundering offences (see *R v Everson* (2002) 1 Cr App R(S)132 and *R v Basra* (2002) 2 Cr App R(S) 100).

(14) Mode of trial decisions

26.112 As these offences are triable either way, justices will be called upon to make decisions as to mode of trial. The fact that in both *Hanna, O'Meally and Morgan*, and *Greenwood* the Court upheld sentences considerably in excess of the justices' powers of punishment in respect of comparatively modest sums of money laundered by relatively unsophisticated means, suggests that rarely, if ever, will summary trial be appropriate. Further, the complexity of the case should also be taken into consideration. Money laundering cases frequently involve a detailed analysis of complex financial documentation which, together with the volume of evidence necessary to prove the case, means that any trial can be lengthy.

D. The EC Money Laundering Directives

26.113 On 10 June 1991 the Council of the European Communities issued a Directive (91/308) on the prevention of the use of the financial system for the purpose of money laundering. The Directive was issued because, in the words of the preamble:

> . . . lack of Community action against money laundering could lead Member States, for the purpose of protecting their financial systems, to adopt measures which could be inconsistent with completion of the single market; whereas in order to facilitate their criminal activities launderers could try to take advantage of the freedom of capital movement and freedom to supply financial services which the integrated financial area involves if certain co-ordinating measures are not adopted at Community level.

26.114 The Directive required Member States, by 1 January 1993, to introduce certain measures to prevent the financial system being used for money laundering. These included ensuring that money laundering is prohibited (Article 2); requiring credit and financial institutions to obtain evidence of identification of their customers (Article 3) and retain that evidence, together with records of transactions, for at least five years (Article 4); requiring such institutions to disclose to law enforcement authorities transactions which might be an indication of money laundering (Article 6) and that they refrain from carrying out transactions they know or suspect relate to money laundering (Article 7); and ensuring these institutions establish adequate procedures for internal control and communication in order to forestall and prevent money laundering transactions and for making their employees aware of the provisions of the Directive.

26.115 The definition of 'money laundering' in Article 1 covers only the proceeds of drug trafficking and not those of any other crime. The reason for this is that Article 1 defined 'criminal activity' as being a crime specified in Article 3(1)(a) of the Vienna Convention. As this Convention is concerned with measures to combat drug trafficking, the definition of 'criminal activity' is confined to such offences. Article 15 of the Directive however allowed Member States to adopt stricter measures to prevent money laundering and the preamble expressed the hope that they will extend it to cover other crimes. In consequence, certain countries, including the UK, have taken the opportunity to adopt 'all crime' money laundering legislation. Similarly, some countries, while not going so far as to extend the legislation to cover all crimes, have adopted legislation that covers other criminal activity, as well as that relating to drugs.

(1) UK legislation to implement the Directive

26.116 The legislation introduced to compel disclosure of transactions relating to money laundering and the establishment of systems within financial institutions to prevent money laundering comprise of the Money Laundering Regulations 1993, SI 1993/1933, the Money Laundering Regulations 2001, SI 2001/3641, Pt III of the DTA 1994, and Pt 7 of POCA 2002.

(2) The Money Laundering Regulations

26.117 The Money Laundering Regulations 1993, SI 1993/1933 give effect to Articles 3, 4, 10, and 11 of the Council Directive (EC) 91/308 on prevention of the use of the financial system for the purpose of money laundering. These regulations came into force on 1 April 1994. The Regulations require that where business relationships are formed, or one off transactions are carried out in the course of relevant financial business, the persons carrying out that business are required to maintain certain procedures for the purposes of forestalling or preventing money laundering (see regs 7, 9, 12, and 14). The Regulations also require relevant financial businesses to train their employees in procedures that will forestall or prevent money laundering, and in the recognition of money laundering transactions and the law relating to money laundering.

26.118 The Money Laundering Regulations 2001, SI 2001/3641 supplement the provisions of the Money Laundering Regulations 1993 and give effect to Articles 12 and 13 of Council Directive (EC) 91/308 on prevention of the use of the financial system for the purpose of money laundering. These Regulations, together with those introduced by the 1993 Regulations were considered in the first edition of this book.

(3) The new Regulations

26.119 The Proceeds of Crime Act 2002 and Money Laundering Regulations 2003 (Amendment) Order 2006, extended important obligations upon professional advisers from a wide range of sectors, including tax advisers, accountants, auditors, insolvency practitioners and legal advisers. Professionals who carry on relevant business are required to fulfil a range of obligations to prevent money laundering. The 2003 Money Laundering Regulations came into force on the 1 March 2004. The regulated sector, including, but not limited to, accountants and auditors; tax advisers; dealers in high value goods (including auctioneers); casinos; estate agents; some management consultancy services; company formation agents; insolvency practitioners; legal advisers; and bureau de change; are all included within the regulated sector which requires those businesses to establish procedures to confirm the identity of new clients and appoint a money laundering nominated officer to whom money laundering reports must be made. They should also establish systems and procedures to forestall and prevent money laundering and provide relevant individuals for training or money laundering awareness courses.

26.120 The Money Laundering Regulations 2003 replaced the Money Laundering Regulations 1993 and 2001 with updated provisions which reflect Council Directive (EC) 2001/97 and amend Council Directive (EC) 91/308 on the prevention of the use of the financial

D. The EC Money Laundering Directives

system for the purpose of money laundering. Where business relationships are formed, or one off transactions are carried out, in the course of relevant business (defined in reg 2), persons carrying out such relevant business are required to maintain certain identification procedures (see reg 4), record keeping procedures (see reg 6) and internal reporting procedures (reg 7).

26.121 Businesses are also required to establish other appropriate procedures for the purpose of forestalling or preventing money laundering (reg 3(1)(b)). They are also required to train their employees in those procedures and, more generally, in the recognition of money laundering transactions and the law relating to money laundering (see reg 3(1)(3)).

26.122 The 2003 Regulations also revoked the Financial Services and Markets Act 2000 (Regulations relating to Money Laundering) Regulations 2001, SI 2001/1819). As stated, the 2003 Regulations came into force on 1 March 2004, although reg 10, insofar as it relates to a person who acts as a high value dealer, came into force on 1 April 2004. It will be noted that solicitors are not 'deposit-taking bodies' operating an account they maintain, as a result of amendments introduced by SOCPA.

26.123 A person who fails to maintain the procedures or carry out the training is guilty of a criminal offence (reg 3(2)). Casino operators, for example must obtain satisfactory evidence of the identity of all people using their gambling facilities (reg 8).

26.124 Regulation 9 requires Revenue and Customs to keep a register of money service operators and a register of high value dealers. Regulations 10 and 11 state the registration requirements placed on such persons and reg 12 list the grounds on which registration may be refused by Revenue and Customs, including where information which has been supplied is incomplete, false or misleading. Furthermore, reg 13 lists the circumstances in which registration may be cancelled by Revenue and Customs. Under regs 15-19 the Revenue and Customs have various powers in relation to money service operators and high value dealers, including a power to enter and inspect premises, where there are reasonable grounds for believing that an offence under the regulation is being, has been, or is about to be, committed by a money service operator or high value dealer. In such circumstances the Commissioners may seek a court order requiring any person in possession of certain information to allow them access to it. (See reg 19.)

26.125 Regulations 20 and 21 give the Commissioners of Revenue and Customs various powers imposing penalties and conducting reviews. Regulation 22 sets out the appeal procedure (which is to a VAT and Duties Tribunal). Regulation 23 allows Revenue and Customs to prosecute offences and reg 25 requires people who are authorised by the FSA to inform the FSA before they operate a bureau de change.

(4) Relevant businesses

26.126 Regulation 2(2) defines 'relevant businesses' as including dealing in investments; managing investments; arranging deals in investments; advising in investments; the business of operating a bureau de change; transmitting money by any means; estate agency work; operating a casino; the activities of a person appointed to act as an insolvency practitioner; the provision by way of business of accountancy services; the provision by way of business of audit services; the provision by way of business of legal services; the activity of dealing in goods of any description by way of business (including dealing as an auctioneer) whenever a transaction involves accepting a total cash payment of Euro15,000 or more, (see SI 2003/3075).

(5) Other amendments

26.127 The Proceeds of Crime Act 2002 and Money Laundering Regulations 2003 (Amendment) Order 2006, came into force on the 21 February 2006. It makes various amendments to s 330 of the Proceeds of Crime Act 2002 to encompass not only professional legal advisers but other relevant professional advisers as well (see reg 2(2)). Section 330 of POCA 2002 requires a person to make a disclosure in accordance with s 330(4) (as substituted by s 104(3) of the Serious Organised Crime and Police Act 2005) where he knows or suspects, or has reasonable grounds for knowing or suspecting, that another person is engaged in money laundering and the information or other matter came to him in the course of a business in the regulated sector. Schedule 9 to that Act (as amended by the Proceeds of Crime Act 2002 (Business in the Regulated Sector and Supervisory Authorities) Order 2003, SI 2003/3074 has the effect of determining what is a business in the regulated sector (see para 27.14 of Chapter 27). Failure to make such a disclosure is an offence under s 330(1).

(6) The Third European Money Laundering Directive

26.128 The Third European Money Laundering Directive came into effect on the 15 December 2005 (see the EU Official Journal L 309 25 November 2005 at pp 15-36). The Directive requires EU members to bring into force the laws, regulations and administrative provisions necessary to comply with the new Directive by 15 December 2007. It is likely that the Money Laundering Regulations 2003 and the Proceeds of Crime Act 2002 will require amendment by that date in order to comply with the requirements of the 2005 Directive. New requirements will include that there be due diligence procedures in relation to existing clients and customers at appropriate times on a risk-sensitive basis. There will also be a requirement for the supervision and monitoring of all institutions and persons operating in the regulated sector. This supervision and monitoring may be undertaken by government or by professional bodies, such as the Institute of Chartered Accountants or the Law Society. This will mean that new arrangements will need to be developed before the end of 2007 for the monitoring and supervision of those businesses within the regulated sector which are not currently subject to supervision, including estate agents and unqualified accountants.

27

DISCLOSURE OF SUSPICIOUS TRANSACTIONS

A.	**Introduction**	27.01	(7) 'POCA clauses'	27.63
	(1) Background	27.05	(8) Protection for judges	27.69
B.	**Disclosure of Suspicious Transactions Under POCA**	27.10	D. **Suspicious Activity Reports: 'SARS'**	27.70
	(1) Failure to disclose: regulated sector	27.10	(1) Review	27.70
			(2) Form and manner of disclosures	27.72
			(3) Submitting reports	27.73
	(2) Businesses in the regulated sector	27.14	E. **Tipping Off**	27.76
	(3) Excluded businesses	27.17	(1) The offence of tipping off under POCA	27.76
	(4) Defences to failing to disclose in the regulated sector	27.19	(2) Defences available	27.80
	(5) What tests should the court apply?	27.26	(3) Maximum penalty under ss 330, 331, 332, and 333	27.82
	(6) Legal privilege	27.29	(4) Consent	27.84
	(7) 'Suspects'	27.32	(5) Protected and authorised disclosures	27.85
	(8) Failure to disclose: nominated officers in the regulated sector	27.33	(6) Threshold amounts	27.86
	(9) Defence available	27.38	(7) Mode of trial decisions	27.87
	(10) Considerations for the court	27.39	F. **Disclosure of Suspicious Transactions Under the DTA**	27.88
	(11) Failure to disclose: other nominated officers	27.40	(1) Failure to disclose knowledge or suspicion of drug money laundering	27.89
	(12) Protected disclosures	27.41	(2) Legal professional privilege	27.92
	(13) Defence available	27.42	(3) Defences	27.94
C.	**Professional Legal Advisers**	27.43	(4) Tipping off	27.95
	(1) Introduction	27.43	(5) Defences to tipping off	27.97
	(2) *Bowman v Fels*: the facts	27.45	(6) Tipping off under the CJA 1988	27.98
	(3) *Bowman v Fels*: the issues	27.47	(7) Penalties	27.103
	(4) *Bowman v Fels*: the judgment	27.50		
	(5) *Bowman v Fels*: conclusion	27.57		
	(6) Consensual resolution in a litigious context	27.60		

A. Introduction

Money laundering and confiscation law can only be truly effective if banks, financial institutions, and professionals who handle money on behalf of clients, are compelled to disclose suspicious transactions to law enforcement authorities. The provisions of POCA 2002, the DTA 1994, and the CJA 1988 (examined in Chapter 26) encourage such disclosure by providing certain exemptions from criminal liability for money laundering and civil liability at the suit of the customer for any breach of confidentiality. **27.01**

27.02 In this chapter we consider the thrust of the provisions of POCA in relation to disclosure of suspicious transactions in relation to the professions – one of the hottest topics since the introduction of the Act.

27.03 The POCA provisions came into force on 24 February 2003, however, like much of POCA, the transitional provisions (SI 2003/120) provide:

> The new failure to disclose offences shall not have effect where the information or other matter on which knowledge or suspicion that another person is engaged in money laundering is based, or which gives reasonable grounds for such knowledge or suspicion, came to a person before 24 February 2003 and the old failure to disclose offences shall continue to have effect in such circumstances.

27.04 It will be seen that POCA has been substantially amended in relation to money laundering and the disclosure of suspicious transactions by virtue of the Serious Organised Crime and Police Act 2005 (SOCPA). According to the explanatory notes that accompany SOCPA, these amendments are designed to improve the effectiveness of the civil recovery scheme and ease the money laundering reporting requirements on the regulated sector.

(1) Background

27.05 The Proceeds of Crime Act legislation originates from two European directives: Council Directive (EC) (1991/308) (the 1991 Directive) and Council Directive (EC) (2001/97) (the 2001 Directive). The express purpose of the 1991 Directive was the prevention of the use of the financial system for the purpose of money laundering. Article 2 provides that 'member states shall ensure that money laundering as defined in this Directive is prohibited'. Article 1 explained the phrase 'money laundering' embraced four different types of intentional conduct. These may be described as 'conversion or transfer', 'concealment or disguise', 'acquisition, possession or use' and 'participation'.

27.06 The 2001 Directive, for its part, amended the 1991 Directive in a number of important ways. Paragraphs 1-15 of its recital explain the reasons why the steps required to combat money laundering needed to be enlarged. Paragraph 13, refers to evidence that the tightening of controls in the financial sector had prompted money launderers to seek alternative methods for concealing the origin of the proceeds of crime. Paragraph 14 speaks of trends towards the increased use by money launderers of non-financial businesses. And paragraph 15 states that the obligations of the 1991 Directive concerning customer identification, record keeping and the reporting of suspicious transactions, should be extended to a limited number of activities and professions, which had been shown to be vulnerable to money laundering.

27.07 Article 1 of the 1991 Directive, as amended by the 2001 Directive, defines money laundering as meaning the following conduct when committed intentionally:

(a) The conversion or transfer of property, knowing that such property is derived from criminal activity or from an act of participation in such activity, for the purpose of concealing or disguising the illicit origin of the property or of assisting any person who is involved in the commission of such activity to evade the legal consequences of his actions;

B. Disclosure of Suspicious Transactions under POCA

(b) The concealment or disguise of the true nature, source, location, disposition, movement, rights with respect to, or ownership of property, knowing that such property is derived from criminal activity or from an act of participation in such activity;

(c) The acquisition, possession or use of property, knowing, at the time of receipt that such property was derived from criminal activity or from an act of participation in such activity;

(d) Participation in, association to commit, attempts to commit and aiding, abetting, facilitating and counselling the commission of any of the actions mentioned in the foregoing indents;

(e) Knowledge, intent or purpose required as an element of the above-mentioned activities may be inferred from objective factual circumstances.

27.08 These issues are considered in more detail in Chapter 26. They were also considered by Brooke LJ in *Bowman v Fels* who stated that the 1991 and 2001 Council Directives were important to the Act's proper understanding. As a result the Court interpreted 'so far as possible, the Act in the light of the wording and the purpose of the Directives in order to achieve the result pursued by the latter' (see also Case C-106/89 *Marleasing SA v LA Comercial Internacional de Alinentacion SA* [1990] ECR I-4135, para 8).

27.09 In his Lordship's judgment it was open to the UK Parliament to go further than the Directives and in some respects, in the Court's opinion, they did (see para 44). Particularly, the UK legislation defined money laundering to include property known 'or suspected' to constitute or represent a benefit from criminal activity and apply it to the benefits of any type of criminal conduct (see s 330(3) of the 2002 Act). The extended definition of money laundering in the UK legislation (to embrace circumstances of suspicion) involved abandoning the distinction drawn in the Directives between money laundering and the requirement that the institutions and persons subject to the Directives should 'refrain from carrying out transactions which they know or suspect to be related to money laundering'.

B. Disclosure of Suspicious Transactions under POCA

(1) Failure to disclose: regulated sector

27.10 Under s 330 of POCA 2002 a person commits an offence if each of the following conditions are satisfied:

(2) The first condition is that he-
  (a) knows or suspects, or
  (b) has reasonable grounds for knowing or suspecting,
that another person is engaged in money laundering.
(3) The second condition is that the information or other matter-
  (a) on which his knowledge or suspicion is based, or
  (b) which gives reasonable grounds for such knowledge or suspicion,
came to him in the course of a business in the regulated sector.

27.11 By s 104 of SOCPA, s 330 is amended and new conditions have been added. The new conditions are as follows:

(3A) The third condition is (a) that he can identify the other person mentioned in section 330(2) or the whereabouts of any of the laundered property, or (b) that he believes, or it is reasonable to expect him to believe, that the information or other matter mentioned in section 330(3) will or may assist in identifying that that other person or the whereabouts of any of the laundered property.

(4) The fourth condition is that he does not make the required disclosure to (a) a nominated officer, or (b) a person authorised for the purposes of this Part by the Director General of the Serious Organised Crime Agency, as soon as is practicable after the information or other matter mentioned in sub-section (3) comes to him.

(5) The required disclosure is a disclosure of (a) the identity of the other person mentioned in sub-section (2), if he knows it, (b) the whereabouts of the laundered property, so far as he knows it, and (c) the information or other matter mentioned in section 330(3).

27.12 Section 330 replaces s 52 of the DTA and is intended to create an obligation to report suspicion of money laundering to the authorities. In so doing it widens the scope of the offences that it replaces under s 52 beyond reporting drug money laundering to reporting the laundering of the proceeds of *any* criminal conduct. The second limb of the first condition, 'has reasonable grounds for knowing or suspecting', introduces a negligence test which means that the failure to disclose an offence would be committed if a person had reasonable grounds for knowing or suspecting that another person is engaged in money laundering (even if they did not actually know or suspect).

27.13 The laundered property is the property forming the subject matter of the money laundering that the individual knows or suspects, or has reasonable grounds for knowing or suspecting, that the other person is engaged in (see s 330(5)(a)). An individual does not commit an offence under this section if he has a reasonable excuse for not making the required disclosure; or he is a professional legal adviser and if he knows either of the things mentioned in s 330(5)(a) because the information or other matter came to him in privileged circumstances; or the information or other matter mentioned in s 330(3) came to him in privileged circumstances; or s 330(7) applies to him. (Subsection (7) states that this subsection only applies if the individual does not know or suspect that the person is engaged in money laundering, and he has not been provided by his employer with such training as is specified by the Act.)

(2) Businesses in the regulated sector

27.14 The original definition of the 'regulated sector' in Appendix 9 of the 2002 Act was replaced by the Proceeds of Crime Act 2002 (Business in the Regulated Sector and Supervisory Authorities) Order 2003, SI 2003/3074 under Pt 3 of Appendix 9. The activities defined as constituting business in the regulated sector are, basically, activities in the financial and property sectors, including provision by way of business/or services by a body corporate or unincorporate or, in the case of a sole practitioner, by an individual and which involves participation in a financial or real property transaction.

27.15 A business is in the regulated sector to the extent that it engages in any of the following activities in the UK:

(a) a regulated activity specified in subpara (2);
(b) the activities of the National Savings Bank;
(c) any activity carried on for the purpose of raising money authorised to be raised under the National Loans Act 1968 under the auspices of the Director of Savings;

B. Disclosure of Suspicious Transactions under POCA

(d) the business of operating a bureau de change, transmitting money (or any representation of monetary value) by any means or cashing cheques which are made payable to customers;
(e) any of the activities in points 1 to 12 or 14 of Annex 1 to the Banking Consolidation Directive when carried on by way of business, ignoring an activity falling within any of paragraphs (a) to (d);
(f) estate agency work;
(g) operating a casino by way of business;
(h) the activities of a person appointed to act as an insolvency practitioner within the meaning of s 388 of the Insolvency Act 1986 or Art 3 of the Insolvency (Northern Ireland) Order 1989, SI 1989/2405 (NI 19));
(i) the provision by way of business of advice about the tax affairs of another person by a body corporate or unincorporate or, in the case of a sole practitioner, by an individual;
(j) the provision by way of business of accountancy services by a body corporate or unincorporate or, in the case of a sole practitioner, by an individual;
(k) the provision by way of business of audit services by a person who is eligible for appointment as a company auditor under section 25 of the Companies Act 1989 (c. 40) or Article 28 of the Companies (Northern Ireland) Order 1990, SI 1990/593 (NI 5));
(l) the provision by way of business of legal services by a body corporate or unincorporate or, in the case of a sole practitioner, by an individual and which involves participation in a financial or real property transaction (whether by assisting in the planning or execution of any such transaction or otherwise by acting for, or on behalf of, a client in any such transaction);
(m) the provision by way of business of services in relation to the formation, operation or management of a company or a trust;
(n) the activity of dealing in goods of any description by way of business (including dealing as an auctioneer) whenever a transaction involves accepting a total cash payment of 15,000 euro or more.

(2) These are the regulated activities—
  (a) accepting deposits;
  (b) effecting or carrying out contracts of long-term insurance when carried on by a person who has received official authorisation pursuant to Article 4 or 51 of the Life Assurance Consolidation Directive;
  (c) dealing in investments as principal or as agent;
  (d) arranging deals in investments;
  (e) managing investments;
  (f) safeguarding and administering investments;
  (g) sending dematerialised instructions;
  (h) establishing (and taking other steps in relation to) collective investment schemes;
  (i) advising on investments;
  (j) issuing electronic money.

27.16 POCA intends therefore that the businesses listed above will employ a higher level of diligence in handling transactions than businesses that fall outside of the types of businesses listed in Sch 9. It will be noted that the Proceeds of Crime 2002 (Business in the Regulated Sector) Order 2006, SI 2006/2385 amends para 2(g) of Pt 1 of Sch 9 so as to add to the list of excluded activities the arranging and advising on regulated home reversion plans and home purchase plans, (see also the consequential amendment in SI 2006/2383).

(3) Excluded businesses

27.17 The duty to report under s 330 is restricted to those businesses in the regulated sector listed as amended by SOCPA.

27.18 A business is not in the regulated sector to the extent that it engages in any of the following activities (as per the Schedule attached to the Proceeds of Crime Act 2002 (Business in the Regulated Sector and Supervisory Authorities) Order 2003):

(a) the issue of withdrawable share capital within the limit set by section 6 of the Industrial and Provident Societies Act 1965 by a society registered under that Act;
(b) the acceptance of deposits from the public within the limit set by s 7(3) of that Act by such a society;
(c) the issue of withdrawable share capital within the limit set by s 6 of the Industrial and Provident Societies Act (Northern Ireland) 1969 by a society registered under that Act;
(d) the acceptance of deposits from the public within the limit set by s 7(3) of that Act by such a society;
(e) activities carried on by the Bank of England;
(f) any activity in respect of which an exemption order under s 38 of the Financial Services and Markets Act 2000 has effect if it is carried on by a person who is for the time being specified in the order or falls within a class of persons so specified;
(g) the regulated activities of arranging deals in investments or advising on investments, in so far as the investment consists of rights under a regulated mortgage contract;
(h) the regulated activities of dealing in investments as agent, arranging deals in investments, managing investments or advising on investments, in so far as the investment consists of rights under, or any right to or interest in, a contract of insurance which is not a qualifying contract of insurance.

(4) Defences to failing to disclose in the regulated sector

27.19 A person does not commit an offence under s 330 if:

(6) (a) he has a reasonable excuse for not disclosing the information or other matter;
(b) he is a professional legal advisor and the information or other matter came to him in privileged circumstances;
(c) subsection 7 applies to him.
(7) This subsection applies to a person if—
(a) he does not know or suspect that another person is engaged in money laundering, and
(b) he has not been provided by his employer with such training as is specified by the Secretary of State by order for the purposes of this Section.

27.20 Under s 330(6)(b) legal professional privilege survives POCA, but see para 27.30 below. It is also a reasonable excuse for an employee to raise that his employer has not given him adequate training, although the employers themselves may then find themselves in jeopardy

B. Disclosure of Suspicious Transactions under POCA

of the money laundering regulations discussed in Chapter 26. Statutory Instrument 2003/171 specifies training for the purposes of POCA 2002.

27.21 Section106(2) of SOCPA also amends s 330 of POCA to insert a new subsection (7A), after s 106 (7), which states:

Nor does a person commit an offence under this section if – (a) he knows, or believes on reasonable grounds, that the money laundering is occurring in a particular country or territory outside the United Kingdom and (b) the money laundering – (i) is not unlawful under the criminal law applying in the country or territory, and (ii) is not of a description prescribed in an order made by the Secretary of State.

27.22 New s 106(9A) stipulates:

(9A) But a disclosure which satisfies para's (a) and (b) of sub-section (9) is not to be taken as a disclosure to a nominated officer, if the person making the disclosure (a) is a professional legal adviser, (b) makes it for the purpose of obtaining advice about making a disclosure under this section and (c) does not intend it to be a disclosure under this section.

27.23 Section 330(6)(b) (as substituted by s 104(3) of SOCPA) provides a defence to this offence where the person is a professional legal adviser and the information or other matter came to him in the circumstances set out in s 330(10). In order to give full effect to Council Directive (EC) 2001/97, Art 2(2) of this Order amends s 330(6)(b), (9A)(a) and (10) to extend the persons to whom the defence applies to a 'relevant professional adviser', as defined by s 330(14), which is inserted by Art 2(5). The amendments made by Art 2(3) and (4) provide a defence for a person who is employed by (or in partnership with) the professional legal adviser or other relevant professional adviser to provide assistance or support.

27.24 The effect of these amendments are to extend the defence available to a professional legal adviser under s 330(6)(b) for failing to make a disclosure (contrary to s 330(1)) and to provide a defence for a person employed by, or in partnership with, a professional legal adviser or a relevant professional adviser to provide that adviser with assistance or support. They came into force on 21 February 2006.

27.25 As a result, the obligation to disclose suspicions of money laundering will apply only if the person required to make a disclosure knows the identity of the person engaged in the money laundering offence, or the whereabouts of any of the laundered property, or the information which would have to be reported discloses, or may assist in uncovering, the identity of the person engaged in that offence, or the whereabouts of any of the laundered property.

(5) What tests should the court apply?

27.26 Section 330(8) reads:

(8) In deciding whether a person committed an offence under this section the court must consider whether he followed any relevant guidance which was at the time concerned
   (a) issued by a supervisory authority or any other appropriate body,
   (b) approved by the Treasury and
   (c) published in a manner it approved as appropriate in its opinion to bring the guidance to the attention of persons likely to be affected by it.

27.27 Under s 330(8) an appropriate body is any body which regulates or is representative of any trade, profession, business, or employment carried on by the alleged offender (see s 330(13)).

27.28 The British Bankers Association has set up a Joint Money Laundering Steering Group which has produced guidance notes on money laundering since 1990. It should be noted that guidance notes are just that, and cannot be supplanted by the letter of the law, which the courts are bound to follow. Nevertheless s 330(8) provides that the court must at least take account of guidance notes issued by any supervisory authority providing that they have been approved by the Treasury.

(6) Legal privilege

27.29 Section 330(10) states:

Information or other matter comes to a professional legal advisor in privileged circumstances if it is communicated or given to him—

(a) by (or by a representative of) a client of his in connection with the giving by the advisor of legal advice to the client,
(b) by (or by a representative of) a person seeking legal advice from the advisor, or
(c) by a person in connection with legal proceedings or contemplated legal proceedings.

27.30 However, s 330(10) does not apply to information or other matter that is communicated or given to the legal adviser with the intention of furthering a criminal purpose (see s 330(11) and *Francis and Francis v Central Criminal Court* [1988] 3 All ER 775 (HL)).

27.31 The important decision of *Bowman v Fels* [2005] EWCA Civ 226 in relation to professional legal advisers is considered in detail at para 27.45 below.

(7) 'Suspects'

27.32 The meaning of the word suspects/suspicion is considered at para 26.13 of Chapter 26.

(8) Failure to disclose: nominated officers in the regulated sector

27.33 Section 331 of POCA criminalises conduct where a nominated officer receives a report under s 330 which causes him to know or suspect, or gives reasonable grounds for knowledge or suspicion, that money laundering is taking place, and where that nominated officer does not disclose that report information 'as soon as practicable' after it comes to him. See para 26.62 in Chapter 26 for the definition of 'nominated officer'.

Section 331 states:

(1) A person nominated to receive disclosures under section 330 commits an offence if the conditions in subsections (2) to (4) are satisfied.
(2) The first condition is that he—
 (a) knows or suspects, or
 (b) has reasonable grounds for knowing or suspecting,
  that another person is engaged in money laundering.
(3) The second condition is that the information or other matter—
 (a) on which his knowledge or suspicion is based or
 (b) which gives reasonable grounds for such knowledge or suspicion,
  came to him in consequence of a disclosure made under section 330.

27.34 The required disclosure must be made to either a person authorised by SOCA or in the form and manner prescribed under s 339 (see s 331(5)).

B. Disclosure of Suspicious Transactions under POCA

27.35 Section 104(4) of SOCPA substitutes s 331(4) to (6) of POCA by introducing amended conditions to the original Act. Section 3A states that the third condition is that the individual knows the identity of the other person mentioned in subsection (2), or the whereabouts of any of the laundered property, in consequence of a disclosure made under s 330 and that that other person, or the whereabouts of any of the laundered property, can be identified from the information or other matter mentioned in subsection (3); or that the individual believes, or it is reasonable to expect him to believe, that the information or other matter will or may assist in identifying that other person or the whereabouts of any of the laundered property. The fourth condition is that he does not make the required disclosure to a person authorised for the purposes of Pt 7 of POCA as soon as is practicable, after the information or other matter comes to him, (subsection 4).

27.36 The 'required disclosure' is a disclosure of: (a) the identity of the other person mentioned in s 3A(2), if disclosed to him under the applicable section, (b) the whereabouts of the laundered property, so far as disclosable to him under the applicable section, and (c) the information or other matter mentioned in s 3A(3).

27.37 By s 3A(5A), the 'laundered property' is the property forming the subject matter of the money laundering that the individual knows or suspects that other person to be engaged in.

(9) Defence available

27.38 A person does not commit an offence under s 331 if he has a 'reasonable excuse' for not disclosing the information or other matter (see s 331(6)).

Similarly, a new subsection (6A) has been inserted after subsection (6) which is in identical terms to the new defence available under s 330.

(10) Considerations for the court

27.39 In deciding whether a nominated officer has committed an offence under s 331, the court must consider whether he followed any relevant guidance which was at the time concerned issued by a supervisory authority or any other appropriate body and approved by the Treasury (see s 331(7)). An 'appropriate body' is a body which regulates or is representative of a trade, profession, business, or employment (see s 331(9)).

(11) Failure to disclose: other nominated officers

27.40 Under s 332, it is an offence where a nominated officer receives a report under either s 337 or 338, (protected disclosures or authorised disclosures (see Chapter 26, paras 26.73 and 26.58 respectively, and para 27.41 below), which causes him to know or suspect that money laundering is taking place, and notwithstanding that, he does not disclose the report as soon as the information comes to him. The offence is committed if the following three conditions under s 332(1) to (4) are satisfied:

(1) that the person nominated knows or suspects that another person is engaged in money laundering;
(2) that the information or other matter on which his knowledge or suspicion is based came to him as a consequence of disclosure made under ss 337 or 338;

(3) that he does not make the required disclosures 'as soon as is practicable' after the information or other matter comes to him.

Under s 332(5) a nominated officer is required to disclose to SOCA in the form prescribed by s 339. The role of nominated officers is further discussed at para 26.69 of Chapter 26, and the meaning of the word 'suspects' in considered at para 26.13 of Chapter 26).

(12) Protected disclosures

27.41 Pursuant to s 104(7) of SOCPA, s 337 of the Proceeds of Crime Act (Protected Disclosures) has inserted after subsection (4) the following:

(4A) Where a disclosure consists of a disclosure protected under sub-section (1) and a disclosure of either or both of – (a) the identity of the other person mentioned in sub-section (3), and (b) the whereabouts of property forming the subject matter of the money laundering that the discloser knows or suspects, or has reasonable grounds for knowing or suspecting, that other persons to be engaged in,

the disclosure of the thing mentioned in para's (a) or in (b) (as well as the disclosure protected under subsection (1)) is not to be taken to breach any restriction on the disclosure of information (however imposed).

(13) Defence available

27.42 It will be noted that under s 332(6) of the substituted Act, an individual does not commit an offence if he has a reasonable excuse for not making the required disclosure. SOCPA inserts a new defence in the guise of s 332(7), which is in identical terms to that set out in s 330 above.

C. Professional Legal Advisers

(1) Introduction

27.43 It will be noted that professional legal advisers continue to be exempt from the reporting obligations under this section if the information or other matter came to them in legally privileged circumstances. The defence of lack of training under s 330(7)(B) also remains, as does the defence of 'reasonable excuse'. Section 330(9)(A) confirms that legal professional privilege is not lost when professional legal advisers, including solicitors and barristers, discuss matters with the nominated officers in their firms. Legal professional privilege remains intact whether or not the nominated officer is himself a professional legal adviser or not. The new provision allows professional legal advisers to take advice from their nominated officers, without formal disclosure being made to the nominated officer. This amendment has the effect of giving some comfort that the client's legal professional privilege rights are protected.

27.44 The related case of *Bowman v Fels* [2005] EWCA Civ 226 raises important issues relating to the ambit of POCA and its application to the legal profession. Because of its importance the Bar Council, the Law Society and the former National Criminal Intelligence Service were all granted permission to intervene in the appeal.

(2) Bowman v Fels: the facts

27.45 The underlying facts were relatively straightforward. The claimant lived with the defendant for 10 years in a house that was registered in the defendant's sole name. After their relationship

C. Professional Legal Advisers

ended she asserted a right to the beneficial interest in the property arising out of a constructive trust. Her case was that before the house was purchased the defendant had expressly agreed with her that they would buy the property jointly. The defendant resisted her claim and the matter was listed for trial at the Central London County Court. The claimant's solicitors notified NCIS prior to the hearing of their suspicion that the defendant had included the cost of the work he had carried out at the property within his business accounts and his VAT returns, even though these were unconnected with his business. The claimant's solicitors believed that s 328 of the 2002 Act obliged them to make this disclosure and that it also prevented them from telling either their client or the defendant's solicitors what they had done.

27.46 The claimant's solicitors proceeded to make a 'without notice' application to the judge for an order vacating the trial date, after they had been told by NCIS that it was unlikely that the requisite consent would be granted before the trial started. The judge granted their application. The defendant's solicitors were informed of the terms of the order, but not on what basis it had been made. They responded with an application that the judge's order should be set aside and the claimant's solicitors should be directed to disclose the basis of their application and the evidence they had tendered in support of it. They had guessed, correctly, why the application had been made, (see para 4 of the judgment).

(3) Bowman v Fels: *the issues*

27.47 The Court was invited to determine whether s 328 means that as soon as a lawyer acting for a client in legal proceedings discovers or suspects anything in the proceedings that may facilitate the acquisition, use or control (usually by his client or his client's opponent) of 'criminal property', he must immediately notify NCIS of his belief if he is to avoid being guilty of the criminal offence of being concerned in an arrangement which he knows or suspects facilitates such an activity (by whatever means), (see para 20). Section 328 is set out at para 26.43 of Chapter 26.

27.48 *Bowman v Fels* focused on the applicability or otherwise of s 328 of POCA in a case where information comes to the attention of the lawyer for one of the parties in the course of legal proceedings leading him to know or, more likely, suspect that the other party was engaged in money laundering. Potential issues arose from the decision and guidance given by the President of the Family Division in *P v P (Ancillary Relief Proceeds of Crime)* [2004] Fam1.

27.49 The issue at the centre of the appeal in *Bowman v Fels* was whether s 328 applied to the ordinary conduct of legal proceedings at all. There was also a narrower issue, namely if it did, whether Parliament can be taken, without using clear words to that effect, to have intended to override the important principles underlying legal professional privilege and the strict terms on which lawyers are permitted to have access to documents disclosed in the litigation process (para 24 of the judgment delivered by Brooke LJ).

(4) Bowman v Fels: *the judgment*

27.50 The Court (Brooke LJ) found that s 330 was only relevant where information or other matters coming to the attention of a person in the course of a business in the regulated sector led him to know or suspect, or have reasonable grounds for knowing or suspecting, that another person is engaged in money laundering (see para 55).

27.51 Where legal professionals learn of information in privileged circumstances they are exempt from any obligation of disclosure, and this suggests that they may continue to act as legal professionals, and continue the conduct of any legal proceedings or the giving of any legal advice, without making such a disclosure, although clearly caution should be exercised.

27.52 In *Bowman*, the Court held:

> ... There seems to us to be considerable room for argument, although it is unnecessary to express any concluded view on this, that the protection intended in respect of the giving of legal advice must have been intended to cover advice given in the context of a transaction which the client was about to undertake; it cannot, in other words, have been envisaged that a legal professional would be "carrying out a transaction" merely because he had advised in relation to it. (Para 16.)

The Court went on to state:

> It cannot in our view have been conceived that the ordinary conduct of litigation to its ordinary conclusion, resolving the rights and duties of two parties according to law, could be said to involve the "carrying out" of a "transaction" related to money laundering. This would remain the case even if assets which happen to be the proceeds of money laundering might be the subject of claims in the proceedings, or be retained or used to satisfy any liability according to the outcome of the proceedings. The purpose of litigation – to resolve rights and duties according to law – and the public scrutiny to which it is subject, together with the presence and role of the judge, also distinguish legal proceedings from any "transaction" that the European legislator can have had in mind, as well as offering safeguards against misconduct. (See para 62.)

27.53 The absence from s 328 of any equivalent protection to that contained in respect of the regulated sector in s 330(10) is a strong argument for a restricted understanding of the concept of 'being concerned in an arrangement' in s 328(1). The Court held that although s 328 applies to any person and is not limited like s 330 to the regulated sector, s 328 only applies if a person 'enters into or becomes concerned in an arrangement' which he knows or suspects facilitates the acquisition, retention, use or control of criminal property. In the Court's view, it was improbable that Parliament had the ordinary conduct of legal proceedings in mind when drafting s 328 (or indeed ss 327 and 329).

27.54 The Court in *Bowman v Fels* commented that in *P v P* no distinction had been drawn between acting for a party in litigation (or, as it was put, seeking an arrangement from the court) and negotiating the settlement of a financial dispute (para 64). It was also assumed in *P v P* that a legal professional could become concerned in an arrangement prior to its execution, by, for example the act of negotiating it (see para 48 of *P v P*). However, in *Bowman v Fels* the Court held that a judgment or order is not an arrangement within the section and they found the word 'arrangement' to be a most unnatural use of language in the legal context (para 65). They stated that in s 328 the nature of the act is either entering into an arrangement or the vaguer concept of becoming concerned in an arrangement. To enter into an arrangement involves a single act at a single point in time; so too, on the face of it, does 'to become concerned' in an arrangement, even though the point at which someone may be said to have 'become' concerned may be open to argument.

C. Professional Legal Advisers

As a result, the court rejected the notion that the ordinary pursuit or conduct of legal proceedings could give rise to an 'arrangement' which facilitated the acquisition, retention, use or control of criminal property under s 328, (para 68), and thus distinguished and rejected *P v P*. **27.55**

The court held that so far as UK domestic law was concerned, it was elementary that when a lawyer is advising a client or acting for him in litigation, he may not disclose to a third part any information about his client's affairs without his express or implied consent (see para 78 and *R v Derby Magistrates' Court ex p B* [1996] 1 AC 487 at pp 503-508 and *Three Rivers DC v Bank of England (No 6)* [2004] 3 WLR 1274, where the House of Lords re-stated emphatically that legal advice privilege was just as important as litigation privilege, and that for good policy reasons the law affords a special privilege to communications between lawyers and their clients which it denies to all other confidential communications. **27.56**

(5) Bowman v Fels: *conclusion*

The Court concluded that the proper interpretation of s 328 is that it is not intended to cover or affect the ordinary conduct of litigation by legal professionals. That included any step taken by them in litigation, from the issue of proceedings and the securing of injunctive relief or a freezing order up to its final disposal by judgment. Legal proceedings were defined as a state provided mechanism for the resolution of issues according to law. **27.57**

The Court went on to consider the narrower issue of whether, on its true construction, s 328 had the effect of overriding legal professional privilege and the terms upon which lawyers are permitted to have access to documents disclosed in the litigation process. The Court concluded that there was nothing in the language of s 328 to suggest that Parliament expressly intended to override such privilege and formed the firm opinion that it would require much clearer language than is contained in s 328 and its ancillary sections, before a parliamentary intention could be gleaned to the effect that a party's solicitor is obliged, in breach of his implied duty to the court, and in breach of the duty of confidence he owes to his own client as the litigation solicitor, to disclose to SOCA a suspicion he may have that documents disclosed under compulsion by the other party raised an issue under s 328. **27.58**

As a result, the Court concluded that s 328 was to be interpreted as including legal proceedings within its purview, and could not be interpreted as meaning that either legal professional privilege is to be overridden or that a lawyer is in breach of his duty to the court by disclosing to a third party, external to the litigation, documents revealed to him through the disclosure processes, (see para 90). **27.59**

(6) Consensual resolution in a litigious context

In *Bowman v Fels*, the Court of Appeal considered the position where parties agreed to dispose of the whole or any aspect of legal proceedings on a consensual basis. The consensual resolution of issues is an integral part of the conduct or ordinary civil litigation. There is also within the Civil Procedure Rules a need to encourage cooperation and the value of consensual settlement is underlined. **27.60**

27.61 The Court commented that:

> any consensual agreement can in abstract dictionary terms be called an arrangement. But we do not consider that it can have been contemplated that taking such a step in the context of civil litigation would amount to "becoming concerned in an arrangement which . . . facilitates the acquisition, retention, use or control of criminal property" within the meaning of s 328. Rather it is another ordinary feature of the conduct of civil litigation, facilitating the resolution of a legal dispute and of the parties' legal rights and duties according to law in a manner which is a valuable alternative to the court imposed solution of litigation and judgement.

27.62 The Court went on to state that the position could be different if one were concerned with a settlement which did not reflect the legal and practical merits of the parties' respective positions in the proceedings, and was known or suspected to be no more than a pretext for an agreement relating to the acquisition, retention, use or control of criminal property.

(7) 'POCA clauses'

27.63 The Court in *Bowman v Fels* left open the permissibility or possibility of a POCA clause, whereby an arrangement might be entered into but expressly made subject to it 'not taking effect until authorised disclosure has been made pursuant to s 328 of POCA and appropriate consent is given or deemed to be given under s 335 of that Act'. The Court commented that a question could arise whether the making of such an arrangement, even though its validity or implementation were to be made subject to the condition, could itself be a prohibited act within ss 328(1) and 338.

27.64 The Court stated (at para 103) that it remained uneasy about a clause which would disclose to all concerned (including the other party, who might well be the person suspected of money laundering activity) that money laundering was suspected.

27.65 It commented that curiously, the prohibition on tipping off under s 333 only applied once a disclosure to the authorities has been made. In *Bowman v Fels*, the Court stated that both s 330(3)(c) and (4) and s 342(3)(c) and (4) preserve a broad freedom to make disclosure not merely to a client when giving legal advice, but to any person in connection with actual or contemplated legal proceedings, so it may be that a POCA clause would create no problem in the context of legal proceedings (see para 104), but clearly caution should be exercised.

27.66 The Law Society's view in relation to consensual resolution of issues appears to be that the logic of the Court's conclusion in relation to both litigation and consensual resolution must also apply to alternative dispute resolution. The Law Society, in their guidance issued to solicitors, state that in their view solicitors will not be committing s 327 or s 329 offences as a result of their Lordships' judgment in *Bowman v Fels* if they are conducting litigation in its preparatory stages (including pre-action) where settlements, negotiations, out-of-court settlements and ADR are involved, but again caution should be exercised because it is submitted that general litigation remains within the ambit of s 328 and a lawyer may fall within the ambit of s 330 if he is undertaking non-contentious advisory work which falls within the regulated sector, although in those circumstances there is the express defence for legal professional privilege.

27.67 It is also important to note that whilst the litigation in related processes may fall outside of the ambit of the offences, the property itself remains criminal property for the purposes of s 340(3) of POCA. Therefore any future dealings with the property after the terms of any

D. Suspicious Activity Reports: 'SARS'

judgment or settlement are carried out, will require a re-examination of whether a report to SOCA is required. Solicitors will also need to advise their clients about their own position if ownership of criminal property by them falls outside a court order or other type of settlement covered by the exclusion. The s 329 offence of acquisition, use and possession may be particularly relevant in these circumstances.

27.68 It should further be noted that neither common law legal professional privilege nor the s 330(6) exemption apply to communications made with the intention of furthering a criminal purpose.

(8) Protection for judges

27.69 In relation to judges who suspect that the subject matter of the dispute may be criminal property, the Court of Appeal has made it clear that their judgments and orders will not constitute an 'arrangement' for the purposes of s 328 (see para 65 of their judgment). Although it will be noted that the Court of Appeal does not expressly address the position of either arbitrators or mediators, it must be implied that the same consideration will be applied.

D. Suspicious Activity Reports: 'SARS'

(1) Review

27.70 A review of the SAR regime was commissioned in July 2005, its terms of reference requiring it to be conducted in consultation with those who would be affected by its outcome. Its weaknesses were found to be familiar ones: an absence of any single organisational focus for the work; inconsistent training; poor dialogue between the reporting sectors on the one hand and users on the other; a lack of feedback from law enforcement agencies on the successes achieved; a limited ability to access and manipulate the central database of SAR; and uneven law enforcement exploitation of the opportunities presented by the disclosures made.

27.71 Nevertheless, despite these weaknesses, the regime was clearly delivering benefits stated in both the terrorist and money laundering contexts, and there was recognition within the Report that NCIS's performance had improved. The Report recommended that SOCA should take over day-to-day responsibility for the effective functioning of the regime. Statistically, HM Revenue and Customs indicated that around one in five SARS received identified a new subject of interest and a quarter led to new inquiries in relation to direct taxation matters. Furthermore, about 20-30 per cent of SARS disseminated to the National Terrorist Financial Investigation Unit, either led to a longer term investigation, or added substantially to an existing investigation. (See Sir Stephen Lander's Report on the review of the SARS regime – 'Review of the Suspicious Activity Reports Regime, March 2006'.)

(2) Form and manner of disclosures

27.72 Section 339 of POCA is amended by s 105(5) to substitute s 2(2) and (3) as follows:

(1A) A person commits an offence if he makes a disclosure under s 330, 331, 332 or 338 otherwise than in the form prescribed under sub-section (1) or otherwise than in the manner so prescribed in (1(b)), but a person does not commit an offence under sub-section (1A) if he has a reasonable excuse for making the disclosure otherwise than in the form prescribed under sub-section (1) or (as the case may be) otherwise than in the manner so prescribed.

(3) Submitting reports

27.73 According to the Serious Organised Crime Agency's website (<www.soca.gov.uk>) a SAR should be made as soon as the knowledge or suspicion that criminal proceeds exist has arisen, especially if consent may be required, or at the earliest opportunity thereafter.

27.74 A SAR can be downloaded from SOCA's website. SOCA also prefers these forms to be submitted electronically. Any reporter choosing not to use one of the electronic reporting methods is advised to obtain a copy of the SOCA preferred form. Those wishing to complete reports on their own computer should download the forms from the SOCA website. Alternatively, to request versions of the forms (for completion by hand) and for guidance on completing the form, a telephone help line is available: 020 7238 8282. Hard copy reports should be sent to: UK FRU, P.O. Box 8000, London. SE11 5EN. There is also a money web support team on 020 7238 2888.

27.75 SOCA will not acknowledge any SAR sent by fax, post or by letter. Electronic submissions through the SAR online system will receive an acknowledgement which will include an automatically generated reference number.

E. Tipping Off

(1) The offence of tipping off under POCA

27.76 If a person was to disclose to the subject of an investigation the fact that law enforcement authorities had commenced an enquiry into his affairs, or that a production order had been obtained in relation to his bank accounts, or that a financial institution had disclosed a suspicious transaction, this could seriously prejudice the outcome of the enquiry. Accordingly, under s 333(1) of POCA a person commits an offence if:

(a) he knows or suspects that a disclosure falling within s 337 or s 338 has been made, and
(b) he makes a disclosure which is likely to prejudice any investigation which might be conducted following the disclosure referred to in para (a).

27.77 This offence, together with s 342 (an offence prejudicing an investigation) replaces s 53 of the DTA 1994 and s 93D of the CJA 1988. It makes it an offence to disclose information that is likely to prejudice a money laundering investigation or an investigation that may be undertaken by law enforcement authorities.

27.78 The difficulties encountered by virtue of the tipping off provisions were highlighted in *Bank of Scotland v A* [2001] 1 WLR 751, where the Court of Appeal stated:

> The tipping-off legislation which was the source of the problem with which this appeal deals, gave extensive powers to the police. Properly used they were beneficial. Misused they could create unintended consequences. It is of the greatest importance that the use of those powers is confined to situations where it is appropriate. Institutions such as banks need to be able to ensure that they are not affected adversely or unnecessarily because of the existence of the police's powers.

E. Tipping Off

27.79 For banks duties in relation to tipping off see *BS v A* [2001] 1 WLR 751, considered below at para 27.101.

(2) Defences available

27.80 A person does not commit the offence of tipping off if:

(a) he did not know or suspect that the disclosure was likely to be prejudicial;
(b) the disclosure is made in carrying out a function he has relating to the enforcement of any provision of POCA or of any other enactment relating to criminal conduct or benefit from criminal conduct;
(c) he is a professional legal advisor and the disclosure falls within s 333(3).

Section 333(3) states:

A disclosure falls within this subsection if it is a disclosure—
(a) to (or to a representative of) a client of the professional legal advisor in connection with the giving by the advisor of legal advice to the client, or
(b) to any person in connection with legal proceedings or contemplated legal proceedings.

27.81 However, disclosure does not fall within s 333(3) if it is made with the intention of furthering a criminal purpose (see s 333(4) and *Francis and Francis v Central Criminal Court* [1988] 3 All ER 775 (HL)).

(3) Maximum penalty under ss 330, 331, 332, and 333

27.82 A person guilty of an offence under ss 330, 331, 332, or 333 is liable:

(a) on summary conviction, to imprisonment for a term not exceeding six months or to a fine not exceeding the statutory maximum or to both, or
(b) on conviction on indictment, to imprisonment for a term not exceeding five years or to a fine or to both.

27.83 It will also be noted that under SOCPA, s 334 of POCA (penalties) has inserted a new subsection (3) which states that a person guilty of an offence under s 339(1A) is liable on summary conviction to a fine not exceeding level 5 on the standard scale.

(4) Consent

27.84 For definitions on the appropriate consent and consent from a nominated officer see Chapter 26, paras 26.64 and 26.69.

(5) Protected and authorised disclosures

27.85 For definitions of protected disclosures under s 337 of the Act and authorised disclosures under s 338, and the form and manner of disclosures under s 339, see Chapter 26, para 26.73, 26.58, and 26.76.

(6) Threshold amounts

27.86 After s 339 of Pt 7 of POCA (Money Laundering) there is inserted, by virtue of s 103(5) of SOCPA, a new section that relates to threshold amounts. See para 26.37 of Chapter 26.

(7) Mode of trial decisions

27.87 See Chapter 26, para 26.112.

F. Disclosure of Suspicious Transactions under the DTA

27.88 As mentioned above, the POCA failure to disclose offences do not have effect where the information or other matter on which knowledge or suspicion that another person is engaged in money laundering is based, or which gives reasonable grounds for such knowledge or suspicion, came to a person before 24 February 2003. In those circumstances the 'old Acts' still apply. Like many of the transitional arrangements this will mean that the three Acts, the DTA, the CJA, and POCA will run side by side for some time to come.

(1) Failure to disclose knowledge or suspicion of drug money laundering

27.89 By s 52(1) of the DTA a person is guilty of an offence if:

(a) he knows or suspects that another person is engaged in drug money laundering,
(b) the information, or other matter on which that knowledge or suspicion is based came to his attention in the course of his trade, profession, business or employment, and
(c) he does not disclose the information, or other matter to a constable as soon as reasonably practicable after it comes to his attention.

27.90 'Drug money laundering' means doing any act which is an offence under ss 49, 50, or 51 of the DTA, or which would constitute such an offence if done in England and Wales (see s 52(7) of the DTA 1994).

27.91 This section is drawn in very wide terms and is by no means limited to banks and other financial institutions. It would, for example, extend to solicitors acting in conveyancing transactions, where they know or suspect the transaction is being funded through the proceeds of drug trafficking, or a car dealer selling an expensive motor vehicle to a client. In order to escape liability it is important that all businesses likely to attract the custom of money launderers should make their staff aware of the provisions in thissection and instruct them to report such transactions to a designated person (referred to in the Act as the 'appropriate person') immediately. Information that comes to a person's attention other than in the course of his employment is not caught by the section.

(2) Legal professional privilege

27.92 By s 52(2) of the DTA, it is not an offence if a professional legal adviser fails to disclose any information or other matter that has come to him in privileged circumstances. Section 52(8) provides that information comes to a professional legal adviser in privileged circumstances if it is communicated or given to him:

(a) by, or by a representative of, a client of his in connection with the giving by the adviser of legal advice to the client;
(b) by, or by a representative of, a person seeking legal advice from the adviser; or

F. Disclosure of Suspicious Transactions under the DTA

(c) by any person—
  (i) in contemplation of, or in connection with legal proceedings; and
  (ii) for the purpose of those proceedings.

27.93 Section 52(9) contains an important proviso to the effect that such information shall not be treated as having come to the professional legal adviser in privileged circumstances if it is communicated or given with a view to furthering any criminal purpose (for whether documents are held with a view to furthering a criminal purpose see *Francis and Francis v Central Criminal Court* [1988] 3 All ER 775 (HL); for solicitors and money laundering see *R v Duff* (2003) 1 Cr App R(S) 466 (88) CA).

(3) Defences

27.94 By s 52(3) of the DTA it is a defence that the person charged had a reasonable excuse for not disclosing the information or other matter in question. Section 52(5) provides that, in relation to a person who is in employment at the time in question, it is a defence that he disclosed the information or other matter concerned to the appropriate person in accordance with the procedure established by his employer for the making of such disclosures. Where proper disclosure is made in accordance with the section, it shall not be treated as a breach of any restriction imposed by statute or otherwise.

(4) Tipping off

27.95 Section 53 of the DTA creates a number of offences in relation to 'tipping off' others. By s 53(1) a person is guilty of an offence if:

(a) he knows or suspects that a constable is acting, or is proposing to act, in connection with an investigation which is being, or is about to be conducted into drug money laundering, and
(b) he discloses to any other person information or any other matter which is likely to prejudice that investigation or proposed investigation.

A person is guilty of an offence under s 53(2) if:

(a) he knows or suspects that a disclosure has been made to a constable under s 50, 51, or 52 of this Act ('the disclosure'), and
(b) he discloses to any other person information or any other matter which is likely to prejudice any investigation which might be conducted following the disclosure.

Finally, under s 53(3) a person is guilty of an offence if:

(a) he knows or suspects that a disclosure of a kind mentioned in section 50(5), 51(8) or 52(5) of this Act ('the disclosure') had been made, and
(b) he discloses to any person information or any other matter which is likely to prejudice any investigation which might be conducted following the disclosure.

27.96 It is thus essential that great care be taken to ensure strict confidentiality is maintained to prevent any unauthorised disclosure taking place. In order to minimise the risk of someone within the disclosing organisation tipping off the customer, it is advisable that only those employees with a need to know should be told of the position. It should particularly be borne in mind, it is submitted, that employees who deal on a day to day basis with the customer whose affairs are subject to investigation, might have developed a good rapport, or even friendship with him.

(5) Defences to tipping off

27.97 It is a defence under s 53(6) of the DTA for the person charged to prove he did not know or suspect the disclosure was likely to be prejudicial to the investigation. Section 53(7) gives constables and others exemption from liability in respect of anything done in the course of acting in connection with the enforcement, or intended enforcement, of any provisions of the Act relating to drug trafficking or the proceeds of drug trafficking. Section 53(4) provides a similar exemption in relation to matters subject to legal professional privilege to that provided by s 52.

(6) Tipping off under the CJA 1988

27.98 A similar offence of tipping off is created by s 93D of the CJA 1988 (as added by s 32 of the CJA 1993) in respect of investigations into the laundering of the proceeds of criminal offences other than those relating to drug trafficking:

93D—
(1) A person is guilty of an offence if—
   (a) he knows or suspects that a constable is acting, or is proposing to act, in connection with an investigation which is being, or is about to be, conducted into money laundering; and
   (b) he discloses to any other person information or any other material which is likely to prejudice that investigation, or proposed investigation.
(2) A person is guilty of an offence if—
   (a) he knows or suspects that 'the disclosure' has been made to a constable under Section 93A or 93B above; and
   (b) he discloses to any other person information or any other matter which is likely to prejudice any investigation which might be considered following the disclosure.
(3) A person is guilty of an offence if—
   (a) he knows or suspects that a disclosure of a kind mentioned in Section 93A(5) or 93B(8) ('the disclosure') has been made; and
   (b) he discloses to any person information or any other matter which is likely to prejudice any investigation which might be conducted following the disclosure.

27.99 In proceedings against a person for an offence under s 93D(1), (2), or (3), it is for the defence to prove that he did not know or suspect that disclosure was likely to be prejudicial in the way mentioned in the relevant subsection (see s 93D(6).

27.100 In *A Bank v A Ltd (Serious Fraud Office, Interested Party)*, The Times, 18 July 2000 (first instance), Laddie J held that a bank does not become a constructive trustee of money deposited with it merely because it entertains suspicions as to the provenance of the money. If a bank, being aware that a money laundering investigation was being conducted into the affairs of its customers, made an ex parte application for an order freezing the customer's funds on deposit with itself, such order should not be made if the effect of the tipping off legislation (s 93D of the CJA) would be to prevent the order, skeleton arguments, witness statements, or transcripts from being disclosed to the respondent. The Court held that it was a fundamental principle that no-one should be tried or deprived of his property without being told of the claims against him and having the opportunity to be heard, and the court should protect the rights and interests not only of those who were innocent, but also of those not proved to be guilty. The bank appealed Laddie J's decision.

F. Disclosure of Suspicious Transactions under the DTA

The Court of Appeal (reported as *BS v A* [2001] 1 WLR 751) considered a situation where the police informed the bank that money laundering investigations were being conducted into activities closely associated with one of its customers, in consequence of which the bank was put in a dilemma: if it paid out, it might be liable to third parties as a constructive trustee, whereas if it did not, an action could be brought against the bank and it would be unable to defend itself because the police would object to the bank revealing what it had been told. The Court held that the question of what information could be revealed should have been capable of agreement between the bank, the police, and the Serious Fraud Office (SFO). Failing such agreement, the appropriate remedy was not to seek an ex parte order freezing the customer's account, but to seek an interim declaration under the Civil Procedure Rules 1998 r 25.1(1)(b). **27.101**

In such an application the SFO would be the defendant and the court could set out what information it would be proper for the bank to rely on. The making of the application would protect the bank from criminal proceedings. In *BS v A* it was also held that the ability of the court to give directions would ensure that banks were not adversely affected by the 'tipping off legislation' which gave extensive powers to the police, it being of the greatest importance that those powers were only used in situations where it was appropriate. The Court of Appeal added that the powers of the court were discretionary and an application should only be made where there was a real dilemma requiring the court's intervention: the making of an application should not be regarded as a substitute for a decision within the area of the bank's commercial responsibility. **27.102**

(7) Penalties

Offences of failing to disclose knowledge or suspicion of money laundering and tipping off are punishable on indictment with a maximum penalty of five years' imprisonment and an unlimited fine or, on summary conviction, with six months imprisonment and a fine up to the statutory maximum (see s 54(2) of the DTA and s 93D(9) of the CJA). **27.103**

28

COSTS AND COMPENSATION

A. Introduction	28.01	(19) *Capewell*: conclusion	28.56
(1) Costs and compensation distinguished	28.03	(20) Receiver's costs: Crown Court	28.59
B. Costs		(21) Release of restrained funds to cover legal expenses under the DTA and CJA	28.60
(1) Costs: High Court/civil cases	28.04	(22) Legal expenses and third parties	28.70
(2) Court's discretion and circumstances to be taken into account when exercising its discretion as to costs	28.06	(23) Release of restrained funds to cover legal expenses under POCA	28.71
		C. Compensation	28.78
(3) Basis of assessment	28.07	(1) Compensation for the acquitted defendant under the DTA and CJA	28.78
(4) Factors to be taken into account in deciding the amount of costs	28.09	(2) Other conditions	28.80
(5) Interim costs orders	28.10	(3) Compensation for third parties	28.81
(6) Costs: Crown Court	28.13	(4) How much compensation and by whom is it paid?	28.83
(7) The power of the magistrates' court to order costs	28.15	(5) Procedure on applications	28.84
(8) The acquitted defendant and costs	28.22	(6) Compensation for the acquitted defendant under POCA 2002	28.85
(9) Orders for the payment of costs in confiscation order cases	28.23	(7) When a confiscation order is varied or discharged under POCA	28.91
(10) Confiscation orders: prosecution costs	28.24	(8) Other powers to order compensation under POCA	28.93
(11) Costs of receivers	28.26	(9) Compensation in relation to interim receiving orders and property freezing orders	28.96
(12) Receiver's costs in litigation	28.29		
(13) Payment of receiver's costs: High Court	28.34		
(14) Civil Procedure Rules 69	28.36	(10) Compensation for recovery of cash in summary proceedings	28.99
(15) The judgment in *Capewell*	28.43		
(16) Remuneration, not expenses	28.46	(11) Compensation and the victims of crime	28.103
(17) *Capewell*: analysis	28.48		
(18) Indemnities	28.55		

A. Introduction

Restraint orders are made when the High Court, and now under POCA the Crown Court, **28.01** is satisfied that there is reasonable cause to believe that the defendant has benefited from the criminal activity with which he is charged. When the case comes to trial, however, the jury has to be satisfied of the defendant's guilt beyond reasonable doubt in order to record the conviction that is an essential prerequisite to a confiscation order being made. Sometimes a defendant who has been subject to a restraint order for a substantial period of time will be acquitted.

Then the restraint order will promptly be discharged, but he may have incurred costs in defending the High Court or Crown Court proceedings and, together with other parties holding realisable property, have suffered loss in complying with the terms of the restraint order.

28.02 The purpose of this chapter is to consider the rights of the defendant to seek costs and compensation against the prosecuting authority. We have divided it into two parts, the first dealing with issues relating to costs, including legal fees; the second dealing with compensation for the acquitted defendant, and the powers to award compensation under POCA. There has necessarily been some overlap from other chapters to give the reader a complete overview of the costs and compensation regime under asset forfeiture law. We are acutely aware that many dealing with this area of law for the first time will be criminal practitioners who are perhaps unfamiliar with civil procedure. With that in mind we have included some reference to the Civil Procedure Rules (CPR) and interim costs orders, although detailed consideration of the same is beyond the ambit of this book.

(1) Costs and compensation distinguished

28.03 It is important to appreciate the distinction between an order for costs and an order for compensation. An order for costs is confined to ordering the payment of legal costs incurred by the defendant in restraint order proceedings, which may extend to related contempt or receivership hearings, but does not extend to any other costs or expenses he may incur as a result of the order. An order for compensation on the other hand seeks not to recompense the defendant for legal costs, but to compensate him for any loss he has suffered as a result of complying with the order. Persons other than the defendant who hold realisable property may seek a compensation order.

B. Costs

(1) Costs: High Court/civil cases

28.04 The general rule, as in all civil cases, is that costs follow the event, ie the acquitted defendant is entitled to have his costs of the restraint order proceedings paid by the prosecutor, there being no power to direct their payment from central funds (see *Re W (Drug Trafficking) (Restraint Order: Costs)* The Times, 13 October 1994). The question of costs remains a matter of discretion and where it can be shown that the defendant has behaved in such a way as to bring the proceedings upon himself, he can properly be left to pay his own costs.

28.05 If, of course, the defendant makes an unmeritorious application to either the High Court or the Crown Court in restraint proceedings (eg for a variation of the order) he can properly be ordered to bear not only his own costs, but also those of the prosecution, in respect of that one application.

(2) Court's discretion and circumstances to be taken into account when exercising its discretion as to costs

28.06 Rule 44.3 of the CPR 1998 reads as follows:

(1) The court had discretion as to—
   (a) whether the costs are payable by one party to another;

(b) the amount of those costs; and
(c) when they are to be made.
(2) If the court decides to make an order about costs—
    (a) the general rule is that the unsuccessful party will be ordered to pay the costs of the successful party; but
    (b) the court may make a different order.
(3) ...
(4) In deciding what order (if any) to make about costs, the court must have regard to all the circumstances, including
    (a) the conduct of the party;
    (b) whether a party has succeeded on part of his case, even if he has not been wholly successful; and
    (c) any payment into court or admissible offers to settle made by a party which is drawn to the court's attention (whether or not made in accordance with Part 36).
(5) The conduct of the parties includes—
    (a) conduct before, as well as during, the proceedings, and in particular the extent to which the parties followed any relevant pre-action protocol;
    (b) whether it was reasonable for a party to raise, pursue or contest a particular allegation or issue;
    (c) the manner in which a party has pursued or defended his case or a particular allegation or issue;
    (d) whether a claimant who has succeeded in his claim, in whole or in part, exaggerated his claim.
(6) The orders which the court may make under this rule include an order that a party must pay—
    (a) the proportion of another party's costs;
    (b) a stated amount in respect of another party's costs;
    (c) costs from or until a certain date only;
    (d) costs incurred before proceedings have begun;
    (e) costs relating to particular steps taken in the proceedings;
    (f) costs relating only to a distinct part of the proceedings; and
    (g) interest on costs from or until a certain date including a date before judgment.
(7) ...
(8) Where the court has ordered a party to pay the costs, it may order an amount to be paid on account before the costs are assessed.

(3) Basis of assessment

28.07 Under r 44.4 of the CPR, where the court is to assess the amounts of costs (whether by summary or detailed assessment) it will assess those costs either on the standard basis, or on an indemnity basis, but the court will not in either case allow costs which have been unreasonably incurred or are unreasonable in amount.

28.08 Where the amount of costs is to be assessed on the standard basis, the court will:

(a) only allow costs which are proportionate to the matters in issue; and

(b) resolve any doubt that it may have as to whether costs were reasonably incurred or reasonable and proportionate in an amount in favour of the paying party.

(4) Factors to be taken into account in deciding the amount of costs

28.09 Rule 44.5 of the CPR states:

(1) The court is to have regard to all the circumstances in deciding whether costs were—
   (a) if it is assessing costs on the standard basis—
      (i) proportionately and reasonably incurred; or
      (ii) were proportionate and reasonable in amount, or
   (b) if it is assessing costs on the indemnity basis—
      (i) unreasonably incurred; or
      (ii) unreasonable in amount.
(2) . . .
(3) The court must also have regard to—
   (a) the conduct of all the parties including in particular:
      (i) conduct before as well as during the proceedings, and
      (ii) the efforts made, if any, before and during the proceedings in order to try and resolve the dispute;
   (b) the amount or value of any money or property involved;
   (c) the importance of the matter to all the parties;
   (d) the particular complexity of the matter or the difficulty or novelty of the question raised;
   (e) the skill, effort, specialised knowledge and responsibility involved;
   (f) the time spent on the case; and
   (g) the place where and the circumstances in which work or any part of it was done.

(5) Interim costs orders

28.10 Most orders will include a provision for costs. Where the court makes an order that does not mention costs, the general rule is that no party is entitled to costs in relation to that order (see r 44.13(1)(a) CPR).

28.11 The Costs Practice Direction that supplements the Civil Procedure Rules sets out the meanings of common interim costs orders (see s 8):

(1) Costs in any event or simply 'costs': the party in whose favour the order is made is entitled to the costs in respect of the part of the proceedings to which the order relates, whatever other costs orders are made in the proceedings.
(2) Costs in the case, or costs in the application: the party in whose favour the court makes an order for costs at the end of the proceedings is entitled to his costs of the part of the proceedings to which the order relates.
(3) Costs deferred: the decision about costs is deferred to a later occasion, but if no later order is made the costs will be 'costs in the case'.

(4) Claimant's/defendant's costs in the case at application: if the party in whose favour the costs order is made is awarded costs at the end of the proceedings, that party is entitled to his costs of the part of the proceedings to which the order relates. If any other party is awarded costs at the end of the proceedings, the party in whose favour the final costs order is made is not liable to pay the costs of any other party in respect of the part of the proceedings to which the order relates.

(5) Costs thrown away: where, eg a judgment or order is set aside, the party in whose favour the costs order is made is entitled to the costs that have been incurred as a consequence. This includes the costs of:
  (a) preparing for and attending any hearing at which the judgment order which has been set aside has been made;
  (b) preparing for and attending any hearing to set aside the judgement or order in question;
  (c) preparing for and attending any hearing at which the court orders the proceedings or the part in question to be adjourned;
  (d) any steps taken to enforce a judgment or order which has subsequently been set aside.

(6) Costs of and caused by: where eg the court makes an order on an application to amend a statement of case, the party in whose favour the costs order is made is entitled to the costs of preparing for and attending the application and the costs of any consequential amendment to his own statement of case.

(7) Costs here and below: the party in whose favour the costs order is made is entitled not only to his costs in respect of the proceedings in which the court makes the order but also his costs in the proceedings in any lower court. In the case of an appeal from a divisional court the party is not entitled to any costs incurred in any court below the divisional court.

(8) No order as to costs or each party to pay his own costs: each party is to pay his own costs of the part of the proceedings to which the order relates whatever costs order the court makes at the end of the proceedings.

(9) Where, under r 44.3(8), the court orders an amount to be paid before the costs are assessed:
  (a) the order will state that amount, and
  (b) if no other date for payment is specified in the order r 44.8 (Time for Complying with an Order for Costs) will apply.

Two further costs order are:

(10) Costs in the receivership: such a costs order implies that the costs of the application will be borne as part of the receivership, ie the receiver will be entitled to claim the costs of the hearing and related legal expenses out of the receivership funds which they manage or control. Where an issue remains over the amount to be paid these costs will be expressed as 'Costs in the receivership, subject to taxation'.

(11) Costs not to be enforced without further leave of the court or 'It is further ordered that the costs of this claim be paid by the claimant/defendant, but the determination of the claimant's/defendant's liability to pay such costs shall be postponed pending further order'. Sometimes referred to as the 'pools coupon' order, it is primarily designed to deal

with legally aided claimant's/defendant's who lose an application or matter. The order for costs anticipates that should, at some future point, the claimant/defendant come into funds, then the successful party would be at liberty to get the matter restored and seek their litigation costs.

Appendix 6 of this book sets out where LSC funding is available in restraint and confiscation matters.

28.12 Further comments about costs are beyond the scope of this work. However Pts 43–48 of the CPR deal fully with applications for costs and related procedure. These rules are supplemented by a High Court Practice Direction on costs (PD) that sets out the scope of the costs rules and definitions. The background information to be included in a bill of costs is set out at paras 4.5 and 4.6 of the PD. Under para 12.2, an order for costs will be treated as an order to be decided by detailed assessment unless the order provides otherwise or states that fixed costs are to be paid. Detailed assessments generally take place once proceedings are concluded. There is generally no longer any need for a certificate for counsel unless the court is asked to state an opinion as to whether or not the hearing was fit for representation for one or more counsel (see para 8.7 of the PD).

(6) Costs: Crown Court

28.13 The power of the Crown Court to award costs in restraint and receivership proceedings is now contained within the Criminal Procedure Rules.

Rule 61.20 states:

(1) Where the Crown Court has made an order for costs in restraint proceedings or receivership proceedings it may either—
  (a) make an assessment of the costs itself; or
  (b) order assessment of the costs under rule 78.3.
(2) In either case, the Crown Court or the taxing authority, as the case may be, must—
  (a) only allow costs which are proportionate to the matters in issue; and
  (b) resolve any doubt which it may have as to whether the costs were reasonably incurred or reasonable and proportionate in favour of the paying party.

Rule 61.21 states, in relation to the time allowed for complying with an order for costs:

(1) A party to restraint proceedings or receivership proceedings must comply with an order for the payment of costs within 14 days of—
  (a) the date of the order if it states the amount of those costs;
  (b) if the amount of those costs is decided later under rule 78.3, the date of the taxing authority's decision; or
  (c) in either case, such later date as the Crown Court may specify.

28.14 Rule 61.20(5) of the Criminal Procedure Rules states that the court must have particular regard to:

(a) the conduct of all the parties, including in particular, conduct before, as well as during, the proceedings;
(b) the amount or value of the property involved;
(c) the importance of the matter to all the parties;
(d) the particular complexity of the matter or the difficulty or novelty of the questions raised;
(e) the skill, effort, specialised knowledge and responsibility involved;

(f) the time spent on the application; and
(g) the place where and the circumstances in which work or any part of it was done.

Costs in the Crown Court generally are dealt with at r 76 of the Criminal Procedure Rules (representation orders); r 77 of the Criminal Procedure Rules (recovery of defence costs orders); and r 78 of the Criminal Procedure Rules (costs ordered against the parties).

(7) The power of the magistrates' court to order costs

28.15 The power of magistrates to award costs on the hearing of a complaint is contained in s 64 of the Magistrates' Courts Act 1980:

> On the hearing of a complaint, a Magistrates' Court shall have the power in its discretion to make such order as to costs:
> (a) on making the order for which the complaint is made, to be paid by the Defendant to the Complainant;
> (b) on dismissing the complaint, to be paid by the complainant to the Defendant, as it thinks just and reasonable . . .

Under s 64(2) the amount of any sum ordered to be paid under s 64 (1) above shall be specified in the order, or order of dismissal, as the case may be. The costs ordered to be paid under this section shall be enforceable as a civil debt (s 64(3)).

28.16 Clearly the sum ordered should not be in excess of the proper costs incurred, nor should it be a penalty in the guise of costs (see *R v Highgate Justices ex p Petrou* [1954] 1 All ER 406).

28.17 The amount of the costs must be fixed by the courts 'as part of the adjudication' (*R v Pwllheli Justices ex p Soane* [1948] 2 All ER 815) and may include the expenses of the claimant's witnesses, as well as the fee of his solicitor. It follows that the same justices who reached the decision on hearing the complaint must make the award for costs.

28.18 An award for costs made by the magistrates' court under s 64 is not enforceable by the magistrates' court, but in effect becomes a civil debt enforceable by the successful party on application to the county court.

28.19 Under s 52 of the Courts Act 1971 magistrates are entitled to award costs where an information or complaint has not been proceeded with (s 52(3)(b)). Where a complaint is not proceeded with, a magistrates' court may make such order as to costs to be paid by the complainant to the defendant as it thinks is just and reasonable.

28.20 The power to award costs is limited to making an order as to the costs of proceedings on the complaint in question and does not give authority to award costs which may have been incurred in other proceedings. For example, the power to award costs in a forfeiture application would only relate to the costs and hearings which occurred after the lodging of the application for forfeiture. It would not extend to the continued detention hearing that had taken place prior to the application for forfeiture. Each continued detention hearing is a separate application supported by an information in its own right, and costs should be applied for and dealt with at the time of the continued detention hearing (see *R v Magistrates' Court at Dover ex p Customs and Excise Commissioners* (1995) 160 JP 233).

28.21 There is no right to appeal to the Crown Court against a costs order by the magistrates (see *R v Crown Court at Lewis ex p Rogers* [1974] 1 All ER 589).

(8) The acquitted defendant and costs

28.22 In deciding whether the acquitted defendant has brought the proceedings and related hearings upon himself, the High Court and now the Crown Court will no doubt be influenced by the manner in which the defendant has conducted his defence, in particular if the circumstances that led to the defendant's acquittal could have been raised by the defendant at an earlier stage of proceedings. In DTA and CJA restraint cases in the High Court, the judge is likely to be influenced by the findings of the judge below. If the Crown Court judge, having heard all the evidence during a lengthy trial, forms the view that it is appropriate to award the acquitted defendant his costs from central funds, it is unlikely that the High Court would take the view that the defendant should bear the entire costs of the restraint order proceedings.

(9) Orders for the payment of costs in confiscation order cases

28.23 Orders for the payment of costs should only be made where the defendant has the ability to pay them following a confiscation hearing. If a confiscation order is made in what the court finds to be the full value of the defendant's realisable property, no order for costs should be made. In *R v Szrajber* [1994] Crim LR 543 the defendant's benefit from the offences was found to be £524,000, but his realisable property was valued at £407,188 and a confiscation order accordingly made in this lesser sum. In addition, an order for the payment of costs was made in the sum of £65,428. The Court of Appeal quashed the order for costs on the basis that a confiscation order had been made in the full amount of the defendant's benefit from the offence, and accordingly he had no further assets at his disposal from which the order for costs could be made.

(10) Confiscation orders: prosecution costs

28.24 In *R v Ghadami* [1997] Crim LR 606 the Court of Appeal held that when it came to considering the question of an order to pay the costs of the prosecution, other debts should be taken into account, (eg a confiscation order). It could then be seen if the appellant was a man without assets. On that basis, in *Ghadami,* the order to pay the costs of the prosecution was quashed.

28.25 In *R v Smart* (2003) 2 Cr App R(S) 384, the Court determined that where a judge, having passed sentence, adjourned the proceedings in contemplation of a confiscation hearing and subsequently said he was reserving the question of costs until the issue of confiscation had been decided, he was exercising his lawful power to postpone part of the sentence, and the fact that he subsequently decided that there could be no confiscation proceedings because of a failure to meet the statutory pre-conditions for such, did not deprive him of his power to award costs.

(11) Costs of receivers

28.26 As with all questions of costs, it is a matter for the discretion of the court as to whether these should be met by the defendant. In most cases, costs will follow the event and the defendant

B. Costs

will be required to pay. It is common for the court to order that the costs of the receiver (and, indeed, the prosecutor) be 'Costs in the receivership'—that is to say, met out of the sums realised by the receiver. This empowers the receiver to realise sufficient assets to pay the confiscation order, his costs, and those of the prosecutor. In most cases, the receiver will assess his fees on a time cost basis in accordance with the grade and experience of the fee earner employed.

There may be cases in which the defendant considers that the fees charged are excessive. The defendant's interests can be adversely affected by a large bill from a receiver; if he has assets available, they will usually be realised in addition to those necessary to satisfy the confiscation order. If no such assets are available, the receiver's costs will normally be met out of the assets that have been realised in satisfaction of the confiscation order. The effect of this is that the amount of money available from the proceeds of realisation to meet the confiscation order will be reduced, rendering the defendant vulnerable to serve a portion of the default sentence imposed for non-payment, unless a certificate of inadequacy is sought. **28.27**

One of the remedies for the aggrieved defendant is to seek an order from the court that the proper remuneration of the receiver be assessed by a costs or district judge. The defendant should not, however, embark upon this course unless satisfied that he has a reasonable prospect of reducing the receiver's charges substantially, because an unsuccessful application is likely to result in a further award of costs against him. The defendant would therefore be well advised to obtain expert evidence (preferably from a licensed insolvency practitioner) before seeking an order for taxation. **28.28**

(12) Receiver's costs in litigation

Often a court appointed receiver will become embroiled in litigation as a third party and sometimes by default. Costs are often said to be 'in the receivership' when either the prosecuting authority or the receiver is successful in litigation, although this expression is rarely, if ever, properly defined. The receiver will often have costs beyond merely instructing solicitors and counsel, they also have to incur costs in preparing witness statements and time in conference, giving instructions etc. Costs have often been awarded 'in the receivership' even when the receiver has been unsuccessful in litigation and this once again gives rise to the question as to who truly should bear those costs. In *Re Nossen's Letter Patent* [1969] 1 WLR 683, Lloyd-Jacob J stated that the established practice of the courts was to disallow any sums claimed in respect of the time spent by the litigant personally in the course of instructing his solicitors, but that, in the case of litigation by a corporation, that practice had not been strictly applied, it being recognised that, if expert assistance is properly required, it may well occur that the corporation's own specialist employees may be the most suitable or convenient experts to employ and that the direct costs incurred, but not a contribution to overheads, should, in principle, be recoverable. He expressed (at p 644) his conclusion this way: **28.29**

> When it is appropriate that a corporate litigant should recover, on a party and party basis, the sum in respect of expert services of this character performed by its own staff, the amount must be restricted to a reasonable sum for the actual and direct costs of the work undertaken.

28.30 In *London Scottish Benefit Society v Chorley* (1884) 12 QBD 452; 13 QBD 872 (CA), Sir Gordon Willmer went further and stated that the professional skill can be measured and recognised by law. In his judgment at pp 37–38, he said that costs are '*intended to cover remuneration for the exercise of professional legal skill*'. In relation to other skills he said:

> Other professional people, who become involved in litigation and conduct their own case, may recover something in respect of their own professional skill in so far as they qualify as witnesses and are called as such. Nobody else, however, except a solicitor, has even been held entitled to make any charge, as I understand it, in respect of the exercise of a professional legal skill . . . .

28.31 In *Sisu Capital Fund Ltd v Tucker and Wallace* [2005] EWHC 2321 (Ch), Warren J accepted that there may be cases where, in the fulfilment of his duties as an office holder, a receiver has to bring or defend litigation:

> The fact that he does so does not mean that it is part of his profession to conduct litigation in the way that it is part of the profession of a solicitor to do so. An office holder is not unique in this respect: trustees of family trusts or of pension funds have fiduciary duties, the fulfilment of which may required them to bring or defend proceedings. That sort of duty on the part of an office holder or other fiduciary does not, in my judgement, afford any basis for a difference in treatment, vis-à-vis payment of costs by an opposing party, from any other litigant.

(Paragraph 40 of the judgment.)

28.32 Nor in his Lordship's judgment did the fact that an office holder's remuneration was ultimately under the control of the insolvency court make any difference to the result. The real reason he was not able to recover his costs was because he was not a professional seeking to recover costs for time spent in respect of his area of expertise.

28.33 It therefore appears that if a receiver has costs that are incurred doing work as an expert as part of the litigation (for which, if he was not in office, an expert would have to be employed to carry them out) then those costs are recoverable out of the costs award/the receivership estate.

(13) Payment of receiver's costs: High Court

28.34 In *Capewell v Customs and Excise Commissioners* [2005] EWCA Civ 964, the Court of Appeal departed from the historic jurisprudence that maintained that a receiver's costs should be drawn from the estate that they managed. For example, in *Hughes v Customs and Excise Commissioners* [2003] 1 WLR 177, it was held that, in the absence of any special statutory rules, the receiver appointed under the CJA was to be treated in the same way as his common law counterpart appointed under order of the court. It followed that a receiver was in principle entitled to recover his costs from the assets under his control, even where there had been no conviction and no confiscation order had yet been made. In *Hughes* the Court had followed the decision of the Court of Appeal in *Re Andrews* [1999] 1 WLR 1236. In that case, the defendant and his son had been charged with offences relating to their joint business, and restraint orders had been made. The son was convicted, but the defendant was acquitted and awarded his costs out of central funds. The taxing officer held that such costs did not include the costs of the receivership (amounting to some £10,000). The receiver sought to recover those costs out of the assets under her control. The defendant applied for an order that they be paid by the prosecutor. That application failed. The Court felt bound to apply the established common-law practice that the costs of a court appointed receiver were paid out of realised assets, following *Boehm v Goodall* [1911] 1 Ch 155, at pp 161-162, where Warrington J stated:

> 'I think it is of the utmost importance that receivers and managers in this position should know that they must look for their indemnity to the assets which are under the control of the Court. The Court itself cannot indemnify receivers, but it can, and will, do so out of the assets so far as they extend, for expenses properly incurred; but it cannot go further.'

28.35 The Court in *Andrews* held that its discretion in relation to 'the costs of and incidental to proceedings in the High Court' (Supreme Court Act 1981 s 51) did not extend to the costs of a receivership. Ward LJ said that he reached this conclusion with 'unfeigned reluctance', because it was 'manifestly unfair' that the defendant, having been paid his trial costs out of public funds, should not be indemnified for the loss caused by the ancillary receivership proceedings (pp 1244B - 1246H).

(14) Civil Procedure Rules 69

28.36 Both *Andrews* and *Hughes* were decided under the Rules of the Supreme Court, where the provision dealing specifically with court appointed receiver's remuneration was set out in Ord 30 r 3. This provided that a receiver 'shall be allowed such proper remuneration if any as may be authorised by the court'.

28.37 That rule was replaced by r 69.7 CPR (which applies from December 2002). Part 69 and the corresponding Practice Direction provide (in the words of the White Book):

> ... a comprehensive procedural code dealing with appointment by the court of receivers and managers including provisions relating to their application for appointment, evidence required on such applications, security and remuneration.

28.38 Rule 69.7 is headed 'Receiver's Remuneration'. It provides that a receiver may only charge for his services if the court so directs and specifies the basis on which he needs to be remunerated. Rule 69.7(2) provides:

> ... The court may specify—(a) who is to be responsible for paying the receiver; and (b) the fund or property from which the receiver is to recover his remuneration.

28.39 Paragraph 4 provides that the court is to award 'such sum as is reasonable and proportionate in all the circumstances', and sets out the factors which are to be taken into account.

28.40 Paragraph 9 of the Practice Direction which accompanies CPR 69 confirms (at para 9.2) that the court will normally determine the amount of the receiver's remuneration in accordance with the criteria set out in r 69.7(4) and adds, 'Parts 43-48 (Costs) do not apply to the determination of the remuneration of the receiver'.

28.41 Paragraphs 9.4-5 of the same Practice Direction set out procedural provisions relating to the determination of the amount of the receiver's remuneration. Paragraph 9.6 provides:

> Paragraphs 9.1 to 9.5 do not apply to expenses incurred by the receiver in carrying out his functions. These are accounted for as part of his account of the assets he has recovered, and not dealt with as part of the determination of his remuneration.

28.42 The detailed provisions for controlling the level of a receiver's remuneration appear to stem from the report of a working party under Ferris J in 1998, which was set up in response to apparent public concern at the levels of remuneration and legal fees paid in insolvency cases. The Court of Appeal in *Capewell* found that r 69.7(2) CPR appeared to go beyond the scope of that report, since it enabled the court, not merely to control the amount of remuneration, but to determine who is to be responsible for payment, (see para13 of the judgment). In so finding it cast into question whether *Hughes* and *Andrews* could still be considered good law in CPR 69 receivership cases.

(15) The judgment in Capewell

28.43 The Court in *Capewell* found that on its face, r 69.7(2) gave the court a much wider discretion than under the previous RSC 30 (as applied in *Andrews* and *Hughes*). In *Capewell* the Court of Appeal had determined in a previous judgment ([2004] EWCA Civ 1628), that the receivership in question should have come to an end on 1 June 2004. The issue therefore arose as to who should pay the remuneration and expenses of the receiver after that date, the receivership having run until October before it was discharged by consent. The Court concluded that *'Justice would seem to require that they should not come out of Mr. Capewell's assets, but should be borne by Customs. The question is whether we have power to achieve that result.'*

28.44 The Court of Appeal found that on the face of it, r 69.7(2) gave the court an unlimited discretion in respect of a receiver's remuneration. They reined back from this position by stating that they were not prepared to assume that the rule was intended to make a radical change from the previous practice under RSC 30 without more detailed information as to the background that led to the rule change (para 23). Nevertheless, Carnwath LJ giving the judgment of the Court, stated that the new Rules were clearly designed to give the court some discretion in the matter, at least in special circumstances where application of the ordinary rule would cause unfairness or hardship.

28.45 As a result they ordered that Customs should bear the receiver's costs from 1 June 2004.

(16) Remuneration, not expenses

28.46 The Court in *Capewell* went on to hold that r 69.7 was dealing with the 'remuneration' of the receiver. In ordinary language, they commented that that would not include his expenses. The Court held that although r 69.7(2)(a) refers simply to responsibility for 'paying the receiver', which in a different context might include payment of expenses, it was not possible to read that into the relevant subparagraph.

28.47 The Practice Direction confirms that the distinction between remuneration and expenses is deliberate. Ordinarily, the Court stated, one would expect the same person to be responsible for paying both remuneration and expenses, however Carnwath LJ stated he did not think that he could properly stretch the language of the rule beyond its natural meaning. Accordingly, the Court ordered that the expenses should be met from the realisable assets in the ordinary way.

(17) Capewell: analysis

28.48 The judgment in *Capewell* signified an important departure from the way in which receivers were to be remunerated. Longmore LJ, while agreeing with the judgment, emphasised the importance that courts keep a close control over those it appoints to act as receivers on its behalf and that costs are not too readily incurred, particularly before any confiscation order is made (quoting from Simon Brown LJ in *Hughes v Customs and Excise Commissioners* [2003] 1 WLR 177). He commented that it was only by making, in appropriate cases, orders of the kind that the Court of Appeal did in *Capewell*, that courts can exercise the sort of control envisaged by Simon Brown LJ in *Hughes*.

28.49 The decision of the Court of Appeal in *Capewell* has received a mixed reception. On one view it has been argued that the plain intention of the confiscation legislation was that a receiver's remuneration should be met out of the proceeds of the confiscation order, and if no confiscation order were made, either because of an acquittal or because no proceedings were instituted, then the remuneration should fall to be paid by the prosecutor or the person on whose application the receiver was appointed. Similarly it has been submitted that the decisions in *Hughes* and *Andrews* led to injustice in terms of acquitted defendants having to pay enormous receivership bills while they awaited trials. Conversely, it has been argued that the decision in *Capewell* overlooks important public policy arguments, the effect of the statutory schemes and Parliament's intention. Not only does it represent a departure from earlier decisions, but also it introduces an uncertainty in receivers' remuneration (in relation to those appointed by the High Court), in that the parties will not know who is to be responsible for paying the receiver until the matter is considered ex post facto. This position is to be contrasted with the position under the Proceeds of Crime Act 2002, which enables receivership orders to be made in respect of offences committed after 23 March 2003. Under the 2002 Act the receiver must receive his remuneration from the assets under his control. Thus, the effect of the Court of Appeal judgment in *Capewell* is to create a two-tier structure for receiver's remuneration: one for orders made under the 2002 Act and one for orders made under the 1988 Act and the 1994 Act.

28.50 This unsatisfactory situation is likely to be compounded in receivership cases that begin in the Crown Court, but which are subsequently transferred to the High Court, eg where it is discovered that the offences under consideration were committed before 23 March 2003. Similarly, a two-tier structure is likely to develop in the High Court itself. Receivers appointed under the 2002 Act in relation to interim receiving orders will, under the Serious and Organised Crime and Police Act 2005, have to draw their remuneration from assets from within the receivership estate.

28.51 The uncertainty as to whether prosecuting authorities or the defendant's assets will bear the receiver's costs in cases under the 1988 Act or the 1994 Act will have certain public policy ramifications.

28.52 As the Court of Appeal recognised in its judgment in the substantive appeal, the use of management receivers is a vital tool in the court's ability to restrain and preserve the value of realisable property. The existence of uncertainty as to whether the prosecuting authority will be required to bear the costs of the receiver is likely to deter applications for receivership orders and this in turn may have a detrimental affect on the fight against financially motivated crime.

28.53 Moreover, it may be argued that the retrospective element of the Court of Appeal judgment is likely to cause further unfairness.

28.54 The Court of Appeal's judgment has the scope to generate collateral litigation. The Court did has not attempt to define 'special circumstances' other than unfairness and hardship (which themselves are not defined) and it is therefore likely that defendants may wish to make applications for prosecuting authorities to pay the receiver's costs in cases where the Crown offers no evidence; the receivership comes to an end by consent; the defendant is acquitted; or where the receivership is discharged for other reasons. Courts will also be alive to the possibility that defendants may look to construct reasons for discharge in an attempt to pass the costs on to the prosecuting authority. The House of Lords are shortly due to rule on the *Capewell* judgment which should clarify a number of these issues.

(18) Indemnities

28.55 While prosecuting authorities have in the past offered an indemnity to receivers in circumstances where the assets within the receivership estate are insufficient to meet the receivers costs, that indemnity has always been a private contractual arrangement between the prosecutor and the receiver, which only has application if the defendant no longer has any assets from which the receiver may draw. It is therefore questionable whether Customs or a prosecutor has any liability to the receiver beyond that arrangement.

(19) Capewell: *conclusion*

28.56 While the Court of Appeal in *Capewell* suggest that it is only by making, in appropriate cases, orders of this kind that the courts can exercise a close control over those it appoints, it is not immediately clear why other methods of control such as regular reporting, regular directions/reviews, scrutiny on appointment etc, would not go in some way to fulfil this requirement of close control. Arguably, as a result of the *Capewell* judgment, the close control and policing of the court appointed receiver is more likely to be overseen by the prosecuting authority, who stand to lose the most financially in circumstances where a lower court's decision is overturned on appeal. This, it is submitted, does not necessarily sit comfortably with the independent and impartial role a receiver is expected to perform.

28.57 The decision in *Capewell* has been appealed to the House of Lords and a decision is due in early 2007. (A summary of the House of Lords judgment is at Appendix 23.)

28.58 Because of the introduction of POCA and the corresponding rules which dictate that under POCA a receiver's remuneration must come from the assets within the receivership estate, whatever their Lordships' decision, the effect of *Capewell* is likely to be relatively short-lived, bearing in mind that the CJA and DTA will gradually become more out of date as the new Act becomes fully introduced.

(20) Receiver's costs: Crown Court

28.59 The position in the Crown Court refelects the common law rules established in *Andrews* and *Hughes*, namely for POCA receiverships the receiver must look to the assets within his control for his remuneration. Rule 60.6(5) of the Criminal Procedure Rules states:

(5) A receiver appointed under section 48 of the 2002 Act is to receive his remuneration by realising property in respect of which he is appointed, in accordance with section 49(2)(d) of the 2002 Act.

Rules 60.6 (6) and (7) state:

(6) A receiver appointed under section 50 of the 2002 Act is to receive his remuneration by applying to the magistrates' court officer for payment under section 55(4)(b) of the 2002 Act.

(7) A receiver appointed under section 52 of the 2002 Act is to receive his remuneration by applying to the Director for payment under section 57(4)(b) of the 2002 Act.

(21) Release of restrained funds to cover legal expenses under the DTA and CJA

28.60 Most restraint orders contain provision for a defendant to spend money on legal expenses actually, reasonably, and properly incurred in the restraint proceedings and the related criminal proceedings provided that, before any monies are released for this purpose the defendant notifies the prosecuting authority in writing of the following matters:

(a) the source of the fund to be used to pay the said costs;
(b) the general nature of the costs incurred;
(c) the time spent and by whom in incurring the said costs;
(d) the hourly rate applicable to the costs incurred.

28.61 In the event the prosecuting authority considers the claim to be in respect of costs that have not actually, reasonably, or properly been incurred then the entitlement to draw such costs is usually restricted to 65 per cent of the amount claimed, and the whole claim for costs is then subject to detailed assessment on an indemnity basis in accordance with Pt 48 CPR (but without the provisions of s 48.8(2)(a) and (b) applying).

28.62 One of the difficulties that has arisen under the DTA and the CJA with the above provision is where a defendant wishes to draw upon restrained funds in preference to claiming Legal Service Commission funding (formerly legal aid). In principle a defendant may draw upon restrained funds to pay reasonable legal costs (see RSC 115 r 4(1) and *Re Peters* [1988] QB 871). In *Re L (Restraint Order, Legal Costs)* The Times, 19 July 1996 Latham J held:

> while His Lordship saw the force of that argument it seemed to give inadequate expression to the Defendant's rights to use the funds which were prima facie his for the purposes of defending himself.

28.63 In *Customs and Excise Commissioners v Norris* [1991] 2 All ER 395, the Court of Appeal held that a defendant was entitled to have monies released from a restraint order for the purpose of funding an appeal against conviction, including the making of a confiscation order. If funds were not so released, the defendant would be forced to seek legal aid, and in this regard, Lord Donaldson MR commented as follows (at p 397):

> But it would be an odd position if the court was forcing somebody to qualify for legal aid who would not otherwise qualify for legal aid. There is also this policy consideration (which might appeal to the Customs and Excise rather than Mr Norris) that, if he is forced onto legal aid, then the costs of the defence will come out of public funds whether the conviction is sustained or whether it is not. If, on the other hand, this money is released and is spent on the costs of his appeal, there will be that much saving for the legal aid fund and, if the appeal succeeds, it will be Mr Norris's money that paid for the appeal subject, of course, to any order for costs which might be made by the Criminal Division of this court.

This rationale was recently upheld by Wilkie J in *Briggs-Price* [2006] who started:

> I am bound by authority to disregard the availability of public legal funding when considering whether to . . . release restrained funds for the purpose of funding the defendant's legal representation . . .

28.64 It should be noted that in *Norris*, the Court was dealing with a situation where the defendant had been both convicted and the confiscation order had been made. *Norris* concerned an appeal from both of those matters. It is not impossible that prior to a confiscation order being made, an unscrupulous defendant may conclude that it would be in his interests to spend as much of the money as he could prior to the confiscation hearing taking place in order not only to avoid a large confiscation order, but also to avoid the enhanced sentence in default that would accompany it. The legislative steer is intended to give the High Court powers to restrain any of the defendant's assets with a view to ensuring that the realisable property held by the defendant will, following a confiscation order being made, remain available to allow for that realisation. Section 31(2) of the DTA 1994 imports a protectionist principle over restrained funds:

> (2) Subject to the following provisions of this Section, the powers [to grant restraint orders] shall be exercised with a view to making available for satisfying the confiscation order or, as the case may be, any confiscation order which may be made in the Defendant's case, the value for the time being of realisable property held by any person, by means of the realisation of such property.

28.65 In *A v C (No 2)* [1981] 1 QB 961 Goff J considered an application by certain defendants to vary a Mareva/freezing injunction for the purpose of obtaining a payment of £65,000 from assets subject to the injunction in order to pay legal costs likely to be incurred in the proceedings. Goff J held that there was evidence before the court that the defendants were likely to incur substantial costs in the forthcoming proceedings and it was on that basis they had applied for the release of money to pay those costs. However, no evidence had been placed before the court concerning the other assets of the defendants; it was not therefore possible, Goff J found, for the court to assess whether any other assets of the defendants were available to pay the costs or, if they were still available, why the defendants were seeking to make use of the assets which were subject to the Mareva injunction for this purpose. He said there was a basic principle he had to apply which was that he could only permit a qualification to the injunction if the defendant satisfied the court that money is required for a purpose that does not conflict with the policy underlying the jurisdiction. In so doing, therefore, he firmly placed the burden of proof upon the defendant:

> I do not know, on the evidence, whether they have assets freely available or not—it would be open to Counsel for the Plaintiffs to submit, on the evidence, that it would be wrong for the Court to vary the Mareva Injunction. All I can say is that at present on the evidence before the Court the Defendants have not discharged the burden of proof that rests upon them.

28.66 In *Re P* (QBD, 6 November 1998), the defendant sought to have release of funds under a restraint order following his conviction and a confiscation order being made on the grounds that he had lodged a complaint with the Criminal Cases Review Commission and also an application with the European Court of Human Rights. He wanted funds released from the bite of the restraint order and the receiver's powers so as to enable him to meet expenses associated with those two applications. The Court held that it was:

> clear beyond any doubt that none of these matters should justify a variation of the Restraint Order. The fact is that so far as the domestic criminal litigation is concerned in this case, Mr P is well past the end of the road.

Laws J went on to hold that:

> ... the Commission may, of course, investigate a matter after all other criminal legal processes have been exhausted, indeed that is their very role. However, it is quite clear to me that while they are doing so, and the fact that they are doing so, are no basis for altering, suspending or varying the effect of a Restraint Order and therefore, in effect, the execution of a Confiscation Order once that has been made. The same applies in relation to the application to the European Court of Human Rights.

The release of funds therefore to assist with litigation is limited and the authorities to a degree are at odds with one another.

28.67 While the Proceeds of Crime Act has curtailed the use of restrained assets to fund legal costs in restraint proceedings, the Serious Organised Crime and Police Act reverses this rule in civil recovery cases to allow, once again, respondents to draw upon restrained funds. Similarly, in existing cases under the CJA and DTA, restrained funds may still be utilised in order to fund legal proceedings.

28.68 While there are arguments which go both ways in relation to the release of restrained funds/frozen assets, some guidance may be drawn from a recent freezing order case heard in the Chancery Division: *Polly Peck International v Nadir* (Ch D, 25 January 2006) in which the court was considering whether to release funds for the payment of legal costs, and it held, although not a strict pre-condition to determine the issue, it was helpful to know what other funds the applicant could have used to meet his costs. The Court found it was not merely a question of the other assets the applicant might have available to him in the jurisdiction or outside, but the issue was the court's reluctance to weaken the protection given to a party seeking a freezing order without knowing what other funds might be available. This rationale may be extended to the availability of Legal Services Commission funding.

28.69 In *Re R* (2005) 154 NLJ 581 Stanley Burnton J held that under s 82 of the CJA (exercise of powers by the High Court or receiver), the court had the power to make an order permitting payment of the defendant's legal expenses by a receiver appointed under s 77 of the Act, out of the assets subject to a restraint order, and such order may be made both before and after the making of a confiscation order and it may relate to costs to be incurred in appealing such an order. Section 77(2) made express provision for the payment of legal expenses by way of an exception to a restraint order and the reference in s 77(8) providing for the appointment of a receiver following the making of a restraint order, 'subject to such limitations and conditions as the court may direct' had to be construed on the basis that there could be a corresponding 'exception' to a receivership order as, under s 77(2) there could be to a restraint order. Burnton J stated that an order for payment out of the restrained property could be made if that was necessary to avoid the prosecution and the receiver from acting unethically; both being subject to the supervisory jurisdiction of the court. He viewed legal costs as an exception to the general position that the power under s 82 should not be used to make payment of unsecured debts as to do so would be inconsistent with the legislative steer.

(22) Legal expenses and third parties

28.70 For commentary on the release of restrained assets to fund the legal expenses of third parties see para 22.21 of Chapter 22 and *Re D* [2006] EWHC (Admin) 1519.

(23) Release of restrained funds to cover legal expenses under POCA

28.71 The above discussion about the release of funds under the DTA and CJA is somewhat circumvented by the introduction of s 41 of POCA. Under s 41(3) a restraint order may still be subject to an exception to allow for reasonable legal expenses; however such an exception must not make provision for any legal expenses that relate:

(a) to an offence which falls within s 41(5) and
(b) are incurred by the defendant or by a recipient of a tainted gift.

Under s 41(5) the offences include:

(a) The offence mentioned in s 40(2) or (3) if the first or second condition (as the case may be) is satisfied.
(b) The offence (or any of the offences) concerned if the third, fourth or fifth condition is satisfied.

28.72 Section 40(2) states that the first condition is that a criminal investigation has been started in England and Wales with regard to an offence, and there is a reasonable cause to believe the alleged offender has benefited from his criminal conduct; and s 40(3) states that the second condition is that proceedings for an offence have been started in England and Wales and not concluded, and there is reasonable cause to believe the defendant has benefited from his criminal conduct.

28.73 The third condition applies where an application by the prosecutor or the Director has been made under ss 19, 20, 27, or 28 of POCA and not concluded; or the court believes that such an application is to be made, and there is reason to believe the defendant has benefited from his criminal conduct (s 40(4)). (Section 19 applies when no order has been made and the court is reconsidering the case; s 20 applies when no order has been made and the court is reconsidering the benefit; s 27 applies where the defendant absconds and he has been convicted or committed; s 28 applies where the defendant absconds and he has been neither convicted nor acquitted.)

28.74 The fourth condition is that an application by the prosecutor or the Director has been made under s 21 and not concluded, or the court believes that such an application is to be made, and that there is reasonable cause to believe the court will decide under that section that the amount found under the new calculation of the defendant's benefit exceeds the relevant amount (see s 40(5)).

28.75 The fifth condition is that an application by the prosecutor or the Director has been made under s 22 and not concluded, or the court believes that such an application is to be made, and there is reasonable cause to believe the court will decide under that section the amount found under the new calculation of the available amount exceeds the relevant amount (see s 40(6)). (Section 21 applies where the confiscation order has been made and the court

C. Compensation

is reconsidering benefit, and s 22 applies where a confiscation order has been made and the court is reconsidering the available amount.)

In all of these circumstances, there is no opportunity for a defendant to avail himself of assets under restraint in order to fund his legal representation. He must therefore look to LSC funding, or assets elsewhere (the effect of the POCA provisions being confirmed in *Re S* [2005] 1 WLR 1338). **28.76**

There remains however provisions for other legal costs to be met, eg legal charges in relation to conveyancing of property or litigation costs in ongoing proceedings, which are not connected to the criminal matters in question. **28.77**

C. Compensation

(1) Compensation for the acquitted defendant under the DTA and CJA

Section 18 of the DTA 1994 and s 89 of the CJA 1988, which are worded in identical terms, give the High Court jurisdiction, on an application by a person who held realisable property caught by an order, to order compensation to be paid to the applicant if, having regard to all the circumstances, it considers it appropriate to do so. The provisions thus enable not only the defendant, but also any person holding realisable property to make an application for compensation. An application for compensation can only be made where criminal proceedings have been instituted against the defendant for a drug trafficking offence or an offence to which Pt VI of the CJA applies, as appropriate, and either: **28.78**

(a) the proceedings do not result in his conviction for any such offence, or
(b) where he is convicted of one or more such offences—
   (i) the conviction or convictions concerned are quashed, or
   (ii) he is pardoned by Her Majesty in respect of the conviction or convictions concerned.

Section 18(1) of the DTA and s 89(1) of the CJA read as follows:

(1) The High Court may, on an application by a person who held property which was realisable property, order compensation to be paid to the applicant if, having regard to all the circumstances, it considers it appropriate to make such an order.
(2) The High Court shall not order compensation to be paid in any case unless the court is satisfied—
   (a) that there has been some serious default on the part of the person concerned in the investigation or prosecution of the offence or offences concerned, being a person mentioned in subsection (5) below; and
   (b) that the applicant has suffered loss and consequence of anything done in relation to the property by or in pursuance of—
     (i) an order of the High Court or the County Court under this part of the Act [DTA ss 26–29]; or
     (ii) (applicable only in Scotland).
(3) The High Court shall not order compensation to be paid in any case where it appears to the Court the proceedings would have been instituted or continued even if the serious default had not occurred.
(4) The amount of compensation to be paid under this section shall be such as the High Court thinks just in all the circumstances of the case.

28.79 It is thus essential that the defendant should have been acquitted of all offences to which the restraint order proceedings relate. It is not sufficient that the court did not consider it an appropriate case for a confiscation order; there must be an acquittal before an application for compensation can be entertained.

(2) Other conditions

28.80 An acquittal by itself will not be sufficient to found an application for compensation because, under s 18(2) of the DTA and s 89(2) of the CJA two other conditions must also be satisfied. Firstly, it must be shown that there has been some 'serious default' on the part of a person mentioned in subs (5). Secondly, it must be shown that the applicant for compensation has suffered loss in consequence of anything done to the property as a result of an order made under the Acts. Subsection (3) imposes a further important restriction on the power of the court to award compensation in that it provides that the court shall not order the payment of compensation where it appears that the proceedings would have been instituted or continued even if the serious default had not occurred. Rule 56.6 of the Criminal Procedure Rules deals with compensation on acquittal, and allows for notice of the acquittal to be served on the High Court.

(3) Compensation for third parties

28.81 In *R v Glatt* (2006) the Court of Appeal considered the issue of compensation and confiscation. It stated that the 1988 Act contemplates that both a compensation and confiscation order may be made against the same person in the same proceedings (as per s 71(7)), but where the court does that, the compensation takes priority in the event that the defendant's means are insufficient.

28.82 The Act does not in terms contemplate that it shall operate as a means of compensating the Crown where the Crown is the victim, eg by the evasion of duties and taxes, although a confiscation order may in practice have that effect. Compensating the Crown would only be necessary in cases where the Crown had suffered a loss and does not have a civil claim against the defendant. Such a purpose will be unnecessary in most cases, since the Crown remains entitled to the duties and taxes evaded, and perhaps to other civil remedies whether or not the defendant has been convicted, (see *R v Smith (David)* [2001] UKHL 68). See para 28.103 below for victims of crime.

(4) How much compensation and by whom is it paid?

28.83 Subsection (4) gives the court a wide discretion as to the amount of compensation it may award, providing that the amount to be paid 'shall be such as the High Court thinks just in all the circumstances'. Subsection (5) deals with payment and provides:

(5) Compensation payable under this section shall be paid—
    (a) where the person in default was or was acting as a member of a police force, out of the police fund out of which the expenses of that police force are met;
    (b) where the person in default was a member of the Crown Prosecution Service or acting on behalf of the service, by the Director of Public Prosecutions;
    (c) where the person in default was a member of the Serious Fraud Office, by the Director of that Office;

C. Compensation

(d) where the person in default was an officer within the meaning of the Customs and Excise Management Act 1979, by the Commissioners of Revenue and Customs.

(5) Procedure on applications

28.84 The procedure for making compensation applications is dealt with in RSC Ord 115 r 10 provides that the application must be made in accordance with CPR Part 23, ie on an application notice served together with any supporting evidence, on the person alleged to be in default and on the relevant authority not less than seven days prior to the date of the hearing. The witness statement in support (see CPR Part 22) should, of course, state all the facts relied on in support of the application including full details of the 'serious default' alleged. Any relevant documentation should be exhibited to the witness statement.

(6) Compensation for the acquitted defendant under POCA 2002

28.85 Section 72(1) of POCA sets out the three conditions that need to be satisfied before the Crown Court may make an order for payment of compensation. The amount the Crown Court may order to be paid is described as an amount 'it believes is just'.

28.86 The first condition is satisfied if a criminal investigation has been started with regard to an offence and proceedings are not started for the offence. Under POCA it is possible for a restraint order to be made as soon as the criminal investigation has been started, as distinct to under the DTA, where it was only possible to obtain a restraint order when proceedings had been started or were about to be. One of the main changes of POCA is that compensation will now be payable not only from when proceedings have been started, but from the beginning of the investigation itself. The first condition is also satisfied if proceedings for an offence are started against the person and they do not result in his conviction for the offence, or he is convicted of the offence but the conviction is quashed or he is pardoned in respect of it (see s 72(3)).

28.87 If a criminal investigation has been started with regard to an offence, and proceedings have not or are not started for that offence, the second condition is that in the criminal investigation there has been serious default by a person mentioned in s 72(9) of POCA and the investigation would not have continued if the default had not occurred (s 72(9) is in almost identical terms to subs (5) of the corresponding provisions of the DTA and CJA).

28.88 If proceedings for an offence are started against a person and they do not result in his conviction for the offence, or he is convicted of the offence but the conviction is quashed or he is pardoned in respect of it, the second condition is that in the criminal investigation with regard to the offence or in its prosecution there has been a serious default by a person who is mentioned in subs (9) and the proceedings would not have been started or continued if the default had not occurred.

28.89 The third condition is that an application is made under this section by a person who held realisable property and has suffered loss in consequence of anything done in relation to it by or in pursuance of an order under Pt 2 of the Proceeds of Crime Act (see s 72(6)).

28.90 Section 72 reflects largely the legislation under the DTA and the CJA, save that the provisions have been extended to cover the situation where the investigation is started but proceedings have not been brought. It provides for compensation to be paid to a person whose property has been affected by the enforcement of the confiscation legislation. 'Serious default' is not defined in the Act and therefore each case will need to be determined on its own merits. It is not intended that compensation should be paid on acquittal as a matter of course.

(7) When a confiscation order is varied or discharged under POCA

28.91 Under s 73(1) where a court varies a confiscation order under s 29 of POCA (ie where a defendant has absconded) or discharges a confiscation order under s 30 (where an absconded defendant is later tried for an offence and is acquitted on all counts) and application is made to the Crown Court by a person who held realisable property and has suffered a loss as a result of the making of the order, the court may order the payment of such compensation it believes is just.

28.92 In those circumstance compensation is payable to the applicant by the Lord Chancellor (s 73(3)). It should be noted that this provision is not limited to serious default as in s 72.

(8) Other powers to order compensation under POCA

28.93 Under s 283 of POCA the scheme allows for compensation to be paid under Pt 5 of the Act (civil recovery of the proceeds etc of unlawful conduct). Under Chapter 2 of POCA, Civil Recovery in the High Court, where any property to which an interim receiving order or property freezing order has at any time applied and the court does not in the course of the proceedings decide that the property is recoverable property or associated property, the person whose property it is may make an application to the court for compensation.

28.94 Section 283(1) does not apply if the court has made a declaration in respect of the property under s 281 (Victims of Theft etc), or makes an order under s 276 (Consent Orders) (see s 283(2)).

28.95 If the court has made a decision by reason of which no recovery order could be made in respect of the property, the application for compensation must be made within the period of three months beginning, in relation to a decision of a High Court, with the date of the decision or, if any application is not made for leave to appeal, within the date on which the application is withdrawn or refused or on which any proceedings on appeal are finally concluded (see s 283(3)). If the proceedings in respect of the property have been discontinued, the application for compensation must be made within the period of three months beginning with the discontinuance (see s 283(4)).

(9) Compensation in relation to interim receiving orders and property freezing orders

28.96 As stated above if the court is satisfied that the applicant has suffered loss as a result of a PFO or IRO it may require the enforcement authority to pay compensation to him. The amount of compensation to be paid under s 283 is the amount the court thinks reasonable having regard to loss suffered and any other relevant circumstances (see s 283(9)).

C. Compensation

28.97 This section deals with cases where there has been a loss to owners of property in circumstances where that property has been made subject to a PFO or IRO but has not in the end been deemed to be recoverable or associated property for two reasons:

(1) because the court has so determined, or
(2) because the claim or application has been withdrawn.

Under subs (1) the person whose property it is may apply to the court for compensation for any loss relating to that property. In those circumstances the court may order compensation to be paid by the enforcement authority under subs (5).

28.98 The measure of the compensation to be paid is at the court's discretion, having regard to all of the circumstances including any quantifiable losses suffered. If a claimant has himself contributed to the losses, for example through delays caused by himself, the court is entitled to take those facts into account.

(10) Compensation for recovery of cash in summary proceedings

28.99 Under s 302 of POCA when no forfeiture order is made in respect of any cash detained under Chapter 3 the person to whom the cash belongs or from whom it was seized may make an application to the magistrates' court for compensation. If the seized cash was not paid into an interest bearing account at the first opportunity following its initial detention, the court may make an order for compensation to be paid to the applicant (see s 302(2)).

28.100 The amount of compensation to be paid in those circumstances is an amount which the court thinks would have been earned in interest in the period in question if the cash had been held in an interest bearing account. It is therefore likely to be of relatively nominal value (see s 302(3)).

28.101 If the court is satisfied that the applicant has suffered any other loss as a result of the detention of the cash and that the circumstances are 'exceptional', the court may order compensation or additional compensation to be paid to him (see s 302(4)). In those circumstances the amount of compensation to be paid is the amount the court thinks reasonable, having regard to the loss suffered and any other relevant circumstances. Where Revenue and Customs officials seize the cash, the compensation is to be paid by the Commissioners of Revenue and Customs (s 302(6)). If the cash was seized by a constable, the compensation is to be paid by the relevant police force.

28.102 It should be noted that if a forfeiture order is made in respect of any part of the cash detained under ss 294 and 295 of POCA, the person to whom the cash belongs or from whom it was seized is entitled to claim compensation in relation to any part of the cash that is not ordered to be forfeited (see s 302(8)).

(11) Compensation and the victims of crime

28.103 In *R v Dorrian* (2001) 1 Cr App R(S) 135, the appellant submitted that the court had no power to make a compensation order outside the period of 28 days following sentence in the absence of an expressly stated decision to postpone the compensation order as part of the sentence (s 47(2) of the Supreme Court Act 1981). It was conceded that there was a common-law power in the court to postpone any part of the sentence, but it was submitted that it must be expressly stated. In *Dorrian* there had been no express statement but the making of the compensation order was postponed. The Court of Appeal was satisfied that s 72(5)(b) did not exclude compensation orders from the consideration of the court making the confiscation order and that the sentencer had power to make a compensation order or to postpone the making of an order at the time of sentence. It also held that the appellant was correct in his submission that the section dealt with the manner in which funds were allocated if both of the orders were made. The exclusion of compensation orders from s 72A(9) provided protection for victims of crime. It meant they could benefit from a compensation order, where a confiscation order was made within the time limit provided. It was not however open to the Crown Court to make a compensation order 26 months after conviction where no common-law power had been exercised to postpone the making of such an order at the date of sentence. No reference was made at the time to the making of a compensation order, or postponing the making of such an order at the time, and accordingly the Crown Court had no power to do so more than two years after conviction. For those reasons the compensation order was not lawful and was quashed.

28.104 It follows that compensation orders may be made under s 130 of the Powers of the Criminal Courts (Sentencing) Act 2000 at the time of the confiscation hearing, provided that the court has postponed the making of such an order at the time of passing sentence using its common law jurisdiction. If at the time it postpones the confiscation order it is silent as to whether or not a compensation order will be made, it is not able to make one after the 28 day time limit has expired. There may be, in the light of the recent decisions concerning the purpose and intention of the legislation that a failure to postpone is not as fatal as it may once have been (see *Sekhon* [2003] 3 All ER 508), although in relation to compensation orders this is untested territory. There should nevertheless be some acknowledgment as to the harsh consequences that *Dorrian* may have for a victim of crime on what may merely amount to a procedural irregularity.

28.105 For further discussion on third parties and compensation see para 28.81 above.

29

CONDEMNATION AND RESTORATION

A.	Introduction	29.01
B.	The Condemnation and Forfeiture of Goods	29.07
	(1) The statutory basis	29.07
	(2) Duty payable, unless for own use	29.09
	(3) Importations for a commercial purpose	29.10
	(4) Civil proceedings	29.15
	(5) Legislative background	29.18
	(6) The revised legislative scheme	29.20
	(7) Gifts	29.24
	(8) Transfers for money's worth	29.25
	(9) EU reaction	29.27
	(10) What factors define 'commercial purpose'?	29.29
	(11) What are the minimum indicative levels?	29.37
	(12) Travelling to the UK from outside the EU	29.44
C.	Detention, Seizure and Condemnation	29.45
	(1) The forfeiture provisions	29.46
	(2) What does 'liable to forfeiture' mean?	29.48
	(3) Secondary forfeiture	29.51
	(4) More than one person involved	29.58
	(5) Proof of certain other matters	29.59
	(6) Stops at Coquelles	29.60
D.	Condemnation: Practice and Procedure	29.61
	(1) Initial seizure	29.61
	(2) Possible criminal proceedings	29.67
	(3) Notice of claim—the one month time limit to appeal	29.70
	(4) Six month time limit on HM Revenue and Customs once notice lodged	29.72
	(5) Preparation for the hearing—service of evidence	29.75
	(6) Preparation for the hearing—dutiable goods	29.79
	(7) The hearing—commercial purpose v own use	29.80
	(8) Court procedure: preliminary matters	29.86
	(9) Court procedure: condemnation by complaint	29.90
	(10) Order of speeches	29.92
	(11) The burden and standard of proof	29.97
	(12) Hearsay in civil cases	29.102
	(13) Previous convictions	29.106
	(14) Reasons for stopping the traveller	29.109
	(15) Power to stop the traveller	29.111
E.	Condemnation: Costs and Compensation	29.112
	(1) Costs	29.112
	(2) LSC funding	29.120
	(3) Compensation	29.122
F.	Condemnation Appeals	29.124
	(1) Procedure	29.125
	(2) Pre-hearing review	29.128
	(3) Pending the hearing of an appeal	29.129
G.	Condemnation in the High Court	29.130
H.	Condemnation and the ECHR	29.131
I.	Red Diesel Cases	29.135
	(1) Introduction	29.135
	(2) The legislative provisions	29.137
	(3) Excepted vehicles	29.143
	(4) Compounding	29.147
	(5) Procedural requirements	29.148
	(6) The vehicle and the fuel	29.150
	(7) The civil burden	29.152
	(8) Criminal offences	29.153
J.	Delivery Up	29.156
	(1) Introduction	29.156
	(2) The legislative provisions	29.157
	(3) Practice	29.161

K. Restoration	29.162	(5) Disclosure	29.206
(1) The statutory basis	29.162	(6) Witness statements	29.212
(2) Appeals against non-restoration	29.164	(7) Ongoing criminal proceedings	29.216
(3) Burden and standard of proof	29.165	(8) Failure to comply with directions	29.217
(4) Test of reasonableness	29.167	(9) Pre-hearing reviews	29.219
(5) Proportionality	29.173	(10) Preparation for the hearing	29.222
(6) Jurisdiction	29.177	(11) The hearing	29.223
(7) Personal/commercial use	29.180	(12) Judgment	29.229
(8) Case law	29.192	M. Restoration Appeals	29.231
L. Restoration: Practice and Procedure	29.198	N. Restoration: Costs and Compensation	29.233
(1) Formal departmental reviews	29.198	(1) Compensation	29.233
(2) Tribunal procedure	29.199	(2) Costs	29.234
(3) Time limits	29.200	O. The ECHR and Restoration	29.237
(4) Lodging the appeal and the statement of case	29.202		

A. Introduction

29.01 In this chapter we give an overview of the law in relation to what some still describe as 'Bootlegging'. While not strictly within the ambit of a book that has as its central focus the proceeds of crime, there is, nevertheless a nexus between the two. Cigarette and tobacco smuggling has been successfully deployed by criminal organisations to raise funds for many years, and the extremes to which individuals will go in order to evade the authorities are becoming increasingly sophisticated.

29.02 Nowadays the condemnation of goods covers a vast area in terms of legislation and, as a result, we have sought to concentrate on those areas that are typical of matters that regularly come before the courts. The bifurcated jurisdiction adopted by the legislature in relation to the seizure, forfeiture and condemnation of excise goods and vehicles under ss 49, 139, 141 and Sch 3 to the Customs and Excise Management Act 1979 (CEMA) on the one hand; and on the other, the discretionary power vested in the Commissioners of Revenue and Customs to restore, subject to such conditions (if any) that they think proper, anything forfeited or seized under s 152(b) of CEMA was recognised by Pill LJ in *Gora v Customs and Excise Commissioners* [2003] EWCA Civ 525, at para 57.

29.03 The present system in relation to forfeiture and restoration has not been without its critics. In *Customs and Excise Commissioners v Weller* [2006] EWHC 237 (Ch), Evans-Lombe J called for a 'statutory rationalization of the procedure governing the forfeiture of goods by the Commissioners' (para 24). He stated that:

> It seems to me that the present system is confusing to the public and pregnant with the possibility of substantial injustice.

29.04 The problem of the two-track system of condemnation and forfeiture followed by restoration was also subject to scrutiny by the Court of Appeal in *Gascoyne v Customs and Excise Commissioners* [2005] 2 WLR 222, para 5, where Buxton LJ said:

> The procedure has a number of elements which appear to have grown up over the years and which do not always easily fit with each other.

B. The Condemnation and Forfeiture of Goods

29.05 The courts merely seem to be highlighting the practical and very real problems that both appellants, magistrates sitting in their civil jurisdiction and VAT and Duties Tribunals have experienced. One proposal, which may or may not find favour in years to come, would be to introduce a unified condemnation and restoration procedure, which is less formal, less associated with the criminal courts as well as the magistrates (most first instance appeals are currently dealt with by the Crown Court), that perhaps operates under the auspices of the Tribunals Service.

29.06 Pursuant to s 50 of the Commissioners for Revenue and Customs Act 2005, references to Commissioners of HM Customs and Excise, and HM Customs and Excise generally, have been amended to Commissioners of HM Revenue and Customs, and HM Revenue and Customs respectively.

B. The Condemnation and Forfeiture of Goods

(1) The statutory basis

29.07 The statutory basis for the forfeiture of goods improperly imported derives from s 49 of CEMA. Section 49(1) sets out the circumstances under which goods shall be liable to forfeiture where they have been imported contrary to HM Revenue and Customs restrictions and where the goods in question are chargeable with duty:

49(1) Where—
(a) except as provided by or under the Customs and Excise Acts 1979, any imported goods, being goods chargeable on their importation with customs or excise duty, are, without payment of that duty—
 (i) unshipped in any port,
 (ii) unloaded from any aircraft in the United Kingdom,
 (iii) unloaded from any vehicle in, or otherwise brought across the boundary into, Northern Ireland, or
 (iv) removed from their place of importation or from any approved wharf, examination station or transit shed; or
(b) any goods are imported, landed or unloaded contrary to any prohibition or restriction for the time being in force with respect thereto under or by virtue of any enactment; or
(c) any goods, being goods chargeable with any duty or goods the importation of which is for the time being prohibited or restricted by or under any enactment, are found, whether before or after the unloading thereof, to have been concealed in any manner on board any ship or aircraft or, while in Northern Ireland, in any vehicle; or
(d) any goods are imported concealed in a container holding goods of a different description; or
(e) any imported goods are found, whether before or after delivery, not to correspond with the entry made thereof; or
(f) any imported goods are concealed or packed in any manner appearing to be intended to deceive an officer,
those goods shall, subject to subsection (2) below, be liable to forfeiture.
(2) Where any goods, the importation of which is for the time being prohibited or restricted by or under any enactment, are on their importation either—
 (a) reported as intended for exportation in the same ship, aircraft or vehicle; or
 (b) entered for transit or transhipment; or
 (c) entered to be warehoused for exportation or for use as stores,
the Commissioners may, if they see fit, permit the goods to be dealt with accordingly.

29.08 These broad ranging provisions cover, subject to their own particular legislative provisions, the forfeiture of cigarettes, tobacco (see s 2 of the Tobacco Products Duty Act 1979), alcohol (the Alcoholic Liquor Duties Act 1979, particularly s 5 (spirits), s 36 (beer), s 54 (wine) and s 62 (cider)). They also cover a multitude of other excise goods, including bullion and coins (see *Allgemeine Gold-und Silberscheideanstalt v Customs and Excise Commissioners* [1980] 2 All ER 138 (CA)), pornography, vehicles, as well as goods prohibited from importation by virtue of matters as diverse as trade descriptions and UN sanctions orders.

(2) Duty payable, unless for own use

29.09 UK excise duty is generally payable at the point of importation (see reg 12(1) of the Tobacco Products Regulations 2001, SI 1712/2001 for tobacco; reg 15(1) of the Beer Regulations 1993, SI 1228/1993 for beer; and reg 4(1) of the Excise Goods (Holding, Movement, Warehousing and REDS) Regulations 1992, SI 3135/1992 for wines and spirits. As a result of the Divisional Court's decision in *R (Hoverspeed) v Customs and Excise Commissioners* [2002] 4 All ER 912, these Regulations were amended in 2002, pursuant to the Excise Goods, Beer and Tobacco Products (Amendment) Regulations 2002, SI 2002/2692 and the Channel Tunnel (Alcoholic Liquor and Tobacco Products) (Amendment) Order 2002, SI 2002/2693 to insert a sub-regulation (1A) which makes provision for the cross channel shopper who acquires and transports goods for his own use. This provides that no duty will be payable unless and until the goods are held or used for a commercial purpose by any persons. Sub-regulation (1B) provides the definitions and criteria to be applied when considering whether (1A) applies (the Regulations are set out at para 29.20 below).

(3) Importations for a commercial purpose

29.10 Excise duty only becomes payable if the goods are being imported for a commercial purpose (ie forward sale or for money's worth or for profit). Article 8 of Council Directive (EC) 92/12 provides:

As regards products acquired by private individuals for their own use and transported by them, the principle governing the internal market lays down that excise duty shall be charged in the Member State in which they are acquired.

29.11 The amendment Regulations confirm that duty and tax must be paid on the goods in the Member State in which they are acquired (see subreg (1B(d)).

29.12 In *R v Customs and Excise Commissioners ex p Emu Tabac SARL* [1998] All ER (EC) 402, the European Court of Justice held that on its true construction Article 8 of Directive 92/12 made no provision for the involvement of a third party and therefore it was not applicable where the purchase and/or transportation of goods subject to duty was effected through an agent. The Court went on to hold that although Article 6 of the Directive provided that duty would be chargeable at the time when goods were released for consumption in a Member State, that did preclude excise duty from being subsequently levied in another Member State pursuant to Articles 7, 9 or 10, whereupon duty paid in the first member state could be reimbursed. In *The Netherlands v Joustra* C5-05 (ECJ, 23 November 2006), the Court held that for Article 8 of Directive 92/12 to be applicable excise goods must have been acquired by private individuals for their own use and transported by them (para 332 of the judgment).

The Court rejected the argument that because the wine acquired by Mr Joustra was for his own use and that of members of the wine club, of which he was president, it fell within Article 8 of Directive 92/12 and therefore was not subject to Dutch excise duty on its importation since French excise duty had already been paid on the goods. The ECJ found that the condition that goods are for an individual's own use precludes acquisition of goods for the use of other private individuals. Where any goods have been acquired for the use of others those goods cannot be considered to be held for strictly private purposes by the individual who has acquired them (see para 35 of the judgment). This condition means that the goods must have been transported personally by the individual who purchased them. Article 8 is not applicable where the purchase and/or transportation of excise goods is effected through an agent (para 41 of the judgment). The Court went on to conclude that Article 7(2) of the Directive applied to Mr Joustra. The Court stated that the Directive proceeded on the basis that goods not held for a private purpose must necessarily be regarded as held for a commercial purpose. As Mr Joustra was not holding the goods acquired for the wine circle for his own private purpose he was to be regarded as holding them for a commercial purpose in the Netherlands. This was the case even though he was not acting with a view to making a profit (para 51). Accordingly excise duty was due in the Netherlands. Mr Joustra was however entitled to repayment of the French excise duty paid by him (see para 52 of the judgment).

29.13 Article 9 of the same Directive adds:

(1) Without prejudice to Article . . . 8, excise duty shall become chargeable where products released for consumption in a Member State are held for a commercial purpose in another Member State.

29.14 In *Hoverspeed* [2002] 3 WLR 1219, the Divisional Court held that the 1992 Order correctly transposed the Directive in its definition of own use. Either goods were held for personal use within the meaning of Article 8 of the Directive or they were held for a commercial purpose under Article 9. The Court of Appeal's decision in *Hoverspeed* [2003] 2 WLR 950 confirmed this first instance decision, and this was followed in the Divisional Court case of *Customs and Excise Commissioners v Newbury* [2003] EWHC (Admin) 702. Hale LJ (approving the reasoning of Advocate General Ruis-Jarabo Colomer in *Emu Tabac* [1998] QB 791) held that:

> The object of the rules (in Directive 92/12) is to determine whether duty is payable in the country of origin or the country of destination. The general principle is the latter and Article 8 is an exception in which three conditions must be fulfilled: the products must be acquired by a private individual; the products must be acquired by private individuals for their own use; and the products must be transported by private individuals.

(4) Civil proceedings

29.15 Actions for forfeiture and condemnation are actions *in rem* (against the property as opposed to the individual). Nobody stands in jeopardy and the action is by way of complaint heard, in the first instance, usually before a magistrates' court.

29.16 Paragraph 8 of Sch 3 to CEMA confirms that the proceedings are civil, and this was further confirmed in both *Goldsmith v Customs and Excise Commissioners* The Times, 12 June 2001 and *Mudie v Kent Magistrates' Court* [2003] EWHC (Civ) 237, 2 All ER 631, where the

Courts held that condemnation matters do not involve the determination of a criminal charge and that none of the usual consequences of a criminal conviction apply. As a result Article 6 of the ECHR has no application.

29.17 This is therefore one of the rare examples of the magistrates' court's civil jurisdiction and because the proceedings are civil, the burden of proof is on the *balance of probabilities* and not the higher criminal test of 'beyond reasonable doubt'. Civil rules of evidence apply, including the admissibility of hearsay evidence and there is no necessity for compliance with the Police and Criminal Evidence Act 1984.

(5) Legislative background

29.18 There have been various legislative changes in this area of the law over the years. For several years the Excise Duties (Personal Reliefs) Order 1992, SI 1992/3155 was followed, before it was amended by the Excise Duties (Personal Reliefs) (Amendment) Order 1999, SI 1999/1617. However, both of these Orders were revoked by the Excise Duties (Personal Reliefs) (Revocation) Order 2002, SI 2002/2691 on 1 December 2002 and replaced with a new set of Regulations following the Divisional Court's ruling in *R (Hoverspeed) v Customs and Excise Commissioners* [2002] 4 All ER 912 which held the original Orders had failed to implement the EC Directive (EC) 92/12 and had wrongly reversed the burden of proof by requiring the individual importing the goods to prove that they were for his own use.

29.19 It is as a result of these legislative changes, particularly the revocation of the 1992 Order, (which included a presumption in favour of Customs), that requires case law before 1999 to be viewed with some caution. For example, *Customs and Excise Commissioners v Carrier* (1995) 4 All ER 38 and references to the presumption under Article 5(3) in the case of *R v Customs and Excise Commissioners ex p Kenneth Stephen Boxall* (15 February 1996) (CO 1902/95) should be read in the light of the amended 1999 Order.

(6) The revised legislative scheme

29.20 The Excise Goods, Beer and Tobacco Products (Amendment) Regulations 2002, SI 2002/2692 came into force on 1 December 2002. It sought to correct any deficiency in the previous Regulations by amending the existing Excise Goods (Holding, Movement, Warehousing, and REDS) Regulations 1992, SI 2002/3135 by inserting a specific provision in relation to 'own use':

(1A) In the case of excise goods acquired by a person in another member State for his own use and transported by him to the United Kingdom, the excise duty point is the time when those goods are held or used for a commercial purpose by any person.

29.21 In other words, excise duty only becomes payable on the goods when they are held for a commercial purpose, or at the point in time when they become held or are used for a commercial purpose. This applies to both the traveller who imported them and/or by any other person who has possession or control of them.

29.22 SI 2002/2692 also amended the Beer Regulations 1993, SI 1993/1228 and the Tobacco Products Regulations 2001, SI 2001/1712 in identical terms.

B. The Condemnation and Forfeiture of Goods

29.23 The effect of these amendments is to reassert that goods being brought into the UK for a traveller's 'own use' are not subject to excise duty. This should ensure that goods purchased on cross-border shopping trips for an individual's own personal use are not subject to the payment of any excise duty (see the Divisional Court's judgment in *R (Hoverspeed) v Customs and Excise Commissioners* [2002] 4 All ER 912 at paras 107-109).

(7) Gifts

29.24 The Excise Goods, Beer and Tobacco Products (Amendment) Regulations 2002 also altered the pre-existing Regulations to define 'own use' as including use as a personal gift (para (1B)(b)). It is therefore permissible for a traveller to bring in larger than expected consignments of excise goods, if he intends to give them away as personal gifts. Much will depend on the credibility of the traveller's story, the likelihood of the assertion, and the evidence the traveller is able to produce to support the claim.

(8) Transfers for money's worth

29.25 Paragraph (1B)(c) of the Excise Goods, Beer and Tobacco Products (Amendment) Regulations 2002 states that:

If the goods in question are—
(i) transferred to another person for money or money's worth (including any reimbursement of expenses incurred in connection with obtaining them), or
(ii) the person holding them intends to make such a transfer,
   those goods are to be regarded as being held for a commercial purpose.

29.26 This comprehensive provision has the effect of catching any importation where the goods concerned are passed on in return for any payment, including any travel expenses. The transaction does not have to be for profit (indeed the legislation is broad enough to cover receiving payment at a loss), and it does not need to be for money, eg payment as a 'thank you' such as a dinner out would make the transfer commercial.

(9) EU reaction

29.27 In recent years the EU Commission has expressed dissatisfaction with the UK in relation to its application of the forfeiture provisions, particularly against travellers who are bringing in items such as cigarettes and alcohol on behalf of friends and not for profit.

29.28 Such transactions only amount to minor fiscal offences and individually represent only a small loss to the Revenue. As a result the Commission sent to the UK a 'reasoned opinion' on the basis that in certain circumstances the penalties for smuggling tobacco and alcohol were disproportionate and represented an obstacle to the free movement of goods. This is part of the pre litigation procedure set out in Article 226 of the EC treaty. Although the UK Government's initial reaction appeared to be one of defending their existing policies, anecdotally a slightly more relaxed approach has been adopted by officers at the ports, often resulting in first time offenders being given warnings, rather than having their goods seized in circumstances where the intended destination of the goods is to friends and family at cost price. (See *Hoverspeed Ltd* [2003] 2 WLR 950).

(10) What factors define 'commercial purpose'?

29.29 Paragraph (1B)(e) of the Excise Goods, Beer and Tobacco Products (Amendment) Regulations 2002 sets out a list of matters that may be taken into account by both Revenue and Customs and, ultimately, the magistrates' court, in making their determination as to whether the goods in question were being imported for a commercial purpose. These considerations are:

(a) the person's reasons for having possession or control of the goods;
(b) whether or not the person is a Revenue trader (as defined in s 1(1) of CEMA 1979);
(c) the person's conduct, including his intended use of the goods or any refusal to disclose his intended use of the goods;
(d) the location of the goods;
(e) the mode of transport used to convey the goods;
(f) any document or other information whatsoever relating to the goods;
(g) the nature of the goods, including the nature and condition of any package or container;
(h) the quantity of the goods; and in particular whether the quantity exceeds the guideline quantities (see para 29.37 below);
(i) whether the person personally financed the purchase of the goods in question; and
(j) any other circumstance which appears to be relevant.

29.30 Revenue traders, in the context of (b) above, are persons carrying on a trade or business involving the buying, selling, importation, exportation or dealing in or handling of excise goods. If the person importing the goods had an obvious outlet through which he could sell the goods then that would clearly be a matter that the court/Customs may wish to take account of.

29.31 Regard should be particularly given to (h), the quantity of the goods. If an individual is importing into the UK 100,000 cigarettes (eg in the boot of their car), there is a strong inference that they will not all be for personal use. Although that inference may be rebutted if the individual is a heavy smoker, rarely travels abroad, or has sufficient means or another legitimate non-commercial reason for bringing the cigarettes in, eg gifts for family members at Christmas.

29.32 It should further be noted that under (j) this list is not intended to be exhaustive.

29.33 In *R v Customs and Excise Commissioners ex p Mortimer* [1999] 1 WLR 17 the Court held that Customs officers must take account of the above reasons when considering whether or not they should seize goods. As a result, in practice, what is commonly referred to as an 'A to J interview' will take place at the initial point of interception.

29.34 In *Mortimer* Lord Bingham stated at p 22:

> .... fairness demands that the importer has a fair opportunity to satisfy the Customs & Excise, despite the quantity of the goods involved, that he is not importing them for a commercial purpose. It is plain that the Customs & Excise have no discretion whether or not to give such a fair opportunity: it is something they must do.

29.35 *Mortimer* was decided under the now defunct Excise Duties (Personal Reliefs) Order 1992. As a result the mandatory presumption referred to therein no longer applies. Under the new regulations, the fact that the goods in question now exceed the Minimum Indicative Levels (the quantity guidelines) is something which HMRC and the court are merely

B. The Condemnation and Forfeiture of Goods

entitled to have 'regard to'. The assertion however that the importer must have a 'fair opportunity' to satisfy Revenue and Customs of his case remains, it is submitted, good law.

29.36 In the Divisional Court's judgment of *R (Hoverspeed) v Customs and Excise Commissioners* [2002] 4 All ER 912, Brooke LJ stated that 'if no satisfactory explanation is forthcoming, then the national official may well conclude that the goods were indeed held for "commercial purposes".'

A refusal to provide an explanation, or a misleading explanation, may both be factors that a Court may ultimately take into account in deciding the issues it has to determine (see (c) in the A-J list).

(11) What are the minimum indicative levels?

29.37 The 'Minimum Indicative Level' is now a fairly dated term that relates to the guideline quantities set by the EU.

29.38 In January 2007 when travelling within the EU the quantities were:

- 10 litres of spirits
- 90 litres of wine
- 20 litres of 'intermediate products'
- 110 litres of beer
- 3200 cigarettes
- 400 cigarillos
- 200 cigars
- 3kg of any other tobacco products

(See subreg (1B)(e) of the Excise Goods, Beer and Tobacco Products (Amendment) Regulations 2002.)

29.39 The levels set out mirror the minimum levels that may be adopted by member states in EC Directive (EC) 92/12, (except those for cigarettes and hand rolling tobacco, which are four and three times respectively above the levels set out in the original Directive).

29.40 While difficult to quantify, the cigarette and tobacco levels represent around six months usage for an average smoker (20 cigarettes a day x 182 days = 3640 cigarettes).

29.41 Intermediate Products are defined in Article 17(1) of Council Directive (EC) 92/83.

29.42 It should be emphasised that these levels are only a guide. There are no limits. Genuine shoppers are entitled to bring back greater quantities for their own use. Nor is it unheard of for bootleggers to bring back quantities below the guidelines or matching the guidelines, in an attempt to avoid having their goods being seized. In *Harrison v Revenue and Customs Commissioners* (2007) The Times, 8 January 2007, Lightman J held that where quantities less than the presribed amount were brought into the UK, they could still lawfully be seized where there were ample other circumstances that justified Customs decision.

29.43 It should further be noted:

- If a traveller has over these limits he should declare the goods in the red channel.
- If the importer is under 17 the tobacco and alcohol allowances do not apply (ie there are no allowances).

- On transfer flights to other EU countries, it is only necessary to declare what is in hand luggage. Hold baggage contents need only be declared at the final destination.
- From certain EU countries (namely the Czech Republic, Estonia, Hungary, Latvia, Lithuania, Poland, Slovakia and Slovenia) other limits currently apply.
- For Bulgaria and Romania, see SI 2006 N. 3157.

(12) Travelling to the UK from outside the EU

29.44 Similar (albeit more restrictive) levels exist when travelling from a non-EU country (including the Canary Islands and the Channel Islands). Gibraltar is part of the EU, but is outside the EU customs territory, and therefore the 'outside the EU' levels apply. Similarly, although Cyprus is a member of the EU, any importation from an area not deemed under the control of the Government of the Republic of Cyprus is treated as a non-EU import. In January 2007 the 'outside the EU' levels were:

- 200 cigarettes or 100 cigarillos or 50 cigars or 250g of tobacco
- 2 litres of still table wine
- 1 litre of spirits or strong liqueurs over 22% in volume or 2 litres of fortified wine, sparkling wine or other liqueurs
- 60cc of perfume
- 250cc of eau de toilette
- £145 worth of other goods, including gifts and souvenirs

(See the schedule attached to the Traveller's Allowance Order 1994, SI 1994/955. The sum of £145 was substituted by SI 1995/3044 Art 2.)

C. Detention, Seizure and Condemnation

29.45 Section 139 of CEMA details the provisions as to detention, seizure and condemnation of goods, with s 139(6) referring to Sch 3 to the Act as having effect for the purpose of forfeiture and condemnation proceedings.

(1) The forfeiture provisions

29.46 Schedule 3 to CEMA sets out the relevant provisions relating to forfeiture, including notice of seizure, notice of claim, and condemnation. A copy of Sch 3 may be found at Appendix 20.

29.47 Paragraph 7 of Sch 3 states that the forfeiture shall have effect as from the date when the liability to forfeiture arose.

(2) What does 'liable to forfeiture' mean?

29.48 The expression 'liable to forfeiture', which is littered throughout the relevant forfeiture Acts and statutory provisions, denotes something different to 'shall be forfeited' or 'shall automatically be forfeited'. 'Liable' implies some form of discretion by those considering forfeiture, either at the time of seizure or later at court.

29.49 However, that initial elasticity may be somewhat illusory. Paragraph 6 of Sch3 to CEMA (see Appendix 20) states that if the court finds that the thing was at the time of seizure 'liable to forfeiture', the court shall (meaning must) condemn it as forfeit. The draconian

C. Dentention, Seizure and Condemnation

nature of these provisions appears to be analogous to strict liability/absolute offences in the criminal sphere, where intention or state of mind is irrelevant. This was confirmed in the case of *De Keyser v British Railway Traffic and Electric Co Ltd* [1936] 1 KB 224, where it was held that the justices were bound to condemn prohibited goods and that they possessed no discretion to refuse to do so, eg on the grounds of hardship of an innocent owner.

While Sch 3(6) offers no discretion, it must now be read in the light of recent decisions, particularly *Customs and Excise Commissioners v Newbury* [2003] 2 All ER 964 (DC), where arguments in terms of proportionality when condemning a vehicle as well as the goods seized were successfully raised. **29.50**

(3) Secondary forfeiture

Section 141(1) of CEMA states where anything has become liable to forfeiture under the Customs & Excise Acts: **29.51**

(a) any ship, aircraft, vehicle, animal, container (including any article of passengers' baggage) or other thing which has been used for the carriage, handling or concealment of the thing so liable to forfeiture, either at a time when it was so liable or for the purposes of the commission of the offence for which it later became so liable; and
(b) any other thing mixed, packed or found with the thing so liable, shall also be liable to forfeiture.

This section once again highlights the draconian nature of the forfeiture provisions by setting out the consequences for property found and used in connection with goods liable to forfeiture – hence the term 'secondary forfeiture'. **29.52**

Any vehicle used in the transportation of excise goods where no duty has been paid will itself be liable for forfeiture. Many travellers' motorcars have been forfeited as a result. Similarly, smaller quantities of goods that accompany larger importations of, eg tobacco or cigarettes, are themselves liable. So, where for example 60,000 cigarettes are being imported, together with 3 litres of gin and 1 litre of Bacardi, although the 3 litres of gin and the 1 litre of Bacardi may be understandably considered for personal use, because of s 141 and the provision as to any other thing mixed, packed or found with the thing so liable, the spirits are also liable to forfeiture. **29.53**

In *Travell v Customs and Excise Commissioners* (1997) 162 JP 181 the Divisional Court held that s 141(a) and (b) are be read disjunctively. **29.54**

The reference to 'any other thing' should be interpreted to include only things of a like kind. So for example, where 90 kgs of hand rolling tobacco are discovered in the suitcase of an individual, together with their travel alarm clock, the alarm clock is not an excise good, nor sufficiently similar to justify its forfeiture (see *R v Uxbridge Magistrates' ex p Webb* (1998) 162 JP 198 (DC)). **29.55**

The application of the 'mixed, packed or found' rule must always be a question of fact and degree upon which the Court must find. This is illustrated by *Travell*, where the Crown Court held that 365 obscene magazines found 'all over the Defendant's one bedroom flat', were also liable to forfeiture because they had been 'found with' 15 imported magazines containing indecent pictures of children. In *Webb* the defendant had imported six obscene videos in a suitcase. The magistrates fast forwarded through two of them and concluded **29.56** that their content was obscene. They condemned all six videos on the basis that the other four were 'packed with' the two videos liable to forfeiture that had been viewed.

29.57   In *Customs and Excise Commissioners v Jack Bradley (Accrington) Ltd* [1959] 1 QB 219, the Court held that where kerosene oil had been discovered in the fuel tanks of vehicles, the vehicles themselves would be liable to forfeiture since they had been 'used for the carriage' of the oil.

(4) More than one person involved

29.58   Where excise goods belonging to two people are seized as being liable to forfeiture, the fact that one of them makes no claim under Sch 3 cannot trigger the operation of s 141(1)(b) of the Act so as to preclude the other person from arguing that none of the goods were liable to forfeiture. In *Fox v Customs and Excise Commissioners*, The Times, 20 July 2002, Lightman J held:

> As a matter of common sense and as a matter of common justice it must be open to the owner of the seized goods (in this case Mr. Fox) to challenge the facts relied on to establish the liability to forfeiture of the other party's (in this case Mr. Everett) goods. It adds nothing to the point that the other party (in this case Mr. Everett) declined to make a claim or attend the hearing.

Transfers for money's worth and the gift provisions are considered at paras 29.24–29.25 above.

(5) Proof of certain other matters

29.59   Section 154 of CEMA deals with proof of certain other matters. Section 154(1) states:

> An averment in any process in proceedings under the Revenue and Customs Acts
>
> (a) That these proceedings were instituted by the Order of the Commissioners shall, until the contrary is proved, be sufficient evidence of the matter in question.
> (b) Where in any proceedings relating to Revenue and Customs any question arises as to the place in which any goods have been brought or as to whether or not any duty has been paid or secured in respect of any goods, then the burden of proof shall lie upon the other party to the proceedings.

(6) Stops at Coquelles

29.60   British Revenue and Customs also operate in Coquelles France as a result of agreements reached in relation to the Channel Tunnel. As a result, condemnation law also applies to this 'satellite port', pursuant to the Channel Tunnel (Alcoholic Liquor and Tobacco Products) (Amendment) Order 2002, SI 2002/2693.

D. Condemnation: Practice and Procedure

(1) Initial seizure

29.61   In the case of *R v Customs and Excise Commissioners ex p Mortimer* [1999] 1 WLR 17, it was determined that:

- fairness required Customs officers to give the importer a full opportunity to satisfy them that the importation was not for a commercial purpose; and to alert the traveller to the consequences of his failure to take that opportunity,

D. Condemnation: Practice and Procedure

- officers were obliged to make plain the purpose of any interview they conducted,
- where their purpose was both to investigate the possible commission of crime and to form a judgement for the purposes of forfeiture, they were required to inform the suspect accordingly, (including cautioning him and informing him of his right to remain silent in respect of the criminal investigation),
- officers should explain that under the forfeiture regulations, in the absence of a satisfactory explanation of the traveller's intentions, the goods might be seized

29.62 In *Mortimer*, the Court held that giving the traveller a fair opportunity meant two things: (1) it meant that the importer must have a full opportunity to say anything he wanted about his intentions in relation to the goods with a view to showing that his intentions were non-commercial, because he proposed to use them himself or give them to friends or relations as the case may be, and (2) it means that he must be alerted to the possible consequences if he does not take advantage of the opportunity to satisfy Customs that the goods are not being imported for a commercial purpose.

29.63 This should mean, in practice, that he is told in general terms of the existence of the Guideline quantities and of the consequence that the goods will be seized if Revenue and Customs are not satisfied with the explanation they are given.

29.64 These requirements are usually adhered to when the Revenue and Customs officer reads to the traveller what is referred to as the 'Commerciality Statement', which states:

> You have excise goods in your possession (control) which appear not to have borne UK duty.
>
> Goods may be held without payment of duty providing they have been acquired and are held for your own use. I suspect that you may be holding goods for a commercial purpose and not for your own use. I intend to ask you some questions to establish whether these goods are held for a commercial purpose.
>
> If no satisfactory explanation is forthcoming or if you do not stay for questioning it may lead me to conclude that the goods are not held for your own use but held for a commercial purpose and your goods (and vehicle) may be seized as liable to forfeiture.
>
> You are not under arrest and are free to leave at any time. Do you understand?

If yes, the officer should proceed to the A–J interview (see para 29.29 above), or explain the commerciality statement again. Furthermore, the person intercepted will also be issued with a Notice 1, which sets out the guidelines in terms of the Minimum Indicative Levels.

29.65 It is submitted that best practice dictates that a note of any conversation should be made, preferably contemporaneously. The 'Commerciality Statement' should be used and a copy exhibited/referred to in any statement made by the stopping officer, along with a copy of Notice 1, which should be handed to the traveller, preferably before questioning, with the opportunity being given to read it.

29.66 The case of *R v Customs and Excise Commissioners ex p Kenneth Stephen Boxall* (15 February 1996), although decided before the 1999 amendment, is useful in confirming the procedure of how travellers found with excise goods in their possession should be treated. It repeats that the Revenue and Customs must give the importer the opportunity to tell them why he has the goods in his possession and what he intends to do with them and to produce any document that relates to them. All of this must be done before they make any determination as to whether to seize the goods in question as liable to forfeiture (see p 4F of the judgment). It should be emphasised, as it was in *Boxall*, that natural justice obliges the Revenue and Customs to give the person concerned an opportunity to satisfy them that the goods were not imported for a commercial purpose. Not to do so would render the seizing of any excise goods as unlawful.

(2) Possible criminal proceedings

29.67 Section 139 of CEMA anticipates the possibility of criminal proceedings. There is the scope for charging individuals with an offence of evading duty contrary to s 170(1) and (2) of CEMA or the common law offence of cheating the Revenue. Within the statutory scheme each offence is punishable by up to seven years' imprisonment. If such proceedings are contemplated the codes and regulations set out in the Police and Criminal Evidence Act 1984 (PACE) should be followed.

29.68 However, it should be noted that for the purposes of a forfeiture hearing, a failure to follow PACE is not fatal, as the jurisdiction is civil and therefore falls outside of PACE's remit.

29.69 In *Mortimer*, Lord Bingham identified the practical difficulty Revenue and Customs officers may find themselves in if they were also investigating the possible commission of a crime. In such circumstances they would be obliged to caution the suspect and that would include the suspect being told that he does not have to say anything. The converse problem is that when dealing with the forfeiture aspect of the seizure, the importer is being actively encouraged to say anything that he wants to about the goods with a view to him showing that his intentions are non-commercial. Lord Bingham said there was no entirely simple answer to this practical problem. It would be incumbent on the interviewing officers to make plain the purposes of any interview, and if and when there are two purposes to explain them both. There must be no watering down of the caution, nor must there be any watering down of the officers' duties in respect of warning the traveller about his failure to not take advantage of the opportunity to satisfy Customs that the goods are not being imported for a commercial purpose.

(3) Notice of claim—the one month time limit to appeal

29.70 Schedule 3 to the CEMA states, at para 3, that:

> ... any person claiming that anything seized as liable to forfeiture is not so liable shall within one month of the date of notice of seizure or, where no such notice has been served on him, within one month of the date of the seizure, give notice of his claim in writing to the Commissioners at any office of Revenue and Customs.

29.71 Paragraph 4 of the same Schedule states that any notice under para 3 should specify the name and address of the claimant and, in the case of a claimant who is outside the UK, shall specify the name and address of a solicitor in the UK who is authorised to accept service of process and to act on behalf of the claimant.

(4) Six month time limit on HM Revenue and Customs once notice lodged

29.72 Paragraph 6 of Sch 3 to CEMA (see Appendix 20) states that where a notice of claim in respect of anything is duly given in accordance with paras 3 and 4 of the same Schedule, the

D. Condemnation: Practice and Procedure

Commissioners shall take proceedings for the condemnation of that thing, and if the court finds that the thing was at the time of seizure liable to forfeiture, the court shall condemn it as forfeited.

Accordingly, s 127 of the Magistrates' Court Act 1980 states: **29.73**

... a magistrates' court shall not try an information or hear a complaint unless the information was laid, or the complaint made, within 6 months from the time when the offence was committed.

In *Customs and Excise Commissioners v Venn* The Times, 24 January 2002, the Divisional Court held that CEMA drew a distinction between the detention of goods and the provisions of Sch 3 in respect of forfeiture. Forfeiture depended on there being a seizure of the goods. Where a person gave notice under paras 3 and 4 of Sch 3, claiming that goods seized as liable to forfeiture were not so liable, it was incumbent on the Commissioners to take proceedings for the condemnation of that thing by a court; and where such proceedings were instituted by way of a complaint in a magistrates' court, time ran for the purposes of s 127 of the Magistrates' Court Act 1980 from the date of service of the notice, not from the date of seizure. **29.74**

(5) Preparation for the hearing—service of evidence

There are no rules for service of evidence in the magistrates' court in respect of civil complaints. In the absence of such rules the court is able to regulate its own procedure (*Simms v Moore* [1970] 3 All ER 1). If legally relevant all evidence is admissible, unless excluded by some other rule. **29.75**

Prior to the hearing of any application for forfeiture at the magistrates' court, it is open to Revenue and Customs to either make voluntary disclosure of the evidence upon which it seeks to rely (although they are not obliged to do so), or, by correspondence with the defence, to ask for and arrange mutual disclosure. **29.76**

Voluntary disclosure is useful in cases where, eg the issues are straightforward, little is challenged, or where the witness in question, giving the statement, is unavailable to attend court. It enables his evidence to be agreed prior to the hearing. **29.77**

Mutual disclosure can equally be of assistance where the issues are not straightforward and matters are challenged, so as to expedite matters at Court and crystallise the arguments. This entails Revenue and Customs and the other side coming to an agreement that Revenue and Customs will reveal their case to the defence, ie statements, exhibits, interviews, etc, in return for the defence revealing to Revenue and Customs their case, including proofs of evidence of the defendant. This has the advantage of both parties knowing what the other will say before the case comes to court and avoids ambushes and costly adjournments. **29.78**

(6) Preparation for the hearing—dutiable goods

In *Boxall*, (p 6E), the Court held that para 6 of Sch 3 made it clear that it is for the court to consider whether the thing seized was at the time liable to forfeiture. Read with s 49(1), para 6 obliges the court to decide whether the goods are dutiable. On this question, the **29.79** burden lies on Revenue and Customs and, the proceedings being civil, the court must be satisfied on the balance of probabilities (in the majority of cases there is little issue over the fact that the goods are dutiable, as they generally relate to excise products like cigarettes and tobacco).

(7) The hearing—commercial purpose v own use

29.80 It will be incumbent upon the court to consider the evidence and determine the issue, namely whether the goods were imported for a commercial purpose, or for personal use. In so doing they should consider the criteria set out in at para 29.29 above (the A-J points under subreg (1B)(e)).

29.81 The inclusion of 'any other circumstance that appears to be relevant' (j) covers a multitude of matters, including frequency of travel. On one view an individual who travels abroad frequently does not need to 'stock up' on duty goods such as cigarettes because they know they will have the opportunity to purchase more cigarettes on their next trip. Similarly, an individual who makes regular day trips with the sole purpose of bringing back excise goods may have difficulty persuading a court it is not for a commercial purpose, particularly if, for example, they do not smoke heavily, or are purchasing a variety of brands of cigarettes (smokers tend to stick to the same brand); or if they are using a hire car (in the knowledge that it will avoid their own vehicle being seized – see (e) in the A–J list).

29.82 The court may also consider whether the defendant has been stopped before, or had knowledge of the Minimum Indicative Levels, whether there had been any attempt to hide or conceal the items in question, and whether the traveller's story had changed since the initial stop.

29.83 Conversely, if the 'aggravating' matters outlined above do not feature in the defendant's case, or, for example, he has receipts for the purchases, it is a first time stop, and has verification that the goods are intended for a family party or similar, the court may consider that the importation lacks commerciality (see (f) of the A–J list).

29.84 As has already been observed, the wording of the provisions are mandatory, akin to a strict liability office, and no discretion is afforded to the court in relation to the goods themselves if the court is satisfied on the balance of probabilities they were imported for a commercial purpose, as per *Fox v Customs and Excise Commissioners* (2002) 166 JP 578 at para 16, where Lightman J held:

> . . . the statutory language is mandatory: where the goods are liable to forfeiture the Court is bound to condemn them.

29.85 However, in relation to secondary forfeiture under s 141, eg a traveller's vehicle, the court is entitled to reach its independent judgment on proportionality, weighing up the evidence and the facts. In *Customs and Excise Commissioners v Newbury* [2003] 2 All ER 964 (DC), para 35, the Court held:

> . . . whether forfeiture would be so disproportionate as to be in breach of the particular claimant's rights under Article 1, Protocol 1, to the Convention . . . can be resolved by the court. This is not strictly a question of discretion but a matter upon which the court is entitled to reach its own independent judgment.

D. Condemnation: Practice and Procedure

(8) Court procedure: preliminary matters

29.86 Paragraphs 10(1) and (3) of Sch 3 to CEMA require that the claimant of the goods, ie the defendant, swears on oath that the thing seized was, or was to the best of his knowledge and belief, his property at the time of the seizure (his solicitor may also take the oath on his behalf for the purposes of this section). Paragraph 10(3) states that if any part of that procedure is not complied with, the court shall (meaning must) give judgment for the Commissioners.

29.87 This means that if the defendant is not prepared to state on oath that the goods seized in fact belonged to him and were his property, then the application for forfeiture on behalf of Revenue and Customs must succeed. There is no discretion to continue the hearing.

29.88 It is highly advisable that para 10(1) of Sch 3 to CEMA be dealt with at the outset of proceedings because it would be pointless to sit through an entire case if the defendant was not prepared to swear on oath that the goods belonged to him or, alternatively, that he declared that the goods belonged to another for whom he was acting.

29.89 In giving judgment for Revenue and Customs in such circumstances the court will not have considered the facts of the matter. It in effect becomes condemnation by default. A question therefore arises whether or not s 141 would apply, it only having application where there is a finding that the goods are liable for forfeiture. In such circumstances it will be necessary to invite the court to consider the facts and decide whether any of the goods were so liable, in order for the secondary forfeiture provisions of s 141 to bite (see *Fox v Customs and Excise Commissioners* (2002) 166 JP 578).

(9) Court procedure: condemnation by complaint

29.90 The procedural rules in relation to the hearing of a complaint and the jurisdiction of the magistrates' court are set out at s 51 et seq of the Magistrates' Courts Act 1980.

29.91 Section 52 confirms jurisdiction; s 53 deals with procedure, and states that at the hearing of a complaint, the court shall, if the defendant appears, state to him the substance of the complaint. Section 54 sets out the adjournment provisions, which may take place 'at any time'; and s 55 confirms that if a defendant does not appear the court may proceed in his absence. Similarly, under s 56 where at the time and place appointed for the hearing or adjourned hearing of a complaint the defendant appears but the complainant does not, the court may dismiss the complaint or, if evidence has been received on a previous occasion, proceed in the absence of the complainant. Section 57 states that where neither party attends, the court may dismiss the complaint; and s 58 deals with the transfer of proceedings.

(10) Order of speeches

Once ownership of the goods has been established, the procedure to be followed is set out in the Magistrates' Court Rules 1981 at r 14.

29.92 The order of evidence and speeches in a complaint are as follows:

(i) On the hearing of a complaint, the complainant shall call his evidence and before doing so may address the court.

(ii) At the conclusion of the evidence, for the complainant, the defendant may address the court, whether or not he afterwards calls evidence.
(iii) At the conclusion of the evidence, if any for the defence, the complainant may call evidence to rebut that evidence.
(iv) At the conclusion of the evidence for the defence and the evidence, if any, in rebuttal, the defendant may address the court if he has not already done so.
(v) Either party may, with the leave of the court, address the court a second time, but where the court grants leave to one party, it shall not refuse leave to the other.
(vi) Where the defendant obtains leave to address the court for a second time, his second address shall be made before the second address, if any, of the complainant.

29.93 It follows from the above that Revenue and Customs only has one opportunity to address the court on the facts without further leave; and that is at the beginning of their case.

29.94 It should be noted that either party may, with the leave of the court, address the court a second time or, as in any proceedings, either party may address the court on a point of law at any stage.

29.95 Although the defendant is free to make a submission of no case to answer after the applicant's case, some caution should be exercised, because if it fails and the defendant has been asked to choose between calling evidence and making a submission, he will not be entitled to call evidence thereafter. See *Boyce v Wyatt Engineering* The Times, 14 June 2001.

29.96 It should also be noted that Revenue and Customs has the opportunity to call evidence in rebuttal should it wish to do so. This may occur in forfeiture cases where something has been suggested during the course of the defence case that is either new or was not put to the officer in the case at the first opportunity, and where the officer in the case knows that that aspect of the defence's case needs correcting.

(11) The burden and standard of proof

29.97 It is for Revenue and Customs to satisfy the court, on the balance of probabilities, that the goods were imported for a commercial purpose (*R (Hoverspeed) v Customs and Excise Commissioners* [2002] 4 All ER 912 (DC) para 130/10).

29.98 This was illustrated in the VAT and Duties Tribunal case of *Bevins and Pyrah v Customs and Excise Commissioners* [2005](EO00903) where the Tribunal held that Customs had misapplied the law by incorrectly imposing the burden of proof on the travellers. Both the decision to seize the goods and the decision not to restore had been made on the basis that the travellers had not made out a satisfactory case that the goods were for their own use. It was held that following the decision in *Hoverspeed* such a positive burden could no longer apply; the burden in the first instance was on Customs to show that the goods were for a commercial use.

29.99 It is useful when addressing the court to remind them that they are sitting in their civil jurisdiction and that the burden of proof is that of the 'balance of probabilities' and not that which they may be more familiar with, namely beyond reasonable doubt.

29.100 In other words, the defendant does not have to satisfy the court beyond reasonable doubt that the goods were for his personal use, but only that it is more likely than not that they

D. Condemnation: Practice and Procedure

were. Equally however, HM Revenue and Customs does not need to make them sure that the goods were being imported for a commercial purpose, but only satisfy them that it was more likely than not that that was the case.

29.101 In many civil cases the degree of probability required to establish proof may vary according to the allegation to be proved (see *Hornal v Neuberger Products Ltd* [1957] 1 QB 247) and the court is often reluctant, when considering claims by the Crown, to apply merely a 51/49 per cent test where an individual's property or other assets are in jeopardy (see *Bater v Bater* [1950] 2 All ER 458 and *B v Chief Constable of Avon and Somerset* [2001] 1 All ER 562).

(12) Hearsay in civil cases

29.102 The Magistrates' Courts (Hearsay Evidence in Civil Proceedings) Rules 1999, SI 1999 No 681 set out the rules applying to hearsay in magistrates' courts.

Those rules provide as follows:

3 (1) Subject to paragraphs (2) and (3), a party who desires to give hearsay evidence at the hearing must, not less than 21 days before the date fixed for the hearing, serve a hearsay notice on every other party and file a copy in the court by serving it on the justices' clerk.
3 (2) Subject to paragraph (3), the court or the justices' clerk may make a direction substituting a different period of time for the service of the hearsay notice under paragraph (1) on the application of a party to the proceedings.
3 (3) The court may make a direction under paragraph (2) of its own motion.
3 (4) A hearsay notice must-
  (a) state that it is a hearsay notice;(b) identify the proceedings in which the hearsay evidence is to be given;(c) state that the party proposes to adduce hearsay evidence;(d) identify the hearsay evidence;(e) identify the person who made the statement which is to be given in evidence; and(f) state why that person will not be called to give oral evidence.
3 (5) A single hearsay notice may deal with the hearsay evidence of more than one witness.

These Rules also make provision for:

- the procedure to call a witness for cross-examination on hearsay evidence (r 4);
- a notice requirement where a party tenders hearsay evidence but does not call the person who made the statement to give oral evidence, and another party wishes to attack the credibility of the person who made the statement or allege that he has made another statement inconsistent with it (r 5)
- the service of documents required by the Rules (r 6).

29.103 However, a failure to comply with the duty to give notice should not affect the admissibility of hearsay evidence (see s 1(1) of the Civil Evidence Act 1995 and s 1(2) which is specifically adopted by r 2(2)). It then becomes a question of weight for the justices to determine. In assessing the weight, all the relevant circumstances should be considered including that the individual who makes the statement has not been tendered in cross-examination and therefore has not been tested. The desirability of serving a hearsay notice is obvious as a party may find itself liable for costs if a witness statement tendered at the hearing reveals new evidence that the other side has not had the opportunity of exploring, or fresh evidence that amounts to an ambush.

29.104 Section 4(2) of the Civil Evidence Act 1995 gives some guidance that may assist the Court when assessing what weight should be given to hearsay evidence. That guidance includes:

(i) Whether it would have been reasonable and practicable to have produced the person who made the statements rather than relying on a hearsay report;

(ii) Whether the person who originally made the statements made them contemporaneously with the matters stated;

(iii) Whether the evidence is multiple hearsay, in other words whether the hearsay witness is in fact repeating something which itself is hearsay;

(iv) Whether anyone involved has a motive to conceal or misrepresent matters;

(v) Whether the original statement was made for some purpose or produced in collaboration with others;

(vi) Whether the attempt to rely on hearsay rather than calling the person who made the original statement is designed to prevent a proper valuation of its weight by the Court.

29.105 In the Crown Court the position is slightly different, although the same principle appears to apply. In *R v Wadmore and Foreman* [2006] EWCA Crim 686, a case that concerned an application for an anti-social behaviour order, the Court of Appeal held that ASBOs amounted to civil proceedings in a criminal court. The Criminal Procedure Rules 2005 did not apply to civil cases. The Civil Procedure Rules 1998 do not apply in criminal courts. The Magistrates' Courts (Hearsay Evidence in Civil Proceedings) Rules 1999 did not apply to the Crown Court. The Court of Appeal therefore assumed that as the case was civil in nature, hearsay evidence was admissible under s 1 of the Civil Evidence Act 1995. There were no applicable procedural rules and the Court thought that the Magistrates' Court Rules should be applied by analogy.

(13) Previous convictions

29.106 In *Halford and Brooks [Senior]* The Times, 3 October 1991 the Court confirmed that in civil proceedings a different approach to allegations of criminal behaviour may be taken, in that there is no right to silence and evidence of 'bad character' can be admitted (see also *Ali v Best* (1997) 161 JP 399H).

29.107 Previous convictions can be proved by the production of a certificate of conviction, which is admissible by virtue of ss 11 and 12 of the Civil Evidence Act 1968, (in force by virtue of the Civil Evidence Act 1968 (Commencement No 1) Order 1968, SI 1968/1734 and not repealed by the Civil Evidence Act 1995).

29.108 Where an individual is acquitted in criminal proceedings the evidence of those proceedings is admissible (see *Customs and Excise Commissioners v T* (1998) 162 JP 193, citing *Hunter v Chief Constable of West Midlands* [1982] AC 529 (HL)).

(14) Reasons for stopping the traveller

29.109 The only issue before the court is that concerning commercial or personal use. The action is against the goods, *in rem*, and not against the individual. As a result the reason why an individual was stopped falls away as being irrelevant to the matter the court has to decide.

29.110 Similarly, the seizure of the goods cannot be regarded as axiomatically invalid, merely because it occurred as a result of a check that was invalid or unlawful. See *Customs and Excise Commissioners v Atkinson, Dore and Binns* [2003] EWHC Admin 421; *Customs and Excise Commissioners v Newbury* [2003] 2 All ER 964 (DC) (at para 5) and *Hoverspeed v Customs and Excise Commissioners* [2002] EWCA Civ 1804 at paras 44-49. The Court of Appeal ruled in the case of *Hoverspeed* that no link between the legality of the stop and the legality of any subsequent seizure: '. . . can or should in our view be read into the provisions of CEMA' (para 48). In so finding the court held that it did not "see any unfairness in the seizure of the goods liable to forfeiture, even though their presence happens only to be discovered in the course of unlawful check. That may be bad luck, but it is not unfair.

(15) Power to stop the traveller

29.111 The power of Revenue and Customs to stop and search an individual and their vehicle derives from ss 78, 163A and 164 of CEMA.

E. Condemnation: Costs and Compensation

(1) Costs

29.112 Under s 64(1) of the Magistrates' Courts Act 1980:

(1) On the hearing of a complaint a Magistrates' Court shall have power in its discretion to make such order as to costs—
   (a) on making the order for which the complaint is made, to be paid by the Defendant to the Complainant;
   (b) on dismissing the complaint, to be paid by the Defendant to the Complainant,
   as it thinks just and reasonable . . .

29.113 Pursuant to s 62(2) the amount ordered to be paid shall be specified in the Order and s 62(3) confirms that the costs ordered shall be enforceable as a civil debt. In other words, not administered by the magistrates' court.

29.114 It is always advisable to apply for costs on the same day and at the same time as the hearing of the forfeiture application. This is because such an order has to be made by the same Bench who made the order in relation to the forfeiture application. Like all civil matters, costs follow the event, sometimes expressed as 'winner takes all', unless there are justifiable reasons why costs should not follow the event.

29.115 Defence solicitors should advise their clients very cautiously about this aspect of the proceedings. Revenue and Customs are known to seek their full commercial costs in forfeiture proceedings which can amount to several thousand pounds. Clearly it will sometimes be advisable to take a commercial view on whether to pursue litigation in cases where the value of the goods is not particularly high or where any prospective costs order is likely to make pursuing the claim prohibitive.

29.116 Equally, if the Revenue and Customs application was not successful, the defendant would be able to ask for his legal costs in defending the matter. Again some caution should be exercised when advising on this aspect, as Revenue and Customs would be entitled to object to such an order if, for example, the defendant had raised matters in the magistrates' court for the first time in dealing with the application for forfeiture which he had not mentioned, either at the time of seizure or subsequently in correspondence.

29.117 In exercising its discretion the court can take into account that Revenue and Customs are exercising their statutory function in condemnation matters. See *R v Uxbridge Justices ex p Metropolitan Police Commissioner* [1981] 1 QB 829; *Bradford City Metropolitan District Council v Booth* The Times, 31 May 2000; and *R (Chief Constable of Northamptonshire) v Daventry Magistrates' Court* [2001] EWHC (Admin) 446.

29.118 Importantly, costs must not be used as a device to overcompensate the successful party, or punish the unsuccessful party *(R v Highgate Justices ex p Petrou* [1954] 1 All ER 406*)*.

29.119 The power of the magistrates' court to make a wasted costs order is governed by s 145A of the Magistrates' Court Act 1980 and SI 1991/2096.

(2) LSC funding

29.120 Legal Service Commission funding is not generally available for civil proceedings, although pursuant to the Access to Justice Act 1999 (AJA), a person may apply for public funding as part of the Community Legal Service. Section 6(6) of the AJA however does not permit the funding of services within Sch 2, and para 2(3) prohibits the funding of advocacy in any proceedings in the magistrates' court. Condemnation proceedings in both the magistrates' court and the Crown Court therefore appear to be excluded.

29.121 In *R (Mudie) v Kent Magistrates' Court* [2003] 2 All ER 631, the Court of Appeal confirmed that condemnation proceedings could not be extended to criminal proceedings, and therefore Criminal Defence Service funding was not available. Although, as Laws LJ observed in *Mudie*, there was nothing to prevent solicitors entering into conditional fee agreements in condemnation proceedings (para 6).

(3) Compensation

29.122 Under s 144:

(1) Where, in any proceedings for the condemnation of any thing seized as liable to forfeiture under the customs and excise Acts, judgment is given for the claimant, the court may, if it sees fit, certify that there were reasonable grounds for the seizure.

(2) Where any proceedings, whether civil or criminal, are brought against the Commissioners, a law officer of the Crown or any person authorised by or under the Customs and Excise Acts 1979 to seize or detain any thing liable to forfeiture under the customs and excise Acts on account of the seizure or detention of any thing, and judgment is given for the plaintiff or prosecutor, then if either—

(a) a certificate relating to the seizure has been granted under subsection (1) above; or

(b) the court is satisfied that there were reasonable grounds for seizing or detaining that thing under the customs and excise Acts,

the plaintiff or prosecutor shall not be entitled to recover any damages or costs and the defendant shall not be liable to any punishment.

29.123 In the event of not succeeding with a forfeiture application, Revenue and Customs will always be anxious to ensure that the 's 144 certificate' as to the reasonableness of their original seizure is signed, to preclude any claim for compensation. This is equally so where the court has condemned (for example) tobacco, but refused to condemn the vehicle that was used to transport it (secondary forfeiture).

F. Condemnation Appeals

29.124 Both Revenue and Customs and the defendant may appeal from the magistrates' court decision to the Crown Court, or in the alternative invite the Court to state a case for the High Court on a matter of law (see paragraph 11 of Sch 3 to CEMA). The Crown Court's jurisdiction and powers of disposal are set out in ss 45-48 of the Supreme Court Act 1981.

(1) Procedure

29.125 On appeal to the Crown Court the hearing is de novo (s 79(3) of the Supreme Court Act 1981) and involves a complete rehearing of the original case, including oral evidence. Rule 63.2 of the Criminal Procedure Rules sets out the time limit (21 days) and the procedure (written notice to the magistrates' court), appears to have been adopted for use in complaint appeals, albeit the appeal is civil.

29.126 The procedure adopted at the hearing is the same as set out in the Magistrates' Courts Rules above. Pending the rehearing, there is no restriction on either Revenue and Customs or the defence obtaining more evidence and adducing new evidence at the appeal.

29.127 In *R (Customs and Excise Commissioners) v Maidstone Crown Court* [2004] EWHC (Admin) 1459, Customs sought judicial review of two decisions of the Crown Court in relation to granting permission to appeal out of time. The original applications had been made without notice and were made after several months of delay. There was no proper explanation as to why there had been a delay and the Judge granted permission without giving any reasons. Newman J held that it was incumbent on a judge in the proper exercise of his discretion to consider the reasons given for any delay and to address the proposed merits of the appeal in the light of said delay. Furthermore, a judge should in the interests of justice give reasons for the grant or refusal of permission and communicate that decision to any affected party.

(2) Pre-hearing review

29.128 It is advisable to have some form of Pre-hearing Review at the appeal stage. There are a multitude of reasons for this, which include:

- To assist the court with a time estimate; eg if there are four Revenue and Customs officers being called and two defendants that is likely to occupy a day, if not two days, of court time;
- To determine which witnesses are required, and ascertain their availability to give evidence;
- To notify any points of law that may prolong matters at the appeal hearing; and
- To deal with other matters that may or may not be relevant to the particular case, for example, whether or not an interpreter is required, etc.

(3) Pending the hearing of an appeal

29.129 It should be noted that Art 12 of Sch 3 to CEMA states that pending the final determination by way of appeal of the matter, the goods in question should be left with Revenue and Customs (see Appendix 20).

G. Condemnation in the High Court

29.130 Although rare, as HMRC nearly always commences proceedings in the magistrates' court, condemnation cases may be brought in the High Court. In such cases procedure is by Claim Form and follows the Civil Procedure Rules. Costs are dealt with in CPR Part 44.

H. Condemnation and the ECHR

29.131 The legitimacy of forfeiture proceedings was considered in *Goldsmith v Customs and Excise Commissioners* The Times, 12 June 2001. In that case, the Divisional Court considered what application, if any, Article 6(2) of the European Convention of Human Rights had in relation to Sch 3 to CEMA. The Court found that because proceedings for the condemnation of goods as liable to forfeiture do not involve the determination of a criminal charge, none of the usual consequences of criminal conviction follow on from such proceedings. Therefore, even if the proceedings were proceedings to which the presumption of innocence in Article 6(2) of the European Convention of Human Rights applied, the burden of proof imposed on the importer of excise goods to rebut Customs' assertion that the importation was for a commercial purpose was proportionate, reasonable and justified.

29.132 This issue was also considered in *Salabiaku v France* (1988) 13 EHRR 379, where the Court held that there was nothing particularly unfair in imposing a burden of proof on someone where the subject matter was something that he was particularly well placed to prove. See also *The Netherlands v Joustra* C5-05 (ECJ, 23 November 2006).

29.133 It will be noted that pursuant to Article 1 of Protocol 1 the right to property is not absolute and the State is permitted to secure property in order to control the use of it in accordance with the general interest or securing the payment of taxes and other contributions or penalties. Condemnation proceedings have also been found to be compliant with the ECHR and Article 6 in *Air Canada v UK* (1995) 20 EHRR 150, para 61–63.

29.134 In relation to the condemnation of a vehicle and Article 1, see *Hopping v Customs and Excise Commissioners (EOO 170) (2001),* at para 29.240 below.

I. Red Diesel Cases

(1) Introduction

29.135 Section 139 and Sch 3 to CEMA is intended to cover a myriad of circumstances where Revenue and Customs are entitled to bring proceedings for the condemnation of goods as forfeit.

29.136 Revenue and Customs are allowed, by law, to examine any vehicle, any oil in or on it, and to inspect, test or sample any oil in the fuel supply. They are also entitled to require vehicle

I. Red Diesel Cases

owners or anyone in charge of a vehicle to open a fuel tank or other sources of the fuel supply so that the fuel can be located and inspected or tested or sampled. If there is anything in the supply that might hinder this, it can be removed. They are also entitled, by law, to require anyone in charge of the vehicle to produce any books or documents relating to the vehicle or about the oil carried on it. They are entitled to enter and inspect any premises (except private dwelling-houses) and inspect test and sample any oil on the premises whether in a vehicle or elsewhere. In short, their powers are wide reaching.

(2) The legislative provisions

29.137 Red diesel is gas/heavy oil that carries a lower (rebated) rate of duty. It is commonly referred to as 'red diesel' because of the red dye used in its production. The relevant law is found in the Hydrocarbon Oils Duties Act 1979 at ss 12(2) and 13(6). Section 12(2) reads:

No heavy oil on whose delivery for home use rebate has been allowed . . . shall:
(a) be used as fuel for a road vehicle; or
(b) be taken into a road vehicle as fuel . . .

Section 12(3) states:

(a) Heavy oil shall be deemed to be used as fuel for a road vehicle if, but only if, it is used as fuel for the engine provided for propelling the vehicle or for an engine which draws its fuel from the same supply as that engine; and
(b) heavy oil shall be deemed to be taken into a road vehicle as fuel if, but only if, it is taken into it as part of that supply.

29.138 Derv (fuel for a diesel engine road vehicle) is heavy oil that carries a higher rate of excise duty than other heavy oils such as aviation kerosene, fuel oil, gas oil, and kerosene. It has now been replaced by the more environmentally friendly ultra low sulphur diesel (ULSD), which is also defined as a heavy oil.

29.139 By definition any oil which does not meet the criteria for classification as a light oil is a heavy oil: see s 1(3) and (4) of the Hydrocarbon Oils Duties Act 1979.

Section 13(6) states:

Any heavy oil—
(a) taken into a road vehicle as mentioned in s 12(2) above or supplied as mentioned in sub-section 12(2) or (3) above; or
(b) taken as fuel into a vehicle at a time when it is not a road vehicle and remaining in the vehicle as part of its fuel supply at a later time when it becomes a road vehicle,
shall be liable for forfeiture.

29.140 Because these matters, like the matters dealt with elsewhere in this chapter, are similar to strict liability offences (although not criminal), the defendant's state of mind or mitigating circumstances tends to be irrelevant. The action is against the fuel, as opposed to the individual.

29.141 In *Customs and Excise Commissioners v Jack Bradley* [1959] 1 QB 219 (one of the few reported cases on red diesel) Lord Parker held that where oil was being carried and was being consumed it became liable to forfeiture. Lord Parker held (at p 224):

> The offence is the use of oil . . . one thing at least is clear, that oil is used when it is consumed . . . .

29.142 It appears to follow therefore that even a vehicle that is shunted stands liable for forfeiture if the fuel is being used, for example, to create pressure, as opposed to propelling the vehicle.

(3) Excepted vehicles

29.143 Excepted vehicles to the provisions of the Hydrocarbon Oils Duties Act are set out in Sch 1 to the Act.

Schedule 1 reads:
(1) A vehicle is an excepted vehicle where—
  (a) it is not used on a public road, and
  (b) no licence under the Vehicle Excise and Registration Act 1994 is in force in respect of it.

Public roads are roads repairable at public expense.

Schedule 1(para 12) states as follows:
(1) A vehicle is an excepted vehicle if it is—
  (a) a road construction vehicle, and
  (b) used or kept solely for the conveyance of built-in road construction machinery (with or without articles or material used for the purposes of the machinery).
(2) In sub-paragraph 1 above "road construction vehicle" means a vehicle:
  (a) which is constructed or adapted for use for the conveyance of built-in road construction machinery, and
  (b) which is not constructed or adapted for the conveyance of any other load except articles and material used for the purposes of such machinery.
(3) In sub-paragraphs (1) and (2) above "built-in road construction machinery", in relation to a vehicle, means road construction machinery built-in as part of, or permanently attached to, the vehicle.
(4) In sub-paragraph (3) above "road construction machinery" means a machine or device suitable for use for the construction or repair of roads and used for no purpose other than the construction or repair of roads".

29.144 Provided the vehicle a defendant operates satisfies all of the criteria at subss 1-4 above, it may be classed as a road construction vehicle and is able to use rebated heavy oil (red diesel) as fuel when travelling on a public road.

29.145 Depending on circumstances, vehicles excepted under the scheme include tractors, agricultural vehicles, gritters, mobile cranes, digging machines, work trucks, road construction vehicles and road rollers (a question mark remains over street-lighting vehicles). In terms of penalties the Misuse of Rebated Oil levy now has the maximum civil penalty of £500.

29.146 In *Renfrewshire BC v Revenue and Customs Commissioners* (E00963) (2006) a VAT and Duties Tribunal held that a tractor was an 'excepted vehicle' when it was being used on a public road, within the meaning of Sch 1, when it was either travelling on its way to a site to perform an agricultural activity or its use on the road had some relationship or connection with such an activity (Lawtel, 24 August 2006).

(4) Compounding

29.147 Often in red diesel cases Revenue and Customs will offer to settle the matter upon the payment of a settlement sum. This is known as compounding. The purpose of a compound settlement is to save time and money for them and the defendant, and avoid the need for

I. Red Diesel Cases

legal proceedings. It is important to note that Revenue and Customs are only likely to offer a compound settlement where they have sufficient evidence to proceed to court. It is equally important to note that a compound settlement will not be offered in every case, and much will depend on what is being alleged.

(5) Procedural requirements

Schedule 5 sets out the procedure that must be followed when a person takes a sample from the motor vehicle for these purposes. **29.148**

Section 32 of that Schedule states:

Without prejudice to the admissibility of the evidence of the analyst [who analyses the sample and certifies it as red diesel] such a certificate shall not be admissible as evidence—
(a) unless a copy of it has, not less than 7 days before the hearing, been served by . . . the Commissioners on all other parties; or
(b) if any of those other parties, not less than 3 days before the hearing . . . serves notice on the Commissioners requiring the attendance at the hearing of the person by whom the analysis was made.

The main court procedural requirements for complaints, including appeals, are set out within the condemnation part of this chapter above, and apply equally to red diesel matters.

It is commonplace for somebody who is subject to a seizure to invite HMRC to conduct a review of its decision, as a part of which the person whose property has been seized will have the opportunity to set out his reasons for disagreeing with the decision to seize the property as liable to forfeiture. **29.149**

(6) The vehicle and the fuel

Section 141 of CEMA applies, so if the fuel is liable for forfeiture, the vehicle being used to carry it also becomes liable to forfeiture (secondary forfeiture). (See *Customs and Excise Commissioners v Jack Bradley (Accrington) Ltd* [1959] 1 QB 219, where the Court held that where kerosene oil had been discovered in the fuel tank of a vehicle, the vehicle itself would be liable to forfeiture since it had been 'used for the carriage' of the oil.) **29.150**

Similar arguments in relation to 'bootlegging' matters arise here in terms of proportionality, and whether it would be proportionate to condemn a vehicle with a value of eg £20,000, which was carrying a tank load of red diesel (value eg £35). See para 29.85 above and particularly *Customs and Excise Commissioners v Newbury* [2003] 2 All ER 964 (DC). Much will depend on the circumstances of the seizure: whether it is a first time 'offence', whether warnings have been previously given, the quantities involved, whether HMRC officials/the court were deliberately misled; or whether there exist other 'aggravating' features. Conversely, if such circumstances do not exist, this may amount to a compelling reason not to order secondary forfeiture. **29.151**

(7) The civil burden

If the court finds on the balance of probabilities (these being civil proceedings) that the vehicles were carrying, handling or concealing oil liable to forfeiture, then it has no discretion and must order forfeiture: see Sch 3(6) to CEMA (Appendix 20 of this book). **29.152**

(8) Criminal offences

29.153 While outside the auspices of this book, it is worth noting that the criminal law creates certain offences in relation to the use of oil (other than Derv) to fuel 'road vehicles'. This includes using any oil on which the Derv rate of duty has not been paid. Similarly it forbids the use of fully rebated kerosene to propel a vehicle, or fuel an engine (except one only providing heat); or supply other oils which a defendant may have reason to believe will be used to fuel 'road vehicles'.

29.154 The law goes further in that it makes it an offence to remove any designated chemical marker or dye from any oil (although how commonplace this is, is questionable). Similarly the law makes it an offence to obstruct any officer from Revenue and Customs from obtaining a sample of oil. For completeness, it is also an offence to mix any rebated or duty free oil with any oil on which no rebate has been allowed. In *R v Owens and Owens* (2006) 150 SJ 1188, it was held that any sample must be taken in the presence of the person concerned.

29.155 In the majority of cases the vehicle in question will be restored to the defendant on payment of an amount of money known as the 'restoration amount'. This amount will consist of a penalty for any additional offence committed (a penalty of £250 may be imposed for each offence, see s 13(1)(a) and (b) of the Hydrocarbon Oils Duties Act 1979) and an assessment for the duty rebate. If the offence is considered serious the vehicle may be seized and forfeited and may not be restored to the defendant.

J. Delivery Up

(1) Introduction

29.156 The seizure of goods as liable to forfeiture does not mean that the individual from whom they were seized or the owner of the goods will be unable to regain control of the goods, even if that individual has accepted (or it has been found) that the goods were imported for a commercial purpose.

Revenue and Customs are afforded a discretion to either restore the goods/thing seized or offer 'delivery up'.

(2) The legislative provisions

29.157 The power to offer delivery up is found in para 16 of Sch 3 to CEMA, (see Appendix 20).

29.158 This enables Revenue and Customs, prior to the condemnation of the goods/thing that has been seized, to return it upon payment of a sum, not exceeding the value of the thing seized (including any duty or tax that was due).

29.159 The amount paid for delivery up is in effect a deposit. If the thing is later condemned by the court (or because a valid notice of claim/appeal is not received) the amount paid is forfeited. On the other hand, if the appeal is successful and the court finds in favour of the original owner, Revenue and Customs must return the sum. The benefit for the owner is that they have the use of the thing seized while the appeal against seizure is pending.

K. Restoration

In terms of most goods/things, Revenue and Customs do not usually seek payment of more than the retail value of the thing. The retail value can often be established from valuation guides eg, for vehicles, Glass's Guide. **29.160**

(3) Practice

It should be noted that in practice Revenue and Customs do not normally offer 'delivery up' if they would not subsequently be prepared to restore it (see below). Customs would argue that to do differently would negate the purpose of forfeiture. Nor should the offer of delivery up be construed as an admission by Revenue and Customs that they were wrong to seize the thing in the first place. The fact that the goods/thing is delivered up will not avoid the court proceedings or a final determination by the magistrates. Revenue and Customs will undoubtedly pursue the court proceedings, not least because they would be liable for repayment of the sum paid (by way of refund) if they were not to. **29.161**

K. Restoration

(1) The statutory basis

Section 152(b) of CEMA allows for the restoration of goods that have been seized or forfeited: **29.162**

The Commissioners may, as they see fit—
(b) restore, subject to such conditions (if any) as they think proper, any thing forfeited or seized under [those] Acts.

Unlike 'delivery up', restoration will normally only take place once a seized thing has been condemned, either following a hearing or because the thing has been deemed forfeit because no valid notice of claim/appeal has been lodged (see para 5 of Sch 3, Appendix 20). Revenue and Customs are entitled to impose such reasonable conditions 'as they think proper' as part of the agreement to restore. Common examples include the payment of a sum; production of an import licence (where one is required to import the thing); or re-labelling (where goods were seized under the Trades Description Act because they have false marks of origin). Unlike 'delivery up', a restoration amount is non-refundable. As can be seen, restoration is not automatic. Revenue and Customs may refuse to restore the goods/thing concerned. That refusal is likely to lead, in certain cases to complaint. The remedy is by way of an appeal to the VAT and Duties Tribunal. **29.163**

(2) Appeals against non-restoration

Appeals against decisions not to restore the goods/thing are dealt with by the VAT and Duties Tribunal. The Tribunal derives its jurisdiction from s16(1) of the Finance Act 1994, which gives the Tribunal the power to review Commissioners'/Revenue and Customs' decisions in a number of areas. **29.164**

(3) Burden and standard of proof

In *Golobiewska v Customs and Excise Commissioners* The Times, 25 May 2005, the Court of Appeal held that the effect of s 16(6) of the Finance Act 1994 was to impose the burden of **29.165** proof on the appellant to establish, on the balance of probabilities, grounds showing that the vehicle should be restored. Such a burden was to the civil standard. See also *Szukala Trans Pthu Export-Import v Revenue and Customs Commissioners* (2006) 150 SJ 571 (below).

29.166 However, a distinction must be drawn where one of the factual issues is the question of own use/commercial purpose. In *Bevins and Pyrah v Customs and Excise Commissioners* [2005](EO00903) the Tribunal held that Customs had misapplied the law by incorrectly imposing the burden of proof on the travellers. Both the decision to seize the goods and the decision not to restore had been made on the basis that the travellers had not made out a satisfactory case that the goods were for their own use. Following the decision in *Hoverspeed* such a positive burden could no longer apply. The burden in the first instance was on Customs to show that the goods were for a commercial use.

(4) Test of reasonableness

29.167 Section 16(4) of the Finance Act 1994 introduces a question of reasonableness for the Tribunal to consider and states:

> (4) In relation to any decision as to an ancillary matter, or any decision on the review of such a decision, the powers of an Appeal Tribunal on an appeal under this section shall be confined to a power, where the Tribunal are satisfied that the Commissioners could not reasonably have arrived at it.

29.168 Appeals against non-restoration are ancillary (see Sch 5 para 2(r) of the Finance Act 1994; and s 14(1)(d) of the Finance Act 1994). It is the ancillary decision of HMRC not to restore the thing/goods that are subject to forfeiture, which is secondary in time (and thus ancillary) to the decision to condemn the goods as forfeit.

29.169 In short, the Tribunal is asking itself whether or not the Commissioners/HMRC acted reasonably in deciding to refuse to restore the goods/thing concerned. In *Szukala Trans Pthu Export-Import v Revenue and Customs Commissioners* (2006) 150 SJ 571, the Tribunal held that it was for the appellant to show that the decision was unreasonable. In order to be reasonable, a decision must be soundly based factually; and in this regard the Tribunal had a fact finding function. Since facts were not a matter of discretion but of evidence, if the decision of the reviewing officer was found to have been based on facts that were materially incorrect, his decision would be unreasonable and the Tribunal should direct a fresh review under s 16(4).

29.170 In *Ware v Customs and Excise Commissioners* (E00735) the Tribunal recognised a generally accepted test for what is reasonable: (para 18).

- Is this a decision that no reasonable panel of Commissioners could have come to?
- Has some irrelevant matter been taken into account?
- Has some matter which should have been taken into account been ignored?
- Has there been some error of law? (see *Customs & Excise Commissioners v J H Corbitt (Numismatists) Ltd* [[1980] STC 231).

29.171 In *Gora* the Court of Appeal held that the issue of whether Customs reasonably arrived at their decision raised questions of *Wednesbury* reasonableness, as identified in *Customs and Excise Commissioners v J H Corbitt (Numismatists) Ltd* [1980] STC 231.

K. Restoration

29.172 The case of *Associated Provincial Picture Houses Ltd v Wednesbury Corp* [1948] 1 KB 223 is reported extensively and it is not proposed to go into it in any detail within this chapter, the main principles being espoused by Lord Greene MR at p 229 of the judgment, which are also commented upon by Lord Lane at p 663 of his judgment in the case of *Corbitt*. (See also the Court of Appeal decision of *John Dee Ltd v Customs and Excise Commissioners* [1995] STC 941.)

(5) Proportionality

29.173 In *Lindsay v Customs and Excise Commissioners* [2002] EWCA Civ 267, the Court of Appeal considered the circumstances in which a failure to offer restoration to a person of his or her vehicle that was found to have carried forfeited excise goods would be unreasonable and disproportionate. Lord Phillips MR held that the aim of the Commissioners' policy was the prevention of the evasion of excise duty that was imposed in accordance with European Community law. He stated that was a legitimate aim under Article 1 of the First Protocol of the Convention, (para 55). He went on to note that the trade in smuggled cigarettes was massive and the free movement of persons under Community law greatly facilitated the elicit importation of excise goods, making the smuggler's detection less likely. He also stated that the public were warned that if vehicles were used for smuggling, those vehicles might be forfeited and therefore anybody using their vehicle for smuggling is taking a calculated risk.

He added that as a general policy those who used their vehicles for commercial smuggling could not be heard to complain if they then lost their vehicles. In those circumstances, the value of the vehicles did not need to be taken into account (see paras 60-63 of the judgment). However, he also stated that where the importation was not for profit each case had to be considered on its own facts, and introduced a proportionality test. In setting out the factors that should be taken into account, Lord Phillips MR stated at para 64:

> 'The Commissioners' policy does not, however, draw a distinction between the commercial smuggler and the driver importing goods for social distribution to family or friends in circumstances where there is no attempt to make a profit. Of course, even in such a case the scale of importation, or other circumstances, may be such as to justify forfeiture of the car. But where the importation is not for the purpose of making a profit, I consider that the principle of proportionality requires that each case should be considered on its particular facts, which would include the scale of the importation, whether it is a "first offence", whether there was an attempt at concealment or dissimulation, the value of the vehicle and the degree of hardship that will be caused by forfeiture.'

29.174 In *Aykut Ates v Customs and Excise Commissioners* (2002) (EOO 188) the Tribunal held that the Commissioners had not acted proportionately when refusing to restore a vehicle used for smuggling to its owner, in circumstances where it was accepted that the owner had lent the car to a friend, and was himself innocent of any smuggling and did not know the use to which the vehicle was being put. The facts suggested that the appellant had been duped into lending his vehicle. Customs had taken the view that in lending his vehicle the appellant had taken a risk that the third party concerned would take the vehicle abroad, and as such there were no exceptional circumstances that justified departing from the policy that vehicles used in smuggling would not be restored to the owner.

29.175 The appellant appealed on the basis that that was an unreasonable decision because it did not enable his exceptional circumstances to be taken into account, circumstances which he maintained had been unreasonably rejected because of Customs stated policy. Secondly, he maintained that the seizure of his car was disproportionate in relation to the amount of duty evaded.

29.176 The Tribunal held that it was right for the Commissioners to have a policy, provided that they did not fetter their discretion when applying it. In exercising that discretion, the Commissioners must strike a fair balance between the demands of the general interest of the community and the requirements for the protection of the individual's fundamental rights. In the Tribunal's judgment it was unreasonable to refuse to restore a vehicle in circumstances where the owner was unaware that it was being used for smuggling. Once it had been accepted that the appellant was innocent, the amount of the alcohol imported and the other circumstances relating to the driver became irrelevant.

(6) Jurisdiction

29.177 It should be noted that the above is the limit of the Tribunal's jurisdiction. It is not entitled to, and will not, act as a court of appeal from the magistrates' decision on the question of forfeiture itself. It may however hear evidence about the seizure if it is relevant in assisting with the question of whether the ancillary non-restoration decision was correct (see the guidance provided by the Court of Appeal in *Gascoyne* below).

29.178 In *Lindsay*, the Tribunal purported to direct that if a vehicle could not be restored, the Commissioners should pay compensation. On appeal, Lord Phillips MR stated (para 607):

> 'The Tribunal directed that Mr. Lindsay's vehicle should be restored to him and that, if this were not possible, the Commissioners should pay him compensation. In so doing they purported to be exercising jurisdiction conferred by s 16(4) of the 1994 Act. That sub-section expressly spells out the powers of the Tribunal in the circumstances of this case. They include the power to direct that the decision appealed against ceased to have effect and to require the Commissioners to conduct a further review of the original decision in accordance with the Directions of the Tribunal. [Counsel] sought to persuade us that was all that the Tribunal had done. The decision appealed against was that the vehicle should not be restored. If that decision ceased to have effect, it followed, inevitably, that the vehicle would have to be restored and the Tribunal had done no more that give this Direction. I do not agree. The Tribunal have done more than direct that [the Customs officer's] decision ceased to have effect. They have purported to reverse it. That is something that they have no jurisdiction to do.'

29.179 However, the Tribunal's power to direct that a payment should be made when restoration of the goods was not possible was re-visited in *Powell v Revenue and Customs* (2005) (EOO 900) (see para 29.234 below).

(7) Personal/commercial use

29.180 The Tribunal is not directly concerned with the question of personal use or commercial importation. That is an issue principally within the confines of the condemnation proceedings/the magistrates' court. (See *Gora v Customs and Excise Commissioners* [2003] EWCA Civ 525 (CA) where Pill LJ recognised that the Tribunal procedure was not intended to enable the appellant to challenge the deemed condemnation of forfeit goods if no claim had been made under Sch 3 to CEMA (see para 58)).

In *Gascoyne v Customs and Excise Commissioners* [2005] 2 WLR 222 (CA), Buxton LJ held (at para 46 et seq): **29.181**

> I do not think it can have been intended that the exporter before the Tribunal would have a second bite at the cherry of lawfulness, having failed in condemnation proceedings or let them go by default ... the reason why the importer cannot have that liberty is not because of the terms of the statute, but because of normal English law rules of res judicata or abuse of process.

The reasoning in *Gascoyne* was confirmed by Lindsay J in *Customs and Excise Commissioners v Demack and Eatock* [2005] EWHC 330 (Ch), in which the Court found that VAT Tribunals should not undo findings of fact made by the magistrates in earlier forfeiture proceedings. In *Johnstone v Customs and Excise Commissioners* [2005] EWCA Admin 115, the High Court established that if an appellant advances grounds of appeal against non-restoration based on personal use then he has neither advanced a valid ground for restoration nor a valid ground of appeal before the VAT and Duties Tribunal. Moses J stated (at para 12 et seq.): **29.182**

> Unfortunately, as I have said, they went on to consider that which has been advanced by Mr. Johnstone, namely that these cigarettes were not for commercial use; they were for personal use. That was not a matter for the Tribunal at all. It is no ground for restoration to say to the Commissioners: these cigarettes were for personal use. This is not a ground upon which restoration can be made.
>
> In the instant case no ground whatever for restoration was advanced. All that was said was that the cigarettes were for personal use. But that issue was solely a matter for the Magistrates' or an appeal to the Crown Court. It was not a matter for the reviewing officer; it was not a matter for the Tribunal; and it is not a matter for the court. If all someone importing cigarettes such as this does is to persist in saying they are for personal use, the correct response is to say: 'You have advanced no ground whatever for restoration in the exercise of powers under section 152(b)'. That, in my judgment, is the view which the Tribunal ought to have taken. But unfortunately, in an excess of kindness, they did look yet again at the issue of whether the grounds were for personal use and decided yet again that they were not. That, as I have said, was not a matter for them.

The judgment of Buxton LJ in *Gascoyne* raises the question of how a Tribunal should proceed where the appellant has not been afforded a hearing at the condemnation proceedings stage. While most appellant's have their 'day in court' at the condemnation hearing, and thus have had the opportunity to make and to argue points on own use/commercial purpose etc. (ie a fair hearing pursuant to the ECHR), in cases when no condemnation proceedings have taken place the position will be different. In *Gascoyne* Buxton LJ held (at para 49 et seq): **29.183**

> The ECHR jurisprudence itself creates a great deal more difficulty in relation to the deeming provisions under paragraph 5 of Schedule 3. One's instincts, if no more, suggest that the extent to which it was held in *Gora v Customs and Excise Commnrs* [2004] QB 93 CA that those provisions necessarily prevent any further consideration of the legality of the seizure was an excessive limitation ... Lord Phillips in *Lindsay* at paragraph 64 of his judgment (states) that the principle of proportionality requires that each case should be considered on its particular facts ... As it seems to me, for an importer to be completely shut out in the only Tribunal before which he has in fact appeared from ventilating the matters that are deemed to have been decided against him because of paragraph 5 of Schedule 3 does not adequately enable him to assert his Convention rights. In my view, therefore, in a case where the

deeming provisions under paragraph 5 are applied the Tribunal can re-open those issues: so that a Tribunal will always have very well in mind considerations of, or similar to, abuse of process in considering whether such issues should in fact be ventilated before it. The mere fact that the Applicant has not applied to the Commissioners, and therefore there have been no condemnation proceedings, would not in my view be enough. But in my judgment it goes too far to say that the deeming provisions have always, in every case, got to be paramount.

29.184 Lindsay J in *Customs and Excise Commissioners v Demack and Eatock* [2005] EWHC 330 (Ch) suggests, following *Gascoyne*, that in deemed seizure cases the Tribunal could re-open the evidence and make findings of fact on the matter. See also *William McGuiness v Customs and Excise Commissioners* [E00793], and *Customs and Excise Commissioners v Dickinson*, The Times, 3 December 2003, where the Court held it remained open to an importer to raise the issue of personal use for the purposes of seeking to invoke the discretionary procedure of restoration.

29.185 Anecdotally, Tribunals have appeared reluctant to see their jurisdiction curtailed in the way that the decision in *Gascoyne* anticipates. Part of the problem is the conflicting messages being sent out in terms of case law. The position was re-examined once again in detail by Evans-Lombe J in the case of *Customs and Excise Commissioners v David Weller* [2006] EWHC 237. In *Weller* the Tribunal proceeded on the basis that it had jurisdiction to consider whether the seized goods were for the appellant's personal use, in a case where there had been no condemnation proceedings and condemnation had not been challenged (para 1).

29.186 His Lordship described the present system as being two track. The first track was to challenge the lawfulness of the forfeiture to the magistrates' court with an appeal to the Crown Court and then to a Divisional Court of the High Court. The second track was to seek the return of the goods forfeited with an appeal to the VAT and Duties Tribunal and thereafter to the High Court if unsuccessful (para 10).

29.187 His Lordship proceeded to review both the cases of *Gascoyne* and *Gora*. He noted that Buxton LJ took the view that where there had been deemed forfeiture it was a potential breach of the importer's rights under Article 6 of the European Convention to prevent him from seeking to re-open the issue of whether the original forfeiture was lawful as a reason, or one of the reasons, why his forfeited goods should be returned to him. Buxton LJ had not sought to limit what sort of facts would be relevant to the decision, beyond a recommendation that a Tribunal *'will always have very well in mind considerations of, or similar to abuse of process'*.

29.188 In *Weller* Evans-Lombe J referred specifically to the case of *Revenue and Customs Commissioners v Smith* (QBD, 17 November 2005). In *Smith*, Lewison J was dealing with a case where an importer was stopped at Dover by Customs officers with 2000 litres of beer, 250 litres of wine and four litres of spirits in a Toyota Land Cruiser, without having paid duty. He did not give a notice of appeal to the Commissioners under para 3 of Sch 3 to CEMA, but sought to raise the validity of the seizure on appeal with the VAT and Duties Tribunal following the Commissioners' refusal to review its decision not to return the forfeited goods to him.

29.189 The Tribunal permitted him to raise such an argument. Lewison J however, set aside the Tribunal's ruling. Having referred to Buxton LJ's judgment in *Gascoyne* at para 76, Lewison J stated:

K. Restoration

It is, in my judgment, clear from that passage that in the run-of-the-mill case where there has been a failure to give a paragraph 3 notice invoking the condemnation proceedings, the [provisions] will operate against the applicant in any subsequent appeal to a Tribunal. The Tribunal's function, therefore, is analogous to a sentencing court once a defendant has been convicted. No matter that the defendant still protests his innocence of the charge against him, the function of a sentencing court is to accept mitigation but not to question the original conviction.

Lord Justice Buxton's reference to abuse of power or to considerations analogous to abuse of process are, in my view, references to the well-known principle that it may be an abuse of process to raise in one Tribunal matters that could and should have been raised in another. So the relevant questions will always be, first, could the applicant have raised the question of lawfulness of forfeiture in other proceedings and, if the answer to that question is yes, why did he not do so? In the light of his reasons for not raising the matter in condemnation proceedings, the Tribunal can then answer the question, should he have done so and if the answer to the question is 'yes', then it will be, in most cases, an abuse of process for him to raise the question before the Tribunal.

29.190 Evans-Lombe J agreed with this approach. Whether an importer is able to raise the validity of the forfeiture on a review to a Tribunal will depend on two questions:

(1) Did the importer have a realistic opportunity to invoke the condemnation procedure?
(2) If he did, are there nonetheless reasons, disclosed by the facts of the case which should persuade the Commissioners or the Tribunal to permit him to re-open the question of the validity of the original seizure on an application for return of the goods?

29.191 Evans-Lombe J stated in *Weller* that the first question would almost always be answered in the affirmative, since facts would have to be very unusual to base a conclusion that the importer was prevented, in the 30 days succeeding forfeiture, from giving notice to Customs to initiate condemnation procedure in the magistrates' court (see para 16). It would appear, therefore, that the issue in relation to the Tribunal's jurisdiction has been both clarified and curtailed as a result of the judgments in *Weller* and *Smith*. In the recent case of *Harrison v Revenue and Customs Commissioners* (2007) The Times 8 January 2007, Lightman J held that the prescribed limit was not decisive, and that goods could be lawfuly seized, though under the Minimum Indicative Level, where there were ample other circumstances to justify such a course.

(8) Case law

29.192 In *Robert Brookes v Customs and Excise Commissioners* (2005) (E00847) the Tribunal found a materially different set of facts on the evidence to those previously established by Customs. The Tribunal took the view that because the facts that they found were so different to those found by Customs, and because the new facts might have impacted upon Customs' decision not to offer restoration, it could only be concluded that the earlier review had been unreasonably arrived at within the meaning of s 16(4) of the 1994 Act.

29.193 In *Crocker v Revenue and Customs Commissioners* (18 October 2005) (EO0926) the appellant had her motor vehicle intercepted at Dover Docks on 5 May 2001. Travelling in the vehicle were the appellant's husband and two others. The three men concerned were found to be carrying over 20 kg of hand-rolling tobacco as well as some other excise goods. Both the vehicle and the goods were seized. The appellant maintained that while she had been aware that her husband and the others had been making a trip abroad, she was unaware that her vehicle was to be used for the trip.

29.194 Customs refused to offer unconditional restoration of the vehicle because it believed that the appellant knew her vehicle was to be used; and furthermore that she was not a genuine third party owner because the car had shared insured drivers and the appellant did not have sole and absolute control over the vehicle (although it was registered in her name).

29.195 The Tribunal accepted the appellant's evidence that she did not know her vehicle was to be used and that she would not have consented had she have known. They also accepted that the appellant needed use of the vehicle for herself and her children (including on the day it was seized) and therefore would not have let her husband use it had she had known.

29.196 The Tribunal found that Customs had formed its view on 'remarkably scanty information' (para 23 of the judgment). It dismissed the suggestion that the appellant had not made it clear that the vehicle had been taken without her permission and the mere fact that her husband was bringing something back for her did not mean and could not be taken to imply that she knew her vehicle was being used.

29.197 In relation to the ownership of the vehicle, the Tribunal acknowledged that Customs do not want vehicles being returned to 'wrong doers' (para 24 of the judgment). This, they said, was a perfectly reasonable aim for the Commissioners to have. However, it went on to state that all policies must bend to the facts and be capable of being enforced with sufficient flexibility to take account of the facts of each case. Lady Mitting found:

> ... the situation which we have, because the Respondents have disposed of the vehicle, is that Mrs. Crocker has lost an asset worth £2,775 and received just £306 in lieu. Surely it cannot be right that she should be penalized merely because to give her her vehicle back unconditionally would have a side effect of allowing her husband to regain access to it? If this is the view which (Customs) took, then we consider this to have been unreasonable.

On the above basis the Tribunal found that the decision to offer only conditional restoration of the vehicle to Mrs Crocker was unreasonable and directed that a further review be carried out.

In *Frost and Mason v Customs and Excise Commissioners* (2005) (72) (E00872) the Tribunal found that the review officer's decision was unreasonably arrived at because of the hardship suffered by the loss of the vehicle. The vehicle in question was required by the traveller's wife to care for her grandchild and her father-in-law. The Tribunal ordered further reviews to consider the question of exceptional hardship.

L. Restoration: Practice and Procedure

(1) Formal departmental reviews

29.198 Appeals to the Tribunal are against a formal review decision by the Revenue and Customs. Appeals will only be brought by a person who has first requested a formal department review (see the Finance Act 1994, s 16(2)). Persons able to request a review include those affected by the decision, or persons who are liable to pay any duty or penalty in relation to it; together with persons on behalf of whom an application is made (see s 14(2) of the Finance Act 1994).

L. Restoration: Practice and Procedure

(2) Tribunal procedure

29.199 The procedure before the VAT and Duties Tribunal is governed by the Value Added Tax Tribunal Rules 1986, SI 1986/590 (as amended on 22 January 2003 (see <http://www.financeandtaxtribunals.gov.uk/rules_procedure/The_Value_Added_Tax_Tribunals_Rules_1986.pdf>).

(3) Time limits

29.200 Section 14(1) requires a request for a review to be made in writing within 45 days from the date of the original decision (s 14(3)). While the Commissioners are not obliged to carry out a review if the request is received outside the 45 day limitation period, s 16(1)(b) does afford some scope for out-of-time requests where the Commissioners have agreed to undertake a review after the end of the 45 day period.

29.201 Within 45 days of receiving the request for a review, HMRC must complete their formal review (Finance Act, 1994 s 15(2)). Once the 45 day period expires, the original decision shall be assumed to be upheld and the individual looking to appeal will have an immediate right to pursue that appeal. The 45 day period afforded to Customs cannot be extended. The appeal itself must be served within 30 days of the date of the document containing the disputed decision (r 4(1)). This can be extended for up to a further 21 days with Revenue and Customs consent (r 4(2)). It may also be extended by r 19(1) which specifically allows the Tribunal to extend the time for service of the notice of appeal.

(4) Lodging the appeal and the statement of case

29.202 Rule 3 of the VAT Tribunal Rules states an appeal to the Tribunal should be brought by a notice of appeal served at the appropriate Tribunal centre and that the notice of appeal should be signed by or on behalf of the appellant and should state the name and address of the appellant; the date, if any, with effect from which the Appellant was registered for tax and the nature of his business; the address of the office of HM Revenue and Customs from where the disputed decision was sent; the date of the document containing the disputed decision; and should set out the grounds of appeal. Any other relevant documents should also be attached.

29.203 Pursuant to r 3(2)(e) it is essential that the notice reveals a ground of appeal that is recognised in law. In practice Revenue and Customs usually write and ask for further and better particulars if they have concerns about the grounds of appeal. If there is no response to such a request then the Revenue and Customs are entitled to seek directions; an unless order under r 9; or seek what amounts to a striking-out application under r 6.

29.204 Where such a problem does not arise then the Revenue and Customs will prepare a Statement of Case which will set out in terms why they believe that their decision was reasonable in all the circumstances.

29.205 The Statement of Case will set out all the matters and facts upon which Customs rely, together with any relevant statutory provisions. It should be served within 30 days of receipt of the appeal (see r 8). Customs are entitled to rely on new arguments that did not form part of the decision in their Statement of Case (see *Customs and Excise Commissioners v Alzitrans SL* [2003]

All ER (D) 288 and *Lama Ltd v Customs and Excise Commissioners* (COO 189) – where Customs raised arguments at the time of the hearing for the first time).

(5) Disclosure

29.206 Obligations in relation to disclosure are set out at r 20 of the Tribunal Rules. Rule 20 states:

> 20(1) Each of the parties to an appeal . . . shall, before the expiration of the time set out in paragraph (2) of this rule, serve the appropriate Tribunal centre a list of the documents in his possession, custody or power which he proposes to produce at the hearing of the appeal or application.

29.207 The time limit within which the documents should be served is the period of 30 days after the date of notification of the notice of appeal (see r 20(2)).

29.208 In addition, a Tribunal may, where it appears necessary for the fair disposal of the proceedings, and upon an application of one of the party's to the appeal, direct that the other party should serve within such period as it may specify a list of the documents (or any class of documents) which are or have been in its possession, custody or power, that relate to a question in issue (see r 20(3)). At the hearing of the appeal, a party should produce any document included in the list of documents served by him which is in his possession and which is not privileged from production (see r 20(6)).

29.209 While Tribunal procedures tend to be less formal than court procedures, failure to disclose a certain document may lead to it being excluded from the hearing (see *David Kirk v Customs and Excise Commissioners* (14042)). The risk in non-disclosure is that if the Tribunal is minded to admit any late document, the Revenue and Customs are likely to ask for more time to consider it and that may lead to an adjournment and a possible costs award (see *Customs and Excise Commissioners v Gus Merchandise Corp* [1992] STC 776 at 781-782).

29.210 Requesting further and better particulars is dealt with by r 9 and *Taylor v Commissioners of Customs & Excise* (1975) VAT TR 147 at 163(a).

29.211 In terms of disclosure generally, legal privilege applies (see *Three Rivers DC (Respondents) v Governor of the Bank of England* [2004] UKHL 48 at 114-117 and *Alfred Crompton Amusement Machines Ltd v Customs and Excise Commissioners* [1974] AC 405 in relation to internal correspondence between officers and the legal section of Customs).

(6) Witness statements

29.212 Pursuant to r 21, a party to an appeal should serve witness statements containing the evidence proposed to be given by any person at the hearing of the appeal. Rule 21(2) states:

> (2) A witness statement shall contain the name, address and description of the person proposing to give the evidence contained therein and shall be signed by him.
>
> (3) A proper officer shall send a copy of a witness statement served at the appropriate Tribunal centre to the other party to the appeal and such copy shall state the date of service and the date of notification of the witness statement and shall contain or be accompanied by a note to the effect that unless a notice of objection thereto is served in accordance with paragraph (4) of this rule, the witness statement may be read at the hearing of the appeal as evidence of the facts stated therein without the person who made the witness statement giving oral evidence thereat.

L. Restoration: Practice and Procedure

(4) If a party objects to a witness statement being read at the hearing of the appeal as evidence of any facts stated therein, he shall serve a notice of objection . . . not later than 14 days after the date of notification of such witness statement, whereupon a proper officer shall send a copy of the notice of objection to the other party and the witness statement shall not be read or admitted in evidence at such hearing but the person who signed such witness statement may give evidence orally at the hearing.

(5) Subject to paragraph (4) of this rule, unless the Tribunal should otherwise direct, a witness statement signed by any person and duly served under this rule shall be admissible in evidence at the hearing of the appeal as evidence of any facts stated therein of which oral evidence by him at that hearing would be admissible.

29.213 The time limit within which a witness statement may be served is 21 days after the date of notification of the Commissioners' Statement of Case (see r 21(6)(c)). The proper officer referred to in this rule is the administrator who carries out their duties on behalf of the Tribunal's President (see r 2). An extension of time may be sought under r 19(1).

29.214 It will be noted that because of the civil nature of these proceedings, hearsay is regularly included in witness statements and is itself admissible.

29.215 The Tribunal is entitled to refuse to hear evidence where the procedures have not been complied with, particularly in relation to witness statements and evidence (see *Hossain v Customs and Excise Commissioners* [2004] EWHC 1898 (Ch) at para 18).

(7) Ongoing criminal proceedings

29.216 Pursuant to r 19(3) it is possible to ask for an appeal to be stood over where, for example, criminal proceedings are currently ongoing or if the appeal concerns an important point of law which is presently before a higher court. The decision to stand an appeal over rests with the Tribunal (see *Ex p Brindle* [1994] BCC 297).

(8) Failure to comply with directions

29.217 Extensions of time may be sought under r 19(1), however the importance of complying with the directions of the Tribunal and the requisite time limits was emphasised by *Customs and Excise Commissioners v Young* [1993] STC 394 where the Commissioners lost the appeal because they had served documents 12 days late.

29.218 The consequences for failure to comply by the Commissioners was further emphasised in *Freight Transport Leasing Ltd v Customs and Excise Commissioners* (1992) VAT TR 120 where the Court considered other consequences such as fines and penalties pursuant to Sch 12(10) of the VAT Act 1994 and *Purves v Revenue and Customs Commissioners* (2005) (EOO 924).

(9) Pre-hearing reviews

29.219 Pre-hearing reviews are not uncommon in non-restoration appeals and these may be ordered by the Tribunal of its own volition, or following a request of one of the parties. Often, however, directions are agreed by consent and this can avoid the necessity of a hearing.

29.220 Where directions cannot be agreed or where there is a matter of substance which needs to be dealt with, a hearing can be arranged that will usually be heard before a single chairman/Tribunal judge.

29.221 Pre-hearing reviews may deal with many matters from witness requirements and witness availability to length of hearing, interpreters, notification of complex matters of law (particularly with reference to the ECHR) and disclosure issues. Pre-hearing reviews are usually in private (see r 24(2)).

(10) Preparation for the hearing

29.222 Each party is responsible for preparing its own bundle for the hearing, although in practice Revenue and Customs usually take a lead in relation to this. Rule 23(3) requires that there must be at least 14 days' notice to the parties before the Tribunal hearing takes place. Any further arguments, authorities or chronologies should therefore be served in good time and where possible prior to the listing of the hearing.

(11) The hearing

29.223 The full hearing (unless the Tribunal directs otherwise) is in public (r 24(1)). The correct terms of address for the Chairman/Tribunal judge and any lay members are Sir or Madam, as appropriate. It is not usual for counsel to stand when addressing the Tribunal.

29.224 Rule 25(1) permits appellants to have friends or other associates to represent them at the hearing. The procedure at the hearing is provided for by r 27 which states:

(1) At the hearing of an appeal or application . . . the Tribunal shall allow –
 (a) the Appellant or Applicant or his representative to open his case;
 (b) the Appellant or Applicant to give evidence in support of the appeal or application and to produce documentary evidence;
 (c) the Appellant or Applicant or his representative to call other witnesses to give evidence in support of the appeal or to produce documentary evidence, and to re-examine any such witness following his cross-examination;
 (d) the other party to the appeal or application or his representative to cross-examine any witness called to give evidence in support of the appeal or application (including the Appellant or Applicant if he gives evidence);
 (e) the other party to the appeal or application or his representative to open his case;
 (f) the other party to the appeal or application to give evidence in opposition to the appeal or application and to produce documentary evidence;
 (g) the other party to the appeal or application or his representative to call other witnesses to give evidence in opposition to the appeal or application or to produce documentary evidence and to re-examine any such witness following his cross-examination;
 (h) the Appellant or Applicant or his representative to cross-examine any witness called to give evidence in opposition to the appeal or application (including the other party to the appeal or application if it gives evidence);
 (i) the other party to the appeal or application or his representative to make a second address closing his case; and
 (j) the Appellant or Applicant or his representative to make a final address closing his case.

29.225 Pursuant to r 28(2) witnesses who have been called to give live evidence will take the oath or affirm and are liable to be cross-examined.

29.226 During the hearing the Chairman and any other member of the Tribunal may put any question to any witness called to give evidence (r 27(3)). A Tribunal may regulate its own procedure as it may think fit (r 27(4)), and special allowance may be made where an appellant is unrepresented (see *Kwik Fit (GB) Ltd v Customs and Excise Commissioners* [1998] STC at pp 167-169).

29.227 While officers are entitled to refer to their notebooks when giving evidence, they should make it clear whether the notes were made contemporaneously or not *(Mori Mohal Indian Restaurant v Customs and Excise Commissioners* (1992) VAT TR 188).

29.228 Under r 26(2) if neither party or if only one party attends, then the Tribunal is entitled to go on and hear the matter in any event. Shorthand writers may only be present if permitted by the Tribunal (see *Empire Stores Ltd v Customs and Excise Commissioners* (1992) VAT TR 271).

(12) Judgment

29.229 A decision will not necessarily be given immediately and it is usual for there to be a delay while the Tribunal Chairman/judge prepares his judgment. While there has been complaint in the past about the length of the delay, Moses J held in *R v Customs and Excise Commissioners ex p Dangol* [2000] STC 107 (QBD) that a party could only seek judicial review of a delay in issuing a decision if they could demonstrate that the delay caused an injustice.

29.230 Parties are entitled to have a decision set aside if, eg there is a procedural irregularity. However, that must be done within 14 days of the release of the decision and there is no power to set a decision aside outside of that period, the only recourse then being to appeal (see *Mohammed Razaq v Customs and Excise Commissioners* (14949)).

M. Restoration Appeals

29.231 Appeals to the High Court pursuant to s 11(1) of the Tribunal Inquiries Act 1992 must be filed with the High Court by lodging Form N161, within 56 days of the date of the decision (see CPR Part 52 and its accompanying Practice Direction). The High Court may exercise its jurisdiction in a number of ways including making any decision or order in relation to the appeal, such as re-directing a fresh hearing (see *Customs and Excise Commissioners v Barratt* [1995] STC 661).

29.232 The Civil Procedure Rules (r 30A) also permit the Tribunal to consider a leapfrog appeal provided the Tribunal certifies that the decision it has made concerns a point of law related to the construction of an enactment or statutory instrument or Community legislation which has not been fully argued before. See s 86 of the VAT Act 1994. All parties are required to consent to such a course.

N. Restoration: Costs and Compensation

(1) Compensation

29.233 Traditional thinking has always maintained that the VAT and Duties Tribunal does not have any jurisdiction to entertain claims for compensation and such matters are entirely within the remit of the county court (see *Lindsay*, considered above at para 29.178). However, this was called into question by *Powell v Revenue and Customs Commissioners* (2005) (EOO 900), where the Tribunal held that a power to pay compensation when restoration was no longer possible was a necessary part of the structure of the legislation, pursuant to s 152(b) of CEMA. The Tribunal found (at paras 102, 109, 112 and 113) that there is a right of appeal to the VAT and Duties Tribunal on the question of quantum of compensation and the reasonableness of the payment offered in restoration proceedings where goods have been destroyed. The Tribunal's power would be to return the decision to Customs for review if it found the offer to be unreasonable. It has no power to make its own order in substitution of Customs' decision. It only has the power to keep reviewing the decisions of Customs and if they are unreasonable then returning them for further re-review.

(2) Costs

29.234 Costs are dealt with by r 29 CPR. As with all civil proceedings costs usually follow the event (since 'winner takes all'), provided that they are reasonable and have been properly incurred. The Tribunal may decide that costs are not reasonable where the conduct of a party has been improper or where issues have been raised late in the day and without proper notice.

29.235 The withdrawal of a party from an appeal will not usually save them from having to pay costs unless, for example, they do so as a result of new evidence of which they were previously unaware (see *JJ McGinty v Customs and Excise Commissioners* (1995) V&DR 193).

29.236 Pursuant to *Burgess v Stafford Hotel Ltd* [1993] 3 All ER 222 costs may be awarded on an indemnity basis where the conduct of a party has been unconscionable.

O. The ECHR and Restoration

29.237 It is now trite law that pursuant to s 2(1) of the Human Rights Act 1998, a court or tribunal 'must take account' of decisions of the European Commission and Court. Guidance on how matters should be approached is provided by *Hoverspeed Ltd* [2002] EWHC Admin 1630 at paras 186-189 and for the court's approach in relation to proportionality, see *Lindsay v Customs and Excise Commissioners* [2002] EWCA Civ 267.

29.238 In *Gora* the Court of Appeal upheld the conclusions of the tribunal that a decision not to restore seized goods did not involve a criminal charge for the purposes of Article 6 of the Convention (para 48).

29.239 In *Hopping v Customs and Excise Commissioners* (2001)(EOO 170), the Tribunal held that the policy of 'use it and lose it', namely seizing and refusing to restore to the owner a vehicle used for bootlegging was proportionate in that a fair balance existed between the legitimate aim pursued and the means employed. The Tribunal commented that seizure and the refusal to restore the vehicle are, on first impression, direct violations of the owner's fundamental right of peaceful enjoyment of his vehicle (Article 1 of Protocol 1 of the ECHR); and that the Commissioners' policy was capable of being arbitrary to the point of being

O. The ECHR and Restoration

extravagant (para 28), particularly where the financial loss resulting from the refusal to restore an expensive car could many times exceed the loss of revenue sought from the smuggling operation.

29.240 Nevertheless, the Tribunal found that there were factors which tended to balance up the means employed with the aim pursued:

(1) The policy was a suitable way of preventing smuggling. Take away the vehicle and it can be no longer used for bootlegging.
(2) To refuse to restore is even-handed. It is the course of action that is blind to the value of the vehicle and to the financial means of the owner. It treats all bootleggers alike.
(3) The owner who makes a bootlegging trip to France and whose vehicle is taken will know the score before he embarks on his smuggling operations. In a real sense he ventures his vehicle as one of the stakes of his dishonest enterprise. He foregoes his claim to any unqualified fundamental right of peaceful enjoyment of the vehicle before he sets off on his trip.
(4) So long as the seizure and refusal to restore the vehicle does not cause physical suffering or result in excessive inconvenience to defenceless third parties, its impact will be directed at the owner (see para 28).

Steven Oliver, QC added at para 29:

> 'Every case will have to be dealt with on its own facts. But in principle we do not see a lack of balance when the factors set out above are brought into the reckoning. Where the owner is the driver he risks losing the vehicle when he sets out to bootleg. He takes the risk and loses when he is caught.'

APPENDICES

1	Restraint Order	689
2	Management Receivership Order	695
3	Enforcement Receivership Order	699
4	Letter of Agreement between Prosecutor and Receiver	703
5	Variation of Restraint Order	707
6	LSC Funding Arrangements	709
7	Application Notice by Defendant seeking a Certificate of Inadequacy	711
8	Certificate of Inadequacy	715
9	Claim Form (CPR PART 8)	717
10	Extract from the Practice Direction on POCA 2002 Parts 5 and 8: Civil Recovery: section III	719
11	Extract from the Practice Direction on POCA 2002 Parts 5 and 8: Civil Recovery: section IV	721
12	Schedule 6 to POCA 2002 Sections 247 and 257	725
13	Draft Restraint, Disclosure and Repatriation Order under POCA	727
14	Certificate of Service	733
15	Interim Receiving Order under s 246 of POCA	735
16	Useful Websites on POCA 2002	743
17	Property Freezing Order	745
18	Civil Recovery by Consent Order	751
19	Guidance to solicitors and applicants seeking Community Legal Service funding for proceedings under the Proceeds of Crime Act 2002 involving the Assets Recovery Agency	755
20	Condemnation and Forfeiture of Goods	761
21	ARA: Settlement of Civil Recovery and Tax Cases	765
22	Guidance by the Secretary of State to the Director of the Assets Recovery Agency	767
23	The House of Lords Decision in *Capewell*	769

APPENDIX 1

RESTRAINT ORDER

Claim DTA No. 1234 of 2006

IN THE HIGH COURT OF JUSTICE
QUEEN'S BENCH DIVISION
Administrative Court
Before the Honourable Mr. Justice Bullingham   sitting in Private

IN THE MATTER OF ALFREDO GERMONT (DEFENDANT)

AND

IN THE MATTER OF THE DRUG TRAFFICKING ACT 1994

RESTRAINT ORDER PROHIBITING THE DISPOSAL OF ASSETS

TO:

1. Alfredo Germont (the Defendant)
2. Violetta Valery
3. Giorgio Germont
4. Traviata Trading Enterprises Limited.

PENAL NOTICE

If you, Alfredo Germont, Violetta Valery, Giorgio Germont and Traviata Trading Enterprises Limited disobey this order you may be held to be in contempt of court and may be imprisoned, fined or have your assets seized.

Any other person who knows of this order and does anything which helps or permits the Defendant (or Violetta Valery, Giorgio Germont and Traviata Trading Enterprises Limited) to breach the terms of this order may also be held to be in contempt of court and may be imprisoned, fined or have their assets seized.

THE ORDER

1. This is a restraint order made against Alfredo Germont ("the Defendant") and Violetta Valery, Giorgio Germont and Traviata Trading Enterprises Limited by Mr. Justice Bullingham on the application of the Revenue and Customs Prosecutions Office ("the prosecutor"). The judge read the witness statements listed in Schedule A and accepted the undertakings set out in Schedule B at the end of this order.
2. This order was made at a hearing without notice to the Defendant or to Violetta Valery, Giorgio Germont and Traviata Trading Enterprises Limited. The Defendant and Violetta Valery, Giorgio Germont and Traviata Trading Enterprises Limited has a right to apply to the court to vary or discharge this order—see paragraph 23 below.

DISPOSAL OF OR DEALING WITH ASSETS

3. The Defendant must not:
   (a) remove from England and Wales any of his assets which are in England and Wales whether in his own name or not and whether solely or jointly owned; or

(b) in any way dispose of or deal with or diminish the value of any of his assets whether they are in or outside England and Wales whether in his own name or not and whether solely or jointly owned.

4. Paragraph 3 applies to all the Defendant's assets whether or not they are in his own name and whether they are solely or jointly owned. For the purpose of this order the Defendant's assets include any asset which he has the power, directly or indirectly, to dispose of or deal with as if it were his own. The Defendant is to be regarded as having such power if a third party holds or controls the asset in accordance with his direct or indirect instructions.

5. These prohibitions include the following assets in particular:
   (a) Anytown Bank PLC account number 12345678 in the name of the Defendant;
   (b) Anytown Bank PLC account number 98765432 in the name of the Defendant and Violetta Valery;
   (c) Anytown Bank PLC account number 22334455 in the name of Giorgio Germont;
   (d) Anytown Bank PLC account number 66778899 in the name of Traviata Trading Enterprises Limited;
   (e) The Defendant's interest in all that property and land known as "The Heights" Marbella, Spain;
   (f) The Defendant's interest in a Rolls Royce motor vehicle registered number AG 123 registered in the name of the Defendant;
   (g) The Defendant's interest in a motor vessel named "Hispaniola" registered in the names of the Defendant and Violetta Valery;
   (h) A racehorse named "Nabucco" registered in the names of the Defendant and Giorgio Germont;
   (i) A quantity of cash found on the defendant when arrested totalling £175,000 in Sterling bank notes.

6. Giorgio Germont must not:
   (a) remove from England and Wales; or
   (b) in any way dispose of or deal with or diminish the value of any of
       (i) Anytown Bank PLC account number 22334455 in the name of Giorgio Germont;
       (ii) A racehorse called "Nabucco" registered in the names of the defendant and Giorgio Germont.

7. Violetta Valery must not:—
   (a) remove from England and Wales; or
   (b) in any way dispose of or deal with or diminish the value of any of
       (i) Anytown Bank PLC account number 98765432 in the names of the Defendant and Violetta Valery;
       (ii) All that property and land known as "The Heights", Marbella, Spain;
       (iii) A motor vessel named "Hispaniola" registered in the names of the Defendant and Violetta Valery.

8. Traviata Trading Enterprises Limited must not:—
   (a) remove from England and Wales; or
   (b) in any way dispose or deal with or diminish the value of
       (i) Anytown Bank PLC bank account number 66778899 in the name of Traviata Trading Enterprises Limited.

9. The prosecutor shall be at liberty to pay the sum of £175,000 in cash referred to in paragraph 5 (i) above into an interest bearing bank account save in so far as the same may be required as an exhibit in criminal proceedings against the Defendant.

Charging Order

10. The Defendant is not prohibited from disposing of, or dealing with the property known as "Traviata" 123 The Esplanade, Torquay, Devon but this property shall be charged with immediate effect for securing payment to the Crown of an amount equal to the value from time to time of the property (subject to prior charges).

Provision of Information

11. The Defendant must:
    (i) inform the Revenue and Customs Prosecutions Office in writing within 72 hours of service of this Order on the Defendant of all his assets whether in or outside England and Wales and whether in his own name or not and whether solely or jointly owned, giving the value, location and details of all such assets;
    (ii) confirm the information in a witness statement which must be verified by a statement of truth and served on the Revenue and Customs Prosecutions Office within 14 days after this Order has been served on the defendant.

The information in the witness statement must include:
   a. the name and address of all persons including financial institutions holding any such assets;
   b. details of the Defendant's current salary or other form of income, identifying the amount paid, by whom it is paid and the account or accounts into which it is paid;
   c. the names and numbers of all accounts held by or under the control of the Defendant, together with the name and address of the place where the account is held and the sums in the account;
   d. details (including addresses) of any real property in which the Defendant has any interest, including an interest in any of the proceeds of sale if the property were to be sold. These details must include details of any mortgage or charge on the property;
   e. details of all National Savings Certificates, unit trusts, shares or debentures held by the Defendant in any company or corporation wherever incorporated in the world, owned or controlled by the Defendant or in which he has an interest;
   f. details of all trusts of which the Defendant is a beneficiary, including the name and address of every trustee;
   g. particulars of any income or debt due to the Defendant including the name and address of the debtor;
   h. details of all assets over £5,000.00 in value received by the Defendant or anyone on his behalf since the 22nd July 2001 identifying the name and address of the person from whom such asset was received;
   i. details of all assets over £5,000.00 in value transferred by the Defendant or anyone on his behalf to others since 22nd July 2001 identifying the name and address of all persons to whom such property was transferred.

12. (1) Subject to any further order of the court any information given in compliance with this order shall only be used—
    (a) for the purpose of these proceedings;
    (b) if the Defendant is convicted, for the purposes of any confiscation hearing that may take place; and
    (c) if a confiscation order is made, for the purposes of enforcing that order, including any receivership proceedings.
    (2) There shall be no disclosure of any material disclosed in compliance with this order to any co-defendant in the criminal proceedings.
    (3) However, nothing in this paragraph shall make inadmissible any disclosure made by the Defendant in any proceedings for perjury relating to that disclosure.

Repatriation

13. (1) The Defendant must within 21 days after service of this order upon him bring any moveable asset in respect of which he has an interest, which is outside England and Wales, to a location within England and Wales.
    (2) The defendant must inform the Revenue and Customs Prosecutions Office of the location within England and Wales within 7 days of the arrival of the assets.

(3) If the asset is cash or credit in a financial institution it must be paid into an interest bearing account and the account holder, location and account number be notified to the Revenue and Customs Prosecutions Office within 7 days.

EXCEPTIONS TO THIS ORDER

14. This Order does not prevent the Defendant, as long as he is not in prison, Mr. Giorgio Germont and Miss Violetta Valery from spending £350 per week towards their ordinary living expenses and also £500 each on legal advice and representation. But before spending any money for such purposes the Defendant, Mr. Giorgio Germont and Miss Violetta Valery must tell the Revenue and Customs Prosecutions Office where the money is to come from.

15. The Defendant, Mr. Giorgio Germont and Miss Violetta Valery may agree with the Revenue and Customs Prosecutions Office that the above spending limits for living expenses should be increased or that this Order may be varied in any respect, but any such agreement must be in writing.

16. The Defendant may spend further money on legal expenses actually, reasonable and properly incurred in these proceedings and the criminal proceedings to which these proceedings are ancillary PROVIDED THAT before any monies are released for this purpose the Defendant shall notify the Revenue and Customs Prosecutions Office in writing of the following matters:

    a. the source of the fund to be used for the said costs;
    b. the general nature of the costs incurred;
    c. the time spent and by whom (whether partner, assistant solicitor or otherwise) in incurring the said costs;
    d. the hourly rate applicable to the costs incurred.

AND in the event that the Revenue and Customs Prosecutions Office consider the claim to be in respect of costs that have not actually, reasonably or properly been incurred then the entitlement to draw such costs shall be restricted to 65% of the amount claimed and the whole claim for costs shall be subject to a detailed assessment on an indemnity basis in accordance with CPR Part 48.8 without the provisions of CPR Part 48.8 (2) applying.

17. This Order does not prevent the Defendant, Giorgio Germont and Violetta Valery from spending any money they receive by way of state benefit from the Department of Work and Pensions.

18. This order does not prohibit the Defendant from spending towards his ordinary living expenses any sum earned by him whilst he is in prison.

19. This order does not prohibit Traviata Trading Enterprises Limited from spending up to £1,000 on legal advice and representation. But before spending any money Traviata Trading Enterprises Limited must tell the prosecutor where the money is to come from.

20. This Order does not prevent Traviata Trading Enterprises Limited from dealing with or disposing of any of its assets in the ordinary and proper course of business, including operating account number 66778899 at the Anytown Bank PLC for this purpose. However, to be permitted to do this, the Company must supply to the Revenue and Customs Prosecutions Office within 7 days after it is requested:

    a. the following accounting records of the Company—
        (i) entries from day to day of all sums of money received and expended by the Company and the matters in respect of which the receipt and expenditure takes place;
        (ii) a record of the assets and liabilities of the Company, including debts owed to and by the Company; and
        (iii) if the Company involves dealing in goods, statements of stock held by the Company.
    b. bank statements, cheque stubs, paying-in books, bank transfer documentation and any correspondence with the Bank in relation to the Company bank account.

Appendix 1: Restraint Order

21. This Order does not prevent:
    (a) any person from paying any money in satisfaction of the whole or part of any confiscation order which may be made against the Defendant; or
    (b) the levy of distress upon any goods subject to this order for the purpose of enforcement of any confiscation order which may be made against the Defendant.

Costs

22. The costs of this order are reserved.

Variation or Discharge of this Order

23. Anyone affected by this order may apply to the court at any time to vary or discharge this order (or so much of it as affects that person), but they must first inform the Prosecutor and the Defendant (and Violetta Valery, Giorgio Germont and Traviata Trading Enterprises Limited) giving two clear days' notice. If any evidence is to be relied upon in support of the application, the substance of it must be communicated in writing to the Prosecutor in advance.

Interpretation of this Order

24. A person who is an individual who is ordered not to do something must not do it himself or in any other way. He must not do it through others acting on his behalf or on his instructions or with this encouragement.

25. A person who is not an individual which is ordered not to do something must not do it itself or by its directors, officers, partners, employees or agents or in any other way.

Parties other than the Defendant

26. **Effect of this order** It is a contempt of court for any person notified of this Order knowingly to assist in or permit a breach of this Order. Any person doing so may be sent to prison, fined or have his assets seized. He is also at risk of being prosecuted for a money laundering offence.

27. **Set off by banks** This Order does not prevent any bank from exercising any right of set off it may have in respect of any facility which it gave to the Defendant before it was notified of this Order.

28. **Withdrawals by the Defendant** No bank need enquire as to the application or proposed application of any money withdrawn by the Defendant if the withdrawal appears to be permitted by this Order.

29. **Parties outside England, Wales and Scotland**
    (1) Except as provided in paragraph (2) below, the terms of this order do not affect or concern anyone outside the jurisdiction of this court or Scotland.
    (2) The terms of this order will affect the following persons in a country or state outside the jurisdiction of this court or Scotland—
        a. a person to whom this Order is addressed or an officer or an agent appointed by power of attorney of such a person; or
        b. a person who—
            (i) is subject to the jurisdiction of this court or Scotland;
            (ii) has been given written notice of this order at his residence or place of business within the jurisdiction of this court or Scotland; and
            (iii) is able to prevent acts or omissions outside the jurisdiction of this court or Scotland which constitute or assist in a breach of the terms of this Order.
        c. any other person, only to the extent that this order is declared enforceable by or is enforced by a court in that country or state.

Enforcement in Scotland

30. This order shall have effect in the law of Scotland, any may be enforced there if it is registered under section 35 of the Proceeds of Crime (Scotland) Act, 1995.

Assets Located Outside England and Wales

31. Nothing in this order shall, in respect of assets located outside England and Wales, prevent any third party from complying with—

(1) what it reasonably believes to be its obligations, contractual or otherwise, under the laws and obligations of the country or state in which those assets are situated or under the proper law of any contract between itself and the Respondent; and

(2) any orders of the courts of that country or state, provided that reasonable notice of any application for such an order is given to the Applicant's solicitors unless those assets are situated in Scotland and this order has been registered there in which case this order must be obeyed there.

Communications with the Court

32. All communications to the Court about this Order should be sent to the Administrative Court Office, Royal Courts of Justice, Strand, London WC2A 2LL quoting the case number. The offices are open between 10am and 4.30pm Monday to Friday. The telephone number is 020-7947-6653.

Schedule A

The judge read the following witness statement before making this Order:

Witness statement of (insert name) dated 22nd November 2006.

Schedule B

Undertakings given to the Court by the Prosecutor

1. The prosecutor will serve upon the Defendant, Mr. Giorgio Germont, Miss Violetta Valery and Traviata Trading Enterprises Limited—

(a) a copy of this Order; and
(b) a copy of the witness statement containing the evidence relied on by the Prosecutor, and any other documents provided to the court on the making of the application.

2. Anyone notified of this Order will be given a copy of it by the prosecutor.

3. The Revenue and Customs Prosecutions Office will pay the reasonable costs of anyone other than the Defendant, Mr. Giorgio Germont, Miss Violetta Valery and Traviata Trading Enterprises Limited which are incurred as a result of this Order including the costs of ascertaining whether that person holds any of the Defendant's assets, save that the prosecutor will not pay any legal or accountancy costs so incurred without first giving their consent in writing.

Address of the Prosecutor for Service and any Communication in Respect of these Proceedings

[Address, reference fax and telephone numbers]

APPENDIX 2

MANAGEMENT RECEIVERSHIP ORDER

DISOBEDIENCE OF THIS ORDER IS A CONTEMPT OF COURT WHICH IF YOU ARE AN INDIVIDUAL IS PUNISHABLE BY IMPRISONMENT OR IF YOU ARE A BODY CORPORATE IS PUNISHABLE BY SEQUESTRATION OF YOUR ASSETS AND BY IMPRISONMENT OF ANY INDIVIDUAL RESPONSIBLE

Claim DTA No. 1234 of 2006

IN THE HIGH COURT OF JUSTICE
QUEEN'S BENCH DIVISION
Administrative Court
Before the Honourable Mr. Justice Featherstone   sitting in Private

IN THE MATTER OF ALFREDO GERMONT (DEFENDANT)
AND
IN THE MATTER OF THE DRUG TRAFFICKING ACT 1994

Order Appointing a Management Receiver

IMPORTANT: NOTICE TO THE DEFENDANT, ALFREDO GERMONT, MR. GIORGIO GERMONT, MISS VIOLETTA VALERY AND TRAVIATA TRADING ENTERPRISES LIMITED AND ANYONE IN POSSESSION OR CONTROL OF THE DEFENDANT'S ASSETS

1. This Order appoints a Receiver to manage the assets of the Defendant subject to the Restraint Order made by Mr. Justice Bullingham in the High Court on 25th November, 2006.
2. This order varies the Restraint Order made against the Defendant, Mr. Giorgio Germont, Miss Violetta Valery and Traviata Trading Enterprises Limited by Mr. Justice Bullingham on 25th November, 2006.
3. If the Defendant or any person in possession or control of his assets disobeys this order or obstructs the Receiver he or she may be guilty of contempt of court and may be sent to prison or fined or have his assets seized.
4. There is an interpretation section at page 4 of this Order.

The Order of Appointment

An application was made today by the Revenue and Customs Prosecutions Office to the High Court for the appointment of a Management Receiver over the assets of the Defendant to enforce the Restraint Order made against him by Mr. Justice Bullingham in the High Court on 25th November, 2006.

An application was made today by the Revenue and Customs Prosecutions Officeto the High Court for a variation of the Restraint Order made against the Defendant by Mr. Justice Bullingham in the High Court on 25th November 2006.

The Judge read the witness statement of [insert name] made on the 5th day of December, 2006.

Appendix 2: Management Receivership Order

As a result of the application **THE COURT APPOINTS** [insert name and address of receiver] as Management Receiver ["the Receiver"] of the realisable property of the Defendant including those listed in the Schedule to this Order and including the assets and the business and undertakings of Traviata Trading Enterprises Limited.

And it is Ordered that:—

1. The assets of Traviata Trading Enterprises Limited be treated as the personal assets of the Defendant.
2. The Receiver shall have the following powers without prejudice to any existing powers vested in her whether by statute or otherwise:—
    a. Power to take possession of, preserve, manage, collect, let charge and sell the assets of the Defendant and Traviata Trading Enterprises Limited.
    b. Power to appoint solicitors, counsel, attorneys, accountants or other agents to advise and/or act on behalf of the Receiver in any part of the world.
    c. Power to discharge all and any costs, charges and expenses of the receivership out of the assets and/or the proceeds of realisation thereof.
    d. Power to bring proceedings in the name of or on behalf of the Defendant and/or Traviata Trading Enterprises Limited, within or without the jurisdiction, against any person having possession of the realisable property of the Defendant and/or Traviata Trading Enterprises Limited for possession thereof or for the payment or delivery up thereof.
    e. Power to execute all such documents in the name of and on behalf of the Defendant and/or Traviata Trading Enterprises Limited as may be necessary to take possession of, preserve manage, collect, let, charge and/or sell realisable property.
    f. The Defendant, Traviata Trading Enterprises Limited and all other persons in possession of the assets of the Defendant shall take all such reasonable and necessary steps as may be required by the Receiver to enable the receivership to be conducted and the sale of the Defendant's assets to proceed, including but without prejudice to the generality of the foregoing:—
        (i) Providing the Receiver forthwith upon request by the Receiver with such information and documents relating to the management of he said assets as the Receiver so requires.
        (ii) Signing and delivering to the Receiver in accordance with the instructions of the Receiver letters of authority to financial institutions or any other person or body holding any asset of the Defendant authorising the Receiver to receive information or effect the transfer of any asset to the Receiver's control.
        (iii) Executing and delivering within 4 days of being instructed to do so by the Receiver powers of attorney to the Receiver in such form and in such manner as the Receiver directs.
4. Paragraph 12 and 13 of the Restraint Order of 25th November 2006 be varied as follows:
    (a) Paragraph 12 to the extent that the Defendant and/or Mr. Giorgio Germont and Miss Violetta Valery may agree with the Receiver, that the spending limits identified in the said Order for living expenses should be increased, but any such agreement must be in writing; and
    (b) Paragraph 13 to the extent that the Defendant may spend further money on legal expenses actually, reasonably and properly incurred in these proceedings and the criminal proceedings to which these proceedings are ancillary PROVIDED THAT before any monies are released for this purpose the Defendant shall notify the Receiver in writing of the following matters:
        (i) the source of the fund to be used for the said costs;
        (ii) the general nature of the costs incurred;
        (iii) the time spent and by whom (whether partner, assistant solicitor or otherwise) in incurring the said costs;
        (iv) the hourly rate applicable to the costs incurred.

AND in the event that the Receiver considers the claim to be in respect of costs that have not actually, reasonably or properly been incurred then the entitlement to draw such costs shall be restricted to 65% of the amount claimed and the whole claim for costs shall be subject to a detailed assessment on

Appendix 2: Management Receivership Order

an indemnity basis in accordance with CPR Part 48.8 without the provisions of CPR Part 48.8 (2) applying.

5. No information provided to the Receiver under the powers conferred on the Receiver by this Order shall be used in evidence in the prosecution of an offence alleged to have been committed by the person required to make that disclosure or by any spouse of that person.
6. The costs of the Receivership shall be paid in the Receivership in accordance with the letter of agreement as exhibited to the witness statement of (insert name) made on the 3rd day of December 2006.
7. The Receiver shall act in accordance with the letter of agreement as exhibited to the witness statement of (insert name) made on the 3rd day of December 2006 and the Receiver shall supply to the Defendant copies of the accounts and reports supplied to the Revenue and Customs Prosecutions Office in accordance with the said letter of agreement.
8. In this Order the realisable property of the Defendant or the Defendant's assets include but is not limited to the assets specified in the Schedule to this Order.

Effect of this Order on Persons Outside England, Wales and Scotland

9. The terms of this Order do not affect or concern anyone outside England and Wales or Scotland until it is declared enforceable or is enforced by a court in the relevant country and then they are to affect him only to the extent they have been declared enforceable or have been enforced, UNLESS such a person is:
   a. a person to whom this Order is addressed or an officer or an agent appointed by power of attorney of such a person; or
   b. a person who is subject to the jurisdiction of this court or Scotland and (i) has written notice of this order at his residence or place of business within the jurisdiction of this court or Scotland and (ii) is able lawfully to prevent acts or omissions outside the jurisdiction of this court or Scotland which constitute or assist in a breach of the terms of this Order.

The Costs of this Order

10. Costs reserved.

Duration of This Order

11. This Order shall remain in force until is is varied or discharged by further Order of this Court.

Interpretation of this Order

12. In this Order "the Defendant's assets" or "assets of the Defendant" means any property in which the Defendant has any interest or to which the Defendant has any right and any property held by any other person to whom the Defendant has made a gift caught by the Drug Trafficking Act 1994, including but not limited to all property set out in the Schedule hereto.
13. Reference to selling a property includes charging, disposing, transferring, or conveying the legal and/or beneficial interest in the property to the purchaser of it.
14. Reference to the Receiver means [insert name and address of the receiver]
15. Reference to the Defendant means ALFREDO GERMONT.

Variation or Discharge of this Order

The Defendant (or anyone notified of this Order) may apply to the court at any time to vary or discharge this Order (or so much of it as affects that person), but anyone wishing to do so must first

Appendix 2: Management Receivership Order

inform the Receiver and the Revenue and Customs Prosecutions Office giving 2 clear days notice in writing.

DATED this the 5th day of December, 2006.

All communications to the Receiver about this Order should be sent to [insert name, address and telephone number of the receiver]

All communications to the Court about this Order should be sent to the Administrative Court Office, Royal Courts of Justice, Strand, London WC2A 2LL quoting the case number. The offices are open between 10am and 4.30pm Monday to Friday. The telephone number is 020-7947-6000.

The address for service and telephone number of [insert name of prosecutor] for any communication in respect of these proceedings is:
[insert address and telephone number of the prosecutor]

Schedule to the Receivership Order Made on 5th December 2006

(a) The Defendant's interest in a company known as Traviata Trading Enterprises Limited;
(b) Anytown Bank PLC account number 12345678 in the name of the Defendant;
(c) Anytown Bank PLC account number 98765432 in the name of the Defendant and Violetta Valery;
(d) Anytown Bank PLC account number 22334455 in the name of Giorgio Germont;
(e) Anytown Bank PLC account number 66778899 in the name of Traviata Trading Enterprises Limited;
(f) The Defendant's interest in all that property and land known as "The Heights" Marbella, Spain;
(g) The Defendant's interest in a Rolls Royce motor vehicle registered number AG 123 registered in the name of the Defendant;
(h) The Defendant's interest in a motor vessel named "Hispaniola" registered in the names of the Defendant and Violetta Valery;
(i) A racehorse named "Nabucco" registered in the names of the Defendant and Giorgio Germont;
(j) A quantity of cash found on the defendant when arrested totalling £175,000 in Sterling bank notes.

APPENDIX 3

ENFORCEMENT RECEIVERSHIP ORDER

DISOBEDIENCE TO THIS ORDER IS A CONTEMPT OF COURT WHICH IF YOU ARE AN INDIVIDUAL IS PUNISHABLE BY IMPRISONMENT OR IF YOU ARE A BODY CORPORATE IS PUNISHABLE BY SEQUESTRATION OF YOUR ASSETS AND BY IMPRISONMENT OF ANY INDIVIDUAL RESPONSIBLE

DTA No. 1234 of 2006

IN THE HIGH COURT OF JUSTICE
QUEEN'S BENCH DIVISION

Administrative Court
Before the Honourable Mr. Justice Bullingham   sitting in private

IN THE MATTER OF **ALFREDO GERMONT** (Defendant)
AND IN THE MATTER OF THE DRUG TRAFFICKING ACT, 1994

Order Appointing a Receiver Over the Assets of the Defendant

IMPORTANT: NOTICE TO THE DEFENDANT AND ANYONE IN POSSESSION OR CONTROL OF HIS ASSETS OR NAMED IN THIS ORDER

1. This order appoints a Receiver over the assets of the Defendant to enforce the confiscation order made against the Defendant at the Crown Court sitting at Southwark on 7th January, 2007. This means that the Receiver must, subject to the terms of this order, collect the Defendant's assets and sell enough of them to pay the confiscation order.

2. If the Defendant or any person in possession or control of his assets disobeys this order or obstructs the Receiver he or she may be guilty of contempt of court and may be sent to prison or fined or have his assets seized.

3. There is an interpretation section at page 5 of this order.

The Order of Appointment

An application was made today by the Revenue and Customs Prosecutions Office to the High Court for the appointment of an Enforcement Receiver over the assets of the Defendant to enforce the Confiscation Order made by the Crown Court at Southwark on 7th January, 2007 in the sum of £1,000,000.

The Revenue and Customs Prosecutions Office and the Defendant were represented by Counsel. Violetta Valery was represented by Counsel.

The Judge read the witness statements of [insert name of prosecutor] made 1st April, 2003, Alfredo Germont made on 10th April, 2006 and Violetta Valery made on 12th April 2006.

As a result of the application **THE COURT APPOINTS** [insert name of Receiver] to act as an Enforcement Receiver to take possession of, or otherwise deal with, all the assets of the Defendant including, but not limited to, those listed in the Schedule to this Order.

Appendix 3: Enforcement Receivership Order

It is Ordered that:

1. The Defendant, Violetta Valery and all other persons having possession of the Defendant's realisable property do forthwith deliver up to the Receiver possession of all such realisable property, together with all deeds, books, documents and papers relating thereto, but without prejudice to the rights of any encumbrancer.

2. The Receiver shall have the following powers without prejudice to any existing powers vested in him whether by statute or otherwise:—

    (a) Power to take possession of, preserve, manage, collect, let, charge and sell the assets of the Defendant;
    (b) Power to apply the net proceeds of the realisation of the Defendant's realisable property towards satisfaction of the Confiscation Order made against the Defendant by the Crown Court sitting at Southwark on 7th January, 2007.
    (c) Power to appoint Solicitors, Counsel, Attorneys, Accountants or other Agents to advise and/or act on behalf of the Receiver in any part of the world.
    (d) Power to discharge all and any costs, charges and expenses of the Receivership out of the assets and/or the proceeds of realisation thereof.
    (e) Power to institute, defend or compromise proceedings in connection with the realisation of the Defendant's assets.
    (f) Power to bring proceedings in the name of or on behalf of the Defendant, within or without the jurisdiction, against any person having possession of the realisable property of the Defendant for possession thereof or the payment or delivery up thereof.
    (g) Power to execute all such documents in the name of and on behalf of the Defendant and Violetta Valery as may be necessary to take possession of, preserve, manage, collect, let, charge and/or sell realisable property.
    (h) After satisfaction of the Confiscation Order power to apply out of the realisable property such sum as is required in satisfaction of the legal costs of then Revenue and Customs Prosecutions Office ordered by Paragraph 9 of this Order.
    (i) Power to settle debts and liabilities of the Defendant from the assets of the Defendant.
    (j) Power to manage the realisable property of the Defendant including the leasing, letting and/or granting of a licence in any real property forming part of the realisable property.

3. The powers of the Receiver shall not be exercisable in relation to any gifts made by the defendant to Violetta Valery until agreement between the parties or further order and that part of the application by the Revenue and Customs Prosecutions Office for the appointment of a receiver in respect of such gifts do stand adjourned generally with the following directions:—

    (a) Any evidence from Violetta Valery to be served by 3rd May, 2007;
    (b) Any evidence from the Revenue and Customs Prosecutions Office in reply to be served within 14 days thereafter;
    (c) The application be listed on the first open date thereafter on a date fixed through the list office at the convenience of the parties.

4. The Defendant, Violetta Valery and all other persons in possession of the assets of the Defendant shall take all such reasonable and necessary steps as may be required by the Receiver to enable the receivership to be conducted and the sale of the Defendant's assets to proceed, including but without prejudice to the generality of the foregoing-

    (a) Providing the Receiver forthwith upon request by the Receiver with such information and documentation relating to the said assets as the Receiver requires.
    (b) Signing and delivering to the Receiver in accordance with the instructions of the Receiver, Letters of Authority to financial institutions or any other person or body holding any assets of the Defendant authorising the Receiver to receive information or effect the transfer of any asset to the Receiver's control.

(c) Executing and delivering within four days of being instructed to do so by the Receiver power of Attorney to the Receiver in such form and in such manner as the Receiver directs.

5. The costs of the receivership shall be paid in the receivership in accordance with the letter of agreement as exhibited to the witness statement of [insert name of prosecutor]

6. The receiver shall act in accordance with the letter of agreement as exhibited to the witness statement of [insert name of prosecutor] and the Receiver shall supply to the Defendant copies of any accounts and reports supplied to the Revenue and Customs Prosecutions Office in accordance with the said letter of agreement.

7. The Receiver shall be allowed remuneration in accordance with the aforesaid letter of agreement.

8. In this order the realisable property of the Defendant or the Defendant's assets include but are not limited to the assets specified in the Schedule to this Order.

The Costs of this Order

9. The costs of and occasioned by the orders made on 25th November, 2006, 5th December, 2006 and by this application shall be paid by the Defendant to be subject to detailed assessment by a costs judge if not agreed.

Efeect of this Order on Persons Outside England, Wales and Scotland

10. The terms of this order do not affect or concern anyone outside England, Wales and Scotland until it is declared enforceable or is enforced by a court in the relevant country and then they are to affect him only to the extent they have been declared enforceable or have been enforced, **UNLESS** such person is:

(a) A person to whom this order is addressed or an officer or an agent appointed by power of attorney of such a person; or
(b) A person who is subject to the jurisdiction of this court and-
  (i) Has been given written notice of this order at his residence or place of business within the jurisdiction of this court and
  (ii) Is able lawfully to prevent acts or omissionjs outside the jurisdiction of this court which constitute or assist in a breach of the terms of this order.

Duration of this Order

11. This order will remain in force until it is varied or discharged by further order of this Court.

Iinterpratation of this Order

12. In this order "the Defendant's assets" or "assets of the Defendant" means any property in which the Defendant has any interest or to which the Defendant has any right and any property held by any person to whom the Defendant has made a gift caught by the Drug Trafficking Act, 1994 including but not limited to all property set out in the Schedule hereto.

13. Reference to selling a property includes charging, disposing transferring or conveying the legal and/or beneficial interest in the property to the purchaser of it.

14. Reference to the receiver means [insert name and address of the receiver].

15. Reference to the defendant mean Alfredo Germont.

DATED this the 15th day of April, 2007.

Appendix 3: Enforcement Receivership Order

Schedule
[List all known realisable assets of the Defendant subject to the order]

APPENDIX 4

LETTER OF AGREEMENT BETWEEN PROSECUTOR AND RECEIVER

Claim DTA No. 1234 of 2006

Dear

RE: REGINA -v- ALFREDO GERMONT
APPOINTMENT OF RECEIVER—DRUG TRAFFICKING ACT, 1994

I am writing to enquire as to whether you would be prepared to act as receiver in the above case of which the Revenue and Customs Prosecutions Office has the conduct under the provisions of the Drug Trafficking Act, 1994.

Mr. Germont has been arrested and charged with alleged drug trafficking offences contrary to the Customs and Excise Management Act 1979. He is currently awaiting trial at the Crown Court sitting at Southwark. The Revenue and Customs Prosecutions Office wishes to apply for your appointment as a management receiver under section 26 (7) of the Drug Trafficking Act 1994 for the purpose of managing and preserving his realisable property pending the determination of these proceedings.

Mr. Germont owns a company known as Traviata Trading Enterprises Limited which apparently operates as an import and export business. He is now in prison on remand and the appointment of a receiver is sought so as to ensure the business is properly managed. We would expect you to report to the Court within 28 days of your appointment making recommendations as to whether it is commercially viable for the business to continue trading and, if so, provide an estimate of the costs you would incur in managing the business as a court appointed receiver. Mr. Germont is the owner of other assets that are currently unmanaged including a property known as "Traviata" 123 The Esplanade, Torquay, Devon and a racehorse named "Nabucco". Again we would wish you to report to the Court with your recommendations as to how these assets can be effectively managed and the likely costs involved.

You will appreciate that your appointment is dependent on an order being made by the High Court. On appointment you become an officer of the Court and accordingly draw your authority and powers from the Court. In this connection I would refer you to Part 69 of the Civil Procedure Rules and Order 115 of the Rules of the Supreme Court (incorporated in Schedule 1 to the Civil Procedure Rules) which you may find helpful.

As a condition of being nominated by the Revenue and Customs Prosecutions Office your consent to adhere to a standard practice is requested, the provisions of which appear below. We request that you agree to:—

1. Records

(a) keep separate financial records for each matter or estate in respect of which you are appointed;
(b) keep such other financial records as are required to explain the receipts and payments entered in the records described in paragraph (a) above, including an explanation of the source of any receipts and the destination of any payments, and from day to day enter in those records all the receipts and payments you make;
(c) obtain and keep bank statements relating to any bank account held relevant to your appointment.

2. Report Findings

You must comply with the following reporting requirements:-

(a) In the event that at any time it appears to you that receivership costs (including lawyers and other agents' fees and expenses) will be greater than any estimate you have given or that the costs are increasing, or are likely to increase, to a disproportionate level, you msut immediately file a written report with the Court and serve a copy on the Revenue and Customs Prosecutions Office and the Defendant.

(b) You must in any event file and serve on the Revenue and Customs Prosecutions Office and the Defendant a written report within 28 days afer your appointment and every quarter thereafter. This report should summarise your finds and steps taken in the administration of the receivership. It should also include-
  (i) The costs incurred to date;
  (ii) The work done;
  (iii) The projected costs until the next report;
  (iv) A summary of how those costs attach to the matters that led to your appointment or have arisen since then;
  (v) If appropriate, a final outcome statement; and
  (vi) A statement that you believe that your costs are reasonable and proportionate in all the circumstances.

(c) In the event that you are unable to fufil any of the above reporting requirements, you must as soon as reasonably practicable file and serve a written report giving an explanation as to why this is the case.

3. Produce Accounts

Produce on demand, without prior notice and at any time, to any officer of the Revenue and Customs Prosecutions Office or HM Revenue and Customs any accounts, books or other records kept by yourself and allow him to inspect them. This duty shall extend to:—

(a) production and inspection at your premises and,
(b) production and inspection of any financial records of the kind described in paragraph 1 above; and any such demand may require you to allow an officer of the Revenue and Customs Prosecutions Office or HM Revenue and Customs to remove or take copies of any accounts or financial or administrative documents kept in relation to the administration of the matter or the estate regardless of where they may be situated.

4. Lodge Accounts

Every report should be accompanied by a receipts and payments account for the period to which it relates.

5. Your Powers

Your powers will be set out in the order appointing you. It is intended to ask for sufficient powers to enable you to take possession of and manage the property and draw your remuneration.

6. Instructing Lawyers and Other Agents

In the event that you consider it necessary or desirable, you may instruct lawyers or other agents. If so:-

(a) You must inform the Revenue and Customs Prosecutions Office and the Defendant immediately thereafter, unless it is not reasonably practicable or not in the interests of justice to do so.

Appendix 4: Letter of Agreement between Prosecutor and Receiver

(b) You must request monthly bills and/or fee notes from lawyers and agents and must take all reasonable steps to ensure that bills and fees are reasonable and proportionate.

7. REMUNERATION

It is proposed to seek an order from the Court that your costs in this matter should be costs in the receivership; that is to say that your costs shall be paid out of the monies you bring in during the course of this receivership. Before drawing any remuneration you shall obtain the written approval of the Revenue and Customs Prosecutions Office and give the opportunity to the Defendant to make representations as to the amount claimed. In all cases the Revenue and Customs Prosecutions Office reserves the right to insist upon a detailed assessment of all your costs and the costs of any lawyers instructed by you. You will be allowed to draw any remuneration and pay any disbursements from any realisations within 14 days after service by you of the reports required by this letter.

In the event that your remuneration and expenses exceed the amount brought in by you under this receivership, the Revenue and Customs Prosecutions Office is prepared to indemnify you to the extent of *[insert amount]* inclusive of your remuneration, costs, expenses and disbursements although exclusive of VAT, less any sums available to you from the property under your management.. Should you find yourself in a position where you need to rely upon the indemnity, immediate written notification must be given to the Revenue and Customs Prosecutions Office and written authority must be obtained before the additional costs, expenses and disbursements which will result in the indemnity being utilised are incurred.

8. SECURITY BOND

You are asked to confirm that you have in place sufficient security or insurance to cover any and all liability that you may incur for any actionable act or omission carried out by you as a receiver and, if necessary, or the court directs, to provide evidence of such security or insurance.

You are also asked to confirm the nature of the insurance, namely whether it is in the form of either a bond under the Insolvency Practitioner Regulations 1990 extended to cover appointment as a court appointed receiver, a guarantee with a clearing bank or insurance company or in some other form and, if so, what form.

9. CONFIDENTIALITY

(a) You will undertake to abide and procure that any of your employees, servants and agents abide by the provisions of:—
  (i) the Official Secrets Acts 1911 to 1989; and
  (ii) section 182 of the Finance Act, 1989.
(b) You will keep secret and not disclose and shall procure that your employees, servants and/or agents keep secret and do not disclose any information of a confidential nature obtained by you by reason of the receivership except information which is in the public domain otherwise than by failure by yourself to comply with the requirement to retain confidentiality aforesaid.
(c) the duty described in paragraph 9 (b) to keep secret and prohibiting the disclosure of confidential information shall not apply to disclosure of such information to an employees, servant and/or agent who needs to be in possession of that information to enable yourself as Receiver to discharge and fulfil your duties under the receivership and provided always that such disclosure is made in confidence and is subject to a duty of confidence which is enforceable in law by the Receiver in the event of a threatened or actual breach.
(d) You will ensure that all your employees, servants and/or agents so far as appropriate, are aware of, and comply with the requirements in paragraphs 9 (a) & (b) and in any instance of a threatened or actual breach of confidence mentioned in paragraphs 9 (b) & (c) you will at your own cost apply for appropriate civil process, relief and remedy, to protect the confidentiality of the information or

restrict its further dissemination and disclosure and, shall inform and keep fully informed the Revenue and Customs Prosecutions Office of any such instance and of the proceedings and their progress.
(e) The duty of confidentiality shall not determine with the conclusion of the receivership.
(f) Further, in paragraph 9 (b) "information of a confidential nature obtained by you by reason of the receivership" includes information coming to the knowledge of yourself or your employees, servants, agents and/or sub-contractors prior to your formal appointment as Receiver, by virtue of any dealings with the Revenue and Customs Prosecutions Office including visits and/or meetings with members of the Revenue and Customs Prosecutions Office and/or investigating officers in the employ of HM Revenue and Customs or the Serious Organised Crime Agency.

10. Variation of Standard Provisions

Any variation of these provisions must be consented to in writing by the Revenue and Customs Prosecutions Office.

11. Discharge

Upon concluding the receivership you will inform the Revenue and Customs Prosecutions Office and, in conjunction with that Office, apply to the High Court for your discharge.

Finally, we would require a letter from you confirming acceptance of the terms of this proposed appointment.

Yours sincerely

[Prosecutor]

APPENDIX 5

VARIATION OF RESTRAINT ORDER

DISOBEDIENCE OF THIS ORDER IS A CONTEMPT OF COURT WHICH IF YOU ARE AN INDIVIDUAL IS PUNISHABLE BY IMPRISONMENT OR IF YOU ARE A BODY CORPORATE IS PUNISHABLE BY SEQUESTRATION OF YOUR ASSESTS AND BY IMPRISONMENT OF ANY INDIVIDUAL RESPONSIBLE

Claim DTA No. 1234 of 2006

IN THE HIGH COURT OF JUSTICE
QUEEN'S BENCH DIVISION

Administrative Court

Before the Honourable Mr. Justice Featherstone   sitting in Private

IN THE MATTER OF ALFREDO GERMONT (DEFENDANT)
AND
IN THE MATTER OF THE DRUG TRAFFICKING ACT 1994

Order

UPON HEARING Counsel for the Defendant and Counsel for the Revenue and Customs Prosecutions Office.

AND UPON READING the witness statement of Alfredo Germont made on the 30th day of November, 2006.

It is Ordered that

1. The restraint order made by the Honourable Mr. Justice Bullingham on the 25th day of November, 2006 ("the Restraint Order") be varied to the following extent—
   (a) The amount payable to the Defendant by way of general living expenses pursuant to paragraph 11 of the order be increased from £350 per week to £500 per week, to be paid from account number 12345678 held in the name of the Defendant at Anytown Bank PLC;
   (b) The period for compliance with paragraph 8 (ii) of the Order be extended to 1600 hours on Friday, 20th December 2006.
2. The Defendant has permission to sell all that property and land known as "Traviata" 123 The Esplanade, Torquay, Devon ("the property")

Provided that

(i) The Defendant must provide the Revenue and Customs Prosecutions Office with two independent valuations in respect of the property. The Revenue and Customs Prosecutions Office reserves the right to obtain further independent professional property valuations if it wishes to verify those provided by the the Defendant;

(ii) The Defendant must not sell the property for an amount less than its market value as confirmed by the highest valuation obtained under sub-paragraph (i) above;

(iii) The Defendant shall not pay any fees and charges from the gross sum obtained from the sale of the property (including but not limited to legal fees, agents fees, search fees and charges) without obtaining the prior written consent of the Revenue and Customs Prosecutions Office. The Revenue and Customs Prosecutions Office may withhold its consent for the payment of fees and charges that are unreasonable or are improperly incurred

(iv) The Defendant will instruct Messrs. Thorn and Partners, Solicitors, 1a High Street, Torquay, Devon to act for him on the sale of the property and undertakes not to terminate their retainer in respect thereof save with the written consent of the Revenue and Customs Prosecutions Office or the permission of the court;

(v) The gross proceeds of the sale of the property less:

    a. The total amount required to discharge any mortgages and charges that were registered in relation to the property prior to 25th November, 2006; and

    b. The amount required to pay any fees and/or charges for the prior consent of the Revenue and Customs Prosecutions Office has been obtained in accordance with sub-paragraph (iii) above

must be paid into an interest bearing account in the name of Messrs. Thorn and Co. The net proceeds will be subject to the terms of the restraint order.

(vi) Within two working days of receiving the net proceeds of sale into their interest bearing account, Messrs. Thorn and Co will inform the Revenue and Customs Prosecutions Office in writing of the date on which the net proceeds of sale were received and the amount of those proceeds. Messrs. Thorn and Co will also provide the Revenue and Customs Prosecutions Office with a completion statement in relation to the said sale.

(vii) Within three working days of the Revenue and Customs Prosecutions Office receiving written confirmation that the net proceeds of sale have been paid into an interest bearing account subject to the terms of the restraint order, the Revenue and Customs Prosecutions Office will apply to HM Land Registry for the removal of the restriction registered against the property.

3. The restraint order will remain in force in relation to the net proceeds of sale pending the conclusion of these proceedings.

4. Paragraph 2 of this Order will cease to have effect if the sale of the property does not take place by 4pm on 31st March, 2007.

2. Costs reserved.

DATED this the second day of December, 2006.

APPENDIX 6

LSC FUNDING ARRANGEMENTS

Before and after the Proceeds of Crime Act 2002 for Confiscation, Restraint and Receivership

Type of proceedings	Funding position	Notes
Criminal Justice Act 1988 and Drug Trafficking Act 1994 Proceedings for confiscation, restraint and receivership arising from criminal proceedings (in the Crown Court or the civil courts)	Considered ancillary to the proceedings from which they arise, so covered by any current Representation Order	This covers work for the defendant only. See *Focus on CDS* 15 (August 2004) for more details. CLS funding may be available for third parties if the application is in the civil courts and the firm has a civil contract. Work for third parties in the criminal courts can only be covered by exceptional funding (apply to the Special Cases Unit)
Enforcement proceedings in the magistrates court for confiscation orders	Fresh criminal proceedings: apply for Representation using Form A to the court hearing the matter. There is no means test.	Bill under General Criminal Contract as for a normal magistrates court case (non-standard fee) at the usual rates.
Application for certificate of inadequacy (in the High Court)	Fresh criminal proceedings: apply for Representation using Form A to the court hearing the matter. There is no means test but form B may be required as the court may make a Recovery of Defence Costs Order at the end of the proceedings.	Bill the court directly using rates in the Criminal Defence Service Funding Order 2001 (same as Crown Court rates). Pre-order work can be covered under the order if it is urgent and the application is made promptly.
Proceeds of Crime Act 2002 Proceedings under Part 2 of the Act for confiscation, restraint and receivership arising from criminal proceedings (in the Crown Court) after the defendant has been charged	Considered ancillary to the proceedings from which they arise, so covered by any current Representation Order (extended to Crown Court if necessary). If the original substantive proceedings have ended or there is no Representation Order in place, then you should apply to the Crown Court for a fresh Representation Order using Form A	This covers work for the defendant only. Billed as (part of) a Crown Court bill at the usual Crown Court rates.

Continued

Appendix 6: LSC Funding Arrangements

Type of proceedings	Funding position	Notes
Proceeds of Crime Act 2002 Proceedings under Part 2 of the Act for confiscation, restraint and receivership arising from criminal proceedings (in the Crown Court) before the defendant has been charged, or where the client is not the defendant; Proceedings under Part 5 of the Act ('civil confiscation proceedings') for confiscation, restraint and receivership (in the Crown Court), whether the work is for the defendant or someone else. Cash forfeiture proceedings under Part 5 of the Act (in the magistrates court)	In so far as the work relates to a criminal investigation in which the client is involved, the CDS Advice and Assistance scheme should be used until the defendant is charged. In other circumstances CLS funding may be available. Legal Help covers work excluding advocacy and may be self-granted. For representation, apply to the Commission using form CLSAPP1. Emergency Certificates may be granted in some circumstances. A means test will apply.	All civil proceedings under the 2002 Act are classed as Associated CLS Work under the General Criminal Contract, so CDS firms may undertake it whether or not they also hold a General Civil Contract. Some of these proceedings will be brought by the Assets Recovery Agency. In some cases the CLSAPP1 application will be dealt with by our Special Cases Unit and guidance is available on our website. For all other cases the CLSAPP1 should be sent to the London regional office and any queries should be directed to that office.

APPENDIX 7

APPLICATION NOTICE BY DEFENDANT SEEKING A CERTIFICATE OF INADEQUACY

Application Notice

! You must complete Parts A **and** B, **and** Part C if applicable.

! Send any relevant fee and the completed application to the court with any draft order, witness statement or other evidence; and sufficient copies of these for service on each respondent.

Part A

I, Alfredo Germont,

Intend to apply for the following (a draft order is attached):

A certificate of inadequacy under section 17 of the Drug Trafficking Act, 1994

Because

The value of my realisable property is insufficient to satisfy the confiscation order made against me in the sum of £1,000,000 by the Crown Court sitting at Southwark on 15th January, 2006.

Part B

We wish to rely on: *[tick one box]*

The attached witness statement   √   My statement of case

Evidence in part C overleaf in support of my application

Signed ....Position or Office held

(Applicants Solicitor)

Address to which documents about this claim should be sent (including reference if appropriate)[4]

The court office at The Crown Office, Royal Courts of Justice, Strand, London is open from 10am to 4pm Monday to Friday. When corresponding with the court please address forms or letters to the Court Manager and quote the claim number.

Appendix 7: Application Notice by Defendant Seeking a Certificate of Inadequacy

Part C

We wish to rely on the following evidence in support of this application:
The enclosed witness statement of Alfredo Germont dated 1ˢᵗ April, 2007

Statement of Truth

*(I believe) (The Claimant believes) that the facts stated in these particulars of claim are true.

Full name

Name of claimant's solicitor's firm

signed _____ position or office held

*(Claimant)(Claimant's solicitor) (if signing on behalf of firm or company)

*delete as appropriate

Appendix 7: Application Notice by Defendant Seeking a Certificate of Inadequacy

N244A

Notice of Hearing of Application

Notice of Hearing of Application

To (Claimant's)('s Solicitor)
The hearing of the Defendant's application for an order in terms of the enclosed draft

(see copy attached) will take place at   (am)(pm) on the   day
of 2007 at The Royal Courts of Justice.

The court office at Room 315, Royal Courts of Justice, Strand, London WC2A 2LL is open between 10am and 4pm Monday to Friday. When corresponding with the court, please address forms or letters to the Court Manager and quote the claim number.

APPENDIX 8

CERTIFICATE OF INADEQUACY

Claim DTA No. 1234 of 2005

IN THE HIGH COURT OF JUSTICE

QUEEN'S BENCH DIVISION

Administrative Court

Before the Honourable Mr. Justice Vosper   sitting in Private

IN THE MATTER OF ALFREDO GERMONT (DEFENDANT)

AND

IN THE MATTER OF THE DRUG TRAFFICKING ACT 1994

ORDER

UPON HEARING Counsel for the Defendant and Counsel for the Revenue and Customs Prosecutions Office

AND UPON READING the witness statement of Alfredo Germont made on 1st April, 2007.

IT IS CERTIFIED THAT the value of the Defendant's realisable property is inadequate for the payment of the amount remaining to be recovered pursuant to the confiscation order ("the order") made against him in the sum of £1,000,000 by the Crown Court sitting at Southwark on 15th January, 2006 for the following reasons:—

(a) By order of this Honourable Court made on 30th January, 2007 it was determined that Violetta Valery had a 50% interest in all that property and land known as "Traviata", 123 Esplanade, Torquay and in consequence thereof only 50% of the proceeds of sale were available to meet the order;

(b) The Crown Court in making the order determined that the Defendant's Rolls Royce motor vehicle registration number AG 123 was valued at £75,000 whereas upon sale by the Receiver realised only £35,750.

There be no order for costs.

DATED this the 14th day of June, 2007.

APPENDIX 9

CLAIM FORM (CPR PART 8)

**Claim Form
(CPR Part 8)**

In the

Claim No.

Claimant

SEAL

Defendant(s)

Does your claim include any issues under the Human Rights Act 1998? ☐ Yes ☐ No

Details of claim *(see also overleaf)*

	£
Court fee	
Solicitor's costs	
Issue date	

Defendant's name and address

The court office at

is open between 10 am and 4 pm Monday to Friday. When corresponding with the court, please address forms or letters to the Court Manager and quote the case number.

N208 Claim form (CPR Part 8) (10.00) *Printed on behalf of The Court Service*

	Claim No.	

Details of claim *(continued)*

Statement of Truth
*(I believe)(The Claimant believes) that the facts stated in these particulars of claim are true.
* I am duly authorised by the claimant to sign this statement

Full name _____

Name of claimant's solicitor's firm _____

signed_____ position or office held_____

*(Claimant)(Litigation friend)(Claimant's solicitor) (if signing on behalf of firm or company)

*delete as appropriate

Claimant's or claimant's solicitor's address to which documents should be sent if different from overleaf. If you are prepared to accept service by DX, fax or e-mail, please add details.

APPENDIX 10

EXTRACT FROM THE PRACTICE DIRECTION ON POCA 2002 PARTS 5 AND 8: CIVIL RECOVERY: SECTION III

SECTION III—APPLICATIONS UNDER PART 8 OF THE ACT

How to Apply for an Order or Warrant

8.1 An application by the Director for an order or warrant under Part 8 of the Act in connection with a civil recovery investigation must be made—
   (1) to a High Court judge;
   (2) by filing an application notice.

8.2 The application may be made without notice.

Confidentiality of Court Documents

9.1 CPR rule 5.4 does not apply to an application under Part 8 of the Act, and paragraphs 9.2 and 9.3 below have effect in its place.

9.2 When an application is issued, the court file will be marked "Not for disclosure" and, unless a High Court judge grants permission, the court records relating to the application (including the application notice, documents filed in support, and any order or warrant that is made) will not be made available by the court for any person to inspect or copy, either before or after the hearing of the application.

9.3 An application for permission under paragraph 9.2 must be made on notice to the Director in accordance with Part 23.

(Rule 23.7(1) requires a copy of the application notice to be served as soon as practicable after it is filed, and in any event at least 3 days before the court is to deal with the application.)

Application Notice and Evidence

10.1 The application must be supported by written evidence, which must be filed with the application notice.

10.2 The evidence must set out all the matters on which the Director relies in support of the application, including any matters required to be stated by the relevant sections of the Act, and all material facts of which the court should be made aware.

10.3 There must also be filed with the application notice a draft of the order sought. This should if possible also be supplied to the court on disk in a form compatible with the word processing software used by the court.

Hearing of the Application

11.1 The application will be heard and determined in private, unless the judge hearing it directs otherwise.

Variation or Discharge of Order or Warrant

12.1 An application to vary or discharge an order or warrant may be made by—
   (1) the Director; or
   (2) any person affected by the order or warrant.

12.2 An application under paragraph 12.1 to stop an order or warrant from being executed must be made immediately upon it being served.

12.3 A person applying to vary or discharge a warrant must first inform the Director that he is making the application.

12.4 The application should be made to the judge who made the order or issued the warrant or, if he is not available, to another High Court judge.

APPENDIX 11

EXTRACT FROM THE PRACTICE DIRECTION ON POCA 2002 PARTS 5 AND 8: CIVIL RECOVERY: SECTION IV

SECTION IV—FURTHER PROVISIONS ABOUT SPECIFIC APPLICATIONS UNDER PART 8 OF THE ACT

Production Order

13.1 The application notice must name as a respondent the person believed to be in possession or control of the material in relation to which a production order is sought.

13.2 The application notice must specify—
   (1) whether the application is for an order under paragraph (a) or (b) of section 345(4) of the Act;
   (2) the material, or description of material, in relation to which the order is sought; and
   (3) the person who is believed to be in possession or control of the material.

13.3 An application under section 347 of the Act for an order to grant entry may be made either—
   (1) together with an application for a production order; or
   (2) by separate application, after a production order has been made.

13.4 An application notice for an order to grant entry must—
   (1) specify the premises in relation to which the order is sought; and
   (2) be supported by written evidence explaining why the order is needed.

13.5 A production order, or an order to grant entry, must contain a statement of the right of any person affected by the order to apply to vary or discharge the order.

Search and Seizure Warrant

14.1 The application notice should name as respondent the occupier of the premises to be subject to the warrant, if known.

14.2 The evidence in support of the application must state—
   (1) the matters relied on by the Director to show that one of the requirements in section 352(6) of the Act for the issue of a warrant is satisfied;
   (2) details of the premises to be subject to the warrant, and of the possible occupier or occupiers of those premises;
   (3) the name and position of the member of the staff of the Agency who it is intended will execute the warrant.

14.3 There must be filed with the application notice drafts of—
   (1) the warrant; and
   (2) a written undertaking by the person who is to execute the warrant to comply with paragraph 13.8 of this practice direction.

14.4 A search and seizure warrant must—
   (1) specify the statutory power under which it is issued and, unless the court orders otherwise, give an indication of the nature of the investigation in respect of which it is issued;
   (2) state the address or other identification of the premises to be subject to the warrant;
   (3) state the name of the member of staff of the Agency who is authorised to execute the warrant;
   (4) set out the action which the warrant authorises the person executing it to take under the relevant sections of the Act;

Appendix 11: Extract from the Practice Direction on POCA 2002 Parts 5 and 8

  (5) give the date on which the warrant is issued;
  (6) include a statement that the warrant continues in force until the end of the period of one month beginning with the day on which it is issued;
  (7) contain a statement of the right of any person affected by the order to apply to discharge or vary the order.
14.5 An example of a search and seizure warrant is annexed to this practice direction. This example may be modified as appropriate in any particular case.
14.6 Rule 40.2 applies to a search and seizure warrant.

(Rule 40.2 requires every judgment or order to state the name and judicial title of the person making it, to bear the date on which it is given or made, and to be sealed by the court.)

14.7 Upon the issue of a warrant the court will provide to the Director—
  (1) the sealed warrant; and
  (2) a copy of it for service on the occupier or person in charge of the premises subject to the warrant.
14.8 A person attending premises to execute a warrant must, if the premises are occupied produce the warrant on arrival at the premises, and as soon as possible thereafter personally serve a copy of the warrant and an explanatory notice on the occupier or the person appearing to him to be in charge of the premises.
14.9 The person executing the warrant must also comply with any order which the court may make for service of any other documents relating to the application.

Disclosure Order

15.1 The application notice should normally name as respondents the persons on whom the Director intends to serve notices under the disclosure order sought.
15.2 A disclosure order must—
  (1) give an indication of the nature of the investigation for the purposes of which the order is made;
  (2) set out the action which the order authorises the Director to take in accordance with section 357(4) of the Act;
  (3) contain a statement of—
    (a) the offences relating to disclosure orders under section 359 of the Act; and
    (b) the right of any person affected by the order to apply to discharge or vary the order.
15.3 Where, pursuant to a disclosure order, the Director gives to any person a notice under section 357(4) of the Act, he must also at the same time serve on that person a copy of the disclosure order.

Customer Information Order

16.1 The application notice should normally (unless it is impracticable to do so because they are too numerous) name as respondents the financial institution or institutions to which it is proposed that an order should apply.
16.2 A customer information order must—
  (1) specify the financial institution, or description of financial institutions, to which it applies;
  (2) state the name of the person in relation to whom customer information is to be given, and any other details to identify that person;
  (3) contain a statement of—
    (a) the offences relating to disclosure orders under section 366 of the Act; and
    (b) the right of any person affected by the order to apply to discharge or vary the order.
16.3 Where, pursuant to a customer information order, the Director gives to a financial institution a notice to provide customer information, he must also at the same time serve a copy of the order on that institution.

Appendix 11: Extract from the Practice Direction on POCA 2002 Parts 5 and 8

Account Monitoring Order

17.1 The application notice must name as a respondent the financial institution against which an account monitoring order is sought.

17.2 The application notice must—
  (1) state the matters required by section 370(2) and (3) of the Act; and
  (2) give details of—
    (a) the person whose account or accounts the application relates to;
    (b) each account or description of accounts in relation to which the order is sought, including if known the number of each account and the branch at which it is held;
    (c) the information sought about the account or accounts;
    (d) the period for which the order is sought;
    (e) the manner in which, and the frequency with which, it is proposed that the financial institution should provide account information during that period.

17.3 An account monitoring order must contain a statement of the right of any person affected by the order to apply to vary or discharge the order.

APPENDIX 12

SCHEDULE 6 TO POCA 2002
SECTIONS 247 AND 257

POWERS OF INTERIM RECEIVER OR ADMINISTRATOR

Seizure

1 Power to seize property to which the order applies.

Information

2 (1) Power to obtain information or to require a person to answer any question.
  (2) A requirement imposed in the exercise of the power has effect in spite of any restriction on the disclosure of information (however imposed).
  (3) An answer given by a person in pursuance of such a requirement may not be used in evidence against him in criminal proceedings.
  (4) Sub-paragraph (3) does not apply—
    (a) on a prosecution for an offence under section 5 of the Perjury Act 1911, section 44(2) of the Criminal Law (Consolidation) (Scotland) Act 1995 or Article 10 of the Perjury (Northern Ireland) Order 1979 (false statements), or
    (b) on a prosecution for some other offence where, in giving evidence, he makes a statement inconsistent with it.
  (5) But an answer may not be used by virtue of sub-paragraph (4)(b) against a person unless—
    (a) evidence relating to it is adduced, or
    (b) a question relating to it is asked, by him or on his behalf in the proceedings arising out of the prosecution.

Entry, search, etc.

3 (1) Power to—
    (a) enter any premises in the United Kingdom to which the interim order applies, and
    (b) take any of the following steps.
  (2) Those steps are—
    (a) to carry out a search for or inspection of anything described in the order,
    (b) to make or obtain a copy, photograph or other record of anything so described,
    (c) to remove anything which he is required to take possession of in pursuance of the order or which may be required as evidence in the proceedings under Chapter 2 of Part 5.
  (3) The order may describe anything generally, whether by reference to a class or otherwise.

Supplementary

4 (1) An order making any provision under paragraph 2 or 3 must make provision in respect of legal professional privilege (in Scotland, legal privilege within the meaning of Chapter 3 of Part 8).
  (2) An order making any provision under paragraph 3 may require any person—
    (a) to give the interim receiver or administrator access to any premises which he may enter in pursuance of paragraph 3,
    (b) to give the interim receiver or administrator any assistance he may require for taking the steps mentioned in that paragraph.

Management

5 (1) Power to manage any property to which the order applies.
   (2) Managing property includes—
       (a) selling or otherwise disposing of assets comprised in the property which are perishable or which ought to be disposed of before their value diminishes,
       (b) where the property comprises assets of a trade or business, carrying on, or arranging for another to carry on, the trade or business,
       (c) incurring capital expenditure in respect of the property.

APPENDIX 13

DRAFT RESTRAINT, DISCLOSURE AND REPATRIATION ORDER UNDER POCA

DISOBEDIENCE OF THIS ORDER IS A CONTEMPT OF COURT WHICH IF YOU ARE AN INDIVIDUAL IS PUNISHABLE BY IMPRISONMENT OR IF YOU ARE A BODY CORPORATE IS PUNISHABLE BY SEQUESTRATION OF YOUR ASSETS AND BY IMPRISONMENT OF ANY INDIVIDUAL RESPONSIBLE.

POCA No. 123 of 2006

IN THE CROWN COURT
SITTING AT EXETER

Before the Her Honour Judge Butterfly   sitting in Private

IN THE MATTER OF Mr ALFREDO GERMONT

The Defendant

AND

IN THE MATTER OF THE PROCEEDS OF CRIME ACT 2002

RESTRAINT ORDER PROHIBITING THE DISPOSAL OF ASSETS

TO:

1. Mr Alfredo Germont (the Defendant)
2. Mrs Alfreda Germont
3. ABC Ltd

PENAL NOTICE

If you, Mr Alfredo Germont disobey this order you may be held to be in contempt of court and may be imprisoned, fined or have your assets seized.

Any other person who knows of this order and does anything which helps or permits the Defendant, Mrs Alfreda Germont or ABC Ltd to breach the terms of this order may also be held to be in contempt of court and may be imprisoned, fined or have their assets seized.

IMPORTANT: NOTICE TO THE DEFENDANT, MRS ALFREDA GERMONT AND ABC Ltd

This Order prohibits the Defendant from dealing with his assets. It prohibits Mrs Alfreda Germont from dealing with the assets identified in paragraph 6 of this order. It prohibits ABC Ltd from dealing with the assets identified in paragraph 7 of this order. The Order is subject to the exceptions at the end of this Order. You should read it all carefully.

You are advised to consult a solicitor as soon as possible. Under Paragraph 2 of Schedule 2 of the Access to Justice Act 1999, as amended by Paragraph 36 of Schedule 11 of the Proceeds of Crime Act 2002, you may be entitled to Community Legal Service funding in respect of this Order. Your solicitor will be able to provide you with the appropriate forms. Such application should be submitted to the Legal Services Commission, Special Cases Unit, 1st Floor, 85 Gray's Inn Road, London WC1 8TX. In relation to LSC funding (formerly Legal Aid) geenral enquiries may be directed to the free LSC telephone helpline: 0800 085 6643.

Appendix 13: Draft Restraint, Disclosure and Repatriation Order under POCA

You have a right to ask this court to vary or discharge this Order. If you do wish to do this you must serve on the Revenue and Customs Prosecutions Office and all other affected parties a copy of the application and any witness statement in support at least two working days before the date fixed for the hearing.

There will be a further hearing of this matter on x/y/2007 ("the return date") when the Prosecutor will apply for the continuation of this order. The Defendant, Mrs Alfreda Germont and ABC Ltd and any other person affected by the order are entitled to appear and to object to the continuation of this order or to ask for it to be varied.

THE ORDER

1. This is a restraint order made against Mr Alfredo Germont ("the Defendant") by Her Honour Judge Butterfly on the application of the Revenue and Customs Prosecutions Office ("the Prosecutor"). The judge read the witness statement listed in Schedule A and accepted the undertakings set out in Schedule B at the end of this order.
2. This order was made at a hearing without notice to the Defendant, Mrs Alfreda Germont or ABC Ltd. The Defendant, Mrs Alfreda Germont and ABC Ltd have a right to apply to the court to vary or discharge this order—see paragraph 18 below.

DISPOSAL OF OR DEALING WITH ASSETS

As a result of this application **IT IS ORDERED** by Her Honour Judge Butterfly that until further Order of the Court:

3. The Defendant must not:
   (a) remove from England and Wales any of his assets which are in England and Wales whether in his own name or not and whether solely or jointly owned; or
   (b) in any way dispose of or deal with or diminish the value of any of his assets whether they are in or outside England and Wales whether in his own name or not and whether solely or jointly owned.
4. Paragraph 3 applies to all the Defendant's assets whether or not they are in his own name and whether they are solely or jointly owned. For the purpose of this order the Defendant's assets include any asset which he has the power, directly or indirectly, to dispose of or deal with as if it were his own. The Defendant is to be regarded as having such power if a third party holds or controls the asset in accordance with his direct or indirect instructions.
5. These prohibitions include the following assets in particular:
   (a) The assets of a company called ABC Ltd (Company number 000 000 000), registered address 325 Marine Parade, Paignton;
   (b) NatEast Bank PLC account number 00000000 held at 23 Under Street, London, EC1 1AA, sort code 00-00-00 in the name of ABC Ltd;
   (c) NatEast Bank PLC account number 0000000 held at 311 St Marychurch Road, Torquay, Devon, sort code 00-00-00;
   (d) Le Banque bank account number 000000000 held in Bordeaux, France in the name ABC Ltd;
   (e) Le Banque bank account number 00000000000 held in the name of ABC Ltd;
   (f) Le Banque bank account number 0000000000 in the name of the Defendant and Mrs Alfreda Germont;
   (g) The Defendant's interest in a Volvo estate C70 motor vehicle, index plate Y111 MEE.
      AND IT IS ORDERED THAT:—
      The assets of ABC Ltd be treated as the personal assets of the Defendant.
6. Mrs Alfreda Germont (wife of the Defendant) must not:—
      (a) remove from England and Wales; or
      (b) in any way dispose of or deal with or diminish the value of any of
   (a) The assets of a company called ABC Ltd (Company number 0000000), registered address 325 Marine Parade, Paignton;

Appendix 13: Draft Restraint, Disclosure and Repatriation Order under POCA

    (b) NatEast Bank account number 00000000 held at 23 Under Street, London, EC1 1 AA, sort code 00-00-00 in the name of ABC Ltd;
    (c) Le Banque bank account number 000000000 in the name of the Defendant and Mrs Alfreda Germont.
7. ABC Ltd (a company in the control of the Defendant) must not:—
    (a) remove from England and Wales; or
    (b) in any way dispose of or deal with or diminish the value of any of
    (a) The assets of a company called ABC Ltd (Company number 0000000), registered address 325 Marine Parade, Paignton;
    (b) Le Banque Bank account number 00000000 held at 23 Under Street, London, EC1 1AA, sort code 00-00-00 in the name of ABC Ltd;
    (c) Le Banque account number 0000000000 held in Bordeaux, France in the name ABC Ltd;
    (d) Le Banque bank account number 0000000 held in the name of ABC Limited.

PROVISION OF INFORMATION

8. The Defendant must:
    (i) inform the Revenue and Customs Prosecutions Office in writing within 72 hours of service of this Order on the Defendant of all his assets whether in or outside England and Wales and whether in his own name or not and whether solely or jointly owned, giving the value, location and details of all such assets;
    (ii) confirm the information in a witness statement which must be verified by a statement of truth and served on the Revenue and Customs Prosecutions Office within 21 days after this Order has been served on the defendant.

The information in the witness statement must include:
    a. the name and address of all persons including financial institutions holding any such assets;
    b. details of the Defendant's current salary or other form of income, identifying the amount paid, by whom it is paid and the account or accounts into which it is paid;
    c. the names and numbers of all accounts held by or under the control of the Defendant, together with the name and address of the place where the account is held and the sums in the account;
    d. details (including addresses) of any real property in which the Defendant has any interest, including an interest in any of the proceeds of sale if the property were to be sold. These details must include details of any mortgage or charge on the property;
    e. details of all National Savings Certificates, unit trusts, shares or debentures held by the Defendant in any company or corporation wherever incorporated in the world, owned or controlled by the Defendant or in which he has an interest;
    f. details of all trusts of which the Defendant is a beneficiary, including the name and address of every trustee;
    g. particulars of any income or debt due to the Defendant including the name and address of the debtor;
    h. details of all assets over £5,000.00 in value received by the Defendant or anyone on his behalf since the x/y/2001 identifying the name and address of the person from whom such asset was received;
    i. details of all assets over £5,000.00 in value transferred by the Defendant or anyone on his behalf to others since x/y/2001 identifying the name and address of all persons to whom such property was transferred.
9. (1) Subject to any further order of the court any information given in compliance with this order shall only be used—
    (a) for the purpose of these proceedings;
    (b) if the Defendant is convicted, for the purposes of any confiscation hearing that may take place; and
    (c) if a confiscation order is made, for the purposes of enforcing that order, including any receivership proceedings.

Appendix 13: Draft Restraint, Disclosure and Repatriation Order under POCA

(2) There shall be no disclosure of any material disclosed in compliance with this order to any co-defendant in the criminal proceedings.
(3) However, nothing in this paragraph shall make inadmissible any disclosure made by the Defendant in any proceedings for perjury relating to that disclosure.

REPATRIATION

10. (1) The Defendant must within 21 days after service of this order upon him bring any moveable asset in respect of which he has an interest, which is outside England and Wales, to a location within England and Wales.
    (2) The defendant must inform the Revenue and Customs Prosecutions Office of the location within England and Wales within 7 days of the arrival of the assets.
    (3) If the asset is cash or credit in a financial institution it must be paid into an interest bearing account and the account holder, location and account number be notified to the Revenue and Customs Prosecutions Office within 7 days.

EXCEPTIONS TO THIS ORDER

11. This Order does not prevent the Defendant, as long as he is not in prison, and Mrs Alfreda Germont from spending £350 per week towards their ordinary living expenses. But before spending any money for such purposes the Defendant and Mrs Alfreda Germont must tell the Revenue and Customs Prosecutions Office where the money is to come from.
12. The Defendant and Mrs Alfreda Germont may agree with the Revenue and Customs Prosecutions Office that the above spending limits for living expenses should be increased or that this Order may be varied in any respect, but any such agreement must be in writing.
13. This Order does not prevent the Defendant and Mrs Alfreda Germont from spending any money they receive by way of state benefit from the Department of Work and Pensions.
14. This order does not prohibit the Defendant from spending towards his ordinary living expenses any sum earned by him whilst he is in prison.
15. This Order does not prevent:
    (a) any person from paying any money in satisfaction of the whole or part of any confiscation order which may be made against the Defendant; or
    (b) the levy of distress upon any goods subject to this order for the purpose of enforcement of any confiscation order which may be made against the Defendant.

COSTS

16. The costs of this order are reserved.

VARIATION OR DISCHARGE OF THIS ORDER

17. Anyone affected by this order may apply to the court at any time to vary or discharge this order (or so much of it as affects that person), but they must first inform the Prosecutor and the Defendant, Mrs Alfreda Germont and ABC Ltd giving two clear days' notice. If any evidence is to be relied upon in support of the application, the substance of it must be communicated in writing to the Prosecutor in advance.

INTERPRETATION OF THIS ORDER

18. A person who is an individual who is ordered not to do something must not do it himself or in any other way. He must not do it through others acting on his behalf or on his instructions or with this encouragement.
19. A person who is not an individual which is ordered not to do something must not do it itself or by its directors, officers, partners, employees or agents or in any other way.

Appendix 13: Draft Restraint, Disclosure and Repatriation Order under POCA

20. Reference to the "Defendant" means Mr Alfredo Germont. Reference to an asset belonging to the Defendant includes any property in which the Defendant has an interest and any property to which the Defendant has a right.

PARTIES OTHER THAN THE DEFENDANT

21. **Effect of this order** It is a contempt of court for any person notified of this Order knowingly to assist in or permit a breach of this Order. Any person doing so may be sent to prison, fined or have his assets seized. He is also at risk of being prosecuted for a money laundering offence.
22. **Set off by banks** This Order does not prevent any bank from exercising any right of set off it may have in respect of any facility which it gave to the Defendant before it was notified of this Order.
23. **Withdrawals by the Defendant** No bank need enquire as to the application or proposed application of any money withdrawn by the Defendant if the withdrawal appears to be permitted by this Order.
24. **Parties outside England, Wales and Scotland** (1) Except as provided in paragraph (2) below, the terms of this order do not affect or concern anyone outside the jurisdiction of this court or Scotland.
(2) The terms of this order will affect the following persons in a country or state outside the jurisdiction of this court or Scotland—
    a. a person to whom this Order is addressed or an officer or an agent appointed by power of attorney of such a person; or
    b. a person who—
        (i) is subject to the jurisdiction of this court or Scotland;
        (ii) has been given written notice of this order at his residence or place of business within the jurisdiction of this court or Scotland; and
        (iii) is able to prevent acts or omissions outside the jurisdiction of this court or Scotland which constitute or assist in a breach of the terms of this Order.
    (c) any other person, only to the extent that this order is declared enforceable by or is enforced by a court in that country or state.

ENFORCEMENT IN SCOTLAND

25. This order shall have effect in the law of Scotland, any may be enforced there if it is registered under the Proceeds of Crime Act 2002 (Enforcement in different parts of the United Kingdom) Order (SI No 2002/3133).

ASSETS LOCATED OUTSIDE ENGLAND AND WALES

26. Nothing in this order shall, in respect of assets located outside England and Wales, prevent any third party from complying with—
    (1) what it reasonably believes to be its obligations, contractual or otherwise, under the laws and obligations of the country or state in which those assets are situated or under the proper law of any contract between itself and the Defendant; and
    (2) any orders of the courts of that country or state, provided that reasonable notice of any application for such an order is given to the Applicant's solicitors

unless those assets are situated in Scotland and this order has been registered there in which case this order must be obeyed there.

COMMUNICATIONS WITH THE COURT

27. All communications to the Court about this Order should be sent to the Administrative Office, Southwark Crown Court quoting the case number. The office is open between 10am and 4.30pm Monday to Friday.

Appendix 13: Draft Restraint, Disclosure and Repatriation Order under POCA

SCHEDULE A

The judge read the following witness statement before making this Order:

Witness statement of Peter Pickle dated   December 2006.

SCHEDULE B

Undertakings given to the Court by the Prosecutor

1. The prosecutor will serve upon the Defendant, Mrs Alfreda Germont and ABC Ltd—
   (a) a copy of this Order; and
   (b) a copy of the witness statement containing the evidence relied on by the Prosecutor, and any other documents provided to the court on the making of the application.
2. Anyone notified of this Order will be given a copy of it by the prosecutor.
3. The Revenue and Customs Prosecutions Office will pay the reasonable costs of anyone other than the Defendant, Mrs Alfreda Germont and ABC Limited which are incurred as a result of this Order including the costs of ascertaining whether that person holds any of the Defendant's assets, save that the prosecutor will not pay any legal or accountancy costs so incurred without first giving their consent in writing.

ADDRESS OF THE PROSECUTOR FOR SERVICE AND ANY COMMUNICATION IN RESPECT OF THESE PROCEEDINGS

[Name, address and telephone number of the prosecutor]

APPENDIX 14

CERTIFICATE OF SERVICE

IN THE CROWN COURT AT EXETER   CASE NO: 123 OF 2006

IN THE MATTER OF ALFREDO GERMONT (DEFENDANT)

AND IN THE MATTER OF THE PROCEEDS OF CRIME ACT 2002

CERTIFICATE OF SERVICE

RULE 57.14 Criminal Procedure Rules 2006

I, [*insert full name*] an Officer of HM Revenue and Customs, of [*insert address*] do hereby certify that on 15th April, 2006 at HM Prison, Exeter I served upon Alfredo Germont the following documents-

(a) A true copy of the restraint order made by His Honour Judge Butterfly on the 14th day of April 2006;

(b) A true copy of the witness statement of Peter Pickle made on 11th April, 2006 together with the exhibits thereto

Dated this the 16th day of April 2006

SIGNED:

_____

APPENDIX 15

INTERIM RECEIVING ORDER UNDER s 246 OF POCA 2002

CO No. 123 of 2007

IN THE HIGH COURT OF JUSTICE
QUEEN'S BENCH DIVISION

Before the Honourable Mr Justice Bellini sitting in Private
         IN THE MATTER OF MR ALFREDO GERMONT

(Respondent)

AND

IN THE MATTER OF THE PROCEEDS OF CRIME ACT 2002

INTERIM RECEIVING ORDER

Penal Notice

IF ALFREDO GERMONT FAILS TO COMPLY WITH THE TERMS OF THIS ORDER HE MAY BE HELD IN CONTEMPT OF COURT FOR WHICH HE MAY BE FINED AND BE IMPRISONED OR HAVE HIS ASSETS SEIZED

ANY OTHER PERSON WHO KNOWS OF THIS ORDER AND DOES ANYTHING WHICH HELPS OR PERMITS ALFREDO GERMONT TO BREACH THE TERMS OF THIS ORDER MAY ALSO BE HELD TO BE IN CONTEMPT OF COURT AND MAY BE IMPRISONED, FINED OR HAVE THEIR ASSETS SEIZED.

    To: **ALFREDO GERMONT**

An application having been made to the High Court pursuant to section 246 of the Proceeds of Crime Act 2002 by the Director of the Assets Recovery Agency ("the Director").

And upon reading the witness statement of **Tony Foot** dated 22 July 2007,

And Upon Hearing Counsel for the Director,

THE COURT IS SATISFIED that the relevant requirements for making an interim receiving order are fulfilled.

Appendix 15: Interim Receiving Order under s 246 of POCA 2002

Important Notice

TO THE RESPONDENT ALFREDO GERMONT AND TO ANYONE IN POSSESSION OR CONTROL OF THE RESPONDENTS PROPERTY

A. This Order appoints an Interim Receiver over certain property of the Respondents, limited to the property specified in Schedule 2 to this Order. This Order prohibits the Respondents from dealing with that property.
B. The Order is subject to the exclusions at the end of this Order.
C. You should read all of this Order carefully. You are advised to consult a solicitor as soon as possible.
D. You may be entitled to Community Legal Service Funding in respect of this Order. You are referred to section 6 of the Access to Justice Act 1999 and the Guidance to solicitors and applicants seeking Community Legal Service funding for proceedings under the Proceeds of Crime Act 2002 involving the Assets Recovery Agency.
E. Subject to the provisions of section 245C of the Proceeds of Crime Act 2002 and the Proceeds of Crime Act 2002 (Legal Expenses in Civil Recovery Proceedings) Regulations 2005, you may be entitled to the release of restrained funds to pay for legal representation in connection with this Order. A request for the release of a sum in respect of reasonable legal expenses must be made in writing to the Director of the Assets Recovery Agency and before any release can be made certain conditions must be fulfilled. You and your legal adviser are referred to Part 3 of the Proceeds of Crime Act 2002 (Legal Expenses in Civil Recovery Proceedings) Regulations 2005 (SI 3382 of 2005).
F. Further to the provisions of section 245C of the Proceeds of Crime Act 2002, you may be entitled to the release of restrained funds to meet your reasonable living expenses or to carry on any trade, business, profession or occupation. A request for the release of property or an asset to meet reasonable living expenses or to carry on any trade, business, profession or occupation can either be made to the Director of the Assets Recovery Agency, in the first instance or to the Court pursuant to section 245B of the Proceeds of Crime Act 2002.
G. You have a right to ask this Court to vary or discharge this Order.
H. If the Respondent or any person in possession or control of the property specified in Schedule 2 to this Order disobeys this Order or obstructs the Receiver he or she may be guilty of contempt of court and may be sent to prison or fined or have their assets seized.
I. There is an interpretation section at page x of this Order.

AS A RESULT OF THE APPLICATION THE COURT MAKES THE FOLLOWING ORDERS: -

The Order of Appointment:

1. THE COURT APPOINTS Ivan I. Dere as Interim Receiver ("the Receiver") of the property listed in Schedule 2 to this Order.

Order for the detention, custody, preservation and possession of property:

2. The Respondent must not:
    (i) remove from England and Wales any Schedule 2 property which is in England and Wales whether in their own name or not and whether solely or jointly owned; or
    (ii) in any way dispose of or deal with or diminish the value of any of the Schedule 2 property whether it is in or outside England and Wales whether in the Respondents own name or not and whether solely or jointly owned.
3. Pursuant to section 250 of the Proceeds of Crime Act 2002, the Respondent shall as soon as reasonably practicable:
    (i) on the demand in writing of the Receiver co-operate in procuring the transfer of the monies specified as item iv of Schedule 2 to this Order to such account as is specified by the Receiver;

(ii) bring such property as is specified by the Receiver to the offices of the Receiver at Blueberry House, Strawberry Lane, London N1 1AA or to such other place as the Receiver specifies or place it in the custody of the Receiver; and

(iii) do anything he/she is reasonably required to do by the Receiver for the preservation of the property.

4. Unless otherwise agreed in writing by the Receiver, the Respondent and all other persons having possession of the Schedule 2 property shall forthwith deliver up to the Receiver possession of all such assets, together with all deeds, books, documents and papers relating thereto, but without prejudice to the rights of any encumbrancer and SAVE THAT any person in lawful occupation of any real property is not required, until further order, to give physical possession of the real property to the Receiver.

Disclosure:

5. Within 72 hours of personal service of this order, to the best of his ability, the Respondent must inform the Receiver in writing of all of his assets worldwide exceeding £500 in value whether in his own name or not and whether solely or jointly owned, giving the value, location and details of all of his assets. The Respondent must then provide this information in a witness statement certified by a statement of truth within 14 days after being personally served with this Order.

6. Nothing in this Order shall make inadmissible any disclosure made by the Respondent in any proceedings for perjury relating to that disclosure.

7. If the provision of the information required by paragraphs 5 is likely to incriminate the Respondent, he may be entitled to refuse to provide it, but he is recommended to take legal advice before refusing to provide the information. Wrongful refusal to provide the information is a contempt of court and may render the Respondent liable to be imprisoned, fined or have his assets seized.

Powers of the Receiver:

8. In accordance with Schedule 6 to the Proceeds of Crime Act 2002, the Receiver shall have the following powers without prejudice to any existing powers vested in him whether by statute or otherwise:-

(i) Power to seize property to which this Order applies;

(ii) Power to take possession of and manage any property to which this Order applies;

(iii) Power to enter and search any premises in the United Kingdom in which the Receiver believes or has reasonable grounds to believe that material relevant to his duties under the Act may be located and take the following steps:

(a) carry out a search for or inspection of anything described in this Order, which shall include, but not be limited to, Suite 1, 2 Commercial Road, Torquay TQ1 1RR;

(b) to have Police assistance, if required, when carrying out service of this Order and a search for or inspection of anything described in this Order;

(c) make or obtain a copy, photograph or other record of anything so described in this Order;

(d) remove anything which he is entitled to take possession of in pursuance of this Order or which may be required as evidence in proceedings for civil recovery;

(e) effect and maintain insurance.

(iv) Power to appoint solicitors, counsel, attorneys, accountants or other agents to advise and/or act on behalf of the Receiver in any part of the world;

(v) Power to bring proceedings in the name of or on behalf of the Respondent and any other person within or without the jurisdiction, against any person having possession of the property of the Respondent for possession thereof or for the payment or delivery up thereof;

(vi) Power to execute all such documents in the name of and on behalf of the Respondent and any other person as may be necessary to manage Schedule 2 property;

(vii) Power to require the Respondent, and all other persons in possession of the property of the Respondent to take all such reasonable and necessary steps as may be required by the Receiver

to enable the receivership to be conducted, including but without prejudice to the generality of the foregoing:
   (a) providing the Receiver forthwith upon request by the Receiver with such information and documents including any questions put to them by the Receiver relating to the management of the said property as the Receiver so requires;
   (b) to sign and deliver to the Receiver in accordance with the instructions of the Receiver letters of authority to financial institutions or any other person or body holding any asset of the Respondent authorising the Receiver to receive information or effect the transfer of any such property to the Receiver's control;
   (c) to execute and deliver within 4 days of being instructed to do so by the Receiver power of attorney to the Receiver in such form and in such manner as the Receiver directs.
9. Nothing in this Order shall prevent any person claiming legal professional privilege in relation to the matters set out therein, particularly in relation to communications between the legal adviser and his or her client, or communications made in connection with or in contemplation of legal proceedings and for the purposes of those proceedings. However in such circumstances any person claiming legal professional privilege must still give to the Receiver access to any premises he may enter in pursuance of paragraph 8 and give to the Receiver any assistance he may require pursuant to this order.

Duties of the Receiver:

10. Pursuant to section 247(2)(a) of the Proceeds of Crime Act 2002, the Receiver shall consider such information and documents as are obtained by him in pursuance of this Order to establish whether or not the Schedule 2 property is recoverable property or associated property, and if the latter, to what extent the property comprises associated property.
11. Pursuant to section 247(2)(b) of the Proceeds of Crime Act 2002, the Receiver shall take all reasonable and necessary steps to establish whether or not any other property is recoverable property (in relation to the same unlawful conduct), and if it is, who holds it.
12. In accordance with section 255(1) of the Proceeds of Crime Act 2002, the Receiver must inform the Director and this Honourable Court as soon as reasonably practicable if he thinks that:
   (i) any property to which the Order applies by virtue of a claim that it is recoverable property is not recoverable property;
   (ii) any property to which this Order applies by virtue of a claim that it is associated property is not associated property;
   (iii) any property to which the Order does not apply is recoverable property (in relation to the same unlawful conduct) or associated property; or
   (iv) any property to which the Order applies is held by a person who is different from the person it is claimed holds it, or if he thinks that there has been a material change in circumstances.
13. In accordance with section 255(2) of the Proceeds of Crime Act 2002, the Receiver shall provide to this Honourable Court a report of his findings and shall serve copies of that report on the Director of the Assets Recovery Agency and on any other person who holds any property to which the Order applies or who may otherwise be affected by the report.

Orders relating to service:

14. Permission is given to the Assets Recovery Agency to comply with their undertaking relating to service on the Respondent by serving a copy of the Application Notice, the witness statement of Tony Foot dated 1 July 2007, and this Order on the last known solicitors for the Respondent, namely Messrs Tryitt and See, Green House, Blue Road, Torquay TQ1 1LN.

The Receiver's liability:

15. If the Receiver deals with any property which is not property to which this Order applies, and at the time he deals with the property he believes on reasonable grounds that he is entitled to do so in pursuance of the Order, the Receiver will not be liable to any person in respect of any loss or damage resulting from his dealing with the property except so far as the loss or damage is caused by his negligence.

16. The Receiver is required to have sufficient security or insurance to cover any liability for their acts or omissions as a Receiver. If the Receiver has appropriate insolvency practitioners' bond or guarantee, then no specific order concerning the security will be necessary from the Court. If, however, the insurance comes in some other form, then provided this form is acceptable, the Court will need to make some direction that the security can be given in this other form.

The effect of this Order:

17. A person who is an individual who is ordered not to do something must not do it himself or herself or in any other way. He or she must not do it through others acting on his or her behalf or on his or her instructions or with his or her encouragement.
18. A person which is a corporation and which is ordered not to do something must not do it by its directors, officers, employees or agents or in any other way.
19. Pursuant to Schedule 6(2) to the Proceeds of Crime Act 2002, no answer given by a person to the Receiver in pursuance of paragraph 6 above shall be used in evidence in criminal proceedings against the person, SAVE:
    (i) on a prosecution for an offence under section 5 of the Perjury Act 1911, section 44(2) of the Criminal Law (Consolidation) (Scotland) Act 1995 or Article 10 of the Perjury (Northern Ireland) Order 1979 (false statements); or
    (ii) on a prosecution for some other offence where, in giving evidence, he or she makes a statement inconsistent with it. (But an answer may not be used against a person unless evidence relating to it is adduced, or a question relating to it is asked, by him or her or on his or her behalf in the proceedings arising out of the prosecution).

Third parties:

20. It is a contempt of court for any person notified of this Order knowingly to assist in or permit a breach of this Order. Any person doing so may be sent to prison, fined or have his or her assets seized. He or she is also at risk of being prosecuted for a money-laundering offence.

The effect of this Order on persons outside England, Wales and Scotland

21. The terms of this Order do not affect or concern anyone outside England, Wales and Scotland until it is declared enforceable or is enforced by a court in the relevant country and then they are to affect him or her only to the extent they have been declared enforceable or have been enforced, UNLESS such person is:
    (i) a person to whom this Order is addressed or an officer or an agent appointed by power of attorney of such a person; or
    (ii) a person who is subject to the jurisdiction of this court and (i) has been given written notice of this Order at his or her residence or place of business within the jurisdiction of this court and (ii) is able lawfully to prevent acts or omissions outside the jurisdiction of this court which constitute or assist in a breach of the terms of this Order.

Undertakings:

22. The Director gives to the Court the undertakings set out in Schedule 1 to this Order.

Duration of this Order:

23. This Order will remain in force until it is varied or discharged by further Order of this court.

Variation or discharge of this Order:

24. The Respondent (or anyone notified of or affected by this Order) may apply to the court at any time to vary or discharge this Order (or so much of it as affects that person), but anyone wishing to do so must first inform the Assets Recovery Agency giving at least 2 clear days' notice in writing.

The costs of the Receivership:

25. The Receiver may charge for his services and shall prepare and serve accounts in accordance with the letter of nomination as exhibited to the witness statement of Tony Foot dated 1 July 2007.

Appendix 15: Interim Receiving Order under s 246 of POCA 2002

The costs of this Order:

26. The costs of this Order are reserved.

Communications with the Receiver:

27. All communications to the Receiver about this Order should be sent to Ivan I. Dere of Blueberry House, Strawberry Lane, London N1 1AA, telephone number 0207 000 1111 quoting the Respondents name.

Communications with the Assets Recovery Agency:

28. All communication to the Director of the Assets Recovery Agency about this Order should be sent to the Assets Recovery Agency, PO Box 39992, London, EC4M 7XQ, telephone number 020 7029 5700, fax 020 7029 5896 quoting reference: **GERMONT**.

Communications with the Court

29. All communication to the Court about this Order should be sent to Administrative Crown Office, Royal Courts of Justice, Strand, London, WC2A 2LL quoting the case number. The office is open between 10am and 4:30pm Monday to Friday. The telephone number is 020 7947 6000.

Interpretation of this Order:

30. "Property" is all property wherever situated and includes:
    (i) money;
    (ii) all forms of property, real or personal, heritable or moveable,
    (iii) things in action and other intangible or incorporeal property.
31. Any reference to a person's property (whether expressed as a reference to the property he or she holds or otherwise) is to be read as follows:
    (i) In relation to land, it is a reference to any interest which he or she holds in the land.
    (ii) In relation to property other than land, it is a reference –
        (a) to the property (if it belongs to him or her), or
        (b) to any other interest which he or she holds in the property.
32. "The Respondents recoverable property" or "recoverable property of the Respondent" means property that has been obtained through unlawful conduct, or property that represents such property.
33. "Associated property" means property of any of the following descriptions (including property held by the Respondent) which is not itself recoverable property –
    (i) any interest in the recoverable property,
    (ii) any other interest in the property in which the recoverable property subsists,
    (iii) if the recoverable property is a tenancy in common, the tenancy of the other tenant,
    (iv) if (in Scotland) the recoverable property is owned in common, the interest of the other owner,
    (v) if the recoverable property is part of a larger, but not a separate part, the remainder of that property.
34. "Unlawful conduct" includes conduct occurring in any part of the United Kingdom which is unlawful under the criminal law of that part.
35. The power to 'manage any property' includes:
    (i) selling or otherwise disposing of assets comprised in the property which are perishable or which ought to be disposed of before their value diminishes;
    (ii) where the property comprises assets of a trade or business, carrying on, or arranging for another to carry on, the trade or business;
    (iii) incurring capital expenditure in respect of the property;
    (iv) in respect of any illegitimate business, ceasing the operation of that business.
36. "Dealing" with property includes (1) disposing of it, (2) removing it from the United Kingdom, (3) relinquishing or cancelling or varying any signing authority over any bank accounts over which he has signing authority or in respect of which he is a signatory on the mandate irrespective of whether there is any money in such accounts, (4) relinquishing or cancelling or varying any power of attorney, directorship, office as trustee or other arrangement pursuant to which he has control of

any asset which is not held in his name, or (5) relinquishing, cancelling or varying any arrangements whereby he is empowered to deal with assets which are not in his own name.
37. "Document" means anything in which information of any description is recorded.
38. Reference to selling or otherwise disposing of assets comprised in the property which are perishable, or which ought to be disposed of before their value diminishes, includes charging, disposing, transferring or conveying the legal and/or beneficial interest in the property to the purchaser of it.
39. "Act" refers to the Proceeds of Crime Act 2002.

Reference to the Receiver means:

Ivan I. Dere of Blueberry House, Strawberry Lane, London N1 1AA.

Reference to the Respondent means:

MR ALFREDO GERMONT

DATED this 20th day of July 2007.

Schedule 1

Undertakings given to the Court by the Director of the Assets Recovery Agency

1. The Director will arrange to serve on the Respondent, ALFREDO GERMONT, a copy of this Order together with a copy of the witness statement containing the evidence relied on by the Applicant when obtaining this Order. Service will take place as soon as practicable after the Order is sealed.

Schedule 2

(i) The proceeds derived from the sale of the land and property situated at 1 Royal Road, Brixham BX2 1PP registered at HM Land Registry in the name of A Germont with title number TQ11111, and any property acquired from said proceeds.

(ii) The following motor vehicles:
 (a) Mercedes SL500 with number plate ALFREDO 1 registered in the name of Mr Alfredo Germont;
 (b) BMW X5 with number plate ALFY 2 registered in the name of Mr Alfredo Germont;

(iii) The boat currently being constructed by Boatworks Ltd and located at its premises at Haven Quay, New Road, Brixham BX2 1TT.

(iv) Monies which have been credited to or have passed through the following accounts:

Account holder	Institution	Sort Code	Account
Mr Alfredo Germont	Lloyds TSB	00-00-00	12131415
Mr Alfredo Germont	Halifax	00-10-00	654321
Mr A & Mrs T Germont	Lloyds TSB	00-99-02	000011111
Mr A & Mrs T Germont	Co-Op Bank	00-11-11	22223333

AND

(v) Any other such property that the Interim Receiver may believe to be either Recoverable or Associated Property within the meaning of the Act, so long as the Interim Receiver gives notice of this Order to the appropriate person holding or in control of said property.

APPENDIX 16

USEFUL WEBSITES ON POCA 2002

Assets Recovery Agency
http://www.assetsrecovery.gov.uk/

CPS Guide to the Proceeds of Crime Act 2002
http://www.cps.gov.uk/legal/section21/chapter_a.html#_Toc40070607

Criminal Procedure Rules
<http://www.dca.gov.uk/criminal/procrules_fin/rulesmenu.htm>

Criminal Procedure Rules Practice Direction
<http://www.dca.gov.uk/criminal/procrules_fin/contents/practice_direction/pd_consolidated.htm>

Explanatory Notes to Proceeds of Crime Act 2002
<http://www.opsi.gov.uk/acts/en2002/2002en29.htm>

HM Revenue and Customs Guidance on Money Laundering
<http://www.hmrc.gov.uk/specialist/moneylaundering.htm>

Proceeds of Crime Act 2002 (C. 29)
http://www.opsi.gov.uk/acts/acts2002/20020029.htm

Proceeds of Crime Act 2002 (External Requests and Orders) Order 2005
<http://www.opsi.gov.uk/si/si2005/20053181.htm>

Explanatory Memorandum to The Proceeds Of Crime Act 2002 (External Requests And Orders) Order 2005
<http://www.opsi.gov.uk/si/em2005/uksiem_20053181_en.pdf>

APPENDIX 17

PROPERTY FREEZING ORDER

IF YOU, ALFREDO GERMONT, OR YOU, VIOLETTA VALERY (OTHERWISE VALERY VIOLETTA), DISOBEY THIS ORDER YOU MAY BE HELD TO BE IN CONTEMPT OF COURT AND MAY BE IMPRISONED, FINED OR HAVE YOUR ASSETS SEIZED.

ANY OTHER PERSON WHO KNOWS OF THIS ORDER AND DOES ANYTHING WHICH HELPS OR PERMITS THE RESPONDENTS TO BREACH THE TERMS OF THIS ORDER MAY ALSO BE HELD TO BE IN CONTEMPT OF COURT AND MAY BE IMPRISONED, FINED OR HAVE THEIR ASSETS SEIZED.

<u>PROPERTY FREEZING ORDER</u>

(Section 245A of the Proceeds of Crime Act 2002)

POCA no. 107 of 2007

<u>IN THE HIGH COURT OF JUSTICE</u>
<u>QUEEN'S BENCH DIVISION</u>
<u>ADMINISTRATIVE COURT</u>

Before the Honourable Mr Justice Bullingham Sitting in Private

Between

THE DIRECTOR OF THE ASSETS RECOVERY AGENCY

Applicant

and

ALFREDO GERMONT

First Respondent

and

VIOLETTA VALERY
(OTHERWISE VALERY VIOLETTA)

Second Respondent

TO THE FIRST REPONDENT
AND TO THE SECOND RESPONDENT

Upon reading the witness statement of **Tony Foot** dated the **10th** day of January 2008,
And Upon Hearing Counsel for the Director of the Assets Recovery Agency ("the Director"),
THE COURT IS SATISFIED that the relevant requirements for making a **Property Freezing Order** are fulfilled.

This Order

1. This is a Property Freezing Order made against Alfredo Germont 'the First Respondent' and Violetta Valery (otherwise Valery Violetta) 'the Second Respondent' on 11th January 2008 by Mr Justice Bullingham following an application on behalf of the Assets Recovery Agency ("the Agency").
2. This Order prohibits the First Respondent and Second Respondent from dealing with the property and assets set out herein.
3. The Order is subject to the exclusions at the end of this Order.
4. You should read all of this Order carefully. You are advised to consult a solicitor as soon as possible.
5. Subject to the provisions of section 245C of the Proceeds of Crime Act 2002 and the Proceeds of Crime Act 2002 (Legal Expenses in Civil Recovery Proceedings) Regulations 2005, you may be entitled to the release of restrained funds to pay for legal representation in connection with this Order. A request for the release of a sum in respect of reasonable legal expenses must be made in writing to the Director of the Assets Recovery Agency and before any release can be made certain conditions must be fulfilled. You and your legal adviser are referred to Part 3 of the Proceeds of Crime Act 2002 (Legal Expenses in Civil Recovery Proceedings) Regulations 2005 (SI 3382 of 2005).
6. Further to the provisions of section 245C of the Proceeds of Crime Act 2002, you may be entitled to the release of restrained funds to meet your reasonable living expenses or to carry on any trade, business, profession or occupation. A request for the release of property or an asset to meet reasonable living expenses or to carry on any trade, business, profession or occupation can either be made to the Director of the Assets Recovery Agency, in the first instance, pursuant to paragraph 12 of this Order, or to the Court pursuant to section 245B of the Proceeds of Crime Act 2002.
7. The First Respondent and Second Respondent and any other person affected by this Order have a right to apply to the Court to vary or discharge it.

Disposal of or dealing with assets

8. The First Respondent must not until further order of this Court:-
    (a) remove from England and Wales any of the property or assets set out in paragraph 9 below, whether in his own name or not and whether solely or jointly owned; or
    (b) in any way dispose of or deal with or diminish the value of any of the property or assets set out in paragraph 9 below, whether in his own name or not and whether solely or jointly owned.
9. Paragraph 8 applies to the following property and assets:
    i. The proceeds of the sale of the property situated at 6 Simpson Avenue, Springfield, Torquay TQ1 1AB, previously registered at HM Land Registry in the name of the First Respondent, with title number TQ123456;
    ii. The property situated at 12 Marge Way, Springfield, Torquay TQ2 2AB, and registered at HM Land Registry in the name of the First Respondent, with title number TQ98765;
    iii. Vehicle Registration No. TS02 ACB, a BMW X5 Sport Automatic registered to the First Respondent at Flat 1, 22 Seaview Rise, Paignton TQ6 1PT;
    iv. The following bank accounts
        a. National Westminster Bank account number 12345678 sort code 00-10-00 in the name of the First Respondent;
        b. HSBC account number 98765432 sort code 10-00-10 in the name of the Second Respondent;

Appendix 17: Property Freezing Order

10. The Second Respondent must not
    (i) remove from England and Wales; or
    (ii) in any way dispose of or deal with or diminish the value of any of
        i. The proceeds of the sale of the property situated at 6 Simpson Avenue, Springfield, Torquay TQ1 1AB, previously registered at HM Land Registry in the name of the First Respondent, with title number TQ23445;
        ii. The property comprising the land at the back of 12 Marge Way, Springfield, Torquay TQ2 2AB, and registered at HM Land Registry in the name of the First Respondent, with title number TQ98765;
        iii. Vehicle Registration No. TS02 ACB, a BMW X5 Sport Automatic registered to the First Respondent at Flat 1, 22 Seaview Rise, Paignton TQ6 1PT;
        iv. The following bank accounts
            a. National Westminster Bank account number 12345678 sort code 00-10-00 in the name of the First Respondent;
            b. HSBC account number 98765432 sort code 10-00-10 in the name of the Second Respondent;

Disclosure of information

11. The First Respondent must:
    (i) inform the Agency in writing within 72 hours of service of this Order on the First Respondent of all his assets whether in or outside England and Wales and whether in his own name or not and whether solely or jointly owned, giving the value, location and details of all such assets;
    (ii) confirm the information in a witness statement which must be verified by a statement of truth and served on the Agency within 21 days after this Order has been served on the First Respondent.

The information in the witness statement must include:

a. the name and address of all persons including financial institutions holding any such assets;
b. details of the First Respondent's current salary or other form of income, identifying the amount paid, by whom it is paid and the account or accounts into which it is paid;
c. the names and numbers of all accounts held by or under the control of the First Respondent, together with the name and address of the place where the account is held and the sums in the account;
d. details (including addresses) of any real property in which the First Respondent has any interest, including an interest in any of the proceeds of sale if the property were to be sold. These details must include details of any mortgage or charge on the property;
e. details of all National Savings Certificates, unit trusts, shares or debentures held by the First Respondent in any company or corporation wherever incorporated in the world, owned or controlled by the First Respondent or in which he has an interest;
f. details of all trusts of which the First Respondent is a beneficiary, including the name and address of every trustee;
g. particulars of any income or debt due to the First Respondent including the name and address of the debtor;
h. details of all assets over £2,000.00 in value received by the First Respondent or anyone on his behalf since the 11th January 2001 identifying the name and address of the person from whom such assets were received;
i. details of all assets over £2,000.00 in value transferred by the First Respondent or anyone on his behalf to others since 11th January 2001 identifying the name and address of all persons to whom such property was transferred.

12. The Second Respondent must:
    (i) inform the Agency in writing within 72 hours of service of this Order on the Second Respondent of all her assets whether in or outside England and Wales and whether in her own name or not and whether solely or jointly owned, giving the value, location and details of all such assets;

Appendix 17: Property Freezing Order

(ii) confirm the information in a witness statement which must be verified by a statement of truth and served on the Agency within 21 days after this Order has been served on the Second Respondent.

The information in the witness statement must include:
   a. the name and address of all persons including financial institutions holding any such assets;
   b. details of the Second Respondent's current salary or other form of income, identifying the amount paid, by whom it is paid and the account or accounts into which it is paid;
   c. the names and numbers of all accounts held by or under the control of the Second Respondent, together with the name and address of the place where the account is held and the sums in the account;
   d. details (including addresses) of any real property in which the Second Respondent has any interest, including an interest in any of the proceeds of sale if the property were to be sold. These details must include details of any mortgage or charge on the property;
   e. details of all National Savings Certificates, unit trusts, shares or debentures held by the Second Respondent in any company or corporation wherever incorporated in the world, owned or controlled by the Second Respondent or in which she has an interest;
   f. details of all trusts of which the Second Respondent is a beneficiary, including the name and address of every trustee;
   g. particulars of any income or debt due to the Second Respondent including the name and address of the debtor;
   h. details of all assets over £2,000.00 in value received by the Second Respondent or anyone on his behalf since the 11th January 2001 identifying the name and address of the person from whom such assets were received;
   i. details of all assets over £2,000.00 in value transferred by the Second Respondent or anyone on his behalf to others since 11th January 2001 identifying the name and address of all persons to whom such property was transferred.

13. Subject to any further Order of the court any information given in compliance with this Order shall only be used for the purpose of these proceedings and any subsequent civil recovery proceedings.
14. However, nothing in this paragraph shall make inadmissible any disclosure made by the Respondents in any proceedings for perjury relating to that disclosure.

Costs

15. The costs of this Order are reserved.

Variation or Discharge of this Order

16. The First Respondent or the Second Respondent may agree with the Agency that this Order be varied in any respect but any such agreement must be in writing.
17. Anyone affected by this Order may apply to the Court at any time to vary or discharge this Order (or so much of it as affects that person), pursuant to section 245B of the Proceeds of Crime Act 2002, but they must first inform the Agency and anyone named on the first page of this Order giving 2 clear days notice. If any evidence is to be relied upon in support of the application it must also be served giving 2 clear days notice.

Interpretation of this Order

18. A person who is an individual who is ordered not to do something must not do it himself or herself or in any other way. He or she must not do it through others acting on his or her behalf or on his or her instructions or with his or her encouragement.
19. A person that is a corporation and which is ordered not to do something must not do it by its directors, officers, employees or agents or in any other way.

Appendix 17: Property Freezing Order

Parties other than the Respondents

20. *Effect of this order.* It is a contempt of court for any person notified of this Order knowingly to assist in or permit a breach of the Order. Any person doing so may be sent to prison, fined, or have his assets seized. He is also at risk of prosecution for a money laundering offence.
21. *Set off by banks.* This Order does not prevent any bank from exercising any right of set off it may have in respect of any facility which it gave to the Respondents before it was notified of the Order.
22. *Withdrawals by the respondent.* No bank need enquire as to the application or proposed application of any money withdrawn by the Respondents if the withdrawal appears to be permitted by this Order.
23. *Persons outside England Wales and Scotland.*
    (1) Except as provided by in paragraph (2), the terms of this Order do not affect or concern anyone outside the jurisdiction of this court or Scotland.
    (2) The terms of this Order will affect the following persons in a country or state outside the jurisdiction of this court or Scotland:-
    a. a person to whom this Order is addressed or an officer or an agent appointed by power of attorney of such a person; or
    b. any person who:-
        i. is subject to the jurisdiction of this court,
        ii. has been given written notice of this Order at his residence or place of business within the jurisdiction of this court, and
        iii. is able lawfully to prevent acts or omissions outside the jurisdiction of this court which constitute or assist in a breach of the terms of this Order.
    c. any other person only to the extent that this Order is declared enforceable or is enforced by a court in that country.
24. *Assets located outside England and Wales.* Nothing in this Order shall, in respect of assets located outside England and Wales, prevent any third party from complying with:-
    a. what it reasonably believes to be its obligations, contractual or otherwise, under the laws and obligations of the country or state in which those assets are located or under the proper law of any contract between itself and the Respondents or any of them, or
    b. any Orders of the courts of that country or state, provided that reasonable notice of any application for such an Order is given to the Agency.

Communications with the Court

All communications to the court about this order should be sent to The Administrative Court Office, Royal Courts of Justice, Strand, London WC2A 2LL quoting the case number. The office is open between 10am and 4pm Monday to Friday. The telephone number is 020 7947 6653.

Appendix 17: Property Freezing Order

Undertaking given by the Agency to the Court

The Agency will as soon as practicable serve upon the First and Second Respondents:-

a. A copy of this Order,
b. The witness statement containing the evidence relied on by the Agency and any other documents provided to the Court on the making of the application.

ADDRESS AND TELEPHONE NUMBER OF THE AGENCY FOR SERVICE AND ANY COMMUNICATION IN RESPECT OF THESE PROCEEDINGS

The Director
Assets Recovery Agency
PO Box 39992
London, EC4M 7XQ

Tel: 020 7029 5700
Fax: 020 7029 5896

APPENDIX 18

CIVIL RECOVERY BY CONSENT ORDER

IN THE HIGH COURT OF JUSTICE   CLAIM NUMBER: CO/0000/2007

QUEEN'S BENCH DIVISION
ADMINISTRATIVE COURT

IN THE MATTER OF A RECOVERY ORDER
PURSUANT TO SECTION 266
OF THE PROCEEDS OF CRIME ACT 2002

BETWEEN

THE DIRECTOR OF THE ASSETS RECOVERY AGENCY

Claimant

and

ALFREDO GERMONT

First Respondent

VIOLETTA VALERY

Second Respondent

TRAVIATA TRADING ENTERPRISES LTD

Third Respondent

GIORGIO GERMONT

Fourth Respondent

Order for Disposal by Consent

UPON THE APPLICATION of the Director of the Assets Recovery Agency issued on [*insert date*]
AND BY THE CONSENT of the Claimant and the First, Second and Third Respondents,
AND UPON READING THE FIRST WITNESS STATEMENT of Ivor Edake dated / /08
AND THE SETTLEMENT AGREEMENT DATED / /08, attached hereto marked Schedule Two

Appendix 18: Civil Recovery by Consent Order

It is Ordered that

1. A Recovery Order is made in respect of the property listed in the first schedule to this Order, marked Schedule One (the "**Scheduled Property**").
2. The Scheduled Property shall vest in the Trustee for Civil Recovery (the "**Trustee**"), namely Tony Foot of the Assets Recovery Agency, 55 Ludgate Hill, London EC4M 7JW forthwith upon the making of this Order.
3. The Trustee shall have the following powers without prejudice to any other powers he may have by virtue of statute or by implication of law:
    a. power to transfer, convey and/or sell the Scheduled Property or any part of it or interest in it;
    b. power to incur expenditure for the purpose of:
        i. acquiring any part of the Scheduled Property, or any interest in it, which is not vested in him; and
        ii. discharging any liabilities, or extinguishing any rights, to which the Scheduled Property is subject;
    c. power to manage the Scheduled Property including:
        i. selling or otherwise disposing of assets comprised in the Scheduled Property which are perishable or which ought to be disposed of before their value diminishes;
        ii. where the Scheduled Property comprises assets of a trade or business, carrying on, or arranging for another to carry on, the trade or business;
        iii. incurring capital expenditure in respect of the Scheduled Property;
    d. power to start, carry on or defend any legal proceedings in respect of the Scheduled Property;
    e. power to make any compromise or other arrangement in connection with any claim relating to the Scheduled Property;
    f. for the purposes of, or in connection with, the exercise of any of his powers, power by his official name to do any of things mentioned in sub-clause (g) below and power to do any other act which is necessary or expedient;
    g. the things mentioned in sub-clause (f) above are:
        i. holding, entering or seizing the Scheduled Property;
        ii. entering into contracts;
        iii. suing and being sued;
        iv. employing agents; and
        v. executing a power of attorney, deed or other instrument.
4. Upon the Trustee taking possession of the Scheduled Property, the Interim Receiving Order made by this Court on 1 April 2007 shall be discharged and the proceedings brought under case number CO/0000/2007 shall be stayed as against all the Respondents.
5. There be no order for the costs of these proceedings or for the costs of the proceedings relating to the Interim Receiving Order obtained on 1 April 2007 (case number CO/1912/2003).

Dated this   day of October 2008

_____   _____
For the Claimant   For the First Respondent

_____   _____
For the Second Respondent   For the Third Respondent

Appendix 18: Civil Recovery by Consent Order

SCHEDULE ONE

Property subject to a Recovery Order pursuant to Section 266 of the Proceeds of Crime Act 2002

1. The sum of £15,000 held in an account numbered [*insert number*] in the name of the [*insert respondent*] at [*insert location*] branch of [*insert bank*].
2. Zurich Investment Bond 00000 held in the name of the First Respondent
3. Scottish Provident Investment Bonus Growth policy number 000000 held in the joint names of the First Respondent and the Second Respondent
4. Funds held by Traviata Trading Enterprises Ltd to the order of the First Respondent with a value at April 2007 of £100,000 plus any interest accrued since that time.
5. AMP Pearl policy held in the name of the First Respondent
6. Northern Rock policy number 000000 held in the name of the Second Respondent as trustee with a value as at 1st September 2003 of £5000
7. 5.99% of the current value of the Mercedes 220CE with licence plate numbered TY06 MSW
8. The real property situate at 11 Simpsons Lane, Springfield, Torquay under Land Registry Number TQ12345678.

APPENDIX 19

GUIDANCE TO SOLICITORS AND APPLICANTS SEEKING COMMUNITY LEGAL SERVICE FUNDING FOR PROCEEDINGS UNDER THE PROCEEDS OF CRIME ACT 2002 INVOLVING THE ASSETS RECOVERY AGENCY

Note: this guidance note is primarily intended to provide greater information to solicitors acting for defendants in proceedings brought by the Assets Recovery Agency. If you are a defendant in these proceedings, please contact a solicitor at the earliest opportunity and take a copy of this note with you. If you need assistance locating a suitable solicitor, you can contact CLS Directory Line (tel: 0845 608 1122).

INTRODUCTION

The Proceeds of Crime Act 2002 established the Assets Recovery Agency (ARA), an agency dedicated to investigating and recovering the proceeds of crime. Among the functions of the ARA is a role in the new civil recovery scheme, created by the Act, to recover the proceeds of alleged unlawful conduct in cases where a criminal conviction has not been obtained and is unlikely to be obtained.

The purpose of this paper is to provide general guidance to defendants in proceedings brought by the ARA and their solicitors regarding the availability of Community Legal Service (CLS) funding for these proceedings and the procedures used to consider applications for funding in these cases.

AVAILABILITY OF LEGAL AID IN CIVIL RECOVERY PROCEEDINGS

Proceedings for which CLS funding is available

All High Court proceedings under Part 5 of the Proceeds of Crime Act 2002 and all proceedings under Parts 2, 5 or 8 of the Act that are listed in paragraph 3 of Schedule 2 of the Access to Justice Act 1999 are civil proceedings for which CLS funding is available, subject to meeting the required means and merits tests (these are discussed in greater detail below).

CIVIL RECOVERY BY THE ASSETS RECOVERY AGENCY

Proceedings for civil recovery in the High Court under Chapter 2 of Part 5 of the Proceeds of Crime Act can only be brought by the Assets Recovery Agency. CLS funding is available for these proceedings. This can apply to both a respondent against whom the agency is proceeding or a third party who claims to be an innocent owner of property.

Investigations by the Assets Recovery Agency under Chapter 2 of Part 8 the High Court can make a range of orders to support investigations into whether a person has benefited from criminal conduct, holds recoverable property or has committed a money laundering offence. CLS funding is available for the following proceedings under Part 8:

(a) Application under section 351(3) to discharge or vary a production order or an order to grant entry;
(b) Application under section 362(3) to discharge or vary a disclosure order;
(c) Application under section 369(3) to discharge or vary a customer information order;
(d) Application under section 375(2) to discharge or vary an account monitoring order.

Exclusions

In some cases, despite the fact that the type of proceedings is within the scope of CLS funding, they may nevertheless be excluded from funding under paragraph 1 of Schedule 2. This paragraph lists particular types of proceedings that cannot be funded under CLS. In reality none of the proceedings listed in this paragraph are likely to arise in the proceedings brought by the ARA.

The exclusion in this paragraph that would have arisen most often, which excludes all matters arising out of the carrying on of a business, has been avoided by way of a Direction made by the Secretary of State on 24 May 2004. This Direction states that the Commission is authorised to fund services on behalf of a defendant in Proceeds of Crime Act 2002 proceedings that are in the scope of the scheme, despite the fact that the provision of those services may be excluded by reason of paragraph 1(h) (matters arising out of the carrying on of a business) of that Schedule.

Funding Criteria

Where CLS funding is available for proceedings under the Proceeds of Crime Act 2002 as specified above, applications for Legal Representation will be subject to the normal CLS criteria for scope, means and merits. The Commission has, however, ensured that account is taken of the special nature of these proceedings when considering applications in these cases.

Merits

The proceedings for which CLS funding is available are defined as civil proceedings under the Proceeds of Crime Act 2002. However, as these proceedings are new, and are likely to raise a number of important issues in the period during which an amount of precedent develops in this area, the Commission has set a more flexible merits test for these proceedings, than for other civil proceedings within the scope of CLS funding.

Therefore, the Commission applies an "interests of justice" test to determine whether an application should be funded on merits. This test is essentially whether it is in the interests of justice to provide funding to the client. In deciding whether it is in the interests of justice to fund any particular applicant, we will take into account:

(a) The importance of the issues to the applicant; that is, how seriously the client will be affected by the court making or not making the order in question.
(b) Whether there are complex legal and factual issues that could not fairly be determined without legal representation for the applicant.
(c) Whether the applicant suffers from any lack of understanding of the issues, including any language problem or disability.
(d) Whether the case requires extensive legal preparation, for example in the tracing of witnesses, or advocacy skills.

Means

CLS funding for these proceedings will only be available to applicants who are financially eligible for such funding in accordance with the Commission's standard financial eligibility limits, as set out in the Community Legal Service (Financial) Regulations 2000 as amended. In order to determine whether or not an applicant qualifies financially the Commission will require them to complete a Means Assessment Form setting out their full financial circumstances.

In assessing disposable income and capital the Commission will not take into account any assets that have already been frozen under the Proceeds of Crime Act. However all the applicant's (and their partner's, if they have one) other disposable income and capital will be taken into account. The regulations provide that if an applicant has a partner (whether married or not) their means are aggregated, unless the partner is established to have a contrary interest in the proceedings.

Appendix 19: LSC Guidance on Funding under POCA 2002 Proceedings

The Commission's experience to date has shown that defendants in proceedings brought by the ARA generally have complex financial circumstances. The Commission therefore refers all applications for funding in these cases to our Special Investigations Unit (SIU) in order to determine the financial eligibility of the applicant. The Commission is authorised, by the applicant's and their partner's Declaration and Authorisation on the application form, to seek information on the applicant's, or their partner's financial circumstances from third parties. That includes the ARA.

If funding is provided, and proceedings are successfully defended, the statutory charge will apply. The statutory charge means that any property that is recovered or maintained for a funded client must be used to repay the cost of the case to the CLS fund. Where seized assets have not been taken into account on the basis that they are the subject matter of the dispute, success in the proceedings resulting in the release of assets to the client will be treated as a recovery or preservation. Any assets so recovered must therefore be paid to the solicitor and on to the Commission - see Regulations 18 and 20 of the CLS (Costs) Regulations 2000.

Procedures

CLS funding for Legal Representation in these proceedings is Licensed Work. Both suppliers with a civil franchise in any category, and those with a criminal franchise are licensed to undertake work in relation to these proceedings. Application must therefore be made to the Commission for certificates to authorise such work. All applications must be submitted to the Commission's Special Cases Unit (SCU) at 29-37 Red Lion Street, London WC1R 4PP, DX 170 London/Chancery Lane. Normal CLS means and merits forms must be supplied (CLS APP1 for merits and the appropriate means forms).

Processes within SCU

Once an application is received by SCU, it will make an in principle merits decision in respect of the application as soon as possible. The target time for this decision is 5 days from receipt of the application. However, should any additional information be required before a decision can be reached, this will be delayed. We aim to ensure such information will be sought within 5 days.

Once notified of the merits decision, solicitors will be asked to submit a costed case plan. Upon receipt of this plan, SCU will agree the level of funding and an appropriate work package through the case plan, or raise further queries, again with a target time of within 5 days. Should a dispute arise over work plans or merits refusals, this will be referred to the Commission's Funding Review Committee (FRC).

As stated above, the Commission refers all applications for funding in these cases to SIU in order to determine the financial eligibility of the applicant. It is expected that SCU will refer cases to SIU as soon as possible after receipt in order that both units are able to consider the application at the same time. Once SIU has received an application, SIU will review the client's declared income and determine whether the application is out of scope on that basis.

The application may be refused at this stage.

If the client indicates that they or their partner are in receipt of a passported benefit (Income Support or Income based Job Seekers Allowance) SIU will confirm this with the Department for Work and Pensions. If confirmation is received the application will usually be approved on means at that time.

In all other cases, SIU will write to relevant sources of information, including the ARA, to seek financial information from them in relation to the applicant. Upon receipt of all information initially sought, SIU will determine whether the client is likely to have a partner or assets available from other sources. If such assets appear unlikely then a decision may be made at that time to discontinue the investigation and to approve the means on the basis of the client's income/assets alone. Otherwise all parties will be notified that a full SIU investigation will commence. During any investigation SIU has a target time to deal with all correspondence of within 10 days of receipt.

Emergency Funding

In some cases it will be necessary to provide services to an applicant while the investigation of the applicant's means are on going. Emergency Funding may be available for this work.

Under the existing rules, suppliers who hold a contract (whether civil or criminal) with the Commission are able to self-grant emergency Legal Representation under the usual emergency criteria (see section 12 of the Funding Code Guidance). However, due to the complex nature of these cases, the Commission would prefer that individual applications for emergency funding be made directly to SCU, on the appropriate CLS App 6 form. The Commission has undertaken that in relation to proceedings brought by the ARA, any application for emergency funding will be viewed in as favourable light as possible pending a decision on means.

Solicitors must bear in mind that an emergency application must satisfy the standard Criteria for Legal Representation together with the Criteria for Full Representation contained in the General Funding Code. In addition, where an application for emergency representation is made the solicitor must advise the client about the nature and consequences of emergency representation.

In particular, they must be told:

(a) an emergency certificate will only help a client about urgent matters and will not be a substitute for full Legal Representation;
(b) the client's means will still have to be assessed by the Commission, so:
  (i) if the client does not co-operate, this may result not only in no grant of full Legal Representation but also in withdrawal of the emergency certificate.
  (ii) if the client turns out to be outside the eligibility limits or fails to accept an offer of Legal Representation and pay any assessed contribution, the emergency representation will be withdrawn and in either case this may mean the client having to pay all the legal costs personally and having no costs protection in relation to the opponent's costs;
(c) the emergency certificate will only cover urgent legal work and will be strictly limited as to scope and duration.

Providing information to the ARA

The ARA is able, as a party to these proceedings, to seek updates from the Commission on the progress of a legal aid application. Where such a request is made, the Commission will provide the ARA with confirmation that a grant has been made, or not, and also any chronological information regarding the progress of the application. The Commission will not, however, disclose any information that has been received by the Commission in connection with any individual application for funding to the ARA.

WORKING WITH THE COMMISSION

It should be noted that any failure to co-operate with the Commission's investigations, or a failure to disclose any relevant fact, may lead to a refusal or withdrawal of funding at any time. In addition, whether during assessment or after funding is granted, Regulation 13 of the Community Legal Service (Financial) Regulations 2000 provides that the Commission must be informed of any change in the applicant's (or their partner's) financial circumstances, which might affect the terms on which the applicant is assessed as eligible for funding.

FURTHER INFORMATION

- The leaflet A Practical Guide to Community Legal Service funding explains how the Commission (LSC) funds civil legal services, how to apply and the tests which you need to be able to meet to qualify. Section 5 of the leaflet deals with legal representation in the High Court, where cases under these Parts of the Act are heard.

Appendix 19: LSC Guidance on Funding under POCA 2002 Proceedings

- The Commission's Funding Code, which sets out the decision-making guidance of the Commission, is available on the Commission's website: <www.legalservices.gov.uk>
- The Commission also has an on-line financial eligibility calculator, to assist applicants in determining whether they may be financially eligible for funding. The results of the calculator are indicatie only, and it can be found on the Just Ask website: <http://www.justask.org.uk/legalhelp/calculator>

APPENDIX 20

CONDEMNATION AND FORFEITURE OF GOODS

SCHEDULE 3 OF THE CUSTOMS AND EXCISE MANAGEMENT ACT 1979
PROVISIONS RELATING TO FORFEITURE

Sections 139, 143, 145

Notice of seizure

1

(1) The Commissioners shall, except as provided in sub-paragraph (2) below, give notice of the seizure of any thing as liable to forfeiture and of the grounds therefore to any person who to their knowledge was at the time of the seizure the owner or one of the owners thereof.

(2) Notice need not be given under this paragraph if the seizure was made in the presence of —
   (a) the person whose offence or suspected offence occasioned the seizure; or
   (b) the owner or any of the owners of the thing seized or any servant or agent of his; or
   (c) in the case of anything seized in any ship or aircraft, the master or commander.

2

Notice under paragraph 1 above shall be given in writing and shall be deemed to have been duly served on the person concerned—

(a) if delivered to him personally; or
(b) if addressed to him and left or forwarded by post to him at his usual or last known place of abode or business or, in the case of a body corporate, at their registered or principal office; or
(c) where he has no address within the United Kingdom [or the Isle of Man], or his address is unknown, by publication of notice of the seizure in the London, Edinburgh or Belfast Gazette.

Notice of claim

3

Any person claiming that any thing seized as liable to forfeiture is not so liable shall, within one month of the date of the notice of seizure or, where no such notice has been served on him, within one month of the date of the seizure, give notice of his claim in writing to the Commissioners at any office of [revenue and customs].

4

(1) Any notice under paragraph 3 above shall specify the name and address of the claimant and, in the case of a claimant who is outside the United Kingdom [and the Isle of Man], shall specify the name and address of a solicitor in the United Kingdom who is authorised to accept service of process and to act on behalf of the claimant.

(2) Service of process upon a solicitor so specified shall be deemed to be proper service upon the claimant.

Condemnation

5

If on the expiration of the relevant period under paragraph 3 above for the giving of notice of claim in respect of any thing no such notice has been given to the Commissioners, or if, in the case of any such notice given, any requirement of paragraph 4 above is not complied with, the thing in question shall be deemed to have been duly condemned as forfeited.

Appendix 20: Condemnation and Forfeiture of Goods

6

Where notice of claim in respect of any thing is duly given in accordance with paragraphs 3 and 4 above, the Commissioners shall take proceedings for the condemnation of that thing by the court, and if the court finds that the thing was at the time of seizure liable to forfeiture the court shall condemn it as forfeited.

7

Where any thing is in accordance with either of paragraphs 5 or 6 above condemned or deemed to have been condemned as forfeited, then, without prejudice to any delivery up or sale of the thing by the Commissioners under paragraph 16 below, the forfeiture shall have effect as from the date when the liability to forfeiture arose.

Proceedings for condemnation by court

8

Proceedings for condemnation shall be civil proceedings and may be instituted—

(a) in England or Wales either in the High Court or in a magistrates' court;
(b) in Scotland either in the Court of Session or in the sheriff court;
(c) in Northern Ireland either in the High Court or in a court of summary jurisdiction.

9

Proceedings for the condemnation of any thing instituted in a magistrates' court in England or Wales, in the sheriff court in Scotland or in a court of summary jurisdiction in Northern Ireland may be so instituted—

(a) in any such court having jurisdiction in the place where any offence in connection with that thing was committed or where any proceedings for such an offence are instituted; or
(b) in any such court having jurisdiction in the place where the claimant resides or, if the claimant has specified a solicitor under paragraph 4 above, in the place where that solicitor has his office; or
(c) in any such court having jurisdiction in the place where that thing was found, detained or seized or to which it is first brought after being found, detained or seized.

10

(1) In any proceedings for condemnation instituted in England, Wales or Northern Ireland, the claimant or his solicitor shall make oath that the thing seized was, or was to the best of his knowledge and belief, the property of the claimant at the time of the seizure.
(2) In any such proceedings instituted in the High Court, the claimant shall give such security for the costs of the proceedings as may be determined by the Court.
(3) If any requirement of this paragraph is not complied with, the court shall give judgment for the Commissioners.

11

(1) In the case of any proceedings for condemnation instituted in a magistrates' court in England or Wales, without prejudice to any right to require the statement of a case for the opinion of the High Court, either party may appeal against the decision of that court to the Crown Court.
(2) In the case of any proceedings for condemnation instituted in a court of summary jurisdiction in Northern Ireland, without prejudice to any right to require the statement of a case for the opinion of the High Court, either party may appeal against the decision of that court to the county court.

12

Where an appeal, including an appeal by way of case stated, has been made against the decision of the court in any proceedings for the condemnation of any thing, that thing shall, pending the final determination of the matter, be left with the Commissioners or at any convenient office of customs and excise.

Provisions as to proof
13

In any proceedings arising out of the seizure of any thing, the fact, form and manner of the seizure shall be taken to have been as set forth in the process without any further evidence thereof, unless the contrary is proved.

14

In any proceedings, the condemnation by a court of any thing as forfeited may be proved by the production either of the order or certificate of condemnation or of a certified copy thereof purporting to be signed by an officer of the court by which the order or certificate was made or granted.

Special provisions as to certain claimants
15

For the purposes of any claim to, or proceedings for the condemnation of, any thing, where that thing is at the time of seizure the property of a body corporate, of two or more partners or of any number of persons exceeding five, the oath required by paragraph 10 above to be taken and any other thing required by this Schedule or by any rules of the court to be done by, or by any person authorised by, the claimant or owner may be taken or done by, or by any other person authorised by, the following persons respectively, that is to say—

(a) where the owner is a body corporate, the secretary or some duly authorised officer of that body;
(b) where the owners are in partnership, any one of those owners;
(c) where the owners are any number of persons exceeding five not being in partnership, any two of those persons on behalf of themselves and their co-owners.

Power to deal with seizures before condemnation, etc
16

Where any thing has been seized as liable to forfeiture the Commissioners may at any time if they see fit and notwithstanding that the thing has not yet been condemned, or is not yet deemed to have been condemned, as forfeited—

(a) deliver it up to any claimant upon his paying to the Commissioners such sum as they think proper, being a sum not exceeding that which in their opinion represents the value of the thing, including any duty or tax chargeable thereon which has not been paid;
(b) if the thing seized is a living creature or is in the opinion of the Commissioners of a perishable nature, sell or destroy it.

17

(1) If, where any thing is delivered up, sold or destroyed under paragraph 16 above, it is held in proceedings taken under this Schedule that the thing was not liable to forfeiture at the time of its seizure, the Commissioners shall, subject to any deduction allowed under sub-paragraph (2) below, on demand by the claimant tender to him—
    (a) an amount equal to any sum paid by him under sub-paragraph (a) of that paragraph; or
    (b) where they have sold the thing, an amount equal to the proceeds of sale; or
    (c) where they have destroyed the thing, an amount equal to the market value of the thing at the time of its seizure.
(2) Where the amount to be tendered under sub-paragraph (1)(a), (b) or (c) above includes any sum on account of any duty or tax chargeable on the thing which had not been paid before its seizure the Commissioners may deduct so much of that amount as represents that duty or tax.
(3) If the claimant accepts any amount tendered to him under sub-paragraph (1) above, he shall not be entitled to maintain any action on account of the seizure, detention, sale or destruction of the thing.
(4) For the purposes of sub-paragraph (1)(c) above, the market value of any thing at the time of its seizure shall be taken to be such amount as the Commissioners and the claimant may agree or, in default of agreement, as may be determined by a referee appointed by the Lord Chancellor

Appendix 20: Condemnation and Forfeiture of Goods

(not being an official of any government department [or an office-holder in, or a member of the staff of, the Scottish Administration]), whose decision shall be final and conclusive; and the procedure on any reference to a referee shall be such as may be determined by the referee.

(5) The Lord Chancellor may make an appointment under sub-paragraph (4) only with the concurrence—
   (a) where the proceedings referred to in sub-paragraph (1) were taken in England and Wales, of the Lord Chief Justice of England and Wales;
   (b) where those proceedings were taken in Scotland, of the Lord President of the Court of Session;
   (c) where those proceedings were taken in Northern Ireland, of the Lord Chief Justice of Northern Ireland.

(6) The Lord Chief Justice of England and Wales may nominate a judicial office holder (as defined in the Constitutional Reform Act 2005) to exercise his functions under this paragraph.

(7) The Lord President of the Court of Session may nominate a judge of the Court of Session who is a member of the First or Second Division of the Inner House of that Court to exercise his functions under this paragraph.

(8) The Lord Chief Justice of Northern Ireland may nominate any of the following to exercise his functions under this paragraph—
   (a) the holder of one of the offices listed in the Justice (Northern Ireland) Act 2002;
   (b) a Lord Justice of Appeal (as defined in section 88 of that Act).]

APPENDIX 21

ARA: SETTLEMENT OF CIVIL RECOVERY AND TAX CASES

Issues for Consideration

Issue

1. To outline a non-exhaustive set of factors which the Director may wish to consider in deciding whether or not a case referred to the Agency for civil recovery or tax action is amenable to or suitable for settlement.

Background

2. The Director will have regard to the Agency's strategic aims.
3. The Director is prepared, in principle, to consider settling any civil recovery or tax case which has been referred to it with the respondent or tax payer, as the case may be. In considering whether to settle a case and the terms of any such settlement the Director will act in ways which support these aims and are not capable of being interpreted in ways which would lead to those aims being undermined, for example, settlements being routinely at such a level as to be capable of being paid without disrupting criminal enterprises, or derived from unknown funds.

Settlement Issues

4. In considering the possible and actual settlement of a case, the Director will take account of the specific circumstances of the case and, in addition, the public perception that would be created by knowledge of the settlement in both the law enforcement and criminal communities, and of the wider public at large.
5. In considering whether or not to settle, the Director will consider any factors which are relevant. These may include the following factors but this is not an exhaustive list, nor should it be regarded as a checklist:
   - The scale and nature of the criminality;
   - The likely disruption by settlement as opposed to otherwise of an organised criminal enterprise and the reduction of crime;
   - The value and nature of the assets thought to have been derived by the respondent;
   - The value and nature of the assets subject to recovery or tax action;
   - The assets available to the respondent, including any assets available outside of the jurisdiction;
   - The amount likely to be recovered if the matter proceeds;
   - The interests of third parties;
   - Whether the settlement would promote confidence with other key stakeholders;
   - The crime reduction and community impact of settlement;
   - Whether the proposed settlement demonstrates value for money (taking account of the resources already committed by the Agency and its partners, and the resources which are likely to be committed, in the event of the settlement not being agreed to);
   - What steps the respondent might be required to take in relation to specified assets as a condition of the settlement;
   - The degree to which the respondent has co-operated with the Agency and made a full disclosure of their affairs;
   - The degree to which settlement would affect public confidence in the Agency.

Appendix 21: ARA: Settlement of Civil Recovery and Tax Cases

Application of These Considerations

6. To enable the effective application of this policy:
   - The decision on whether or not to entertain and then embark on settlement negotiations is a matter for the Director, supported by Operational and Legal teams;
   - The conduct of settlement negotiations will be the responsibility of the Director, although the Director may delegate his day to day conduct to members of the Agency;
   - The Director may consider, without prejudice, entering into settlement negotiations in any case where the respondent is prepared to negotiate; and
   - The Director will normally require that, as a condition of the settlement, any claims for compensation and any other legal claims against the Director or the agency, are withdrawn, with the respondent meeting his own costs.

Form of Settlement

7. If a matter is settled, the terms of the settlement should be reduced to writing and signed by the Director and the respondent. The terms of the settlement should include an undertaking by the respondent to do anything that is reasonably in his or her power to give effect to the settlement.
8. If a matter is settled at a time when recovery or tax proceedings are still before a court or tribunal, the court or tribunal should be asked to make consent orders to give effect to the settlement*. That will resolve the outstanding proceedings and will also ensure that third parties are not denied rights they may otherwise have under law.
9. The terms of the settlement should be on the basis that full disclosure of assets has been made by the respondent. (If further property came to light, which was the proceeds of the same or different unlawful conduct, the Director will consider commencing new proceedings against that other property. In relation to tax, if the Agency were to discover more taxable income or gains which accrued in a given tax year the Director will consider raising a further tax assessment to cover the "new" income or taxable gain uncovered, even if the Agency has already had an assessment in respect of income/gain accrued in that same year).
10. The settlement agreement will include the terms on which any property or other assets are to be disposed of and the beneficiaries of the proceeds. This may include the appointment of a third party with power of attorney to dispose of property, where it is not vested in the receiver.
11. If a matter cannot be settled after negotiations have commenced, the Director will seek to progress the matter through the courts.
12. The Director will, within the legislative constraints imposed by the requirement for taxpayer confidentiality, seek publicity that a matter has been settled making clear the terms of the settlement and the assets which have been recovered. Any media material will explain clearly to stakeholders and the general public the reasoning behind the decision and ensure that the Agency is still seen to be working towards crime reduction and not just maximising the amounts recovered.

Approved by the Director

2 September 2004

* See section 276 of the Proceeds of Crime Act 2002 for the settlement of civil recovery claims by consent order. Tax enquiries (under the Self Assessment regime) and investigations (other than under Self Assessment) can be settled in a number of different ways. Details of these are set out in the Inland Revenue Enquiry Manual (EM) see EM3800 et seq, EM5650 et seq and EM6000 et seq.

APPENDIX 22

GUIDANCE BY THE SECRETARY OF STATE TO THE DIRECTOR OF THE ASSETS RECOVERY AGENCY

Proceeds of Crime Act 2002

Section 2 (Directors Functions: General)

Guidance by the Secretary of State to the Director of the Assets

Recovery Agency on how she should best exercise her functions so as best to contribute to the reduction of crime.

Introduction

1. Under section 2 of the Proceeds of Crime Act 2002 the Director must exercise her functions in the way she considers is best calculated to contribute to the reduction of crime. Under section 2(5) she must have regard to any guidance given to her by the Secretary of State in making that consideration. Under section 2(6) the guidance must indicate that the reduction of crime is in general best secured by means of criminal investigations and criminal proceedings. This memorandum sets out the Secretary of State's guidance.

The Importance of Prosecuting Offenders where Possible

2. In accordance with section 2 (6) the Secretary of State considers that the reduction of crime is in general best secured by means of criminal investigations and criminal proceedings. This principle must therefore underpin the way in which the Director exercises her asset recovery functions and she must do her best to facilitate and promote criminal investigations and criminal proceedings. This guidance does not prohibit a criminal investigation by a law enforcement authority being carried out at the same time as either a civil recovery and/or tax investigation is carried out. Nor does it prevent civil recovery and/or tax proceedings being instituted where a criminal investigation by a law enforcement authority is being carried out at the same time into unrelated criminality. Similarly this Guidance does not prohibit criminal proceedings being instituted or carried on a by a law enforcement authority at the same time as either a civil recovery and/or tax investigation is carried out. In no circumstances may criminal and civil/tax proceedings be instituted or carried on at the same time in relation to the same criminality.
3. It follows that the Secretary of State considers that the Director should for the purposes of contributing to the reduction of crime:
   (A) not normally act without a referral from the law enforcement or prosecution authorities:
   (B) consult the relevant law enforcement or prosecution authority before exercising any of her operational functions, in order to enquire whether doing so would prejudice a criminal investigation or criminal proceedings and give due weight to any advice so received:
   (C) keep under review the extent to which taking, continuing or refraining from any course of action has a potential to prejudice a criminal investigation or criminal proceedings and avoid such prejudice where possible:
   (D) Ensure where possible that information relevant to a criminal investigation or criminal proceedings is disclosed to the relevant law enforcement or prosecution authority at the earliest practical opportunity.

4. The Secretary of State also considers that memoranda of understanding and co-operation between the Director and law enforcement and prosecution authorities will help to give effect to the matters set out in paragraph 3.

The respective potential of methods of targeting the proceeds of crime to contribute to the reduction of crime

5. Where a criminal conviction has been obtained, the Secretary of State considers that criminal confiscation of the proceeds of crime will best contribute to the reduction of crime.

Home Office

7 February 2005

APPENDIX 23

THE HOUSE OF LORDS DECISION IN *CAPEWELL*

[2007] UKHL 2

1. In January 2007 the House of Lords gave its opinion in the appeal of *Capewell v HM Revenue and Customs*. The central issue concerned whether the case of *Hughes* remained good law as a result of the introduction of CPR 69.7. The Court of Appeal below had held that Rule 69.7(2) was designed to give the Court some discretion in relation to who would pay the court appointed receiver's remuneration, and accordingly had made an order requiring that Customs should be responsible for payment of the receiver's remuneration for part of the period of the receivership.

2. In upholding Customs appeal, and giving the judgment of the Court (with which all of their Lordships concurred), Lord Walker stated:

    27. In my opinion CPR 69.7 has not had that far-reaching and surprising result. The function of CPR 69 is to set out a procedural code applicable to the generality of receiverships of all types. Its text gives no indication that its draftsman had particularly in mind the new species of receiverships in support of restraint orders and confiscation orders. No doubt its provisions do in general apply to such receiverships but they cannot override the scheme inherent in the detailed provisions of CJA 1988. That scheme is for the receiver's remuneration and expenses to be paid out of the receivership assets, but in a way which counts towards satisfaction of any confiscation order, and subject to the statutory long-stop already mentioned. If an individual subject to a restraint order is not ultimately convicted and made subject to a confiscation order, section 89 of CJA 1988 gives a statutory right to compensation in some circumstances. But Parliament has deliberately framed the right to compensation in narrow terms. That is an aggrieved individual's only right to compensation as such. He would not normally have the benefit of an undertaking in damages since (as Simon Brown LJ observed in *Hughes* at para 50) a prosecutor cannot be required to give an undertaking in damages as a condition of obtaining the appointment of a receiver. An aggrieved individual's only other recourse would be to challenge the amount of the receiver's remuneration, as the respondent has done in this case. There is a similar scheme under POCA 2002 and the Crown Court (Confiscation, Restraint and Receivership) Rules 2003 (SI 2003/421) made under that Act, but in these new provisions it is made perfectly clear that receivership expenses and remuneration are to come out of the assets subject to the receivership.

    28. The Court of Appeal was in my opinion wrong to suppose that CPR 69.7 has made (or could have made) a fundamental change either in the general law of receiverships, or in the position of receiverships under CJA 1988 and the other comparable statutory powers. I would allow this appeal on that ground. There is also a further, narrower ground for concluding that the order of the Court of Appeal cannot be upheld. In the original order appointing Mr Sinclair as receiver, Jackson J directed that "the costs of the receivership" (which in this context must mean expenses and remuneration) were to be paid in accordance with the agreement letter of 21 November 2002. That order was not appealed at the time (although it was contemplated that an early application would be made for discharge of the receiver) nor has there been any subsequent application for permission to appeal from it out of time. A receiver takes on heavy responsibilities when he accepts appointment, and he is entitled to the security of knowing that the terms of his appointment will not be changed retrospectively—even if an appellate court later decides that the receivership should have been terminated at an earlier date . . . .

Appendix 23: The House of Lords Decision in Capewell

3. As a result, the common law position in *Hughes* has now been re-affirmed, and all receiverships under the DTA, CJA, and POCA legislation will proceed on the basis that the overall costs of the receivership will be drawn from assets within the receivership estate, even if the Defendant is subsequently acquitted, not proceeded against, or the receivership is successfully discharged.
4. His Lordship defined 'remuneration' as the professional fees of the receiver and his own staff, confined 'costs' to litigation costs and 'expenses' to all other expenditure necessarily or properly incurred by the receiver in the performance of his duties (para 7).
5. He also re-affirmed the duty of the receiver as an officer of the court, which was to act impartially and in accordance with the directions of the court (para 19). In terms of purpose, he stated:

    20. In short, the appointment of a receiver was in many cases the most effective way of 'holding the ring' between warring litigants until the disputed issues could be finally determined.

6. In conclusion, as a result of this judgment one of the basic principles of receivership survives, namely that the receiver is entitled to be indemnified in respect of his costs and expenses, and his remuneration, out of the assets in his hands as receiver. It is further apparent that the Capewell Guidelines, drafted for the first Court of Appeal judgment in this matter, also survive.

INDEX

absconding defendants 16.77–16.108
  compensation: confiscation order made
      against absconder 16.105–16.107
  defendant later returning 16.89
  discharge of order 16.98–16.104
    procedure 16.102–16.104
  increase in term of imprisonment in default 16.108
  post-conviction 16.79
  powers of court 16.96, 16.97
  pre-conviction 16.84
  procedure 16.80–16.83, 16.86–16.88
  relevant period 16.93
  two year rule 16.85
  variation and discharge of orders 16.90
  variation of order 16.91, 16.92
    procedure 16.94
account monitoring orders 23.55–23.57
agents
  employment by management receiver 3.36–3.38
ancillary orders 4.01–4.51, 8.49 *see also* **disclosure orders; repatriation of assets; seizure of assets**
appeals 24.01–24.120
  applications to vary distinguished 24.02, 24.03
  condemnation 29.124–29.129
  confiscation hearings under DTA, and 10.167–10.171
  confiscation orders, *see* **confiscation order appeals**
  contempt of court 6.39
    Crown Court, from 24.118, 24.119
    High Court, from 24.115–24.117
  Criminal Procedure Rules 24.05
  forfeiture orders, appeals against, *see* **forfeiture order appeals**
  Part 6 of POCA, under 24.111, 24.112
  Proceeds of Crime Act 2002 (Appeals under Part 2) Order 2003 24.85–24.97
    appeals to Court of Appeal 24.85
    general provisions 24.96
    groundless applications, disposal of 24.88, 24.89
    initiating procedure 24.86
    preparation of case for hearing 24.90, 24.91
    references to European Court of Justice 24.97
    right of defendant to be present 24.92
    rules of evidence in Court of Appeal 24.93–24.95
  receivership orders, *see* **receivership order appeals**
  recovery and seizure of cash under POCA 21.187–21.194
  restoration cases 29.231, 29.232

  restraint order, *see* **restraint order appeals**
  thumbnail guide 24.120
  transfer of powers from High Court to Crown Court 24.04
Assets Recovery Agency 1.17–1.22, 19.03, 19.07, 20.03–20.07
  guidance by Secretary of State to Director App 22
  proceedings involving
    guidance for CLS funding App 19
  recovery orders, *see* **recovery orders**
  reduction of crime 20.07
  settlement of civil recovery and tax cases App 21
associated property
  meaning 19.30–19.33
assumptions
  CJA confiscation hearings, *see* **confiscation hearings under the CJA**
  confiscation hearings under POCA, *see* **confiscation hearings under POCA**
  DTA confiscation hearings, *see* **confiscation hearings under the DTA**
  reconsideration of confiscation orders under POCA, *see* **reconsideration of confiscation orders under POCA**
available amount
  meaning 15.34–15.37

banks
  property adjustment orders, and 22.135–22.145
benefit
  meaning 2.34–2.39
  pecuniary advantage 2.38
benefit from drug trafficking 10.11–10.62
  assessing proceeds of drug trafficking 10.49–10.51
  conspiracies 10.47, 10.48
  drugs seized from defendant
    payment or reward, whether 10.33–10.36
  joint 10.59–10.62
  joint apportionment 10.19–10.32
    guilty plea 10.24
    involvement in series or chain 10.29
    professional agents 10.30, 10.31
    trust principles, and 10.28
  knowledge that payment comes from drug trafficking 10.44–10.46
  money laundering 10.22
  multiple defendants 10.19–10.32

Index

benefit from drug trafficking (*cont.*)
  payment or other reward must be received in connection with drug trafficking 10.37, 10.38
  payments 10.18
  proceeds not profits 10.21, 10.52–10.58
  rewards 10.18
  section 63(2) DTA 10.39–10.43
  statutory provisions 10.16, 10.17
benefit under the CJA 12.25–12.68
benefit under POCA 15.11–15.19
bootlegging, *see* condemnation, forfeiture and restoration
businesses
  restraint orders 2.91, 2.92

Capewell **guidelines** 3.15
cash
  meaning 21.17–21.19, 21.199, 21.200
cash seizures, *see* recovery and seizure of cash under POCA
certificate of benefit 10.79–10.81
certificate of inadequacy 13.36–13.58, 16.49–16.76
  application notice by defendant seeking App 7
  form App 8
certificate of increase 13.18–13.26, 13.35, 16.39–16.48
certificate of service
  form App 14
charging orders
  applications to vary or discharge 2.100, 2.101
  circumstances in which made 2.94–2.96
  meaning 2.93
  property which can be charged 2.97, 2.98
  protecting 2.99
  purpose 2.02
  restraint orders, relationship with 2.102
civil recovery 19.01–19.234
  accruing profits 19.36
  associated property 19.30–19.33
  civil legal aid 19.234
  civil proceedings 19.14, 19.15
  consent order, by App 18
  definitions within POCA 19.19
  distinction between recovery and confiscation proceedings 19.16, 19.17
  European Convention on Human Rights, and 20.99–20.118
    Article 1–interference with property 20.100
    Article 6(1) 20.101
    Article 6(2) 20.102, 20.103
    Article 7 – civil proceedings 20.104–20.107
    Article 7 –criminal penalty 20.108–20.114
    Article 7 –retrospectivity 20.115–20.117
    Article 8 20.118
  granting interests 19.37
  High Court 19.18
  legal expenses 19.177–19.234
    assessed if not agreed 19.195
    background to new provisions 19.189, 19.190
    basis for assessment 19.227–19.233
    commencement of proceedings, at 19.201–19–204
    conclusion of proceedings, at 19.192–19.194
    consideration for court 19.205–19.208
    costs judge assessment 19.226
    Director's response 19.213–19.215
    evidence for purpose of meeting legal costs 19.218
    following making of recovery order 19.222
    new regulations 19.191
    ongoing opportunity 19.219
    Part 4 of Regulations 19.224
    practice and procedure 19.197–19.200, 19.209–19.212
    release of interim payment 19.216, 19.217
    statement of assets 19.220, 19.221
    two month time limit 19.196
  mixed property 19.35
  pension schemes 20.119–20.142, *see also* **pension schemes**
  power vested only in ARA 19.07
  Practice Directions App 10, App 11
  proceedings even on acquittal 19.08
claim form (CPR Part 8) App 9
cohabitees 22.79–22.118
companies
  restraint orders 2.53–2.63
  winding up, *see* **insolvent defendants**
compensation 28.78–28.105
  acquitted defendant 28,78–28.80, 28.85–28.90
  amount 29.83
  confiscation order varied or discharged, where 28.91, 28.92
  costs distinguished 28.03–28.77
  interim receiving orders 28.96–28.98
  POCA, under 28.93–28.95
  procedure on applications 28.84
  property freezing orders 28.96–28.98
  recovery of cash in summary proceedings 28.99–28.102
  third parties, for 28.81, 28.82
  victims of crime 28.103–28.105
condemnation and forfeiture of goods 29.07–29.44
  civil proceedings 29.15–29.17
  'commercial purpose' 29.29–29.36
  duty payable unless for own use 29.09
  EU reaction 29.27, 29.28
  gifts 29.24
  importations for commercial purpose 29.10–29.14
  legislation background 29.18, 29.19
  minimum indicative levels 29.37–29.43
  revised legislative scheme 29.20–29.23
  statutory basis 29.07
  statutory provisions App 20
  transfer for money's worth 29.25, 29.26
  travelling to UK from outside EU 29.44

Index

condemnation, forfeiture and restoration
    29.01–29.240
  condemnation and forfeiture of goods,
    see **condemnation and forfeiture of goods**
  condemnation appeals 29.124–29.129
  condemnation: costs and compensation
    29.112–29.123
  condemnation: practice and procedure
    29.61–29.111, see also **condemnation:**
    practice and procedure
  delivery up, see **delivery up**
  detention, seizure and condemnation,
    see **detention, seizure and condemnation**
  High Court 29.130
  human rights, and 29.131–29.134
  red diesel cases, see **red diesel cases**
  restoration 29.162–29.240 see also **restoration**
condemnation: practice and procedure
    29.61–29.111
  burden of proof 29.97–29.101
  court procedure 29.90–29.96
  hearing – commercial purpose v own use
    29.80–29.85
  hearsay in civil cases 29.102–29.105
  initial seizure 29.61–29.66
  notice of claim – one month time limit to appeal
    29.70, 29.71
  possible criminal proceedings 29.67–29.69
  power to stop traveller 29.111
  preparation for hearing 29.75–29.79
    dutiable goods 29.79
    service of evidence 29.75–29.78
  previous convictions 29.106–29.1–8
  reasons for stopping traveller 29.109, 29.110
  six month time limit 29.72–29.74
  standard of proof 29.97–29.101
confiscation hearings
  Criminal Justice Act 1988, under, see **confiscation**
    hearings under the CJA
  Drug Trafficking Act 1994, under, see **confiscation**
    hearings under the DTA
  Proceeds of Crime Act 2002, under, see **confisca-**
    tion hearings under POCA
confiscation hearings under the CJA
  amendments made by Proceeds of
    Crime Act 1995 12.01
  amount to be recovered 12.69
  appeal pending 12.04
  application of Act 11.05, 11.06
  appointment of benefit 12.23
  assests not restricted to those derived from
    criminal activity 12.73–12.75
  benefit 12.25–12.68
    assumptions applied, when 12.46
    assumptions not applied, when 12.52–12.54
    assumptions that can be made 12.49–12.51
    calculating 12.25

    contract services 12.65
    defendant does not have to be able to realise gift
      12.58–12.60
    determining amount that might be realized 12.66
    distinction between realizable property and gifts
      12.61–12.64
    extended 12.44, 12.45
    gifts caught by Act 12.55–12.57
    hidden assets 12.67
    offences of relevant description 12.29, 12.30
    pecuniary advantage 12.31–12.43
    qualifying offences 12.47
    relevant criminal conduct 12.26–12.28
    relevant period 12.48
    valuing property 12.68
  burden of proof 12.11–12.16
  circumstances in which held 11.08
  confiscation orders and sentencing for the
    offence 12.88–12.97
    human rights, and 12.96, 12.97
    power to vary sentence 12.91, 12.92
    prosecution costs 12.93
    third parties 12.94
    time to pay 12.90
  consequences of defendant failing to respond 11.78
  considerations to be applied 11.44–11.47
  conspiracies 12.24
  content 11.59–11.61
  costs of sale 12.81
  court may still proceed 11.23
  date of conviction, running from 11.48
  defence statements 12.17–12.19
  defendant's acceptance conclusive 11.71–2
  defendant's statement 11.63–11.68
  exceptional circumstances 11.39–11.43
  failure to give notice 11.20–11.22
  form 11.59–11.61
  further statements by prosecutor 11.79
  importance of defendant's reply 11.69–70
  imprisonment in default 12.83–12.86
  inflationary adjustment 12.77–12.79
  jurisdiction of Crown Court following
    committal 11.30–31
  jurisdiction to hold 12.07–12.24
  more than one allowable 11.38
  multiple defendants 12.23
  obtaining information from defendant
    'at any time' 11.73–11.75
  offences of relevant description 11.09–11.32
  offences where Act applies in
    magistrate's court 11.32
  pleas, basis of 12.20–12.22
  postponement of proceedings 11.33–11.54
  preliminary matters 11.07
  preparing for 11.01–11.82
  procedure leading to 12.03
  proceeds not profits 12.76

Index

confiscation hearings under the CJA (*cont.*)
  prosecutor's acceptance conclusive 11.76–11.77
  prosecution statement 12.17–12.19
  purpose 11.01–11.04, 12.02, 12.10
  qualifying offences under Section 72AA
    11.24–11.27
  realizable assets 12.69–12.87
  realizable property 12.70–72
  relationship between disclosure statements
    and confiscstion hearings 11.81
  relevant criminal conduct 11.11
  requirement to give notice 11.18–19
  section 73 prosecutor's statements 11.55–11.82
  securing attendance witnesses 11.80
  self incrimination, risk of 11.82
  sentence pending hearing 11.52–11.54
  serving default sentence does
    not extinguish debt 12.87
  service 11.62
  standard of proof 11.13, 11.14, 12.11–12.16
  statutory provision 11.33
  victims, problems of 11.28, 11.29, 12.09
  when to hold proceedings 12.05, 12.06
confiscation hearings under the DTA
  appeals 10.167–10.171
  application of Act 9–01
  assumptions 10.63–10.124
    application 10.73
    assets held overseas 10.107
    assets jointly held with third parties 10.105
    authorities, review of 10.82–10.90
    burden of proof 10.92
    certificates of benefit 10.79–10.81
    costs of sale 10.104
    determining amount to be realized 10.91
    effect of applying 10.75, 10.76
    forfeiture of drugs, confiscation
      orders and 10.122
    gift caught by Act, when 10.109–10.113
    gifts 10.108
    hidden assets 10.94–10.99
    margin for error 10.103
    market value 10.121
    matrimonial homes 10.106
    no other assumptions may be made 10.72
    obligations having priority 10.114, 10.115
    property held by defendant 10.101, 10.102
    prosecutor's statement, and, 10.123
    public interest immunity 10.124
    realizable property, meaning 10.100
    rebutting 10.77, 10.78
    stage at which applied 10.74
    valuing property 10.116–10.120
    when not applied 10.65–10.71
  basis of plea 10.10
  benefit from drug trafficking, *see* **benefit
    from drug trafficking**
  burden of proof 10.04–10.109
  confiscation orders 9.05
  defendants who die or abscond 10.153–10.165
    post-conviction orders 10.154
    pre-conviction cases 10.155–10.157
    procedural matters 10.164, 10.165
    Rules of the Supreme Court 10.158–10.163
  index of defined expressions 10.166
  making confiscation order 10.125–10.152
    costs, orders for payment 10.143
    default penalties 10.133–10.137
    forfeiture orders, relationship with 10.126
    human rights, and 10.145–10.152
    imprisonment in default 10.133–10.137
    relationship with sentence 10.127–10.132
    time to pay 10.138–10.142
    unreasonable delay in enforcement 10.144
  objective of DTA proceedings 9.02–9.04
  offences which constitute drug trafficking
    offences 9.11
  postponement of proceedings pending further
    enquiries 9.12
  postponing determination 9.13–9.48
    absence of defendant 9.34
    appeal pending 9.45, 9.46
    application procedure 9.47, 9.48
    case law applied 9.43
    conviction, not sentence 9.16
    discretion of sentencing judge 9.19
    exceptional circumstances 9.17–9.32
      enquiry into 9.22, 9.23
      failure to properly postpone 9.38–9.42
      further, no requirement to find 9.33
      lengthy trial of co-defendant 9.21
      purpose: further information 9.36, 9.37
    six month rule: no retrospective
      extension 9.35
  preparatory steps 9.54–9.94
    consequences of defendant failing to respond to
      prosecutor's statement 9.87–9.91
    defendant's acceptance conclusive 9.77–9.80
    defendant's statement 9.71
    drafting 9.74
    form and content of section 11 statements
      9.60–9.68
    further provision of information by defendant
      9.83–9.86
    further statements by prosecutor 9.93
    prosecutor's statement 9.56
    purpose of 9.57–9.59
    requiring defendant to respond to prosecutor's
      statement 9.72, 9.73
    section 11 statements 9.55
    securing attendance of witnesses 9.94
    self-incrimination, risk of 9.81, 9.82
    statements relating to drug trafficking 9.54
    time for service of prosecutor's statement 9.69

Index

confiscation hearings under the DTA (*cont.*)
  preparatory steps 9.54–9.94 (*cont.*)
    upon whom prosecutor's statement
      should be served 9.70
    valuing drugs 9.92
  preparing for 9.01–9.94
  procedure leading to 10.03
  purpose 10.01, 10.02
  sentence 9.49, 9.50
  standard of proof 9.51–9.53, 10.04–10.09
  time for 9.06–9.10

confiscation hearings under POCA
  appeals 15.79, 15.80
  assumptions 15.20–15.30
    date of conviction 15.27
    not applying, when 15.28–15.30
    relevant day 15.25, 15.26
  basis of pleas 15.06
  burden of proof 15.07–15.10
  consequences of defendant failing to respond to
    prosecutor's statement 14.87–14.91
  criminal conduct and benefit 14.33
  criminal lifestyle 14.25
    relevant benefit not less than £5000 14.30
  defendant's acceptance conclusive 14.81, 14.82
  defendant's statement 14.77–14.80
  disclosure evidence admissible 14.74
  duty of full and frank disclosure 14.71
  expert evidence 14.108
  failure to provide information ordered 14.103
  failure to respond by defendant 14.83–14.86
  further provision of information by defendant
    14.96–14.100
  further statements by prosecutor 14.104, 14.105
  joint control of assets 14.107
  multiple defendants 14.107
  prosecutor's acceptance conclusive 14.102
  securing attendance of witnesses 14.106
  self incrimination, problem of
    14.92–14.95, 14.101
  service of documents 14.109
  service of prosecutor's statement 14.75, 14.76
  defendant's benefit 15.11–15.19
    double counting, rule against 15.14, 15.15
    general criminal conduct 15.13
    particular criminal conduct 15.16
    proceeds not profits 15.18
    recent case law 15.17
    value of property obtained from
      criminal conduct 15.19
  defendant's conduct forming part of
    criminal activity 14.37
  definitions 15.81
  effect of order on sentence 15.71–15.76
    importance of following provisions of POCA
      15.74, 15.75

  relationship between confiscation order and
    compensation 15.72, 15.73
  evolution 14.01–14.05
  general criminal conduct 14.34
  gifts and recipients 15.55–15.58
  guiding principles 14.24–14.44
    transitional provisions 14.40–14.44
  human rights, and 15.77, 15.78
  lifestyle offences 14.26–14.29
  magistrates' courts 15.05, *see also* **magistrates'
    court, confiscation in**
  mandatory regime 15.03–15.06
  particular criminal conduct 14.35
  person benefiting from criminal conduct
    14.38, 14.39
  postponement 14.45–14.62
    appeal, pending 14.59
    beyond two years 14.50–14.55
    court failing to follow provisions 14.57, 14.58
    date of conviction 14.48
    further 14.49
    permitted period 14.47
    power to vary sentence 14.62
    who may apply for 14.56
  preparatory steps 14.63–14.109
  preparing for 14.01–14.109
  proceeding by court 14.24
  recoverable amount 15.31–15.47
    available amount 15.34–15.37
    hidden assets 15.45
    market value 15.38–15.44
    reasons given by court 15.46
    victims 15.33
  relationship between general and particular
    conduct 14.36
  relevant benefit, meaning 14.31, 14.32
  requirement for 14.06
  section 16 statements 14.63, 14.64
    content 14.67–14.70
    purpose 14.65–14.66
    service 14.72m, 14.73
  sentencing 14.60, 14.61
  standard of proof 15.07–15.10
  steps to confiscation 15.82
  tainted gifts 15.48–15.60
    value of 15.59, 15.60
  time for payment 15.61–15.70
    imprisonment in default 15.65–15.68
    interest on unpaid sums 15.69

confiscation law
  reasons for enactment 1.02–1.08

confiscation order appeals 24.50–24.84
  appeal by prosecutor or Director of ARA
    24.67–24.69, 24.72
  Attorney-General's appeal 24.50
  Criminal Cases Review Commission 24.61, 24.62
  Crown Court proceeding afresh 24.82–24.84

775

Index

confiscation order appeals *(cont.)*
  Crown Court 'slip rule' 24.59, 24.60
  fresh evidence 24.63
  House of Lords, to 24.78–24.81
  judge's discretion, involving 24.57
  leave 24.66
  POCA, under 24.64, 24.65
  right of 24.55, 24.56
  steps which court must take 24.73–24.76
confiscation regime
  object 1.09, 1.10
conspiracy
  benefit from drug trafficking, and 10.47, 10.48
  money laundering, and 26.16–26.24
contempt of court 6.01–6.39
  appeals, 6.39, *see also* **appeals**
  burden of proof 6.06
  commencing proceedings 6.07
  contents of application notice 6.08–6.10
  defendant's response 6.19, 6.20
  discontinuance of application 6.27
  effect of being in contempt 6.36
  evidence in support of application 6.11
  hearing 6.21–6.39
    case management directions 6.22
    legal representation 6.24
    procedure at 6.28, 6.29
    striking out application 6.25
  issuing application 6.17, 6.18
  procedure on applications 6.05–6.20
  proving breach 6.16
  proving service of order 6.12–6.15
  purging 6.37, 6.38
  sentence 6.30–6.34
  serving application 6.17, 6.18
  standard of proof 6.06
  strict compliance necessary 6.05
  suspended committals 6.35
continued detention hearings; cash seizures 21.65–21.104
  application for early release by victims or other owners 21.91–21.93
  applications for return of cash: standard of proof 21.100, 21.101
  correct forms not served, where 21.75–21.82
  early release of cash 21.84–21.86
  Form A 21.65–21.69
  Form B 21.70, 21.71
  Form C 21.72
  Form D 21.87–21.90
  Form E 21.95
  Form F: order for release under s 301(4) 21.98
  insolvency, and 21.83
  joinder 21.99
  objection to release from person from whom cash was seized 21.97
  officers agreeing to release of cash 21.102

  procedure at continued detention hearing 21.74
  proper procedure not followed, where 21.75–21.82
  service of documents 21.73
  third party applications/other owners 21.96
  transfer of proceedings 21.103, 21.104
  victims of unlawful conduct 21.94
costs 28.01–28.77
  acquitted defendant 28.22
  basis of assessment 28.07, 28.08
  compensation distinguished 28.03–28.77
  confiscation orders, and 10.143, 28.23, 28.24
  Crown Court 28.13, 28.14
  discretion of court 28.06
  factors to be taken into account in deciding amount 28.09
  High Court/civil cases 28.04, 28.05
  interim costs orders 28.10–28.12
  property freezing orders, and 19.87
  property, meaning 19.20–19.23
  property obtained through unlawful conduct 19.24–19.26
  recoverable property 19.29
  recovery and seizure of cash under POCA 21.165–21.178
  release of restrained funds to cover legal expenses 28.60–28.69
    POCA 27.71–28.77
    third parties, and 28.70
  restoration 29.234–29.236
  standard of proof 19.10–19.13
  tracing of property 19.34
  unlawful conduct 19.27, 19.28
creditors
  restraint orders, and, *see* **third parties**
Criminal Cases Review Commission 24.61, 24.113, 24.114
criminal conduct
  meaning 14.33, 26.31, 6.32
criminal investigation
  meaning 8.15, 8.16
criminal lifestyle
  meaning 14.25
criminal property
  meaning 26.29, 26.30
Crown Prosecution Service 1.23
customer information orders 23.48–23.54
  discharge 23.53
  offences 23.54
  requirements for making 23.51, 23.52
  variation 23.53

death of defendant 16.78
delay
  restraint orders, and 2.40–2.48
delivery up 29.156–29.161

Index

legislative provisions 29.157–29.160
  practice 29.161
detention, seizure and condemnation 29.45–29.60
  Coquelles, stops at 29.60
  forfeiture provisions 29.46, 29.47
  'liable to forfeiture' 29.48–29.50
  more than one person involved 29.58
  proof 29.59
  secondary forfeiture 29.51–29.57
director's receivers 17.92–17.95
disclosure of suspicious transactions 27.01–27.103
  background 27.05–27.09
  POCA, under 27.10–27.42
    businesses in regulated sector 27.14–27.16
    considerations for court 27.39
    defence available 27.38, 27.42
    defences to failing to disclose 27.19–27.25
    excluded businesses 27.17, 27.18
    failure to disclose: nominated officers 27.40
    legal privilege 27.29–27.31
    nominated officers in regulated sector 27.33–27.37
    protected disclosures 27.41
    regulated sector 27.10–27.13
    'suspects' 27.32
    tests which court should apply 27.26–27.28
  professional legal advisers 27.43–27.69, *see also* **professional legal advisers**
  SARS 27.70–27.75
    form and manner of disclosures 27.72
    review 27.70, 27.71
    submitting reports 27.73–27.75
  tipping off 27.76–27.87
    consent 27.84
    defences available 27.80, 27.81
    maximum penalty 27.82, 27.83
    offence under POCA 27.76–27.79
    protected and authorized disclosures 27.85
    threshold amounts 27.86
  transactions under DTA 27.88–27.103
    defences 27.94
    failure to disclose knowledge or suspicion of drug money laundering 27.89–27.91
    legal professional privilege 27.92, 27.93
    penalties 27.103
    tipping off 27.95, 27.96
    tipping off under CJA 1988 27.98–27.102
disclosure orders 4.06–4.41, 23.58, 23.59
  advising defendant or third party required to disclose 4.33–4.41
  contents of statement 4.37–4.39
  improper use, and 4.40
  initial disclosure 4.34, 4.35
  preparation of witness statement 4.36, 4.39
  timescale 4.34
  drug trafficking cases 4.11–4.14
  form 4.29

jurisdiction to make 4.07–4.14
  notice of 4.10
  power of court 4.08
  prosecutor, cannot be ordered against 4.31, 4.32
  self incrimination, and 4.15–4.28
    ancillary or collateral purpose 4.27
    'Chinese Wall' 4.19, 4.20
    condition, wording of 4.22–4.25
    drug trafficking, and, 4.18, 4.19
    human rights, and 4.23
    undertaking by prosecutor 4.15, 4.16
  third parties, and 4.30
dissipation, risk of 2.40
distress warrants 17.64
drug trafficking
  benefit from, *see* **benefit from drug trafficking**
  meaning 2.17, 2.18
drug trafficking offences
  meaning 2.11
enforcement of confiscation orders 17.01–17.111
  magistrates' courts, *see* **magistrates' courts**
  Proceeds of Crime Act 2002 17.88–17.103
    director's receivers 17.92–17.95
    implementing default sentence 17.110, 17.111
    powers 17.89–17.91
    procedure on application 17.96–17.103
    seized money 17.104–17.108
  voluntary satisfaction by defendant 17.03–17.12
enforcement of external confiscation orders 25.26–25.39
  application of proceeds of realisation 25.39
  registration of order 25.27–25.30
  procedure 25.30–25.38
enforcement receivers 17.13–17.61
  ancillary orders 17.29, 17.30
  challenge to validity of confiscation order, and 17.16
  CJA cases: 'proceedings have not been concluded' 17.19
  dealing with proceeds of realization 17.57–17.60
  discharge 17.61
  discretionary remedy 17.15
  DTA cases: 'a confiscation order is not satisfied' 17.18
  matrimonial home 17.50
  powers 17.27, 17.28
  procedure on applications 17.31–17.48
    defendant's response 17.36–17.39
    evidence in support 17.33–17.35
    order of court 17.49
    third parties 17.40–17.48
  realization of property 17.52
  remuneration 17.53–17.56
  status on appointment 17.51
  statutory provisions 17.14
  'subject to appeal', meaning 17.20–17.26

enforcement receivership order
  form App 3
Enforcement Task Force 1.33–1.35
European Convention on Human Rights and Civil Recovery, *see* **civil recovery**
excepted joint owner
  meaning 20.53, 20.54

financial reporting orders 23.62–23.73
  duration 23.67
  effect 23.68–23.71
  failure to comply with 23.73
  jurisdiction 23.63, 23.64
  offences 23.65, 23.66
  revocation 23.72
  variation 23.72
forfeiture order
  confiscation order, relationship with 10.126
forfeiture order appeals 24.98–24.110
  magistrates' court, from 24.106–24.110
  POCA, under 24.98–24.105
freezing orders
  charging orders distinguished 2.03–2.07
  restraint orders distinguished 2.03–2.07

general criminal conduct
  meaning 14.34
gifts 12.55, 15.48–15.59

hearsay evidence
  magistrates' courts, in 21.143–21.147
hidden assets 12.67, 15.45
High Court procedure 7.01–7.60
  additional matters which should be disclosed 7.25, 7.26
  application to discharge restraint order 7.42–7.60
    appeals 7.60
    applying to court 7.46, 7.47
    costs 7.56
    drafting order 7.50
    drafting witness statement or affidavit 7.48, 7.49
    hearing 7.54, 7.55
    issuing application 7.51
    proof of service 7.53
    service of application 7.52
    serving order 7.57
  application to vary restraint order 7.42–7.60
    appeals 7.60
    applications by prosecutor 7.58, 7.59
    applying to court 7.46, 7.47
    consulting prosecutor 7.43–7.45
    costs 7.56
    drafting order 7.50, 7.57
    drafting witness statement or affidavit 7.48, 7.49
    hearing 7.54, 7.55
    issuing application 7.51
    proof of service 7.53
    service of application 7.52
    serving order 7.57
    variation by consent 7.43–7.45
  applications for restraint order 7.13–7.33
    allocation of business 7.13
    claim form 7.16
    draft order 7.17, 7.18
      third parties 7.18
    duty of full and frank disclosure 7.23, 7.24
    evidence 7.09–7.12
    hearing 7.34–7.41
      oral 7.36
      proceeding without notice 7.35
    non-disclosure, consequences of 7.27–7.33
      breakdown of communication, and 7.33
      discharge of restraint order 7.28, 7.29
    'overriding objective' 7.04
    preparation of documentation 7.15
    service of order 7.39–7.41
    structure of civil procedure rules 7.07
    terminology 7.08
    title of proceedings 7.14
    witness statement 7.19–7.22
      contents 7.19–7.22
  Woolf Reforms 7.03–7.12
HM Revenue and Customs 1.27
human rights
  civil recovery, and, *see* **civil recovery**
    condemnation, and 29.131–29.134
  confiscation orders, and 10.145–10.152
    legality of use 10.151, 10.152
    presumption of innocence, and 10.148
  confiscation procedures, and 12.96, 12.97
  confiscation proceedings, and 15.77, 15.78
  forfeiture provisions, and 21.217
  restoration, and 29.237–29.240

insolvent defendant 18.01–18.24
  bankruptcy order, and 18.04, 18.05
  interaction with restraint proceedings 18.19–18.22
  POCA 2002 18.12–18.18
    floating charge 18.16
    limited liability partnerships 18.17
    protection of insolvency practitioners 18.18
    winding up of companies 18.14, 18.15
  position under DTA and CJA 18.01–18.11
  professional advisers, and 18.23, 18.24
  voluntary arrangement 18.06
  winding up of companies 18.08–18.10
interest
  meaning 20.65
interim receiving orders 19.91–19.176
  application
    practice and procedure 19.101–19.104
  application for 19.92–19.94
  application to clarify receiver's powers 19.140
  application to vary or discharge 19.150–19.152

Index

interim receiving orders (cont.)
  applications for directions 19.141
  compensation 19.170–19.172
  conditions 19.97, 19.98
  contents 19.126–19.132
  contents in terms of reporting by
    receiver 19.137
  exclusion of property which is not recoverable
    19.154, 19.155
  expedition, need for 19.107
  expenses 19.157
  form App 15
  good arguable case 19.99, 19.100
  High Court, powers of 19.123
  independence of interim receiver
    19.142–19.146
  insolvency, and 19.120
  insolvent respondent 19.115–19.119
  interim receiver, functions of 191.24, 19.125
  land, over 19.159
  legislative steer 19.108–19.114
  loss of power to investigate 19.95, 19.96
  made before commencement of claim for
    civil recovery 19.105
  non-specified recoverable property 19.153
  power to vary or set aside 19.147–19.149
  protection for receiver 19.139
  purpose 19.97, 19.98
  reporting 19.167–19.169
  restriction on existing proceedings and
    rights 19.162–19.166
  restrictions on dealing with property
    19.133–19.136
  role of interim receiver 19.142–19.146
  self-incrimination, protection against 19.138
  stand alone claim 19.121, 19.122
  test which court should apply 19.175, 19.176
  time limit for compensation application
    19.173, 19.174
international assistance under DTA and CJA
  25.03–25.15
  ancillary orders 25.24
  applications for variation and discharge
    of orders 25.25
  appropriate authorities 25.06
  enforcement of DTA and CJA confiscation
    orders overseas 25.40–25.42
  enforcement of external confiscation orders,
    see **enforcement of external
    confiscation orders**
  evidence in support 25.19–25.23
  letter of request 25.17, 25.18
  Northern Ireland 25.43–25.45
  obtaining restraint orders in UK on behalf of
    designated countries 25.07–25.15
  procedure 25.16–25.25
  Scotland 25.43–25.45

international co-operation under POCA
  25.46–25.68
  action to be taken on receipt of external
    request 25.49
  ancillary orders 25.54
  appeals 25.56, 25.66
  application, discharge and variation of restraint
    orders 25.55
  application to give effect to external orders
    25.59–25.63
  enforcement of order 25.67
  hearsay evidence 25.57
  management receivers 25.58
  powers of Crown Court to make restraint orders
    25.50–25.53
  procedure on application 25.68
  registration of order 25.64, 25.65
international element 1.37, 25.01–25.70
  co-operation under POCA 25.46–25.68,
    see also **international co-operation under
    POCA**
  designated countries and territories 25.05
  enforcement of POCA confiscation orders
    in different parts of UK 25.69, 25.70
investigations 23.01–23.73
  Code of Practice 23.61
  courts, jurisdiction 23.09
  defining 23.06
  judges, jurisdiction 23.07, 23.08
  legislative provisions 23.03–23.05
  overseas 23.46, 23.47
  statements made in response to orders 23.60

leasehold interests
  restraint orders 2.69–2.72
legal advisers, see professional legal advisers
legal aid 19.234, App 6
legal expenses
  and civil recovery 19.177–19.234
  restraint orders 2.89, 2.90, 8.40
legal professional privilege
  production orders, and 23.16–23.18
Legal Services Commission
  funding 21.174–21.177
  funding arrangements App 6
legislation
  agencies responsible for enforcement
    1.17–1.36
  legislative steer 5.27–5.46, 8.64, 19.108–19.114
letter of agreement between prosecutor
    and receiver
  form App 4
lifestyle offences
  meaning 14.26–14.29
limited companies
  restraint orders, see **restraint orders;
    third parties**

Index

magistrates' courts
  confiscation in 14.07–14.23
    circumstances where magistrates' court may commit 14.12, 14.13
    committal practice and procedure 14.22, 14.23
    discretion to commit 14.14–14.21
    section 70: committal by magistrates' court 14.09–14.11
  confiscation orders 15.05
  enforcement of confiscation orders 17.62–17.86
    delay by prosecutor 17.78–17.86
    distress warrants 17.64
    third party debt orders 17.65
    warrants of commitment 17.66–17.77

management receivers 3.01–3.68
  accounts 3.39–3.42
  agents, employment of 3.36–3.38
  Criminal Justice Act 1988, under 3.01–3.68
  discharge 3.61–3.63
  Drug Trafficking Act 1994, under 3.01–3.68
  duties 3.22–3.42
    negligence, and 3.32–3.35
  exercising discretion to appoint: *Capewell* Guidelines 3.14–3.17
    agents 3.15
    appointment, upon 3.15
    defendant, role of 3.17
    factors to be considered 3.14–3.17
    lawyers 3.15
    objective 3.16
    prosecutor, application by 3.15
    reporting requirements 3.15
  jurisdiction to appoint 3.07–3.13
  liabilities 3.22–3.42
    negligence, and 3.32–3.35
  need for 3.01–3.03
  officer of court, as 3.19–3.21
  Order App2
  persons who may apply for appointment 3.13
  powers 3.12, 3.22–3.42
    common law 3.26
    intangible property 3.24, 3.25
    interference by court 3.31
    sale 3.27–3.30
  Proceeds of Crime Act 2002, *see* **management receivers under Proceeds of Crime Act 2002**
  recent developments in law 3.04–3.06
  remuneration 3.43–3.60
    Capewell, and 3.55–3.60, App 23
    court, approval by 3.49–3.60
    CPR 69.7 3.53, 3.54
    human rights arguments 3.46–3.48
    liability for 3.43–3.60
  restraint order, where 3.10, 3.11
  status on appointment 3.18–3.21
  suitability 3.18
  taxation, and 3.64–3.68
  personal liability 3.65–3.68

management receivers under Proceeds of Crime Act 2002 8.57–8.68
  accounts 8.90
  application for appointment 8.82, 8.83
  application for conferment of powers on receivers 8.84, 8.85
  applications to vary or discharge orders 8.86
  court documents 8.103
  disclosure of documents 8.102
  enforcing 8.123–8.127
  evidence 8.92–8.121
    expert 8.100, 8.101
    writing, in 8.96–8.98
  hearings 8.92–8.121
  inspection of documents 8.120
  legislative steer 8.64–8.68
    maintaining value of assets 8.64, 8.65
    order that property is not to be sold 8.67, 8.68
  non-compliance 8.91
  powers 8.59–8.61
  procedure 8.81–8.91
    change of solicitor 8.116
    consent orders 8.110
    costs 8.117–8.121
      assessment 8.119, 8.120
      time for complying with orders 8.121
    omissions 8.111
    preparation of documents 8.114, 8.115
    slips 8.111
    supply of documents from court records 8.112, 8.113
  remuneration 8.89
  restriction of use of powers 8.62, 8.63
  security 8.87, 8.88
  service of documents 8.104–8.109
    alternative method 8.107
    outside jurisdiction 8.108
    proof of 8.109

management receivership order
  form App 2

mass spec reports 21.151

matrimonial home 22.85–22.118
  developing case law 22.100–22.118
  enforcement receiver, and 17.50
  equitable interests in 22.131, 22.132
  MCA 22.93–22.99
  Re Norris 22.88–22.92

money laundering 1.38, 26.01–26.128
  criminal conduct 26.31, 26.32
  'criminal property' 26.29, 26.30
  criminalization 26.06
  DTA 1994 and CJA 1988 26.79–26.112
    acquisition, possession or use of proceeds of drug trafficking 26.98, 26.99
    assisting another person to retain benefit of drug trafficking 26.84–26.89

money laundering (cont.)
   concealing or transferring proceeds of drug
      trafficking 26.81–26.83
   criminal conduct, meaning 26.106
   defences 26.95, 26.96, 26.103
   defences: adequate consideration
      26.100–26.102
   disclosure of transactions to constable
      26.90, 26.91
   disclosures by persons in employment 26.97
   drafting indictment 26.92–26.94
   laundering proceeds of other crimes under
      Criminal Justice Act 26.104, 26.105
   mode of trial decisions 26.112
   proceeds of drug trafficking 26.79, 26.80
   sentencing 26.107–26.111
   EC Directives 26.113–26.128
      Money Laundering Regulations 26.117–26.125
      relevant businesses 26.126
      Third European Money Laundering
         Directive 26.128
      UK legislation to implement 26.116
   first offence: concealing etc 26.25–26.28
   meaning 26.05
   methods 26.07–26.10
   POCA, under 26.11–26.78
      appropriate consent 26.64, 26.65
      consent from nominated officer
         26.69–26.71
      conspiracy 26.16–26.24
      defences to section 327(1) 26.33–26.36
      defences to section 328(1) 26.45–26.51
      defences to section 329(1) 26.52–26.56
      disclosure to nominated officer 26.62, 26.63
      disclosure under s 338 26.58–26.61
      form and manner of disclosures 26.76, 26.77
      inchoate offences 26.15
      maximum penalty 26.57
      mens rea 26.13, 26.14
      moratorium period 26.67, 26.68
      notice period 26.66
      prohibited act 26.72
      protected disclosures 26.73–26.75
      second offence: arrangements 26.43–26.44
      threshold amounts 26.37–26.42

Northern Ireland
   reciprocal enforcement 25.45

offences of relevant description
   meaning 11.09
overseas assets
   restraint orders 2.76, 2.77
overseas investigations 23.46, 23.47

particular criminal conduct
   meaning 14.35

pecuniary advantage
   benefit 2.38
   meaning 12.31–12.43
pension schemes
   civil recovery, and 20.119–20.142
      calculation and verification of value
         20.127–20.132
         approval of manner of 20.133, 20.134
      consent order 20.141, 20.142
      consequential adjustment of liabilities
         20.138–20.140
      costs of trustees or managers 20.137
      pension scheme, meaning 20.123, 20.124
      Regulations 2003 20.126
      time for compliance with pension recovery
         order 20.135, 20.136
      trustees or managers 20.125
postponement of confiscation hearings 9.12–9.45,
   11.33–11.52
Proceeds of Crime Act 2002 1.14–1.16
   confiscation hearings, *see* **confiscation hearings
      under POCA**
   draft restraint, disclosure and repatriation order
      App 13
   management receivers under, *see* **management
      receivers under Proceeds of Crime Act 2002**
   reconsideration of confiscation orders under,
      see **reconsideration of confiscation**
   recovery and seizure of cash under, *see* **recovery
      and seizure of cash under POCA**
   restraint orders under, *see* **restraint orders under
      Proceeds of Crime Act 2002**
   Schedule 6
   text App 12
   websites App 16
production orders 23.10–23.38
   complying with 23.31–23.35
   excluded material 23.19
   failure to comply with 23.36–23.38
   government departments 23.20
   judicial discretion 23.40–23.45
   jurisdiction 23.10, 23.11
   legal professional privilege 23.16–23.18
   procedure applications 23.21–23.28
   requirements for making 23.12–23.15
   who may apply for 23.29, 23.30
professional legal advisers
   disclosure of suspicious transactions 27.43–27.69
      Bowman v Fels 27.45–27.59
      consensual resolution in litigious context
         27.60–27.62
      POCA clauses 27.63–27.68
      protection for judges 27.69
property
   meaning 2.74, 2.75, 19.20–19.23
property adjustment orders
   third parties, and, *see* **third parties**

Index

property freezing orders 19.38–19.90
  ancillary orders 19.75
  application to vary or set aside 19.88–19.90
  criteria for granting 19.53–19.56
  definition 19.42
  duty of full and frank disclosure 19.46–19.52
  exclusions 19.60–19.64
  exclusions: legal costs 19.87
  factors giving rise to risk of dissipation 19.44, 19.45
  form App 17
  further SOCPA amendments 19.72–19.74
  legislative steer 19.65, 19.66
  practice and procedure 19.78–19.86
  restriction on proceedings and remedies 19.68–19.71
  setting aside 19.57–19.59
  undertakings for damages 19.76
  variation 19.57–19.59, 19.60–19.64
  without notice 19.43
public interest immunity
  confiscation proceedings, and 10.124
  recovery orders, and 20.96–20.98
receivers 28.26–28.59
  Capewell 28.43–28.58, App 23
  Civil Procedure Rules 69 28.69–28.42
  Crown Court 28.59
  director's receivers 17.92–17.95
  enforcement receivers *see* **enforcement receivers**
  High Court 28.34, 28.35
  indemnities 28.55
  interim measures 19.137–19.146
  litigation, in 29.29–28.33
  management receivers, *see* **management receivers**
receivership order appeals 24.29–24.49
  appeals by financial investigators under POCA 24.47–24.49
  Court of Appeal, to 24.29–24.44
    hearing appeal 24.40–24.42
    leave 24.36–24.39
    powers of Court of Appeal 24.44
    Proceeds of Crime Act 2002 (Appeals under Part 2) Order 2003 24.43
  House of Lords, to 24.45, 24.46
receivership orders
  Capewell App 23
  enforcement 6.01–6.39
  sanctions available for breach 6.03, 6.04
  ways in which breaches may be committed 6.02
reconsideration of confiscation orders under POCA 16.01–16.76
  assumptions 16.30–16.37
    changes in value of money 16.36
    exception to rule 16.35
    procedure: applications under ss 19, 20 or 21 of Act 16.37
    revised benefit 16.31–16.33
    status of previous orders of court 16.34

  compensation 16.18–16.20
  confiscation order made, when 16.21–16.29
    date of conviction 16.29
    reconsideration of benefit 16.21–16.29
    relevant amount 16.28
    relevant time 16.27
  inadequacy of available amount 16.49–16.76
    application by Justices' Chief Executive to discharge order 16.74–16.75
    assets difficult to realize 16.65
    bankruptcy cases 16.54
    burden of proof 16.64
    certificate of increase 16.48
    changes in value of money 16.46
    confiscation order made, where 16.39–16.43
    court must give reasons 16.60
    discharge of confiscation order 16.68, 16.69
    procedure 16.55
    procedure: applications under s 22 of Act 16.47
    procedure where Crown Court discharged order 16.76
    relevant amount under s 22 16.44, 16.45
    route to appeal, not 16.56–16.63
    small amount outstanding: discharge of confiscation order 16.72
    specified reasons 16.70, 16.71
    standard of proof 16.64
    variation of confiscation order 16.49–16.53
  increase in available amount 16.39–16.48
  no confiscation order originally made, where 16.02–16.17
    date of conviction 16.06, 16.07
    reconsideration of benefit 16.11–16.17
    relevant date 16.06, 16.07
    statements of information 16.10
    time limit 16.05
  statements of information 16.38
recoverable property
  meaning 21.25, 21.26
recovery and seizure of cash under POCA 21.01–21.217
  48 hour rule 21.51–21.55
  appeals 21.187–21.194
    costs 21.193
    forfeiture, against 21.187
    funding 21.192
  applications for forfeiture of detained cash 21.105–21.112
    Form G 21.106–21.112
  burden of proof 21.129–21.131
  cash, meaning 21.17–21.19
  circumstances in which cash may be seized 21.13
  civil proceedings 21.10, 21.11
  compensation 21.179–21.186
  continued detention hearings, *see* **continued detention hearings**
  costs 21.165–21.178

Index

recovery and seizure of cash under POCA (*cont.*)
  direct evidence of unlawful conduct 21.137
  Drug Trafficking Act 1994, and 21.03, 21.04
  first detention hearing for seized cash 21.43–21.46
  Form H 21.160
  hearing 21.113–21.128
    directions 21.113–21.118
    procedure 21.120–21.123
  hearsay 21.143–21.147
  human rights, and 21.217
  inferences 21.138–21.142
  initial enquiry 21.35–21.38
  interest 21.58, 21.59–21.63
  joint owners 21.163, 21.164
  judicial review 21.194
  Legal Services Commission Funding 21.174–21.177
  lies told by defendant 21.148–21.150
  Mass Spec expert reports 21.151–21.158
  matters to be sworn under oath 21.128
  minimum amount in possession of single person 21.15, 21.16
  minimum amount that may be seized: £1000 21.14
  mixed property 21.29
  ongoing criminal proceedings 21.34
  order of evidence and speeches 21.124–21.127
  POCA regime 21.05–21.09
  practice and procedure 21.35–21.64
  preliminary matters 21.12
  previous convictions, admissibility 21.132–21.136
  procedure prior to first hearing 21.39–21.42
  property not recoverable 21.30–21.32
  record of proceedings 21.159
  recoverable property defined 21.25, 21.26
  release of money over which no suspicion attached 21.64
  re-seizure of cash 21.33
  rules of evidence 21.129–21.164
  searches and seizure of cash 21.195–21.216, *see also* **searches and seizure of cash**
  sensitive evidence 21.161, 21.162
  standard of proof 21.129–21.131
  test applied by court of further detention hearings 21.56, 21.57
  tracing of property 21.28
  unattended dispatches 21.47–21.50
  unlawful conduct 21.20
  unlawful conduct specified 21.21–21.24
  venue 21.39–21.42
recovery orders 20.08–20.98
  associated and joint property 20.51–20.64
    agreements about 20.55–20.57
    calculation of amount 20.58–20.62
    default of agreement 20.63, 20.64
    excepted joint owner 20.53, 20.54
    practice and procedure 20.11–20.13
  confiscation orders, and 20.76, 20.77
  consent orders 20.16–20.19
  exceptions 20.66, 20.67, 20.83–20.92
  exclusions 20.66, 20.67
  exemptions 20.66, 20.67, 20.83–20.92
    declaration of 20.80–20.82
  financial threshold 20.10
  forfeiture of cash 20.74
  insolvency, and 20.93–20.95
  interest, meaning 20.65
  matters which Director of ARA needs to prove 20.29–20.38
  pre-emption, rights of 20.46–20.49
  procedure which ARA must follow 20.14
  public interest immunity 20.96–20.98
  related property 20.70–20.73
  settlement agreements 20.15
  summary judgments 20.20–20.28
  supplementary provisions to s 278 20.78, 20.79
  trustee for civil recovery 20.39–20.44, *see also* **trustee for civil recovery**
  twelve year limitation 20.45
  vesting of recoverable property 20.50
  victims of criminal conduct 20.75
  where court must not make 20.68, 20.69
red diesel cases 29.135–29.155
  civil burden 29.152
  criminal offences 29.153–29.155
  compounding 29.147
  excepted vehicles 29.143–29.146
  legislative provisions 29.137–29.142
  procedural requirements 29.148, 29.149
  vehicle and fuel 29.150, 29.151
Regional Asset Recovery Teams 1.36
relevant benefit
  meaning 14.31, 14.32
relevant criminal conduct
  meaning 11.11
realisable property
  meaning 10.100
repatriation of assets 4.42–4.49
  form of order 4.49
  international cooperation, and 4.43
  jurisdiction to make repatriation orders 4.44–4.48
    discretion of court 4.48
    inherent jurisdiction of court 4.44–4.47
restoration 29.162–29.240
  appeals 29.231, 29.232
  burden of proof 29.165, 29.166
  case law 19.192–29.197
  compensation 29.233
  costs 29.234–29.236
  human rights, and 29.237–29.240
  jurisdiction 29.177–29.179
  non-restoration, appeals against 29.164
  personal/commercial use 29.180–29.191
  practice and procedure 29.198–29.230

Index

restoration (*cont.*)
    disclosure 29.206–29.211
    failure to comply with directions 29.217, 29.218
    formal departmental reviews 29.198
    hearing 29.223–29.228
        conclusion of proceedings, on 5.03
    judgment 29.229, 29.230
    lodging appeal 29.202–29.205
    ongoing criminal proceedings 29.216
    pre-hearing reviews 29.219–29.221
    preparation for hearing 29.222
    statement of case 29.202–29.205
    time limits 29.200, 29.201
    tribunal procedure 29.199
    witness statements 29.212–29.215
  proportionality 29.173–29.176
  reasonableness, test of 29.167–29.172
  standard of proof 29.165, 29.166
  statutory basis 29.162, 29.163
restraint order appeals 24.06–24.28
  Court of Appeal, to 24.06, 24.26
  hearing appeal 24.23–24.25
  High Court, from 24.07–24.12
  House of Lords, to 24.27, 24.28
  leave 24.19–24.22
  Proceeds of Crime Act 2002 (Appeals under Part 2) Order 2003 24.26
restraint orders
  appeals, *see* restraint order appeals
  applications to vary 5.09–5.26
    burden of proof 5.25
    businesses 5.24
    companies 5.24
    full and frank disclosure 7.23
    general living expenses 5.20–5.23
    'legislative steer' 5.27–5.46
      application 5.31
      claim by unsecured third party creditor 5.33–5.40
    luxurious lifestyle 5.41
    payment of expenses on term by term basis 5.32
    preservation of assets 5.29, 5.30
    legal expenses 5.10–5.19
      access to unrestrained funds, and 5.19
      assessment by costs judge 5.13
      dispute by prosecutor 5.13–5.15
      legal aid, and 5.17, 5.18
      proportionate expenditure 5.16
      specific sum 5.11
    Mareva jurisdiction, and 5.43–5.45
    principles on which court acts 5.27–5.46
  businesses 2.91, 2.92
  charging orders, relationship with 2.102
  companies 2.53–2.63
  conditions 2.82–2.92
  contempt of court, *see* **contempt of court**
  costs and expenses incurred in complying with 2.84–2.88

  Criminal Justice Act 1988 (*see* **restraint orders under Criminal Justice Act 1988**)
  delay, and 2.40–2.48
  discharge, applications for 5.02–5.08
    conclusion of proceedings, on 5.03
    failure to give full and frank disclosure 5.07, 5.08
    procedural irregularities by prosecutor 5.04–5.06
  Drug Trafficking Act 1994 (*see* **restraint orders under Drug Trafficking Act 1994**)
  duration 2.78–2.81
  enforcement 6.01–6.39
  freezing orders distinguished 2.03–2.07
  leasehold interests 2.69–2.72
  legal expenses 2.89, 2.90
  legitimately acquired assets 2.67, 2.68
  limited companies 2.53, 2.63
    lifting corporate veil 2.54–2.62
  management receiver, and 3.10, 3.11
  overseas assets 2.76, 2.77
  parties restrained by 2.50–2.52
  procedure on application, *see* **High Court procedure**
  Proceeds of Crime Act 2002, *see* **restraint orders under Proceeds of Crime Act 2002**
  property, meaning 2.74, 2.75
  property not realizable under legislation 2.73
  property restrained by 2.64–2.66
  purpose 2.02
  release of funds after conviction 5.52–5.58
    appeals, and 5.56
    contingency plans 5.55
    enforcement receiver, and 5.57, 5.58
  risk of dissipation of assets 2.40–2.48
  sanctions available for breach 6.03, 6.04
  scope 2.50–2.77
  standard of proof 2.49
  source of payment of legal fees and living expenses 5.47–5.51
    assets not legitimately acquired 5.48
    assets which are prosecution exhibits 5.49–5.51
  terms 2.82–2.92
  third parties, and, *see* **third parties**
  variation
    form App 5
  ways in which breaches may be committed 6.02
restraint orders under Drug Trafficking Act 1994 2.08–2.22
  conditions 2.08
  drug trafficking 2.17, 2.18
  drug trafficking offences 2.11
  proceedings instituted or application made 2.09, 2.10
  risk of dissipation 2.40
  section 25(1)(b): proceedings not concluded 2.12–2.14
  section 25(1)(c): reasonable cause to believe defendant has benefited from drug trafficking 2.15, 2.16
  section 25(3): proceedings to be instituted in future 2.19–2.21

Index

restraint orders under Criminal Justice Act 1988
    2.23–2.39
  benefit 2.34–2.39
  conditions 2.24
  offences to which applies 2.26
  proceedings instituted in England and Wales 2.25
  proceedings not concluded 2.27–2.33
  proceedings resulting in conviction for offence from which defendant may have benefited 2.33
restraint orders under Proceeds of Crime Act 2002
    8.01–8.127
  ancillary orders 8.49, 8.50
  application of Act 8.03–8.11
  applications 8.70–8.72
    prosecutor's witness statement 8.72
  charging orders, and 8.56
  conditions for obtaining 8.12–8.32
    application for reconsideration to be made 8.23–8.26
    criminal investigations 8.13–8.16
    criminal proceedings already started 8.17–8.22
    reconsideration of available amount 89.29–8.32
    reconsideration of benefit 8.27, 8.28
  court documents 8.103
  discharge 8.55
  discharge applications
    person who applied for order, by 8.80
  disclosure of documents 8.102
  enforcing 8.123–8.127
  evidence 8.92–8.121
    expert 8.100, 8.101
    writing, in 8.96–8.98
  exceptions 8.38, 8.39
  hearings 8.92–8.121
  inspection of documents 8.102
  legal expenses 8.40–8.48
    human rights, and 8.44–8.46
  making order 8.33–8.37
  offences straddling commencement date 8.04–8.11
  order 8.73, 8.74
  procedure:
    change of solicitor 8.116
    consent orders 8.110
    costs 8.117–8.121
      assessment 8.119, 8.120
      time for complying with orders 8.121
    omissions 8.111
    preparation of documents 8.114, 8.115
    slips 8.111
    supply of documents from court records 8.112, 8.113
  procedure on applications 8.69–8.80
  protecting in relation to real property 8.122
  restrictions 8.51–8.54
  service of documents 8.104–8.109
    alternative method 8.107
    outside jurisdiction 8.108
    proof of 8.109
  variation 8.55
  variation applications 8.75–8.79
    person who applied for order, by 8.78, 8.79
    persons affected, by 8.75–8.77
Revenue and Customs Prosecutions Office
    1.24–1.26
risk of dissipation of assets
  restraint orders, and 2.40–2.48

SARS 27–70–27.75
Scotland
  reciprocal enforcement 25.44
search and seizure warrants 23.39
searches and seizure of cash 21.195–21.216
  cash, meaning 21.199, 21.200
  cash on premises 21.196
  cash on the suspect 21.201–21.203
  Code of Practice 21.211–21.214
  judicial discretion 23.40–23.45
  minimum amount: £1000 21.197, 21.198
  procedure at hearings 21.215
  safeguards 21.205–21.209
seizure of assets 4.02–4.05
  dealing with seized assets 4.04, 4.05
  standard of proof 4.03
self incrimination
  disclosure orders, and 4.15–4.28, *see also* **disclosure orders**
sentence
  confiscation order, relationship with 10.127–10.132
Serious Organised Crime Agency 1.30–1.32
Serious Fraud Office 1.28, 1.29
subject to appeal
  meaning 17.20–17.26

taxation
  management receivers, and 3.64–3.68
third parties 22.01–22.150
  cohabitees 22.79–22.118
  confiscation orders 22.59–22.78
    defendant, role of 22.73
    hearing 22.74
    order of court 22.75–22.78
    powers of court and receiver 22.70–22.72
    receivership proceedings 22.62, 22.63
    right to be given notice of proceedings 27.64
    right to make representations 22.65, 22.66
    seeking adjournment 22.68, 22.69
    steps to be taken on receipt of application to appoint enforcement receiver 22.67
  property adjustment orders 22.119–22.149
    application of sums 22.134
    banks 22.135–22.145
    equitable interests in matrimonial home 22.131, 22.132
    insolvent defendant 22.146–22.149

Index

third parties (*cont.*)
  property adjustment orders (*cont.*)
    MCA, and 22.127
    POCA and *MCA* 22.125, 22.126
    property should form part of confiscation order 22.128–22.130
    Re Norris, and 22.127
    trusts 22.133
  restraint orders 22.03–22.58
    assets, use of 22.57
    corporate veil 22.23–22.28
    jurisdiction 22.03–22.06
    legal expenses 22.21
    limited companies 22.22–22.28
    living expenses 22.19
    obligations 22.07–22.10
    person who denies that defendant has interest in restrained asset 22.57
    prosecutor does not have to give undertaking in damages 22.29
    reasonable costs and expenses 22.12–22.15
    rights 22.11
    unsecured third party creditors 22.30–22.56
    wife of defendant 22.16–22.18, 22.79–22.118
third party debt orders 17.65
tipping off 27.76–27.87
trustee for civil recovery 20.39–20.44
  functions 20.41, 20.42
  meaning 20.39, 20.40
  powers 20.43, 20.44

unlawful conduct
  meaning 21.20

variations to confiscation orders under DTA and CJA 13.01–13.60
  applications by defendant for decrease 13.36–13.60
    assets difficult to realize 13.54
    burden of proof 13.38, 13.39
    certificate of inadequacy and legitimate expectation 13.58–13.60
    certificates of inadequacy 13.36, 13.37
    certificates of inadequacy: procedure 13.55, 13.56
    court must give reasons 13.57
    Crown Court stage 13.40
    route to appeal, not 13.41–13.53
    standard of proof 13.38, 13.39
  applications by prosecutor in drug trafficking cases 13.05–13.17
    procedure on 13.16, 13.17
    section 13: where court has not proceeded under Act 13.07–13.09
    section 14: where court determines defendant has not benefited from drug trafficking 13.11–13.13
    section 15: revised assessment of proceeds of drug-trafficking 13.14, 13.15
    time limits 13.10
  CJA cases 13.27–13.35
    increase in realisable property 13.35
    section 74A: review of cases where proceeds of crime not assessed 13.28–13.31
    section 74B: revision of assessment of proceeds of crime 13.22, 13.33
    section 74C: revision of assessment of amount to be recovered 13.34
  increase in realisable property 13.18–13.26
    certificates of increase 13.26
    practice 13.19–13.22
    procedure on applications 13.24, 13.25
    unfettered discretion 13.23
voluntary satisfaction by defendant 17.03–17.12

warrants of commitment 17.66–17.77
websites App 16
wife of defendant
  restraint orders, and 22.16–22.18
wives 22.74–22.118
Woolf reforms 7.03